AN ENCYCLOPA

Chinese–Engl

C000066997

An Encyclopaedia of Translation

Chinese–English · English–Chinese

Edited by
Chan Sin-wai
David E. Pollard

The Chinese University Press

An Encyclopaedia of Translation
  Edited by Chan Sin-wai and David E. Pollard

© **The Chinese University of Hong Kong,** 1995, 2001

ISBN 962–201–997–8 (Paperback edition)

First hardcover edition 1995
First paperback edition 2001

THE CHINESE UNIVERSITY PRESS
The Chinese University of Hong Kong
SHA TIN, N.T., HONG KONG
Fax: +852 2603 6692
     +852 2603 7355
E-mail: cup@cuhk.edu.hk
Web-site: www.chineseupress.com

Printed in Hong Kong

Table of Contents

Preface

When three years ago we conceived the idea of putting together a conspectus of the field of translation we already foresaw the problem of giving it a suitable title. As we planned to muster as much help as possible with it (and in the end recruited close to a hundred contributors), the word "conspectus" itself — or the near synonym "survey" — had the weakness of suggesting both very limited authorship and extreme brevity of treatment. "Handbook" and "guide" suggested rather more ready reference than we intended to provide. "Encyclopaedia" had the advantage of indicating multiple headings and essay-length entries, hence its eventual adoption. However, we are only too aware that this title is presumptuous. Translation studies is too immature a field to justify the authoritativeness implied in "encyclopaedia". Compared with say the wisemen of the *Princeton Encyclopaedia of Poetry and Poetics* we are children sporting on the shore: we have nothing like the same historical scholarship behind us. On the other hand, we did feel the time had come to attempt to sum up what had been achieved in our field, to enable us and our confrères elsewhere to take stock of where we had got to so far, so that we could go on to do better in future.

"Elsewhere" begs the question, where? Being who we are, where we are, we naturally have a particular interest in translation between Chinese and English. The two meet in almost every classroom and on every street corner in Hong Kong, and our job is to make the meetings more fruitful. Given this interest, the language-specific and culture-specific entries in this volume relate to interaction between the Chinese-speaking and English-speaking worlds.

We have called upon many colleagues in China and sinological circles worldwide to help us deal with aspects of this interaction. For disciplinary, universalist topics we have drawn heavily on the goodwill of European and North American experts in translation, including several leading theorists. In an age when the universities are dominated by mercantilism we have been greatly encouraged by the willingness of our contributors to give of their labour without recompense.

Some peculiarities in this Encyclopaedia will be immediately obvious. Of these, the taking of more than one bite at the same cherry follows from our dual concern with both the local and the universal, which has led us to ask for a Chinese and a Western perspective on the same subject. Less frequently we have allowed some overlap in developing areas where views tend to differ widely. It will also be noticed that entries vary greatly in length, and the length is not strictly proportionate to the notional importance or magnitude of the subject. Some contributors presented very economical summaries, others full-length academic papers. Despite editorial efforts to coax more on the one hand and rein in on the other hand, with some success it may be said, the remaining disparities bespeak our lack of ruthlessness. More positively, we were inclined to give room to longer articles that dwelt on relatively untrodden ways and went into interesting detail; for that we do not apologize.

It goes without saying, however, that not all detail will be of interest, or even meaningful, to all readers. Some of the force of the Chinese examples will be lost on the non-sinophone readers, and contrary-wise citation of European language usage (excluding English) may not mean much to our local readers. But multiplicity of languages is the foundation of translation practice and translation studies, and we have to cope as best we can.

Some topics were dropped from our inventory because of contributors failing to deliver; others planned never found contributors at all; some gaps were filled late in the day, but at the cost of keeping waiting those who had delivered their manuscripts promptly. That sad history is common to compilations of many hands; only the scale of our enterprise is unusual. Yet however generous the scale in time and in length, a line has to be drawn somewhere and you have to make do with what you have got. We regret the lack of balance that remains, but are far from discontented. On the contrary, the quality of a substantial number of the entries seems to us to have fully justified our plan.

To end with a little local flagwaving, the "plan" referred to was conceived as a departmental project for the Department of Translation at The Chinese University of Hong Kong. Most of our colleagues interested in translation at CUHK have contributed, as have several from other tertiary institutions. Hong Kong has probably the highest concentration of translation departments in the world. We hope that this compilation will help to strengthen their academic footings, and at the same time be of more than passing interest to those who plough a like furrow everywhere.

Apart from the authors of the entries, we wish to acknowledge the help of Miss Ngai Lai Man, Miss Gabriella Chow Ngar See, and Mrs Chan Cheung Mei Ling, who acted at different stages as editorial assistants, and we thank Mr. T. L. Tsim, Director of The Chinese University Press, and his colleagues Mr. Patrick Kwong, Mr. Y. K. Fung and Mr. Kingsley Ma for their production of this volume.

The editors

Acknowledgement

The editors gratefully acknowledge the permission given by the author and publisher to reprint the following copyrighted articles:

Carl James. "Perspectives on Transfer and Translation." *The Linguist*, Vol. 27, No. 1 (1988), pp. 45–48.

Wolfram Wilss. "Cognitive Aspects of the Translation Process." (Translated by Roger C. Norton). *Language and Communication*, Vol. 10, No. 1 (1990), pp. 19–36, Pergamon Press PLC.

Acknowledgement is also made to the Elite Engineering Company and to the Hui Yeung Shing Fund, which donated HK$110,000 and HK$30,000 respectively, for the production of this book.

List of Contributors

Contributors, together with their affiliations, are listed in alphabetical order, followed by the titles of their entries printed in italics.

Almberg, S. P. E.
Department of Translation
The Chinese University of Hong Kong, Hong Kong
Retranslation, pp. 925–30

Ames, Roger T.
Department of Philosophy
University of Hawaii, Honolulu, U.S.A.
Translating Chinese Philosophy, pp. 731–46

Bassnett, Susan
The Centre for British and Comparative Cultural Studies
University of Warwick, Coventry, U.K.
Translation Theory in the West: An Historical Perspective, pp. 388–92

Birch, Cyril
Department of Oriental Languages
University of California, Berkeley, U.S.A.
Yuan Zaju, pp. 172–82

Blum-Kulka, Shoshana
Communications Institute
Hebrew University, Jerusalem, Israel
Discourse Analysis, pp. 142–49

Brislin, Richard W.
Institute of Culture and Communication
East West Center, Honolulu, Hawaii, U.S.A.
Back-translation: A Tool for Cross-cultural Research, pp. 22–40

Cayley, John
Wellsweep Press, London, U.K.
Chinese Classical Poetry, pp. 758–72

Chan, Man Sing
Department of Chinese
University of Hong Kong, Hong Kong
Arthur Waley, pp. 423–28

Chau, Simon S. C.
Department of English
Hong Kong Baptist College, Hong Kong
Translation Education, pp. 190–208
Voice, pp. 317–23

Cheng, Y. P.
Member, AIIC, Hong Kong
Interpreting, pp. 464–71

Cheng, Zhenqiu
Department of Translation and Interpretation
Ministry of Foreign Affairs, Beijing, China
Translation of Chinese Political Writings, pp. 827–34

Dai, Liuling
Department of Foreign Languages and Literature
Zhongshan University, Guangzhou, China
Children's Literature, pp. 83–86

Deeney, John J.
Department of English
The Chinese University of Hong Kong, Hong Kong
Biculturalism and Ambiculturalism, pp. 110–26
Transcription, Romanization, Transliteration, pp. 1085–1107

Dent-Young, John
Department of English
The Chinese University of Hong Kong, Hong Kong
Translating Chinese Fiction: The Shui Hu Zhuan, pp. 249–61

Delabastita, Dirk
Department of English

Facultés Universitaires Notre-Dame de la Paix, Belgium
Translation and Mass Communication, pp. 639–50

Dong, Zhendong
BGL Computer Co. Ltd.
Beijing, China
TRANSTAR: An English-Chinese Machine Translation System, pp. 628–38

Duff, Alan McConnell
Member, Slovenian Translators Association, Slovenia
Overtranslation, pp. 716–30
Undertranslation, pp. 1108–1117

Feleppa, Robert
Department of Philosophy
Wichita State University, Kansas, U.S.A.
Translation as a Basis for Cultural Description, pp. 127–41

Fong, Gilbert C. F.
Department of Translation
The Chinese University of Hong Kong, Hong Kong
Translated Literature in Pre-modern China, pp. 580–90

Freimanis, Carolina
Centre for Interpretation and Translation Studies
The University of Hawaii, Monoa, Hawaii, U.S.A.
Back-translation: A Tool for Cross-cultural Research, pp. 22–40

Fung, Mary M. Y.
Department of Chinese
University of Hong Kong, Hong Kong
Translation of Metaphor, pp. 658–71

Golden, Séan
Faculty of Translation and Interpreting
Universitat Autonoma de Barcelona, Barcelona, Spain
Professional Translator and Interpreter Training Programmes, pp. 1074–1084

Gottlieb, Henrik
Center for Translation Studies and Lexicography

University of Copenhagen, Copenhagen, Denmark
Subtitling pp. 1004–1011

Guo, Jianzhong
Department of Foreign Languages
Hangzhou University, Hangzhou, China
Translatability in CE/EC Translation, pp. 1057–1067

Hartmann, Reinhard R. K.
Language Centre
University of Exeter, Exeter, U.K.
Contrastive Textology, Bilingual Lexicography and Translation, pp. 505–18

He, Ziran
Department of Linguistics
Guangzhou Institute of Foreign Languages, Guangzhou, China
Pragmatics, pp. 835–45

Ho, Wai Kit
Department of Chinese, Translation and Linguistics
City Polytechnic of Hong Kong, Hong Kong
Media Translating, pp. 651–57

House, Juliane
Zentrales Fremdspracheninstitut
University of Hamburg, Hamburg, Germany
Translation Quality Assessment, pp. 982–98

Huang, I-min
Department of English
Tamkang University, Taipei, Taiwan
Puns, pp. 918–24

Huang, Jianhua
Guangzhou Institute of Foreign Languages
Guangzhou, China
Translating for International Conferences, pp. 459–63

Huang, Yushi
Qinghua University, Beijing, China
Form and Spirit, pp. 277–87

Hung, Eva
Research Centre for Translation
The Chinese University of Hong Kong, Hong Kong
Translation Editing, pp. 183–89

Hutchins, W. J.
Library, University of East Anglia, Norwich, U.K.
Machine Translation, pp. 591–602

Hwang, Mei-shu
Graduate School of Western Languages and Literature
Tamkang University, Taipei, Taiwan
Allusions, pp. 14–21

Ivir, Vladimir
Department of English, Faculty of Philosophy
University of Zagreb, Zagreb, Croatia
Formal Correspondence, pp. 288–300

James, Carl
Department of Linguistics
University of Bangor, Wales, U.K.
Transfer and Translation, pp. 1048–1056

Jin, Di
Foreign Languages Institute
Tianjin, China
Equivalent Effect in Translation, pp. 231–34

Jin, Serena S. H.
Department of Translation
The Chinese University of Hong Kong, Hong Kong
Colour Terms, pp. 87–94

Jones, Francis Redvers
Language Centre
University of Newcastle Upon Tyne, U.K.
Translation in Language Teaching, pp. 487–504

Kao, George
Maryland, U.S.A.
Translation of Humorous Writings, pp. 393–400

Knechtges, David R.
Asian Languages and Literature
University of Washington, Seattle, U.S.A.
Problems of Translating the Han Rhapsody, pp. 794–806

Lai, Chui Chun Jane
Department of English
Hong Kong Baptist College, Hong Kong
Drama Translation, pp. 159–71

Lam, Jacqueline K. M.
Language Centre
University of Exeter, Exeter, U.K.
Thinking-aloud Protocol, pp. 904–17

Lang, Margaret F.
Department of Languages
Heriot-Watt University, Edinburgh, U.K.
Discourse Analysis and the Translator, pp. 150–58

Larson, Mildred L.
Summer Institute of Linguistics, Dallas, U.S.A.
Factors in Bible Translation, pp. 41–53

Lau, Joseph S. M.
Department of East Asian Languages and Literature
University of Wisconsin-Madison, Wisconsin, U.S.A.
Author as Translator, pp. 949–59

Lee, Thomas H. C.
Department of Asian Studies
The City College, New York, U.S.A.
Western History, pp. 361–72

Lefevere, André
Department of Germanic Languages
University of Texas at Austin, Texas, U.S.A.
Factors of Poetic Translation, pp. 747–57

Lie, Raymond S. C.
Department of English

Hong Kong Baptist College, Hong Kong
Commercial Translation, pp. 95–109

Liu, Bingshan
Department of Foreign Languages
Zhongshan University, Guangzhou, China
Translation of English Essays, pp. 235–41

Liu, Ching-chih
Centre of Asian Studies
University of Hong Kong, Hong Kong
Western Music, pp. 678–705

Liu, Miqing
Department of Translation
The Chinese University of Hong Kong, Hong Kong
Aesthetics and Translation, pp. 1–13
Grammar and Translation, pp. 301–16
Translation Theory from/into Chinese, pp. 1029–1047

Liu, Zhongde
Department of Foreign Languages
Hunan Normal University, Changsha, China
English Attributive Clauses, pp. 971–81

Loh, I-Jin
United Bible Societies Asia Opportunity Program
Bible Society in the Republic of China, Taipei, Taiwan
Chinese Translations of the Bible, pp. 54–69

Lorscher, Wolfgang
Institute of Applied Linguistics
University of Hildesheim, Hildesheim, Germany
Pyscholinguistics, pp. 884–903

Ma, Zuyi
Oceanic Literature Institute
Anhui University, Hefei, China
History of Translation in China, pp. 373–87

McDougall, Bonnie S.
Department of East Asian Studies

University of Edinburgh, U.K.
Contemporary Chinese Poetry: Poems by Bei Dao as an Example, pp. 773–82

Neubert, Albrecht
Department of English and Translation Studies
Karl-Marx University, Leipzig, Germany
Textlinguistics, pp. 1016–1028

Newmark, Peter
Department of Linguistic and International Studies
University of Surrey, Guildford, U.K.
Translation Procedures, pp. 871–83

Nida, Eugene A.
American Bible Society, New York, U.S.A.
Dynamic Equivalence in Translating, pp. 223–30

Nkwenti-Azeh, Blaise
Centre for Computational Linguistics
University of Manchester Institute of Science and Technology, U.K.
Terminology, pp. 610–27

Pfister, Lauren F.
Department of Religion and Philosophy
Hong Kong Baptist College, Hong Kong
James Legge, pp. 401–22

Pollard, David E.
Department of Translation
The Chinese University of Hong Kong, Hong Kong
Body Language in Chinese-English Translation, pp. 70–77
Empty Words: Modal Adverbs, pp. 216–22

Pong, Lam Shuk-lin
Willowdale, Canada
Simultaneous Interpreting, pp. 472–75
Training of Conference Interpreters, pp. 1068–1073

Qian, Feng
Department of Computer Science and System Analysis

University of Salzburg, Austria
Computational Linguistics, pp. 546–58

Rose, Marilyn Gaddis
Center for Research in Translation
State University of New York at Binghamton, U.S.A.
Text Typology and Translation: Across Languages, pp. 1012–1015

Schlepp, Wayne
East Asian Studies
University of Toronto, Toronto, Canada
Sanqu, pp. 807–26

Schulte, Rainer
Center for Translation Studies
University of Texas at Dallas, Dallas, U.S.A.
Interpretation, pp. 448–58

Shen, Dan
Department of English
Peking University, Beijing, China
Literalism, pp. 568–79

Shih, Hsio-yen
Department of Fine Arts
University of Hong Kong, Hong Kong
Translation of Chinese Texts on Calligraphy and Painting, pp. 267–76

Sinn, Elizabeth
Department of History
University of Hong Kong, Hong Kong
Yan Fu, pp. 429–47

Snell-Hornby, Mary
Institute of Translator and Interpreter Training
University of Vienna, Austria
Lexicography and Translation, pp. 533–45

Tan, Cheng Lim
English Language Proficiency Unit
National University of Singapore, Singapore
Language Teaching and Translation, pp. 476–86

Tsai, Frederick
Hong Kong Translation Society, Hong Kong
Book Titles, pp. 78–82
English Fiction, pp. 262–66
Europeanized Structure in English-Chinese Translation, pp. 242–48

Wang, Zongyan
Department of Foreign Languages
Zhongshan University, Guangzhou, China
Linguistic Aspects of CE/EC Translation, pp. 559–67

Wang, Zuoliang
Beijing Foreign Studies University, Beijing, China
Translation Standards, pp. 999–1003

Watson, Burton
Department of East Asian Languages and Culture
Columbia University, New York, U.S.A.
Chinese History, pp. 347–60

Wilss, Wolfram
Universitat des Saarlandes, Saarbrucken, Germany
Cognitive Aspects of the Translation Process, pp. 846–70

Witzleben, John L.
Department of Music
The Chinese University of Hong Kong, Hong Kong
Chinese Music, pp. 672–77

Wong, Ian P. K.
Hong Kong Translation Society, Hong Kong
Translating Empty Words, pp. 209–15

Wong, Kin Yuen
Department of English
The Chinese University of Hong Kong, Hong Kong
Hermeneutics and Translation, pp. 333–46

Wong, Siu Kit
Department of Chinese
University of Hong Kong, Hong Kong
Arthur Waley, pp. 423–28

Wu, Jingrong
Department of English
Foreign Affairs College, Beijing, China
Chinese-English Dictionaries, pp. 519–32

Yan, Qingjia
The Institute of Scientific and Technical Information of China
Chongqing Branch, China
Scientific Translation, pp. 942–48

Yang, Guobin
Beijing Foreign Studies University
Beijing, China
English Poetry, pp. 783–93

Yu, Lisan
Department of Foreign Languages
Shantou University, shantou, China
Rhetoric, pp. 931–41

Yu, Yungen
Foreign Languages University
Luoyang, China
Onomatopoeia, pp. 706–15

Zeng, Xiancai
Department of English
Guangzhou Institute of Foreign Languages, Guangzhou, China
Semantics, pp. 960–70

Zhang, Liangping
Department of Foreign Languages
Qinghua University, Beijing, China
Practical Considerations of Machine Translation, pp. 603–609

Zhang, Peiji
University of International Business and Economics
Beijing, China
Translation of English Letters as Shape Describers, pp. 324–32

AESTHETICS

Aesthetics and Translation

Liu Miqing
Department of Translation
The Chinese University of Hong Kong, Hong Kong

Historical Ties between Aesthetics and Translation

As in the West, China's exploration of translation artistry drew close the ties between classical aesthetics and translation studies. The exploration can be dated back to A.D. 220–230, when translators of Buddhist scriptures were seeking for philosophical backup. The first exploration in this direction can be found in Zhi Qian's 支謙 writing in which he quoted Lao Zi's 老子 maxim that "beautiful words are not faithful, and faithful words not beautiful" 美言不信，信言不美 ("Preface to Dhammapada" 〈法句經序〉), the time-honoured aesthetic controversy of "beauty vs truth", and introduced into translation studies a topic which hung on for seventeen centuries in China. It is no exaggeration to say that traditional studies of translation have never ceased to seek theoretical reference from Chinese classical aesthetics, chiefly in the area of literary aesthetics.

Commonness in Values

Aesthetics and translation share similar values. Traditional translation studies have long accorded with classical aesthetics in Chinese literature and philology in their exploration of the relationship between the following binaries:

1. "Beauty vs Truth" in Aesthetics and "Gracefulness (Elegance) vs Faithfulness" in Translation

The nature of beauty and the relationship between beauty and truth have always been the major problems in aesthetics. In China, aesthetic thought began with Confucius (551–497 B.C.) who advocated that the perfect harmony lies in the integration of "supreme beauty and supreme good" 盡善盡美 . Confucius and his followers asserted that in the light of "the Doctrine of the Mean" 中庸之道 , "beauty is concord and concord, beauty" 中和之美 . Lao Zi stood for the antagonism between the beautiful and the true, a point of view in opposition to that of Mencius (372?–289 B.C.) who followed Confucius in defense of the unity between beauty and truth. Other great thinkers in Chinese philosophy such as Zhuang Zi 莊子 (369?–286 B.C.) and Han Fei 韓非 (280?–233 B.C.) all pursued enthusiastically their studies on aesthetic subjects. Han Fei held that outward beauty and inward content "is an antagonistic binary", the two being related both in opposition and in compensation, and what he advocated was "the inward content not the outward gracefulness" 好質而惡飾 . Nourished by the aesthetic legacy, early explorers of translation in China readily took over these topics in their discussion of the art of translation.

2. "Content vs Form" in Aesthetics and "Substantialness vs Embellishment" in Translation

The topic of "content vs form" has also been handed down from ancient times. Its long history began with Xun Zi 荀子 (313?–238 B.C.), the first aesthetic thinker who stressed the significance of form without neglecting the content. Xun Zi asserted that paying sole attention to the content and neglecting the form would inevitably result in "philistine speech" 鄙夫之言 . His conclusion, therefore, was that "to get across the message of the content, embellished language is indispensable" 文以致實 . Xun Zi's stress on "form" to assure the expression of the content was at variance with the views of Confucianists who contended that the beauty of the content is always first and foremost. Obviously enough, the old controversy of "substantialness" 質 versus "embellishment" 文 in translation was but an extension of the debate in the area of classical aesthetics.

It must be noted that as far as the binary of "content vs form" is concerned the main trend in classical Chinese aesthetics was the Confucian Doctrine of Concord. Confucius' interpretation of "concord" was 彬彬 in

文質彬彬, which means a perfect integration of form/embellishment 文 and content/substantialness 質. To achieve this, he also stressed "expressiveness", saying that "expressiveness is of vital importance in the use of words" 辭達而已矣. This has been regarded as the origin of Yan Fu's 嚴復 "Three-Character Criteria" (信達雅, "Faithfulness, Expressiveness and Gracefulness"). Zhuang Zi put the emphasis on substantialness, affirming that it is "the very nature of everything" 本然之性, and "all doctrines will be reduced to nothing if substantialness falls short of embellishment" 既盡其文，未盡其實，不能得道. Zhuang's point of view was later rebutted by Liu An 劉安 (179–122 B.C.) in *Huainanzi* 《淮南子》 when he stressed the interrelation of the two in the light of Confucianism, saying that "in as much as substantialness exists, so it is expressed in embellishment 必有其質，乃爲之文. Explorers of translation artistry after the Eastern Han Dynasty (25–220) brought in almost automatically the topic from literary aesthetics of "content vs form" after much further discussion by Yang Xiong 揚雄 (53 B.C.–18 A.D.), Wang Chong 王充 (27–97?) and Cao Pi 曹丕 (187–226).

3. *"Spirit vs Form"* 神與形

This binary has been another much talked-about translation principle in Chinese traditional translation studies since the 1920s, especially in the 1950s when Fu Lei 傅雷 (1908–1966) put forward an open advocacy of spirit closeness over formal closeness. Yet again, this was a borrowing from a typical subject in Chinese classical aesthetics in reference to landscape painting. The first philosopher who advanced the binary in philosophical as well as aesthetic areas was Xun Zi, who affirmed that "spirit comes into being as soon as the form takes shape" 形具而神生. But it was as late as the period of The Three Kingdoms (220–280) that artists and critics came to realize the importance of spirit over form as expounded and specified by Lu Ji 陸機 (261–303), Gu Kaizhi 顧愷之 (345?–406) and Liu Xie 劉勰 (465–532?). For example, Gu Kaizhi, a painter in the Eastern Jin Dynasty, interpreted his approach as "expressing spirit by means of form" 以神馭形. As a matter of fact, this approach to the subject of "spirit vs form" has become a long-standing and well established tradition of the philosophy of art not only pertaining to painting and other forms of fine arts but to literature and writing in general. In the 1960s when Qian Zhongshu 錢鍾書 explained his idea of "sublimation" 化境 as "the transmigration of souls", he was again expounding his theory in line with the Chinese heritage founded on a classical aesthetic value.

Commonness in Methodology

Methodologically, Chinese classical aesthetics likewise exerted a decisive influence on Chinese translation studies. The influence is especially remarkable in the following aspects.

1. Emphasis on Intuition and Empirical Appreciation

Influenced by the heritage of the Chinese traditional philosophical thinking, traditional studies of translation in China tend to pay too much attention to perception 感悟 and appreciation 了悟 of the aesthetic subject (i.e., the translator) instead of structural analyses of the aesthetic object (i.e., the original to be rendered) and investigation of its aesthetic elements. Traditional studies usually concentrate on the aesthetic subject's intuition and empirical insight instead of systematic verification based on linguistics. In short, they tend to pay too much attention to the translator's subjectivity rather than the source language objectivity.

2. Fuzziness in Definition

Confined by the limitations of the aesthetic subject's intuition and appreciation and weakness in objective analysis, traditional studies of translation are characterized by their narrowness of theoretical vision and fuzziness and ambiguity in logical intension. They tend to regard the art of translation as nothing more than a series of abstract aesthetic values such as 神、形、文、質、情采、豐姿、風姿 etc. Take 風姿 for example: presumably owing to the fact that its meaning is imprecise, its seemingly equivalent terms are virtually inexhaustible. There are 風姿、風華、風采、風節、風骨、風操、風志、風韻 and so forth. Their interpretations are so fluid that no practitioner in translation is very sure which is exact and how to proceed.

Reorientation of Aesthetic Exploration of Translation

The 1980s saw a reorientation in the exploration of the interrelationship between aesthetics and Chinese translation theory. Renewed attempts are intended to push traditional studies toward a scientific schema covering major topics in translation in the light of modern aesthetics.

Translation: Its Aesthetic Features as a Bilingual Communicative Activity

From the aesthetic angle of vision, translation is a bilingual aesthetic activity 審美活動 characterized by the following features:

Source Language as the Aesthetic Object

Anything in the objective world may come into our aesthetic vision and any object with aesthetic value must have the basic nature of perceptibility 可感知性 . In translation the aesthetic object is the source language, which may be written in beautiful as well as in plain language. Whatever language it is written in, it must be put under our aesthetic scrutiny if it is to be translated as effectively as the way the original is put. The possibility of our success is due to the source language's basic nature of perceptibility.

Given its basic nature, any text of the source language as an aesthetic object can be observed and assessed by the translator in terms of aesthetic values. And, any aesthetic object can be evaluated in terms of aesthetic constituents.

1. Formal/Material Constituents

Any aesthetic object has its holistic characteristics 整體特徵 . The source language as an aesthetic object possesses a system of holistic characteristics which fall into two groups. The first group comprises formal hence material aesthetic elements. They are visually or audibly perceptible. Therefore we call them the SL's formal/material constituents.

The audio-visual perceptibility of the source language aesthetic elements makes it possible for the translator to do a scanning of the source language text with a view to singling out all the formal/material constituents in the form of stylistic devices in the broadest sense, including devices in the SL letter-system (1st Level), phonology (2nd Level), figures of speech and other stylistic devices (3rd Level) and textual/syntactic arrangements (4th Level). The translator's task is to explore all the aesthetic elements in the source language form at the four levels.

What is vital in translation theory is to set aesthetic norms for bilingual transfer so as to recapture as much as possible the source language's perceptible holistic characteristics in the receptor language. The general norms are as follows:

i. Dependence 依附性

Theoretically, the beauty in the RL form ("form" is also in the broadest sense) is dependent on that in the source language. In practice, however, dependence raises a two-fold requirement. Positively, the receptor language must live up to the SL aesthetic values and intended aesthetic effect. To this end, the translator has to do his utmost to give full play to his aesthetic originality. Negatively, the translator is by no means free from all the restrictions of the SL formal devices and licensed to create the RL beauty regardless of the SL restrictions. The translator's originality is bound to be stunted to square with the SL aesthetic values. In both cases, dependence determines what the receptor language should be.

ii. Relativity 相對性

Aesthetic relativity in translation is derived from the limits of translatability, which put obstacles in the way of "equal value translation" 等值翻譯 or "equal effect translation" 等效翻譯 . Most limits stem from the disparities in the areas of letter-system, phonology, usage, syntax and culture between the source language and receptor language. In all these cases, the aesthetic constituents in the form are without exception subject to the RL translatability and social acceptability. For example, the translator's margin to allow for phonological beauty equal to 重重疊疊山，曲曲環環路，丁丁冬冬泉，高高下下樹 in the receptor language is almost nil.

iii. Unity 統一性

This is the norm by virtue of which the translator can strive to give full play to his aesthetic originality and experience to reproduce the beauty of the SL text. Here, the meaning of "unity" is multi-dimensional: (a) the unity of the SL form and the RL form; (b) the unity of the RL form and the SL content; (c) the unity of the source language author's aesthetic performance and the translator's aesthetic empathy; and (d) the unity of the author's and translator's aesthetic devices and the potentialities of the "receptor's aesthetic fusion" 接受者的審美融合 .

iv. Gradation 層級性

It must be noted that language is gradable in aesthetic value. In terms of functional stylistics, poetical/fictional prose may be graded much higher than technical/scientific prose, inasmuch as the former abounds in aesthetic constituents. When poetic narration and factual exposition are compared, their respective beauty is clear:

(a) 日落江湖白，潮來天地青。(王維:〈送邢桂州〉)
(b) 日落後，空中只有散射餘光，因此水面呈灰白色；潮漲時，天空與水面似乎更接近，此時水天均呈藍青色。

Obviously enough, there is an abundance of aesthetic devices in (a) at the above-mentioned four levels of language, while the aesthetic value of example (b) lies in its clarity and matter-of-factness. It is in this sense that we say "the beauty of language is found in its social function."

2. Non-formal/Non-material Constituents

The characteristics of these kinds of aesthetic constituents are as follows:

i. Fuzziness

Fuzziness is a non-quantitative element that exists in the source language to call forth aesthetic appeal in a pervasive manner. While formal/material constituents of a SL text are "countable", i.e., each and every one of them is not only visible but audible, non-formal constituents are "uncountable", i.e., they exist not in quantity but in quality, because they are of a non-material nature that cannot be felt by intuitive association 直覺聯想 alone but by intuitive imagination 直覺想像 — the upgraded intuitive association. Take a line from Su Shi's 蘇軾 (1037–1011) poem 〈赤壁懷古〉 "To the Tune of Niannujiao" 〈念奴嬌〉: 大江東去，浪淘盡千古風流人物 . The beauty of the poem cannot be felt unless the receptor is affectively moved to make use of his/her ability to think of and form pictures or ideas of things in connection with Chinese history and geographical charm as well as the poet's unlucky life story. Obviously, the beauty of the poem lies not in the individual words and not even in the language itself but in the overall power and appeal to arouse the receptor's thoughts on things remote. The fuzziness in the poem is conveyed in the description of Liu Xizai 劉熙載 (1863): 字字無華，字字生華 (Every word is plain but there is colour in its plainness).

ii. Collective Perceptibility

As has been exemplified above, the nature of these aesthetic constituents, though non-formal hence non-material, is fuzzy but they are still perceptible as "a collective". This quality in the aesthetic object is called "non-quantitative collectivity of fuzziness" 非定量模糊集合 . This means that the beauty of fuzziness is not built upon individual words; its captivation resides in the whole, to which every word contributes. Moreover, it does not mean that quantity means nothing to the whole. The key to it is appropriateness.

iii. Openness

The non-formal aesthetic element is characterized by openness to imagery 意象 . The mechanism of fuzziness in man's thinking leads to amazing flexibility and dynamism of his imagination. The ability to imagine, starts from intuitive association, then develops into imagery (intuitive imagination) by virtue of the fuzzy information 模糊信息 existing in the outside world (the aesthetic object). This process of development is always open to the receptor (reader/hearer/translator).

Needless to say, it is in this respect that the difficulty in translation lies. For example, flexibility and dynamism of the imagery make an expression of Li Qingzhao's 李清照 (1084–1151?) poem 人比黃花瘦 ("To the Tune of Zuihuayin" 〈醉花陰〉) too pervasive to render. It seems that no receptor language would have words for it.

Translator as the Aesthetic Subject

In aesthetics, the translator is not just a language user. He must be an aesthetician of language before he can say he is a good language user. To live up to this requirement, he is expected to strive to be qualified in the following aspects:

1. Artistic Accomplishments

Good taste and judgement result from training. Artistic accomplishment is acquired from cultivation. By the same token, the translator as the aesthetic subject must be constantly exposed to prismatic phenomena of the desirable language environment. Then, through the process of long exposure and diversified aesthetic practice, the translator comes to be capable of aesthetic performance. The translator as an aesthetician of language is expected to be able to do much scanning to extract the aesthetic value from the source language. To achieve this, he is also expected to have encyclopaedic knowledge, the knowledge of a "specialized generalist" 雜家 . Without such a knowledge, the translator would unavoidably be colour blind.

2. Aesthetic Ideal in Translation

Aesthetic judgement and values are attained from aesthetic experiences 審美體驗 which are, generally, guided by the subject's aesthetic ideal. In translation, however, the translator's aesthetic ideal is subject to (a) the SL author's aesthetic inclinations manifested in the SL text; (b) diachronic and synchronic adjustments (e.g., Yan Fu's "gracefulness" refers to the elegant style in the Qin and Han Dynasties, which has long since been regarded as out of date); and (c) translatability.

3. The System of Aesthetic Consciousness in Translation

In general, the system of aesthetic consciousness 審美意識系統 refers to the aesthetic subject's overall reflection on and reaction to the outside world pertaining to its "beauty". It is in this system that man, the aesthetic subject, acquires and experiences and performs his aesthetic ability in the light of his aesthetic ideal. In translation, the mechanism of the system of aesthetic consciousness functions in the whole process of bilingual transfer. The process can be described in a schema as follows:

Levels of the System of Aesthetic Consciousness in Translation
翻譯審美意識系統的層次圖式

Level A Perceptional Stage 感性階段
- The aesthetic object (the source language): The mechanism of formal/material elements functions.
- The aesthetic subject (the translator): The mechanism of intuitive association functions.
- Result: The formation of non-self-conciousness based on aesthetic sentiments, feelings, desires, etc.

Level B Cognitional Stage 知性階段
- The aesthetic object (the source language): The mechanism of non-formal/non-material elements functions.
- The aesthetic subject (the translator): The mechanism of intuitive imagination functions.
- Result: The formation of non-self-consciousness based on aesthetic attitudes, ideas, concepts, etc.

Level C Rational Stage 理性階段
- The aesthetic object (the source language): The mechanism of inte-grated aesthetic elements functions.
- The aesthetic subject (the translator): The mechanism of aesthetic judgement, values and ideals functions.
- Result: The formation of aesthetic self-consciousness that makes the receptor language take the aesthetically desired shape.

Level D The aesthetic subject's readjustment according to the receptor's "fusion of vision"

In the light of the aesthetics of reception, the translator must be cognizant of the aesthetic potential of the receptor (reader/hearer) 接受者的審美潛勢 in the process of the development of the system of aesthetic consciousness. He must be ready to provide a "fusion of vision" (Holub, 1984) to make his system of aesthetic consciousness more adaptable to produce an effect similar to that of the source language for the source language receptor.

4. General Law of Aesthetic Experience in Translation

The general law of the translator's aesthetic experience in translation 翻譯者審美體驗的一般規律 functions in the following steps corresponding to the levels of the system of aesthetic consciousness:

Step 1 (the system of aesthetic consciousness: Level A and Level B)
The aesthetic subject (the translator) uses his perception and cognition to scan out the SL aesthetic constituents to form intuitive association and imagination.

Step 2 (the system of aesthetic consciousness: Level C)
The aesthetic subject (the translator) uses his self-consciousness to trans-form what he/she has experienced in Step 1 into RL aesthetic information.

Step 3 (the system of aesthetic consciousness: Level D)
The aesthetic subject (the translator) adapts what he has experienced in Step 2 to accord with the RL receptor's "fusion of vision", taking into account the receptor's aesthetic potential.

Needless to say, for any translator with an aesthetic purpose, "Step 1" in his aesthetic experience is of primary importance. And of all the aesthetic elements, the formal and material constituents are likewise of primary importance. Therefore, it is imperative for him to be cognizant of the types of aesthetic devices in the source language referable to translation:

   i.   Graphological aesthetic devices
        e.g., antithesis, couples, chiasmus, etc.
   ii. Phonological aesthetic devices
        e.g., alliteration, assonance, rhyme, rhythm, etc.
   iii. Lexical aesthetic devices
        e.g., simile, metaphor, metonymy, pun, irony, oxymoron, etc.
   iv. Syntactic aesthetic devices
        e.g., anastrophe, repetition (tautology), aposiopesis, contrast, etc.
   v.   Textual aesthetic devices
        e.g., humour, symbolism, represented speech, stream of consciousness, flashback, flash language, etc.

Special attention must be paid to obtain an image as sharp as possible of the general (holistic) aesthetic characteristics in the source language and the author's workmanship. The source language beauty in fuzziness can only be obtained through the translator's assiduity in striving to give full play to the mechanism of the system of aesthetic consciousness.

Referential Norms Pertaining to Aesthetic Translation

Relevance

For a translator with an aesthetic purpose, relevance must be his/her first and foremost concern when it comes to the process of perception-cognition-translation aesthetic experience. Languages in bilingual transfer may belong to different families, and their basic characteristics may differ sharply in graphology, phonology and morphology. Disparities in syntax may lead to conflicting artistic values (e.g., tautology is very common in Chinese in view of phonological beauty, but in English it is not a very common aesthetic device). Accordingly, the translator's aesthetic performance must be subject to diachronical and synchronical conditioning.

Values

Aesthetic values vary not only in language itself but differ from culture to culture. And culture improves side by side with the development of society. What seemed beautiful in Yan Fu's time is no longer acceptable today. Values change with the passage of time. A translator must develop a sensitiveness to artistic beauty so that he can treat his aesthetic object in a diachronical and synchronical manner.

Openness

Aesthetic performance is a highly individualized kind of behaviour. The appreciation of the source language beauty is bound to differ from translator to translator. So is the receptor's "fusion of horizon". Accordingly identical interpretation and reproduction of the beauty of the same source language text is impossible. It is openness that makes translation a fascinating and endless endeavour and the exploration of its artistry a real charm.

Polyphony

Language is not only structurally stratified but aesthetically graded. From the point of view of functional stylistics, literary style in poetical and fictional prose is highly "aesthetical", while the least so are documentary and legal writings. In the latter cases, the translator's concern should be the very basic one of language readability. Their fundamental requirements in aesthetics are (a) grammaticality, (b) clarity, (c) idiomaticness, (d) organization and (e) stylistic adaptability. From the angle of sociolinguistic function, the beauty in language is a polyphonic compound.

References

Chu, K. T. 朱光潛. 《悲劇心理學》 (*The Psychology of Tragedy*). Hefei: Anhui Education Press 安徽教育出版社, 1989.

Croce, Benedetto. *Aesthetics as Science of Expression and General Linguistics.* New York: Noonday Press, 1953.

Holub, Robert C. *Reception Theory: A Critical Introduction* (Chinese Translation). 1984.

Jauss, Hans Rober. *Toward an Aesthetic of Reception* (Chinese Translation). 1983.

Li, Zehou 李澤厚. 《中國美學》 (*Chinese Aesthetics*). Hong Kong: Joint Publishing Co. 三聯書店, 1988.

Liu, Changyuan 劉昌元 . 《西方美學導論》 (*An Introduction to Western Aesthetics*). Taipei: Lien-ching Publishing Enterprise 聯經出版事業公司 , 1986.

Liu, Miqing 劉宓慶 . 〈翻譯基本理論構思〉 (Aesthetics and Translation: A Theoretical Outline). 《中國翻譯》 (*Chinese Translators Journal*), No. 4 (1986), p. 20.

Liu, Wentan 劉文潭 . 《現代美學》 (*Modern Aesthetics*). Taipei: The Commercial Press 商務印書館 , 1991.

Read, Herbert. *The Meaning of Art*. New York: Penguin Books, 1949.

Yang, Xin 楊辛 and Gan Lin 甘霖 . 《美學》 (*Aesthetics*). Beijing: Peking University Press 北京大學出版社 , 1983.

ALLUSIONS

Allusions

Hwang Mei-shu
Graduate School of Western Languages and Literature
Tamkang University, Taipei, Taiwan

An allusion (典 or 典故) is a direct or indirect reference to a person, place, event, or character, usually well-known in history, literature, legend, mythology, or books like the Bible. In his *The Art of Chinese Poetry* (1962), James Liu calls these kinds of references "specific" allusions and those made to common knowledge and beliefs "general" allusions. He says well that "in dealing with allusions we should ask not so much whether they are original or conventional, popular or abstruse, but rather whether they have any purpose or justification"; that is, if an allusion adds anything to the meaning or effect of a work or if it simply shows off the writer's learning. This is a useful principle for the translator to bear in mind. Liu's words also imply that some allusions are meaningful whereas some others are really superfluous — in fact, there are also misused allusions.

Like proverbs, allusions are very common in everyday speech as well as in works of literature. Usually the older a culture is, the richer it is in such references. Successful allusions of all kinds are economical and effective means for presenting an analogical situation or providing a contrast, which may strengthen the tragic, comic, ironic, or other desired effects in a work or speech because, through our association and imagination, skillfully employed allusions can summon up rich images in our minds and thus add the authority of past experience to the present occasion.

With perhaps the exception of those from such universally read books as the Bible, allusions are deeply rooted in the soil of a particular culture and can hardly be transplanted into a foreign land and bear the same fruit. In other words, the translation of allusion is not only difficult but often impossible. Yet, they are very often too significant to be ignored.

Exactly equivalent expressions are hard to find in any two languages. It is therefore impossible to find completely identical references in the target language for "specific" allusions growing out of the soil of the source language. This is to say that the non-existence of the referent and reference in the target language constitutes the main difficulty in allusion translation. The translator's most common practice is to use footnotes to "explain" the references and implications of the allusions. As long as the "explanations" are good and the reader is willing and patient enough to stop to consult the notes in the reading of poetry, fiction, and drama, such a practice may work fairly satisfactorily. However, footnoting an allusion is not a simple matter of providing source information. It is an art. First of all, there is the problem of how much detail to supply. Except for students of literature, most readers would be bored by footnotes, especially long ones. Secondly, the translator has to consider the function of the allusion according to the context and, sometimes, even the psychological background of the writer as well. Take for instance two footnotes for Xi Shi 西施 :

a. The famous beauty instrumental in the ruin of Wu, 5th century. (*The Rainbow Pass*, in *Famous Chinese Plays*, translated by L. C. Arlington and Harold Acton)

b. A famous beauty of the 5th century B.C. From a humble family, Hsi Shih [Xi Shi] was taken and trained by the king of Yueh [Yue] and afterward used to seduce the king of Wu and cause his defeat. (*Two Men on a String*, in *Classical Chinese Plays*, translated by Josephine Huang Hung)

In 〈虹霓關〉 *The Rainbow Pass*, a general has a dream of ill omen which makes him feel that he may die on the battlefield. He reveals his mind to his wife. When his wife promises to take care of the Pass while he is away, he says to her, "That's all very well, but have you forgotten the old story of Xi Shi?" He is killed and the wife swears to avenge his death, but ends up by marrying the man who killed her husband. Example two is from 〈鳳儀亭〉 *Two Men on a String*: A beautiful maiden offers to help her master to bring about the downfall of an evil prime minister. According to their plan, she is called to wait on the minister at a feast and the minister is immediately bewitched and says "... she is as alluring as Xi Shi." Neither footnote has emphasized the point that Xi Shi is remembered by the Chinese as a trustworthy heroine who willingly sacrificed herself for the good of her own country. She is not simply a great legendary beauty. Bearing this in mind, we can see that the first allusion to Xi Shi is a bad or wrong use in the original. It is obvious that no husband would say such a stupid thing to his wife whom he trusts. The translator should provide a more detailed explanation than a simple footnote like the one quoted above. He does not have to point out whether or not it is a wrong use of the allusion; but he has to give sufficient information to enable the reader to form his own conclusion. A more informative note like the following for the wutong tree may offer a better service to the reader. It is for the imagery in the line "The wu-t'ung [wutong] tree locked in a golden courtyard." (*Ssu Lang Visits His Mother*, in *Traditional Chinese Plays*, Vol. 1, translated by A. C. Scott.) The note reads: "The wu-t'ung tree was the only one on which the sacred phoenix roosted according to the Chinese legend. Ssu Lang uses the title in poetic reference to himself."

The second Xi Shi example shows a quite successful use of the allusion. Besides serving as a means of foreshadowing the development of the story, it is an especial irony that the playwright puts the line into the mouth of the minister — the victim himself, who at the moment thinks of nothing but his animal desire for the maiden and compares her beauty to that of Xi Shi, forgetting the fate of the king of Wu. So the allusion here achieves double levels of meaning. The footnote should give information related to the appreciation of the line, not simply historical background. By the way, the word "alluring" is an interesting choice of the translator in terms of the "writing footnotes into the translation" method to be discussed a little later.

There are also translators who like to use similar references in the target language instead of translation and/or transliteration with footnotes. For instance, a translator used Hamlet for a Chinese prince of irresolute character. At the first glance, this seems a clever invention. But such an invention may often cause confusion in the minds of readers/audiences in the target language when they, consciously or unconsciously, think of the identity or nativeness of the character. In like manner, when an allusion is not a proper noun or a phrase, but a well-known line, it is also dangerous to approximate it with a line of similar meaning and popularity. Such an approximation may sometimes appear a natural and happy equivalent, but more often than not it will be misleading. When the translator who uses Hamlet for the

Chinese prince puts "… ay, there's the rub!" into his mouth (though in terms of literal, verbal meaning of the original it is a correct approximation), he is tinting the Chinese character with the hue of Shakespeare's Hamlet, which would very likely create a wrong impression to English-speaking people.

The third difficulty of footnoting is that it is sometimes hard to ascertain the real source of an allusion of which the writer or speaker was actually thinking. For example, many modern English and Chinese people know Romeo and Juliet as a couple of young lovers. But when they allude to these characters, they may think of Shakespeare's play, or simply movies and other secondary sources based upon the story. This means that in the course of time "specific" allusions may become "general" references and, then, become mixed up with proverbs. And writers and speakers are not thinking of the original specific sources at all when they come to use them. In such a case, it seems advisable that the translator's first job is to footnote the function of an allusion, with or without an explanation of the source. Sometimes when the source is of no importance, he may translate such an allusion with a common expression. It is, for instance, better to put " 說曹操曹操就到 " into "Speak of the devil and he will appear," rather than "Speak of Cao Cao and Cao Cao will be here (there) right away." Happy translations like this are not found very often and translators have to be specially conscientious in making sure if, to use the above example, the Cao Cao in the original is a kind of devil and if the devil in the English expression is a devil, both in the ordinary sense of the words as well as in application and connotation.

But what should a translator do when he has to render something for the ears, like a play for the stage? The speaker cannot stop to explain the meaning of an allusion. To deal with this, Peter Arnott's approach of "writing footnotes into the translation" is a necessary evil, if it is not a satisfactory answer. And the writing in of such information would mean the taking of greater pains than producing the alternative of separate footnotes. Arnott has clearly demonstrated this method when he says that though Fitts makes a major concession to the audience by translating *Andromeda* into "That play by Euripides, *Andromeda*," yet it is not good enough. Fitts has not indicated the nature of the play — a new, exotic type of tragedy, and this information is significant to the appreciation of Aristophanes' attitude toward Euripides in his *Frogs*. So Arnott himself revises it as "That play by Euripides, *The Perils of Andromeda*," and he hopes that the audience will associate it "with *The Perils of Pauline*, or, even if they do not, that the title will be self-explanatory." (Arrowsmith, 1961) Arnott's comment on Fitts is certainly justified. But would his revision risk the danger of misleading the audience to mistake *The Perils of Andromeda* as Euripides' original title? To most modern audiences not familiar with Euripides' works, very likely it would. Facing such a problem, if the translator cannot think of any better method, he should at least ask himself the following questions before he makes his decision: (a) what harm would such a risk do the audience? and (b) how much would the added information help the audience? If the benefit is greater than the harm, it may be worth the risk.

Generally speaking, this built-in type of footnoting would make lines more comprehensible for the listener in the target language, and should be as brief as possible in order to avoid misleading or affecting the rhythm of the original. Therefore we can perhaps say that since *The Perils of Pauline* is not a very popularly known work, Arnott's rendering might well be shortened to "Euripides' exotic play *Andromeda*" or "That exotic tragedy *Andromeda*." In this light, the above-mentioned "alluring" is also a good example of the built-in explanation, since in the Chinese original the phrase used to modify Xi Shi is a neutral one without any bewitching and seductive connotation. So far we can say that careful employment of this method is very useful not only in translating plays for production or poetry for recitation, but also in rendering materials for reading pleasure only. The detailed footnotes may co-exist, even in translating for the stage, because information or explanation in some detail may save time for actors in the creation of their roles and directors in the preparation of the production. In addition to indicating the nature or characteristics of allusions, the built-in footnoting can also be adopted for providing essential information for proper names, special plants and animals, proverbs and terms peculiar to the source language, and referents non-existent in the target language. It should not cause any complication or confusion if a translator adds "the Capital" to "I persuaded him to go to Nanjing" and makes it "I persuaded him to go to Nanjing, the Capital." The translator may also use parenthesis to indicate his own addition like "I have studied all the classics, astronomy, geography, and the three doctrines [of Confucianism, Taoism, and Buddhism]."

So much for the problems of translating allusions without referents and references in the target language, and the considerations of footnoting. But a greater problem, and possibly a trap too, lies in the existence of the same referent in the target language, but without the same association and/or symbolical meaning. Take the mythological animal 龍 in Chinese, which has often been rendered into English as "dragon." But in Chinese tradition the 龍 is believed to be a heavenly being or creature, whereas a dragon is generally associated with evil in Western folktales and literature. A Chinese 龍 can be evil only when it is qualified by adjectives of evil nature or implication: for examples, 惡龍 (evil or wicked 龍) and 蛟龍 (a serpent-like 龍 or dragon). Of ordinary animals, the bird 鴛鴦 of the aix genus is conventionally taken as a symbol for happily married couples in Chinese. A cuckoo bird of the cuculus genus known as 杜鵑 is a favourite image of Chinese poets and playwrights; and to most Chinese, who know or do not know its literary source, the crying of the bird symbolizes heart-breaking sorrow. The 布穀 bird of the same genus has also a very different association in Chinese from what is usually associated with cuckoos in English. If these two birds are translated into "mandarin ducks" and "cuckoos," they will lose their original colour virtually and symbolically, even to the English-speaking people who have seen such birds in the zoo or park. Images developed from such references are perhaps even more difficult to appreciate in the target language (e.g., 野鴛鴦 , meaning "wild mandarin ducks" for illicit lovers).

Allusions with such referents and references are common in Chinese literature and everyday speech, and some of them have long passed from the "specific" into the "general." Now, no matter whether such allusions are of the "specific" kind or the "general," since any zoologically faithful translation would not work, any invention is better than omission. For instance, on many occasions "lovebirds" would be better for 鴛鴦 than "mandarin ducks." Special consideration would also be required in footnoting such allusions.

There is another aspect worth our attention. In modern literature there is a new type of allusion — allusions from the target language. A very common example is the use of Romeo and Juliet as a symbol for devoted young lovers in Chinese short stories and novels by contemporary writers. It looks very easy to render such an allusion — simply by changing the Chinese words for these two names back into English. But such a "restoration" is very often tasteless; it is somehow like "translating" pidgin English expressions of Chinese origin (e.g., "people mountain people sea" and "long time no see") back into Chinese. All the interesting "strangeness," both good and bad, is lost and the peculiar flavour of pidgin English in the text of normal English is completely gone. The original interestingness in the source language becomes flat and plain in the "translation back to the original." Though an indication of some kind — a separate footnote or a built-in-one — may let the reader/audience of the target language "know" the fact, it can never make them "feel" the same thing the reader/audience of the source language would enjoy. In facing such a difficulty, theoretically the best solution is perhaps to sacrifice the literal fidelity in favour of the aesthetic function of the allusion. In practice, to replace it with a similar new "foreign" allusion known to the people of the target language may not be a bad way to achieve the original function in the work. An accompanying footnote is essential to explain the translator's invention for the benefit of the conscientious readers.

Last but not least is the problem of translating allusions originally footnoted, like those in T. S. Eliot's "The Waste Land," which, as some scholars have pointed out, are in part "guying" the reader. In rendering such a poem *and* the original notes into Chinese, additional footnotes are often essential not only to indicate that they are Eliot's own notes but also to provide some explanation about the context of the event, meaning, or tone each of the allusions calls up. The most unusual example of the use of allusion and footnote in a Chinese work one may come across is perhaps the popular expression " 道高一尺 / 魔高一丈 " (meaning literally "the 道 [or good] is a foot high, but the 魔 [or evil] is ten feet high") in the revised Acting Edition of *The Red Lantern* 〈紅燈記〉 of 1970, which is in nature a propaganda drama of the Chinese communists. Here, the captured Chinese hero is arguing with a Japanese officer and the hero uses it to suggest that though the Japanese army is strong for the time being the Chinese will prove ten times stronger at the end. But no Chinese who considers himself on the just side of a battle would identify himself with the 魔 or evil. The authors of the play must know this too, and that must be why they add a long footnote to explain that the 魔 means the Japanese and the 道 means the Chinese against the Japanese invaders. One English translation of the line reads: "The evil is strong, but the good is ten times stronger," without the original note (*Five Chinese Communist Plays*). Though the translation has correctly expressed the original "intention" it has lost the interesting complication rising from the unusual use of the phrase, especially if it is heard in the theatre. Another translation reads: "The law is strong, but the outlaws are ten times stronger," with the original note (*China on Stage*). It might be more "faithful" if an additional one is added to explain that this footnote was provided in the original text and also that it is an unusual or abnormal use of the expression.

All in all, no matter what approach or method the translator chooses to use to approximate an allusion, pun, or other image peculiar to the source language, he has to have the context and the total text of the work in mind. He must also be clear in his mind for whom his translation is intended, as this concerns his choice of diction, the nature and detail of footnotes, etc. He should ponder on the individual expressions in the light of the work as a whole in order to preserve the original meaning, spirit, rhythm, and atmosphere. And when it proves impossible to reproduce the total significance of the original, he must invent something to save its spirit — and invention is better than complete omission.

References

Arrowsmith, William and Roger Shattuck, eds. *The Craft and Context of Translation*. Austin, Texas: University of Texas Press, 1961.

Birch, Cyril. "Translating and Transmuting Yuan and Ming Plays: Problems and Possibilities." *Literature East and West*, Vol. 14, No. 4 (1970).

Brower, Reuben A., ed. *On Translation*. Cambridge, Mass.: Harvard University Press, 1959.

Chao, Yuen Ren. "Dimensions of Fidelity in Translation with Special Reference to Chinese." *Harvard Journal of Asiatic Studies*, Vol. 29 (1969), pp. 109–30.

Forster, Leonare. "Translation: An Introduction." In *Aspects of Translation*, edited by The Communication Research Centre, University College of London. London: Secker and Warburg, 1958.

Hwang, Mei-shu. "Peking Opera: A Study on the Art of Translating the Scripts with Special Reference to Structure and Conventions." Doctoral dissertation, Florida State University, 1976.

BACK-TRANSLATION

Back-translation: A Tool for Cross-cultural Research

Richard W. Brislin
Institute of Culture and Communication
East West Center, Honolulu, Hawaii, U.S.A.

Carolina Freimanis
Center for Interpretation and Translation Studies
The University of Hawaii, Manoa, Hawaii, U.S.A.

Language is the basic tool for communication and yet it can also be a source of misunderstanding, even between people who share the same linguistic and cultural background. Communication across cultures has the added problem of transferring meanings and concepts to peoples of diverse languages and cultures, and the potential for misunderstandings under these circumstances can be staggering. Translation serves as an aid to cross-cultural communication but the problems encountered in the translation process are such that some authors have said that it is "probably the most complex type of event yet produced in the evolution of the cosmos." (Richards, 1953:247–62)

Several translation methods have been proposed for cross-cultural research purposes, and among them the one that is most recommended is back-translation, for several reasons: (1) it is particularly useful in the case when the researcher has little knowledge of the target language and has to rely upon the translators, since they cannot read the target version and make a judgment concerning the quality of the translation; (2) because it has the advantage of "decentering" the questionnaire away from the original language form; decentering is a translation concept that will be presented in more detail later; and (3) because experience with back-translation has yielded a set of guidelines to write research instruments in a more translatable English, not only to ensure good translations but also to create and modify items that will be understandable to respondents. The first part of this article will present an overview of the different translation theories, the problems encountered in the process of translating cross-cultural research instruments, and the different types of translation methods that can be used in conjunction with back-translation. The second part will present the back-translation method, its problems and variations, and finally the set of guidelines that was developed for writing translatable English.

Translation Theories

There have been many attempts to create a comprehensive theory of translation that takes into account the many elements involved in the translation process and thus provides the translator with a system that could be applied to all types of texts. For example, Casagrande (1954:20, 335–40) classified translation into four types: (1) *pragmatic translation*, concerned mainly with translating information accurately into the target language, paying little attention to stylistic matters; an example is the translation of technical documents or instruction manuals in which translators have no concern other than getting the information across in the second language; (2) *aesthetic-poetic translation*, concerned not only with the message but also with the effect, emotion, and feelings of the original language version, the aesthetic form used by the author (e.g., sonnet, heroic couplet, dramatic dialogue) as well as the message. The clearest examples are in the translation of literature; (3) *ethnographic translation*, which regards translation more as a communication process and strives to include the cultural context of the source and target language versions. Translators have to be sensitive to the way words are used and must know how they fit into the cultures which use the source and the target languages; and (4) *linguistic translation*, concerned with the grammatical and linguistic aspects of the text, striving to achieve an equivalent target language version, not only in meaning but also in structure. According to Chau (1984), translation is a process of code transference where the translator looks for lexical equivalents in code B and arranges them according to its syntactic rules. For example, a sentence like: "You, he, and I have won a prize each" should be translated into Chinese as "I, you, and he have won a prize each" in order to sound natural, because the order of the first, second and third persons are expressed differently in English and Chinese. Another case is the use of the passive voice in different languages. For example, if the sentence "He was sent to America to study" were translated directly into the Thai language, it wouldn't have much sense because the passive "was sent" implies doing something against one's will and in Thailand, going to America is considered a pleasant experience. In order to eliminate this incongruity, the sentence should be translated as "He was sent to school."

Translators know that it is almost impossible to classify a text into any one of those categories since a text may contain elements from most, if not all, of those categories. An important step in the creation of a unified theory of translation was Nida's sociolinguistic model of translation, similar to Casagrande's ethnographical model, which regards translation as an act of communication and analyses the source of the discourse taking into consideration "who said what, to whom, under what circumstances, for what reasons and for what purpose." (Nida, 1964) Given that the main concern of cross-cultural psychology is to obtain behavioral data from different cultures in order to test the generality of psychological concepts as well as to establish differences across cultures, the sociolinguistic model of translation is also a useful guide for solving the problems encountered in translations for cross-cultural purposes.

Translation Problems in Cross-cultural Research

According to Sechrest, Fay and Zaidi (1972:41–56), cross-cultural researchers need to translate four types of materials from their original English-language: (1) the translation of orientations or introductions given to the subjects about the research that will be carried out; (2) the translation of instructions for the tasks and measures being used; (3) the translation of the research instrument (questionnaires, interviews, inventories, etc.); and (4) the translation of responses when limited response alternatives (true-false, etc.) are not used.

The basic problem translators have to deal with in this, as in any other type of translation, is that of equivalence, i.e., whether the target text is equivalent in meaning to the original or source text. Judgements about translation quality can be guided by giving emphasis on meaning, but this is very difficult to do since there are no specific criteria for translation quality and there can be many possible good translations of any one text. However, a rule of thumb has been suggested by Nida (1964:164) who stated that one of the requirements of translation is to "produce a similar response" from readers of a source and target version. As in behavioristic psychology, an observable, verifiable response may be the standard for an ultimate criterion of translation equivalence and quality.

In general, translators have to deal with problems of linguistic equivalence and of cultural and psychological equivalence. Linguistic equivalence problems can be categorized as follows.

Vocabulary Problems

It is generally believed that the best way to find equivalent terms in the target language is using dictionaries, but quite often, these are a poor source of information and can even be a source of confusion. Words, as they are used in any given target culture, seldom appear in dictionaries and the translator must be knowledgeable of, or have access to, the terminology used by the target audience. Butcher and Garciá (1978:473) make reference to the importance of the target audience in an example of the translation of an item on the Minnesota Multiphasic Personality Inventory (MMPI) which includes the word "hobbies." A first translation into Spanish used the word *distracciones*, but they found that word "had vague connotations and was too imprecise." Given that most Spanish-speakers use the English word hobbies, the translators of a second version decided to leave it untranslated because it conveyed the meaning intended in the original. It should be noted, however, that translators are usually discouraged to use foreign words or anglicisms in their work, and yet translations for cross-cultural research purposes must make allowances for, and indeed encourage, the use of such words if they are commonly used in the target culture.

Similar problems are found in Chinese. For example, in Taiwan the word "taxi" is translated as *ji cheng che* 計程車 . However, in Hong Kong, where the English influence is greater, the term *di shi* 的士 in Cantonese, a close phonetic approximation of the English word, is used. If *di shi* 的士 were used in Taiwan, the term would have no meaning.

Word choice can be a serious problem in cases where there is a wide variation of terminology across cultures that use the same language. In

Spanish-speaking cultures, for example, a word that is used in one country might be totally unknown or used differently in another. If translators are not aware of these nuances, they might run the risk not only of making meaning errors, but also of using terms that might be incomprehensible or even offensive in the target culture. Take the word "bug," for example: if the target audience were Venezuelan, translators could use the word *bicho*, but they better not use the word for a Puerto Rican audience, because in their language culture that term is an obscenity. Likewise, translators could use the word *chinche*, but that would work only in Mexico since in most other countries that word refers to a specific insect and not to "bugs" in general. This example puts in evidence another problem with word choice, namely, that of register. In the above example, "bug" is used as a colloquialism for "insect," and translators must strive to maintain that same register in the translated version rather than use the higher-register term *insecto*.

Another problem with dictionaries is that they offer many choices for one word and it is not always easy to know which term to use in any given case. In the above example, the word "bug" might not refer to an insect at all but to a listening device, so it is important to know the context in which the word appears. The importance of context in the translation process cannot be over-emphasized and it has been cited by researchers in this area as having major effects on the quality of a translation. Werner and Campbell (1969) pointed out that a word is translated least adequately when it is translated as a single item, that translation improves when a word is a part of a sentence, and is even better when the sentence is a part of a paragraph. Thus a good translator will never give equivalents for terms without asking first questions like: "What is the context?" or "What exactly do you mean?" Researchers should be prepared to supply this context for their translators.

Evidently, there can be terms in one language for which there are no equivalents in the other. For example, during a research seminar, the authors recently asked members of different cultures to give three examples of mentor's advice in their respective cultures. The word "mentor" was problematic for some of the participants since the concept of "mentor" is not as common in other cultures as it is in the United States. The term was explained as someone who is wise and offers advice and the variety of examples given by the participants ranged from advice given by "old people" in oriental cultures like China, to that given by "parents" and *padrinos* in Latin American cultures.

Shi Xiaojing, formerly a conference interpreter at the United Nations and currently teaching at the Center for Interpretation and Translation Studies at the University of Hawaii at Manoa, was part of this research seminar and she reported the difficulties in translating the concept of "mentor" into Chinese. The dictionary gives several variations: *liangshi yiyou* 良師益友, which translates back into "good teacher, helpful friend," or *siren jiaoshi* 私人教師 (private tutor) and 輔導教師 which means "instructing" or "guiding teacher." In all these meanings, the Chinese concept and relationship of "teacher" and "student" are paramount and the sense of respect, obedience and subordination is strong. In English, the word has more connotations of "counsellor" and "guide" than outright "teacher". Depending on which connotations are required, different translations would be needed. If the mentor were someone in a higher position, the term used in the PRC, *lao shangji* 老上級, literally "old superior" (in the familiar respectful sense) could be used. If the sense of "older and more experienced" is needed, *zhangbei* 長輩 ("elder" or "senior") would be more appropriate. If the experience aspect is to be emphasized, *jingyan fengfude ren* 經驗豐富的人 ("person with rich experience") is a possible version. If a study was to be done in the United States and China that dealt with advice given to young people, the phrase "advice given by a person with rich experience" could be used in the English language version of the research instrument. The English language choice would be influenced by the availability of a better translation in Chinese than the word "mentor."

A final note with respect to vocabulary equivalence has to do with the common belief that problems are more serious between pairs of languages whose cultural and linguistic differences are larger. In fact, languages that are close culturally and linguistically present problems that are just as serious. Languages like English and Spanish have words that share the same etymological roots and while these words may have the same form and look the same, their meaning is quite different. Word pairs like "compromise-*compromiso*," "actual-*actual*," and "adequate-*adecuado*," are examples of cognates, or "*faux amis*," and translators must be always on guard in order to avoid them because it is easy to fall into the trap and make a type of error that is, unfortunately, quite prevalent. These errors can be avoided if the translator assumes that when a word looks the same in Spanish and in English, it will almost always have different meanings.

Idiomatic Problems

Translators often find that idioms in one language seldom translate into another. In a series of guidelines to write research instruments with "translatable English" in mind, Brislin (1986:137–64) argues that it is advisable to avoid metaphors and colloquialisms since they are less likely to have equivalents in other languages and the translator would have to resort to explain the concept using many words in order to convey the meaning. However, according to Sechrest, Fay and Zaidi (1972:45) that would "produce a highly stilted, pedantic form of discourse that would be utterly unsuitable for research efforts with the general population in any culture." Although colloquialisms can be avoided when writing or modifying research instruments, that is not always possible, especially in the case of verbal responses of subjects. The translator must then find an equivalent of the expression, in meaning if not in form. For example, the English expression: "A stitch in time may save nine" has an idiomatic equivalent in Spanish, *más vale prevenir que lamentar*, which is closer to the English: "Better safe than sorry." Even though the two expressions are not equivalent in terms of vocabulary or in terms of the image they elicit, the meaning is the same and the language register is maintained.

Grammatical-syntactical Equivalence

Most languages differ in grammar and syntax, and problems may arise because there are no equivalent parts of speech, for example the use of gender in Spanish nouns and verb forms, and its absence in their English counterparts. Problems with verbs are also very common when striving to achieve equivalence in translations, because "not all languages deal with the problems of verb mood, voice, or tense in the same way, and it is sometimes very difficult in a given language to put expressions which have the same verb form or meaning in English." (Sechrest, Fay and Zaidi, 1972:46)

Syntactical differences might also affect the meaning in translations. For example, the use of negative wordings in English sentences might create problems in other languages, specially in items that require a true or false answer, in which case the wording of the item as well as the scoring key could be changed. For example the phrase "I can read a long time without tiring my eyes" may not translate smoothly into other languages and to avoid any possible misunderstanding, it could be reworded as "My eyes get tired when I read for a long time."

The problems of cultural equivalence are somewhat different because, besides the linguistic component, translators must take into account the cultural and psychological background of the target population. These types of problems can be classified as experiential and conceptual.

Experiential

Translations of research instruments must use terms that refer to things and experiences that exist in the cultures under study. In cross-cultural terms, translations should strive to preserve both the *etic* or core component, which refers to "a phenomenon, or aspects of a phenomenon, which have a common meaning across the cultures under investigation," (Brislin, 1986:140) as well as the *emic* component, or the aspects that are specific of any given culture. Emics are not necessarily shared by the cultures under study but they are related to a shared etic, so translators must know what psychological construct is being studied and search for its emic manifestation in the target culture. Sechrest, Fay and Zaidi (1972:47) give the example of an item *intended* to test femininity (etic component) which reads: "I like the work of a florist." In some cultures, most florists are women and thus a florist (emic) conveys an effeminate outlook. However, there might be countries where the concept of a florist or even a flower shop does not exist so the task of the translator is to find an equivalent activity that is carried out mainly by women in the target country in order to adapt the item for that culture.

Experiential variations are not limited to instances where cultures differ so much that finding an equivalent is difficult, if not impossible. Problems may also arise because the cultural arrangements are different in the target culture. For example, the experience students have in universities in the United States in terms of classroom behaviour, classroom management, student-teacher relationships, and even social interactions differ greatly from the experience students of other cultures may have, so statements about student life are unlikely to be equivalent for two different cultures. (Sechrest, Fay and Zaidi, 1972:48)

Conceptual

The problem here is to ensure that the concepts used in the original and the translated instrument have equivalent connotations. For example, both cultures might use a word that when translated seem to be in agreement, and yet the concepts behind them are not equivalent. For example, in English, the word "discussion" can be translated into Spanish as *discusion*, without many problems with respect to vocabulary equivalence. However, in Spanish, *discusion* almost always implies an argument or a fight, whereas in English that is not necessarily the case.

Another problem may arise when a concept that is common in one culture does not exist in another, making it difficult to have instruments that are conceptually equivalent for both cultures. Using once again the example of the experiences of students in different cultures, it would be difficult to find a concept or a term that has the same connotations as the concept of a fraternity or a sorority in an American university. If an item in a test made reference to the social experience of students in fraternities, for example, translators would have to explain that fraternities are "clubs" for male students only, that they are named after letters from the Greek alphabet, that they perform strange initiation rituals, and that the social implications of belonging to one of those "clubs" are important.

Shi Xiaojing was involved in a research project in which the difficulty of translating some concepts into Chinese was obvious. For example, the concept of "privacy" presents difficulties because all versions have connotations at variance with the concept as it is used in non-oriental cultures, e.g., the "right to privacy" as in the Universal Declaration of Human Rights. The terms *siren shenghuo* 私人生活 , "private life" or *geren shenghuo* 個人生活 , "personal life," do not cover the whole scope of "privacy;" *siyin* 私隱 often means "secret" or "private matter one wants to hide" and implies something indecent, illicit or embarrassing. For the older generation, these terms have a derogatory meaning, but younger people are more used to them. In Taiwan, the "right to privacy" is called *siyin quan* 私隱權 , and although it is coming into use in the PRC, its connotation is still sexual.

Another concept that presents difficulties is "dating." In Chinese, "dating" means literally going out with someone, and it does not necessarily have the connotation of courting or "falling in love." The Chinese equivalent of "dating" is *you yuehui* 有約會 , but to include the meaning of "courting" or "falling in love," other terms must be used. A more serious kind of relationship is called *tan lian'ai* 談戀愛 (literally "talk romance") or *jiao pengyou* 交朋友 (establish "friendship" relations).

Many translations are equivalent only in an abstract sense while their specific meanings are quite different. Werner and Campbell give the following example of the different implications a simple sentence can have when we know the cultural background in which it is found. The sentence "John plants corn" is not totally equivalent to the sentence "Ashkii plants corn" if we know that John is a farmer in Iowa who has all the latest technology and Ashkii is a traditional Navaho, who plants corn by hand, following sacred rituals and singing sacred songs to assure a plentiful harvest. These connotations can be crucial in translation, specially in translations of cross-cultural research instruments that test, for example, the impact of technological change. Thus, "translation is not simply code switching, where one code is unambiguously retrievable if the other is given. The world of different speakers is not just the same world with different labels attached." (Werner and Campbell, 1970:403)

Most of the problems that arise in the use of cross-cultural research instruments stem from the fact that these are usually developed in one culture and the content and structure of personality that they are testing do not necessarily transfer to other cultures. One solution is to adapt the existing instruments, or write new ones in order to have a decentered or symmetrical translation. In this process, the original version is changed according to the results obtained in the analysis of its back-translations. The final result is a source language version that is not centered around any specific culture or language, and a target language version that is smooth and natural-sounding and also maintains the meaning and the tone of the original.

In many types of translations (e.g., of the Bible), modifying the original is almost impossible but in the case of translations for cross-cultural research purposes, decentering, and therefore the modification of the already existing materials, is almost always necessary. Butcher (1982; Butcher and García, 1978; Butcher and Clark, 1979) has worked on the cross-cultural applications of the MMPI and the basic rule for item modification is to maintain the infrapsychology of the item which may or may not be apparent from its content and can be different from what it suggests. Thus, translators must "know the empirical connotations of an item as well as its linguistic and literal referents." For example, the item "I think Lincoln was greater than Washington," found on the MMPI must be modified because it does not have any meaning outside the United States. Translators must find a substitute for those historical figures in the target culture, maintaining "the differences between the images of these two historical figures (i.e., one a humanist and the other a militarist or liberator)." (Butcher and García, 1978:474)

There is a close relation between the modification of existing items, the creation of new ones and their subsequent translation into other languages. Several methods have been proposed which include checks on the translation quality needed for research in cross-cultural psychology. These methods can be used separately or combined according to the needs of any one research project.

1. *Back-translation*, which will be discussed in greater detail later in this entry.
2. The *bilingual technique*, in which bilinguals take the same test, or different groups take different halves of a test, in the two languages that they know. Items yielding discrepant responses, or differing frequency of responses, can be easily identified. The advantage of the technique is its preciseness and the potential for using sophisticated statistics and test concepts such as item analysis and factor analysis (Drasgow and Hulin, 1990). The disadvantage is that the research instrument is being developed on the basis of responses from an atypical group, bilinguals.
3. The *committee* approach, in which a group of bilinguals translates from the source to the target language. The mistakes of one member can be caught by others on the committee. The weakness of the method is that committee members may not criticize one another, and may even unite against the researcher.
4. *Pretest* procedures. After a translation is completed, it should be field tested to ensure that people will comprehend all the material to which they will be expected to respond. There is no weakness *per se* with this method. Indeed, all translated material should be field tested. But, of course, the technique will only be as effective as the interviewers doing the pretesting.

Werner and Campbell (1970:402) have suggested that the "trick" of translation is the mapping procedure, particularly the mapping of the semantic structure of the target language. The recommended type of translation method is back-translation, which is a special case of the mapping of equivalent sets of sentences in one language onto a set in another, and also has the advantage of decentering the research instrument from the original language.

Back-translation

In back-translation, a researcher prepares material in one language and asks a bilingual to translate it into the target language. A second bilingual, who has not seen the original version, then translates the material back into the original language. The sequence would be: original–target–original (back-translation). The purpose of back-translation is not to obtain a polished version in the original language (back-translated version) but a literal version of the translation (e.g., the example below) in order to be able to check its quality, and to later allow tests of meaning equivalence. The advantage of this process is that a person who does not know the target language can examine the two source language forms (original and back-translation) and make a preliminary judgement about the quality of the translation.

Mildred Larson (1984) gives the following example of a source text that was translated into the Aguaruna language of Peru and then back translated into English:

Source text: Title: The Orphan Boy

There once was a man who lived alone with his wife. They had no children. He said to his relatives, "Please have pity on me. I want a child to raise so that I will have someone to go with me when I go to work." Then one of his relatives named Wampukus answered, "There is a child at my house who has no parents. He is nearly grown up. I will give him to you, but be careful. He will pester you all the time asking to go and swim across the river. On the other hand he is an obedient child." Then he went and brought the child to the man …

Back-translation: Title: An Orphan Child Which Was Brought Up

A married man who was childless, just the two of them living together, asked his relatives, "You pity me, I want to be able to have a child in order to raise the child, in order that he accompany me while I am working." He saying that, Wampukus answered, "At my house there lives a child who is motherless, almost grown-up. That I will give to you, but be careful, he will cause you to suffer, being one who desires to swim in the river in order to go across. However, he is one who obeys what he is told." Advising like that he brought him …

As can be seen, even though the meaning is maintained in the back-translation, it sounds awkward. In order to eliminate this awkwardness, the differences between the original and the back-translation could be analyzed, and idiomatic phrases such as "He will pester you," which was back-translated as "He will cause you to suffer" could be eliminated or changed in the original until a satisfactory target language version is obtained. This is the beginning of the decentering process: the analysis of the back-translated version would give insights as to the nature of the Aguaruna language which in turn would determine the changes that should be made in the English version. This rewritten version would be then back translated again until a smooth, natural sounding version in the second language is obtained.

Therefore, when back-translation is properly applied, it is an iterative process, i.e., after the first sequence of original to target to original is made, the back-translated version is examined and corrected, and then it is back-translated again, revised, etc. Translators at every stage must be very critical of their work to ensure that this iterative process yields a better and better approximation to the original.

Here is how the decentering procedure works in actual practice. (Brislin *et al.*, 1973:38–39) An original language version of a question or test item such as the following is given to a translator. This item is from the Marlowe-Crowne Social Desirability scale (Crowne and Marlowe, 1964); respondents would answer "true" or "false" as the item applies to them.

> I don't find it particularly difficult to get along with loud-mouthed, obnoxious people.

Brislin (1970:185–216) had this translated into Chamorro, the language of Guam and the Marianas Islands and then back-translated into English. The terms "particularly" and "obnoxious" were not in the back-translation, and the bilinguals explained that there were no good Chamorro equivalents. The first back-translated version was given to another bilingual (not the original version, as above). The decentering process had started, as the nature of the Chamorro language determined the decisions made about the English language version. In the second back-translation, "get along with" was replaced by "talk with," the bilinguals pointing out that the Chamorro term for the latter would be more understandable to the projected population of respondents.

Another translation and back-translation showed word-for-word equivalence and the final version was:

It is not hard for me to talk with people who have a big mouth.

Since this revised version led to a good Chamorro translation and the original version did not, it was subsequently used for the cross-cultural study comparing English-speaking and Chamorro-speaking people and for the actual data gathering process. Back-translation can then guide the final decisions about the wording of the original language version through the decentering process which determines the changes that must be made.

When the researcher compares the last back-translated version with the original version and finds a concept that "survives" the decentering procedure, it is assumed to be etic since there must be readily available words and phrases in the two languages which the translators could use. If a concept is not in the final back-translated version, the reason could be that it is emic, i.e., the concept might be readily expressible in only one of the languages. At this point, there should be extensive discussions with the bilinguals who can indicate reasons why materials were and were not translatable. For instance, Phillips (1960:188) found it very difficult to have this sentence stem translated into the Thai language: "Sometimes a good quarrel is necessary because ..." He wrote, "After much discussion the translators decided that although it was conceivable that an American might enjoy a quarrel for its cathartic effect, the notion would be incomprehensible to a Thai." To use the terms already introduced, "having a good quarrel" is not an etic. Rather, the translation procedure has pointed up a very important difference which can be built into cross-cultural investigations of interpersonal relationships.

Problems with Back-translation and Variations on the Method

As with any type of translation method, care should be taken in the use of back-translation. Problems may arise in the different stages due to the quality of the translators being used. For example, if the translator who did the back-translation is careless or lacks experience, the result could be a bad back-translation of a good translation. The obvious solution is to work with professional translators who are knowledgeable of the subject matter as well as of the target language and culture.

According to Sechrest, Fay and Zaidi (1972:51), the first back-translation usually shows discrepancies between the two original versions. This, however, should not be regarded as a flaw in the method but as a way to control the quality of the translation as well as a source of information as to which items can and cannot be transmitted in the target culture. Indeed, back-translation serves as "a filter through which non-equivalent terms will not readily pass. If there is not an appropriate word or phrase in a target language for one in the source language, that fact has a high probability of being discovered. The investigator will be able to decide fairly accurately just what concepts he can employ in the two languages. He need not speculate; he can act on the bases of the back-translation results." (Sechrest, Fay and Zaido, 1972:51)

Like any single method or approach, back-translation is no panacea and researchers should not depend solely on it. All materials should be pre-tested with respondents similar to those in the proposed main sample since there will always be items which simply do not work well in actual use. Also, there could be errors that go undetected without the pre-test procedure and this might help researchers devise means to solve them not only for the present instrument but also for future use. For example, problems can occasionally arise if a highly skilled bilingual can make sense out of a mangled target version. Just as all readers of this entry can make sense out of broken English when interacting with visitors from other countries, back-translators can sometimes take very rough materials and polish them so much that they appear as "diamonds" in the final version. To avoid this, a fourth step in the back-translation is suggested in which one of the best translators could be asked to read a translation and tell the writer if (1) the grammar was good, (2) if words are used which most native speakers would understand, and (3) if he felt that other people would have any problem reading the material and answering questions about it. In such a case, the four-step sequence would be: original to target; target to target (check); and target to original. This procedure assumes that the translation checker is willing to be critical, an assumption probably not possible in some cultures.

When this suggested procedure is not possible, another related variation of the back-translation procedure could be used, in which researchers could ask monolinguals similar to the respondents to rewrite the material instead of using a translator to check the target version. In such a case, the sequence would be: original to target (bilingual 1); target to target rewrite (monolingual); target rewrite to original (bilingual 2). Although adding the target check or rewrite steps minimizes the possibility of errors, pre-testing is still necessary. Indeed, it is always desirable to use multiple methods when translating research instruments, and the use of back-translation and pre-testing gives favourable results.

Another variation involves the use of a monolingual to rewrite the original items. This would ensure a better understanding of the original English version by the translators since it would be written in a "translatable English," thus avoiding many errors in the back-translated version. The sequence in this case would be: original to original rewrite (monolingual); original rewrite to target (bilingual); and target to original (bilingual).

Another method was proposed by Werner and Campbell (1972:412) which is particularly useful when the researcher knows very little of the target language and wants to know the quality of the translators he or she is employing. The technique involves the use of two translators: one translates the first half and the other the second half of the material; then each translator works back into English using the translated version done by the other, the end result being also two translated versions. In this way, if there are discrepancies, the researcher can go through each problem with both translators, discussing both the translations and the back-translations to find their cause and this will enable the researcher to select good translators and thus obtain the best target version of the instrument.

Working with Translators to Produce a More "Translatable English"

One of the results of the back-translation procedure was the development of a set of guidelines useful for any sort of item preparation, whether for new items or modification of existing items, which has been presented in the cross-cultural literature as "guidelines for writing material which is readily translatable." (Brislin, Lonner and Thorndike, 1973; Brislin, 1986) These rules were developed by giving a wide variety of English language materials to bilinguals competent in English and in a variety of other languages, and then determining the successes and failures in their translation efforts. The purpose of these guidelines is to assure that translators will:

1. Have a clear understanding of the original language item;

2. Have a high probability of finding a readily available target language equivalent so that they do not have to use convoluted or unfamiliar terms;
3. Be able to produce target language items readily understandable by the eventual set of respondents who are part of the data gathering stage of the research project. (Brislin, 1986:143)

The suggested guidelines are as follows:

1. Use short simple sentences of less than sixteen words.
2. Employ the active rather than the passive voice.
3. Repeat nouns instead of using pronouns.
4. Avoid metaphors and colloquialisms.
5. Avoid the subjunctive, for example verb forms with "could," "would," "should."
6. Add sentences to provide context for key ideas.
7. Avoid adverbs and prepositions telling "where" or "when" (e.g., frequently, beyond, upper).
8. Avoid possessive forms where possible.
9. Use specific rather than general terms (e.g., the specific animal such as cows, chickens, or pigs rather than the general term "livestock").
10. Avoid words indicating vagueness regarding some event or thing (e.g., probably, maybe, perhaps).
11. Use wording familiar to the translators.
12. Avoid sentences with two different verbs if the verbs suggest two different actions.

After writing the items following these suggestions, the next step would be to translate the material into another language. Assume that a questionnaire is to be translated; if the back-translation technique is used, it has the additional advantage of "decentering" the questionnaire away from the original language form. The result of decentering contrasts with the awkward, stilted versions common when material in one language is taken as the final content that must be translated with minimal change into another language.

Conclusions

Translation serves as an aid to cross-cultural psychology and researchers have become aware of the difficulties of the translation process by using research instruments in different cultures. The goal of translation is to achieve linguistic, cultural and psychological equivalence and judging its quality is a great concern, especially since there are no specific criteria to guide that process. Of the translation methods proposed for cross-cultural research purposes, back-translation, used in conjunction with pre-testing procedures, has proven to be useful not only to obtain a target language version that is equivalent to the source in meaning and in tone, but also to judge the quality of a translation. When correctly applied, back-translation also "decenters" the research instrument and through this decentering process, it provides insights as to what can and cannot be conveyed in the target culture. In this way, the back-translation procedure can also point to cultural differences which can later be included into other cross-cultural investigations.

References

Brislin, Richard W. "Back-translation for Cross-cultural Research." *Journal of Cross-cultural Psychology*, Vol. 1, No. 3 (1970), pp. 185–216.

———. "The Wording and Translation of Research Instruments." In *Field Methods in Cross-cultural Research*, edited by W. Linner and J. Berry. Newbury Park, Ca: Sage, 1986, pp. 137–64.

———, W. J. Lonner and R. M. Thorndike. *Cross-cultural Research Methods*. New York: Wiley Interscience, 1973.

Butcher, J. N. and R. E. Garciá. "Cross-national Application of Psychological Tests." *Personnel and Guidance Journal*, No. 56 (1978), pp. 472–75.

Casagrande, J. "The Ends of Translation." *International Journal of American Linguistics*, No. 20 (1954), pp. 335–40.

Chau, Simon S. C. "What Does a Translator Learn?" Paper presented at the Monterey Institute of International Studies, Monterey, California, 1984.

Drasgow, F. and C. Hulin. "Item Response Theory." In *Handbook of Industrial and Organizational Psychology*, edited by M. Dunnette and L. Hough, Vol. 1. Palo Alto, Ca: Consulting Psychologists Press, 1990, pp. 577–636.

Larson, Mildred L. *Meaning-based Translation: A Guide to Cross-language Equivalence*. Lanham, MD: University Press of America Inc., 1984.

Nida, Eugene A. "Translating Means Communicating: A Sociolinguistic Theory of Translation." Paper presented at American Translators Association, 1964.

Phillips, H. "Problems of Translation and Meaning in Field Work." *Human Organization*, Vol. 18 (1960), pp. 184–92.

Richards, I. A. "Toward a Theory of Translating." In *Studies in Chinese Thought*, edited by Arthur Wright. Chicago: University of Chicago Press, 1953, pp. 247–62.

Sechrest, L., T. Fay Zaidi and S. M. Hafeez. "Problems of Translation in Cross-cultural Research." *Journal of Cross-cultural Psychology*, Vol. 3, No. 1 (1972), pp. 41–56.

Seleskovitch, Danica. "Zur Theorie des Dolmetschens." In *Probleme von theorie und praxis in der Ausbildung zum Übersetzer und Dolmetscher*, edited by V. Kapp. Heidelberg: Quelle & Meyer, 1974.

Werner, O. and D. T. Campbell. "Translating, Working through Interpreters, and the Problem of Decentering." In *A Handbook of Methods in Cultural Anthropology*, edited by R. Naroll and R. Cohen. New York: Columbia University Press, 1970.

BIBLE TRANSLATION

Factors in Bible Translation

Mildred L. Larson
International Academic Consultant
Summer Institute of Linguistics, Dallas, U.S.A.

Introduction

Translation is the process of communicating the meaning of the source text
in a target language in such a way that the same meaning is communicated
in that language as well. This definition applies to all types of texts. Most of
the factors which are important for other types of translation are also
applicable for Bible translation. However, there are some additional considerations when translating a document which was written long ago, which
has been variously interpreted by many scholars over many years, and
which has a high level of religious connotations as well.

Other books are sometimes translated into several other languages, but
the Bible has been translated into over 270 languages and the New Testament section of the Bible into another 600 languages. Translation is currently in progress in over 1,000 more languages. In addition, hundreds of
commentaries and thousands of books have been written giving scholarly
opinions on the meaning of the Hebrew and Greek texts. The result is that
Bible translation is a unique type of world-wide translation activity. Those
more general factors which have to do with discovering the meaning of a
text which is to be translated will be reviewed first, then the factors which
are especially in focus in translating the biblical texts, and third, those
factors which have to do with sociolinguistic aspects of the target language readership. Finally, the types of translations which result from the

interaction of these factors in making any particular translation are discussed.

Linguistic and Pragmatic Factors

Differing Grammatical Structures

Translation, by definition, is the transfer of the meaning of a text in one language (the source language) into a second language (the target language). The grammatical structures of languages differ, sometimes only slightly, if the two languages are closely related, but more often radically, if the two languages are from differing language families. Until rather recent times, most translations of biblical texts were based on a formal correspondence between the two languages. If the source text used a noun, a noun was used in the target language. If a passive construction was used in the source text, so also in the target language translation. The results were translations which reflected the structure of the biblical texts but which were unnatural and hard to understand in the target translations.

Linguistic studies have had a profound effect on translation. As more and more languages have been described, and the sometimes radical differences in their structures noted, so translators have become more and more aware of the need to use the natural grammatical structures of the target languages in the translations, rather than attempting to keep the forms of Greek and Hebrew. For example, the Greek text abounds in nouns such as *forgiveness*, *faith*, *righteousness*, and *redemption* which actually refer to actions. Many languages of the world do not have equivalent nominal forms but rather only verbs which express the actions mentioned. Even if a nominalized form is available in the target language it may be used in very limited contexts. In either case, verbs, not nouns, would then be used in the translation.

There are certain linguistic features which are peculiar to the biblical texts. For example, two nouns may be joined by *kai* "and", but the meaning is not that of coordination but, rather, a meaning in which one noun modifies the other. For example, Acts 23:6 uses the phrase *of the hope and resurrection* meaning "hope of the resurrection." Luke 2:47 uses the phrase *his understanding and answers* meaning "his intelligent answers". It is unlikely that other languages would have a coordinating word functioning in this same way. Therefore different constructions would be used.

Another well known linguistic structure found especially in the

Gospels is what is known as the Semitic Passive. The passive construction is used in order to avoid pronouncing the name of God. For example, Matt. 13:12 has the expressions *to him shall be given* and *from him shall be taken away* in which the passive in the Greek source text is used to avoid saying *God shall give to him* and *God shall take away from him*. In order for such passages to make sense in the translation the active form will often need to be used.

The above are only a few examples. There are many linguistic contrasts between any two languages. The target translation will likely differ from the source text in use of nouns, use of pronouns, connectors, verb aspects and tense markers, passive constructions, word and phrase order, length of sentences, and other grammatical choices. (For further biblical examples see Beekman and Callow, 1974:212–28.) In order to communicate accurately the meaning of the source text, a translator will carefully consider the linguistic differences between the two languages by comparing the classes of words and the grammatical constructions.

Secondary Meanings

Much of the complication encountered in the process of translating results from the secondary meanings of words and secondary functions of grammatical constructions. A single form in the biblical text, for example, may have various meanings depending on the context. A study of the Greek lexicon makes this quickly evident. It is likely that only the primary meaning will be translated by a literal equivalent in the target language and all the secondary meanings will call for translation by different forms. Thus translation necessitates a careful study of the meaning of words in each of their contexts. For example, the Greek word *sarks* has the primary meaning of "flesh". However, it also has various secondary meanings. The American Standard Version translates all occurrences with *flesh* in English. However, the New English Version translates the secondary meanings with appropriate English terms. (See Nida and Taber, 1974:15–19 for more examples.) Note the following comparison taken from Nida and Taber, page 17:

	ASV	NEB
Luke 24:39	*flesh*	flesh
2 Cor. 7:5	*flesh*	poor body
Rom. 11:14	*flesh*	men of my own race
Acts 2:17	*flesh*	everyone

Rom. 8:3	*flesh*	lower nature
2 Cor. 10:3	*flesh*	weak men
1 Cor. 1:26	*flesh*	human standard

However, secondary meanings are not restricted to the meanings of words. Phrases, and even whole sentences, often have more than one meaning, each meaning being determined by the context in which the phrase or sentence is used. For anyone translating from the Greek New Testament texts, the meanings of the Greek genitive phrases present a variety of problems. For example, the phrase *love of God* sometimes means, "God's love for people", sometimes "people's love for God". (See Chapter 16 of Beekman and Callow, 1974, and pages 35–39 of Nida and Taber, 1974, for more examples.)

The translation of questions found in the Greek texts also presents special problems for the Bible translator. Sometimes the questions are real questions but often they are rhetorical and may have one of several meanings or functions. Beekman and Callow (1974:238) list four functions of questions which are not real questions: (1) a statement of certitude; (2) a statement of incertitude; (3) a statement of evaluation or obligation; and (4) to highlight and introduce a new subject or a new aspect of the same subject. For example, in Matt. 9:26 the sentence *"Why are ye afraid?"* carries the meaning of rebuke, that is, "You shouldn't be afraid." In many languages a question form would not carry the meaning of rebuke. (For more example see Chapter 15 of Beekman and Callow, 1974.) Few languages would have these same functions for the question form. Appropriate ways to communicate the correct meaning will need to be found in the target language.

Figurative Meanings

All languages use figurative language but the types and usages will vary from language to language. The biblical texts abound in metonymies, euphemisms, similes and metaphors, to name just a few types of figures of speech. If translated literally wrong meaning often occurs because the target language may not use the same figures in the same way. For example, the euphemism *those who are afar off* (Eph. 2:13, 17), if translated literally would probably not carry the meaning of the Greek text, i.e. *Gentiles*. All languages abound in idioms. However, the idioms used in one language do not match the idioms of another language. Most languages have metaphors, but the meaning and comparison may be quite different in each of them. The Gospels have many extended metaphors, or parables, which challenge the translator since part of the comparison may have been left implicit. For example, *the tongue is a fire* (James 3:6) is a metaphor but the point of comparison is not indicated in the text. (For a full discussion of the translation of figures of speech found in biblical texts see Beekman and Callow, 1974:128–50.)

Implicit Meanings

Bible translators have long recognized the fact of implicit information in the source texts. Grammars of Greek and Hebrew regularly discuss the types of ellipsis found in these two languages. It has also been recognized that at least some of this implicit information must be made explicit if there is to be understanding of the translation. The Bible translator must account for this implied information. Since languages differ from one to another as to which information may be left implied in a text and the text still be understood, and which needs to be made explicit for good communication, the translator must take careful note of all implied information. What of this information will need to be expressed overtly in the target text will depend on the structure of the target language and what is understood by the speakers of that language. "… translators need to take into careful consideration the presence of implicit information in the original, so that it may be used explicitly when it is needed in the receptor language version." (Beekman and Callow, 1974:47).

Perhaps no source language constructions contain more implicit information than the Greek genitive constructions. (For examples see Beekman and Callow, 1974, Chapter 16.) The challenge to the Bible translator is to determine what information has been left implicit, in order to make an appropriate adjustment in the translation. For example, note the following comparisons in which the first column is translated literally from the Greek and the second gives the full meaning:

Mark 15:47	*Mary of Joses*	"Mary, Joses' mother"
Luke 6:16	*Judas of James*	"Judas, James' son"
John 19:25	*Mary of Clopas*	"Mary, Clopas' wife"

The implicit information becomes even more crucial in Greek genitive constructions when the construction represents a whole clause. Compare the following:

| Rom. 2:3 | *the judgment of God* | "God will judge (people)" |
| Col. 1:10 | *the knowledge of God* | "(people) know God" |

Some of the implied information is easily supplied from the immediate context. For example, in Matt. 26:4, 5 the italicized words may need to be supplied in the translation: "... and consulted that they might take Jesus by subtility, and kill him. But they said, *Let us* not *take him* on the feast day lest ..." The original Greek only has the phrase "Not on the feast day". However, the context makes it easy to fill out the implied information, thus giving a clearer English version. Often, however, the implicit information is derived from a more remote context or even from the culture of biblical times. Perhaps one of the most difficult tasks in translating is that of deciding what implicit information is needed for communicating the meaning, that is, when is it legitimate to make implied information explicit in the translation. If it is required by the grammar of the target language then the choice is simple. However, in other instances, it is often hard to judge when it is actually needed in other instances, in order to communicate the same meaning as the source text.

Cultural Differences

The culture of the people who speak the target language is often very distinct from that of the people about whom and for whom the source text was written. Language is part of culture and therefore translation from one language to another cannot be done adequately without a knowledge of the two cultures involved. Meaning is culturally conditioned. The culture of the source text determined the meaning of that text. The culture of the target language speakers will determine what they understand from the translation. The translator is the one who must understand both cultures and bridge the gap of misunderstanding which will occur if adjustments are not made to account for the cultural differences.

The writers of the biblical texts assumed the beliefs, attitudes, values, and rules of the audience for which they wrote. The translator will need to understand these matters in order to adequately understand the biblical texts and adequately translate them for people who have a different set of beliefs, attitudes, values, and rules. For example, both languages may have a word for *priest*. But the whole system of religious activity must be studied in order to be sure that the religious role of the Jewish *priest* will be adequately communicated by the target language word and to avoid negative connotations. Sometimes a modification will be necessary to communicate correctly. Languages can combine terms in new ways in order to express new concepts or to avoid negative connotations. Finding lexical equivalence for terms which carry heavy cultural information is a special challenge for a Bible translator.

The Purpose of the Author

All texts are written in a communication context. The biblical texts were also written in such a context. The authors had information and attitudes which they wished to communicate to a particular audience. Matthew's purpose in writing the gospel was different from John's purpose, which again was different from that of Luke and Mark. When studying the texts to be translated, the translator is interested in discovering the author's purpose and as much information as possible about the audience to whom he was writing. In order to do this it is often necessary to study the history of the time of writing, including the political, social, and religious dynamics as a backdrop to understanding the message intended. The characteristics of the audience for whom the message was intended provide understanding of the text itself.

An author makes many choices in order to communicate his or her purpose to the intended audience. These choices include such matters as the genre to be used, the order in which the information is presented, the length of sentences, the use of highly emotive words rather than less emotive words, and the style of the text. All such features of the source text are the choice of the original author. However, a formal matching of these devices in the target translation will not always result in communicating the same message to the target audience. Matters of style and text structure are not universal, but rather they are language specific. What is appropriate to get across a certain point in one language may not result in the same understanding in another language. For example, the Greek New Testament generally has short sentences in the gospels which are narratives and long complicated Greek sentences in the Pauline Epistles which are expository. However, some languages in South America and in Papua New Guinea have just the opposite structure with long narrative sentences, and with expository text consisting of short argumentative sentences. The difference between a mediocre translation and a brilliant one is often dependent on how clearly the translator communicates the intent of the original author through choices which affect style.

Factors Related Specifically to Biblical Texts

Multiple Versions of the Source Texts

Most translations are dealing with a single text which is the text to be translated. However, in Bible translation there is an added complexity which is the result of the fact of multiple versions of the source texts as well as many translations already available in major languages. Concerning the first matter, there are still places in the Greek New Testament, for example, where there is difference of opinion among scholars as to the intended reading of the text. The original documents do not exist. The source documents are all copies and there is some inconsistency, perhaps due to errors in copying. The specialized branch of study which compares and evaluates these variant readings is called "textual criticism". The translator is, therefore, faced with the problems resulting from this variety in the source texts and the variety of opinions concerning them.

In addition to the variety of texts in the biblical languages, the translator also often has access to a variety of translated versions in one or other major languages. All of these versions claim to be translations of the biblical languages but they are often very different from one another in grammatical and lexical form and sometimes in meaning. The translator is faced with sorting out information from these sources and coming to a conclusion about the meaning to be communicated in the target language. This process of exegesis is a major aspect of biblical translation. In all types of translation one must discover the meaning of the source text. However, for the Bible translator, exegesis, that is, "the critical study of the Bible according to hermeneutical principles with the immediate purpose of interpreting the text ..." (Toussaint, 1966:2) is of major importance.

The Source Text Communication Situation

The biblical texts, and the information contained in them, were set in a particular culture at a particular time in history. Because these texts are the foundation of Christianity which is firmly rooted in history, the translator must become acquainted with the culture and world view of the Israelites of the Old Testament and the Jewish people of the New Testament.

An understanding is also needed of the other nations which existed at the time of the biblical writings, especially the Greek and Roman world of New Testament times. The historical framework of the biblical texts must be kept in focus if the translation is to be historically accurate. Beekman and Callow (1974:35) state that "objects, places, persons, animals, customs, beliefs, or activities which are part of a historical statement must be translated in such a way that the same information is communicated by the translation as by the original statements."

There will always be a partial match between the source culture and the target culture. But more often there will be notable differences. The meaning connected with specific items will be different. Frequently there will be objects, classifications of persons, animals, customs, etc. which do not exist in the target culture and therefore are not found in the target language. (These matters are discussed in detail in Beekman and Callow, 1974:175–211 and in Larson, 1984:153–85.)

The translator is faced with a tension between being historically faithful and being faithful to the didactic, or teaching, aspects of the source text. "Scripture is not merely a historical record of events of the past;… (it) is replete with commands, illustrations, parables, and similitudes, all of which have a didactic function which in a faithful translation must be preserved." It is not always an easy matter to be faithful to both historical and didactic aspects of the biblical text.

Church History and Literature

Translators of non-biblical material are usually left on their own, with their dictionaries and perhaps a few books related in some way to their project. They decide what the author intended and, for the most part, their decision will not be challenged. If the author is living, they can telephone and ask what the intended meaning was for a given paragraph. Not so with the Bible translator. Not only is there the fact of the long distance in time since the texts were written, which does not allow for author verification, but there is the long history of the development of the Christian church which has interpreted Scripture over the centuries. There is also a large body of literature — commentaries, lexicons, Bible dictionaries, and treatises of various kinds. The translator is not alone. He has 2,000 years of scholarship which cannot be ignored. This increases his task as he cannot afford to make decisions without consulting this scholarship lest his translation be rejected outright by the very people for whom he is translating.

Religious Connotations of Key Words

Any text which is to be translated will have key words. These are words which are used over and over in the text and are crucial to the theme of the text. The translator will take special care in choosing a lexical equivalent in the target language for these words. In Bible translation, the matter of key words takes on an additional focus because of the religious connotation of many of them. If the translation is to be used by the general Christian public such key words as *baptism, salvation, priest,* and *temple* will need to be checked carefully for negative connotations and to be sure they are acceptable to all Christian groups. There are also words such as *cross, blood,* and *bread* and *wine,* which have special symbolic meaning. Even though *bread,* for example, may not be the main food in the target culture as it was in New Testament times, it may be necessary to introduce it by a loan word in the translation because of the symbolic meaning and religious connotation which it has in the Christian church. The choice of key words is crucial to the acceptance of a translation by the target audience.

Target Language Sociolinguistic Factors

In the above, linguistic and cultural matters affecting the translation were discussed, including some matters related to the target language and culture. There are other factors concerning the target audience which also have implications for the translator. These are sociolinguistic in nature.

Bible translation is carried on in a great variety of sociolinguistic situations. Some translations are in major languages for very large groups of highly literate people. Others are done for minority groups, some very small in number and with very little education. The choice of grammatical forms and vocabulary will be different for a highly literate, well educated audience than for newly literate people or those with only limited education. In the second case, less technical vocabulary may need to be used and less complicated structures. If the translator hopes that the translation will be read by all members of a society it may be necessary to present the translation in a "common language" which will overlap between all groups in the society.

Sometimes there are dialects which must be considered. Such dialects may vary because of the amount of bilingualism in a major language. If the translation is written for people who are highly bilingual many more borrowings from the major language may be included. If the translation is for the less bilingual then there is likely to be less borrowing, that is, fewer loan words might need to be used. A given language may also have several dialects, completely apart from matters of bilingualism. The translator than faces a decision as to which dialect to use, or how to accommodate to the various dialectical differences.

Some translations will be for people with no background in biblical matters whatsoever. Other translations are done for groups of people with a long history of Christianity. Sometimes people of minority languages develop a strong emotional attachment to the major language translation which they encountered first. They will compare any translation into their mother tongue with the forms of the major language translation. Vocabulary will have developed which is accepted by them as the "right word", but in fact it may come far from communicating the meaning of the source text. The translator is then faced with a dilemma.

Often the target audience does not have an understanding of the principles of translation. They do not understand the priority given to meaning. Rather, they are looking for the same grammatical and lexical forms. Sometimes the problem is complicated by the fact that target audiences may have come to think of the Bible as a "magic" book which is not meant to be understood by ordinary people. It might even be possible that the church leaders do not want the Bible to be too clear. They want to be the ones to tell the people what it means. Pressure from the church leaders is a factor which may cause some translators to translate more literally then they might otherwise care to do.

Types of Translations Resulting from These Factors

All who have been involved in Bible translation would indicate that they are striving to obtain the closest possible equivalence in their translation. Nevertheless, the results show a wide variety of translation types depending on the focus of the equivalence. The following chart (Larson, 1984:17) shows the span from very *literal* to *unduly free* which characterizes Bible translation. Each translation will fall someplace along this continuum. How a given translation would be classified will depend on how the various factors discussed above are taken into consideration in the translation process.

very literal	literal	modified literal	inconsistent mixture	near idiomatic	idiomatic	unduly free

TRANSLATOR'S
GOAL

An interlinear gloss of the source text is a completely *literal* translation. Such translations are very useful in presenting texts for linguistic purpose since they represent the structure of the source language. The Greek-English Interlinear New Testament with the Nestle's Greek text and an English gloss is an example of a completely *literal* translation and is very useful for studying the source text.

Translators who tend to translate literally actually would not normally translate completely literally. But there are many examples of Bible translations which are *modified literal* translations. The translators have modified the order of the words to match the order of the target language and made other obligatory grammatical modifications. However, very often the lexical items are translated literally, not taking into account secondary senses and figurative senses. Occasionally they will change a word to avoid complete nonsense or in some way improve communication, but nevertheless, the result is more an equivalence of forms than of meaning.

An *idiomatic translation*, on the other hand, gives priority to the meaning rather than to the grammatical and lexical forms. The goal of the translator is to use the natural forms of the target language. Grammatical forms which are the natural forms of the target language are used. Lexical items are adjusted so as to carry the meaning intended by the source text author. A good *idiomatic* translation does not sound like a translation. It is natural and clear and reads like a text originally written in the target language. Most translations fall someplace on the continuum between *modified literal* and *idiomatic*. Some parts will be truly *idiomatic* and in other places the translator is strongly influenced by the forms of the source text and translates more literally.

Only occasionally are translations made which are *unduly free*. The translator adds extraneous information which was not in the source text, or in some way changes the meaning. Some translations distort the historical and cultural facts in order to communicate to a particular audience. Normally these translations would not be considered acceptable translation.

Most translations of the Bible which were done before this century would be classified as *modified literal*. These translations contained ambiguities and obscure phrases, and they were unnatural in style and difficult to understand. Such translations are often considered adequate for people who are motivated to read and study and have access to reference works to resolve the lack of clarity. During the last five decades the emphasis has shifted to *idiomatic* translations which are easy to understand because they use the natural receptor language grammatical structures. However, there is still an ongoing debate as to whether the translation should follow more closely the source language structures and lexicon, or be more idiomatic, using only natural target structures and adjusting lexical items. (Glassman, 1981) Nevertheless, translation principles developed during recent decades have radically changed the approach used by most Bible translators.

Nida set the stage for much of the more *idiomatic* translation which has been done in these past several decades. He stated the goals of the translator in his early book (Nida, 1947:13) by listing "three basic requirements: (1) the translation must represent the customary usage of the native language, (2) the translation must make sense, and (3) the translation must conform to the meaning of the original." These can be summarized as *natural, clear* and *accurate*. A Bible translation project which takes into account the requirements suggested by Nida will result in a translation which communicates the meaning of the biblical texts to the target audience.

References

Beekman, John and John Callow. *Translating the Word of God.* Grand Rapids, Michigan: Zondervan Publishing House, 1974.

de Waard, Jan and Eugene A. Nida. *From One Language to Another: Functional Equivalence in Bible Translating.* Nashville, Tennessee: Thomas Nelson, 1979.

Glassman, Eugene H. *The Translation Debate: What Makes a Bible Translation Good?* Downers Grove, Illinois: Intervarsity Press, 1981.

Larson, Mildred L. *Meaning-based Translation.* Lanham, Maryland: University Press of America, 1984.

Nida, Eugene A. *Bible Translating.* New York: American Bible Society, 1947.

Nida, Eugene A. and Charles R. Taber. *The Theory and Practice of Translation.* Leiden: E. J. Brill, 1969.

Toussaint, Stanley D. "A Proper Approach to Exegesis." *Notes on Translation,* Vol. 20 (1966), pp. 1–6.

Chinese Translations of the Bible

I-Jin Loh
United Bible Societies Asia Opportunity Program
Bible Society in the Republic of China, Taipei, Taiwan

Strictly speaking, the more academically respectable Chinese translations of the Bible are not those from the English, but rather those from the original Hebrew (Old Testament) and Greek (the New Testament). However, influence from the major English versions, such as King James Version (1611), Revised Version (1885), Revised Standard Version (1952), Today's English Version (1976), etc., has been enormous.

Early History

Christianity was introduced into China in A.D. 635 during Taizong's reign by the Nestorians. From the reference found in the Nestorian Tablet unearthed in Xi'an in 1623, it is evident that the New Testament or parts of the Bible was translated into Chinese during the first half of the seventh century. There were also reports of translations done by Catholic missionaries from the 13th to the 16th centuries. Unfortunately, none of these translations has ever been found. The earliest extant text is the Slone Manuscript (#3599) now housed in the British Museum. It is the translation done by Jean Basset (1662–1707), a French priest from Paris, and contains a Harmony of the Gospels, the Acts of the Apostles, the Letters of Paul, and the first chapter of the Letter to the Hebrews. This is the manuscript which Robert Morrison, the first Protestant missionary to China, copied and took with him to Guangzhou in 1807, and from which he apparently learned his Chinese. Morrison's transcript is now kept in the Morrison Collection in the Hong Kong University.

Wenli 文理 (Literary) Versions

Morrison and Marshman Versions

The first translations of the Bible into Chinese were all in literary language, intended primarily for the literate and educated Chinese. Interestingly, two translations of the Bible went on simultaneously, one by Joshua Marshman, and the other by Robert Morrison. Marshman, an associate of the famous William Carey of the Serampore Mission in Calcutta, assisted by Johannes Lassar, an Armenian born in Macao, published the first complete book of the Bible, *The Gospel according to Matthew*, in 1810 in Serampore. A few weeks later, Morrison published his first portion, *The Acts of the Apostles*, in Guangzhou. China was so hostile to Christianity at that time that the covers of this edition had to be camouflaged in order to escape notice by the Chinese authorities. Morrison's New Testament came off the press in 1814. However, the honour of issuing the first complete Chinese Bible went to Marshman and Lassar when they published their version in 1822. Morrison, joined by William Milne in 1813, and with his assistance on part of the Old Testament, finished his translation of the complete Bible in 1819, but he was not able to publish it until 1823.

Although Marshman's translation of the New Testament was based on the Greek text, the draft was prepared by Lassar from the King James Version. Morrison's translation was based on the original texts, but its dependency on the King James Version as a textual base and for interpretation, and on the Roman Catholic Basset Version especially as a guide to receptor language is also evident. Both versions used 神 for "God" and 聖風 for "Holy Spirit". Marshman, being a Baptist, employed 蘸 (literally, to dip in) for "baptism", while Morrison used 洗 (to wash). Even though Marshman's version came out first, Morrison's translation won wider acceptance. For one thing, his is a better translation: unlike Marshman's, his translation was done in China and had more adequate help from Chinese scholars. For another, being the first missionary to China, he was held in greater reverence, so naturally was his translation also. It is no surprise therefore that his translation was later used as the basis for other revisions and versions.

The Medhurst-Gutzlaff-Bridgman Version

In spite of the fact that the Morrison-Milne Version was well received, it became evident that a revision was desirable. Not long after Morrison's death in 1834, his son James Morrison presented a plan for a revision. And with his assistance the project was undertaken by William Medhurst, Karl F. A. Gutzlaff, and Elijah Bridgman — the trio were to be key figures in other versions later. The New Testament Revision, with Medhurst taking the lead, was finished in 1835 and printed in 1836. The Old Testament, mainly the work of Gutzlaff, was published between 1838 and 1840.

Gutzlaff Version and the Taiping Rebellion

Karl Gutzlaff was an extraordinary person. He inspired the formation of the Chinese Evangelization Society which sent out Hudson Taylor, the founder of the China Inland Mission. He was a prolific writer, with more than sixty Chinese publications to his credit. In addition to assisting in the Delegates' Version, he also made his name in translating the Bible into other languages such as Thai and Japanese. In fact, his translation of the Letters of John inaugurated the history of Protestant Bible translation in Japan. He also published his own version of the whole Bible, having revised the New Testament of the Medhurst-Gutzlaff-Bridgman Version and added his own translation of the Old Testament, which was eventually printed in 1855. Interestingly, this is the version adopted by Hong Xiuquan 洪秀全 of the Heavenly Dynasty of Great Peace 太平天國 when he published, with considerable changes in places, portions of the Bible with the title *The Sacred Book of the Newly Bequeathed Oracles* 《新遺詔聖書》 in 1853.

The Delegates' Version

With the cession of Hong Kong to the British, as the result of the Nanjing Treaty, Hong Kong became the centre of Protestant missionary activity. On August 22, 1843, twelve American and British missionaries, representing various missionary societies and agencies, met and decided to undertake a revision of the Bible. The meeting resolved that a committee of missionaries should be set up in each of the five treaty ports, namely Fuzhou, Guangzhou, Ningpo, Shanghai and Xiamen. The New Testament would be divided among the groups for revision. Each of the five committees would submit its work to the other four for review and comments. The finalization would be made by the general committee, consisting of five delegates, one from each committee — hence the "Delegates' Version". The original delegates were William Medhurst and Elijah Bridgman (both had worked on the Morrison-Milne revision), W. J. Boone, Walter M. Lowrie and John Stronach. Lowrie was thrown overboard by pirates on the way from Hangzhou to Ningpo on August 19, 1847, and thus became the first Protestant martyr in China. On Lowrie's death, W. C. Milne, son of Morrison's associate William Milne, took his place. Then in 1850, when Boone retired because of ill health, M. S. Culbertson replaced him.

Controversy soon erupted over the so-called "term question", namely the question about the proper rendering of "God", "Spirit", and "to baptize/baptism". For "God", both Marshman and Morrison used 神 . Medhurst, Gutzlaff, and Stronach favoured 上帝 , while others in the committee wanted to keep 神 . For "Holy Spirit", both Marshman and Morrison employed 聖風 , Medhurst and Gutzlaff favoured 靈神 , while some Americans supported 聖靈 . Unable to reach a consensus, the delegates decided to leave blank spaces to be filled by the respective publishers: the American Bible Society used 神 and 聖靈 , while the British and Foreign Bible Society favoured 上帝 and 聖神 . The delegates finished the New Testament in 1850, but because of the inability to resolve the term controversy it was not published until 1852.

In the meantime, the revision of the Old Testament continued with the same group of revisors. But the group realized soon that it would be impractical to continue the procedures followed in the revision of the New Testament. Instead of local committees, they decided to form a committee consisting of representatives from the six port cities. They were Bridgman from Guangzhou, James Legge (the famous Sinologist) and H. Hamburg from Hong Kong, Stronach from Xiamen, S. Johnson and M. C. White from Fuzhou, Culbertson from Ningpo, as well as Boone, Medhurst, and J. L. Shuck from Shanghai. Unfortunately, controversy arose again regarding principles and style of translation and the committee was split into two groups. The British delegates Medhurst, Stronach, and Milne, with help from Legge, proceeded to finish the Old Testament in 1853, following the principles used in the newly completed New Testament, and had it printed in 1854. In 1855 the complete Bible was published and it became known as the Delegates' Version. It is generally agreed that the literary style of this version, which had the benefit of help from a Chinese scholar by the name of Wang Tao 王韜 , was superior to the rival version.

Post Delegates Wenli Versions

The other group, the American members of the reconstituted committee, principally Bridgman and Culbertson, went ahead and produced a new version of the whole Bible. Their New Testament, based on the original Delegates' Version, but revised to correspond to the principles and style adopted for their Old Testament project, appeared in 1859, the Old Testament in 1863, and the complete Bible known as the Bridgman-Culbertson Version in 1864. The translators placed priority on strict literal fidelity to the original, rather than stylistic elegance in the receptor language. As to the "term question", the translators used 神 for "God" and 聖靈 for the "Holy Spirit". This version was published by the American Bible Society and was widely circulated for many years.

Another splinter group from the Delegates' Version was the Baptists. They withdrew from the committee, not long after its constitution, over the rendering of "to baptize/baptism", and decided to ask Josiah Goddard to do a revision of the Marshman Version. The revised New Testament was published in 1853. This edition was subsequently revised by E. C. Lord and printed in 1873. In the meantime, the Old Testament translation started by Goddard was finally finished by Lord, with assistance from William Dean, and the complete Bible was published in 1868. Another Baptist, T. H. Hudson, produced his own New Testament in 1866, again a revision of the Marshman Version.

There are some other versions worth mentioning. The Russian Ecclesiastical Mission published a New Testament in 1862. In this version, they adopted 天主 for "God", the term used by the Catholics. John Chalmers and Martin Schaub, who were among those selected in 1890 to do a revision of the Delegates' Version, produced their own tentative version of the New Testament edition in 1897. Of special interest is the translation of chapters 1 to 4 of *The Gospel according to Mark* by the distinguished Chinese scholar and translator Yan Fu 嚴復 . He was not a Christian, but hoped to make the Bible a great classic for the Chinese. His translation, based on the English Revised Version of 1885, was published in Shanghai in 1908.

The Wenli Union Version

The General Conference of the Protestant missionaries met in Shanghai in 1890. Distressed by the large number of rival versions, the Conference made a momentous decision to initiate translation of one Bible in three Union Versions, namely in Wenli, Easy Wenli, and Mandarin 官話 . The translators could use all existing versions, especially the Delegates' Version, but the original text underlying the English Revised Version was to be the basis of their work. The original members elected to the Wenli Union Bible Committee were John Chalmers, Joseph Edkins, John Wherry, D. Z. Sheffield, and Martin Schaub. Later, upon the death of some members, L. Lloyd and T. W. Pearce were added to the Committee. The work was hampered by the constant struggle between literalism and style, but the Committee was able finally to publish the New Testament before the Centenary Conference in 1907. The translation of the Old Testament was finished in 1915, but the complete Wenli Union Version Bible was not published until 1919, one month after the appearance of the Mandarin Union Version Bible.

Individual Catholic Versions

There are several published Catholic Wenli translations worth mentioning, all by individuals. The first published work is the Four Gospels, translated by Fr. J. Dejean, published in 1892. Another is also a New Testament by Fr. Laurence Wen-yu Li 李問漁 , published in 1897. Of special interest is a translation of the Psalms and the New Testament by Mr. Wu Jingxiong 吳經熊 , published in 1946 and 1949 respectively at the expense of Chiang Kai-shek 蔣介石 . Mr. Wu, a Catholic layman, was a former Ambassador of the Republic of China to the Vatican. His Psalms are paraphrastic renderings, and in isosyllabic and metrical lines.

Easy Wenli Versions

Easy Wenli is a simpler form of the literary style used and understood by people of limited classical education. It was the style employed in government documents as well as in popular novels before the May Fourth Movement.

Individual Translations

1. The Griffith John Version

Griffith John, an evangelist always concerned to reach the common folk with the Christian gospel, was the first one to employ the easy Wenli style in translating Scriptures. His New Testament appeared in 1885. The translation was based on the Greek text underlying the King James Version, but referred to the Beijing Mandarin and the Delegates' Versions. He used 上帝 for "God", and 聖神 for "Holy Spirit".

2. *The Burdon-Blodget Version*

John S. Burdon and Henry Blodget (who were to be involved in other versions later) produced a New Testament in 1889. In this case, they based their translation on the Beijing Mandarin Version. They adopted 天主 for "God", and 聖靈 for "Holy Spirit".

3. *The Schereschewsky Version*

Of special interest and significance is the translation done by Joseph I. J. Schereschewsky. He was of Jewish descent, but converted to Christianity. He went to a Seminary, and upon graduation was offered a professorship, but declined the offer and decided to dedicate himself to translation of the Bible into Chinese. He came to China in 1859, became a Bishop, and founded the St. John's University in Shanghai. But since his major interest was in Bible translation, he set himself single-mindedly to this arduous task. He started with the Mandarin Old Testament first and published it in 1874. He was stricken with paralysis in 1881 and returned to America in 1886. While there, still unable to walk and speak properly, he revised his Mandarin translation, and in the meantime started working on an easy Wenli version. Unable to hold a pen, and with the use of only one finger of each hand to type with, he finished the translation, came back to Shanghai in 1895, transcribed the Roman text into Chinese characters, published a tentative edition of the New Testament in 1898, and finally the complete Bible in 1902. This Bible became fondly known as the "Two-finger Edition". At first, Schereschewsky used 天主 for "God" and 聖神 for "Holy Spirit", but later he changed 天主 to 上帝 .

Easy Wenli Union Version

As already indicated, the Easy Wenli Union Bible Committee was called into being by the resolution of the General Conference of the Protestant missionaries in 1890. The original translators selected included J. S. Burdon, H. Blodget, R. H. Graves, J. C. Gibson, and I. Genaehr. J. W. Davis was added later. After a number of tentative editions, the New Testament was published in 1904. It was increasingly realized that the two Wenli Versions were so close as to make one unnecessary, and that the future lay with the Mandarin Version, and so at the Centenary Conference held in 1907 the decision was made to discontinue further work on the Easy Wenli Union Version.

Mandarin Versions

Mandarin, translated as 官話 (official language), is sometimes referred to as 國語, 白話, or 普通話. Basically a spoken language based on the Beijing vernacular, it was eventually adopted as the written language as the result of the May Fourth Movement started by Hu Shi 胡適 and others in 1917.

Pre-Union Version Translations

1. The Nanjing Mandarin Version

Following the appearance of the Delegates' Version New Testament, two of its translators, W. Medhurst and J. Stronach, proceeded to adapt it into the "southern" or "Nanjing" Mandarin. The initial draft was prepared by an unknown young Chinese scholar. The New Testament first came out in 1857, and thereafter it was reprinted several times.

2. The Beijing Committee Version

The Committee included William A. P. Martin, Joseph Edkins, S. I. J. Schereschewsky, J. S. Burdon, and H. Blodget. It apparently used the "Nanjing Mandarin" Version as the basis of adaptation into the Beijing dialect. The New Testament was printed in 1872. Because of the term controversy, four editions had to be printed: one with 上帝 and 聖神, a second with 天主 and 聖神, a third with 天主 and 聖靈, and a fourth with 神 and 聖靈. Another noteworthy thing about this version is the fact that Marie Taylor, wife of the founder of the China Inland Mission, starting in 1869, transcribed the Gospels, Acts, and Epistles into roman script. This is the first record of a lady being involved in the translation of the Bible. Yet another noteworthy fact is that this version was apparently the first Testament to be published in a diglot form (with the King James Version) in 1885.

3. The Schereschewsky Mandarin Version

Joseph Schereschewsky, a member of the Beijing Committee and the person who produced the influential "one man translation" in Easy Wenli, produced a Mandarin Old Testament on his own, based on the Hebrew text, with reference to the King James Version and De Wette's German Bible. It was published in 1874. Later on, this translation, printed with the Beijing Committee New Testament in 1878, became the standard Mandarin Bible until the appearance of the Mandarin Union Version Bible in 1919.

4. The Griffith John Version

For fear that the Beijing Mandarin would not be easily understood by those living in central China, Griffith John was asked to make a fresh translation. He did this by making an adaptation from his Easy Wenli Version published four years earlier. The New Testament was printed in 1889.

The Mandarin Union Version

The problem with the Wenli and the Easy Wenli Versions was that the language was too difficult for the ordinary readers. The only alternative was to prepare a Mandarin version, in the language within reach of the majority of the people. The revision of the Bible into Mandarin took more than 27 years. The project was supported by the British and Foreign Bible Society, the American Bible Society, and the National Bible Society of Scotland, all three societies working in China. Selection of suitable and competent translators was not an easy task, as it was desirable to have representatives from different nations and denominations, as well as from the different Mandarin-speaking areas. Altogether twenty-seven translators were nominated, but only seven were chosen: Henry Blodget, C. W. Mateer, Chauncy Goodrich, J. L. Nevius, George S. Owen, and J. R. Hykes, and Thomas Bramfitt. Later on, in various stages, Henry M. Woods, S. R. Clarke, F. W. Baller, Spencer Lewis and E. E. Aiken were added. From the very beginning it was painstaking and exacting work. It aimed at fidelity to the original and simplicity in style, easy enough to be understood by the ordinary people. Every word, phrase, and sentence was subjected to the closest possible scrutiny by the committee. One report says that a thousand new expressions and eighty-seven new characters had to be found to render fully the meaning of the original. The New Testament was first published in

1907, and revised later before it was printed with the Old Testament as part of the complete Bible in 1919. Of the original translators, only Goodrich survived to see the complete Bible in print.

This Mandarin Union Version Bible was published in two editions, one with 上帝 and the other with 神 for "God", but both had 聖靈 for "Holy Spirit". It was immediately recognized as a great achievement and quickly superseded all previous versions. It became the Bible for Chinese Christians everywhere, and continues to be so even today. Its continuing popularity has been enhanced by the publication of an edition with modern punctuation by the United Bible Societies in 1988, and a simplified script edition, also with new punctuation, in 1989 by the China Christian Council. This epoch-making version is generally believed to have made a significant contribution to the Mandarin Vernacular Movement.

Post-Union Version Translations

1. Protestant Versions

The first New Testament after the Union Version appeared in 1929. This is the translation done by Absalom Sydenstricker, father of the novelist Pearl Buck, with the assistance of Zhu Baohui 朱寶惠 . The translation was based on the Greek text, but every effort was made to express the plain sense of the original in clear and idiomatic vernacular.

The next New Testament, which appeared in 1933, was the work of Mr. Wang Yuande 王元德 (Xuanchen 宣忱), a professor at Qilu University. He had served as an assistant to C. W. Mateer, the chairperson of the Mandarin Union Version Committee. Apparently not entirely satisfied with the style of the Union Version (the work primarily of the Westerners), he began his own translation in 1930, based on the Latin text of 1916 and the American Standard Version of 1901, with emphasis placed on the readability of the text. This is the first private translation done solely by a Chinese Protestant scholar.

The translation of the complete Apocrypha (the Deuterocanonicals) appeared for the first time in 1933. This is an adaptation prepared by H. F. Lei, based in part on earlier portions in Easy Wenli translated by M. H. Throop and Wang Yiqiu 王一秋 (Waung Yih-tsieu).

In 1939, "The Bible Treasury New Testament" appeared. This version, the work of H. Ruck and Zheng Shoulin 鄭壽麟 , is based on the Greek original, and is a concordant type of translation, that is, each word in the original language is given one and the same rendering in Chinese irrespective of context. It uses 神 for "God", 洗禮 for "baptism", and 召會 for "church".

Lü Zhenzhong 呂振中 (Lü Chen-chung) published his private translation of the New Testament in 1946, based on the Greek text edited by A. Souter. The complete Bible appeared in 1970. Lü at times placed too much emphasis on literal fidelity to the original at the expense of the Chinese style, and therefore his version is very close to the crib type of translation. His translation has the distinction of being the first and only "one man version" of the complete Bible in Chinese by a Chinese. The name "Jehovah" in the Old Testament is rendered as 永恆主 .

Another private version of the New Testament appeared in 1964, translated by Xiao Tiedi 蕭鐵笛 (Theodore E. Hsiao) and revised by Zhao Shiguang 趙世光 (Timothy S. K. Dzao). There is an introduction to each book.

2. Catholic Versions

Fr. Xiao Jingshan 蕭靜山 (Joseph Hsiao Ching-shan) published his translation of the Four Gospels in 1919, and then in 1922 the New Testament, both based on the Latin text. It became a popular edition widely used by the Catholics. In 1948, a revised version based on the Greek original was issued.

The next New Testament to appear was a translation by a committee of four, including a Chinese by the name of Xiao Shunhua 蕭舜華 , led by Fr. George Litvanyi. This version, based on the Latin text, was published in 1949.

The most important Catholic version is the work of the Studium Biblicum Franciscanum. It had more than ten Western and Chinese scholars, under the leadership of Fr. G. M. Allegra, working for sixteen years to finish the translation. The New Testament came out in 1961, and the complete Bible in 1968. This has the distinction of being the first Catholic translation of the whole Bible, including the Deuterocanonicals. It follows scientific principles of translation, and is the only Catholic translation based entirely on the original Hebrew and Greek texts.

Recent Versions

In the mid 1970s, four new translations prepared by various Protestant groups came out. Here we observe an extremely important shift taking place in the history of Chinese Bible translation: all are committee translations, and all are by Chinese translators.

The first to appear was the Chinese Living New Testament in 1974, a version prepared by a committee led by Joseph Chiang, and sponsored by the Living Bibles International. This is a translation based on the English Living Bible — a paraphrase of the American Standard Version of 1901 by Kenneth Taylor. The complete Bible, identified as "The Contemporary Bible", came out in 1979. It used "the newest 'living translation method'", thus justifying clarification of ambiguities as well as explanation of peculiar customs and backgrounds in the text.

Almost simultaneously, another paraphrase appeared. This was a translation by the Asian Outreach and published by the China Bible Publishers. The New Testament was published in 1974, and the complete Bible, also named "The Contemporary Bible", came off the press in 1979.

The Today's Chinese Version New Testament, sponsored by the United Bible Societies, appeared in 1975. The complete Bible came out in 1980. The translators include Moses Hsü 許牧世 , Chow Lien-hwa 周聯華 , Martin Wang 王成章 , Evelyn Chiao 焦明 , and I-Jin Loh 駱維仁 , assisted by a panel of reviewers. The translation is based on the Hebrew and Greek original, but uses the Today's English Version (Good News Bible) as the model. Applying the translation theory developed by Eugene A. Nida, it marks a significant shift in the approach of translation. Instead of the prevalent formal correspondence approach, this translation aims at reproducing the meaning of the original with functional equivalent words in the receptor language. The name "Jehovah" in the Old Testament is rendered 上主 . Some Catholic scholars were involved in the review process, and a Catholic edition of the New Testament was issued in 1986 with only two substitutions: namely 天主 for 上帝 , and 聖神 for 聖靈 .

Another New Testament, which appeared in 1976, is by the New Chinese Bible Commission, sponsored by the Lockman Foundation. This translation, known as "The New Version", was done by several groups of Chinese scholars from various countries and locations. It follows two guiding principles, namely, fidelity to the original and employment of the modern Chinese style. The translation is based on the Greek original, and is more literal than other recent versions. The Old Testament is expected to be completed soon.

Moving into the 1980s, two interesting translations appeared. The first was the translation of the Deuterocanonicals/Apocrypha of the Today's English Version, entitled 聖經後典 . This is a translation done by Zhang Jiuxuan 張久宣 , a member of the Religious Research section of the Chinese Academy of Social Sciences, and published in Beijing in 1987.

Another New Testament known as "The Restoration Version" was published in 1987. This translation, headed by Li Changshou 李常受 , tries to keep the flavour of the Union Version, but does not hesitate to incorporate good renderings found in existing English and Chinese versions. It has copious notes aiming at bringing out the spiritual meaning of the original. There are a number of new terms used. For example, it has 神言者 for 先知 (prophet), 話 for 道 (word/logos), 奴隸 for the traditional 奴僕 (servant), 浸 for 洗 (to baptize), etc.

Current Translations in Progress

In 1986, Bishop Jin Luxian of Shanghai published his translation of the Four Gospels. It is based on the French "Jerusalem Bible", adapting its notes and adding new ones. The New Testament is expected to come off the press sometime in 1991.

One of the most important developments in the history of Chinese Bible translation was the official launching of the Interconfessional Translation Project in 1987, after years of preparatory work, including drawing up a list of common terminologies. This first *bona fide* cooperative effort between the Catholics and the Protestants is sponsored by the United Bible Societies. There are Translation Committees working in Hong Kong and Taiwan, coordinated by an Editorial Committee consisting of Mark Fang 房志榮 , Chow Lien-hwa and I-Jin Loh. A trial edition of *The Gospel according to John* appeared in 1990, and it is expected that the New Testament will roll off the press in 1993.

Chinese Dialect Versions

Any discussion of Chinese translations of the Bible will be incomplete without reference to dialect versions. Relatively early in the history of Chinese Bible translation, Protestant missionaries began to translate the Bible into various Chinese dialects, some using Chinese characters, others Roman. Records show that portions of the Bible have been translated into twenty-four different dialects to date, not counting the Beijing Mandarin.

1. From the Mandarin Group

The Zhili dialect had its only portion, Luke, in Wang Chao phonetic system in 1925. The Nanjing dialect had its New Testament in 1857, an adaptation of the Delegates' Wenli Version by a Chinese. The Shandong dialect had Luke and John in 1892, and Matthew in 1894. The Jiaodong dialect had Mark in Wang Chao phonetic system in 1918 and Matthew in 注音 phonetic system in 1920.

2. From the Wu Group

The Hankou dialect had Mark in Wang Chao phonetic system in 1921. The Hangzhou dialect had its John in 1879 and Matthew in 1880, both in Roman script. The Jinhua dialect had John in Roman script in 1866. Ningpo dialect had the first portion (Luke) in 1852, first New Testament in 1868, and the whole Bible in 1901, all in Roman script. The Shanghai dialect had its first portion John in Chinese characters in 1847, first New Testament in Roman script in 1871, and second New Testament in Chinese characters in 1881, plus various portions of the Old Testament. The Suzhou dialect had its first portion in 1879, New Testament in 1881, and Bible in 1908, all in Chinese characters. The Taizhou dialect had its New Testament in 1881, and Bible in 1914, all in Chinese characters. The Wenzhou dialect had its first portion Matthew in 1892, and New Testament in 1902, all in Roman script.

The Hainan dialect had its first portion Matthew in Roman script in 1891. Thereafter some portions from both the Old and New Testaments were published.

3. From the Yue Group

The Guangdong dialect had its first portions Matthew and John in 1862, New Testament in 1886, and complete Bible in 1894. Another version of the Bible appeared in 1907. The Sanjiang dialect had its first portion Matthew in 1904, followed by Mark, Luke, and John in 1905, all in Chinese characters.

4. The Kejia Group

The Dingzhou dialect, which possibly belongs to the Kejia family, had its only portion Matthew in Roman script in 1919. The Kejia dialect had its first portion Matthew in 1860, and New Testament in 1883, both in Roman script; revised New Testament in 1913, and Bible, both in Chinese characters, in 1916. The Wujingfu Kejia had its New Testament in Roman script in 1916. A new version of the New Testament for the Kejia people in Taiwan is being finalized. It should appear later in 1991. It is a functional equivalent translation sponsored by the Bible Society in Taiwan. The chief translator is Peng Deh-hsiu 彭德修 , with help from John Chong-fat Chen 曾昌發 , Paul Mclean, and others.

5. *From the Min Group*

The Xiamen dialect (known as Taiwanese in Taiwan) had its first portion John in 1852, New Testament in 1873, complete Bible in 1884, both in Roman script. In 1933, a revised edition appeared. This edition is still being used in Taiwan. In Taiwan, the Catholic church published a new translation of the Four Gospels in 1967. This functional equivalent translation is the work of Chek-hoan Ko 高積煥 and Pang-tin Tan 陳邦鎮 , with some assistance from some Protestant scholars, namely T. S. Chang 張德香 , T. L. Kuo 郭得列 , J. L. Tsai 蔡仁理 , and Martin Wang. A new translation of the New Testament, also a functional equivalent version, is underway in Taiwan. The translators include T. S. Chang, L. K. Cheng, Paul Liao, H. K. Weng, Martin Wang, and I-Jin Loh. A trial edition of Mark appeared in 1988 and 1-3 John in 1990. It is expected that the New Testament will be published by 1992. One of the distinctive features of this edition will be the employment of the combined Chinese-Roman text.

6. *Still from the Min Group*

The Fuzhou dialect had its first portion Matthew in 1852, New Testament in 1856, Bible in 1891, all in Chinese characters. A Roman script edition of the New Testament appeared in 1905 and Bible in 1906. The Jianning dialect had its first portion Matthew in 1896, and New Testament in 1896, both in Roman script. The Jianyang dialect had its Mark in 1898 and Matthew in 1900, both in Roman script. The Shantou dialect had its first portion Ruth in 1875, portions of the Old and New Testament afterwards, and New Testament in 1898, all in Chinese characters. Another version of the New Testament in Roman script appeared in 1905. The Shaowu dialect had the James portion in Roman script in 1891. And finally, the Xinghua dialect had its first portion John in 1892, New Testament in 1901, and Bible in 1912.

References

Broomhall, Marshall. *The Bible in China*. San Francisco: Chinese Materials Center Inc., 1977.

Kramers, R. P., ed. *Chinese Bible Translation*. Hong Kong: The Council on Christian Literature for Overseas Chinese, 1965 (in Chinese).

Nida, Eugene A., ed. *The Book of a Thousand Tongues*. New York: United Bible Societies, 1972.

——— and Jan de Waard. *From One Language to Another: Functional Equivalence in Bible Translating*. Nashville: Thomas Nelson Publishers, 1986.

Spillett, Hubert W. *A Catalogue of Scriptures in the Language of China and the Republic of China*. London: British and Foreign Bible Society, 1975.

Strandenaes, Thor. *Principles of Chinese Translation as Expressed in Five Versions of the New Testament and Exemplified by Mt. 5:1–12 and Col. 1*. Coniectanea Biblica, New Testament Series 19. Uppsala: Almqvist and Wiksell International, 1987.

BODY LANGUAGE

Body Language in Chinese-English Translation

David E. Pollard
Department of Translation
The Chinese University of Hong Kong, Hong Kong

> Xiangwen did not answer. Her shoulders jerked spasmodically. She cried even more bitterly. Li … figured out what had happened. He clenched his fists and bit his lip hard.

This is a quotation from a respectable Taiwan writer of fiction. To the Chinese reader it is entirely unremarkable, standard fare. It could have come from the pen of any number of authors, from Hong Kong, Taiwan or mainland China. But to the foreigner it marks itself out as typifying a peculiarity of Chinese fiction, namely the great attention that is paid to the outward manifestations of emotions. Add to this the description of bodily sensations that are not apparent and gestures or expressions that convey attitude, and you have a body of vocabulary that presents the translator with problems.

Now some physical sensations must be universal because they arise from glandular action: sweating from fear, flushing with anger, heart pounding with excitement. With these one can make a close match. The same applies to reactions that are reflexive or involuntary — such as the mouth dropping open in astonishment, though there are some cultural refinements here (in the traditional Chinese phrase, a person who is so thunderstruck sticks out the tongue as well as opens the mouth). The main difficulties arise from:

A. a specifically Chinese view of the functioning of the internal organs: not surprisingly, they do not follow Galen;
B. a set of expressions and gestures that are either peculiar to the Chinese or signify different things from the Western ones;
C. the remarking of physical reactions that Western authors do not normally discern: what is conventional to the Chinese reader may be strange or even alarming to the English reader.

The most colourful descriptions of physical effects are found in old fiction. With these the translator can have a lot of fun. For example:

洪太尉⋯嚇得三十六個牙齒捉對兒廝打，⋯渾身卻如中風，兩腳一似鬥敗公雞，口裡連聲叫苦。

Commander Hung was so frightened that his thirty-six teeth chattered together in pairs, his whole body went numb as if he had suffered a stroke, his two legs were as limp as the defeated contender in a cockfight, while his mouth ceaselessly uttered moans and groans.

And, to describe the state of internal turmoil brought on by extreme nervousness:

那心頭一似十五個吊桶，七上八落的響。

His heart was like fifteen buckets clashing together in a well as seven went up and eight went down.

Modern Chinese fiction's focus on physicality is probably derived from this tradition, but is a lot tamer. On the whole it causes the translator more headaches than enjoyment.

Category B is probably easiest to talk about as it comprises a closed, though fairly large, set. Fortunately, physical sign language between Chinese and Anglo-Saxon (other European habits may differ somewhat) overlaps to a great extent. Nodding and shaking the head mean the same. But to a Chinese the waving of a hand (搖手) is not done to attract attention; it is a sign of dismissiveness. If we look at the way translators have dealt with this gesture we will see that we have a range of strategies that can be applied generally.

Our source text may say 甲搖手說:「不⋯」: "X waved her hand and said 'No....'."

Strategy (1) is to give a bald translation, and hope the reader will twig if not this time, then the next time round, that the gesture also means "no." You add nothing, you falsify nothing.

Strategy (2) is to elaborate: you add "negatively" or "dismissively" to "waved her hand". Bearing in mind that your reader may be reading Chinese fiction for the first and possibly only time, there is a lot to be said for this strategy if you do not want to take a chance on him/her misunderstanding. But to add an adverbial may make for a cumbersome construction if you already have an adverbial, e.g. "smilingly", "with a smile", "sourly", "irritatedly".

Strategy (3) is to convert the Chinese gesture to the nearest equivalent in the target-language culture: for instance, "raised a protesting hand". Intrinsically there is nothing wrong with this: the significance is very nearly the same, and you have made a perfectly natural English statement. But extrinsically you have misled the reader, who if burdened with a good memory may hold it against you when he mixes with Chinese people and finds they don't do as you have described.

Strategy (4) is to leave the waving out, and justify the omission on the ground that you already have a negative in the answer "no". As a partial remedy you might transfer some of the message of the gesture to the verb: "X *protested*, 'No'."

The same options are available for all gestures where there is an equivalent or near-equivalent in the target-language culture. Another example would be the apparently simple and unambiguous act of pointing a finger at someone while addressing them; but to the Anglo-Saxon this is a sign of accusation, while to the Chinese it signifies reprimand. The Chinese to English conversion here would involve the substitution of wagging a finger.

Sometimes there is no equivalent. As far as I know there is no equivalent of 羞 , "to shame". It consists of drawing the finger repeatedly across the cheek to indicate that the other person has done something for which he ought to be blushing. Here strategy (1) is out: a bald translation like "stroking the cheek" would not convey anything. We have already said that strategy (3) — conversion — does not apply. So we are only left with strategies (2) and (4).

David Hawkes uses strategy (2) — elaboration — in a big way when girl chides boy in *The Story of the Stone*:

> ... smiling mockingly, and stroking her cheek with her finger — which in sign language means "You are a big liar and ought to be ashamed of yourself."

Everything after the dash is added. Fortunately it harmonizes well with the surrounding text. Strategy (4) could offer no more than minimal compensation in these cases: you could only reinforce the idea of "teasing" or "chiding". The loss of the playfulness of the gesture would be serious.

The expression 轉眼睛 "turn the eyes", "roll the eyes", whose significance would be similarly unclear to the Western reader, takes us on the category C: because involuntary, it is not culture specific, but it is not normally remarked on or recognized by Anglo-Saxon writers. It indicates that a cunning thought has struck the owner of the eyes: he is going to get up to no good. (Perhaps we should all look out for this sign, which seems to really exist.) The nearest common expression to it in English I can think of is "a shifty look came into his eyes," but that does not have the momentary quality of 轉眼睛 : a shifty look tends to be prolonged.

To continue with involuntary physical effects, Chinese writers talk of panic causing sweat to exude from the whole head or scalp. This is in fact a quite accurate description — you do indeed sweat all over the scalp in extremis — but Western writers tend to note only the visible outbreak of sweat on the forehead, so in turn Western readers would suspect exaggeration if the Chinese phrase is translated literally. As the translation of a novel cannot be used as an occasion to instruct the reader in physiology, the translator has to choose between challenging or conforming to the readers' preconceptions.

The first sign of tearfulness is described in Chinese as a smarting or pricking sensation in the nose (鼻酸), again quite factually. But normally one refers in English only to the eyes: "tears pricked her eyes"; or one leaves the location unspecified: "she felt the sting of tears." This may be because reference to what goes on in the nasal passages is considered indelicate.

It is rather more difficult to determine the facts of the matter with regard to the hairs which are said to spring erect with horror or terror. Both languages have the same phrase for the hair on the head standing on end, but what about the hairs on the back? English usage tends to be contradictory, as shivers are said to go down the spine, and it is this goose-pimpling that presumably causes the hair to stand on end, but reference to hair in that region is to the nape of the neck, not the whole length of the spine. In contrast, Chinese writers quite freely refer to "hair on the back" standing up. Perhaps the Western mind sees a logical objection to hairs standing on end under the pressure of clothes — assuming that the people who undergo this sensation are not stripped to the waist.

Contortions of the features probably get more mention than any-thing else. They can be of two kinds. If reflexive they may be universal, and the only thing that separates the Chinese from the Anglo-Saxon may be that Chinese has a word for a certain contortion and English does not; or they may be conventional, that is, whether conscious or not they may be imitated, and therefore possibly culture-bound. In any case, from the frequency with which they occur the foreign reader of Chinese fiction will soon be disabused of the notion that the Chinese are inscrut-able.

The most mobile of the features are of course the eyebrows and the mouth. Eyebrows are most commonly drawn together in concentration, pain or disapproval; there is no translation problem there. The twitching of the eyebrows from disquiet can also be accommodated. Such simple de-scriptions are child's play to Chinese writers. When they really want to show what they are made of they produce phrases like 眉尖聳動著 , to show profound indecision. Literally this means "the tips of the eyebrows going up and down repeatedly" (or "heaving"). I confess I do not know how to put this into acceptable English.

Coming down the face, we pass the cheeks, which are given to trem-bling (again quite truly), and arrive at the mouth. Chinese vocabulary is very extensive in the area of doing things with the mouth. English, on the other hand, has a fairly limited range of verbs. To "pout" or "purse" the lips is about all the average translator can think of. The more resourceful may run to "pucker", or even "moue", but there we come to an end. As far as I know, there is no equivalent to 努嘴 — to push out the lips and motion with them, for instance when you want to point somebody out without alerting them; this sign would usually be made among Anglo-Saxons with the inclination of eye or head. Similarly unfamiliar, 撇嘴 means to protrude the lower lip and pull down the corner of the mouth, to show disgust. As before, if the main thing is to convey the significance of the expression, one could do a cultural transfer and translate as "curled the lip"; or seek neutral ground and leave it up to the reader's imagination by using a formula like "his lips set in an expression of disgust." 努嘴 in the above usage is deliberate sign language (and so belongs to category B), while 撇嘴 is unconscious (and so belongs to category C), but together they typify contortions that are familiar to the Chinese reader but strange to the English reader. A general principle of translation is that what is normal in the source language should be translated into what is normal in the target language, but to follow that principle in such cases would compromise the fact — a distortion of the contortion, so to speak.

To return to our first category now, which refers to the distinctive functioning of the internal organs. There is quite a lot of common ground between the Chinese and the European view: both consider the heart as the seat of the emotions in general and the bowels as the seat of pity or tenderness in particular; to both the gall stands for boldness, and so on. But Chinese physiology has a lot of refinements unknown to Europe. In literature this is reflected in set phrases (such as that associating the lungs with sincerity), which being purely rhetorical only challenge the translator to match the level of language — to meet picturesque with picturesque, for example. But extended metaphors deriving from peculiar views of the functioning of internal organs obviously present difficulties. To take a simple example, in the Chinese view, the heart is the seat of thought as well as of feeling. Usually the translator will convert "heart" to "mind". But consider this passage:

> 作者聽他數說自己時，忽然起一個不快意的念頭，梗在心中，像胃裡消化不了的硬東西。
>
> When the author heard him criticizing him, an unhappy thought struck him, blocking his heart like something hard and indigestible in the stomach.

The writer of this can make an easy transition from heart to stomach because of their propinquity; it is more of a jump from mind to stomach. Furthermore, it is easier to imagine the vessels of the heart being blocked than the mind (or brain) being blocked. It seems that some cutting is necessary to achieve an acceptable translation: perhaps

> … an uncomfortable thought struck him, lying on his chest like some indigestible lump of food.

Modern authors, understandably, make less reference to the function or malfunction of internal organs than their forebears, but they retain some of the traditional flamboyance. It is fairly common for people to hear booming or buzzing noises in the head, and when the subject is on the verge of fainting this is acceptable universally, but Wang Anyi takes the effect a stage further:

> 見了這情景，母親腦子裡轟的一響，雖然什麼都不明白，可卻又什麼都明白了。
>
> When his mother saw this sight, something went boom in her head, and although she understood nothing, at the same time she understood everything.

Here the mother is confronted by the unexpected return home of her son from school in Shanghai, from where he has been expelled — a fact which he conceals from her. The boom in her head marks a sudden intuitive understanding of the truth. The Western writer would probably convey this kind of experience in terms of light rather than sound.

The same author lends extra force to the common metaphor of the blood freezing in this description:

他渾身的血液都凝固了
His whole-body blood all congealed (lit.)

By the addition of "whole-body", or "throughout his body", the reader is called upon to visualize the blood vessels as actually clogging up. Things that go on in the internal cavities of throat, chest and abdomen are also described in detail and with imagination by Chinese writers, and are taken in their stride by their readers. To the foreign reader they may seem alarming. For instance, this to describe some boys who are encouraged to jeer at an unfortunate pair of adults, but at the same time know they should not be so rude:

難禁的笑聲，憋在喉嚨裡咕咕作響
Their irrepressible laughter, trapped in their throats, made gurgling sounds

At times like these one might reasonably think a doctor is called for.

There is one problem of a different nature. This one is language driven. Verbs in Chinese are rarely left unsupported by adverbials or complements. Writers go along with this trend willingly: it gives them a chance to add to the description. So people are said to "struggle vigorously"; unless a writer in English wanted to make the special point that someone was struggling weakly, they take it for granted that struggling implies vigour. Translators of Chinese (especially academic translators) fail to make allowance for this phenomenon, and so over-translate. And of course this applies to body language. So for example you have this description of a girl in conversation with her boy friend:

吳芬芬輕咬住嘴唇
Wu Fenfen bit her lip softly/lightly

The Chinese reader, being prepared for some kind of adverb, takes the word "softly" innocently as an extra, meant to show that the girl is well brought up, not given to extravagant gestures, gentle in her ways. But the reader of English does not expect the biting of lips to be anything other than soft, unless emotion is running so high that the lip is made to bleed, which certainly does not pertain here. So the explicit mention of "softly" rouses suspicions that the action might be calculating, i.e. deliberately soft, which would do the poor girl an injustice. Similarly:

臉上布滿憂戚神色
On face spread-full misery expression (lit.)

Here the word "full" is a verb complement: if not this word, then some other complement would have been used. But translators think they have to account for the idea of fullness, so "His face was filled with misery." According to English descriptive convention, unless it is intended that only a *hint* of emotion showed, it goes without saying that the expression is not partial but full. If the form of a description is language driven, transfer should be made to the language drive in the target language, which may be differently geared. It would be perfectly reasonable to reach for "His face was a picture of misery." But a closer fit would be made if one resorted to "write" as the verb, because that also takes a complement for linguistic reasons:

Misery was written all over his face.
(You cannot comfortably dispense with "all".)

As I have said, translations from the Chinese tend to be made by academics, and academics tend to read the more intellectual type of fiction in their own language, where emotions are kept under fairly tight control. They therefore suffer from two handicaps when it comes to body language. Both can be relieved: the first by shedding not necessarily their posts but their academicism; the second goes without saying.

Body language may give rise nowadays to headaches rather than pleasure, but occasionally one comes across a description it is a pleasure to translate. I include this among that limited collection:

洩了氣的肉就像放下的簾子，鬆鬆耷拉在臉上
His flesh was as it were deflated, and hung like a curtain, loosely on his face.

Book Titles

Frederick Tsai
Honorary Fellow
Hong Kong Translation Society, Hong Kong

When I read the Rev. Father Albert Chan's *The Glory and Fall of the Ming Dynasty*, a classic, I was struck by the fact that almost all the titles of the Chinese books in the notes and the bibliography were transliterated. Even titles which could be translated without apparent difficulty are treated in the same way. Excerpts quoted in the book are excellently translated, and Father Chan's erudition is legendary. Why then did he not translate the titles? I can only conclude that this is the usual practice among sinologists, and Father Chan simply follows it. My inference has since been confirmed by checking other English books where Chinese book titles appear.

After considering a few titles, I came to realize that there is good reason not to translate such titles. It is often not only a strenuous but also a futile task. However good a translator may be, he or she cannot do the impossible. One can of course translate any title, but the translation may not always convey what the original meant to native readers. He will have to give an explanation, or more like an argument, amounting in length to a short article. For instance, the title of a Chinese book like 《春在堂全書》 (*The Complete Works of Yu Yue* 俞樾), to me defies translation. It draws upon his famous line: 花落春仍在 (Though flowers have fallen, spring is still with us). We can translate *The Complete Works of the (Owner of the) Hall of Spring Being Still Here*, but it fails miserably to tell the readers a beautiful literary anecdote behind the whole line. When, in 1850, Yu sat for an imperial examination he came out top of the list. And this is the first line of his poem on *A Day with Light Mist, Sprinkling of Rain, and Fallen Flowers*, which was tremendously admired by one of the examiners, Zeng Guofan 曾國藩 , himself a poet and scholar, whose favorable comment on it was: "It conveys no decadent implications where fallen flowers are concerned." Zeng recommended to his fellow-examiners that they award Yu the first place. Today we can say that Yu's line is imbued with what Dr. Norman Vincent Peale calls positive thinking. Yu was so grateful for and happy over Zeng's appreciation that he named his house 春在堂 . Even if we add "Flowers Fallen" to the title, we still have not told the entire anecdote. All Chinese literati are supposed to know it, and can appreciate Yu's feeling of elation when the title is read. Can any translation of the title arouse such a shared feeling among its foreign readers?

I might add that Zeng's comment also argues that Yu's poem is similar to the meaning of a poem by "Song Minor" on fallen flowers. "Song Minor" was Song Qi 宋祁 (996–1061), a successful candidate for the highest imperial examination, together with his elder brother, Song Xiang 宋庠 . Since they were both notable literary figures of the day, they were known as Song Major and Song Minor. The poem is a masterpiece and was regarded by Xia Song 夏竦 , the brothers' patron and an erudite scholar, as a sign indicating that some day Song would become a minister of the highest rank at court. He was right in his prediction, for Song later rose to various important positions. The poem is a 律詩 , a poem of eight lines with seven characters to each line, the form most strict in rules governing such things as tonal pattern, rhyme scheme, and the use of allusions and antitheses for the two middle pairs of lines. It is a real poser for the translator. The general idea of the poem is that although it is sad that flowers should fall, they still dance in the wind and are beautiful; like the tears of a sea monster, they can turn themselves into pearls and still retain their fragrance.

If only one title is involved a translator can insert a note to tell a story. But in a book like Father Chan's hundreds are referred to; notes like this will cover more pages than the text, and readers will soon be sated with them. They will find that they are unable to read the book. In fact, no writer of such a book could complete it if he were bogged down by the research and the compilation of hundreds of notes to book titles.

We might say that it is interesting to be acquainted with an anecdote like the above. There are, however, other titles, the key to which can turn out to be very dull. Let us take 《湧幢小品》 (*Essays Written in Yong*

Chuang) by Zhu Guozhen 朱國禎 (1557–1632) for example. The title is so impenetrable that the author had to write a short article to explain it. In it he tells among other things that he built a wooden hexagonal pavilion, which resembled a stone tablet (幢), capable of being put anywhere, folded or unfolded, like something springing up from the ground (湧). What he called 小品 (essays) are not essays, but miscellanies. The book is so entitled because he read his books and wrote his short articles in the pavilion. No translator can condense a story like this into a title; he can only tell it, at best in a brief note.

Not every writer is so considerate as to let his readers know how he chose his titles. The research can be considerable, sending the translator to concordances, encyclopedias, large dictionaries, dictionaries of quotations, and so forth. Often he needs to consult more learned friends or scholars who specialize in a certain period or a certain author. He can never be quite sure of his findings. Query: is it worthwhile for a translator to spend so much time in such an endeavor?

I can cite many Chinese book titles which show how ticklish they can be to translators. Suffice it to say, many such titles, like Chinese personal names, contain a quotation or part of a quotation, or a quotation in disguise from the most ancient classics, or the *bon mot* of a literary giant. Often only an accomplished scholar can identify its source. Transliteration seems to be the only choice.

In one area alone can translators enjoy complete freedom in disregarding the original, and that area is the translation of book titles. But the danger here is they are quite likely to misrepresent the author and mislead their readers. When a translator acts as editor, he may be either a judicious one or a dangerous one. A century ago, Lin Shu 林紓 , who knew no foreign language whatever, but depended on others to interpret for him, translated over 150 European books into Chinese. It is not our concern here to discuss his contribution to translation; it is his translation of book titles that interests us. They are all traditionally Chinese, elegant and classical, but some may also be misleading. For instance, he gave 《塊肉餘生述》 (literally, *A Narration of the Survival of an Orphan*), as the title of Charles Dickens's *David Copperfield*. To those who have read the book, it cannot pass muster. The story is not limited to the hero's survival, but covers his life from childhood to his success as a writer. It is true, however, that he was an orphan.

Another questionable translation is Fu Donghua's 傅東華 title, 《飄》

for Margaret Mitchell's *Gone with the Wind*. We can hardly associate this, which signifies *float in the air*, or *flutter*, with the novel; we would suggest that 逝 , which means *pass away*, fits much better. Unfortunately, these two translations, Lin's and Fu's, are well established, and have become standard, even though never regarded by people of taste as acceptable.

Now let us see if English titles are any less troublesome. Any student of English literature can recognize that Thomas Hardy's *Far from the Madding Crowd* is a quotation from Gray's *Elegy*, so that failure to produce the whole line and mention the poet's name and the title of the poem would be an inexcusable omission. But there are other titles which may conceal something hard to uncover. Max Beerbohm's *And Even Now* is one. This is his last volume of essays. The title is simple, but I am afraid that unless one reads the book, one would be unable to tell what the author intended to convey. On page 10, in the essay *A Relic*, the incomparable Max, as George Bernard Shaw called him, says, through Mlle. Angélique, the heroine of the piece: "To think what I once was, monsieur, — what, but for him, I might be, even now!" To understand its relation to the title, we have to refer to Max's short "Note" in place of a preface: "perhaps a book of essays ought to seem as if it had been written a few days before publication." Here, I presume, but am not absolutely sure, that he meant that all the essays in it, "written in the course of the past ten years," (his own words) are fresh even now. If a translator had to translate this title, could we expect him to find and go through the whole book to solve its enigma? What if he has to deal with hundreds of titles?

Other European book titles may also require some research. H. Sienkiewicz's *Quo Vadis* may lead us to regard it as a quotation from the Vulgate version of The Gospel according to St. John 16: 5, but in point of fact, it is not. In the last chapter of the novel, the author tells of Peter the apostle, who reluctantly disguised, flees from Rome through the gate, and sees the Lord entering Rome. "Lord, where are you going?" he asks. The Lord replies, "I am going to Rome to be crucified." With the Lord's epiphany, Peter comes to himself, and returns to Rome, ready to be a martyr. This story is not found in the canon of the Bible, but in the apocryphal *Acts of Peter*. And at the end of the novel we read: "Quo Vadis Domine?"

We all know that an English translator does not have to do anything when he runs into a French or German book title; he lets the original stand in his translation with perfect legitimacy. Only a title in an entirely different language like Chinese or Arabic calls for translation or transliteration. His readers cannot complain if they do not read French or German; but what about transliteration of Chinese or Arabic titles? Can they charge the translator with dereliction of duty? Translators are, however, human beings. To ask them to translate 《春在堂全書》 is no less a thing to ask them than to "stride over the North Sea with Mount Tai under their arms", if I may borrow a phrase from Mencius. (I am using Professor D. C. Lau's translation.) It is a genuine case of impossibility to satisfy. Their readers will be more understanding if they know that not only book titles, but strictly speaking, many other things also, resist translation.

References

Cao, Congsun 曹聰孫 . 〈關於翻譯作品的譯名〉 (On the Translation of Titles). In 《翻譯論集》 (*Essays on Translation*), edited by Luo Xinzhang 羅新璋 . Beijing: The Commercial Press 商務印書館 , 1984, pp. 993–95.

Feng, Huazhan 豐華瞻 . 〈漫談書名的翻譯〉 (On the Translation of Book Titles). In 《翻譯論集》 (*Essays on Translation*), edited by Luo Xinzhang. Beijing: The Commercial Press 商務印書館 , 1984, pp. 999–1002.

Jovanovic, Mladen. "On Translating Titles." *Babel*, Vol. 36, No. 4 (1990), pp. 213–22.

Wu, Xueshu 伍學書 . 〈書名翻譯雜談〉 (The Translation of Book Titles). 《中國翻譯》 (*Chinese Translators Journal*), No. 2 (1986), pp. 57–58.

Yang, Qishen 楊豈深 . 〈漫談書名人名的翻譯〉 (On the Translation of Book Titles and Personal Names). In 《當代文學翻譯百家談》 (*Views on Translation by One Hundred Contemporary Literary Translators*), edited by Wang Shoulan 王壽蘭 . Beijing: Peking University Press 北京大學出版社 , 1989, pp. 333–38.

Children's Literature

Dai Liuling
Department of Foreign Languages and Literature
Zhongshan University, Guangzhou, China

Children's literature was in its proper sense scarcely known in China less than a hundred years ago. The recognition it gradually gained was due mainly to extensive translation of foreign literature of which books for children formed an appreciable percentage. Lin Shu 林紓 (1852–1924) headed the list of translators of the recent past. Among his early translations was Mrs Stowe's *Uncle Tom's Cabin* in 1901. It caused a great stir at that time. The depiction of Uncle Tom's experiences moved Chinese children profoundly. China was then suffering repeated humiliating defeats at the hands of foreign aggressors. The story's anti-slavery and anti-racism sentiment thus likewise fired Chinese intellectuals with patriotism. Lin Shu appreciated the story probably both for its entertaining content and its moral teaching. Anyway, it marked the beginning of the introduction from the West of a literary work intended primarily for children. Lin's *The Fables of Aesop* was done in 1903 possibly from an English version. His *Robinson Crusoe* appeared in 1905 and *Gulliver's Travels* in 1906, both counted for a long time among his finer productions. A little earlier, in 1904, when he brought out Charles and Mary Lamb's *Tales from Shakespeare*, he had scored less success. He missed somewhat the light and graceful touch in the original. But with regard to his *Tales from Chaucer* by Charles Cowden Clarke, he simply made a wrong choice for his labour. Much worse was his *Tales from Spenser* by Sophia H. MacLehose. He has been much criticized

for translating many of the adventure romances by Haggard, being generally considered a second-rate author. But Haggard's *King Solomon's Mines*
is justly famous. And Lin did it admirably. With equal success, he rendered
Irving's *Sketch Book* which contains the two diverting pieces, *Rip Van
Winkle* and *The Legend of Sleepy Hollow*.

Lin Shu knew no foreign languages. He translated through oral interpreters. To compensate for this obvious shortcoming, he had the gift of
story-telling. Being a master of classical Chinese prose, he opposed
strongly the use of the language of the common people in writing. With the
reform in language and education, Lin's translations of books for children
have become utterly unintelligible to children of the new age.

In 1922, two years before Lin's death, Chao Yuen Ren 趙元任 (1892–
1982) published his *Alice's Adventures in Wonderland* by Lewis Carroll.
Chao's approach differs completely from Lin's. A linguist by profession, he
knew thoroughly the lexical and structural features of English and Chinese.
He was convinced of the limitations of antiquated literary Chinese so dear
to Lin. In his opinion English books could be best translated into spoken
Chinese. In the case of a book like *Alice in Wonderland* which was written
chiefly for children, this is particularly true. It is difficult for traditional
literary Chinese to recapture the childlike simplicity and naturalness in
speech characterizing its pages. For this reason he preferred living, everyday speech based on the Beijing dialect. The whole book, rich in innocent
fun, parodies and nonsense rhymes, was satisfactorily rendered into Chinese. He wrote a foreword to his translation. In this way he showed by
example and precept how books for children should be translated and what
was the suitable linguistic medium to be used.

The supremacy of spoken Chinese over literary Chinese was one of
the necessary results of the May Fourth Movement which, in its turn, led to
the New Culture Movement. The years following this may be said to be a
long flowering of translation. Nearly all translators favoured the use of
spoken Chinese. There were several new renderings of *Robinson Crusoe*
and *Gulliver's Travels*. Lin Shu's renderings of the same works had become
outmoded. Familiar titles never done into Chinese before were consequently made legitimate objects of pursuit. Lin Shu only put forth Stevenson's *New Arabian Nights*. It was up to the new generation of translators to
attend to his *Treasure Island, Kidnapped, The Black Arrow* and *A Child's
Garden of Verses*. They succeeded in making up for what Lin had left
undone. In a similar manner, *Through the Looking-glass*, a sequel to *Alice*

in Wonderland, could now stand beside the latter as sister volumes in Chinese.

It is no exaggeration to say that nearly all important English books for children brought out in the last century, and a great many in the present, have been touched by Chinese translators. Besides those mentioned above and those we shall speak of below, we need only here name a few authors of such books: Wilde, Grahame, C. S. Lewis, Alcott and Hawthorne.

Veteran translators like Wu Guangjian 伍光建 (1866–1943) and Zhou Xuliang 周煦良 (1905–1984) did not think it beneath them to contribute their share here. Wu was a cadet at the Royal Naval College in Greenwich from 1886–1891. His translations include stories from Kipling's *Jungle Books*. His language is homely, terse and lively. Unlike Chao Yuen Ren, he loves to intersperse his colloquialisms with borrowings from old Chinese storybooks. Sometimes he resorts to free rendering of a passage in the original defying literal translation. His aim is to make every expression read like a native speaker's Chinese, unaffected by foreign idioms. Zhou Xuliang is closely related to Wu in style. During his student days in Edinburgh, he studied under Herbert Grierson and developed a fine taste in English prose and poetry. His seemingly amateurish and yet scholarly contrastive analysis of Chinese and English usage stands him in good stead. His Maugham, Galsworthy and especially A. E. Housman are models of delightful accuracy. The same quality is to be found in his *The Water-Babies* by Kingsley, except that here simple vocabulary and expressions are used.

One thing claiming our attention is the immense labour spent on individual works or authors by a translator. Zhang Wanli 張萬里 (1913–1986), a college teacher of English, studied Mark Twain's *The Adventures of Huckleberry Finn* with great earnestness. Before his translation of the novel was published in its finished form in the early fifties he had polished and repolished it for nearly thirty years. Another excellent Chinese version of the same novel was made by Zhang Yousong 張友松 (1903–?). It also appeared in the fifties. With great gusto Zhang Yousong did many of Mark Twain's books, including such pieces for children as *The Prince and the Pauper* and *The Adventures of Tom Sawyer*, besides the one mentioned above. The case of Mark Twain points to China's growing interest in children's books of quality and also increasing specialization in translation.

But when so many translations rush helter-skelter into print, it is natural that Chinese children will respond favourably to some and take little interest in others. Barrie's *Peter Pan* is a case in point. Though translated twice into Chinese, it seems never to have been very popular. The reason is perhaps that Chinese boys and girls are not yet used to the play's sophisticated mysteriousness.

Children's literature has since 1949 received considerable attention from the Chinese educational and cultural authorities. They deem it necessary to provide children with wholesome books for entertainment and edification as well. Great caution should therefore always be exercised in the selection of such books to be translated. The prevalence of scenes of violence and brutality in contemporary Western children's books is strongly objected to. Meanwhile there are now more and more publishers in China catering for the intellectual food of children.

We can safely predict in conclusion that translation of children's literature produced in the English-speaking world will continue to thrive.

References

Klingberg, Gote, Mary Orvig and Stuart Amor, eds. *Children's Books in Translation: The Situation and the Problems*. Stockholm: Almqvist and Wilsell International, 1978.

Lin, Liang 林良. 〈爲孩子們翻譯〉 (Translating for the Children). In 《翻譯因緣》 (*On Translation*), edited by Hu Tsu-tan 胡子丹. Taipei: Renditions Monthly Press 翻譯天地出版社, 1979, pp. 187–91.

Puurtinen, Tiina. "Assessing Acceptability in Translated Children's Books." *Target*, Vol. 1, No. 2 (1989), pp. 201–13.

Ren, Rongrong 任溶溶. 〈我要一輩子爲兒童翻譯〉 (I Want to Translate for Children for My Entire Life). In 《當代文學翻譯百家談》 (*Views on Translation by One Hundred Contemporary Literary Translators*), edited by Wang Shoulan 王壽蘭. Beijing: Peking University Press 北京大學出版社, 1989, pp. 207–10.

Shavit, Zohar. "Translation of Children's Literature as a Function of Its Position in the Literary Polysystem." *Poetics Today*, Vol. 2, No. 4 (1981), pp. 171–79.

Xu Jiarong 徐家榮. 〈兒童文學翻譯對譯文語言的特殊要求〉 (Special Requirements of Target Languages for Children's Literature). 《中國翻譯》 (*Chinese Translators Journal*), No. 5 (1988), pp. 15–19.

Colour Terms

Serena S. H. Jin
Department of Translation
The Chinese University of Hong Kong, Hong Kong

The problem of translating colour words arises in two quite distinct forms. The first occurs where the colour word is employed in a purely descriptive and literal sense. Here the solution depends upon visualizing the exact colour meant by the word in the source language and knowing the correct equivalent in the target language by which to translate it. The second case confronts the translator in the form of an entirely metaphorical use of a colour, e.g., "black despair". Here the solution may lie either in replacing the original colour word by an altogether different colour in the target language, or by employing the equivalent idiom which may not necessarily involve any colour word at all, e.g., a "black sheep" in English becomes 害群之馬 in Chinese, an expression that means approximately the same but involves no reference to a colour. In this instance the accuracy of the translation depends primarily upon a full understanding of the English idiom, followed by identification of the appropriate Chinese equivalent.

Colour is, in fact, probably the most common factor employed in the formation of metaphors in all languages. But the symbolic or metaphorical significance of any given colour varies from language to language. Thus to the Chinese white is one of the two colours of mourning, whereas in European usage it represents purity or, in certain cases, nullity or neutrality as in the term "white noise". Such contradictions constitute one of the major problems in the translation of metaphors, a feature of particular importance in the translation of poetry.

Both Chinese and English are rich in colour terms. However, colour terms can be divided into two major categories: (1) basic colours such as black, white, red, green, yellow, blue, brown, purple, pink, grey, orange, etc.; and (2) colours derived from objects, such as apple, rose, grass, lilac, primrose, peacock, raven, amber, ivory, steel, cream, indigo, flame, snow, etc.

The first category seems more universal in nature. Though each basic colour may have different metaphorical significance in different languages, the colour itself is generally perceptible, in other words, people of different countries and races share more or less the same visual sense. The second category is much more complicated. When colour terms are derived from the exact colour of objects in the environment, green in one language may become "leaf-coloured" in another language. A Western reader may just manage to accept the colour "cream" becoming "rice" in Chinese, but how can he visualize the human face as being the "colour of soya sauce"? He will also have difficulty accepting the colour of sky at dawn as "fish-belly white".

In tackling the problem of translating colour terms, we should perhaps begin with the basic colours. The colour most frequently used with a metaphorical significance in English is probably blue. The fact blue occurs with a wide range of meaning, sometimes positive, sometimes negative, certainly causes a lot of trouble in translation. While blue refers to the positive aspects of blue sky and blue sea as indicated by the film title "Blue Hawaii", and to nobility as in "blue blood", it also has an entirely negative connotation in phrases like to "have the blues" (to be depressed) and to "sing the blues" (to complain).

A Chinese reader would be totally baffled if a translator were to translate literally the following terms related to the colour blue. They would hardly understand why a "blue book" is an important official document, whereas "blue films" are pornographic films. Nor would the Chinese reader realize that a "blue coat" means a policeman, "blue-collar" indicates a manual worker as opposed to a "white-collar" or clerical worker, a "blue-jacket", a sailor, and a "blue-stocking", an intelligent but over-academic lady.

Another problem arises from differences in the colour terms employed in different languages to describe the same physical realities. Thus "blue in the face" becomes "ash grey" in Chinese, while "blue fur" becomes the more accurate "bluish grey". The phrase "his face was blue with cold" normally becomes "his face was purple with cold." Whereas someone may be beaten "black and blue" in English, the French phrase is "*battre quelqu'un tout bleu*," while in Chinese, it becomes "blue and purple".

Certain metaphorical phrases make use of a colour in a way that would be totally incomprehensible to speakers of other languages. For instance, the expression to be "in a brown study" meaning to be lost in thought, a Victorian English turn of phrase already somewhat archaic, would be meaningless to anyone not already familiar with it.

Black and white are relatively simpler to translate. Black seems usually to have negative connotations, such as evil, wicked, bad, notorious, sullied, stained whereas white denotes positive attributes, such as pure, spotless, clean, innocent, chaste, virtuous. The Chinese reader can readily understand the connotation of the English expression "to blacklist", but the term "white-haired boy", meaning a special favourite and implying someone with blond or "golden-hair", would have to be rendered by a phrase devoid of any colour reference, since all Chinese have black hair until they are old, and white hair, especially when it is referring to a young boy, could not have a positive connotation.

Black is used with a wide variety of negative connotations, e.g., without hope, gloomy; angry or resentful as in "black look"; pessimistic or macabre as in "black comedy"; wicked or harmful as in "a black lie" or "black-hearted".

Red is also a colour of interest from the point of view of English-Chinese translation. In English, red is often connected with passion or rage, as in the sentence "he saw red". It also indicates left-wing politics. In Chinese, red is generally the most favoured colour, and is always used in traditional architecture and on festive occasions such as weddings, birthdays and New Year's Day. Thus, "red-carpet" can be easily translated into Chinese with the same colour word. "Red-tape", on the other hand, is translated into a Chinese idiom without a colour word.

In Chinese one says of a jealous person that he is "red-eyed" whereas in English "red-eye" is a slang term for cheap whisky, while the colour for jealousy is green (the "green-eyed monster") instead.

Green also has many other symbolic meanings in English, of which hope is perhaps the most important. Related to "hope" but mainly derived from the fact that it is the predominant colour of nature is its use in connection with the ecology or environmental movement, which remains exactly the same in Chinese.

Yellow seems to be a colour that is not very much favoured in English. It usually means cowardly, but also offensively sensational, as in the phrase the "yellow press" for cheap, sensational newspapers. But the Chinese being called "people of the yellow race," have no such unpleasant associations with the colour yellow. On the contrary, since yellow is related to gold, it signifies wealth and status. The imperial robe, for example, is yellow in colour.

"Yellow journalism" becomes in Chinese "peach-coloured" journalism, though modern usage tends to employ the same colour word "yellow" to translate this term. The reasons why the Chinese turn "blue movies" into "yellow movies" are quite unclear.

Other colours which have different symbolic meanings in English and Chinese are purple and pink. While in both the Chinese and the English cultures, purple is the colour of royalty, it has a special connotation in English in the expression "a purple passage" or "purple prose" meaning a passage of writing that is excessively elaborate or full of imagery. The Chinese regard purple as even more intense or precious than red, as in the phrase 紅得發紫, meaning literally "from red to purple" indicating that someone has become "extremely popular or well-known." Pink in Chinese is expressed as "light-red", and has no special status as in English. In English, pink is a much favoured colour. When someone is "the pink of perfection," it means he is hundred per cent perfect. The Chinese has no such connotation in relation to "pink", which generally has the implication of "romantic".

The fact that modern Chinese tends to use compound words rather than monosyllabic words makes the translation of colour terms a great challenge to most translators.

An experiment carried out with students at The Chinese University of Hong Kong in 1985 produced a variety of renderings for the English phrase "blue eyes", which became in Chinese:

湖水藍的眼睛	(lake-blue eyes)
碧眼	(blue eyes but using another Chinese word for "blue")
藍藍的眼睛	(blue, blue eyes)
藍色的眼睛	(blue-coloured eyes)

藍眼晴	(blue eyes)
晶藍的眼睛	(crystal blue eyes)
藍澄澄的眸子	(blue, blue eyes, using reiterated locution to modify "blue")

Only in two instances was "blue" translated by a single-word colour term.

A more sophisticated example is "snow-white hair". Translations varied as follows:

白髮	(white hair)
雪白的頭髮	(snow-white hair)
銀白的頭髮	(silver-white hair)
頭髮斑白	(grizzled hair)
雪白的頭髮	(hair white as snow)
滿頭花白	(a head of grey/grizzled hair)
頭髮白雪雪	(hair snow, snow white)
斑斑白髮	(grizzled hair)
頭髮雪白	(hair snow-white)
滿頭霜白的頭髮	(full of frost-white hair)
一頭銀絲	(hair of silver threads)
白皚皚的頭髮	(white, white hair, using reiterated locution)
斑斑白白的頭髮	(grizzled, grizzled and white, white hair)
白髮蒼蒼	(grey-haired)
白髮如霜	(white hair like frost)

In the back translation, it is clear that "grizzled hair" has a different connotation than "snow-white hair". While the former is drab in colour and unpleasant to look at, the latter is shiny and can be quite appealing. But what leads a translator to change "snow-white" into "silver" or "frosty" is not only a matter of taste, but a choice based on the context of the original piece of writing.

As previously mentioned, both English and Chinese are rich in colour terms. All colours have many potential qualities. White can be pallid, cadaverous or bright as snow, pure as a lily. Off white can be dull as chalk or lustrous as pearl. There are also many varieties of black. While raven and sable are sombre, ebony and jet are shiny. Thus, a famous Black magazine in the States is called "Ebony". When basic colour terms are translated into another language, they may be expressed in simple basic terms, or qualified by reference to objects of a specific colour. On the other hand, colours related to objects may be converted into basic colours in the course of translation.

Since modern Chinese has a tendency to use compound words, the simple basic colour terms in English are usually translated into double-words or multi-words in Chinese. Examples can be drawn from Irving Stone's *Lust for Life*. This book has been translated by three different translators. All three translators have tried to match the original colour terms with comparable terms in Chinese, but, one of the translators, Professor Yu Kwang-chung, stands out as exploiting most fully the expressive resources of the Chinese language. For example, he has translated "black" as 黝黑, "red" as 火紅, "orange" as 橙黃, "lilac" as 淡紫, rather than merely 黑、橙、紅、紫 and so on.

Reverse situations can be found when translating colour words from Chinese into English. While Chinese writers tend to use more complicated forms in rendering colours, English writers usually express colours more directly. Chosen at random from *Renditions*, we can find examples as follows:

Chinese	*English Translation*
黑烏烏的大眼睛	big *dark* eyes
(*Renditions*, 1981)	
一樣的天, 為什麼紅的紅,	strange, how could the same sky be
青的青, 黑的黑呢?	so *pink*, so *grey*, so *black*?
(Ibid.)	
那綠茸茸的夢	The dream of *green* growth
(*Renditions*, 1983)	
紫紅色荊叢	a grove of *purple* thorns
(Ibid.)	

Certain Chinese colour terms vary in meaning according to the context. Thus, *bi* 碧 can mean "green" as well as "blue", *cang* 蒼 can mean deep blue, dark green, grey or greyish-yellow. *Qing* 青 is a colour word of many facets. Referring to sky, it means "blue", while referring to vegetables it is "green"; of hair it means "black", of complexion it means "ghastly pale". There are also many Chinese colour terms which are often used in Chinese classical literature and thus have a special flavour of elegance. Stephen Soong 宋淇 mentions in his article on "Translation of Colours" that using

縞素 when describing a woman in mourning is much more vivid and arresting than using the simple term "white". Similarly, terms such as 青翠 are more appealing than a mere "green". Other colours which have a strong Chinese flavour are 豆沙色 (colour of red-bean paste), 蝦肉色 (colour of shrimp), 蟹青色 (crab-green), 魚肚白 (fish-belly white), 鵝黄 (goose-yellow), 蔥綠 (onion-green), 菱色 (colour of water caltrop), 藕色 (colour of lotus root), etc., which will give Western translators a hard time.

A special device employed in Chinese rhetoric must be mentioned in connection with the problem of translating colour terms. That is, the use of reiterated locutions. As previously stated, all colours have many different qualities and shades. Instead of using such words as deep, dark, light, pale, bright, rich, vivid, dull, murky, drab, to describe the colours concerned, or suffixes such as "ish" to indicate the degree of intensity of colour, Chinese writers tend to use reiterated locutions that combine with particular colour words to denote different shades. Thus *bai ai-ai* 白皚皚 is snow-white, *bai liang-liang* 白亮亮 is shiny-white, whereas *bai mang-mang* 白茫茫 is misty and murky. *Hei sen-sen* 黑森森 is dark black, *hei you-you* 黑油油 is shiny black. *Hong du-du* 紅嘟嘟 is ruddy, *hong yan-yan* 紅焰焰 means flaming red. *Lü wang-wang* 綠汪汪 has to do with an expanse of water, whereas *lü you-you* 綠油油 is lustrous green, and usually used to describe trees and grass. There are numerous similar examples and mastery of such reiterated locutions will certainly make the Chinese translations of colour terms more vivid and expressive.

References

Bennett, T. J. A. "Translating Colour Collocations." *Meta*, Vol. 26, No. 3 (1981), pp. 272–80.

Berlin, B. and P. Kay. *Basic Color Terms*. Berkeley: University of California Press, 1969.

Kao, George 喬志高. 《美語新詮》 (*On Connotations in American English*). Taipei: Pure Literature Press 純文學出版社, 1974, pp. 17–31.

Lin, Yi-liang 林以亮. 《林以亮論翻譯》 (*Lin Yi-liang on Translation*). Taipei: Chih-wen Press 志文出版社, 1974, pp. 91–95.

Yao, Shaoping 姚少平. 〈基本顏色詞理論述評─兼論漢語基色色詞的演變史〉 (A Theoretical Introduction to Basic Colour Terms — With a Discussion on the Development of Chinese Basic Colour Terms). 《外語教學與研究》 (*Foreign Language Teaching and Research*), Vol. 73 (1988), pp. 19–28.

Zhang, Peiji 張培基 . 《英語聲色詞與翻譯》 (*English Onomatopaetic and Colour Terms and Their Translation*). Beijing: The Commercial Press 商務印書館 , 1964.

Zhang, Yinquan 章銀泉 . 《色彩描寫語語例釋》 (*Examples and Explanations of Expressions Describing Colours*). Yinchuan: Ningxia People's Press 寧夏人民 出版社 , 1983.

COMMERCIAL TRANSLATION

Commercial Translation

Raymond S. C. Lie
Department of English
Hong Kong Baptist College, Hong Kong

What is Commercial Translation?

This entry attempts to pinpoint some of the major issues and problems of commercial translation, with reference to the translation market in Hong Kong. Commercial translation, defined simply, is any translation work undertaken and required directly or indirectly for any commercial purpose. Since the commercial field covers a diffuse range of activities (e.g., administrative, industrial, legal, scientific and technical), the label "commercial translator" can be inclusively applied to anyone engaged in translation work relating (even remotely) to any of these activities. Thus, a legal translator working for industry and commerce can justifiably call himself a "commercial translator," or a "legal-commercial translator." This pragmatic definition of the term primarily distinguishes the commercial translator from his traditional counterpart, the literary translator, in the mainly factual or practical (rather than literary, aesthetic, poetic, or belletristic) nature of the material he works with.

Commercial translation, as understood in this sense of the term, has a rather short history. It has, within the international context, become a recognized profession in its own right only during the past few decades, since the establishment of the United Nations and UNESCO and their numerous international governmental and inter-governmental agencies with the consequent increase in the need for highly trained linguists, bilingual and multilingual experts, and translators and interpreters in all fields of human activity. On top of the translation services of governments and international organizations, translating agencies and industrial or commercial translation departments are the other major providers of commercial translation services.

The post-1984 burgeoning in Hong Kong of commercial translating activities — 1987 statistics show that the number of local translating agencies (including one-man or two-men operations) soared to nearly a hundred in that year — seemed to have been significantly heralded both by China's Open Door Trade Policy in the late 1970s and by the signing in 1984 of the Sino-British Joint Declaration on the Future of Hong Kong. The post-1984 period witnessed a sharp rise in the volume of translation work emanating from China Trade-related activities — public corporations and multi-nationals, large firms of solicitors, patent agents have all established their own translation departments to handle their China Trade contracts. Previously, commercial translators had never existed on such a great scale, on either the corporate or the individual levels. Concomitant with this has been an increased public awareness of the importance of the commercial translating profession. Accordingly, many local tertiary institutions have been competing with one another in actively launching professionally-oriented translator/interpreter training programmes to produce graduates to meet the urgent historic demand for local commercial translators. Among the local prominent organizations that employ commercial translators on their staffs are China Light, Cable and Wireless, Hong Kong Federation of Industries, Trade Development Council, Productivity Council, Vocational Training Council, with the Hong Kong Government being the biggest employer of so-called "Chinese Language Officers."

The existence of translating agencies offering commercial translation services depends partly upon the popularity of foreign languages in the region concerned. For example, translating agencies have always been more prominent in the United Kingdom than in countries such as the former Federal Republic of Germany, the Netherlands, or Switzerland, where more people are familiar with foreign languages. This is so because foreign languages are something quite alien in the United Kingdom, and many people in industry and commerce there are glad to relegate this part of their work to translating agencies. Thus it can be seen from the above examples that a demand for commercial translators can be prompted by many factors, including political and cultural developments, international commerce with concomitant technology transfer, popularity of foreign languages, etc.

Text-types and the Source Language Text

Given their conglomerate nature, commercial texts encompass the whole range of subjects that relate centrally or peripherally to the commercial world. Miscellaneous texts (e.g., scientific and technical, medical, legal) that would be otherwise classified can, therefore, be subsumed under the rubric of "commercial" texts, provided that their translation ties in with any commercial need. This broad pragmatic categorization may seem unorthodox or rather strange to non-professionals steeped in the conventional dichotomy of literary versus technical translation text-typologies. It can be imagined, then, that the variety of so-called "commercial" texts handled by both governmental and company translation departments as well as translating agencies can be quite enormous, ranging from average run-of-the-mill texts (e.g., memoranda, reports, contracts and tenders, patents, academic papers, advertising copy and slogans, signs and notices, personal letters and certificates, instructional manuals, catalogues, film scripts, restaurant menus) to exigent types of text of a highly specialized or exotic nature (e.g., legal documents involving specialized technical knowledge or ancient Chinese deeds).

Perhaps the most distinguishing feature of commercial texts in general is their poor textual quality. Many texts are poorly written in the source language, which can be manifested in problems such as linguistic and stylistic infelicities, sloppy and incorrect syntax, tautologies, idiolects, non-sequiturs, howlers, etc. Coupled with these linguistic inadequacies are other problems like obscurities, ambiguities, errors of facts and figures, misprints, miscopying, orthographic errors, and poor physical form, etc. Certificates, for example, are often faded and tattered with pieces missing at the edges and along the folds, presenting the problem of physical clarity for the translator. This is often compensated, fortuitously, by their standard phrasing and format; accordingly their translation in terms of both content and form will not pose much of a problem. The linguistic problems found in these source-language texts are so caused because writers of commercial texts are mostly non-linguists who are either ignorant or unconcerned about the mechanics of good writing and communication theory. It can be further detected that the quality of originals is text-specific: for example, the problem of loose phrasing can often be found in drafts and working documents, whereas that of inaccurate terminology is found in situation-specific texts.

These linguistic inadequacies inherent in the source text pose a great problem for the commercial translator, in contrast to the literary translator who normally works with well-written, finely polished texts. As a consequence of the poor overall textual quality, either communication breaks down altogether, or the translator is confronted with the question of whether or not to fill in the gaps in the source text by, for example, correcting the obvious errors or oversights of the source-language writer and normalizing other source-language features. What happens is that the pragmatic duty of getting the intended message across will compel the beleaguered translator to decipher, correct, recast or even generally improve upon the source-language text. The professional rule of ethics that the translator has no right to "doctor" the source-language text in his charge is conditionally modified in view of the more urgent pragmatic need for accuracy, clarity and intended utility. Nevertheless, it still remains a moot point whether the translator has this moral/immoral right or duty — a solution to this dilemma is for the translator to correct them and bring their treatment to the user's attention in a translator's note. The resultant target-language text will often prove to be a great improvement on the original with a greater pragmatic impact.

As many commercial texts are inadequately written in the source language, the translator must try to cultivate a sense of source scepticism and not stick slavishly to the source text. To translate warts and all would result in a defective target-language version that fails to achieve the purpose for which it is intended. He should recognize that in general terms, the structures, style and other features of the source text are not sacrosanct and that he will probably need to produce a freely re-arranged translated text rather than a literal reproduction of the original, complete with any infelicities, solecisms, ambiguities, obscurities, etc. For example, the following letter of invitation, written by a charity requesting the honour of the presence of the British Royal couple at a formal function, contains so many linguistic and stylistic infelicities that it must be completely rewritten before it can be translated:

敬啓者：一九八九年十一月八日至十日，爲王子查理斯及王妃戴安娜訪問香港的好日子。

如果能出席本中心「金榜題名慈善家」頒獎大會主禮的話，這是一個極
好的消息，對於發揚鼓勵各慈善家繼續以「善中行樂樂在善中」之精神
行善，打了一支強效興奮針，無疑亦是一有力的鼓舞，更為各慈善家為
此感到相當榮幸及高興，同時，有助於……，並鼓吹各慈善家實踐「善
中行樂樂在善中」行善精神，必可得到預期美滿之成功，敬希應允出席
函覆為荷，好消息我們是樂於聽到的。……

Firstly, in the above formal letter appealing directly for the honour of
the Royal presence at a function, the anonymous address 敬啓者 would
seem to be unceremoniously infelicitous in style. If rendered literally into
English as, say, "Dear Sir/Madam," this address would sound unbearably
impersonal and might even alienate the Royal couple, thus failing to
achieve the pragmatic purpose for which the translation is intended. Moreover, with the Royal couple as the direct readership in mind, the unintended
(?) use of the third person vocative in the first paragraph 王子查理斯及王妃
戴安娜 would seem to be inappropriate, though in Chinese the use of such
third person vocatives in polite contexts often indicates an appropriate
degree of aloof respectfulness. Secondly, the absence at the beginning of the
second paragraph of the grammatical subject denoting the Royal couple
如果能出席 ... also appears to be unjustified, though again, in the Chinese
sentence the grammatical subject can sometimes be omitted. Nonetheless
the inadvertent omission of such a grammatical word smacks of abruptness
amidst the flow of the text. Thirdly, the text is also quite tautologous in
places. For example, in the expression 打了一支強效興奮針，無疑亦是一有
力的鼓舞 the second phrase is obviously redundant. The expression near the
end of the second paragraph 並鼓吹各慈善家實踐「善中行樂樂在善中」行
善精神 also needlessly repeats another phrase 發揚慈善家繼續以「善中行樂
樂在善中」之精神行善 at the beginning. Fourthly, the afterthought at the
end of the second paragraph 好消息我們是樂於聽到的 is also stylistically
inept in that it is unnecessary and even sounds a little patronizing. Finally,
another serious stylistic error is the indiscriminate use of the punctuation
mark, the comma. Commas are sprinkled all over the second paragraph,
producing clusters of run-on sentences verging on unintelligibility in
places. (e.g., Is the phrase 必可得到預期美滿之成功 a predicate of the
absent grammatical subject or does it refer to something else?)

Translation Procedure, Methods and Quality

Ideally and as a generalization, the translation procedure for commercial texts, as for most other types of text, should be as follows: (a) Read through source-language text; (b) Research subject; (c) Translate in draft; (d) Put draft translation aside for at least twenty-four hours; (e) Check, revise and edit target-language text. Firstly, read the document right through to get an overall idea of its subject-master, terminology, etc. Then decide on the translation strategies, style and register, etc. by considering the status of the source-language text, the purpose and the readership for which the translation is intended. Secondly, research the subject if it does not already fall within the specialism of the translator; verify or clarify any information in the source-language text by consulting relevant reference material (e.g., glossaries, textbooks, directories, complete texts, diagrams), end users, personal informants, specialists, etc. Thirdly, translate in draft, jotting down the translated terms for the sake of terminological consistency and noting any problems encountered, etc. Fourthly, put the draft translation aside for as long as possible, as in translating one will invariably be mesmerized into producing translationese, slips, and other errors. Finally, return to check, revise and edit the target-language text. This last stage, having been performed by the translator himself, should be repeated again by the in-house team of revisers. Here a reviser who has the target language as his language of habitual use should be employed to pick up any loose ends in grammar, usage, style, etc. in the translated text, if the target-language text is made by someone to whom the target language is not their language of habitual use. Then another subject specialist should be brought in to check for terminological accuracy, comprehensibility and appropriateness of style in the draft translation. Collectively, the revisers are to keep a close watch on possible textual omissions, correction of facts and figures, and any other problems in the target-language text.

Unfortunately, this somewhat idealized and theoretical account of translation procedure diverges from much common practice in the "real" world of commercial translation, especially where the local scene is concerned. Under the constraint of time and cost-effectiveness, the commercial translator often bypasses stages (a), (b), (c) and (d): namely, he plunges straight into the text without reading it first or researching the subject beforehand, revises the draft translation right after translation and commits himself as little as possible to checking, revising and editing. The work of both language and subject experts is often performed perfunctorily by a general reviser. Frequently, staff and freelance translators do not even have their translations revised.

Particularly in translating standardized texts with an emphasis on standardized terms, common syntactic structures, and a minimum of figurative language, a standardized in-house translation version will often be imposed on the source-language texts. The imposition of a standardized target-language version can also result, for example, from the repetitive nature of legal translation work. The translation of legal documents such as notices of writ is restricted to only the short statement which contains details (e.g., the names of the parties) specific to each case; the bulk of the document will be identical to other notices of writ and will normally only require standardized translation. The same applies to other texts of a repetitive nature such as memoranda, articles of association of English companies, tenders, contracts, etc. The gap between theory and practice in commercial translation can be further seen in the translation of instructions: the translator can hardly be expected, for example, to put his hands on the large piece of equipment in question and follow the process through before translating. The fact that commercial translation assignments are often demanded at short notice means also that the translator cannot allow unlimited time for more and more delicate polishing of his product. In short, everything will be dictated by commercial expedience.

Different types of commercial text with their respective pragmatic purposes require different methods of translation. In general terms, "informative" texts (e.g., textbooks, technical reports, memoranda, minutes or agenda of a minute) constitute the vast majority of the commercial translator's work, to be followed by "vocative" texts (e.g., notices, instructions, publicity) and "expressive" texts (e.g., speeches given by VIPs, personal correspondence, declarations) respectively. Since typical "informative" and "vocative" texts are loyal to the truth and the target-language readership respectively whilst the writer's status remains anonymous, they both normally require communicative rather than semantic translation to achieve the pragmatic impact desired. Conversely, typical "expressive" texts, namely writer-centred documents irrespective of any reader's response, normally require semantic translation, in which the expressive components (e.g., linguistic idiosyncrasies) have to be kept intact. The distinction between semantic and communicative translation is that the former tries to preserve both the linguistic and other formal features of the source-language text, whereas the latter aims at producing pragmatic, equivalent effect on the target-language readership through a dynamic adjustment of the source-language features to their corresponding target-language norms.

The oscillation between semantic and communicative translation can be illustrated with examples of specific pragmatic impact to be achieved by particular text-types. For example, legal documents translated for information purposes only (e.g., wills, agreements) normally require purely semantic treatment. In such translated legal texts, "translation equivalence" is mostly achieved through word for word, phrase for phrase, sentence for sentence translation — this rigid adherence to the source-language formal grammatical structures will be required, because the target-language texts are often to be used as secondary or reference documents in conjunction with the source-language texts. For example, in an agreement on the distributorship of a certain product the following clause will, inevitably, have to be "faithfully" translated into some kind of rather unreadable Chinese prose: (Clause: "If this Agreement is terminated under (a), (b) or (c) the (PRODUCER) may, at its sole option, require the DISTRIBUTOR to return to the (PRODUCER) or its designee any products then in possession of the DISTRIBUTOR upon payment to the DISTRIBUTOR of the amount paid by the DISTRIBUTOR for such PRODUCTS.")

Translation:

若此契約於（甲）、（乙）、（丙）任何一種情況下取消，則（廠商）擁有買賣獨權，可付經銷商爲貨品所付之貨款予經銷商，要求經銷商將經銷商當時所擁有之任何貨品歸還（廠商）或其指定人。

The pendulum swing will, however, be pulled in the other direction of communicative approach in translating such "vocative" texts as advertising copy or slogans where differences in national mentality, cultural values, etc. can cause advertisements to misfire when transferred from one culture to another. For example, in a pamphlet advertising a certain Chinese medical product the culture-bound expression 滋陰補陽 cannot be semantically translated as, say, "nourishing Yin and supplementing Yang" but rather must be communicatively translated as, say, "nourishing." And in translating certain "expressive" texts where the form is as important as the content, perhaps a mixed semantic-communicative approach would be preferred over a purely semantic or communicative one. Thus, the text of an important speech given by a world leader for an international readership can be communicatively translated, with the quirks and sports of idiolect preserved.

Few commercial texts, however, are purely "expressive," "informative" or "vocative": these epithets are used only to show the emphasis or "thrust" of a text. Accordingly, there can be different approaches to a certain source-language feature (e.g., cultural components) found in the different stretches ("expressive," "informative" and "vocative") of a single text. For example, in a travel brochure containing expressive, informative and vocative descriptions of exotic Chinese festivals, these cultural elements can then be translated differently. Hence, in the expressive stretch, 中元節 , for example, can be transferred intact (e.g., "Zhong Yuan Festival," perhaps with an annotation?); in the informative stretch, 媽祖誕 , for example, transferred and explained with culturally neutral terms (e.g., "a Chinese festival commemorating a protectress of wrecked ships"); in the vocative stretch, 七夕 , for example, replaced with a cultural equivalent (e.g., "St Valentine's Day").

In general terms, the quality requirements for translation will vary according to the many different purposes for which commercial texts are translated. In-house "read and discard" notice-type translations, for example, will normally be roughly made, whereas high quality will be expected of camera-ready work for immediate publication (e.g., technical reports). The translation of a dubbed film script may warrant scrupulous care over the synchronization of lip movements, often at the expense of content. What constitutes a good translated commercial text is one that meets the user's immediate need whether it is to provide information quickly, to market a product or to achieve any other commercially motivated purpose. In its final version the target-language text may not be an exact reproduction of the source language, as in the case of "improved" translations of advertising copy, with input from target language culture specialists to achieve equivalent pragmatic impact on the target readership. Thus, there are many levels of equivalence, any of which can be successful at a certain level of practical functioning.

Language/Subject Combinations and Translation Rates

Ideally, translators work into their own language of habitual use but in reality, the commercial translator is often required to work out of his own language as well in the course of his professional life. The adoption of the language of habitual use for the target language is based on its merit of native fluency, though some scientific and technical translators have argued that because translation accuracy is more crucial than fluency in their work, it makes more sense for them to be more proficient in the source language. The languages handled by the commercial translator in Hong Kong are chiefly English and Chinese, followed by Japanese, German, French, Arabic, Korean, Thai, etc. English-Chinese translators are manifestly in greatest demand and supply; there is, however, a lesser demand for and also a lesser supply of native translators (consequently with a relatively lower performance standard) for Chinese-English translation. A serious pinch is developing especially in Japanese-English and English-Japanese translation (because of trade links with Japan) and other rare language-language (e.g., Arabic-Thai) and language-subject (e.g., Arabic-fung shui) combinations.

Translation rates are normally calculated on the basis of text-types, rarity of languages, urgency, technical difficulty, and other jobs involved (e.g., editing, artwork, typesetting, publishing). As in 1989, the "going rate" on the local translation market was about HK$600 per 1000 words/ characters in source language on average charged to the client for general texts, with a higher rate of $1 per word/character for more difficult areas (e.g., legal documents) or an even higher rate for highly demanding, specialized texts (e.g., texts dealing with advanced technologies). Higher rates will also be charged for odd language-language or language-subject combinations. A surcharge of up to 100 per cent will be charged for overnight rush deliveries. There will also be extra charges for editing, typesetting, publishing, artwork, etc. which many established local translating agencies take on to maximize their own profits. Some local agencies offer special discounts to their regular clients.

Client-translator Relationship

Generally speaking, clients or end users of a translated commercial text seem to be rather ignorant about the different aspects of commercial translation. This inevitably influences their view on the value and degree of professionalism of the translating profession, as well as the way in which they deal with its practitioners. For example, unaware of the "invisible" para-translation activities (e.g., scanning for information and research), they only willingly pay for the seen product of translation. They also have the misguided view that anyone with a smattering of source language and target language and common sense can undertake translation work — they are sure they (or rather their personal secretary) could do it better than professional translators if only they had the time. Thus, uninformed about the degree of technical knowledge and skills required, they tend to offer work to the lowest priced translators. And to aggravate the situation, despite their lack of linguistic expertise upon which to base their own judgements, they often indulge in flaunting their linguistic ego: their often misguided judgement about a particular translated text submitted to them often leads to the superimposing upon it of an objectively inadequate version of their own.

The foregoing account, though somewhat cynical, is however not meant to disparage every single client. There are certainly enlightened clients or end users, who fully appreciate that they are not just passive recipients of a translation but are expected to help the translator by providing the latter with the technical background information, a complete text, the diagrams, the background information, the earlier documents, or the other things that make it possible for the translator to understand what he is asked to translate. Experience shows that this co-operative approach can be highly fruitful for both sides.

Electronic Aids to Commercial Translation and Presentation

In response to the increasing use of electronic aids to commercial translation and presentation, governmental and company translation departments as well as translating agencies are becoming quite capital-intensive with electronic communications and typesetting and printing equipment these days. Increasing numbers of clients and end users now require the transmission of source-language texts and translations as well as presentation by electronic means. The professional commercial translator can now no longer legitimately submit his draft typescript with hand-written corrections and offer the explanation, "I'm a translator, not an electronics expert." There is a particularly marked trend towards presenting finished translation in a professional form acceptable to the client, e.g., on diskette or via electronic mail, or in other machine-readable form. However, the type of presentation will be dictated by factors such as the deadline imposed, the purpose for which the translation is intended, etc. For example, in the case of urgent meetings or hearings, draft copy or transient translated texts will probably be the appropriate presentation, whereas camera-ready copy will be required for immediate publication of important documents. To cope with this contemporary trend, the more sophisticated breed of commercial translators are therefore now fully equipped with modern electronic aids to translation and presentation like dictaphones, personal computers, terminological data banks, reference data banks, computerized glossaries, telex, facsimile machines, word processors, etc. This has considerably improved their productivity and enhanced the degree of their professionalism.

Commercial Translators and Professionalism

Commercial translators fall into two broad categories: staff translators and freelance translators; freelance translators can be further classified into those working full-time professionally and those working part-time professionally. Staff translators have, by and large, to be all-rounders, as they will usually have to tackle work in a wide range of subjects, whereas free-lancers can usually limit themselves to a fairly narrow specialization in which they have a particular personal interest. Freelance translators who claim a narrow specialization will, however, be disadvantaged because translating agencies tend to pigeon-hole them. Because of the diversity of subjects involved, staff translators will need to be able to translate several texts at the same time and may have difficulty in switching from one type of document to another. They can, moreover, be asked to do a certain amount of administrative work as part of their duties, e.g., marketing, contacting, chasing free-lancers' work or informally acting as interpreters for foreign visitors. The majority of commercial translators also complain that they find their jobs repetitive and humdrum, and that they have a rather low professional status because they are at everyone's beck and call. And this is despite the fact that a staff translator job is generally regarded as a career ultimate. While staff translators work in a secure, social environment and are paid a regular salary, their freelance counterparts lead a rather solitary existence and unless established, suffer from an irregular work flow and income. Yet regardless of their respective category, both must face the same professional realities, i.e., having to work under the stress of deadlines and to deal with both inferior originals and superior clients.

Among the qualities commercial translators have to bring to their job are linguistic competence, shrewdness, perceptiveness, exceptional common sense, meticulousness, a developed sense of responsibility and professional ethics, etc. They also need to recognize their own limitations as a translator in terms of linguistic ability, subject knowledge, resources, time, etc. But despite their lack of appropriate subject knowledge or resources, staff translators may still be called upon to work with texts that are outside their own specialism in the absence of other qualified translators. Nonetheless, they (especially those working at the grass-root level) remain undervalued, underpaid and unrecognized. This applies particularly to local commercial translators who enjoy both a rather low status and an extremely low degree of professionalism. For example, contrary to Japan which regards commercial translation as a major intellectual discipline in its own right and highly rewards its practitioners in monetary terms, present-day Hong Kong views, in some quarters, commercial translation as a menial, clerical task and pays its practitioners accordingly. On the one hand, they are not registered, certified or regulated by the local authorities, and on the other hand, no significant efforts have yet been made to promote and uphold a professional ethics, educate the general public about the importance and particularities of the profession and defend their material and moral interests. They are sadly disorganized and undervalued. Nonetheless, a mention can perhaps be made of the Hong Kong Translation Society in Hong Kong, which, despite its non-statutory and independent status, has been trying in recent years to ameliorate the above unsatisfactory state of affairs.

A survey of the professional organization of our western counterparts will convince us that we certainly lag far behind in the aspect of professionalism. For example, a register called "The Register of Translators and Translating Agencies in the United Kingdom" was published in the United Kingdom in 1987, fulfilling a long-felt need for a national directory of the diffuse profession of translating. In addition to being an indispensable reference guide for all those engaged in the practice of translating in its many facets, the register will be invaluable to information offices, chambers of commerce, embassies, professional and trade organizations, etc. and to anyone requiring the services of a translator for whatever purpose. The core of the register is an alphabetic directory of the translators and translating agencies listed. Details (e.g., name, address, telephone number, fax number, languages involved, subject specialisms) are given for each entry. Also in the former GDR, all full-time freelance translators had to have valid licences, which were issued according to their qualifications, specifying languages, directions of translation, and different categories of translating. Fees were prescribed on the basis of language group, direction, type of translation, degree of difficulty, tasks involved (e.g., translating, editing, typing, proof-reading) and any complicating factors. The professional translating field in the West now has its own highly developed training courses, examinations, career structures, and professional organizations — such as the American Translators' Association, the Translators' Guild of the Institute of Linguists, and the Fédération Internationale des Traducteurs. Several central organizations have now also developed to coordinate information about the availability of translations and to facilitate their accessibility, once they are made — notably the International Translation Centre at Delft (The Netherlands) and the National Translation Center in Chicago.

It would seem that in the circumstances outlined above, the professionalism of commercial translation worldwide can be enhanced in two ways. First, its practitioners should try to win the public recognition that their profession requires high standards of work and specialized skills acquired by considerable training. They themselves must have an adequate self-esteem as manifested in a solid internal organization and the solidarity of its members. Secondly, to complement the public recognition and its self-esteem, the profession itself should also strive for better protection, regulation and greater improvements in all its facets. In this regard, an urgent need has been identified for professional societies for the protection of commercial translators, their work, and their legal, social, and fiscal status; guidelines, such as codes of professional ethics and conduct (e.g., the document written by the UNESCO-sponsored FIT), model contracts and agreements, and local legislation; colloquia for the exchange of professional information and knowledge, etc.

References

Crystal, David. *The Cambridge Encyclopedia of Language*. Cambridge: Cambridge University Press, 1987.

Henderson, J. A. *Personality and the Linguist*. Bradford: Bradford University Press, 1987.

Keith, Hugh and Ian Mason, eds. *Translation in the Modern Languages Degree*. London: Centre for Information on Language Teaching and Research, 1986.

Kongrat-Butlar, Stefan, ed. *Translations and Translators*. New York: R. R. Bowker Co., 1979.

Morris, Philip, *et al.*, eds. *The Register of Translators and Translating Agencies in the U.K.* London: Merton Press, 1987.

Newman, Patricia E., *et al*. *First North American Translators Congress*. Medford, New Jersey: Learned Information, Inc., 1986.

Newmark, Peter. *A Textbook of Translation*. Hertfordshire: Prentice Hall, 1988.

Picken, Catriona, ed. *ITI Conference 1: The Business of Translation and Interpreting*. London: Aslib, 1987.

———, ed. *Translation and Communication*. London: Aslib, 1985.

———, ed. *Translating and the Computer 7*. London: Aslib, 1986.

———, ed. *Translating and the Computer 8*. London: Aslib, 1987.

———, ed. *The Translator's Handbook*. London: Aslib, 1989.

Van Slype, G. *Better Translation for Better Communication*. Oxford: Pergamon, 1983.

CULTURE

Biculturalism and Ambiculturalism

John J. Deeney
Department of English
The Chinese University of Hong Kong, Hong Kong

This essay is about the role of the *cultural component* in translation which I subdivide into a *bicultural attitude* and an *ambicultural practice*. There is another coinage by Talat S. Halman which I also wish to introduce: "Cultranslation" (Halman, 1978:11). This compact invention sums up the inseparability of the translation process from its cultural contexts. This is true of any communication medium, and as Federico Fellini put it when talking about the impossibility of making a film in any language but Italian: "A language is not just a dictionary of words, sounds and syntax. It is a different way of interpreting reality, refined by the generations that developed that language.... How can I express in English the sentiments of another way of looking at life, of other myths, of other rites, of other philosophies and another history?" (Fellini, 1986:37)

The cultranslator is one who tries to turn Fellini's attitude of impossibility into a respectable approximation and, at least, minimize the losses in the process. The translator's need for cultural awareness may seem obvious today. It has not always been so. Therefore, it must not be taken for granted even though it adds an additional burden to the already busy and harassed translator. There was a time in the not too distant past when translators were often considered mere word merchants, to be paid for the relatively easy drudgery of looking up linguistic equivalents in a dictionary. Fortunately, the acceptance of the importance of comparative cultural studies as well as the role of social sciences in this century, makes the point of this essay relatively easy to establish: complete bilingualism must include a broad cultural dimension. Eugene Nida, for instance, insists on the essential relationship between culture and language and lists the cultural categories under which problems of translation occur: (1) ecology, (2) material culture, (3) social culture, and (4) linguistic culture.

I leave it to others to take up some of the more technical aspects of this question (see, for instance, Robert Feleppa's "Translation as a Basis for Cultural Description," also in this volume). Neither shall I go into the vast amount of literature by linguists, philosophers of language, anthropologists, psychologists, etc., on translation theory, nor the controversies aroused, for example, by the Sapir-Whorf hypothesis. The reader interested in investigating this and other hypotheses about how language influences and shapes thought patterns and cultural perspectives of the world or vice versa, may care to consult some of the bibliographical suggestions at the end of this essay (e.g., Bloom, Whorf, etc.).

I am not so much interested in *how* language influences culture or vice versa, as I am in underscoring the fact *that* it is so, and "compleat" translators will reflect this in their work. My approach to translation is a common sense one based on examples, but needs repeating for emphasis and because it is still neglected in some training programs. If my tone is a bit hortatory, it is because anyone who wishes to improve his or her translation ability must go beyond the world of dictionaries, and proceed resolutely into the world of other cultures. My text will be laced with many illustrations, many of them quite homey, both from others as well as my own personal experience. Many more examples can be found in the citations given in the bibliographical section at the end of this essay.

In the introduction to a recent collection of essays edited by Susan Bassnett and André Lefevere, all the writers illustrate the central concept of the book through a variety of case studies about the "cultural turn" that has taken place in translation studies. For instance, the editors refer to Mary Snell-Hornby's contribution in which she "exhorts linguists to abandon their 'scientistic' attitude and to move from 'text' as a putative 'translation unit', to culture — a momentous step that would go far beyond the move from the word as a 'unit' to the text" (Bassnett and Lefevere, 1990:4). The editors go on to say:

"Faithfulness", then, does not enter into translation in the guise of "equivalence" between words or texts but, if at all, in the guise of an attempt to make
the target text function in the target culture the way the source text functioned
in the source culture. Translations are therefore not "faithful" on the levels
they have traditionally been required to be — to achieve "functional equivalence" a translator may have to substantially adapt the source text.... Translation as an activity is always double contextualized, since the text has a place in
two cultures.... Since languages express cultures, translators should be bicultural, not bilingual. The object of study has been redefined; what is studied is
the text embedded within its network of both source and target cultural signs
and in this way Translation Studies has been able both to utilize the linguistic
approach and to move out beyond it. (Bassnett and Lefevere, 1990:10–12)

I would like to begin my own discussion with some examples indicating the inseparability of language and culture and how they are part and
parcel of one another (ignoring the "chicken or the egg" debate over which
came first). My first two examples take language in the broad sense to
include body language which is often very culture-specific. For instance,
there is the story of the white African missionary who was distressed at the
nudity of the blacks he was working with. He expostulated with one,
insisting that decency demanded that all but the face should be covered. The
native replied, "But my whole body is my face!"

Another "face" example (in more ways than one) is taken from the field
of consecutive interpretation in Hong Kong, where the one doing the
interpreting mistakenly thought that his verbal proficiency was sufficient
while the rest of his demeanor and behavior were irrelevant. In fact, his lack
of the appropriate body language undermined almost everything he was
saying and disgraced his profession. This particular male court interpreter
was translating from Chinese into English on behalf of a very frightened
and embarrassed young girl plaintive in a sexual harassment case. While
translating for the English magistrate, he kept his hands in his pocket,
nonchalantly walked back and forth, sometimes casually leaning on the
magistrate's desk, and wore an expression of insolent indifference, looking
right through the girl. His unspoken message seemed to be: "I've got
complete power over you. I hope you are scared. You ought to be. I really
don't take your case seriously, I handle hundreds of cases like this all the
time." His manner was so arrogant and undignified that it all but destroyed
the meaning of these serious proceedings. Needless to say, the girl lost her
case.

One of the most difficult problems in communicating another culture through translation is the associations certain words have in one culture that are completely absent in another. For instance, non-Chinese (and some Chinese as well) might regard the exorbitant sums paid by the Cantonese of Hong Kong for certain combinations of lucky numbers on licence plates as the height of superstition. The same could be said for certain words which are homonyms or near-homonyms with life and death situations (some Chinese buildings will not have a number four (*si* 四) floor because the number is homonymous with the word for death (*si* 死)). There are many other ways of dealing verbally with good or bad luck which really indicate cultural concepts. For instance, in Hong Kong and many parts of the world where Chinese live, there is also the all-important issue of finding an acceptable *fengshui* 風水 . This is a term from Chinese geomancy which refers to the proper lay of the land, a building, furnishings of a house, etc., and is of crucial importance in maintaining harmony with the world. Similar examples, of course, could be found in Western culture (e.g., the lucky number 7, the unlucky number 13, etc.).

Hong Kong, incidentally, is one of the world's most exciting cross-cultural cities and illustrates a number of language/culture problems. It is not only faced with what could be termed a tricultural situation (strong local Cantonese identity, its passing colonial status as Britain's "Crown Colony," and its return to the China Mainland in 1997), but also a challenging trilingual crosscurrent of languages: Cantonese, English, and Mandarin (the Chinese common vernacular — *putonghua* 普通話). Spoken Cantonese and Mandarin are mutually incomprehensible, but that great cultural constant, the written character, is virtually the same for all Chinese dialects. Hong Kong is truly in a cultural crisis: maintaining its own strong Cantonese identity; living down its colonial past; and preparing for the difficult transition of life with China after 1997 while trying to maintain its prosperous international connections with the rest of the world. Just the legal problems alone (translating British common law into Chinese) are daunting, to say nothing of the more pedestrian issue of changing the streets named after British colonials to appropriate Chinese "liberated" titles.

Another example of how impenetrable one culture may seem to be to another is how inadequate merely translated words are in certain situations. For instance, there are levels of communication where it is always difficult to find the right emotive or affective words when trying to comfort someone over the loss of a beloved member of the family. We are at a loss for words and resort to all kinds of indirect euphemisms, even in one's native culture, to say nothing of the restrictions and taboos we feel when dealing with another culture. For a Christian, the pain of loss may be mitigated by referring to a better after-life of happiness with God, but of what comfort would a translation of John Donne's "Death Be Not Proud" poem be to a non-Christian Chinese? In the face of such cultural differences, mere text-book "mastery" of a language will often be inadequate and leave one tongue-tied.

Allow me to cite two more brief examples in order to dispose of two facets of literary culture that are so difficult for the translator to handle without extensive notes or explanations: allusions and puns. Allusions are virtually impossible to translate because they are often capsule summaries of an entire history of a given culture in miniature. Imagine the associations that come to the Western mind with the name Cleopatra (immortalized best, perhaps, in the title of Dryden's play: *All for Love, or, the World Well Lost*). Similarly, there is a world of associations stirred in Chinese hearts when they hear the name of Yang Guifei 楊貴妃 , also immortalized in Po Juyi's 白居易 long narrative poem, 〈長恨歌〉 (The Song of Everlasting Sorrow) or, more recently, Mao's disastrously misnamed, 文化大革命 Cultural Revolution (1966–1976). Mere dates can also reverberate with vast cultural resonances: 1492 (Columbus discovered America), 1812 (Tchaikovsky's *Overture* and the Napoleonic War in Russia); 五四 May Fourth (1919 Literary Revolution Movement in China), 六四 June 4th (1989 Tiananmen massacre in Beijing, China); etc.

As for puns, there is the interesting example of a verbal clash of cultures in the case of a Western man married to a Chinese woman. One day he was about to share a pear with his Chinese wife. As he started to cut the pear in two, his wife shouted in horror: "You mustn't cut the pear!" He was completely bewildered until she explained that a married couple never cut a pear in two because the Chinese words for "cut a pear," 分梨 are exact homonyms for 分離 , meaning "to separate." Although one might think such a pun untranslatable, the famous linguist, Zhao Yuanren (Chao Yuen Ren) 趙元任 , rendered the phrase brilliantly with a matching pun in English: "Don't split a pear (pair)."

Before getting into a more detailed discussion of biculturalism and ambiculturalism, it will be useful to review some descriptive definitions of the complex term, "culture." The unabridged *Random House Dictionary of the English Language* is as good a place as any to begin. Some of the meanings listed under "culture" — and, more or less, the composite meanings used throughout my discussion — are: "1. the quality in a person or society that arises from an interest in and acquaintance with what is generally regarded as excellent in the arts, letters, manners, scholarly pursuits, etc.; ... 3. a particular form or stage of civilization ...; 4. *Sociol.*: the sum total of ways of living built up by a group of human beings and transmitted from one generation to another." In discussing biculturalism and ambiculturalism in translation, my point is that good translators not only strive for perfect bilingualism but, more importantly, they must be dedicated to the life-time task of becoming bicultural and, as I shall explain in part two, ambicultural.

Biculturalism

Very simply, biculturalism is being at home in two cultures. As noted in the previous section, we know the importance of context in trying to translate words, but translation itself is part of a wider context — the culture out of which every language derives its life and sustenance. Beginning translation students, in particular, have to be constantly reminded of this fact. Therefore, we are not only concerned with the art of translating the components of one language into another language, but we must strive to develop the habitual disposition or attitude of thinking and feeling in two cultures.

Bassnett and Lefevere, in their essay referred to earlier, make a useful distinction: "If neither the word, nor the text, but the culture becomes the operational 'unit' of translation, it might be wise to distinguish between 'intracultural' and 'intercultural' translation" (Bassnett and Lefevere, 1990:8). The latter refers to the usual translation process of moving from one culture to another; the former represents texts belonging to the language of the same culture but based on knowledge gleaned about a different culture through materials published in the native language, such as plot summaries, commentaries, histories, criticism, and even film versions of popular novels. The authors cite an interesting example from cinema:

> The movie based on *Un amour de Swann* is likely to have represented Proust to many more people than any of the other forms of representation.... This, then, would be the 'intercultural' translation, which we propose to call, 'rewriting', with the proviso that certain texts originally translated from another culture (the Bible, Lenin, Shakespeare) can become naturalized to such an extent that they are given the same 'intercultural' treatment as texts which

have originally been generated within the culture in question. (Bassnett and Lefevere, 1990:9)

Under the "intercultural" rubric, one might also include the role of textbooks written in the original language. It would seem to be far more important for foreign translators to know how a famous Chinese novel is perceived and interpreted at middle-school level in China than to be familiar with a deep-structure analysis of the work. Bassnett and Lefevere then go on to make some useful observations about the importance of pop culture and its implications for the future of translation studies:

> Since "our common culture, however much we might wish it were not so, is less and less a book culture and more and more a culture of cinema, television and popular music" (Hillis Miller, 1987:285), literature reaches those who are not its professional students much more by way of the "images" constructed of it in translations, but even more so in anthologies, commentaries, histories and, occasionally, critical journals, than it does so by means of "originals", however venerable they may be, and however much professors of literature and its students who approach it in a "professional" way may regret this state of affairs. What impacts most on members of a culture, we suggest, is the "image" of a work of literature, not its "reality", not the text that is still sacrosanct only in literature departments. It is therefore extremely important that the "image" of a literature and the works that constitute it be studied alongside its reality. This, we submit, is where the future of "translation studies" lies. (Bassnett and Lefevere, 1990:9–10)

The task of mastering one's own native culture in all its complex ramifications is already quite difficult for a cultranslator to achieve. We are often called upon to have at least a passing acquaintance with the humanities and the social sciences as well as many technologies and even the natural sciences. The chore is further complicated by the fact that there are vast shifts in translation sensibility over different periods of time. Homer decked out in Pope's heroic couplets might have been fine for eighteenth-century England, but hardly suitable today. Herbert Giles's translations of Chinese poetry might have suited his audience and Ezra Pound his, but brilliant originals will always require a re-translation for a contemporary, ever-changing cultural readership.

An interesting set of examples is cited by teachers of English as a foreign language (TEFL) in China to dramatize cross-cultural misunderstanding. Two teachers at the Nanchang Teachers' College of Vocation and

Technology, Wu Song-chu and Harold A. Stephens, list and analyze a number of culture-based communication problems most foreigners in China have experienced at one time or another. The authors' italicized parenthetical remarks are useful markers which pinpoint the cultural ambiguities; the comments in square brackets are some interpolations based on my personal experiences which corroborate the examples.

> *Example 1.* Two people meet on the street.
> Chinese student: Hello! Where are you going?
> American teacher: Oh, to the market.
> CS: (*cheerfully*) What for?
> AT: (*a bit defensively*) To do some shopping.
> CS: (*smiling*) What do you plan to buy?
> AT: (*somewhat sullenly*) Er …

Persons of different cultures may have different norms. Example 1 illustrates the conflict caused by these different norms. According to Chinese norms, "where to" and "what for" inquiries are merely casual greetings and do not warrant specific answers. In cultures other than Chinese, however, they might be considered offensive, "nosy" questions, and invasions of privacy [a particularly difficult word-concept to translate into Chinese]. Similarly, questions regarding age, salary, family status [and number and sex of children], and other personal matters are generally inappropriate. In cultures other than Chinese, the "small talk" of greetings is generally limited to very impersonal subjects.

I recall a personal example from my callow youth, mentioned in an earlier article on "Biculturalism and Translation," where the reverse situation occurred. I was the American student (AS) taking a class in Mandarin from my Chinese teacher (CT). I had engaged the teacher to come for an extra class on a Saturday morning. I lost track of time but, around noon time, he made motion to make a graceful exit and said, "Why don't you come over to my place for lunch?" Rather naively and brashly I replied: "O.K. That sounds terrific!" The poor teacher became visibly embarrassed, thinking apprehensively of his wife's reaction when, unannounced, he brought home a foreign student. It hadn't occurred to me that this was not really an invitation, but rather his way of making me feel at home, so to speak, in announcing that it was lunchtime and he had to go. It would not have been polite from his point of view, to tell me that he was getting hungry without inviting me along for lunch! When he realized my awkwardness, he gave us both a way out by saying: "You look tired after such a long class; maybe you should take a little rest first." Notice, the invitation was not withdrawn, but an alternative way out was offered. Not being altogether culturally illiterate, I replied: "Yes, I am a bit tired. Let me take up your kind invitation some other day."

The ability of Chinese to find pat expressions to maintain smooth interpersonal relationships is quite sophisticated and indicates a cultural sensitivity towards the other which we do not always experience — or find desirable or necessary — in the West. I am reminded of two examples in *ave atque vale* situations for which it would be difficult to find equivalents through translation. Both examples involve a situation where an individual is actually, or perceived to be, one's superior. It is often difficult or awkward to break the ice in initiating a serious conversation with such a person.

The expression 請教 (literally, "to ask/request/beg information/instruction/teaching") is often used in a deferential way by someone initiating a conversation, in order to put the other person immediately at ease and even extend to that person a superior status. This polite expression is very commonly used among Chinese (especially if the question is directed to an older person) in order to smooth interpersonal relationships. It is even more important, I suggest, when non-Chinese wish to begin a serious discussion with their Chinese counterparts, because it reveals an attitude of mind where the guest genuinely wishes to learn from a native of the host culture. Depending on circumstances, one's manner would indicate the unspoken (but presumed) preamble leading up to the expression: "There's something I'm not sure about and I am confident that your experience and superior intelligence can help me to solve my problem." Then, the actual query: "May I ask you something?"

My second example often occurs when two persons — say at the beginning or the end of a meal or a meeting — are about to pass through a door and it is a question of who should go first. Westerners are often amused and bemused at the interminable number of polite expressions of deference that can go back and forth between the two rivals in ritual, especially if there is a series of doors to pass through. It is finally settled when one comes up with an expression that allows the other person a graceful exit. One of these expressions is, 恭敬不如從命 (loosely translated as, "paying my respects to your superior status must defer to taking your words as my very command").

But to return to the series of examples from the TEFL experience:

Example 4. Two persons have just been introduced and are engaging in "small talk."
AT: You speak quite good English.
CS: Oh, no. My English is very poor.
AT: *(at a loss for words)* Er …

Example 7. A guest is intending to leave his host's house.
CS: I'm going now. You must be tired. I'm sorry to have wasted your time.
AT: *(completely puzzled)* Er …

To paraphrase the authors' analyses of these last two dialogues, the examples point up the Chinese inclination to "put themselves down" out of a false sense of modesty and a lack of confidence. Generally speaking, Chinese do not publicly pride themselves on achievements based on self-reliance, personal achievement, independent demonstration of one's skills, positive self-esteem and legitimate promotion of one's self-image, etc. In the seventh example, "this attempt at humility serves to humiliate all participants involved…. The Chinese student, because of his deprecation of his worth, and the American teacher, because of the impression he gains of having no worthwhile impact on his visitor."

Another example involving cultural conflict is when one is invited to a Chinese home for a meal. Frequently, the wife cheerfully slaves away in the kitchen not only before the meal, but during the meal (since this "personal touch" shows esteem for the guest and assures that the fresh, top-quality food is served hot). When viewing the beautifully appointed and overladen table just before the meal begins, the Westerner is often completely nonplussed at Chinese etiquette. First of all, the fact that the hostess is not present during most of the meal is a source of embarrassment. But imagine one's state of baffled befuddlement at what to say when she toasts the guest of this sumptuous banquet with the words, 沒甚麼菜 (roughly, "I'm so sorry that there's really nothing much to eat"), before hurriedly disappearing back into the kitchen!

Here is another typical example, with the authors' analysis and a few comments of my own:

Example 6. The American teacher is a guest for dinner in a Chinese home.
[CS: *(heaping generous portions on guest's plate)* More sea slugs?]
[AT: *(hesitantly)* Well …]
CS: More wine?
AT: No, thank you. I've had plenty. You're a very gracious host.

CS: (*persistently*) Well, if you really think so, you'll have one more!
AT: All right, in that case …
[CS: (*gleefully*) Another toast!]
[AT: (*in his cups by now*) Why not! …]

A Western host typically encourages his guest to help himself, whereas the Chinese host insists on keeping his guest's plate and glass filled at all times. As a result, an impossible situation develops — the Westerner, thinking it impolite to leave food on his plate or drink in his glass, overeats and overdrinks. Meanwhile, the Chinese host, although aware that his guest has exceeded reasonable limits [and, perhaps, with a bit of mischievous pride in having drunk his "foreign friend" under the table], has a cultural compulsion to continue forcing food and drink on his guest.

The authors summarize their research: "Misunderstandings, inaccurate assumptions, and, at times, offensive confrontations" of TEFL students (and translators, I might add) "stem from their lack of cross-cultural awareness rather than weakness in knowledge of the language".

Ambiculturalism

In the first part of this essay, I have used the term bicultural to stress the importance of a well-informed but also sympathetic and tolerant *attitude* toward another culture. It is necessary for really competent translators always to cultivate this attitude of mind in order to grasp the complex and comprehensive nature of another culture. Otherwise, they will never be able to translate that culture successfully in words. In this section, I wish to be a bit more practical by talking about the translator's *performance*.

I should begin by elaborating on my choice of words, biculturalism and ambiculturalism and say something about their Latin prefixes, "bi-" and "ambi-." The former usually designates "two" or "double," as in bilingual, biplane, etc. The latter not only means "both," but also has the implication of practical ability, as in the term, ambidextrous (literally, both are right, as in having the ability to perform a task as if one had two right hands). In other words, ambicultural translators must have an ambidextrous mentality which enables them to translate with equal facility as if they had two right hands or two right-minded cultural mentalities.

Sometimes the translator's ambidexterity might require taking some creative liberties (a bit of legerdemain, perhaps) with the original text. This may be necessary to avoid sticking to the original text so closely that the wrong impression is created. J.C.P. Liang of the University of Leiden characterizes these mis-cultranslations under the rubric, Acceptability of Tone. Liang was looking into translation problems regarding the booklets published in Chinese as part of Taiwan's series on its Chinese Cultural Heritage. Ironically, some of the translations provided for different Western countries are counter-productive. As Liang points out, there are certain cultural mind-sets which characterize and condition the reception of information. These mind-sets are quite varied even within the same European community; for instance, Germans, Dutch, and English are considered to be rather reserved in temperament when compared with the more demonstrative French, Spanish, and Italians. As Liang puts it, "the linguistic expression of the first group of people is plainer, more reserved in tone, and more inclined to understatements than superlatives" (Liang, 1990:4). Therefore, the translator(s) of the same Chinese text into these different Western languages, must cultivate and apply a multi-cultural mentality in order to preserve an acceptable tone for each receptor readership. Liang gives an example and then analyzes the problem:

C-1: 中華文化是今日世界上最博大精深、歷史悠久的文化。

T-1: In the world of today, Chinese culture is the most comprehensive, refined and profound, with the longest history.

Aside from the truth value of the Chinese sentence above, its expression of a good measure of national pride is perfectly acceptable and, indeed, quite usual within the Chinese context. Yet, as this "national" pride is not easily shared by another people for the simple reason that it is not their nation, a direct and literal translation of such a sentence into a western language could conceivably be counter-productive. A French reader could find T-1 extremely offensive, for he is accustomed to thinking that French culture is indeed the most comprehensive and refined in the world. For a Dutch reader, T-1 is also not acceptable because it has clearly trespassed upon their range of sensibility. The down-to-earth Dutchman, returning from a great theatre performance, would more likely proclaim to his company "pretty good, eh?" than exclaim "c'est formidable!" The effusive American could nearly somersault on the same occasion and shriek "the greatest thing I even saw in my entire life!"

Liang would undoubtedly be willing to make a distinction between written Chinese and its oral expression. In the latter, most Chinese — especially when speaking among themselves — would be likely to tone down what otherwise might be taken as chauvinism. They do this by making use of the many understatements or expressions of doubt and hesitation which abound in their language. Liang gives a second translation of the same passage and then goes on to comment:

> T-2:   In the world of today, traditional Chinese culture is still very much alive. In the course of forty centuries, it has developed into a civilization of great complexity and refinement.

T-2 is a rewriting of the ideas in the original Chinese sentence. It is faithful to the original in substance (though not in form) and presents the information in a way palatable to a western public. There may of course be many more ways to rewrite a given passage, but that is not the central point of this paper. (Liang, 1990:4–5) Liang concludes: "The original text should be edited and rewritten in such a way that the story is faithfully told, but in words and formulas digestible to the projected reader." (Liang, 1990:8)

This mental dexterity does not come naturally but must be cultivated by constant exercise and training just as in sports. Unfortunately, some individuals believe that because they have a fairly good command of the linguistic aspects of a language, this automatically qualifies them to be good translators. They are no more likely to succeed than those bilingual literature teachers automatically qualify as overnight comparative literature scholars.

The exercises I recommend in order to cultivate this ambiculturalism are based on a *habit of individual research* and an *interdisciplinary approach*. As that great British author and thinker, Samuel Johnson (1709-1784) put it, "Knowledge is of two kinds; we know a subject ourselves or we know where we can get information upon it" (Johnson, 1991:163). This research dimension is common to all professionals, of course, and is no less important for the translator who wishes to rise above mediocrity. Truly professional translators are those who are research scholars at heart and know how to continue educating themselves about cultural issues through independent research. A good reason for motivating us to do research is the fact that the best translators are those who have approached the cultural translation task as a challenge which is interdisciplinary.

One of the first basic research problems with interdisciplinary implications lies in choosing a standard text out of a plurality of choices. In other words, one often has to do a considerable amount of research simply to ferret out which text is the most reliable and authentic; otherwise it might not be worth translating. This textual criticism approach requires, on the part of the translator, both historical sense and philological skills in order to make sure s/he is working on the best text. And yet it is not uncommon to find scholars taking whatever popular version is at hand, often using unedited reprints in an anthology or some bowdlerized edition of a text which has been tampered with in some way.

Crossing disciplines is also necessary when we reflect on the fact that complex cultures can only be thoroughly understood if we approach them from several angles. Not to take advantage of disciplines such as linguistics, psychology, anthropology, political science, sociology, etc., is to relegate ourselves to a partial view of the culture in question. Some years back, an article by James P. Soffietti appeared in the *Journal of Educational Psychology*, entitled, "Bilingualism and Biculturalism." Two paragraphs from the article are of particular interest for the translator:

> At times ... a cultural accent may be so subtle that all we can say is that there is something 'foreign' about the person in question without our being able to put our finger on the distinguishing feature involved.

> Learning to behave in conformity with the non-verbal cultural pattern of another society can be as much of a task as learning its verbal patterns, i.e., its language. To get rid of cultural accents can be just as difficult as getting rid of linguistic ones: both are based on deep-rooted systems of habit, some of which have strong emotional basis. (Soffietti, 1955:224)

Yes, for the cultranslator, learning to detect and communicate a "cultural accent" can be as important as finding some way to bring out Cantonese colloquialisms or Beijing slang in English translation or — to reverse the challenge — certain dialects used in British or American novels.

Understandably, the interdisciplinary aspect of ambi- and bi-culturalism cannot be presupposed even among otherwise very sophisticated translators. Many have never learned to make a systematic use of the numerous academic tools available to dig out and examine the cultural implications of given document. Obviously, this is even more true for beginners. Unfortunately, one of the most disconcerting aspects of translation teaching is the students' lack of appreciation for the need to do basic research. This is especially important if a learner has no opportunity for direct contact with the receptor culture.

I remember a passage I once included in an examination for postgraduate-level students of Chinese-English translation. The passage mentioned the city of Bilbao and described a battle in the area. Not one out of the thirty students bothered to inquire about the cultural contexts: what was the occasion of the battle? When did it occur? Where in the world is the city mentioned in the text? Is there a map which would give some idea of the terrain and the scale of the battle? Is the writer of the passage objective or prejudiced toward one side or the other? How does this affect the tone and style of one's translation? etc. The students were content simply to translate the words, not the essential cultural components.

Fortunately, there are two modern developments which can be an enormous help to translators who wish to break out of their cultural isolation by crossing disciplines: the audiovisual media and computers. Films, videotapes, television and music programs, plus many other visual aids (transparencies, slides, filmstrips, etc. on painting, architecture, scenes from nature and the environment, etc.), can give us a "feeling" — not mere intellectual understanding — for another culture and assist in communicating aspects of an alien world that words find difficult to encompass and describe.

In addition, "on hands" experience with the computer has and will continue to supply us not only with short-cuts to information (e.g., online databases, CD ROM disks, etc.) all over the world. Furthermore, Computer Assisted Learning (CAL) can enable us to learn a subject at our own pace and also give us access to a marvelous array of audio-visual materials to help us cross cultural barriers in informative and even entertaining ways (e.g., laser videodisks of illustrated dictionaries, encyclopedias, etc.).

Translators of the future will be able to make use of an increasing range of computer networking opportunities. For instance, they can easily tap into library computer systems to search card catalogs all over the world for information on a variety of topics requiring research. Then they can up-date themselves by using their computers to call up the latest information on a subject by accessing an electronic bulletin board kept buzzing by like-minded colleagues. In short, just as in so many other fields, the microchip has enabled translators to make a macro leap forward in their discipline.

Finally, regarding the actual manuscripts they are working on, all translators need is a good word processing program. After as many revisions and reprintings (on a wide variety of typefaces and graphics) as necessary, they can bring out the camera-ready document themselves with one or other of the many desktop publishing software programs now available. Further correspondence and revisions can be handled inexpensively and efficiently by fax and electronic-mail connections. For translators, an additional bonus might well be the development of more sophisticated uses related to machine translation in order to help them access certain types of data more efficiently (especially mathematics, science, etc.).

To sum up then, I will list some of the most important qualities which describe ideal translators. These dedicated conveyers of the human spirit are not only forever striving to attain a perfect bilingualism but, more importantly, are committed to the life-time job of becoming bicultural and ambicultural. They achieve their goals by means of a stringent objectivity about the positive aspects of the receptor culture; an open and welcoming attitude about other life styles which may have certain features that could complement their own culture; an insatiable intellectual curiosity; and an honest humility which actively wishes to become acquainted with another culture's often strange but enriching features. Furthermore, they must not only overcome ignorance and intolerance about other cultures, but also avoid imposing their preconceptions and false assumptions as well as their prejudices and stereotypes on that culture and its people.

Ideally, all this is best done by an actually lived experience in the receptor culture through contact with people on all levels of life. If this is not possible, then there is still much that can be learned through research in library-supplied hard copy information as well as audiovisual media and computer services. In any case, ambitious translators must take the initiative and actively seek out opportunities for fuller comprehension of other cultures in all their complexity. In short, ideal translators — through the cultivation of a bicultural attitude and an ambicultural perform- ance — must learn to so verbally authenticate, for their readers or listeners, the cultural experience of the source language that it becomes, as fully and richly as possible, the cultranslation experience of its fortunate beneficiaries.

References

Bassnett, Susan and André Lefevere, eds. *Translation, History and Culture*. Lon- don: Pinter Publishers, 1990.

Bloom, Alfred H. *The Linguistic Shaping of Thought: A Study of the Impact of Language on Thinking in China and the West*. Hillsdale, N.J.: Laurence Erlbaum Associates, 1981.

Deeney, John J. "Biculturalism and Translation." *The Asian Messenger*, Vol. 2, No. 2 (1977), pp. 30–35.

Fellini, Federico. "A World Going Down the Tube." *Time*, 27 January 1986, pp. 36–37.

Halman, Talat Sait. "'Cultranslation' — A New Technique of Poetry Translation." *Council of National Literatures: Quarterly World Report*, Vol. 1, No. 2 (1978), pp. 10–11.

Johnson, Samuel. *James Boswell: The Life of Samuel Johnson*, edited by John Canning. London: Methuen, 1991.

Liang, J.C.P. "Cultural Transposition in Translation." Paper delivered at the International Conference on the Translation of Chinese Literature, Taiwan, 1990. (Publication in preparation).

Nida, Eugene A. "Linguistics and Ethnology in Translation-problems." *Word: Journal of the Linguistic Circle of New York*, Vol. 1, No. 2 (1945), pp. 194–208.

Snell-Hornby, Mary. "Linguistic Transcoding or Cultural Transfer? A Critique of Translation Theory in Germany." In Bassnett and Lefevere, pp. 79–86.

Soffietti, James P. "Bilingualism and Biculturalism." *Journal of Educational Psychology*, No. 46 (1955), pp. 222–27.

Whorf, Benjamin. *Language, Thought, and Reality: Selected Writings of Benjamin Lee Whorf*, edited by J. B. Carroll. Cambridge, Mass.: The MIT Press, 1956.

Wu, Song-chu and Harold A. Stephens. "Be Bicultural to Be Bilingual." *English Teaching Forum*, Vol. 29, No. 2 (1991), pp. 28–31.

Translation as a Basis for Cultural Description

Robert Feleppa
Department of Philosophy
Wichita State University, Kansas, U.S.A.

How can interpretation enable one to understand the most basic and general conceptual categories of foreign languages? Of particular interest here are the radically foreign languages of cultures bearing relatively little prior relationship to cultures already familiar to anthropologists. These cases are particularly interesting because they hold out the possibility of discovery of new varieties of conceptual organization. Most intriguing here is the variation possible at the most fundamental cognitive levels. Cultural anthropologists who rest cultural studies heavily on translation, whom I shall broadly term "interpretive anthropologists", or simply "interpretivists", often view this sort of discovery as the most important kind that they can contribute to human knowledge. For not only do we discover that some particular culture has organized their thought differently, but we discover new possibilities of organizing our own thought differently in the process.

But just where and how "in the process" of translation we learn this is extremely important. The translator necessarily begins with the conceptually familiar. He tries to equate terms in the language being studied (the source language) with terms in another (the receptor language). Genuine translation succeeds, it seems, just insofar as the translator can adapt his own conceptual scheme to express the ideas in the scheme of the individual or group he is trying to understand. And clues about how the inquirer's mind is to be stretched must be drawn from the data of translation. Contact with another culture could so stimulate us intellectually that we come to think about the world in new ways. But this alone would not be discovery that cultural participants themselves think in these novel ways.

For instance, Pike (1954) contends that the study of a single culture (ethnography) must begin with concepts with which the anthropologist is familiar. Then, gradually, the anthropologist *approximates* the concepts of the source-language speakers. The final product is an understanding of a culture from what is often termed the "cultural insider's" point of view. From there, genuine cultural comparison (ethnology) can proceed — and only from there, interpretivists contend. We must find out what cultures are really like to their participants before we can compare them.

But how do we achieve this approximation of the unfamiliar? Earlier anthropology is full of examples of anthropologists who failed finally to distance themselves sufficiently from their own conceptual-cultural heritage. And interpretive anthropologists remain haunted by the fear (a healthy one, they contend) that insufficiently sensitive translation will show false similarities between source and receptor languages. So the approximation of concepts cannot be the result of the inquirer *imposing* rather than *discovering* them. Otherwise he runs the risk of simply seeing his own concepts "writ large" on the rest of humanity. He is thus condemned, and blind, to ignorance about the real conceptual divergences exhibited in other cultures. However, imposition is not so easily escaped, as we shall see.

The Interdefining Character of Concepts

Major figures in the interpretivist tradition, such as Boas and Malinowski, insisted that culture be understood from the point of view of the cultural participant, or the "cultural insider." Many anthropologists follow Pike's advice that we apply "emic analysis" to culture (or study culture "emically"). Pike derives this term from the phonological study of "phonemics," that is, of sound comparisons and contrasts that are significant to cultural insiders. On the other hand there is "etic analysis", which is derived from the phonological concept of "phonetics", or the study of linguistic sound from the point of view of a universally imposed system of sound classifications. Emic analysis tries to understand concepts, practices, and institutions as they are understood to interrelate with each other by cultural insiders. Etic analysis looks for intercultural similarities and sometimes willfully imposes categories of external origin on a culture. (For fuller discussions of these sometimes controversial notions see Harris 1976, Fisher and Werner 1978.)

Pike himself explains the distinction with the help of the following analogy: We can give an emic analysis of an automobile if we "describe the structural functioning of a particular car as a whole, ... showing the parts of the whole car as they function in relation to one another." An etic analysis would "describe the elements one at a time as they are found in a stock room where ... [they] have been systematically 'filed' according to general criteria." (1954) Emic analysis makes sense of behavior in terms of concepts that subjects themselves understand. It fits a given concept, practice, or institution into a "cultural puzzle", as it were. It insists on sensitivity to the fact that a culture does not have an "election" unless it also has interrelated concepts such as "electorate", "decision", "majority", etc. On the other hand, if a Western observer saw enough in a culture's group decision making process to liken it to voting, he could make enlightening comparisons of this process to, say, Western democratic processes, even though he did not see how the process fits into the cultural puzzle generally. This would be an etic approach.

Pike sees the two forms of analysis as complementing each other. Cultural comparison is to be viewed as based on successful emic analysis of individual cultures. Once culturally specific items have been discovered, they can be compared to similar items in other cultures. This is, for many anthropologists, the most important purpose of cultural anthropology.

If this is to be the interpretive basis of anthropological theory, however, then it is the basis for cross-cultural comparisons and categorizations. But taken at face value, a very clear dilemma emerges. If every concept and institution in a culture gets its meaning from its fit within specific cultural puzzles, and if all cultures constitute different puzzles, then cross-cultural comparison is impossible!

One classic response to this problem may be found in Kluckhohn (1953): He proposed that we consider as the basis for genuine cross-cultural comparison the "fairly definite limits within which cultural variation is constrained by panhuman regularities in biology, psychology and the processes of social interaction." In effect, as Berry (1969) notes, this problem shifts the burden of discovering universals to other disciplines. However, one problem with this is that other disciplines will tend, if anything, to be less sensitive to intercultural variation.

Another way in which this problem has been approached has been to acknowledge that cultures, understood purely from within, are not comparable. On such approaches, etic analysis will pay relatively little attention to the results of emic analysis. Similarities in institutions and behavior will be described in terms of concepts that are imposed by the inquirer and like nothing that is understood by the cultural insider. Approaches such as functionalism and cultural materialism compare cultures in terms of how they resolve common biological, environmental, and social problems. The common problems they attribute to cultures have a certain parallelism to Kluckhohn's bases for cultural universals. However, they do not share the concern of Kluckhohn to combine emic analysis and cross-cultural comparison. Kluckhohn wants to compare concepts *as understood within* cultures.

Many interpretivists share the suspicions of etic anthropologists concerning emically based cross-cultural comparison. However, since they value interpretation and emic understanding, their advice is to avoid comparison and anthropological theory-formation generally. However, such so-called "descriptivists" or "relativists" may not easily escape the problems of concern here. For while they might not explicitly try to compare cultures, they seem to burden themselves with a comparative task in the very process of translation. If a complete successful translation is the matching of ideas expressed by source- and receptor-language terms, this implicitly asserts the sharing of concepts by two cultures.

The interdefining character of concepts seems to present the interpreter with a self-contained system of concepts and a problem of how to move from his own self-contained conceptual scheme to another. This problem is worsened, as we shall now see, by considering the effect of unconscious and historically distant factors on learning and meaning.

The Sapir-Whorf Hypothesis

The interpretive anthropologist can thus be seen as opposing both those who try to base ethnography on translation, but do a poor job of it, and those who don't place very much importance on understanding from the insider's point of view. Extensive and at times bitter theoretical disputes have raged over such issues as whether interpretivists are too ingenuous if they trust what their informants say about their customs. It has been argued, for instance, that informants might convey their own self-deceptions about their behavior: They report what they *ought* to be doing instead of telling what they *actually* do. (Harris, 1979)

But the fact that subjects might not be fully conscious of the rule-governed patterns they follow brings up a much broader problem. Edward Sapir, though an interpretivist, stressed the often unconscious and unreflective nature of linguistic structure. (Sapir, 1949) Sapir here exemplifies the beginning of a divergence in concern among interpretive anthropologists toward sometimes incompatible aims (1) to understand what people actually think and believe and (2) to probe areas of their thought and behavior exhibiting patterns of which they are not aware. Insofar as the latter aim distances itself from what subjects actually report, it may hopelessly blur the distinction between analyses that impose (say, psychoanalytic) conceptions and those that discover unconsciously grasped elements of the cultural insider's point of view.

Sapir and his influential student Benjamin Lee Whorf authored a hypothesis that has greatly exercised the theoretical imagination of anthropologists, linguists, and psychologists. The thesis asserts that patterns and structures in one's native language have a strong influence on a person's world-view. As Sapir himself remarks:

> It is quite an illusion to imagine that one adjusts to reality essentially without the use of language and that language is merely an incidental means of solving specific problems of communication or reflection. The fact of the matter is that the "real world" is to a large extent unconsciously built up on the language habits of the group. No two languages are ever sufficiently similar to be considered as representing the same social reality. The worlds in which different societies live are distinct worlds, not merely the same world with different labels attached. (Sapir, 1949)

Sapir and Whorf gave particular attention to the ways in which fundamental linguistic categories underlay differences in world view. Differences in Hopi tense structure were seen to yield differences in conceptions of time. The absence of mass-terms in the Hopi language was tied to a pluralistic metaphysics since no sense could be made of such things as "matter" or "substance" as the common stuff of which all things are made.

The deeper one goes into a conceptual scheme, the more serious the problem of imposition. Commenting on the problems faced by the "Standard Average European" (SAE) anthropologist in translating native American Indian languages and native languages of Africa, Sapir remarks:

> Such categories as number, gender, case, tense, mode, voice, "aspect" and a host of others, many of which are not recognized systematically in our Indo-European languages, are, of course, derivative of experience in the last analysis, but, once abstracted from experience, they are systematically elaborated in language and are not so much discovered in experience as imposed upon it because of the tyrannical hold that linguistic form has upon our orientation in

the world. Inasmuch as languages differ very widely in their systematization of fundamental concepts, they tend to be only loosely equivalent to each other as symbolic devices and are, as a matter of fact, incommensurable in the sense in which two systems of points in a plane are, on the whole, incommensurable to each other if they are plotted with reference to differing systems of coordinates. (Sapir, 1931)

The vision here is of the possibility of a conceptual scheme organized in its most basic fundamentals along different lines than those familiar to the SAE mind. And yet our ignorance of our own conceptual relativity makes imposition an extremely likely pitfall. The familiarity of SAE concepts takes the form of a "tyrannical hold" on our imagination, and it is a tyranny that must be overcome. This conceptual relativity, Sapir argued (1949), is "generally hidden from us by our native acceptance of fixed habits of speech as guides to an objective understanding of the nature of experience." A carefully considered "calibration" had to be made between the conceptual schemes of inquirer and subject. He contended that language had to make contact with the world in order to be useful and learnable, but under fuller elaboration it becomes "a self-contained conceptual system which previsages all possible experience in accordance with certain accepted formal limitations". (Sapir, 1949)

But if we add the key elements of the Sapir-Whorf position together with those stemming from the interrelationship of items in a conceptual scheme, we find a more severe problem than Sapir acknowledges. If patterns of linguistic and cultural conditioning structure our world view, to the degree that the SAE and Hopi "live in different worlds," how does any "calibration" or translation between them succeed? The qualitative enrichment needed by the SAE anthropologist must spring, somehow, from translational data-acquisition. But Sapir and most anthropologists, psychologists, and philosophers maintain that sense experience itself is filtered by one's socially conditioned set of concepts. If so, how can the interpreter's observations ever be sufficiently objective to determine what a radically different conceptual scheme might be like? If the linguist's only means of access to a native language is through relating observed subject verbal behavior with associated nonverbal stimulation, and if the linguist's perceptions of the immediate environment reflect cultural conditioning, then there seems to be little the linguist can share with the subject. It seems that the linguist can share with the subject the grasp of a common attribute only if he uses a receptor-language expression that applies to experience discriminated in the same way as by the speaker of the source-language expression it translates. Coming to share a conceptual scheme seems to depend critically on successful translation, which latter depends on having similar perceptions of the world. Yet having such similar perceptions depends on sharing a conceptual scheme. This condition, characterized by Dilthey as the "hermeneutic circle", has a history of concern, notably in the Western biblical scholarly tradition, much older than anthropology. However, it is particularly acute in the anthropological contexts of Sapir's concern.

Imposition in Translation

The philosophical worries here are well articulated by the philosopher W. V. Quine (1951):

> The relevant features of the situation issuing in a given utterance are in large part concealed in the person of the speaker, where they are implanted by his earlier environment.... If we could assume that our speaker and our English speaker, when observed in like external situations, differed only in how they say things and not in what they say, so to speak, then the methodology of synonymy determinations would be pretty smooth.... But of course the trouble is that not only the narrowly linguistic habits of vocabulary and syntax are imported by each speaker from his unknown past.

> Theoretically the ... difficulty is that, as Cassirer and Whorf have stressed, there is in principle no separating language from the rest of the world, at least as conceived by the speaker. Basic differences in language are bound up, as likely as not, with differences in the way in which the speakers articulate the world itself into things and properties, time and space, elements, forces, spirits, and so on. It is not clear even in principle that it makes sense to think of words and syntax as varying from language to language while the content stays fixed; yet precisely this fiction is involved in speaking of synonymy, at least as between expressions of radically different languages.

Indeed, as translation gets further away from reference to observable features, Quine argues, the interpreter "comes to depend increasingly on a projection of himself, with his Indo-European *Weltanschauung*, into the sandals of his ... informant." (1951) And this brings the key problem to the surface: If there are concepts that the interpreter attributes to subjects simply on the *assumption* that the subject's concept is the same as the interpreter's, this seems to cost us our basis for objectively ascribing that concept to the subject. This seems to be a form of the conceptual "tyranny" against which Sapir warns us. We can *start* that way, following Pike; but we are not to end up that way. But what Quine suggests is that we never escape this sort of imposition of the familiar concept, and that we must therefore reconsider some of the key assumptions we make about interpretation.

To put his point briefly (for fuller elaborations see his 1960), he maintains that it is a mistake to try to explain the fact that individual words or sentences make sense by theoretically assigning to them mental or abstract objects such as "propositions" or "concepts". Only confusion results if we posit the existence of these objects to explain translation and communication. In Quine's view, Sapir is getting at a very important point in saying that we cannot view translation as a matter of matching differing linguistic labels to an otherwise shared reality. But Quine goes one step beyond this claim in saying that it is just as much a mistake to think that there is a set of propositions, concepts, or ideas shared by subject and translator, which their languages label differently.

There are a number of considerations that motivate Quine's view. One is to acknowledge that empirical data (indeed, even all imaginable data) severely underdetermine interpretation. As the concepts being investigated get more abstract, the number of alternative, empirically adequate translations multiplies, and the more the linguist must rely on "projecting himself into his informant's shoes". But, agreeing in effect with interpretive anthropologists who say that imposition is incompatible with objective discovery of concepts, Quine maintains that since imposition is essential to translation, the "objective discovery" such anthropologists are after may just be *impossible*.

While Quine raises a concern about all interpretation and theory-formation, he is decidedly not a skeptic about interpretation. That a set of assumptions makes translation impossible is a *reductio ad absurdum* of those assumptions. However, if this negative attack succeeds in showing us what objectivity in translation is not, it does not say much about what it *is*. However, he does provide the clues to an answer. He explores the limits of translation to show us what it cannot do. By exploring those same limits we can see what is the best that it can do, and derive our ideas about objectivity from there.

We should emphasize the point that we depend on imposing familiar concepts in order to translate. After all, translation *is* a process of relating unfamiliar terms and behavior to familiar ones. In a very fundamental way it is a *coordination* of languages, not a description of one in the terms of another. In fact, as Quine notes, translation rests heavily on a principle of *charity*. This principle bids us to translate so that most of a speaker's beliefs turn out to agree with those of the translator. This extends beyond the beliefs expressed in actual utterances. According to this principle, the translator must also view as shared the most basic logical rules that connect these beliefs to others. For instance, Quine's influential student Donald Davidson argues:

> The methodological advice to interpret in a way that optimizes agreement should not be conceived as resting on a charitable assumption about human intelligence that might turn out to be false. If we cannot find a way to interpret the utterances and other behaviour of a creature as revealing a set of beliefs largely consistent and true by our own standards, we have no reason to count that creature as rational, as having beliefs, or as saying anything. (Davidson, 1984)

Alternatively:

> Crediting people with a large degree of consistency cannot be counted mere charity: it is unavoidable if we are to be in a position to accuse them meaningfully of error and some degree of irrationality. Global confusion, like universal mistake, is unthinkable, not because imagination boggles, but because too much confusion leaves nothing to be confused about and massive error erodes the background of true belief against which alone failure can be construed. (Davidson, 1980)

There are two important claims here: (1) Agreement in belief is not an empirical result. It is an *a priori* deduction from reflection on the nature of translation. (2) Unless we assume a considerable amount of agreement between subject and translator, we have no basis for thinking the subject is in error.

Davidson, like Quine, has objectives here that extend beyond questions of interpretation. These passages contain the germ of a position that makes massive error itself, not just the attribution of it to others, impossible. His general idea is that if we can interpret each other, then we cannot be living in a world about which we have largely mistaken beliefs. That is, he is here addressing the traditional Western philosophical problem of skepticism. However, whatever the virtues of this broader position, I think that we have our fingers here on the source of a vague feeling of oddness in all the earlier discussions of the challenges of interpretive anthropology.

We saw there positions that challenged us to get inside the conceptual schemes of others, but threatened to make the challenge insurmountable. What made it seem insurmountable was that there were reasons to think we might be largely mistaken about what subjects mean, despite our successes in translation. This seemed especially so when we started to realize that imposition of the familiar was impossible to avoid. This in turn seemed to carry the consequence that all translation was ethnocentric and the goal of discovering deep conceptual diversity was therefore inaccessible. We might, in our discoveries that some languages such as the Hopi's were extremely difficult to translate, base our claims of divergence on the degree of difficulty involved. But there seemed a very real fear that for all our efforts, the *real* structure of Hopi and the real divergences from SAE languages would be forever undetectable.

However, such errors cannot be forever undetectable. Our empirical methodology of translation provides our only warranted basis for attributing difference in belief, or speaker error, of any kind. If this methodology *requires* charity in order to work, then *this* form of imposition of familiar belief and concept cannot provide reason to think that the source-language speakers beliefs differ from what we think they are. If they differ too much, we will have before us not a speaker with whom we disagree, but a speaker whom we do not *understand*.

Let us review the important steps that lead to this point. We should consider very carefully the interdependence of beliefs and the interdependence of beliefs and meanings. The interpretation of a particular sentence, the revelation of a single belief, cannot be done in isolation from the interpretation of other sentences and expressions. I understand a sentence only when I understand the words in it; and I understand those words only when I know how to use them correctly in other sentences. Put in broader terms, akin to those used in discussion of emic analysis above, I genuinely understand a practice as a kind of "scientific inquiry" if I have evidence that the practitioners have notions of "evidence", "cause", "prediction", and so forth. And I can attribute these concepts to them only if I am ready to attribute other concepts in turn. (For instance, one views something as "evidence" for something else only if one sees certain happenings as giving "reasons" to believe things.) As Davidson remarks, a belief gets its very *content* from its place in an overall pattern. (1980)

But then how do translators break in to this overall pattern? Consider the most basic cases: that is, where they translate utterances of the source-language speakers about things evidently in the immediate environment. As Davidson remarks, the translator "interprets sentences held true (which is not to be distinguished from attributing beliefs), according to the events and objects in the outside world that cause the sentence to be held true" (Davidson, 1983). The source-language speaker's beliefs must be seen as about the things that cause them in these cases. A source-language sentence that seems to report the perception of a tree, after suitable efforts have been made to be sure it is not about some particular feature of a tree, should be translated as a perception about a tree. Now the empirical data does not force this on us. We can translate people as really talking about spirits manifesting themselves as solid, leafy objects, or in any number of other ways consistent with their linguistic behavior. Or, with respect to their "logic" of belief, nothing in the data forces us to say they relate beliefs to beliefs according to the same basic logical inference patterns that we do. Logical inference patterns are not manifest in the data! What is manifest is that certain utterances, translated a certain way, follow others. Or that certain kinds of non-verbal behavior (the assumption of a defensive posture) follow utterances translated in a certain way ("an enemy is approaching"). There seems to be no other way to break in to the closed circle of belief and meaning. The inquirer must take the conditions that make receptor-language sentences true for him in these basic situations as the correlates of source-language sentences that seem to have the same truth conditions. This is not to say that source-language speakers cannot be in error. A speaker might call a tree a shrub. But it is only insofar as we know that "shrub" does not mean "tree" for him that we can safely say he has mistakenly labeled a shrub. And it is only on the basis of a large number of other correct attributions of the term we are translating as "tree" to trees that we can have an empirical basis for saying that the term in question is correctly so translated. Thus we can only attribute difference or error in belief on the basis of the attribution of a large number of other correct beliefs, and similarly for meaning.

Pike and other proponents of emic analysis are quite well aware of the ways in which beliefs depend on each other, and the ways in which meanings depend on each other. But they seemed to think that we could make sense of a conceptual scheme as distinct from the factual claims about the world it could be used to make. But this is to overlook the dependence of meaning and belief on *each other*. A mistake or difference about meaning can always be treated as a mistake about belief. If the subject used the word we have translated as "tree" to apply to a shrub, we might judge that he does not know what the term we have translated as "tree" means. But we can always say he does use language correctly here and is instead just mistaken in thinking it *is* a tree. But by the same token, a mistake or difference in belief can always be viewed instead as concerning meaning. The mistaken belief about the tree can become a correct belief about a tree by changing the translation of the source-language word previously translated as "shrub".

The only way to break into this circle of meaning and belief is to get a fix on belief by translating in accordance with the charity principle. Our beliefs about obvious things become their beliefs about them. From there, and only from there, can translation proceed.

Translation, by its very nature, involves the blending of languages. It must force conformity of the source-language to the receptor language because its primary task is to make sense of the verbal and non-verbal behavior of source-language speakers. It is not surprising, then, that a careful look at the methodology of translation shows that we can have no empirical basis for saying that we have entirely *discovered* a match of source- and receptor-language meanings or beliefs.

There is of course some place for psychology and other disciplines to discover cognitive deviance in individuals and groups. We can only ask that we be rational *by and large*. We count others largely correct and rational, but it is difficult to give an exact measure to how "largely". The point is, however, that the methodology of translation places severe constraints on how much error and how much cognitive divergence we can find in a person.

So on the one hand there is no need to follow Kluckhohn in seeking to discover cultural or biological universals as a basis for cultural comparison (and recall that translation itself implies cultural comparison). Nor do we have to give up on interpretation because we cannot find such things. Translation is possible, and it is possible only if there is imposition of familiar patterns on the source-language.

Translational Objectivity in a New Light

This kind of resolution to the problem raises some questions. (1) What defines the difference between "objective" and "ethnocentric" translation, if translation has a kind of ethnocentrism built into it? (2) What is the point of interpretive anthropology if it cannot reveal underlying meaning? (3) Can interpretive anthropology achieve its goal of revealing new, perhaps surprising levels of cognitive divergence?

1. Translation will be unfairly ethnocentric if it overlooks data that would disconfirm translations that make subjects look similar to us on some score. Sapir and his followers garnered very clear evidence that the imposition of certain familiar SAE categories on native American Indians would do an inadequate job of translating them. A related point would be that attribution of beliefs to people would have to bear some relationship to careful translations of what they say. Attribution of concepts of standard Western economic thinking to foreign traders, say, could not be based simply on the fact that it would lead to correct predictions of what they do. Discussion of the exact nature of this complex relationship is beyond the scope of this paper. (Recall that we must allow for the existence of cultural concepts which even cultural insiders themselves do not fully or explicitly grasp.)

2. Interpretive anthropology better enables communication with source-language speakers than other forms of cultural anthropology. This is not to value it over those others. Valuable purposes are also served by noting similarities in the function of cultural institutions in meeting common human needs. Also, the position I have defended is a position about interpretive objectivity. It does not conclude with a deep skepticism about what people "really mean": it concludes that our notion of "real meaning" leads to contradictions that signal a need to revise that notion. The accepted standards of interpretation, including charity, give us all the "real meaning" there is.

3. Discovery of conceptual divergence is discovery that translation can succeed only with difficulty: with creative play and perhaps difficult reconceptualization of *receptor*-language translations and grammatical analyses in order to accommodate the linguistic data of field translation. The measure of cognitive difference is to be found, as Quine suggests at one point, in the "sheer degree of difficulty of intertranslation, the degree of elaborateness of the interlinguistic

manual." (1970) There is, however, a limit on conceptual divergence. The belief systems and the most basic levels of the logics of different cultures must have considerable overlap. For unless we presume this, translation cannot get off the ground. Moreover, the identification of error or the *specification* of divergence at any subsequent stage of translation rests on the assumption that most other beliefs are correct. For it is only under that assumption that we fix belief sufficiently to get a hold on what people mean. Too much error makes them *uninterpretable*.

There may remain the strong intuition that what we are actually left with is the possibility of other minds so alien to our own that we are unable to grasp their content. However, it may be that the better lesson to learn is that the mind is not the sort of thing we think it is. Or, better still, that talk about "the contents of minds" just *is* talk about the possibilities of interpretation. Changing our attitudes about the mind is something that is also encouraged in other quarters, such as psychology.

Why is it better to revise our notions of translational objectivity to accommodate relativism (to our own schemes), as opposed to conceding ethnocentrism and skepticism? The answer, again, is that the possibility of massive difference that the skeptic wishes to hold open is one that makes translation impossible. Thus these skeptical doubts undercut themselves.

If something in this seems still to grate on our intuitions, perhaps this is a signal of an error in the position. But perhaps it also signals a deep *empiricism* that has become commonplace in our thought. Such an empiricism carries a typically healthy suspicion of using "inward" reflection on methods of analysis to discover things about the world "out there." Thus we have our inclination to follow Kluckhohn and *try to* discover with the help of psychology the common elements that make understanding possible. However, what we take to be an *object* of discovery may instead be a *precondition* for it.

References

Davidson, Donald. "A Coherence Theory of Truth and Knowledge." In *Kant oder Hegel?*, edited by D. Henrich. Stuttgart: Klett-Cotta, pp. 423–38.
––––––. "Mental Events." In *Essays on Actions and Events*, edited by Donald Davidson. Oxford: Clarendon Press, 1980, pp. 207–27.

————. "Radical Interpretation." In *Inquiries into Truth and Interpretation*, edited by Donald Davidson. Oxford: Clarendon Press, 1984, pp. 125–39.

Fisher, Lawrence E. and Oswald Werner. "Explaining Explanation: Tension in American Anthropology." *Journal of Anthropological Research*, Vol. 34 (1978), pp. 219–28.

Harris, Marvin. *Cultural Materialism: The Struggle for a Science of Culture.* New York: Random House, 1979.

————. "The History and Significance of the Emic-etic Distinction." In *Annual Review of Anthropology*, Vol. 5, edited by B. J. Siegel, *et al.* Palo Alto, Calif.: Annual Reviews, Inc., 1976, pp. 329–50.

Pike, Kenneth. *Language in Relation to a Unified Theory of the Structure of Human Behavior*, Part 1. Glendale, Calif.: Summer Institute of Linguistics, 1954.

Quine, Willard V. "Philosophical Progress in Language Theory." *Metaphilosophy*, Vol. 1 (1970), pp. 2–19.

————. "The Problem of Meaning in Linguistics." In *From a Logical Point of View*, edited by Willard V. Quine, 2nd ed. New York: Harper and Row, 1951, pp. 47–64.

————. *Word and Object.* Cambridge, Mass.: M.I.T. Press, 1960.

Sapir, Edward. "Conceptual Categories in Primitive Languages." *Science*, Vol. 74 (1931), p. 578.

————. *Selected Writings of Edward Sapir in Language, Culture, and Personality*, edited by D. G. Mandelbaum. Berkeley and Los Angeles: University of California Press, 1949.

DISCOURSE ANALYSIS

Discourse Analysis

Shoshana Blum-Kulka
Communications Institute
Hebrew University, Jerusalem, Israel

Discourse analysis is used to describe a wide range of research activities in disciplines as diverse as sociolinguistics, language philosophy, pragmatics, text-linguistics and semiotics (Brown and Yule, 1983). Though differing in method and focus, all studies of discourse share a common interest in the analysis of texts beyond the sentence, in language as communication and in the ways the process of communication is embedded in socio-cultural contexts. Since the sixties, developments in the various fields of discourse analysis have had a profound though often fragmented impact on studies of translation. Translation scholars came to recognize that "no adequate general theory of translation can be developed before scholars have turned from a sentence-restricted linguistics to produce a full theory of the nature of texts. Such a theory will devote extensive attention to the form of texts — how their parts work together to constitute an entity —, to the ways texts convey often very complex patterns of meaning, and to the manner of which they function communicatively in a given socio-cultural context." (Holmes, 1972: 100) In default of such a "full theory of discourse" to date, scholars of translation have drawn on the insights gained with regard to the nature of texts through studies in discourse analysis in explaining and describing the process of translation, in setting up models for translation quality assessment and in carrying out empirical research on processes and products of translation.

The impact of discourse-analysis on the field of translation is already noticeable from a cursory look at the way the scope of topics discussed in theoretical introductions to the field has changed over the last decade. Parallel to a similar development in introductions to linguistics, while the seminal works of Rabin (1958), Nida (1964), and Catford (1965) discuss the linguistics of translation in terms of semantics and syntax only, more recent works (e.g., Bassnett-McGuire, 1980; Snell-Hornby, 1988) include discussions of translation issues on the textual level and go beyond semantics to consider translation equivalence in terms of "functional" or "pragmatic meaning". Other works on translation announce their discourse oriented approach already in their title (e.g., *Text and Translation*, Neubert, 1985; *Discourse and the Translator*, Hatim and Mason, 1990). The linguistic education of students of translation has thus come to incorporate a "discoursal" component. Yet both the theory of discourse drawn on and the uses it is being put to within translation studies remain highly diverse and controversial.

Text and Discourse

One of the central questions of translation theory has to do with establishing the scope of linguistic units (words, sentences, texts) to be examined and the types of equivalence to be sought for (formal/functional) between source and target texts. In seeking equivalence on the textual level, translation studies draw on discourse-analysis to reveal the systematic, though potentially language specific ways in which texts cohere to form whole entitities. This field of inquiry, known as contrastive discourse-analysis, continues the contrastive tradition laid down by Vinay and Darbelnet (1958) in their classic *Stylistique comparée du français et de l'anglais*. But while Vinay and Darbelnet focus on words and sentences only, in discourse-analytical oriented studies the base-line for comparison are the textual norms governing specific text-types, or the types of linguistic devices used for establishing the text's interconnectedness. This type of work has shown for example that Hebrew and English differ in preferences shown for types of cohesion markers used, and that translated texts show traces of transfer on the textual level, yielding texts that deviate from textual norms in the target language (Levenston, 1973). Weizman's (1984; 1986) work on the discourse structure of journalistic texts in French and Hebrew similarly reveal that differences in discoursal norms in regard to the use of quotation marks serve as an important baseline for understanding shifts in translation. It follows from this line of work that a discourse-oriented translation-paradigm has to be based on a three-step analysis: a contrastive study of discourse norms governing the structure of comparable, specific text-genres between two languages, an explanation of the criteria used and functions achieved by the structural devices used in each, followed by an analysis of the solutions observed in actual translations (Weizman, 1986; House and Blum-Kulka, 1986).

The second facet of the "equivalence" issue in translation relates to both prescriptive and descriptive attempts to set up criteria for translation quality assessment. The understanding of the nature of texts and their functions, achieved through advances in discourse-analysis, allows for textual-type and function considerations to enter the debate about "quality assessment." (Reiss, 1973; Wilss, 1982) The notion of "functional equivalence" (House, 1977) or "communicative equivalence" (Neubert, 1985) used by discourse-analytically oriented translation scholars relates both to the level of the units compared for assessment, as well as to the levels of meaning taken into account in the comparison. The units by definition are textual, since it is assumed that it is always the text which is the input and the output of the translation model. It is the communicative status and role of the source text which needs to be established at the outset of the translation process, to be followed by a retrospective analysis of the translated target language text. In House's (1977) model of translation assessment, it is the linguistic-situational features of the source text and target texts, as determined following work in systemic linguistics (e.g., Halliday, 1973), which serve as the basis for analysis. In Neubert's case (1985) the criteria for the text-analysis followed derive from the textlinguistic tradition, represented by de Beaugrande and Dressler (1981). But in both cases, as in many others, the units of analysis are texts, and the criteria for evaluation and/or description look for functional meanings at the level of texts.

Text and Context

If a focus on global text structure, derived from advances in textlinguistics in the broadest sense, enriches the study of translation by providing the necessary "tertium comparationis" for translation oriented contrastive discourse-analysis, a focus on the complexity of meaning and interpretation in communication, derived from pragmatics and sociolinguistics, anchors the field of translation firmly within the study of communication. In Nida's formulation: "Because translating always involves communication within the context of interpersonal relations, the model for such activity must be a communication model, and the principles must be primarily sociolinguistic in the broad sense of the term" (Nida, 1976:78). Claims for the need to see translation in the wider socio-cultural context as an act of cross-cultural communication have also been made by Mounin (1963), who talks of "communication through translation", House and Blum-Kulka who view translation "as an interdisciplinary enterprise in the broad sense of studies in communication" (1986:7) and Toury (1980), who proposes a "cultural semiotic perspective" for studies on translation. But the general theoretical perspective advocated by such statements has been only rarely backed up by empirical translation studies grounded in advances in the fields of pragmatics and interpretive sociolinguistics. Insights from pragmatics on the intricacies of the interdependence between meaning and context, have found their ways into linguistic theories of translation (e.g., House, 1977; Neubert, 1985), and some textual studies (e.g., Blum-Kulka, 1981; 1986; House and Blum-Kulka, 1986; Tirkonnen-Condit, 1985), but their impact is still felt mainly in text-books for translators (e.g., Delisle, 1980; Hatim and Mason, 1990).

Consider the issue of pragmatic meanings. It is widely accepted that while semantics studies the relationships between signs and their references, pragmatics is the study of the explicit and implicit functions or purposes for which utterances are used, as related to the contextual conditions under which the utterances acquire their specific functions (Levinson, 1983). In the context of translation studies, the distinction made in pragmatics between explicit and implicit means for achieving communicative acts helps explain shifts of pragmatic meaning derivable from incongruences in the structure of such communicative acts (cf. "speech acts", Levinson, 1983). Indirect speech acts may differ between cultures and language both in structure and conventions of use, and translations may err both by failing to interpret indirect meanings or by deviating from conventions of use in expressing them in the target language (Blum-Kulka, 1981).

Furthermore, the interpretation of implicit meanings in the source text may heavily depend on textual cues interpretable in terms of a network of socio-cultural presuppositions available to source language, but not target language audiences (Blum-Kulka, 1986). Misreadings of textual cues may also occur as a result of the process of translation, as when the translator fails to render in the target language cues necessary for the interpretation of narrative point of view (Levenston and Sonnenschein, 1986).

Discourse and Interpretation

For studies of translation, "discourse" can signify a given text in the particular context of the situation (House, 1977), and/or the focal unit of translation analysis (Neubert, 1985; Toury, 1980; Stern, 1980). In a broader semiotic sense, "discourse" or "discourses" can be seen as conventionalized modes of talking and writing typifying interaction in specific social domains. Communication scholars have drawn attention to the power-potential inherent in differential access to "discourse" conventions of any specific domain (Kress, 1985; Foucault, 1972). Translators and interpreters often fulfill the role of mediators and gate-keepers in situation governed by specific discourse conventions, such as in interpretation for immigrants in institutional settings (Knapp-Potthoff and Knapp, 1987) and bilingual courtrooms (Berk-Seligson, 1987). This line of work suggests that the issues of power involved in bilingual gate-keeping encounters provides a new direction to be explored from the perspective of discourse and translation.

This brief review can hardly do justice to the topic of discourse and translation. Yet it does suggest some general principles in regard to the ways in which a discourse-oriented approach to translation may proceed in the future. Such an approach works on the premise that translation is an act of communication. This means that, as in the case of all processes of communication, we should be concerned both with the preconditions which can ensure successful communication, and with the effects which the communicated message has on its audience. In the case of translation, preconditions include the conventions governing the textual, pragmatic and socio-cultural systems of the languages and cultures involved. Textually, contrastive discourse-analysis can reveal the discourse conventions typifying specific discourse genres in the two languages involved, and the findings of such analyses can serve as the framework for contrastive analysis of source and target language texts. On the pragmatic level, since pragmatic meanings are one of the most evasive and intricate systems of meaning to be defined and delimited, studies in translation need to to be especially attentive to findings in the areas of pragmalinguistics (e.g., the way certain linguistic markers indicate pragmatic meanings) and cross-cultural pragmatics (e.g., the way cultures differ in conveying similar pragmatic functions). On the other hand, the fine-grained analysis of source and target texts, specific to translation studies, may enrich the field of pragmatics by revealing points of pragmatic incongruence not apparent in other ways. Consider the socio-cultural dimension. Scholars in translation have always been aware of limits on translatability imposed by the uniqueness of socio-cultural systems. A discourse-analytically oriented approach to translation may perhaps refine our understanding of this dimension by drawing attention to the intricate ways in which presupposed socio-cultural knowledge is contextually exploited in both literary and nonliterary texts to convey implicit meanings. The issue of translation "effects" can be approached in widely different ways. One path is to study the role of translation in a given culture from a historical perspective, in a way that illuminates critical instances of cultural contact and their effects on the development of the culture under study. Another much less studied way is to try and trace experimentally the processes and levels of interpretation involved in the decoding of translated texts, as compared to interpretation of the original, as a way of estimating the role of translation in processes of communication. Finally, "effects" may be understood as a sociological construct, calling for the study of the social role of the translator/interpreter as a cross-cultural mediator.

References

Bassnett-McGuire, Susan. *Translation Studies*. London and New York: Methuen, 1980.

Beaugrande, Robert de and Wolfgang Dressler. *Introduction to Text Linguistics*. London: Longman, 1981.

Berk-Seligson, S. "The Intersection of Testimony Styles in Interpreted Judicial Proceedings: Pragmatic Alteration in Spanish Testimony." *Linguistics*, Vol. 25 (1987), pp. 1087–25.

Blum-Kulka, Shoshana. "Shifts in Cohesion and Coherence in Translation." In *Interlingual and Intercultural Communication*, edited by Juliane House and Shoshana Blum-Kulka. Tübingen: Gunter Narr, 1986, pp. 17–37.

———. "The Study of Translation in View of New Developments in Discourse Analysis." *Poetics Today*, Vol. 2, No. 4 (1981), pp. 89–95.

Brown, Gillian and George Yule. *Discourse Analysis*. Cambridge: Cambridge University Press, 1983.

Catford, J. C. *A Linguistic Theory of Translation: An Essay in Applied Linguistics.* London: Oxford University Press, 1965.

Delisle, Jean. *Translation: An Interpretive Approach*, translated by P. Logan and M. Creery. Ottawa: University of Ottawa Press, 1988.

Foucault, M. *The Archaeology of Knowledge*, translated by M. Sheridan. London: Tavistock, 1972.

Halliday, M.A.K. *Explorations in the Functions of Language.* London: Arnold, 1973.

Hatim, Basil and Ian Mason. *Discourse and the Translator.* London and New York: Longman, 1990.

Holmes, James S. "The Name and Nature of Translation Studies." In *3rd International Congress of Applied Linguistics Abstracts.* Copenhagen: 1972.

House, Juliane. *A Model for Translation Quality Assessment.* Tübingen: Gunter Narr, 1977.

────── and Shoshana Blum-Kulka. *Interlingual and Intercultural Communication: Discourse and Cognition in Translation and Second Language Acquisiton Studies.* Tübingen: Gunter Narr, 1986.

Knapp-Potthoff, A. and K. Knapp. "The Man (or Woman) in the Middle — Discoursal Aspects of Non-professional Interpreting." In *Analyzing Intercultural Communication*, edited by K. Knapp, W. Ennenger and A. Knapp-Potthoff. The Hague: Mouton, 1987.

Kress, G. *Linguistic Processes in Sociocultural Practice.* Victoria: Deakin University Press, 1985.

Levenston, Edward A. "Towards a Comparative Stylistics of English and Hebrew." In *Chaim Rabin Jubilee Volume* (in Hebrew), edited by B. Z. Fischler and R. Nir. Jerusalem: 1973, pp. 59–67.

────── and G. Sonnenschein. "The Translation of Point-of-view in Fictional Narrative." In *Interlingual Communication*, edited by Juliane House and Shoshana Blum-Kulka. Tübingen: Gunter Narr, 1986, pp. 49–61.

Levinson, Stephen. *Pragmatics.* Cambridge: Cambridge University Press, 1973.

Mounin, Georges. *Les problèmes théoriques de la traduction.* Paris: Galimard, 1963.

Neubert, Albrecht. *Text and Translation.* Leipzig: VEB Verlag Enzyklopädie, 1985.

Nida, Eugene A. "A Framework for the Analysis and Evaluation of Theories of Translation." In *Translation: Applications and Research*, edited by Richard W. Brislin. New York: Gardner Press, 1976, pp. 47–91.

──────. *Towards a Science of Translating, with Special Reference to Principles and Procedures Involved in Bible Translating.* Leiden: E. J. Brill, 1964.

Rabin, Chaim. "The Linguistics of Translation." In *Aspects of Translation*, edited by A. H. Smith. London: Secker and Warburg, 1958, pp. 123–45.

Reiss, K. "Der Texttyp als Ansatzpunkt für die Losung von Übersetzungsproble-
men." *Linguistica Antverpiensia*, Vol. 7 (1973), pp. 111–27.

Snell-Hornby, Mary. *Translation Studies: An Integrated Approach.* Amsterdam:
John Benjamins, 1988.

Stern, D. *Theoretische Grundlagen der Übersetzungswissenschaft.* Tübingen:
Gunter Narr, 1980.

Tirkonnen-Condit, Sonja. *Argumentative Text Structure and Translation.* Doctoral
thesis, Studia Philologica Jyvaskylaensia, University of Jyvaskyla, 1985.

Toury, Gideon. *In Search of a Theory of Translation.* Tel-Aviv: The Porter Institute
for Poetics and Semiotics, 1980.

Vinay, Jean-Paul and J. Darbelnet. *Stylistique comparée du français et l'anglais.*
Paris: Didier, 1958.

Weizman, E. "An Interlingual Study of Discourse Structures: Implications for the
Theory of Translation." In *Interlingual Communication*, edited by Juliana
House and Shoshana Blum-Kulka. Tübingen: Gunter Narr., 1986, pp. 115–29.

―――. "Some Register Characteristics of Journalistic Language: Are They Universals?" *Applied Linguistics*, Vol. 5, No. 1 (1984), pp. 39–50.

Wilss, Wolfram. *Science of Translation.* Tübingen: Narr, 1982.

Discourse Analysis and the Translator

Margaret F. Lang
Department of Languages
Heriot-Watt University, Edinburgh, U.K.

Introduction

Discourse linguistics has led to the development of an approach to translating which draws on the work of researchers in many disciplines: sociolinguistics, semiotics, pragmatics, cultural studies in their broadest sense (history, politics, literature, psychology, philosophy, etc.), and language studies. It has provided the possibility of creating a model of the translating process, that is, creating a set of categories or parameters which can assist in ensuring consistency and accuracy in translating and translation. The method derived from this model is discourse analysis.

The term discourse analysis has a wide range of acceptations. It has been used, for example, to refer to the interaction of translation and language studies, and to the view of language not as an isolated phenomenon but related to the world around and to other disciplines. Discourse analysis in translating refers to a method that is holistic, dealing not with single words or sentences but with entire constituents of an act of communication in so far as these can be determined by the translator. It is a method which studies a discourse (a) in its context of situation, taking into account participants, purpose, field, culture, etc. of both source and target texts and (b) in terms of its structure and its individual constituents, and by interpretation of context and structure and constituents assists in determining the meaning of the source text and fulfilling the requirement of the target text.

Before defining the components of discourse analysis, it is apposite to summarize what the appropriateness of such a method is in relation to translating. Discourse analysis provides for the teacher, student, and professional translator resources for achieving objectivity and for making and justifying decisions. It provides a strategy for relating the problems and processes of discourse and the specific concerns and objectives of the translator. It can be applied in translating to all kinds of texts, whether scientific, legal, religious, etc.

The Components of Discourse Analysis

The following definitions of the components of discourse analysis have a dual purpose: to describe the material on which the translator works — the source text, and to define the components of the method he will put into practice.

The basic unit of language which is the material for the translator is the text. This is a complex multi-dimensional structure of varying length which may be defined as an expression of culture, situation, and language. A text is rarely composed of only one type of writing. It is rather an amalgam of various *text types*, for example, narration, exposition, argumentation, instruction. To illustrate the hybrid nature of the structure of a text, consider the composition of an advertisement. This is typically exposition (description of the product), followed by argumentation (statement of why it is a good product), followed by instruction (recommendation to purchase the product). Texts are, however, seldom as straightforward as this in their structure, nor are text types always so easily identifiable.

A text has *texture*, which is provided by cohesive relations within the text. These are established when the interpretation of one element is dependent on the interpretation of another. Texture reflects the *coherence* and *cohesion* of the text.

Context and *co-text* are essential constituents of a text and are indispensable factors in determining its purpose. The former term is used to refer to the combined influences of participants, purpose, particular situation, environment or circumstances, and culture, from which the text is produced. Hatim and Mason (1990) define context in terms of three essential dimensions: communicative, pragmatic, and semiotic.

The communicative dimension includes *field, mode* and *tenor*. The pragmatic dimension includes *intentionality, speech acts, implicature*, and *inference*. The semiotic dimension includes *texts, discourses, genres, signs, intertextuality*. It is important to bear in mind that while such categories can be identified as discrete components, they are nevertheless mutually dependent and combine to form a unit, the unit being the text. Co-text is the text surrounding a single word or phrase or sentence. Its importance lies in the fact that meaning is derived from or constrained by co-text. Indeed, in attempting to interpret a text when contextual details concerning time, place or purpose are not available, the translator may from the co-text be able to reconstruct some part of the original context.

Frequently, the term *discourse* is used interchangeably with the term text. It is perhaps useful to distinguish the two as follows: text is a structured sequence of language, whereas discourse is, more precisely, language in use. Discourse analysis is, then, the analysis of language in use. Thus the translator is processing language in use, in communication. Discourse is the amalgam of constituents of a communicative act. Discourses are ways of communicating which are identifiable because they manifest similar patterns of lexical and formal features. Hence one can identify bureaucratic discourse, racist discourse, trade union discourse, feminist discourse, diplomatic discourse, etc.

Discourses contain different types of text. Political discourse, for example, typically contains a variety of text types: exposition, persuasion, refutation, etc. Moreover, because the language of politics often conceals a purpose different from that which is apparent from a cursory reading of the text; one might find that one text type conceals another. Exposition may mask persuasion, for instance. To this can be added a further and related characteristic of discourse. Typically, discourses express participants' involvement or attitude to a particular subject. Thus, a politician may appear in some policy document to be following the ideology related to his political party, but he may, in reality, be using narration to mask disagreement with the particular policy, or aspects of it. He has achieved this by shifting from one text type to another within the political discourse. Awareness of the change of focus is vital for the translator in the effort to achieve accuracy and fidelity concerning the source text and the target text. It would perhaps be more appropriate, since the translator is processing language in use, to talk of source discourse and target discourse rather than source text and target text, but the latter are in general use in the literature, and there seems to be no good reason to alter the usage.

Two further text-related types of communicative acts which are important concepts in translating are *genre* and *register*. Certain types of texts have similar generic constituents — specific forms and meanings which have been established by social convention. Thus, obtaining information about train times at a railway information desk has a recognizable and distinctive pattern of exchanges. A business letter has a particular set of constituents which have to be matched in the target text with the set of constituents obtaining in this genre in the target language. Texts, in other words, have generic constraints, which need to be observed in the appropriate form in the target text.

Registers are varieties of language within a whole language and are determined according to situations of use. One can discern different patterns of grammatical and lexical features used in different types of communicative activity. The discoursal variables involved in register identification are field, or area of language activity, mode, or medium of language activity, and tenor, or level of formality involved or required in the specific language activity. The three aspects of language use are interdependent.

Hatim and Mason (1990) distinguish between field and subject matter. To illustrate this, they give the example of the political field of discourse which may deal with various subject matters such as law and order, taxation, foreign policy.

For the translator the three variables assume particular significance if they have to be altered according to the task that he is required to carry out. A translator may be asked to write an abstract in a target language from a conference paper delivered in a different language. In such a situation, the changes involved in the shift in mode and tenor, from oral code to written code, and subjective tenor to impartial tenor, would have to be carefully observed.

To a certain extent, the pragmatic dimension of language has been covered, since it refers to language in use, language in context. Pragmatics may be defined as the communicative use of language, which means that it involves discoursal aspects of language. In addition, pragmatics refers to aspects of the communicative act which are related specifically to the participants and how they use and react to a particular communicative act. These are aspects such as implicature, inference, assumption, presupposition, etc. These discourse constituents describe what participants are thinking and doing, that is, inferring, assuming, etc. not what the relation is between one sentence and another. The participant can be certain of rules and conventions in language communication and knows that if deviated from, then there is a need to infer, to assume, etc. in order to determine the implicature.

For the translator, however, this aspect of language use poses a problem in that with a written text the communicative activity is typically delayed since the writer and reader are not present when the text is being processed by the translator. Consequently, the interpretation by the translator risks being only partial. The purpose of the translator/discourse analyst in this situation is to determine as much as possible of the context. This is essential since the translator is moving into the realms of uncertainty and is compelled to turn to the identifiable and secure components of pragmatic discourse such as co-text, cohesion, etc.

Within the pragmatic dimension is included the concept of speech acts, which occur when certain types of sentences can be regarded as the performing of an act. For example, if a user promises that he or she will be with someone at 2:30, the promising indicates an action the user intends to undertake. If the verb is omitted the speech act might, depending upon the context, be a threat, a warning, an apology, and indeed one speech act may perform a variety of functions.

Various classifications of speech acts have been offered, for example, that of Traugott and Pratt (Hatim and Mason, 1990), who categorize speech acts as representatives (state, tell, insist), expressives (admire, define), verdictives (assess, estimate), directives (order, request), commissives (promise, pledge), declaratives (baptize, dismiss). The translator must ensure that the meaning of a speech act identified in a source text is conveyed, appropriately, in the target text. Once again, the translator has to rely on available co-text and context in the attempt to achieve an accurate interpretation, and to preserve the speech act of the source text in the target text. Ambiguity resulting from error in determining a speech act, for instance, where a command (directive) is given to a young police officer but is perceived by him as a different speech act, say admiration (expressive), could have awkward consequences. If such intentions or purposes of language are not recognized for what they really are, misinterpretations can occur.

For a text to be perceived as text it must exhibit characteristics which reflect its coherence, that is, its well-formedness, its logical relations, its continuity. Coherence is the term used to describe the conceptual relations underlying the surface text, relations that are evident in devices of cohesion present in the surface text.

Coherence is generally assumed to exist by participants involved in communication. Participants perceive coherence through a range of cohesive devices such as reference, substitution, ellipsis, and through the cohesion evident in lexical fields, and syntactic and grammatical structures. (Brown and Yule, 1983)

There are also markers of cohesion which indicate that the text producer is expressing concession, reservation, consequence, etc. (however, but, consequently). Such cohesive devices are not necessarily explicit, however, and a text can be totally coherent, despite their absence. When this type of cohesive device is lacking, the translator has to rely on co-text to interpret the logical direction of the text, just as he must when these devices are used, perfectly acceptably, with a meaning which differs from that contained in a dictionary definition. To put it slightly differently, idiolectal or deviant use of such cohesive devices may pose a problem for the translator. A further problem lies in the fact that different languages have different ways of expressing cohesion.

Together, coherence and cohesion constitute *texture*: texture indicates that a text is cohesive and coherent.

The third dimension of context is the semiotic dimension. Semiotics is the study of *signs*. These may be paintings, musical notes, road signs, morse code, etc. Above all, for the translator they are words, and more precisely, words used meaningfully. Hence, a text is understood as a system or structure of verbal signs manifesting coherence through cohesion. An individual sign occurs within a system, or text, and derives its meaning through interaction with other signs, or words, in that text.

Interdependence of the Dimensions of Context

People communicate within a context. Hatim and Mason (1990) describe the relation between the dimensions of context surrounding and influencing a text as follows: there are lexical and syntactic choices made within the field (mode, tenor, etc.) of a given discourse ... determined by pragmatic considerations to do with the purposes of utterances, real world conditions ... to perceive the full communicative thrust of an utterance, we need to appreciate not only the pragmatic action, but also a semiotic dimension which regulates the interaction of ... various discoursal elements as "signs". The interaction takes place ... between various signs within texts and ... between the producer of these signs and the intended receivers. In other words, pragmatics and semiotics are interdependent. The translator interprets and processes the intentions of the writer of the source text by analysis of the pragmatic values — such as field, mode, tenor, of individual items and then of entire sequences in the text. The organizing principle of a text, which by definition is the result or product of some communicative need and action, brings into play a whole network of meanings acquired when interaction occurs between one sign and another and between the newly acquired meaning, the new sign and another sign or signs. Thus there is a constant process of development and accumulation of meanings. But these entities are always the product of co-textual and contextual influences and of reference back to previous texts or discourse. The association and interaction of present text and previous texts is known as intertextuality. The difficulty for the translator is precisely that there exists the tendency for producers of texts to be influenced by texts they have experienced. Such influences add yet another complication as the translator attempts to determine the meaning of the signs of which the text is composed.

The Translator/Discourse Analyst

The translator acts as an intermediary whose responsibility it is to interpret the meaning of a source text and transfer that meaning to a target text. He is, therefore, working with two, or three, cultures — those of the source language, his own, and perhaps a third, if the target language is not his mother tongue. His processing of the source text is likely to be at a more detailed level than that of the average reader. He is more alert to possible ambiguities, and he has to maintain impartiality in his task.

The translator is a discourse analyst throughout the process of translating — identifying and interpreting contextual, linguistic, and co-textual features which influence the texts on which he is working — the focus moving from the processing and understanding of the source text towards the processing and creating of the target text. Working at both macro and micro levels, the translator exercises caution in interpretation as the texts unfold. There are bound to be areas of dissimilarity between texts, since cultures, and, consequently, perceptions of reality, differ, and since languages are never identical systems.

The pragmatic dimension of discourse analysis is in play when the translator makes assumptions about the source text. He is dealing with possible implications, he is inferring meaning. He is working with a writer's references, references to something with which only the writer is totally familiar. It is important that register is identified, that is, that context is reconstructed through identification of field, mode, and tenor. The problem is to find equivalent means in the target language so as to convey appropriately the elements of register.

Discoursal attitudes in the source text must be observed as far as is possible, as must any cultural constraints of the target language. The process of translating is not a matter of matching source speech act with target speech act, but rather transferring the entire act of discourse from source to target language, and this furthermore, according to the requirements of the client for whom the translator is working. He may, for example, be asked to translate an advertisement, the purpose of which is to sell a product. But the client may wish only to have information concerning the product: he may not be interested in the "sales pitch". The communicative purposes of the source and target texts are quite different. The translator has to decide what the communicative priorities of the texts are and adjust the target text accordingly. Thus it can be said that his choices, his decisions, are influenced or motivated. This can lead to omissions, additions, and modifications, in order to achieve semiotic equivalence. Such alterations are acceptable only in terms of (a) the meaning intended in the source text, and (b) the constraints of the purpose of the target text. To identify the meaning and the constraints the translator needs to be able to rely on secure and well-founded means of interpreting texts, such as are provided by discourse analysis. Discourse analysis offers resources to determine the communicative intention, the pragmatic factors, and the semiotic relations within texts — source and target — which are the translator's material.

Conclusion

There are two fundamental advances in translation studies provided by discourse analysis: it holds that the relevant language unit for translating is the entire text, not the single word or sentence, and that context — communicative, pragmatic, and semiotic — and co-text are, quite simply, indispensable constituents for interpreting and processing the source and target texts.

Discourse analysis has then moved on from former approaches which perceived translating as applying grammatical rules and referring to a dictionary. In a sense, it has indicated the limitations of the bilingual dictionary as a tool in translating. Until dictionaries are able to provide a full contextual reference for each item in all contexts including uses that are figurative, metaphorical, idiolectal, they form only a preliminary stage in the interpreting and processing of text.

Discourse analysis may be said to constitute a successful attempt to deal with a web of relationships in which the meaning of single items is determined according to their relations to each other and within the broader context of two cultures and two languages. Hence, discourse analysis is not an approach which analyses in order to separate and detach, but which analyses in an attempt to see items in their textual and contextual unity in order to determine their true meaning. The approach does not offer solutions to problems in translating, but it surely assists in their solving. Through insights into the amalgam that is language, it offers the possibility of processing text, objectively, and making decisions about translating which involve omission, addition, and modification, which can be justified and defended.

References

Brown, Gillian and George Yule. *Discourse Analysis*. Cambridge: Cambridge University Press, 1983.

Edmondson, W. *Spoken Discourse: A Model for Analysis*. London and New York: Longman, 1981.

Hatim, Basil and Ian Mason. *Discourse and the Translator*. London and New York: Longman, 1990.

Sinclair, John McH. and R. Malcolm Coulthard. *Towards an Analysis of Discourse*. Oxford: Oxford University Press, 1975.

Snell-Hornby, Mary. *Translation Studies: An Integrated Approach*. Amsterdam and Philadelphia: John Benjamins, 1988.

DRAMA

Drama Translation

Jane Lai Chui Chun
Department of English
Hong Kong Baptist College, Hong Kong

There is a two way traffic in the translation of drama between Chinese and English, though the nature of the traffic in each direction is different. Attempts to bring early Chinese drama to the West consist of translations of traditional Chinese opera lyrics, intended as literature for reading rather than performance. These include *The Western Chamber* and a number of Yuan dynasty operas. A rare exception was the experiments of Fr. Sheridan in Hong Kong in the 1950 to perform Chinese operas in English. Among the modern classics in Chinese speech drama in English translation are Cao Yu's 曹禺 *Thunderstorm* 《雷雨》 by Wang Zuoliang 王佐良 , and *Wilderness* 《原野》 by James Liu 劉若愚 . Since the late 1970's, many new plays from China have been collected in anthologies of translations of contemporary Chinese literature. (Hsu Kai-yu, 1980; *Renditions*, 1983)

The introduction of Western speech drama to China began in 1907 with an adaptation of *Uncle Tom's Cabin*. From the 1930s a number of translations from plays in English were published. These include the works of English dramatists Shakespeare, George Bernard Shaw and Oscar Wilde. Of these Shakespeare attracted most interest, and there are over five versions to some of the plays. Some of the translations were intended for performance while others were not.

In the 1960s, the busy publishing industry in Taiwan helped to bring out translations of Western post-war drama. The lively theatre scene in Hong

Kong since the 1960s, and in China since the late 1970s, have encouraged translations and adaptations of plays from many countries around the world — classic, modern classic, contemporary or avant garde. These served mainly performances, and not all the translations have appeared in print.

Translation of Drama

In translating drama, one is confronted with most of the difficulties encountered in translating other literary genres in terms of linguistic, cultural, historical, socio-political differences. The consideration of style and register of language is made more complex by the acting style of theatrical performance. The meaning of words and sentences can change in the light of speech rhythm, tone and intonation which may be indicated or merely implied in the text.

The translation of a play often has to serve three masters: the playwright, the actor and the reader/audience, and if one is translating for a particular stage performance, a fourth master, the director, for the fine tuning in interpretation. To serve the playwright, or his text, one attempts to present as much as possible of the text itself, but also the message encoded in such additional elements as stage scenery, lights, music, make-up, costumes, movements, postures, and gestures. A translation of a play for performance has to render the lines actable for the actor, in terms of readability, rhythm, and the cohesion of the dialogue. The audience at a performance has no access to footnotes or explanations, so the translated text has to be understood directly and immediately.

André Lefevere (1980) advocated the profitability of operating with a certain concept of "norm". He distinguished between the following norms:

1. Preliminary norms: the translator asks himself what kind of translation he wants to produce.
2. Initial norms: the translator decides on whether to adopt the code of the source text or that of the target text.
3. Operational norms: the translator makes use of the linguistic, contextual and intertextual instrumentation described above.

This concept is useful in an analysis of the operation involved in translating drama.

Preliminary Norms

What kind of translation?

1. A choice between producing a reading text or a text for performance. A translated text intended as a reading text can be treated much as other literary texts, with the use of explications, footnotes, and need not yield to other priorities which constrain a text for performance. An acting text has to forego details which do not transpose well, or immediately, to the target language. It has to have the appropriate speech rhythm for the message of the particular utterance to facilitate consonance between the spoken speech and the acting and gesture.

2. A choice between "bringing the reader to the source text or bringing the source text to the reader." This choice entails an attitude towards the source text. It ranges from the source text as the authority (or maximizing the chance of an encoded preferred reading) in a literal translation, to a direct translation, to a free translation and so on to an adaptation, or a drastic rewriting of the text which might be called a "version". The objective may range from giving the reader/audience an idea of the source text/performance in its own cultural environment to taking the plot or a message from the source text, giving it a different cultural and/or chronological context, for comment via the juxtapositions. Ortrun Zuber draws attention to the legal consideration in adapting a source text by citing a court case in 1974 involving changes made to *A Streetcar Named Desire*. One shift was from an encoded socio-cultural message to a racial one. (Zuber, 1980)

Initial Norms

Which code to use?

1. The choice between adopting the code of the source text or that of the target text in terms of cultural, historical, socio-political considerations. A translation of a play written at about the same time as the translation need not go through as many of the items on this list. But a play written in an earlier period may be translated into a time code contemporaneous with the translator, or into a fictitious contemporaneity in some past or future era when its language is not that of the

audience/reader. A Shakespearean play may be translated using the social, cultural code of the Tang dynasty, or of a particular decade in the twentieth century, or of some future projection. A translator working on an acting script for a particular stage production makes this choice in consultation with the director to achieve harmony between the language and the style of the production. Differences in customs, assumptions, attitudes and vocabulary are factors to be considered.

2. The choice of codes in terms of the form and the interpretation of the source text. The first applies especially to verse drama: whether one translates it into prose or verse, and what kind of verse. One could, of course, translate prose drama into verse. The second applies where one sees a cluster of encoded messages, or a number of interpretations, in a play. The choice is which ones to bring into prominence. In a production this is likely to depend on the director's choice of interpretation of the play. Another code in the source text that should be considered is the distinctive quality of the text which one might choose to, or not to, highlight in the translation — like the diversity of styles within a Shakespearean play, the ritual choric quality of a Greek tragedy, the deliberate slow staccato of a Pinter piece, or the subtle tonal variations within the apparently monotonous repetition of Beckett.

Operational Norms

The use of linguistic, contextual and intertextual instrumentation.

Translators and critics have pointed out the problem areas of difficulties encountered.

1. Reba Gostand (1980) mentions idioms, slang, tone, irony, double entendre, word-play and puns. Terms of endearment and abuse may provoke inappropriate audience response when rendered too literally in another language. Topical allusions could be substituted but that may be out of character with the whole work.

2. Franz H. Link (1980) comments on the levels of speech used in drama which serve different functions. Contemporary speech gives immediacy and familiarity; poetic or ritual language characterizes the reality in which the performance and audience participate as fictitious or as something outside or "beyond" every-day reality;

colloquial speech or slang might be used to keep characters as close to reality as possible, and should be translated to the correspondent language at the time of their performance. Dialect localizes the characters speaking it, but if it is no longer understood, it should be neutralized or translated into another dialect.

3. Unidentifiable or obscure allusions, and information irrelevant to certain audiences should be cut. Some topical or comic references in comic passages can be substituted for additional comic effect.

4. Susan Bassnett (1980) stresses the theatrical aspect of drama, and argues, "... a theatre text, written with a view to its performance, contains distinguishable structural features that make it performable, beyond the stage directions themselves. Consequently the task of the translator must be to determine what those structures are and to translate them into the target language, even though this may lead to major shifts on the linguistic and stylistic planes." One example is found in the translation of an exchange between Kent and Oswald in Shakespeare's *King Lear* (II ii).

Oswald. What dost thou know me for?

Kent. A knave, a rascal , an eater of broken meats; a base, proud, shallow, beggarly, three-suited, hundred-pound, filthy worsted-stocking knave; a lily-livered, action-taking, whoreson, glass-gazing, super-serviceable, finical rogue; one-trunk-inheriting slave; one that wouldst be a bawd in way of good service, and art nothing but the composition of a knave, beggar, coward, pander, and the son and heir of a mongrel bitch: one whom I will beat into clamorous whining if thou deni'st the least syllable of thy addition.

奧斯華德: 你認識我是誰？

肯特：一個無賴；一個惡棍；一個吃剩飯的家伙；一個下賤的、驕傲的、淺薄的、叫化子一樣的、只有三身衣服、全部家私算起來不過一百鎊的、卑鄙齷齪的、穿毛絨襪子的奴才；一個沒有膽量的、靠著官府勢力壓人的奴才；一個婊子生的、顧影自憐的、奴顏婢膝的、塗脂抹粉的混賬東西；全部家私都在一隻箱子裏的下流胚，一個天生的忘八胚子；又是奴才，又是叫化子，又是懦夫，又是忘八，又是一條雜種老母狗的兒子；要是你不承認你這些頭銜，我要把你打得放聲大哭。（朱生豪）

In such a passage, the value attached to having three suits, or a hundred pounds or the wearing of worsted stockings is not likely to come across to the audience of a different culture and a different time. Keeping these items in the translation for performance is likely to call up unexpected audience response, and possibly momentary confusion in the mind of the audience as it tries to transpose the information into its contemporary situation. Such momentary distraction detracts from the performance. Moreover, in the target language of Chinese, the customary syntax for speech, especially in hurling abuse with gusto, would forego the use of 一個 for the article "a". The excessive use of it in speech would create an impression that there is a horde of rascals on stage, or that the speaker is stammering while struggling for the next image or phrase.

5. Susan Bassnett-McGuire also quotes Robert Corrigan (1961), who maintains that at all times the translator must *hear* the voice that speaks and take into account the "gesture" of the language, the cadence, rhythm and pauses that occur when the written text is spoken. The consonance of speech and gesture is vital for an actor, if his acting is to synchronize with what he says. Take the example of the outburst of King Lear (I i) when Lear, mad with rage, warns Kent not to plead for Cordelia:

Lear: The bow is bent and drawn; make from the shaft.

  1. 弓已經引滿待發，儘早離開我的箭。（梁實秋）
  2. 箭已在弦上且已經扯滿了，快離開這射線。（曹未風）
  3. 弓已經彎好拉滿，你留心躲開箭鋒吧。（朱生豪）
  4. 弓已經引滿，弦絲已經繃緊，快躲開這枝箭。（孫大雨）
  5. 利箭上急弦，你避開。（黎翠珍）
  6. 弓已經彎足，引滿；快避開箭鋒！（卞之琳）

A wordy translation would slow down the pace of the acting, and dampen the fire in that utterance, or the actor would find himself still speaking the line seconds after he had make an angry gesture to sweep away Kent from his view. Or, perhaps, it might serve well if the director had wanted a dotard for a Lear, and the utterance to be one of mealy-mouthed muttering of suppressed rage. The length, even syllable count, of the utterance may be crucial for the actor to do his job.

The dynamics of sound in acting is an interesting topic which has not received much attention or analysis. The following example is taken from the source text and translations of Oscar Wilde's *The Importance of Being Ernest*. In the last act, Lady Bracknell demands of Miss Prism information about a baby Miss Prism had lost:

Lady Bracknell: Prism, where is the baby?

1. 姓勞的！那小孩哪兒去了？（余光中）
2. 普麗斯姆，那個嬰兒在哪裏？（錢之德）
3. 肖布露紫，嬰兒在哪裏？（張南峰）

Translation 1 uses a double iambic metre in the first phrase, yet uses only three syllables leaving the second stress silent. The energy and the anticipation which builds up is just right for lending significance and value to a movement or a gesture that goes with the utterance. Translations 2 and 3 both use a four-syllable utterance, but these leave no pause, no energy or anticipation for any movement or gesture. If Lady Bracknell makes a menacing move towards Prism while speaking the line, the movement is weaker. If she makes a move after the four-syllable transliteration of the name, it creates a pause. The pace is slower, more ponderous, though more deliberate.

To create an actor-friendly translation, even the type of discourse in a line can make a difference for acting with. In the opening scene of *The Importance of Being Ernest* Jack teases Algernon:

Jack ... Eating, as usual I see, Algy!

1. 我看你哪，好吃如故。（余光中）
2. 阿爾杰農，我看到，你老是在吃！（錢之德）
3. 嗄，奧哲能，又在吃哪！（張南峰）

Translation 1 is a statement; 2 is a reprimand and 3 is good humoured teasing. That nature of the utterances, to some extent, prescribes the possible responses of the person spoken to. When a statement is made about one's habit of constantly eating, one could respond with more or less grace in acceptance or denial, but enthusiasm is less likely. When one is reprimanded, however mildly, one can at best shrug it off. But when one is teased, one could cheerfully agree and carry the conversation a step further. The nature of the utterances, therefore, prescribes the reactions of the actor playing Algy, and the interpretation he can bring to the role of Algy. An

Algernon who merely shrugs is not likely to be the scintillating character intended as a foil for Jack's wit.

A survey of six Chinese translations of an excerpt from Shakespeare's *King Lear* may be useful as an illustration of the elements, considerations, approaches and strategies mentioned above.

Original Text

Shakespeare: *King Lear* V: iii
Lear: No, no, no, no! Come, let's away to prison;
         We two alone will sing like birds i' th' cage:
         When thou dost ask me blessing, I'll kneel down,
         And ask of thee forgiveness: so we'll live,
         And pray, and sing, and tell old tales, and laugh
         At gilded butterflies, and hear poor rogues
         Talk of court news; and we'll talk with them too,
         Who loses and who wins; who's in, who's out;
         And take upon's the mystery of things,
         As if we were God's spies: and we'll wear out,
         In a wall'd prison, packs and sects of great ones
         That ebb and flow by th' moon.

Chinese Translations

1. Liang Shiqiu 梁實秋 (published about 1936)
   李爾王：
   不，不，不，不！來，我們到監牢去；只我們兩個要像籠裏的鳥一
   般歌唱：你要我祝福時，我便跪下，求你饒恕：我們便這樣活著，
   祈禱，歌唱，講老故事，笑那些納姱的廷臣，聽窮人談朝中事；我
   們也和他們交談，誰得寵，誰失勢；誰在朝，誰下野；冒充了解一
   切事情的內幕，好像是上帝的暗探一般：我們就在監牢壁下，忘記
   那些無數的權貴結黨營私，時而飛騰時而消逝。

2. Cao Weifeng 曹未風 (published about 1946)
   李：
   不，不，不，不！來吧，我們到囚牢裏去：
   祇有我們兩人在一起，像籠中鳥雀一樣的歌唱：
   在你請求我祝福的時侯，我就也跪下，
   去請求你的原諒：我們將如此生活，

禱告，懂唱，講著往日的故事，看見
金碧的蝴蝶而歡笑，去聽那些可憐的貧賤人
談講宮廷裏的新聞；那時我們也加入，
談說誰得勝了，誰又失意；誰升官，誰被黜，
然後我們再專心去探索萬物的隱密，
同上帝的探子一樣：那樣，在那高牆的
囚牢裏，我們都可以比得上無數偉大的人物，
他們隨著月亮的圓缺而升降。

3. Zhu Shenghao 朱生豪 (published in 1947)

李爾：

不，不，不，不！來，讓我們到監牢裏去。我們兩人將要像籠中之
鳥一般唱歌；當你求我爲你祝福的時候，我要跪下來求你饒恕；我
們就這樣生活著，祈禱，唱歌，說些古老的故事，嘲笑那班像金翅
蝴蝶般的廷臣，聽聽那些可憐的人們講些宮廷裏的消息；我們也要
跟他們談話，誰失敗，誰勝利，誰在朝，誰在野，用我們的意見解
釋各種事情的秘奧，就像我們是上帝的耳目一樣；在囚牢的四壁之
內，我們將要冷眼看那些朋比爲奸的黨徒隨著月亮的圓缺而升沉。

4. Sun Dayu 孫大雨 (published in 1948)

黎琊：

不要，不要，不要，不要。來罷，
讓我們跑進牢裏去；我們父女倆，
要像籠鳥一般，孤零零唱著歌。
你要我祝福的當兒，我會跪下去
懇請你饒恕。我們要這麼過著活，
要禱告，要唱歌，敘述那些陳年的故事，
笑話一班金紅銀碧的朝官們，
聽那些可憐的東西說朝中的聞見；
我們也要和他們風生談笑，
議論那個輸，那個贏，誰當權，誰失勢，
還要自承去參透萬象底玄機，
彷彿上帝派我們來充當的密探。
我們要耐守在高牆的監裏，直等到
那班跟月亮底盈虧而昇降的公卿
徒黨們都雲散煙消。

5. Lai Chui Chun, Jane 黎翠珍 (performed in 1983, unpublished)

李：

唔去，唔去，唔去，唔去！嚟啦，我地去監牢。我地兩人高歌好似

係籠中鳥。你若求我祝福，我就會下跪向你求寬恕。我地可以咁樣
渡日，祈禱、唱歌，重可以講故事，笑一吓啲披金戴銀嘅蝴蝶，聽
一吓閒人閒語話當朝，同佢地高談闊論朝中事，誰勝誰負，誰人失
勢，邊個當權。傾吓普天之下的奧妙事，好似得天獨厚知天意。要
坐喺監牢四壁內，冷眼看朋黨浮沉於官宦潮。

6. Bian Zhilin 卞之琳 (published in 1989)
   里：
   不，不；不，不！來吧，我們進監獄去。
   我們倆要像籠中鳥一樣的唱歌；
   你要我祝福的時侯，我會跪下去
   求你寬恕。我們就這樣過日子，
   祈禱，唱歌，講講古老的故事，
   笑蝴蝶披金，聽那些可憐蟲閒話
   宮廷的新聞；我們也要同他們
   漫談誰得勝，誰失敗，誰當權，誰垮台；
   自認能滲透和解釋事態的秘密，
   儼然是神明的密探；四壁高築，
   我們就冷看這一幫、那一派大人物
   隨月亮圓缺而升沉吧。

Cao's translation attempts a line-for-line transposition, keeping the
form of the blank verse without much attempt to convert it into any
recognizable verse form or linguistic familiarity in Chinese. It is not intended to cater for the actor. Both Liang and Zhu have chosen to translate
the text into prose to obviate the restrictions of verse form. Zhu's translation
shows signs that it is intended for performance, both in the fact that he uses
no footnotes and annotation, and in his attempt at fluent speech rhythms.
Liang's translation aims at linguistic fluency as well, but it also aims at
being a scholarly text in that, elsewhere in the translation, he uses footnotes
for explication, and the translation is enriched with commentary. It is the
element of the scholarly text which takes precedent. Sun's translation is an
elaborate effort, consisting of two volumes, one of which is dedicated to
scholarly research, analysis and commentary on the text, and the other
contains the translation and translator's preface explaining his procedures.
He translates the blank verse into a version of blank verse in Chinese,
attending to metrical arrangement, sense and details, adding in occasional
footnotes for elucidation. All four of these translations choose a modern
form of spoken Chinese as the linguistic element, reproducing a basically

Christian concept in the reference to God. Lai's translation, commissioned
for performance in the Cantonese dialect in Hong Kong, is written in
Cantonese which deviates a little from standard Chinese. As the production had an unspecified Western archaic setting, the language used
bears a resemblance to classical poetry in Chinese for a sense of the
archaic. That choice of language determines its own style which resembles
rhythmic prose, a recognizable genre in Chinese. The aim is familiarity,
the archaism an attempt to create another reality on stage. It has its
own rhythm, and is actor-friendly; but it is not Shakespeare's blank
verse. Bian attempts the sophistication of moulding the modern Chinese
language into Shakespeare's blank verse. The exercise shows a variety of
possibilities.

These extracts also provide interesting examples for other types of
consideration.

1. The Phonetics of Stage Utterances

   In the Chinese language, the tones of words dictate the meaning.
   These tones have their own dynamics the mystery of which awaits
   exploration in further research. These tones have their own movements and momentum. Tone 2, for instance, does not allow the
   speaker to say a word with as much force and flamboyance as Tone
   4. Lai's exit word may, in Putonghua, be a Tone 2 word; but not so
   in the Cantonese dialect. This observation may help to draw attention to sound quality in translated acting scripts.

   The way speech sounds are used in a Western play for performance require more study from the translators. King Lear's cry of
   pain at the discovery of the death of Cordelia in the last scene is
   given meaning in the words "Howl, howl, ..." Zhu's rendition of the
   words were given appropriate grammatical markers: 悲嚎吧 !
   悲嚎吧 .... The interruption of the grammatical marker 吧 makes it
   impossible for the actor to use the words in the way they were
   intended. The introduction of the marker 吧 also turns the utterance
   into an invitation (to the cast, and the audience) to howl. The actor
   playing Lear would be fortunate to escape ridicule.

2. Cultural/Mythological

   The Source Text's use of the word "Gods'" indicates a polytheistic
   cultural context, consonant with earlier appeals to such "pagan"
   gods as Jupiter and Juno. Rendering the word into 上帝 gives the

translations a Christian cultural background which is at odds with the earlier invocations.

3. Literary Aesthetics and Form

   In a well-constructed dramatic text, individual utterances and speeches are part of a design, much as musical phrases are part of the architecture of a piece of music. Translators have to attend to the whole while working on the parts. The deliberate design of the aria solo pieces for the major characters in Eugene O'Neill's *Long Day's Journey into Night* is a notable example. In the context of *King Lear* this excerpt comes at the end of a series of scenes of pain, madness, intrigue and fighting. The intricate patterning of parallels in the mid-line caesurae, and the run-on lines creates a sense of concealed order (unlike the overt sense of order in a heroic couplet) to smooth balm over the laceration of the earlier scenes. Failure to capture this subtle patterning of order in form, syntax and figurative rather than plain language would reduce this key passage to the level of ordinary utterance and destroy the form of the theatrical experience.

References

Bassnett-McGuire, Susan. *Translation Studies.* London: Methuen, 1980.

Corrigan, Robert. "Translating for Actors." In *The Craft and Context of Translation*, edited by William Arrowsmith and Robert Shattuck. Austin: University of Texas Press, 1961.

Gostand, Reba. "Verbal and Non-verbal Communication: Drama as Translation." In *The Language of Theatre: Problems in the Translation and Transposition of Drama*, edited by Ortrun Zuber. Oxford: Pergamon Press, 1980, pp. 24–50.

Hsu, Kai-yu, ed. *Literature of the People's Republic of China.* Indiana: Indiana University Press, 1980.

Lefevere, André. "Translating Literature/Translated Literature: The State of the Art." In *The Language of Theatre: Problems in the Translation and Transposition of Drama*, edited by Ortrun Zuber. Oxford: Pergamon Press, 1980, pp. 153–61.

Link, Franz H. "Translation, Adaptation and Interpretation of Drama Texts." In *The Language of Theatre: Problems in the Translation and Transposition of Drama*, edited by Ortrun Zuber. Oxford: Pergamon Press, 1980.

Zuber, Ortrun. "Problem of Propriety and Authenticity in Translating Modern Drama." In *The Language of Theatre: Problems in the Translation and Transposition of Drama*, edited by Ortrun Zuber. Oxford: Pergamon Press, 1980, p. 94.

Zuber-Skerritt, Ortrun, ed. *Page to Stage: Theatre as Translation.* Amsterdam: Rodopi Press, 1984.

Yuan *Zaju*

Cyril Birch
Department of Oriental Languages
University of California, Berkeley, U.S.A.

Introduction: Characterization of Yuan *Zaju*

The word *zaju* 雜劇 literally means something like "variety show," and when first used in the Song period indicated a theatrical potpourri that included juggling, sword-dancing and acrobatics as well as singing and comedy routines. Later the term was reserved for the type of play which dominated the stage for the hundred years or so of the Yuan dynasty, and relinquished its popularity only gradually during the Ming. This flourishing of *zaju* made the Yuan the first (and in the eyes of many, the greater) of the two golden ages for Chinese plays as works of literature. The second flowering took place during roughly the period 1550 through 1700, when the long, involved plays known as *chuanqi* 傳奇 , "dramatic romances," were the preferred form for the poet-playwrights.

The shape of a *zaju* play is confined within some of the strictest bounds of convention known to literature. Over 160 plays survive, a surprisingly large number, and they display a surprising uniformity of length and format. Much of this uniformity may be due, however, to the fact that the plays as we know them today are the products of revision by late-Ming editors, with only partial versions of some thirty plays available in texts printed during Yuan times. The standard *zaju* may be described as follows: four acts, each act consisting of a set of arias sung by a single character, with interspersed spoken dialogue among all the characters and occasional short verses spoken on entrance and exit. The contents of the four acts will often follow the sequence exposition — development — climactic action — denouement, almost in Aristotelian fashion. In addition to the four acts there may be a "wedge", used as prologue to the play or inserted between acts. This "wedge" will contain either no arias or just one, and is no more than a functional convenience to explain the dramatic situation, often through the dialogue of minor characters in a manner familiar to the Western world from the sort of opening scene frequently used by Shakespeare.

The set of arias which comprises the backbone of each act uses the form of lyric poem known as *qu* 曲 , "song", which enjoyed the sort of popularity during Yuan times that the *ci* 詞 , "lyric" had known during the Song dynasty. *Yuan qu* 元曲 is in fact an alternative term for *zaju*, and critics distinguish between *xiqu* 戲曲 , "dramatic songs" or arias appearing in plays, and *sanqu* 散曲 , "free-standing songs"; numbers of the latter type of poems have been published in English versions by such translators as J. I. Crump Jr., A. C. Graham and Wayne Schlepp. All the dramatic arias use existing melodies belonging to a given musical mode, the mode itself changing from act to act. The language of the arias varies from vernacular to a loosely classical lyric style, often rich in poetic imagery and capable of intense emotional effects. The dialogue is based on vernacular speech, and may include contemporary slang, invective and obscenities, but when officials or emperors are speaking a more elevated semi-classical diction is usually employed.

The stories acted out in Yuan plays are very seldom original, but are taken from a variety of sources. These include the standard histories; accounts of the lives of Buddhist and Daoist saints; old tales and legends; and in particular the story-cycles which were eventually worked up into the great novels of Ming times, works like *Romance of the Three Kingdoms* 《三國演義》 and *Outlaws of the Marsh* 《水滸傳》 . The subject-matter of Yuan plays is quite colourfully and comprehensively described in a classification under twelve headings from a critical text dated 1398. James I. Crump translates the twelve headings as follows:

1. Gods, immortals and transfiguration.
2. Withdrawal and enjoyment of the Way.
3. Wearing court robes and grasping scepters.
4. Faithful ministers and men of honour.
5. Filial piety, righteousness, and purity.
6. Abuse of the traitorous and denunciation of the traducer.
7. Cast-off ministers and orphaned children.
8. Pikeswords and quarterstaves.
9. The wind on flowers and the moon on snow.
10. Sorrowful partings and joyful reunions.
11. Powder and eyeshadow.

12. Ghosts and spirits.

From some of these categories very few plays if any have ever been translated, and the list would be more helpful if it included a special section for a common theme-type, the "courtroom" melodrama in which courageous resistance defeats a rich and powerful bully backed by a corrupt magistrate. Plays of this kind may have served a topical purpose in expressing Chinese detestation of Mongol overlords, and such a historical interest would explain their popularity with translators. Other favourite subjects for translation have been the plays about romantic love indicated by the categories nine through eleven above.

Chinese lovers of the drama have always prized Yuan *zaju* for the poetic excellence of their arias more than anything else. This is clearly illustrated by the fact that the surviving versions of plays printed during the Yuan dynasty contain little more than the arias themselves, since the dialogue evidently was regarded as of secondary importance, and in any case the story of the play was most probably from a source already well-known to the audience or reader. In contrast to this situation, the first Western translators of Chinese plays, lacking previous familiarity with the stories, found these the most appealing aspect of the plays, and so in many cases translated the dialogue fairly fully but severely abridged the arias, which seemed in their view superfluous — and incidentally were considerably harder to interpret.

Early English Versions of Yuan *Zaju*

Before and even into the twentieth century, English versions of Yuan plays were usually made from existing translations by French or German scholars and almost invariably offered a text abridged to some extent. The very first Chinese play to appear in English guise was *The Orphan of the Zhao Family* 〈趙氏孤兒〉. Though not regarded as one of the greatest masterpieces of Yuan drama, this is a moving play about a tyrant's attempt to exterminate a rival clan and the devotion of friends and retainers who sacrifice their lives to ensure the survival of the heir (it will be apparent that the play contains elements of the third through seventh of the categories listed above). The text of the play, or at least its dialogue, was translated into French by the Jesuit father Prémare and published in 1735 in Du Halde's *Description de l'empire de la Chine*. Several English adaptations of Prémare's work appeared in due course, the first by William Hatchett in

1741 under the title *The Chinese Orphan*, but part of the reason this particular piece captured popular attention in Europe was the stage success of the play by the great Voltaire which was based on the *The Orphan of the Zhao Family* story and was entitled *L'Orphelin de la Chine*.

One of the outstanding tragedies among Yuan plays is *Autumn in the Han Palace* 〈漢宮秋〉. This is the story of Wang Zhaojun 王昭君 , beautiful consort whom the Han emperor loved to distraction but was forced for reasons of state to send out into the desert wilds to marry the Tartar khan. *Autumn in the Han Palace* was translated directly from Chinese into English, though only in partial form, by John Francis Davis in 1829 under the title *The Sorrows of Han*. Davis had published the first directly translated *zaju*, *An Heir in His Old Age* 〈老生兒〉 in 1817. *Matching the Shirt* 〈合汗 衫〉 uses the old folkloric motif of the tracing of a long-lost child by fitting together two token pieces previously torn or broken from a single object. The play was translated from the French by S. Wells Williams under the title *The Compared Tunic* and published in 1849. Another domestic drama, in which a clever magistrate establishes the identity of the true mother in a case of disputed custody, is *The Circle of Chalk* 〈灰蘭記〉. This was turned into English from the nineteenth-century French of Stanislas Julien as late as 1954, by Frances Hume; there is also a 1929 English translation by James Laver and numerous English versions of the famous play by Bertold Brecht, *The Caucasian Chalk Circle*, based on earlier German translations of *The Circle of Chalk*.

English Translations of the Modern Period

A popular English translation of a Yuan play was S. I. Hsiung's *Romance of the Western Chamber*, published in 1935. The Chinese original, *Xixiang ji* 〈西廂記〉, consists of five parts each of four acts, and so although it forms a single organic whole it resembles a sequence of five plays rather than a single *zaju*. It is the most famous and best-loved of all Chinese plays, telling of the love of the young student Zhang for the beautiful, passionate but enigmatic Yingying 鶯鶯 , the ultimate embodiment of the mystery of womanhood for romantically-inclined Chinese audiences. The progress of their love is assisted by Hongniang 紅娘 , the epitome of the pert, witty maid-confidante, who in later dramatic versions of the *Xixiang* theme just about takes over the play. The translation by S. I. Hsiung, himself a dramatist, has a rather flowery, old-fashioned flavour as we read it today, but it is quite clear, mostly accurate and shows more respect for the original text than we can find in the earlier translators. We may compare Hsiung's version of a famous passage from the last act of the second part of the play with the translation recently made by Wilt Idema and Stephen West under the title *Story of the Western Wing*. This new translation uses the earliest and most authentic text of the play published in 1498, and though no less "poetic" than Hsiung's is more specific and precise, as we shall see, in rendering the imagery of the original.

(Yingying in the temple garden listens to young Zhang as he plays his lute to give voice to his lovesickness. In Hsiung's version:)

這是什麼響。倒蠻好聽。鶯鶯云。
你猜咱。紅娘沉吟云。

（天淨沙）
是步搖得寶髻玲瓏。是裙拖得環佩丁冬。是鐵馬兒簷前驟風。
是金釣雙動。吉丁當敲響簾櫳。

（調笑令）
是花宮。夜撞鐘。是疏竹瀟瀟曲檻中。是牙尺翦刀聲相送。
是漏聲長滴響壺銅。

鶯鶯云。都不是的。你仔細再聽者。
紅娘假意再聽科。半晌云。
我潛身再聽。在牆角東。原來西廂理絲桐。
鶯鶯點首云。對了對了。好一手琴音呵。

（禿廝兒）
其聲壯。似鐵騎刀鎗冗冗。其聲幽。似落花流水溶溶。
其聲高。似風清月朗鶴唳空。其聲低。似兒女語小窗中喁喁。

（聖藥王）
他思已窮。恨不窮。是為嬌鸞雛鳳失雌雄。他曲未通。
我意已通。分明伯勞飛燕各西東。盡在不言中。

Yingying says:

Hongniang, what is that sound?

Hongniang says:

Guess, my Young Mistress.

Yingying sings:

Is it the tinkling sound of the head-ornaments as their wearer walks?

Or is it the ringing sound of the ornaments of her skirt as it sweeps along?

Is it the creaking of the iron hinges as gusts of wind blow under the eaves?

Or is it the ding-dong sound of the gilt hooks knocking against the curtain frame?

Is it the evening bell that is being sounded in the Buddhist monastery?

Or is it the rustling sound of the few bamboos in the winding balustrade?

Is it the sound of the ivory foot-measure and the scissors that is being wafted here?

Or is it the incessant dripping sound of the water-clock as the water falls into the receptacle?

Concealing myself, I listen again

At the eastern corner of the wall,

And find that it is indeed the sound of the strings of the lute coming from the Western Chamber.

The sound is powerful, like the sabres and spears of the mailed horsemen;

The sound is gentle, like flowers falling into rushing water;

The sound is high, like the cry of the crane at moonlight in the pure breeze;

The sound is low, like the whisper of lovers at the casement.

He is at his wits' end, but his sorrow is endless

Because he is separated from the young person he loves.

Before the tune is ended, already I realize its meaning,

Which distinctly expresses the separation of two lovebirds.

It is entirely music without words!

And now the same passage in the Idema-West translation. Notice that these translators follow the original text in using the actor's role-type rather than the name of the character to indicate the speaker or singer; also, they take care to provide the individual melody-titles for the successive arias, which are unidentified and all run together by Hsiung (as, in other plays, by most earlier translators):

(*Female lead speaks*): What's that sound?

(Reddy [i.e., Hongniang] acts out a comic routine.)

　　([Tune title] 〈天淨沙〉) (*Female lead sings*):

Could it be that our precious hair-ornaments are set a-jangling by our steps as we walk?

Could it be that our girdle pendants clink and tinkle as we trail our skirts?

Could it be that the iron horses [wind chimes] are stirred by the wind before the eaves?

Could it be that the golden curtain hooks hung in pairs

Are jingling and chinking as they beat against the door posts?

(〈調笑令〉) (*Female lead sings*):
Could it be the night-struck bell in the Brahma Palace?
Could it be the scattered bamboos rustling behind the curved balustrade?
Could it be the sound of ivory rulers and scissors keeping time?
Could it be the long dripping of the clepsydra echoing in catchpot's bronze?
Hiding myself, I listen again east of the wall,
All the time it was someone tuning the zither near the Western Wing.

(〈禿廝兒〉) (*Female lead sings*):
When the sounds are virile, they are like the cacophony of the blades and
    spears of iron-clad cavalry,
When the sounds are serene, they are like the rippling of fallen flowers on
    flowing waters,
When the sounds are raised, they are like a crane's cry in a void of clear breeze
    and bright moon,
When the sounds are lowered, it is like hearing the cooing of lovers' whispers
    through a small window.

(〈聖藥王〉) (*Female lead sings*):
There, his longing is limitless,
Here, I have already understood his intentions:
The lovely simurgh and fledgling phoenix have lost their mates.
Before his song is finished,
My feelings have grown intense,
But alas, the shrike goes west and the flying swallow east —
It's all told in what's unspoken.

Before leaving the Western Wing we should note that the twelfth-
century "chantefable" or "medley," from which the Yuan play was developed, has been translated by Li-li Ch'en under the title *Master Tung's
Western Chamber Romance*.

The most prolific and most highly-regarded of the Yuan dramatists was
undoubtedly Guan Hanqing 關漢卿. In 1958 the indefatigable husband-
and-wife team of Yang Hsien-yi 楊憲益 and Gladys Yang published a
volume entitled *Selected Plays of Kuan Hanching*, which presents eight
plays including the celebrated tragedy *The Injustice to Dou E* 〈竇娥冤〉,
also known as *Snow in Midsummer* 〈六月雪〉, which is the title used by
the Yangs. Dou E, falsely accused and wrongly convicted of the murder of
her step-father, is the perfect type of the young woman whose virtue and
courage triumph (even in death) over the abuse of vicious and corrupt men
in positions of power over her. It is a type Guan Hanqing was particularly

fond of, and used in plays like 〈望江亭〉 and 〈救風塵〉 (*The Riverside Pavilion* and *Rescued by a Coquette*, as the Yangs in their *Selected Plays* translate these titles).

A superior English version of *Dou E yuan* was made by Chung-wen Shih and published in 1972 together with a critical study, a word-for-word English rendering and the original text in Chinese characters and in a romanized form reflecting Yuan dynasty pronunciation. Two other less satisfactory versions of the play appeared in this same year of 1972: Richard F. S. Yang's "Tou O Was Wronged" in his volume *Four Plays of the Yuan Drama*, and Liu Jung-en's "The Injustice Done to Tou Ngo" in his *Six Yuan Plays*. The latter volume contains a useful selection of plays including "The Orphan of Chao" and "Autumn in the Han Palace," but unfortunately reverts to the old unforgivable habit of abridging their arias: Liu excises over one hundred lines, including nine arias in their entirety, from his translation of *Dou E yuan*.

J. I. Crump has contributed more than any other Western scholar to the study of Yuan drama and his translations are the liveliest yet made. His version of *Li Kui Carries Thorns* 〈李逵負荊〉 appears in the anthology of Chinese literature edited by Cyril Birch. Li Kui is a major character of the picaresque novel *Outlaws of the Marsh,* and the events of the play are exactly paralleled in the fiction text as mistaken identity leads to blood-thirsty but uproarious comedy. The lusty slapstick of *Li Kui Carries Thorns* comes across very vividly from the Crump translation, which is reprinted in Crump's *Chinese Theater in the Days of Kublai Khan*, together with his versions of *Rain on the Xiaoxiang* 〈瀟湘雨〉 and *The Moheluo Doll* 〈魔合羅〉. The latter play is a courtroom drama in which a case of poisoning is resolved; *Rain on the Xiaoxiang* is a characteristic "partings and reunions" play notable for its heart-rending portrayal, in arias such as the following, of the ordeal of a woman convict travelling under guard to slavery on Shamen Island:

> (Cuiluan sings to the tune *Xi Qianying*:)
> So great
> The rain I'll never reach a refuge.
> (Who knows
> Which of Hell's gates is found on Shamen Island?)
> Alas, alas!
> The very air condenses into cloudy brume.
> As I walk,

Drowned wheelruts work pitfalls to trap and seize my legs
And soon will
Wrench a thighbone from its socket.
How will I stand either
The gleaming, streaming rain upon my head
Or the sliding, subsiding mud beneath my feet?

Also included in the Birch anthology is a translation by Donald Keene of *Autumn in the Han Palace*. Keene uses English blank verse for the arias of this play, and although this is clearly not the most appropriate choice to represent the very varied meters of *qu* this new translation improves greatly upon its predecessors and achieves fine lines in rendering such arias as the following:

> (*The Emperor sings*) [he is on horseback, hence the effective imagery of reins and whip:]
> Now she will put aside her Chinese clothes
> And change to robes of fur and coarse brocades.
> I must look at her portrait once again.
> Old pleasures are as short as golden reins;
> New grievances outreach jade-handled whips.
> We who were once a pair of mandarin ducks
> Dwelling in golden chambers, never dreamt
> That we should fly apart on lonely wings.

Another accurate and effective translator of Yuan *zaju* is George A. Hayden. His monograph *Crime and Punishment in Medieval Chinese Drama* contains translations of three courtroom dramas, *Selling Rice at Chenzhou* 〈陳州糶米〉, *The Ghost of the Pot* 〈盆兒鬼〉 and *The Flower of the Back Courtyard* 〈後庭花〉. The awesome figure of the incorruptible magistrate Judge Bao looms over the action of each of these plays, but in fact *The Ghost of the Pot* is a black comedy in which the ashes of a corpse are baked into a pot which is then purchased by a crotchety old man for use as a chamberpot. When he tries to use the pot, the ghost of the murdered man teases him in a passage which offers splendid opportunities for mime:

> [*The old man is speaking*]: … and now I have to get up to relieve myself. There's that pot Zhao the Jug gave me: I might as well test it out. (Urinates.) (Ghost takes the pot away.) Why is it I don't hear anything hitting the pot? It's landing on the ground instead! (Feels about him.) Damn! I really am getting stupid in my old age. The pot's over there, and here I am peeing over here!

(Crosses over.) (Ghost takes the pot away again. Zhang feels about him once more.) (Startled:) How did it get over there now? (Ghost puts the pot on his head. Zhang gropes about.) Ai-ya! Now it's dangling in midair!

Before leaving the subject of George Hayden's volume of translations we should note that his appended twelve-page bibliography includes a comprehensive listing of the most useful Chinese sources for glossing terms found in Yuan dramatic texts. The multi-volume Beijing compilation 《元曲釋辭》, by Gu Xuejie and Wang Xueqi, did not begin publication until 1983 and should be added to Hayden's list.

William Dolby, author of the most comprehensive history of Chinese drama yet to appear in English, is himself an accomplished translator and includes an early Yuan *zaju*, *Qiu Hu Tries to Seduce His Own Wife* 〈秋胡戲妻〉 in his volume *Eight Chinese Plays*.

Prospects

Taiwan and mainland Chinese scholars in recent years have made great strides towards establishing texts for Yuan plays which may come as close as possible to what the original authors wrote, and in providing glossaries for the vernacular phrases peculiar to dramatic and a few other texts. With such help, and with the emergence of translators who combine scholarly competence with a true sense of the stylistic possibilities of English, we may hope to see more satisfactory versions of Yuan *zaju* in the future. Among plays for which no adequate translation exists are *The Orphan of the Zhao Family* (still, after 250 years!), the comedy *Over the Wall from Horseback* 〈牆頭馬上〉, the moving ghostly romance *The Soul Journey of Qiannü* 〈倩女離魂〉, and all of Guan Hanqing's plays with the exception of *The Injustice to Dou E.*

Some Yuan *zaju* are run-of-the-mill potboilers, trite pieces lacking interest as literary or even as historical documents, and many, perhaps most of the plays that have survived may never see print in English. But it is still a matter for real regret that there still exists in English no single volume offering a representative sampling of Yuan *zaju* in the kind of translation that will give a true impression of the liveliness and beauty of the originals.

References

Birch, Cyril. *Anthology of Chinese Literature*. New York: Grove Press, 1965.

Crump, J. I. *Chinese Theater in the Days of Kublai Khan.* Tucson: University of Arizona Press, 1980.

Dolby, William. *Eight Chinese Plays.* New York: Columbia University Press, 1978.

Hayden, George A. *Crime and Punishment in Medieval Chinese Drama: Three Judge Pao Plays.* Cambridge, Mass. Harvard University Press, 1978.

Hsiung, S. I. *The Romance of the Western Chamber.* New York: Columbia University Press, 1968.

Idema, Wilt and Stephen H. West. *The Moon and the Zither: A Translation and Study of the Hongzhi Edition of 1498 of Wang Shifu's Story of the Western Wing.* Berkeley: University of California Press, 1992.

Liu, Jung-en. *Six Yuan Plays.* Harmondsworth, Middlesex: Penguin Books, 1972.

Shih, Chung-wen. *The Golden Age of Chinese Drama: Yuan Tsa-chü.* Princeton: Princeton University Press, 1976.

———. *Injustice to Tou O.* London: Cambridge University Press, 1972.

Yang, Hsien-yi and Gladys Yang. *Selected Plays of Kuan Han-ching.* Peking: Foreign Languages Press, 1958.

Yang, Richard F. S. *Four Plays of the Yuan Drama.* Taipei: The China Post, 1972.

EDITING

Translation Editing

Eva Hung
Research Centre for Translation
The Chinese University of Hong Kong, Hong Kong

Translation editing is also a kind of copy-editing, but with a difference: the editor here deals with not one, but two languages, and all the attendant social and cultural differences inherent in the languages involved. The editor of a translation has to come to grips with the intention, the style, and the success and failure of not just one person, but at least two — the original author and the translator(s). Just as translation differs from creative writing primarily in that it imposes more restrictions on the practitioner, so a translation-editor finds himself answerable to more than one person who has the right (if not exactly the ability) to question his decisions.

Ideally, a translation editor, like a translator, should be thoroughly bilingual; he should have read the original (and, ideally, liked it); he should understand the translator's approach and make corrections and suggestions which are in line with this particular approach; when faced with an unpublishable script he should reject it; when he comes across a valid translation the style of which does not suit his journal/publishing house, he should advise the translator to send it to another house.

Unfortunately, the world is far from ideal, particularly when we are talking about the translation of Chinese literature into English. The interest in "things Chinese" shown by some major publishers in recent years, which has resulted in an increase in the number of books translated from the Chinese, only reveals more clearly the weaknesses in every link of the translation-publishing chain. In one of the very few articles on translation editing, Denver Lindley (1961) talks about this endeavour from the publisher's point of view, and the problems of editing translations for a commercial publisher he describes are still relevant. To sum up the problems revealed in Lindley's paper is therefore a useful starting point for a discussion of translation editing. First, editors who cannot read the language in question — in this case, Chinese — have to rely completely on outside reports when they decide on which books to translate, and they are often reluctant to rely on specialists in the field because they feel that these people lack publishing experience. Second, the translator is again chosen by editors (who have no knowledge of Chinese) probably on the strength of a short sample translation. Third, the editor reads the finished translation to see if it is English. "Even if he is competent to check the translation line by line, time will usually not allow him to do so." (Lindley, 1961: 157–59)

Now we come to the "editing". Since no editor in any U.S. or U.K. commercial house knows any Chinese, all the "editing" that is done concerns one language and cannot be called translation-editing at all. It is such an "editor", working without restrictions and compunction, who is responsible for the following passage (the editor's contribution, including the addition of two whole paragraphs, is in italics):

> But *what of this child?* ... what could he do for *her? How could he comfort her? She needed to start all over again.* "Listen," *he said, looking directly into her face.* "I can see *very clearly* that you look just like a little girl."
>
> "Really? *Can you see that?" she asked with a calmer voice.* Her tears and sobs stopped at once.
>
> "Yes," *he said with great conviction. "There is no question: You are yourself, a girl, and you can see perfectly well. You can be strong."*
>
> She looked up. Her *red,* tear-stained face was *transparent,* like a clear sky after rain. She folded her arms in front of her chest and peered through the *openings in the* branches at the patients still *watching* so eagerly from the balcony.
>
> "They're waiting for their visitors," she explained quietly.
>
> "Yes, they're waiting," he replied *softly.*
>
> *They were no great distance from the balcony, yet far enough to see the path which had brought them both to the bench beneath the hawthorn. They stopped to listen ...*
>
> *And without even being aware of it, Wu Cangyun had found at last, within his compassion, the beginnings of his story.* (Jenner, 1986: 31)

This is Zhang Jie's story "Under the Hawthorn" and the translation is attributed to William Jenner who, as we can see from the disproportionately long sections in italics, cannot really be held responsible.

I am not saying that editors should not make stylistic changes to a translation; in many cases this is almost essential. When, for example, several stories by the same author are translated by different hands to form a single book, the editor may have to make many stylistic changes in order to give the author a single, recognizable voice. But to do so, the editor would need the understanding and consent of the translators in question. The case quoted above does not fall into this particular category, and neither the translator nor the author had been consulted before (or, for that matter, after) the translation was published.

Even Lindley's claim that an editor reads a translation first to check its English because "on this subject he is competent to judge, whether he knows the original language or not" seems to ring hollow in the face of the unspeakable English which abounds in translations published in the U.S. and the U.K. The following examples are taken from four stories or novellas translated *and* edited by native speakers of English:

"Have you eaten?" "*Eaten.*"

He *was knitting his thick eyebrows* and staring intently at ...

The *seventh belly,* no problem — he was thinking, she was just like a mother hen dropping another egg.

Making clicks, he grabbed my hand and stretched it toward the darkness.

This is too large a gift. (My Italics)

The first and the last examples represent one of the most common kind of "translationese" — in the last of course the author does not mean that the gift is too large in size. In the second example the man's eyebrows seem to have turned into something similar to a sweater-in-progress, and of course no editor in his right mind can blame this on Chinese peculiarity. Nor can we blame the "seventh belly" or "making clicks" on a "literal" approach towards translation. In fact terms such as "free translation" and "literal translation" have never been clearly defined, and have frequently been used as the bolt-holes of incompetent translators. To be exact we can perhaps call the first example quoted here a "word-for-word translation", which is what some machines do. The "seventh belly" is not some monster, it is just a woman's seventh pregnancy. However, the word *du* 肚 cannot be given any credit for enriching the English language here, because the Chinese text actually says "*di qi tai*" 第七胎 . As for the man "making clicks" in the fourth example, he should in fact be "munching noisily". And what is it that he is munching? Human internal organs in the form of grapes. Here one can see how, by misconstruing a single phrase, the translator can spoil the effect of the original (though in this particular case it may come as a relief for the readers).

Even without any knowledge of Chinese the editors in question should have spotted these awkward phrases. If they had cared to point these out to the translators, and if the translators had been conscientious enough to check them against the original, the mistakes could have been avoided. When you find mistakes and editorial slips like these on every page of a translation, the problem is not minor at all. Moreover, such problems point to a general editorial approach or trend. Editors who know no Chinese tend to let awkward and misleading phrases through the net because they think that these are exotic, while the translators' genuine attempts to convey local flavour are frequently struck out for being too outlandish.

And then there are publishers whose editors are not expected to (and are unable to) check whether a translation reads like English. Fingers have pointed to the Foreign Language Press, but the FLP is in fact in very good company. Many university and academic presses operating in East Asia do not have on their staff anyone capable of editing an English manuscript, and yet they regularly publish works written in or translated into English. In the case of an original work readers will at least know on whom to blame the bad English, but in the case of a translation the author is simply made to sound ridiculous. The university presses probably take comfort in the thought that their books are "refereed". The question is of course: who do they get as referee? As for some well known non-academic publishers in Hong Kong and their sister presses in America, there is even less quality control to speak of.

All that has been said above seems to indicate that translation editing either does not exist, or the editors are doing such a bad job that they might as well forget about it. That is of course not the whole truth. Some translations are checked not just line by line, but word by word, and the translators are saved many an embarrassing moment because of this. (Readers, I am afraid, have been deprived of a few good laughs.) I offer as evidence the following "translation bloopers" which have been prevented from seeing the light of day:

A filial girl who treats her aunt well. (孝婦善視其姑 i.e., a filial woman who treated her mother-in-law well.)

Ambitious scholars have a midnight mind/For a good horse plain daylight is enough. (志士終夜心/良馬白日足 i.e., a man with ideals cannot put his mind to rest at night, just as a fine steed cannot rest its legs in the daytime.)

Amid the *days of war and calamity that followed, people could scarcely live their lives.* (兵燹之下，民救死不給 i.e., amid the ravages of war, people could scarcely survive.)

Whatever may be the natural conditions and happenings in human life, nothing can alter man's true feelings. He would make utterances out of his mind. (天時人事，胥無足易其心，誠於中而有言 The published version reads: Yet no events, be they natural or human, can alter a man's true feelings so long as he speaks from his heart.)

She accused me of having forgotten all the favours her husband had done me while his corpse was still warm.

While cases such as the last example cited are just a matter of oversight, most of the above mistakes are the result of the translator's inability to understand the original text. But the translation sometimes sounds so ludicrous as English that one wonders why the translator considers it publishable. We all accept that even the best translators make mistakes. The most famous example is probably Arthur Waley's "red-legged immortal" for 赤腳大仙 in *Monkey*, which, from the point of either an editor or a reader, is really no big deal. After all it is very easy to correct, and even as it stands it tells the reader that there is something strange about the lower limbs of this particular immortal. This is clearly a mistake resulting from oversight rather than incompetence, and it is the latter which should concern us the most.

There are translations so heavily edited that the translator is really getting credit which should belong to someone else. Such heavy editing, or re-translation, happens in the world of commercial publishing, as described by Lindley:

> When ... a translation appears without a translator's name attached, this may not indicate callous disregard of the translator's rights but simply the fact that so much re-writing has been necessary that to attribute the result to the original translator would be, in effect, dishonest and misleading. (Lindley, 1961: 159)

In the field of Chinese-English translation, cases in which originally unusable translations are salvaged through heavy editing or even re-translating are mostly limited to specialist journals. Sometimes these would appear as co-translations, but more often than not the credit goes to the translator alone, for various reasons: the editing may have been done by two or three people, which makes the attribution of credit rather trouble-some; the editor may not be happy enough with the final version to put his name down as co-translator; or the translator, though happy enough to have someone improve on his work, is unwilling to acknowledge such help.

Competence in the area of English-Chinese translation editing should be higher, if only because the number of native speakers of Chinese with a reasonable command of English is much higher than in the Chinese-English situation. However, precisely because of this, the danger of complacency is also higher. On the whole, the problems discussed in Lindley's article still apply. First, with commercial publishers, there is hardly ever the time to check any translation thoroughly, if at all. This is particularly true of book series consisting of twenty or thirty volumes published over two or three years, as is the case with the translation of many foreign-language literary works in Taiwan. Second, few publishers recognize the need for careful editing in the case of translations. The assumption that all translators can be trusted to do a competent job is of course a fallacy, and can prove particu-larly dangerous when students of English with little more than three or four years of study behind them begin to translate major works of literature, sociology and philosophy with the help of dictionaries and little else, as was the case in mainland China in the 1980s, a period which witnessed a sudden boom in translation activities. There have also been cases where individual works are divided up amongst a group of translators. One translation of *Noble House*, published in Shanghai, boasts of seven translators. Logically, considerable editing would be necessary to unify the style of the whole book, but it is doubtful whether such attention is ever given to any English-Chinese translation. This is perhaps why, in literary translation at least, the best Chinese translations from the English are still those done by scholars.

The deficiency in translation editing is a universal phenomenon result-ing from a general lack of expertise in foreign languages. So-called bilin-gualism takes many forms; for example, one would not expect much if one advertises for a bilingual girl-Friday. Instead of bilingual, perhaps we should from now on refer to translation as a bi-cultural activity. The com-mon, and no doubt very wise, attitude is that if one can translate, why should one spend one's time improving other people's work? After all, one gets much more credit as a translator than a mere mention in the acknow-ledgement name list. It is therefore small wonder that translation editing is still very much an exchange of a favour amongst scholars and serious translators.

Lastly, it must be pointed out that not all translators can be editors. While a translator must have a thorough understanding of the author he translates, his rendition will always represent just one possible way of interpreting or conveying the original in a foreign language. People differ substantially in their linguistic and stylistic preferences, but many translators tend to overlook this fact when they judge other people's translations. What a good translation editor needs above all else is the ability to differentiate voices and styles. The editor may disagree with the translator's approach, but he must be able to draw a line between what is wrong and what is just not to his own liking.

References

Lindley, Denver. "The Editor's Problem." In *The Craft and Context of Translation*, edited by William Arrowsmith and Roger Shattuck. Austin: University of Texas Press, 1961, pp. 157–62.

Jenner, W.J.F. "Insuperable Barriers." *Renditions*, No. 25 (1986), pp. 18–35.

EDUCATION

Translation Education

Simon S. C. Chau
Department of English
Hong Kong Baptist College, Hong Kong

Evolution

> Translation training in the past has not demonstrated sufficient purpose, plan-
> ning and objectivity. It was left to individual genius, hard work and self-taught
> technique. There were amateurs but few devotees. (Pan, 1977:51)

> Although translation has been practised for thousands of years and there
> have always been schools for translators and interpreters which, with greater
> or lesser success, have trained their students for the work of translation, there
> is still no systematic method of teaching translation. In all fields of knowledge
> — and not least in this sphere — it is today becoming urgent to find suitable
> methods of teaching, since with the ever-growing flood of translations and the
> huge demand for training for translation work, the efficiency of this training
> must be increased as much as possible. (Reiss, 1976:329–30)

> The development of learner group-specific, text-typologically differenti-
> ated methods of TT is still in its infancy. It is symptomatic of the present
> unsatisfactory state of affairs that the term Übersetzungsdidaktik (translation
> pedagogy) is a fairly new coinage and that the manifold problems associated
> with this term have only recently provoked noticeable interest among linguists
> engaged in TT. (Kapp, 1974, quoted in Wilss, 1982:77)

Like translating itself, translation teaching (TT) has been going
through a process of professionalization since the Second World War, in
response to a universal need for specialization. It is gradually evolving from
piecemeal individual insights relevant to local immediate situations to

explicit, empirical, and systematic procedures based on up-to-date data and theories from adjacent disciplines, aiming at certain degrees of universal validity. Apart from describing the situation with admirable precision, the significance of the three quotations above lies no less in the fact that they were published as late as the mid-seventies, a testimony to the slowness of this professionalization process. As far as I know, no experimental data or serious survey findings have been published to date, despite efforts to establish the empirical nature of translation teaching.

The provision of institutionalized training for translators and interpreters is hardly a novel idea. Various methods were tried out in the training of the Egyptian dragoman, the Greek hermeneus, and the Latin interpres (Schmitt, 1982:96). In the West, at least three well-known schools for translators existed prior to modern times: one in Toledo in the Middle Ages, one in Baghdad during the Arab hegemony, and one in Paris at the Ecole d'Etudes Orientales (Arjona, 1980). In China, large-scale projects of translating Buddhist scripts imported from India were sponsored by succeeding governments between the first and the seventh century A.D. The projects involved hundreds, and at times thousands, of professional translators, and were accompanied by schemes of formal training.

Even so, there is little evidence of the legacy of these ancient programmes inspiring modern ones either in the West or in the East. Rather, translation pedagogy, or the theories of translation teaching, in the modern time is, with few exceptions, limited to the description and rationalization of designs by individual educators, mostly founders of prestigious programmes.

The scene changed since around 1980, as described below.

Legitimacy

One important factor which delayed the development of translation teaching must be the general lack of confidence in its usefulness within and outside the profession. Even today, there are practitioners who believe that translators are born, not made, pointing to their own successful careers as concrete proof of such a conviction: "Look, here I am, getting along pretty well without a single lesson in translating."

Despite the important role played by translators and interpreters in the modern world, there has been, until recent years, an astonishing lack of translation and interpreting education in most parts of the world: "There is

no formal training for translators in this country [Britain] and no set syllabus of what translators should know." (Cook-Radmore, 1964:34) In 1974,
it was reported that "99% of US translators have not been trained through a
formal course of training. Many of these are nevertheless making successful
careers for themselves. In view of this, the ATA [American Translators
Association] rather paradoxically stated that training is not absolutely necessary." (Caille, 1974:137). Speaking in 1980, G. Toury stated that "Most of
the translators who have been working 'in reality' have never gone through
a systematic course of training."

Even when there was formal training of some kind, translation teaching
was far from being sophisticated or systematic: "Although language teachers and foreign language departments at universities and colleges have
traditionally used translation as a teaching technique they have not shown
any marked proclivity to help students become professional translators. So
far, the training of translators has been left to the few schools, most of them
outside the U.S., which specialize in translation and interpretation, or, more
often, it has been left to personal interest, ingenuity, experience, and
chance." (Tinsley and Horn, 1971:10)

The presence of articles with titles like "Should We Teach Translation?" (Hendrickx, 1975), "Are Translators Born?" (Ozerov, 1979), "Translators — Made, Not Born?" (Healey, 1978), "Peut-on enseigner à
traduire?" (Waltz, 1944) and "Peut-on former des traducteurs techniques?"
(Gravier, 1967) reminds one that translation teaching was not taken for
granted. In fact, this challenge to the legitimacy of translation teaching is far
from a rhetorical one.

Objections to translation teaching usually take two forms: that translating is an art whose proficiency cannot be profitably formalized, and that
translation and interpreting involves qualities which are untrainable. In the
lack of detailed reasoning on the untrainability of such qualities, these
statements of Schmitt's deserve careful consideration:

> Most translators are the product of a combined accident that find them bi- or
> multilingual and untrained in those courses which are required for such occu-
> pations as law, engineering, medicine — or plumbing. In brief, they are self-
> taught. By the nature of its membership, the translating profession is thus akin
> to public relations, advertising, creative writing or politics where innate ability
> plus experience are the major qualifications. (1966:123)

A certain amount of scepticism in a new discipline like translation teaching is healthy and could be ignored, if it did not stem from the very persons for whom everything is designed: the translators and translator trainees themselves. On the one hand, it is common to hear graduates from translation and interpreting courses complaining that they have not learnt many useful things, and that their competence, if any, comes from post-graduate efforts. On the other hand, self-taught translators seldom consider formal training necessary. As no survey of any scale concerning this matter has been carried out to date, one can only resort to episodic records.

The scarcity of writings opposed to formal training must not be taken as a sign of universal support. It might well be that the opposition does not bother to write. Being "practical" professionals, translators and interpreters on the whole do not have the habit of theorizing.

In this respect, C. Schmitt, who published "The Self-taught Translator" (1966), is an exception — if indeed he was self-taught. As the subtitle "From Rank Amateur to Respected Professional" implies, it is possible to reach that goal by self-tuition — and that is precisely what is explained in the paper. According to him, none of the basic requirements of a profes-sional translator has to be acquired through anything like formal training. Reading through autobiographical accounts of successful translators, it is the norm to find that these geniuses became translators simply by a turn of fate, and there was invariably no formal training involved. M. Bullock's "How I Became a Translator" (1966) is an archetype of these.

So far, the most explicit anti-institutionist view was probably expressed in 1961 by A.T. Pilley. In his address to the Translators' Guild (U.K.), he argued that interpreter's schools could be "a snare and a delusion." Accord-ing to him, the number of professional interpreters produced by such institutions was "infinitesimal". It is almost impossible for anyone to inter-pret simultaneously if he learned his second language at the school or university rather than being bilingual by birth or accident of upbringing (1962). As a matter of fact, things have changed since his time, for the proportion of practising interpreters trained in translation and interpreting schools has been steadily increasing.

While writings on interpreter training emphasize the importance of some inborn abilities, such as audio comprehension and oral delivery (Longley, 1978), earlier works on translating often maintain that it takes a poet to translate a poet. According to this view, translation teaching is irrelevant, as few would believe that poets can be trained (Ozerov, 1979:11). While many translation educators would argue that this is only true of literary translating, E.A. Nida points out that some inborn qualities are indispensable. In a paper entitled "Translators Are Born Not Made," he says: "When I have had the opportunity to discuss fully with experienced translators and teachers of translation what the key element in translation success is likely to be, it has seemed that ultimately the most important factor is creative imagination. Some people have this capacity, and others simply do not have it." (1981:402). On a different occasion, after describing some successful translators he wrote: "Having met these men and many others who have become outstanding translators and interpreters, I have been forced to conclude that in a sense translators are not made, they are born." (1979:214)

L. Ozerov, summing up his article "Are Translators Born?", states that a happy combination of many circumstances and components is required for literary translators. Ultimately, "the individual, the creative individual, is what matters." His verdict on the nature vs. nurture controversy is quite even-handed: "The answer to the question in the title is that translators are born in much the same way as poets are born. But a born translator must study, that is, make himself — create himself, I would say." (1979)

With the establishment of translation and interpretation as a profession in the seventies, and as formal translation teaching gains almost universal recognition, anti-institutionist views are becoming less visible. While few would deny that some inborn qualities are indispensable for a successful translation and interpretation career (as is true of any profession), it is now difficult to argue that the reliance on inborn qualities and self-tuition is the optimal access road to the profession. The vigorous development of translation teaching as a discipline since 1980 in various parts of the world itself is a proof of the value of formal training. This statement of F. Healey's must be representative of the convictions of most translation educators today: "I would say that the good translator ... must be born with certain necessary qualities but needs a modicum of training to reach full stature." (1978:58)

Aims

As W. Wilss pointed out, there are widespread disagreements over the aims of translation and interpreting courses as well as the means to implement these aims. He summarized the problem under three headings: it is difficult to assess the need of individual organizations which eventually employ the graduates, not to mention catering for their individual needs, it is difficult to predict the trend of the future market, and there is disagreement among translation educators as to what can and must be achieved within the framework of a translation and interpreting course (1977:117–18).

An examination of the views of prominent translation educators on this topic reveals a consensus something like this: translation and interpreting courses are to provide trainees with the following:

1. In depth studies of the languages involved;
2. Orientation of general backgrounds of the cultures involved;
3. Insights into the operations of human communication;
4. Decoding and re-encoding competencies;
5. Familiarity with the ethos of the profession;
6. A "general liberal arts" education;
7. Familiarity with the fields the future translator/interpreter will be engaged in.

It goes without saying that each programme has its own focus and preoccupation, depending on its context and "givenness". For example, a postgraduate course training engineers to translate can perhaps do without "6" and "7", while concentrating on "3", "4", and "5". An undergraduate programme for students with poor Language 2 competence cannot but spend a lot of time on "1", at the expense of most of the others, perhaps regrettably.

Together or Separate?

Should translator and interpreter training be concurrent, consecutive, or separate?

Most of the translation teaching writers argue that the two are very different, thus the teaching methods must differ, as should the assessment of performance. Keiser (1978:17) points out that although both belong to the family of language communication, the practitioners are not often inter-changeable. The temperament of translators and interpreters often differs. The factor of speed and sheer physical stress in interpreting has prevented many otherwise gifted translators from becoming conference interpreters. So, "translation should definitely not be part of the curriculum during the actual period of interpreter training." Healey (1978:57) also explained that the interpreter must be able to make mental interlingual transpositions rapidly and accurately, and to sound convincing, and his work is usually not subjected to detailed scrutiny or analysis. The translator has more time to ponder and his work has greater permanency and is open to scrutiny and criticism. To achieve this kind of fidelity, the translator must be able to digest the source text thoroughly, and represent it naturally in his own words. B. Harris (1981:155–59) gave a theoretical justification for teaching translator and interpreter separately: while translators work on TEXTS, interpreters work on UTTERANCES. This point is taken up by H. Keith (1983), who explained that although the ultimate aim of the interpreter is the same as the translator, the skills required and processing problems involved are different.

Despite these arguments, translation and interpretation are, more often than not, taught in the same programmes to the same students (Coveney, 1971; Ferenczy, 1977). The published course outlines bear witness to this fact.

In her comprehensive study, Arjona (1980:59–61) identifies six types of translator and interpreter training arrangements based on three basic models:

1. The Linear Model — Translation certification precedes interpreting studies. The philosophy behind this model is that translation studies can lay a solid terminological basis and facilitate linguistic skills useful for interpreting. Hidden in this approach may be the bias that interpreting work is superior to or more difficult than translating.
2. The Parallel Track Model — Translator and interpreter training conducted on a parallel basis. Students can enter by either track, and switch to the other later. No one can receive both concurrently.
3. The Forked Track Model — Students complete a core programme before branching off to translation or interpretion. The degree granted at the end is either.

As it is now, the particular model adopted in a translation and interpretation institute or programme is invariably the result of tradition, local context, and personal conviction of the founders.

The Teachers

Who should be teaching in translation and interpretation programmes? Who are actually now teaching?

Among the literature on translation teaching, there is no lack of repeated emphases that translation teaching must be practised by "professionals". The following argument of Keiser's is typical:

> Strangely enough, while nobody would claim that medicine should be taught by somebody who has never seen an ill person, or music by somebody who has never been to a concert, there are, still now, quite a number of schools pretending to train interpreters where there is not one conference interpreter among the faculty, and where most if not all teachers have never been in an international conference let alone seen interpreters at work. They buy well known texts by Herbert, Rozen and Van Hoof, and off they go happily training interpreters. They know languages, have an idea of translation, and that, for them, is enough. But it is not enough, alas, for the students, and what comes out of those schools ... are precisely those poor people we have seen being shot down in flames in the selection tests of international organizations.... (1978:13)

The recurrence of such laments reflects the fact that although the ideal (that only professionals should teach) is generally accepted, it is not often put into practice.

There is also a body of opinion against full-time translation and interpreting teaching, as this would divorce the teacher from the market reality. Longley, for example, insists that he should be practising his art concurrently, as "there are some things that only a professional can teach." (1978:53)

As it is now, translation and interpreting teachers fall into three categories, each with their very different upbringing and approach to the art or "business" of translating and interpreting:

1. The Literature Academics — Graduates of classical, foreign or comparative literature programmes, these fine ivory-tower criticism specialists typically indulge in the "art" of translating, and translate a poem/play/novel or two in their spare time. Rarely do they see the need to break down the wall between town and gown. They are the people who are most prepared to argue that Translators Are Born Not Made, and defend their teaching as indirect orientation ("sensitivity enhancement", etc.) rather than "translation training".

2. The Linguisticians — Self-proclaimed scientists eager to test the latest model of linguistic hypothesis on the activity of translating and interpreting. Hardly ever tempted to translate any kind of

writing or to spend time in the booth, their only interest in the "real world" is, in most cases, the use of translators and interpreters and their performances as specimens for academic research.

3. The Practitioners — After a fairly long career in the booth or practising as translators, these veterans leave the market temporarily or permanently to nurture the new generation in the profession. Many of them were self-taught, though the proportion of formally trained ones is increasing. With their faith in the effectiveness of practice and experience sharing, they are prone to take anti-academic and/or anti-theory stands.

As more and more translation and interpreting education is now being conducted in universities, the "battle" between the academics and the practitioners becomes all the more heated because universities are inclined to employ people with higher academic rather than professional qualifications, and few translation and interpreting practitioners bother, or can afford the resources, to obtain the former.

Yet there is ground to be optimistic in this respect, as the wall between town and gown is coming down, and the social recognition of the profession enables or even requires the practitioners to gain academic recognition. More and more of the translation and interpreting teachers will come close to the ideal, namely that they should —

a. have bi- or multilingual competence;
b. have bi- or multicultural competence;
c. have a fair amount of experience as practitioners in the market;
d. be knowledgeable in the art of educating, such as curriculum planning, classroom skills, assessment, and the psychology of learning;
e. be knowledgeable in the operations of human communication;
f. have a love and passion for teaching.

Usefulness of Theory

One of the hotly debated topics which often divide translation teachers is: Should theories of translation be taught?

"Theory" seems to be a dirty word for many. It seems to be fashionable to argue that "a practical linguist is better than a theoretical one". Similarly, it is common to find in reports on translation and interpreting programmes that theories are deliberately avoided. Ferenczy's on the Budapest programme is typical: "No theoretical instruction is given; the training consists entirely of practical sessions." (1977:182)

There is no lack of anti-theorists who see theory and practice as opposing entities: "Much that has been written about translating, especially since the war, and in particular about the translation of scientific or technical documents, has been far too theoretical and has only confused the issue. No doubt, information theory and research in terminology have their place in academic research; nevertheless, these must surely be elements of long-term research, and can, in my opinion, contribute little at the moment, at any rate, to the solutions of day-to-day problems which face us." (Readett, 1958:138)

Following such logic, the absence of theoretical training in translation teaching is a virtue. Hence "pragmatic" and "practical" have become favourite adjectives to describe and sell translation and interpreting courses.

Themselves theorists, many translation teaching writers are in favour of teaching theories. As their titles suggest, P. Fawcett's "Teaching Translation Theory" (1981) and I. Mason's "The Role of Translation Theory in the Translation Class" (1982) unequivocally affirm the place of theory in translation teaching. Fawcett gives reasons which account for the lack of enthusiasm for formal translation theory courses (1981:141–42). Mason examines the relation between translation theory and translation teaching, and concludes that when theory stops short at the word-group level (as is the case with contrastive linguistics, for example), the student may fail to link it with practice. Only by applying it to actual texts can insights at abstract level be seen as relevant. He explained in concrete terms how this can be done in the curriculum.

Keiser (1969:5) considers the "theory of translation" an important part of the syllabus. His approach is one which is practised by many translation teachers. The idea is to make short exposés (15 to 20 minutes) dealing with a vast range of subjects. Theoretical instruction would not necessarily be given in a pre-established order, but as practical problems arise or whenever questions put by the student warrant a more thorough explanation.

Wilss, who favours teaching theory, completes his programme by a course in "the science of translation" with lectures, tutorials and pro-seminars. Not devoted to "practical learning aims", this course serves to help the students to think about translating and interpreting analytically: "To investigate the various factors involved in interlingual synchronization processes, to integrate those therefrom processual regularities (and non-regularities) which then can be exploited for a number of theoretical and practical purposes." (1977:120)

While the debate on theory goes on, the fact remains that most translation and interpreting programmes are far from theoretical. As R.P. Roberts reported: "Most translation programmes have only one three-credit 'theory of translation' course in an approximately ninety-credit programme." (1981:193). As Perkins pointed out: "The translation of selected texts [of differing style and content] remains the principal activity within the translation class." (1978:241) There are some, like C.W. Frerk, who compromise and favour a period of "theoretical training" at school, and another one of practical training in the translation department of a large organization (1963:365–66). Wendland underlines the importance of both: "Just as theory without practice is dead, so also practice without continual direction and stimulation from theory profits little." (1982:125)

As translation studies became more and more sophisticated, and the application of modern linguistics insights to translating proves increasingly rewarding (see Chau, 1984: Ch. 3), linguistic theories as well as translation theories are gradually establishing a permanent place in translation teaching curricula. The foundation of regular postgraduate programmes in translation theory and the establishment of professorial chairs in translation theory in American and European universities in recent years are both indicators of this trend.

General versus Specialized Training

"Knowledge of languages, however comprehensive, is not enough. Personal, ... intellectual, ... and more qualities are also required, but even these essential qualities will not make for a good interpreter unless they are backed up by solid knowledge of the subject in hand." (Herbert, 1952, quoted in and translated by Fraser, 1983:87)

This comment on the utmost importance of subject competence in interpreting can be equally applied to translating. While hardly anyone questions this view, opinion is divided among translation and interpreting educators as for the desirability and practicability of providing specialized subject training within the translator and interpreter curriculum. The fact remains that some schools aim at producing "general" linguists, others train specialized translators and interpreters.

Full-scale specialization is uncommon due to three reasons:

a. the schools do not always have the necessary resources, especially qualified teaching staff;
b. it is difficult to predict the requirements of future jobs;
c. translators will go through in-house on the job training anyway.

These are reflected in Hendrickx's report:

> Obviously, no school can provide tuition and training in all the fields of knowledge a translator may need to be familiar with; it should, however, be possible for schools to provide basic tuition of such quality and scope that the translator or interpreter is capable of adapting himself to new circumstances in a limited period of time. (1975:103)

This view is affirmed by Citroen, who also envisages that some translation and interpreting schools will differentiate their programmes, each school giving the type of course "in harmony with its character". While no detailed study of any particular subject is provided, students can be equipped with a sound basic knowledge of a few broad fields such as science, technology, law, and economics (1966:143–44). Judging from the outlines of many programmes, this is in fact the case.

These orientations in various fields are advocated in Hendrickx's report:

> The teaching of languages and of translation should be supplemented by a 'general' education covering a wide range of subjects such as economics, politics, law, technology. This again should be complemented by some kind of specialization, e.g., in electronics, medicine, commerce, agriculture, chemistry, the fine arts. Whether this specialization should take place before, during or after the actual tuition period remains an open question, since conditions may vary quite considerably as regards both the available facilities for language study and the nature of demand of translation. (1975)

There are, however, translation and interpreting educators who fear that while specialization is absolutely necessary for technical translators (though not WITHIN the translation and interpreting programme itself), there is a danger that the specialized translator will have a lack of "universal knowledge", and lose interest in the search for it (see, for example, Suchodolski, 1962:18).

In a sense the debate about specialized training is not about its necessity, but its quantity. It is worth noting that one Unesco report pointed out that "There must be a level of technical competence beyond which any increase will not improve the quality of the translated material." Thus the urgent need is to determine the level, and devise means to test it. (1957:167–68)

Arguing for the provision of specialized training, Longley explained that this is not the same as producing subject experts. Rather, the aim is to break down the barrier of alien language and ideas of the specific subjects, especially when the students have hitherto received language training and little else. After this training, students can use the same language as the experts they translate or interpret, and above all not "be afraid to understand" (1978:49). In Reiss's translation teaching model, translational specification with career-oriented special training becomes the last of four translation teaching stages, following the first three which form the "basic studies" (1976:336ff). Napthine, in her survey of translation teaching, points out that the aim of modern translation training is to combine the skills of a subject specialist and a linguist, so subject training should have a place in the curriculum (1983:21–24). At Heriot-Watt University, for example, translation and interpreting students are offered a choice of 25 to 30 elective subjects taught by another department, such as economics, business organizations, and industrial relations (Fraser, 1983:87).

Apart from practical needs, there are theorists who link subject training with education ideals. E. Lippmann, after stating that quality education means exposing students to a wide range of education opportunities providing them with various kinds of learning experience, recommends a closer link between schools and employers:

> novel learning experiences which may be the product of an exciting dialogue between language education and industry have not been exploited in translation — not even in translation workshops dealing with a variety of material under the supervision of experienced professional translators. It is precisely such learning experiences which could be achieved by including in the curricula not only translation-oriented courses, but also courses which may be on the periphery of translation, and courses which essentially contribute to an enhancement of the translator's role as an influential factor in business and society." (1976:163)

Curriculum Content

What do translation and interpreting schools do to their trainees, and in what sequence?

Unlike undergraduate programmes in physics, medicine or linguistics which usually have a common body of knowledge to be introduced to the students in a generally accepted order, translation and interpreting course outlines from different schools are often strikingly dissimilar in their contents and sequencing. Some provide practically no language training, while others apparently devote more than half of their effort to upgrading the languages involved. Some place heavy emphasis on cultural orientation, others simply neglect it. Topics like linguistics, translation theory, the history of translation, literary criticism, professional orientations, computer literacy, target language writing training, terminology training, etc. find their place in some of the curricula, but not others.

Despite this diversity, there is evidence that translation and interpreting educators are learning from each other, thanks to the increasing number of international conferences and seminars on translation pedagogy and faculty exchange programmes, enabling the concerned teachers to compare notes and enrich their curriculum with experience and insights from elsewhere.

If one has to find common denominators of translation and interpreting programmes worldwide, it is possible to group their contents under the following headings:

(1) General education — helping the student to grow intellectually and become a mature person with a critical mind and intellectual curiosity, well-equipped with the skills to conduct research to solve problems.
(2) Translating competence training — including
    a. Language orientation: perfecting the languages involved;
    b. Cultural orientation: familiarity with the cultures involved, and understanding of the role culture plays in human communication;
    c. Communication orientation: understanding how language works (linguistics, communication theories, semiotics, literary criticism, discourse analysis, language philosophy, text typology, etc.);
    d. Mastery of decoding and re-encoding competencies (practices, orientations in procedures and problem-solving methods, reading efficiency training, etc.),
    e. Reflections on the activity of translating (translation theory, history of translation, translation criticism, etc.).

(3) Interpreting competence training — including a to d above;
    e. Training in public oration, memory, note-taking and other supporting skills.
(4) Subject competence training — providing students with basic knowledge in some fields (economics, journalism, technology, etc.) which they might be working in during their working life.
(5) Professional training — including
    a. Orientations in professional ethics and code of practice;
    b. Formats of presentation and styles for publication;
    c. Training in communication technology (word processing, machine-aided translating, on-line research skills), copy-editing, vetting;
    d. Orientations in dealing with clients, team work as professionals, and understanding of market ethos.
(6) Placement — or internship, in translator and interpreter user organizations, under faculty supervision.

No two translation training curricula can or should be identical. There is no such thing as an ideal translation and interpreting curriculum. The actual shape of each programme is determined by many factors, among which the following are usually most important:

(1) The need of the society and the demand of the job market — the language situation, socio-economic climate, national policies, the present state of translator and interpreter service, etc.
(2) Aspiration and ability of the trainees — their level of education, language and cultural competence, preference and motivation, etc.
(3) Resources of the school — availability of expertise among faculty, facilities for research, possibility of sending students abroad for brief stays or of placements in translator and interpreter user organizations, etc.
(4) The translation educators' philosophy — their visions and knowledge.

The New Scene

An observer from outside who examines the state of translation teaching would probably be struck by two of its features: firstly, its subordination to local situations, i.e. how it is done depends primarily on the local language situation, job market, tradition, etc., and secondly, the existence and mutual ignorance of two groups of translation and interpreting educators who dominate the business — the self-made veteran practitioners who set up their course based on individual intuition and experience, and the academics who have little translation and interpreting experience and build their curriculum around linguistics or translation theories.

Both of these factors are perhaps the greatest obstacles to the establishment of the discipline of translation teaching. It is a cliché to emphasize the importance of combining theory and practice, yet, as always, it is easier said than done. When local demands overrule everything, the construction of a curriculum based on rational and comprehensive theories is often a luxury, to the frustration of the dedicated educator. As long as translation teaching is in the hands of the veterans with the paradoxical attitude of "I didn't have to go through all these — I know exactly how best to train you", or academics who have practised little but believe that academic training of whatever kind cannot be a waste of time, the professionalization of translation teaching, as advocated by distinguished educators like Wilss, Reiss, and Arjona, might not go very far.

Nevertheless, the tide is visibly on the turn. As the demand for professional translation teaching grows, as the proportion of formally trained translators and interpreters (and therefore that of educators who are formally trained translators/interpreters) goes up, as the relevance and contribution of language studies and translation theories to translation teaching increases, and as educators communicate academically more often, translation teaching is becoming an entity as it was never before. All these are tangibly demonstrated by the rapidly growing numbers of papers, researches, and conferences focusing on translation pedagogy. It is such efforts that are gradually nullifying the statements quoted at the beginning of this article, to the benefit of the trainees and the profession.

References

Arjona, Etilvia. "Translator and Interpreter Training in Europe and the U.S.A." Unpublished manuscript, School of Education, Stanford University, 1980.

Bullock, Michael. "How I Became a Translator." *Author*, Vol. 77, No. 2 (1966), pp. 18–22.

Caille, Pierre-Francois. "Translators and Translation: 1974 Survey." *Babel*, Vol. 20, No. 3 (1974), pp. 130–41.

Chau, S.S.C. "Aspects of Translation Pedagogy: The Grammatical, Cultural and Interpretive Teaching Models." Doctoral thesis, University of Edinburgh, 1984.

Citroen, I.J. "Targets in Translator Training." *Meta*, Vol. 11, No. 4 (1966), pp. 139–44.

Cook-Radmore, D. "What is a Translation?" *The Incorporated Linguist*, Vol. 3, No. 2 (1964), pp. 34–37.

Coveney, J. "Schools of Modern Languages. The Bath University Post-graduate Diploma in Language Studies." *Babel*, Vol. 17, No. 2 (1971), pp. 21–25.

Dunlop, D.M. "The Work of Translation at Toledo." *Babel*, Vol. 6, No. 2 (1960), pp. 55–59.

Fawcett, Peter. "Teaching Translation Theory." *Meta*, Vol. 26, No. 2 (1981), pp. 141–47.

Ferenczy, G. "Postgraduate Short-term Training of Interpreters and Translators at the Faculty of Liberal Arts, Budapest University." *Babel*, Vol. 23, No. 4 (1977), pp. 181–82.

Fraser, J. "Vocational Training in Modern Languages at Heriot-Watt University, Edinburgh." *The Incorporated Linguist*, Vol. 22, No. 2 (1983), pp. 86–87.

Frerk, C.W. "Training Translators." In *Quality in Translation: Proceedings of the Third Congress of the International Federation of Translators (FIT), Bad Godesberg, 1959*, edited by E. Cary and R.W. Jumplet. New York: MacMillan, 1963, pp. 363–68.

Gravier, M. "Peut-on former des traducteurs techniques?" *Babel*, Vol. 13, No. 2 (1967), pp. 73–76.

Harris, Brian. "Prolegomenon to a Study of Differences Between Teaching Translation and Teaching Interpreting." In *L'Enseignement de l'Interprétation et de la traduction de la théorie à la pédagogie*, edited by Jean Delisle. Ottawa: University of Ottawa Press, 1981, pp. 153–62.

Healey, F. "Translators — Made, Not Born?" *The Incorporated Linguist*, Vol. 17, No. 3 (1978), pp. 54–58.

Hendrickx, Paul V. "Should We Teach Translation?" *Babel*, Vol. 21, No. 3 (1975), pp. 101–106.

Herbert, Jean. *Manuel de l'interprète*, 2nd ed. Geneva: Georg, 1952.

Hu, Shih. 〈佛教的翻譯文學〉 (The Translation of Buddhist Literature). In 《翻譯論集》 (*An Anthology of Essays on Translation*), edited by C. T. Huang 黃嘉德. Shanghai: West Wind Press 西風出版社, 1940, pp. 273–93.

Kapp, V. "Probleme von Theorie und Praxis in der Ausbildung zum Übersetzer und Dolmetscher." In *Übersetzer und Dolmetscher: Theoretische Grundlagen, Ausbildung, Berufspraxis*, edited by V. Kapp. Heidelberg: 1974, pp. 7–13.

Keiser, W. "Selection and Training of Conference Interpreters." In *Language Interpretation and Communication, NATO Conference Series III. Human*

Factors, V. 6, edited by David Gerver and H. Sinaiko. New York: Plenum Press, 1978, pp. 11–24.

————. "A Syllabus for Advanced Translation Courses." *L'Interprète*, Vol. 24, No. 2 (1969), pp. 2–6.

Keith, Hugh A. "Liaison Interpreting — An Exercise in Linguistic Interaction." Paper presented at the AILA Colloquium, Saarbrucken, 1983.

Lippmann, E. "How Can Schools Enhance the Professional Relance of the Translator?" *Babel*, Vol. 22, No. 4 (1976), pp. 131–42.

Longley, Patricia E. "An Integrated Programme for Training Interpreters." In *Language Interpretation and Communication, NATO Conference Series III. Human Factors*, Vol. 6, edited by David Gerver and W. H. Sinaiko. New York: Plenum Press, 1978, pp. 45–56.

Mason, Ian. "The Role of Translation Theory in the Translation Class." *Quinquereme*, Vol. 5, No. 1 (1982), pp. 18–33.

Napthine, A.M. "Training of Translators." In *The Translator's Handbook*, edited by C. Picken. London: Aslib, 1983, pp. 21–32.

Nida, Eugene A. "Translations and Translators." *Babel*, Vol. 15, No. 4 (1979), pp. 214–15.

————. "Translators Are Born Not Made." *The Bible Translator*, Vol. 32, No. 4 (1981), pp. 401–5.

Ozerov, L. "Are Translators Born?" *Babel*, Vol. 25, No. 1 (1979), pp. 11–12.

Pan, Francis K. "Towards a Formal Training Program." In *The Art and Profession of Translation: Proceedings of the Asia Foundation Conference on Chinese-English Translation*, edited by T. C. Lai. Hong Kong: Hong Kong Translation Society, 1977, pp. 38–51.

Perkins, C.R.B. "Towards the More Systematic Teaching of Translation." *English Language Teaching Journal*, Vol. 32, No. 3 (1978), pp. 236–41.

Pilley, A.T. "The Training, Qualifications and Professional Status of Interpreters." *The Incorporated Linguist*, Vol. 1, No. 3 (1962), pp. 69–70.

Readett, A.G. "The Training of Translators." *Aslib Proceedings*, Vol. 10, No. 6 (1958), pp. 131–46.

Reiss, Katharina. "How to Teach Translation: Problems and Perspectives." *The Bible Translator*, Vol. 27, No. 3 (1976), pp. 96–102.

Roberts, Roda P. "The Role of the Practicum in Translator Training Programmes." In *L'Enseignement de l'Interprétation et de la traduction de la théorie à la pédagogie*, edited by Jean Delisle. Ottawa: University of Ottawa Press, 1981, pp. 193–203.

Schmitt, C. "The Self-taught Translator — From Rank Amateur to Respected Professional." *Meta*, Vol. 11, No. 4 (1966), pp. 123–26.

————. "Translating and Interpreting, Present and Future." *The Incorporated Linguist*, Vol. 21, No. 3 (1982), pp. 96–102.

Suchodolski, P. "The Quality, Training and Professional Status of the Technical Translator." *The Incorporated Linguist*, Vol. 1, No. 1 (1962), pp. 17–22.

Tinsley, Jr., R.L. and S.F. Horn. "The Role of the University in the Training of Translators." *American Translator*, Vol. 3 (1971), pp. 10–15.

Toury, Gideon. "The Translator as a Nonconformist-to-be, or: How to Train Translators so as to Violate Translational Norms." In *Angewandte Übersetzungswissenschaft, Internationals Übersetzungswissenschaftliches Kolloquium an der Wirtschafts Universitat Aarhus, Denmark, 19–21 Juni 1980*, edited by S.O. Poulson and Wolfram Wilss. Danemark: Aarhus, 1980, pp. 190–94.

Ts'an, H. 〈佛經的傳譯人數和譯本補述〉 (The Number of Interpreters and Works Translated in the Translation of Buddhist Texts). 《翻譯通報》 (*Translation Bulletin*), Vol. 3, No. 1 (1951), pp. 22–25.

UNESCO. *Scientific and Technical Translating*. Paris: UNESCO, 1957.

Waltz, R. "Peut-on enseigner à traduire?" In *Bibliotheque de la Faculté Catholique des Lettres de Lyon*, Vol. 3, edited by M. J. Saunier, 1944.

Wendland, Ernst R. "Receptor Language Style and Bible Translation — III: Training Translators About Style." *The Bible Translator*, Vol. 33, No. 1 (1982), pp. 115–27.

Wilss, Wolfram. "Curricula Planning." *Meta*, Vol. 22, No. 2 (1977), pp. 117–24.

———. *The Science of Translation: Problems and Methods*. Tübingen: Gunter Narr Verlag, 1982.

EMPTY WORDS

Translating Empty Words

Ian P. K. Wong
Vice-president
Hong Kong Translation Society, Hong Kong

Introduction

Here we will not define "empty words" 虛詞 as a Chinese grammarian would in a grammar book. Our aim is rather to help the reader understand the importance of "empty words" in translating Chinese into English.

The Function of "Empty Words"

Strictly speaking, there are no morphological changes in the Chinese language. Word order and the use of "empty words" are critical, because they are the basis of word formation and sentence construction.

"Empty Words" (虛詞) and "Solid Words" (實詞)

In the Chinese language, all words can be divided into two categories: "solid words" and "empty words." Traditionally, 名詞 (nouns), 動詞 (verbs), 助動詞 (auxiliary verbs), 形容詞 (adjectives), 數詞 (numerals), 量詞 (measure words) and 代詞 (pronouns) have been regarded as "solid words," and 副詞 (adverbs), 介詞 (prepositions), 連詞 (conjunctions), 助詞 (particles), 嘆詞 (interjections) and 象聲詞 (onomatopoeia) as "empty words."

Most Chinese grammarians define "solid words" as words which can be used independently and "empty words" as words that cannot. In fact, this is somewhat oversimplified. In the following sentences:

1. 你跟我一塊兒來，好嗎？ — 好！
   Will you come with me? — O.K.
2. 你要買我的畫？ — 全部！
   You want to buy my paintings? — All of them!
3. 你愛我嗎？ — 永遠，永遠！
   Do you love me? — Always!

好 (fine, O.K.,) 全部 (all) and 永遠 (always) are "empty words" or adverbial phrases, yet they are used independently. In such cases, they are classified by certain unconventional grammarians as "semi-solid."

Some words can be classified as "semi-empty" too, for example:

誰先到達終點，誰先拿獎杯。
He who finishes first wins the cup.

The word 誰 (any person) is a noun, which is a "solid word," but it does not stand for a specific person, and thus it is not solid. Furthermore, the two 誰 connect the two sentences and in a sense play the role of conjunctions. A conjunction is an "empty word," and therefore we have reason enough to classify 誰 in this sentence as "semi-empty."

The Number of "Empty Words"

Although there are innumerable "solid words," the number of "empty words" is comparatively small. Besides approximately 600 adverbs, many of which can be considered "semi-empty," there are perhaps one hundred more.

However, adjectives which Chinese grammarians classify as "solid words" can in many cases be adverbs or adverbial phrases which are part of "empty words." For example, 一點兒 (a bit, a little) can be both an adjective and adverbial phrase. The following sentences demonstrate the use of 一點兒 as an adjective:

1. 她爲了減肥，每天只吃一點兒東西。
   She only takes a few bites every day in order to lose weight.
2. 他這人一點兒頭腦也沒有。
   He is a man without a grain of sense.
3. 他的證供一點兒眞實性也沒有。
   There is not a shred of truth in his statement.

4. 她這個人一點兒幽默感也沒有。

She is a woman entirely lacking humour.

5. 他每天晚上都喝一點兒威士忌。

He drinks a dram/a tot of whisky every evening.

6. 我有一點兒感冒了。

I've got a touch of flu.

7. 這湯欠了一點兒鹽。

The soup can do with a touch more salt./The soup needs a trifle more salt.

一點兒 can be used adverbially as follows:

1. 他這人有一點兒愛拍。

He is something of a soft-soaper.

2. 她今天似乎好一點兒了。

She looks a shade better today.

3. 他對衣著一點兒也不講究。

He doesn't care a whit about his clothes.

4. 他恐怕有一點兒醉了。

I'm afraid he's had one too many/he's a wee bit drunk.

5. 他差一點兒就破產了。

He was within an ace of ruin. /He was all but bankrupt. /He was on the brink of bankruptcy.

6. 她說的話一點兒真的都沒有。

There is not an iota of/a scintilla of truth in what she says.

7. 我一點兒也不喜歡這幅畫。

The painting has no appeal for me whatsoever/ doesn't appeal to me at all.

Some adjectives and numerals, especially the ordinal numbers 序數詞 and the approximate numbers 概數詞 are, in a broad sense, "empty words." For instance, the ordinal numbers:

頭 in 頭賽 (the first half of the game)

末 in 末班車 (the last bus)

初 in 初小 (the junior primary school)

高 in 高中 (the senior middle school)

大 in 大兒子 (the eldest son)

小 in 小女兒 (the youngest daughter)

and the approximate numbers:

多 in 六十多歲 (over sixty)
幾 in 幾天 (a few days)
來 in 二十來個雞蛋 (about two dozen eggs)
多少 in 多少有點失望 (feeling somewhat disappointed)
上下 / 左右 in 六十上下 / 左右 (about sixty)

Why Are "Empty Words" Difficult to Translate?

Generally speaking, "solid words" are not difficult to deal with in Chinese-English translation. For example, in a sentence like 她昨天要我跟她去看電影 : 她 – she, 昨天 – yesterday, 要 – want, 我 – me, 去看 – go to see, 電影 – movie are all "solid words," and the Chinese sentence can be easily rendered into English: "Yesterday she wanted me to go to the movies with her." However, if we add emphasis with the adverbial phrase 非…不可 (simply must), the Chinese will read 她昨天非要去看電影不可 . Here the emphatic and commanding tone of the Chinese phrase 非…不可 is relatively difficult to translate. Some possible renderings are: "Yesterday she insisted on my going to the movies with her" or "Yesterday she thought I just had to go to the cinema with her." As 非…不可 expresses an emphatic tone, the English translation should vary accordingly, and equivalent emphatic expressions should be used. For example, 在輿論的壓力下他們非讓步不可。 — "Under the pressure of public opinion they will have no alternative but to yield." English expressions such as "to have no alternative/choice/option but" suggest the same degree of emphasis as the Chinese 非…不可 .

Other examples can show how English translations vary according to different degrees of emphasis in Chinese:

1. 香煙像瘋了似的加價，我相信你能明白，現在是非戒煙不可了。

Here 非…不可 is not specially emphatic; it can be rendered as follows: "As the price of cigarettes shoots up, I trust you realize the need to give up smoking."

2. 你要是把車子開得那麼快，到頭來非進醫院不可。

Here 非…不可 is not so emphatic, and it can be translated in this way: "You'll wind up in hospital if you drive so fast."

3. 現在你非向她道歉不可了。

Here 非⋯不可 is strongly emphatic, so the English equivalent should maintain the same tone: "All you can do now is offer her an apology."

4. 他既然是發起人，那他今天非到場不可。

Here 非⋯不可 is rather emphatic, and the phrase should be translated similarly: "Since he is the man who initiated it, he is bound to be present today."

5. 我看這事情不見得非你去幹不可。

Here 非⋯不可 is less emphatic: "I don't think you're the only person who can do the job."

6. 我是作者，所以我對出版商說：你們編輯方面加工，但要改動手稿內容，非得我同意不可。

Here 非⋯不可 is specially emphatic, so it can be translated in more formal language: "As the writer of the manuscript, I told the publisher he could do some editorial polishing on it, but any changes in content could only be made subject to my consent."

Mastering "Empty Words"

As "empty words" present an immense challenge, it is important for a Chinese-English translator to make a thorough study of them. He should first of all study Chinese grammar, especially 連詞 (conjunctions) 關聯詞 (correlatives) and 複句 (complex sentences).

In English a conjunction often joins two sentences or clauses, but in Chinese there may be no conjunction in between. For example:

1. 他是教師，我是學生。
   He is a teacher, and I am a student.
2. 他剛走，她就來了。
   As soon as he had left, she arrived.
3. 風停了，雨也就小了。
   When the wind had stopped, the rain was letting up.
4. 他們下午來，我在家等著。
   As they are coming this afternoon, I'll wait at home.

According to some Chinese grammarians, the above examples are

意合法 (implied correlatives). Chinese-English translators should familiarize themselves with this construction and insert an appropriate conjunction.

All the correlatives are "empty words," as they consist of conjunctions connecting clauses and adverbs that have the function of linking more than one phrase and sentence, such as 又…又… (both … and …), 越… 越… (the more … the more …), 因爲…所以… (because), 不但… 而且… (not only … but also …), 既然…也就… (now that …), 一邊…一邊… (at the same time as …), etc. Some are difficult to deal with and may baffle Chinese-English translators in some contexts. For example: 忽而…忽而… in 她的情緒忽而好忽而壞，這又使她的男朋友忽而高興忽而灰心；一方面… 〔另〕一方面… in 一方面行賄，一方面敲詐，他弄了一大筆錢；與其…，不如… in 與其說她漂亮，不如說她迷人 and so on.

Complex sentences include a wide range of "empty words." They comprise both coordinate complex sentences (並列複句) and subordinate complex sentences (偏正複句). The following table gives the different relations between all the clauses in complex sentences:

Complex Sentence 複句	
Coordinate Complex Sentence 並列複句	Subordinate Complex Sentence 偏正複句
Coordinative relation 聯合關係	Adverse relation 轉折關係
Successive relation 承接關係	Causative relation 因果關係
Progressive relation 遞進關係	Conditional relation 條件關係
Alternative relation 選擇關係	Hypothetical relation 假設關係 Purposive relation 目的關係 Preference relation 取捨關係

Various "empty words" are used to describe the nature of all the relations in complex sentences.

Conclusions

Perhaps it may be helpful to restate the following points:

1. "Empty words" are not defined here as they would be in a Chinese grammar book. They are viewed in the light of translating Chinese into English.

2. The use of "empty words" together with word order are the basis of word formation and sentence construction.

3. "Empty words" can sometimes be used independently.

4. "Empty words," though relatively small in number compared to "solid words," present an immense challenge. They are difficult to deal with and may baffle Chinese-English translators in some contexts.

5. It is essential that a Chinese-English translator make a thorough study of "empty words." He should study Chinese grammar, especially conjunctions, correlatives, including "implied correlatives", and complex sentences.

Empty Words: Modal Adverbs

David E. Pollard
Department of Translation
The Chinese University of Hong Kong, Hong Kong

The Chinese language has a class of adverbs that are described as 語氣詞 (modal words, or literally "tone of voice words"). Their function is not structural, i.e. they do not mark sequence or logical connection; they can in fact be left out without impairing the sense or progress of a passage. They serve instead to convey the speaker's or writer's comment on what he is saying — for instance to express concession, reservation, confidence — or to anticipate a reaction from the listener or reader. They therefore occur in sentences which pass judgement, express feelings and opinions, or are argumentative. To give a preliminary example, in the sentence 你想知道，我也想知道, "You want to know (and) I also want to know," the adverb 也 "also" has the structural function of associating two identical propositions; but in 那也無所謂 "that does not matter," there is no comparator: 也 only adds a "colouring" to the statement. It is the latter kind of usage we are concerned with.

Broadly speaking, these Chinese modal adverbs can be regarded as discourse markers, as they signal the speaker's/writer's position or attitude rather than convey concrete information. Their counterparts in English separate fairly easily into different registers: the colloquial (well, now, you know, I mean, come to think of it, now you mention it, etc.) and the formal (I wouldn't say, presumably, admittedly, in point of fact, etc.). The Chinese modal adverbs (也 , 又 , 倒 , 總 , 還 etc.) are common to both registers. They all have lexical meaning, but this meaning may shade off into nothingness depending on the unit of discourse within which they occur.

The Chinese modal adverbs are not distributed haphazardly. By virtue of the fact that they are adverbs, they must modify verbs or other adverbs, but they tend to cluster at certain strategic points in a sentence. These include:

1. the copula 是 , when it follows a long noun-phrase or clausal subject, where they serve to strengthen a syntactically weak link; or
when 是 follows a demonstrative pronoun that sums up a proposition after lengthy preliminaries, as in:

> It is counted by some a weakness in princes to have favourites;
> but it is of all others the best remedy against ambitious great-
> ones. (Bacon)
> 以爲國君有寵臣，是一個弱點，殊不知在對付野心勃勃的大人物
> 一切法門之中這倒是最上乘的妙法。

2. negatives, where they inject some animus into an utterance, as in:

> 「你呀，還眞有點『造反』的味兒。」
> 「我可不敢『造反』了。」
> "It's true, you really do talk like the 'rebel faction'."
> "I (–) wouldn't dare to rebel."

3. modal verbs, as in:

   a. 那（——）可以
   "That (—) would be all right"
   where the gap (—) would normally be filled by either 倒 , or 也 ,
   or 還 , or 總 .

   b. 他竟敢侮辱我
   "He (—) dares to insult me"

4. fixed expressions. For example:

> 我對他眞是推心置腹。

This sentence is used to translate "I had the utmost confidence in
him." The fixed phrase 推心置腹 , literally "extend one's heart into
someone else's belly," already conveys the idea of "utmost confidence;" 眞 ("really") has two functions: grammatically it is a signal
that a fixed expression is coming, and semantically it indicates how
far the speaker's feelings measure up to the classic description.

5. words of feeling, thinking. For example:
   我終覺得大可不必。
   I (—) feel that would be quite unnecessary

In all these cases a form of words in English could be found to reflect the force of the modal adverbs to a certain extent, but I have chosen
in my translations to leave them entirely unaccounted for. The English

nevertheless seems complete as it is, whereas without them the Chinese would very often give the feeling of "something missing." There is in other words a sense of gaps to be filled in the Chinese sentences. This marks a difference between the two languages: adverbial reinforcement is more often felt desirable in Chinese than in English.

Gapfillers, or reinforcers, pose a question when it comes to translation: how far should words used at least partly for syntactical or stylistic reasons be accounted for, if the syntactic and stylistic reasons do not apply in the target language? In practice they are often simply left out, as we have deliberately done above. However, one suspects that the reason why they are left out may be that the translator, if a foreigner, does not fully understand their function, or if a native speaker, looks upon the word as truly "empty," and therefore not worth bothering with, or has not the address to supply a good rendering.

For classical Chinese 虛詞 ("empty" or functional words) have formed the backbone of the "grammar" for centuries; modern Chinese 虛詞 have only relatively recently claimed the attention of grammarians. A number of handbooks have been published, as have some articles on individual words, but is still difficult to find a concise summary of the essential message individual 語氣詞 carry: there is still too much reliance on vague explanations like "adding emphasis," "strengthening" and the like.

We will now look at three modal adverbs, 也 , 總 , and 又 , describe the role they play, and discuss how they may be coped with in translation.

也 : full lexical meaning: "also, as well." In discourse, the modal 也 normally signals that the speaker demurs at or disagrees with the previous speaker's words, or their tenor; the speaker claims that the facts support his view, not the other person's, or that the truth is on his side. 也 therefore has to do with claiming validity for one's statement, and as such may apply to something admitted to oneself as well as pointed out to another person.

1. 你這麼說也太武斷了。

    (In saying this) you are jumping to conclusions.

2. 這也不是沒有道理的。

    That wouldn't be unreasonable.

The force of 也 might be rendered with parentheticals in English: for (1) "I must say," or "You must admit;" for (2) "Mind you," "the truth is," or negatively "I wouldn't say," "I couldn't claim." But other more subtle means may be found of doing the same job.

總 : full lexical meaning: "always." The use of parentheticals would be very cumbersome in this case. From discrete data one can see that 總 variously conveys the ideas of necessity, of general truth or fact, and disregard of detail (regardless of person, time or place). From these data one can extract the chief element of inevitability (or ineluctability) allied to imprecision or indefiniteness about circumstance or detail. Once the semantic burden of 總 has been clarified, the word lends itself more docilely to manipulation. A small example would be the often heard 我總覺得… : this can be translated confidently as "I can't help thinking …," because the English expression conveys the looked-for ineluctability (you are driven to think) plus a vagueness as to the reasons why you so think (somehow or other).

Of more elevated status, since it has been included in a collection of *100 World's Great Letters*, is this from a letter of Ellen Terry to George Bernard Shaw:

Well, somehow you will be rewarded, I doubt not.

The translation nicely matches the English "empty" words with Chinese ones:

不過，你總會得到報答的。

The 總 carries the implication both of "bound to be" and of vagueness as to means: "somehow (or other)." And the final 的 underscores the imputation that the claim is not be doubted.

又 : full lexical meaning: "again." In its 語氣 function, 又 is used with a negative to deny a supposition that might have been made (1) thoughtlessly, (2) spitefully, (3) fancifully. The supposition has not been stated: it is either taken as implied or is anticipated. Hence the construction finds a match in "not as if …" in English. " 他又不會吃人，你怕甚麼？ " would go into English as "What are you afraid of? It's not as if he will eat you."

The "not as if …" formula does not always work, however. This may be seen from this utterance:

朱丹生氣了，我又沒有講要造集中營式的圍牆，鋼骨水泥和電網都是你們加上去的。

Here the speaker is described as "angry," and the "not as if …" expression is not compatible with impetuous delivery; it would hold up the rush of words. There may be no alternative to trusting to stress:

I *didn't say* we had to build a concentration-camp type of wall; the reinforced concrete and the electric fence was all your idea.

The 又 used to strengthen rhetorical questions essentially performs the same function as that described above. "這點花招又能騙誰？" "Who would be taken in by this tomfoolery?" means the same as "It's not as if anyone would be taken in by this tomfoolery." Exclamations can similarly accommodate 又 : the following Chinese sentence aptly translates a typically flamboyant utterance of Ellen Terry in the same letter to George Bernard Shaw:

不過，歸根結底，又有甚麼要緊的呢？
And, after all, as if anything mattered!

All of the adverbs looked at so far are capable of different interpretations in other situations: we have concentrated on particular usages, to illustrate the need to go deeper into understanding the subtle functions of a relatively neglected class of words. This neglect has led to uncertain, inadequate or even misconstrued renderings. We will not continue in this vein, as we cannot hope to be comprehensive. The time has come to take stock.

Discourse markers are used very commonly in both the Chinese and English spoken languages. In written composition, however, they tend to be suppressed, but because in English they either take the form of parentheticals belonging to a low register or are verbose, the suppression is more severe than in Chinese. Where they are retained in significant numbers in writing, it is by stylistic choice: in English to make one's writing loose, or animated; in Chinese either for similar reasons, or oddly enough, in imitation of classical rhythms. But in Chinese they are used additionally to reinforce syntactically weak constructions.

Whatever the factors involved might be, there certainly exists an imbalance between the two languages in their way of indicating attitude to what one is saying, and to the other person and his expectations: English places less reliance than Chinese on adverbials for this purpose. One means to which English has recourse (which we have noticed in passing) is phonetic stress: the writer expects the reader sympathetically to reproduce the right stress in order to appreciate the precise strength with which the idea is maintained. Intonation (as distinct from tonal pitch) is of course a feature of the Chinese language, but speech delivery is comparatively flat and expressionless: individual words and phrases are not marked out to the same extent as in English by pause and stress. Particles and adverbs, as well as overall sentence construction, are called upon to signal the main thrust of an utterance or the relative weight of its component parts.

A nice example of this contrast is quoted by Fu Fen 傅玢 in an article in 《中國翻譯》 (*Chinese Translators Journal*) (though with a different intention in view). The source text is Arthur Miller's *Death of a Salesman*. Willy says

> Biff Loman is lost. In the greatest country in the world a young man with such personal attractiveness, gets lost.

While the first "is lost" is unemphatic, the second cannot be so: preceded as it is by a long adverbial and complex noun construction, the delayed verb "gets lost" demands a special intonation because of its very brevity. Presumably it would be pathetically long drawn-out in stage delivery. Ying Ruocheng's 英若誠 translation recognizes the desirability in Chinese of indicating verbally Willy's attitude to what he is saying — and incidentally bolstering this lonely verb syntactically:

> 比夫洛曼居然找不到路子，在全世界最偉大的國家裡，這樣一個年輕人 —— 這麼招人喜歡的年輕人，居然找不到路子。

The interpolated 居然 (actually) puts into words Willy's incomprehension. In my opinion, however, while it thereby conforms to Chinese expressive practice in the second sentence, in the first it is redundant, as the tone is flat, there are no prominences to draw attention to, and it is not called for syntactically.

We have looked at ways in which Chinese modal adverbs can be translated by English parentheticals. The traffic can of course go in the opposite direction. Too often, however, Chinese translations resort to awkward literal rendering, like 驚人的是 for "surprisingly," 無疑地 for "no doubt" and, as in this example, 請注意 for "mind you:"

> I never knew such a strange creature, yet harmless, mind you, as the babe unborn.
> 我從來沒有見過這樣的怪傢伙，但是請注意，它完全無害，簡直像未生的嬰兒一樣無害。

Could not the idea of "mind you" be conveyed by 也 : " 但是它也全無害，簡直… " etc.?

The "little words" we have been discussing are the kind that spring spontaneously to the lips. They do not only not require thinking about, they even almost defy thinking about: very often the speaker would be hard put to it to explain what he means by them. Similarly in writing, they (perhaps a slightly different set of them) probably flow from the pen without much conscious reflection. If the translator can cope with them in the same kind of semi-automatic fashion, well and good, but that happy condition would depend on perfect bilingualism. For less fortunately endowed translators, their function has to be reasoned out. In the end they might not require to be rendered by expressions of corresponding status, they might not even need translating at all, but to neglect rendering them out of inattention or to misrender them out of ignorance is hardly the best response to their presence.

References

Lü, Shuxiang 呂叔湘 , ed. 《現代漢語八百詞》 (*800 Contemporary Chinese Functional Words*). Beijing: The Commercial Press 商務印書館 , 1980.

Pollard, David E. "The Use of 'Empty' Words in Chinese and English." In *Interpreting Culture Through Translation*, edited by Roger T. Ames, Chan Sin-wai and Ng Mau-sang. Hong Kong: The Chinese University Press, 1991, pp. 207–25.

Sun, Ruihe 孫瑞禾 , comp. 《漢語虛詞英譯》 (*English Translation of Chinese Empty Words*). Beijing: The Commercial Press 商務印書館 , 1981.

EQUIVALENCE

Dynamic Equivalence in Translating

Eugene A. Nida
American Bible Society, New York, U.S.A.

The traditional focus in discussions of translating has been the verbal comparison of the source and target (or receptor) texts. In some cases the differences or the motivations for producing differences have been discussed in terms of bringing the reader back to the source text or bringing the source text to the reader (Higham, 1938), but generally arguments about the legitimacy of a translation have dealt almost exclusively with the issue of literal versus free correspondences. In recent years, however, the issues of acceptability in translating have moved from the discipline of philology into quite new areas in which linguistics, psychology, communication theory, game theory, and semiotics are playing an increasingly important role. This can be readily seen in such volumes as Brower (ed.) 1959, Nida 1964, Ladmiral 1979, Wilss 1982, Tatilon 1986, and especially the highly insightful volume by Snell-Hornby 1988. In all these contributions to the principles and procedures of translating the focus is on the issue of equivalence, although it is described from a number of different perspectives. One thing is clear: the old distinctions about form versus content and literal versus free are no longer valid since they imply quite false dichotomies.

Since all communication moves from source to receptors, what is strategically important is the message received by the audience. But reception involves more than mere comprehension. Messages which are significant in both form and content need not only to be understood but also to be appreciated, and if there is a failure in either aspect of the communication event, there can be no real equivalence. The real issue, however, is in defining the nature of "equivalence," and especially in stating those features which make it "dynamic."

Even though at present it seems better for a number of reasons to speak of "functional equivalence" rather than "dynamic equivalence," there is an important scientific basis for the concept of dynamic equivalence. This can be readily seen from an examination of the following standard model of translation:

$$S_1 - M_1 - R_1 - R_1S_2 - M_2 - R_2$$

The symbols S, M, and R represent the source, message, and receptors respectively, while the subscript 1 marks the initial communication, the combined SR is the translator, and the subscript 2 marks the translating of the message and its reception by the audience. But these are by no means the only factors in interlingual communication. One must also reckon with the settings of the original communication and of the translation, the intent and purpose of the author and of the translator, matters of noise (both physical and psychological) which may influence the transmission and reception of the message, the kinds of receptors of the original and translated messages, and the differences of culture and language which may significantly alter the comprehension of and appreciation for the text.

With so many factors involved in interlingual communication there is no way to arrive at a precise definition of what an ideal equivalent might be, but it is possible to describe a maximal and minimal level of equivalence. The maximal level, though never realized in actual performance, would be one in which the receptors of the translated text could respond to it with comprehension and appreciation in essentially the same manner and to the same degree as the original receptors of the message. This maximal level of equivalence can never be attained since language usage and cultural experience are never that close.

The minimal level of equivalence would be one in which receptors of the translated text would be able to understand and appreciate it to the point of being able to comprehend how the original receptors must have understood and appreciated the message. Most good translations lie somewhere between the maximal and minimal level of equivalence.

The dynamic aspect of equivalence exists in the differences and similarities of the respective languages and cultures. The greater the similarities in language and culture the greater the degree of comprehension and appreciation, and conversely the greater the differences in language and culture the greater the difficulties in comprehension and appreciation. In all cases one must measure both the designative and associative meanings, not merely in terms of lexical and syntactic features but also in terms of the total rhetorical impact and the complete communication event.

Despite the relatively wide acceptance of the principle of dynamic equivalence, there are a number of reasons to describe precisely the same principles in terms of "functional equivalence." Unfortunately, some persons have misunderstood the significance of the term "dynamic" and have thought that if a translation carries a great deal of impact, it is justifiably regarded as dynamic and therefore acceptable. But impact and dynamic equivalence are two quite different matters. What is crucial is the degree to which the original and the translated texts are able to perform essentially the same functions. Equivalence of meaning can only be stated in terms of performing similar functions.

Since the languages do not differ significantly in what they can communicate but in how they do so, the test of adequacy in translating depends upon the degree to which the translated text performs essentially similar functions. In some languages the type of repetition which occurs in Hebrew liturgical poetry appears to be nothing more than boring tautology, and the elaborate periodic sentences of traditional academic German are regarded by many as ways to conceal clarity of thought. Because of wide differences in culture it is often necessary to render culture-specific figurative expressions by means of nonfigurative words or phrases. If, however, too many such shifts from figurative to nonfigurative expressions occur, then it may be necessary to introduce other figurative expressions so that the overall function of the text can be made at least somewhat equivalent.

A further problem is involved in the use of the term "equivalence." In mathematics "equivalence" implies complete identity of sum or proportion. In speaking of language such a meaning is quite impossible, since there are no two words in any two languages which are absolutely identical in meaning nor are there two languages in which rhetorical patterns have precisely the same functions. The term "equivalence" must, therefore, be understood in a broad sense of "having essentially the same function" although never possessing an identical function.

The implications of functional equivalence may be illustrated by examining nonlinguistic isomorphisms, as are so well illustrated by Hofstadter in his fascinating volume entitled *Goedel, Escher, and Bach: An Eternal*

Golden Braid. The physical forms of the acoustic waves in the vocal mechanism, through the air, on the ear drum, in the bones of the ear, through the liquid of the ear, against the cilia of the cochlea, and in the electro-chemical transmission to the brain of the hearer are quite distinct, but since they preserve the shape, amplitude, and frequency despite the different mediums, there is no loss in information. In various respects the forms are quite different, but the functions are essentially the same. Similarly, in language a person may use English *one, two, three*, Spanish *uno, dos, tres*, German *eins, zwei, drei*, or Chinese *yi, er, san*, and though the sounds are significantly different, the series are isomorphic since they perform essen-tially the same functions within their respective language-culture systems.

The concept of functional equivalence in translating profits greatly from some of the important insights coming from sociosemiotics, the science of signs in human societies. In the first place, verbal signs are always defined by other signs within each code, i.e., a specific system of signs. This means that there is no universal system of signs or meanings to which all specific signs can be compared or evaluated.

In the second place, signs are not neatly circumscribed and delimited units in a mosaic of language and culture. Rather, they all have indefinite boundaries and are parts of fuzzy sets of meanings. As a result, the relations between meanings in two different languages are never one-to-one, and not even one-to-many, but many-to-many. There is never a perfect translation, and because languages are constantly changing, no translation can retain its value for very long.

In the third place, signs only have "meaning" in terms of the real, imagined, or language worlds which they represent. A word such as *rabbit* has meaning since it represents or stands for a particular animal. Similarly, the term *mermaid* has meaning since it represents a creature in an imagined world. And the word *noun* has meaning because it represents a class of signs in the language world. In fact, languages are special codes in that they have signs to represent parts of themselves.

In the fourth place, verbal signs may have quite distinct levels of meaning. A word such as *cross* may on one level represent the instrument on which criminals were executed in biblical times, but on a second level it may represent the death of Jesus, and on a third level it may represent Christendom, as in the phrase "the conflict between the Crescent and the Cross," a way of speaking about the wars between Muslims and Christians.

Discussions of translational equivalence usually focus upon lexical and syntactic correspondences, but increasingly people's attention has shifted to the more complex and crucial aspects of the discourse structure. In many languages it seems quite appropriate to begin a narrative in the middle and then to introduce flashbacks so as to provide the necessary background information. But in other languages such a procedure is both misleading and frustrating. In the Orient it is generally not the practice to state one's thesis first and then to back it up with reasons or evidence, but rather to state the reasons and to describe the circumstances with the hope that the receptors will readily come to the proper conclusions. Such a procedure seems to Orientals to be so much more polite and considerate. In Latin America it is the usual practice in business correspondence to begin and end letters with rather effusive expressions of praise and gratitude, but North Americans interpret such statements as flattery and deception. On the other hand the rather formal nature of business letters dictated by North American businessmen to business contacts in Latin America is frequently judged by Latin Americans as being impersonal, cold, and even arrogant. Culturally alert secretaries soon learn how to delete in their translations the misleading expressions from Latins and to add the necessary expressions of friendliness which North American businessmen seem never able to master.

Very serious problems have occurred in some translations of the Bible, because some translators insist that they should not employ a poetic format, even though the translation is poetic in terms of parallelisms and measured lines. Unfortunately, for many persons poetic format suggests immediately that the contents are only imaginary and hence not true. In fact, in one instance a reader expressed her great satisfaction that some of the Bible text looked like poetry and the rest did not. In this way she could know that the parts of the Bible in prose really came from God and that sections printed as poetry came only from some writer's own imagination.

Translators generally do not hesitate to make radical adjustments on the level of sounds since preserving rhyme and alliteration is almost impossible. They also seem to realize that frequent adjustments must also be made in dealing with figurative language and syntax. But adjustments on the level of discourse are generally avoided, since such modifications would seem to be an intrusion into the realm of an author's stylistic preferences and distinctiveness. Gradually, however, more and more translators are beginning to realize that nothing in a text is "untouchable" if one wishes to produce a true functional equivalent.

Translators should not make adjustments in a text in a random or haphazard fashion since there are a number of valid ways of evaluating the degrees of divergence between the source and receptor texts and of deciding what type of adjustments seem reasonable under the circumstances. The application of these principles differs considerably depending upon the discourse types, e.g., from lyric poetry to commercial contracts. One may, however, use with considerable justification the following principles when there are significant problems in rendering a text more or less literally:

1. When a literal or close translation is likely to result in serious misunderstanding because of difficulties in designative and/or associative meaning, it is legitimate (a) to alter the text, especially if the contents are figurative or nonfactive or (b) to translate more or less literally and to add a footnote to explain the meaning of the literal rendering.

2. When a literal or close translation makes no sense (except in instances in which the source text is purposely meaningless), it is legitimate (a) to alter the text so as to make sense of the contents if it appears from the document that the author genuinely wanted to make sense and if there seems to be a reasonable probability of determining the intended meaning or (b) to leave the translated text more or less meaningless, but to indicate in a footnote that the original text does not make sense.

3. When a literal or close translation would be so difficult that the readers for which the translation is being made would be likely to give up reading the text since it would require too much effort, it is legitimate to alter the level of language and to build in necessary redundancy unless the original purpose of the text was to impress readers with the esoteric nature of the contents or with the intellectual pretensions of the author.

4. When the setting in which a translation is to be used differs greatly from the setting and use of the original communication, it is legitimate to call attention to such matters in an introduction or footnote and to specify the types of alterations which have been introduced, e.g., deletions of footnotes, summaries of content, and background information with respect to the original use.

5. When a translation is made to accompany nonlinguistic codes, e.g., lip synchronization in television or the cinema, words set to music

(songs or recitatives in opera), and expressions adjusted to match different types of actions in a drama, it is not only legitimate but necessary to match the accompanying codes.

There are a number of practical implications in making the above types of adjustments so as to produce a satisfactory functional equivalent of the original text. First, the greater the cultural specialties between source and receptor cultures, the greater the number and types of adjustments, e.g., unusual artifacts (e.g., Papua New Guinea), a rather distinct ecology (the Sahel), and a highly evolved social structure with corresponding levels of honorific language (Thailand). Second, the greater the linguistic differences between the source and receptor languages, e.g., rhyme patterns, order of subordinate clauses, arrangements of narrative contents, and systems of measured lines in poetry, the greater the number and types of adjustments. Third, the more idiosyncratic the author's style, i.e., the distinctive manner in which he or she exploits the rhetorical resources of the source language, the greater the number of adjustments which must be introduced.

Many translation theorists and even some translators clamour for well-defined, rigid rules for producing functional or dynamic equivalents in a receptor or target language, but no such comprehensive rules will ever be forthcoming. Languages are entirely too creative a means of communication to ever be subjected to precise and absolute formulations of rules and regulations. Natural language is not mathematical language, and even mathematical language is no more the exceptionless entity which it was formerly considered to be. Chance and chaos loom constantly larger in all aspects of science, and in the interest of aesthetics, creativity constantly breaks all the traditional rules about what people can and should say. Verbal communication is essentially a "game" with its broad rules and its endless series of strategies constantly challenging the rules at the fuzzy boundaries of language. Language is not so much a rigid mosaic covering the experience of its speakers but a constantly changing mass of bubbles floating on a moving current.

References

Brower, Reuben A. ed. *On Translation*. Cambridge, Mass.: Harvard University Press, 1959.

Higham, T. T. *Oxford Book of Greek Verse in Translation: Introduction II*. Oxford: Oxford University Press, 1938.

Hofstadter, Douglas R. *Goedel, Escher, Bach: An Eternal Golden Braid*. New York: Basic Books, 1979.

Ladmiral, J.-R. *Traduire: théoremes pour la traduction*. Paris: Payot, 1979.

Nida, Eugene A. *Toward a Science of Translating*. Leiden: E. J. Brill, 1964.

────── and Charles R. Taber. *The Theory and Practice of Translation*. Leiden: E. J. Brill, 1969.

Snell-Hornby, Mary. *Translation Studies: An Integrated Approach*. Philadelphia and Amsterdam: John Benjamins, 1988.

Tatilon, Claude. *Traduire: pour une Pédagogie de la Traduction*. Toronto: Editions du GREF, 1986.

Wilss, Wolfram. *The Science of Translation: Problems and Methods*. Tübingen: Gunter Narr Verlag, 1982.

EQUIVALENT EFFECT

Equivalent Effect in Translation

Jin Di
Foreign Languages Institute
Tianjin, China

The principle of equivalent effect in translation means that the effect produced by a translation on its receptors (readers or listeners) should be as close as possible to the effect produced by the original work on *its* receptors.

This is the only way to be really faithful to the original text. The traditional idea of "faithfulness" usually means resemblance to the source-language text in formal (lexical, syntactic, or stylistic) or semantic elements. But owing to the complicated linguistic and cultural disparities between different languages, a formal or semantic similarity does not often coincide with proximity in meaning, even in very simple expressions. Nobody would translate the phrase 狗咬人 into "dog bite man," though each of the three English words seems to correspond to its counterpart in the original nicely and the structure seems to be identical with that of the original. It would be completely against the genius of the English language. For one thing, since English verbs in finite positions must be conjugated, the unconjugated "bite" produces an uncertainty of meaning unknown in the Chinese. But even "dog bites man" would not do, unless the talk were in hypothetical generalities (e.g., in a humorous discussion about "dog bites man" or "man bites dog"). Depending on the context, the translation would have to vary from case to case. As a warning, it could be "The dog bites." Spoken by the owner of a dog who has done such a thing, it might be "He bit someone." In both cases the translations deviate from the source-language text not only in formal but also in semantic elements, yet they carry the same messages in the English-speaking environment. The dropping of the object in the first example is required by the genius of the English language in such general statements, while the use of the personal pronoun in the second is natural with English-speaking people who love their dogs.

The concept of "effect" covers, in this definition, not only the aesthetic effect, but the whole message conveyed by the text and the way it is received. It refers to the overall impression a translation produces on the mind of the receptor, involving the spirit and the substance (including alleged and imagined facts, questions, commands, etc.) as well as the aesthetic effect.

The formation of an effect depends not only on the message delivered, but also on the mind which receives the message. Individual *responses* to messages may be unpredictable because they can be controlled by individual circumstances, but the way a message may be expected to be generally *understood* in a language community is predictable because it is in the nature of such a community that its members will share their linguistic peculiarities and cultural backgrounds. In order to produce a desirable effect on the receptor's mind, the translator has to be thoroughly acquainted with those peculiarities and backgrounds and be sensitive to the subtle changes which they may bring into the implications of the message. Then he or she must adjust the text of the translation in such a way as to produce the closest effect despite the linguistic and cultural disparities.

The principle of equivalent effect is applicable to all kinds of translation (commercial, scientific, legal, political, journalistic, etc.), since all translation involves linguistic and cultural adaptation, and every translator is obliged to convey the message in question, whatever its nature is, with the desired effect. But it is particularly important for literary translation, where the needs of a work of art often call for creative transformations. Not all creative transformations, however, are necessarily conducive to the desired effect. Only those which achieve it better than untransformed or less transformed versions are justifiable, as are many instances in David Hawkes's translation of the classic Chinese novel 《紅樓夢》. A good example is his handling of the lisping passage from Chapter 20 of that work:

The original text:

……湘雲走來，笑道："愛哥哥，林姐姐，你們天天一處玩，我好容易來了，也不理我理兒。"黛玉笑道："偏是咬舌子愛說話，連個'二'哥哥也叫不上來，只是'愛'哥哥'愛'哥哥的。回來趕圍棋兒，又該你鬧么'愛'三了。"……湘雲笑道："這一輩子我自然比不上你。我只保佑著明兒得一個咬舌兒林姐夫，時時刻刻你可聽'愛'呀'厄'的去！阿彌陀佛，那時才現在我眼裡呢！"

說的寶玉一笑，湘雲忙回身跑了。

Hawkes's English translation:

Just then Xiang-yun burst in on them and reproved them smilingly for abandoning her:

"Couthin Bao, Couthin Lin: you can thee each other every day. It's not often I get a chanthe to come here; yet now I have come, you both ignore me!"

Dai-yu burst out laughing:

"Lisping doesn't seem to make you any less talkative! Listen to you: 'Couthin!' 'Couthin!' Presently, when you're playing Racing Go, you'll be all 'thicktheth' and 'theventh'!"

…

"I shall never be a match for you as long as I live," Xiang-yun said to Dai-yu with a disarming smile. "All I can thay ith that I hope you marry a lithping huthband, tho that you have 'ithee-withee' 'ithee-withee' in your earth every minute of the day. Ah, Holy Name! I think I can thee that blethed day already before my eyeth!"

Bao-yu could not help laughing; but Xiang-yun had already turned and fled.

(David Hawkes [trans.], The Story of the Stone
[Penguin, 1973], Vol. 1, pp. 412–13.)

One seemingly important fact is altered in this translation: the phonemic fault of pronouncing the *er* syllable like *ai* (peculiar to speakers of a southern dialect in China) is replaced by a typical English lisping. Consequently the original words with those syllables are simply left out in the translation, where all English words with *s* sounds are pronounced with *th* sounds instead. Thanks to this basic change and the consequential alterations, the fun of the quibble and the characters of the two contending girls become fully accessible to English readers. This remarkable success is achieved despite some minor shortcomings in the passage, including a mistranslation about the sentence with the "blethed day".

Translational equivalence is a relative value. Hawkes's version can be regarded as an equivalent effect translation because no other versions could achieve a closer effect. Possible alternative versions include: (1) one retaining the Chinese *er/ai* pair by giving their sounds, with a footnote to explain their meanings, as was actually done by other translators; (2) a still more academic version with a technical term to define the speech defect accurately, explaining how different it is from a typical case of lisping in English. But those versions would neither convey the fun of the passage, nor show the characters of the protagonists. Both the spirit and the beauty of the passage would be lost.

The translator must also avoid overtransformation, which is apt to occur when he or she neglects the potential capability of the receptor to perceive unfamiliar ideas and images with the help of the context.

References

Jin, Di 金隄 . 《等效翻譯探索》 *(Exploring Equivalent Effect)*. Beijing: China Translation and Publishing Corporation 中國對外翻譯出版公司 , 1989.
———. "The Great Sage in Literary Translation." *Babel*, Vol. 35, No. 3 (1989).

ESSAYS

Translation of English Essays

Liu Bingshan
Department of Foreign Languages
Zhongshan University, Guangzhou, China

In 1907, Lin Shu 林紓 published his translation of Washington Irving's *The Sketch Book* 《拊掌錄》, which was modelled on 18th century English essayists. In 1911, the Commercial Press in Shanghai published a selection of Addison's and Steele's essays with Chinese notes, *Sir Roger De Coverley Papers* 《阿狄生文報捃華》. So we may say English essays were first introduced to China at the beginning of the present century. But it was only after the May Fourth Movement of 1919 and under the necessity of the development of the new vernacular literature that Chinese writers and scholars began to comment on, translate, select and annotate English essays in a big way. Zhou Zuoren's 周作人 short article "Belles Lettres" 〈美文〉, published in *Literary Supplement to the Morning Paper* 《北京晨報副刊》 (Peking, June 8, 1921), which mentions Addison, Lamb, Gissing and Chesterton, called on Chinese writers to learn something from English essayists in creating the modern Chinese prose. In 1923–1924, Zhou Zuoren rendered into Chinese two of Swift's essays, "A Modest Proposal" 〈育嬰芻議〉 and "Directions to Servants" 〈婢僕須知〉. His translation was very well done and full of flavour. In 1925, Lu Xun 魯迅 made a translation of two articles on English essays by the Japanese critic Kuriyagawa Hakuson 廚川白村, "Essay" and "Essay 與新聞雜誌", and published, in 1928, in his magazine *Rushing Torrents* 《奔流》 Chinese versions of essays by W. H. Hudson and L. P. Smith. The encouragement

and recommendation of the Zhou brothers, being two masters of modern
Chinese prose themselves, exercised a great influence on the men of letters
all over the country. At the turn of the twenties and thirties many were the
writers and scholars who enthusiastically wrote about and translated English essays. The most outstanding among them was Liang Yuchun 梁遇春
who published successively three books of selection and translation from
English essayists 《英國小品文選》, 《小品文選》 and 《小品文續選》,
which include writings of Steele, Addison, Goldsmith, Lamb, Hazlitt, Hunt,
Chesterton, Belloc, Lucas, Lynd, Gardiner and others. Liang Yuchun also
wrote a brilliant article on Charles Lamb entitled 〈查理斯・蘭姆評傳〉
and many familiar essays in the Lambian fashion, which earned him the
name "the Elia of China." From then on, English essays have always been
favourite reading for Chinese readers with higher culture, and, as Yu Dafu
郁達夫 wrote, their influence "became a potential force among our intellectuals, that will not disappear even after ten or twenty more years."

During the years of 1937–1949, when the austere struggles for national
salvation and for China's destiny were being carried on, the introduction
and translation of English essays were uninterrupted, though pushed
into a somewhat unobtrusive nook. Essays of Bacon, Addison, Goldsmith,
Lamb, Stevenson, Lynd and Beerbohm still found their way into the
classroom readings of English courses. It was also in these years that
two classics of English essays, Bacon's *Essays* 《培根論說文集》 and
George Gissing's *The Private Papers of Henry Ryecroft* 《四季隨筆》, were
done into Chinese, the former by Shui Tiantong 水天同 and the latter by Li
Jiye 李霽野.

Love of English essays continued after the founding of the People's
Republic of China. In the fifties, Lamb's "Dream Children: A Reverie" was
used as a text for the students of English in universities (徐燕謀:《大學
四年級英語》). In early sixties, selected essays from Bacon, Addison,
Goldsmith, Lamb, Hazlitt and V. Woolf were published with Chinese notes
and commentaries as outside readings (王佐良、李賦寧、周玨良主編:
《英美文學活頁文選》). In 1961, *World Literature* 《世界文學》, Beijing,
published Wang Zuoliang's 王佐良 translation of Bacon's "Of Studies"
〈談讀書〉, "Of Beauty" 〈談美〉 and "Of Great Place" 〈談高位〉. Only
when the Cultural Revolution broke out did English essays altogether
disappear, along with all other fine writings of the world.

The studies and translation of English essays revived with the new
period of reform and "openness". From 1979 to now, journals of foreign

literature like *World Literature* 《世界文學》 and *Foreign Literature* 《外國文學》 in Beijing, and *Foreign Literature and Art* 《外國文藝》 in Shanghai, magazines of prose like *Familiar Essays* 《隨筆》 in Guangzhou, *World of Prose* 《散文世界》 in Beijing, and *Prose* 《散文》 in Tianjin, and other literary periodicals have published English essays rendered into Chinese, including those of De Quincey, Lamb, Chesterton, A. C. Benson, Lynd and V. Woolf. With the flourishing of contemporary prose-writing in China, a need has been felt to draw on the experience of foreign essayists. Hence the publication of many collections of foreign essays, a considerable number of which are selections of English essays in Chinese translation, such as *Sixty British and American Prose-writers* 《英美散文六十家》, selected and translated by Gao Jian 高健, published by Shanxi People's Press 山西人民出版社, 1983; *A Selection of English Essays* 《英國散文選》, translated by Liu Bingshan 劉炳善, published by Shanghai Translation Press 上海譯文出版社, 1985–1986; *A Selection of Modern English Essays* 《現代英國散文選》, translated by Lan Renzhe 藍仁哲 and others, published by Chongqing Press 重慶出版社, 1986; *A Selection of 18th Century English Essays* 《英國十八世紀散文選》, translated by Zhang Guozuo 張國佐 and Huang Shaoxin 黃紹鑫, published by Hunan People's Press 湖南人民出版社; and *The Best Essays of English Romantics* 《英國浪漫派散文精華》, edited by Gu Zhengkun 辜正坤 and published by Beijing Writers Press 北京作家出版社. Shui Tiantong's 水天同 translation of Bacon's *Essays* 《培根論說文集》 appeared in a new edition by Beijing Commercial Press 北京商務印書館. *The Private Papers of Henry Ryecroft* has now two Chinese versions, one of which is a new edition of Li Jiye's 李霽野 translation as 《四季隨筆》, published by Shaanxi People's Press 陝西人民出版社, and the other a new rendering by Zheng Yitang 鄭翼棠 as 《四季隨筆》 and published by Hunan People's Press 湖南人民出版社. Other special collections of English essayists published in recent years include Ruskin's *Sesame and Lilies* 《芝麻與百合》, translated by Liu Kunzun 劉坤尊, published by Hunan People's Press 湖南人民出版社; De Quincey's *Confessions of an English Opium Eater* 《英國癮君子自白》, translated by Liu Zhongde 劉重德, published by Hunan People's Press 湖南人民出版社 and my translation of Lamb's *Essays of Elia* 《伊利亞隨筆選》, published by Joint Publishing Company in Beijing 北京三聯書店.

During the past eighty or ninety years, the translation of English essays has made significant headway, which has in turn provided models from abroad for modern and contemporary Chinese prose-writers. But, generally speaking, there is still much to be desired in the width and depth of the work in this field, which calls for greater attention and effort from our translators, scholars, editors and publishers.

The challenge which a translator of English essays is first of all confronted with is: How to attract the reader's attention? An essay is merely a piece of prose with neither the vivid stories of a novel to stir the reader's heart nor the metre and rhyme of a poem to please his ear. An essay is the author's monologue: he talks in a gossipy fashion, making a clean breast of himself and indulging in digressions, with no more restraint than a cloud in the sky or the flowing water of a stream. It is hard for a translator to turn such free discourse into another language without losing its charm and flavour. What should a translator do to secure the reader's appreciation?

Literary translation is a labour of love. A translator had better choose for a foundation of his work an author whom he loves or at least feels akin to, so that he can throw his own feeling into the work and grasp the author's thought and sentiment with his own heart and mind. Literary translation should be done like literary creation, because it is a process of the re-creation of some work of art. A good essay is a little masterpiece. After being translated, it should still be a fine piece of writing. So the translating of an English essay resembles to some degree a famous painting as being engraved by another artist. Though the work done is reproduction in nature, an engraver cannot regard it as a mere matter of technique. He has to go about his task as if he himself is carrying out an artistic creation, in accomplishing which he must gather his energies, muster his artistic talent, improve his work by elaborate touching and retouching until the result of his reproduction becomes such a fine work of art by itself that a spectator might mistake it for the original work engraved by the painter himself. A translator of literary works should work as an engraver of famous paintings does. I am of the opinion that a translator of essays should write some essays himself, so that he can apply his own experience of literary creation to his work of literary translation.

Since literary translation is a kind of artistic re-creation, it is clear that in translating English essays one cannot rely solely on dictionaries. Dictionaries and reference books of all sorts must be consulted, and consulted very carefully if need be. But after consulting them, one must beware of being fettered by the set definitions of words in them. It is advisable to adopt Lin Yutang's position of regarding the meaning of a whole sentence of the original as the basic unit and not to fall under the domination of isolated words, otherwise the translation would become a conglomeration of broken fragments and pleasant essay turn into something unreadable.

Essayists are often scholars who have read many rare books, ancient and modern, and seen much of the world in their life-times. Their writings are full of quotations and allusions which form obstacles for a translator. Lamb's essays, for example, are interspersed with allusions to classical, European and English literatures and histories, references to his kith and kin, anecdotes about many personages in the political, legal and commercial circles of England at the turn of the 18th and 19th centuries, as well as several hack writers and minor authors who were then active in the literary or journalistic world of London but have since been all relegated to oblivion. Most of the allusions cannot be found in ordinary books of reference, but one must clear up these problems before embarking on the translation of Lamb.

Above are some general remarks about translating English essays. There remain three important elements of English essays, i.e., personality, style and humour.

Personality is the soul of the essay. Montaigne's famous saying, "It is myself I paint," is the motto of every essayist. The secret of the charm of an essay lies in the author's personality which reveals itself "between the lines." "He (Lamb) tells all sorts of trifling things about himself so pleasantly because he can show his whole character by his gossip." (Liang Yuchun). In order to show the characteristics of the essayist's personality, a translator has to make himself familiar with the former's life, career and character. Lamb's essays are full of autobiographical elements, but he conceals them under the pseudonym of "Elia". He changes people's names and identities and shifts the times of events so as to blend fact with fiction, creating a complicated and confusing impression on the reader's mind. It is an inescapable prerequisite for a translator to distinguish between truth and artistic creation in *The Essays of Elia* and find Lamb's real personality by careful studies before doing anything else.

Every essayist is a stylist. Style is the free revelation of a writer's personality and temperament as developed under certain social, intellectual and cultural conditions and expressed through certain forms of language art. The translator of an essayist must first study, and then communicate in his translation, the latter's style. Of all the styles of English essayists, Lamb's is the queerest, which can be called the-moon-hidden-by-clouds sort of style 雲遮月式的風格 , if we may describe it by a Chinese idiom. He likes to cover up "the kernel of his writing" 文心 under a special shell of language, i.e., an imitation archaic style which blends the classical with the conversational manner of writing. It is, for a translator, a hard nut to crack. But only when one can break it through will he be able to enjoy the pleasure of reading the Elian essays and start on the happy labour of translating them. Needless to say, one cannot translate the essays written in such a fantastic style with ordinary colloquial Chinese. I have sprinkled a little classical Chinese in my version in order to produce some half-archaic and half-comical effects. I hope I have not profaned Lamb in the process. Another thing I have done is to repeatedly revise my translation of the first paragraph in each essay until I find Lamb's special tone of writing, which is the key-note of the whole essay.

The last but not the least important feature of English essays is humour. Chinese readers usually comprehend humour as some happy remark which hits the point or some witticism which makes one smile 談言微中，妙語 解頤 . But it has much more delicate meanings in it. Humour is one of the distinguishing features in the national character of the English people. It is also one of the striking characteristics of English essays. Whenever one reads English essays, one always feels it there. Moreover, the humour of each essayist carries with it his own tinge of character. So it is impossible to give humour an all-embracing definition. It is wise not to give it any. Lamb's humour is said to be inimitable. Then, how could a translator communicate it into another language? When I translated *The Essays of Elia*, I spent two and a half years on solving the riddle of Lamb's humour. I studied the many explanations of humour in general and the various analyses of Lamb's humour in particular. Finally I accepted the conclusion that Lamb's humour is a kind of "laughter in tears". Like other humorists, Lamb could tell a ridiculous story in the most solemn tone. He was also a master of puns and jokes. But at the core of his humour lies an honest, good soul, the "gentle-hearted Charles", pressed by domestic tragedy and wearied by daily drudgery "at the desk's dull wood", who struggled first to prevent himself from being crushed by mental illness and then to fulfill his responsibility to his unhappy family. So, in his essays laughter is mingled with tears and there is sadness underneath his humour. This kind of humour is not so difficult to comprehend for Chinese intellectuals who have gone through all sorts of hardships and sorrows. Based on this understanding of Lamb's humour, I managed to translate thirty-two essays of Elia. Needless to say, not every essayist's humour is "laughter in tears". We should make independent "qualitative analysis" in each case.

The great difficulty in translating English authors is the rendering of their puns. Up to now, there has never been an ideal way of dealing with them. But sometimes there may be coincidences. When I translated from *The Last Essays of Elia* the short piece "That Home is Home though it is never so Homely", the adjective "Homely" in the title, which quibbles with "Home", greatly embarrassed me. Of course, I could translate it as 寒傖 but then the effect of punning in the original would be lost. In my dilemma, a line of Tang poetry, 西望長安不見家(佳), which has been quoted by the famous Chinese writer Lao She 老舍 , flashed into my mind, and I translated the title into 〈家雖不佳仍是家〉, which can render the meaning correctly and at the same time happily communicate the quibbling of "Homely" with "Home". This "happy stroke", however, is an unexpected coincidence which a translator might meet with once in a while but cannot hope to obtain by conscientious effort.

References

Liu, Bingshan 劉炳善 . 〈英國散文與蘭姆隨筆翻譯瑣談〉 (How I Translated English Essays and *Essays of Elia*). 《中國翻譯》 (*Chinese Translators Journal*), No. 1 (1989).

Ma, Ji 馬驥 and Gan Yonglong 甘永龍 , annotated. 《阿狄生古文報捃華》 (*Sir Roger De Coverley Papers*). Shanghai: The Commercial Press 商務印書館 , 1911.

Yu, Dafu 郁達夫 . 《中國新文學大系：散文二集導言》 (Introduction to *A Serial Anthology of Chinese New Vernacular Literature, 1917–1926, Second Collection of Essays*). Beijing: Liang You Book Company, 1935.

Yu, Yuangui 俞元桂 , ed. 《中國現代散文理論：資料匯編》 (*Modern Chinese Prose Theories: A Collection of Reference Materials*). Guilin: Guangxi People's Press 廣西人民出版社 , 1984.

Zhou, Zuoren 周作人 , tr. 《冥土旅行》 (*A Trip to the Nether World*). Beijing: Beixin Book Company, 1927.

———. 《中國新文學大系：散文一集導言》 (Introduction to *A Serial Anthology to Chinese New Vernacular Literature, 1917–1926 — First Collection of Essays*). Beijing: Liang You Book Company, 1935.

EUROPEANIZED STRUCTURE

Europeanized Structure in English-Chinese Translation

Frederick Tsai
Honorary Fellow
Hong Kong Translation Society, Hong Kong

The source language of a translation seems reluctant to make its exit; it prefers to seek reincarnation in the target language. If it is English, it will prevail upon the translator to anglicize Chinese, if the target language is Chinese. Since China opened her door a century and a half ago, hundreds of European books, predominantly English, have been translated into Chinese, and Europeanized, or to be more accurate, anglicized, structure in translation has caused sweeping changes in Chinese. (There is some justification in the use of *Europeanized*, for English shares with other European languages some linguistic features non-existent in Chinese.)

Europeanization would not have been so much tolerated in China had the early translators or writers who read a European language not deemed it a reformation or even a revolution to introduce it to the Chinese language, thus making it, as they thought perhaps erroneously, more precise, more logical, and more in conformity with Western thinking. It should also be noted that classical Chinese, which is too well established in its usage to allow any foreign influence, was, in the early nineties, losing its hold on Chinese literati, and writing in the vernacular, which translators had taken up, was still in too early a stage of experiment for regular and extensive use, and therefore vulnerable to the sway of a foreign language. Besides, translators are naturally attracted by the gravity of the source language, especially a civilized one, and in the process of translation are apt to let it have its head, and at the same time want to win favour among their readers with novelties of expression.

Chinese translators firmly believe, not altogether without foundation, that Europeanized structure will in time be naturalized, crude though it might be when it first appears to Chinese readers. But when it becomes a vogue in which to indulge, we can hardly blame purists who condemn it for the corruption of Chinese. Europeanization can go too far, as we will see later.

Let us examine now what strikes us most as Europeanized structure in translation.

Connected vs. Disconnected Speech

A few words about the most fundamental difference between Chinese and European languages would not be out of place here. Chinese, in contrast with European languages, is a disconnected language, at least in appearance. Indeed, there are conjunctions, such as 因為 (because), 和 (and), 或 or 或者 (or), etc; and prepositions, such as 在 … 的上面 (on), 在 … 的下面 (under), 在 … 的裡面 (in), and so on; but they are not as necessary as in English. Very often words in a Chinese sentence are like beads on a plate without any string or chain to link them.

An English sentence like:

> It is a curious fact of which I can think of no satisfactory explanation, that enthusiasm for country life and love of natural scenery are strongest and most widely diffused precisely in those European countries which have the worst climate and where the search for the picturesque involves the greatest discomfort.

> (Aldous Huxley: *The Country*)

when translated into Chinese will lose almost all of its links like *which, of, that, for, and, in, where,* in their Chinese equivalents. It is a mistaken concept that they should be faithfully translated into Chinese as far as possible. In so doing, the translation will be in a tangle and even unintelligible. Understandably, it will be a difficult task to retain the original structure. A clever translator would rearrange the order of words, which can serve as invisible links, in such a way as to make the relation between words self-explanatory, and cut the long sentence into two or more sentences.

If, When

The equivalents of the conjunctions are not as much needed in Chinese for their grammatical functions as in English. Conditional clauses are very often left unmarked in Chinese, simple sequence being relied upon to suggest the logical connection. And the frequent appearance of 當 ... 的時侯 ... (when) in a piece of Chinese writing can be tiresome, although it is normal in English. The reason is simple; there is no need in Chinese to point out at what juncture something will happen or did happen. This is a link that should be done away with when the English language is translated into Chinese.

Similarly the use of the copula 是 , where it is not required in Chinese, is a sure mark of Europeanization. Thus, 他是聰明 (He is clever), grammatically faultless, sounds exotic to native ears. For although we say in Chinese "He is a clever man," we never say "He 'is' clever." We would say so only when we want to emphasize that he *is* clever, not dumb as you may think. There is no need to connect *he* and *clever*. We may say 他很聰明 ; here 很 (very), an adverb, may serve as a quasi copula, scarcely signifying *very*.

Definite and Indefinite Articles

Chinese, like Latin, requires no articles, definite or indefinite, to point to a noun. It is, therefore, both wasteful and ugly to pollute a piece of translation (or original writing in Chinese) with a plethora of the equivalents of both these articles. The curse is it is not wrong to use them, but idiom shuns their random use. Take 他是一個好人 (He is a good man). We may retain 個 , a classifier, but not 一 (one). In "He has the unusual capacity for making friends," the definite article *the* in its Chinese equivalent 那 or 那個 , is not required. Translators with blind faith in English grammar who do not guard against unnecessary words in Chinese always retain their equivalents.

Europeanization can be ridiculous. The translation of a longer sentence may contain more than one indefinite article to point to a single object. "She is pretty, clever, energetic, and a high-class lady" can be rendered in Chinese as 她是一個漂亮、聰明、精神飽滿的一個上流女子 . Even in original Chinese vernacular writing or talking, such repetition is not uncommon in China today.

Only when you have to add a large number of articles to point to the majority of nouns in translating a piece of undefiled Chinese writing into

English do you realize why such articles should be ignored when you translate English into Chinese.

Prefixes and Suffixes

The equivalents of many English prefixes and suffixes cannot be as freely used in translation. For instance, the equivalent of non- 非 , is a poor substitute in such words as non-conformist 非國教徒 , non-human 非人性 , or non-profit 非牟利 . Translators of such compounds have to work a little harder to find other ways to produce a more acceptable translation, 不信奉 國教的人 for non-conformist, for instance.

Likewise, the Chinese equivalent for -er, -or, -ist 者 , is archaic, but translators like to use it for convenience. Today only a few compounds like 帝國主義者 (imperialist), 讀者 (reader), 作者 (writer), have lingered in the Chinese language.

Quite often no such suffixes are required to show a trade or status in Chinese, like 裁縫 , that is, to cut (cloth) and stitch, therefore, a tailor.

Particular care must be taken in the use of 性 for -ness, -ty, -cy. The Chinese are especially averse to abstract nouns suffixed with 性 . Indifferency 中性 , legality 法律性 materiality 物質性 , etc., are all offensive, and political writers go a step further than translators by using 性 for nouns when no such prefixes could be found in its English equivalents. For instance, *zeal* can be translated with 積極性 (zealness? Of course we have *zealousness*.) Europeanization knows no bounds.

Excessive Use of Nouns

It is interesting to observe that while excessive use of nouns is censured in such an authoritative book as the Fowler brothers' *The King's English*, it is popular in China today among innovative writers, as a result of Europeanization. The Chinese language by its very genius rejects in particular the use of an abstract noun as the subject of a sentence. Up to now only a few like 失敗是成功之母 (Failure is the mother of success) are accepted in China. A literal translation of "Honesty is the best policy" is utterly a foreign saying. A good translator would find a different way to say it in Chinese. Since some modern Chinese writers are deeply engrossed in the use of nouns, translators have good reason to translate literally, thinking that they can impress their readers with claptrap by so doing. A sentence like "His absurdities horrify me" would grate on Chinese ears if rendered word-for-word.

Omission of Subjects

In Chinese the subject of a sentence can often be omitted, particularly if it is the same as that of the sentence preceding it. Julia Mills, in her diary, omits the pronoun "I" (Ch. XXXVIII, *David Copperfield*) which is somewhat peculiar in English style, but this happens to be the norm in the literary, and particularly epistolary, mode in Chinese. In general, not all Chinese sentences require a subject, and possessive pronouns are not always used either. Thus, "I am reading my book" when translated into Chinese will best become 讀書 (read book). There is nothing grammatically wrong if it is literally translated into Chinese, but it would sound silly. It is only legitimate when one answers an impertinent question by stressing that it is *I*, not someone else, who is reading *my* book, not someone else's or *your* book.

As the pronunciation of the Chinese characters for he, him, she, her, it, 他、她、牠 is the same *ta*, they are not as useful as their English counterparts. A simple sentence like "He likes her, but she doesn't like him" if translated literally into Chinese would be confusing when read aloud to a listener. Europeanized structure can be defective, if adopted without prudence.

Singular and Plural

There is no need to indicate whether a noun is in the singular or in the plural in Chinese. Influenced by the English grammar, Chinese writers, as well as translators, have begun to be over-observant of number. The character 們 signifies the plural. Thus, 我們 (we), 他（她）們 (they). But it is not always necessary to use it to indicate plurality. 律師 can be a lawyer or lawyers; similarly 童子軍 may be a boy scout or boy scouts. The addition of 們 to such nouns in the plural is not grammatically wrong, but sounds weird, because it is superfluous. An over-scrupulous and over-conscientious translator can out-English English by adding 們 to "latter" in his translating it into Chinese as 後者們 , if the second mentioned of two something is in the plural, little remembering that "latter" is an adjective.

Passive Voice

The passive voice is used in Chinese, but never as extensively as in English. Translators tend to translate English sentences in the passive voice into Chinese in the same voice, running the risk of making the translation awkward. It should be pointed out that many Chinese transitive verbs are also deceptively intransitive (cf. the English word *look*). For instance, 釋放 (release) can both be transitive and intransitive; so that we can say 警方釋放了嫌疑犯 (The police have released the suspect), and can also say 嫌疑犯釋放了 (The suspect has released, that is, been released). To add the Chinese character 被, a passive auxiliary, is redundant, a fact often overlooked by many translators who aspire to be accurate and faithful to the original. The unnecessary 被 makes the sentence unidiomatic and unChinese.

Possessive Case

There is no absolute need to use the possessive case in Chinese. 我家 (I home) is the usual way to express 我的家 (my home). It is not incorrect to say 我的家, but it is unnecessarily wordy. "My father and my mother" when translated into idiomatic Chinese will become 我父母 (I father mother). A literal translation of "my father and my mother," preferred particularly by those who want to translate every word in the source language whether it is required in the target language or not, represents one of the worst kinds of Europeanized structure.

Feminine You

Chinese is a gender-free language. Contact with European languages has initiated the use of not only the feminine pronoun of the third person 她 (she, her), but also of the *second* person 妳 (you). This is a step too far forward, never popular among more thoughtful translators and writers. When a movement is initiated one never knows where it will stop. (Incidentally, these two characters were not coined for the new occasions; they were old ones given new meanings.)

Punctuation Marks

Only two punctuation marks, the full stop and the comma, were used in Chinese before the revolution of 1911. Even these two were not systematically used in most ancient Chinese writings, and full stops often took the place of commas, or no marks whatsoever were used throughout a book. Thanks to translation of European books into Chinese, punctuation marks began to appear in Chinese, although it took some time before early Chinese writers became proficient in using them. Their universal use now makes reading much easier and has even in some measure changed the structure in Chinese writing. No aspect of Europeanization in Chinese deserves more of an accolade.

Conclusion

It is unbecoming to accuse Europeanization of having defiled or corrupted the Chinese language, and it is futile to try to avoid this linguistic tide. No one, not even the government, nor the most authoritative literary groups, can do anything to keep Chinese utterly pure. To the dismay and chagrin of purists and traditionalists, Europeanized structure will remain. To be fair, it has enriched and given new features to Chinese, although it has also made Chinese cumbersome, cacophonous, and sometimes ugly. We are not sure whether Gresham's law can apply to languages, namely, whether inferior changes will predominate over superior ones as some evidence have shown, but happily, we also find that the better sense of the majority has accounted for the disappearance of some of the most incongruous innovations. On the other hand, time irons out the jaggedness of alien expressions. What was peculiar thirty years ago may become native by frequent use, and may even be considered stale a couple of generations from now. We are certain that Chinese will for better or worse never be written or spoken as it was a century, or half a century, or even a decade ago. Trail-blazing translators and writers are both culprits and heroes.

FICTION

Translating Chinese Fiction:
The *Shui Hu Zhuan*

John Dent-Young
Department of English
The Chinese University of Hong Kong, Hong Kong

These remarks are based on our experience in producing an English version of the *Shui Hu Zhuan*. We start with a basic premise — that it is justifiable to try to render a work which is popular (in various senses) in the original by a text which also aims at being popular. Of course there is no formula for achieving popularity — or at least, none which is compatible with the aims of the translator — but this premise provides a criterion for some of the many choices that have to be made in translating.

The first and most important question to decide was style. I shall say more about this later, but in general terms what we decided to aim at was a straightforward style without fustian, but with a slight touch of archaism at times — for example in the court scenes at the beginning, in people's elaborate exchanges of courtesy, or occasionally for purposes of irony. For the basic narrative we use very simple syntax — no Walter Scott, for example — but play around with word order a good deal, and use participles and relative clauses to speed up the routine patches (rather as a journalist does to condense information). We try to vary sentence length a good deal however, and to shape each individual incident in order to maximize its interest.

We have tried also to characterize our narrator, by allowing him a slightly more high-flown style in descriptive or sentimental moments. Just occasionally we cut something when the original has it repeated verbatim in adjacent sentences, but where possible we deal with repetition by means of what is usually referred to in English as elegant variation. This is of course used by critics of style as a term of abuse, but if challenged we would pass the blame to our slightly naive narrator, whose presence throughout the novel we feel quite strongly.

Much the same can be said of the verse passages, mostly either jingles or pretentious description. We have retained them because we feel they help to establish the sense of narrator and audience. We make no excuses for dealing with them very freely; we imagine that readers will skip them anyway, but we want them to be noticed as a characteristic of the text. At the same time we have sometimes tried to vary the verse according to the mood of the narrative where it occurs. This may seem contradictory, but we want the verse at the very least not to destroy the mood created in the narrative; in fact if possible we would like it to reflect a sense of the narrator's own interest or excitement in the things he is describing. In the case of the chapter headings and songs that occur as integral parts of the text (i.e. when a character comes on stage singing them) we have sometimes made major changes to the wording, in the interests of rhyme or rhythm, while maintaining a relevant sense.

Verbal abuse plays a big part in the novel and we tried to make this both realistic and comic but not absurd (avoiding for example expressions like "filthy beast!" which belongs more in the vocabulary of children, or "wretched varlet!" which belongs in no one's vocabulary). We also make use of irony and understatement, which often seems the best way in English to convey the pithiness of Chinese.

I shall now try to deal in more detail with the problem of translating fiction, and I shall attempt to put some order into my ideas by supposing that there are three aspects which it will be profitable to examine:

1. cultural and social background.
2. psychology and motivation.
3. literary and linguistic conventions.

These are overlapping categories and I am using them only as signposts to indicate general areas of concern within the pragmatics of translation.

Ultimately the translator's problem can be described as a single, essentially stylistic one: how to create a text which works for the English reader, and which parallels at least some important qualities of the original.

Cultural and Social Background

These problems are the most straightforward and familiar, and at the same time perhaps the most intractable. Inevitably in translation there are terms which are problematic because they refer to objects or systems that are not present in the culture of the target language. Typical problems in the *Shui Hu* are terms connected with government and administration, with professions, domestic life, the natural environment and so on.

Any attempt to solve such problems is a compromise. In many cases the most accurate method might be to transliterate the original word or use some esoteric English term and provide explanatory notes, but our basic principle rules that out: notes place a barrier between the reader and the text, a barrier, moreover, which did not exist for reader of the original. For some items the problem may be that relatively close English parallels exist, but only in some era long past, so that the terms are no longer familiar to modern readers. The paraphernalia of fighting, for example, can be paralleled in mediaeval or Renaissance Europe, but distinctions between, say, halberds and guisarmes, will mean nothing to most contemporary readers. Jacques Dars in his French translation uses many old French words which he explains in a glossary but again, our principle seem to rule this out. In some cases, however, it may be an advantage to use terms which are no longer familiar, because the reader will not be sensitive to anachronisms like the co-existence of weapons from different periods.

A related problem is that a term may be still fairly well known in English but so tied to a particular historical period that it can only be used comfortably if one is prepared to transpose the whole work to that period. We have rejected the word "vassal", for instance, a fairly good equivalent of 莊客 , because it has mediaeval connotations which would require us to mediaevalize more of the setting — something we wanted to avoid because of its distancing effect. The distinction is somewhat arbitrary, but it seemed to us that a character who speaks with a relatively modern voice can wield a staff or a pike, but cannot comfortably be served by "vassals". Our solution has been to translate 莊客 variously as *farmers, peasants, servants, members of the household* or *the rest*. In other cases the problem is with an English word which drags in irrelevant or sometimes absurd modern connotations: Gao Qiu's "football", for example, seems a potential danger, though in the context it probably explains itself sufficiently.

Two general points seem to me important. Firstly, and obviously, there is no such thing as a "correct" translation for any of these problematic terms. You can never say that X in the original means Y in the target language (though it is surprising how often people do approach a translated text in this way). If any notion of "correctness" is valid at all, it has to be the idea of "correctness" within the context of a specific translation: any given term must bear the right meaning and implications relative to all the other terms that appear in the translation. Secondly, what the translator ideally needs is a heightened awareness of the multiple implications in any text and then some ad hoc principles for deciding what is more important, and above all what is more important for the text he is *producing*. For example, the monstrous snake which frightens the Marshal on the Dragon-Tiger Mountain, is described as being "as big as a bucket". A bucket however is typically rather a small object, so we have changed this to "big as a barrel". Another example: the characters in *Shui Hu* all have nicknames, most of which have martial or heroic connotations. To take just one example: the robber chief Chen Da , "the Gorge-Leaping Tiger" (Shapiro, 1980). In our version we have changed this to "River-jumping Tiger". Undoubtedly gorge can translate 澗 . But "Gorge-Jumping" is harder to say and we feel that an essential part of a nickname is that it should be as easy to pronounce as possible. And in the context, is there any important difference between a gorge-jumping tiger and a river-jumping tiger?

While I'm on the subject of names, Chinese ones are a particularly difficult problem because English readers find them all confusingly similar. In some cases one can get round this with a liberal use of titles, including military ranks, or nicknames. However, English is not very well supplied with titles. Some that do exist, like "Sir" as in Sir Francis Drake, seem more or less unusable because the combination of title, first name and family name is so specifically English. "Sir" with a family name alone, which sometimes occurs in translations from Chinese (e.g., Sir Chang) merely sounds illiterate (though in contemporary Hong Kong Sir + initials seems to have become accepted). On the other hand some "incorrect" usages may be useful to characterize uneducated speakers: the servants can address a monk as "Reverend", but their master should not do so. When names are used, there is a problem about whether to transliterate or translate. I am never too happy with "Golden Lotus" type names because it is alien to the English system for names to have meanings that have not been erased by conventional use. The un-English Adj+N combination seems inevitably to draw attention to a name's meaning. On the other hand I think one has to bear in mind the relation of the story-teller to his characters. There seems to be a certain point in referring to Lu Zhishen as Profound Wisdom when he is behaving in a particularly unenlightened and disreputable manner. When a name recurs often I think a combination of transliteration and translation may be best.

Social and interpersonal forms connected with systems of etiquette, forms of address and reference to self, markers of politeness and so on, are particularly crucial in Chinese-to-English translation. Here I believe one has to assume that some basic universals of social relations exist, for example the varying requirements of politeness and intimacy, but that they are realized differently in different languages or cultures. I think Chinese speaker's-humility must normally be translated into English markers of politeness, often in the form of indirection or formality. However, it is not only a matter of differing realizations. In some cases politeness may be realized in both languages by relatively similar forms (as for example in expressed reluctance to accept a gift) but the lengths to which the "politeness" is taken or the situations in which it occurs may differ. And one has to remember that the deliberately excessive or inappropriate use of conventional forms may be meaningful as a way of marking criticism or rejection by the speaker. Translation of politeness (or rudeness, for that matter) therefore requires special attention to situational factors in the context.

These considerations lead us into the next section. But before we move on, there is one more type of problem that needs mentioning: regional variation and other types of variation in the target language. For example, the word county means something different, and has I think different connotations, in American English and British English. The terms *prefect* and *prefecture* probably mean much the same to both British and American readers, but have a distancing effect because of their foreignness. There is quite a range of administrative terms connected with the British colonial experience, but some of these may be unfamiliar to American readers or even to younger British ones. This is not to say that such terms cannot be appropriated: their unfamiliarity may be useful. But it is an element that has to be borne in mind.

Psychology and Motivation

If a novel is to work it must represent an internally consistent world. Everything should be explainable in terms of this world, and the reader should not be confronted with actions or speeches which are inexplicable. It is after all a basic assumption of all but the most wilfully experimental types of fiction that characters are motivated. This is not to say that the characters' motives must necessarily be transparent. They may speak or behave in ways which strike the reader as strange: one of the purposes of reading foreign novels (or perhaps any novel) is to gain an insight into other people's worlds and it would be disappointing if they contained only what is completely familiar and everyday. But there has to be a basic assumption of something universal both in the behaviour of the characters and in the technique of the writer. The things they say and do (both the characters and the writer) have to make sense.

A work as distanced historically and culturally from the contemporary English reader as the *Shui Hu* naturally contains some puzzles, but I believe the translator's job is to provide explanations, i.e. to translate in a way that reveals the motives behind what is said and done in the story. This does not mean that the translated version should be more explicit, but that care should be taken to ensure that it conveys relevant rather than irrelevant implications. A fine line also needs to be drawn between this and interpretation. It is not the translator's job to smooth out genuine ambiguities in the original or to provide an interpretation of the work, but I think he probably has to work with an interpretation in the back of his mind. One must not attempt, for example, to make the violence of the *Shui Hu* disappear, however distasteful some of it may be to the Western reader. But it does seem to me appropriate to aim at presenting it as much as possible in a Rabelaisian context, as a slightly humorous exaggeration, rather than as a purely heroic ideal. Of course all these remarks on making things understandable for the reader presuppose that the writer has done his job properly and not produced a work which is flawed with inconsistencies or sensationalism. In translating a classic I think one must start from the assumption that it makes valuable sense.

Such considerations, combined with the kind of facts about language use which have been studied intensively in pragmatics, sanction a considerable degree of license with regard to the actual words of the original. Fiction shows language very much in action, often in dialogue and in describing sequences of events that are causally connected. As in ordinary speech, many of the meanings and many of the connections are not explicit, and one must search for the English linguistic forms which provide equivalent implied meanings while not suggesting any which are irrelevant.

I shall try to give a few examples, though it is difficult to exemplify a process which is more or less continuous in the business of translating, and not necessarily conscious. It is also rather frustrating that any individual case I pick on by itself seems trivial. I am convinced however that the effect of the sum of such cases, which occur on every page, is far from trivial.

In Chapter 5 Lu Zhishen arrives at Peach-blossom Hall and receives a mixed reception because of something unpleasant which is due to happen there in the evening. The servants threaten him, but the master when he appears apologizes and treats him with great respect. Guest and host exchange civilities in the usual fashion. Zhishen now becomes even more curious to know what his host is so worried about, and inquires: 敢問貴莊今 夜有甚事？ In our version this is "Forgive me for asking, but ..." We assume that this first inquiry is polite. If the question is translated as "Would you mind telling me what is going on here?" (Shapiro, 1980) it sounds not polite but irritable. Zhishen then assumes that the old man's anxiety is caused by his unexpected arrival and request for lodging, so he says he is going to pay. The old man replies that he always gives alms to monks and one more makes no difference. This reply of his begins, 師父聽說 literally, as Shapiro has it, "Hear me ..." (p. 84). However, this sounds like the opening of a plea, whereas one expects him to be indignantly rejecting the idea that he needs to be paid for his hospitality, so we prefer: "I can assure you ...". A little later Zhishen offers to wait for the robber in the bridal chamber and "persuade" him, by reasoning, to give up the idea of forcibly marrying the old man's daughter. The old man accepts this proposal somewhat doubtfully and warns Zhishen not to pluck the tiger's whiskers. Zhishen replies 不是性命？ If one interprets that as "I want to live too, don't I ?" (Shapiro) it sounds unheroic, which is not in character. Dars has "Do you think I'm afraid to die?" ("Croyez-vous donc que nous ayons peur de la mort?") which is theoretically quite different in meaning, but also makes it sound as if Zhishen lacks confidence. We have translated it as "I can take care of myself", in order to remove any idea that Zhishen even contemplates losing.

This example may seem insignificant, but in fact the episode is carefully shaped and the dialogue has important effects. For the reader Zhishen's bravado is contrasted with the old man's fear of the robbers, but on the surface both are engaged in social behaviour which involves a good deal of concealment. The old man is at first too polite to involve his guest, supposedly a holy man, in his own troubles. The dramatic irony is that we know Zhishen is not the unworldly monk the old man takes him for. More precisely we know what he is: just the sort of person who will be able to solve the old man's problem with a few well-aimed blows. The irony continues: we must surely be suspicious of Zhishen's suggestion that he will "reason" the robber out of his plan. Whether or not you regard this irony and these contrasts as humorous (we do), they are of the essence of effective story-telling and should not be lost. The gap between words and intentions is an essential part of the scene and the reader's chief pleasure is in what he can read into it.

Here is an example of something we find a problem. During the jousting in Chapter 13, Yang Zhi has just defeated his opponent with the lance; a contest with bow and arrow is about to begin. Before starting, Yang Zhi speaks to the governor. He points out that arrows can be fatal, and asks for instructions, and the governor replies. In Dars' version the exchange is as follows:

> "Votre Grâce, s'il faut maintenant décocher des
> flèches, les traits ne connaissent ni ami ni
> ennemi, et il y a risque de blessure!
> Veuille Votre Grâce faire savoir Ses instructions!"
> "Est-ce que les soldats qui se battent doivent
> se soucier de possibles blessures? Que chacun montre
> ce qu'il sait faire! Une raillonade, même mortelle,
> ne saurait être prise en considération!"

In Shapiro this is:

> "Excellency, an arrow in flight knows no mercy. It can cause a grievous wound. Please issue your instructions."
> "When warriors fight, who thinks of wounds? Even if death results, there will be no consequences."

The problem here is to decide on the illocutionary force of the governor's reply: is he issuing a rebuke, making a promise, or simply philosophizing? A rhetorical question sounds like a rebuke, as if he is accusing Yang Zhi of cowardice, but in view of the fact that the governor himself has organized the contest to provide a pretext for promoting Yang Zhi, whom he seems to recognize as a hero, it is unlikely that he would interpret Yang Zhi's speech this way. Most probably therefore he wants to imply that Yang Zhi will not be blamed if he kills his opponent. This is perhaps what the second sentence of Shapiro's version is meant to imply, but the disconnectedness between the two sentences makes it difficult to interpret. We have tried to retain ambiguity while eliminating irrelevance with:

> "Your Excellency, when arrows fly, it's a serious business and someone may get hurt. I request your instructions."
> The Governor said: "When soldiers compete, they should not take wounds into account. Think not of death but only of doing your best."

What we wanted was to avoid any suggestion that the governor is rebuking Yang Zhi and to leave his words open to the interpretation that he is covertly reassuring Yang Zhi about the consequences, while ostensibly pontificating about a soldier's honour.

I hope to have shown with these examples the kind of problem which I think the translator of fiction ought to address. In particular I believe it is a responsibility to try to remove non sequiturs. Attention to bad joins, badly connected sentences, can often reveal mistranslations.

Clichés are particularly dangerous in this respect. Often a cliché seems to be an exact translation of the original, but it has treacherous connotations. There is an example in Shapiro's version, page 139, when the prisoner Lin Chong, who is suffering extremely because he has been beaten, had his feet scalded in boiling water by one of the guards, and been forced to march a long distance, says "My feet are killing me." The idiom suggests someone on a shopping expedition, rather than a man who has been severely beaten and is about to be victim of an assassination attempt.

Literary and Linguistic Conventions

A text of any kind is a highly artificial product, shaped by conventions as well as the demands of an audience. When translating, one has to decide what to do about conventional aspects: whether to retain them more or less intact or whether to render them by different conventions of the target audience.

In any case the final result of translating a work of fiction must be a text which has the same kind of logic in narrative as I have argued for in the dialogue and characterization. What this principally means is that each sentence should be motivated from the point of view of the text: that is to say, it must connect meaningfully with what went before and what follows.

In one particular aspect there is an important difference between Chinese and English texts. Chinese tolerates a degree of repetition which is not acceptable to the English reader. This is especially serious with the *Shui Hu* where routine narrative elements recur endlessly, where characters exhaustively recapitulate their experiences to each other, and where whole episodes mirror preceding ones with different heroes. We felt it essential therefore to exploit to the full the various cohesive devices of English (anaphora, substitution, etc.) and to vary sentence structure and sentence length wherever possible. In doing so we found it natural to distinguish between repetitive routines which could often be dealt with through subordination, and the meaningful episodes which needed to be shaped climactically. This part of the translation task, which we had regarded with misgivings, turned out to be in some ways the most challenging and rewarding.

We may have laid ourselves open to an accusation of putting into our translation a variety which is not in the original. But I believe that this difference is a *conventional* difference and that it is justifiable to alter such conventional aspects in pursuit of our primary aim of producing a readable text. If one had to argue the point, one would say that a convention is transparent to those for whom it is a convention, but is obtrusive to those for whom it is not.

On the other hand, this principle cannot be applied blindly. One might argue that the continual references to eating and drinking are conventional, and undoubtedly tedious for the English reader. To leave these out, however, would be to obscure an important cultural point. In general we have tried to do nothing to obscure the original narrator's sense of what is interesting to his audience. This is, incidentally, another reason for including at least some of the verse passages of the longer versions. However repetitive the descriptions of temples, mountains, cosy country inns, the clothes people wear and the courtesies they show to each other when they meet, they reveal something of the interests and mentality of the society which gave birth to the novel. But what we have tried to do, as I said above, is reduce the monotony by stylistic means.

A similar point can be made about viewpoint. Early fiction in general, not just Chinese, is less careful about consistency of viewpoint than modern fiction. But for the modern reader it is important that a character should not, for example, think his thoughts in language which is too formal or too complicated — on the whole the modern reader/writer assumes that people think in the language of everyday speech. It would be wrong, however, to suppose that viewpoint is a modern discovery. Interestingly enough, viewpoint is sometimes more literally identified in the *Shui Hu* than it normally is in English: a scene is commonly introduced with a reference to somebody *seeing* it. We have reduced this explicitness, often omitting mention of the observer when it is obvious who he is. But we have tried to retain a certain naivety of tone in the narration as a reminder of the oral tradition which is still so visible in the Chinese text.

For the same sort of reasons as above, we felt it necessary to give as much variety as possible to the speech of different characters, to characterize all official proclamations and to vary the tone of the narrative according to the scene it describes: for example, in the opening passage which deals with the emperor and his court we tried to give a suggestion of eighteenth century formality. We have tried to pick up this elegance and formality elsewhere from time to time, whilst keeping the language in all more active parts of the story straightforward and modern so that it will be easier to read. It is a convention of modern English that different characters speak with different voices.

Another point about style concerns the translation of figurative language. There is not a great deal in the *Shui Hu* and it seems a pity to lose what there is. On occasions we have deliberately not followed the principle of translating the intention rather than the words. That is to say, we have tried to stick closely to the words. For example, in Chapter 1, when the Taoists are describing to the Marshal the great holiness of the Heavenly Master and the impossibility of getting him to descend from his mountain peak, they say 蹤跡不定, in our version "his footsteps are not fixed". Shapiro has "Nobody knows exactly where he is". This undoubtedly captures the Taoists' meaning; but they are Taoists, and the Master's powers are miraculous, and much of the effectiveness of this episode lies in the Marshal's increasing frustration and bewilderment as he tries to deliver the Emperor's edict to the elusive Master. We prefer to allow the Taoists a more mystic way of expressing themselves, and believe that the reader can grasp the intention from the contextual effects.

Quite an important principle is at stake here. Translating a work of fiction into English requires attention to the contemporary English literary climate. At present there are various factors in English-speaking literary culture that encourage tolerance for unconventional uses of language, from the experimentation of modernism to the success in recent years of writers from non-English-speaking cultures making some use of local dialects, and the current popularity of fantasy or science fiction novels. I think therefore that some element of unconventional or "exotic" language is needed to render a world which is undoubtedly distanced in time and place. Otherwise one commits the kind of absurdity that Ursula Leguin ridicules in her collection of essays on the language of fantasy novels, *Language of the Night*. Ultimately, as I said at the outset, the problem of translating fiction is a problem of style. What one must aim for is a kind of consistency. Only consistency here is a relative affair, not an absolute. Fiction is illusion and one is tempted to say that translated fiction is a double illusion. That is not quite true, however. It is better to say that a translator is likely to be more calculating and conscious of the illusion because he must constantly consider what he can and cannot get away with. Complete historical or stylistic consistency is not possible, nor is it necessary. Writers may suggest, for example, non-standard forms of speech to characterize speakers, but they do not render dialect with accurate detail or consistently, because the added burden for the reader would outweigh the advantages. Instead they selectively use a limited number of deviant forms and allow the reader's imagination to do the rest. The translator, however, must be on the alert for linguistic choices which might betray the illusion. At one point, for example, we found something in the Chinese which might have been rendered by: "If ..., then I'm a Dutchman!", but we decided this mixture of nationalities would be as absurd as a badly mixed metaphor.

As for the audience we envisaged for this translation, we believe that the *Shui Hu* is interesting enough to attract a variety of readers in English, but we particularly had in mind readers who would value completeness and would like to be assured that the version they are reading is reasonably close to the original and can tell them something about the culture from which it sprang. We assumed, since this is such a long work, that readers will be prepared to skip, but we wanted there not to be passages that are so dead they have to be skipped. And finally, any emphases or distortions there may be in our version are the result of trying to make it accessible to contemporary English readers. The literary translator must be involved in communicating his or her pleasure in the work. This is particularly so with classics, which, if worthy of the name, are more alive and communicate more directly with the reader than the many writings of critics which have accumulated around them.

References

Buck, Pearl S., tr. *All Men are Brothers*. London: Methuen, 1937.

Dars, Jacques, tr. *Au bord de l'eau*. Paris: Gallimard, 1978.

Dent-Young, John and Alex, tr. "The Marshes of Mount Liang: Excerpts." *Renditions*, No. 40 (1993), pp. 32–60.

Jackson, J. H., tr. *Water Margin*, edited by Fang Lo-tien. Shanghai: The Commercial Press, 1937.

Leguin, Ursula K. *The Language of the Night*. New York: Berkeley, 1982.

Shapiro, Sidney, tr. *Outlaws of the Marsh*. Beijing: Foreign Languages Press, 1980.

English Fiction

Frederick Tsai
Honorary Fellow
Hong Kong Translation Society, Hong Kong

If someone asks "Is it possible to translate English novels into Chinese?" the answer is "Yes," but the translation may not agree with the name, though it may be readable and enjoyable. Even the best translator cannot make of it what it ought to be, for the difficulties are of great variety and some are insuperable.

Dialogue on the lowest level is the highest hurdle. While the use of two or three negatives is now a sign of poor education, it is not a solecism committed by Chinese illiterates. As to provincial accents, Chinese may be guilty on that score, but they can never be as offensive as their counterparts in England. Very important persons from various provinces may try hard to speak Mandarin, the standard spoken Chinese language, but few, except those who are born in Beijing, or are gifted linguists, can be successful; people respect them nonetheless. Chinese never drop their h's, even if some of them mix l's with n's. Thus, the uncommonly picturesque speech of a Yarmouth fisherman, Daniel Peggotty, in Charles Dicken's *David Copperfield*, makes adequate translation absolutely impossible. For in China, even the most unlearned speak with few grammatical mistakes. Not that they all have good grammar; the truth is the Chinese grammar is much simpler. There is no inflexion of nouns (no gender, no cases), verbs (no voices, moods, tenses, aspects, numbers, and person), adjectives and adverbs (no degree).

A Chinese coolie may not be able to use literary and elegant words and phrases, and quote the classics or famous authors, but his speech level is different from that of an English unskilled laborer. He never says anything like "I ain't get no call to go," "me pencil," "He growed ...," "You was ...," "He don't want them books," and so forth. In almost all Chinese novels, classical and modern, the speech of all kinds of characters is never too conspicuously different. Anyone who translates Peggotty's speech can only compromise, for he is unable to do a satisfactory job.

There are other difficulties. The comprehension of English is one. The person who translates an English novel into Chinese is generally a Chinese who can write Chinese well. Certainly he can have a library of reference books, the largest of dictionaries, encyclopaedias, various concordances, and what not, but these can never be quite enough. They are helpful and indeed indispensable, but they are not prepared for his particular needs. Even notes especially compiled for a particular novel, like *David Copperfield*, cannot provide him with *all* the information he wants, for the simple reason that what may be plain to an educated Englishman is beyond his comprehension. He can only consult a native if he is fortunate enough to know one. But a highly educated native may not be infallible. Unless he or she is a professor of English literature, there are difficulties natives may not be able to help a foreigner comprehend. Research can be formidable and inexhaustible. A translator has often to go so far as to contact English professionals, consuls, merchants, scholars of various disciplines, on knotty points. He may still be open to error, because what looks to the translator innocent of any ambiguity may mean something different from what he thought. Further, annotators may omit notes that should be furnished for the uninitiated. In Chapter XLV of *David Copperfield* there is a phrase "put hair in papers" which can be puzzling if a foreigner is not told that in those days ladies used curl paper, instead of plastic hair-rollers, to twist their hair into curls.

Supposing that the translator's comprehension of English is perfect, he may still often face the difficulty of finding an equivalent fit for use. A theological term like *justification* has been translated by both Chinese Roman Catholic and Protestant churches, but their translations are still Greek to non-Christians, and the translator must give a lengthy explanation whatever translation he may choose to use. Now for a text book or an academic paper, it is quite in order to do so when the need arises, but a novel is different. It is to be enjoyed, to be read without a second's interruption. Frequent reference to extended notes, without which the reader is left in the dark, can be most annoying. A translator can only claim that in translating an English novel, he is also doing another important job, namely, that of familiarizing his readers with English (including European) culture and civilization. His notes will touch upon English history, geography, arts, music, stage, folklore, custom and manners, religion, aristocracy and various social strata, justice and judicial systems, famous battles, popular sports and games, economic structure, social and environmental conditions, personalities, Greek and Roman mythologies ... All of these may require elucidation. He can be proud with good reason because he not only entertains but also instructs his readers. If such notes are interesting readers will like them; if interrupting, readers will ignore them when they read the novel the second time. But after all, notes should be as scanty and brief as possible. A novelist may freely quote a famous poet like Shakespeare, directly or indirectly. The translator has the obligation of identifying the source of the quotation. Readers will enjoy it more if they know it. No translator is learned enough to trace all such quotations in a novel. He will rely on concordances, which, however, are not all-inclusive. Quotations can be disguised, and *only* those who have read the original and still remember its authorship can spot them. Writers may also misquote, and it is the translator's job to point that out. They may paraphrase a quotation or quote only in part, and the whole saying may be unintelligible without producing the original or the missing part of it.

In Chapter XXIII of *David Copperfield*, David mentions his aunt "being firmly persuaded that every house in London was going to be burnt down every night." This alludes to the great London fire of 1666, which lasted for five days and virtually destroyed the city. Such a casual statement requires a note. In Chapter XXXI of the same novel, Mrs Gummidge says within quotation marks that "As you have done it unto one of the least of these, you have done it unto me." This is familiar to every Christian, but may not be so to non-Christian Chinese. Readers should therefore be referred to Mt. 25:40. In Chapter XXXIII when David Copperfield says "I don't think I had any definite idea where Dora came from, or to what degree she was related to a higher order of beings," here Dickens is alluding to the nine classes of angels from the highest seraphim to the lowest. It calls for a note.

Any seemingly insignificant point can be important in translation. The ringing of the door bell may be performed either by button or by bell-rope, but the novelist may not say whether the ringer's hand is on the button or on the bell-rope. The translator's task is to find it out for himself.

A genius like Dickens could be faulty in his English. In Chapter XIX David Copperfield writes: "so I shook my head, as much as to say, I believe you!" This is bewildering. Did he mean "I *nodded* my head?"

A novel translated with ample annotation can never be the same as its original. It may still be enjoyable because the Chinese may be very good, but it may have lost some connotations and word-play in the source language, although it may have added other desirable qualities in the target language. Puns resist translation; a clever translator may produce a new pun, if he is lucky, in the target language, but one can only chance upon it, not expect it.

Notes in an annotated edition may occasionally leave one in doubt. For instance, in the World Class edition of *David Copperfield*, published by the Oxford University Press, a note in Chapter XXXII concerning an Irish giant, given by Nina Bergis, the editor, reads: "Charles Byrne (1761–83) whose skeleton, measuring eight foot four inches...." But in Dr Brewer's *Dictionary of Fables and Phrases*, under *Giants*, there is Murphy, who "was 8 ft. 10 in. in height. An Irish giant of the late 18th century...." This giant was six inches taller than Charles Byrne, and so we do not know which was the one Dickens spoke of. Since Dickens died in 1870, the same year Dr Brewer's dictionary appeared, could he have known the name of Murphy?

One difficulty confronts a translator from English into Chinese, that is, the transliteration of personal names. Chinese is not a phonetic language, nor does it use an alphabet; all Chinese characters, which are used for transliteration, have meanings. The transliteration of a foreigner's name can range from reverential to the most vilifying. In China, a person's name often shows what his breeding, social status, and profession are. What characters a translator chooses to represent the sounds of an Englishman's name calls for some learning as well as care. In Chinese as in English, masculine and feminine names are distinct. When a baby is born, its parents usually ask a scholar to give it a good name. So transliteration of personal names becomes a task. Chinese novelists often reveal the characteristics of their characters by a subtle nomenclature. For characters in an English novel, the translator should have the ingenuity to hint at what kind of a character is by giving him or her a suitable name. There was an old tradition to use characters that would not bear any meaning with which to transliterate names of foreigners. The purpose was to let the readers know that they are foreigners. This device is clearly not popular among translators today.

Chinese may speak their own dialects, but when they transliterate, they must uniformly use Mandarin. This can be very difficult to those who are unable to speak it, because they are not necessarily familiar with a phonetic alphabet. Transliteration of English names can always show how excellent or inadequate a translator is.

Translation of an English novel into Chinese can enlarge the intellectual sphere and enrich the mental life of its Chinese readers. If the translator cannot make an exact facsimile of the original, he nevertheless may render a great service to his readers.

FINE ARTS

Translation of Chinese Texts on Calligraphy and Painting

Shih Hsio-yen
Department of Fine Arts
University of Hong Kong, Hong Kong

Chinese literature on the two fine arts (in Chinese cultural terms, which may include music as well) is so voluminous, increasing exponentially with the years/centuries, that translators have only been able to deal with works up to and including the Yuan dynasty adequately. Even this claim cannot be made for texts on calligraphy, but for painting alone. And, for painting, theoretical content has attracted more attention.

The Shanghai shuhua chubanshe 上海書畫出版社 is presently producing a new compilation of Chinese texts on painting in three volumes — one for texts proper, one for excerpts or references in other writings, and finally an index volume. However, it is projected that this will take ten years to complete. In the meantime, we must depend on editions of varying quality, some punctuated and with explanatory notes (most published by Shanghai wenwu chubanshe 上海文物出版社), and others without such aids and often containing multiple misprints. For the most useful available collections of texts on painting, see "Bibliography A" in Susan Bush and Hsio-yen Shih, comps. and eds., *Early Chinese Texts on Painting* (Cambridge, Mass. and London, England: Harvard University Press, 1985), p. 363. The Bush and Shih collection of excerpted translations includes in its "Bibliography B" (pp. 363–70) a guide to Chinese texts on painting which have been translated, and in "Bibliography C" (pp. 371–72) published translations.

Missing are translations submitted as part of postgraduate dissertations, of which American and French universities appear to have a number.

Among the many translators, special attention should be given to Professor Alexander Soper who was not only a pioneer in the field but also a scholar of high standards in research on classical Chinese terminology. That not all translations are equal in value becomes evident if one were simply to compare various versions of a single text — e.g., Zong Bing 宗炳 (373–443), *Introduction to Painting Landscape*〈畫山水序〉— in chronological order translated by Arthur Waley 1923, Osvald Sirén 1936, William Acker 1954, Shio Sakanishi 1957, Lin Yutang 林語堂 1967, Leon Hurvitz 1970 and Susan Bush 1983.

In recent years exhibition catalogues have become increasingly significant in their use of translated texts, particularly so for calligraphy, as well as for Ming and Qing texts on painting. While their translations will rarely be of complete writings, they often remain our only ones for specific works. The collaboration of Marilyn W. Fu and Fu Shen 傅申 has been especially fruitful, producing *Studies in Connoisseurship: Chinese Painting from the Arthur M. Sackler Collection*, 2nd rev. ed. (Princeton: The Art Museum, Princeton University, 1976), and *Traces of the Brush: Studies in Chinese Calligraphy* with other contributors (New Haven: Yale University Art Gallery, 1977). Ming texts on painting are generously cited in the Dong Qichang 董其昌 exhibition catalogue about to be published by the Nelson Gallery — Atkins Museum in Kansas City (April 1992). Zhou Ruxi 周汝熙 at the University of Arizona and the Phoenix Art Museum have made available many Qing texts on painting in the symposium papers for the exhibition "Chinese Painting under the Qianlong Emperor," 2 vols., *Phoebus* 6:2 (1988).

In addition, journal articles on specific subjects or painters often include translated passages, but these are more difficult of access. Various special issues of *Renditions* published by The Chinese University of Hong Kong should be consulted. Otherwise, the *Art Index* may provide guidance.

One should draw attention to French and German translations, generally of very high quality, e.g., Nicole Vandier-Nicolas's *Le Houa-che de Mi Fou (1051–1107)* 《米芾畫史》 (Paris: Presses universitaires de France, 1964).

Literature on calligraphy has been less carefully studied, but such texts are available in a number of compendia. 《歷代書法論文選》 (Shanghai:

Shuhua chubanshe, 1980) includes 95 works by 66 authors, but has no annotations. Its 《續編》 (1989) added another 120 texts by 102 authors. The 美術叢書, compiled by Huang Binhong 黃賓虹 and Deng Shi 鄧實 (Taibei: Yiwen chubanshe 藝文出版社, 1975) includes texts on calligraphy. Finally the encyclopaedic 《佩文齋書畫譜》, commissioned by the Kangxi Emperor, comp. Sun Yueban 孫岳頒 ca. 1708, exists in various editions. There is also, of course, the extremely helpful 《書道全集》 in 26 volumes, 3rd ed. (Tokyo: Heibonsha, 1966–1969).

Some recently edited and/or annotated texts can also be most useful — e.g., Deng Sanmu 鄧散木, 《書法學習必讀 — 續書譜圖解》 (Hong Kong and Taibei: Taiping shuju, 1962); Zhu Jianxin 朱建新, 《孫過庭書譜箋證》 (Beijing: Zhonghua, 1963); Zhu Jia 朱嘉, 《書學格言疏證》 (Hong Kong: Zhonghua, 1978); Ma Guoquan 馬國權, 《書譜譯法》 (Shanghai: shuhua chubanshe, 1980).

The following is a bibliography of articles and books on or including calligraphy that contain passages of translated texts, arranged in chronological order:

1. Zürcher, Eric. "Imitation and Forgery in Ancient Chinese Painting and Calligraphy." *Oriental Art*, n.s. 1 (1955), pp. 141–45.

2. van Gulik, Robert H. *Chinese Pictorial Art as Viewed by the Connoisseur*. Rome: ISMEO, 1958.

3. *Chinese Calligraphy and Painting in the Crawford Collection*. New York: Metropolitan Museum of Art, 1962.

4. Barnhart, Richard M. "Wei Fu-jen's *Pi-chen Tu* and the Early Texts on Calligraphy," *Archives of the Chinese Art Society of America*, 18 (1964), pp. 13–25.

5. Driscoll, Lucy and Kenji Toda. *Chinese Calligraphy: An Introduction*, 2nd ed. Chicago: University of Chicago, 1964.

6. Ch'en, Chih-mai. *Chinese Calligraphers and Their Art*. Melbourne: Melbourne University, 1966.

7. Lin, Yutang. *The Chinese Theory of Art: Translations from the Masters of Chinese Art*. New York: Putnam, 1967; London: Heinemann, 1967.

8. Soper, Alexander C. *Textual Evidence for the Secular Arts of China in the Period from Liu Sung through Sui*. "Artibus Asiae Supplementum", Ascona, 1967.

9. Ledderose, Lothar. *Die Siegelschrift (Chuan-zhu) in der*

*Ch'ing-zeit: Ein Beitrag zur Geschichte der Chinesischen Schrift-
kunst.* Wiesbaden: F. Steiner, 1970.

10. Ecke, Tseng Yu-ho. *Chinese Calligraphy.* Philadelphia: Museum of Art, 1971.

11. Ledderose, Lothar. *Mi Fu and the Classical Tradition of Chinese Calligraphy.* Princeton: Princeton University, 1979.

12. Fong, Wen. *Images of the Mind.* Princeton: Princeton University, 1984.

13. Chang, Léon L.Y. and Peter Miller. *Four Thousand Years of Chinese Calligraphy.* Chicago: University of Chicago, 1990.

14. Billeter, Jean Francois. *The Chinese Art of Writing.* New York: Rizzoli, 1990.

Of the works listed above, No. 14 supplies the most bibliography, as well as the most translations. Its only drawback is that the translations were originally into French, and so the English edition offers translations at "second-hand."

In so far as possible, the following list offers the names of Chinese calligraphy texts and their translations as presented in the bibliography given above. Pre-Tang and some Tang works were collected by Zhang Yanyuan 張彥遠 (ca. 815–after 875) in his 《法書要錄》, just as painting texts appear in his 《歷代名畫記》.

1. Cai Yong 蔡邕 (133–192). 〈書論〉 (On Calligraphy). See 10: Intro.

2. Zhao Yi 趙一 (end 2nd–early 3rd century). 〈非草書〉 (Polemic against the Grass Script). See William Acker. *Some Tang and Pre-Tang Texts on Chinese Painting.* Leiden: E. J. Brill, 1954, I: LIV–LVIII.

3. Wei furen 偉夫人 (272–349) attributed. 〈筆陣圖〉 (Chart of Brush Manoeuvres). A fake text probably of Tang date. See 4; 14: 162–63, 186–87, 203.

4. Yang Xin 羊欣 (370–442). 〈古來能書人名〉 (Names of the Great Calligraphers of the Past). See 11: 15, 76.

5. Yu He 虞龢 (5th century). 〈論書表〉 (A Memorial on Calligraphy). Postscript of 470; memorial on calligraphy submitted to Sung Mingdi 宋明帝 (r. 463–473). See 1: 142; 11: 37, 41–42.

6. Tao Hungjing 陶弘景 (452–536). 〈論書〉 (On Calligraphy). Letter to Liang Wudi 梁武帝 (r. 502–549). See 11: 38.

7. Yu Shinan 虞世南 (558–638). 〈筆髓論〉 (On the Quintessence of the Brush). See 14: 165, 243.

8. Tang Emperor Taizong 唐太宗 (r. 627–650). 〈論書〉 (On Writing). See 14: 125–26.

9. Sun Guoting 孫過庭 (ca. 648–703). 〈書譜〉 (Treatise on Calligraphy). Preface of 687. See 10: Intro.; 11: 39; 13: 97; 14: 104, 111, 127–28, 132, 192, 205. Also for a German translation, see Roger Goepper, *Shu-pu. Der Traktat zur Schriftkunst des Sun Kuo-ting.* Wiesbaden: F. Steiner, 1974.

10. Xu Hao 徐浩 (703–782). 〈古跡記〉 (Record of Ancient Remains). See 1: 143.

11. Xu Hao. 〈論書〉 (On Calligraphy). See 14: 203–204.

12. Zhang Huaiguan 張懷瓘 (act. first half of 8th century). 〈議書〉 (A Discussion of Calligraphy). See 1: 142; 13: 419.

13. Zhang Huaiguan. 〈書斷〉 (Evaluations of Calligraphy). See 13: 35; 14: 203.

14. Zhang Huaiguan. 〈文字論〉 (On the Chinese Written Language). See 14: 183.

15. Dou Ji 竇臮 (8th century). 〈述書賦〉 (Rhymed Prose on Calligraphy). Postscript of 769. See 13: 34.

16. Han Yu 韓愈 (768–824). 〈送高閑上人序〉 (Farewell Letter to Abbot Gaoxian). See 14: 191, 273.

17. Su Shi 蘇軾 (1036–1101). Numerous statements. See 10: Intro.; 13:2, 4, 32, 195; 14: 127, 203, 238, 265–66.

18. Zhu Changwen 朱長文 (1039–1098). 〈續書斷〉 (Addendum to *Evaluations of Calligraphy*, see [13] above), preface of 1074. See 14: 183.

19. Huang Tingjian 黃庭堅 (1045–1105). 〈山谷題跋〉 (Inscriptions and Colophons by Huang Tingjian). See 6: 202; 13:4.

20. Mi Fu 米芾 (1051–1107). 〈書史〉 (History of Calligraphy). See 11: Appendix A, 1103–1107.

21. Mi Fu. 〈海岳名言〉 (Famous Sayings of Mi Fu) and 題跋 (Inscriptions and Colophons by Mi Fi), compiled by Mao Jin 毛晉 (1599–1659). See 11; 13: 2, 33, 193–94, 211; 14: 116, 122, 238.

22. Song Emperor Gaozong 宋高宗 (r. 1127–1162). 〈翰墨志〉 (Random Notes on Calligraphy). See 13: 2.

23. Jiang Kuei 姜夔 (c. 1155–1221). 〈續書譜〉 (Addendum to the Treatise on Calligraphy, see [9] above). See 14: 104, 110, 126, 204,

239; also Lin Shuen-fu, "Chinag K'uei's Treatises on Poetry and Calligraphy," in *Theories of the Arts in China*, edited by Susan Bush and Christian Murck (Princeton: Princeton University, 1983).

24. Yue Ke 岳珂 (1183–1234). 〈寶晉英光集〉 (Collection of the Bao-jin Studio of the Ying'guang Hall). See 11: 1086.

25. Yue Ke. 〈寶眞齋法書贊〉 (Colophons on Calligraphy Exemplars in the Baozhen Studio), cited in the 《永樂大典》 (*Yongle Encyclopaedia*), completed in 1407. See 14: 126.

26. Zhu Yunming 祝允明 (1460–1526). Miscellaneous sayings. See 14: 204–205.

27. Dong Qichang 董其昌 (1555–1636). 〈論用筆〉 (On the Way of Using the Brush). See 13: 32.

28. Bao Shichen 包世臣 (1775–1855). 〈安吳論書〉 (On Calligraphy), preface of 1868. See 6: 210.

29. Zhou Xinglian 周星蓮 (mid-19th century). 〈臨池觀見〉 (Notes of a Calligrapher). See 14: 173.

30. Liu Xizai 柳熙載 (1813–1881). 〈藝概〉 (Outline of the Arts), Pt. 5, 〈書概〉 (Outline of Calligraphy). See 14: 84, 133, 134, 203–204, 250, 266.

31. Kang Youwei 康有爲 (1858–1927). 〈廣藝舟雙輯〉 (Two Compilations from the Boat of Great Artistry). See 14: 122.

32. Li Ruiqing 李瑞清 (1866–1920). Cited in 13: 31.

33. Hu Guangwei 胡光煒 (1888–1962). 〈書藝樂論〉 (On the Art of Calligraphy). See 13: 3.

34. Ding Wenjun 丁文雋 (1906–?). 〈書法精論〉 (Essential Principles of Calligraphy). First published 1938, Beijing: Zhongguo shudian, 1983. See 14: 117, 126.

Beyond the usual problems of reproducing literary expression of one linguistic mode in another, translation of Chinese texts on the visual arts presents several additional pitfalls. One lies in the different course of Chinese art history, so that developmental patterns accepted for European art do not necessarily apply to chronologically equivalent Chinese art. Interpretation of Chinese texts requires full awareness of their historical particularities. Another is posed by Chinese aesthetic terminology, much of which is shared for analyses and critiques of literature itself, as well as music, calligraphy and painting, yet with varying signification for each art form. Underlying the concepts of aesthetics in China (as elsewhere) are, of course, the philosophical currents distinctive to different periods in the history of thought.

A good example of the difficulties a translator might encounter in Chinese texts on calligraphy and/or paintings is presented by the frequently quoted "Six Laws" of Xie He 謝赫 (act. ca. 500–535). The 六法 are also translatable as the "Six Canons, Maxims, Principles or Elements" of painting. As they have been transmitted (the earliest printed version available to us being a Ming Jiajing reign, 1522–1566, woodblock reproduction of a Song Dynasty edition), six groups of four graphs each are usually read as comprising six complete statements. Literally translated these could be:

1. 氣韻生動 breath/spirit harmony/resonance born/produce movement
2. 骨法用筆 bone law/method use brush
3. 應物象形 responding/corresponding to material thing/object image form
4. 隨類賦綵 following/suiting type spread/apply colour
5. 經營位置 dividing planning position placement
6. 傳移模寫 transmission conveying model describe/write

William R.B. Acker's translation in *Some T'ang and Pre-T'ang Texts on Chinese Painting* (Leiden: E.J. Brill, 1954, XIV–XLV, 4) differs from earlier attempts in assuming the first two graphs of each statement to be a binome and the subject, the second two also a binome and the object, with the verb "is" being implied. Such a reading has been arrived at independently by both Chinese and Japanese scholars. Thus, his translation reads:

1. Spirit Resonance which means vitality.
2. Bone Method which is (a way of) using the brush.
3. Correspondence to the Object which means the depicting of forms.
4. Suitability to Type which has to do the laying on of colours.
5. Division and Planning, i.e., placing and arrangement.
6. Transmission by Copying, that is to say the copying of models.

James Cahill questioned Acker's reconstruction, in "The Six Laws and How To Read Them" (*Ars Orientalis*, Vol. 4 (1961), pp. 372–81), maintaining grammatical parallelism in couplets of four graphs to each line, certainly a popular literary convention long before the 6th century A.D. Thus, Cahill's translation offers:

1. Engender (a sense of) movement (through) spirit consonance.
2. Use the brush (with) the bone method.
3. Responding to things, image (depict) their forms.
4. According (adapting?) to kind, set forth (describe) colours (appearances).
5. Dividing and planning, positioning and arranging.
6. Transmitting and conveying (earlier models, through) copying and transcribing.

Another approach to understanding Xie He's recommendations is in recognising that Six Dynasties painting was focussed on living beings, human or divine, and that Xie himself is known otherwise as a critically not much admired but fashionable portrait-painter of his time in Nanjing. Thus, all his statements should be applied to figural subjects. Painted images attain spirit resonance through life-movement or an effect of vitality. Figural forms gain structural strength (boniness) through brushwork. The remainder of the Six Laws present no special problems.

The term 六法 first referred to poetry (in the *Zhou Li* 《周禮》, but without definition), being then named by Wei Hong 衛宏 in A.D. 25 in the "Great Preface" to the *Shijing* 《詩經》. *Feng* 風, *ya* 雅 and *song* 頌 seem to have been poetic genres — the song, ode and hymn. *Fu* 賦, *bi* 比 and *xing* 興 functioned more as compositional methods — description, comparison and allegory or narrative, metaphor and allegory (the last as explained by Liu Xie 劉勰 (465–523) in the *Wenxin diaolong* 《文心雕龍》). Liu Xie, however, also suggested another interpretation for 風 — "It is the source of transformation, and the correlate of emotion. He who would express mournful emotions must begin with 風, and to organize his linguistic elements he must above all emphasize bone (*gu*) ..." (Vincent Y. C. Shih, *The Literary Mind and the Carving of Dragons by Liu Hsieh*. New York: Columbia University Press, 1959, p. 162). Here we find in a nearly contemporary analysis of literary creation a sequence of terms very close to Xie He's first two laws. Moreover, *feng* could signify a distinctive, nameable attribute or quality of a human being. It might also signify popular customs, but equally denote an invisible, life-giving energy. As an intangible power, it could be an influence or suasive force. In this, it is a correlative of *qi* 氣. Literary theory developed a critical vocabulary before the visual arts, but even its aesthetic terms were preceded by philosophical concepts.

Aesthetic vocabulary for literature, music, calligraphy and painting depended on a Chinese system of natural philosophy systematized by the 陰陽五行 or Five Phases School, and known now as transmitted in Confucian and Daoist writings. Phenomena, their organization and significance, in the cosmic order as well as the human consciousness, were repeatedly examined between the fourth and second centuries B.C., adapted by the Han Dynasty's orthodoxy and redefined in Song Neo-Confucianism.

In the post-Han period painting was already recognized as an art going beyond formal representation and mimesis. Inevitably painting theory became increasingly involved with non-formal, non-technical aspects of the art. Xie He's First Law could be translated as "Sympathetic responsiveness of the vital spirit effecting animation" (Alexander Soper, "The First Two Laws of Hsieh Ho," *The Far Eastern Quarterly*, Vol. 8 (1949), pp. 412–23), with the "vital spirit" responding to that of nature. His Second Law of "Structural method in the use of the brush" borrows its appreciation of "boniness" from a criterion generally more in use for assessment of calligraphy.

This connection between calligraphy and painting was explicitly stated by Zhang Yanyuan 張彥遠 (ca. 815–after 875) in his exegesis of Xie He's Six Laws in the first book of the 《歷代名畫記》 :

> The painters of antiquity were sometimes able to transmit formal likeness while endowing it with a noble vitality (骨氣). They sought for what was beyond formal likeness in their painting.
>
> Now, the representation of things necessarily consists in formal likeness, but likeness of form requires completion by a noble vitality. Noble vitality and formal likeness both originate in the definition of a conception and derive from the use of the brush. That is why those who are skilled in painting often excel in calligraphy as well.
> (Bush and Shih, *op. cit.*, 54)

Post-Tang discussions tended to revise the Six Laws for contemporary usage. Jing Hao 荊浩 (late 9th–early 10th century) substituted the "Six Essentials" 六要 in his 〈筆法記〉, these being — Spirit or *qi*, Resonance, Thought, Scene, Brush and Ink. The outward appearance and the inner reality of a depicted object, together could convey life or vitality. Guo Ruoxu 郭若虛 (act. first half 11th century) thought that the last five of the Six Laws were instructive or learnable techniques, but the first was "an innate knowledge", "an unspoken accord, a spiritual communion; 'something that happens without knowing how.'" Guo's 〈圖畫見聞志〉 associates this gift with the Confucian gentleman 君子 , and quoting Yang Xiong 楊雄 (53 B.C.–A.D. 18) concludes:

> Words are mind-sounds, and calligraphy is mind-painting. When the sounds and the painting are formed, the gentleman or the small man is revealed.
> (Bush and Shih, *op. cit.,* 96)

From the painting to the painter, the object to the subject, Xie He's First Law could bear a new focus and fresh content. And so, in translation, we have also to be conscious of the continuing yet changing theoretical tradition behind each text.

Form and Spirit

Huang Yushi
Qinghua University, Beijing, China

If one runs through the Chinese literature about translation, he will find that the one topic discussed by our predecessors at greater length than anything else is that of the difficulties or even impossibility of translation. They laid out a great many reasons (not all quite to the point, I should say) why it was so. One of them even made such a terrible comparison as likening translation to making openings in the head of the legendary queer creature Hundun, and concluded that "the Hundun would have died as soon as the openings were made" 竅成而混沌終矣 . Another likened it to "chewing food for others: as a result, the food not only would lose its taste for them, but would make them nauseous" 有似嚼飯與人，非徒失其味，乃令人嘔穢 . These vividly represent their glum sentiments about translation.

The above statements were all made by persons who were regular translators of Buddhist scriptures in the Tang Dynasty (618–907). How is it that while on the one hand they were going about the work in earnest, they should, on the other hand, be so dissatisfied with, and even feel intolerant of, what they had done?

The reason, I believe, is rather simple.

It seems that all our early predecessors instinctively felt that translation must necessarily keep all the original forms unchanged, or, better yet, match the original word for word exactly, not knowing that this was impossible. Here one can hardly refrain from thinking that it is just like a person who, wanting to go forward along a road, first blockades it, and then complains of its being impassable. This being the case, it is surely no wonder they have arrived at such a conclusion. And most unfortunately, this has constituted the most outstanding feature of our history of translation as a whole. The mistaken concept has not only influenced the thought of our predecessors one generation after another, but persists even today.

Here of course, we cannot go on without saying something about Yan Fu 嚴復, the famous scholar and most important translator and (considered by some as) the greatest translation theorist of China, who was active at the turn of the 19th and 20th centuries. It is beyond doubt that he made numerous indelible accomplishments in introducing many new Western thoughts into China, and in ushering in a new epoch of translation in the country, but equally beyond doubt is the fact that great harm has been done by him to the general undertaking of translation in the country, through a rather flippant statement made by him near the end of the last century: "the (three) difficulties in translation lie in: trueness, intelligibility, and elegancy" 譯事三難信達雅. Was he just drawing a conclusion from what his predecessors had thought about translation, or really trying to set forth, on the basis of his predecessors, a theory of his own? I think it was the former, (for which I could give more than one reason) though he has all along been considered to have done the latter, and thus been held up as the greatest authority in the field.

The question certainly has little to do with our discussions here, only my view of it would relieve him of the chief responsibility therefore and let it fall on those who misunderstood him. But that of course is beside the point.

As it is, the greatest harm done by Yan Fu lies in the fact that his statement of "three-difficulties" reaffirmed the mistakes of his predecessors, and even lent them renewed energy.

For example, with him trueness meant nothing but slavishly adhering to the original forms, just as his predecessors had done, as is proven by his statement that "in case a true translation fails to make clear the original meaning, and thus actually fails to be a translation at all, then, intelligibility must take precedence" 顧信矣不達，雖譯猶不譯也，則達尚焉.

When we say trueness, it can only mean either one of two things: (1) keeping all the forms (i.e., the grammatical structures, means of expression, etc.) of the original in the translation — that is, true to form; (2) making the translation conform to the original in ideas, meaning, or content — that is, true to the spirit. The first kind is to be achieved supposedly by "literal" translation, the second, supposedly by "liberal" translation. A third one does not exist. Now what does Yan Fu's trueness actually mean? If we take it to mean trueness in the second sense, his statement here would be tantamount to saying that the translation of a sentence, though it means the same thing as the original, is nevertheless intelligible to none. And that would be totally absurd. For, if one cannot make out its sense, how can one tell whether it means the same thing as the original or not? Therefore, it is quite clear that Yan Fu's trueness could not but fall into the first category, i.e., true to form, as only this kind of trueness can possibly make translation "true" to the original, but at the same time totally unintelligible.

To take all in all, the brief statement made by Yan Fu may be safely paraphrased as: "translation is very very difficult, because a translator has to make first the translation exactly the same as the original in form, and at the same time make it mean the same thing as the original to the readers, etc., but as this trueness may render the translation entirely unintelligible, then, his priority must be intelligibility."

But can that be considered a sensible argument? Can one gather from it in what relation exactly this trueness and intelligibility stand to each other? Nobody can tell. It seems as if he were saying, trueness to the original form is of course very important, but in case this trueness becomes a hindrance to intelligibility, then, forget about it! Is it governed by logic? As this trueness would more often than not become a hindrance to intelligibility and have to be discarded, then how is one to account for its importance?

But anyway, because of a blind belief in the trueness to forms, which they could neither find a way to do with, nor to do without, our predecessors appear to be all confused as to questions of its true relation to intelligibility.

Take the famous scholar Liang Qichao 梁啓超 for example. A little before Yan Fu made his "three-difficulties" theory, he had said that "there are two catches in translation (from Western languages into Chinese), one is that, if one has the Chinese version written in the Chinese way, it would lose the original sense of the Western languages; the other is that, if one has it written in the ways of the Western languages, it would be entirely unreadable" 譯書有二弊，一曰徇華文而失西義，二曰徇西文而梗華讀 . Now everyone can see that to have the Chinese version written in a Western language's way, it would nine times out of ten be entirely unreadable, but how is one to understand that the Chinese version written in Chinese ways would necessarily lose the meaning of the original Western language?

Could the Chinese version written in Chinese ways not be made to express the original meaning of a Western language? In that case how could a translation be concocted?

In view of the aforesaid, I think it would be not far wrong to say that, to our early predecessors, the forms of a language, for some groundless reasons, just could not be separated from the meaning, so much so that they just couldn't be made to believe that the English "How old are you, granny?" means exactly the same as the Chinese 您高壽，老奶奶？, or the English "It is anybody's for the taking," means exactly the same as the Chinese 誰要誰拿去 simply because their forms are so widely apart.

I even vaguely suspect that the same is true with the famous French-Chinese translator Fu Lei 傅雷. At least when he said that "Even the best translation couldn't be just the same in flavour as the original, but must be either excessive or inadequate" 即使最優秀的譯文，其韻味較之原文仍不免過或不及, what was actually in his mind was still these differences in forms between the original and the translation. Or the statement would be as meaningless an affirmation as to say that there are no two leaves of a tree exactly the same, which of course is true.

To put it in a nutshell, this belief in the trueness to forms was the greatest mistake our predecessors have ever committed, and is the greatest mistake a theorist of translation could ever commit. But most unfortunately it has from the very beginning till today run as a "black thread" through all our translation history and theory, and in many recently published books is still preached as the first principle of translation.

There might be other reasons accounting for the unsatisfactory level of our translation from English into Chinese in general, but I should hold this mistake primarily responsible.

First of all, we must know that in any translation, trueness to form is but an illusion, and can never be achieved.

Let's look at a few examples.

We may translate:

1. "I am your friend" into Chinese as 我是你的朋友 and
2. "I saw a boy" into Chinese as 我見到一個男孩

Most people, I think, might take them to be good examples of translation true to the original forms, or word-for-word translation, and believe them to be entirely different from such so-called liberal translations as:

3. "How do you do?" being translated 你好? and
4. "How old are you?" being translated 您多大年歲?

But in actuality, are the two groups of translation really so different from each other as to make it possible for us to believe that they are really done in two different ways, or by two different methods — the literal method and the liberal method respectively? Certainly not.

First of all, logically speaking, if we say that there are two different methods of translation, it must mean that any one sentence, or at least most sentences in English, can be easily done into Chinese *either* way, as the translator would prefer. But in the case here, not only can't we have the examples (3) and (4) done word for word as 如何做你做? and 如何老是你?, which obviously make no sense whatsoever, but we cannot even imagine how the examples (1) and (2) could be translated in a liberal way without arbitrarily altering the ideas of the original. Is there much sense in calling them two different methods?

Secondly, perhaps one may say that the two methods are not to be used at liberty, but to be applied separately to different cases. That is of course possible. But, as a matter of fact, we see that almost all the simple sentences used in daily talk, such as "Good morning?" "How do you do?" "How are you?" "What is your name?" "How old are you?" "Where do you come from?" "Good-bye!" etc., cannot be translated in a word-for-word way, and that if we take any English book and open it at random to any page, I don't believe that we can find more than two or three sentences, if any at all, that we can really do literally. Then, what sense is there in setting the two apart as distinct methods, even if there are some differences between them?

What is more, if we look into the matter further, we can't help asking, are the above first two examples, 我是你的朋友 and 我見到一個男孩 really translations done in a word-for-word way? If so, couldn't the sentence (2) "I saw a boy," be very reasonably translated into 我鋸一個跑堂的 ("I [cut with a] saw a [serving] boy") and still make perfect sense? Why would everybody consider it wrong? Could there be any other explanation for it than that the translator who put it into 我見到一個男孩 did not at all do it one word after another separately, though it looks like it; but did it just in the same way as he dealt with the other two examples, namely, to grasp the meanings of the whole sentences first and then put them into the Chinese versions accordingly? So it is very clear that if there is any difference between the two groups of translation, it is only that in the first group, the Chinese way of saying the things is just the same as the English, while in the second group it is not; it has nothing whatever to do with the translation methods! Isn't it so? How regrettable so many people should have wasted so much energy and time in pursuance of something that is a mere illusion!

All in all, in order to lay bare the whole matter, I think we must first of all be very clear on two points: (1) What exactly is the relation between languages and human thoughts and feelings, and (2) Do thoughts and feelings vary from race to race, or are they all the same? Obviously here lies the root of the above-said mistakes of our predecessors, and here also lies the basis of the theory of translation.

What I mean is that our predecessors didn't know that languages, spoken or written, are mere instruments to convey man's thoughts and feelings, neither more, nor less. They don't mean anything by themselves. This point is of paramount importance. For example, in English one may say "He was killed by a robber," or "A robber killed him"; these two sentences though very different in form can't be said to be a whit different in meaning. The same is true with the English version "I was born in the year of ..." and the Chinese version 我生於某年 .... Besides being in different languages, the different forms they are in (the English being in the passive voice, the Chinese in the active voice) do not at all prevent them from having exactly the same meaning. Here it would be ridiculous to talk about which of the two is better, or which is more scientific, etc.

But, of course, to know all this certainly needs a more thorough knowledge of languages than our early predecessors could have had.

As for the second question, I am afraid they were all the more totally in the dark. Even as late as on the eve of the Opium War, we find in a petition written by a noble to the emperor of Qing Dynasty the Westerners 洋人 being described as "stiff at the waist, with unbending legs, and so very liable to fall down at the slightest blow, and therefore not for a moment to be feared." According to this description, we see it was even doubtful to some Chinese of the time whether the Westerners belonged to the same mankind as the Chinese did. How could they know what was in the Westerner's mind and heart, or whether they had the same thoughts and feelings as we Chinese had?

But that time has long passed. Seeing that the people of different races have been living in the same environment (on the same earth), have gone through the same stages of development, have got along with the same modes of production and ways of living, and have been making use of the same principles of logical inference, by nature all seeking for pleasure and avoiding pain, and they are the same in their physiological requirements, in their superstition of ghosts and gods out of ignorance and fear, and with their ideas of good and evil basically the same, etc., we know that generally speaking all the races in the world could not be very different in their thoughts and feelings. And owing to more and more frequent and intimate contacts with persons of various races, we've become aware that no matter how different and queer the languages are that different races may use, the substance of what they talk about will never come from outside the general stock of thoughts and feelings, so to speak, common to all races.

From this simple but very important basic fact we can at least draw the following conclusions:

1. It is this similarity or rather identity in thoughts and feelings that makes it possible for one person to communicate with another. Languages are of but secondary importance. As we see, two persons speaking entirely different languages, if thrown into a very special situation, can manage by mere cries and gestures to communicate with each other; while two persons speaking the same language won't be able to communicate with each other on questions of painting if one of them is colour-blind, nor on questions of music if one of them is hard of hearing.

2. That means, on the contrary, that had there been no similarity or identity in thoughts and feelings between persons of different races, they would never be able to communicate with each other, however hard they might try; the languages they used, be they as expressive as can be in themselves, would be totally useless. And in that case, it would be definitely impossible for a person of one race to learn the language of any other race, let alone translate it. But fortunately, we can be certain that such is not the case.

3. Thus we see that communication between one person and another is carried on merely through exchanges of ideas or thoughts and feelings between them, and the languages they use, similarity or dissimilarity in forms notwithstanding, are but tools, or conveyers, which do not actually *participate* in the communication at all. In other words, as soon as one of them gets the idea of what the other

wants to make clear, he will throw the language, including its strange or not strange forms, into oblivion right away.

4. Since the thoughts and feelings are all the same among all races, and therefore, the substance of what a person of any race talks about can never be entirely apart from the common thoughts and feelings, it naturally follows that no unsurmountable difficulties could be there to thwart communication between any two races, nor translation from any one language into another. In that case, to say translation is impossible is as much as to say that the same and common thoughts and feelings that persons of *A* race can express freely in *A* language, persons of *B* race would be unable to express in their *B* language.

Now, may we say that if we totally throw away trueness to forms, translation would suddenly become something very easily done? Probably not, for one has to get the mastery of both the primary and the target languages first, especially the latter, the one he translates into. That is no easy matter. But at any rate, with the mastery of the two languages accomplished, we can say, as our great author Mao Dun 茅盾 would have it, one would be not far from being a competent translator.

Here another question calling for our attention is that, with trueness to forms being repudiated, shall we take trueness to the spirit (i.e., to the ideas, the meaning, or the contents) of the original as the only guide to translation? Well, yes. But it certainly does not mean that one may, with a bit of the general idea of the original in mind, go on to concoct his translation as freely as he likes, so as to translate, to give an extreme (but not very extraordinary in actuality) example, "Leave it to me," into Chinese as 老兄公務繁忙，些須小事自有小弟代勞，何勞費心 — though obviously the translator who did it might well unflinchingly argue that his translation is very true to the original spirit.

Nor does it mean that, since it is only the spirit a translator has to be true to, he must have a very wide scope to exercise his imagination, which would allow him to translate "Can man change his nature?" into Chinese as 本性難移 or to translate "Am I my brother's keeper?" into Chinese as 我不應該留我兄弟在此 (Examples of this kind can be easily found in some well-sold books, teaching "translation techniques").

These are not translations, I am sorry to say, but rather parodies.

At any rate, as the term "trueness to spirit" came into being merely as an opposite to "trueness to form," now with the one being negated, the other must have lost its justification for existence, and as the term itself is so vague as easily to cause new misunderstandings, I think we'd better throw this lame term away with its counterpart, and return to the simplest but also clearest idea — true to the original.

Here I especially appreciate the principle proposed by Ma Jianzhong 馬建忠 , the first grammarian of China, of the last century. He once wrote that a translator should "try to make his translation exactly the same as what he is translating." 使譯成之文適如其所譯 . But of course, we shall hasten to add, not including the form.

This principle, though it sounds rather abstract, is nevertheless quite to the point, and I believe a better concept is hard to find.

To make it more concrete, I'd like to explain in what important respects one should "try to make his translation exactly the same as what he is translating".

Firstly, in general ideas, or the substantial meaning. It goes without saying that in a translation the general idea must be exactly the same as the original. This failing, nothing is to be said about the other aspects. One may say this is the foundation which decides whether a translation is right or wrong. The above-cited translations of "Leave it to me," "Can man change his nature?" and "Am I my brother's keeper?" may be said to have all failed in this respect.

Here attention should also be paid to the tenses used and logical relations implied in the original text. For it is quite obvious, if a translation does not rightly reproduce the original tense sequence and logical relations, it cannot be said to have reproduced the general ideas of the original.

Secondly, in the ways of expression. We know from experience that with the same idea in mind, one can express it in many different ways. One may say it, for example, simply or verbosely, boringly or wittily, reservedly or exaggeratingly, etc. And a translator must keep in mind which way is used in the original, and try to write the translation accordingly. This is no doubt the main reason why the above-mentioned Chinese version of "Leave it to me" cannot be deemed a proper translation.

Thirdly, in effectiveness. The famous linguist Professor Chao Yuen Ren 趙元任 once wrote: "To take the French saying 'Ne vous dérangez pas, je vous en prie!' for example, it can be literally translated into English as 'Do not disturb yourself, I pray you!' but in consideration of its effect, the French sentence ought to be translated into English as 'Please don't bother.'

Because this is just what an English man would say, in places where the French saying is used...." Here Professor Chao Yuen Ren undoubtedly propounded a very important principle that a translator should never neglect.

In English-Chinese translation, countless examples of the kind may be given. But perhaps the best one I can think of is the word "stop". This single-word English sentence can be used in nobody knows how many ways to tell a person to stop what he is doing. I mean no matter whether he is reading, singing, writing, eating, swimming, or what not, you can always tell him "Stop!" But obviously, none of the regular Chinese translations of the word, such as 停!停止!停住! or 停下! will bring about that effect with a Chinese doing any of these things, no matter how loud you cry.

Why? It is obviously because none of the Chinese versions, though seemingly the same as the original in meaning, has the function in Chinese that the original has in English. In Chinese, in place of "Stop", we always say, 別念了!別唱了!別寫了! or 別吃了! (Read no more! Sing no more! etc.) as the case requires.

In other words, when we translate anything into Chinese, we must always take into consideration what is the idiomatic Chinese way of saying it, otherwise even if a translation may seem all right in other respects, it will never be acceptable to the readers.

Fourthly, in the undertone. As everybody knows, when a person wants to say something, his mind must have come into action beforehand, and as a rule, what is in his mind will always be more than he can, or cares to, speak out. In other words, a part of his thought will often, for various reasons, be left unsaid. But this part of thought, though omitted in his speech, can hardly be suppressed altogether, but will have been hinted at by him, whether consciously or unconsciously, hence the undertone. This is of course also true with writings, especially in literary works, whose purpose it is to imitate life.

Just because of this particular way of coming into being, naturally it would be something rather subtle and complicated in any one piece of speech or writing, and I should say that the flavour or 韻味 so cherished by Fu Lei would be mainly this.

Generally speaking, the undertone is important in that through it we can detect what is left unsaid in a speaker's or writer's mind: what his real position was, what sentiments he wanted to conceal, or what he would like to make known in a roundabout way.

Fifthly and lastly, in the style or type of writings. We may say that all writings must fall into a special kind of style. For example, judging from their different uses, they may be distinguished as narrative, descriptive, epistolary, dialogical, or the style of a dissertation, etc., and from their special tones, they may be distinguished as being light or serious, delightful or sad, humorous or melancholic, chatty or pompous, etc.

We know that a special style of a piece of writing usually creates a special atmosphere for all the sentences therein to run harmoniously and swimmingly, and thus make the writing as a whole all the more vivid and vigorous. Now, how could the translation that is a fair representation of the writing be deprived of it?

I am not certain whether there are any more aspects. Anyway, as far as I can see, if we can make our translation similar to the original in all these five respects, we can be almost sure that the translation, if not yet perfect, is at least not far from it.

These five aspects can all be said to be the spirit of the original, as they obviously do not have much to do with forms. But of course they are all integral parts of the original.

References

Bates, E. S. *Modern Translation*. Oxford: Oxford University Press, 1936.

Huang, Yushi 黃雨石 . 《英漢文學翻譯》 (*Explorations into English-Chinese Literary Translation*). Shaanxi: Shaanxi People's Press 陝西人民出版社 , 1988.

Liu, Ching-chih 劉靖之 . 《翻譯論集》 (*Essays on Translation*). Hong Kong: Joint Publishing Company 香港三聯書店 , 1981.

Luo, Xinzhang 羅新璋 , ed. 《翻譯論集》 (*Collected Essays on Translation*). Beijing: The Commercial Press 商務印書館 , 1984.

Tytler, A. F. *Essay on the Principles of Translation*. London: J. M. Dent, n.d.

FORMAL CORRESPONDENCE

Formal Correspondence

Vladimir Ivir
Department of English, Faculty of Philosophy
University of Zagreb, Zagreb, Croatia

Formal correspondence is a term used in two separate yet not unrelated linguistic disciplines — translation studies and contrastive analysis. In fact, it is precisely the concept of formal correspondence that links the two disciplines: in one, translation, it provides the starting point in the search for equivalence; in the other, contrastive analysis, it is the product of comparison of linguistic units in pairs of texts held together by translational equivalence. The linkage is quite strong, given the fact that translational equivalence is judged with reference to formal correspondence and that the necessary *tertium comparationis* for the establishment of formal correspondence in contrastive analysis is provided by translational equivalence.

(1) The adjective "formal" in the term formal correspondence refers both to the (superficial) form and to the semantic content of linguistic units. In a chapter devoted to principles of correspondence, Nida recognizes that "there can be no absolute correspondence between languages," (Nida, 1964:156) and goes on to note that there are two basic orientations in translating and hence two different types of (closest, not absolute) equivalence — formal and dynamic (Nida, 1964:159). Formal equivalence, also called structural equivalence, is typified by "gloss translation", in which the translator "attempts to reproduce as literally and meaningfully as possible the form and contents of the original," (Nida, 1964:159) preserving (1) grammatical units, (2) consistency in word usage, and (3) meanings in

terms of the source context. The term "formal equivalence" is replaced by "formal correspondence" in Nida and Taber (1969:22, 27–28), where it is explicitly opposed to "dynamic equivalence".

While Nida saw formal correspondence as textually realized in translation (which explains why he first called it "equivalence"), Catford distinguished clearly between textual and systemic correspondences: he called the former translation equivalents and the latter formal correspondents. Thus, translation is defined as "the replacement of textual material in one language (source language) by equivalent textual material in another language (target language)" (Catford, 1965:20), whereas formal correspondence is defined as identity of function of correspondent items in two linguistic systems, so that a formal correspondent is taken to be "any target-language category which may be said to occupy, as nearly as possible, the 'same' place in the economy of the target language as the given source-language category occupies in the source language." (Catford, 1965:32) It is noteworthy that for Nida, the establishment of formal correspondence is an act of translation, involving a source-language text and a particular version of its target-language translation (one that preserves, as far as possible, the form and content of the linguistic units of the original); for Catford, on the other hand, formal correspondence is established by comparing paired linguistic systems to find categories (items, units) which occupy the "same" places in their respective economies.

Both approaches face considerable difficulties when challenged to operationalize their definitions. If Nida's formal correspondence is typified by gloss translation, it is obvious that it is not to be found in normal translation done for non-metalinguistic purposes. Where it is found is in one of the stages of the "multiple stage translation" (Voegelin, 1954:271–80), in which it serves to highlight the semantic and structural relationships between the source and the target language prior to making the changes (rearrangement, addition, deletion) necessitated by the target language. The explicit listing of source-text morphemes and faithful reproduction of its structures yields a checklist of linguistic means with which the original author communicated his intended message. The target language may not be able to use the same means for either linguistic or communicative (say, pragmatic) reasons. Linguistically, the target language may not have the particular means of expression that the source language has (for instance, Croatian has distinct forms for the masculine, feminine and neuter gender of third-person plural personal pronouns — *oni* m pl, *one* f pl, *ona* n pl, while English has only *they* for all three genders), or it may have and obligatorily use a means that the source language does not have (for instance, English expresses the link between the beginning of an action in the past and its continuation up to the moment of speaking by relying on the Present Perfect Tense in an example like *I have been here for half an hour*, while no such link is expressed by the Present Tense in the Croatian translation *Ovdje sam pola sata* "I am here half-an-hour").

Communicatively, some of the formal structural and semantic features of the source text get abandoned and/or replaced by features not present in the source text but required to ensure communication in the new context of situation (involving a different language, different culture, different sender, i.e. translator, different purpose, and different receivers). Thus, since gloss translation is possible only as a metalinguistic exercise and not as normal translation, the identification of formal correspondents in translated texts is somewhat arbitrary.

The task is made more difficult, if anything, when "sameness" of the economies of two linguistic systems is invoked, as it is not at all clear how paired items can occupy the "same" place in the economies of their respective languages. Can, for instance, even such closely related items as the English and German definite articles be said to play the same role in the economies of English and German? Or the English progressive tense and the Slavic verbal aspect? Of course, the likelihood of there being "same" items (linguistic units, categories) in different languages decreases with genetic distance. The likelihood is even smaller for the more rigorous requirement of congruence, characterized by the presence, in the two languages, of the same number of equivalent formatives arranged in the same order (Martin, 1968; Krzeszowski, 1971). For that reason, one of the proponents of the concept of congruence later focused on the relation of equivalence, which he, however, defined as sameness of deep structure (Krzeszowski, 1972:80), so that equivalent sentences were also congruent at the level of deep structure, but their congruence disappeared on the way to the surface structure.

(2) The problem of formal correspondence is twofold — one of methodology and one of relevance. Methodologically, the problem boils down to that of the *tertium comparationis* on the basis of which correspondence is established, and for which there are three possible candidates: functional systemic identity, common metalanguage, and translation equivalence. The first two are *langue*-based and the third is *parole*-based. In the former case,

paired linguistic units of two languages are held together as correspondents by their functional (formal and semantic) and/or metalinguistic identity as elements of two linguistic systems. It has already been shown that working with arbitrarily isolated linguistic units does not promise usable results: in the first place, it is not obvious how, and which, units of a given language are chosen for comparison; secondly, it is not clear on what grounds particular units of another language are recognized as formal correspondents (since, belonging to a different language, they display a different form, and since there is no objective way of ascertaining the identity of their meaning; metalinguistic labels may look like an excellent *tertium comparationis* until one remembers that they, too, are language-specific and that the same category names are applied to very different phenomena — a definite article is not the same in English and Hungarian, for instance); thirdly, it is not easy to say what place a given unit occupies in the economy of a given language, and it is even more difficult to say whether a given counterpart unit occupies the same place in another language — if "sameness" of place is at all conceivable across languages.

As for relevance, especially relevance for translation theory and practice, formal correspondence established systemically and built on a non-translational *tertium comparationis* would not seem to be very useful — even if it were practically feasible. (Its usefulness for language pedagogy is also questionable, but this is not our concern at present.) Students of translation have stressed repeatedly that translation involves not the comparison of languages but the production of texts: Jakobson (1959:235) speaks of the substitution of messages in one language, "not for separate code-units, but for entire messages in some other language." Bolinger (1966:130) makes the distinction between the two operations in Saussurean terms: "Translation may be viewed amorphously as the rendition of a text from one language to another. This is translation from the standpoint of *la parole*: the text, the act of speech or writing is the thing. Or it may be viewed as a systematic comparison of two languages: this is translation from the standpoint of *la langue*." Wilss (1982:60) clearly separates translational performance from systematic competence: "The classification of the science of translation as performance linguistics is an important precondition for separating it from /.../ contrastive (confrontative) linguistics and bi- or plurilingual structural comparison of languages." And, of course, there are those translation theorists who explicitly reject linguistic insights as a basis for a realistic theory of translation: "La théorie de la traduction n'est donc pas une linguistique appliquée." (Meschonnic, 1973, quoted in Steiner, 1975:x) They thus directly contradict those who claim with Mounin (1963:17) that "/toute opération de traduction /.../ comporte à la base une série d'analyses et opérations qui relèvent spécifiquement de la linguistique /.../"

The discussion of the relevance of formal correspondence for translation theory and practice is inextricably linked with the understanding of the nature of translation equivalence by a particular theorist or practitioner. Two extreme views are possible and have indeed been adopted throughout the history of translation: one is that linguistic correspondences are what translation is all about and that translating means matching linguistic units across languages; the other is that the *raison d'être* of translation is to convey to the ultimate receiver the sender's communicative intention, achieving the same communicative effect that the sender's original achieved on its receivers, using to this end not the original sender's means of expression but the linguistic means that would guarantee such an effect given the requirements of the new communicative situation (involving a different language, different culture, different receivers, different purpose of communication). No references are needed for the two views: suffice it only to say that the first gives rise to translations that go under the names such as literal, source-language oriented, sender-oriented, author-oriented, and the second to translations dubbed as free, target-language oriented, receiver-oriented, reader-oriented. The theory of translation built on the first view would be essentially linguistic, and that built on the second view essentially communicative.

The opposition between the two views is not as stark in real life as it is here presented, as both practitioners and theorists of translation recognize that linguistic correspondences have a role to play in translation, but that their role is limited and other factors intervene: "Ainsi une linguistique de la traduction, si la lingistique proprement dit en constitue un élément essentiel, doit s'ouvrir à une sémiologie qui n'étudie seulement les signes porteurs de signification dans le cadre des structures linguistiques en question, mais leur rôle dans l'acte de communication et dans la vie sociale." (Vernay, 1974:211) Degrees of "extremism" vary, with some authors giving up the idea of language being an object of translation and others recognizing that language is involved but is subsumed under the more important, actually dominant, factor of the purpose of translation. Thus, Holz-Mänttäri (1986) has no qualms about excluding language from the business of translation: "Für 'translatorisches Handeln' ist es wesentlich, den Gedanken fallen zu lassen, dass Texte oder Teile davon oder gar Sprachen 'übersetzt' werden." Reiss and Vermeer (1984) do not deny the role of language, but they see it as subservient to the purpose for which the translation is done: "Die Dominante aller Translation ist deren Zweck." (Reiss and Vermeer, 1984:96) And the (communicative) end justifies the (linguistic) means: "Der Zweck heiligt die Mittel." (1984:101)

(3) Much of the discussion of the role of interlingual relationships in translation is inspired by the participants' failure to establish a link between *langue* and *parole*. Systemic relations are established between languages as abstract objects but are then found to be inadequate for the reality of human communication involving translation. Consequently, they are abandoned wholesale by the more radical proponents of translation as "communicative transaction" (involving the original sender, translator and receiver, but not the relationship between their languages; cf. Harris, 1983; cf. also Seleskovitch, 1990:529: "La traduction s'intéresse aux discours et non aux langues.") or accepted as an initial step in the process of "text-induced text production" (Neubert, 1985:18). On the other hand, linguists do not seem eager to utilize normal human translations (produced for non-metalinguistic purposes) for the establishment of contrastive correspondences. Their reluctance is due to their inability to isolate the systemic (*langue*) relationships from what they see as random, *ad hoc* communicative (*parole*) relations resulting from a variety of other than linguistic factors. It is not surprising, therefore, that their analyses are based on translations of isolated sentences done for non-communicative (i.e. meta-linguistic) purposes and that in each instance the contrastive correspondences that are exhibited are one-to-one. Thus, a vicious circle is established: formal correspondence is seen as irrelevant in the search for translation equivalence, while translation equivalence for its part is ignored in the establishment of correspondences between linguistic (sub)systems.

The vicious circle can be broken only by re-establishing the link between translation and contrastive analysis. Notice in this connection that the term "contrastive correspondence" is to be preferred to "formal correspondence", both because of the ambiguity of the adjective "formal" and because the term is thus firmly rooted in contrastive linguistics. This also guarantees that *langue* features will be discussed with reference to *parole*, and vice versa.

(4) The main characteristics of the procedure for the establishment of

contrastive correspondence to be presented here (developed in Ivir, 1969, 1970, 1981) are the following: (1) The analyst works with a corpus consisting of a source and a target text which are assumed to stand in a relation of translational equivalence. (2) Formal elements are isolated from the source text and their counterparts are sought in the target text. (3) The counterparts are recognized as contrastive correspondents if they satisfy the back-translation test (cf. Spalatin, 1967; Ivir, 1988). Back-translation differs from translation in that it is restricted, semantically bound (meaning-preserving), non-communicative, and metalinguistic. (4) Correspondences are typically one-to-many rather than one-to-one. (5) The absence of correspondences in equivalent texts is ascribable either to linguistic (ultimately cultural) differences between the languages involved or to differences between the two contexts of situation.

The above characteristics require further specification. As regards the relation of equivalence, the analyst takes it for granted, accepting the authority of the translator as a competent bilingual speaker and competent communicator, as well as the fact that the translation served its purpose, however approximately and imperfectly, of communicating the original sender's intention to the ultimate receivers. This approach rests on the view of translation as a highly relative undertaking. In fact, all communication is relative rather than absolute, and translational communication is only more so. This is due to the factors that make up the context of situation in which communication takes place. These factors include the extralinguistic content to be communicated, the language chosen for communication (L1), the original sender as a linguistic person (speaker of L1), the spatio-temporal channel of communication, the nature of the sender's relation to his receivers, the receiver as a linguistic person (speaker of L1); in the case of translation, the (usually unintended) receiver is the translator, who is also a particular linguistic person (speaker of L1), then the language into which translation is done (L2), the translator as a linguistic person in that language (speaker of L2), the nature of the translator's relation to the ultimate receiver, the second channel of communication, and the ultimate receiver as a linguistic person (speaker of L2). Each of these factors participates in the process of communication and affects its result, and any change in any of the factors changes the communicative effect.

The infinitely changing nature of the factors which make up the communicative context of situation is responsible for the relativity of all communication — within a single language and across languages.

Communication involving translation is only more relative than that without the need for translation, because there are two contexts of situation in
the latter case and each factor acts twice instead of only once. The source
language (L1) is equipped in a particular way to deal with the extralinguistic content to be communicated. Its potential is relatively constant (even
though it, too, changes over time and place), but, what is more important, it
is certainly different from the potential that L2 puts at its speakers' disposal
to deal with that extralinguistic content. Speakers can only express what
their languages enable them to express. What the original sender's language
will enable him to express is certainly not the same as what the translator's
language will enable the translator to express. The sender acts as a speaker
of L1: his command of that language differs from that of any other speaker
of L1 and from his own command at other points in time (for instance, he
does not control the resources of his language in the same way in different
periods of his life, or when he is fresh as against when he is tired, when he
is sober as against when he has had a drink or two, when he has been
exposed to particular manifestations of that language as against when he has
not, etc.). Similarly, his coding will vary with his perception of the receivers
with whom he intends to communicate. In face-to-face communication, he
will adjust his wording in response to the feedback reaction from the
receivers, while in his communication with receivers who are not actually
present the imagined feedback guides his coding process. The point to note
is that the speaker is quite willing to concede the non-absolute status of his
message and is prepared to modify it so as to reach his receivers more
effectively. (Notice that while variation caused by the sender's particular
qualities as a linguistic person is for the most part unconscious, variation
caused by feedback from the receivers is often conscious and deliberate.
But in either case the effect is to make communication relative — the price
that the communicants readily pay, knowing that this is the only way that
communication can be achieved.) The changes that the transmitted message
undergoes in the channel of communication owing to the phenomenon of
noise and the variable decoding of the received message by the receiver as
a particular linguistic person add further to the relativity of communication.
Precisely the same considerations apply to the translator as receiver, translator as sender, the second channel of communication, and the ultimate
receiver, thus only compounding the relative nature of translational communication. One should note also a more pervasive factor, namely, culture:
the purpose of communication, in most general terms, is to convey culture,

but equally, and more importantly, all communication takes place against the background of culture. The original sender shares the same culture with receivers (who thus belong to an in-group), but he does not share it with the receivers of the translation (who are members of an out-group), and the extent of cultural distance is yet another factor making for the relativity of communication.

(5) The process of translationally effected communication sketched here is actually the process of achieving equivalence. Equivalence is thus seen to be relative and not absolute, achievable only in the communicative context of situation and having no existence outside that context; it is created anew in each new context as defined by the interplay of all the factors described above and is not stipulated in advance by an algorithm for the conversion of linguistic units of L1 (including whole texts as linguistic units of the highest order) into linguistic units of L2. There are only two points in that process at which languages as systems, with their repertoires of units and rules for their functioning, become operative. One is the original sender's choice of a particular language for communication and the other is the translator's choice of another language for translation.

The two languages are different systems, each offering its users a different set of expressive means for particular extralinguistic contents, each having a different potential on the level of *langue* — irrespective of the use to which a given speaker as a particular linguistic person is able to put it in the act of *parole* in a particular context of situation. Being different systems, they map the extralinguistic reality differently, and individual speakers have little control over what a given language can or cannot, must or must not, say. Also, they have little choice: they must accept the language as they find it, warts and all, or abandon the attempt to communicate. Fortunately, most speakers readily accept the preferred ways of expression offered by their languages, blissfully unaware of any limitations. Only an occasional poet will complain of the inadequacy of his language as a vehicle for the expression of what he would like to communicate. It is only when a speaker confronts his language with another language that he begins to appreciate that there are different possible ways of mapping the same extralinguistic reality and that his language obligatorily expresses certain features of that reality which the other language does not, and *vice versa*. The translator, being bilingual by definition, contrasts his two languages and is very much aware of the differences between them.

The systematic contrasting of L1 and L2 serves to establish correspondence (and their absence) between the two systems and to compare the expressive potentialities of the two languages. Contrasting can be, and has been, attempted in different ways: One approach is to take an L1 unit and contrast it with an L2 unit having the same form. This can be illustrated by internationalisms, say German *eventuel* and English *eventual,* and by identical abstract structures, such as the German Perfekt, *Ich habe gegessen,* and the English Present Perfect *I have eaten.* The formally identical units thus established are taken as formal correspondents and then compared semantically/functionally. Another possible approach is to take independently defined semantic categories and identify their realizations in L1 and L2. Examples would be, for instance, Definiteness in English and Russian, Iterativeness in Croatian and Italian, expression of Instrument in Spanish and English, etc. The third approach relies on metalinguistic labels as *tertium comparationis,* and units or processes are contrasted in pairs of languages — for instance, Adjectives in English and Croatian, Reflexivization in Russian and Italian, Nominalization in French and German, the Instrumental Case in Russian and Polish, etc.

Objections can be raised in connection with each of these approaches: the first approach relies on the identity of form, but that identity is an exception rather than the rule across languages; the second approach is jeopardized by the lack of a language-independent semantic system (we do not know what its categories are) and of any reliable criteria of class membership for any given category; the third approach presupposes a consistent linguistic theory with a fully developed metalanguage in terms of which both languages have been described to the same degree of exhaustiveness — an ideal that can hardly be said to have been achieved for any pair of languages. A more general objection valid for all three approaches is that they limit themselves to *langue* and take no account of *parole,* which is responsible for the relative paucity of the insights thus gained and their limited usefulness for the practice of translating.

A different approach has therefore been proposed (Ivir, 1969, 1970, 1981), one which relies on translation and assumes — in view of the concept of translation equivalence outlined above — that contrastive correspondents are potentially present in translationally paired texts, but that since the contrastive relationship between linguistic systems in only one of the factors participating in the translational context of situation, the translated text will fail to display some of the linguistic units present in the source text, while at the same time displaying certain linguistic units not present in the source text. The reasons for the translator's departure from the linguistic makeup of the source text (Ivir, 1983) are twofold: the shift is necessitated either by the difference between the linguistic systems or by the communicative needs arising from the action of some other factor in the context of situation.

The approach advocated here can be illustrated with the English correspondents of the Croatian Instrumental Case. The source text will yield a number of instances of use of that formal element, and for each of these uses the translation will have either zero or some L2 unit(s) relatable to it: *rezati nožem* — cut with a knife, *doći sa ženom* — come with one's wife, *doći vlakom* — come by train, *doći popodnevnim vlakom* — come on an afternoon train, *doći automobilom* — come by car/in a car, *doći biciklom* — come on a bicycle, *šetati parkom* — walk in the park, *prolaziti poljem* — walk across the field, *prolaziti šumom* — walk through the forest, *putovati prvim razredom* — travel first class, *letjeti Lufthansom* — fly Lufthansa, *odbiti s indignacijom* — refuse indignantly/with indignation, *predavati utorkom* — lecture on Tuesday/on Tuesdays/Tuesdays, *pisati tintom* — write in ink, etc. An example of the Instrumental having no counterpart in the translated text is found when the instruction *Pište štampanim slovima* "Write in block capitals" is translated as *Use block capitals*. The difference between the last example and the preceding ones is one between contrastive correspondents and a non-correspondent. The procedure to establish the difference and isolate contrastive correspondents in translationally equivalent texts is that of back-translation, which serves as a check on the semantic content: the translation *Use block capitals* back-translates as *Upotrijebite štampana slova,* showing that the Instrumental Case of the original *Pišite štampanim slovima* has not been preserved.

The identification of contrastive correspondents in the way described here achieves two things: while recognizing that both are involved, it separates *langue* and *parole* aspects of translation and thereby makes for a neater theoretical study of the translation process; second, it not only provides a more or less exhaustive list of correspondents (depending on the size of the corpus) but also enables generalizations to be made about the particular functions of the L1 unit that the different correspondents reflect (in our example, the Croatian Instrumental has different English correspondents for functions such as Instrument, Company, Manner, Mode, Means, Place, Time, etc.). Practical uses of such contrastive statements for translation pedagogy are not negligible, while a full-scale analysis of pairs of languages would result in bilingual dictionaries of correspondent linguistic units with specifications of the functions of each L1 unit covered by a particular L2 correspondent. In this way, contrastive correspondence and translation equivalence, though separated methodologically as they should be, would remain firmly linked, just as they are in translation itself: contrastive correspondents would be established on the basis of equivalent texts and would in turn be used by translators in their search for translation equivalence.

References

Bolinger, D. "Transformulation: Structural Translation." *Acta Linguistica Hafniensia*, Vol. 9 (1966), pp. 130–44.

Catford, J. C. *A Linguistic Theory of Translation*. London: Oxford University Press, 1965.

Harris, B. "Co-writing: A Canadian Technique for Communicative Equivalence." In *Semantik und Übersetzungswissenschaft*, Vol. 6, edited by G. Jäger and Albrecht Neubert. Übersetzungswissenschaftliche Beiträge Leipzig, 1983, pp. 121–32.

Holz-Mänttäri, J. *Translatorisches Handeln. Theorie und Methode*. Annales Academie Scientiarum fennicae, B 226. Helsinki, 1986.

Ivir, V. "Contrasting via Translation: Formal Correspondence vs. Translation Equivalence." Yugoslav Serbo-Croatian — English Contrastive Project. *Studies*, Vol. 1 (1969), pp. 13–25.

———. "Formal Correspondence vs. Translation Equivalence Revisited." *Poetics Today*, Vol. 2, No. 4 (1981), pp. 51–59.

———. "Reasons for Semantic Shifts in Translation." In *Semantik und Übersetzungswissenschaft*, Vol. 6, edited by G. Jäger and Albrecht Neubert. Übersetzungswissenschaftliche Beiträge, Leipzig, 1983, pp. 62–67.

———. "Remarks on Contrastive Analysis and Translation." Yugoslav Serbo-Croatian — English Contrastive Project. *Studies*, Vol. 2 (1970), pp. 14–26.

———. "Translation and Backtranslation." In *Yugoslav General Linguistics*, edited by M. Radovanovic. Amsterdam/Philadelphia: John Benjamins, 1988, pp. 131–43.

Jakobson, R. "On Linguistic Aspects of Translation." In *On Translation*, edited by R. A. Brower. Cambridge, Mass.: Harvard University Press, 1959, pp. 232–39.

Krzeszowski, T. P. "Equivalence, Congruence and Deep Structure." In *Papers in Contrastive Linguistics*, edited by G. Nickel. Cambridge: Cambridge University Press, 1971, pp. 37–48.

————. "Kontrastive Generative Grammatik." In *Reader zur kontrastiven Linguistik*, edited by G. Nickel. Frankfurt: Athenäum Fischer Verlag, 1972, pp. 75–84.

Marton, W. "Equivalence and Congruence in Transformational Contrastive Studies." *Studia Anglica Posnaniensia*, Vol. 1 (1968), pp. 53–62.

Meschonnic, H. "Poétique de la traduction." *Pour la poétique II*. Paris: Gallimard, 1973.

Mounin, G. *Les problèmes théoriques de la traduction*. Paris: Gallimard, 1963.

Neubert, A. *Text and Translation*. Übersetzungswissenschaftliche Beiträge 8. Leipzig, 1985.

Nida, E. A. *Toward a Science of Translating*. Leiden: E. J. Brill, 1964.

Nida, E. A. and C. R. Taber. *The Theory and Practice of Translation*. Leiden: E. J. Brill, 1969.

Reiss, K. and H. J. Vermeer. *Grundlegung einer allgemeinen Translationstheorie*. Tübingen: Max Niemeyer Verlag, 1984.

Seleskovitch, D. "La contribution de l'interprétation à la théorie de la traduction," *Übersetzungswissenschaft: Ergebnisse und Perspektiven, Festschrift für Wolfram Wilss zum 65 Geburtstag*, edited by A. Arntz and G. Thome. Tübingen: Gunter Narr Verlag, 1990, pp. 528–35.

Spalatin L. "Contrastive Methods." *Studia Romanica et Anglica Zagrabiensia*, Vol. 23 (1967), pp. 29–45.

Steiner, G. *After Babel: Aspects of Language and Translation*. London: Oxford University Press, 1975.

Vernay, H. *Essai sur l'organisation de l'espace par divers systèmes linguistiques: Contribution à une linguistique de la traduction*. München: 1974.

Voegelin, C. F. "Multiple Stage Translation." *International Journal of Applied Linguistics*, Vol. 20 (1954), pp. 271–80.

Wilss, W. *The Science of Translation: Problems and Methods*. Tübingen: Gunter Narr Verlag, 1982.

GRAMMAR

Grammar and Translation

Liu Miqing
Department of Translation
The Chinese University of Hong Kong, Hong Kong

Grammar is generally regarded as "a practical and instrumental means" by translators as well as translation teachers. Although people may argue about how relevant it is to the development of translation theory, one point in grammar is beyond question, that is, it is a key to linguistic analysis in source language syntax and text and a key to verification of the target language quality in equivalence to the source language meaning and form.

Grammar as a Cognitive Means of Meaning Acquisition in Translation

The first step to take in doing translation is to acquire the meaning of the source language. Grammar serves as a very useful means to help the translator to "break down" the source language sentence for meaning acquisition.

Grammatical Componential Analysis

Componential analysis based on source language grammar plays a decisive part for the translator in his attempt to obtain the semantic relationships of a source language sentence which, under any circumstances, is made up of syntactic components, namely, S (Subject), V (Verb), O (Object), C (Complement) and A (Adverbial). To make logical sense, these components must fall into sentence patterns with SV collocation as the kernel. These patterns are SV/SVO/ SVO_1O_2/SVOC/SVA/SVOA/SVC. The distribution of syntactic components in the form of patterns is so closely related to the meaning of the sentence it gives the translator a key to the semantic structure of that sentence. Hence:

He(S) that(S) is(V) too clever(C) is(V) not clever(C) at all(A) = S(SVC)VCA

gives an English-Chinese translator a basically corresponding sentence like

太聰明的人畢竟是不聰明的。

The next step for the translator, if he is sensitive enough, is just to refine, reshuffle or recast the "base" 句坯 into a sentence more acceptable while at the same time equivalent in meaning:

聰明反被聰明誤。

Therefore it is by and large correct to say that the more a translator knows about the source language grammar (lexicology, syntax and text-discourse), the greater is his ability to unfold the meaning of a source language sentence, the very first step in translation. It is even more the case when the source language is a highly inflected language in which the forms of S, V, O, C, and A are marked by specific inflectional systems.

For less or non-inflected languages like Chinese, the method of componential analysis is also instrumental for fixing grammar functions in different cases. For Chinese, syntactic functions of grammatical components are basically determined by word order and "empty words" (虛詞 , Cp., structural words or form words). For example, the sentence

人不可以無恥。無恥之恥，無恥矣。

The syntactic functions of the components in the above sentence are fundamentally determined by the linear order of SVO and the "empty word". Here, the word 無恥 (meaning "shameless"; its basic part of speech is adjective) has been used three times without any change in form but with different syntactic functions. The first is used after an auxiliary 可以 , hence is a "verbal adjective" 謂詞性形容詞 used as the predicate of the first sentence. The second is used before the empty word 之 (meaning "of"), therefore it is a noun, while the third one is again a "verbal adjective" used as the predicate. This analysis shows to some extent the peculiarities of the

Chinese grammar yet reveals again how it is instrumental in the translator's effort to bring out and shape up the meaning of the Chinese source language text into English:

> A man must not be without shame. Being without shame is a shame in itself.

Obviously enough, without resorting to sentence analysis of grammatical components, the translator will be at a loss and find no way to break down the surface structure of the source language sentence and dig out its meaning in general.

Semantic Implications Analysis

Very often an acquisition of meaning in general is not enough for translation. The translator is from time to time expected to dig out the meaning in particular. For example in an inflected language, grammatical forms chiefly derived from verb inflections (i.e., changes in the form of a verb to mark voice, tense, aspect and mood) may carry implications a translator cannot afford to neglect. Take voice in English.

1. He shaved this morning.
2. He had his beard shaved this morning.

The verb "shaved" in both sentences is the same in form but the voice is different. In (1), it is used in the active voice, while in (2) the passive voice. A grammatical change brings about different implications: in (1), "he" did the shaving himself while in (2), "he" caused somebody to shave for him. In Chinese, (1) and (2) may share the same equivalent — 他今早 刮過臉 , as "shaving" is an insignificant action. However, in the following cases, the fact "who did it" is so important that it can lead to different convictions:

3. He killed the man.
4. He had the man killed.

In that case the translator must be very careful to bring out the implications caused by the different grammatical functions of the two words of "killed", and express the differences properly in Chinese:

5. 他殺了那個人（他把那個人殺了）。
6. 他叫人把那個人殺了。

The same caution has to be employed in Chinese-English translation as the Chinese speakers usually do not pay any attention to this kind of implication:

    7. 她說她要把鋼琴搬到樓上去。

As analyzed above, the speaker is actually meaning to say:

    8. She said she would have the piano moved to upstairs.

Aspects of the English verb may also carry implications that are too subtle to be rendered in words yet should not be overlooked by a conscientious translator. Here grammatical category is again vested with subtle implications.

    9. He lives in Hong Kong.
       他住在香港。

But,

    10. He is living in Hong Kong.
       他目前住在香港。

And,

    11. Some people complain.
       有些人發牢騷。

But,

    12. Some people are always complaining.
       有些人總是愛發牢騷。

While (9) and (11) are simply "factual", (10) implies temporarity and (12) reveals a resentful feeling. For an English-Chinese translator, he must be careful enough to detect the implication nuance and try to express it in Chinese.

    But then implication by way of grammatical mechanism (inflection, category shift, etc) is always a problem in bilingual transferring, the crux being the subtlety in semantic content and the limited means of conveying it. Very often it is a case of " 增一字則嫌多，減一字又嫌少 " (One word more would be excessive, one word less too little). The difficulty usually results from the basic disparities between the Chinese and English grammar. In Chinese, grammatical categories may be covertly indicated by lexical means 詞匯手段 or by nothing at all; but in English, inflections, an overt grammatical functional system, still play a decisive role in semantic structure.

Grammar as a Check-up Means for Correct Translation

It is quite possible for one to get some understanding of a source language text by his language experience or simply by intuition. But no thorough and correct comprehension of a source language text can be achieved without exercising one's systematic knowledge of source language grammar. In translation, the simple truth is, a good knowledge of source language grammar not only leads to a thorough and correct understanding of the source language but also results in an appropriate and exact paraphrase in the target language. In other words, grammar plays a two-fold role for the translator: a cognitive means for the source language and a check-up means for the target language.

As a check-up means, grammar can be applied to find out mistranslations, thus enhancing the target language quality. Chinese-English/English-Chinese mistranslations which occur most frequently can be grouped as follows:

Group A: Mistranslations due to incorrect analysis of the source language syntactic structure.

13. It's as likely that he'll damn you as say "Good morning".
他好像是向你問好，實際上是在罵你呢。(wrong)
他很可能向你道聲「早安」，也可能罵你一頓。(right)

The incorrect translation seems basically to result from incorrect analysis of the source language sentence structure. The translator would have done better if he had figured out the complete structure: It is as likely that he will damn you as that he will say "Good morning".

14. 他這個人年年舉債，天天酒肉。(雖然年年舉債，仍舊天天酒肉)
He is in debt every year, because he is always indulging himself in food and wine. (wrong)
He is in debt every year; nevertheless he keeps on indulging himself in food and wine. (right)

Chinese text tends to be loosely connected, favouring what is called "parataxis" 意合, and the "case-gap" of conjunction (coordinate or subordinate) is always a problem. Correct analysis of syntactic relationship is often based on sound logic in Chinese-English text translation.

Group B: Mistranslations due to incorrect analysis of tense, voice, mood, or aspect of the verb in source language sentence.

15. She was sitting beside his desk now in an aroma of perfumes, smoothing the handle of her umbrella and nodding the great black feather in her hat. Mr Alleyne *had swivelled* his chair round to face and thrown his right foot jauntily upon his left knee. (J. Joyce)

    此刻她正坐在他的寫字桌邊，全身散發出濃郁的香味，她撫摸著傘把，帽子上的一枝大的黑色羽毛不斷地顫動著；於是阿連恩先把轉椅轉過來面對著她，逍遙自在地將右腳擱在左膝上。(wrong)

    此刻她正坐在他的寫字桌邊，全身散發出濃郁的香味，她撫摸著傘把，帽子上的一枝大的黑色羽毛不斷地顫動著。這時，阿連恩先已把轉椅轉過來面對著她，逍遙自在地將右腳擱在左膝上。(right)

16. 有一天，世界上的人一半白，一半黑；那不用說就不成其為世界了。

    If the human species is divided 50-50 into black and white, it goes without saying it will not be the world we know. (wrong)

    Were the human species divided 50-50 into black and white, it goes without saying that it would not be the world we know. (right)

Group C: Mistranslations due to incorrect analysis of the modifier-modified relationship in the source language.

17. The new suit needs a white shirt and a pair of black shoes to match.

    這套新裝需要配件白襯衣和一雙合適的黑皮鞋。(wrong)

    這套新裝需要配白襯衣和黑皮鞋。(right)

18. 那是一棟新職工宿舍。(新〔的〕＋〔職工宿舍〕)

    That is an apartment house for new staff members. (新職工＋宿舍)
    (wrong)

    That is a new apartment house for staff members. (right)

Group D: Mistranslations due to incorrect analysis of reference and coherence.

19. Anna told Lucy that Ruth was going to leave, but she didn't believe her.

    安娜對露西說，魯絲要走了，但安娜并不信魯絲眞的要走。

    (wrong)

安娜對露西說，魯絲要走了，但露西不信安娜的話。 (right)

20. 旁觀者清，當局者迷。（旁觀者清，而當局者迷）

Although outsiders can see clearly, the persons concerned are often in the dark. (wrong)

Outsiders see more of the truth. (right)

Lexical mistranslations in English/Chinese-Chinese/English transfer are, needless to say, the most frequent in occurrence. It is more of a semantic than a grammatical problem.

Grammatical Theories and Translation

Some critics in the past have rather rashly asserted that grammatical theories of modern linguistic schools "have little to do with translation." (SIL, 1977) As a matter of fact, we can say with some confidence that translation studies may benefit from not a few linguistic schools which concern themselves with grammar. The point is, grammatical theory is advanced to enunciate propositions about language mechanisms, not about translation. It is the task of translators and translation theorists to bring forth the value for translation studies from various grammatical theories, not vice versa.

Translation Studies and Structuralist Grammar

Structuralism contributes methodologically to translation studies. American Structuralism, together with its European pioneers, the Prague Group and the Copenhagen School, carries on Ferdinand de Saussure's preponderant attention to synchronic analysis of language structure without neglecting its diachronic development.

Translators and translation studies benefit from Structuralism methodologically. Despite the general neglect of meaning (Bloomfield, 1955; Harris, 1963), Structuralists' close and systematic observations of the *form* of language help translators and translation studies to pay particular attention to language *structure* to grasp source language meaning instead of relying heavily on the translators' intuitive appreciation or general impression, which, more often than not, only catches the drift of what the source language really means. The shift, though a methodological change in nature, has brought about a remarkable improvement in translation quality since the fifties of this century not only in China but the world over.

In the wake of Structuralism, translators and translation studies have begun to pay much attention to analysis of morphemes, the distribution pattern of "sememe" 義素 (Bloomfield, 1955) and "sentence patterns" 句型 (C. C. Fries). In China, the American Structuralists' method of IC (Immediate Constituent) Analysis (Bloomfield, 1933; Well, 1947) has contributed immensely to the progress of translation studies along with the enhancement of translation quality. As a matter of fact, the Structuralist approach to sentence analysis by means of IC subdivision is still held by most translators in China as the most feasible way to get to the bottom of the syntactic and semantic structure of a source language sentence.

What is ironical is the fact that except for Fries, A. Gleason (1955) and Eugene Nida (1951), almost all structuralists play down the role of "meaning" in structural analysis, but then their methods (chiefly substitution, comparison, distribution and IC analysis) turn out to be effective ways to bring out the "meaning". Things do not always turn out the way one claims. The same seems true of linguistics and translation studies.

Translation and Semantic Analysis of the London School

The London School in linguistics is generally regarded as the group of modern linguists represented by J. R. Firth, B. Malinowski and M. A. K. Halliday. The grammatical theory of the London School which has proved very helpful to translation studies relates chiefly to the basic principles pertaining to "meaning inference" 意義推斷 , the fundamental task in translation.

Linguists of the school mostly concern themselves with problems of meaning and the factors that determine meaning. Coincidentally, a translator's basic concern in doing translation is to handle all those factors that determine meaning. His next step, theoretically, is to put all the meaning he has grasped from the source language into target language, which is usually called "expression" in translation studies. Obviously, successful expression is based on "an exact and thorough grasp" of the source language meaning. The point here is how to make the grasp of source language meaning "exact and thorough" in order to put it into exactly equivalent expression in the target language. A poor translator would stick to each and every individual word and carefully put them together. This seemingly close translation will often end in mistranslation, if not absurdity. The principle maintained by Malinowski (1923) to ensure meaning inference involves a set of premises: (1) the meaning of a language is geared to the environment of the language;

(2) the meaning of a language must not be found in itself alone, but in the context of culture and the context of situation; (3) thus, meaning inference is to be done in specific reference to *social function*. According to Malinowski, the meaning of a word is not in the word itself but in the context to which it is geared. This is the first reference to meaning inference from the functional point of view.

Firth accepted Malinowski's principle (1957), and specified "context of situation" by pointing out that language is a social process which can be described in terms of "speech act", by which he means "an act" including participants, the environment and the effect. Therefore, the meaning of a speech act is bound to be heterogeneous: it contains the meaning in the context of situation, which is the exterior factor that determines the meaning, and contains the meaning in the context of structure which is the interior factor that determines the meaning.

Malinowski's and Firth's approach to meaning is so significant for meaning inference in translation that it has been widely accepted as a very practical as well as theoretical way of translation not only of words but also of sentences. Firth's formula of "meaning is determined by collocation" is kept in mind as a golden rule by many translators in China.

Halliday's systemic-functional grammar began to attract the attention of translation scholars in China late in the 1970's. His studies in cohesion in English (1976) bear much relevance to translation studies due to the great disparities between Chinese and English. Descriptions of different use of "cohesive ties" are of great help to Chinese translators in their translation of "text" 語段 from Chinese into English in particular.

Translation and Functional Grammar

Translators and translation theorists have found that the basic approach of Functional Grammar has noticeable relevance to bilingual transfer in practice as well as in theory. As a matter of fact, functional grammarians, or functionalists, do not at all unanimously identify themselves with the Functional School, which is also called Prague Group represented by V. Mathesius (1882–1945) and Roman Jakobson (1896–1982). Functional Grammar is widely regarded as a general approach to the mechanism of *communicative functions* of language rather than a specific system of grammatical rules.

Functions of language in communication play a decisive role, because both *meaning* and *form* are subject to language function. Under any circumstances, language in communication must serve a function which helps to shape up, readjust and determine the semantic and syntactic structure. This functional approach to language was initiated by Saussure and was developed by A. Meillet (1866–1936) and A. Martinet (1908–   ). Since function is always performed and fulfilled in communication, present-day functional grammar runs parallel with communicative grammar, which has been widely maintained by Halliday, R. Quirk, J. Svartvik, S. U. Philips, E. Nida and transformational-generative grammarians.

As stated above, a language-in-action, which carries meaning and takes form, is always motivated by function. A shift in function in communication is bound to bring about change in form or syntactic structure without changing the semantic content. This is a point that has much to do with translation. Take for example the potential of the two semantic units 你 and 好 in Chinese to form sentences. Note just how a change in function leads to a change in sentence structure:

Function	*Form of Utterance*
1. Greeting: 你好！	Hello, hi, Morning, etc.
2. Enquiring: 你好嗎？（近來怎樣？）	How are you keeping?
3. Assessing: 你（很）好。（我認爲你是個好人）	You're a nice guy.
4. Reassuring: 你（是）好（的）。（他不怎麼樣）	You're all right.
5. Rebutting: 你（這算）好（哇）？！	As if you were all right!
6. Reproaching: 你（眞夠）好的！	What a terrible fellow you are!

From the functional point of view, any variation in the structure of an utterance must imply a shift of function of the language in communication. In translation, accordingly, what looks important in form is actually determined not only by the semantic content but by the content flexibly adapted for a specific communicative purpose. This role played by function has been called by functionalists "sifting of function" 功能的篩選過程 . Relevance of functional grammar to translation also includes aspects such as registers, text and textual function of language, semantic macro-functions 宏觀語功能 (Halliday, 1973, 1975), and speech level and language situation.

Translation and Transformation-generative Grammar

The relevance of transformation-generative grammar to translation has long been a controversy in the circles of translation and translation studies. The controversy is still under way in China as well as in countries with English as their mother tongue (Newmark, 1988). Obviously enough, any "yes" or "no" answer to such a complicated question like this would be an oversimplification of the contradictions. A cautious approach would immediately admit the following points:

1. Since transformation-generative grammar contains a set of rules pertaining to *intralingual* transformation and generation, its relevance to *bilingual* transfer is inherently limited;
2. Since transformation-generative grammar deals with transformational and generative rules of *language*, though intralingually, its relevance to bilingual transfer is, again inherently, evident.

This analytic approach obviously has an advantage, for it allows us to maintain readiness to draw on the strength of transformation-generative grammatical theory for the promotion of Chinese-English/English-Chinese translation studies.

Deep Structure, Surface Structure and Translation

Noam Chomsky's transformation-generative grammatical theory has undergone four stages in its development since its founding in 1957, when Chomsky published his *Syntactic Structure*. Throughout the stages, transformation-generative grammar has consistently concerned itself with the mechanism of language generation of the human race. The four-stage development signifies transformation-generative grammar's process of continuous refinement. According to Chomsky's REST (Revised Extended Standard Theory), the perfected formula of language transformation and generation, the mechanism can be illustrated in Diagram One.

This diagram of the whole of process of human language transformation and generation from concepts in the brain (inner speech) to verbal expression (speech), gives some enlightenment for bilingual transfer.

Diagram One

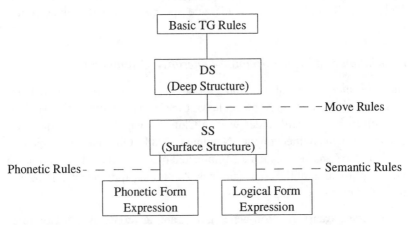

Basically, the process of translation is all the way from source language comprehension to target language expression. According to Chomsky's REST, the process of bilingual transfer can be illustrated in Diagram Two.

Diagram Two

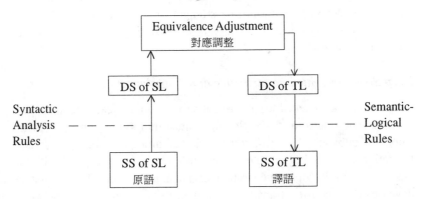

As is shown in this diagram, the movement of translation thinking starts from surface structure of source language, goes forward to deep structure of source language and gets into the most dynamic, selective and productive domain of thinking, namely, Equivalence Adjustment. The result of the dynamic selection and production is the surface structure of target language processed upon the target language semantic-logical rules. This description of bilingual transfer in the wake of transformation-generative grammar may offer us a basic clue to the theory of translation procedures 翻譯程序論 , and provide a fact to show that in translation the decisive task in the whole process is Equivalence Adjustment. And this task, theoretically, is supposed to be fulfilled basically in the domain of the deep structure.

Translation and Case Grammar

Case Grammar was first put forward by C. J. Fillmore in 1968 in his article "The Case for Case" as a branch of transformation-generative grammar. In his works Fillmore defines "case" as a concept different from traditional grammar. For Fillmore a "case" suggests the grammatical relationships of a syntactic component in deep structure. Case grammar concerns itself with the "syntactic-semantic relationship" 句法語義關係 of every noun or noun phrase in terms of "case", such as agentive, objective, dative 與格 , factitive 使成格 , locative 處所格 and instrumental 工具格 . As for the verb in deep structure, it is characterized by the linear arrangement of a "case frame", indicating the grammatical relationship of the verb and the noun in a specific frame. For example, the verb "remove" is usually put in the "frame" of an animate agentive (A) plus objective (O), namely, "– O + A." Similarly, the verb "give" is usually put in the frame of "– O + D (dative) + A". With the help of case frames, the translator, hopefully, will be able to work out the arrangement the "syntactic-semantic relationships" of the source language sentence in deep structure, and, from that "base", he will be able to work out the configuration of the sentence components in target language surface structure. Take for example cases in a deep structure: Tom(A, i.e., agentive), the log(O, i.e., objective), an axe(I, i.e., instrumental) and the verb "chop", which is usually put in the case frame of "– O + I + A". Based on the frame, the sentence in the deep structure would be: "Tom chopped the log with an axe." Then, based on the deep structure, the surface structure of the Chinese target language would be 湯姆用斧子砍木頭 .

Other aspects of application of case grammar in translation have been illustrated by Newmark (1988) such as filling in "case-gaps" and making options of "case-partners". In China, researchers and technicians of machine translation are turning to case grammar after attempts to make use of transformation-generative grammar rules for transformation, including "deleting" 刪除 , "copying" 復寫 , "adding" 添加 and "reordering" 位移 , proved virtually fruitless.

Translation and the Reorientation of the Studies in Chinese Grammar

The 1980s saw a reorientation of the basic approach to the study of contemporary Chinese grammar. A group of Chinese grammarians, chiefly from central and southeast China, issued vigorous challenges to the traditional approach to grammatical studies initiated by Ma Jianzhong, who wrote *Ma's Grammar* 《馬氏文通》 from 1882 to 1896. Published in 1898, it is a very influential monograph on Chinese grammar, based on Latin grammatical rules. Though an unprecedented breakthrough which started an effort to analyze the Chinese language grammatically in a *linguistic* way, its weaknesses and limitations have been pointed out by Luo Changpei 羅常培 , Wang Li 王力 , Zhao Yuanren 趙元任 , Lü Shuxiang 呂叔湘 , Gao Mingkai 高名凱 and many other veteran linguists. The basic problem has been made crystal clear: historical-comparative linguistics makes possible the groupings of languages into language families, and different language families have developed different grammatical systems worlds apart from one another. Accordingly, the Chinese language can hardly be properly analyzed in the light of a grammatical system basically deduced from the Indo-European family, as it belongs to a very different group, the Han-Tibetan language family.

Proceeding from the arguments and in the wake of the pioneers' analyses, the reorientation of grammatical studies concerns itself with the primary aspects of the language and grammatical features of present-day Chinese:

1. Reassessing the necessity of the transliteration of Chinese characters into the Chinese phonetic alphabet 漢語拼音化 .
2. Embarking on a comprehensive undertaking of constructing a new framework for the grammar of the Chinese language based on the following principles: (a) the necessity of renewed investigation of the grammatical function of the system of the Chinese character 漢字的語法功能體系 ; (b) a systematic understanding of the *flexible* nature of Chinese grammar free from analogical inferences from and mechanical comparison with inflected languages; (c) full

attention to be paid to the connection between the Chinese style of thinking and the structure of Chinese language and mode of expression.

3. Embarking on an interdisciplinary investigation with a view to developing a new subject of "Chinese Cultural Linguistics" 中國文化語言學 , a subject which "combines the source material of Chinese language with various problems in the history of Chinese culture, so that the interrelationship between Chinese language and the history of Chinese culture can be better defined."

The new effort to reorientate the approach to Chinese grammatical studies proves helpful to translation and bilingual contrastive studies, which has been regarded as one of the foundation subjects of translation theory. Efforts made for the reorientation will prove of service to Chinese-English/English-Chinese translators in the following areas:

1. Defining the meaning — especially the connotation — of the Chinese word thus making it possible for the translator to achieve exact or more appropriate target language equivalence. For example in present-day Chinese 吹噓 is used in a derogatory sense. Investigation made from the diachronical and cultural angle proves that it is used in a complimentary sense in Du Fu's 杜甫 poem 揚雄更有河東賦，唯待吹噓送上天 (Yang Xiong wrote his "He Dong Fu", expecting our extolment.) This stress on diachronical and cultural research of the semantic content of Chinese lexicon will help the translator to avoid one-sidedness of morpheme analysis.

2. Breaking away from rigid classification of parts of speech, syntactic components and sentence patterns in the framework of Indo-European languages and grammatical norms. Textual flexibility based on pragmatic mechanisms characterizes the structure of the Chinese language especially at the syntactic level. A typical sentence like 花生米下酒 is just as normal in SVO-pattern in present-day Chinese as "I like Chinese wine" in the English SVO sentence. In translation a sub-categorization of the subject is therefore absolutely necessary in order to put the Chinese subject in proper syntactic place in the target language.

3. Paying attention to the *style* of Chinese thinking and finding expression for it in the forms of a language characterized by tense, voice, mood, etc. Thus a sentence like 活幹完了 in the active voice is just

as normal in Chinese as "The job has been done" in English in the passive voice. From the point of view of the new approach, the use of voice in Chinese is more of a stylistic nature than a grammatical norm and a logical inference.

References

Feng, Zhiwei 馮志偉.《現代語言學流派》 (*Schools of Contemporary Linguistics*). Shaanxi: Shaanxi People's Press 陝西人民出版社, 1984.

Fillmore, C. J. "The Case for Case." In *Universals of Linguistic Theory*, edited by E. Bach and R. T. Harms. New York: Holt, Rinehart and Winston, 1968.

Firth, J. R. *Papers in Linguistics*. London: Oxford University Press, 1951.

Halliday, M.A.K. *Explorations in the Functions of Language*. London: Arnold, 1968.

Newmark, L. *Grammatical Theory and Teaching of English*. NASFA Papers, 1964.

Newmark, Peter. *A Textbook of Translation*. Hertfordshire: Prentice Hall, 1988.

Nida, Eugene A. *Componential Analysis of Meaning: An Introduction to Semantic Structures*. The Hague: Mouton, 1975.

Quirk, Randolph, *et al*. *A Grammar of Contemporary English*. London: Longman, 1972.

Shen, Xiaolong 申小龍.《中國文化語言學》 (*Chinese Cultural Linguistics*). Jilin: Jilin Education Press 吉林教育出版社, 1990.

Voice

Simon S. C. Chau
Department of English
Hong Kong Baptist College, Hong Kong

Voice, according to some modern grammarians, is the relation between the participants and the event indicated in the verb. Examples:

active (he went)
passive (he was hit)
middle (he did it to her)
reflexive (he did it for himself)
reciprocal (they hit each other)
benefactive (she worked for him)
transitive (hit him)
intransitive (he came)
instrumental (he hit her with it)
agentive (he sent it through her)
causative (he caused it to happen)

In translating from English to Chinese, the main problem with voice seems to be that of the use of the passive in English and its realization in Chinese.

Even good multilinguists are not always aware of the fact that not every language makes use of the passive in the same way and to the same extent. Translators often make mistakes when they keep the voice (active or passive) of the source language in their target language translation "automatically".

There are languages with no passive constructions formally. Others use these by different rules. In many languages from East Africa to Southeast Asia, the passive is used only in a bad or unpleasant sense. Sometimes it communicates the negative feeling of the speaker. At other times it casts an undesirable value on the content of the message. For example, in Thai, a sentence like

— He was sent to America to study.

sounds incongruous, because this is considered a very pleasant experience. But

— The boy was sent to school.

is acceptable, meaning that he is being forced against his will to attend school. The following sentences are not acceptable:

— We are loved by God.
— We were invited to the party by the mayor.

Certain verbs in Thai can most readily be used in the passive voice, such as "to kill, to hit, to blame".

Obviously, the same is not true of Chinese, but the English-Chinese translator would do well to remember:

1. Not every passive construction ought to be retained in the target language translation.
2. While the passive in English is almost always realized by the use of the preposition "by", the equivalent Chinese ones are far more flexible.

Failure to observe these two points results in "translationese".

Statistically, there is a marked gap. Comparing a number of Chinese vs. English texts of the same register will reveal that passive constructions are notably more common in English. Many ideas expressed in the passive in English turn up as active in equivalent Chinese texts, while the opposite rarely happens. So the problem for the translator is when to retain the passive, and how.

The idea of using the passive form with English-speaker is fundamentally different from that with the Chinese. In Chinese, the passive form is usually employed together with the agent of the action, otherwise the notional passive is used instead.

In English, on the other hand, when the agent or doer of the action expressed by the predicate verb is to be emphasized, we make it the subject of the sentence which is thus in the active form. Or when the object of the action is to be emphasized, we make the object of the verbal action the subject of the sentence which is thus said to be in the passive form. So the agent of the action is usually not expressed in an English sentence in the passive form, just contrary to the Chinese construction.

While the passive form is comparatively rare in Chinese, it plays a very important role in English. The English-speaker considers it necessary to put the verb in the active in some cases, and in the passive in others. Typically:

1. When the active subject is known and need not be mentioned:
   — All the counter-revolutionaries *will*, sooner or later, be *arrested* and *punished* accordingly. (i.e. by the government or the police.) Typical Chinese equivalent: retain passive, supply agent as object of sentence.
   — Visitors *are requested* to wait a little. (i.e. by the host, managers, etc.) Typical Chinese equivalent: turn into active, with active subject dropped.
2. When the active subject is unknown or cannot be readily stated:
   — The doctor *was* immediately *sent for*. Chinese: turn into active, supply agent ("someone").
   — New factories, schools and hospitals *are being built* in the city. Chinese: turn into active, with no agent as active subject.
3. When the active subject is self-evident from the context:
   — The toast *was* duly drunk. Chinese: turn into active, supply subject ("the host and guests", "everyone", etc.)
4. When the active subject is not mentioned for some special reasons (tact or delicacy of sentiment):
   — Some things have *been said* here tonight and ought not to have been spoken. Chinese: turn into active; supply subject ("someone").
5. When the active subject is less important than the object:
   — A child *was run over* by a car. Chinese: retain passive with 被 or similar unpleasant prepositions, see below.
6. When the active subject is avoided for stylistic reasons (e.g. to avoid incoherence on account of shifting construction):
   — *I was asked* several questions in the oral exam and answered every one correctly. (instead of "The teacher asked me several questions in the oral exam and I answered correctly".)

Chinese: turn into active, with the active subject dropped.
— Larry actually loved her and *was loved* in return.
Chinese: turn into active with active subject supplied.

It is clear from the above examples that there is no single rule of handling passive constructions when translating, instead there are a few standard strategies.

Here are a few features relevant to English-Chinese translation:

1. Unlike English, there is at times no sharp distinction between an active and a passive construction in Chinese, syntactically as well as semantically. A line like
   — 不覺青林沒晚潮。

   not aware green forest cover/disappear evening tide
   can be interpreted as "gradually, the green forest fades out in the evening tide". The very force of the expression lies in the ambiguity of the image.

2. Obvious semantically passive ideas are expressed in syntactically "neutral" forms, without passive markers:
   — 狡兔死走狗烹。

   wild rabbits dead, hunting dogs boil.
   (After all the wild rabbits are hunted, the dogs are put into the pot to be boiled and served as meals.)
   — 書還沒有看完。

   book yet not have been read through.

3. Untutored translators tend to retain the passive form in Chinese blindly, thus either make the target language translation sound unnecessarily marked, or utterly unnatural:
   — He was deeply loved by her. 他是被她深深地愛著的。
   — We were given a hearty welcome.? 我們被給以熱誠的歡迎。
   — What are you called?* 你被叫什麼名字？
   (An asterisk before a sample sentence cited denotes unacceptable grammatical construction; a question mark indicates doubt in grammaticality.)

4. Untutored translators tend to put down 被 as passive marker every time when constructing passive sentences, thus resulting in translationese. They have to be reminded that there are other legitimate passive markers, each with slightly different functions and tones. A

wrong choice of alternative preposition for the English "by" may result in stylistically unacceptable or ungrammatical sentences. For example, some prepositions can only be used in positive contexts, others the opposite:

— He was criticized by the management.

    He- 被 — the management-criticized.

    He- 挨 — the management-criticized.

    * He- 蒙 — the management-criticized.

— He was praised by the management.

    He- 被 — the management-praised.

    * He- 挨 — the management-praised.

    He- 蒙 — the management-praised.

And there are other semantic restrictions on different equivalents of "by":

— He was betrayed by his friends.

    He- 給 — friends-betrayed.

    He- 被 — friends-betrayed.

    He- 由 — friends-betrayed.

    * He- 受 — friends-betrayed.

    He- 挨 — friends-betrayed.

— He was replaced by her.

    ? He- 給 — her-replaced.

    He- 被 — her-replaced.

    He- 由 — her-replaced.

    * He- 受 — her-replaced.

    * He- 挨 — her-replaced.

— He was given a beating.

    He- 給 — others-beaten.

    He- 被 — others-beaten.

    * He- 由 — others-beaten.

    He- 受 — others-beaten.

    He- 挨 — others-beaten.

On the whole, 被 is the constant while others are all variables with different shades of meaning. It should also be pointed out that where several alternatives are possible, there are usually stylistic nuances. For example, in "He was given a beating", the use of 挨 is more emotionally charged than the more neutral 給 or the unmarked 被 . The examples given above are by no means exhaustive. The choice of another alternative 爲 , for instance, introduces a formal and archaic flavour.

1. There are times when it is more desirable to retain the original passive construction, especially when the same idea can be expressed in the passive in Chinese in a natural way, or when changing into active would alter the meaning:
   — Members agreed that the declaration would be drafted by Mr Lee, revised by the Secretariat, and approved by the Presidium.
     會員公議宣言由李君草擬，由秘書處修正，再經主席團批准。
   — His suggestions were not accepted.
     他的建議沒有受到接納。
   — The murderer was arrested on the scene.
     兇手當場就捕。

2. In a large number of cases, the translator is obliged by Chinese grammar or stylistic considerations to change the passive construction in English into active Chinese expressions:
   — He was given a banana.
     他得到一隻香蕉。 (He got/received a banana.)
   — It was learned that …
     據聞 … (One learns that …)
   — Have your hands been washed?
     手洗了沒有? (Hands already washed?)
   — I was warned that …
     我聽人警告說 … (I heard others warning me that …)
   — She was not surprised when she was told the news.
     她聽到消息沒覺得驚奇。 (She heard the news and did not feel surprising.)
   — I am convinced that he embezzled public funds.
   — I am satisfied that he embezzled public funds.
     (both should become) 我確信他盜用了公款。 (I surely believe that he embezzled public funds.)
   — The patient's pulse is returning to normal. It is hoped that he will come out of the coma soon.
     病人脈搏漸回復正常，希望很快就會從昏睡中醒過來。
     (The patient's pulse is returning to normal. Hope he will come out of the coma soon.)

The English-Chinese translator is also warned to watch out for past participles used as adjectives in English. They must not be mistaken for passive constructions. This is not an uncommon mistake made by careless translators:

— a *trained* horse (a horse which has been trained, NOT a horse under training or being trained by someone.)
— a *burnt* house, the bread is *burnt*. (in both cases, "burnt" is an adjective qualifying the noun, and not a passive verb.)
— This Shakespeare is *bowdlerized*. (same as above.)

GRAPHIC TRANSLATION

Translation of English Letters as Shape Describers

Zhang Peiji
University of International Business and Economics
Beijing, China

The 26 letters of the English alphabet, which represent speech sounds in English and in which we write English words, are often used to describe the shapes of things. Each of these letters, from A to Z, especially when capitalized, possesses a distinct and unique shape of its own, and is thus capable of performing the function of shape description in both spoken and written English. It is a common practice for English-speaking people to name different things from their distinctive shapes or appearances. For instance, anything shaped like a horseshoe is often named *a horseshoe* (The town stood in the mouth of a *horseshoe*/The central plains were surrounded by a vast *horseshoe* of hills.) A radio or TV antenna with two movable, branched metallic rods shaped like two rabbit ears is called a rabbit-ear antenna. Likewise, the English letters are often used as one of the handy means for naming things, e.g.:

A-tent	A 形帳篷
C-spring	C 形發條
D-valve	D 形活門
F-hole	提琴上的 F 形孔眼
H-post	H 形電桿
I-beam	I 字樑

J-bolt	J 形螺釘
K-frame	K 形架
L-iron	L 形鐵
S-hook	S 形鈎
T-bone	T 骨牛排
U-tube	U 形管
V-belt	三角皮帶
Y-gun	Y 形雙筒炮
Z-crank	乙字曲柄

Moreover, because of their shape-describing function, the English letters are used not only for naming things, but also as a common stylistic device. See the following lines quoted from the prologue of Shakespeare's history play *Henry the Fifth*:

But pardon, gentles all,
The flat unraised spirit that hath dar'd
On this unworthy scaffold to bring forth
So great an object: can this cockpit hold
The vasty fields of France? or may we cram
Within *this wooden O* the very casques
That did affright the air at Agincourt?
但，諸位貴客們，請原諒
我們這些拙劣的演員，不自量力，
竟敢在簡陋的戲台上扮演
這齣大戲。難道這圓劇院容納得下
廣闊無垠的法蘭西沙場？難道這
木製圓形場裝得下
那些當年震撼阿琴古爾的勇士們？

In the sixth line, *the wooden O* refers to the Globe Theatre, a famous London playhouse erected in the summer of 1599 during the Elizabethan age. Standing outside the city of London, the Theatre was a roundish wooden structure of three stories, so high for its size that it looked more like a clumsy tower than a theatre. Shakespeare made clever use of the shape-describing letter *O,* calling the Theatre this *wooden O* instead of this *roundish wooden building.* Besides, *O* also meets the requirement of sound and rhythm in the said line and makes the language more witty, hinting at the narrowness and limitations of the stage in the Theatre and matching and supplementing the metaphor *cockpit* in the fourth line (which is also suggestive of such narrowness and limitations).

The following poem is quoted from the first chapter of *A Dream of Red Mansions* 《紅樓夢》:

時逢三五便團圞，滿把清光護玉欄；天上一輪才捧出，人間萬姓仰頭看。

The translation made into English by David Hawkes is:

In thrice five nights her perfect *O* is made,
Whose cold light bathes each marble balustrade.
As her bright wheel starts on its starry ways,
On earth ten thousand heads look up and gaze.

Let us compare it with the translation made by Yang Hsien-yi and Gladys Yang:

On the fifteenth *the moon is full*,
Bathing jade balustrades with her pure light;
As her bright orb sails up the sky
All men on earth gaze upwards at the sight.

In the first line of the Chinese original, 團圞 , meaning *to become circular*, refers to the full moon. While Yang Hsien-yi and Gladys Yang put it into English literally: *the moon is full*, David Hawkes picked on the shape-describing letter *O* to express the same idea.

Next is an example quoted from Chapter Three of Thomas Hardy's *Tess of the d'Urbervilles*:

Joan Durbeyfield, as she spoke, curved a sodden thumb and forefinger to *the shape of the letter C*, and used the other forefinger as a pointer.
瓊‧德伯維爾一邊說，一邊把笨拙的大姆指和食指彎曲成C字形，並用另一隻手的食指來指點。

According to the novel, Tess' father went to see a doctor, who diagnosed the old man's illness as heart trouble and said that his heart was enclosed by fat except for a little space still open. In the cited example, Joan Durbeyfield, who was Tess' mother, repeated what the doctor had said with the help of her fingers. Hardy made effective use of the letter *C* to picture graphically the two curved fingers and the little open space in-between.

The following are two sentences quoted from two different sources:

魯鎮的酒店的格局，是和別處不同的：都是當街一個曲尺形的大櫃台，櫃裡面預備著熱水，可以隨時溫酒。（魯迅：〈孔乙己〉）

The layout of Luzhen's taverns is unique. In each, facing you as you enter, is *a bar in the shape of a carpenter's square* where hot water is kept for warming rice wine.

錫箔店幾乎佈滿全城，茶館和有著<u>曲尺形櫃台</u>的小酒店也隨處都可以看到。（王士菁：《魯迅傳》）
Tinfoil-paper shops, teahouses and small taverns with their *L-shaped bars* could be found all over the city.

The expression 曲尺形櫃台 , which appears in both passages, has been put into two different English versions by using two different methods respectively. The first has been done literally: *a bar in the shape of a carpenter's square*. The second is more concise because a shape-describing letter has been used: *L-shaped bars*.

Another two examples, one from James Aldridge's novel *The Diplomat*, the other from Herman Wouk's novel *The Winds of War*, are given below along with their respective translations:

They went over a modern bridge and turned along the white river and into the open *U drive* of the British Embassy.
他們走過一座現代化的橋，沿著一條白色的河流轉彎駛入英國大使館的空闊的<u>U字形</u>的車道。

Ugly *X-shaped* wooden braces disfigured the windows.
難看的<u>交叉型</u>木條使窗戶變了樣。

The first sentence describes the open drive in front of the British Embassy as resembling the letter *U* in form. The second sentence shows how wooden braces had been put up on the windows in the form of the letter X, like so many crosses.

The last two examples are quoted from *G. I. Joe*, a book written by Ernie Pyle, the famous American war correspondent during the Second World War:

The company was bivouacked around the hedgerows of a large grassy *L-shaped* pasture.
連隊沿著青草蔥蔥的<u>L形</u>大牧場周圍的灌木樹籬露營。

We drove into the tiny town of Le Mesniltore, a sweet old stone village *at the "T" of two gravel roads*.
我們驅車進入辣曼斯尼托小鎮，這是一個位於<u>丁字形石子路中間的</u>、秀麗古老的小鄉鎮，房子都是一些石頭建築物。

When used as shape-modifiers, the 26 letters stop being mere signs for spelling English words, but are a part of the English vocabulary with definite lexical meanings. As such, they are either nouns or adjectives, depending upon their syntactical functions. For instance, the *V* in *to form a V* (成V形) is a noun while the *V*'s in *in V formation* (成V形隊伍) and *V-shaped* (成V形) are both adjectives. The *S* in the sentence *The flares illuminated the sky, one, two ... altogether twelve, forming a huge S* is a noun while the *S*'s in *Hanging from the beam was a large S-hook* and *Geographically the country of Korea is an S-shaped peninsula* are both adjectives. Again, the *U* in *Ages ago, the river had formed a natural bend, in the shape of a U* is a noun while the *U* in *The freighter had to make a U-turn in the river* is an adjective. Generally speaking, a shape-describing letter can be flexibly used in three different ways, namely: (1) used alone as a noun; (2) followed by a noun; (3) followed by the word *shaped.*

What deserves our particular attention is that not only do shape-describing letters serve as an effective means of expression in both oral and written English, they are also very useful and even indispensable in Chinese-English translation. The reasons are as follows:

1. Sometimes a shape expression in the Chinese original may baffle a translator simply because it allows of no literal translation at all or because, when literally translated, it is far from being readable. Under such circumstances, the appropriate use of a shape-modifying letter may be of great help. It may turn out to be a very effective labor-saving and word-saving device. Here are some examples:

   a. 一個馬鞍形，兩頭高，中間低。（劉少奇：〈1958年中共八屆二次會議上的工作報告〉）

   The development is *U-shaped*, i. e., high at the beginning and the end, but low in the middle.

The Chinese shape expression has been aptly rendered into U-shaped. The literal translation *saddle-shaped*, a seeming alternative, would be misleading and inaccurate because the form of a saddle could indicate in English the idea of something low at both ends, but high in the middle, which is just the reverse of U-shaped.

   b. 高大的威虎山前懷，抱著 ∴ 山形的五個小山包，名叫五福嶺。（曲波：《林海雪原》，第17章）

   Backed by the high towering main peak were five lower peaks

— the so-called Five Happiness Peaks situated *in an "X" formation*.

To illustrate the position of the five lower peaks, a sketch map formed of five little spots is used in the original sentence for lack of an appropriate Chinese shape expression. The translator, however, is fortunate in having at his disposal the shape-modifier *X* to express the same idea.

c. 一切安排妥當了，只見楊子榮手一揮，三個戰士成〝三三制〞小組戰鬥隊形滑下來。（曲波：《林海雪原》，第35章）

When all was ready, Tzu-jung waved his hand, and the first three men started down *in fighting "V" formation*.

The Chinese expression 成〝三三制〞小組戰鬥隊形 is also impossible of literal translation, so the translator resorted to the shape-modifier *V*.

d. 船頭激起的白浪有尺許高，船左右捲起兩條白練拖得遠遠的。
（茅盾：《子夜》，第17章）

White foam churned up a foot high around the cutwater, and the bow-wave trailed out far across the river in *a long white V*.

The phrase *a long white V* in the English version gives a graphic description of 左右捲起兩條白練 in a most economical way.

2. As we know, characters, instead of letters, are used in the Chinese writing system. However, since one of the six principles of Chinese character formation is by picturing visible forms or shapes, some Chinese characters, being picture-like signs (pictographs), are likewise often used as shape-describing elements. For example, the character 口 in 口字樓 illustrates the shape of 樓 ; the character 山 in 山牆 illustrates the shape of 牆 . Other characters like 丁、工、八、乙、之、金 , etc. are also commonly used shape-modifiers. Since some of these characters resemble certain English letters in shape, they can be easily translated into English, or vice versa, e.g.:

丁   T
山   (horizontal) E
工   I
八   (inverted) V
人   (inverted) Y
乙   Z

Some further examples are as follows:

a. 此外，分佈在潼關到寶雞、咸陽到延安〝丁〞字形交通線上的有十二個旅。（《毛澤東選集》，第1290頁）

The remaining 12 brigades are distributed along the *T-shaped* communication lines from Tungkuan to Paoki and from Hsienyang to Yenan.

b. 愛姑便坐在他左邊，將兩隻鉤刀樣的腳正對著八三擺成一個〝八〞字。（魯迅：〈離婚〉）

Ai-ku sat on his left opposite Pa-san, her scythe-shaped feet fanning out *to form a V*.

c. 他在青龍橋車站附近，設計了一條〝人〞字形鐵路。

He designed *a Y-track* near Blue Dragon Bridge station.

d. 大粒的汗，從額上滾下，夾襖也帖住了脊心，兩塊肩胛骨高高凸出，印成一個陽文的〝八〞字。（魯迅：〈藥〉）

Beads of sweat stood out on his forehead, his lined jacket was sticking to his spine, and his shoulder blades stuck out so sharply, *an inverted V* seemed stamped there.

The Chinese character 之 , similar in form to 乙 , is often used to indicate more twists than the latter. Therefore, although both characters can be represented by the English letter Z as a shape-modifier, it is considered more appropriate to use the English word *zigzag* as the English equivalent of 之 in translation, e.g.:

打黑槍的傢伙放一槍以後，轉到小屋的後面，傍著柳樹叢子，順著〝之〞字路，一會歪曲，一會偏東，飛也似地往北頭跑去。

（周立波：《暴風驟雨》）

Meanwhile the hidden gun man had run into a willow grove and escaped north along *a zigzag path*.

Similarly, *zigzag* is to be expressed by 之 in English-Chinese translation, e.g.:

Two or three lamps were rained out and blown out; so both saw the lightning to advantage as it quivered and *zigzagged* on iron tracks. (Charles Dickens: *Hard Times*, Book the Second, Chapter XI)

有兩三盞燈被風雨搞熄了，所以她倆能更清楚地看見那閃閃的像之字形的電光在鐵路上閃動著。

3. Since the May 4th Movement of 1919 in China, more and more Chinese writers have made a practice of borrowing English letters for shape description in their own works. When it comes to translating Chinese literary works into English, all that a translator

has to do is to transplant the same letters to the English text. See the following sentence quoted from Lu Xun's short story 〈幸福家庭〉 (*A Happy Family*) and its English translation:

> 就在他背後的書架的旁邊，已經出現了一座白菜堆，下層三株，中層兩株，頂上一株，向他疊成一個很大的<u>A字</u>。

> Beside the bookcase behind him had appeared a mound of cabbages, three at the bottom, two above and one at the top, confronting him like a large *letter A*.

Sometimes, instead of directly using shape-describing English letters in their writings, Chinese writers transliterate them into Chinese characters, substituting, for instance, 愛字形 for A 字形 , 皮字形 for B 字形 , 西字形 for C 字形 , etc. Here is an interesting example taken from Chapter Eight of Mao Dun's novel 《子夜》 (*Midnight*):

> 噯，還是梳一個橫<u>愛司</u>嗎？

In the English edition of the novel now available, 愛司 has been restored to the letter *S*. The whole sentence reads:

> Now, what about doing you a horizontal *S*, madam?

4. Sometimes, while a shape-describing term is used to name an object in Chinese, a non-shape-describing term or a non-letter shape-describer is used instead to name the same object in English. The proper thing for us to do in Chinese-English translation is to employ the ready-made English terminology instead of shape-describing letters. For instance, it is absolutely unnecessary to translate 人字針 into *V-patterned stitch* because there is already a special English term in use, i.e., *herringbone stitch*, which is a non-letter shape-describing term. Nor is it necessary to translate 人字屋頂 into a *roof in the shape of an inverted V* because the existing English special term *gable roof* is good enough for the same purpose. As is known to all, the English equivalent of 金字塔 is *pyramid*. To translate 金字塔 into something like *a tower in the shape of an inverted V* would be quite an absurdity.

To sum up, as effective picture-giving signs, the English letters are very useful in translation as well as in oral and written English. They are vivid and clear in form, simple and handy to use, and make for economy of expression too. But they also have their limitations, and translators, in using them, must always take the context into consideration. For instance, 八字鬍子 sometimes means just a neatly-trimmed moustache. A word-for-word translation with the help of the letter *V* like *a V-shaped moustache* or *a moustache in the shape of an inverted V* would not only be clumsy, but also sound facetious or even pejorative. Sometimes, in order to meet the need of more detailed and exact description, it is necessary to have the shape-describing letters preceded by such qualifiers as *inverted, horizontal, reverse, large, small, fat, thin, long, short* and so on, like the above-mentioned *inverted V, horizontal E* and *horizontal S*. Furthermore, the 26 letters of the English alphabet, though none too small in number, are far from enough to satisfy the need of picturing all the diverse objects under the sun. English sometimes uses Arabic figures as shape-describers, like *She glided very confidently backwards in a large figure 8*. Also very commonly used as shape-modifiers in English are the names of many concrete objects, such as:

butterfly valve	蝶形閥
butterfly stroke	蝶式游泳
crow's feet	眼睛外角的皺紋
claw hammer	羊角榔頭
dog-ear	書頁的折角
drumstick	鼓槌形的東西（如雞腿等）
globe valve	球形閥
hairpin	髮夾狀的東西
hairpin bend	陡路上的急轉彎
horseshoe	馬蹄形的東西
horseshoe table	蹄鐵形桌
pincer movement	鉗形運動
pigtail	辮子
rabbit-ear faucet	兔耳形自閉水龍頭
sandwich	三明治形物
sandwich man	身前身後掛著廣告牌的人
scissortail	鋏尾鳥
shoestring potato	細長的土豆絲
swallow dive	燕式跳水
sword lily	劍蘭
tile tea	茶磚

Hermeneutics and Translation

Wong Kin Yuen
Department of English
The Chinese University of Hong Kong, Hong Kong

Introduction

In recent years there has been an upsurge of interest in translation studies as to how translation can be related to modern hermeneutics, especially in the attempts to raise its status from a practice craft to an independent and academically respectable discipline. Despite the fact that the significance of the relationship between these two fields and the nature of their mutuality have been generally recognized, the all too easy claim that doing translation is necessarily doing hermeneutics is either too vague to mean anything and thus tautological, or it can be misleading in assuming that there is absolutely no difference between the two. To be sure, any adequate theorization of translation has to concern itself with modern hermeneutics, especially with the kind of hermeneutics practised by thinkers such as Heidegger and Gadamer; and an exploration of their interarticulated relationship will not only enable us to better understand how one reinforces the other, but will also help us to construct a paradigm for the ontological status of translation.

Translation is in a broad sense a metaphor borrowed by hermeneuticians to capitulate the interpretive process such as in the case where one is to translate classical texts to the modern language, from the divine to the vernacular, from the written to the spoken and vice versa, and so on. When George Steiner begins his mammoth study *After Babel* with the idea of the interpreter being a translator, he is making use of this metaphorical element of the word "translation". He says: "When we read or hear any language-statement from the past, be it Leviticus or last year's best seller, we translate. Reader, actor, editor are translators of language out of time." However, we will have to be careful, even at this early stage of our discussion, in handling the intriguing relation between the literal and figurative meaning of language, especially as it affects the theory of translation, and the role metaphoricity plays in the process of interpretation. After beginning our discussion with an early note on the metaphorical function of translation within the framework of hermeneutics, we will circle around and eventually engage the issue of how metaphor can serve as a paradigm for both interpretation and translation. Not until then will we have a fuller understanding of the fact that identity of any kind has to base itself on some fundamental analogies or configurations, and that any interpretation of ourselves and the world is "a basically figurative process of seeing something *as* something." (Armstrong, 1990:58) Meanwhile, we should deal with the question of how the structure of translation was discovered by modern hermeneutics as expounded by Heidegger and Gadamer and how it is useful in delineating a process of understanding and interpretation of our being-in-the-world.

Hermeneutics in Translation

Richard E. Palmer, one of the earlier explicators of modern hermeneutics in the English speaking world, makes it clear that "modern hermeneutics finds in translation and translation theory a great reservoir for exploring the 'hermeneutical problem.'"

His usage of the word "translation" apparently originates from what is ascribed to Hermes, the Greek messenger god who is said to "transmute" what is beyond human understanding into a secular form of human intelligence. In modern times, the dynamic interchange between understanding and our linguistic translation should be attributed to Heidegger, especially in his later emphasis on language as that which embraces the presencing of being. In a Foreword to the French translation of *Was ist Metaphysik?*, Heidegger says: "Through translation, the work of thinking is transposed into the spirit and outlook of another language and thus undergoes an inevitable transformation. But the transformation can become fertile because it makes the fundamental way of posing the question appear in a new light." Here, translation is given a function of challenging thinking to be aware of the uniqueness of both the original and the translated language in their capacity to harbour philosophical premises.

Heidegger's linking translation to his central thought on hermeneutics enables later hermeneuticians to include translation as one of the major forms of interpretation. One such theorist is Gadamer who makes specific use of the interplay between translation and historicity when he develops his philosophical hermeneutics in terms of the concept of fusion of horizons. In the third part of *Truth and Method*, where the primacy of language as the ontological framework for hermeneutics is brought forward, Gadamer speaks of language as "the middle ground in which understanding and agreement concerning the object takes place between two people." (Gadamer, 1975:345–46) The significance of translation lies in the fact that it exemplifies "situations in which understanding is disrupted or made difficult." The structure of translation is "especially informative" to hermeneutic understanding since the translator has to preserve the meaning of the foreign text but it "must be expressed within it in a new way," and therefore "every translation is at the same time an interpretation." As Gadamer writes:

> Let us again start by considering the extreme case of translation from a foreign language. Here no one can doubt that the translation of a text, however much the translator may have felt himself into his author, cannot be simply a re-awakening of the original event in the mind of the writer, but a recreation of the text that is guided by the way the translator understands what is said in it. No one can doubt that we are dealing here with interpretation, and not simply with reproduction. A new light falls on the text from the other language and for the reader of it. The requirement that a translation should be faithful cannot remove the fundamental gulf between the two languages. (Gadamer, 1975: 346–47)

But we have to bear in mind that translation is not Gadamer's major concern in this part of *Truth and Method*; he is using it to demonstrate first, that language is the universal medium of hermeneutical experience and the object of interpretation is linguistic in nature, and second, that, as opposed to the romantic hermeneutics which takes the text as an object, the conversation process in which two partners open themselves up to each other, both "falling" into the dynamics of verbal exchange, is paradigmatic of his concept of fusion of horizons. A close look at the reasons for Habermas to focus on Gadamer's discussion on translation in his famous review on *Truth*

and Method will give us a clearer picture as to how translation can specifically serve as an ideal model for the hermeneutical problem. Habermas, to
begin with considers Gadamer's insight into the situatedness of all understanding instructive in working out a "dialectical concept of translation."
(Wachterhauser,1986:246) For Habermas, Gadamer's model of translation
is invaluable in preserving "the unity of reason in the pluralism of
languages" by the fact that ordinary languages are "in principle inter-
translatable." (Wachterhauser, 1986:245) Translation involves learning to
recreate in one's own language what is said in another, not by discarding the
primary language in order to resocialize oneself in the foreign language
game, but by recognizing "the full value of what is alien" through the lens
of one's language structure. (Gadamer, 1975: 348)

Translation is useful in explaining the act of interpretation in that it
involves the bringing into relationship of at least two sets of language rules,
fore-structures, cultural "prejudices" and so on, to forge a consensus of
meaning. Understanding is achieved through the very involvement of the
translator/interpreter in the convergence of two horizons. Gadamer believes
that a translator has to emerge from his own horizon in order to assimilate
what is foreign in a "new light," the fusion of horizons can only be achieved
through a readiness on the part of the interpreter of a written text to accept
the fact that his present horizon also counts in the irreducibly plural enterprise of meaning. Thus a temporal distance is always an integral part of the
hermeneutical phenomenon in the sense that a text, once written, is "de-
tached both from the writer or author and from a specially addressed
recipient or reader," and such a detachment "has given it a life of its own."
(Gadamer, 1975:353) Even the basic structure of translation has a built-in
element of distance in time, since "translation is always *after*, supplementary, with a gap, an unbridgeable gulf, *nach* or *zurück*." (Leavey, 1990:73)

Hermeneutic Circle

This built-in element of temporal distance in interpretation/translation has
far-reaching implications in relation to the famous hermeneutic circle
which is the central concept in modern hermeneutics. In fact it provides
a paradigm in terms of which the possibility of translation can be discussed. At the same time it also serves as a departure into an analysis of the
relation between theory and practice of translation as the transmission of
culture. According to Heidegger, the circular structure of interpretation is

manifested by the analogous relation between Being and time, in which his ideas of involvement, facticity and historicity all point to the temporality of *Dasein* which is already always in the world, in the situatedness of interpreting. "What is decisive," Heidegger emphasizes, "is not to get out of the circle but to come into it in the right way ... In the circle is hidden a positive possibility of the most primordial kind of knowing." (Heidegger, 1962: 195) One of the most significant implications of this hermeneutic circle is that there is no presupposition less understanding. It is always the case that an interpreter "finds what 'stands there' in the first instance is nothing other than the obvious undiscussed assumption (*Vormeinung*) of the person who does the interpreting." (Heidegger, 1962:192)

That Gadamer's fusion of horizons has direct bearing on the theory of translation is manifested by the fact that the German word for tradition (*Überlieferung*) has the same prefix as *Übersetzen*; and it is really the transmission of culture — here with an unmistakable emphasis on the flow of time — that both the carrying on of tradition and the carrying over of translation set in motion within the hermeneutic circle. Such a fusing of the past with the present can be considered the fundamental structure upon which the interarticulatedness of translation and tradition is based. It is obvious that the very act of translation involves some element of time. This is why Steiner points out for us that "strictly speaking, every act of translation except simultaneous translation as between earphones, is a transfer from a past to present." (Steiner, 1975:334) Thus, without a firm grasp of the importance of the hermeneutic circle, a translator may easily succumb to the axiomatic of fidelity by aiming at faithful "equivalence" or "*tertium comparationis*" which functions according to a linear and one directional movement under the original — copy structure. Such a situation, however, is redeemed by the circular structure of interpretation which makes possible a reciprocal enhancement between the source language and target language, as we are reminded by Gadamer that "the translator's task of re-creation (*Nachbildungsaufgabe*) differs only in degree, not qualitatively, from the general hermeneutical task presented by any text; (Gadamer, 1975:349) and that translation is a transfer from one language to another which is "already interpretation (*Auslegung*)." In fact the circularity of interpretation is such that the hermeneutics of translation rests squarely on Gadamer's premise that any understanding is always an interpreting; and that is how "a translating process can help us understand the basic structure of all interpretation." (Schmidt, 1990:85) Therefore when Steiner talks about the transfer from a past to a present of translation under his four hermeneutic movements, he is fully aware of the circular structure of time, and this is evident in his quoting Borchardt who said that "true archaicism is not antiquarian pastiche, but an active, even violent intrusion on the seemingly unalterable fabric of the past." (Steiner, 1975:339) Later, he notes that "the hermeneutic of appropriation is meant not only to enrich the translator's native inheritance but to change it radically. Translation is made metamorphosis of the national past." (Steiner, 1975:341)

The hermeneutic circle does not limit itself to temporality or historicity in its contribution to translation theory. Structurally speaking, this concept in modern hermeneutics also manifests itself in the very circularity of language which in turn touches on some fundamental aspects in the act of translation. First of all, Gadamer's historicity dictates that there is no metalanguage which is ontologically neutral; and in interpreting our world in relation to ourselves, we can never transcend the fundamental linguisticality (*Sprachlichkeit*) of understanding. All of our pre-understanding, as has been emphasized by Heidegger, is linguistically mediated and there is always a reciprocity between language and reality. This has important bearing on translation, for it provides an account of the actual process of how the very idea of ourselves has been mediated by our native language and how the second language acquisition enhances our understanding not only of ourselves and the world, but the very linguisticality of our own being. We are reminded by a hermeneutician that "the self is not chosen but always finds itself already somewhat determined by virtue of the fact that it exists, so to speak, in *medias lingua*, that is, in the midst of a native language, spoken in a certain cultural context with certain implicit understandings of the meaning of selfhood and its possibilities. This implies that the self as a linguistically mediated reality is both determined and awaiting further determination and definition." (1986:225)

Translation Dialectics and Hermeneutic Structure

It is at this point that the reason for Gadamer to consider translation helpful in our understanding the structure of hermeneutics becomes obvious. When he says that translation is "an extreme case that doubles the hermeneutic process," (Gadamer, 1975:362) he is pointing to the readiness of the interpreter to make room for what is foreign in its mode of expression he finds in another language which is a pre-requisite in coming to an understanding in conversation. Also, Gadamer reminds us that "the case of translation makes us conscious of linguisticality as the medium in which understanding is achieved; for in translation understanding must first be artfully produced through an explicit contrivance." (Gadamer, 1975:362) This is the case because, as we have learned from Habermas, second language acquisition has a unique element which highlights for us the linguisticality of our hermeneutical experience. It is therefore this "dialectical concept of translation" Habermas finds most important in Gadamer's hermeneutics; and this may well have been the main reason for Habermas to start his review on *Truth and Method* with an unmistakable emphasis on Gadamer's idea on translation. For Habermas, translation is first based on the fact that any language has a built-in potential to transcend itself, to be translated into other languages. In other words "the first grammar that we learn to master already puts us in a position to step out of it and to interpret what is foreign." (Wachterhauser, 1986:243) Then the linguistic nature of our interpretive act enters the hermeneutic circle, as again uniquely exemplified by translation, by virtue of the fact that "hermeneutics insists that we learn to understand a language from the horizon of the language we already know," and it "starts with the idea that learning language games can never succeed abstractly but only from the basis of the language games that the interpreter has already mastered." (Wachterhauser, 1986:253) On the other hand, however, translation is also an exemplary case for hermeneutical problems in general, since its dialectical structure is such that it is "only where we lack transformation rules permitting the establishment of a deductive relation between languages through substitution and where an exact 'translation' is excluded do we need that kind of interpretation that we commonly call translation." (Wachterhauser, 1986:244) In other words, the very translatability in translation is what allows and indeed makes any hermeneutical experience possible in the first place, since "hermeneutic understanding (*Verstehen*) is applied to the point of rupture; it compensates for the brokenness of inter-subjectivity." (Wachterhauser, 1986:250)

It is this unique dialectic of translation which cuts right into the inner structure of modern hermeneutics. Gadamer's point that translation makes us conscious of our linguisticality being *the* medium of understanding is further developed in the so-called "linguistic turn" (Schmidt, 1990:5) by contemporary theories of translation. This shift is set in motion with Habermas's idea that language has an innate self-transcending nature from its particularity to universals, since "in translation, language is experienced with a peculiar intensity, an intensity that opens us up to ourselves anew."(Schmidt, 1990:8) This circularity in the structure of our linguistic being is highlighted by Stephen David Ross when he draws our attention to the "transgressive" nature of translation in the article mentioned above. By drawing upon Benjamin's radical idea of translation which is marked by the "promise in the multitude of languages" in their after-life of unending renewals, Ross points to the fact that "translation is at the point where languages turn back on themselves, where representation circles back to disrupt and affirm itself," and that "translation here occupies the neighborhood in which language and being *circle* around each other, holding each other in the proximity of their openness." (Schmidt, 1990:33–34)

It should be clear by now that even though Gadamer at one point uses translation as an exceptional or extreme case to demonstrate generally the difficulty of hermeneutical experiences, (Gadamer, 1975:349) and even though he considers translation unnecessary when understanding is achieved in his conversation model, (Gadamer, 1975:345) translation is still given paramount importance when the circularity of language is put forward as the basis of all interpretation. When he reiterates his idea that all understanding is interpretation, he takes pains to add that "all interpretation takes place in the medium of a language which would allow the object to come into words and yet is at the same time the interpreter's own language." (Gadamer, 1975: 350) And then later he pursues the point by noting that "in order to be able to express the meaning of a text in its objective content we must translate it into our own language. This however, involves relating it to the whole complex of possible meaning in which we linguistically move." (Gadamer, 1975:357) This is of course another "metaphorical" use of the word translation as has been described earlier on in this article. Nevertheless, the implication of the argument is that interpretation in general has to be translation; and this is what John P. Leavey, Jr. arrives at in his analysis of what he calls the "hermeneutics of translation":

> All understanding is interpretation; but all interpretation, not just its limit case, is translation, the translation or transformation of what brings the object to *Sprache* — i.e., *Sprache* itself in the universality of sense — and of the *Sprache* of the interpreter; and so all understanding of speech and writing, contrary to Gadamer's prior discrimination, is translation. (Schmidt, 1990:74)

Finally, speaking from the perspective of Gadamer's fusion of horizons, Lawrence K. Schmidt sums it up:

The fusion of horizons occurs when the interpreter is able to express, i.e., translate, what the text has to say into his or her own linguistic horizon. The main point of the secret of our agreed understanding of the world is that all understanding involves a translating from one language horizon to another. (Schmidt, 1990:88)

Turns in Translation

Indeed, the hermeneutic circle, both in its temporal/historical dimension and its linguistic circularity as delineated above, has a paradigmatic significance for translation theory. On top of the "linguistic turn" mentioned by Dennis J. Schmidt, there are at least, I venture to suggest, two other "turns," namely, the "translator's turn" and the "cultural turn," which dominate the recent development of both theory and practice of translation. Within the Western tradition these two turns are essentially part of the whole post-modernist movement which is characterized by a special attentiveness to language, culture and ideology, by calling into question several long-standing convictions such as instrumentalism of translators and the principle of the same or *tertium comparationis* in translation. That translators have been regarded as mere instruments or agents through which two languages or cultures meet has long been an acknowledged fact. Marginalized by the romantic fallacy of authorship, translation itself has been treated as secondary and subsidiary to literary creation as a result of the privileging of individual originality. Good translation is judged by its fluency, by its "giving the appearance that it is not translated, that it is the original of the foreign text." (Venuti, 1992:4) To counter such a "valorization of transparency" Douglas Robinson has proposed a strategic shift by announcing the coming about of a "translator's turn" under paradigms which subvert the "structure of equivalence" that has alienated translators from the human contexts. By translator's turn, Robinson means "translator's liberation," liberation from instrumentalism. (Robinson, 1991:109) By grounding his theory in what he calls the "somatics of translation" — that translation is fundamentally not mental but physical, bodily, rooted in feelings and a gut-level sense of one's being-in-language — Robinson develops further the idiosomatic and ideosomatic conditioning or programming to account for the "pretexts" all translators have to carry over in their work. He then traces back to the Western tradition long-standing concepts such as dualism of mind/body, spirit/flesh, original/copy and meaning/word, and also instrumentalism as well as perfectionism, which all dictate that translators should be "a transparent window to the original text and that good translation should not sound like translation at all." (Robinson, 1991:54–60)

But just as the fact that language is deeply entrenched in history within the circular structure of our linguistic being, a translator is also thoroughly situated in the circle of interpretation. The hermeneutic circle stipulates that it is a mistake to assume that a translator is merely a *medium* through which two languages meet, and his or her job is to objectively provide a passage for the meaning of source language (SL) to be conveyed to the target language (TL). In the same way the messenger of gods Hermes is not only a messenger, since "his appearance itself could be the message," and "the medium could be the message" itself. (Hoy, 1978:1) With Heidegger's emphasis on situatedness and thrownness, and with Gadamer's iteration that all interpretation necessarily implies praxis and application, it is the central argument of modern hermeneutics that any understanding has to include self-understanding. Whereas Gadamer would say that understanding "is not so much an activity performed by a 'subject' as it is the very being of the subject," (Madison, 1988:96) Ricoeur comes close to hammering home the point by saying that "To understand is not to project oneself into the text but to expose oneself to it; it is to receive a self-enlarged by the appropriation of the proposed worlds which interpretation unfolds." (Ricoeur, 1981:94)

In his attempt at "a synthesis of the feeling theory and the use-theory," Robinson firmly takes a "hermeneutical and dialogical" approach by drawing upon first Martin Buber's I-Thou relationship and then Bakhtin's dialogism in his structuring of the translator's engagement in both the SL and TL. For Robinson, "the act of translation involves the unidirectionalizing of the bilingual confluence, a channeling of internal heteroglossia into a current from one (SL) to the other (TL)." (Robinson, 1991:107) For him, the translator turns him/herself in, as it were, placing his/her translation act well within the hermeneutic circle.

What Robinson calls "the Ideosomatics of translation" receives fuller attention by cultural critics and the consequence thereof constitutes the cultural turn in recent development of translation theory under the influence of modern hermeneutics. In fact the term "cultural turn" is used by André Lefevere and Susan Bassnett in their introduction to a collection of essays entitled *Translation, History and Culture* published in 1990. In one of the articles collected here, Mary Snell-Hornby advocates an integrated approach to translation by turning to culture as the operational unit of translation. (Bassnett and Lefevere, 1990:84–85) As "verbalized point of a socio-culture," the text "is embedded in a given situation, which is itself conditioned by its sociocultural background." (Bassnett and Lefevere, 1990:83) Also, the concept of "pre-text" advanced by Palma Zlatera, i.e., the cultural assumptions or pre-judgment within the translator's horizon already determine the choice of materials, the particular way of approaching the task as well as the success or failure of a translated text. In other words, the turning to culture as the focus of translation studies shows that "translation, like all (re)writing is never innocent. There is always a context in which the translation takes place, always a history from which a text emerges and into which a text is transposed." (Bassnett and Lefevere, 1990:11)

Whenever the subject of socio-cultural criticism is brought up in connection with modern hermeneutics one has to hark back to Habermas's review of Gadamer's *Truth and Method*, particularly if one has in mind how translation is relevant to such a connection. The critique Habermas launches at Gadamer has of course become well-known nowadays, but few have noticed the fact that Habermas again made use of the concept of translation to get his point across. Habermas starts his critique in the second half of his review by pointing out that "hermeneutic understanding is structurally oriented toward eliciting from tradition a possible action-orienting self-understanding of social groups." (Wachterhauser, 1986:265) Complaining that Gadamer "fails to appreciate the power of reflection," (Wachterhauser, 1986:268) hence "unwittingly obliges the positivistic devaluation of hermeneutics," (Wachterhauser, 1986:266) Habermas aims at turning Gadamer's structure of prejudgments to a more radical use by reflecting on "the repressive character of social power relations." (Wachterhauser, 1986: 273) Again, this critique is possible only through "the hermeneutic self-reflection of language analysis," (Wachterhauser, 1986:271) since language is "a medium of domination and social power; it serves to legitimate relations of organized force." Language is also "ideological," since the legitimation and institutionalization of these power relations are not articulated, and hence "hermeneutic experience that encounters this dependency of the symbolic framework on actual conditions changes into critique of ideology." (Wachterhauser, 1986:272) And it is here, as in Gadamer, that Habermas makes use of the model of translation to reiterate how hermeneutics can turn to social critique:

What we have called communicative experience will normally take place within a language whose grammar fixes a connection of such schemata. But the brokenness of intersubjectivity renders the continuous coordination of views in a common schema a permanent task. Only in extreme cases does this inconspicuously ever-present transformation and development of transcendental schemata of world interpretation become a problem that has to be explicitly mastered through hermeneutic understanding. Such cases appear when traditions are disrupted or foreign cultures are encountered — or when we analyze familiar traditions and cultures as if they were foreign. A controlled distanciation (*Verfremdung*) can raise understanding from a prescientific experience to the rank of a reflected procedure. In this way hermeneutic procedures enter into the social sciences. (Wachterhauser, 1986:266)

Adding Wittgenstein's sociolinguistic self-reflection of linguistic analysis to Gadamer's historical hermeneutics, Habermas finally announces in the review the interarticulation of tradition and translation. His conclusion is that at the historical stage of reflection:

the interpreter and his object are conceived as elements of the same complex. This objective complex presents itself as tradition or historical influence. Through it, as a medium of linguistic symbols, communications are historically propagated. We call this process "historical" because the continuity of tradition is preserved only through translation, through a large-scale philology proceeding in a naturelike manner. The intersubjectivity of ordinary language communication is broken and must be restored again and again. This productive achievement of hermeneutic understanding, whether implicitly or explicitly carried through, is for its part motivated by the tradition that it further develops in this way. Tradition is not a process that we learn to master but a transmitted language in which we live. (Wachterhauser, 1986:271)

Habermas's appeal to social critique as the necessary development of what he calls a "depth hermeneutics" exerts an obvious influence on recent translation theories; and a collection of essays with the title *Rethinking Translation: Discourse, Subjectivity, Ideology* published in 1992 should be considered a direct result of such a trend of cultural turn. With their collective aim of challenging the "marginal status of translation in language and literature departments," (Venuti, 1992:3) contributors join forces to call into question some of the most powerful conventional concepts in this field by advocating a rethinking of it both philosophically and politically. They take into account social, cultural and ideological dimensions as well as question of the circularity of language. And also a range of topics from gender subversion in terms of cultural hegemony and postcolonial discourse attests to the fact that the cultural turn of translation theory goes hand in hand with the post-modernist movement worldwide in political discourses such as psychoanalysis, Marxism and feminism. It is here that the concept of hermeneutic circle finds its most radical version strongly propagated:

> A text is a heterogeneous artifact, composed of disruptive forms of semiosis like polysemy and intertexuality, but it is nonetheless constrained by the social institutions in which it is produced and consumed, and its constitutive materials, including the other texts that it assimilates and transforms, link it to a particular historical moment. It is these social and historical affiliations that are inscribed in the choice of a foreign text for translation and in the materiality of the translated text, in its discursive strategy and its range of allusiveness for the target-language reader. And it is these affiliations that permit translation to function as a cultural political practice, constructing or critiquing ideology-stamped identities for foreign cultures, contributing to the formation or subversion of literary canons, affirming or transgressing institutional limits. (Venuti, 1992:9)

Such a "thorough-going historicization" of translation reinforces the translator's turn discussed above, and "such a translation hermeneutic assumes a notion of agency that allows for the full complexity of the translator's work" which "emerges as an active reconstitution of the foreign text mediated by the irreducible linguistic, discursive, and ideological differences of the target-language culture." (Venuti, 1992:10–11) It is clear by now that the translator's turn, linguistic turn and cultural turn have amalgamated into one, all circling back upon each other within the round-about orbit of the hermeneutic circle; and one is eventually tempted to call it the hermeneutic turn which cultivates an acute sense of the constituted character of all social, historical and linguistic structures in modern translation theory.

References

Armstrong, Paul B. *Conflicting Readings: Variety and Validity in Interpretation.* London: North Carolina University Press, 1990.

Bassnett, Susan and André Lefevere, eds. *Translation: History and Culture.* London: Pinter, 1990.

Gadamer, Hans Georg. *Truth and Method.* London: Sheed and Ward, 1975.

Habermas, Jurgen. "A Review of Gadamer's *Truth and Method.*" In *Hermeneutics and Modern Philosophy*, edited by Brice R. Wachterhauser. Albany: New York State University Press, 1986.

Heidegger, Martin. *Being and Time*, translated by John Macquarrie and Edward Robinson. New York: Harper and Row, 1962.

Hoy, David Couzens. *The Critical Circle: Literature and History in Contemporary Hermeneutics*. Berkeley: California University Press, 1978.

Leavey, Jr., John P. "Bold Counsels and Carpenters: Pagan Translation." In *Hermeneutics and the Poetic Motion*, edited by Dennis J. Schmidt. New York: New York State University Press, 1990, pp. 69–82.

Lefevere, André. "Introduction: Proust's Grandmother and the Thousand and One Nights: The 'Cultural Turn' in Translation Studies." In *Translation, History and Culture*, edited by Susan Bassnett and André Lefevere. London: Pinter, 1990.

Madison, G.B. *The Hermeneutics of Postmodernity*. Bloomington: Indiana University Press, 1988.

Palmer, Richard. *Hermeneutics: Interpretation Theory in Schleiermacher, Dilthey, Heidegger, and Gadamer*. Evanston: Northwestern University Press, 1969.

Ricoeur, Paul. "Metaphor and the Central Problems of Hermeneutics." In *Paul Ricoeur: Hermeneutics and the Human Sciences*, translated and edited by John B. Thompson. London: Cambridge University Press, 1981.

Robinson, Douglas. *The Translator's Turn*. London: Johns Hopkins University Press, 1991.

Ross, Stephen David. "Translation as Transgression." In *Hermeneutics and the Poetic Motion*, edited by Dennis J. Schmidt. New York: New York State University Press, 1990, pp. 25–42.

Schmidt, Dennis, J. ed. *Hermeneutics and the Poetic Motion*. New York: New York State University Press, 1990.

Schmidt, Lawrence K. "The Exemplary Status of Translating." In *Hermeneutics and the Poetic Motion*, edited by Dennis J. Schmidt. New York: New York State University Press, 1990.

Snell-Hornby, Mary. "Linguistic Transcoding of Cultural Transfer? A Critique of Translation Theory in Germany." In *Translation, History and Culture*, edited by Susan Bassnett and André Lefevere. London: Pinter, 1990.

Steiner, George. *After Babel: Aspects of Language and Translation*. London: Oxford University Press, 1975.

Venuti, Lawrence, ed. *Rethinking Translation: Discourse, Subjectivity, Ideology*. London: Routledge, 1992.

Wachterhauser, Brice R. *Hermeneutics and Modern Philosophy*. Albany: New York State University Press, 1986.

HISTORICAL WRITINGS

Chinese History

Burton Watson
Department of East Asian Languages and Cultures
Columbia University, New York, U.S.A.

From very early times the Chinese have been tireless keepers of historical records. The oldest examples of narrative writing in Chinese are found in such historical works as the *Book of Documents* 《書經》 or the *Spring and Autumn Annals* 《春秋》, or in inscriptions on bronze vessels that relate the illustrious deeds of the owner's ancestors. Indeed, in a culture dominated by ancestor worship as was that of traditional China, it is only natural that great attention should have been paid to the compiling of historical records, and that historical literature appeared earlier, and in the early centuries reached a far higher level of development, than did literature in the fiction and drama forms.

This historical literature of traditional China takes many different forms. Some works, such as the so-called dynastic histories, attempt to cover the history of no more than a single dynasty, and were often compiled under official auspices. Other works such as the general histories 通史 or continuous histories deal with a longer period of time and trace the changes that took place over a succession of dynasties. Still others focus on a particular geographic region, institution, or social group, or are in biography form.

Chinese historical works are on the whole marked by two notable characteristics. With the exception of a few texts of a specifically religious nature, they are fundamentally humanistic in outlook. Though reference may at times be made to a vague force called Heaven or Destiny that appears to influence human affairs, the principal cause determining the course of history is almost always sought in the actions of human beings themselves. It follows, therefore, that history's ills are capable of being corrected through adjustments in human behaviour, and that in theory at least, the Golden Age, which most Chinese historians believe actually existed long ago in the half-legendary past, can to some extent be recreated in the present.

This leads us to the second dominant characteristic of Chinese historical writing: its strongly didactic tone. History in the Chinese view is not merely a record of past events, but a guide to what is likely to occur in the future if similar courses of action are pursued. From earliest times the Chinese have compared history to a mirror in which one can view the past and, by learning from its successes and failures, adopt a wiser course in the future.

The Chinese historian customarily attempts to arrange his material in such a fashion that the patterns of cause and effect, the didactic message of his text, will be apparent to the thoughtful reader without the need for overt comment. He therefore seldom breaks into his narrative to inject any type of personal remark or conjecture. If he wishes to offer such comments, he will usually reserve them for a special section at the conclusion of a chapter or passage of narrative and preface them with some conventional term that sets them off clearly from the narrative itself. For this reason, the body of his text is likely to have a rather dry and impersonal tone, particularly in comparison with early works of Western historiography such as the writings of the Greek and Roman historians.

In addition, while early works of history in the West were often designed to be read aloud, Chinese histories were written primarily for the eye, and accordingly favour a highly compressed and economical style. Though the Chinese historian, like his counterpart in ancient Greece or Rome, at times invents speeches or dialogues in order to lend greater interest and verisimilitude to his narrative, he is usually more sparing in his descriptive passages, particularly when dealing with events of a violent or sensational nature such as battles or natural disasters. This difference in the two historiographical traditions probably derives from the fact that early Western historians were writing under strong influence from the epic tradition, whereas their counterparts in China, where the epic form does not exist, were guided by the principles of Confucian decorum, which shuns undue attention to events of a violent or prodigious nature. As a result, Chinese historical works often appear less colourful and dramatic in tone, though because of their compression of language they are capable of conveying a staggering wealth of data in a relatively short space. In addition, whereas Western historians, particularly when dealing with a much earlier period, will more often summarize their sources or recast them in a modern idiom, Chinese historians usually prefer to quote their sources verbatim. They are able to do this with relative ease because the written language in use in China in pre-modern times remained relatively unchanged over a period of many centuries.

Selection of Material for Translation

With these introductory remarks in mind, we turn now to the practical problems that confront a translator who undertakes to put Chinese historical writings into English. Though texts such as the *Book of Documents* and *Spring and Autumn Annals* that are numbered among the Confucian Classics were translated long ago, only a small fraction of the Chinese historical literature has so far been put into English, or into any other Western language, for that matter (though much of it exists in Japanese translation). One reason for this, as will become apparent from the discussion that follows, is that many of the works are very lengthy, and it is difficult to find a translator or team of translators with the time and interest needed to carry a large-scale translation project to completion.

Some scholars, in fact, question whether there is any real need to translate these voluminous texts into English, pointing out that specialists who read Chinese can extract what data may be needed from the originals, and that non-specialists would find the material, if it were translated in full, too narrow in scope, repetitious, or biased in outlook to be of real interest.

Many of the texts, particularly the dynastic histories that were compiled under official auspices, are of course mainly concerned with the men and affairs connected with the ruling house, and in this sense are rather narrowly political in nature. In addition, their approach to many matters such as foreign relations is understandably China-centered and biased to some extent — what nation has ever left an open-minded and unbiased account of the foreign peoples with which it had dealings? But despite these drawbacks, the Chinese histories contain a great wealth of information on the social and cultural life of the Chinese people, though it may be scattered around in many different parts of the text. And the chapters on foreign countries such as Korea, Japan, and Vietnam, or on non-Chinese peoples such as the Xiongnu, biased though they may be, often constitute the earliest, if not the only, written record on the subject, and hence are of enormous significance. Nowadays, when so much attention is turning to studies in comparative history, it is particularly important that material of this type be made available to scholars who do not have access to the original sources.

In addition, it should be noted that many of the historical works, especially the early and more famous ones such as the *Records of the Historian* 《史記》 or *History of the Former Han Dynasty* 《漢書》 have in the past been read and revered as literary masterpieces, and constituted an indispensable part of a traditional style education, not only in China but in other countries such as Korea, Japan, and Vietnam that were under strong Chinese cultural influence. They thus occupy a position of prime importance in the Chinese literary tradition. It is these early historical texts that established the themes and motifs, the character stereotypes, the narrative techniques and plot patterns that would characterize Chinese fiction and drama when these forms appeared in later centuries.

When all this has been said, however, the translator must of course adopt a realistic approach when he or she comes to decide just how much and what parts of this vast body of historical literature he will undertake to render into English. Experience has shown that grandiose projects that set out to translate complete works into English and begin hopefully with Chapter One of the original are very likely to grind to a halt long before they reach completion, due usually to lack of funding or loss of interest on the part of the persons involved. What results, therefore, is a partial translation that, because of its approach or incomplete nature, is difficult to utilize.

Less ambitious projects that undertake to translate only a section of a historical work, such as one of the chapters dealing with foreign nations or peoples, a treatise on some special subject such as economics, religion, or geography, or the biography of a particular individual or group of individuals, are likely to fare much better, and many successful translations of this type have been produced so far and published in monograph form. Such selected translations, on the other hand, face the difficulty that, though a single chapter or group of chapters of the original may present most of the pertinent data on a subject or individual, much background and subsidiary material relating to the subject is inevitably scattered throughout other sections of the historical work. In order to give full coverage to the subject, therefore, the translator must, in addition to translating the main chapter or chapters, gather together the relevant data from other chapters of the original and present it to the reader along with the translation, either in an introduction or appendix to the translation, or in the form of annotation. Generally speaking, therefore, the shorter the selection one chooses to translate, the greater the amount of supplementary data the translator must supply in order to make the coverage complete and meaningful.

Annotation

This brings us to the question of how much annotation, and of what type, is necessary or desirable when presenting translations of Chinese historical texts. Some people seem to feel that when offering works of poetry in translation, or even of prose works whose interest is primarily literary, if the translator appends too much annotation, it can distract from or impair the reader's appreciation of the work. But in the case of translations of historical texts, such objections are seldom raised, and the general opinion would seem to be that the more annotation provided, the better. There are, however, distinct dangers involved when annotation is allowed to pile up without limitation.

Some years ago, a project was set up to produce an English translation of all or part of the *Hanshu* or *History of the Former Han*, the first of the dynastic histories and one of the most famous and influential of all Chinese historical works. The work is in one hundred chapters, and the team of translators understandably began with the first chapter, little by little working their way through the first section of the history, the *diji* or "Imperial Annals", which presents a year by year record of the official acts and pronouncements of the reigning emperors. But because this section of the history contains no more than a dry outline of official acts, almost every entry requires a great deal of background and supplementary information in order to be fully understandable. Most of this information was available in other parts of the history itself, and if the *Hanshu* had been translated in its entirety, the reader could have been referred to such other parts for the information. But the translators in this case chose to supply it in the form of introductions and appendices, or in footnotes appended to the translation.

Because of the elaborate annotation and explanatory material thus required, the translators were able to translate only the twelve chapters that make up the "Imperial Annals" section of the history, plus one chapter from the biography section, when their project came to an end. Thus they hardly touched upon the treatise or biography sections of the history, which contain the most interesting and important data and have been of greatest influence upon later Chinese literature. Moreover, in an attempt to reduce the amount of annotation needed at the foot of each page of the translation, they decided to relegate biographical information on persons mentioned in the text to a glossary that was to have appeared at the end of the translation. The glossary, however, was never completed, or at least was never published, so that the carefully inserted instructions to the reader to "See Glossary" that appear in the annotation are now meaningless. The project, which lasted for many years, resulted in the publication of three magnificent volumes containing a vast amount of scholarly information. But the translations themselves give almost no impression of the scope and variety of the material contained in the *Hanshu*, its ingenious method of organization, or its literary grandeur.

Examples such as that just described suggest that annotation, while desirable in the ideal, should be kept within bounds that are practicable for the scale and purposes of the particular translation project. Technical terms or points of special historical interest in the translation offer opportunities for an eager annotator to write footnotes that are in fact whole essays on the subject in hand. But before appending such footnotes, one should stop to ask whether the reader really needs, or wants, such a wealth of information on the subject at that point, or whether a much briefer note would not serve the purpose as well. Should footnotes attempt to bring the reader fully up to date as to the latest views on particular historical problems, or is it enough to refer the reader to some place where that information can be obtained? Footnotes describing the exact location of a place mentioned in the text may be of great interest to readers who have an intimate knowledge of the geography of the area under discussion, but how useful or meaningful can they be to those who have no such knowledge? How can one best handle material dealing with purely textual or philological matters such as emendations to the text or adoption of textual variants, material that may be needed by someone who is comparing the translation with the original, but which is quite meaningless to readers who know no Chinese? Should one in fact append two sets of notes, one for the general reader and one for specialists in the language?

These and similar questions should be carefully considered when deciding how much and just what type of information to provide in annotation. A translation, no matter how heavily annotated, is of no practical use if the translator for one reason or another was never able to complete it, nor is a completed translation which the translator never got around to annotating. The translator should therefore try to gauge how much time he or she will be able to give to the project, and adjust the length of the translation and the degree of annotation accordingly. We have already seen too many unhappy examples of translators who failed to do so.

I myself, in my translations from historical texts such as *The Zuo Commentary on the Spring and Autumn Annals* 《左氏春秋》, *Records of the Historian* 《史記》, and *History of the Former Han Dynasty* 《漢書》, have in most cases kept my annotation to a minimum, on the grounds that, by doing so, I can therefore translate a larger proportion of the original text than I could if I took time to provide copious annotation. I have also argued that my translations are designed primarily for readers who are interested in the literary appeal of the originals and hence do not need detailed annotation concerning other aspects of the material. But ideally, of course, a translation should be able to satisfy the needs of many different kinds of readers, not just those attempting to trace literary themes, for example, but those pursuing political, economic, or philosophical lines of investigation, or approaching the text with some rather special interest such as materia medica or the status of women in early China. For readers in such categories, my annotation is no doubt inadequate and I have been duly castigated as a result. My only defense would be to point out that my translation projects have at least been practicable in their dimensions, and I have yet to expire in the middle of one or otherwise fail to carry it through to completion.

Names, Titles, Technical Terms

Chinese historical texts customarily refer to major persons in the narrative by a bewildering variety of family and personal names, official titles, and posthumous names. Though the particular manner in which the historian employs these various names customarily follows definite rules and may even imply value judgements of the individual, it is usually too much to ask the English reader to cope with all these variations in nomenclature. In most cases, therefore, it seems best to choose one name by which to refer to a given individual in the translation, and explain the other methods of refer-ring to the person in notes or introductory matter to the translation.

Even when such steps are taken to smooth the reader's way, one should be prepared to find that average readers of English — that is, those with no special knowledge of China — experience great difficulty in remembering Chinese names or distinguishing one name from another. Partly the prob-lem lies with the brevity of Chinese names, particularly surnames, and the fact that so many of them look very much alike in romanized form. The difficulty is of course compounded by the daunting appearance of the systems of Chinese romanization in use in English. Readers in the past have been puzzled enough by the apostrophes and diacritical marks of the Wade-Giles system, and as pinyin, with its baffling "x"s and "q"s, gains increas-ingly wide use in English, they are sure to become more perplexed than ever. I do not know anything to be done about this problem other than providing readers with a guide to the pronunciation of the system used, but one should keep in mind that it is a factor that inevitably limits the appeal and effectiveness of English translations from Chinese. Some years ago, when I assigned portions of my *Shiji* translation as readings for the Ameri-can students of an undergraduate course on Asian literature, I was distressed to find that they could not seem to cope with or remember even the names of the leading figures in the narrative.

Another problem facing translators from Chinese historical texts is whether to translate official titles and technical terms, and if so, how. Most translators choose to translate official titles rather than merely romanizing the Chinese titles since, as I have just pointed out, Chinese words in romanized form present special difficulties for English readers, but the methods of translating such titles may vary greatly. Fortunately there are now reference works such as Charles O. Hucker's *Dictionary of Official Titles in Imperial China* (Stanford University Press, 1985) which hopefully will insure greater uniformity in translation of official titles in future, though no comparable guides as yet exist for the handling of technical terms.

In dealing with technical terms, and with terms or concepts that are peculiar to Chinese history or culture, one must always consider the type of reader who is likely to be utilizing the translation and the degree of background knowledge of China such a reader is likely to possess. There is surely no need to supply a lengthy description of the overall nature of Confucianism, Taoism, or Buddhism whenever these religions or philosophical systems are alluded to in the text; but on the other hand one cannot assume that readers will have any detailed knowledge of Buddhist or Taoist or Confucian terminology or ritual. Perhaps the best way to approach the problem is to ask just how much information the reader needs in order to understand the particular term or allusion that appears in the text one is translating. One should by all means avoid trying to get around difficulties of translation merely by adopting facile equivalents from Western thought or culture — for example, by employing terms associated with Christianity when translating passages dealing with Buddhism or Taoism — since such terminology in the long run may seriously confuse or mislead the reader.

Language of the Translation

Finally we come to the question of what type of language or what tone is best aimed for in an English translation from a Chinese historical text. A few translators, because the originals are for the most part products of ancient or medieval China, argue that they should be rendered into English that has an appropriately old-fashioned tone to it. In fact, however, many of the masterpieces of the Chinese historiographical tradition such as the *Shiji* and *Hanshu* were written many centuries before the English language even came into existence, so no amount of old-fashionedness in the translation can possibly match the antiquity of the original. Moreover, unless one is extremely skilled in the use of language, such efforts to create a deliberately archaic tone in translation are almost certain to end in failure, and may even produce a ludicrous effect. Most translators therefore elect to write in modern English, of whichever variety, British, American, or whatever, that they are most at home in.

Modern English, however, is a product and reflection of modern English-speaking society, and that society is often very different in its structure and outlook from the society portrayed in Chinese historical works. We today are not in the habit of speaking with elaborate deference to persons who are vastly superior to us in social position, or of referring to ourselves in language indicative of extreme humility. Yet such hierarchical language appears constantly in Chinese historical texts, particularly in matters pertaining to the emperor, who in Chinese is addressed or referred to as a veritable deity. The translator, therefore, while working within the diction of modern English, must somehow devise translations that will convey to the reader these vast differences in social status. He must also find ways to express in English the subtle nuances in tone conveyed by a whole host of Chinese pronouns or terms of address — *zuxia, qing, jun, zi, ruo* — that range in tone from highly polite to familiar or even contemptuous. As is also the case when translating works of fiction, passages of dialogue perhaps present the greatest difficulty, challenging the translator to find language that will not only convey the meaning and tone of the original, but at the same time will read like something that someone might conceivably say in English.

Not all translators of Chinese historical texts, it should be noted, are particularly concerned about creating translations that read like natural, idiomatic English, however. There are many different schools of translation, and many practitioners of the art believe it is far more important to capture the exact semantic content and flavour of the words in the original Chinese than to worry about how the translation may sound as English. In order to achieve their aim, they do not hesitate to invent neologisms, based on Greek or Latin roots, that they claim convey the meaning of the Chinese better than could any normal English word, or employ translations that one reviewer has aptly characterized as "brutally literal". Translators of this type claim that only by resorting to such methods can they be truly faithful to the original, and perhaps they are right. But if as the result of such methods the translation becomes so awkward or difficult to follow that readers are repelled by it, then their efforts would seem to be self-defeating. Mere readability is certainly not the only criterion by which a translation should be judged, but neither is it one that can be completely ignored without serious consequences.

The above remarks, impressionistic and personal in nature though they may be, will, it is hoped, be of help to persons undertaking an English translation of Chinese historical texts. A vast amount of such work remains to be done. Large portions of the *Shiji* are now available in English translation, as are a number of chapters from the *Hanshu*, but few English translations have been made from the other dynastic histories, and the continuous histories such as the mammoth *Comprehensive Mirror for Aid in Government* 《資治通鑑》 and the institutional histories are virtually untouched. Funds to support the work of translation and publication pose a serious problem, and there are questions as to how much readership, and of just what kind, there would be for future translations. But there can be no doubt that much more of this Chinese historical literature deserves to be put into English, and that skilled translators will be needed to do the job.

Bibliographical Note

It is impossible here to give an exhaustive list of all the English translations of Chinese historical literature that have been produced in recent years, but it seems appropriate to mention certain works of key importance in the field and to suggest something of the nature and range of the translations that have appeared.

"The translation of Chinese historical texts is not a very prestigious undertaking," the American sinologist Michael Rogers notes regretfully in the introduction to his translation of a biography from one of the dynastic histories. As he goes on to explain, in the past it has been assumed that a really first-rate scholar in Chinese studies will cull what information he needs from the Chinese sources, subject it to suitably rigorous critical examination, and then present the results to readers in a form commensurate with the latest standards and approaches of present-day scholarship. Any-one who spends time producing a "mere translation" of the Chinese sources is therefore thought to be engaging in a decidedly inferior activity. This attitude unfortunately persists today, and has made it difficult to interest scholars in the task of translating Chinese historical texts or to obtain funds for such undertakings.

Despite this lack of prestige and financial support, however, a number of very valuable translations from Chinese historical literature have ap-peared in recent times. Probably the first to come to mind, though hardly a recent work, would be the monumental French translations from the *Shiji* produced by Édouard Chavannes. Chavannes' translations of this, one of the earliest and most influential of all Chinese historical works, are a model of scholarship, scrupulously faithful to the original and provided with copious annotation. Beginning with the first chapter of the 120-chapter history, Chavannes translated all of the annals, chronological tables, and treatise sections of the work, and had nearly completed the section entitled hereditary houses when other duties obliged him to set aside what, in a moment of exasperation, he termed "cette interminable affaire". His trans-lation of the first 47 chapters appeared in five volumes under the title *Les Mémoires Historiques de Se-Ma Ts'ien* (Paris: E. Leroux, 1895–1905), and a sixth volume published in 1969 brought the translation up to chapter 51. Thus he translated almost half of the original work, though he never got as far as the 60-chapter biography section, which in some ways is the most interesting part.

Subsequent translations in English from *Records of the Historian*, such as those by Derk Bodde, *China's First Unifier* (Leiden: E. J. Brill, 1938) and *Statesman, Patriot, and General in Ancient China* (New Haven: American Oriental Society, 1940); the volume by Gladys and Hsien-yi Yang, *Records of the Historian* (Hong Kong: Commercial Press, 1974); and my own volumes, *Records of the Grand Historian*, 3 vols: Han Dynasty I, II, Qin Dynasty (revised edition. Hong Kong: The Chinese University Press and New York: Columbia University Press, 1993) include many of the chapters left untranslated by Chavannes, so that now almost all of the *Records of the Historian* is available either in French or English translation.

The *Hanshu* or *History of the Former Han Dynasty*, a work second only to the *Shiji* in fame and importance, is also available now in partial English translation. The project described above resulted in the publication of three volumes of translation covering the imperial annals, plus one very important chapter from the biography section, that dealing with the usurper Wang Mang: Homer H. Dubs, tr. *The History of the Former Han Dynasty*, 3 vols. (Baltimore: Waverly Press, 1938–55). Translations of ten chapters from the biography section of the same work have appeared in my *Courtier and Commoner in Ancient China: Selections from the History of the Former Han by Pan Ku* (New York: Columbia University Press, 1974), and translations of a few other chapters, as will be mentioned below, have come out as monographs.

In the early 1950s a series entitled Chinese Dynastic Histories Translations was launched at the University of California. The translations were done mainly from the *Jinshu* (*Chin shu*) and the Tang dynastic histories and pertained to the period A.D. 220–960. In all, ten monographs appeared, published by the University of California Press over the years 1952–1968, each containing a translation of a chapter or chapters from one of the dynastic histories dealing with a particular individual or ethnic group, along with extensive annotation and introductory material.

The treatises in the dynastic histories, which deal with specialized subjects such as economics, geography, religious affairs, or the bureaucratic system, are an especially rich source of information on traditional Chinese society. Some of these have been translated in the volumes by Chavannes or myself cited above, while others have appeared in monograph form. Of particular note among the latter are the French translations by Robert des Rotours, *Le Traité des Examens, tr. de la nouvelle histoire des T'ang* (Paris: E. Leroux, 1932) and *Traité des fonctionnaires et Traité de l'armée, tr. de la nouvelle histoire des T'ang* (Leiden: E. J. Brill, 1947–48); the translation by Nancy Lee Swann of the treatise on economics from *The History of the Former Han, Food and Money in Ancient China: Han Shu 24* (Princeton: Princeton University Press, 1950); that by A. F. P. Hulsewé of the *Han shu* treatises on the penal code, *Remnants of Han Law* (Leiden: E. J. Brill, 1955); and Leon Hurvitz's translation of the Buddhist section of the *History of Wei* 魏書 treatise on Buddhism and Taoism, *Wei Shu: Treatise on Buddhism and Taoism* (Kyoto: Kyoto University Press, 1956), all of which are provided with elaborate annotation.

The continuous histories and institutional histories, no doubt because of their formidable size, have so far barely been touched upon, though a few translations have appeared from the most famous of them, Sima Guang's 354-chapter *Comprehensive Mirror for Aid in Government* 《資治通鑑》. The translation by Achilles Fang, *The Chronicle of the Three Kingdoms* 《三國志》 (Chapters 69–78 from the *Tzu chih t'ung chien by Ssu-ma Kuang*, Harvard-Yenching Institute Studies VI. Cambridge: Harvard University Press, 1952) not only presents a translation of Sima Guang's narrative for the Three Kingdoms period, but carefully examines the sources from which the historian drew his material, thus constituting an invaluable study of Chinese historical method. Another important section of the same historical work is translated in Rafe de Crespigny, *The Last of the Han* (*Chapters 58–68 of the Tzu-chih t'ung-chien*), Monograph 9. Canberra: Centre of Oriental Studies, Australian National University, 1969.

A translation of one other type of Chinese historical work, a *shilu* 實錄 or "veritable record," is represented in the translation by Bernard S. Solomon of *The Veritable Record of the T'ang Emperor Shun-tsung* (*Han Yu's Shun-tsung shih-lu* 《順宗實錄》, Harvard-Yenching Institute Studies XIII. Cambridge, Mass.: Harvard University Press, 1955). This text represents the oldest extant example of a *shilu*, a detailed chronological account of the activities of an emperor which served as an important source for historians in compiling the imperial annals sections of the dynastic histories.

As this brief survey indicates, a vast amount of work remains to be done in getting over into English the most important texts of the Chinese historiographical tradition. Impressionistic and personal though they may be, it is hoped that the remarks offered here will prove of assistance to persons who are contemplating a project in this field.

Reference

Rogers, Michael C. *The Chronicle of Fu Chien*. Chinese Dynastic Histories Translation No. 10. California: University of California Press, 1968, p. ix.

Western History

Thomas H. C. Lee
Department of Asian Studies
The City College, New York, U.S.A.

Traditional historiography in China differs from that in the West in a few significant ways, and these differences affect the translation of Western historical works into Chinese. First of all, from very early on, Chinese historical writings were sponsored and controlled by the government; particular sets of vocabulary and style were developed for historical writings. Although early works, such as Sima Qian's 司馬遷 *Records of the Historian* 《史記》, effectively incorporated fictional elements and have significant literary value, most standard histories produced by the state's history bureaus are of a more record-keeping nature, often highly stereotyped, with the historians' style or personality suppressed. The Chinese idea of historical works therefore reflects such a clearly defined interest and purpose. Few great Western historical works could meet the immediate approval of professional Chinese historians. Translators of major Western historical works have consequently been more generalists, or students of Western thought or literature than professionally trained historians.

Another characteristic of Chinese historical writing that has a bearing on how Western historical works are translated is the moral imperative in historical thinking and interpretation. It is perhaps inevitable that in selecting major Western historical works for translation into Chinese, Chinese translators will tend to choose those that reveal overriding concern for moral purpose by their authors. A Tacitus or a Toynbee appeals more to the Chinese reader than, say, a Thucydides or a Ranke.

In general, the translation of Western histories into Chinese is an underdeveloped field, and except for perhaps a small group of scholars whose interest has been to translate books of intellectual import into Chinese, and hence certain types of historical works, nobody can discuss authoritatively the problems involved in translating Western historical works, especially those available in English, into Chinese. What follows are therefore some preliminary reflections on the purpose and actual problems of my own experience as an occasional translator.

The Lesson of Historical Experience versus History as What Actually Happened

In the past half century, the most widely circulated Western historical work translated from English is Arnold J. Toynbee's *Study of History* which has appeared in various abridged translations. His other works, including *Half the World* and *Civilization on Trial* have also been translated into Chinese. Although most Western historians dismiss Toynbee as not a serious scholar, his popularity in China (and Taiwan) says a lot about the Chinese fascination with the moralist or generalist approach to history. Indeed, Oswald Spengler (English abridged edition is available in Chinese translation) has appealed to Chinese readers, clearly for the same reason. One could perhaps also include such works of historical philosophical interest as Thomas Carlyle's *Heroes, Hero-Worship and the Heroic in History* (available in two complete translations) or H. W. Van Loon's *Story of Mankind* (complete translation).

As a contrast, the purely narrative type of history, such as Guicciardini's *History of Florence* (complete translation), which has received much praise from Leopold von Ranke, does not seem to excite Chinese readers and has only recently been translated into Chinese. The same could be said of Thucydides' *Peloponnesian War* (complete translation), Caesar's *Gallic Wars* (complete translation), or the histories produced by Christian writers of more narrative nature, such as Gregory of Tour's *History of the Franks* (complete translation). Translators and readers alike seem to find the *Odyssey* or Shakespeare's *Cleopatra* more exciting than, say, Herodotus' *Persian Wars* (complete translation), however literary and informative the latter also is.

In fact, the penchant in the English world for historical novels does exist in China, witnessed by the fact that some of the nineteenth century novels, such as *A Tale of Two Cities* and *The Three Musketeers*, were quite popular, at least in the thirties. However, modern Chinese people do not seem to find great English narrative historians, such as Thomas B. Macauley and George M. Trevelyan, instructive, much less interesting. Their works are selectively available in Chinese translations but seldom discussed. Similarly, Edward Gibbon's *Decline and Fall of the Roman*

Empire is available also only in selected translations. Likewise, while Paul Kennedy's *Rise and Fall of the Powers* has been translated not only once, but twice within two years of its publication, Simon Schama is not represented by any translation of his *Embarrassment of Riches* or *Citizens*.

Some history textbooks are translated, but even so, H. G. Wells' *Outline of History* has remained widely used, and was still reprinted in China only a couple of years ago, whereas William McNeill's *Rise of the West* remained untranslated for more than twenty years. Other recent works, such as those by L. S. Stravianos, Robert Lopez *et al.* also are still not translated.

Thus, factual knowledge as such does not appeal to Chinese translators and readers. This is most evident in the translation of R. G. Collingwood's *Idea of History*, which is available in four different Chinese translations. The fact alone shows how philosophical history appeals to Chinese translators. More importantly, at least in one of the four translations, the part on the history of Western historiography, written from Collingwood's viewpoint (history as thought), is left untranslated.

The discussion above serves to show that there is a pragmatism in all the translating efforts related to historical works. The Chinese translators and readers seem to be above all looking for quick answers to historical questions from the more interpretative and philosophically minded historians. Although the Commercial Press 商務印書館 in China has supported a respectable and carefully organized project to translate major Western historical works into Chinese and has actually published quite a number of them (ranging from Herodotus to G. P. Gooch,) more work is done, even though sporadically, by private translators who flock to books of interpretative interest.

The problems arising from such a preference in purpose naturally affect the ways translators do their work. We move to these in the next section.

History as Philosophy Teaching by Examples

Bolingbroke's famous dictum certainly reflects the central belief of Chinese historical thinking. If history works are translated mainly for didactic or interpretative purposes, then translators would be more concerned with the philosophical interest than how to provide a good introduction to the issues that interest historians. Let me again take Edward Gibbon's *Decline and Fall of the Roman Empire* as an example. The most carefully translated and annotated part of the book undoubtedly belongs to his famous chapters 15 and 16 dealing with the rise of Christianity. The translator provides copious notes, largely based on the famous J. B. Bury commentaries, to help readers to understand better the historical background. But the reason that they are chosen for translation must be that the translator was primarily interested in their interpretative nature. The two chapters are also the least narrative in Gibbon's famous work.

My personal opinion is that philosophical histories, such as Karl Löwith's *Meaning in History* (complete translation) or Karl Popper's *Poverty of Historicism* (two complete translations) are less difficult to translate because the translators need not provide careful annotations to the extensive number of names, places and chronological information that certainly will appear in more strictly narrative histories. To translate Will Durant's *Lessons of History* (complete translation) is certainly easier than to translate any of his other volumes, because the translator, and his readers as well, do not have to grapple with too much information and could still delude themselves into believing that they have learned something from "history".

Furthermore, interpretative types of historical works, Toynbee and Spengler coming to my mind again immediately, are often not strictly philosophical, that is to say, not as philosophically oriented as, say, Hegel's *Philosophy of History* (complete translation), Arthur Danto's *Analytical Philosophy of History*, or Hayden White's *Metahistory*, because historians are less rigid in their choice of vocabulary for writing. Translators find it much freer and easier to use regular vocabulary to translate a Burckhardt (whose *Force and Freedom* has a complete translation) or a Herbert Butterfield (whose *History and Faith* has a complete translation.) Translators will inevitably have to deal with certain key words which are more often used in historian's works than in philosophical works; these are like "virtu" (*dexing* 德行 or *caoshou* 操守), "fortuna" (*mingyun* 命運), "providence" (*shenming lun* 神命論), "historism" (*lishi zhuyi* from German *Historismus*), "historicism" (also *lishi zhuyi*, but better *lishi dingming lun* 歷史定命論), "Zeitgeist" (*shidai jingshen* 時代精神), "climate of opinion" (*sixiang de fengshang* 思想的風尚), etc. Most of these terms challenge their translators, and require the translators to have a good understanding of their intellectual context. My feeling is that, fortunately, there are relatively few terms which are like those mentioned above that need special annotations. Certainly, "Zeitgeist" or "climate of opinion" are not necessarily more difficult than "Hesiod of Ascra" to annotate. Some words, such as "society" (*shehui* 社會), "culture" (*wenhua* 文化), "civilization" (*wenming* 文明), "-ism" (*zhuyi* 主義), or "historical materialism" (*lishi weiwu zhuyi* 歷史唯物主義), are so well established in Chinese vocabulary that they no longer create problem in translation.

In short, translating the interpretative type of historical works is a relatively less challenging job and the preference of Chinese translators to concentrate more on them is not without its pragmatic rationale; concrete historical examples in such books, often selective and well known, certainly are easier to explain in relatively plain language than philosophical ideas (such as Hegel's "Idea"), and after all, "history is philosophy teaching by examples" is very Chinese, too.

Books on Historiography

Books on historical method are of course attractive to translators. James H. Robinson's *New History* was translated into Chinese almost immediately after it came out in the U. S.. Ernst Bernheim's *Lehrbuch der historischen Methode* has also served almost like a classic for nearly a century since it was first translated into Chinese. Some of the important conceptions related to historical investigation, such as "evidence" (*zhengju* 證據), "external and internal criticism" (*waizheng* 外證 and *neizheng* 內證) or analysis (*fenxi* 分析) are standard in Chinese discussions on historical methods.

Similarly, the history of historiography has been a useful subject, although little studied. James Thompson's huge *History of Historical Writings*, however, is becoming available in a complete translation with a carefully compiled list of Chinese and English names and index. Obviously, the translator must have learned something from Thompson's book. J. B. Barnes' shorter one of the same title, which is actually better and more concise than that of Thompson's, is, on the other hand, available only in a much abridged translation.

The tradition of Western historical writings also means the history of important concepts and the creation of terms which need careful translation. Seventeenth century "Erudition" immediately comes to my mind. My translation of it into "tongru" 通儒 is mainly for "erudite". "Textual criticism" (à la Lorenzo Valla and Guillaume Bude, etc.) is another term that requires annotation, because of the legal nature in the early phase of its development in the West, which is quite different from the eighteenth-century Chinese *kaozheng* 考證 , although *kaozheng* is almost uniformly used to translate "criticism" or "textual criticism".

Similarly, "annals" and "chronicles" as terms are easy to translate, but what they actually are is little known in Chinese historical circles. Famous Chinese historical works have been given the names of "annals" (*The Spring and Autumn Annals: Chunqiu* 《春秋》) or "chronicles" ("The Chronicle of Fu Chien" 〈符堅載記〉), because the Chinese historiography seems to have developed similar writing styles: to record events chronologically. But from the Biblical times, annals and chronicles have been compiled under strong religious influence, and medieval annals are marked by religious festivals and rites. Even though early Roman annals record state affairs, most annals known in Western historiography are religious in nature. Since very few chronicles (selections of Froissart's *Chronicle* are available in my anthology) have been translated into Chinese, the use of "niandai ji" 年代記 for "annals" and "biannian" 編年 for "chronicle" can mislead Chinese readers, and some annotation will be necessary.

Historical periodization is another issue that is related to historiography in general. The tripartite scheme first developed by Joachim of Flora, but brought to wide circulation in the Renaissance, is probably the most difficult to accept for Chinese readers. The Chinese scheme of periodization has been political in nature, and Chinese historical thinking, at least before the nineteenth century, had little to do with the idea of progress. Up to the present day, as a result, "modern" has been translated into either "jindai 近代" or "xiandai 現代," with "jindai" probably implying that the period has been completed, and that therefore China does not have to seek to enter it. The different translations reflect a Chinese ambivalence about the Western idea of linear time and progress and whether China necessarily has to become "modernized".

In the same vein, the "Middle Ages" have been known to the Chinese with the "Dark Age" connotation, and the term is hence often equated with "Feudal Ages" when things were "feudal", meaning backward and detrimental to progress (more on this later). The "Middle Ages" could therefore be any time before the 1949 Communist Revolution, and so fairly recent, or perhaps the "Period of Disunion" (220–589 A.D.) in Chinese history, when China was considered to be quite "dark" or "chaotic" (*luan* 亂). The usual Western definition, say, between the fourth and the fifteenth centuries, gets easily lost in translation.

"Early modern" is another difficult term to translate, almost as difficult as defining it in Western historiography. "Jingu" 近古 is the preferred translation, although "jindai zaoqi" 近代早期 , which is cumbersome, seems to be a more logical rendering. Indeed, almost all the names denoting the major eras in Western civilization have their respective difficulties in translation. The "Renaissance" comes immediately to mind: it has been translated as "Wenyi fuxing" 文藝復興 for almost one hundred years now, but the "nascence" part of the name gets lost in the translation, as the Chinese rendering only emphasizes the "restoration" part, and it is well-known that in Chinese historical thinking, "fuxing" (or "zhongxing" 中興) did mean exactly that and not more. When "Renaissance" first entered the Chinese vocabulary, Burckhardt's "modernist" interpretation perhaps had yet to prevail. Scholars before him had traditionally stressed the revival of antiquity especially in the fields of art and literature. It is only natural that such aspects of the culture received emphasis when the first translators (perhaps Chinese translators adopted it from the Japanese) pondered over a good rendering.

Fortunately, the popularity in recent times of "revolution" as a name for historical eras ("Scientific Revolution", "Commercial Revolution", and even "Historical Revolution", as well as French Revolution, Russian Revolution, etc.) creates little problem for the Chinese who have consistently used "geming" 革命 to translate "revolution"; etymologically, *geming* (change of cosmic/heavenly mandate, taking place in cyclic sequence) and "revolution" are very similar, and when this ancient Chinese term was revived and regained popularity in the early twentieth century, the idea that there should be a "revolution" to overthrow the last imperial Chinese dynasty was gaining ground. The revolutionaries certainly learned from the French Revolution, and by design or by accident, put *geming* back into circulation.

The issues touched on in this section are common enough, and one sees that some of them originated from different interpretations of a similar historical event or phenomenon in Western historiography. While a name for an historic epoch or event, once coined, usually stays unchanged in its original language, even if interpretations of it may vary over time, translators of different generations are more likely to adopt new renderings. Renaissance, Enlightenment and democracy have all been translated differently in the past one hundred years. My conclusion is that, therefore, a responsible translator should attend to the needs of readers in terms of helping them understand key terms in Western historiography.

History as Social Science

Recent historical works in the English-speaking world have been markedly social-science oriented. Many books come with pages of statistics, tables, and charts. Works of this nature pose new problems for translators. Jargon borrowed from economists, political scientists and, above all, anthropologists needs special treatment in translation if the translators wish the translated works to be understandable to the educated layman.

In a way, the problem with technical jargon is similar to that of translating philosophers' works on historical philosophy. But some terms in social sciences have their origin in historical writings, and these terms now need careful rethinking after they had been "universalized" in theory-construction. The spectrum of meanings in "capitalism" is one good example. Translated as "ziben zhuyi" 資本主義, this is supposedly a conception or historical phenomenon the Chinese readers could understand readily, after forty years of Communist rule, but when employed by Max Weber, it could mean quite a different thing. Charles Beard had his own definition of this term, too. In translating their respective works, one has to take into consideration whether "ziben zhuyi" is adequate for all of them. A more interesting term is "middle class" which has been an English translation of "bourgeoisie". The latter was once transliterated into Chinese as "Bu'erqiaoya" 布爾喬亞. Lately, "zhongchan jieji" 中產階級 or "zichan jieji" 資產階級 has replaced "Bu'erqiaoya", and the new translation perhaps carries a more neutral connotation than that of Marxist derogatory usage. The same could be said of translating "bureaucracy" which has traditionally been rendered as "guanliao zhidu" 官僚制度, carrying a negative "bureaucratic" connotation. Social scientists are suggesting that it should be translated into "keceng zuzhi" 科層組織. It is believed that the new translation is also more neutral in nature (and hence more scientific). But the new translation means almost nothing to a non-professional reader.

"Feudalism" is also a term that requires a lot of explanation when translated into Chinese: this term traditionally has been translated into Chinese as "fengjian" 封建 which itself is a name for an ancient Chinese system of government. The choice of "fengjian" to translate it is bad enough, but what has complicated the situation is that the Chinese Communists chose to accept Marx's theory and argued that China was "feudal" (hence "fengjian") until 1949, when it was then liberated by the Communists. "Fengjian" therefore was something detrimental to progress, and to be condemned. I can imagine that translators of Marc Bloch or F. L. Ganshof shall please many readers who continue to respect traditional Chinese historiography, considering China as feudal only in the Zhou times (ca. 1121–221 B.C.), but those who abide by Communist orthodoxy will find these works confusing and troubling. Whether "fengjian" is a good translation, however, remains unresolved. Another example is "class", which for quite a long time has been translated into *jieji* 階級 . It is now increasingly been translated as *jieceng* 階層 , especially in Taiwan and Hong Kong. The changing translation again probably comes form the desire to get rid of the Marxist connotation for "jieji". One last example is "chengbang" 城邦 for "city-state". Both "cheng" and "bang" are conceptions that went back to the first millennium B.C. But when Greek "city-states" first appeared in Chinese books, they were translated into "chengbang". A recent writer has insisted that only the ancient Chinese state system should be properly called "chengbang", and warns his readers against equating this "chengbang" with the Greek "city-state".

Chinese vocabulary can be poor in dealing with the distinctions between "slave" and "serf", "peasant and "farmer", "nation" and "state", or "lineage" and "clan". The Chinese readers also are not familiar with such notions as "social mobility", "meritocracy", "elite", "gentry" or "mentalité" (as used by Annales historians). To translate them, new Chinese terms have to be created. This is not an easy job. Readers are not professional historians; they will find these terms troublesome. Providing them with notes may be very helpful.

Another problem is the complexity of highly technical historical works. Fernand Braudel's *Mediterranean World* and *Civilization and Capitalism* are cases in point. Both remain untranslated, but have been commented and reported on, and written about frequently. Not only do his terms like "structure" connote a range of meaning which conventional rendering cannot properly convey (*jiegou* 結構 is the common translation for "structure"), but his interpretations of statistical materials, accompanied by the kaleidoscopic range of units of length, weight and volume, could also frustrate the most industrious translator. That Braudel is admired but not read is not simply because of the length of his book, but also because of the relatively technical nature of his presentation. In contrast, *On History*, which is a collection of his less substantial essays, was translated into Chinese almost immediately after its English translation was published.

One cannot deny that the length of a book influences the decision of translators, but this is not always true. I think it is rather the pretentiousness of books, especially if burdened with professional jargon and statistical charts, etc., that scares away translators. Unfortunately, many modern historical works belong to this category.

Outstanding technical works are thus often reported in Chinese, but rarely translated; most readers are content with summaries of the works. Marc Bloch, Max Weber or Emile Durkheim are often cited or discussed, but their more substantial works (like Weber's *Economy and Society*, Bloch's *Feudal Society* and Durkheim's *Suicide* as opposed to *Protestant Ethics, Historian's Craft* and *The Rules of Sociological Method* which are all available in Chinese translation) have remained untranslated since they were published more than half a century ago. Clearly, their technical nature must have been the restraining factor. It goes without saying that recent clinometrical works will have even fewer translators.

This leads me to the problem of "abridged/summary translation". Often the translation is to introduce the main arguments; the main body of the work is then left untranslated. But before moving on to that issue, let me summarize what I have discussed above. In general, recent historical works have been greatly influenced by social sciences, in methods and in the adoption of technical terms. Most technical terms are extremely difficult to render into Chinese, but little effort has been given to coordinating or unifying their translation. Many translators are content with introducing the methodological aspect of the historical writings and care less about translating the most important part of the work, that is, the basic facts and information. That this should be the case is perfectly understandable.

Anthologies of Historical Writings and History as Literature

There have been some useful anthologies of major Western historical works or works in the philosophy of history. For university students studying the Western historical tradition, such publications are useful indeed. The Commercial Press project also includes selected translations of major historians; for example, Livy, Gibbon and Ranke (*History of the Popes*) are available only in selected translations, perhaps with the intention that these partial translations should serve the immediate need of teaching, while the complete translations could come out later. As a result, a good range of major Western historians are now available in just partial translations. Modern writers on historical thinking, such as Dilthey, Meinecke, Croce, and Carl Becker, are also available in selected translations.

The problem with "abridged/summary translation" is that the very essence of historical writings is often left out in the process. One gets to know something about Tacitus by reading selections of his works, but if one wishes to have a good knowledge of the first century Roman Empire, then one needs to have the entire compass of Tacitus' *Agricola, Germania, Histories* and *Chronicle* (all are now fully translated).

Pragmatism certainly dominates the minds of translators. Still, no great historical work can do without the narrative component. How to tell a great story in translated language therefore remains the central task of the translator. The issues involved here are not much different from those encountered by all translators, but translators of historical works have a unique problem to tackle. This is whether, in choosing the right words and tone, to reflect the concerns of the original author or to stick to faithful rendering of the narrative. As is well known to all historians, history is inevitably the images as caught and conceived by the historians themselves. A translator has to comprehend the personality as reflected in the narrative, in order to reproduce faithfully the images in the Chinese language: a Burckhardt is different from a Leopold von Ranke; E. H. Carr's *History of the Soviet Union* is not the same as E. H. Carr's *What Is History?* (complete translation).

My experience has been mixed in this regard, and most translators seem to be also torn between the two. This difficulty is compounded by the fact that especially in Communist China, scholars have been cut off from the mainstream of historical scholarship and hence could not utilize the most up-to-date studies to help their translations. The translator of Voltaire's *Age of Louis XIV* did not mention J. H. Brumfit. Similarly, the translators of Thucydides did not mention C. N. Cochran or J. H. Finlay and that of Caesar ignored M. Rambaud or F. E. Adock. On the other hand, some translators do make special efforts to study the historical thinking of the authors, and are able to capture the spirit at work behind the narrative. For example, at least one of the two translators of Burckhardt's famous *The Culture of the Renaissance in Italy* has taken pains to employ a particularly elegant language which seems to me to convey quite successfully Burckhardt's sensitivity to beautiful things which only a handful of elite scholars or thinkers could actually appreciate. The ambivalence as seen in Burckhardt's desperate appreciation of *Gewaltmenschen*, hoping that they could support artistic creativity, is evident even in the Chinese translation. Not many translators are as good. To make up for the inadequacy of more pedestrian rendering, it would be desirable to prepare a detailed introductory essay to provide the readers with reliable background knowledge. The translator of *The Peloponnesian War* does just that, and thereby more than offsets the clumsiness of his Chinese language which does little justice to Thucidides' terse, but precise and often forceful exposition.

The ability to capture the spirit of the original authors does not come easily, and it almost requires that the translator be first a historian. But this is a demand not easily met. Then, a good historian may be a poor writer, not always knowing how to choose the correct language. The dilemma will continue for as long as historical works have to be translated.

Concluding Remarks

The discussion above is not more than some very personal reflections on my experience as an occasional translator. The concerns raised above are primarily those of a practising historian. The panorama of ideas and experiences of Western historical writing, even if only partly manifest in the English originals and translations, is complex enough, and the Chinese translator is confronted with a whole spectrum of terminology/ nomenclature and theories and ideas which could easily exasperate him. Occasionally, the Chinese language, a product of a very different cultural and historical tradition, simply betrays the translator. At other times, the difficulty is in not quite being able to enter the inner world of the historian one is translating. As a result, a wonderful narrative may be reduced to a horrible aggregate of disparate words, which is void of the message and nuance of the original author.

A responsible translator may therefore wish to provide occasional annotations or introductory essays, but then we are asking him to be more than just a translator. He also has to be a historian. The translation of Western historical works demands that the translator is one who has the historical perception and training and is also a sensitive connoisseur of the nuances of both the English and Chinese languages.

HISTORY OF TRANSLATION

History of Translation in China

Ma Zuyi
Oceanic Literature Institute
Anhui University, Hefei, China

Translation in China has a very long history. According to the *Rites of Zhou* 《周禮》 and the *Book of Rites* 《禮記》 , as early as in the Zhou dynasty (c. 11th century–221 B.C.), there was established a sort of institute for foreign affairs, provided with interpreters or translators. It was also stipulated that at intervals of seven years the official interpreters or translators from the feudal states should gather at the capital of Zhou kingdom to undergo a training course. After that, each dynasty in China maintained the same organization with different names, and the official interpreters or translators played an important role in foreign affairs. A special translation organ for foreign affairs was first set up in the Sui dynasty (581–618). It was called Sifang Guan 四方館 , which was later adopted in both Tang and Song dynasties. The first foreign languages institute for training interpreters or translators in China was called Siyi Guan 四夷館 established in the Ming dynasty (1368–1644), in which such languages as Mongolian, Tibetan, Indian, Burmese, Thai and Arabic were taught and studied. The second one was called Tongwen Guan 同文館 (Interpreters' College) set up in 1868 at Beijing, the then capital of the Qing dynasty (1644–1911). There, English, French, German, Russian and Japanese were taught and studied. Its teachers and students like W. A. P. Martin, A. Billequin, S. M. Russell, Wang Fengzao 汪鳳藻 , Yang Shu 楊樞 , Lian Fang 聯芳 and Qing Chang 慶常 translated a number of foreign works such as Wheaton's *International Law*,

Fawcett's *Political Economy*, *Code Napoleon*, *Guide Diplomatique*, *Outline of the World's History*, etc.

The first translated version of poetry in China is *Song of the Yue Girl* 〈越人歌〉 It was in the period of Spring and Autumn (770–476 B.C.). A lord named Ejun Zixi 鄂君子皙 in the state of Chu, was one day travelling in blue-plumed boat with a kingfisher awning. A Yue girl in the same boat fell in love with the lord and sang a song as she plied the oars. The lord did not know her Yue language, so he asked someone to translate it for him. Deeply affected and filled with desire, he raised his embroidered quilt and covered the girl. This Song can be found in Liu Xiang's 劉向 *Shuo Yuan* 〈說苑〉, with 32 Chinese characters attached to record the sounds of its original.

The second one is a *Folk Song of Xiongnu* 〈匈奴歌〉, which only has four lines. Its translator is unknown. The Song expresses the Xiongnu people's grievance at the loss of the Yinshan Mountain 陰山 during their war with the Western Han dynasty (206–24 B.C.). As the ancient Xiongnu people had no written language, it is the only piece of their literature recorded.

In addition, there were three Odes by Tang Zou 唐菆, king of Bailang 白狼, in praise of the Mingdi emperor of the Eastern Han dynasty. The Odes were composed in the period of 58–74 and put into Chinese by Tian Gong 田恭, a petty government official. Each translated version of the Odes has 56 Chinese characters attached to it to record the sounds of its original text, which is a valuable source for linguistic studies.

The two Songs and three Odes are the only translations extant before the activities of translating the Buddhist sacred literature, which began in 148 in the Eastern Han dynasty and ended in the Northern Song dynasty (960–1127). During the 980 years, more than 150 translators were identified as taking part in this task. Among those translators, the first one without dispute is An Qing 安清 (or An Shigao 安世高), who immigrated to China in 148 and in the remainder of his life put into Chinese 35 items of Buddhist scriptures in 41 volumes, by using the method of literal translation.

In the history of Chinese Buddhism there are four great translators, of whom the most famous two are Kumarajiva 鳩摩羅什 (334–413) and Xuan Zang 玄奘 (600–664).

Born in the country of Qiuzi 龜茲 (modern Kuche in Xinjiang), Kumarajiva entered Buddhist orders at the age of seven and became a well-known scholar. When the Qiuzi country was overthrown by general

Lü Kuang's 呂光 troops in 385, Kumarajiva was transported to Liangzhou (modern Wuwei in Gansu), where he lived for 15 years and learned and mastered the Chinese language. Then, in 401, Yao Xing 姚興, ruler of the late Qin state (one of the Sixteen Kingdoms in north China), invited the scholar to his capital Chang'an (modern Xi'an in Shaanxi). Before his death, Kumarajiva put into Chinese 74 items of Buddhist scriptures in 383 volumes. He was the first one who used the method of free translation. A Chinese scholar Chen Yinke 陳寅恪 compared Kumarajiva's translations with their original text and found that he had put to use these three techniques: (1) to simplify the text by weeding out superfluities and repetitions, (2) to avoid being restricted by the original literary form, and (3) to make the translated version idiomatic, so as to be easily understandable. On his deathbed, Kumarajiva vowed that none of his translations had misrepresented their original texts in essentials. It is generally acknowledged that Kumarajiva's translations marked an epoch in the history of Buddhist scriptures translation in China.

Xuan Zang, the founder of Weishi Zong 唯識宗 (the Mere-Ideation school) in China, was born in Goushi 緱氏 (modern Yanshi in Henan) and entered Buddhist orders at thirteen. In 629, he made a celebrated trip to India in search of Buddhist scriptures. His journey took him across the dreadful deserts of Central Asia and the towering, snow-capped mountains of Northwest India before he arrived in the holy land of Buddhism in 633, where he stayed about 10 years. His fame became so widespread that he was even honoured and respected by the powerful king Harsa, ruler of North India. He returned to China in 645 with over 657 items of Buddhist scriptures, packed in 520 cases. In the remainder of his life, Xuan Zang only translated 75 items in 1335 volumes. Besides, he also put *Lao Zi* into Sanskrit and sent it to India. The account of his travels *Records on the Western Regions of the Great Tang Empire* 《大唐西域記》 has proved to be most useful to historians and archaeologists working on Central Asian and Indian history. In his translation, Xuan Zang put forward and carried out the five principles of transliteration. He mastered such techniques of translation as omission, addition, transposition, substitution, division or combination and restoration of nouns for pronouns, which was proved by P. Pradhan and Zhang Jianmu 張建木, Indian and Chinese scholars, who had compared Xuan Zang's translations with the Sanskrit texts. Without doubt, Xuan Zang is one of the world's greatest translators.

The other notable figures in the field of Buddhist scriptures translation are Dao An 道安 (312–385), Fa Xian 法顯 (337?–422?), Xie Lingyun 謝靈運 (385–433), Yan Zong 彥琮 (557–610) and Yi Jing 義淨 (634–713). Among them, Xie Lingyun was not a monk himself, but a poet who was the first noted for his contribution to the mountains-and-rivers poetry in Chinese literature. Few people know that he was also a translator. Dao An compiled the first catalogue of the translated Buddhist scriptures in China and summarized the early experience of Buddhist scriptures translation by pointing out that there were three difficulties which the translators could hardly overcome and five cases in which the Chinese version could not adhere to its Sanskrit original. Yan Zong made a further summing up of such experiences and put forward the eight requirements for his fellow translators. Fa Xian and Yi Jing were not only translators but also travellers. Together with Xuan Zang, they are known as the three high-ranking monks who made a pilgrimage to the holy land, India. The account of Fa Xian's travels *Records of Buddhist Kingdoms* 《佛國記》 parallels Yi Jing's *Records of Buddhism in the Southern Overseas Kingdoms* 《南海寄歸內法傳》 in its value for historical and geographical studies.

Dao An helped Zhao Zheng 趙政 , an official of the Jin state, to take care of the translation workshop 譯場 and Yan Zong was sent by the Wendi emperor 文帝 of the Sui dynasty to take charge of the workshop for Buddhist scripture translation 翻經館 . Formerly, the translations of Buddhist scriptures were only individual activities. They were usually done by two or three persons working together. The translation workshop was set up in the Eastern Jin dynasty (317–420) and lasted to the Song dynasty. After its establishment, the translation of Buddhist scriptures became an official undertaking and was done through collective effort. In the translation workshop, when a scripture was to be translated, there had to be a symposium presided over by the chief translator, with a number of assistants and hundreds of attendants. Of course, the attendants were monks and Buddhist disciples, who only lent a willing ear to the chief translator. When the chief translator, like Xuan Zang or Yi Jing, read out the Sanskrit text and gave his oral translation, his assistants carried out their respective duties, to record the sounds of Sanskrit with Chinese characters, put down his oral translations, polish the translated version, compare the translated version with its original text and do some rectification and then chant the final version. It is recorded that when Xuan Zang was doing his oral translation, the words flowed from his mouth as from the pen of a master.

Now almost all the Buddhist scriptures in Sanskrit have been lost in

India, but most of their Chinese texts still remain intact. In the history of translation in China, the translation of Buddhist scriptures is considered the first high tide of translation. No kind of translation in the world can match it in length of duration, in immensity of scale, in multitude of participants and in profundity of influence.

In the history of China there were many nationalities whose upper classes once ruled a part or the whole of China. During the Song dynasty, the ancient nationality Qiang established the Western Xia kingdom (1023–1227) in the western part of China and the ancient nationalities Qidan and Nuzhen founded the Liao dynasty (916–1125) and the Jin dynasty (1271–1365) early or late in north China. Those nationalities all had their own languages into which they translated a great number of Chinese historical books, Confucian scriptures and literary works. For example, Li Yuanhao 李元昊, founder of the Western Xia kingdom, put *The Book of Filial Duty* 《孝經》 into Western Xia language; Yelu Longxu 耶律隆緒, emperor of the Liao dynasty, translated into Qidan language some of the Tang poet Bai Juyi's 白居易 verses; and according to the *History of the Jin Dynasty*, in 1183, the governmental translation organ finished translating into Nuzhen language these nine Chinese works: *The Book of Changes* 《易經》, *The Book of History* 《書經》, *The Confucian Analects* 《論語》, *Mencius* 《孟子》, *Lao Zi* 《老子》, *Yang Zi* 《楊子》, *Wenzhong Zi* 《文中子》, *Lie Zi* 《列子》 and *The New History of the Tang Dynasty* 《新唐書》. As for the Yuan and the Qing dynasties, they were separately set up by the upper classes of Mongol and Manchu nationalities who once reigned over the whole China. In both dynasties, there were a lot of translations done from Chinese into Mongolian or Manchu and vice versa.

The second high tide of translation in China rose between the late Ming and the early Qing dynasties. It centred on science and technology translations, which were done by both Chinese scholars and foreign Jesuit missionaries. In the 16th century, China, with its big population, was an area that Christian missionaries, especially the Jesuits, wished to enter. When Matteo Ricci (1552–1610), an Italian Jesuit, was admitted to Beijing, the then capital of the Ming dynasty, and given the right to reside there, in 1601, the door of the old China was finally knocked open and then entered in succession a host of Jesuit missionaries sent by the Society of Jesus. The noted ones among them totalled over 70, such as Italian Jesuits Nicolaus Longobardi (1559–1654), Julius Aleni (1582–1649), Jacobus Rho (1593–1638) and Sabbathinus de Ursis (1575–1620), German Jesuits Johannes

Adam Schall von Bell (1519–1666) and Ignatius Kogler (1680–1740), Portuguese Jesuit Franciscus Furtado (1587–1652), Swiss Jesuit Jean Terrenz (1576–1630), French Jesuits Franciscus Gerbillon Jean (1656–1730) and Michel Benoist (1715–1774), Belgian Jesuit Ferdinand Verbiest (1623–1688), *et al.* As the missionary strategy of Jesuits had undergone modification and put great stress on the importance of knowing the Chinese language and acquiring knowledge of the culture, the efforts made by those Jesuits to attract and convert the Chinese intelligentsia brought them into contact with many outstanding personalities like Xu Guangqi 徐光啓 (1562–1633), Li Tianjing 李天經 (1579–1659) and Li Zhizao 李之藻 (1565–1630). In the late Ming dynasty, the scholar-officials represented by Xu Guangqi all had cherished the hope of making the country rich and building up its military power. They also had a keen interest in the scientific and cultural achievements of the Renaissance Europe, which were imparted by the Jesuits as a part of their approach to the missionary work. It was all the more natural for both sides to cooperate in the work of translating Western science and technology.

It is recorded that the noted Jesuit missionaries compiled and translated over 300 works with or without the help of the Chinese scholars. Among them there were about 200 works of science and technology, of which 75 were compiled and translated by Matteo Ricci, Johannes Adam Schall von Bell, Jacobus Rho and Ferdinand Verbiest. Those 200 works may be classified into such categories as astronomy, mathematics, physics, mining and metallurgy, physiology and anatomy, biology, military technology and cartography.

When Xu Guangqi and then Li Zhizao took charge of composing the official Chinese calendar, the Jesuits Nicolaus Longobardi, Jean Terrenz, Adam Schall von Bell and Jacobus Rho were all invited to take part in the task. As a result, 135 volumes of the new almanac were completed in 1664, of which 59 volumes were compiled and translated by the four Jesuits and their Chinese assistants.

While in Italy, Matteo Ricci studied science under the noted mathematician Christopher Clavius. In 1606, Ricci and Xu Guangqi started translating Euclid's *Elements* but only finished 6 of its 15 volumes in 1607. Xu Guangqi set great store by this work and regretted that the rest could not be put into Chinese. However, 200 odd years later, that task was accomplished by Li Shanlan 李善蘭 (1810–1882) and Alexander Wylie, who translated the rest of *Elements* from English. The Kangxi emperor 康熙 of the Qing dynasty loved natural science and had a special interest in astronomy and mathematics, so he asked Franciscus Gerbillon Jean and Joachin Bouvet, Jesuits sent by Louis XIV, King of France, to teach him geometry. It is said that the two Jesuits translated some 20 books on astronomy and mathematics into Manchu or Chinese and Kangxi put one of them from Manchu into Chinese. At the same time, an Italian Jesuit Ludovicus Buglio compiled two booklets about lions and hawks for Kangxi. It is said they were translated from Aldrovandi's biological works.

As a scientist, Xu Guangqi was good at imbibing the essence of Western science and putting it into practice. When he was to build water conservancy projects, he asked Italian Jesuit Sabbathinus de Ursis to help him translating a book on the advanced Western methods of water conservancy. The book was completed in 1612. Then he used those methods to reclaim wasteland in Tianjin, thereby turning it into a high-yield paddy field.

Wang Zheng 王徵 (1571–1644) was also a scientist who studied mechanics and made 55 kinds of machines. In 1627, he helped Jean Terrenz to compile a book of Western mechanisms. He selected the most useful machines for illustrating. According to a Chinese scholar Fang Hao's 方豪 textual research, the book was translated from Victruvins' *De Architectura*, Agostino Ramalli's *Le Diverse et Artificiose Machine*, Georgius Agricola's *De Re Metallica* and Simon de Bruges' *Hypomnemata Mathmatica*.

Having adopted the suggestion put forward by Xu Guangqi, the Xizong emperor advertised for skilled foreign workers to make Hongyi (red cloth) cannons. In a battle against the Qing troops, a cannon shell hit Nuer Hachi 努爾哈赤, founder of the Qing dynasty, who was seriously injured and died later. So, in 1643, Adam Schall von Bell and Jiao Xu 焦勗 translated and published a book concerning the methods of cannon-making. Then in the early Qing dynasty, the Kangxi emperor appointed Ferdinand Verbiest to supervise the cannon-making so Verbiest translated another book on this subject. Those cannons showed their might during the war against Russian invaders.

Besides, Jean Terrenz and Wang Gongzhen 王拱震 translated a book of physiology and anatomy; Franciscus Furtado and Li Zhizao translated a book of logic. It was the first time that Aristotle's logic was introduced into China. Many of the Jesuit missionaries also put into Western languages a number of Chinese Confucian scriptures and historical and literary works.

They certainly did an excellent job in the cultural exchange between China and the West.

Xu Guangqi, born in Shanghai, was a great translator in this period. He spent his whole life in scientific research. His masterpiece is *The Complete Works of Agriculture* 《農政全書》. He planned to launch an academic movement centred on science and technology so as to give impetus to the development of Chinese science. But unfortunately his proposal did not find support in the feudal court.

In 1723, the Yongzheng emperor of the Qing dynasty laid a ban on Christianity and drove out the Jesuit missionaries, thus putting an end to the translation of science and technology. It was only after the time of China's defeat in the Opium War of 1840 that those who wanted to overcome China's weakness began to learn conscientiously from the West and introduce its new knowledge, which gradually pushed the translation activities to another upsurge.

In this period the first one who encouraged and sponsored the activities of translating materials of new knowledge from the West was Lin Zexu 林則徐 (1785–1850). Lin was accepted as a national hero because of his courage and feats in opposing the British before the Opium War. When he was posted to Guangzhou to stop the opium trade, he set up a translation institute to put into Chinese the news and reviews from *Canton Press*, *Canton Register* and *Singapore Free Press*, De Valtet's *Laws of Nations*, Thelwall's *Pamphlet Against Opium* and a part of Murray's *Cyclopaedia of Geography*. His slogan, as Wei Yuan put it, was "the use of foreign superior techniques to control the foreigners".

Impressed by the strength of warships and guns displayed in the imperialist aggressive wars and supported by the Manchu nobles Yi Xin 奕訢, Gui Liang 桂良 and Wen Xiang 文祥 in Beijing, the anti-Taiping generals Zeng Guofan 曾國藩, Li Hongzhang 李鴻章 and Zuo Zongtang 左宗棠 launched a Westernization movement with the aim of preserving the feudal regime of the Qing government by introducing techniques of capitalist production. In the first period of the modern industrial development (1861–72), the effort was focussed on the manufacture of firearms and machines and the most important enterprises were the Jiangnan Arsenal (established in 1865), the Tianjin Machine Factory (established in 1867) and the Fuzhou Shipyard (established in 1866). Each of these enterprises had a translation institute attached to it. But the biggest one was the translation institute attached to the Jiangnan Arsenal, which started its translation from 1867. It was directed by Xu Shou 徐壽 (1818–1884), a well-known scientist who made the first steamer in China. Those who took part in such activities were Chinese scientists like Li Shanlan, Hua Hengfang 華蘅芳 (1833–1902) and Xu Jianyin 徐建寅 (1845–1901), and foreign scholars and missionaries John Fryer, Young J. Allen, L. L. Kreyer, Alexander Wylie and D. J. MacGowan. As these Chinese scientists did not know foreign languages, the foreigners mentioned above acted as oral translators. It was recorded that they put 163 Western works into Chinese, most of which were of natural science and technology, such as J. D. Dana's *System of Mineralogy* and Charles Lyell's *Principles of Geology* translated by Hua Hengfang and D. J. MacGowan, John Frederich William Herschel's *Outline of Astronomy* translated by Li Shanlan and Alexander Wylie, *Methods of Gunpower-making* translated by Ding Shutang 丁樹堂 and John Fryer, etc. At the same time, there were other translation and publication institutes set up by the Christian Church, like the London Mission Press, the School and Text Book Series Committee, Tenchow College and Christian and Literature Society of China. They translated hundreds of books concerning astronomy, mathematics, physics, chemistry and others.

After the Sino-Japanese War of 1894, China was placed on the brink of being partitioned. It aroused a keen sense of crisis, in which the Hundred Days of Reform of 1898 was staged. The reformists laid stress on institutional or ideological changes and felt confident that only by learning from the West could China be modernized and that since the Japanese had successfully learned from the West, the Chinese should also learn from the Japanese. The outstanding reform leaders Kang Youwei 康有爲 (1858–1925) and Liang Qichao 梁啓超 (1873–1929) emphasized the importance of translating materials of new knowledge from the West, and suggested that such translation could be done by using Japanese versions as Japan had published thousands of books concerning Western political science, economics, philosophy and sociology since its Meiji Restoration. Their suggestion was then widely accepted. According to Yang Shouchun's 楊壽椿 statistical data, in the last years of the Guangxu emperor's reign, there were 533 translated books in print, of which 321 were put into Chinese from Japanese. In 1896, Liang Qichao compiled a catalogue of books translated between 1840–1894 and then put forward three measures to remedy the shortcomings in the translations of the previous stage. They were the selection of books worth translating, the standardization of translated terms and the training of qualified translators. Ma Jianzhong 馬建忠 (1845–1900),

a scholar who knew Latin, Greek, English and French, suggested that translation institutes should be set up for training translators and for doing translation work in a planned way. He also set out the requirements for a good translation. At this stage translation was in full swing and a number of capable translators emerged. The most famous one was Yan Fu 嚴復 (1853–1921), who, for the first time, introduced Western philosophy systematically into China. Born in Houguan (modern Fuzhou in Fujian), he was sent to England to study naval techniques in 1877 but he soon became interested in government, economics and sociology. He returned to China in 1879. China's humiliating defeat by Japan in 1895 prompted him to advocate liberal social and political reform, so he translated into Chinese T. H. Huxley's *Evolution and Ethics and Other Essays*, J. S. Mill's *On Liberty* and *A System of Logic*, Herbert Spencer's *The Study of Sociology*, Adam Smith's *An Inquiry into the Nature and Cause of the Wealth of Nations*, C. L. S. Montesquieu's *The Spirit of the Law* and E. Jenks' *A History of Politics*, in an attempt to show the Chinese intellectuals that the secret to Western wealth and power did not lie in special Western techniques, but in the institutions that lay behind these techniques. Yan's translation of the first two chapters of T. H. Huxley's *Evolution and Ethics and Other Essays* was first carried in the *National News* 《國聞報》, which started publication at Tianjin in 1897. As Fan Wenlan 范文瀾 says in his *Modern History of China*, "The translation of *Evolution* expounded the generally acknowledged truth of the law of the jungle, the survival of the fittest and the preservation of species through unceasing efforts. The book brought a new hope to people who had felt disappointed and disheartened. It became popular with the whole country and was regarded as the best of the translation works. It played an important role in the Reform Movement. The Shanghai *News of Current Affairs* 《時務報》 and the Tianjin *National News* held the leading position of public opinion respectively in the South and North. The influence of Yan Fu's thoughts was no less than that of Liang Qichao's." In the history of translation in China, it was Yan Fu who first proposed faithfulness, expressiveness and elegance as the criteria of translation, which are still widely accepted by Chinese translators, although their interpretation of "elegance" is different from his.

A coup d'état carried out by the Empress Dowager ended the Reform Movement. The nationalists and revolutionists represented by Sun Yat-sen 孫逸仙 took another road to save the crisis-ridden China. Their aim was to overthrow the feudal dynasty and establish a republic. Sun and his comrades had their most enthusiastic and numerous supporters among the Chinese students in Japan, whose numbers increased rapidly between 1900 and 1906. In 1896, only 13 students were sent to Japan for the first time; the figure rose to about 1,000 in 1903 and to some 8,000 in 1905–1906. Many of these students began to organize themselves for propaganda and immediate action for the revolutionary cause. The Western and revolutionary thoughts diffused easily and widely by means of journals and pamphlets published in Tokyo, Shanghai and Hong Kong. These publications began to mushroom at the turn of the 20th century. Most of the translators in this stage were returned students and most of their translated books and pamphlets were originally written or translated by the Japanese, such as the *History of Greece's Independence, Lincoln, Imperialism,* the *Documents of Young Italy, Declaration of the Rights of Man and of the Citizen, Declaration of Independence,* etc. The best-known translator at that time was Ma Junwu 馬君武 (1882–1939), who knew English, German and Japanese, and studied in Japan and Germany. While in Japan, he translated into Chinese the *History of the French Revolution,* J. S. Mill's *On Liberty,* Herbert Spencer's *The Principles of Sociology* and Charles Robert Darwin's *On the Origin of Species.* In literary translation, like the poet Su Manshu 蘇曼殊 (1884–1918), he also did a good job: he introduced G. G. Byron, Thomas Hood, J. C. F. Schiller and J. W. von Goethe to Chinese readers.

The establishment of the Republic did not change China's semi-colonial and semi-feudal status. It showed that the theory of evolution, the theory of natural rights and the bourgeois republic could by no means save China. Then, the Russian Revolution of 1917 awakened the Chinese people and they learned something new, Marxism-Leninism. In 1919, the May Fourth Movement took place in China, and in 1921 the Communist Party of China was founded. To seize state power, the Communists in China had to first whip up revolutionary opinion by spreading knowledge of Marxism-Leninism. Therefore, the fourth high tide of translation in China, the translation of Marxist-Leninist works, started to flow. As early as in 1906 and 1908, excerpts from the *Communist Manifesto* were translated by Zhu Zhixin 朱執信 (1885–1920) and by Min Ming 民鳴 . It was Chen Wangdao 陳望道 (1890–1977) who put the whole of the *Communist Manifesto* into Chinese in 1920. Together with Chen Duxiu 陳獨秀 (1880–1942), Chen Wangdao set up the first society for Marxist studies in China. In 1912 and 1920, excerpts from Engels' *The Development of Socialism from Utopian to Scientific* were translated by Shi Renrong 施仁榮 and by Zheng Cichuan

鄭次川, but its two complete Chinese versions by Wu Liping 吳黎平 and by Bo Gu 博古 were published separately in 1938 and in 1943. Marx's *Critique of the Gotha Programme* was translated by Xiong Deshan 熊得山 in 1922 and by Li Chunfan (Ke Bainian 柯百年) in 1925. Excerpts from Engels' *The Origin of the Family, Private Property and the State* were introduced by Xiong Deshan in 1923 and later two complete Chinese versions were published, one by Yang Xianjiang 楊賢江 in 1929 and the other by Zhang Zhongshi 張仲實 in 1939. From 1930 to 1934, Chen Qixiu 陳啓修 , Wang Shenming 王慎明 and Hou Wailu 侯外廬 , Pan Dongzhou 潘冬舟 , and Wu Bannong 吳半農 all translated the first volume of Marx's *Capital*. It was in 1938 that Guo Dali 郭大力 and Wang Yanan 王亞南 put the three volumes of *Capital* into Chinese. Before the establishment of the People's Republic of China, the main part of Marx's and Engels' works all had their Chinese versions. Leninism was first introduced into China in 1920. There were over 70 translators who took part in translating Lenin's and Stalin's works. From 1921 to 1949, over 500 Marxist-Leninist works were translated and published. In 1953, the Communist Party of China set up its Translation and Edition Bureau for Marx, Engels, Lenin and Stalin's works, provided with 200 odd translators. Up to 1984, it translated and published 50 volumes of Marx-Engels' *Complete Works*, 39 volumes of Lenin's *Complete Works* and 13 volumes of Stalin's *Complete Works*.

In parallel with the high tide of Marxist-Leninist translation ran the other high tide of translation, the foreign literatures translation. It began to rise in the later period of the Qing dynasty. According to *Hanfen Lou Catalogue of the Classified New Books* 《涵芬樓分類新書目錄》 , the translated novels in this period, including those printed in 1911, amounted to some 400, which is by no means the exact figure, as A Ying 阿英 put it, because only in the year of 1906 there were already 87 translated novels in print. It is acknowledged that Liang Qichao had something to do with the rapid advance of foreign fiction translation. In his articles, Liang stressed the importance of fiction-writing and translating while overstating the significance of "political fiction". His opinion found an echo in the men of letters at that time. Through the language they learned, the Chinese students in Japan had access to the Western literature which had been translated into Japanese since the Meiji Restoration, and to the "political fiction" written by Japanese authors. Therefore, a great number of literature translations were made from Japanese versions, such as E. de Amicis' *Coeur* by Bao Tianxiao 包天笑 (1875–1973), A. Pushkin's *The Captain's Daughter* by Ji

Yihui 戢翼翬 , A. Tchehov's *The Black Monk* by Wu Tao 吳檮 , etc. Bao
Tianxiao, Ji Yihui, Wu Tao and the others like Zhou Guisheng 周桂笙
(?–1926), Zeng Pu 曾樸 (1871–1935), Xu Nianci 徐念慈 (1874–1908), Wu
Guangjian 伍光建 (1866–1943), Su Manshu (1884–1918), Zhou Shoujuan
周瘦鵑 (1895–1968) etc. were all noted for their translating foreign fiction
or poetry. As far as the introduction of foreign literatures into China is
concerned, the contributions made by Lin Shu 林紓 (1852–1924) were the
most remarkable. Born in Minxian (modern Fuzhou in Fujian), Lin was a
man of letters who made available to Chinese readers 184 works of Western
literature, even though he himself had no first-hand knowledge of any
foreign language. Working through 19 oral interpreters, he translated fiction
from England, the United States, France, Russia, Switzerland, Belgium,
Spain, Norway, Greece and Japan. Because of the second-hand nature of his
translations — indeed, many are translations of translations — they are not
completely accurate and have been severely criticized for their errors. But
Lin Shu's skilled use of the Chinese literary language 文言 has been highly
praised, and his translations remain important for their role in introducing
Western literature to China.

The activities of those translators represented by Lin Shu were the
prelude to the high tide of literary translation. The cultural reform movement which grew out of the May Fourth Movement pushed forward China's
literary revolution and at the same time carried the translation of foreign
literatures to a new stage. After 1919, there mushroomed a number of
literary societies such as Literature Studies Society 文學研究社 , Creation
Society 創造社 , Unnamed Society 未名社 , New Moon Society 新月社 ,
Sunken Bell Society 沉鐘社 , etc. Members of the societies were engaged in
both producing new-vernacular literature and translating foreign literatures.
All of the societies had their own journals. Literature Studies Society edited
Fiction Monthly 《小說月報》 and published a series of books. From 1921
to 1926, *Fiction Monthly* carried a great number of foreign literary works,
of which 33 belong to Russia, 27 to France, 13 to Japan, and 6 to India and
England respectively. As for the series published, there were near 100 books
of fiction, prose, poetry and drama by foreign authors. Literature Studies
Society made efforts to introduce realistic foreign literature and literatures
of weak and small nations in the world. The translators of the Society
numbered over 100. Creation Society started its translation activities in
1922. The members of the Society dedicated themselves to introducing
romantic foreign literature and other schools of literature like symbolism,

futurism and expressionism. Unnamed Society was set up in 1925. Their translations were noted for introducing Russian literature and especially Soviet literature after the October Revolution. The members of New Moon Society were all poets who were good at translating foreign verses into Chinese. From 1919 to 1927, the translated foreign literatures printed in book form totalled 187 titles, of which 65 belong to Russia, 31 to France, 24 to German, 21 to England, 14 to India and 12 to Japan.

In 1930 the Chinese Left-wing Writers' Union was founded and soon became the centre of translating the works of Marxist literary theory, Soviet literature and the progressive literature of other countries. In 1934, *Translation Text* 《譯文》 started publication. It was the first journal for introducing foreign literatures in China. In 1935 and 1936, 12 volumes of the complete collection of World Literature 世界文庫 were published. Zheng Zhenduo 鄭振鐸 was the editor-in-chief and more than 100 writers and translators were on the translation and editorial board. In the 12 volumes they introduced more than 100 literary masterpieces from 12 foreign countries. During the years of 1930–36 there appeared a host of articles on translation. Lu Xun 魯迅 , Qu Qiubai 瞿秋白 and Lin Yutang 林語堂 (1895–1976) all voiced their opinions on the principles, methods and requirements of translation, which were conducive to developing the Chinese theory of translation.

It is recorded that from 1919 to 1949 the translated foreign literature printed in book form amounted to more than 1,700 titles and from 1949 to 1978 the figure of such publications came up to 5,677 titles, including 503 of different versions or different editions of the same work. After 1949, the literary works by 1,909 foreign writers from 85 countries were put into Chinese. In fact, many of those writers can by no means be ranked high and their works seem not to be worth translating. Nevertheless, through those works the Chinese readers can, more or less, deepen their understanding of other peoples. Now, the Chinese translators, old and new, are making efforts to put into Chinese some 3,000 kinds of famous world literary works.

References

Chen, Yugang 陳玉剛 , ed. 《中國翻譯文學史稿》 (*A Tentative History of Literary Works Translation in China*). Beijing: China Translation and Publishing Corporation 中國對外翻譯出版公司 , 1989.

Lin, Hui 林輝 , *et al.*, comp. 《中國翻譯家辭典》 (*A Dictionary of Chinese Transla-tors*). Beijing: China Translation and Publishing Corporation, 1988.

Ma, Zuyi 馬祖毅 . 《中國翻譯簡史 — 「五四」運動以前部份》 (*A Brief History of Translation in China — Before the May Fourth Movement*). Beijing: China Translation and Publishing Corporation, 1984.

Translation Theory in the West:
An Historical Perspective

Susan Bassnett
The Centre for British and Comparative Cultural Studies
University of Warwick, Coventry, U.K.

The earliest statements on translation and translating practice date from ancient Rome, and of particular importance are Cicero's *Libellus de optimo genere oratorum* (46 B.C.) which offered the famous precept not to translate "verbum pro verbo" (word for word) and Horace's *Ars Poetica*. (*c*. 12–8 B.C.) Also significant are discussions on translation by theoreticians of the Roman Empire, such as Quintilian. (1st century A.D.) Implicit in Roman theories of translation is the notion of enrichment of the Latin literary system, for translation took place from Greek into Latin and Latin authors were therefore concerned with developing Greek models in their own language. The principal responsibility of the translator was to his target language readers, who were familiar with both languages, and translation was effectively a stylistic exercise. It is from the Romans that the distinction between "word for word" and "sense for sense" translation derives.

As the Roman Empire declined and Christianity spread rapidly northwards and westwards across the Mediterranean, a principal task for translation now became the dissemination of the Word of God. There were numerous translations of the New Testament, and St. Jerome (*c*. 347–420 A.D.), the most famous Bible translator of this period, developed the Ciceronian distinction between the undesirability of "word for word" and the desirability of "sense for sense" translation. However, with the translation of sacred texts the problems were doctrinal as well as stylistic, and the debate about the distinction between translation and unacceptable interpretation continued for centuries. At first, attention focussed on the skills of the translator in ancient languages such as Aramaic, and on the problems of establishing a precise notion of the "original" Bible, given the large number of textual variations in circulation, but later, with the development of European vernacular languages from the 10th century onwards, the emphasis shifted. Translators such as King Alfred or Aelfric in England perceived the task of translating the Bible as linked to the task of elevating the status of the newly developing language known as English. By the time of the translation of the first complete Bible into English between 1380 and 1384 (the Wycliffite Bible), translation was explicitly linked to the growth of ideas of nationalism and the decline of the centralization of Church power. Bible translation and the Reformation, during which all kinds of doctrinal matters were thrown into question, resulting in the spread of diverse Protestant religious factions, were inextricably linked. In Germany, Martin Luther published his version of the Bible in 1522, and in his famous *Circular Letter on Translation* (1530) he made a significant distinction between "übersetzen" (literally: to translate) and "verdeutschen" (literally: to germanize). Translations of the Bible appeared in rapid succession throughout Northern Europe, matching the spread of the Reformation: in Danish in 1529, in Swedish in 1526–41, in Czech in 1579–93. A measure of the passions aroused by the debates on Bible translation can be seen by the reaction of the authorities to texts deemed to be subversive. The great English translator William Tyndale was burned at the stake in 1536, following the public burning of his version of the New Testament in 1526, and the French humanist translator Etienne Dolet, author of one of the earliest theoretical statements on the translation process, *La manière de bien traduire d'une langue en aultre* (How to translate well from one language into another) published in 1540, was burned at the stake in 1546. Although the persecution of Bible translators came to an end in the seventeenth century, the fundamental issue of doctrinal "fidelity" and the possibility of heretical "mistranslation" continued to be debated. Significantly, it is from Bible translation and the theoretical statements of contemporary translators such as Eugene Nida, that much of the basis of Translation Studies derives today.

Translation in the Middle Ages was linked to the development of vernacular languages and to the spread of education, through the universities established from the twelfth century onwards. Alongside the translation of sacred texts, translation of literary texts continued and it can be argued that the major shifts in the Western literary system were all due to the impact of translation — the shift from epic to romance in the twelfth century, the advent of the Renaissance from the fourteenth century onwards. Statements on translation from the medieval period are to be found principally in discourses on the art of rhetoric and on education, but by the sixteenth century, with the growth of individualism, the number of explicit theoretical statements on translation increased significantly. Translation was seen as linked to imitation, and theoretical discussion focussed principally on the relationship between source and target texts. Word for word translation was generally seen as undesirable, though translation was often described in terms of "copying" an original. George Chapman (1559–1634), the great English translator of Homer, like Etienne Dolet (1509–1546) before him, argued that the translator should endeavour to reach the "spirit" of the original text, whilst at the same time following the source with scholarly precision and appropriate care. The problem for Renaissance translators was how to strike a balance between the desirability of "copying" an original and also creating a new text with an individual voice, how to remain faithful without being subservient. A great many statements on translation can be found in translators' prefaces, and the preface to the Authorized Version of the Bible in 1611 describes translation as an activity that lets in light, that opens windows onto darkness. This metaphor implies an evangelistic function for translation, whilst other translators describe their work as a process of digestion, a change of clothing or, in keeping with the great age of European expansion into Africa and the Americas, as a voyage of discovery or a search for hidden treasure.

During the seventeenth century, with the development of new theories of languages, the notion of "accuracy" in translation that could somehow be measured on a qualifiable basis began to emerge. It is also during this century that the activity of translation falls into three distinct categories: translation as recovery or imitation of classical texts (most of the theoretical statements involve this kind of translation): translation as language learning exercise (as testified by the development of bilingual dictionaries, grammars and illustrated multilingual textbooks); translation as commercial enterprise (the growth of mass publishing and the spread of new theatres meant that countless texts had to be produced at great speed and frequently of indifferent, or downright poor quality.) Major theoreticians and translators of the late seventeenth and eighteenth centuries include John Dryden (English, 1631–1700), Nicholas Boileau (French, 1636–1711), Johann Gottsched (German, 1700–1766), Alexander Pope (English, 1688–1744), Voltaire (French, 1694–1778), Christoph Wieland (German, 1733–1813), Melchiore Cesarotti (Italian, 1730–1808).

In 1791, the first systematic theoretical volume on translation by the Scot, Alexander Fraser Tytler was published. Tytler was reacting against the tendency that had developed through the eighteenth century of "loose" translation, what Dryden had defined as "paraphrase", which corresponded to the sense for sense approach. Such looseness had resulted in some extraordinary developments, such as Houdar de la Motte's 1714 version of Homer's *Iliad* that reduced the poem by half and justified the exclusion of the twelve books by arguing that he had not omitted anything of any significance to the plot. Tytler's book appeared at the same time as the emergent Romantic discussions on translation that centred around the problem of whether translation could be considered as a creative or a mechanical enterprise. Translators and theoreticians such as Percy Bysse Shelley (English, 1792–1822), Johann Wolfgang von Goethe (German, 1749–1832), Ferenc Kazinczy (Hungarian, 1759–1831), August Wilhelm Schlegel (German, 1767–1845), Vasily Zhukowsky (Russian, 1783–1852) discussed the role of creative imagination in the translation process, raising new questions on the nature of meaning and the genius of a work or art. Moreover, the age of Romanticism is also the age of European nationalism, and the pattern of translation into emergent languages — Hungarian, Polish, Czech, Slovak, Serbo-Croat and many others — was paralleled by a series of revolutionary struggles for independence.

By 1848, the greatest year of revolution in Europe since 1789, theoretical discussion on translation had proliferated and we have a large number of important statements, along with a large number of translated texts. Two basic tendencies can be seen in this period, the one linked to those nations undergoing their revolutionary struggles for identity, and the other linked to nations such as Britain who were engaged in world-wide colonial expansion. The number of translations into English slowed down, and the assumptions of translators such as Edward Fitzgerald (1809–1863) or the American Henry Wadsworth Longfellow (1807–1881) were that English was a superior language and that by translating they somehow upgraded the source texts. This imperialistic notion of translation stands in contrast to the revolutionary model of writers throughout Scandinavia, Central and Eastern Europe, the German states and Italy before unification in 1870, who translated extensively as part of a deliberate policy of enriching their native literatures. In this century also, as a result of developments in philology and linguistic studies generally, important theoretical questions on the language of translation began to be discussed. A key scholar who proposed the creation of a separate sub-language specifically for translated texts is the German Friedrich Schleiermacher (1768–1834).

As the frontiers of Europe opened to influences from the rest of the world, so attitudes to translation changed. Probably the greatest translator and theoretician of translation who bridges the nineteenth and twentieth centuries, as well as bridging East and West and the Ancient and Modern Worlds is Ezra Pound (1885–1972). Pound invented a new concept of translation, the "Homage", a version of work that unifies the creativity of both the original writer and the translator and that he saw as quite distinct from any other type of translation activity. In his theories he prefigures the work of contemporary post-modernist critics, especially Jacques Derrida, who questions the notion of the "original" text and argues that by translating, a translator does not so much depart from an original, but rather produces the "original". Derrida's work has also reclaimed the other great translation theorist of modern times, the German Walter Benjamin, author of the famous essay *Die Aufgabe des Übersetzers* (The Task of the Translator) (1923).

Translation theory in the twentieth century has made great leaps forward. In the 1940s and early 1950s, work in translation was closely bound up with developments in linguistic theory, and for a time, especially after the Second World War, great hope was placed in the future of machine translation. Leading scholars include Jiří Levy, Eugene Nida, Roman Jakobson, George Steiner and, from the 1970s onwards, James Holmes, L. G. Kelly, André Lefevere, Anton Popovic and Gideon Toury. Translation theory during the past two decades has been distinguished by a radical change in terminology: the term Translation Studies is now used to describe the study of translation in its multi-faceted relation to the related disciplines of anthropology, linguistics, literary study, psychology, history, politics and economics. There are clearly distinguishable groups working especially in Belgium, Canada, Czechoslovakia, Israel, the Netherlands and Scandinavian countries where multilingualism has led directly to advanced theoretical discussion. Centres of Translation Studies are developing world-wide, not always along European lines, and the 21st century is certain to see the expansion of theoretical work and translation practice that involves non-European languages and literary systems.

HUMOUR TRANSLATION

Translation of Humorous Writings

George Kao
Founding Editor, Renditions
Maryland, U.S.A.

The translation of humour is like translating other types of literary writing, only more so. It presumes a firm grasp of the two languages at hand and a familiarity with the cultures reflected in these languages. But further, it calls for a special talent, a kind of knack, for inducing mirth in the reader with a certain felicitous arrangement of words.

Humour is not per se a literary form — distinct from prose or poetry, drama or the essay, fiction or non-fiction — but a quality that informs it where appropriate. To appreciate the difficulty of conveying a humorous effect from one language to another, it may be instructive to begin on a non-literary level. Telling a joke, even in one's own language, is an act of translation. It involves transmitting a supposedly funny message to the listener and making him laugh as you have laughed. A sure-fire story clumsily handled can fall flat, eliciting such response as "What's the point?" or, worse, "It ain't funny!"

An oral exercise in humour at least has the aid of voice inflections, facial expressions, gestures, timing, and other tricks of the comic's trade. The translator of humour is without benefit of all this, labouring as he is in cold print and trying to achieve the desired effect in a different language.

Still, translating humour is not always an impossible task. It has been said that human beings are the only laughing animals (except for the hyena), and what tickles the funny bone is basically universal. Since all human emotions and thoughts recorded in literature can be translated with varying degrees of success, humour, when it appears, must need to face the same challenge.

Early Chinese literature, intended as "vehicles of the Way" 文以載道, is not likely to indulge in humour for its own sake. However, there is no lack of witty sayings, bizarre paradoxes, and cautionary tales which will provoke laughter, or a few chuckles, or at least a knowing smile, when rendered into English.

Lao Zi's epigrammatic 信言不美，美言不信 "Truthful words are not beautiful; beautiful words are not truthful," (Lau, 1963) loses nothing in a literal translation. There is actually a contemporary quip in the same vein, sometimes attributed to the French, which happens to concern the art of translation. "Translations are like women," so it goes. "If they are beautiful, they are not faithful; if they are faithful, they are not beautiful." Zhuang Zi's assertion 聖人不死，大盜不止 may be rendered, rhyme and all, "As long as sages are alive, so long will robbers continue to thrive." The seeming illogic of the statement may amuse, until one is acquainted with the moral thesis as it was seriously advanced by the philosopher.

Not all Chinese witticisms are self-evidently funny in Western terms. The quotation 五十步笑百步, from the *Book of Mencius*, baldly put in English ("Fifty paces laughs at a hundred paces"), makes no sense at all, let alone nonsense. In fact it has become an idiomatic phrase employed to this day, a dig at a person who does not realize that he is as guilty as the rest in some offence or other, and that what separates them is only a "difference in degree" — even as a soldier who ran away on the battlefield and paused at fifty paces from the pursuing enemy had no business mocking those who had outrun him and stopped at a more distant hundred paces.

The translator of this phrase, to make it meaningful, may adopt one of two techniques: (a) Interpolate a few words in his piece by way of explanation; or (b) resort to a footnote for more extensive backgrounding of the original context. In either case, the sharp edge of satire would be blunted. It would be like the teller of jokes who is obliged to explain his point.

The late Professor Chao Yuen Ren made a very wise remark when he said, "There are translations and translations." (Chao, 1969) Translation is such an inexact thing that the same text can come out in as many different versions as there are hands to re-cast it in another language. This is nowhere more true than it is in the translation of poetry, but the translation of humour must run a close second.

There is a parable from *Mencius* about the farmer of Song which may be regarded as the forerunner of the present-day moron jokes. The original reads as follows:

宋人有閔其苗之不長而揠之者，芒芒然歸，謂其人曰，今日病矣，予助苗長矣。其子趨而往視之，苗則槁矣。

Here are four English versions: the first two follow closely the spare prose of the text; the others dilate on it somewhat.

(1) There was a man of Sung who was grieved that his growing corn was no longer, and so he pulled it up. Having done this, he returned home, look-ing very stupid, and said to his people, "I am tired today. I have been help-ing the corn grow long." His son ran to look at it, and found the corn all withered.
(Legge, 1895)

(2) There was a man from Sung who pulled at his rice plants because he was worried about their failure to grow. Having done so, he went on his way home, not realizing what he had done. "I am worn out today," said he to his family. "I have been helping the rice plants to grow." His son rushed out to take a look and there the plants were, all shrivelled up.
(Lau, 1970)

(3) A certain farmer planted his rice-shoots. Every day he went to the fields to see how much they had grown; but each day he was disappointed, for there was no perceptible growth. So this day he goes to the fields, and takes hold of each rice-shoot and pulls at it; pulls it up a little from the ground, thinking that this will make it grow more quickly.
That evening he tells his wife and children about his hard day's work on the rice-shoots. The children are delighted with their father's ingenuity. The next morning, they all rush out to see the result: withered and dead rice-shoots.
(Morris, 1981)

(4) A man in the state of Song was anxious day and night that his rice shoots were not growing fast enough. He hit upon an idea one day. He came to his plot and pulled up every one of the young shoots so that they all looked higher. When he returned home, he said to his family, "I'm tired out today. But the rice in the field has grown higher." Puzzled by his words, his son ran to the field and saw that all the young rice shoots had withered.
(Zhao and Tang, 1984)

The substance of the story is in all four versions, but such is the elusiveness of humour that it is hard to say which one of them strikes the reader as the funniest.

Another piquant tale from *Mencius* tells of the man of Qi who loses the respect of his wife and concubine for boasting of his high social connections but is discovered going the rounds of the graveyards begging for food and drink from people's sacrificial leftovers. The incidents are sketched in succinct language culminating in the description of the husband, oblivious to his exposure, coming home "with a jaunty air, carrying himself proudly to his wife and concubine" (Legge, 1895). Or, he "came swaggering in to show off to his womenfolk" (Lau, 1970). However rendered, the adverbial phrase in the sentence 施施從外來，驕其妻妾 is a deft touch that makes the story exquisite.

As the narrative art is developed in the novels and dramas of later ages, humour is more and more enjoyed as part of life itself. It is built into characters and situations, and not just the product of a clever turn of phrase or some outlandish circumstance recounted to make a moral point.

Among the 108 bandit-heroes of the Liangshan Marshes, Lu Zhishen "The Tattooed Monk" is a fully realized Rabelaisian character. If the translator does justice to the work at all, the reader will laugh or cry (mostly tears of laughter) with the hero's picaresque progress through life. (Buck, 1933; Jackson, 1937; Shapiro, 1981) The same can be said of the Monkey King of *The Journey to the West* who styles himself "The Great Sage, Equal of Heaven" and whose adventurous pilgrimage to immortality has made him one of the most lovable and laughable figures in Chinese folklore. (Waley, 1942; Yu, 1977)

Contemporary Chinese writers, under the heavy burden of "national humiliation" and "national salvation", tend to produce sombre stuff. In spite of this, comic relief rears its head from time to time. Lun Xun's famous creation Ah Q has left a searing mark on the national psyche, but on the surface it is a perfect caricature of the village ne'er-do-well. Here is a key passage from the story and two of many English translations:

閒人還不完，只撩他，於是終而至於打。阿Q在形式上打敗了，被人揪住黃辮子，在壁上碰了四五個響頭，閒人這才心滿意足的得勝的走了。阿Q站了一刻，心裡想，「我總算被兒子打了，現在的世界真不像樣……」於是也心滿意足的得勝的走了。

(1) As the idlers [who had been taunting Ah Q about his scabby head] still would not let him alone, a fight usually followed. Ah Q invariably lost and

ended up by being held by the queue while his head was being thumped noisily against the wall. This was of course only an outward defeat. After his adversary had gone with the laurels of victory, Ah Q would say to himself, "I have been beaten by my son. What a world we live in today!" and he too would go off satisfied and spiritually victorious. (Wang, 1941)

(2) If the idlers were still not satisfied, but continued to bait him, they would in the end come to blows. Then only after Ah Q had, to all appearances, been defeated, had his brownish pigtail pulled and his head bumped against the wall four or five times, would the idlers walk away, satisfied at having won. Ah Q would stand there for a second, thinking to himself, "It is as if I were beaten by my son. What is the world coming to nowadays...." Thereupon he too would walk away, satisfied at having won. (Yang and Yang, 1960.)

Despite minor discrepancies in language and style, these two versions bring out Lu Xun's bitter satire of the incorrigible "Chinese character". If the Western reader cannot grasp the author's intent as fully as a Chinese would it is because he does not understand a bit of cultural background wherein calling somebody your "son" is a grave insult.

By the same token, Mr. Pickwick for one would suffer in a Chinese translation on account of the uniquely English setting in which he and his fellow members of the club cavort. Perhaps this is why *The Posthumous Papers of the Pickwick Club* was neglected by the famed late-Qing litterateur Lin Shu, who was largely responsible for initiating his Chinese audience into the rest of the Dickensian world of extraordinary events and grotesque characters. Lin was innocent of any Western language and relied on his collaborators to translate orally for him, while he dashed off in elegant classical prose a veritable library of 19th century English and American authors. His works, widely read at the time, proved the truism that in literary translation, while a good comprehension of the "source language" is important, a native speaker's command of the "target language" is a must.

Qian Zhongshu 錢鍾書 , an erudite scholar at home in a multitude of languages and an admirer of Lin Shu's translations, had somewhat mixed feelings when he discovered that Lin not only communicated Dickens' comic style but at times contributed "his own comic and satiric flourishes" by way of embellishment. Qian called this "an exercise in parasitic or fragmentary creation." (Qian, 1964) Some of the examples cited were from *Nicholas Nickleby*, which Lin, not surprisingly, re-titled 《滑稽外史》 (*An Informal History of Humour*).

Arthur Waley, himself a pioneer translator of Asian literatures, took a more positive view. "Dickens," he wrote, "inevitably, becomes a rather different writer and to my mind a better writer [in Lin Shu's classical Chinese]. All the overelaboration, the overstatement and uncurbed garrulity disappear. The humour is there, but is transmuted by a precise, economical style; every point that Dickens spoils by uncontrolled exuberance, Lin Shu makes quietly and efficiently." (Waley, 1958)

Humour in fiction often resides in the colloquial, in idioms and slang, whether it is the author speaking or, more likely, in the dialogue that he invents. It is in this area that the Chinese-English translator, for instance, meets his greatest dilemma: whether to give his native figures of speech a foreign garb, and risk unconscious humour or not being understood at all, or seize upon an English idiomatic equivalent (sometimes there are remarkably close ones) and thus destroy the illusion of "Chinese-ness" in the story.

A case in point is the sassy, loud-mouthed mama-san of a Taipei carbaret in Pai Hsien-yung's story "The Last Night of Taipan Chin". (Pai, 1982) A sampling of her talk in this English-language version reads like the speech of any American "broad". Such phrases as "toot my own horn" … "shell out their dough" … "that stinking dead-beat" … "way over the hill," and many more, are found cheek by jowl with exotic Chinese expressions rendered literally into English. They seem to blend together to reproduce the tone of the original without a jarring note and help make a colourful tragic-comic character come alive in a modern, big-city setting. But it is a thin line that the translator must walk; a misstep either way could land him in the pitfall of ludicrous incongruity.

In an age of global communication American buzz words and catch phrases like *bottom line, talk show, lame duck, bottleneck, media event,* etc. are quickly assimilated into the Chinese vocabulary. This goes to explain why the Art Buchwald column, with all its in-jokes and slang terms, is regularly purveyed to Chinese newspaper readers in Taiwan and Hong Kong, although its humour cannot but suffer some sea-change in the process.

A more onerous type of humour is that of a play on words. Such verbal or rhetorical tricks as acronyms, dialect, rhymes, malapropisms, portmanteau words and puns defy translation. Mark Twain endures for his manifold genius, while lesser dialect humorists of his day are long forgotten. English-language writers from Lamb to E. B. White have a particular weakness for puns. It happens that the Chinese tongue is rich in homonyms, and translators often find it irresistible, on one hand, to explain their double entendres in terms of English and, on the other, to give an idea of English puns to their own readers. On rare occasions they may achieve a reasonable facsimile; in most cases the effort is fruitless or leads only to confusion.

Chao Yuen Ren, in the early '20s, essayed a translation of *Alice's Adventures in Wonderland*, which aroused considerable interest in Chinese literary and linguistic circles at the time. The first line of the Mock Turtle's Song —

Beautiful soup, so rich and green

is remembered in Chinese as 體面湯，濃又黃 , the change in colour no doubt due to rhyming exigencies. When it comes to the mournful refrain —

Beau — ootiful Soo — oop!
Beau — ootiful Soo — oop!

the broken-down syllables were perforce represented by separate characters thusly: 涕 — 夷 糜 — 厭湯 . This may not have contributed to Chinese phonetics, but it was great fun, and nonsensical too, in the best tradition of Lewis Carroll. (Chao, 1926)

In the Chinese folk theatre there is a comedy act called 相聲 (*xiang-sheng* or "cross-talk") which has as its format a rapid-fire exchange between two stand-up comedians, proceeding from small talk to mutual insults to good-natured ribbing of topical events and personalities. It does not take long before a performance has the audience rolling in the aisles. On the American vaudeville stage a classic routine by the team of Abbot and Costello called "Who's on First?" matches this form of entertainment with a hilarious dialogue about baseball players. It has been translated by Lai Shengchuan, the foremost exponent of *xiangsheng* in Taiwan, to underscore his belief that "comedy speaks a universal language." (Lai, 1990) His readers must have guffawed over the translation because baseball is practically the national game in Taiwan. It is doubtful, however, if a scenario with the same subject could provoke laughter in Chinese-speaking areas unfamiliar with this sport. So differences in culture, even among people using the same language, can affect one's appreciation of humour.

Generally speaking, unless perfect equivalence can be achieved, it is a higher order of literary translation to be faithful to the spirit rather than the letter of the lore. This is even more true when that "slithy" thing called humour is involved.

References

Buck, Pearl S., tr. *All Men are Brothers*. New York: John Day, 1933.

Chao, Yuen Ren 趙元任 , tr. 《阿麗思漫遊奇境記》 (*Alice in Wonderland*). Shanghai: The Commercial Press 商務印書館 , 1926.

———. "Dimensions of Fidelity in Translation, with Special Reference to Chinese." *Harvard Journal of Asiatic Studies*, Vol. 29 (1969), pp. 109–30.

Hsia, C. T. "Chinese Sense of Humor." *Renditions*, No. 9 (1978), pp. 30–42.

Jackson, J. H., tr. *Water Margin*. Shanghai: The Commercial Press, 1937.

Kao, George, ed. *Chinese Wit and Humor*. New York: Sterling, 1974.

———. "*Ku-chi.*" In *The Indiana Companion to Traditional Chinese Literature*, edited by William H. Nienhauser. Jr. Bloomington: Indiana University Press, 1986, pp. 482–84.

Lai, Shengchuen 賴聲川 . 〈誰在一壘？〉 (Who's on First?). 《聯合報》 (*United Daily News*), Taipei, 29 May 1990.

Lau, D. C., tr. *Lao Tzu: Tao Te Ching*, Vol. 2. Hong Kong: The Chinese University Press, 1982.

———, tr. *Mencius*. Harmondsworth: Penguin, 1970.

Legge, James, tr. *The Works of Mencius*. Hong Kong: Hong Kong University Press, 1960.

Morris, Peter T. *Chinese Sayings: What They Reveal of China's History and Culture*. Hong Kong: Po Wen Book Co., 1981.

Pai, Hsien-yung. *Wandering in the Garden, Waking from a Dream: Tales of Taipei Characters*, translated by Pai Hsien-yung and Patia Yasin, and edited by George Kao. Indiana: Indiana University Press, 1982.

Qian, Zhongshu 錢鍾書 . 《文學研究集刊》 (*An Anthology of Literary Studies*). Beijing: 1964.

Shapiro, Sidney, tr. *Outlaws of the March*. Beijing: Foreign Languages Press, 1981.

Tan, Situ, comp. *Best Chinese Idioms*, translated by Zhao Shuhan and Tang Bowen. Hong Kong: Hai Feng Publishing Co., 1984.

Tao, Yin. *Anthology of Chinese Humour*. Hong Kong: Joint Publishing Co. 三聯書店 , 1987.

Waley, Arthur, tr. *Monkey*. London: Allen and Unwin, 1942.

———. "Notes on Translation." *The Atlantic Monthly*, No. 11 (1958), pp. 107–12.

Wang, Chi-chen, tr. *Ah Q and Others*. New York: Columbia University Press, 1941.

Yang, Hsien-yi and Gladys Yang, tr. *The Complete Stories of Lu Xun*. Beijing: Foreign Languages Press, 1981.

———, tr. *Selected Stories of Lu Hsun*. Beijing: Foreign Languages Press, 1960.

Yu, Anthony C., tr. *The Journey to the West*. Chicago: The University of Chicago Press, 1977–1983.

INDIVIDUAL TRANSLATORS

James Legge

Lauren F. Pfister
Department of Religion and Philosophy
Hong Kong Baptist College, Hong Kong

Introduction

Probably the most important and influential sinologist of classical Confucian literature in the nineteenth century, James Legge's (1815–1897) authoritative English translations of *The Chinese Classics* (1861–1872, second edition 1893–1895) and *The Sacred Books of China* (1879–1891) continue till this day to be republished and employed by Western scholars. Because his professional interests as a representative of the London Missionary Society in Hong Kong (1843–1873) and as the first professor of Chinese language and literature at Corpus Christi College in Oxford (1876–1897) involved missiological and comparative religious concerns, Legge's translations also included important contributions in Daoist philosophical and religious literature, early Chinese Buddhist literature, and Nestorian Christianity in China. An intriguing confluence of historical, cultural, intellectual, and religious influences framed his life in preparation for these sinological achievements, making a biographical sketch of his early life as important as it is interesting.

Graduating valedictorian of his class at King's College after rigorously competitive examinations in 1835, Legge spent a year and a half teaching mathematics and Latin at an English secondary school before entering a Nonconformist Seminary for training in a Master of Divinity. By 1838 he had committed himself to the London Missionary Society for work among

Chinese peoples, and began taking Chinese lessons under Samuel Kidd in London. Assigned to work as a teacher in Malacca at the Anglo-Chinese College established by the first Protestant missionary to China, Robert Morrison, Legge completed his seminary training, married a pastor's daughter of the Congregational church which he attended while at seminary, and set off with her on a slow boat bound for Malacca in 1839. During the first year at Malacca, Legge went through intensive language training with a native informant in several Chinese dialects (not always clearly distinguished in Legge's mind), and wrote a simple multilingual language text for use in the College (in English, Malay, and Chinese, including Chinese characters, and tranliterations in Mandarin, Cantonese and Hakka). In the following two years he edited and revised a long two volume novel, *The Rambles of The Emperor Ching Tih In Keang Nan* [sic], translated from Chinese by one of the advanced students at the College, Tkin Shen. By the time these two volumes were published in London in 1843, Legge had taken over responsibility for the College as principal, and had been awarded an honorary doctorate for his work by the University of New York in the United States. The treaty following the conclusion of the Opium Wars opened up the possibility of moving the Anglo-Chinese College to a context closer to China in the new colony of Hong Kong. Legge promoted this plan with the London-based headquarters, and was permitted to make the move in 1843.

Translations During Missionary Career

While in Malacca Legge had already seen the rough text of one of the first Protestant translations of *The Four Books* by an earlier missionary teacher at the Anglo-Chinese College, David Collie. Legge quickly gained an interest in all similar translations that he could locate, partly out of a greater desire to understand, and partly from the pragmatic reality that he was using these same texts as part of the curriculum for the College. By the end of the 1840s he was informed about some of the earlier Jesuit and later French translations, and had gained a vision for the total translation project. The first clear indication of his intentions was written down in a journal of 1847, while he was on the slow boat returning to Hong Kong after a necessary furlough in Scotland due to health problems. (Pfister, 1990a,1990b) By this time Legge was the principal of a new theological school in Hong Kong, was about to become embroiled in a two year public debate (1850–1852) on the "term question" (the problem of identifying the most suitable translation terms for Biblical concepts such as "God," "gods," "spirits," and "souls"), and had apparently already begun his first translations of various Confucian scriptures.

In the prefaces to a number of the volumes of his two major translations projects, *The Chinese Classics* and *The Sacred Books of China*, Legge informally referred to his particular way of preparing translations. Having chosen a specific Chinese text and collected some translations already available from Western sources, Legge would strictly rely on Chinese dictionaries and commentaries to render his translation. Only after having done this independent work would he refer to the Western sources at his disposal. This methodology was rooted in the translation method learned in Scotland of version making from Latin to English, but it also gave him some particular insights into the quality of various other translations and what he might do to improve on them. The first complete translation of a text being finished, he would file it away. Returning to the Chinese text a few years later, Legge would do another independent translation without reference to his earlier draft. Only after completing the whole work would he compare it with his earlier effort, checking to see what had changed, in what ways he had matured, and identifying any further patterns which suggested better ways to handle general problems of ancient grammar or idioms. For any one text, depending on the length, Legge may have done as many as three or four independent versions before preparing the manuscript for publication.

Several factors assisted Legge in maintaining a growing maturity in his understanding of the ancient Chinese and the particular texts. First of all, throughout the 1840s and most of the 1850s he was teaching many of these Chinese texts to different students at the College, making him quite familiar with the Chinese texts themselves. Secondly, Legge maintained a precise discipline of noting down every occurence of a term in the Confucian scriptures in a separate concordance which he made for each text. He recorded in his own hand the locations of individual words, names, and important phrases, identifying their special contexts whenever this might suggest the need for another translation rather than a more obvious one. (The concordances are still kept in manuscript form in the New York Public Library.) These precise recordings became the basis for the last appendix which he published along with each major text of *The Chinese Classics*, suggestively titled, "Index of Chinese Characters and Phrases; intended also to help towards the formation of a Dictionary and Concordance for the Classics." (Preceding this index were also indices for specific subjects and proper names.) Finally, Legge liberally sought help with his translations, sending portions or whole drafts to qualified and interested sinologists, whether missionaries or professional academicians. Missionary educators such as John Chalmers and Frederick Stewart in Hong Kong are specifically mentioned as readers in various prefaces. Another important correspondent was the French academician, Stanislas Julien (180?–1872). Julien, probably the most outstanding sinologist in Europe at the time, had begun corresponding with what became the Hong Kong Branch of the Royal Asiatic Society in the late 1840s; Legge joined the Society in 1852. Julien wrote Legge in very precise detail about his translations in the 1860s, arguing with Legge over particular renderings, even challenging his choice of texts at times. It is not insignificant that a committee of sinologues at the University of Paris chose to honor Legge with the first international Julien Prize in Chinese Literature in 1875, a post-mortem tribute both to their friendship and Legge's sinological contributions. In additon, Legge regularly referred many major technical problems to his scholarly friend, Wang Tao 王韜 (1828–1897), who had arrived in Hong Kong in 1863. Legge's collaboration with Chinese informants and commentarial resources of various sorts will be dealt with in some detail below.

What was so unusual about this translation of the Confucian scriptures? Why were they considered such an important advance over earlier translations? In order to highlight the distinctive features of the translations in *The Chinese Classics*, they will be described from three vantage points of communicative action: the expressive, the cognitive, and the evaluative. Where different levels of response at the cultural, societal and personal level can be perceived, these also will be mentioned within the discussion of each vantage point.

From the expressive vantage point one can easily identify important advances. For the first time in any Western translation, the whole of the Chinese text by itself was presented along with the translation. Works involving the efforts of the Jesuit Prosper Intorcetta in the 1660s did include a bilingual interlinear text of three of *The Four Books* 《四書》, but this did not fully display the Chinese text as a text in itself. (Mungello, 1988; Lundbaek, 1991) Most of the Legge volumes, however, presented the running Chinese text in large characters independently at the top of the page, with the English translation in large Roman type in the middle of the page, and at the bottom in small type came English exegetical and commentarial notes which also frequently contained Chinese characters and phrases. From the angle of the Chinese script, which appeared in large graphs in the text, small characters in the notes, and minuscule figures for numeration of verses, this was a quantum leap in aesthetic presentation. It had been made possible because of the technical innovation of the printer of the London Missionary Society in Hong Kong, a Mr. Dyer, who developed a metallic moveable type in these three sizes for the required Chinese characters. Use of the metallic type made possible clearer printing, a more usable text, as well as a much more rapid process in editing and publication. For the first time in any translation, the Chinese text was presented with its own book and chapter headings, including various important attachments (including the orthodox prefaces and editorial divisions) which were particularly important to Chinese scholars and students of the day. The only text in which this was not the case was *The Spring and Autumn Annals* 《春秋》, which had attached to it the often lengthy orthodox *Zuo Commentary* 《左傳》. In this case the whole of the classical and commentarial texts were printed in Chinese script of two appropriate sizes, followed, sometimes after several pages, by the full page translation of the classical text and, in small type and in two columns, the translation of the *Zuo Commentary* along with exegetical and further commentarial notes.

Distinctive advances were also made in the style of translation for each classic. Many of the early Jesuit renderings were extended paraphrases of the Chinese texts, filled with attempts at accommodating Christian themes in Confucian verbiage. This arose in part because they relied on a specific commentarial tradition for interpreting *The Four Books* — that of the Ming dynasty imperial tutor, Zhang Juzheng 張居正 (1525–1582) — which was easier to employ for their purposes than the orthodox commentaries of Zhu Xi 朱熹 (1130–1200). A notable exception was the slightly less wordy translations of Francois Noël (1651–1729), who had a broader knowledge of the commentarial traditions and favoured Zhu Xi's authoritative commentaries. (Mungello 1988; Lundbaek 1991) Protestant translators in the early nineteenth century were generally far less competent than the Jesuits, and tended to force texts into interpretations which were exegetically questionable. The French academicians were slightly better, but they were also imbalanced by theoretical assumptions about the proper way of interpreting various texts. Representatives of both Protestant and French academic traditions in the first half of the nineteenth century tended to standardize translations for key terms, leaving no room for contextual nuances or connotative differences. (Pfister, 1990a) This kind of error Legge self-consciously avoided. First, Legge sought to translate in a manner consistent with the original text. If its dicta were terse and poignant, he sought ways to emulate these qualities through the use of Western idioms. Where qualities of formal and informal speech were evident, he tried to convey the difference in mode. Poetry was written in stanzas; apothegms in short sentences; prose in connected lines. Secondly, in order to avoid verbosity, Legge saved comments and alternative renderings for the exegetical notes. In this way he could provide a more subtle balance than his predecessors, simply because he could differentiate between authoritative interpretations, genuine alternatives, and problematic renderings. Thirdly, because he was imbued with the variety of the Chinese commentarial traditions, Legge offered many nuances in his translations for the multidimensional key terms. For both Dao, "the Way," and *ren*, "benevolence," he underscored the futility of limiting their meanings to any one standardized translation term. In the case of the Confucian gentleman, 君子 , Legge employed many titles and descriptive terms just to illustrate the different levels of gentlemen there actually were in the text and in Chinese society. (Pfister, 1990a)

From the cognitive vantage point, there are a number of conceptual shifts involved in Legge's appropriation of the rubric of "classics." Legge was the first Western person to refer to the whole of the Confucian Canon by this term, although David Collie of the Anglo-Chinese College in Malacca (d.1828) had referred to *The Four Books* as "the Chinese Classical Work." The French Jesuit scholar of the eighteenth century, Francois Noël, had referred to the same texts as "Les libres classiques de l'empire de la Chine." (Pfister, 1990a) Legge knew perfectly well that the actual canon involved much more than this set of texts, regarded by Zhu Xi as the nucleus of Confucian study and cultivation. The authorized scriptures 經 had grown to thirteen in number during the major dynasty preceding Zhu Xi's influence; the texts for which Zhu coined the term "Four Books" included two texts among these thirteen 經 and two others which were originally chapters in a third 經 , *The Book of Rites* 《禮記》 . This set of four books had become a profound heuristic device for Confucians in the dynasties following that of Zhu Xi, and so were the first to gain the attention of the Jesuit translators who strategically sought out relationships with the literati. By extending the range of reference of the term "Classic" back to the original thirteen 經 , Legge was correcting a possible misperception of the canonical status of various Confucian texts on the part of the Western target audience.

A further conceptual shift, one perhaps more subtle than the former, is found in the order in which Legge translated and published *The Chinese Classics*. When the first Confucian scriptures were canonized in 136 B.C. by Emperor Wu of the Western Han dynasty, there were five *jing* placed in a calculated order of importance: *The Book of Changes* 《易經》; *The Book of Documents* 《書經》; *The Book of Poetry* 《詩經》; a compilation of ritual practices and their interpretations generally referred to as *The Rites Scriptures* 《禮記》; and *The Spring and Autumn Annals* 《春秋》. After the Manchurians had established themselves by conquering the representatives of the Chinese Ming dynasty in 1645, a major imperial project of reorganizing all Chinese literature and evaluating their relative merits was instituted. The resulting *Imperial Catalog* 《四庫全書》 listed the 《經》 in the same order as the Han dynasty canon, adding others in the following sequence: *The Book of Filial Piety* 《孝經》; general works on *The Five Scriptures* 《五經》 (the Han Canon) and *The Four Books*; works on *The Book of Music* 《樂經》 (which had been lost in the pre-Han period); and texts involving 小學, or philology. For Legge to start with *The Four Books* suggested that he was emphasizing the orthodox Confucianism following Zhu Xi. To overlook The *Book of Changes*, however, while translating the other four early classics, presented a very different picture to Westerners of the authority and nature of the canon itself.

Part of the reason for this move was understandable and Legge admitted it: he was not able to fathom the key to translating *The Book of Changes* by the time of the first publications in 1861, even though he had translated the whole text and its appendices for the first time in 1855. Rather than proceed with a text of inferior quality, Legge decided to delay it until he had completed the remaining texts in *The Five Scriptures*. Furthermore, during his debates over the "term question" — that is, identifying the most appropriate Chinese terminology for translating the Christian Bible — Legge had rediscovered traces of monotheistic religion in *The Book of Documents* and *The Book of Poetry*. These particular texts motivated him as a Christian missionary to pursue comparative investigations between the conceptual and cultural backgrounds of China and various ancient civilizations in Europe and the Middle East. Consequently, their prior publication focused his Western audience's attention on the positive cosmological parallels within ancient Confucianism and Christian monotheism.

The conceptual adjustments already mentioned lend understanding to what is perhaps the most important and most critical conceptual shift: translating the term 經 by the English word "Classic." Here the cross-cultural conceptual battle was fully mobilized. The Bible, etymologically derived from the term for "book" in Greek, was one optional category, but none of the Confucian canon claimed to be revealed by the Supreme Lord 上帝 , even though it assumed the existence of such a being. Christian missionaries had agreed to render the name of the Bible by the term 聖經 , the "Holy 經 ." Large editions of the *Thirteen Confucian Scriptures* were also preceded by the same adjective 聖 , "holy." Then by which category of texts should the Confucian scriptures be known? Legge's experience with Latin studies — including pre-Christian, non-Christian, and Christian texts — suggested the category of the Classic.

Troublesome implications bound to the conceptual breadth of this translation term continued to badger Legge throughout his later life. Because he emphasized that *The Chinese Classics* did have an ancient monotheistic tradition — more like the Roman Catholic tradition with its saints and angels than the more austere forms of Protestant Evangelical theology — Legge was charged by various Protestant missionaries with the error of raising the ancient Confucian traditions to an unjustified status equal to that of the Old Testament. On the other hand, a French academician reviewing the Confucian portions of *The Sacred Books of China* (which involved a number of the same texts) claimed, since they contained no revelation at all, Confucianism must be in fact the lowest form of religion ... if it were religious at all. (Pfister, 1990c) Nevertheless, because there was within the texts such a wide variety of content, style, and relative importance, the unwieldy character of the texts themselves seemed to be suited best for this kind of general nomenclature.

The evaluative vantage point presents an even more complex and enriched dimension of the general advances achieved through Legge's work as translator of the Confucian tradition. Although he formally appeared to present the texts of orthodox Confucianism and clearly at times lauded Zhu Xi for his style and insight, Legge's translations and exegetical notes nevertheless quite often contained critical judgments just as clearly opposed to Zhu Xi's translations and justifications. Detailed analysis of the text of the *The Analects* 《論語》 uncovers the independent judgment Legge employed when facing orthodoxy. Sometimes he relied on Zhu's interpretations for the translation in the main text, but he then placed alternative renderings from earlier Han authorities and more recent scholars in the commentarial notes. Othertimes, Legge blatantly opposed Zhu's position in his translation of the main text, but would balance this boldness with a translation of Zhu's reasonings in the exegetical notes. There are even cases in the same dictum where Legge would selectively confirm and oppose Zhu's position. Legge felt justified in doing so because he was aware of the later critical philological studies which challenged the orthodox assumptions underpinning a number of important traditional interpretations. (Pfister, 1991)

Further examples involving more broad evaluative judgments for and against orthodoxy can be located in Legge's texts. The orthodox text of *The Great Learning* 《大學》, was a thoroughly revised text prepared and commented on by Zhu Xi, radically different from the old text found originally in the *The Book of Rites*. In presenting the Chinese text and translation of this initial tome of *The Four Books*, Legge kept the revised form of the orthodox text, but in his commentary beneath the translation he pointed out many of the textual and interpretive problems bound to this revision. In this text as well as in his translation of *The Spring and Autumn Annals* with the *Zuo Commentary*, Legge was very attracted to the revisionist position of Mao Qiling 毛奇齡 (1623–1716), who argued in favour of Wang Yangming's 王陽明 (1458–1527) preference for the old text of *The Great Learning*, and vehemently defended the *Zuo Commentary* against the two other important commentarial traditions. In the former case, Mao opposed the orthodox position; in the latter, he supported it. Legge was so impressed with Mao's arguments regarding the *Zuo Commentary* that he nearly decided to translate one of his texts on this classic. Better judgment prevailed, however, when he thought of the needs of readers and students.

These relatively simple examples must be weighed against the annotated bibliographic support Legge added to the end of the extensive prolegomena he wrote for each classic. Throughout his lengthy commentarial notes in each classic Legge would refer to texts and authors by name, making good use of many of the best texts in his bibliographies and illustrating the problems or failures of other commentators when they seemed pertinent to a particular issue. In the five-volume second edition of *The Chinese Classics* completed two years before his death in 1897, Legge cited over 180 Chinese titles, seventeen dictionaries and lexical tools in Chinese, twenty-two English texts, twenty French and Latin works, and even one unpublished Russian translation of *The Spring and Autumn*

Annals (which he admitted he had not seen). Two of the titles among the Chinese references, the *Imperial Catalog of the Qing Dynasty* and the *Explanations of Classics by the August Qing* 《皇清經解》, were eighteenth century collectanea containing hundreds of separate titles. Legge itemized volumes he found most helpful from within these collectanea and annotated them for the benefit of more diligent readers. The recent discovery of his personal library revealed that Legge also collected sinological texts written in Italian, German and Dutch, along with a few volumes in Japanese and Manchurian. (Pfister, 1991) These, however, did not receive the thorough attention in *The Chinese Classics* which the former texts commanded.

Another addition to the evaluative dimension of Legge's effort during this period is manifest in the erudite and critical prolegomena already referred to above. He not only provided encyclopedic references to the history, authorship, and general themes of each text, but also included extra translations and insightful essays from other sinologists. The former kind of textual sensitivity — involving not only the problem of extant texts, but also interpretive subtraditions within Confucianism which built their justifications through complicated rereadings and realignments of texts — demanded the kind of rational discipline for detail which Legge had learned from both George Buchanan's attempts to reconstruct Scottish history and the Biblical textual criticism in which he was trained during his seminary days. The impact of Legge's reliance on this kind of rationalized empiricist method of textual analysis is generally clearcut: where sizeable doubts arose regarding the historical reliability of texts (as in the case of *The Book of Documents*) Legge joined the side of the skeptics. When claims regarding the authorship of the Classics demanded assessment, especially as they related to Confucius' hand in creating or revising certain texts, Legge felt obliged to point out their lack of foundations (especially regarding the editing of *The Book of Poetry*, Zhu Xi's reconstruction of *The Great Learning*, and Mencius' tradition that Confucius had written *The Spring and Autumn Annals*). Many times this required Legge to draw the line between the myths associated with Confucius and the historical person of Confucius, a theme which had also become more and more prominent within the textual critical studies related to the person of Jesus during the latter half of the nineteenth century. Legge's tendency was to stand against Confucian traditions and deny the reliability of these claims. Yet even when he made this kind of independent judgment, he always sought confirmation within Confucian studies and the commentarial tradition. The remarkable and important consequence was that Legge always did find reputable Chinese Confucian scholarship which had anticipated the more skeptical positions Legge himself had come to defend.

Unlike many translators and scholars, Legge freely adopted the judgment of better qualified scholarship whenever it was available. In part, this was the result of a growing sociological trend in Western academic institutions at large: the phenomenon of research journals and academic serials. An essay by the Rev. John Chalmers, "On the Astronomy of the Ancient Chinese," was published in the prolegomena of *The Book of Documents*, and Legge's translation of "Researches into the Manners of the Ancient Chinese According to the She-king [Shijing]," by the early nineteenth century French academician and sinologist, Edouard Biot, added depth to his evaluations of the complexities involved in *The Book of Poetry*. Furthermore, being ever concerned to portray important alternatives in Confucian interpretive traditions, Legge accrued a number of important translations of representative subtraditions within Confucian history and scholarship. When dealing with the problem of the basic character of human nature, Legge included translations of Xun Zi's (*c.* 313 B.C.–238 B.C.) theory of an evil human nature, Han Yu's (768–824) essay on human nature, the seventh chapter of the 《列子》 containing opinions of the pre-Confucian anarchist Yang Zhu 楊朱 , and an extensive translation and evaluation of Mo Zi's 墨子 (*c.* 468 B.C.–376 B.C.) theory of universal love. Seeking to clarify the many chronological problems of *The Book of Documents*, Legge presented a complete translation of *The Annals of the Bamboo Books* 《竹書紀年》 . Pre-Qin poetry not found in *The Book of Poetry*, culled from a dozen different sources, the famous minor and major prefaces to the same text, as well as *Han's Illustrations to the Shi* 《韓詩外傳》 were all presented in bilingual (Chinese-English) format, sometimes with commentarial notes. The climax came in the volume of *The Spring and Autumn Annals*. After working through the problems of the three major commentaries to the work and justifying his choice in providing a full translation of the *Zuo Commentary* (no full translation of these works had ever been published in any foreign language), Legge proceeded to provide readers with thirty pages of bilingual representative samples from both of the other commentaries, the *Guliang* 《穀梁》 and *Gongyang* 《公羊》 *Commentaries*. When one adds these to the three maps, multiple charts, and appendices in each volume as already mentioned, the overall sense gleaned from this evaluative vantage point is one of immense erudition. It was, and remains today, the standard set of studies on the Confucian Classics.

At this point it is proper to recall and assess more precisely how Legge appeared to his Western audiences. These comments relate specifically to his work on the 《論語》 , for which he coined the title, *The Analects*. (Pfister, 1990a) Nevertheless, most if not all of the following seven comments can be generalized to the other texts in *The Chinese Classics*.

First, being aware that these works were authoritative texts with long histories of traditional commentaries and sub-commentaries, Legge was generally cautious in his translation of questionable materials. In these cases, he would follow standard commentators in his rendering even if he questioned their interpretations, but offered alternatives (including his own preferences) in the notes. If there was evidence for textual corruption, Legge felt himself restrained from making radical judgments unless the text was absolutely unintelligible. Even some of the principles employed in interpreting the texts were identified as being drawn from methods set down by Zhu Xi, the orthodox interpreter of the Classics, rather than from exclusively Western sources and principles. This manifests Legge's respect of the Chinese Confucian tradition, a necessary attitude for those who would translate authoritative texts and wish them to become standards in and of themselves.

Second, in the light of the often laconic style of the Chinese original, Legge attempted to give similar texture to his translations whenever it was possible. In doing so, Legge occasionally recalled Western apothegms which were both witty and archaic, the latter quality making his translations at times a bit too quaint. Nevertheless, this stylistic adaptiveness was an asset in that he sought to portray meaning through both its content and its mode of expression.

Third, Legge did raise in his commentarial notes some questions related to the comparative religious issues of his era, always to shed more light on the religious issues which were related to Confucian religious themes. Persian and Indian religious themes were cited, as well as the expected Biblical references in appropriate places. This was always done, however, for the sake of bringing forth more insight into the original text; Legge guarded against any obvious Christian interpolations or eisegetical misreadings. Because he was seeking to communicate the insights of a culture that were largely outside the scope of most of his readers' immediate experience, he was wise enough as a translator to seek out comparable expressions and approximating imagery in order to unveil unfamiliar expressions within the source texts.

Fourth, it was not outside Legge's scope to offer comparative philological and linguistic comments on various expressions in Chinese. For this purpose, he referred to Greek, Latin, and Hebrew grammar in order to further illustrate the nuances of certain locutions in the classical Chinese. Cross-referencing between the different Classics and precise references within any one Classic made these grammatical comments all the more precise and helpful.

Fifth, whenever the name of a disciple of Confucius or of a new figure within the ancient texts appeared for the first time, Legge took the extra effort to provide a brief biographical sketch in the commentary. He was culturally sensitive and aware enough to provide not only this information, but also the person's honorific and sobriquet (if they were known). In the case of Confucius' disciples, he also mentioned in which place this disciple's spirit tablet stood in the current ordering within the Confucian temple. Even for readers who had no experience of Confucian religious attitudes, these notes provided a wealth of information which assisted them in sensing the value and role of these various characters within the tradition as a whole.

Sixth, wanting to avoid prolixity and at the same time provide a readable text in English, Legge took pains to distinguish which terms were direct translations and which were not. If the addition of a phrase or a qualifying term was essential to portraying the sense of the text, but was in fact not explicitly present in the Chinese original, Legge italicized these terms. The precedent he was following came from Biblical translations in which a similar device was employed for exactly the same purpose.

Finally, Legge was aware of and responsive to his audience as students. Therefore, he conscientiously worked through the grammatical points, identifying similar locutions in other parts of the text. This is why he took the extra effort at times to give literal renderings of phrases — word for word translations — so that particularly unusual or difficult passages might be clearer to those who studied them. Professionally always a teacher, whether as a missionary or a professor, Legge did not lose sight of the dynamic process of communication in which his translations played a major role.

Through these seven methods and principles as well as through the disciplines of the expressive, conceptual and evaluative vantage points employed in the translations of *The Confucian Classics*, Legge's multidimensional texts took on immense stature as standard translations of the highest order.

Translations Before and During Oxford Professorship

From 1873 till his death in 1897, James Legge proceeded to pursue his life goal of providing translations of the traditional Thirteen Confucian Classics. Having taken the chair of the first Professor in Chinese Language and Literature at Corpus Christi College in Oxford in 1876, his mode of delivery changed substantially and his range of interests in translation was expanded. From the perspective of these final years, a period which constituted nearly twenty-five years of further productivity in translations, it is possible to come to some new and different evaluations of Legge's extensive corpus. This can occur because the expressive modes of his translations were radically changed, his conceptual tools were further sharpened by intellectual challenges from colleagues and the lack of previously employed Chinese informants, and his evaluative methods with their attendant conclusions were placed directly into the refining fire of international academic attention.

Already by 1867 a second printing of the complete set of *The Chinese Classics* was begun by Trubner Publishers in London, while the prolegomena related to Confucius and Mencius along with more popularized translations for lay readers were published as independent books (in 1867 and 1875 respectively). Having left the metallic Chinese press in Hong Kong to his Chinese Christian colleagues, Wang Tao and Huang Sheng, Legge in 1872 promised readers that he would complete his life goal of translating the rest of the Classics, whether it would mean producing it in Britain or returning to Hong Kong. Once he left the Orient in 1873, however, he never returned. The prestige of the Julien Prize for Chinese literature catapulted him into the international limelight, so much so that a circle of influential friends presented to Oxford the possibility of a professorship, and then created a fund to provide meager but adequate support for the new chair in 1876.

In the interim period, Legge was fully engaged in a new kind of translation. Having always admired Buchanan's Latin paraphrases of the Psalms, he prepared a complete paraphrase of the Hebrew Psalms in English, with a short but informative introduction. The fact that this long manuscript was never published has been left a mystery; notes on the manuscript, now kept in the library of New College at the University of Edinburgh, contain special directions for the printer. Perhaps it was because Legge had not presented either the long and critical remarks or the extensive apparati which he normally gave readers. Nevertheless, this Psalter was apparently produced for the sake of a stylistic change in translation, one which also affected a second edition of the 《詩經》 Legge did publish in 1876 under the title, *The Chinese Classics: Translated into English, with Preliminary Essays and Explanatory Notes — The She King; Or, The Book of Poetry*. A parenthetical note on the title page explained that the text was "revised and reproduced" from the original translation of 1871. In fact, this work was a completely new kind of project, stimulated by two of Legge's scholarly nephews. Their intention was to produce a metrical 《詩經》, one as faithful to the original meaning as possible, and yet also poetically constructed to express the style, mood, and relative formality or informality of the Chinese language. Only the senior Legge was a sinologist; the three who ended up participating had no similar training, one of them employing two earlier translations of the book in German. After each of the four had produced representative metrical odes for their assigned portions, the results were sent to the senior Legge. He admitted having to rework many, so that three quarters of the poems were in fact his own, and the remaining ones he edited. The preparation now took a further step: having become satisfied with these renderings, Dr. Legge sent the manuscript to a recognized poet, a Mr. Mercer he had known in Hong Kong, receiving his suggestions and rewritings (including several in Latin) before a final reworking of the whole text was done. When the final result was published, it was full of dynamic qualities seldom found in the earlier translation. Some poems were put into Scottish dialect, to reflect the language of the commoner; others were more formal and set in rigorous rhymes. No Chinese text appeared; the prolegomena had been revised and digested into a shorter form; explanatory notes were left to a minimum. Legge had shifted from a more literalistic translation product to a more dynamic and functional one. This was evidently the result of his becoming even more conscious of the aesthetic sensibilities of his audience. The final judgment came from the readership: the volume went through only one printing ... and was never again republished. This flexibility in translation mode, particularly in a poetic medium, could be seen as a welcome change, but there were unfavorable critics, especially among the sinologists who knew Legge's earlier works.

When Legge opted to accept the professorship in 1876, the position augured positive signs for future productivity. Certainly one of the most important formative influences on Prof. Legge during the initial stages of his adjustment was his colleague, F. Max Muller. Through their friendship came a set of arrangements which made possible Legge's final translations of the Confucian classics, set up some new goals in Daoist translations, and challenged Legge most intimately in his evaluation of Confucius and Confucianism. (Pfister, 1991)

Besides publishing elaborations of the *Kang Xi Imperial Maxims* 《聖諭》 in *The China Review* and translating a small Chinese tract for the sake of promoting famine relief in China in 1878, Prof. Legge divided his time between, on the one hand, translations of Confucian, Buddhist, Nestorian, and Daoist texts, and, on the other hand, more philosophically polemical monographs on Chinese religions, texts comparing Christianity and Confucianism, and writings on Chinese literary and historical issues.

Of first importance to Prof. Legge was his lifelong goal of completing the translation of the Confucian Classics. This was achieved in four volumes, subtitled *The Texts of Confucianism* (1879–1885), appearing as the first and major portion of *The Sacred Books of China* in the fifty volume series edited by F. Max Muller, *The Sacred Books of The East*. Since the purpose of the whole series was to present the most representative religious texts within each tradition, Legge agreed to prepare first one volume containing the whole of *The Book of Documents*, selected sections of *The Book of Poetry*, and *The Book of Filial Piety*. Afterwards he dealt with texts which proved to be the most difficult and lengthy translations of his career: those of *The Book of Changes* and *The Book of Rites*.

In comparison to the earlier volumes in *The Confucian Classics*, these tomes in the expressive dimension were far less advanced. On the positive side, Legge had submitted himself to a new transliteration system, the one prepared by Thomas Wade, which would become in its final form in the twentieth century the standard for all Anglo-American sinological works. This factor in providing consistent transliterations of terms and names was eclipsed by a number of less fortunate features. None of the translations contained the Chinese texts, and only in the text on the 《易經》 and its Appendices were there a fairly good number of Chinese characters present in the footnotes. Guided by the precondition that he was to emphasize the religious sections of the Classics, Legge made special arrangements in both the 《書經》 and the 《詩經》 in order to draw readers' attention to the relevant materials. In the former, an asterisk (*) marked any paragraph which referred to religious categories; in the latter, Legge reorganized the order of the canonical text. He explained to readers that it was primarily in the fourth section of the 《詩經》 , the 《頌》 — or "Odes of the Temple and the Altar," that religious themes were embedded in the text; it was the last small portion of this fourth section, the *Shangsong* ("The Sacrificial Odes of Shang") that the oldest themes relating to 上帝 , the ancient monotheism, were found. On the basis of these justifications, Legge placed the fourth section first, translating the whole of it; within the fourth section, he transposed the *Shangsong* from the last to the first, to emphasize its religious importance. Selected poetry from the first three sections of the 《詩經》 followed, displaying aspects of the imperial cult and ancestral worship. Following this came the new translation of the short but important 《孝經》 .

This first volume of translations in *The Sacred Books of China* were new translations, although the 《書經》 and 《詩經》 sections were in fact retranslations and generally followed the earlier renditions found in *The Chinese Classics*. An entirely new factor in their presentation, however, had now appeared: a certain vision of religious life was the determining factor for the order of presentation. Neither the relative order of the Classics as perceived by Confucian orthodox traditions nor the order within the texts themselves was necessarily followed. Legge's profound concern to empha-size the fact of the early monotheistic themes in the Confucian classics actually supported general claims made by Muller and others of a "high god" concept being universally evidenced in all early cultural traditions. The motivations which prodded Legge's interest in this matter were not the same, being more completely bound to his unique way of reinterpreting the relationship between Confucianism and Christianity. (Pfister, 1991) Nevertheless, the order in which the texts appeared — 《書經》 、《詩經》 、《孝經》 — undoubtedly suggested to the target audience an order of priority with regard to the religious worldviews identifiable within Confu-cian traditions. In effect, Legge was promoting a particular evaluative standpoint; it was underscored in *The Religions of China*, Legge's religious and philosophical evaluations of Confucianism and Daoism in China, pub-lished the following year in 1880. In effect, Prof. Legge presented the following assessment: the imperial cult dedicated to 上帝 was the true religion of China, following and fulfilling the oldest religious reflections of all the Confucian traditions. All other forms of religious rituals in all other religious communities and social classes of Chinese society, in spite of their relative popularity and numbers of adherents, were secondary to this higher form of piety. Many of his readers believed this claim, but a few sinologists felt uneasy with it and its justifications. Consequently, they wrote several negative reviews against Legge's "misinterpretations".

In preparing the second volume of *The Sacred Books of China*, Legge had a conceptual breakthrough with regard to understanding translation itself as well as grasping the key to translating the 《易經》 in particular. Jesuit scholars who had tried to render the Classic in a strictly literal manner ended up with a text which was largely unintelligible; this Legge had discovered in the 1850s. That form of rendering simply did not clarify to the target audience how or why the text was a source of reverence and awe among Chinese scholars. The general effect, to the contrary, was to leave the mysteries in a cloud of vague superstition, further supported by its association with divination. So startling was the self discovery of the nature of translation to Legge, and so important was its implications for the translation of the 《易經》 and its Appendices, that he explained it in some detail in his preface to the volume. His reflections went as follows:

> [The Jesuit] version is all but unintelligible, and mine was not less so. How to surmount this difficulty occurred to me after I had found the clue to the interpretation; — in a fact which I had unconsciously acted on in all my translations of other classics, namely, that the written characters of the Chinese are not representations of words, but symbols of ideas, and that the combination of them in composition is not a representation of what the writer would say, but of what he thinks. It is vain therefore for a translator to attempt a literal version. When the symbolic characters have brought his mind en rapport with that of his author, he is free to render the ideas in his own or any other speech in the best manner that he can attain to .... In the study of a Chinese classical book there is not so much an interpretation of the characters employed by the writer as a participation of his thoughts; — there is the seeing of mind to mind. The canon hence derived for a translator is not one of license. It will be his object to express the meaning of the original as exactly and concisely as possible. But it will be necessary for him to introduce a word or two now and then to indicate what the mind of the writer supplied for itself. What I have done in this way will generally be seen enclosed in parentheses, though I queried whether I might not dispense with them, as there is nothing in the English version which was not, I believe, present in the writer's thought. I hope, however, that I have been able in this way to make the translation intelligible to readers.

Legge presented first the text of the sixty four hexagrams and then the traditional *Ten Wings* 《十翼》 in seven appendices, following the order of the traditional texts, but uniting several which were identified as first and second portions of the same Chinese text even though they were counted as separate units. The subjective dimension of translation which Legge realized was part of every translation still required of him the research into commentaries and support from Confucian scholars beyond his own "seeing of mind to mind." After publication, there were a few vigorous attacks on Legge's method, with selective instances cited which made it appear that Legge's mind was more dominant than "the mind of the text." Legge responded with objective support from Chinese sources, and demanded of his critics a text of their own to illustrate their ability to overcome these textual problems. No other text was published before he died which could challenge Legge's renderings or replace his scholarship.

In 1885 the final two volumes, containing the most lengthy of all of the Confucian classics, were published. Legge knew of several other translations in Latin and French of *The Book of Rites*, but all were incomplete. Once more he was performing a pioneer translation, but he admitted it was particularly difficult without the aid of his Chinese scholar friend, Wang Tao, whom he had left in Hong Kong in 1873. Again, the translation appeared without the Chinese text and with only the most essential notes. After a brief but concise introduction to the three texts on Confucian rites, Legge provided the justification for translating the 《禮記》 alone and then provided summaries for each of its chapters, emphasizing any points which pertained to Confucian religiosity and piety. The lack of any translation of either *The Rites of the Zhou Dynasty* 《周禮》 or *The Rites of Etiquette* 《儀禮》, was in fact an important shortfall, since they both were numbered among the traditional Thirteen Classics. Legge nevertheless was pleased with this representative and most important piece among the three, knowing that he had achieved his original purpose.

Prof. Legge rendered all forty-six chapters of the received text including the old texts of *The Doctrine of The Mean* 《中庸》 and *The Great Learning* 《大學》. These additions were important because in many contemporary Chinese renditions of the 《禮記》, these two chapters were left out since they constituted two of *The Four Books*. There were, however, important changes made in their structure and interpretation by Song dynasty scholars of the eleventh and twelfth centuries, especially in the case of Zhu Xi's 《大學》. It is significant that Legge added critical remarks to both chapters, noting these facts (and following a number of other details in the case of the old text of the 《大學》). At the end of the 《禮記》 he provided, in a fashion reminiscent of *The Chinese Classics*, two indices giving subject and proper names for all the Confucian texts of *The Sacred Books of China*.

The Texts of Taoism published in 1891 included the complete text of Lao Zi's 《道德經》, the complete 《莊子》, and a number of selected Daoist religious texts. As before, all the translations appeared without their Chinese originals, and with a minimal amount of Chinese terms printed in the occasional notes. The last set of texts deserve some attention for a number of reasons. First of all, as Daoist religious texts they were completely separated from the Daoist philosophers. Secondly, they were presented as a single text, *The Thai Shang Tractate of Actions and Their Retributions* 《太上感應篇》, with appendices. Both of these editorial arrangements were unfortunate, because, in the first case, Daoist philosophical texts were very often commented on by Daoist priests and so were not considered to be separate traditions by Daoists. Secondly, the seven appendices attached to the *Tractate* were not directly related to it at all: four were other *Daoist* tracts of different periods; two were the translations of dedications to Lao Zi and Zhuang Zi as found in certain Daoist temples; and one, the fifth, was a translation of a Chinese summary of selected chapters of the 《莊子》. Editorial insensitivity may account for part of the causes behind this problem, but it is still worth asking why there was such a misrepresentation.

Part of the reasoning, intimately tied to Prof. Legge's "seeing mind to mind" kind of translation, was that he rendered the Daoist texts from the context of a Confucian point of view. It has been demonstrated elsewhere that Legge had a deep attachment to Han Yu 韓愈; it was Han Yu who scourged Daoist and Buddhist religions as superstitious and unworthy of a gentleman's attention. (Pfister, 1991) In addition, other Confucian scholars lauded Lao Zi and Zhuang Zi while deriding Daoist religion in itself. Prof. Legge, who proclaimed himself a great admirer of Zhuang Zi during a public lecture in Oxford, took this very same position. Casting Daoist religion to the side apart from the Daoist philosophers, even if it were unjustified from within Daoism itself, was precisely the way numerous Confucian scholars dealt with the Daoist tradition.

This is an important reflection on Legge's translations in general, particularly because of the charge that Western scholars create their own version of the Orient quite apart from the actualities of the Orient. (Said, 1978) The Legge of *The Sacred Books* might be culpable of this charge; the Legge of *The Confucian Classics*, however, was scrupulous in following the footsteps of other Confucians.

At this juncture it is appropriate to refer briefly to Wang Tao, Legge's scholarly friend and paid informant from 1863 to 1873. At least seven works written by Wang Tao were directly related to their work, some being commissioned by Legge during this period: one on the 《詩經》, one on the 《易經》, a lengthy compendium of the 《禮記》 and other texts on the rites, and four on *The Spring and Autumn Annals* with its *Zuo Commentary*. Legge had extremely positive evaluations of the text on the 《詩經》 and one of those related to the *Zuo Commentary*. In reference to the value of these two works, Legge gave the following statement: "Whatever completeness belongs to my own work is in a great measure owing to this." In other contexts, Legge professed to have gained much from Wang, but also to have argued often with him, finding Wang too often attached to conservative views of the texts without justification. Legge's standard of an "independent judgment" supported by indigenous scholarship seemed to be the guiding rule in their relationship as it was in the translations at large. The two scholars, men of very different temperament but common faith, maintained mutual respect and a high regard for each other's capabilities.

Besides the Confucian and Daoist texts, Prof. Legge published the following major translations: *A Record of Buddhistic Kingdoms, Being an Account by the Chinese Monk, Fa-Hien of His Travels in India and Ceylon (A.D. 399–414) in Search of the Buddhist Books of Discipline* (1886); *The Nestorian Monument of Hsi-an Fu in Shen-Hsi, China, Relating to the Diffusion of Christianity in China in the Seventh and Eighth Centuries* (1888); and "The Li Sao Poem and Its Author" *in The Journal of the Royal Asiatic Society of Great Britain and Ireland* (1895). Each text published along with the translation the complete Chinese text with introductions and "copious notes." In addition, each text presented involved materials Prof. Legge had known years before, had translated several times in his normally disciplined manner, and had waited to publish only after all the critical factors — textual, linguistic, historical, academic — were sufficiently under his control.

Yet something more than the "old standard" is here: each protagonist in these works — Fa Xian 法顯, Aluoben 阿羅本, Qu Yuan 屈原 — is a pioneer of sorts, a hero against incredible odds, setting out for himself and for his times standards which others had neither conceived or pursued. Fa Xian brought fledgling Chinese Buddhism closer to its roots in India; Aluoben gained entrance to the imperial chambers of Chang'an, and pioneered the transmission and translation of Christian faith into Chinese contexts; Qu Yuan tried to penetrate the mysteries of the universe with the eye of a moral man, and left a tragic monument to personal integrity through his suicide. Each initiated a transformation of his own tradition by extending it to a firmer foundation, far beyond the anticipations of his own contemporaries. In these singular translations, Prof. Legge fused his own Scottish admiration for heroism, his Christian respect for authenticity, and his translator's goal of seeing mind to mind.

References

Lundbaek, Knud. "The First European Translations of Chinese Historical and Philosophical Works." In *China and Europe: Images and Influences in Sixteenth to Eighteenth Centuries*, edited by Thomas H. C. Lee. Hong Kong: The Chinese University Press, 1991, pp. 29–44.

Mungello, David. "The Seventeenth Century Jesuit Translation Project." In *East Meets West: The Jesuits in China, 1582–1773*, edited by Charles E. Ronan and Bonnie R. C. Oh. Chicago: Loyolla University Press, 1988, pp. 252–73.

Pfister, Lauren. "Clues to the Life and Academic Achievements of One of the Most Famous Nineteenth Century European Sinologists — James Legge (A.D. 1815–1897)." *The Journal of The Hong Kong Branch of The Royal Asiatic Society*, Vol. 30 (1990).

————. "Serving or Suffocating the Sage? Reviewing the Efforts of Three Nineteenth Century Translators of *The Four Books*, with Special Emphasis on James Legge (A.D. 1815–1897)." *The Hong Kong Linguist* (Spring/Autumn 1990), pp. 25–56.

————. "Some New Dimensions in the Works of James Legge (1815–1897): Part I." *Sino-Western Cultural Relations Journal*, Vol. 12 (1990), pp. 29–50.

————. "Some New Dimensions in the Works of James Legge (1815–1897): Part II." *Sino-Western Cultural Relations Journal*, Vol. 13 (1991), pp. 33–48.

Said, Edward. *Orientalism*. New York: Random House, 1978.

Wylie, Alexander. *Memorials of Protestant Missionaries*. Shanghae [sic]: American Presbyterian Mission Press, 1867.

Arthur Waley

Wong Siu Kit *and* Chan Man Sing
Department of Chinese
University of Hong Kong, Hong Kong

Author of forty books, eighty-two articles, and almost one hundred and fifty book reviews (Johns, 1988), Arthur David Waley (1889–1966) was arguably the most distinguished Sinologist, Japanologist and translator of his generation.

Coming down from Cambridge where he read Classics, Waley joined the British Museum as assistant keeper in the Print Room in 1913. He continued in this position until 1929 when he resigned in order to engage himself full time in research and translation. Waley's responsibilities in the Museum required some knowledge of oriental languages and in due course he taught himself Chinese and Japanese.

Chinese Poems, Waley's first book, was privately printed in 1916, and distributed among some fifty friends, including W. B. Yeats, Ezra Pound, T.S. Eliot and Bertrand Russell. His second book, *170 Chinese Poems* was published in 1917 and was generally well received. In translating some of the poems in this volume, Waley was, as he acknowledged elsewhere, assisted by a certain Mr. Ting, although to what extent it is now impossible to determine.

By the time Waley left the British Museum he had already published eight books of translations. These included *More Translations from the Chinese* (1919), *The Temple and Other Poems* (1923), *The Pillow Book* 《枕草子》 (1928) and the first four volumes of *Genji Monogatari* 《源氏物語》 (1925–28). When the remaining two volumes of *Genji* were completed in 1933, Waley's interest in the pre-Qin period of China had begun to develop. *The Way and Its Power* was published in 1934, *The Books of Songs* in 1937, *The Analects of Confucius* in 1938, *Three Ways of Thought in Ancient China* in 1939.

During the second world war, whilst engaged in intelligence work,

Waley also found time to transform the 《西遊記》 into the delightful *Monkey* (1942).

Public recognition now came Waley's way. In 1945 he was elected to an Honorary Fellowship by King's College, Cambridge. In 1953 he was awarded the Queen's Medal for Poetry. And in 1959 the Japanese government decorated him with the Order of Merit of the Second Treasure.

Waley's publications continued to be prolific in the twenty years after the war. The four biographies belong to this period: *The Life and Times of Po Chü-i* (1949), *The Poetry and Career of Li Po* (1950), *The Real Tripitaka and Other Pieces* (1952), *Yuan Mei* (1956). Some of the other major works include: *Chinese Poems* (1946), *The Nine Songs* (1955), *Ballads and Stories from Tun-huang* (1960) and *The Secret History of the Mongols and Other Pieces* (1964).

Waley died on 27 June 1966.

Waley was linguistically extremely gifted. Apart from English, he spoke Yiddish and the principal European languages. He could read not only Chinese and Japanese, but also the ancient Syrian script, Hebrew, Sanskrit, Manchu and Mongolian. It was this linguistic knowledge and his familiarity with a wide range of traditional and modern disciplines that made Waley the phenomenal scholar and translator that he had every claim to be.

While Waley's achievements in translation in general are universally acknowledged, it is his rendering of Chinese poetry in particular that must be adjudged artistically significant and historically important. Reacting to, and ultimately abandoning the examples set by earlier practitioners such as Herbert Giles and L. Cranmer-Byng, Waley brought about a number of innovations which revolutionized the concept of poetic translation. Waley had no use for traditional prosody; rhyming he found restrictive and potentially distorting; and blank verse seemed to him unsuitable for the usual two-line unit of Chinese verse. Instead Waley employed a metre in which every syllable of the original line of verse is matched by one stressed syllable (the unstressed syllables are irregular but there are rarely more than two of them between two stresses). The invention was not a conscious one, as it took Waley himself six years to recognize the pattern that evolved, and while the metre resembled G. M. Hopkins' "sprung rhythm" closely, Waley repeatedly denied that it was an imitation.

The metre that Waley developed produced the best effects when used for translating poems in five-character lines. Employed to translate seven-character verses, it could at times become somewhat unwieldy. And, in general, partly because the stresses can be ambiguous, the metre is at times hardly distinguishable from prose.

Prosody belongs to verse, but Waley's main concern was with the reproduction of poetry. To that purpose Waley carefully retained all images he detected in a given poem. This was a consciously adopted strategy. In the Preface to the first edition of *170 Chinese Poems*, Waley already declares that imagery is "the soul of poetry." The same conviction is given expression again in *The Book of Songs*.

Waley's triumphs in the re-creation of images are so numerous and familiar that they do not need to be illustrated here. It would be more interesting to consider how Waley could worry and re-work a difficult image over the years. Take the two lines

上用倉浪天故
下爲黃口小兒

from a 樂府 poem for example. The 1919 translation reads:

Above we have the blue waves of the sky,
Below, the yellow face of this little child.

(Waley, 1919)

The "yellow face" hardly does justice to 黃口 , a circumstance of which Waley must have been aware, for in the 1946 version, the second of the two lines has been improved upon and given more texture:

Below, the face of this child that suckles at my breast.

(Waley, 1946)

The fact that Waley translated very extensively and smoothly can give us the false impression that he went about his business casually. The truth is that he was always fully armed with heavy scholarly paraphernalia. Take his *Confucian Analects* for example. The translation is backed up by far more than the standard commentaries by Xing Bing 邢昺 (923–1010) and Zhu Xi 朱熹 (1130–1200). Waley consulted the later Chinese commentaries by Wang Niansun 王念孫 (1744–1832), Wang Yinzhi 王引之 (1766–1834) and Yu Yue 俞樾 (1821–1907) as well as the Tunhuang fragments of Zheng Xuan's 鄭玄 (127–200) commentary recovered as recently as in 1900s. And he went beyond the Chinese authorities. The work done by scholars such as K. Shiratori 白鳥清 , Y. Ojima 小島祐馬 , M. Granet, H. Maspero and

J. Frazer also contributed to the foundation of Waley's own interpretation of the *Analects*.

Waley's reading was not confined to the commentaries and studies of the ancient Chinese texts themselves. He had a great interest in anthropology and was for instance familiar with the investigations of Margaret Mead and M. Eliade. The result is that he approached the pre-Qin texts from an anthropological angle. The poems in the *Nine Songs* he thought were shamanistic. He believed that the *Book of Songs* 《詩經》, the *Confucius' Analects* 《論語》 and the *Daodejing* 《道德經》 contained facets of life in primitive society. Passages in these texts which have traditionally been regarded as obscure are sometimes forced to yield up their secrets. We must be content with a single example. The poem *Wanlan* 芄蘭 in the *Shijing* (No. 55 in *The Book of Songs*) has baffled a long line of commentators and compelled even Zhu Xi to confess ignorance. Waley convincingly treats it as a courtship poem: he explains the 觽 (knot horn) symbolically as a grown man's right to "undo the knot of a bride's girdle," and 韘 (thimble) as his coming "of age to go to war." (Waley, 1937) The interpretation may not be definitive, but it does provide a reading to a poem otherwise incomprehensible.

Analysts of Waley often ask how closely his translations adhere to the original. This is a difficult question. Waley himself often claims that his translations are "literal." But there are signs of adaptation, suppression, perhaps even invention; and, certainly, in the sense that language writes us, there are moments of subtle transformation which no translator could have entirely avoided.

Take the poem *"Shiyun"* 〈時運〉 by Tao Qian 陶潛 (365–427):

邁邁時運，穆穆良朝。襲我春服，薄言東郊。
山滌餘靄，餘靄微消。有風自南，翼彼新苗。

Here is Waley's translation:

Swiftly the years, beyond recall.
Solemn the stillness of this fair morning.
I will clothe myself in spring-clothing
And visit the slopes of the Eastern Hill.
By the mountain-stream a mist hovers,
Hovers a moment, then scatters.
There comes a wind blowing from the south
That brushes the fields of new corn.

(Waley, 1946)

The original is in four-character lines, and the translation gives us lines with four stresses in each. Every two lines in the translation constitute a sense unit, suggesting the regularity of the original. Rhyme is not employed in the English poem, but the loss is compensated by the assonance in "Swiftly the years" and the alliteration in "… mountain … mist … moment." In these ways the translation imitates and echoes the original.

But both Waley's lyricism and his colloquialism are his own, and are far removed from Tao Qian's archaic style. Also Waley's own are the dramatic description of the mist and the wind in the last four lines, the light and liquid rhythm of "Hovers a moment," the caesura between "moment" and "then," and the emphatic stresses in "fields of new corn." It would be difficult — and perhaps irrelevant — to determine whether the Chinese poem or the English one is superior, but it is important to recognize that they provide quite different kinds of reading experience.

In translating prose and lengthy poems, Waley takes greater — and more conscious — liberty still. *Monkey* is approximately a third in length of the 《西遊記》. Most of the verse in the Chinese novel is suppressed; arcane references to Daoist alchemy and the art of longevity are at best summarized. Whatever is hard for the translator to express or the reader to comprehend, Waley often passes over in discreet silence. Thus in translating 《韓擒虎話本》 (*The Story of Catch-tiger*) from the Tunhuang manuscripts, Waley decides that the descriptions of battle formations are "quite out of his depth" and expunges them. (Waley, 1960)

In Waley's translations there are also instances of skilful improvement on the original. A charming example occurs in Yuan Mei's biography of his mother. The original gives us this description:

枚不覺失聲而慟，太孺人訶曰：人心不足，兒癡耶，天下寧有不死人耶，我年已九十四矣，兒何哭爲？

Waley's account is as follows:

"Don't be silly," she said, "Surely you have had enough of me by now! Everyone has to die sometime, and I am ninety-three. You must not be sad about it. (Waley, 1956)

Ninety-four for the Chinese is of course ninety-three for the English, but the words of interest are "Surely you have had enough of me by now!" The gentle mockery, the sense of humour even, belongs to Waley.

Waley's translations are a monumental success that has had an unmistakable and indelible impact on all subsequent translators of Chinese texts into English. They have also been enjoyed as English literature in their own right. Some of the poems among them have been anthologized more than once. As T. S. Eliot pointed out in the late forties, "in our time, the poetical translations from the Chinese made by … Arthur Waley, have probably been read by every poet writing in English." (Eliot, 1949) Even beyond the confines of English literature, Waley's influence is palpable. Bertolt Brecht's *Chinesische Gedichte* is a product of that influence, and some of the poems in it are German versions of Waley's translations. Brecht's unfinished *Leben des Konfutse*, too, is based on Waley's *Confucian Analects* and refers to *Three Ways of Thought in Ancient China*.

A quarter of a century after his death, Arthur Waley continues to be re-printed and read with exquisite pleasure.

References

Eliot, T.S. *Notes Towards the Definition of Culture*. New York: Harcourt, Brace and Co., 1949.

Eoyang, Eugene. "Waley or Pound? — The Dynamics of Genre in Translation." *Tamkang Review*, Vol. 29 (1989), pp. 441–65.

Johns, F. A. *A Bibliography of Arthur Waley*, 2nd ed. London: The Athlone Press, 1988.

Waley, Arthur. *Ballads and Stories from Tun-huang*. London: George Allen and Unwin, 1960.

———. *The Book of Songs*. London: George Allen and Unwin, 1937.

———. *Chinese Poems*. London: George Allen and Unwin, 1919.

———. *Chinese Poems*. London: George Allen and Unwin, 1946.

———. *Yuan Mei*. London: George Allen and Unwin, 1956.

Yuan, Jinxiang 袁錦翔 .〈從幾篇譯作看 A. Waley 的譯詩〉 (Judging Waley's Translations by a Few of His Works). In 《名家翻譯研究與賞析》 (*Analysis and Appreciation of Famous Translations*). Wuhan: Hubei Education Press 湖北教育出版社 , 1990, pp. 147–66.

Yan Fu

Elizabeth Sinn
Department of History
University of Hong Kong, Hong Kong

Yan Fu 嚴復 (1854–1921) was one of the foremost thinkers of his day and one of the most important Chinese translators in modern times.

Yan was born in Houguan 侯官 county, Fujian Province, the son of a medical doctor. He began his formal education at the age of five and at nine studied with a private tutor who was well versed in both Han Learning and Neo-Confucian doctrines, but his father's early death forced him to abandon his classical education. Instead, he entered the newly established Majiang Naval Academy attached to the Fuzhou Shipyard, on a scholarship which provided maintenance for him and his family. It was fortuitous that of the Academy's two Schools, he chose the School of Navigation, where the language of instruction was English. As the English language gave him access to Western ideas, Great Britain became his model state, and English ideas shaped his world view. During his five years at the Academy which were spent on English and scientific and technical subjects, he continued his Chinese learning, and practised the composition of essays required by the Civil Service Examination.

After graduating in 1871 he worked at the Naval Shipyard until 1877 when he was sent to study in England. At the Greenwich Naval College, Portsmouth, he studied mathematics, physics and naval science. But he also devoted his energy to observing British society and the political system, and throughout his life, he was obsessed with finding the key to the wealth and power of Western states. He returned to China in 1879 and taught for a year at the Fuzhou Naval Academy. In 1881, Li Hongzhang 李鴻章, the Governor-General of Zhili Province who had become chief manager of China's naval affairs, appointed Yan Dean 總教習 of the newly founded Beiyang Naval Academy in Tianjin, where he went on to become Chancellor. But as his foreign education did not qualify him for an important position in the bureaucracy, which many considered the only meaningful career, Yan was determined to take the orthodox avenue for advancement — the Civil Service Examination. In 1885 he purchased the 監生 degree and then sat for the 舉人 examination in Fujian but failed. He made three more unsuccessful attempts in 1888, 1889 and 1893.

Frustrated by his repeated failures, the limitations of his position in the academy and the corruption and incompetence he saw about him, Yan turned to writing and translation. His first translation was published in 1892, a rendering of Alexander Michie's tract *Missionaries in China* — (1891), an attack by a Westerner on the methods of missionaries in China. This, however, seems to have made little impact.

Yan first made his mark in 1895, when China's defeat by Japan caused panic over China's future, prompting many scholars to reevaluate China's social and political system. In the four essays he published in the *Zhi bao* 《直報》 of Tianjin, he presented Western ideas, tracing the source of Western strength beyond technology, beyond commerce and industry, beyond even political institutions to Western thought and culture, and shared with his countrymen what he believed to be the explanation as well as remedy for China's predicament. He showed that *the issue was one of ideas and values*. The effect of these articles was explosive.

He also spent 1895 translating Thomas Huxley's essay "Evolution and Ethics" under the title *Tianyan lun* 《天演論》, an effort started probably a year earlier. The manuscript was circulated among friends and parts of it were published serially in 1897 in the *Guowen bao* 《國聞報》, a newspaper he founded in Tianjin that year. The appearance of these translations as a book in 1898 was a resounding success and won him national fame.

Yan did much to make the *Guowen bao* North China's most influential newspaper. His many articles there showed him to be one of the sharpest and most honest critics of the administration and of what he considered as fossilized Chinese ways. The years 1895–1898 may be regarded as intellectually the most dynamic period of his life.

Despite his intellectual affiliation with reformers, Yan stayed very much outside the constitutional movement of 1898 and never became a political activist. His argument was that the people were not ready for rapid change, and it would take time to educate them for it. He served as Chancellor of the Beiyang Naval Academy until 1900 when the Boxer Uprising broke out. He went to Shanghai, and for several years moved from job to job. In 1901, he became one of the two Chinese members on the board of directors of the Kaiping Mining Company. When Wu Rulun

吳汝綸 , a noted classical stylist and close associate, became Chancellor of Imperial University at Beijing in 1902, Yan was appointed director of the University's newly established Translation Bureau. He held the post without enthusiasm and finally resigned in 1904. He then helped Ma Liang 馬良 establish the Fudan Academy, and in 1906 he served briefly as its principal. He was then invited to supervise the Anhui Higher Normal School, where he stayed one year. In 1908, he was appointed chief editor of the Bureau of Terminology within the Ministry of Education, a post he held until 1911. The Qing government awarded him the 進士 degree in 1909 and appointed him a member of the Advisory Council for Political Affairs in 1910. He was made a rear admiral in the Navy and in 1911 was appointed to the Naval General Staff.

In 1912, Yan became Head of the College of Letters of Beijing University, probably the most responsible position he had held, but he resigned shortly afterwards. In the same year he became Chief Reviser of the Naval Ministry's Translation Bureau and supervised the translation of foreign naval documents. In 1913, he became adviser on legal and foreign affairs to the President of the new Chinese Republic. His part in helping Yuan Shikai 袁世凱 become emperor remains controversial. Yuan doubtlessly respected him greatly as an intellectual. But Yan Fu , while insisting that his part in the Peace Planning Society 籌安會 , organized to draft Yuan as emperor, was purely passive, made no secret of his opposition to republicanism, which again stemmed from his belief that the people were not sufficiently educated for it, or of his advocacy for the return of monarchism. After Yuan's death in 1916, Yan went into complete retirement. The association of his name with the monarchical revival severely damaged his reputation and he was condemned in the official histories of both the Nationalist and Communist parties.

He returned to Fuzhou from Beijing in 1920 and died there in 1921.

Yan Fu's national reputation rested primarily on his role as translator-commentator. His was the first systematic attempt since the Jesuits to present contemporary Western ideas to the Chinese literati, and to demonstrate the high seriousness of these thoughts. Through his translations he introduced many 18th and 19th century Western thinkers to China, covering a broad range of thought — political, economic, social, philosophical, ethical and religious — and provided abundant information about the West. Yan, most likely, knew and understood the West more thoroughly than anyone else in China at the time.

Above all, he introduced to China Spencer's brand of social science which embodied the concepts that human society could be studied "scientifically," and of a law of historical progress universally applicable. While showing the differences between Western and contemporary Chinese thought, Yan was also keen to identify wherever possible common ideas and values in the two cultures, especially Chinese culture of the pre-Qin period. Essentially, he wished to highlight the universality of human experience, upon which was predicated the promise that the present wealth and power of the West would come to China in the future, a concept which eroded the basic Chinese belief in the uniqueness of their own culture and history. Together, these ideas broadened the cultural horizon of Chinese scholars and became essential elements of the intellectual revolution of modern China.

Yan's significance in both the history of intellectual development and of translation in China will be discussed in turn, although it should be noted that, strictly speaking, it is impossible to disentangle his roles as translator, thinker and commentator.

As mentioned, Yan made his debut as a serious writer in 1895. The four essays he wrote that year — "On the Speed of World Change" 〈論世變之亟〉 "The Origin of Strength" 〈原強〉 "On Our Salvation" 〈救亡決論〉 and "Refutation of Han Yu" 〈闢韓〉 — articulated all the basic assumptions underlying his translation and writings of the following years, and blended the ideas of Spencer, Montesquieu, Huxley, Smith and Mill, all of whom he was to translate, with extraordinary consistency despite the great differences in the thinking and historical background of these thinkers.

Yan had read Spencer's *The Study of Sociology* in 1881 and was fascinated by his theory of social evolution and idea of a science of society. Though he did not begin translating it until 1897, and did not publish a complete translation until 1903, Yan's writings, translations and commentaries were all underlined by a Spencerian bias. In "The Origin of Strength," intellectually the most significant of the essays, he gave a succinct summary of the principles of Darwin and Spencer. Darwin, the biologist, had discovered the basic principle of nature to be "things struggled, nature selected" 物競天擇 — things struggled for existence 物爭自存 while nature preserved the fittest species 存其宜種 . Spencer, the sociologist, applied this principle of natural evolution 天演 to the human process — society, as the organic aggregate of individuals, was capable of survival and progress, but by the same token, it was liable to extermination. In essence, social Darwinism as presented by Yan in these works, was a theory concerned with change and adjustment: change was natural and inevitable, adjustment imperative.

Spencer's theory of society, which Yan translated as 群 , and equated readily with the state, helped Yan explain China's weakness. The state's well-being and chances of survival depended entirely upon the physical, intellectual and moral well-being of the individuals. A society in which the people's physical, intellectual and moral energies were developed would be strong, while a society in which these were inhibited would be weak, and it was obvious that when these two societies confronted each other in a struggle for existence, the latter would be vanquished even without a clash of arms.

China was weak precisely because the people's energies had been consciously suppressed, and in "Refutation of Han Yu", Yan Fu lashed out at absolute monarchism as the culprit of China's impotence. For centuries, he wrote, emperors had to secure their positions by keeping the people subjugated with laws and doctrines which "spoilt the people's talents, dissipated their strength and corrupted their morals", and the qualities indispensable for a wealthy and powerful society were deliberately stifled.

Much as Yan wished to criticize absolutism, he was more eager to awaken the Chinese people to the importance of collective strength. The concept of 群 was a double-edged sword. Even as it exhorted rulers to encourage the development of the people's energy as a prerequisite for a powerful state-society, it stirred people from their selfish and complacent unconcern for society as a whole and instilled group consciousness. His ideas were full of revolutionary potentials which others, such as Liang Qichao 梁啓超 and Tan Sitong 譚嗣同 , were to explore. For himself, the collective bias was the basis for an authoritarian tendency which became increasingly pronounced as he grew older. Notably, he departed from Spencer on this point even from the very start: Spencer advocated extreme individualism while Yan saw the liberation of individual energy only as a means to strengthen the collective whole.

The theory of social evolution was presented more systematically in *Tianyan lun*, the most dramatically successful of his works. Liang Qichao, Kang Youwei 康有爲 and others, fascinated by the idea of evolutionary progress, adopted it as theoretical justification for their political reform proposals in the late 1890s and thereafter. Its powerful message dominated a whole generation of Chinese intellectuals. By the 1900s social Darwinism had become so widespread that in 1905, Wang Guowei 王國維 wrote, the names of Darwin and Spencer were on everyone's lips and phrases such as 物竞 and 天择 were found even in popular literature. Hu Shi 胡适 remembered how the book swept the nation in the 1900s, as the idea of the struggle for existence and survival of the fittest became the ideal formula for a people reeling under the traumatic effect of the Boxer troubles. The *Tianyan lun* was so popular that Hu Shi was asked to discuss natural selection in a composition lesson. His own name 适, connoting "fit for survival", suggested by his elder brother, also reflects the climate of the times. Other notable intellectuals who felt the book's impact included Lu Xun 鲁迅 and Cai Yuanpei 蔡元培 .

Tianyan lun manifests the sense of mission underlying all Yan's translations: to find the key to the wealth and power of states among a range of Western social theories to ensure China's national salvation, and to transmit that wisdom to his people.

Yan's decision to translate "Evolution and Ethics" is interesting. This essay, which was Thomas Huxley's Romanes Lectures delivered in 1893, was actually an attack on rather than a defence of social Darwinism. While believing in evolution, Huxley's overwhelming preoccupation was to protect human ethical values against the efforts to create an "evolutionary ethic". The whole tract was directed against Spencer's crass and brutal cosmic optimism. Obviously it ran counter to Yan's pathos at this time, and there were other differences as well. Yan chose to translate it nonetheless probably because it contained the briefest and most vivid account of the main tenets of Darwinism available. Moreover, the lecture also surveyed the whole history of human thought, creating a sense of the essential transcultural unity of mankind which Yan was also eager to establish.

Besides, Yan had his own strategy for dealing with his many differences with Huxley. For example when Huxley wrote,

> So far as that limited revelation of the nature of things, which we call scientific knowledge, has yet gone, it tends, with constantly increasing emphasis, to the belief that, not merely the world of plants, but that of animals; not merely living things, but the whole fabric of the earth; not merely our planet, but the whole solar system; not merely our star and its satellites, but the millions of similar bodies which bear witness to the order which pervades boundless space, and has endured through boundless time; are all working out their predestined courses of evolution.

Yan translated it roughly as:

凡茲運行之理，乃化機所以不息之精，苟能靜觀，隨在可察：小之極於
跂行倒生，大之放乎日星天地；隱之則神思智識之所以聖狂，顯之則政
俗文章之所以沿革，言其要道，皆可一言蔽之，曰"天演"是已。

In this passage, we can see two significant points. First, while Huxley's original was much more related to the natural and cosmic order, Yan stressed the human order. Second, Huxley's attitude toward science was agnostic, tentative and sceptical, calling it "limited revelation" while Yan was convinced of the potency of science, and he added:

此其說濫觴隆古，而大暢於近五十年，蓋格致學精，時時可加實測故也
。且伊古以來，人持一說以言天，家宗一理以論化。

conveying the impression that science had *confirmed* evolution beyond doubt.

Yan also distorted Huxley through omission. Huxley wrote,

The word "evolution", now generally applied to the cosmic process, has had a singular history, and is used in various senses. Taken in its popular significa-tion it means progressive development, that is, gradual change from a condi-tion of relative uniformity to one of relative complexity; but its connotation has been widened to include the phenomena of retrogressive metamorphosis, that is, of progress from a condition of relative complexity to one of relative uniformity.

Huxley thus asserted that evolution was not necessarily a one-way street — from relative uniformity to relative complexity, which was the "popular signification"; but it could also go the other way — retrogressive metamor-phosis, that is of progress from relative complexity to one of relative uniformity. Yan omitted this section altogether, and so precludes in his version any alternative pattern of evolution. Huxley also wrote:

It is very desirable to remember that evolution is not an explanation of the cosmic process, but merely a generalized statement of the method and results of that process.

Huxley obviously questioned the potency of the concept of evolution and Yan, who saw evolutionism as an intellectual panacea, *again omitted* this section. Philosophically, Huxley's agnosticism led him to admit that there was much about evolution, particularly its cause, which could not be known. Yan omitted this presumably because his belief that *evolution was progress* stemmed from a teleological view of the universe which seemed to justify itself.

Perhaps Yan's most blatant intrusion was to bring Spencer into *Tianyan lun*, where he enthusiastically expounded Spencer's ideas not only in the commentaries, but in the text as well. Thus he wrote in the text,

斯賓塞爾曰："天擇者,存其最宜者也。"夫物既爭存矣,而天又從其爭之後而擇之,一爭一擇,而變化之事出矣。

These sentences were naturally absent in Huxley's work. In fact, Huxley would have found Yan's addition objectionable.

These examples from *Tianyan lun* show how Yan's ideological bias interfered with his translation. Evolution might mean the survival of the fittest but Huxley doubted if it necessarily meant improvement or progress, and certainly from an ethical point of view, unrestrained struggle in human society could be extremely destructive. Thus he advocated restraining the struggle by promoting co-operation and harmony instead.

Yan Fu, like Huxley, believed in evolution, but at this point of his life, he, like Spencer, was convinced evolution would only lead to improvement and finally to perfection. Yet, unlike Spencer, Yan believed human effort must be made to intensify the struggle, for this alone could help to mobilize and liberate the moral, intellectual and physical potentials of man. In late 19th century China, Yan's advocacy of a voluntaristic view of human evolution was really a political statement, exhorting China to pull her socks up and meet the challenges of foreign powers.

The fact is that for Yan, translation was *not* an academic exercise but a means to find practical solutions to China's problems. Yet, though he was meticulous in selecting works to be translated there was not one which had all the answers, making it necessary for him to incorporate ideas of other thinkers as well as his own with the authors'. *Tianyan lun* epitomizes this synthesis, and his own interpretation often dominated the original.

This tendency can be seen again in his translation of Adam Smith's *The Wealth of Nations*, entitled *Yuan fu* 《原富》, which he began translating in 1897 and completed by the end of 1900. Here, the translation was less paraphrastic than *Tianyan lun*, but Yan still managed to include his own ideas in the extended commentaries interlaced with the text. Together, they provide a good elementary course on the tenets of classical economics.

To Yan, wealth was a fuel of power. He was impressed by Britain's unprecedented economic power and he believed Smith's book was the key to that power. Though aware that since the book's publication in 1776 other economists had overtaken Smith, he nevertheless chose to translate it partly because much of Smith's criticism of the rulers of his days for their closed-mindedness was applicable to the rulers of contemporary China. He made up the shortfall by referring profusely to more modern economists.

Yan agreed with Smith on the importance of free trade, but he differed from Smith in other aspects. Smith championed economic individualism; Yan's preoccupation was the state's wealth and power. When Smith wrote of "general interest" Yan easily translated it into state interest. The difference can be seen for instance in their views on public debt. Smith deplored the practice of increasing the national debt by funding, and predicted that excessive funding would ruin even England. Yan however was profoundly struck by one fact above all else, that Great Britain had been able to maintain and increase its wealth even while increasing its national debt. The secret to success was that in releasing the economic energies of the people, the state had been able to tap this inexhaustible source of wealth for its own purposes. In Yan's opinion, China's predicament was exactly that the people were so poor that the state could not tap their economic energies without leading to even more abysmal poverty. If the Chinese people could be oriented toward production, the state could assume more and more burdens without fear of impoverishment. In practical terms, in the name of the state's wealth and power, he favoured *laissez faireism*.

Yuan fu challenged traditional Chinese attitudes towards wealth and production. In exalting enlightened self-interest, it questioned centuries of Confucian contempt for material gain as a conscious object of pursuit as well as contempt for merchants as parasites. Moreover, Yan emphasized that the Confucian dichotomy between interest 利 and righteousness 義 was illusory because enlightened self-interest could contribute to the greater interest of the community and ultimately the state's wealth. Thus in Yan's hands, a book preaching economic individualism became one advocating channelling the wealth of society toward the wealth of the state. In typical Darwinian terminology, Yan wrote that "the study of economics, in an immediate sense, concerns the wealth or poverty of China, and in a distant sense the flourishing or decline of the yellow race!"

The Study of Sociology had played a decisive role in shaping his intellectual development. He published two translated chapters of it in 1897 in the *Guowen bao* 《國聞報》, and in 1903, the complete book of 16 chapters was published in Shanghai. Sociology fascinated him because he believed it helped people understand society's past and anticipate the future, and in providing principles for correct moral attitudes, utility and improvement of people's livelihood, it was a source of good and strong government. Yan was especially impressed by its alleged scientific basis, which rested upon principles of cause and effect, and consistent with his intellectualistic approach to all things, he believed science and the scientific attitude would save China. He believed that since China's present problems were deeply rooted in history, it would be useless to introduce reforms without first understanding China sociologically.

But, even here, where Yan followed Spencer so closely, his own orientation was clear. For example Spencer, criticizing the legislature for meddling with the evolutionary process, wrote,

> The ordinary political schemer is convinced that out of a legislative apparatus properly devised and worked with due dexterity may be had beneficial State action without any detrimental reaction. He expects to get out of a stupid people the effects of intelligence and to evolve from inferior citizens superior conduct.

Yan paraphrases this as:

> 恃吾法制，弱民可使爲强國，貧民可使爲富國，愚民可使爲智國，此何異夢食求飽者乎！

Here we see Yan's central preoccupation with the power of the state creeping into his paraphrase of passages which said nothing on the subject. The fact is that Spencer, concerned only with the people's welfare, nowhere introduced the state's wealth and power into his argument. It was not the state as an end but as instrument which was under discussion. In Yan's hands, again, the whole tone changed and society/state became the end.

A wide spectrum of ideas, likewise alien to China, were introduced through Yan's other translations. There was the idea of individual freedom in J.S. Mill's *On Liberty*. Against the growing claims of society and the subtle pressures of democratic "conformism", Mill was anxious to stake out a legitimate area for the operation of individual liberty. Though in true utilitarian tradition, he advocated "the greatest good for the greatest numbers", he was as concerned for human beings becoming "noble and beautiful objects of contemplation". However, in Yan's hands, individual liberty was no longer an end in itself but a means to the advancement of the "people's virtue and intellect", and beyond this to the purposes of the state.

For Mill, freedom of thought provided the only way to reach truth; for Yan, the only truth to which he was committed was the truth of natural and social sciences as revealed by Spencer and Smith. Yan's ideas intruded into the text, and his translation of *On Liberty* is interpretation through translation rather than translation *per se*.

The Spirit of the Law expounds on a whole range of law from civil through the constitutional, and the latter opens onto discussions on political structure. Yan, in translating this work, attempted to present the legal system and legal outlook of Western states as indispensable ingredients leading to their wealth and power. As if to complement Montesquieu's static analysis of the different legal and constitutional forms, Yan went on to translate Edward Jenks's *A History of Politics* and provide an evolutionary framework for change. Spencer had taught Yan to think of human history in terms of the organic growth of social, political systems over time, and Jenks's scheme of historical stages — savage "totemistic" society, followed by "patriarchal" society, and finally by the state, or "political" society — provided the substantiation of the framework. Jenks's work partly enabled Yan to explain why China had not progressed from "patriarchalism" when Western states had reached their modern form, the political state.

Yan's last two major translations looked even further to the source of Western wisdom — logic, often called the science of all sciences. In particular, Yan was devoted to Mill's logic which glorified inductionism. It was a corrective, Yan thought, to the deplorable Chinese tendency to rely on *a priori* knowledge, epitomized in Mencius' assertion "that all things are stored up in me". The attraction of Mill's logic lay in its emphasis on empirical data. Inductionism was a form of activism which mocked the Chinese scholar's preference to find knowledge either in meditation or in classical literature. In the end what Yan obtained from Mill's logic was a programme of action, a plan for conquering nature, including man's nature as embodied in his social history, through the method of induction.

Only half of Mill's *Logic* was translated. Though he considered completing the effort, Yan was too emotionally and intellectually drained by events to continue. He found Mill's work, full of profound and complex ideas, too formidable. Instead, he turned to a much simpler work, W. S. Jevons' *The Primer of Logic*, and he even took a shortcut by translating it very loosely.

Translation was, to a large extent, a vehicle for Yan's own visions, but he was no less serious about translation as a craft. In "Notes to the

Table. Yan Fu's Major Translations

Title of Translation	Original Title	Author	Publication Date of Original	Publication Date of Translation	Date of Translation	Remarks	Length of Translated Work (approx.)
《天演論》	*Evolution and Ethics*	T.H. Huxley (1825–1895)	1893	1898	1894?–1896	Parts of translation first appeared serially in the *Guowen bao* in 1897	50,000 words
《原富》	*An Inquiry into the Nature and Causes of the Wealth of Nations*	Adam Smith	1776	1901–1902	1897–1900		450,000 words
《群學肄言》	*The Study of Sociology*	Herbert Spencer (1802–1903)	1873	1903	1897–1903	2 chapters first appeared in *Guowen bao* in 1897	180,000 words
《群己權界論》	*On Liberty*	J.S. Mill (1806–1873)	1859	1903	1899		70,000 words
《社會通詮》	*A History of Politics*	Edward Jenks (1861–1939)	1900	1904	1903		100,000 words
《法意》	*L'esprit de Lois (The Spirit of the Law)*	C.L. Montesquieu (1689–1755)	1743	1904–1909	1900?–1909		450,000 words
《穆勒名學》	*A System of Logic*	J.S. Mill	1843	1905	1900–1902	Only half the original was translated	270,000 words
《名學》	*The Primer of Logic*	W.S. Jevons (1835–1882)	1879	1909	1908		100,000 words

Translation" in *Tianyan lun*, Yan discussed his criteria and strategy as a translator. He identified three major difficulties in translation — 信, faithfulness to the original; 達, comprehensibility; 雅, elegance of style — which he also saw as the basic requirements of good translation. Although he was not always able to practise what he preached, these have largely been accepted in China as standard criteria for translation for most of the twentieth century.

Yan, recognizing on the one hand the need to achieve both faithfulness and comprehensibility, and on the other the difference between English and Chinese in sentence structure and grammar, overcame the problem by avoiding translating word by word, sentence by sentence. Instead, his strategy was first to digest the spirit and meaning of the original and then write it out spontaneously to eliminate awkwardness. Thus, Yan's translation was chiefly paraphrastic. It was effective too, though as Liang Qichao observed, this method was only able to work because "Yan's knowledge was so close to the authors'". Indeed, Yan's thorough understanding of the original text sets him apart from translators who translated merely mechanically.

Yan continued to defend translating loosely and "selectively". In his "Notes to the Translation" in *Yuan fu* he justified taking the liberty to render only summarily parts of the original which he regarded as too cumbersome, and even to omit whole sections which he considered irrelevant. In "Notes to the Translation" in *On Liberty* 《群己權界論》 he explained that by judicious paraphrasing, he was making the work more comprehensible to the reader. Interestingly, he pointed out that though many readers complained that his translations were difficult to read, they should realize that the originals were actually even more so! By the time he worked on W.S. Jevons' *Primer of Logic*, he treated the original even more casually. While adopting Jevons' general meaning in broad outline, he found it easier to construct his own illustrations. He thought it sufficient for him to convey the meaning without being too concerned about strict adherence to the original text. Thus we see that despite Yan's initial intention to achieve both faithfulness and comprehensibility, it was not always possible to strike a balance between them and Yan often opted to sacrifice faithfulness for comprehensibility.

It has already been shown that some of Yan's "unfaithfulness" had ideological roots; sometimes, his unfaithfulness was stylistic, affecting tone rather than content. For example, when Huxley simply used the phrase "unceasing struggle for existence", Yan wrote:

戰事熾然，強者後亡，弱者先絕，年年歲歲，偏有留遺。

The difference in tone is apparent.

The discrepancy can be illustrated in another passage:

The subject of this Essay is not the so-called Liberty of the Will, so unfortunately opposed to the misnamed doctrine of Philosophical Necessity; but
Civil, or Social Liberty: the nature and limits of the power which can be
legitimately exercised by society over the individual. A question seldom
stated, and hardly ever discussed, in general terms, but which profoundly
influences the practical controversies of the age by its latent presence, and is
likely soon to make itself recognized as the vital question of the future. It is so
far from being new, that in a certain sense, it has divided mankind, almost from
the remotest ages, but in the stage of progress into which the more civilized
portions of the species have now entered, it presents itself under new conditions, and requires a different and more fundamental treatment. (*On Liberty*)

It is translated as:

有心理之自繇，有群理之自繇。心理之自繇，與前定對；群理之自繇，
與節制對。今此篇所論釋，群理自繇也。蓋國，合眾民而言之曰國人
(函社會國家在內)，舉一民而言之曰小己。今問國人範圍小己，小己受
制國人，以正道大法言之，彼此權力界限，定於何所？此種問題，雖古
人之意，有所左右，而爲之明揭究論者稀。顧其理關於人道至深，挽近
朝野所爭，樞機常伏於此，且恐過斯以往，將爲人群大命之所懸。不佞
是篇之作，所爲不得已也，所言非曰新說，但宇內治化日蒸，所以衡審
是非，裁量出入，稍與古殊，非爲討本窮原之論，難有明已。

The historian Wen Xinyuan 溫心園 has pointed out several interesting
points:

that 意志的自由 might be a more accurate rendition of "Liberty of Will"; than
心理之自繇；

that 以正道大法言之 is a rather odd translation of "legitimately";

that to translate "a vital question" as 將爲人群大命之所懸 is cumbersome;

that 雖古人之意，有所左右 and 不佞是篇之作，所爲不得已也 and 衡審是非，
裁量出入 are not in the original;

that 所言非曰新說 does not convey all that "It is so far from being new that in
a certain sense, it has divided mankind, almost from the remotest ages"
conveys.

Wen's verdict is that while Yan Fu had no problem understanding the original, the language he used imposed serious restrictions. Indeed Yan was very concerned with language, and believed it was not enough to achieve faithfulness and comprehensibility; literary elegance was equally essential.

In "Notes to the Translation" in *Tianyan lun* he explained that Huxley's ideas being so profound, only the pre-Han style, which combined precision with richness, terseness with profundity and clarity with elegance, was appropriate, adding that the current literary style was too vulgar to do Huxley justice. We can see here a hint of social and intellectual snobbery. On a later occasion, he wrote scornfully that "to use the vulgar style currently in vogue just to facilitate ignorant people in the market places and isolated villages is cultural dismemberment, not [cultural] revolution."

In fact, Yan's decision to use the pre-Han style is significant. It was partly due to his aesthetic bent. More importantly, he might have been trying to win recognition from the scholar elite; not having earned any degree through the Civil Service Examination, he might have been keen to prove that despite this, he belonged to the same league as they. At the same time, he might have been hoping to sway the style-conscious literati who habitually scorned all non-Chinese things as uncivilized, by demonstrating that Western thought did lend itself to the noblest Chinese prose. Indeed, some conservative literati did read his translation for its beauty of style. Thus, both linguistically and intellectually, Yan did much to raise the status of translators.

A fairly accomplished poet himself, Yan did not hesitate to translate poetry either. Huxley had included Alexander Pope's poem,

> All nature is but art, unknown to thee;
> All chance, direction which thou canst not see;
> All discord, harmony not understood;
> All partial evil, universal good,
> And spite of pride, in erring reason's spite,
> One truth is clear; whatever is, is right.

Yan's translation of this is:

> 元宰有秘機，斯人特未悟，
> 世事豈偶然，彼蒼審措注，
> 乍疑樂律乖，庸知各得所，
> 雖有偏沴災，終則其利溥，
> 寄語傲慢徒，慎勿輕毀詛，
> 一理今分明，造化原無過。

This is probably the first translation of an English poem into Chinese. It is aesthetically pleasing and fairly faithful in tone and substance to the original; the only flaw appears to be the last sentence, 造化原無過 which lacks the positiveness of "whatever is, is right". It is also one of the lesser known of Yan's achievements. There are, however, several collections of Yan's own poems.

Another example of Yan's artistic inclination can be seen in his translation of the preface in Spencer's *The Study of Sociology*:

敘曰：

一・　含靈秉氣，群義大哉，強弱明暗，理有由來。哀此流俗，不知本始，在筌忘魚，操刃傷指。譯《砭愚》。

二・　執果窮因，是惟科學，人事紛綸，莫之掎擵。雖無密合，寧尟大同，籀此公例，彪彼童蒙。譯《倡學》。

三・　眞宰神功，曰惟天演，物競天擇，所存者善。散曰么匿，聚曰拓都，知微之顯，萬法所郛。譯《喻術》。

四・　道巽兩間，物奚翅萬，人心慮道，各自爲楦。永言時位，載占吉凶，所以東聖，低佪中庸。譯《知難》。

五・　難首在物，是惟心所，傳聞異辭，相爲旅距。見者枝葉，孰察本根，以槿議椿，如蝱處褌。譯《物蔽》。

六・　主觀二義，曰理與情，執己量物，哀此心盲。簡不逮繁，小不容大，滯礙僻堅，舉爲群害。譯《智絃》。

七・　懮喜惡欲，皆使衡差，以茲目眚，結彼空花。所嚴帝天，所畏魔蝎，以是言群，幾何能達。譯《情瞀》。

八・　心習少成，由來學最，楊取爲我，墨尙兼愛。偏至之德，所傷實多，曷建皇極，以救厥頗。譯《學詖》。

九・　民生有群，而傅以國，竺我忘人，愛或成賊。反是爲曊，矯亦失中，惟誠無妄，其例乃公。譯《國拘》。

十・　演深治久，群有眾流，以各爭存，乃交相鰌。或怒譸張，或怨施奪，民德未隆，安往不刺。譯《流梏》。

十一・國云天地，基命黔首，云何胥匄，獨責元後。朝有政黨，樂相詆諆，元黃水火，鑒瞂衡迗。譯《政惑》。

十二・天人之際，宗教攸貣，聽神蔑民，群治以衰。舉人代天，教又不可，釋景猶回，皆有負荷。譯《敎辟》。

十三・夫惟知難，學乃殆庶，屬西三科，曰斗間著。斗以觀法，間乃窮因，習著知化，乃凝夫神。譯《繕性》。

十四・一神兩化，大德曰生，咨此生理，群義以明。群實大生，而生之織，欲觀拓都，視此么匿。譯《憲生》。

十五‧我聞佛說，境胥心造，化萬不同，肇於厥腦。主道齊者，民情是
田，不洞幽漠，孰知陶甄。譯《述神》。

十六‧惟群有學，以因果故，去私戒偏，來導先路。蓋勿孟晉，猶懷蓬
廬，譯此懸論，敢告象胥。譯《成章》。

Yan took great pains over the selection and creation of new terms;
many terms simply had no equivalent in Chinese. He warned that translators must not treat these arbitrarily because some terms which might appear
comparable could in fact differ widely in connotation. Sometimes, he
admitted, he "pondered for a month over one term". In "Notes to the
Translation" to *On Liberty*, he went to great lengths to explain why he had
chosen his Chinese title as 《群己權界論》 (lit., the boundary between
one's rights and others') as he felt that none of the many existing terms
connoting freedom completely conveyed the sense of liberty described in
Mill's book.

Avoiding the neologisms created by the Japanese during the previous
decades, he was proud of expressions he created himself, such as 物競天
擇. The difficulty of translating terms is in fact only the manifestation of
the difficulty involved in transmitting ideas and concepts from one
thought system to another, from one culture to another. For instance, one of
the most difficult terms Yan grappled with was "nature" in "Evolution and
Ethics" which he translated as 天. 天 contains the connotation of a
directive, purposive power which might not be entirely identical to the
objective, impersonal and artless nature Huxley wished to portray. Yet,
given the cultural constraints, it was probably the best he could do.

Yan's insistence on the abstruse pre-Han 古文 style, however noble the
motive, made his works inaccessible to many readers, which Liang Qichao
found most regrettable. As later translators began to translate from the
Japanese using much plainer prose, his translations became increasingly out
of date. Many people only knew about his work second hand, and by the
time of the May Fourth Movement, he had become an anachronism. In
addition, many of the neologisms from Japan overtook his carefully chosen
but obsolete terms. Though 物競天擇 remained an integral element of the
new Chinese vocabulary, the term 進化 from Japan overtook 天演. The
Japanese term 經濟 which he discarded as too broad, also found acceptance
over his own creation 計學. Likewise, other terms he chose to use such as
格致 for science, 群 for society and 群學 for sociology were all overtaken by
科學, 社會 and 社會學 from Japan.

Besides translations, essays, lectures and poems, Yan's other major efforts were an annotated edition of *Laozi* 《老子》 and a commentary on *Zhuangzi* 《莊子》. Though Yan frequently asserted that Lao Zi's views are compatible with those of Darwin and Spencer, it is not difficult to see that there are fundamental differences between them. Lao Zi emphasized passivity and quietude, shrinking from struggle and strife and positively fearing the assertion of human vital energies. This contrasts sharply with Spencer and Darwin's belief in energy, dynamism, struggle, self-assertion and the fearless realization of all human potentialities on ever higher levels of achievement. That Yan could accommodate Lao Zi's essentially backward-looking, metaphysical cosmology to Darwin and Spencer's forward-looking and positivist cosmology reflects the complexity and richness of his mind. The intellectual synthesis he undertook defies any simple categorization into Western and Chinese thinking, and he objected strongly to the principle of "Chinese learning for essence and Western learning for utility" 中學爲體，西學爲用.

In his old age, he grew progressively pessimistic about the contemporary situation and looked increasingly to Chinese antiquity for solutions to political and philosophical problems. In 1913, when the Confucian Society petitioned Parliament to adopt Confucianism as the state religion, he gave his support. He believed that Chinese tradition of the pre-Qin period should be perpetuated by teaching it to students of all grades so that the younger generation could cultivate proper moral sentiments and learn to respect the sages of the past. The outbreak of the First World War further undermined his confidence in the West. In 1918 he wrote,

> In my old age, I have seen the Republic during the seven years of its existence and an unprecedented bloody war of four years in Europe. I feel that the evolution of their [Western] races in the last three hundred years has only made them kill one another for self-interest, without a sense of shame. Today, when I reconsider the way of Confucius and Mencius, I feel it is broad enough to cover the whole cosmos and to benefit the entire world.

Among his deathbed injunctions to his children was: "Though the old traditions may be modified, they must never be overthrown."

These views ran counter to ideas then prevalent among intellectuals in China. Yan Fu opposed the May Fourth Movement, whose main aims, science and democracy, he had ironically championed more than a quarter of a century earlier. Chen Duxiu 陳獨秀, Hu Shi and others of their generation had been inspired by him in their youth, and much of their bold new thinking was already present in his synthesis of the 1895–1908 period. Yet, as Benjamin Schwartz observed, "They and he [were] divided from each other not merely by age but by a difference in life experience which lies deeper than the level of conscious intellectual attitudes." Even though the radical iconoclasm of the May Fourth Movement overshadowed his seemingly conservative argument that social and political evolution must be based on the *gradual* re-educating of people's minds, historical hindsight leads us to wonder if his contemporaries did not do China a disservice by not considering his advice more seriously then.

Yan Fu played an important role in directing intellectual trends in a period of transition in modern Chinese history. A pioneer in using translation as a tool to open up new cultural horizons, he showed both the possibilities and limitations of the intercultural exchange of ideas. His writings and translations initiated a re-evaluation of China's own cultural tradition. By absorbing different strands of Western ideas and synthesizing them, and juxtaposing these with Chinese ideas, Yan displayed a richness and complexity of thought that makes him one of the finest minds of modern China.

References

Editorial Division, The Commercial Press 商務印書館編輯部, ed. 《論嚴復與嚴譯名著》 (*On Yan Fu and the Works He Translated*). Beijing: The Commercial Press 商務印書館, 1982.

He, Lin 賀麟. 〈嚴復的翻譯〉 (The Translations of Yan Fu). 《東方雜誌》 (*The Eastern Magazine*), Vol. 22, No. 21 (1925), pp. 75–87.

Ng, Mau-sang. "Reading Yan Fu's *Tian Yan Lun*." In *Interpreting Culture through Translation*, edited by Roger T. Ames, Chan Sin-wai and Ng Mau-sang. Hong Kong: The Chinese University Press, 1991, pp. 167–84.

Schwartz, Benjamin. *In Search of Wealth and Power: Yen Fu and the West*. Cambridge, Mass.: Harvard University Press, 1964.

Sinn, Elizabeth 洗玉儀. "Yan Fu as Translator: A Textual Criticism of the *Tianyanlun*." In 《翻譯新論集》 (*New Essays on Translation*), edited by Liu Ching-chih 劉靖之. Hong Kong: The Commercial Press 商務印書館, 1991, pp. 359–66.

INTERPRETATION

Interpretation

Rainer Schulte
Center for Translation Studies
University of Texas at Dallas, Dallas, U.S.A.

What is the function of interpretation? To provide the reader, listener, and viewer with entrances into a text, whether that text be a literary, visual or musical work. Each artistic work presents a particular view of the world, a way of seeing objects and situations as if it were for the first time. Critics and scholars must help us to find ways of entering into these new perspectives of seeing the world. However, it seems that criticism in the last few years has failed to respond to this need. Often, critical approaches that are meant to bring the reader closer to a text have the exact opposite effect. They distance the reader from the text and close rather than open doors to a better understanding of the particular nature of a given form of artistic insight and expression.

Partly responsible for that phenomenon is the critic's and scholar's attitude toward seeing the text as a springboard for the development of his or her own ways of thinking rather than looking at the text as something that has to be entered and clarified. What we have in this case is criticism of criticism of criticism. A look at many of the books that have been published by scholarly presses in recent years confirms this trend which has as its unfortunate consequence that many students and readers turn away from the act of reading literary works. One should remember that any work of criticism comes into existence only because there is a work that was created by the writer or artist.

To counteract this trend in contemporary criticism, we looked at translation as a possible new way of revitalizing the act of interpretation. At first sight it is difficult to see the immediate relation between interpretation and translation. Seen, however, in the larger context of interpretation as communication with a text, the connection becomes transparent. George Steiner's comment that "all acts of communication are acts of translation" further affirms this way of thinking. There is no communication without translation and the reading of a text is an intense act of translation. The words of the philosopher Hans Georg Gadamer come to mind: "Reading is already translation, translation is translation for the second time .... The process of translating comprises in its essence the whole secret of human understanding of the world and of social communications."

Thus, the methodologies of the art and craft of translation can be seen as one way of revitalizing the complicated act of interpretation not only of the literary work but also for all artistic works. What does this mean? Simply, that we begin to look at a text from the translator's point of view. The translator learns and applies methods of transplanting words, or rather situations, from one language into another. Interpreting a text within the same language can also be considered as an act of translation; and, therefore, an investigation of the translator's methods can shed light on the process of interpretation. What is it that the translator does when confronted with the text in the foreign language?

A few basic considerations might help to clarify the translator's procedure. The word "to trans-late," which gains even a clearer visualization with "über-setzen" in the German language, underlines the notion of interaction and exchange. In its original meaning, "über-setzen" indicates that something is being carried across from one side of the river to the other, yet what is carried across must be modified so that it can be integrated into the laws of the otherness in a new culture. What this means is that the translation process begins in the other. For a communication to take place with the other, a thorough exploration of the dynamics of the situations on the other side of the river must be undertaken. The translator's starting point — and here resides the important link with the act of interpretation — must be anchored in that which he or she has to face in the foreign text. If we transfer this idea to the act of reading within the same language, then each word must be considered a "foreign" entity. To think in the foreign constitutes the first step toward a possible interpretation that can then lead to the actual translation. Let us assume that the English translator reads the simple words "maison" or "jardin" in French and initiates his or her approach to this text by thinking about these two words in terms of "house" and "garden"; then a real entrance into the foreign text is seriously endangered. The English word "garden" creates a totally different atmosphere than the French "jardin." They are the same as far as the dictionary is concerned, but in terms of their cultural and aesthetic ambiance, they are miles apart. The translator who decides to think through the French text in terms of the universe that surrounds the English word "garden" closes the door to any true communication with the foreign in the other language. The translator carries something to the foreign text which its semantic boundaries cannot hold. A mold is imposed on the foreign word that freezes the word's internal energy and destroys its recreative power for the dynamic interchange with other words. The interpretive process ends before it has begun.

The interpretation as translation within the same language requires the same attitude. The reader must approach each word as if it were a word in a foreign language. A writer manipulates words, often modifies and enhances their established connotations, creates new fields of meaning through the interaction with other words, and builds a universe of feelings and emotions that enlarges the reader's/interpreter's way of seeing and understanding the world. Only through the experience of the other can we expand our insights into the human condition.

Practically speaking, the interpreter as translator continuously engages in the question: What kind of research must I undertake in order to do justice to the text I am reading, whether I choose to translate it from a foreign language into my own or whether I translate it into my own frame of mind within the same language? The translator's interpretive act is always rooted in the concreteness of the textual situation and not in some theoretical construct. The translator — in contrast to many critics — does not consider the word as an object that can be described or even frozen into a specific meaning but continuously interacts with the internal of a word's magnetic field. When the interpreter assumes the translator's role, he or she lives inside the word and thereby establishes a dynamic environment rather than a static one. Even when a translation appears in the fixed form of the printed page, it cannot claim to be final. There is no such thing as the definitive translation of any text, as there is no definitive interpretation of any text. Whenever a translator returns to the same text, a different reading will take place and, therefore, also a different interpretation. At every moment, the translator recreates the process of interpretation in the sense of finding new connections between the two sides of the river. That process is in no way different when we read and interpret within the same language. We constantly must transplant ourselves into the foreign so that we build the bridge from there back to our own way of seeing.

The translator who has to anchor the interpretive act in the realities of each word has to develop a certain strategy to do justice to a word as an isolated phenomenon and as the link in the ever-widening circle of connotations that a word gains through its context expansion. Words, as we know, have primary and secondary meanings. No two people will ever take the exact same impression and visualization from a word. Language in itself is quite restricted: in many instances we have one or two words to describe an object. When we use the word "chair," every person immediately creates an image in his or her mind that hardly ever coincides in all its details with the visualization of that object in the mind of another person. The chair comes in multiple shapes: a high or low chair, an easy chair, a reclining chair, a swivel chair, a secretarial chair, etc. It is unlikely that our first association upon hearing the word "chair" would create in our mind the image of an "electric chair," although that might be the connotation of that word when it first appears in a literary text. In that sense, the reader as interpreter and translator must unlearn language before the act of interpretation can be initiated. What we think a word connotes upon a first reading of a text rarely coincides with the connotations that the writer injected into that word. Unlearning could also be characterized as an attitude of openness toward the multiplicity of meanings working within any given word. The tremendous variety inherent in the presence of "chairness" underlines the dilemma that faces all writers: to create through language something that transcends language. Not only does the chair come in many different shapes, but the specific appearance creates varying emotional reactions in the viewer. A French chair built under Louis XIV generates an atmosphere quite different from a contemporary Swedish or Danish chair, not to speak of a chair that was chiselled out of stone. A writer's foremost concern is not to offer statements of meanings to the reader, but to build atmospheres which make it possible for the reader to experience a situation. In order to succeed in this endeavor, writers constantly discover new relationships between words that have to be reconstructed in the interpretive process by the reader/translator. Yet, we must remember that a word does not only exist through its semantic reality. Each word comes to life with a certain specific physicality that includes its meaning possibilities, its sound and rhythm, its link to cultural and historical traditions, its modified uses conditioned by geographical realities, and also its visual appearance on the page, especially in poetic forms of expression. All of these ingredients begin to work on the writer as well as on the reader.

Exploration of the word's internal levels of meanings initiates the reading and translation process. The translator places himself or herself inside the word to think out its magnetic field, to uncover the streams that will flow into the semantic fields of other words. That act — which is the most fundamental one of any interpretation — should be called "visualiza-tion." The American poet W.S. Merwin opens his poem "In Autumn" with the following words: "The extinct animals are still looking for home ..." None of these words pose any serious difficulties for the English-speaking reader. Yet, before any entrance into the line becomes feasible, the reader must undertake an act of visualization. The expression "the animals are still looking" causes in itself no major problems. What initially confuses the reader is the combination of "extinct" with "animals." How can animals who are extinct — which might suggest that they do no longer exist — be engaged in an act of looking? Do we change the meaning if we replace extinct with dead? Very much so. Dead and extinct generate different processes of visualization. The use of dead in that line would derail the poetic as well as the experiential logic: a dead animal has lost the ability to look. That kind of reasoning brings us, the reader/translator, closer to the visualization of "extinct." Even though the animal as a species might be extinct, it possibly can still live as a stuffed animal in a museum. The context of the following lines in the poem seems to suggest that kind of visualization. For the combination of "extinct animals" to come to life, the reader will be forced to assess every possible existing meaning — as speci-fied through entries in philological and etymological dictionaries — and then decipher the evolving meanings in relation to the context of the poem. Again, the process of "über-setzen" as a carrying back and forth is at work, this time within the dynamics of the text itself. Coming from the semantic field of "extinct," the reader relates that field to those emanating from other words in the text, only to come back to the starting point to see whether the context will enrich the connotations of "extinct" even beyond what we have learned about the word from the dictionary entries. That enrichment of words through the contextual progression often affects the decisions a translator of novels has to make. A word that appears on the first page of a given novel is repeated several times throughout the progression of the work. Each time the word reoccurs, the translator realizes that another level of meaning has been added to the word. Finally, in the middle of the novel, the translator comprehends the full impact of that word which then forces him or her to reassess the original translation choice that was made. And since frequently the new language might not have a similar word that allows for all of the nuances that the writer instilled in the word to be incorporated, the translator will choose several different words to carry the situation over into the new language environment.

From the visualization of the individual word, the translator moves to the contextual visualization: the word in relation to the word before and after, to the rest of the sentence, to the paragraph, to the entire text, and finally to the oeuvre. At every step of the translator's work, questions will be asked that come out of the necessity of the word and its placement within the text. Where does the word come from, what semantic and emotional baggage has it acquired through the centuries, what original image lies behind the surface appearance, what role does it play in a given text, how often does it appear in the oeuvre of a given writer, how have other writers of the same period used the word, has the writer revived a meaning-aspect that was prominent in a previous century but not necessarily common today, and how has it been treated, if at all, by other translators and critics? All of these considerations constantly bombard the translator's consciousness, and they should also be the major concerns of any person who approaches the interpretation of a text. A famous critic is said to have interpreted a particular passage in a Henry James story where the word "coil" appeared. The critic, at the time deeply involved in studying Sigmund Freud, constructed an interpretive approach around all the possible Freudian connotations that the word "coil" brings to mind. When the article was published, the author received a short note from the printer who told him that "coil" was actually a misprint and should have been "soil." I have never verified this incident, but even if it did not happen, it illustrates what can happen when an interpretation loses its contextual placement.

Texts from the past that have already undergone the scrutiny of time are in that sense easier to handle. Dictionaries will be able to tell us what certain words meant at a particular time of literary history. The *Oxford English Dictionary* (*OED*) is an indispensable tool for reading English texts of the past. Not only are words explained by themselves, but they are also documented with specific examples from various works written around the same time. The contemporary text, that is to say, a text that has just been written by an author, poses more complicated problems. Whatever linguistic and semantic innovations the poet or writer has brought to the use of his or her language has not yet been reflected in the fixed form of a dictionary. It might show up in a few years, which is of little help for the current reader and interpreter. In that case, the new meaning attributed to a word or an expression can only be illuminated through the process of a rigorous contextual visualization. The English writer Francis Bacon wrote an essay entitled "Of Studies" in 1597. The first sentence of that essay reads: "Studies serve for pastimes, for ornaments and for abilities." For that sentence to regain meaning for the modern reader, a series of scholarly pursuits have to be undertaken. Literary history tells us that this essay, when first published, had a certain impact. Since the words "pastimes, ornaments, abilities" have changed through the centuries, we no longer have immediate access to the power of expression they had in their own time. Thus, a process of translation of these words into the present linguistic and semantic environment has to be initiated. The interpreter explores the foreignness in these words and tries to find equivalents in present-day language. Once again the question has to be asked: "What kind of research do I have to undertake in order to do justice to this line or text? Actually, the investigation of a single word such as "pastimes" or "ornaments" could serve as an agent to reconstruct an entire Zeitgeist of that period. Starting with the exploration of all the immediate connotations associated with those two words, the reader/translator will then pursue the cultural, aesthetic, artistic, social or political nuances that might be working in these words. What becomes clear in this approach is the important recognition that all translation research — in whatever direction it might lead the translator — will always lead the reader back to the text itself. Here lies a major difference between critical and translational practices. In the former case, critics often distance themselves from the text without feeling any obligation to return to it at the end of their interpretations.

Using the dictionary definitions for the word "abilities" might not necessarily provide us with a totally intelligible meaning of how the word is used in the line. Yet, the various choices given generate in the reader ways of thinking about the text that otherwise would not have happened. Here are some definitions given for "ability" in the *OED*: suitableness, fitness, aptitude, faculty, capacity, bodily power, strength, wealth, talent, cleverness, mental power or capacity. The gamut of associations could probably be extended some more. Somewhere in-between all of these definitions lies the meaning of "ability" that the translator must decipher in his or her act of interpretation. The example brings us back to the abovementioned comments about chair and chairness. The plurality of existing chair designs reaffirms that there is such a thing as chair. On a higher level, one could say the multiplicity of existing bible translations throughout the centuries reassures us that there is such a thing as the Bible. With respect to the excursion into the word "ability," the translator must move among all of these dictionary possibilities, since each one of them will force him or her to return to the text and rethink the line in terms of each given meaning. In that sense, the act of interpretation seen through the translator's eyes develops a reader's and student's ability to visualize a text. From the practice of translation we learn above all the art of "situational thinking."

The Bacon example showed how one can approach a text through the exploration of one word with its numerous branches of meanings. That practice can be transferred to the interpretation of texts, especially poems, through multiple translations. A poem can never be fully recreated in another language through one translation. However, the use of multiple translations of a given poem transplanted by several translators opens up a different way of thinking about the poem. A case in point is the opening line of Rainer Maria Rilke's "The Panther." In the original it says "Sein Blick ist vom Vorübergehn der Stäbe ...." The key word in that line is "Blick" which has been translated by "glance, vision, seeing, sight, gaze." The English reader immediately perceives the differences between the words that the translators used to render "Blick." Clear boundaries can be drawn around the semantic fields of "glance" and the other renderings. The activity of visualization contained in "glance" is different from that of "vision." That practice leads the reader/interpreter to an intense interaction with the situations that each one of these words creates as an isolated phenomenon but possibly also in the context of the line. In addition, the comparison of these expressions will automatically force the interpreter to ask the simple question: why did the various translators come up with these diverse solutions? That question takes the reader back to think in the context of the original German poem. Something foreign in that text needs to be uncovered that is responsible for the multiplicity of renderings. Thinking out the word in the German reveals that, indeed, the word comprises two directions of meaning at the same time: On the one hand "Blick" encompasses the content of looking at an object; on the other, it is also the activity of seeing. Thus, the English solutions of "seeing and glance" versus "sight and vision." Naturally, none of the English words contains the double activity at work in the original German text. So far, the interpretive process has only dealt with the dynamics of one single word. Now the reader has to explore whether the two directions of thinking within the word are essential to the further development of the poem. Might this ambiguity emerge as a structuring principle for the entire poem? Thus, the reader/translator will dissect the rest of the poem, only to assemble it again at the end of that process and relate it back to the situational thinking in the word "Blick."

The study of a poem through the medium of various translations displays the complex associations of poetic thinking and induces the reader to ask questions about the nature of the poem that otherwise would not have been asked. Out of all these various interpretations readers can formulate their own ways of seeing and interpreting the poem. This kind of reading offers an extraordinary richness of perceptions, a living inside the poem, which could rarely be reached by reading just one translation of a given poem. As an afterword to these remarks, it is curious to realize that to this day there is no anthology in the English-speaking world that would provide the reader with a selection of multiple translations of the same text. Such a textbook could indeed become one of the most valuable tools to introduce students to the art of reading and interpreting. This kind of reading is always anchored in the reality and the concreteness of the text, which generates its own excitement by forcing the reader to actively recreate the interactions and relationships in a text. The text becomes an experience rather than an object that is being seen by the reader/interpreter from a distance. Participation replaces description.

What then does the reader learn from the methodologies derived from the art and craft of translation? As readers transplant themselves into the atmosphere of a new situation in the foreign text, they realize that the text does not build just one clearly defined reality, but, rather, possibilities of various realities. The readers are left with various options that they can interpret within the context of that atmosphere. The reader/translator reestablishes at every step of his or her work the inherent uncertainty of each word, both as isolated phenomenon and as semiotic possibility of a sentence, paragraph or the context of the entire work. The rediscovery of that uncertainty in each word constitutes the initial attitude of the translator. Reading and thus interpreting become the making of meaning and not the description of already-fixed meanings. The foreign text does not offer the reader a new, comfortable reality, but, rather, places him or her between several realities among which he or she has to choose; the words that constitute the text emanate a feeling of uncertainty. That feeling, however, becomes instrumental in the reader's/translator's engagement in a continuous process of decision-making. Certain choices have to be made among all these possibilities of uncertain meanings. Whatever the translation decision might be, there is still another level of uncertainty for the reader/translator that continues the process of reading not only within the text but even beyond the text. This proliferation of uncertainties must be viewed as one of the most stimulating and rewarding results that the reader/translator perspective finds in the study and interpretation of a text. Reading as the generator of uncertainties, reading as the driving force toward a decision-making process, reading as discovery of new interrelations that can be experienced but not described in terms of a content-oriented language. Whatever questions translators ask with respect to their involvement in a text, these questions have no prefigured answers that would be prompted by outside information brought to the text or content-oriented statements about the text. In the translation process there are no definitive answers, only attempts at solutions in response to states of uncertainty generated by the interaction of the words' semantic fields and sounds. Reading institutes the making of meanings through questions in which the possibility of an answer results in another question: what if?

To look at a text from a translator's point of view changes our way of thinking about interpretation. Thomas S. Kuhn talks in his book *The Structure of Scientific Revolutions* about paradigm shifts as a vital necessity for the creation and the development of disciplines. Translation methodologies and their transferral to the field of interpretation have generated a paradigm shift in how we read and understand texts. When we think within the framework of translation, words such as integration, interactivity, interconnectedness, and interrelationships come to mind. In other words, the translation process establishes a systemic way of looking at a text. Everything is related to everything else in the overall structure of a poem, play or novel. Even though the translator begins with a technique of dissecting every detail of a given sentence or paragraph, he or she will consider all individual insights and discoveries as part of an overall coherent structure. The translator aims at the reconstruction of the totality of a text in its human and historical context. Therein lies the integrating power of the translator's way of looking at works of art. Thus, a study dedicated to the reconstruction of the translation process will provide the reader/interpreter with the tools to change interpretive perspectives that rebuild texts as dynamic rather than static entities. The translator's point of view positions the translator inside the text as a recreator of its complex semantic levels of expression. The composer Aaron Copland distinguishes three ways of listening to music: one where we notice music only when it is no longer played, as for example in department stores; one where we try to impose a specific meaning on any given composition, as with Beethoven's "Moonlight Sonata"; and one where we become involved in listening and interpreting the melodic and structural lines of a piece of music. It is the last one that is the most exciting one, and it is also the one that can be achieved by transferring the methodologies derived from the art and craft of translation to the interpretation of literary texts. The interpreter emulates the author's intensity through an intense form of recreation. At times the pleasures derived from the interpretive act can equal the pleasures experienced by the original writer/artist.

As the translation methodologies change our way of approaching the practice of interpretation, they also innovate our research attitudes. Translation research is always based on the necessity to solve problems. That problem-solving capacity requires that research be anchored each time in the necessity of the actual moment in the text. Translators don't bring anything to the text; they evolve everything from the text. The recurring question remains: what research is necessary to respond to the difficulties encountered in a work? All efforts of defining the course of research thinking are generated from the need of the actual textual situation that the translator has to face. Furthermore, based on the need of a particular moment in the text, the translator's research procedures and tactics will always be of an interdisciplinary nature. The exploration of a word or a situation frequently takes the translator beyond the boundaries of one discipline. In that sense, translation methods can be considered a revitalizing power not only in the literary field but also in the entire spectrum of humanistic and artistic interpretation. The methodologies of translation can be used as a dynamic process that engages the reader or the viewer and listener in a more intense "experience" of the artistic work.

INTERPRETING AND CONFERENCE TRANSLATION

Translating for International Conferences

Huang Jianhua
Guangzhou Institute of Foreign Languages
Guangzhou, China

What Kind of Work Does a Conference Translator Do?

In principle, a conference translator works for international organizations, such as the following:

1. The United Nations Organization and its special agencies, e.g., ILO (International Labour Organization), IMF (International Monetary Fund), FAO (Food and Agricultural Organization of the United Nations), WHO (World Health Organization), etc.
2. Governmental organizations, such as EEC (European Economic Community), EURATOM (European Atomic Energy Community), OAU (Organization of African Unity), etc.
3. Non-governmental organizations, which are almost innumerable, such as PEN (International Association of Poets, Playwrights, Editors and Novelists), IUA (International Union of Architects), INSEA (International Society for Education through Art), etc.

"Conference translator" is a general term for four categories of personnel with different responsibilities:

1. The conference translator proper, who translates foreign language documents into his own native language.

2. The editor, who oversees the presentation of texts and is responsible for having them printed.

3. The précis writer, who takes notes during sessions and produces minutes of the proceedings.

4. The reviser, who checks the work of the three categories above, ensuring co-ordination, and especially revises translations into his mother tongue of conference documents written in a foreign language from the point of view of faithfulness to the original and accuracy of terminology. Moreover, certain translators even take upon themselves the work of terminologists.

Linguistic Combinations for a Conference Translator

As for language used in the United Nations, there is an agreement that the six following languages can be used as official languages of the main organizations in the system of U.N. agencies. They are: Arabic, Chinese, English, French, Russian and Spanish. But the working languages at their headquarters are usually English and French. Generally, the number of languages used in an international organization depends on the needs of its membership. But for a conference translator three languages are almost indispensable:

1. Language A, his native language;
2. Language B, his first foreign language, the "active" one that he can read, write and speak nearly as well as his mother tongue.
3. Language C, his second foreign language, the "passive" one from which he can translate into his native language.

As for a Chinese translator, his mother tongue is, of course, the Chinese language, and he can take English or French as his first foreign language. But at the moment, none of the other languages listed is rated as the first foreign language for a Chinese translator.

Qualities a Chinese Translator Should Have

Emphasis should be put upon the following points for a Chinese translator who takes English as his first foreign language.

1. An excellent command of modern Chinese, preferably the standard Chinese used in the People's Republic of China, which is understood by the Chinese who live in various countries and regions, and by overseas Chinese. The Chinese language used in China's

mainland and that used in other places differ to some degree in orthography, in vocabulary and in usage. For example, simplified Chinese characters and their complex forms are not the same. We know that the English "Madam Thatcher" is translated as 柴契爾 in Taiwan, and 戴卓爾 in Hong Kong, but 撒切爾 in the People's Republic of China. Differences often occur with classifiers (measure words), e.g. in expressing "one school", the people in Beijing say *yi suo* 一所 , but *yi jian* 一間 is used in Hong Kong Cantonese.

2. Good and wide knowledge of languages. Besides English, a Chinese translator should also understand one more tongue as his second foreign language, such as French, Russian, Spanish, or Arabic.

3. A wide range of general knowledge. It is necessary to be quite familiar with common knowledge in the area of international issues, particularly the background and current situation of those organizations for which a Chinese translator usually works.

4. High speed of translation, if it is required. Usually a Western translator should finish 7–8 standard pages daily, but at peak periods, there should be much more. As for a Chinese translator, he should normally complete at least 3–4 standard pages from English to Chinese. At peak periods, he must finish more than that. Sometimes, for certain document translations, a time limit is stipulated and no delay is permitted.

The qualifications mentioned above apply to all four kinds of "conference translator". Specifically, a précis writer must also have a quick mind and develop an ability to synthesize. He should retain the essential parts of a speech and drop its secondary points. Besides, he must have good comprehension of spoken English with different accents, because people working for international organizations come from various parts of the world. As for the editor, he should be very precise about details. Publications remain forever. Any mistakes or omissions, however minimal, will lower the prestige of the organization for which he works.

A big international organization sometimes creates its own terminology. In different organizations the same term is not necessarily to be translated in the same way. For example, "seminar" in English is rendered into French as "séminaire" at UNESCO, but sometimes French delegates prefer "table ronde" to "séminaire". At OIT, it is translated into "cercle d'étude", and at the Université de Genève it is just "cours". Other organizations, however, may use "stage d'étude". Thus, it is important to regard an expression from every point of view. If a temporary staff member has to work for various organizations alternatively, he must become familiar as soon as possible with the conventional terminology of each organization, and do his best to avoid any confusions.

The Organizing of Translation Services

In general, the set-up of translation services depends on the number of languages used in the organization and the amount of material to be translated. Normally, a large international organization has its own translating department, under which are translation sections for each language used, e.g. English section, French section, Chinese section, Russian section, etc. Each section has a section chief, a secretary and translators, the number of whom depends on the amount of work. As for the Chinese section, 50% of the translators take English as their first foreign language and 50% take French. The section chief and the secretary should have either English or French as their first foreign language. However, if the organization is located in an English-speaking country, it will be better if the section chief and the secretary have English as their first foreign language. It is often the case that every two translators share a reviser, i.e. every reviser is responsible for two translators' output. The reviser is responsible for any mistakes in translation. The translation department in some organizations has a staff member responsible for the translation of technical terminology; other organizations may set up a terminology section. The job of the editor or the précis writer is often done by the translator.

UNESCO's latest table of the functions and responsibilities of the reviser and the translator sums up a typical situation:

Functions and Responsibilities of a Reviser	Approx. % (Multiples of 5)
Under the supervision of the Head of the Section, the Reviser has the following functions and responsibilities:	
(1) Considering faithfulness to the original, the correctness of style, and the accuracy of terminology, revise Chinese translations and adaptations of documents or publications of documents or publications written (a) in French and (b) in English;	70%

Functions and Responsibilities of a Reviser	Approx. % (Multiples of 5)
(2) If need be, translate texts from one of the above mentioned languages into Chinese;	5%
(3) Provide for the editing of session reports written in Chinese;	5%
(4) Carry out various kinds of research in terminology and take part in the compiling for glossaries;	10%
(5) Play a role, through observations and advice, in the training of translators/editors;	5%
(6) Carry out any other tasks assigned by the Head of the Section: for example, evaluating translations, participating in reading committees, etc.	5%

(Based on the French version)

Functions and Responsibilities of a Translator	Approx. % (Multiples of 5)
Under the supervision of the Head of the Section, the Translator has the following functions and responsibilities:	
(1) Translate into Chinese UNESCO documents and publications in English or French, either of a general or a technical nature;	65%
(2) If necessary, adapt documents written in one of the above mentioned languages for Chinese-speaking readers;	5%
(3) Write in Chinese analytic reports of meetings;	5%
(4) If need be, review or edit Chinese texts;	10%
(5) Should the occasion arise, translate Chinese texts into English or French;	5%
(6) Carry out various kinds of research work in terminology and take part in the compiling of glossaries;	5%
(7) Carry out any other tasks assigned by the Head of the Section.	5%

Reference

Adenis, J. "Le traducteur de conférence." *Traduire*, No. 53 (1976).

Interpreting

Y. P. Cheng
Member, AIIC
Hong Kong

Introduction

Interpretation is one of the oldest trades in the world and yet it has not been accorded its rightful status as a profession in many parts of the world. The main reason is that most people in the modern world are able to speak at least some foreign language and they tend to think that interpretation can in fact be done by people without proper training.

This is certainly not the case. Interpretation requires special and rigorous training and there is only one class of interpreters — the professionals. A "second-class" interpreter can cause more harm than good, since he who cannot facilitate communication cannot but hinder, if not disrupt, communication.

By definition, a professional interpreter is one who can provide interpretation in a conference either consecutively or simultaneously.

History of Conference Interpretation

Conference interpretation did not begin until after World War I, when the League of Nations came into being. At that time, only interpretations between English and French were necessary, and the only form of interpretation required at the League of Nations was consecutive interpretation, where the interpreter speaks after the original speaker finishes his speech or part of his speech. After World War II, when Nazi war criminals were tried at Nuremberg, simultaneous interpretation was formally introduced. This was because English, French, Russian and German were used for the trial, and the time factor made it virtually impossible to have every speech delivered in one language interpreted consecutively into the other three languages.

When the United Nations (UN) was set up, simultaneous interpretation was also adopted since there were five official languages — Chinese, English, French, Russian and Spanish, with Arabic added on later. However, for the sake of greater accuracy, consecutive interpretation was used in the Security Council for a long time before it was replaced by simultaneous interpretation.

Consecutive Interpretation

Consecutive interpretation is an easily misunderstood term. In its broad sense, any interpretation where the interpreter speaks "consecutively" after the original speaker can be considered consecutive interpretation. Thus, court interpretation, police interpretation, or even interpretation provided by a tourist guide, could be defined as consecutive interpretation.

In the professional and narrow sense of the term, however, consecutive interpretation is applied to situations where an interpreter, with or without taking notes (although most interpreters take notes, there are some who prefer to rely solely on their memory for large chunks of speech), can reproduce a speech of, in theory at least, any length in the other language.

In interpreter schools, consecutive interpretation is usually taught before simultaneous interpretation. This has led to the widespread misconception that consecutive interpretation is easier than simultaneous interpretation. However, most professional interpreters consider consecutive interpretation more demanding than simultaneous interpretation. In simultaneous interpretation, the interpreter has to transform the sound (the original speech) into idea, and then convert the idea back to sound (the interpretation) in another language. In consecutive interpretation, however, one more step is involved. The interpreter has to transform the sound into idea, the idea into notes, and later on convert the notes back to sound in another language. The whole process is therefore more complex.

An interpreter has to have a logical and analytical mind, good short-term memory, composure, broad general knowledge, and a firm grasp of the cultural background of the countries of his working languages.

And because of the demand for greater accuracy in consecutive interpretation, the interpreter has to have a highly developed sensitivity towards his working languages and the communicative situation. He must be alert to the nuances of the language, the slightest shift in tone, the inflexions, pauses, silence, etc.

Differences from Simultaneous Interpretation

Consecutive interpretation is different from simultaneous interpretation in the following areas:

1. consecutive interpretation is done without any equipment except perhaps a microphone and an amplifying system in cases where a large number of delegates are present, therefore it is less expensive;
2. consecutive interpretation provides better security if the meeting is closed-door as people outside the meeting room could pick up simultaneous interpretation signals if they really tried;
3. simultaneous interpretation is done "immediately" into the other language while consecutive interpretation is done at the end of a speech or part of the speech;
4. the speed of simultaneous interpretation is dictated by the speed of the original speaker while that of consecutive interpretation can be determined by the interpreter, within reason;
5. consecutive interpretation is considered to be more accurate than simultaneous interpretation, and that is why for important meetings, such as diplomatic negotiations, the summit meetings of the European Community, to name a few, consecutive interpretation is still used; and
6. a simultaneous interpreter works in a booth and is thus away from the limelight, while a consecutive interpreter works in front of the delegates and is very much part of the conference.

History of Conference Interpretation in Hong Kong

At the end of the 1960's, the people in Hong Kong, most of whom are ethnic Chinese, called for the use of Chinese in government business. The Government appointed a committee, The Chinese Language Committee, under the chairmanship of Kenneth Ping-fan Fung.

The Committee was set up to "examine the use of Chinese in official business and to advise on practicable ways and means by which the use of Chinese might be further extended." The Committee invited A.T. Pilley, an internationally known conference interpreter from Britain, to come to Hong Kong to advise the committee on whether it was possible to introduce simultaneous interpretation between languages as apparently different as

English and Cantonese, and whether there were people who could provide the service.

Pilley first visited Hong Kong in December 1970 and concluded that it was possible to introduce English-Cantonese simultaneous interpretation at the open meetings of the Legislative Council and the Urban Council, and later for other boards and committees with non-English speaking members, as part of the Government's bilingual policy.

The Committee drafted its first report, based on the recommendations of Pilley, and submitted it to the Government. The Government accepted the report and advertised both in Hong Kong and Britain to invite prospective candidates to apply for the post of Simultaneous Interpreters.

Recruitment exercises were conducted under the supervision of Pilley. As a result, one candidate from Britain was offered the post of Chief Interpreter (Simultaneous Interpretation), and three candidates, all of whom civil servants, were recruited as part-time Simultaneous Interpreters. The Simultaneous Interpretation Unit (later Section) was set up in April 1972, when the Chief Interpreter (Simultaneous Interpretation) took up his post.

The first occasion when simultaneous interpretation was officially used was on 18 October 1972, at the first sitting of the 1972/73 Legislative Council session.

Although consecutive interpretation has always been used by Court Interpreters and Police Interpreters in Hong Kong, simultaneous interpretation was the only form of interpretation at top Government level until the end of the 1970s, when there was a gradual thaw in the relationship between Hong Kong and the mainland of China.

A delegation from the Department of Posts and Telecommunications of Guangzhou visited Hong Kong in early 1976, and the then Chief Interpreter of the Hong Kong Government provided, for the first time at top Government level, consecutive interpretation for the Postmaster General.

After this, visits between Hong Kong on the one hand, and Guangzhou and Guangdong on the other, became more frequent. However, consecutive interpretation was needed only for such regional contacts. When Murray MacLehose, the then Governor, visited Beijing in 1982, he went with his advisers but no interpreters. It was not until 1982, when the then Financial Secretary, John Bremridge, led a Hong Kong delegation to Beijing, that interpreters were included in the team. And this has become the standard practice ever since.

In 1982, when Margaret Thatcher, the then British Prime Minister, visited Beijing and reached an agreement with the Chinese that the two sides should begin negotiations on the future of Hong Kong, the then Chief Interpreter was called upon to provide consecutive interpretation for the negotiations whenever necessary.

The substantive negotiations took 22 rounds to conclude, with an agreement to set up a Sino-British Joint Liaison Group and a Land Commission to deal with practical and residual matters for the transition period before China resumed its sovereignty on 1 July 1997.

The Hong Kong Government, foreseeing the heavy demand for consecutive interpretation for the Group and the Commission, set up a Putonghua Interpretation Pool (later Section) in 1985 under the Chinese Language Division, and selected a number of Chinese Language Officers (mostly translators then) with good Putonghua and an aptitude for interpretation to undergo a period of training before joining the Section. The Section has since expanded to an establishment of one Chief Conference Interpreter, three Chief Chinese Language Officers, five Senior Chinese Language Officers and four Chinese Language Officers I. They provide Putonghua consecutive interpretation for meetings of all levels between the British and Hong Kong governments on the one hand, and the Chinese government on the other, as well as top level visits between China and Britain.

Status of Consecutive Interpreters in Hong Kong

There are different types of interpreters within the Government. There are Police Interpreters, Court Interpreters, Chinese Language Officers with some duties of interpretation, Interpreters (Simultaneous Interpretation), and Chinese Language Officers posted to the Putonghua Interpretation Section. While simultaneous interpreters enjoy the status of "Professional Grade" (with Chief Interpreter at the rank of "Senior Professionals") in the Government hierarchy, consecutive interpreters are usually one grade below. The Chinese Language Officers posted to the Putonghua Interpretation Section enjoy the same status as simultaneous interpreters *de facto*.

Private Sector

In Hong Kong, the private sector offers AIIC (see below) rates for interpreters of professional standard. Most of the interpreters required, however, are simultaneous interpreters and not consecutive interpreters. This is because most firms would use one of their own staff with a good knowledge of both English and Chinese (Cantonese or Putonghua as the case may be) as an "interpreter" when necessary. These "interpreters" would accept the assignment as they are under the misconception that consecutive interpretation is easier to handle. This is still the usual practice. The case is different with simultaneous interpretation, though, since not many people without proper training would dare to take up such an assignment.

AIIC

The Association Internationale des Interprètes de Conférence (AIIC) is the internationally recognized association of conference interpreters. It is based in Geneva with a membership of over 2,000 as of 1991.

All AIIC members should be able to provide both consecutive and simultaneous interpretations.

AIIC sets both professional requirements and ethical standards for its members. It is also responsible for maintaining the professional standards of its members. A candidate has to have the endorsement of five members of the Association, and must have worked for at least 200 conference-days prior to admission as a full member.

AIIC also lays down the minimum remunerations for conference interpreters around the world, taking into consideration local costs of living and working environments. They also prescribe the basic standards of working conditions — size of the booths, number of interpreters required for specific language combinations, etc.

Training of Interpreters

The training of interpreters is a relatively new venture.

The first generation of professional interpreters were usually "born" instead of trained. Only in the last thirty years or so has interpretation been formally and systematically taught in institutes though even now there is some controversy on the trainability of interpreters.

Most institutes where interpretation is taught adopt the method best described as "master class" style. In consecutive interpretation training sessions, students take turns to interpret the speeches made by their classmates. The teacher and the class then comment on the interpreter's performance. Each speech usually lasts for three minutes. The theory behind it is that if someone can do a speech of three minutes, he can cope with a speech of practically any length.

The Polytechnic of Central London, the École Supérieure d'Interprètes et de Traducteurs (ESIT) in Paris and the École de Traduction et d'Interprétation (ETI) in Geneva all had, at one time or another, training programmes for Chinese interpreters. But after the People's Republic of China (PRC) and the UN reached an agreement which specified that only interpreters trained in the UN-sponsored training school set up in Beijing in the 1970's were acceptable for full-time employment as Chinese interpreters in the UN, these courses faded out gradually. At present, these institutes only conduct, on an *ad hoc* basis, programmes for a small number of trainees.

As of 1991, only three institutes outside the mainland of China and Hong Kong provide Chinese/English interpretation training: the Monterey Institute of International Studies (MIIS), Monterey, California; the Graduate Institute of Translation and Interpretation Studies (GITIS) in Taipei, Taiwan; and the Center for Interpretation and Translation Studies, University of Hawaii at Manoa. The Chinese programme in MIIS was first set up some thirty years ago and rejuvenated in 1986, while GITIS was set up in 1988. These two institutes offer programmes only at MA level while the University of Hawaii only offers an undergraduate course on interpretation and translation.

In China, the only target-oriented interpretation training programme is the UN Language Training Programme, established in late 1970's, under the Beijing Foreign Studies University. The programme is run jointly by the United Nations and the PRC. The graduates are sent to the UN for a period of, usually, three years.

In China, most "interpreters" are in fact desk officers of the relevant field with a good knowledge of Chinese and at least one foreign language. They are not "professional" in the sense that they work as interpreters only during a certain period of their career, after which they will return to their trained profession. Other than the media, only the Ministry of Foreign Affairs is known to have full-time translators and interpreters.

In Hong Kong itself, as from 1991, all tertiary institutes provide translation courses of one form or another, with different degrees of emphasis on interpretation. There are undergraduate and post-graduate degrees, as well as part-time and full-time courses.

With the impending arrival of 1997, by which time the sovereignty of Hong Kong is to be returned to China, Putonghua (Mandarin) is becoming increasingly important. Most of the tertiary institutes provide separate Putonghua courses for their translation and interpretation students, some compulsory, some elective. The fluency in Putonghua gives the graduates a wider job market.

With the rapid development in the training of interpretation, and with a great number of trained interpreters by 1997, Hong Kong could very well provide the necessary expertise in this field for China.

Simultaneous Interpreting

Pong Lam Shuk-lin
Willowdale, Canada

What is Simultaneous Interpretation?

Simultaneous interpretation refers to interpretation which is provided almost in step with the delivery of a speech. Simultaneous interpreters work from sound insulated booths. They listen to speeches or discussions through headphones, and simultaneously interpret by speaking into a microphone. Sound engineers working in a technicians' booth close by monitor and operate the simultaneous interpretation equipment to transmit the interpretation to receivers. Delegates can listen to interpretation in the language of their choice by tuning in to the appropriate channel in their receivers.

At multilingual conferences, interpretation can be provided at once into several languages by teams of interpreters using the relay method. This is at times necessary because interpreters may not have, as their working languages, one or more of the languages spoken at the conference. For example, in a meeting using English, Chinese and Spanish, interpreters working in English and Chinese may not be able to work into or from Spanish. The arrangement is for Spanish to be interpreted into a common, or pivot language, which in this scenario is English. The Chinese interpreters listen to the interpretation in English, and interpret simultaneously from English into Chinese. The reverse process will take place when Chinese is spoken. In this particular case relay will not be required when English is spoken. There is likely to be some loss in the total message passed on in relay, therefore this method is used only when absolutely necessary.

Consecutive versus Simultaneous Interpretation

Consecutive interpretation refers to interpretation which is provided by an interpreter who interprets after a speaker has spoken for up to a few minutes. This form of interpretation can take place in almost all types of meeting venues without the need for electronic equipment. Consecutive interpretation, however, will prolong meeting time. This is particularly so if interpretation is required into more than one language.

As mentioned above, simultaneous interpretation can be provided in several languages at the same time without prolonging meeting time. Provision of such service is dependent upon the availability of interpreters with the required language combination as well as simultaneous interpretation equipment well suited to the conference venue. In order to procure the best possible services, planning must be made well in advance for booking of interpreters and equipment.

In multilingual meetings, or meetings with a long agenda, simultaneous interpretation is usually used so that matters can be discussed and resolved expeditiously. In meetings or negotiations between heads of states or ministers, or in meetings of drafting committees, consecutive interpretation is the preferred mode. It is estimated that simultaneous interpretation is used in about 95% of meetings requiring interpretation.

Conference interpreter refers to an interpreter providing both consecutive and simultaneous interpretation at conferences, or to an interpreter rendering service in either of these two modes. Most conference interpreters work in both modes.

Simultaneous Interpreters' Booths and Equipment

Interpreters work in a team of at least two in a sound proof booth with glass windows directly facing the conference room. International standards have been adopted to enable interpreters to work effectively for several hours in a constricted environment. These are, among other things, an elevated booth with a good view of the conference room, a booth of adequate dimensions for interpreters to work in, adequate ventilation, comfortable humidity, suitable width and height of working table, optimum illumination, and comfortable chairs. Interpreters also need to have easy access to sound engineers so that defects with equipment can be remedied as soon as possible. They also require direct access from their booth to an area outside of the conference room so that they can obtain extra reference material or pick up papers which may have just become available.

A brief description of simultaneous interpretation equipment has been given. Broadly speaking, there are three types of simultaneous interpretation equipment:

(1) *Wired* — this is fixed equipment wired to provide for a pre-determined number of delegates. Once installed, it requires minimum setting up or dismantling before and after use. However, this type of equipment cannot be easily modified to accommodate more delegates.

(2) *Wireless* — Wireless equipment is more flexible and can be set up in a conference room easily. Equipment, once set up, can be moved around with minimum effort to accommodate subsequent changes in the setup of the conference room. However, this type of equipment is not used for closed door meetings, as it is possible for an outsider to listen in to the discussion by tuning in to the same frequency with a wireless receiver.

(3) *Infra-red* — this type of equipment offers the security lacking in wireless models. Its installation is flexible as more transmitters can be easily installed to accommodate a larger number of delegates. However, this type of equipment is not suited for use in rooms with direct sunlight, due to interference of the equipment's infra-red rays by infra-red rays of the sun. Too many pillars in the room will also hinder transmission.

Working Languages of Conference Interpreters

An interpreter's working languages can be classified into active and passive languages. In the active language category, the A language refers to the interpreter's mother tongue, or another language strictly equivalent to a mother tongue. The interpreter interprets into his A language from all his other working languages. The B language is a language into which the interpreter works from one or more of his other languages and which, though not a mother tongue, is a language of which he has perfect command. Some interpreters work into B languages in only one of the two modes of interpretation. The passive language is a language of which the interpreter has a complete understanding of and from which he interprets.

What is Effective Simultaneous Interpretation

Simultaneous interpreters listen, comprehend and interpret whilst at the same time repeating the same process for what is to follow. To be effective, they must be complete and accurate in their interpretation, and should convey sense and not just words. The interpretation should be a logical account of the original speech and should be delivered in the same register. It should flow smoothly and be easily intelligible. This means that the simultaneous interpreter has to interpret speeches of varying speed on a diversity of subjects. He has to exercise the greatest degree of concentration and be able to perform under great pressure.

As simultaneous interpretation is such a demanding task, rigorous training has to be given to those with demonstrated aptitude. Aside from training, adequate preparation before the meeting and team work by interpreters working at the same meeting are equally important. All these factors combined will ensure provision of effective interpretation which will greatly facilitate conference proceedings.

LANGUAGE TEACHING

Language Teaching and Translation

Tan Cheng Lim
English Language Proficiency Unit
National University of Singapore, Singapore

Introduction

In the past, discussion on translation and translation problems has mostly focused on approaches to translation, which include definitions of translation, theories of translation, controversies over literal translation and free translation, translatability and readability, and preservation and loss of original meanings. The views expressed tend to be overconcerned with problems in translating the Bible, literary works, cultural heritage, and psychological connotations of words and expressions. Few translation theorists have attempted to link translation (including translation problems and techniques) to language instruction (including teaching methods and instructional materials production), though works on analyses of errors on English compositions have often been tied up with language teaching pedagogy (Tan, 1989).

In the eyes of the present writer, *translation problems, translation techniques, and language instruction* need to be combined. Such a tie-up is, in fact, crucial, since translation problems are basically language problems and, according to Newmark (1969), "translation, like language-learning, is partly a discipline in applied linguistics; as a translator, one is a linguist before one is a scientist or a poet." This implies that a translator must possess good linguistic ability, without which he cannot become a good translator. Besides linguistic ability, it is also necessary for a translator to undergo some training so as to be really competent. "Training" includes the learning of translation techniques on the basis of target-language use. It should, however, be pointed out that translation techniques can by no means be separated from language ability, and that learning of translation techniques *per se* may not lead to success in translation if the translator is not competent in the target language. But if the translator already has a good command of the target language, translation techniques will stand him in good stead as added skills. Such techniques will help the translator make syntactic adjustments where the two language systems diverge. Translation techniques are not a substitute for language ability; they are in fact subservient to language ability.

This article will be devoted to three interrelated issues; that is, translation problems, translation techniques, and language instruction.

Translation Problems

The translation problems in this section are based on 200 Chinese-English translation exercises by Singapore secondary-school students of ethnically Chinese origin from one of the three types of high schools:

(1) English-language stream schools where English is taught as the first language and Chinese as the second language.
(2) Chinese-language stream schools where Chinese is taught as the first language and English as the second language.
(3) SAP (Special Assistance Plan) schools where both Chinese and English are taught at the first language level. All the participating students had at least ten years of formal school instruction in Chinese and English.

The 200 Chinese-English translation exercises were thoroughly analyzed according to the error-analysis procedures for the purpose of (1) comparing the frequency and percentage of syntactic errors, vocabulary errors, and semantic errors; (2) comparing the frequency and percentage of various aspects of syntactic errors, vocabulary errors, and semantic errors; and (3) explaining each type of error with illustrations from error-laden sentences.

The analysis shows that, of the three types of translation errors, syntactic errors are the largest in number: 1682 items, or 55.84%, out of all the errors made. Vocabulary errors and semantic errors are about the same: 660

items, or 21.91%, and 670 items, or 22.25%, respectively. The combined numbers of vocabulary and semantic errors are 44.16% as opposed to 55.84% of syntactic errors. This indicates that, though the major problem of Chinese-English translation comes from errors in English syntactic structure, the problems arising from vocabulary and semantic errors, separately or in combination, are of no less gravity.

For syntactic errors, the main difficulty arises from misuses, which consist of 908 items, or 53.98%, of the total number of syntactic errors made. Another difficulty comes from omissions, which consist of 433 items, or 25.74%, followed by awkwardness, with 189 items, or 11.24%, and redundancies comprising 152 items, or 9.04%.

For vocabulary errors, they almost all come from the use of inappropriate words or expressions, consisting of 642 items, or 97.28%, out of all the vocabulary errors found. Only 18 items, or 2.72%, are nonsensical.

In the realm of semantic deviations, wrong interpretations of meanings or total misinterpretations account for 380 items, or 56.72%, as opposed to 290 items, or 43.28%, arising from meanings which are modified or partially misinterpreted.

Problems in translation, as shown by the errors above, boil down to two areas: (1) comprehension and (2) expression. The comprehension problem is mainly caused by semantic errors and partially by vocabulary errors. Semantic errors can be subdivided into two types. One is the complete misunderstanding or non-understanding of the original meaning. The other one is the partial misunderstanding or inadequate understanding of the original meaning. As a result, the meaning is modified or twisted. At times, it is inflated; at other times, it is subdued; at still other times, it is concocted. The expression problem is due to syntactic and vocabulary errors. Like syntactic errors in compositions, syntactic errors in translation are varied and numerous. They are categorized under four headings: omissions, redundancies, misuses, and awkwardness.

The comprehension problem arises from an inadequate knowledge of the source language, including its syntactic structure, vocabulary, and rhetorical features. The expression problem stems from a lack of understanding of differences between the source language and the target language. From these language inadequacies and deficiencies come 1. the interference from the source language; 2. the confusion from the target language; 3. the failure to use suitable translation techniques to help resolve the expression problem pertaining to 1 or 2 or both 1 and 2.

The sources of interference from Chinese, particularly Chinese structure, are (1) Chinese has a system which is different from the English corresponding system in the deep structure; (2) Chinese has a system which is the same as the English counterpart in the deep structure but different from English in the surface structure; (3) Chinese has alternative forms for a certain system, but English has only one obligatory form or has different alternatives. The sources of confusion in English structures include (1) over-generalizations; (2) English has optional structures for a system, but Chinese has only one obligatory form.

Among the three Chinese articles chosen for translation by Singapore secondary-school students, the first one (about 300 words) is the longest and most difficult, the second one (about 130 words), the shortest and easiest, and the third one (about 290 words), second in length and level of difficulty. As a result, the first and third articles produced more problems than the second one. For the 300-word article, there are 41.70% syntactic errors, 58.22% vocabulary errors, and 53.06% semantic errors. For the 290-word article, there are 33.00% syntactic errors, 21.65% vocabulary errors, and 24.52% semantic errors. For the 130-word article, there are only 25.30% syntactic errors, 20.13% vocabulary errors, and 22.42% semantic errors. (Note that syntactic errors include omissions, redundancies, misuses, and awkwardness. Vocabulary errors include wrong and nonsensical words. Semantic errors include wrong and modified meanings.)

Problems in structures were also substantiated by the 200 English-Chinese translation works by the same group of students (i.e. those doing the Chinese-English translation from which the results have just been given above.) The statistical breakdown of the 200 English-Chinese translation works is summarized below:

Like Chinese-English translation, syntactic errors in English-Chinese translation are the largest in number; i.e. 1203 items, or 43.05%, out of all the errors found, followed by semantic errors, which account for 920 items, or 32.91%, and vocabulary errors, which come to 672 items, or 24.04%.

This is a clear indication that the fundamental problem in English-Chinese translation is, like Chinese-English translation, caused by an inability or inadequate ability to use the structure and vocabulary of the target language, which constitutes the "expression" component of rendition. However, the problem posed by misunderstanding or inadequate understanding of the structure and vocabulary of the source language, which constitutes the "comprehension" component of rendition, can by no means be lightly treated or deliberately ignored.

Apart from the above evidence, the findings are further validated by 100 Chinese-English translation assignments by ten first-year students at the National University of Singapore (NUS). These ten students were majoring in Chinese Studies and at the same time taking an English proficiency course at the English Language Proficiency Unit. The analysis of their translation assignments gives the following results:

Syntactic errors: 431 items, or 69.40% out of all the errors, of which 202 items are misuses, 138 items are awkwardness in sentence constructions, 71 items are omissions, and 20 items are redundancies. Vocabulary errors: 145 items, or 23.35%. Semantic errors: 45 items, or 7.25%.

The results reveal very few semantic errors. Hence there are no serious "comprehension" problems. However, the "expression" problem of the undergraduates is as serious as that of the secondary-school students. This is proved by the great number of errors in syntax and vocabulary in English; i.e. 576 items out of 621 items, or 92.75%, out of all the translation errors detected.

Translation Techniques

This section recommends some useful techniques of translation for resolving the expression problem in Chinese-English and English-Chinese translation.

The translation techniques recommended are addition, subtraction, and alteration.

"Addition" means the supplying of syntactic element(s) to the sentence of the target language to make it structurally better or semantically more explicit or both. "Add to the target language words which do not exist in the form but in the meaning of the original" (Lin, 1981). "It is important," says Nida (1964) "to recognize that there has been no actual adding to the semantic content of the message, for these additions consist essentially in making explicit what is implicit in the source language text."

Words can thus be added to increase the fluency of an expression, but a meaning which does not exist in the original content cannot be added. Translation which deviates from the original content is no longer translation but composition. Such a translation work is a breach of fidelity, and a breach of fidelity is a taboo in translation.

In the Chinese-English translation works analyzed, some syntactic elements were omitted because of the carelessness of the translators. Others were left out because the translators were not sure of the meanings of those items, especially content words like nouns, verbs and adjectives, and phrases and clauses. However, words which are syntactically or grammatically required for the target language have also been found missing. For example, the article "a" and the verb "be" are missing from (1) and (2) below; they should be added: (1) "You will realize whether you are in *a* high or low position." (2) "You will know about your position and *be* able to choose the good path." Other areas where the addition technique is often required include "the conjunction, pronoun, subject, object, etc ...," as in (3) 房裡有五、六個人 "There are five *or* six persons in the room." (4) 一天天的冷了 "*It* is getting colder every day." (5) 中文是一種有用的語文，必需學習 "Chinese is a useful language. *We* must learn *it*."

Diametrically opposed to the addition technique is the "subtraction" technique.

Some syntactic elements are necessary and indispensable and cannot be omitted in English but are deemed superfluous and can be omitted in Chinese. On the other hand, some other syntactic elements are necessary and indispensable and cannot be omitted in Chinese but are considered unnecessary and useless and can be omitted in English. English articles "a, an, the" serve as a good case in point. Though vital in English, they are almost non-existent in Chinese. Conversely, there are structural particles in Chinese which have no English counterparts.

In Chinese-English and English-Chinese translation, it is therefore necessary to note that a syntactic element which can be omitted is better omitted through the subtraction technique. "Subtraction" is to omit whatever is not necessary in translation or leave out whatever may be detrimental to the language habit of the language translated into. However, "subtraction" does not mean taking away some of the thought content in the original.

Theoretically, words or other syntactic elements added to English in Chinese-English translation under the "addition" technique may be deducted from Chinese in the English-Chinese translation through the "subtraction" technique, and vice-versa. For instance, the "subtraction" technique is usually applied to those circumstances where English nouns, verbs, connectives, subjects, objects, or even larger units of syntactic elements are not syntactically required, as in: 那是暫時的現象 "That is only transient," where the noun "phenomenon" 現象 is deleted. 家貧出孝子，國亂顯忠臣 "Dutiful children are found in poor families, loyal statesmen in a troubled nation," where the verb "are produced" 顯 has disappeared. 他雖然用功，但是不聰明 "Though he is diligent, he is not intelligent," where the conjunction "but" 但是 is obligatorily dropped.

In addition to "addition" and "subtraction" techniques, the third type of translation technique is the "alteration" technique.

An English sentence may be very long, complicated, and fraught with modifying elements at word, phrasal and clausal levels. Such an English sentence has been compared to "a towering tree overgrown with leaves and branches." A Chinese sentence may be long too, but it is long in a different way. First, it is made up of a string of short sentences, one following another according to the proper word order and a logical semantic sequence. Hence a long sentence in Chinese is likened to "a vast expanse of blue water surging forward." It has also been described as "a bamboo stick with one joint following another joint," as opposed to an English sentence which looks like "a bunch of grapes with some small ones surrounding the big one." In short, English syntax is hypotactical, i.e. the sentence construction is mainly through formal markers like prepositions and connectives, resulting in syntactic preciseness; Chinese sentence structure is paratactical, i.e. the sentence construction is mainly through word order, logical sequencing of elements, resulting in syntactic conciseness.

In the face of syntactic differences between Chinese and English, it is almost impossible to translate either English sentences into Chinese or Chinese sentences into English without making appropriate syntactic adjustments by means of the "alteration" technique, which, like "addition" and "subtraction" techniques, helps solve the expression problem in the target language. For instance, the word order of English is more flexible than that of Chinese. It is therefore necessary to pay attention to the differences in word order between these two languages. Hence the need for inverting specific syntactic elements, converting word classes, transforming different types of phrases and clauses, and restructuring long, complicated sentences by dint of the "alteration technique".

The three techniques of translation — addition, subtraction, and alteration — are complementary. They free the translator from the bonds of peculiarities of the source language and help him say accurately what is said in the target language. It is, however, important to note that there should be no misinterpretation of the original author. As to the individual items used in the reproduction, nobody checks whether they correspond to the original text in specific syntactic elements, word classes, or types of phrases and clauses.

The three translation techniques should therefore be carefully studied and employed. They are not mutually exclusive; they must not be taken separately, independent of other techniques. In translating Chinese into English and English into Chinese, the translator might sometimes be compelled to apply more than one technique to the same sentence at the same time.

Language Instruction

This section will first touch on the question of language teaching methods, then discuss the issues of instructional materials, and finally suggest the adoption of useful classroom activities with reference to the structure and vocabulary of English as the target language.

Structuralists view language learning as habit formation through stimulus and response, practice and reinforcement. Hence, they advocate the audio-lingual method for language teaching. Transformationalists, on the other hand, consider language learning as a kind of cognitive activity, involving the use of a limited number of language rules to generate an unlimited number of sentences to express ideas. As a result, they recommend the cognitive approach to language teaching, hoping to promote active expressive skills in addition to passive perceptive ability and achieve linguistic competence as well as linguistic performance.

Which is preferable, the audio-lingual method or the cognitive approach? Evidence shows that neither is perfect; both display certain inadequacies. Instead, classroom experience supports the advocacy of an eclectic approach involving the employment of various teaching techniques related to language instructional materials serving different purposes. For example, as most Chinese-English translation errors result from translators' inability to handle the structure and vocabulary of English, it is necessary to zero in on the error-prone areas of English structure and vocabulary and devise sufficient materials for constant practice. Specifically, practice materials for English structure should include (1) those which show differences between Chinese and English, as errors tend to surface because of negative transfer; (2) those which are liable to give rise to intralingual errors as a result of confusion in English itself; (3) those which are important for certain purposes but which the learner tries to avoid producing for one reason or another; and (4) those which indicate finer differentiations, as these may sometimes be very difficult to use. As for the materials for vocabulary practice, it is not enough to identify the word class to which a lexical item belongs; nor is it sufficient to explain the meaning a word possesses. It is important, among other things, to keep in view word collocations, which must be semantically congruous and structurally compatible in a sentence. Practice materials for word collocations are particularly important for Chinese students learning English and English-speaking students learning Chinese. The reason is that, while there are word-for-word equivalents between Chinese and English, there are more differences in word combinations between these two languages. In English, for instance, the same verb may be used with more than one noun, as in "to cut *grass*, to cut *the cake*, to cut *the finger-nails*, to cut *a tooth*, to cut *prices*, to cut *a stone figure*, to cut *a record*, etc." In Chinese, these nouns have to be used with different verbs: 割草、切蛋糕、剪指甲、出牙齒、減價、雕刻石像、灌唱片 . On the other hand, the same verb in Chinese may require different verbs in English for different noun collocations. Take the Chinese reduplicative verb 蕭蕭 for example. It may refer to the sound made by *the wind, the rain, the horse*, or *the tree*. In English, these sounds have to be expressed with different verbs. Hence: The wind *whistled*. The rain *pattered*. The horse *neighed*. The tree *rustled*. This type of vocabulary distinction has deep implications for Chinese-English and English-Chinese translation.

With the guidelines for instructional materials decided, the final task left to be considered is the introduction of effective relevant exercises into the classroom.

As a rule, classroom exercises should, first and foremost, be orally done according to a few basic steps, such as repetition, substitution, transformation, and recombination. Repetition and substitution exercises reinforce the sentence patterns taught. Transformation and recombination exercises make the student rethink and re-express his/her thoughts in suitable forms. These oral activities should be accompanied by written practice with a view to better consolidating what has already been orally learned. It is at this stage that composition practice, starting from the guided type and ending in the free mode, assumes an important role. As an intermediary measure, the teacher may design other varied and lively written exercises, culminating, where possible, in Chinese-English translation practice aimed at promoting students' awareness of the similarities and differences between Chinese and English structures.

As misuses of vocabulary constitute a great problem in Chinese-English and English-Chinese translation, and as many language learners lay great stress on vocabulary and vocabulary learning (Tan, 1991), vocabulary exercises should also be made an integral part of English language learning. It is vital to include in an English language programme direct vocabulary teaching in addition to indirect vocabulary learning. Useful vocabulary exercises worthy of recommendation include these six types:

(1) *Guessing meanings of words in context*, e.g., "The power of the Tribune (one million people read it every day) is enormous." What could the thing that one million people read be if it is not a kind of publication? Since this thing attracts one million people, its power should be very great. In this case, the meaning of "enormous" has also become clear.

(2) *Analyzing word formation*, e.g., Fill in each blank with a word derived from the italicized word: "Talented people *innovate* methods and techniques which lead to more — in various fields manned by those with — ideas. (Ans. innovations; innovative.)

(3) *Determining meanings of words and expressions*, e.g., In each pair of sentences below, determine the meaning of the italicized word: "(a) After an *exhausting* search, the police found the missing boy. / (b) After an *exhaustive* search, the police found the missing boy." (Ans. (a) tiring; (b) thorough.)

(4) *Distinguishing the meanings and usage of confusing words*, e.g., Make a sentence with each verb in the pair to illustrate its meaning and usage: "prevent: avoid". (Ans. The rain *prevented* us from going out. / You must *avoid* keeping bad company.)

(5) *Increasing vocabulary by association*, e.g., List five idiomatic expressions related to the organ "eye". (Ans. keep an *eye* on someone, open one's *eyes* to something; see *eye* to *eye* with someone; close one's *eyes* to something; feast one's *eyes* on something.)

(6) *Word collocations*, e.g., Complete each sentence by choosing the most suitable item to fill each blank: "Some Asian ministers met to (make up, draw up, show up, pick up) a common (stronghold, strategy, consultation, setting) for their coming (confrontation,

deadlock, conference, truce) with the Western leaders." (Ans. draw up; strategy; conference.)

Based on the eclectic approach, drawing upon the techniques for analyzing and describing the target language with concentration on linguistic errors in translation, relying on the teacher's wide-ranging knowledge and cumulative experience, and getting the students to play an active role in the learning process, one can open up vast vistas for productive language instruction.

Reference

Lin, Weimin. "Conversion of Word Classes and Sentence Components in English-Chinese Translation of Scientific and Technical English." *Translators' Notes*, No. 2 (1982), pp. 39–43.

———. "On Scientific English and Translation." *Translators' Notes*, No. 5 (1981), pp. 16–21.

Newmark, Peter. *Approaches to Translation.* Oxford: Pergamon Press, 1981.

———. "Some Notes on Translation and Translators." *The Incorporated Linguist*, Vol. 8, No. 4 (1969), pp. 79–85.

Nida, Eugene A. *Toward a Science of Translating.* Leiden: E. J. Brill, 1964.

——— and Charles R. Taber. *The Theory and Practice of Translation.* Leiden: E. J. Brill, 1969.

Tan, Cheng Lim. *English Checklist: A Glossary of Redundancies, Omissions, Misuses & Misinterpretations.* Singapore: EPB Publishers, 1989.

———. *Language and Translation.* Singapore: Hillview Publications, 1990.

———. *200 Hints on Practical English Structures.* Singapore: Hillview Publications, 1989.

Translation in Language Teaching

Francis Redvers Jones
Language Centre
University of Newcastle Upon Tyne, U.K.

Introduction

Translating and foreign language learning are closely linked. In order to translate, one needs to have learnt a second language. But is the reverse also true: in order to learn a second language, does one need to translate?

At first sight, it would appear so. Learners — even young children acquiring two "mother tongues" at once — often ask for and compare meanings across the two languages. Does this mean, however, that translation should be used in the *classroom* for teaching meaning? Even if it does, why use translation to teach the skills of communicating in the foreign language — is it not better to practise skills such as writing and speaking directly, without constantly referring to the mother tongue? And yet, is translation not a useful language skill in itself, and therefore one which needs practising?

These questions have been the subject of fierce debate among teachers and methodologists in recent years. Some see translation as the central activity of a language course, whereas others deny that it has any role to play whatsoever. Relatively few, however, take a middle position, arguing for a "modest but real" presence of translation in the syllabus.

Before continuing, I wish to establish a few key terms. Unless I state otherwise, I assume that "translation" includes "interpreting", in other words that it may involve either spoken or written mode, or a combination of the two. Moreover, I use "second" and "foreign" language interchangeably, and make no distinction between "learning" and "acquisition".

Two Philosophies of Language Learning

The status of translation in language-teaching methodology is closely linked to the status of the mother tongue in the language classroom.

Differing attitudes to the mother tongue result in two distinct approaches to classroom teaching.

Although second-language learning (by adolescents and adults, that is) and first-language acquisition are not exactly the same, many linguists see strong parallels between the two; also, it is a fact that the processes of translating between two languages are very different from the processes of speaking, writing, listening and reading within one language. As a result, a "monolingual" approach to classroom learning aims to teach the second language as a self-contained system, avoiding mother-tongue use where possible. Hence translation (sometimes even of target vocabulary) is excluded from the lesson: translating, it is claimed, does not only waste time which could be better spent on building up foreign-language skills, but translation's focus on accuracy and cross-language work might actually make it difficult to gain fluency in the foreign language.

A "bilingual" approach, by contrast, sees the mother tongue as a useful resource in the classroom. Lexical equivalents are often used as keys to meanings; also, translation exercises may be used for language practice. It is rarer, however, for translation to be taught for its own sake — i.e., in order for the students to become expert translators.

At the moment, monolingual approaches to language teaching seem to have the upper hand. It would be unwise, however, to view the recent successes of the "communicative approach" as signalling the final defeat of bilingual methods: the monolingual-bilingual debate has been going on for much longer than the last few decades, and is likely to continue in the future. The reason for this is that both sides base their arguments on questions not so much of educational fact, but rather of educational philosophy — such as whether more attention should be paid, in the early stages of learning, to fluency (monolingual approaches) or to accuracy (bilingual approaches); or whether we should see the successful student as a near-native speaker of the foreign language (monolingual approaches) or as someone highly skilled in more than one language, including his or her own (bilingual approaches).

The Historical View

In this section I take a brief look (largely from a British perspective) at the history of the relationship between translation and language teaching. This will give us a framework for looking more closely at the different roles which translation can play in language learning. For more detailed histories of language teaching, see Kelly (1969), Stern (1983) and Howatt (1984).

Early Times

Translation as a language-learning means — in Europe, at any rate — is largely unmentioned in ancient and medieval times, although it was briefly fashionable in the late Roman Empire (3rd century A.D.). It reappeared, however, in the late Middle Ages, becoming popular in Renaissance Europe:

> Translation is easy in the beginning for the scholar, and bringeth also much learning and great judgement to the master.
>
> Roger Ascham: *The Schoolmaster*, 1570 (quoted in Kelly, 1969)

At this period, the classical languages (Latin, Greek and Hebrew), as the vehicles of ancient culture, enjoyed much higher status than the "vernaculars" (modern languages such as French and English); moreover, only the classical languages had full grammatical analyses. This resulted in clear differences in classroom methodology: the classical languages preferred to concentrate on written text and grammatical/rhetorical form, whereas the teaching of the vernaculars was based much more on speaking and on real-life communicative needs.

Grammar-translation

As time progressed, however, grammars appeared for the major Western languages (the first for English were Johnson's and Wallace's grammars of 1640 and 1653 respectively), enabling study- and text-based approaches to be used in modern languages too.

The culmination of this process was the 19th century "grammar-translation" method, where grammatical rules (explained in the mother tongue) were practised through the written translation of contextless sentences; little — if any — attention was paid to the spoken language, or even to free writing activities. Translation-based methods — i.e., those where translation exercises form the control element of the course, whether or not grammar is the only area of language studied — have remained popular until the present day, although written translation is now usually supplemented by other exercise-types.

The remarkable survival of grammar-translation is not only due to whatever merits it may have. A major factor was the adoption of translation-based methods by 19th-century university modern-language departments, who were eager to make the study of their languages seem as rigorous and "scientific" as classical-language studies, which still enjoyed higher status.

The resulting dominance of translation did not stop at the university gates: through their control of state examination systems, universities have been (until very recently) the single most important influence on language teaching in secondary schools. In the People's Republic of China, for example, grammar-translation for the teaching of English in secondary and higher education was only replaced (by a more "communicative" approach) in the mid-1980s (《大學英語教學大綱》, 1985). In Britain, by contrast, with its less centralized education system, we now have the curious situation of translation-based methods no longer being used at secondary level, but surviving vigorously in most university modern-language departments.

The Reaction Against Translation

The first wave of opposition to the extreme "bilingualism" of grammar-translation came as early as the beginning of this century. In the so-called "reform" or "direct" methods (Jespersen, 1904), which could be seen as the direct ancestors of today's communicative methodologies, the foreign language became the means of classroom communication; meaning was demonstrated or explained (where possible) in the foreign language instead of being translated; and realistic — often spoken — practice took the place of written translation exercises.

The second challenger was the "audio-lingual" method, which gained world-wide popularity in the 1960s. Here translation — and all conscious attention to language structure, in fact — were rejected in favour of the repetition of sentence patterns until they became automatic.

The third wave, however — the so-called "functional" and "communicative" approaches of the late 1970s and 1980s — seems to have been the most successful in overturning the long dominance of translation. They claim that language is best learnt neither through translation nor through meaningless repetition, but through realistic use. In addition, the opening up of the science of linguistics in the same period has led to a much more complex analysis of what should be taught (Wilkins, 1976; Munby, 1978; 《大學英語教學大綱》, 1985): grammar, vocabulary and pronunciation have been joined by speech-act "functions", discourse, culture, and specific training in the skills of reading, writing, listening and speaking.

The only unchanging thing, however, both in life and in language teaching, is change itself: recent "post-communicative" approaches (Swan and Walter, 1984) are taking a more positive view of cognitive language study, and are beginning to see the mother tongue not as a handicap, but as a useful resource for the learner.

Translation, however, has not yet been rehabilitated, although there are signs that this process may be beginning: a small number of methodologists, for instance, have argued that translation skills should be re-integrated into the modern language syllabus. Even so, most methodologists assume that the genuine defects of the grammar-translation method somehow still justify the complete exclusion of translation from general language classes.

The Roles of Translation

Potentially, translation could be said to play three distinct roles in language learning:

1. as a key to the meaning of new items;
2. as a means of practising, learning and testing production or comprehension;
3. as a skill worth acquiring for its own sake.

In the following sections I examine each use in detail.

Translation as a Key to Meaning

Texts

A popular means of presenting new material is the "glossed text", where the foreign-language text has the mother-tongue equivalents written beneath each line (an "interlinear"), or where a mother-tongue "parallel text" is given alongside or below. The glossed text frequently takes the form of a dialogue, or "colloquy", which helpfully illustrates some aspect of the target culture. In medieval or Renaissance times the colloquy might have been about farming, for instance, or a conversation in an inn; nowadays it is more likely to be concerned with making a telephone call in Britain, or catching a bus in Beijing. The basic format, however, remains unchanged:

三、談語言

句子

21. 你是哪國人？

Which country are you from?

22. 我是法國人。

I'm a Frenchman.

23. 你會說英語嗎？

Can you speak English?

24. 我不會說英語。

No, I can't.

25. 你會不會中文？

Do you know Chinese? Or not?

26. 我會一點兒。

I know a little.

27. 你能看中文書嗎？

Can you read Chinese books?

(Zhang and Mao, 1984)

In the above dialogue, equivalence is assumed to be sentence for sentence rather than word for word. Word-for-word interlinears, by contrast — where each word is translated individually:

你會不會中文？

You know-not-know Chinese?

help understanding by making phrase and sentence construction transparent (indeed, the very strangeness of the resulting phrase may aid memorization!).

There is always a risk in word-for-word translating (both of texts and of individual items) that false parallels may be drawn — for example, the learner may be led to believe that 你 and "you" are exact equivalents. We must not forget, however, that most — if not all — language teachers are fully aware that not all items are translatable. Translation, therefore, is rarely used as the only means of illustrating meaning: hence the teacher or the textbook will put across the number/formality differences between 你好？, 您好？, 你們好？ and 老師好？ by explanation and/or demonstration.

Conversely, very few methodologies actively discourage student translation for explaining and recording purposes; by definition, however, "monolingual" methodologies do not see translation as the role of the coursebook or the teacher. The traditional reason for this view is that use of the mother tongue "interferes" with the establishment of second-language concepts, either because inappropriate concepts are transferred from the first language, or because using the mother tongue for classroom communication means wasting a valuable opportunity for the students to practise hearing and using the second language in a real communicative situation. Even so, banning mother-tongue use altogether can be very disconcerting for beginners, especially where the two languages (Chinese and English, for example) are very different in terms of script, vocabulary and/or grammar.

In recent years, however, a middle position has emerged: "equivalence-seeking" is becoming seen as a useful language-learning technique in its own right. Moreover, it is argued that equivalence-seeking (as opposed to being given the translations on a plate, as it were) also leads to more efficient learning. This is the rationale behind "linguistic problem-solving activities": one way of focussing on key vocabulary, for example, is to give students a list of 10 mother-tongue words and tell them to find the equivalents in a foreign-language text. As yet, however, few bilingual coursebooks use this activity-type, although monolingual problem-solving activities are quite common.

Lexical and Phrasal Meaning

As already mentioned, the meaning of words and phrases can be shown in various ways, of which translation is only one. Moreover, the student may obtain the meaning from various sources: from the teacher or the coursebook, from a dictionary (as the dictionary is a subject in its own right, I will not attempt to describe its use here); alternatively, an item's meaning may be clear from the context in which it is used.

One translation-based method of indicating lexical meaning is to use "occasional glosses" (in the margin or in the form of footnotes) to explain or translate certain items in a longer text. These, however, are more likely to be mentioned by the teacher and/or written in by the student than supplied by the textbook.

The translated vocabulary list is met in a wide range of coursebooks, including many which do not use translation exercises for learning purposes, such as *Chinese 300*:

    2. 法國 (專名) France

3. 會 (動) to be able to; to know how to do sth; can
4. 英文 (名) English
5. 一點兒 a little
6. 能 (助動) can; to be able to
7. 看 (動) to read; to look at
8. 中文 (名) Chinese
9. 書 (名) book

It would seem that most students have a deeply-felt need to study lexical items in isolation as well as using them in context; and once these items are focussed on consciously, students will almost always translate them, whether orally or in writing. Where the mainstream methodologies disagree once more is as to whether it is the coursebook's duty, or even the teacher's duty, to provide translations of new words.

Giving translated vocabulary lists is a problem if the coursebook is designed to be sold in many countries world-wide (as is often the case with English). One way of solving this is by listing target-language vocabulary only, and asking students to fill in their own mother-tongue equivalents (Swan and Walter, 1984).

Grammatical Meaning

Grammatical explanations follow a similar pattern. They may be supplied by the teacher, by the coursebook, or in a separate "grammar"; alternatively, the students can be encouraged to work out grammatical rules as a problem-solving exercise. Bilingual methods frequently provide word-for-word or structure-for-structure equivalents in the mother tongue:

4. The Direct Object always comes before the Indirect Object.
   In Chinese we say
   Give some money (Direct Obj.) to this man (Ind. Obj.).
   俾的錢呢個人
   Instead of
   Give this man some money.

(Chan, 1947)

As with vocabulary items, the student frequently translates a grammatical structure word-for-word into this mother tongue in order to establish or confirm its meaning — even if the teacher or the coursebook has given a foreign-language explanation.

Contrastive analysis of grammatical patterns (comparing structures, rather than translating their contents word for word) has been applied to language teaching at various periods since the Renaissance, although it has rarely played a central role in methodology. Even in "monolingual" methods, the teacher may well compare mother-tongue and foreign-language patterns where appropriate, although she will probably not provide full translation equivalents.

Discourse meaning

Discourse structure seems a very recent concern, its adoption into the language-teaching syllabus coinciding with the growth of communicative methodology. Parallel texts, however, have existed for hundreds of years; by giving idiomatic and stylistic equivalents (instead of word-for-word translations), they manage to illustrate low-level discourse rules, such as the use of "conversational formulae":

3. 你身體好嗎?
   How are you?
4. 很好。
   Very well, thank you.

(Zhang and Mao, 1984)

Word-for-word translation or contrastive discussion may also be used to explain higher-level discourse differences, such as the differences in "politeness" between Chinese and English, or differences in the way that arguments are structured (for further details, see Kaplan, 1972 and Young, 1982). Usually, however, this information is supplied by the teacher rather the coursebook, and thus depends on the individual teacher's knowledge and insight into the cultural and discourse differences between the two languages.

Translation for Language Practice, Learning and Testing

Word-lists

Translated word-lists do not only demonstrate lexical meaning; they can also help in recording, memorizing and testing new vocabulary. Recent approaches stress the fact that it makes more language-learning sense for the learner to assemble the lists her — or himself, and to choose between alphabetical, thematic and lesson-based methods of ordering the items; moreover, translation equivalents should be supplemented by examples of first-language use in context.

It is arguable that word-lists are most useful for learning vocabulary in the early stages of learning, and that monolingual methods (such as extensive listening and reading) become more effective at later stages, when learners are more able to cope with authentic texts and real-life interaction — especially as the latter seems much more fun!

Sentences

During the 19th-century heyday of the grammar-translation method, exercises at all but advanced level consisted of the *translation of isolated, specially-constructed sentences*, which were designed to focus closely on grammatical structure. Although factors such as context or discourse-structure were ignored, grammar-translation did in fact also lay a great deal of emphasis on the acquisition of basic vocabulary, as a glance at primers like *Colloquial Chinese* (Whymant, 1922) will show.

Texts

Translating into the foreign language has long been considered a useful means of learning how to write in the foreign language; it is rarely used as a means of teaching speaking, however. In the early stages, the texts — or, more usually, sentences — tend to be specially constructed; at advanced levels, authentic literary or journalistic texts are more common (or rather, extracts from such texts: translations longer than a page or so are rare).

We see a similar picture with translating into the mother tongue. As it aims to test reading comprehension, the accent has traditionally been on faithfulness to source text structures. Any target-text creativity is usually kept to a minimum: hence almost all translation is of prose texts. The translation of poetry fell out of favour early in the 19th century, when grammar-translation chose to ignore high-level rhetorical structures, and has not yet come back into general fashion (Jones, 1990).

Written translation classes — especially at university level — may also be supplemented by classes in oral interpreting (Altman, 1987; Keith and Mason, 1986). Although some would claim that interpreting exercises help the development of general speaking and listening skills, most teachers would justify these classes in terms of training the skills of oral translation itself.

Translation was widely used in Renaissance Europe to teach rhetoric — what we would now call "discourse" or "textual structure" (such as how to introduce a topic, or how to persuade an audience.) Although grammar-translation methods did introduce real texts (usually of a literary nature) at advanced level, factors such as discourse and context were still ignored: what was still important was to demonstrate one's knowledge of vocabulary and grammar by translating as "literally" as possible. Textual structure only came back into the foreign-language syllabus in the 1970s, by which time translation was very much out of fashion among methodologists.

One of the greatest problems, in fact, in reintegrating translation into the language syllabus is that of the "Great Methodological Divide". On the one hand, most progressive methodologists deny any importance to transla-tion; on the other hand, most modern translation-based methods seem to ignore the far-reaching developments of the last twenty years in the fields of linguistics and language-teaching methodology — which only confirms modern methodologists' misgivings.

With modern translation-based methods, we only begin to see differ-ences from the traditional grammar-translation model at advanced level, as real texts take over from specially-constructed sentences. Although low-level equivalence of words and grammatical structures is still considered important, "stylistic appropriacy" is also taken into account. Moreover, translation exercises are usually supplemented by reading comprehension, written composition and (to a lesser extent) conversation activities — thus mirroring Renaissance rather than nineteenth century practice.

These changes, however, are hardly radical: translation-based methods still concentrate on sentence-level accuracy, with the text-level appropriacy usually coming a very poor second. A recent book of activities by Alan Duff (*Translation*, 1989) attempts to bridge the Great Divide by using translation exercises to explore textual and discourse structure in English. In the following exercise, for example, "literal" translation into the student's own language would almost certainly be inappropriate:

TASK SHEET B

Passive forms are very common in all kinds of materials designed for public information (signs, notices, regulations, etc.). Below are some of those most often seen. With a partner, look at the items in your task sheet and decide where you would be most likely to see each one (in a hotel, on a building site, on a public notice-board, etc.). Decide in each case what would be the usual wording for a similar sign or notice in your own culture. If a direct translation would be out of place, suggest a suitable equivalent.

1. Sorry — NO CREDIT *given*!
2. *Right of admission reserved.*
3. All payment by cheque *must be accompanied* by a valid banker's card.
4. All complaints *should be addressed in writing* to the manager.
5. TRESPASSERS *WILL BE PROSECUTED*.
6. NO PARKING AT ANY TIME — *Your car may be removed.*
7. If you have any complaint concerning this product *it should be returned*, together with your receipt, to the manufacturer.
8. Please check your change, as *mistakes cannot later be rectified.*

Duff's book also looks at a wide range of text types: this contrasts sharply with conventional advanced-translation texts, which, as already mentioned, are usually extracts from newspapers or literary works.

Evaluation

Studies (e.g., Evans, 1988) have shown advanced-level translation classes to be highly popular with students. Although one reason may be that such students have limited experience of other lesson-types, it cannot be denied that translating is a highly satisfying activity for many learners. Moreover, few activities make one pay quite as much attention to exactness of meaning as translation: in free speech or writing it is possible to avoid or paraphrase difficult items, but not in translation. This also means that word-for-word translation is easy to correct, thus explaining its popularity as a testing medium. This explains the popularity of translation exercises in self-study courses, where the student has no teacher to correct her during free speech or writing tasks.

The argument against translation as a means of teaching language, however, is a powerful one: it does little to teach fluent, free production and comprehension within the foreign language, even though most translation-based courses almost always aim to teach *monolingual* foreign-language skills. This, though, is more an argument against the *exclusive* use of translation as a learning means. There may well be a justification, in other words, for using translation as one of a number of language-study techniques.

Translation as Skill

"Communicative Skills" in Language Teaching

The notion of "language skill" is central to modern syllabus design. The division of language for teaching purposes into the four "basic skills" of reading, writing, listening and speaking is nothing new. In modern approaches, however, the separate skills are often split up into a number of "sub-skills" (e.g., for writing: handwriting, spelling, control of vocabulary and grammar, etc.). Alternatively, several different skills may be combined into realistic "integrated-skill" activities (e.g., reading a text, taking written notes on it, and then summarizing it orally in a seminar).

Practice is a central element in modern skills-based lessons, for it is felt that the most effective way of learning how to use a skill is to actually use it. As it is also generally accepted that the main purpose of language learning is to enable the learner to communicate in real-life situations, this practice should, where possible, be "communicative" — in other words, it should involve real communication. This is achieved by such means as communication gaps (where one student has information or opinions unknown to another), pair and small-group work (to increase practice-time per student), role-play (to practise dealing with language in a variety of styles and situations), etc.

Teaching Translation as a Communicative Skill

Translation can also be viewed as a communicative language skill. Recent translation theory (e.g., Stern, Hönig and Kussmaul, Lörscher, 1989) sees translation as a complex communicative act, where a text is interpreted, reshaped, and then used to create another.

There are other language activities besides translation itself which involve reshaping linguistic input to produce output. Moreover, many of these "language transfer activities" are already being practised in the foreign language classroom. These activities involve, for example, transfer of mode (e.g., from read input to spoken output, as in the note-taking activity mentioned above), or transfer of style (e.g., from formal input to colloquial output). At present, though, transfer of code ("translation proper", in other words) is rarely practised in general language classes. The fact that other transfer-types *are* being taught, however, indicates that code-transfer activities could easily be added to the range of "post-communicative" classroom activities — bringing back translation, in other words, need not mean bringing back grammar-translation, as many modern methodologists fear.

And there is evidence that translation is beginning to reappear. Duff, for example, uses recent models of language and of classroom organization (e.g., pair and group work) in his activities. Even so, Duff's exercises still remain traditional in some respects: communication is *about* translation, not *through* translation; and the mode is still only read text to written text, with a concentration on close equivalence of length, content and style.

Translation activities, however, as Tudor (1987) and a few others point out, can involve real communication; moreover (as in real life), change of code may be combined with change of mode and/or text-type. To give an example: a Hong Kong class may be divided into 2 groups, each hearing a different section of the BBC World Service news in English; each student then gets together with a partner from the other group to write a Chinese summary of the broadcast; they then check their summary against the full news broadcast.

Translation activities may also involve transfer of style: for example, a student gives a colloquial explanation of an official notice to a partner who pretends to be unable to read it (real communication would take place, of course, if the speaker does not let the listener see the notice!).

In addition, role-play can be used to explore different real-life uses of translation: for example, a sketch where two students play a Chinese customs officer and a Briton suspected of smuggling, with a third student having to "interpret" their attempts at communication.

In modern syllabus design practice, the amount of classroom attention given to a particular language area or skill is roughly equivalent to its perceived real-life usefulness. Translation is probably a skill which most students find useful to have, but which they will actually use only occasionally; this implies that translation deserves inclusion in general language syllabuses — but as a minor rather than a major skill element.

Translation as a Professional Skill

Most of the teachers and methodologists attempting to make links between modern classroom methodology and translation seem to be working in tertiary-level (college/university) modern-language departments. There appear to be two main reasons for this. Firstly, modern-language departments are slowly becoming aware of communicative, skills-based approaches, though most are reluctant to abandon translation — traditionally the central course element — completely.

Secondly, translating is an important career option for many tertiary-level students. Employers, however, often complain (Keith and Mason, 1986) that their new recruits are too concerned with translating "literally", and have too little experience of producing high-quality target text (in their mother tongues, of course) and of varying the text-type according to user needs (a summary to be circulated internally, for example, does not need to be of the same quality as advertising copy to promote the company).

As a result, many universities and colleges, instead of rejecting translation, are beginning to incorporate translator- and interpreter-training into their undergraduate modern-language courses, with attention being paid to different text-types, readership factors, and target-text quality. In most cases, however, professional translator-training is still left to specialist courses, often at post-graduate level.

Classroom Factors

English language teaching is widely acknowledged to have set the pace of methodological change for much of this century. Although there are more non-native than native teachers of English in the world, most published methodological works have been produced by native English speakers, often working with mixed-nationality classes in Britain or the United States. These are difficult circumstances for translation, and this fact has been a major influence on the "forgetting" of translation by modern methodologists.

Translation-as-skill, however, is perhaps the role of translation where it is least important that the teacher have expert knowledge of the students' mother tongue. As long as the teacher has at least a basic knowledge of the students' language and confidence in the students' mother-tongue judgement (Jones, 1990), then it is possible for rewarding activities to take place:

after all, he or she is teaching equivalence-seeking *skills* rather than the equivalents themselves. Even so, translation activities are inadvisable for classes where the teacher has very little knowledge of the mother tongue of some or all of his/her students.

Level of proficiency in the foreign language will affect the *length and complexity* of foreign-language texts used or produced, but need not restrict the *type* of activity — beginner and elementary students, in other words, can be encouraged to carry out a range of language-transfer activities using short, linguistically simple stretches of language. There is little justification for restricting translation to more advanced classes, as is sometimes proposed.

Direction of translation is a major classroom factor, for there is a great difference in difficulty between translating into and out of one's native tongue (Lam, 1991). Professional translators usually argue that one should only translate into one's mother tongue, which would seem to justify concentrating on this direction in the classroom, especially when there is a professional-training element to the course. In real life, however, one may frequently also have to translate out of one's mother tongue; hence there is a justification for including this direction in the syllabus as a translating "sub-skill". There is, however, the danger that translating into the foreign language, especially in writing, might get bogged down with problems of low-level target-text accuracy — problems which are probably better tackled by non-translation activities.

There are strong reasons for using the foreign language as the language of classroom communication. Translation activities, however, involve discussion of a mother-tongue text — for which it is more logical to use the mother-tongue. If translation is only a relatively minor element in the syllabus, however, and most non-translation activities are carried out in the foreign language, then mother-tongue use in translation activities is unlikely to cause much damage.

Conversely, when translator-training is seen as an important element of a language course, there are strong arguments for improving target-text quality by actually teaching mother-tongue production skills, as some institutions have realized (Keith and Mason, 1986). In language courses where translation is much less prominent, translation activities may still produce "spin-off" improvements in first-language skills: the attention to detail of form and meaning which is encouraged by many translation activities, applies to both source and target texts. In secondary schools this would seem to be a golden opportunity for greater cooperation between foreign-language and mother-tongue departments.

It is here, perhaps, where the reintroduction of translation has the most far-reaching implications for classroom practice (Jones, 1990), for it implies seeing language learning not as the adding on of isolated "language modules", but as a process of developing one's linguistic ability as a whole. But is this not, in the end, the ultimate aim of education — to develop not as a bundle of unrelated knowledges, but as a whole person?

References

Altman, H. Janet, ed. *Teaching Interpreting: Study and Practice*. London: Centre for Information on Language Teaching and Research, 1987.

Chan, Yeung Kwong. *Everybody's Cantonese*. Hong Kong: Chung Yuen Press, 1947.

《大學英語教學大綱》 (*The College English-Language Teaching Curriculum*). Beijing: Higher Education Press, 1985.

Duff, Alan. *Translation. Resource Books for Teachers*. Oxford: Oxford University Press, 1989.

Evans, Colin. *Language People: The Experience of Teaching and Learning Modern Languages in British Universities*. Milton Keynes: Open University Press, 1988.

Howatt, A.P.R. *A History of English Language Teaching*. Oxford: Oxford University Press, 1984.

Jespersen, Otto. *How to Teach a Foreign Language*. London: Routledge, 1904.

Johnson, Keith. *Communicative Syllabus Design and Methodology*. Oxford: Pergamon, 1982.

Jones, Francis R. "Star Goes Bananas: Learner, Translating and Text in the Language Classroom." In *University of East Anglia Papers in Linguistics, Special Issue: The Teaching of Translation 1990*, pp. 31–32.

Keith, Hugh and Ian Mason, eds. *Translation in the Modern Languages Degree*. London: Centre for Information on Language Teaching and Research, 1986.

Kelly, Louis G. *25 Centuries of Language Teaching*. Rowley, Massachusetts: Newbury House, 1969.

Lam, Jacqueline Kam Mei. "An Investigation into the Process of Translating Poetry from Chinese to English and Vice Versa, with Particular Emphasis on What Is on the Translator's Mind." Master's thesis, University of Exeter, 1991.

Lörscher, Wolfgang. "Models of the Translation Process: Claim and Reality." *Target*, Vol. 1, No. 1 (1989), pp. 43–68.

Munby, John. *Communicative Syllabus Design*. New York: Cambridge University Press, 1978.

Stern, H.H. *Fundamental Concepts of Language Teaching*. Oxford: Oxford University Press, 1983.

Swan, Michael and Catherine Walter. *The Cambridge English Course*. New York: Cambridge University Press, 1978.

Tudor, Ian. "Guidelines for the Communicative Use of Translation." *System*, Vol. 15, No. 3 (1987), pp. 365–71.

Whymant, A. Neville J. *Colloquial Chinese*. London: Kegan Paul, Trench and Trubner, 1922.

Wilkins, David A. *Notional Syllabuses*. Oxford: Oxford University Press, 1976.

Young, Susan. "Inscrutability Revisited." In *Language and Social Identity*, edited by John J. Gumperz. New York: Cambridge University Press, 1982.

Zhang, Yajun and Mao Chengdong, eds. *Chinese 300*. Beijing: Sinolingua, 1984.

LEXICOGRAPHY

Contrastive Textology, Bilingual Lexicography and Translation

Reinhard R. K. Hartmann
Language Centre
University of Exeter, Exeter, U.K.

Introduction

Contrastive textology (CT) in its numerous variant forms is a relatively new approach in general and applied linguistics aimed at combining comparative and textual studies. This article sketches the historical background of CT, its contemporary framework, and its relevance to two practical fields, bilingual lexicography and translation.

From very modest beginnings, CT has grown since the early 1980s into a lively specialization. However, because of its internal complexity, diverse orientations and conflicting methodologies it does not lend itself easily to overall reviews. Two such overviews that have been attempted are Volume 3 of the *Annual Review of Applied Linguistics*, edited by Robert Kaplan (1983), on the theme of "contrastive rhetoric", and the state-of-the-art article on "contrasting discourses" by Marie-Paule Pery-Woodley in *Language Teaching Abstracts* (1990). The former summarizes the position of the study of written discourse in English and a number of other languages, the latter surveys the literature as it relates to the teaching of writing in second-language acquisition. Both are thus applied in their vantage point, but they also give us an impression of the very wide range of theoretical stances taken, procedures employed, and languages covered.

There is still no comprehensive bibliography of CT, there are no introductory anthologies of writings on the subject, there is no single periodical devoted to it, and there has never been a conference dealing exclusively with contrastive textological topics. Some language pairs are better served than others.

"Contrastive textology" is only one of the terms used to designate this field. Other competing near-synonyms are:

> comparative stylistics (Jean-Paul Vinay, Alfred Malblanc);
> translation comparison (Mario Wandruszka, Werner Koller);
> contrastive rhetoric (Robert Kaplan, John Hinds);
> comparative discourse analysis (Henry Gleason, Juliane House);
> macrolinguistic contrastive analysis (Carl James, Tsao Feng-Fu);
> contrastive text linguistics (Nils Erik Enkvist, Aleksander Szwedek);
> contrastive pragmatics (Philip Riley, Charles Fillmore);
> cross-cultural discourse grammar (L.K. Jones, Robert Longacre);
> contrastive sociolinguistics (Karol Janicki, R.T. Scollon);
> study of translation shifts (Raymond van den Broeck, Kitty van Leuven-Zwart);
> writing across languages (Ulla Connor, Shirley Ostler);
> cross-language communication analysis (Kari Sajavaara, Jaakko Lehtonen);
> parallel text analysis (John Laffling, John Denton);
> etc.

History of CT

There is as yet no satisfactory historical account of the development of contrastive text studies inside (and outside) linguistics. In my own book *Contrastive Textology* (Hartmann, 1980) I tried to give a chronological outline, including some early pioneers.

It is unlikely that CT could have developed without the knowledge accumulated over many centuries in such fields as classical rhetoric, literary stylistics, and comparative-historical linguistics. Even before Saussure had laid the foundations of modern (general) linguistics, individual scholars showed an interest in the structural properties of texts and the adjustments necessary to translate them into other languages. As early as 1887 and 1912, Henri Weil and Irene Nye, for example, investigated intersentential links in major European languages, especially Latin. In the years between the two

World Wars, Charles Bally, Czech linguists and Russian formalists made important discoveries about stylistic and text typological contrasts between pairs of Romance, Germanic and Slavonic languages.

Not until contrastive analysis (after George Trager, Robert Lado and others) and discourse analysis (after Zellig Harris, Kenneth Pike and others) had been developed separately, was a convergence of these two traditions feasible. One of the first advocates of such a "comparative discourse analysis" was Henry Gleason who argued (in 1968:58) that

> ... we now have a framework that provides a better starting-point than any we have had before for systematic contrastive work. It allows us to focus on what may well prove to be the most interesting of all contrastive problems, the differences in the way connected discourse is organized and the way that organization is signalled to the hearer or reader.

This approach was adopted and adapted in Bible translation circles and the Summer Institute of Linguistics at various centres around the world (Longacre, Grimes, *et al.*) Another impetus came from "contrastive rhetoric". Robert Kaplan and others, especially in the EFL field, had noticed that languages differ markedly in their rhetorical conventions, and then argued that these culturally conditioned conventions are describable, learnable and (therefore) teachable. In their scene-setting essay for the Kaplan volume (1983:4), Diane Houghton and Michael Hoey stressed the need for and value of a contrastive approach to discourse:

> Contrastive rhetoric presupposes two kinds of inter-connected input — work on the development of a universal theory of discourse, and description of the written discourses of individual languages.

Towards the end of the 1970s and in the early 1980s, contrastive linguists regularly questioned the narrow microlinguistic perspective of classical contrastive analysis, and at the same time an emergent discourse and text linguistics began to address issues of "transphrastic" organization and "pragmatic" interaction (e.g., Fisiak, 84). Scholars like Mario Wandruszka in Austria and Rudolf Filipovic in Yugoslavia in addition contributed the idea of "parallel text" corpora, thus providing another indirect link with translation studies that had been anticipated many years previously by Vinay's "comparative stylistics".

Theory of CT

My own book *Contrastive Textology* (Hartmann, 1980) was intended as a first programmatic plea for a systematic synthesis of contrastive analysis and discourse analysis. It also raised some fundamental questions about the status of such a framework in relation to general, descriptive and applied linguistics — and other interdisciplinary areas — and speculated on its methods and its sub-divisions. CT was seen as a compound theory whose double purpose was (a) improved description of the linguistic facts of pairs of languages in contrast (and contact) and (b) improved problem-solving in practical domains such as translation, foreign-language teaching and bilingual lexicography.

Figure 1. A Framework for Contrastive Textology

General (comparative) Linguistics	text theory	← Semiotics (*et al.*)
Descriptive (differential) Linguistics	functions & settings ranks & levels forms & units	← Stylistics (*et al.*)
Applied (contrastive) Linguistics	lexicography translation	← Rhetoric (*et al.*)

(Contrastive Textology)

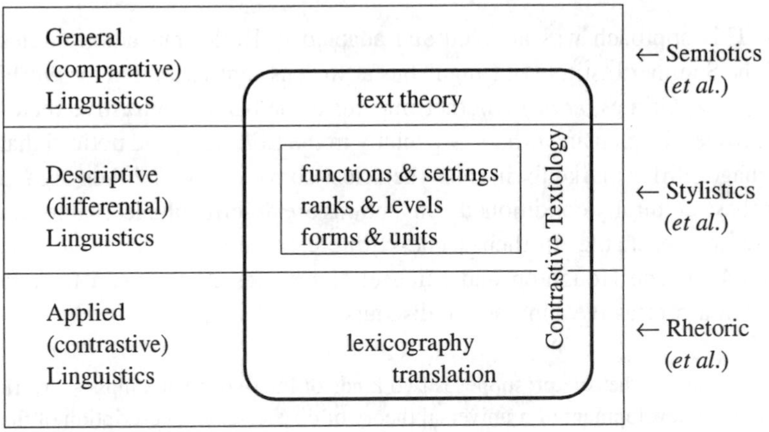

I start with the basic relationships represented in Figure 1. In the most abstract domain of General or Theoretical Linguistics, not only do we need a sufficiently well-developed theory of macrolinguistic organization to account for high-level discourse units from sentence to paragraph and text, embedded in communicative interaction, but also we have to develop a usable notion of "tertium comparationis" so that we can relate like with like. In the domain of Descriptive Linguistics, CT requires information on what the predominant patterns (forms and units, ranks and levels, functions and settings) are in the two languages to be compared, a desideratum that still eludes us for many pairs of languages, especially in the parallel descriptions of their respective varieties (styles, registers, dialects). In the domain of Applied Linguistics, the categories must be appropriate to the problem at hand, be it one of codification (lexicography) or remediation (translation).

What should be the sub-divisions or component parts of a CT? There are two possibilities: either a subject-specific framework which starts with the given concepts of a particular discipline, or a problem-oriented framework which works from a practical task towards appropriate models and solutions. There are many precedents for both subject-specific and problem-oriented approaches to CT. I will just select a few examples, and hint at their inherent limitations.

The obvious candidate for a subject-specific framework would be linguistics, a discipline that has made enormous progress in the last decades, especially in its "macrolinguistic" areas, notably the more sociologically oriented discourse analysis and the more logically based text linguistics. The frontiers have been pushed upwards, as it were, in a multi-layered structural model, from the lower, small and simple patterns (like phonemes and morphemes) to higher, larger and complex patterns (like idioms and sentences), so that a top-level textology has emerged in which such questions as inter-sentence cohesion and theme/rheme development can be addressed. However, it soon turned out that structural linguistic text models were too narrowly conceived and did not even admit facts that had been tackled, however inadequately, by traditional rhetoric and stylistics.

One important improvement to linguistic text models has come from semiotics. The three semiotic dimensions of semantics or paradigmatics, syntax or syntagmatics, and pragmatics (as formulated by philosophers like C.S. Pierce and Charles Morris) have led to a subdivision of textology into text semantics, text syntax and text pragmatics. The study of pragmatic factors has been particularly fruitful, allowing the integration of phenomena previously considered external to language, like "context", "genre" and "presupposition". However, it would be fair to admit that there are many conceptual and methodological difficulties that have not yet been overcome. It now looks as though the way out of the dilemma is through interdisciplinary collaboration with such disciplines as cognitive psychology, ethnomethodology and literary stylistics, especially if the focus is to be contrastive and cross-cultural.

Meanwhile, the problem-oriented view has also shown some promise. It would be impossible and unnecessary to provide a complete catalogue of practical issues that have led to contrastive textological studies and insights, but here is a select list from the fields of (literary) writing, (language) teaching and (bible) translation:

— What are the means available in different languages for anaphora and other forms of cross-reference in text?
— what are the appropriate conventions that guide stylistic variation and repetition?
— what are the signals that delimit successive discourse blocs?
— is theme/rheme progression different from text type to text type?
— what are the factors that govern register and genre ranges in different languages?
— are conversational gambits different in source and target language, and how can they be taught?
— how many learner's errors are due to textural contrasts?
— what are the factors contributing to or inhibiting text cohesion?
— are narrative story lines explicit or implicit?
— what shifts are required in translating particular texts?

Not all these have been explored in detail for all major language pairs (some are summarized, for example, by Michael Clyne for English and German, in the Kaplan 1983 volume). What such studies have in common is a concern for text as performance rather than competence, strategy rather than code, parole rather than langue, process rather than product, active rhetoric rather than passive stylistics, concrete discourse construction rather than abstract text grammar.

Recent Developments in CT

Let us recap. The CT paradigm had emerged in various forms by the end of the 1970s, and was ripe for development in the 1980s in two ways: either by consolidating its methodological apparatus as part of theoretical model-building, or by detailed studies of interlinguistic problem situations. The former was likely to produce elaborate static structures of potential sterility, the latter would risk remaining at the level of episodic engineering.

One mediating factor between the two extremes of discipline-based theoretical models and practical problem-solving efforts is the realization, already hinted at, that text-composition strategies are dynamic processes rather than static taxonomic systems. To illustrate this important point, I will draw on three research frontiers where we have seen influential innovative thinking in the last few years: interlanguage transfer, translation equivalence, and interlingual contact.

The study of "interlanguage" has revolutionized the whole field of language teaching methodology. Instead of naively assuming that a differential comparison of source and target languages will result in a list of interlingual contrasts as learning difficulties, we have come to accept (a) that it is the learner himself/herself who makes the transition from one to the other along an as yet ill-understood path, (b) that errors are not due only to interlingual differences, and (c) that progress depends on many factors over and above any contrasts between the two language systems. Errors are indirect evidence of and unavoidable stepping stones on the way individuals approach the target. The study of these positive transfer and negative interference strategies, notably in terms of text decoding and encoding skills, is therefore likely to be more useful than an abstract classification of micro-linguistic differences. From this vantage point, it seems reasonable for contrastive textologists to show an interest in the (variable) discourse production potential of native speakers as well as foreign-language learners. It is from this perspective of "writing strategies" that Houghton and Hoey (1983) and Péry-Woodley (1990) have reviewed the recent literature on contrastive rhetoric.

The study of "translation equivalence" is another instance where a more open and dynamic approach to comparative text analysis has led to significant new insights. The traditional notion of equivalence related words to their counterparts as corresponding formal units in parallel systems, a view that was strengthened by the apparent ease with which bilingual dictionaries can supply ready-made lexical equations for insertion into the appropriate portion of a text. However, the semantic abstraction that is built into the lexical inventory of the dictionary has deprived each of these words of their natural context, and the translator must compensate for the lack of contextual information from his/her own bilingual discourse competence. More recent research has stressed the approximative nature of these equivalence creation processes. From this vantage point, the contrastive textologist will want to go beyond the mere comparison of given parallel texts as translation products, and search instead for the actual code-switching processes that allowed the translator to "find" a suitable target-language equivalent. Again, we are faced not with static systems, but communicative strategies. I shall return to this theme, and contemporary literature (e.g., Hatim and Mason, 1990), later in this article.

The third source of new, more dynamic ideas for CT is the study of "interlingual contact", which includes bilingualism as well as language mixing in the form of pidginization and creolization. Indeed, the boundaries between interference in language learning, lexical borrowing, code-switching and translation are fluid; in all cases it is the individual (bilingual) speaker who brings about contact, change, or equivalence. From this vantage point, the contrastive textologist will have gained an awareness of the fact that similarities and differences between pairs of languages are not so much obtained from systematic comparisons of corresponding systems, but mediated by interlingual acts which can be skewed, unidirectional, unsymmetrical, multivalent and unpredictable.

Two more recent developments are worth reporting here: protocol analysis and computerized corpora. Both have come from outside the field. Protocol analysis is a technique for observing behaviour in action, developed in the social sciences. Computer corpora have become available as a result of developments in information technology, lexicography and descriptive linguistics. Together, these two techniques are likely to constitute powerful aids in contrastive textology, as they can provide data not available before on the composition and structure of spoken and written discourse.

Protocol analysis, in the form of either thinking-aloud records or diaries, is a method for charting mental processes not normally accessible to direct empirical observation. To overcome the "black-box" syndrome, some scholars (e.g., Hans-Peter Krings) have suggested that factual evidence on such linguistic activities as writing, translating, and dictionary use can be gathered by encouraging performers to verbalize their thoughts, recording them on tape and/or film, and transcribing the result in the form of protocols.

More indirect but comprehensive data can be collected from text corpora. The subject of corpus evidence has recently attracted the attention of linguists, translators, lexicographers and computer scientists, and several projects are on the way to provide large databases and concordances of literary and prose texts for English and other languages. If it were possible to build up parallel text corpora for two or more languages, then the old dream of automatic CT and interlingual equivalence creation would have come a step nearer. Several recent studies have demonstrated the viability of computer-aided parallel-text analysis for the purpose of finding translation equivalents.

A review of recent developments in CT would not be complete without at least hinting at some specific studies that have not reached the international limelight, but nevertheless contributed towards the trend of strengthening comparative discourse analysis. The 1991 Conference on "New Departures in Contrastive Linguistics" at Innsbruck was symptomatic in this respect. It not only reflected the general tendency towards CT as outlined above, but introduced a few new highlights. Most remarkable among these was the (re-)discovery of contrastive analysis for research into linguistic universals and typological comparison. More specific topics were politeness phenomena, conversational strategies and joking in pairs of languages, contrastive idiomatology and other phenomena requiring a CT perspective not previously investigated. Other areas not touched on at Innsbruck, but recently reported in periodicals, include the development of pragmatics in child language acquisition and what could be called "contrastive terminology".

Applications of CT in Translation and Lexicography

As will have become apparent by now, the potential applications of CT are legion. Of those that have been of particular interest to me, translation and bilingual lexicography deserve more detailed treatment here. One important caveat is perhaps in order. Both translation and lexicography are discourse-related practical fields which historically anticipated linguistic scholarship, indeed they could be said to have contributed a great deal to academic speculation on how language works and how interlingual comparison can be achieved in the first place. If it is true that linguistics owes as much to these language-based practices as they in turn depend on linguistic insights, we must recognize a "hermeneutic circle" between them; applied CT in this sense is only a small segment of that circle of very recent vintage. It amounts to an attempt to reinterpret translating and bilingual dictionary-making as exercises in CT, or as processes which can be better understood if they are viewed through the prism of CT.

In the give-and-take relationship between linguistic CT and practical translating, we need to allow for several complexities. For example, it is crucial whether we assume that the former is "discipline-specific" and the latter "problem-oriented" (see above), or whether we equate CT with static models and translation with dynamic processes. Such tensions are, of course, reflected in the theoretical and methodological tools that we may have at our disposal at a particular place or point in time: thus protocol analysis promises a more realistic approach to the facts of the translation process than any based merely on a taxonomy of the textual features of the product of the operation.

What we expect from CT is a framework that will not only specify the linguistic categories involved (as mentioned in Fig. 1 above), but also explain the mediating ability of the translator: what interlingual competence is needed to approximate the text conventions of source and target languages? Figure 2 provides a check-list of the components of the translator's code-switching competence.

In order to convert a source language text into a target language text, a translator needs to have the three basic skills of "decoding" (receiving the message intended by the sender in terms of the verbal units at various linguistic levels and/or the sign in various semiotic dimensions), "recoding" (finding translation equivalents in the target language for the units constituting the source-language message), and "encoding" (recasting the message in terms of the linguistic and/or semiotic conventions of the target language). None of these operations are straightforward, all are approximative processes depending on the code-switching skills and — at least to some extent — on the typological distance between the languages and cultures concerned. The most difficult is the re-coding phase, the crossing point at the border of languages where "equivalence" is established. (Psycholinguistic observation by introspective methods, e.g. think-aloud protocols, has shown these interlingual metaphrase processes to be akin to intralingual paraphrase processes.)

Recent scholarship has confirmed not only that textological contrasts are an important deciding factor in these interlingual approximation acts, but also that several constituent theories are still in need of refinement. Hatim and Mason (1990) give some examples of such theory deficits. They argue, inter alia, for a translation-specific view of text as communicative interaction (not composed of static structures, but evolving from dynamic discourse strategies), text as instance of language variety (not as static typologies of registers, but as dynamic ranges of variable genres), and text as a vehicle of culture (not as static semiotic systems, but as dynamic accounts of contact in action).

Similar observations can be made about the give-and-take relations

Figure 2. Translation as CT Approximation

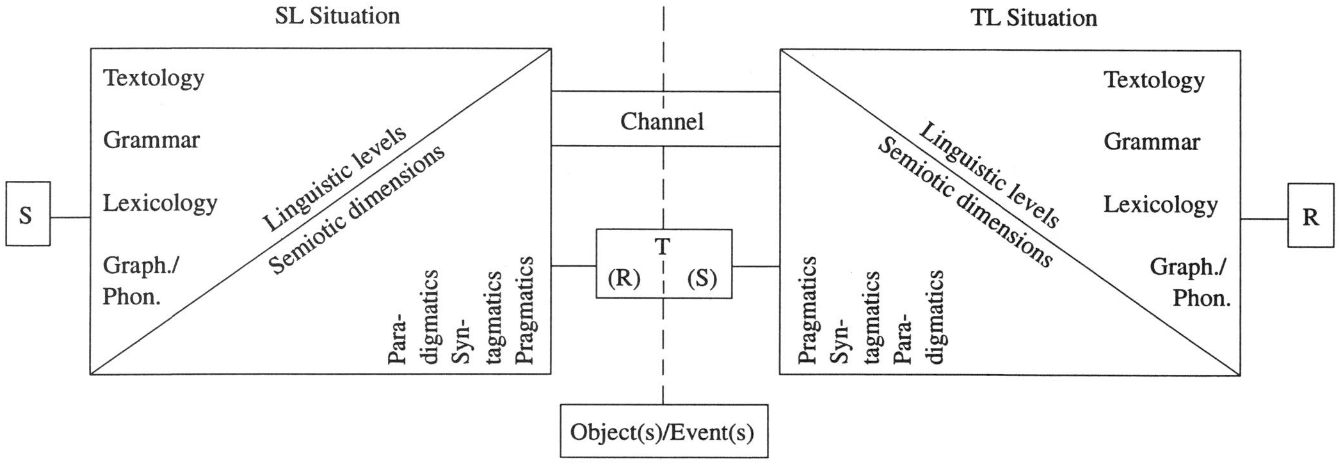

between CT and bilingual lexicography. (That there are indeed strong parallels between translation and lexicography, I have explored elsewhere in terms of the translator as user of dictionaries, on the one hand, and the lexicographer as user of translation, on the other.) Just as the contrastive textologist can provide insights of interest to the dictionary maker, bilingual dictionaries can often constitute a valuable source of data for CT. These two relations of applying knowledge and gathering facts obviously vary considerably from one language pair to another.

The question that has occupied some researchers is whether and how CT can be of help to bilingual lexicography. The obvious answer is that an analysis of parallel texts from any pair of languages could yield candidates for lexical equivalents to be codified in dictionaries, provided that these texts are selected in such a way that they are themselves "equivalent". A practical demonstration that this is a realistic aim has recently been given by John Laffling (forthcoming).

Laffling's detailed study of party political manifestos from Britain and Germany proved that it was possible, by computer-assisted matching of words and phrases in these parallel texts (which are independently composed, not the product of translation), to locate natural equivalents from corresponding genres that had not been listed before in bilingual dictionaries. Of the 7 collocations in the following list, only one, i.e. *Schichten*, appears in this form in one contemporary German-English dictionary, the *Collins/klett Grosswörterbuch*.

> politische Auseinandersetzung // political debate
> Bildungsangebot // educational provision
> Eigentumsstreuung // spread of ownership
> die offentlichen Haushalte // the public purse
> Not und Elend // misery and hardship
> Produktivvermögen // productive assets
> breite *Schichten* der Bevölkerung // large sections of the population

This application of CT to bilingual lexicography and, very recently, to machine translation and various artificial intelligence projects (where it takes the form of "parallel text concordances" or "bilingual text corpus retrieval") not only vindicates the viability of an idea (e.g., Hartmann, 1980), but also illustrates the long delay between the time of its first formulation and its eventual implementation by the means of computer technology.

Conclusion

CT is still in its infancy. However, in several of its theoretical versions and methodological manifestations, it promises us a realistic way of comparing discourse in pairs of languages.

CT has a place in general, descriptive and applied linguistics, where it offers a wider perspective for discourse-based interlingual research, especially if its proponents manage to move on from the more static models of linguistics and semiotics towards more dynamic frameworks which can explain the bilingual speaker's code-switching strategies.

Translation and bilingual lexicography are among the most likely beneficiaries of the application of CT to the solution of practical problems, although much remains still to be done. Introspective observation and computer technology are likely to play an increasingly important role, but inter-disciplinary and international collaboration must also be intensified in the future.

References

Clyne, Michael G. "Linguistics and Written Discourse in Particular Languages: English and German." In *Annual Review of Applied Linguistics*, Vol. 3, edited by Robert B. Kaplan. Rowley, MA: Newbury House/Cambridge University Press, 1983, pp. 38–49.

Fisiak, Jacek, ed. *Contrastive Linguistics. Prospects and Problems.* Trends in Linguistics, Studies and Monographs 22. Berlin: Mouton W. de Gruyter, 1984.

Gleason, Henry A. "Contrastive Analysis in Discourse Structure." In *Report of 19th Annual Round Table Meeting*, edited by J.E. Alatis. Washington D.C.: Georgetown University Press, 1968, pp. 39–63.

Hartmann, Reinhard R.K. *Contrastive Textology: Comparative Discourse Analysis in Applied Linguistics.* Studies in Descriptive Linguistics 5. Heidelberg: J. Groos, 1980.

Hatim, Basil and Ian Mason. *Discourse and the Translator.* London: Longman, 1990.

Houghton, Diane and Michael Hoey. "Linguistics and Written Discourse: Contrastive Rhetorics." In *Annual Review of Applied Linguistics*, Vol. 3, edited by Robert B. Kaplan. Rowley MA: Newbury House/Cambridge University Press, 1983, pp. 2–22.

Kaplan, Robert B., ed. *Annual Review of Applied Linguistics*, Vol. 3. Rowley, MA: Newbury House/Cambridge University Press, 1983.

Laffling, John. *Towards High-Precision Machine Translation — Based on Contrastive Textology*. Distributed Language Translation 7. Dordrecht: W. de Gruyter (forthcoming).

Péry-Woodley, Marie-Paule. "Contrasting Discourses: Contrastive Analysis and a Discourse Approach to Writing." *Language Teaching*, Vol. 23, No. 3 (1990), pp. 143–51.

Chinese-English Dictionaries

Wu Jingrong
Department of English
Foreign Affairs College, Beijing, China

A Historical Perspective

Bilingual dictionaries originate with cultural or language contacts between nations. In China, it was not until the late Qing period that Chinese-English dictionaries began to appear. The Western lexicographers who compiled these dictionaries, however, were no trained scholars and their works were often very crude. According to Jerry Norman,

> The dictionaries of Robert Morrison (1815–1823) and Walter Medhurst (1842–1843) were characterized by serious defects in indicating pronunciation. Morrison, for example, failed to distinguish aspirated and unaspirated stops, and Medhurst, although he recognized the distinction, often inserted aspiration marks in the wrong words. Samuel Williams' *Syllabic Dictionary of the Chinese Language* (1874) was apparently the first dictionary to get this distinction sorted out properly. (Norman, 1988)

Jerry Norman does not mention William Baller (1850–1922), who compiled his *Analytical Chinese-English Dictionary* along the same lines. William Baller and Herbert Giles were followed by R. H. Mathews whose *Chinese-English Dictionary* was first published by the China Inland Mission in 1931 and revised in 1956. This dictionary, as Jerry Norman describes, "scrambled together without differentiation words from the earliest texts of Chinese literature with contemporary neologisms." (Norman, 1988) As a matter of fact, this defect was shared by most or all of his predecessors; it stemmed from their superficial acquaintance with Chinese language and culture. For instance, no one would say anything like 同一火腿也，其美醜判若天淵 . (Giles, 1909) Indeed it was a kind of vernacular and literary mixture totally unacceptable to native speakers of Chinese. Let us cite more examples:

1. 面面相覷 is a simple, common phrase. 覷 and 觀 are of the same radical but different in structure. However, Giles mistook 觀 for 覷 and consequently 面面相覷 became "looking at one another." Baller who changed the character 觀 back to 覷 failed to restore the sense. The meaning of the phrase, as explained in the *Modern Chinese Dictionary* 《現代漢語詞典》 (Chinese Academy of Social Sciences, 1978), indicates a situation where one looks at the other in blank dismay or consternation.

2. 面首 is "male concubine". Giles misinterpreted 面首三十人 as meaning "thirty women with beautiful faces and hair." The phrase, moreover, is a free combination. Its inclusion as an entry is obviously inappropriate.

3. 豪舉 means a bold resolute move. But Baller gave "bullies, ruffians" as its equivalents.

4. 理屈詞窮 , which means "fall silent on finding oneself bested in argument," became "twist one's principle in order to finish an argument" in Mathews' dictionary. Mathews probably translated the idiom word for word: 理 (principle), 屈 (twist), 詞 (argument), 窮 (finish), and then shifted them around to work out this nonsensical version.

5. 沐猴而冠 is an idiom meaning "a monkey with a hat on." Giles' version was "a washed monkey with a hat on." Mathews' version was similar: "A monkey washed and dressed up — no sort of a man." 沐猴 does not mean "wash a monkey" or "a washed monkey." In fact, 沐猴 is a kind of monkey or just a monkey.

Apart from the problem of misinterpretation, these early lexicographers paid little attention to the selection of entries. In fact, their entries were mostly free combinations. It is sad to remember that for so many years translators at home and scholars abroad had sometimes to turn to these works to check up on an English version, as no Chinese-English dictionary of any importance ever emerged during the period to replace these dictionaries. Dr. Lin Yutang's 林語堂 *Chinese-English Dictionary of Modern Usage* 《當代漢英詞典》 (1972) was fairly comprehensive, but it failed to include many of the new words and expressions that had come into use in Chinese society. It is said that Dr. Lin deliberately excluded PRC terms from his work. If so, he was wrong, and Professor Liang Shiqiu 梁實秋 was much wiser. In his Introduction to *A Practical Chinese-English Dictionary* published in Taiwan in 1974, Professor Liang wrote: "Language being what it is, a lexicographer would be faulted for allowing his personal preference to influence his judgement in this respect."

Both Dr. Lin's and Professor Liang's dictionaries had certain obvious defects. First, they contained no illustrative examples, a fact which made them pale by comparison with many other Chinese-English dictionaries. Secondly, while Dr. Lin had an alphabetical system of his own which often proved frustrating for the users, Professor Liang arranged his entries according to the radicals, which was equally frustrating. Furthermore, Professor Liang used as a pronunciation guide the Mandarin Phonetic Symbols, which had become obsolete except in Taiwan. In New China, however, work on the Chinese-English dictionary, of which I was Editor-in-Chief, did not start until 1970. Fortunately, by that time Chinese linguists had not only worked out Pinyin, but also had a medium-sized dictionary ready for publication. This is very important, for the success or failure of a bilingual dictionary is often determined by the source language dictionaries available, their entries, equivalents and illustrative examples.

The Chinese-English Dictionary published by the Commercial Press in 1979 was the first of its kind to put Chinese bilingual lexicography on a relatively sound basis. As a matter of fact, since then no Chinese-English dictionary comparable in scope and thoroughness has been published. However, this Chinese-English dictionary is not entirely free from errors. The most glaring one is an excessive use of tendentious expressions by way of illustrative examples. A dictionary is not a political pamphlet, nor is the lexicographer a moralist.

Moreover, the dictionary suffers from inadequate attention to matters of principle in entry selection, apart from certain inaccuracies and omissions. 沉舟, for instance, has "sunken boat" for translation equivalent, but, it is nothing but a loose free combination. It cannot serve as an entry any more than 病樹 (withered tree) can. It is there merely for the sake of introducing the familiar lines of a Tang poem: 沉舟側畔千帆過，病樹前頭萬木春 (A thousand sails pass by the shipwreck; ten thousand saplings shoot up beyond the withered tree.) These two lines were fairly frequently quoted by writers of political articles in the seventies to show that the new forces were forging ahead while the old world was on the verge of disintegration.

Some explanations and equivalents offered in *The Chinese-English Dictionary* are incomplete or even inaccurate. 觥, for example, is explained as "an ancient wine vessel made of horn." This explanation is based on a definition given in *Ciyuan* 《辭源》, p. 2865. Presumably 觥 was made of horn in primitive times. However, in the Zhou Dynasty, another type of wine vessel made of bronze and in the shape of an animal was introduced, and in such authoritative dictionaries as *Cihai* 《辭海》, 觥 is simply defined as a kind of animal-shaped bronze wine vessel. In classical Chinese, moreover, 觥 is a measure term and is practically synonymous with any ordinary wine vessel. All this seems to have been left out. 戈, for another example, has "dagger-axe" as its equivalent, which is obviously inaccurate. 戈 was a double-edged, hook-like ancient weapon with a long shaft. "Dagger" or "axe" or "dagger" and "axe" put together do not resemble a long-handled weapon. And 菱 has three equivalents in *The Chinese-English Dictionary*: ling, water chestnut, water caltrop. In fact "water chestnut" should be deleted as it also appears as an equivalent of 荸薺.

Alphabetization and the Arrangement of Entries

In the *Modern Chinese Dictionary*, the entries are arranged in the order of Pinyin (the new phonetic alphabet) instead of using the Wade system or the radicals. Pinyin has standardized the transcriptions of all Chinese proper nouns with the exception of a few names such as Confucius 孔子, Mencius 孟子, Dr. Sun Yat-sen 孫逸仙, Madame Soong Ching-ling 宋慶齡, Chiang Kai-shek 蔣介石, Kuomintang 國民黨 and some others which remain unaffected for various reasons. Of course, Pinyin has its obvious advantages, but certain specific details in connection with it are far from satisfactory. For example, we have now the Changjiang River instead of the Yangtze, the Huanghe River instead of the Yellow River, the Zhujiang River instead of the Pearl River, Taishan Mountain instead of Mount Tai, Xizang instead of Tibet, to name only a few, but foreigners would instinctively prefer the old forms, particularly in speech.

It is clear that the arrangement of entries according to Pinyin is much simpler than by radicals, and is in conformity with the principle of alphabetization acceptable to all lexicographers. However, the problem is more intricate than one would expect. In the first place, single-character lexical units are relatively limited in number and they mainly serve as headwords to introduce multi-character items though they have meanings of their own. For example, the character 勾 has several meanings: cancel, delineate, induce, collude with, etc., but in actual usage it is often accompanied by a particle such as 了, 掉, 起, 出. Under 勾 we have a number of multi-character units with 勾 as the first character: 勾搭 (gang up with), 勾劃 (draw), 勾結 (collude with), 勾留 (stop over), 勾引 (induce, seduce), 勾消 (strike off).

It should be noted that the concept of an English word is not exactly the same as that of a Chinese character, e.g. 玫瑰 (rose), 蜻蜓 (dragonfly), 葡萄 (grape), and 蘿蔔 (turnip). None of the first characters of these nouns can be counted as a morpheme, for a morpheme is a meaningful unit, but they are still treated as lexical units. Such characters, however, are few and should be distinguished from the numerous disyllabic and trisyllabic words (multi-character items) in modern Chinese which, as Jerry Norman pointed out, "can be analyzed as strings of monosyllable morphemes." (Norman, 1988)

Entries under each character are arranged according to the traditional order of the four tones. If two characters are alike in form but different in pronunciation and meaning, they are listed under separate letter headings. 朝 *chao* and 朝 *zhao* have different pronunciations and meanings and therefore constitute different items. "朝" *chao* in general means "court" or "dynasty" when used as a noun, but it means "have an audience with (a king or emperor)" or "face" when used as a verb. Both noun and verb forms are characters of the same origin, so they do not constitute separate items in a Chinese dictionary. However, in an English dictionary, "face" as a noun and "face" as a verb are treated as separate items.

There is another aspect to the problem of entries. "Since Ferdinand de Saussure introduced his two-sided model of the sign as the basic linguistic unit," Hartmann pointed out, "specialists in lexical and semantic analysis have adapted and modified it to their own ends. The word as a sign is said to have two related sides or aspects (a) a formal shape or phonetic/graphic image and (b) a semantic content or meaning/sense." (Hartmann, 1983) If a word has different senses, it should have different entries. Thus the word "bank" has five entries — two nouns and three verbs according to *Longman's Dictionary of Contemporary English*. The word "bank" in the "Bank of China" and that in the "bank of a river" are exactly the same in form and pronunciation but entirely different in meaning. In addition, "bank" has three verb forms, which have three different meanings. The same principle applies in a Chinese dictionary. For example, the word 生 has four entries, namely 生計 (livelihood), 吃生的 (eat something raw), 學生 (pupil, student), 生病 (fall ill), and each of them is a separate entry. Of course, in a Chinese-English dictionary this general practice should be allowed if dictionary-making is to be put on a scientific basis.

However, English and Chinese do not always follow the same principle in counting entries. English is a phonetic language which has morphological changes, though they are much less complicated than those of other European languages. In an English dictionary, for instance, a word with the negative prefix un- or dis- is a separate entry. So "honest" and "dishonest" are separate entries and their noun forms "honesty" and "dishonesty" are separate entries too. In a Chinese dictionary, an entry is a minimum lexical unit, which is irreducible. 公平 (fair, just) and 清楚 (clear, distinct) are entry words while 不公平 (unfair, unjust) and 不清楚 (unclear, indistinct) are not, because Chinese is a non-inflectional language and 不 is not exactly like a negative prefix in English but simply an adjective or adverb with a negative sense. However, while 不公平 , 不恰當 , 不理解 and other similar words are not treated as lexical units, 不公 , 不當 , and 不解 are full-fledged entry words. Semantically 不公 is no different from 不公平 any more than 不當 or 不解 is different from 不恰當 or 不理解 . But 不公 , 不當 , 不解 are idioms which become fairly common idiomatic phrases in certain combinations such as 處置不公 , 用人不當 and 迷惑不解 . Similar items are numerous. 不含糊 , 不客氣 , 不簡單 and many others are also entry words. They are not just negative words with 不 loosely attached to them, they have a special connotation of their own which entitles them to separate entries. So 不客氣 is not just "being impolite", though this sense is retained in some cases, but the special connotation is explicit in such collocations as 你如果這樣下去，我可不客氣了。 (I will get tough with you if you go on like this). The same is true of 不含糊 or 不簡單 , which has the idea of "wonderful" or "remarkable" and is therefore entitled to a separate entry. The majority of these lexical items headed by 不 are negative words which have no positive forms such as 不可救藥 (incurable), 不可估量 (inestimable), 不可告人 (not to be divulged), 不可磨滅 (indelible), 不可勝數 (countless) and numerous others.

Permanence and Ephemerality

The compiler of a bilingual dictionary, like that of a monolingual dictionary, must concern himself, first and foremost, with the selection of entries. Language changes. New words appear while old ones disappear. Echoing the sentiment of Dr. Johnson, Dr. Robert Burchfield says in his Preface to *A Supplement to the Oxford English Dictionary*:

... we have kept constantly before us the opposing concepts of permanence and ephemerality, retaining vocabulary that seemed likely to be of interest now and to future generations, and rejecting only those words, phrases, and senses that seemed transitory or too narrowly restricted in currency.

This sentiment is shared by all great lexicographers. "One of the basic problems of lexicography is to decide what to put in and what to exclude." (Tomaszczyk, 1983) In this respect, the compiler of a Chinese-English dictionary faces a peculiarly difficult problem for on the one hand he has to weigh carefully all the new words and expressions to see which of them have the stamp of permanence and, on the other hand, he has to offer equivalents for them, presumably with illustrative examples where necessary. The matter is further compounded by the fact that he has to weed out what are generally regarded as archaisms, which is a formidable task because of the difficulty of establishing where to draw the line. Besides, there is a considerable number of quaint classical expressions which, though they may sound somewhat highbrow to ordinary speakers, are well within the vocabulary of modern Chinese intellectuals.

In fact, the Chinese language is steeped so deeply in classical tradition that the lexicographer had better think twice before making up his mind to discard what he considers rare or archaic, e.g.

作奸犯科　commit offences against law and discipline
擢髮難數　(of crime) be as countless as the hairs on the head
錙銖必較　haggle over every penny
趑趄不前　hesitate to advance
誅心之論　penetrating criticism
運籌帷幄　plan strategies within a command tent
越俎代庖　exceed one's functions and meddle in other people's affairs
一息尚存　so long as one still has a breath left

As these expressions and many more are not necessarily limited to classical essays, they should no doubt constitute an integral part of the Chinese lexicon. In a Chinese-English dictionary, however, those expressions, most of them being culture-bound, are difficult to interpret without reference to historical contexts. If we offer bare equivalents, it may serve the needs of translators, but it will not satisfy those who seek comprehension. If we offer both translation equivalents and background information, the dictionary would become very bulky. It is true that the duty of a bilingual lexicographer is not the same as that of a monolingual lexicographer, but we cannot equate a bilingual lexicographer with a translator either. In a Chinese-English dictionary, in particular, the lexicographer is often called on to translate and explain as well.

Equivalents and Illustrative Examples

The makers of a monolingual dictionary, aside from the selection of entry words, are faced with the difficult task of defining entries. Sometimes, the object to be defined is very simple and plain. The definition of "door" in *Webster's Third New International Dictionary*, for example, is as follows:

> A movable piece of firm material or a structure supported usually along one side and swinging on pivots or hinges, sliding along a grove, rolling up and down, revolving as one of four leaves, or folding like an accordion by means of which an opening may be closed or kept open for passage into or out of a building, room, or other covered enclosure or a car, airplane, elevator or other vehicle.

The definition is scientifically worded, but one wonders whether native speakers of English or foreign learners of the language would care to look up the definition to find out what a door is like or what sort of thing may be properly called a door. Similarly, the definition of 門 (door), as given in *The Modern Chinese Dictionary*, serves no practical purposes either: 房屋、 舟船、或用圍牆、籬笆圍起來的地方的出入口 . (entrance of a house, vehicle, ship, or a place enclosed with a wall or a fence.) The first duty of a bilingual lexicographer, fortunately, is not to define or explain but to give equivalents. In a concise Chinese-English dictionary, the lexicographer may simply offer "door" and "gate" as the equivalents of 門 without going into detail. We might even think that this is a big advantage enjoyed by the bilingual dictionary and that after all an equivalent is simpler and easier to understand than a lengthy, intricate definition, however accurate it may be. But this is only part of the picture. Like many other Chinese characters, 門 is very often used metaphorically. If we say somebody is a 門外漢 , we mean that he is a layman, not a professional. 門戶之見 refers to sectarian bias, and 門當戶對 is a phrase which indicates that a couple are well-matched in social status and wealth. Many more examples which could be added to this list have no practical reference to the physical aspect of a door. We will then probably come to realize that "door" or "gate" is no absolute equivalent of 門 but one of its various senses.

If 門 and "door" are still identical in their primary sense, words like 龍 and 鳳 actually have no equivalents, not even near-equivalents in English. Of course, 龍 and dragon were both legendary animals, large and scaly, but the Chinese dragon was a symbol of royalty and the dragon in Western mythology was a monster which had the power to breathe out fire. 鳳 and phoenix were likewise legendary. 鳳 was the queen of birds with splendid feathers; it was a symbol of prosperity whereas the phoenix in Egyptian mythology was a beautiful lone bird which lived in the Arabian desert for 500 or 600 years and then burned itself and rose renewed from the ashes to start another new life. It was a symbol of rejuvenation. *The Modern Chinese Dictionary* has such entries as 鳳毛麟角 (said of somebody who is very talented and rare, or of something which is very hard to come by.) Ordinary birds pose a problem too. Nightingale, lark, owl — they can inspire an English poet to write the finest verse while Chinese poets, particularly classical poets, are fond of oriole, wild goose, eagle, magpie. It is interesting to note that the wild goose which may not be interesting at all to English poets is, in Chinese poetic vision, regarded as a messenger bird flying from one place to another for friends or lovers who live apart. 杜鵑 is as familiar a name in Chinese poetry as "cuckoo" is in English poetry, but while the former often calls up the saddest feelings in the Chinese poet, the latter is, for the English poet, a harbinger of spring or a symbol of joy, though some people may argue that 杜鵑 and cuckoo are not exactly the same kind of bird.

Even trees and flowers are also culture-specific. Elms, firs, daffodils, roses, lilies — these names are fairly common in English poetry while the Chinese have a special fondness for willows, pines, cypresses, for plum and peach blossoms, for chrysanthemums, lotus flowers, and peonies, all of which have their distinctive qualities and often reflect the moods and aspirations of classical poets. It would seem difficult for non-native speakers of Chinese to understand that the pine and cypress stand for longevity and moral integrity as they can withstand inclement weather and remain evergreen, that the chrysanthemums stand for nobility of character as they come proudly into flower despite the chilly autumn wind, and that the lotus flowers are particularly worth admiring because they merge unsullied from the mud.

Aside from the question of style and that of culture-specificity, there is another question involved, that is, the question of polysemy. If an entry word is polysemous, it has to be explained in different items and illustrated with examples. The situation is even more complicated if the equivalents given are polysemous, as most likely they are, because absolute equivalents are very rare. For example, 動搖 may have three equivalents: shake, sway, and vacillate, none of which coincides completely with the Chinese entry in meaning. However, when these three equivalents are put together, the user may find an area of meaning shared by the three words in common, something that approaches an ideal equivalent or near-equivalent.

The Part-of-speech Labels

Another difficulty which attends the Chinese lexicographer is assigning the part-of-speech labels to the entries. Although Chinese grammarians disagree among themselves about many things, they all agree that Chinese grammar should be explained in terms of the Chinese language rather than modelled on the grammar of any foreign language.

"Early grammarians" Professor Zhu Dexi 朱德熙 pointed out, "looked at the problem of the parts of speech from the point of view of the Indo-European languages. Their argument boiled down to two points. First, they thought neither verbs nor adjectives could occupy the position of subject or object and that the word occupying this position was always of the nature of a noun. Secondly, they considered that any word modifying a noun was necessarily an adjective. In fact, the majority of verbs and adjectives in the Chinese language can function as subject or object, and the word modifying a noun is not necessarily an adjective. Whether in classical or vernacular Chinese, a noun can always qualify a noun." (Zhu, 1982) Should we agree with the earlier grammarians, Professor Zhu argues, it would be tantamount to admitting that in Chinese the noun, verb and adjective can be used interchangeably, and this would lead to the erroneous conclusion that no word can be assigned to a definite part of speech. This is a clear-cut statement, but the problem of the verb-noun-adjective relationship is not merely a problem of Chinese grammar, it exists in English grammar as well. Professor Zhu suggests that Otto Jespersen's idea of "the three ranks" was intended to solve the part-of-speech problem in English grammar, and it was for this reason that both Professor Wang Li 王力 and Professor Lü Shuxiang 呂叔湘 borrowed this idea from Jespersen, though without much success, to try and solve the same problem in Chinese grammar. Of course, it would be unrealistic to deny the existence of part-of-speech distinctions altogether, but it would be equally unrealistic to talk as if the problem did not exist at all. Commenting on the subject-predicate relationship, Simeon Potter quotes from Sapir:

> No language wholly fails to distinguish noun and verb, though in particular cases the nature of the distinction may be an elusive one. It is different with the other parts of speech. (Potter, 1957)

The problem is all the more difficult to solve in the Chinese language which is non-inflectional. "Adjectives", according to Jerry Norman, "can be negated by *bu* 不 and can function independently as predicatives ..." (Norman, 1988) Take 紅 (red) and 綠 (green) for instance. They are adjectives in 紅花綠葉 (red flowers and green leaves). However, in the phrase 酒綠燈紅 (the wine is green and the lanterns red), both 紅 and 綠 are verbs, not predicatives with link verbs omitted. The same is true of 月明星稀 (the moon is bright and the stars sparse.) It is a sentence describing a situation, not just a phrase stating an obvious fact. 紅 may also function as a noun. In Chinese poetry, 紅 is used metaphorically as "flowers" in such combinations as 落紅 (fallen flowers or petals). Moreover, in the Chinese dictionary, it is the multi-character lexical units that predominate, and these items are often verb-object phrases or even complete sentences. In items such as 發展 (develop, development), 建設 (construct, construction), 教育 (educate, education), 訓練 (train, training), 偏離 (deviate, deviation), 背離 (depart, departure). The words are either nouns or verbs depending on the context. Thus many Chinese lexicographers hesitate to assign the noun, verb, and adjective labels to the entries while they have no difficulty in identifying adverbs, prepositions, conjunctions, particles, and onomatopoeia.

A Higher Degree of Overall Fidelity

It must be noted, however, that in a Chinese-English dictionary, an example is often an index of meaning as well as an illustration of usage. Since examples have to be given both in Chinese and English, the problem arises whether the versions of both languages really match. This is a matter of practice as well as a matter of theory. In the past, Chinese translators and translation theorists often argued among themselves about literal and liberal translation, or about the desiderata set up by Yan Fu 嚴復 namely, fidelity 信 , intelligibility 達 and elegance 雅 . Whatever their views, they paid very little attention to the role of the receptor. Their idea of fidelity was, first and foremost, fidelity to the source, to which both the literalists and liberalists claimed loyalty. Since the fifties, translation has been explained in terms of communicative theory. Translation, in modern eyes, is an encoding and decoding process, and the first duty of a translator is to correctly put across a message from the source to the target language. If the message is distorted, there is no fidelity to speak of. This is no doubt true, but translation is more than a lexical transfer; it involves many other factors. In a Chinese-English dictionary, many of the multi-character lexical units are idioms, aphorisms, proverbs, and all kinds of pithy remarks. 無風不起浪 , literally translated, is "there are no waves without wind." But the English version does not seem to match the original in style. "There's no smoke without fire" would be better, for it not only conveys the message but also catches the spirit. Let us take another instance. 養癰貽患 is a kind of aphorism. Should we translate it literally or liberally? The most authoritative version we can get is "a boil neglected becomes the bane of one's life — leaving evil unchecked spells ruin." (Beijing Foreign Languages Institute, 1982) But it sounds flat and didactic without a trace of moral fervour. If we use a figure of speech of the same import as an equivalent, say, "palliatives foment the disease," we would achieve what Dr. Zhao Yuan-ren 趙元任 calls a higher degree of overall fidelity. This principle also holds good in the editing of a bilingual dictionary.

However, we have to be very careful in choosing translation equivalents of this kind. We may often come across what we often call "false friends". 亡羊補牢 seems to have a ready equivalent in English: mend the fold when the sheep is lost. However, despite the apparent similarity in language, the English and Chinese versions convey different messages. In the English eyes, to mend the fold when the sheep is lost is a belated, foolish measure, whereas in the Chinese mind this is proper and wise for one who has learned a lesson from his loss and will take steps to prevent its recurrence.

Special Difficulties Involved in Chinese-English Bilingual Lexicography

In compiling a bilingual dictionary, the lexicographer must, first of all, determine for himself whether his work will serve the needs of source language or target language speakers and whether it is designed for comprehension or for production. This has much to do not only with the number of entries to be included in his dictionary, but with the way the dictionary is to be compiled. A bilingual dictionary compiled for comprehension should include more entries and senses but less syntactical information than one designed for production. This is theoretically and generally true, but the Chinese-English dictionary might be an exception, for even if the user refers to it for the sole purpose of comprehension, he has often to rely on the given examples to make sure that his understanding is correct. It is through these examples that he can best appreciate the syntactic functions of an entry.

It is evident that the compiler of a Chinese-English dictionary should be bilingual, bilingual in the real sense of the word. That is, he should be well versed in both languages and cultures. The idea that a person should be translating into his mother tongue as suggested by Eugene Nida is sometimes misleading. It leaves one with the impression that the target language is of primary importance while the source language is secondary in all cases. This is at least not true of Chinese-English translation or Chinese-English dictionary-making for that matter. The difficulty of the Chinese language is such that the slight misreading of a word or phrase may cause complete misunderstanding. Thus most Western scholars who appreciate Chinese language and culture never fail to give expression to this sentiment. Arthur F. Wright says:

> Translators of Chinese face a range of difficulties which may not be qualitatively different from those of other translators. But each type of difficulty is increased by the almost total absence of common customs, language elements, ideas, and values. And each is further multiplied by a monstrous weight of a millennial literary tradition. (Wright, 1953)

Dr. I. A. Richards remarks, as if with a sigh, about the possible transfer into English of Chinese concepts:

> We have here indeed what may very probably be the most complex type of event yet produced in the evolution of the cosmos. (Richards, 1968)

In Chinese-English dictionary-making, as in the case of Chinese-English translation, Chinese poses special problems and deserves special consideration. It is useful to recall that the early Chinese-English dictionaries compiled by native speakers of English have become worthless not because of the editors' imperfect command of the target language but because of their imperfect understanding of the source language on top of their total disregard for accuracy.

References

Beijing Foreign Languages Institute 北京外語學院 . 《漢英成語詞典》 (*A Dictionary of Chinese Idioms*). Beijing: The Commercial Press 商務印書館 , 1982.

Dictionary Editing Unit, Language Research Institute, Chinese Academy of Social Sciences 中國社會科學院語言研究所編輯室 . 《現代漢語詞典》 (*Modern Chinese Dictionary*). Beijing: The Commercial Press 商務印書館 , 1978.

Giles, Herbert, ed. *A Chinese-English Dictionary*. New York: Paragon Reprinting Company, 1964 (1909).

Hartmann, R. R. K., *Lexicography: Principles and Practice*. London: Academic Press, 1983.

Norman, Jerry. *Chinese*. Cambridge: Cambridge University Press, 1988.

Potter, Simeon. *Modern Linguistics*. Andre Deutsch, 1957.

Richards, I. A. "Towards a Theory of Translating." In *Studies in Chinese Thought*, edited by Arthur F. Wright. New Haven: Yale University Press, 1968.

Tomaszczyk J. "On Bilingual Dictionaries." In *Lexicography: Principles and Practice*, edited by R. R. K. Hartmann. London: Academic Press, 1983.

Wright, Arthur F. *Studies in Chinese Thought*. Chicago: University of Chicago Press, 1953.

Zhu, Dexi 朱德熙 . 〈漢語語法叢書序〉 (Preface to Chinese Grammar Book Series). In Lü Shuxiang 呂叔湘 , 《中國文法要略》 (*Concise Chinese Grammar*). Beijing: The Commercial Press 商務印書館 , 1982.

Lexicography and Translation

Mary Snell-Hornby
Institute of Translator and Interpreter Training
University of Vienna, Austria

History

Both translation and lexicography are among the oldest recorded activities of mankind. And yet, strange as it may seem at first sight, our knowledge of their history is still fragmentary. The history of translation involves a vast mass of material which is scattered among the various traditional language disciplines, making it well-nigh impossible for the individual scholar to obtain a balanced or coordinated overview. Furthermore, there were times when the interest in translation seems to have been so meagre that they have left little recorded evidence of its existence, so that our knowledge will probably always remain patchy. The history of lexicography has only in recent years attracted scholarly interest, and here too research has centred round particular epochs and specialized fields of interest. We can however recognize basic constellations which favour increased activity in both translation and dictionary-making: these presuppose an impact of one culture, and hence its language, on another, whether through religion (hence missionary work), trade, warfare, diplomacy, art or learning.

Ancient Mesopotamia

Such a constellation created the beginnings of lexicography, going back to word lists compiled by the Sumerians in southern Mesopotamia over four thousand years ago. The Sumerians believed that an object only had real existence if it were given a name, and their word lists amount to a complete documentation of the things around them. During the 3rd millennium B.C., Sumer fell into the hands of the Akkadians, Semitic invaders from northern Mesopotamia, who believed they could best consolidate their political supremacy by making the Sumerian cultural heritage their own. (von

Soden, 1974) The impact of the Sumerian culture on the Akkadians gave rise to the oldest bilingual word lists known to us, in which the Sumerian monolingual entries were provided with pronunciation glosses and Akkadian translations — the first bilingual "dictionaries". These were used mainly for the training of future scribes, along with polyglot word lists which included such languages as Hittite and Ugaritic. (Civil, 1976)

The Mesopotamian lexicographical legacy is imposing not only in size (it runs into tens of thousands of entries), but also because of the diversity of its compilation. The areas covered include legal and administrative terminology, trees and wooden artifacts, pottery, hides and metals, domestic and wild animals, parts of the body, stones, plants, birds and fish, textiles, geographic terms, food and drinks, professions, kinship terms and human activities, and extends to lists of compound words, synonyms and antonyms, and a collection of simple signs and compound logograms of the cuneiform script. (Civil, 1976)

A closer look at some of the entries reveals some fascinating insights into the world-view of Ancient Mesopotamia. Examples from the lists of wild animals for instance show clearly that the Sumerian categories in particular by no means correspond to the species familiar to us, while the Akkadian lists tend towards zoological interpretation. Thus the Sumerian "roof-mouse" was interpreted as a kind of dormouse and the Sumerian "mouse of destruction" as a rat. Sumerian categorization involved a good deal of evaluation (the "nasty mouse" appears in Akkadian as a shrew), while the physical categories were frequently interspersed with mythological elements: a Sumerian "giant caterpillar", for example, was understood by the Akkadians to be a dragon. (Landsberger, 1934)

Some points emerge from this brief list which are important both for translation and for the complex relationship between translation and the dictionary. Above all it is clear that the understanding of words varies with a specific world-view and differing cultural backgrounds, making "translation equivalence" a problematic principle. It is also interesting that the vast majority of entries in the Sumerian word lists, and subsequently in the bilingual word lists, denote concrete, static objects or represent nomenclatures, whereas it is the more complex lexeme, such as verbs and adjectives, which often provides the real challenge in translation.

During the course of the centuries Mesopotamia and the surrounding regions developed into a thriving polyglot trading area, and consequently interlingual correspondence was required. Scribes specialized in various languages and were employed to produce foreign language texts, giving rise to the earliest translation bureaus.

Latin as the Language of Scholarship

At the time of the ancient bilingual word lists, Sumerian — probably already a dead language — was the accepted language of scholarship in Akkadian society, which at the same time was consciously absorbing and developing the older, superior culture. A similar constellation was to influence Western lexicography right up into modern times — and that was the situation caused by the overwhelming domination of Latin.

In the Middle Ages Latin was the undisputed lingua franca of scholarship. Of major importance for the development of lexicography is the embryonic form of the future bilingual dictionary as interlinear glosses explaining difficult Latin words. As in Ancient Mesopotamia, here too early lexicography was essentially a one-way track, making the distant and lofty world of scholarship and its strange, archaic terms accessible to an invariably passive learner or recipient. One of the most remarkable lexicons of the Middle Ages is the Latin-French *dictionarius* of the Cartusian prior Firmin Le Ver. Between 1420 and 1440 Le Ver compiled a dictionary covering 45,000 Latin headwords and sub-headwords, providing a mix of Latin equivalents, Latin definitions, French equivalents and French definitions that adds up to a text containing close to half a million words including metalinguistic terms and abbreviations; this is the largest Latin-French lexicon of the Middle Ages. (Merrilees, 1988)

Latin continued to dominate bilingual lexicography right into the 17th century, and also formed the source language for polyglot vocabularies such as the popular *Sex Linguarum* (1537) and Calepino's monumental *Dictionarium* (1585), even though these contained perfectly familiar and concrete everyday words. The change came with the growth of commerce and the rising importance of foreign travel in the 17th century, which both presupposed at least some communicative competence in modern foreign languages. Even with the decline of Latin however, cultural supremacy (conditioned by political power) continued to be a major factor in bilingual lexicography; this explains why dictionaries linking Romance language-pairs have a longer history than those linking the at one time "weaker" Germanic languages English and German. (Hausmann and Cop, 1985)

The domination of Latin was also of vital importance for the development and status of translation. It was not only thought to be a language far superior to the vernacular, but was also a source language for translations of the Bible, and as such represented the "sacred" word of God which was not to be distorted or violated. Thus a translation had to be as close a copy of the original as possible, even if this meant "bending" the natural idiom of the target language.

China

In China too both translation and lexicography have a long history, and here too both are the result of cultural and linguistic impact, particularly through religion, diplomacy and scholarship.

The influence of religious zeal on translation and lexicography made itself felt when Buddhism was introduced to China during the Western Han dynasty (25–220) and missionaries were faced with the difficulty of translating their scriptures into Chinese. Early translations were apparently crude, as Buddhist concepts were not easily rendered from Sanskrit and Pali into Chinese. However, translation bureaus were established, reference works developed and translators trained — and gradually standards improved. A significant breakthrough took place during the Tang dynasty when Chinese Buddhist monks like Yi Jing 義淨 (635–713) made pilgrimages to India to study the Buddhist languages: Yi Jing compiled what was possibly the first reliable Sanskrit-Chinese glossary with the title *Sanskrit One-thousand Character Text* 《梵語千字文》. (Chien and Creamer, 1986)

Apart from glossaries, Buddhist monks also compiled dictionaries. The first prominent example is Xuan Ying's 玄應 *The Sound and Meaning of the Tripitaka* 《一切經音義》 (ca. 650) in 25 chapters. It was based on a collection of sutras, and the purpose in compiling it was to define difficult words, both Sanskrit and Chinese, that appeared in the Chinese translations of the sutras. In that it collects non-Chinese words and defines them in Chinese, it is remarkable as a pioneer attempt at bilingual lexicography. (Chien and Creamer, 1986)

Translation and lexicography were however not solely in the hands of Buddhist monks: in China the two branches of scholarship also had secular support. Officially appointed interpreters were even known to have existed right back to the Zhou dynasty (11th century B.C.–221 B.C.), but it was in 1407 with the establishment of the Bureau of Translators, founded to deal with foreign tribute-bearing nations, that the Chinese government really became active in translation and lexicography. The Bureau of Translators was later combined with the Hui Tong Academy, which produced a number of manuscript dictionaries, most of which were however lost.

The forcible opening of China in the 19th century resulted in an influx of diplomats, traders and missionaries from the West, also in an upsurge in Western scholarship. This led to the foundation of the Interpreter's College (Tongwen Academy 同文館), with its main centre in Beijing, which not only produced dictionaries and glossaries, but also involved itself in standardizing Chinese equivalents for foreign words. In 1901 a department of the Academy even laid out rules for bilingual dictionaries with a view towards standardizing terminology. (Chien and Creamer, 1986)

This was not however the earliest influence of Western culture on Chinese lexicography and translation. Robert Morrison (1782–1834), the first Protestant missionary to China, also compiled the first Chinese-English dictionary, and in 1819 he completed a translation of the Bible into Chinese. At the end of the 19th century (1892) the diplomat Herbert A. Giles, who began his career as an interpreter for the British Consular Service, published his *Chinese-English Dictionary*; this was revised in 1912 and is still used today. (Chien and Creamer, 1986)

The Dictionary and the Translator

In this brief historical overview, the discussion of lexicography centred mainly round the bilingual dictionary. It is important however to note that for the translator the bilingual dictionary is not the only tool, and certainly not the best one. With the real "professional" this even has a long tradition. In the early days of Bible translation no significant part seems to have been played by bilingual lexica: St Jerome evidently had none at his disposal — he learnt Hebrew himself, and for Aramaic he sought the counsel of experts. (Marti, 1974) A similar principle applies for the professional translator of today: a command of both source and target language is essential, and for extremely specialized areas of knowledge expert advice (or parallel literature) can be consulted.

Professional translators, particularly those working in literary translation, agree that, while monolingual learners' dictionaries proliferate, the ideal dictionary for the translator still does not exist. The basic problem is that any dictionary operates with lexemes in isolation but actually functions for words in individual texts and in varying contexts. The conventional bilingual dictionary is even more problematic because it is based on a principle which is now being increasingly probed and called into question: that of interlingual equivalence. The dictionary provides one or more "equivalents" for the foreign language headword, which — according to the current presuppositions of bilingual lexicography — are expected to fit into the translated text. (Zgusta, 1984) It is however common knowledge among professional translators that a translated text is not merely a string of dictionary equivalents, and that the relationship between languages and cultures is far more complex than can be expressed by lexical equivalence. At present translators usually find more useful information in monolingual dictionaries, where words are defined and explained as part of the linguistic and cultural background in which they are embedded.

Interlingual Relationships

The problems, however, vary according to context and text-type, but also with the type of lexeme concerned, and much could be done to help the translator if the rather static concept of equivalence were replaced by the more dynamic principle of varying interlingual relationships.

As a fundamental principle we may say that the simplest interlingual relationship, where the term *equivalence* is still justified, exists at the level of terminology and nomenclature — the very type of word on which the ancient Akkadian word lists were founded. The most complex relationships occur with words expressing sociocultural norms, perception, emotion or subjective evaluation, as is frequently found in certain kinds of adjective or verb, while little or no relationship exists at the level of culture-bound items.

With this in mind, we can distinguish five basic groups (examples are given for the language-pair English-German):

1. *Terminology/Nomenclature*
   e.g., oxygen: Sauerstoff
   reproduktionsfähige Vorlage: camera-ready copy
2. *Internationally known items and sets*
   e.g., Saturday: Sonnabend/Samstag
   typewriter: Schreibmaschine
   but: to type: tippen, mit der Maschine schreiben
3. *Concrete objects, basic activities*

    e.g., chair: Stuhl, Sessel
    cook, boil: kochen
4. *Words expressing perception, emotion or evaluation, often linked to
   sociocultural norms*
   e.g., billow, foreboding, gleam, bleak, nag
   keifen, kitschig, gemutlich
5. *Culture-bound items*
   e.g., haggis, wicket, drugstore
   Pumpernickel, Privatdozent, Sechselauten

In this concept, equivalence in the strict sense of the word is limited to
Group 1 (terminology, nomenclature), and specialized bilingual dictionaries of this kind, as well as electronic data banks, will profitably continue in
alphabetical form with foreign language equivalents. Otherwise our list
shows a gradual transition from more or less approximate "equivalence" in
Group 2 via "equivalence with discrimination" (Group 3) on to "partial
overlapping" (Group 4) and nil-equivalence (Group 5).

These differences should be reflected both in the structure of the dictionary entries and in the design of the dictionary itself. The approximate
equivalence of Group 2 can be indicated simply by labels or glosses indicating regional (Sonnabend: North German, Samstag: South German) or
stylistic (tippen: informal) differences. For Group 3 however, sense discrimination is often required to a far greater degree than most bilingual dictionaries yet provide, and in Group 4, where complex, multi-dimensional
semantic structures are involved which lack any kind of equivalent in the
target language, the traditional alphabetical arrangement might well be supplemented by a thesaurus-type presentation in contrastive semantic fields, to
which the main body of the dictionary would act as index. And for Group 5,
where not only the word, but even the concrete item itself is non-existent in
the target language culture, the only acceptable mode of bilingual presentation is definition or explanation in the target language.

Model for a Translator's Dictionary

As mentioned above, at present monolingual dictionaries usually provide
the translator with more useful information than do bilingual ones — with
the exception of course of specialized terminology. This does not mean
however that lexical material could not be arranged bilingually and
contrastively in such a way that it would help the translator in choosing the

best word or phrase to fit the particular text concerned. The problem is rather that lexicographers are still unfamiliar with the very sophisticated demands and specialized needs of the professional translator, whom they still tend to see as a kind of language learner, and publishers are reluctant to venture into what they see as a risky field with a limited market (although no concrete statistics are provided to support this contention). The result is that translators have to make do with an assortment of other dictionaries designed for other types of user.

There have however been attempts to formulate ideas and work out models for a translator's dictionary, notably from literary translators working at the European College of Translators in Straelen, Germany. There the modern alphabetical bilingual dictionary is rejected in favour of a monolingual thesaurus approach, with entries arranged according to word-fields, and by way of illustration older dictionaries are cited which present the translator with the kind of information he or she needs: quotations and collocations, word behaviour descriptions with additional semantic, pragmatic and stylistic information, and a metalanguage which conjures up the "natural environment" of the word concerned. (Birkenhauer and Birkenhauer, 1988) This thesaurus layout would of course be supplemented by an alphabetical index with precise references.

The Straelen translators have already put their ideas into practice and presented Glossaries based on the above criteria, whereby the field covered is of course limited, but the information offered is varied and detailed enough to meet the sophisticated needs of the literary translator. An exciting prospect might be a bilingual and contrastive thesaurus of the type envisaged above, with synonyms compared through behaviour descriptions and quotations. This is obviously an area which will present a real challenge for the lexicographers of the future.

Modern Chinese-English Lexicography

Seen with reference to Chinese-English lexicography, much of what has been established above emerges in a new light. Of particular interest is the specific impact between the two languages and cultures.

The first Chinese-English dictionary at the beginning of the 19th century was the concrete result of missionary activity. At the end of the 19th century, when Herbert Giles published his *Chinese-English Dictionary*, the political and cultural constellation had radically changed: China had been thrown open to Western influence, and with normal diplomatic and trade relations the type of translation activities could develop which characterize life today. In the meantime of course new Chinese-English dictionaries have been compiled to meet the changing needs of modern society, and one of the most remarkable is the *Chinese-English Dictionary of Modern Usage* 《當代漢英詞典》 by Lin Yutang 林語堂, published in 1972. By then English was the language long since accepted as an international medium of communication (a lingua franca, not only for the scholar and not for supposed reasons of superiority as had been the case with Latin, but for convenience and through general consent), whereas Chinese was the language of over a quarter of mankind. Obviously new types of dictionary were required to meet the demands of a changed world: whereas Giles can still be useful as an explanatory dictionary for students of classical Chinese literature and of Imperial China, the modern user also has active communicative needs, which go far beyond those of the passive recipients of past scholarship.

One problem still remains however in essence unchanged: the radical difference between the two languages — and in particular the two cultures — involved. Formal linguistic differences specific to Chinese-English dictionaries were already overcome by early lexicographers: notable examples are the modern method of marking the tone of a Chinese character, the phonetic arrangement of dictionaries, and romanization systems, first that of Wade-Giles (as used in the latter's dictionary), and then the Pinyin system officially adopted by the People's Republic of China in 1958. What is still a challenge are problems that have been discussed above: interlingual equivalence and the differing cultural backgrounds.

Lin Yutang bases his dictionary on what is called "idiomatic equivalence", whereby the principle of varying interlingual relationships would be applied here too. What Lin Yutang describes in his Introduction as "Western terms" (such as *supersonic speed, lunar modules, atomic power* or *weekend*, which in our grouping vary between terminology and internationally known items) have now been absorbed into Chinese and have specified Chinese equivalents. Levels of speech are indicated by style labels, whereby the attitude of the speaker is noticeably differentiated: beside the usual labels such as *coll.* (colloquial) and *derog.* (derogatory), we find those indicating courteous address, dialect colloquialisms and a whole range of usage from satirical and facetious to abusive, contemptuous and vulgar. The principle called "idiomatic equivalence" again affects culture-bound items and those indicating evaluation and perception. An example of the former is the explanation of *tanhuarng* ("a form of story-telling in rhymes at teahouses, partly sung"), and the latter is illustrated by the entry for *aur-yar*, offering two senses: "(1) (of ancient writings) full of characters that are difficult to make out and pronounce, descriptive of foreign sounds, unpronounceable, crotchety writing; (2) twisting (old trunks); rough (experience)." A final example shows the mingling of the mythical and the zoological, as was found in the word lists of Ancient Mesopotamia: under *niour* (Zoo.) cattle, we also find, besides a phrase explained as "(Chin. myth.) messenger boy of Hell," the cryptic entry: "(Astron.) Sagittarius, one of the twenty-eight Chinese zodiac constellations."

Lin Yutang does not explicitly specify the intended user of his dictionary, though by inference one can assume that he addresses the "modern reader". Yet the scope and variety of treatment in his entries and the abundance of additional material offered does approach what has been suggested above as the type of information needed by the translator. Especially important is what he stresses in the Introduction as the principle of "contextual semantics", defined as "the subtle, imperceptible changes of meaning due to context." Examples of usage are not just illustrations of a given definition; they are rather the raw material of language from which the meanings and nuances derive. The context always modifies the meanings." (1972:xxiv) This insight, along with the numerous examples of usage, the detailed explanations, the meticulous sense discrimination and the variety of style labels add up to those "word behaviour descriptions" which may help to conjure up the "natural environment" of the lexeme. A translator working from Chinese to English might use such information with great profit.

Translation as a Cross-cultural Event

In the linguistically oriented translation theory of the 1960s and early 1970s, translation was viewed as a transcoding process involving the substitution of a sequence of equivalent units. It is now however a truism that the translator does not translate units, be they words or phrases, but texts, and these are by no means merely a linear sequence of sentences, each of which is a string of words and grammatical items. In more recent, culturally oriented theories, the text is viewed as a *Gestalt*, a complex multidimensional structure which is more than the mere sum of its parts, and translation consists in the recreation of that whole. Furthermore, it is not merely a matter of code-switching from one language to another, but is now seen as a form of action, whereby the translated text can be described as the product of a "cross-cultural event". The ritual of greeting, for example, varies greatly from one culture to another, and the rendering of the literal, linguistic meaning in another language need by no means recreate the action of greeting in itself. Similarly the conventions of legal language vary so fundamentally that they are as important in the translation of a contract or any other legal document as the knowledge of individual terms.

The dictionary however, operates by necessity with words and phrases, and the bilingual lexicographer must offer, in one form or another, some kind of rendering of those words and phrases, usually with additional linguistic information. This does not mean however that the dictionary entry can necessarily be taken over wholesale and inserted into the translated text like a coin in a slot. What the translator needs in his or her decision-processes is adequate information to create a text that will function in the target culture. Thus the product of the lexicographer is for the translator a kind of open-ended potential.

The work of the bilingual lexicography and the professional translator is therefore by no means identical, but it is certainly related, and it is no coincidence that lexicographers have also worked as translators and interpreters, and that translators' colleges have also produced glossaries and dictionaries. China has produced pioneer work in this regard: not only were Buddhist monks active long before their colleagues in medieval European monasteries, but even the imperial government established translators' bureaus, academies and specialized departments of a kind not reached in Europe before the twentieth century. Nowadays institutions for translator training, for dictionary production and for the standardization of terminology exist all over the world. Within the multilingual and international communication network of our global community it can only be hoped that Chinese-English lexicography and translation will continue to develop on a basis of mutual enrichment.

References

Birkenhauer, Klaus and Renate Birkenhauer. "Shaping Tools for the Literary Translator's Trade." In *Translation and Lexicography*, edited by Mary Snell-Hornby, Esther Pohl and Benjamin Bennani. Kirksville, Missouri: John Benjamins/Paintbrush, 1989.

Calepinus, Ambrosius, comp. *Dictionarium Decem Linguarum*. Lyon: E. Michel, 1585.

Chien, David and Thomas Creamer. "A Brief History of Chinese Bilingual Lexicography." In *History of Lexicography*, edited by R. R. K. Hartmann. Amsterdam/Philadelphia: John Benjamins, 1986.

Civil, Miguel. "Lexicography." In *Sumerological Studies in Honor of Thorkild Jacobsen*, edited by S. J. Lieberman. Chicago: Chicago University Press, 1976.

Giles, Herbert A., comp. *Chinese-English Dictionary*. London: Kelly and Walsh Ltd., 1892.

Hausmann, Franz J. and Margaret Cop. "Short History of English-German Lexicography." In *Symposium on Lexicography II*, edited by Karl Hyldgaard-Jensen and Arne Zettersten. Tübingen: M. Niemeyer, 1985.

Landsberger, Benno. *Die Fauna des alten Mesopotamien nach der 14. Tafel der Serie Har-Ra = Hubullu*. Leipzig: Hirzel, 1934.

Lin, Yutang. *Lin Yutang's Chinese-English Dictionary of Modern Usage*. Hong Kong: The Chinese University Press, 1972.

Marti, Heinrich. *Übersetzer der Augustin-Zeit. Interpretation von Selbstzeugnissen*. München: Fink, 1974.

Merrilees, Brian. "The Latin-French dictionarius of Firmin Le Fer (1420–1440)." In *ZuriLEX '86 Proceedings*, edited by Mary Snell-Hornby. Tübingen: Francke, 1988.

Morrison, Robert. *Dictionary of the Chinese Language*, 6 vols. Macao: Honorable East India Press, 1815–1823.

Snell-Hornby, Mary. "The Bilingual Dictionary — Help or Hindrance?" In *LEXeter '83 Proceedings*, edited by R. R. K. Hartmann. Tübingen: M. Niemeyer, 1984.

———. "The Bilingual Dictionary — Victim of Its Own Tradition?" In *The History of Lexicography*, edited by R. R. K. Hartmann. Amsterdam/ Philadelphia: John Benjamins, 1986.

———. *Translation Studies: An Integrated Approach*. Amsterdam/Philadelphia: John Benjamins, 1988.

———. "The Unfamiliar Image: Metaphor as a Problem in Translation." In *Anglistentag 1987*, edited by H. W. Ludwig. Giessen: Hoffmann, 1987.

———, Esther Pohl and Benjamin Bennani, eds. *Translation and Lexicography*. Kirksville, Missouri: Benjamins/Paintbrush, 1989.

Soden, Wolfram von. "Leistung und Grenze sumerischer und babylonischer Wissenschaft." *Die Welt als Geschichte*, Vol. 2 (1936). Darmstadt: Wissenschaftliche Buchgesellschaft, 1974.

Xuan, Ying 玄應. 《一切經音義》 (*The Sound and Meaning of the Tripitaka*). Chang'an: Anon, 7th century.

Yi, Jing 義淨 , comp. 《梵語千字文》 (*Sanskrit One-thousand Character Text*). Chang'an: Anon, 1727.

Zgusta, Ladislav. "Translational Equivalence in the Bilingual Dictionary." In *LEXeter '83 Proceedings*, edited by R. R. K. Hartmann. Tübingen: M. Niemeyer, 1984.

LINGUISTICS

Computational Linguistics

Qian Feng
Department of Computer Science and System Analysis
University of Salzburg, Austria

Introduction

Computational linguistics is, in its broader understanding, a division of linguistics which deals with the computer problem-solving of all linguistic endeavors. In a narrower and more or less America-dominated usage computational linguistics is largely equivalent to natural language understanding, the computer modeling of the syntax, semantics and pragmatics of a particular language and the eventual simulation of human understanding of a piece of text in this language by a computer. Translation is a social activity which associates with and has symbiosis with nearly all human commitments, whether commercial, scientific or military. Translation usually falls into two divisions: oral and written. We tentatively call the former interpreting and the written version translation, which is our current topic.

Theoretical linguistics as well as computational linguistics has long ignored problems of, and potential bonus from translation, taking it more as a separate activity with diverse aspects ranging from an everyday task (in the case of commercial or scientific translation) to lofty literary creativity (in the case of translation from, say, Cao Xueqin 曹雪芹 , Shakespeare, Balzac or Goethe) than a linguistic enterprise. To our knowledge very few authors have made theoretical investigations into the interaction between linguistics and translation and still fewer between translation, and computational linguistics. A serious theory of translation in the light of linguistics or particularly of computational linguistics is long overdue. We are thus put in a rather difficult position to address the problem of the relationship, if any, between computational linguistics and translation.

Machine translation is now generally taken as a branch of computational linguistics which deals with loosely the same problem faced by natural language understanding, with the distinction that in machine translation we deal usually with a language pair, for instance, Chinese-English, whereas in natural language understanding the problem is focused on one language. Hutchins (1989) points out:

> Research on Machine Translation began in the 1950's and has largely remained to this day an activity which combines an intellectual challenge, a worthy motive and an eminently practical objective. The challenge is to produce translations as good as those made by human translators. The motive is the removal of language barriers which hinder scientific communication and international understanding. The practical objective is the development of economically viable systems to satisfy a growing demand for translations which cannot be met by traditional means.

We can now discuss the possible interaction between computational linguistics and translation through the channel and orientation of machine translation. Computational linguistics has established and secured its deep influence over translation through a long journey, as discussed in Qian (1983). Machine translation was much earlier than computational linguistics in developing and had been idiocratic until the ALPAC Report. After ALPAC computational linguistics researches took over most machine translation efforts but also eventually shed strong light on machine translation and, consequently, on translation. The sound and rapid advances in computational linguistics are bringing new elements to translation as a human undertaking, and a fresh working style to individual translators as well.

Translation in Common Sense and in Computational Linguistics

A working definition of translation runs as follows: to re-express in correspondence a text of one language, called source language, using another language, called target language, without much loss of all the aspects of information contained in the source language. We will follow our discussion in terms of this definition. First we introduce a schematic model of the process of translations shown in Figure 1. (Johnson and Whitelock, 1987)

Figure 1. A Working Model of the Process of Translation

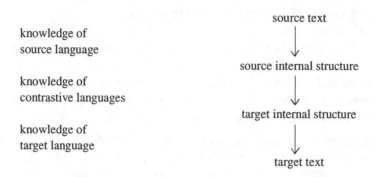

After reading the source text a translator develops a source internal structure from the source text using his knowledge of the source language to capture the aspects of contained information. Then the translator tries to transfer this source internal structure into some target internal structure using his contrastive knowledge of the two languages, still keeping in mind that little information should be lost. Eventually the translator re-expresses the target structure in form of a target text using his knowledge of the target language and thus finishes the process of translation. We argue that any translator should experience this, though maybe in different ways and with different degrees of skill or awareness, however over-simplified this model might be from a first glance. For instance, an expert in technical translation would build an exact source internal structure from the source in no time without much thought to the syntax, semantics or pragmatics (all these make up the source knowledge) before he shifts quickly to the transfer phase, while a novice would be trapped in a struggle with the syntax of a very long sentence. Primarily the first phase means understanding of the source text, the third phase re-expression or sometimes paraphrasing in the target language, while the middle phase is virtual translation.

From the point of view of computational linguistics the above model captures the key mental process involved in the intelligent activity of translation, but this has been realized only recently. It would be clearer to trace a little bit of the historical perspectives of the conceptual design of machine translation as shown in Figures 2(a), (b), and (c) (Batori, 1986; Qian, 1987).

The model in Figure 2(a) is basically a rudimentary word-to-word

Figure 2(a) The Computer Model of Machine Translation

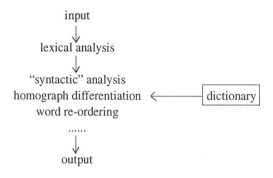

input
↓
lexical analysis
↓
"syntactic" analysis
homograph differentiation ⟵——————— dictionary
word re-ordering
......
↓
output

Figure 2(b) A Computational Linguistics Model of Machine Translation

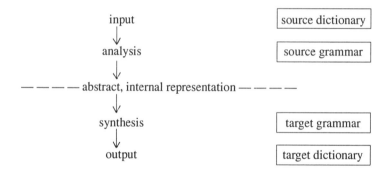

input   source dictionary
↓
analysis   source grammar
↓
— — — — abstract, internal representation — — — —
↓
synthesis   target grammar
↓
output   target dictionary

Figure 2(c) An Artificial Intelligence Model of Machine Translation

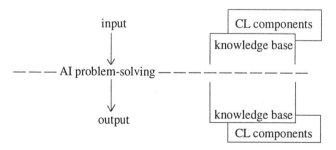

input   CL components
↓   knowledge base
— — — AI problem-solving — — — — — — — — — —
↓
output   knowledge base
                               CL components

version of machine translation, reflecting the naive and over-optimistic outlook of most of the early machine translation workers.

In Figure 2(b) the model represents a remarkable leap-forward, incorporating the significant advances in computational linguistics after the ALPAC Report. To date the dominating framework for most machine translation systems, including nearly all operational systems, is based essentially on this syntax-oriented approach of computational linguistics; and a tremendous amount of technical and commercial documents have been translated from one language to another language in this environment. One only has to compare this scheme and the model in Figure 1. to realize that part of work of a translator has been replaced by a number of sophisticated technical steps of syntactic analysis, semantic analysis, transfer and generation, all deeply rooted in computational linguistics. (Qian, 1990a) It is astounding that an academic theory, once implemented by computer programming, should actually work on that enormous scale and dramatically change the way of life of a human activity.

The third model in Figure 2(c) aims, using recent techniques in Artificial Intelligence (AI), at rather higher approximation to a knowledge-based scheme, a machine translation system which understands before it translates. (Carbonell and Tomita, 1987) The key feature of the last model consists of a simulation of some relevant behaviour of an expert translator. (Qian, 1987)

Difficulties of Human Translation and Machine Translation

If we suppose that our definition of translation is workable, all difficulties, both for human and for machine, are intrinsically contained in the two requirements stated in this definition: i.e. in the rubrics, "in correspondence" and "all aspects of information". We should, in addition, distinguish between two kinds of difficulties: interlinguistic and extralinguistic.

It is well known there are no exact correspondences between any language pair on any linguistic level. On the lexical level even a very common English word, say *act* has no German equivalent; it is not exactly German *Aktion*, nor *Akt*, nor *Handlung*, etc. The English word *to produce* occupies a piece of the lexical space between Japanese *tsukuridasu* and *hikiokosu* that are usually used to translate it. There are at least eight different German translations for the Chinese noun 事 , and more than

twelve distinct German rendering for the Chinese verb 有 . A physical/
mental/social world continuum is segmented when it is described by a
natural language which has only finite number of words and thus is discrete.
No two peoples speaking different languages ever had an agreement to
segment the world in correspondence, thus no exactly corresponding piece
of semantics ever exists. Pure scientific and technical terms are exceptions
but with a lot of "footnotes" (cf. *operator* in "*admittance operator*" and
"*computer operator*", etc.). It is no wonder translators should rack their
brains for such Chinese words as 風流 , 空靈 or 俠客 , to name only a few.

On the level of syntax it seems more correspondences have been found
but this is not actually the case. A simple Chinese sentence pattern subject-
object has to be translated into four different cases. A single Japanese
watashi-wa kinō gakusei-ni atta may correspond to the following four
sentences in English: *I met a student yesterday. I met the student yesterday.
I met students yesterday,* and *I met the students yesterday.* The choice
depends on the corresponding context or it is pragmatic. Syntax reflects
primarily how different peoples have incorporated those logical concepts
into their languages.

Beyond lexical, syntactic, semantic and pragmatic the extralinguistic
problems are even more sophisticated and often intractable. Now the translators should work for preserving "all aspects of information". But what
does this mean? "All aspects" means, besides the above-mentioned linguistic features, a vast territory of cultural, historical and customary issues, etc.
This realm embraces in fact the whole cosmos of all human activities. A
simple English sentence such as *I'll come tomorrow* must be translated into
five different Japanese sentences according to different cultural honorifica-
tion: *asu oukagai itashimasu; asu oukagai shimasu; asu ikuyo; asu ikuwa;
asu ikimasu.* (Tsujii, 1989) One of the key decision points is for the
translator to determine the priority of choices from different environments.
The Shakespearean sentence *Not a mouse stirring* (Hamlet: Act I, Scene I)
is translated into French *Pas un chat.* Did the French Shakespeare student
make no distinction between "mouse" and "cat"? No, he gave a higher
priority to culture than to linguistics. This aspect of information can hardly
be exhausted, thus translation is always lame in one leg.

Loftier still is the contrastive study of different cultural mentalities of
different peoples. To take a case of Chinese vis-à-vis Western. Chinese
people like resorting to synthesis, induction and implication while the
Western mentality prefers analysis, deduction and exhaustive description.

(Fu, 1987) This general characteristic deviation in mentality makes an ideal rendering from one language to another very difficult.

All the difficulties of human translation have been inherited by machine translation. As discussed in Carbonell *et al.*, 1981, machine translation pursues the following dimensions of quality, namely:

1. Lexical invariance;
2. Structural invariance;
3. Semantic invariance;
4. Pragmatic invariance.

while it avoids or ignores other "higher-level" issues. The extralinguistic problems discussed above are thus not so remarkable as they are in the case of human translation. The interlinguistic ones are simply enough for machine translation endeavours.

Machine translation workers once talked about Full Automatic High Quality Translation with the acronym FAHQT, but the practice has long given up this dream. Being much more realistic, the current operational machine translation systems produce very simple grammatical errors which, fortunately, no human translator would make. It is notorious that most systems have difficulties in selecting proper pronouns, prepositions and conjunctions, let alone definite or indefinite articles when dealing with such languages as Chinese and Russian which do not have articles. Other uncomfortable things include dealing with homographs and polysemes; and a no less critical problem has been found with technical vocabulary. Revisers of machine translation output, most of them professional translators, have a generally poor opinion of machine translation systems which often require a great deal of low-level correcting.

To overcome eventually all the difficulties would require some dramatic and keen insight of human beings into the most important means of daily communication and their own invention — natural language. Computational linguistics has been making progress in this connection towards a dual aim: to approximate to the ideal goal in close collaboration with Artificial Intelligence on the one hand (Qian, 1990a), to try to open a new horizon to the human translators on the other hand.

Impact on the Human Translator

Recent developments in computational linguistics have swept away clouds over FAHQT and brought new insight into machine translation research. One realistic attitude now is to take into full account various possible interactions between a human translator and a machine translation system. To distinguish between the different kinds of human interaction, machine translation people use two acronyms, namely HAMT for Human-assisted Machine Translation and MAHT for Machine-assisted Human Translation (usually also MAT for Machine-assisted Translation).

HAMT

Suppose we have a machine translation system which can perform some part of the translation work assisted by a human translator. There are essentially three ways in which the human can intervene during the translation process: before the system starts working, while the system is working, and after the system has finished the work. It is interesting to note that all the three models use computational linguistics methods, more or less, in designing various linguistic components to be integrated in machine translation systems. The horizon of traditional translation is thus expanded.

(1) *Pre-editing*

Typically in a pre-editing environment texts have to be specially drafted, by human translators or editors, in a limited language using a restricted syntax and a restricted vocabulary. For example the length of sentences is limited — a sentence found too long would be split into several shorter ones, or a too complex sentence is "regularized". The machine translation system would then guarantee that it translates any of those texts. It is clear that the human now needs only expert knowledge of handling the restricted language; all other aspects of translation expertise are supplied by the machine.

(2) *Interactive Machine Translation*

A number of current operational machine translation systems display the source text and provide facilities to allow the translator-editor to build up a translation interactively. This is done usually using a second window side by side with the one displaying the original text. The facilities range, as with the products from ALPS — a machine translation firm of Provo, Utah in the States — from on-line bilingual glossaries to window-oriented word-processor in the target language. The real interaction between the machine translation system and the operating translator happens when the systems offers, in addition, an interactive translation working mode. In this scenario the system first attempts a sentence-by-sentence translation, but pauses to allow the translator to choose from among possible options. Of course the Machine Translation modules are usually not so powerful as in the other two cases, but still all the linguistic components, besides the word-processor, are designed using methods of computational linguistics.

(3) *Post-editing*

This is one of the safest ways to organize a man-machine cooperative translation. Typically, as in the case of products of the Chicago-based machine translation firm Worldwide Communications, the machine does the raw translation in a batch mode, consuming thousands and thousands of words at night. The human post-editors of translators then verify the output of the machine translation system in the day time. Post-editing is a highly knowledge-intensive task. The post-editor needs to be an expert in the subject area, in the target language and in the contrastive knowledge. In effect he should be at least as skilled in translating the language-pair as an original translator.

MAT

Carbonell *et al.*, 1987 points out:

> Much of the time of a human translator is wasted in manual lexicographic searches, and in document editing and formatting. Time consuming as they may be, they are the simplest tasks that a translator must perform, and therefore the easiest to automate effectively. Hence, one approach to improving the efficiency of a valuable, experienced human translator is to provide him or her with high-powered computational tools for the more mundane, time-consuming tasks.

Such tools range from split-screen word processor to on-line technical dictionaries and grammar checker. We may introduce the concept of a translator workstation to illustrate better what is a MAT.

At lower level the workstation is used to provide translation aids with the translator producing translation directly from a source text on paper or into a word processor diskette. This level is based on word processing, dictionaries and possibly networking. The translator is encouraged to use a word processor. The translation will first be assisted by a computer diction-ary looking-up. Further facilities include access to remote information sources such as remote term banks and textual databases for monolingual research into the usage of certain terms. All these are available without leaving the word processor.

This mode can be augmented by such advanced options as dictionary scans, concordances, and text-related glossaries. ALP's product Auto Term system is an example. A concordance program can be a good tool for studying a text before translating it and for, say, looking at all occurrences of a difficult word or phrase. (Qian and Wang, 1986) The translator may then decide to translate all occurrences identically, or to vary depending on local context. The text-related glossaries, being a table of words and phrases along with their translation, are most useful for technical texts where translation should be consistent throughout the document.

The prospectives of MAT can be further expanded by such translation aids as context-sensitive searching utilities and automated dictionary up-date interface, etc. A human translator requires fast access to technical terminology, and context-sensitive searching programs would make these far more effective. For instance, if a term has multiple meanings, these could be presented in rank order based on the relevant topic of the source text for choice. On the other hand, no technical dictionary is ever complete, largely due to the rapid evolution of technical vocabularies. The most effective way to stay abreast of a continuous lexical evolution is to enable the translators themselves to up-date the dictionary entries.

Computer Simulation of Human Translation

The real exciting things happen when we talk of using computers to simu-late the human translator. One of the approaches applies knowledge engi-neering techniques to simulate knowledge that human translators possess and make use of in translation, as we discussed in the above, and to overcome or bypass the difficulties. (Qian, 1990)

Earlier versions in this direction added certain Artificial Intelligence components, for instance, an expert knowledge checker to do disam-biguation which no syntactic or semantic analysis could have tackled. (Qian, 1987) One of the recent advanced systems is the design of knowl-edge-based Machine Translation such as presented in, say, Carbonell and Tomita, 1987 and Tomita and Carbonell, 1989. Just as we have pointed out, accurate translation builds in a degree of comprehension, and comprehension requires various kinds of knowledge. Knowledge-based machine translation combines syntactic and semantic information to produce an intermediated knowledge representation abstracted from the source text which is then generated in the target language. Some new advances in computational linguistics methods for combing lexical, syntactic, semantic and pragmatic knowledge promise to make systematic knowledge-based machine translation a practical reality.

A knowlege-based machine translation system builds in the following performance objectives:

1. Semantic accuracy — the translation should maintain semantic invariance above all else;
2. Discourse phenomena — extra-sentential phenomena such as anaphora, ellipsis and speech act should be handled within the framework since a human translator is good at handling them;
3. Multilingual generality — the system should be able to treat any language and any semantic domain;
4. Interactive translation — translation should occur in real time, interacting with the translator/user as required;
5. Multiple utility — the methods should be applicable to multiple natural language interfaces. Especially interesting is that the knowledge-based Machine Translation system should be used to develop a computational linguistics workbench, where different linguistic theories can be subjected to comparative testing across multiple languages and linguistic phenomena.

One of the characteristics of Artificial Intelligence Machine Translation systems is that they do not produce strict translation but rather paraphrase in the target language. The real challenges to computational linguistics, artificial intelligence and knowledge engineering is the modeling of the expertise of translators. If we admit that knowledge engineering techniques can be successfully used in developing various machine translation systems and translation aids, an important task will be developing a knowledge module of translator expertise and integrating it into the operating systems. This expertise consists in the relevant kinds of knowledge as above pointed out, and some heuristics in reasoning, which are still not so well studied to date. Instances of them are human ability to disambiguation, human knowledge to process illogical and vague expressions of natural language, to extract precise meaning from insufficiently explicit, context-bound texts, and human ability to use effective and quick association of one language with another language.

References

ALPAC. *Languages and Machines: Computers in Translation and Linguistics.* Report of the Automatic Language Processing Advisory Committee, Division of Behavioral Sciences, National Academy of Sciences, National Research Council Publication 1416. Washington, D.C.: National Research Council, 1966.

Bátori, I. "Die Paradigmen der maschinellen Sprachübersetzung." In *Neue Ansätze in Maschineller Sprachübersetzung: Wissenrepresentation und Textbezug,* edited by I. Bátori and H.J. Weber. Tübingen: Niemeyer, 1986.

Carbonell, J.G., R.E. Cullingford and A.V. Gershman. "Steps towards Knowledge-based Machine Translation." *IEEE Transactions on Pattern Analysis and Machine Intelligence,* No. 3 (1981).

———— and M. Tomita. "Knowledge-based Machine Translation, the CMU Approach." In *Machine Translation,* edited by Sergei Nirenburg. Cambridge: Cambridge University Press, 1987.

Hutchins, W.J. "Prospectives in Machine Translation." In *Machine Translation Summit,* edited by Makoto Nagao, *et al.* Tokyo: Ohmsha, 1989.

———— and H.L. Somers. *An Introduction to Machine Translation.* London: Academic Press, 1992.

Johnson, R.L. and P. Whitelock. "Machine Translation as an Expert Task." In *Machine Translation,* edited by Sergei Nirenburg. Cambridge: Cambridge University Press, 1987.

Qian, Feng 錢鋒 . "Computer Science Lends Itself to Machine Translation." *Computer Science,* No. 3 (1983).

————. "Introducing CHEMATS: ECNU Chinese-English Machine Assisted Translation System." Paper presented at "Conference on Translation Today," 17–21 December 1987, Hong Kong.

————. *An Introduction to Computational Linguistics — A Multilingual Approach to Some Fundamental Theories and Basic Methods for Computer Understanding of Natural Languages* (in Chinese). Shanghai: Xuelin Publishing House 學林出版社 , 1990.

————. "Knowledge-based Computational Linguistics/Machine Translation Systems and Chinese as a Formal Language." In *ALLC-ACH 90: The New Medium,* Book of Abstract, 4–9 June 1990, University of Siegen, Germany, 1990.

————. "Was There Once an Ancient European Writing System? — Rendezvous with a Prehistoric Europe Using Techniques of Artificial Intelligence." In *Fit '90: Future Trends in Information Technology Fundamentals and European*

Cooperations in Information Systems and Education, Schriftenreihe der österreichichen Computer Gesellschaft, Band 53, edited by V. Haase and P. Zinterhof. Wien, München: Oldenbourg, 1990, pp. 255–74.

—— and Wang Jie. "An Open Database for English Teaching and Research." In *Database in the Humanities and Social Sciences*, Vol. 3, edited by T. Moberg. Osprey, FL: Paradigm Press, 1986.

Schwanke, M. *Maschinelle Übersetzung: Ein Überblick über Theorie und Praxis.* Berlin: Springer, 1991.

Tomita, M. and J. G. Carbonell. "CMU Project." In *Machine Translation Summit*, edited by Makoto Nagao. Tokyo: Ohmsha, 1989.

Tsujii, Jun-ichi. "Machine Translation: Research Trends." In *Computerlinguistik, Ein internationales Handbuch zur computergestutzten Sprachforschung und ihrer Anwendungen*, edited by I. S. Bátori, *et al*. Berlin: Walter de Gruyter, 1989.

Linguistic Aspects of CE/EC Translation

Wang Zongyan
Department of Foreign Languages
Zhongshan University, Guangzhou, China

What are the relations between linguistics and translation? Can linguists be of any service to people whose profession is to put a text in English into Chinese and vice versa?

The answer hinges on one's concept of linguistics.

If by linguistics is meant the study of the language system pure and simple, linguists and translators are at best nodding acquaintances. If it means the study of linguistic performance in its manifold forms and functions, linguists can be said to be blood brothers of translators.

If one sees linguistics as a body of explicit rules regulating language, translators most probably will yawn with boredom. If it signifies the choice of words and locutions, consciously or sub-consciously, to fit the social occasion, there is nothing to stop translators from embracing linguistics.

In this article, *linguistics* is used in the broad sense, free from the trammels of Bloomfield and Chomsky and generally along the lines of Halliday and Dell Hymes.

To a certain extent, the relations between linguistics and translation resemble those between literary theories and creative writing. Linguistics is not and cannot be the sole determinant in translation, but it is an aid if applied within limits and with prudence.

Incidentally, there are linguists who declare that translation is a science. This is a big claim, and should be taken with a grain of salt.

In the following, four topics will be taken up. They are (1) the history of translation in China, (2) the issue of translatability and untranslatability, (3) the criteria of translation and (4) where linguistics can help.

An Unending Wrangle

Over the centuries, there has been an incessant dispute between two schools of thinkers in China. On the one hand, there were the literal translators; on the other, there were the claimants for a measure of freedom. As a matter of fact, it was a debate between perfectionists and soft-liners, between strict teachers and considerate popularizers, or as Eugene Nida puts it, between the scholar and the stylist. (Nida, 1974:103) The one side wants to transplant, root and branch; the other settles for a workable if inadequate paraphrase.

Among the early translators, Kumarajiva 鳩摩羅什 (344–413), an Indian who came to China and mastered the Chinese language, is generally assumed to be a free-hander, while Xuan Zang 玄奘 (602–644), the zealous Chinese learner who defeated all his opponents in philosophical debates in India, is a literalist.

Hu Shi 胡適 (1891–1962), who knew literature and translation well, was an admirer of Kumarajiva, especially for his bold emendations, but he also pointed out that the Indian translator sometimes resorted to borrowings such as 阿耨多羅三藐三菩提 (*anuttarasamyaksambodhi*), which has certainly mystified millions of Chinese Buddhists. (Luo, 1984:67–78) Liang Qichao 梁啓超 (1871–1929), on the other hand, sang the praises of Xuan Zang (Luo, 1984:62), whose dictates, nevertheless, were questioned by such an erudite and discerning critic as Zhu Ziqing 朱自清 (1898–1948).

Beginning some time towards the close of the nineteenth century and continuing up to the 1930s, another controversy was raging. On the one hand, there was Yan Fu 嚴復 (1853–1921), a navy cadet turned social scientist, who put forward the three-in-one principle of faithfulness, intelligibility and elegance (i.e. using the ancient Chinese language). (Luo, 1984:136–138) As a translator, he often, though not always, recast and adapted. On the other hand, Lu Xun 魯迅 (1881–1936), who was famous for his literary skill and revolutionary fervour, promoted the tolerance of clumsy and unidiomatic versions — he was not averse to the advice from Qu Qiubai 瞿秋白 (1989–1935), however. (Luo, 1984:265–88)

Since Lu Xun had a big following, his creed was supposed to carry the day, but many practitioners probably followed their own principles. Those who wished to spread the Marxist doctrine had to catch the ears of the masses, but translations that were too literal were often inexplicable to the ill-educated. In the fifties, the pendulum began to swing to the side of the freehanders. Some time later, students began to pay heed to Chao Yuen Ren 趙元任 (1892–1982) and Lin Yutang 林語堂 (1859–1976), both eminent in the fields of linguistic research and translation. They also rediscovered Wu Guangjian 伍光建 (1866–1943) and even reassessed Lin Shu 林紓 (1852–1924), and listened with respect to Fu Lei 傅雷 (1908–1966) and Qian Zhongshu 錢鍾書 (1910–   ).

When the critics have learned to be open-minded and objective, they can be expected to grow judicious and fruitful.

Are All Texts Translatable?

All conscientious translators, from Kumarajiva to Fu Lei, are dissatisfied with their own works. Most critics, from Dao An 道安 (314–385) to Ke Bonian 柯伯年 , have found fault with the translators. Thus the question arises: Is translation possible? And are all verbal productions equally translatable?

On such questions, opinions may be diametrically opposite.

A. V. Federov, the Russian scholar whose notions were quite influential in China in the 1950s, believes that there is nothing untranslatable. Xuan Zang, who was revered in the seventh century, is positive that there are many expressions that cannot and should not be translated.

The opinion that translation is impossible can hardly be convincing to the common reader. Are business contracts and diplomatic agreements in different versions not signed and acted upon every day? Are Reuters and Associated Press news reports not translated and published in non-English speaking countries? Weren't Arthur Waley's translation of Chinese poems and Martin Luther's translation of the Holy Scriptures well-known successes?

On the other hand, ever since the fourth century, translations of Buddhist classics had been cried down. The unkind critics likened them to a glass of port diluted with water (Luo, 1984:23) or a dish of food chewed up and spoon-fed, both insipid and nauseating.

If one looks at the facts, it should be obvious that people speak and write generally to communicate and inform, not to confuse and mystify. Their discourse may be inexact, ineffectual or otherwise faulty, but such is not their original intention except in the case of swindlers and tricksters.

And the wide reading public believes that, as a rule, what is intelligible should be translatable.

Such sentiments, however, go against the grain of the ancient and modern literalists. To them, *prajnaparamita* could only be borrowed as 般若波羅蜜多 , and *Bolsheviks* should not be rendered as 多數派 but 布爾什維克 .

Are there things untranslatable? Certainly there are, and plenty of them. What is peculiar to a language or culture is resistant to translation. Alliterations, jingles, puns cannot be retained; Chinese antithetical couplets defy rendering, so do English sonnets. Allusions, though familiar to one nation, are incomprehensible to aliens. And of course incantations and taboos are not meant to be interpreted in another language.

Even when the expressions are easily understood, it is often tremendously difficult to give equivalents in another tongue.

As Xuan Zang points out, polysemous words are hard to render. Realism is 現實主義 or 寫實主義 in literary criticism but 實在論 or 唯實論 in philosophy; argument is 辯論 in everyday conversation but 自變量 in mathematics; memory is 記憶 in psychology but 存儲器 in computer science.

Moreover, different words in the source language may appear in the same form in the target language. Both *peasants* and *farmers* are 農民 in Chinese, but a farmer may be a rich man managing 1,000 acres while a peasant is only a poor fellow struggling along on a small piece of land. *Speech acts* are studied by philosophers and *verbal behaviour* by Skinnerian psychologists, but both may assume the form 語言行爲 in Mandarin. In linguistic discussions, *sense* and *meaning*, *use* and *usage* are sharply distinguished, but how do you manage to do so in Chinese unless you provide attributive modifiers?

Words similar in constituents may be wholly unlike in meaning. In Cantonese, 酒家 is a restaurant, while 酒店 is a hotel; in Putonghua, 飯店 is a hotel, while 飯館 is a restaurant. A *drug store* in the U. S. sells a wide variety of merchandise; can it be covered by 藥店 ? At *the chemist's* in the United Kingdom one can get the perfume one's girl friend prefers; is it expected of a 化學藥品店 in China?

It seems justifiable to say that while in a language most expressions are translatable, there are some that defy rendering. This reminds us of modern literature. No doubt most twentieth-century novelists are comprehensible, but can you decipher James Joyce?

What is a Good Translation?

If all things were of the same length, there would be no need for yardsticks. If all sayings were equally translatable or untranslatable, there would be no need for theorists. But the sad fact is that the same saying may be translatable in one context but difficult to render in another. Anybody knows how to translate *We don't hang together*; so does he when he sees *We hang separately*. But how do you put into Chinese *If we don't hang together, we'll hang separately*? If one hangs onto the meaning, one's grip on the form cannot be maintained; if one holds tight to the form, the witty remark will no longer be a witticism.

When one compares Chinese translation theorists with Westerners, one finds a notable difference. The Chinese harp on the linkage between faithfulness and intelligibility; the Westerners focus on equivalence, variously phrased and defined. (Wilss, 1982) The central issue, of course, is the criterion or criteria for translation. By what standard can we grade the quality of discourse put into another language?

Just as among philosophers there are rationalists and agnostics, so among translation theorists there are monists and dualists, even triadists.

On the one hand, there are eggheads who believe in the principles they themselves enunciate. They call translation a science. For them, rules can be formulated and tenets should be preached.

On the other hand, there are quite a bunch of unrepentant unbelievers. In 1981, Cao Jinghua 曹靖華 , a veteran translator of Russian classics, declared that there was no key to success in translation and no criterion for the job. (Luo, 1984:897–99) In 1988, Paul St-Pierre, who teaches translation and semiotics at Université Laval, bemoaned "the lack of consensus about what constitutes a good translation" and decided that "uncertainty and normality go hand in hand." (Hammond, 1988:305–306) It is interesting to note that in 1989, even Eugene Nida, the doyen of the theorizing profession, admitted that "no full-scale theory of translation now exists" and that "we really know so little about what makes translators tick." (Nida, 1989:2–8)

In China, the monists claim that the sole requirement of translation is faithfulness. If a translator is faithful, he will have fulfilled all his obligations. The question is, however, faithful to what and in what way.

If to be faithful is to convey the message, the dualists (who want to be both faithful and intelligible) would rapturously assent. If to be faithful is to retain the morphological and syntactic patterns of the original text, the dualists would ask how common sayings such as *Nothing succeeds like success* or 靠山吃山，靠水吃水 are to be faithfully represented.

The triadists, who insist on elegance (in the current sense, not Yan Fu's), in addition to faithfulness and intelligibility, do not see entirely eye to eye with the dualists. They are stylists who have a genuine care for the idiom. They feel uncomfortable when confronted with such an expression as 如是我聞 . The wording has long been established in the translated Buddhist classics; it can be said to be both faithful to the original and comprehensible to Buddhist scholars; but the triadists ask, "Do you think it is Chinese?"

At present, it seems that most Chinese readers agree with Guo Moruo when he says that faithfulness, intelligibility and elegance are all requisites. (Luo, 1984:500) And since Mao Dun asked for literary flavour in addition to faithfulness and intelligibility in translated literary works, there have been no dissenters. (Luo, 1984:501–17)

The theory of translation equivalence was developed abroad, and has found favour with some Chinese academics. Only one demand is made, so the theorists are monists, but as they are often inconsistent, they look like pluralists.

In a long article published in 1989, one of the advocates of translation equivalence has a profusion of interesting examples arranged under several headings and sub-headings.

"Translation equivalence," says he, "is composed of stylistic equivalence, socio-cultural equivalence and linguistic equivalence, and linguistic equivalence can be subdivided into pragmatic equivalence, grammatical equivalence and semantic equivalence."

So far so good, but what if the equivalences come into conflict like warlords of old China? "It goes without saying," declares the writer, "that linguistic equivalence always comes before either socio-cultural equivalence or stylistic equivalence when the three cannot be attained at the same time."

This decision, however, is easier made than sustained. When the same writer translates *She is no dancer* into 她壓根兒不會跳舞 , there is stylistic resemblance but no grammatical similarity. Does he give precedence to linguistic equivalence? When he recommends rendering *As she worked hard, Mary achieved excellent results* into 瑪麗學習努力，在期終考試取得優異成績 , is the choice based on linguistic equivalence?

One may agree that translation equivalence is a fascinating subject that deserves deep research, but linguistic phenomena are complexities that do not lend themselves to pigeon-holing. Too much compartmentalizing may bedevil the analysts instead of helping them.

Where Linguistics Can Help

When all is said and done, a fair-minded observer would not deny the usefulness of linguistics to translators. It cannot solve all problems, but can show where the problems are (that's exactly what Nida's books are about and we thank him for it) and in what direction we can grope for the solutions.

It would appear that linguistics has proved to be helpful on several counts.

First of all, linguistics has pointed out that different genres require different treatments. As is well-known, legal documents are not translated as lyrical poems are. Peter Newmark stresses that expressive writing (informal letters), informational writing (scientific reports) and communicative writing (advertisements) should be handled in different ways. Wolfram Wilss remarks that "a qualified LSP translator is not necessarily at the same time a qualified translator of literary texts" and vice versa. (Wilss, 1982:134) In China, Professor Jin Yuelin 金岳霖 (1896–1984) noted that even philosophical works are not all the same. Those based on pure logic are easier to translate, he thinks, but those imbued with metaphysics are distressingly intractable. (Luo, 1984:463–79)

Second, a careful translator, in the opinion of linguists, has to take into consideration not only the text but also the linguistic context and the social background. A joke should not be reproduced as a statement of fact; an ironic remark is not to be taken at its face value. In answering questions, the Chinese expressions 是 - 不是 and the English counterparts yes-no operate differently and need careful discrimination.

Third, contrastive linguistics shows that in translation there are only approximations, never exact equivalents. To render is to imitate and to re-create, not to take a photoprint. 他去看病 in essence means *he went to see a doctor*, but the English speaker mentions the doctor, the Chinese doesn't. *He flung his arm around his father* means 他緊緊抱住他的父親 , but it is only in English that one senses the suddenness and force of the limb moving.

Fourth, all translations involve to a degree amplifications, simplifications and omissions, conscious or unconscious. One may think *wishful thinking* is good enough for 如意算盤, but the English phrase is far less graphic. *Love me, love my dog* is roughly 愛屋及烏, but the Chinese proverb is redolent of ancient times. And how do you represent 人走茶涼？Can the sense of loneliness and despondency haunting an ex-apparatchik be fully conveyed by the factual statement *When the guests are off the tea gets cold*?

Fifth, it has dawned upon many critics that a translator is a human being, not a computer. Both process words, but in ways quite different. Moreover, among translators, each goes his own way, and even the same man adopts different styles at different times. As noted by Qian Zhongshu, Lin Shu, who has often been denounced for his unfaithful translation, is at times quite literal. (Luo, 1984:696–725)

We may agree with Gladys Yang that a translator can hardly be undivided in his loyalty. He may be willing to stick to the original, but at the same time he has to keep an eye on the readers. If he is mainly concerned with the text — as was Xuan Zang — he is inclined to be literal and inflexible; if he wishes to be well-understood, he will take some liberties like Kumarajiva's. Among contemporary translators, David Hawkes retained all expressions in *Hong Lou Meng* 《紅樓夢》 puns included, while S. Shapiro snipped off the poems in *Outlaws of the Marsh* 《水滸傳》 because "they are little better than doggerel and ruin the suspense by revealing what is about to follow." (Shapiro, 1981) The literary historian may appreciate Hawkes, but to the common reader, manicures do not lead to haemorrhages.

In order to see how modern linguistics contributed to the making of a better translation , one may take a look at Roger Coleman's report on the revision of the *New English Bible* (1970.) (Coleman, 1989:3–8) In the *Revised English Bible* (1989), the following changes have been made. The obsolete second person singular pronoun is gone (*thou* into *you*); Briticisms have been removed (*ass* is offensive to Americans, so replaced with *donkey*); male-dominated expressions are rephrased (*The wicked* instead of *wicked men*); technical terms are altered (*purification-offering* instead of *sin-offering*).

At 2:Corinthians 8:10 in *The New English Bible*, Paul said, "Here is my considered opinion on the matter. What I ask you to do is in your interests." In the *Revised English Bible*, the wording is, "Here is my advice, and I have your interests at heart." Even to the Chinese ear, the new locution appears to be more informal, more friendly and so more persuasive.

But you never can tell. To native speakers brought up on the *Authorized Version* of 1611, the new version might sound disappointingly undignified if not grossly vulgar.

References

Coleman, Roger. "A Contemporary Bible." *English Today*, Vol. 5, No. 4 (1989), pp. 3–8.

Luo, Xinzhang 羅新璋, ed. 《翻譯論集》 (*Essays on Translation*). Beijing: The Commercial Press 商務印書館, 1984.

Nida, Eugene A. "Theories of Translation." 《外國語》 (*Journal of Foreign Language*), No. 6 (1989), pp. 2–8.

———— and Charles Taber. *The Theory and Practice of Translation*. Leiden: E. J. Brill, 1974.

Shapiro, Sidney. *Outlaws of the Marsh*. Beijing: Foreign Languages Press, 1981.

St. Pierre, Paul. "Criteria for Translation." In *Languages at Crossroads: Proceedings of the 29th Annual Conference of the American Translators Association*, edited by Deanna Lindberg Hammond. Medford, New Jersey: Learned Information, Inc., 1989, pp. 305–306.

Wilss, Wolfram. *The Science of Translation: Problems and Methods*. Tübingen: Verlag Gunter Narr, 1982.

Literalism

Shen Dan
Department of English
Peking University, Beijing, China

The Nature of Literalism

Anyone who is interested in the theory of translation would be familiar with the distinction between literal (word-for-word) and free (sense-for-sense) translation. This distinction, "established within the Roman system, has continued to be a point for debate in one way or another right up to the present" (Bassnett-McGuire, 1980). Literalism in the strict sense refers to the translation of the primary meaning of each individual word, while copying all the syntactic features of the source-language text. The following is an example (Nida, 1964):

> became/happened man, sent from God, name to-him John; this/the-same came-he into/for testimony/witness, that/in-order-that testify/witness-might-he concerning/of/to the light, that/in-order-that all believe-might-they through him, not was he/that-one the light, but that/in-order-that witness-might-he concerning/of/to the light. (Alternative lexical equivalents are marked by slant lines, and translations requiring more than one word are joined together by hyphens, to indicate that they correspond to a single unit in the source text.)

Although a bit out of fashion now, literalism has, however, no lack of believers and practitioners. "Words are still transferred brick by brick from one language to another, and a text reconstructed in a second language piecemeal, in the optimistic hope that the text will come through undistorted because of the conscientious but clumsy efforts of the brick-layer" (Ray, 1976).

Given that a language is a set of *patterned* symbols, and that each language has its own peculiar syntactic patterns, literalism can be defined as word translation plus syntax *transplantation*, imposing the source language's peculiar syntax on words of the receptor language, treating the receptor language as a syntactically unpatterned system. This definition may be clarified by the following diagram:

Given two corresponding systems X & Y, as follows:

(1) X: A   B   C   D
            | | | |
     Y: F   G   I   J

we can say that F, G, I, J are corresponding forms of A, B, C, D respectively.

If, on the other hand, given two systems X & Y as follows:

(2) X: A   B   C   D
            | | | |
     Y:

where in Y no corresponding forms are available, we can come to another conclusion, that in Y the corresponding forms to A, B, C, D in X are the copied A′, B′, C′, D′ respectively, as follows:

(2) X: A   B   C   D
            | | | |
     Y: A′   B′   C′   D′

It is fairly obvious that in the case of (1), where system Y does possess corresponding forms, it will be theoretically infelicitous to leave F, G, I, J aside and make in system Y a copy of A, B, C, D *as system Y's corresponding forms to X*, as follows:

(1) X: A   B   C   D
            | | | |
     Y: (F) (G) (I) (J)
            A′   B′   C′   D′

What is shown here is in fact an abstract formulation of syntactic transplantation in literalism, where the replacement by receptor language's corresponding syntactic patterns is to give way to the copying of source language's original forms, treating the receptor language as a syntactically unpatterned system.

Interestingly, literalism has been formalized in and, to a certain extent, justified by the widely accepted concept of "formal-equivalence" (or "formal-correspondence"), first proposed by Eugene A. Nida in 1964, as follows:

> Such a formal-equivalence translation is basically source-oriented; that is, it is designed to reveal as much as possible of the form and content of the original message. In doing so, a formal-equivalence translation attempts to reproduce several formal elements, including: (1) grammatical units, (2) consistency in word usage, and (3) meanings in terms of the source context. The reproduction of grammatical units may consist in: (a) translating nouns by nouns, verbs by verbs, etc.; (b) keeping all phrases and sentences intact (i.e. not splitting up and readjusting the units); and (c) preserving all formal indicators, e.g. marks of punctuation, paragraph breaks, and poetic indentation.

It is understood that, in translation theory, the term "reproduce" or "preserve" is synonymous with "translate faithfully", hence the concept "equivalence". Clearly, the *un*translated source language's formal features are wrongly treated as the receptor language's equivalent ones, irrespective of the receptor language's own corresponding forms. To put things right, one had better use words like "copy" or "transplant" in place of "reproduce" or "preserve". And instead of saying "translating nouns by nouns …", one ought to say "keeping the part of speech in the source-language text *un*translated". Literalism is not "formal-equivalence" but "formal-transplantation" (Shen, 1989).

The basic assumption underlying "literal or faithful translation" is well understood to be "to adhere closely to the original" (Savory, 1957). Given the Italian sentence "Ha comprato Maria un libro", a literal translator would render it into "Has bought Mary a book" rather than "Mary has bought a book", with the claim that the former is more faithful to the original form. But if "faithfulness" lies in keeping the original elements untranslated, why should one translate words? Literalism is quite inconsistent in its general position. On the one hand, as in the case of syntax, it regards the substitution of receptor-language's corresponding forms as a violation of fidelity; on the other hand, so far as words are concerned, the substitution of receptor-language's corresponding forms is considered right and proper, which substitution is however again subjected to the non-substitution of, among other things, classes of words. Based on such a grossly inconsistent and self-contradictory position, literalism has indeed little claim to theoretical validity as an approach to ("total") translation. Indeed, because of the "faithful" efforts of literal translators, the very object of devotion, the source-language message, has more often than not been in various degrees unconsciously distorted, as Nida and Taber put it: "Formal correspondence: the form (syntax and classes of words) is preserved [untranslated]; the meaning is lost or distorted" (1982). Although literalism, which is only partial translation, often involves severe distortions of the original, it can be justified in terms of its pragmatic function. It reveals or demonstrates, with the help of receptor-language words, the peculiar formal features of the source language, able to serve, among other things, as a tool for language learners (Nida, 1964; Catford, 1965; Savory, 1957).

The Cause of Literalism and the Reason for Its Survival

How did literalism come into being? Why have the unsubstituted source-language's formal elements been wrongly treated as the receptor-language's corresponding ones? It was, first of all, a historical mistake: (1) Treating language as a repertoire (mass) of words instead of as a patterned system, so that words in the receptor language are chosen to be arranged according to the original. (2) Treating the source language as superior or even sacred, as in some religious translation, so that the receptor language is made to conform to the syntactic rules and other formal features of the source language (Nida, 1964; Kelly, 1979; Chen, 1983). The cause, however, is not only historical but also conceptual, otherwise literalism might not have survived into modern times.

Conceptually, literalism is to be accounted for by the following all-too-easily-confused concepts:

(1) "Equivalence" ("correspondence"): the crux of the confusion lies in the two alternative possibilities of "equivalence", which has already been shown by a diagram. In translation, no copied (unsubstituted) source-language form can be regarded as the receptor-language's equivalent *except* where no corresponding (ready-made or derivative) form is available in the receptor language. Failure to realize this *mutual-exclusiveness* rather than simultaneous existence of the two possibilities can all too easily lead to the

indiscriminate acceptance of any copied source-language form as the equivalent in the receptor language.

(2) Source language versus the original: absence of discrimination has given rise to another confusion, namely, mixing up the formal peculiarities of the source language with the formal peculiarities of the original. The two in effect differ fundamentally from each other in the following closely related aspects: (a) the former are to be determined solely in terms of their relation to formal peculiarities in other language systems, the latter mainly in terms of their relation to formal peculiarities in other works in the same genre within the same language system; (b) the former are arbitrary, conventionalized rules, the latter deliberate, personal choices; (c) the former, as the norm for *everybody* in the language system to comply with, have nothing to do with the peculiar thought pattern or intention of the original author, while the latter, as *personal* deviations from the norm, bear the imprint of the original author's style. Failure to make this basic distinction has the consequence that all formal elements in the original, be it norm or deviation, have been indiscriminately treated as expressive of the original author's thought pattern or style, and hence to be transplanted, if possible, one and all, to the receptor language. As Kelly puts it, "Strict formal equivalence outside technical translation often rests on the assumption that style is the man" (1979). Indeed style is the man, but whether one uses "Mary has bought a book" (SVO) or "Ha comprato Maria un libro" (VSO) has nothing to do with the style of the man. The effort of rendering "Ha comprato Maria un libro" into "Has bought Mary a book" conveys very little of either the style or the man. Similarly, if language X is hypotactic and language Y paratactic, and if no necessary adjustments are made, the syntactic aspect concerned in the translation will reflect anything but the man. Given the basic distinction in question, one could at least have substituted receptor-language's norm for source-language's norm while duplicating the formal deviations of the original. Even so it would be only half way towards proper translation, which demands the replacement of the whole source-language message by the closest receptor-language's equivalent, norm by norm, deviation by deviation, in a word, by what the original author would have put down in the receptor language.

Apart from these reasons mentioned above, there are some more objective conditions that may have played some part in the birth and survival of literalism: (1) Similarity of formal features between cognate languages. (2) Similarity of some major syntactic patterns (e.g. SVO) and some other formal elements between different languages. (3) In the translation of some classical or religious works, a laboured effect may add to the elevation or solemnity of the language. Moreover, in the translation of poetry, a genre marked by deviation, unusual syntax might well be expected.

Idiomatic Expression: A Peculiar Case

Where one finds it most difficult to come to terms with the substitution of a receptor-language's equivalent for the source-language message is in the case of idiomatic expressions, for the simple reason that here, unlike elsewhere, the receptor-language's equivalent may bear little resemblance to the original in formation: compare the English "kick the bucket" with its Chinese equivalent "qiao bianzi" 翘辫子 (with one's pigtail erected). The crux of the problem lies in what Nida defines as the "semantically exocentric" nature of these conventionalized expressions:

> there is nothing in the forms of such words as *boy, girl, dish, news,* and *snow* which would tell us their referents. Similarly, there are many combinations of words to whose meaning the constituent parts offer little or no clue. For example, the Hebrew idiom *children of the bridechamber* refers to the wedding guests, and specifically to the friends of the bridegroom; but adding up the component parts of the phrase does not provide a clue to this meaning. The same situation applies to all kinds of so-called idioms, e.g. *heap coals of fire on his head* ... (1964)

With such an essential similarity in formation between a word and an idiom, the conclusion can be drawn that if, in translation, a source-language word is to be replaced by a corresponding receptor-language word rather than by a group of corresponding letters, e.g.:

(A)	source language (English)	"girl"
	receptor language (French)	"fille"
	rather than:	
	source language (English)	g - i - r - l
	receptor language (French)	g - i - r - l

then a source-language idiom is similarly to be replaced by a corresponding receptor-language idiom (or, when unavailable, by the closest plain equivalent) rather than by a group of corresponding words, e.g.:

(B)   source language (English)   "kick the bucket"
       receptor language (Chinese)   翹辮子
       rather than:
       source language (English)   kick-the-bucket
       receptor language (Chinese)   踢這桶子

Clearly, what appears in (B) is in essence by no means a choice between "literal" and "free" translation — no more than in (A) where no one would call the rendering of the English "g-i-r-l" into the French "g-i-r-l" literal and the rendering of the English "girl" into the French "fille" free. Failure to realize fully the semantically exocentric nature of idioms, coupled with a failure to view "translation as semiotic transformation" (Bassnett-McGuire, 1980) has resulted in the misapplication of the "literal vs. free" dichotomy to the idiomatic expression, which is to be treated semantically as a single word. As a matter of fact, in the case of idiomatic expressions, "literal" and "free" translation would amount to the one and the same thing; for both approaches, no matter of "word for word" or "sense for sense", would equally mean replacing the whole source-language idiom (this being "a single word") with a corresponding receptor-language idiom (this again being "a single word") or a plain expression (to take the place of the source-language "word").

A word, generally definable as "the smallest isolable meaningful element of the language" (E. D. Collins), is usually the most basic unit to be substituted in translation. The so-called "literal" rendering of an idiom actually works on a "sub-verbal" level, i.e. replacing, instead of the "single word" (idiom), its constituent parts which may not provide a clue to its meaning. It is clear that this "sub-verbal" approach, like the attempt of rendering the English "girl" into the French "g-i-r-l" rather than "fille", amounts to theoretical absurdity.

Superficially verbal but intrinsically sub-verbal, this duality is to account for one's reluctance in accepting the total replacement of source language by receptor language in the case of idioms. Although one normally may not feel sorry to discard sub-verbal elements in translation, one does want to see receptor-language words correspond, if possible, to those of the original. So, in contrast to one's readiness to abandon "g" (i) "r" (l) while substituting "fille" for "girl", one does find it difficult to come to terms with the discarding of "kick" "the" "bucket" that the substitution of "qiao bianzi" for "kick the bucket" involves, as the latter is, after all, not a group of meaningless letters, but consists of words themselves. However, since the group of letters "d" "i" "e" and the group of words "kick" "the" "bucket" both in essence form the constituent parts of "a single word", sharing with each other arbitrariness and meaninglessness, it is only proper to discard them equally without mercy in translation.

Nevertheless, though hardly any justification can be found for translating the constituent letters of a word rather than the word itself, some justification may be offered for translating the constituent words of an idiom instead of the peculiar "single word" itself. For the constituent words differ from the constituent letters in the following ways:

(1) Possibly not so arbitrary and meaningless: The relative possibility arises from the following two comparisons. First, unlike the constituent letters, the constituent words of an idiom, as words in themselves, are able to convey some sense which may have a certain association with the referent of the idiom. The Hebrew idiom "children of the bridechamber" cited above is a case in point. Despite the fact that the constituent words do "not provide a clue" to the referent of the idiom, they do at least drop a hint of the wedding. Secondly, within the idiomatic kingdom, the constituent words of some idioms are more meaningful than others, especially when contextualized. Many idioms are fossilized metaphors, implying points of similarity between one entity and another. So while "kick-the-bucket" may suggest nothing of the event referred to by the idiom, "beat-about-the-bush" does convey obliquely, in a vivid and striking way, some indirectness of approach, meant to be signified by the whole idiom.

(2) Freedom of formation: A language has a somehow fixed number of word forms, which usually are not susceptible to change short of the transformation of the whole system. In contrast with this is the freedom of formation of idioms which, "presumably coined by one person and diffused through popular speech, writing and later the media" (Newmark, 1981), may come into being at any time, new ones constantly replacing old ones. That is to say, the form of a word is more or less an inherent member of a stable system, while

the form of an idiom is, by contrast, a somewhat contingent member in an open field, that of expression.

(3) Absorbability (into receptor language through translation): What closely ties up with the previous two points is the relative absorbability of the constituent words of an idiom as opposed to the constituent letters of a word. Since the latter is, generally speaking, totally arbitrary and meaningless, and since in each language system the form of a word is somehow stable (so is the number of forms), a source-language word normally may not be able to find its way through translation into the receptor language (to be juxtaposed with receptor-language equivalent(s)), even if corresponding letters are available, and even if the receptor-language audience gets to know what the group of the corresponding letters refers to. In contrast with this exclusiveness of the more or less closed arbitrary sign system itself is the ready receptiveness of the open field of expression, to which idioms belong. For all its peculiarity, a source- language idiom, if vivid as well as somehow "meaningful", may be adopted by the receptor language under given circumstances. This is especially the case where the idiom is free from particular spatial and temporal references, e.g. "beat about the bush".

(4) Local cultural colour: When an idiom does have local cultural references, it may find it more difficult to get itself adopted by the receptor language. The local colour itself, however, may constitute sufficient interest for the receptor-language reader and hence make it worth presenting. This is of course also a point at which the constituent words of an idiom differ from the "non-signifying" constituent letters of a word.

Since the constituent words of some idioms are not very arbitrary and meaningless, but are vivid, striking, carrying local colour, embodying the popular wisdom of the source language and possibly absorbable by the receptor language, the attempt to render them into the receptor language may help provide the receptor language with alternative "energies of meaning" (Steiner, 1975), an effect that is often sought after in translation. Furthermore, this "sub-verbal" approach, by rendering the exact words of an idiom, may prove helpful to language learners. Such pragmatic functions go beyond the capacity of the proper approach.

These two different approaches have been regarded as presenting a choice between "form and content". But actually they do not. Since the constituent words of an idiom (a "single word") are generally and essentially analogous to the constituent letters of a word, if one does not wish to regard the letters of a word as "form" and the word itself as "content", one is practically in no position to call the words of an idiom "form" and the peculiar "single word" itself "content".

What has been said about idioms in effect holds good for words in general. Peter Newmark points out:

> Words are not things, but symbols of things … Words *in context* are neither things nor usually the same symbols as individual words, but *components of a larger symbol* which spans a collocation, a clause or a sentence. (1981; emphasis added)

Idiomatic expressions present an extreme case where the individual symbols are "submerged", as it were, in a larger symbol and consequently become symbols different from individual words. What literal (word-for-word) translators normally do is to treat contextualized symbols as isolated ones and to substitute each of them according to its decontextualized primary sense, e.g. to turn the English phrase "catch cold" into the Chinese "zhuozhu leng" 捉住冷 (seize coldness), which has an entirely different referent from that of the original (Lu, 1959). If pushed to such "an absurd extent", the result may well become "relatively meaningless strings of words" (Nida, 1964).

Regrettably, this "so-called concordance of terminology" has been labeled, together with the "sub-verbal" rendering of idioms, as "formal-equivalence" (ibid.). It is understood that, in both cases, the "form" does not refer to the formation of a word, i.e. the combination of letters, or else the English "cold" will find its French "formal-equivalence" in the shape of "c-o-l-d", and its Chinese (pictographic) "formal-equivalence" a sheer impossibility. What the "form" in question actually refers to is the sense of a word in normal context. As regards the phrase "catch cold", the "form" of "catch" would then be its decontextualized normal sense "seize" and its "content" the contextualized particular meaning "be infected with". The same applies to "cold". Accordingly, the whole phrase "catch cold" will find its Chinese "formal-equivalence" in the shape of "zhuozhu leng" 捉住冷 (seize coldness) and its Chinese "dynamic-equivalence" in the form of "huan ganmao" 患感冒 (be infected with illness of the nose or throat).

There seems little need to go into the theoretical infelicity of labeling the normal *sense* of a word "form" and its contextualized meaning "content": since the former is as much content as the latter.

Given that in translation the basic word form (spelling and sound) is practically unconveyable, the label "form" may well be generally applied to the formal properties of words, such as archaic, elevated or euphemistic. One may regard, for instance, the Chinese "qiao bianzi" 翹辮子 as being formally more equivalent to the English "kick the bucket" than the straight-forward "si" 死 . It is worth noting that this "formal-equivalence" is and can only be based on "content-equivalence", for the formal attributes are to be compared between substitutes for the same source-language word(s), which should share the same referent.

A Full Picture of Literalism

By now a fairly full picture of literalism will have emerged: (1) Insofar as grammatical units are concerned, it keeps them untranslated. (2) In the case of idioms, it takes what might be considered a "sub-verbal" approach. (3) When it comes to words in general, it treats them as isolated symbols and substitutes them irrespective of their contextualized meaning. Although theoretically infelicitous, this approach can fulfil certain pragmatic functions, able to serve, among other things, as a tool for receptor-language learners.

References

Bassnett-McGuire, Susan. *Translation Studies*. London: Methuen, 1980.

Catford, J. C. *A Linguistic Theory of Translation*. Oxford: Oxford University Press, 1965.

Chen, Zhongbao 陳忠保 . 〈翻譯原則古今談〉 (Ancient and Modern Principles of Translation). 《翻譯通訊》 (*Translators' Notes*), No. 3 (1983), pp. 41–43.

Kelly, L. G. *The True Interpreter*. Oxford: Blackwell, 1979.

Loh, Dian-yang 陸殿揚 . *Translation: Its Principles and Technique*. Beijing: The Epoch Publishing House, 1959.

Newmark, Peter. *Approaches to Translating*. Oxford: Pergamon Press, 1981.

Nida, Eugene A. *Towards a Science of Translating*. Leiden: E. J. Brill, 1964.

———— and C. R. Taber. *The Theory and Practice of Translation*. Leiden: E. J. Brill, 1969.

Ray, L. "Multi-dimension Translation: Poetry." In *Translation: Applications and Research*, edited by R. W. Brislin. New York: Gardener Press, 1976, pp. 261–78.

Savory, Theodore. *The Art of Translation*. London: Cape, 1957.

Shen, Dan. "Literalism: NON-'Formal-equivalence'." *Babel*, Vol. 4 (1989), pp. 261–78.

Steiner, George. *After Babel*. Oxford: Oxford University Press, 1975.

LITERARY TRANSLATION

Translated Literature in Pre-modern China

Gilbert C. F. Fong
Department of Translation
The Chinese University of Hong Kong, Hong Kong

The late Qing period in Chinese history witnessed the transformation of a homogeneous, closed society being forced to open its doors to the influx of foreign influence. Politically, China was tottering at the brink of obliteration, and the urgency was felt throughout the nation that something had to be done to fend off the threat of foreign domination. In the confrontations with foreign powers, China had been humiliated in successive military debacles and driven to an admission of its scientific and technological backwardness. But the once proud cultural tradition was reluctant to subjugate itself, still hanging on to the claim of superiority, if only in spiritual matters, over an alien (barbarian) culture. The desire to regain the former glories of the empire gave rise to the bid of pragmatism, thus the Westernization Movement's (*c.* 1860–1890) slogan: "Chinese learning as essence, Western learning for practical use." (中學爲體, 西學爲用)

In an effort to "understand foreign affairs", (Chen, 1989) translation bureaus were set up to teach foreign languages and to translate books on science and technology. For example, the translation office of the Jiangnan Arsenal was established in 1867, which included three sub-divisions of physics, chemistry, and arms production. The office put out a total of 163 books on mathematics, surveying, machine parts, army and navy strategy, ship building, diplomacy, international law, and other practical matters. (Ma, 1984) These books, the result of the first large-scale systematic translation undertaking in the Qing dynasty, were all directed at "knowing the enemy" and building up the nation's military arsenal, or as Zeng Guofan 曾國藩, an advocate for the Westernization Movement, put it, "Translation is the foundation of arms production." (Chen, 1989)

However, a series of military setbacks and subsequent unequal treaties soon caught up with the Westernization proponents and their technocentric views on translation. In the last decade of the 19th century, there were calls among the intellectuals to introduce Western thought and ideology, as technology, in their opinion, had proven ineffective in curing the nation's ailments. In 1897, Liang Qichao 梁啓超, one of the leaders of the ill-fated Reform Movement of 1898, pointed out:

> There are two reasons for China's defeat: first, we had been unaware of the enemies' strength, and then we were unaware of how the enemies had acquired such strength .... Among the books translated by the government offices, nearly half of them are concerned with military matters .... We have to know that even though the Westerners' strength lies in their military prowess, it is not the reason for their strength .... If we understand this fact, then there would be no need to translate any more books on military matters.

He then went on to argue for the urgency to translate books on law, history, and Greek and Roman philosophy for the people's enlightenment. (Liang, 1897)

Yan Fu 嚴復, a Confucian scholar, did not share Liang Qichao's reformist zeal on the political front, yet he did share the view that Western learning was not merely utilitarian, pointing out that it also excelled in the spiritual, and ideas such as liberty and democracy had been pivotal in building up wealth and power in the West. Yan Fu went on to translate T. H. Huxley's *Evolution and Ethics* (1898), Adam Smith's *The Wealth of Nations* (1902), and other studies on law, logic, politics, and sociology. The translations, rendered into beautifully styled classical Chinese, were particularly well received by the literati, making them aware of the urgency to modernize the nation's thinking. In particular, evolutionism became a key concept effecting major changes in modern Chinese intellectual history.

Yan Fu's translations present us with classical examples of how non-literary source texts, when translated, are regarded as literature in the target text community. That they were also practical and message-based further facilitated their induction into the target-language literary polysystem which had been heavily conditioned by didacticism. A similar combination of literary grace and functionalism was also carried over into the translation of literature, a relatively latecomer. Thus to Lin Shu 林紓 , who translated Harriet Beecher Stowe's *Uncle Tom's Cabin* in the classical style of Tang *chuanqi* 傳奇 , the black slaves' agony was a sad reminder of the future destiny of the declining yellow race. (Lin, 1901) And adventure stories such as Defoe's *Robinson Crusoe* and Scott's *Ivanhoe* were popular because they alerted the Chinese readers to the West's adventurism and military spirit, and served to stimulate them into action at a time when the country was suffering from inertia and stagnancy. (Lin, 1907) And after the aborted Reform Movement of 1898, there emerged a wave of "political fiction". Liang Qichao, then living in exile in Japan, insisted (perhaps too readily and naively) that "political fiction" was responsible for the progress made in the foreign countries. (Liang, 1898) Therefore, he launched his *New Fiction Magazine* 《新小說》 in 1902, in which were featured many translated stories politically relevant to the Chinese conditions for his compatriots' edification. In the mean time, Lu Xun 魯迅 and others translated Western and Japanese science fiction, aiming to eliminate superstitions and to provide the readers with scientific knowledge.

Translated literature, despite its popularity, was only accorded a lowly status. As one later critic put it, "Most of the literati at the time only conceded that China was inadequate in its antiquated and corrupted political system. As for Chinese literature, it was still the best and the most beautiful." (Zheng, 1924) In terms of translation process, the preference for the domestic mode, given the deeply entrenched narcissism of Chinese culture, was hardly surprising.

Yan Fu's famous three guidelines for translation, or "difficulties", as he also called them — faithfulness, comprehensibility, elegance (信、達、雅), evince a similar bias for the target language text. In the preface to his translation of Huxley's *Ethics and Evolution*, he relies heavily on the Confucian classics to explain his guidelines, which later formed the basis of modern Chinese translation theory. Among them, only "faithfulness" is directly related to the source text in terms of accuracy in cognitive information; "comprehensibility" and "elegance" are target-text-centred, the principles according to which the source-text information should be remolded and encoded linguistically. Of "comprehensibility", he says: "When the translator had understood thoroughly and digested the whole text he will then be able to rewrite it in the best manner possible." The re-encoding process and its product, the target text, then do not necessarily bear any relation to the modes of presentation, or the ease or difficulty of the source text, and the translator is free to choose his style, which, according to Yan Fu, should strive for refined "elegance". Strangely enough, this is also where "comprehensibility" enters into the picture: "In using the syntax and style of the pre-Han period one actually facilitates the comprehensibility of the profound principles and subtle thoughts, whereas in using the modern vernacular one finds it difficult to make things comprehensible." (Yan, 1898) Archaism certainly lends an air of authority and "elegance", but to the contemporary reader, the pre-Han style of more than two millennia ago, in which the Confucian classics had been written, was very remote and difficult to understand. One wonders whether Yan Fu, himself a scholar of the classical Tongcheng School 桐城派 , was motivated by mere comprehensibility or by his aspiration for respectability, and "comprehensibility" was but a red herring, the rationalization for acceptance by his literati peers of his translations as serious scholarship.

Yan Fu's sinicization was so complete that it raised some eyebrows. Among those who disapproved was Wu Rulun 吳汝綸 , the Tongcheng doyen, who urged Yan Fu to retain the Western mode in the source text, like the Buddhist monks who had translated the sutras in a style independent of that of the Chinese classics. (Wu, 1897) However, on another occasion he also commended Yan Fu for his effective reduplication of the style of the ancients (of the Later Zhou dynasty). (Wu, 1898) Wu Rulun's vacillating between the source and target languages was also observable in Yan Fu's translation career. Critics have pointed out there were three stages of development: he first started with a semantic approach, followed with a comparatively literal procedure, and finally reverted to message-based translation, giving priority to the conventions of the Chinese language, even to the point of adopting Chinese allusions and metaphors as illustrations of Western ideas. He commented that "it is sufficient for my work to be understood by the readers; whether it proffers an exact correspondence with the original is not my concern." (Yan, 1908)

Lin Shu's translations were often compared to the Tang *chuanqi*, the Song *ci* 詞 poetry, and other classical literary writings. He lamented the fact that he did not understand any foreign language, and had to rely on his helpers for interpretations, thus he was unable to reproduce the stylistic excellence of foreign literature. In many of the prefaces to his translations, he attempted to analyse the original stories according to the "rules" prescribed by the Tongcheng School, and came up with the conclusion that there were similarities in structuring principles and techniques between the works by Dickens, Scott, Stowe, Rider Haggard and others and the master-pieces of Chinese narratives such as *Records of the Grand Historian* 《史記》 and *The Zuo Commentary on the Spring and Autumn Annals* 《左傳》. (Lin, 1901 and 1905) Unlike his contemporaries who often looked down upon foreign literatures, Lin Shu at least admitted their merits and regarded them as equals. The claim of parity justified translated litera-ture, and bestowed upon it legitimacy of existence alongside other Chinese classics in the home polysystem. To an extent, the conservative-minded literati welcomed Lin Shu's works despite being mindful of their difference, and they accepted them as *bona fide* literature and "learning" because they found that translations, like their own writings, also conformed to the "rules".

This explains why Lin Shu's translations were often adaptations, not for the sake of simplicity, but with an eye on their literary and cultural relevance to the home tradition. Thus lengthy passages of scenic and psychological descriptions were characteristically deleted from the source texts because they were considered alien to the Chinese narrative tradition. Some critics even claimed that his translations were *chuanqi* stories featur-ing Western themes and subject matters. (Actually he was more "faithful" than many of his contemporary counterparts, whose translations were often merely rewrites, or 演義, with sinicized characters, setting, and syntax.) (Lin, 1990) Naturalization was deliberate, a means to the end of assimila-tion, not so much the incidental result of the lack of a foreign tongue or incompetent interpreters, and it is doubtful that given proper assistance, Lin Shu would have produced more faithful representations of the source texts. Nor was he concerned about "equivalent effect", as he was only interested in the response of the target-language readers. In many prefaces to his translations, he conspicuously shied away from any discussion on "faithful-ness", and admitted that with his insistence on stylistic "elegance", he was willing to compromise "faithfulness" to achieve the refined decorum funda-mental to the Chinese literary style.

The source-language culture was also generally manipulated to avoid a clash with the home culture. Yan Fu, for example, strained to interpret Western concepts in terms of their counterparts in the Chinese classics. And in selection, particularly in the early years of the period, source texts were chosen for their resemblance to existing themes popular among the Chinese readers for thousands of years. Thus romantic love stories and adventures were among the most popular. Translators, burdened with the heavy weight of tradition, remained ambivalent towards the West. And as with Yan Fu, it was common practice to impose Chinese culture onto translated literature, appending such moral norms as loyalty and filial piety. The dominance of the home culture and the general contempt of Western morality (or immorality) led to diminishing the authority of the source texts, which were to be routinely and freely manipulated. In extreme cases, moral concessions prompted translators to censor or even mutilate the source texts. For instance, in 1901 Bao Tianxiao 包天笑 , the famous newspaperman and translator, co-translated Rider Haggard's *Joan Haste*. Only the first part of the story was published, and the translators claimed that they could not locate the second part. But the truth was that it contained the chapters where the heroine gives birth to an illegitimate son. As illegitimacy was morally revolting, the translators had to resort to bowdlerization to avoid disparagement and rejection by their readers who might feel offended. Interestingly, Lin Shu offered a complete version of *Joan Haste* in 1905, and there appeared a controversy arguing for and against the merits of the two translations. To some critics, Lin Shu acted indiscreetly, even presumptuously, in exposing Joan Haste's wrongdoing to censure, and his rendition was an act of defamation, a conspiracy to destroy the good name of the hitherto chaste and innocent heroine. (Yin, 1907)

Modification of the source texts was also observed in the treatment of literary genres nonexistent in the domestic repertory. Translations of fiction were in the majority, as they could be easily adapted to conform with the conventional mode of narration with only minor adjustments. But it appeared that even within a genre, the dominance of a certain structure was also a deciding factor. For example, the "chapter format", which had been the only structure for Chinese fiction written in the vernacular, was retained by Lu Xun, Liang Qichao, and others when the translations were in the colloquial *baihua* 白話 , but was discarded by translators like Lin Shu when they were translating in *wenyan* 文言 , the classical language. In Chinese literature, *baihua* novels were the norm, and there existed no precedent for lengthy *wenyan* stories, which made it easier for Lin Shu to sidestep the convention, and his translations have been deemed a breakthrough in literature written in the classical language. Lin Shu remained a conservative writer in the May Fourth period and Lu Xun became a pioneer of modern literature, and this irony really brings home the immense conforming power of tradition at the time.

Even though the first translated poem (Longfellow's "Psalm of Life") had appeared in 1864 (Qian, 1984), large-scale introduction of Western poetry did not occur until the 1900's. Chinese poetry, historically revered as the best and most prestigious in the hierarchy of literary genres, had a long tradition of excellence, and its various forms and rules had been handed down from generation to generation and persisted even in the late Qing period. And as poetry demands maximum exploitation of the resources in a linguistic system, the differences between languages were either minimized or dismissed totally in the translation process in favour of the formal and aesthetic conventions in the domestic repertory. Thus famous translators such Su Manshu 蘇曼殊 , Ma Junwu 馬君武 , and Lu Xun chose to translate poems by Byron, Shelley, Goethe, Heine, Sienkiewicz, and others according to the classical Chinese versification schemes and using Chinese allusions. As a result, their translations resembled original compositions. "Parodistic" transference of Western poetic forms was introduced only in the May Fourth period with the arrival of vernacular literature, which in effect liberated poetry from the constraints of traditional norms.

There were only few translations of drama, and as no tradition of spoken drama had existed, they were often rewritten, transmuted into other genres in the Chinese tradition. For example, the balcony scene in *Romeo and Juliet* was adapted into 彈詞 , a performance text interspersed with poetry and songs. And even as late as the 1910's, Lin Shu still translated Ibsen's *Ghosts* and some Shakespeare plays into narrative form and published them as novels. Interestingly, the first Chinese spoken drama 話劇 , modelled after the Western-styled presentation in which dialogues (not singing) predominated, was staged in 1907 in Tokyo by the Spring Willow Society 春柳社 organized by a group of Chinese students then studying in Japan. The play was adapted from *La Dame aux camélias*, and was followed by another adaptation of *Uncle Tom's Cabin* in the same year. There were no scripts, and the promptbooks outlining the plots for the actors were based on Lin Shu's translations of the Western novels, confirming that the format of drama written as performance text was uncommon, and inspiration had to be sought from a different, and more familiar literary genre. More significantly, the introduction of a new form, in this case spoken drama, was launched on foreign soil where it would encounter less resistance. As the dominance of home tradition was hostile to nonconformities, any innovation could only be attempted circuitously.

Translation influence is a complex phenomenon for which there is no ready-made explanation. According to Itamar Even-Zohar, translated literature could be categorized as primary or secondary activity. The primary activity, representing the principle of innovation, "participates actively in *modelling the centre* of the polysystem", and the secondary maintains the established code and "constitutes a peripheral system within the polysystem, generally assuming the character of epigonic writing." (Even-Zohar, 1978) In the late Qing period, the majority of translated literature falls into the latter category, in which the translation process was molded and conditioned by the dominant forces established in the home polysystem. As Zhou Zuoren 周作人 says of this period:

> The Chinese were unwilling to imitate, and they did not know how to imitate .... A translator was not motivated by admiration; he translated a certain book only because it resembled us [our writings]. Therefore, the novels by Scott were translatable and readable because they resembled *Shiji*, which is the same as regarding Huxley's *Evolution* as comparable to the Zhou and Qin Classics. Such a feeling was pervasive, thus no reform was possible. They [the late Qing scholars] were unwilling to learn from others; they only wanted others to resemble them. (Zhou, 1918)

Especially in the early years of this period, translation was no more than epigonic writing; its models were the well-established and respected classics, and its aim was to preserve traditional taste. An interesting development emerged: while translated literature strove to be "old", the home literature was experimenting with new norms and modes. For instance, Su Manshu translated Byron's *Childe Harold's Pilgrimage* into 古詩 (ancient poetry), which was even more archaic than the classical poetic forms practised in his time; at the same time, many Chinese poets, those belonging to the New Poetry Movement such as Huang Zunxian 黃遵憲 and Liang Qichao, were developing innovative devices in versification, subject matter, and a new diction. And in fiction, while Lin Shu and others were omitting descriptions of setting and psychology, Wu Woyao 吳沃堯 and other novelists were trying out exactly the same techniques in their stories.

But the picture did not remain static. It was probable that the dynamism in the home literature, especially in the latter years, helped to modify the "reactionary" nature of translation activities by promoting change and familiarizing the new and the foreign, thus lending them legitimacy in the home polysystem. The door was open for translation to assume its role as a "primary activity", and to constitute new models to be imitated. For instance, Zhou Guisheng 周桂笙 retained the time reversal exposition in his translation of a French story which he entitled *Coil of the Poisonous Snake* 《毒蛇圈》 (1904), and in the next year Wu Woyao published his *Nine Murders* 《九命奇冤》 featuring the same technique. (Fong, 1980) And in the process of translation, more and more emphasis was placed on the source-text's mode of style and presentation. For example, Lu Xun and Zhou Zuoren's *Stories from Foreign Lands* 《域外小說集》 was considered the first Chinese translation to adopt the literal approach. The stories were translated in the classical language, but there was still resistance to its Westernized mode of narration which was preserved. Only 21 copies of the book were sold in the ten years after its publication.

Functionalism characterized the translation activities in pre-modern China. The need for information provided impetus and conditioned the selection and translation processes. Thus translations were essentially message-based, and the message was often remolded to accommodate the stylistic and generic modes then prevalent. In imposing domestic conventions onto translations and submitting them to scrutiny and approval according to domestic standards, translations were in effect undergoing a process of "naturalization", whose aim was not to stimulate change, but to maintain the status quo. Translation thus became a conservative force, the means to preserve tradition and to resist changes. Just as the late Qing political reforms were for the survival of the nation, translations could be seen as undertakings targeted to reform traditional culture for its continuation. Western masterpieces were regarded as kindred spirits; their resemblance to the Chinese classics, and their apparent capability and ease of being "naturalized" and absorbed into the main stream were proof of the universality and excellence in a tradition worthy of maintaining. In this respect, translation activities were also an effort of self-preservation on the part of a declining tradition, an attempt directed at cultural and linguistic autonomy (Vossler, 1977) in the face of the encroachment of foreign culture and home-generated demands for change.

In the context of Chinese literary history, translation in late Qing corresponded with the struggle for survival, the last hurrah, so to speak, of old literature. At the end of the period, the grip of tradition began to loosen and there were gaps through which the new and innovative force, in both language and ideology, began to seep through. But universalism, which the conservatives had been using to safeguard the old, just could not be contained behind closed doors, and translations, due to the extraneousness inherent in them, promoted a climate of change and dissatisfaction with the status quo. The feeling became even more widespread especially when translation activities expanded their scope from technical manuals and intellectual treatises to include popular literature. The circumstances were primed for the arrival of new approaches and methods.

In the May Fourth period that followed, translation took on the role of "primary activity", in which source texts were chosen for their compatibility with the fledgling new literature and to provide inspirations and new models. There was a shift towards the emphasis on the source texts and "adequacy" became a major concern. There also emerged a new kind of functionalism. Didacticism was still prevalent, this time directed at forging a new ideology as displacement of the old. And the translators, most of them were also leading writers, rejected the conservatives' rationalization of universality; instead they accentuated the difference between foreign literature and traditional Chinese literature. In comparison, the latter was found wanting, inferior, and no longer effective in promoting a new culture and portraying the new reality. Thus translations also represented a challenge to old literature, to bring it to submission for the ascendancy of the new. The new literature also needed a new language, viz., the vernacular, and translated texts, by retaining foreign linguistic features, became useful in bring in new modes of expression. And functionalism persisted and revealed itself in what Lu Xun called "give-me-ism" 拿來主義 , in that translations were to enrich the linguistic resources of the Chinese language by borrowing from foreign vocabularies, syntax and other linguistic features, and the influence of translation was not only felt culturally but also in linguistic terms.

References

Chen, Yugang 陳玉剛 , *et al.*, eds. 《中國翻譯史稿》 (*History of Translated Literature in China*). Beijing: China Translation and Publishing Corporation 中國對外翻譯出版公司 , 1989.

Even-Zohar, Itamar. "The Position of Translated Literature within the Literary Polysystem." In *Literature and Translation*, edited by James S. Holmes, Jose Lambert, and Raymond van den Broeck. Belgium: Acco Leuven, 1978, pp. 117–27.

Fong, Gilbert C. F. "Time in Nine Murders: Western Influence and the Domestic Tradition." In *The Chinese Novel at the Turn of the Century*, edited by Milena Dolezelova-Verlingerova. Toronto: University of Toronto Press, 1980.

Huang, Lin 黃霖 and Han Tongwen 韓同文 , eds. 《中國歷代小說論著選》 (*Selected Essays on Chinese Novels Through the Ages*), 2 vols. Nanchang: Jiangxi People's Press 江西人民出版社 , 1990.

Liang, Qichao 梁啓超 . 〈論譯書〉 (On Translation). In 《翻譯研究論文集》 (*Collected Essays on Translation Studies*), 1897, pp. 8–20.

———. 〈譯印政治小說序〉 (Foreword to the Publication of Political Fiction) (1898). In Huang Lin and Han Tongwen, Vol. 2, pp. 26–27.

Lin, Shu 林紓 . 〈《黑奴吁天錄》序〉 (Preface to *Uncle Tom's Cabin*) (1901). In A Ying 阿英 , pp. 196–97.

———. 〈《黑奴吁天錄》例言〉 (Introductory Remarks on *Uncle Tom's Cabin*) (1901). In Luo Xinzhang 羅新璋 , pp. 162–63.

Lin, Wei 林薇 . *A Hundred Years of Ups and Downs: A Summary of Lin Shu Criticism*. Tianjin: Tianjin Education Press 天津教育出版社 , 1990.

Luo, Xinzhang 羅新璋 , ed. 《翻譯論集》 (*Essays on Translation*). Beijing: The Commercial Press 商務印書館 , 1984.

Ma, Zuyi 馬祖毅 . 《中國翻譯簡史 — "五四" 運動以前》 (*A Brief History of Translation in China — Before the May Fourth Movement*). Beijing: China Translation and Publishing Corporation 中國對外翻譯出版公司 , 1984.

Niu, Yangshan 牛仰山 and Sun Hongni 孫鴻霓 , eds. 《嚴復研究資料》 (*Research Material on Yan Fu*). Fuzhou 福州 : Haixia Wenyi Chubanshe 海峽文藝出版社 , 1990.

Qian, Zhongshu 錢鍾書 . "Psalm of Life: The First English Poem Translated into Chinese." In Luo Xinzhang, pp. 233–50.

Vossler, Karl. "Translation as Cultural Imperialism." In *Translating Literature: The German Tradition from Luther to Rosensweig*, edited by André Lefevere. Amsterdam: Van Gorcum Assen, 1977, p. 97.

Wu, Rulun 吳汝綸 . 〈答嚴幼陵〉 (A Reply to Yan Youling) (1897). In Niu Yangshan 牛仰山 , pp. 250–51.

Yan, Fu 嚴復 . 〈《天演論》譯例言〉 (Introductory Remarks on Evolution) (1898). In Niu Yangshan, translated by C. Y. Hsu as "General Remarks on Translation." *Renditions*, No. 1 (1973), pp. 4–6.

———. 〈《名學淺說》譯者自序〉 (Introduction to Logic) (1908). In Luo Xinzhang, pp. 145–46.

Yin, Bansheng 寅半生 (Zhong Junwen 鍾駿文). 〈讀《迦因小傳》 (On Reading the Two Translations of *Joan Haste*) (1907). In Huang Lin 黃霖 , Vol. 2, pp. 186–88.

Zheng, Zhenduo 鄭振鐸 . 〈林琴南先生〉 (Mr Lin Qinnan) (1924). In Luo Xinzhang, pp. 184–92.

Zhou, Zuoren 周作人 . 〈日本近三十年小說之發達〉 (The Development of Japanese Fiction in the Last 30 Years) (1918). In Huang Lin, Vol. 2, pp. 542–63.

Machine Translation

W. J. Hutchins
Library, University of East Anglia, Norwich, U.K.

Introduction and Basic Concepts

The term machine translation (MT) refers to computerized systems responsible for the production of translations with or without human assistance. Commercial and operational MT systems are sometimes referred to as systems for computer-aided translation, because human aid is essential for good results. However, the field does not include the development of computer-based translation tools to support translators, e.g. by providing access to on-line dictionaries or remote terminology databanks, the transmission and reception of texts, etc. In an MT system, the basic task of translation is undertaken by a computer program in conjunction with automated dictionaries and grammars.

Although the ideal aim of MT systems might be to produce translation as good as those from the best human translators, in practice the output has to be revised (or "post-edited") for most recipients. In this respect MT does not differ from the output of most human translators which is normally revised by a second translator before dissemination. However, the types of errors produced by MT systems do differ from those of human translators (incorrect prepositions, articles, pronouns, verb tenses, etc.). Post-editing is the norm, but in certain circumstances MT output may be unedited or only lightly revised, e.g. if it is intended only for specialists familiar with the subject field of the text. Unrevised output might also serve as a rough draft for a human translator, often referred to as a "pre-translation".

The translation quality of MT systems may be improved either (most obviously) by developing more sophisticated methods or by imposing certain restrictions on the input. The system may be designed, for example, to deal with texts limited to the "sublanguage" (vocabulary and grammar) of a particular subject field (e.g. biochemistry) and/or document type (e.g. patents). Alternatively, input texts may be written in a "controlled language", which restricts the range of vocabulary, avoids homonymy and polysemy, and eliminates complex sentence structures. A third option is to mark input texts ("pre-edit") to indicate prefixes, suffixes, word divisions, phrase and clause boundaries, or to differentiate grammatical categories (e.g. to distinguish the proper name *Brown* from the adjective *brown*; or the noun *convict* from its homonymous verb *convict*.) Finally, the system itself may refer problems of ambiguity and selection to human operators (usually translators) for resolution during the processes of translation itself, i.e. in an "interactive" mode.

Systems are designed either for two particular languages ("bilingual" systems) or for more than a single pair of languages ("multilingual" systems). Bilingual systems may be designed to operate either in only one direction ("uni-directional"), e.g. from Japanese into English, or in both directions ("bi-directional"). Multilingual systems are usually intended to be bi-directional and to provide translations from any one language into any one or more other languages within the same configuration. In some cases, MT systems are called "multilingual" if they combine a number of bilingual unidirectional systems based on similar principles and sharing some common dictionary and grammatical data.

In overall system design, there have been three basic types of systems. The first (and historically oldest) type is generally referred to as the "direct translation" approach: the MT system is designed in all details specifically for one particular pair of languages, e.g. Russian as the language of the original texts, the "source language", and English as the language of the translated texts, the "target language". Translation is direct from the source language (SL) text to the target language (TL) text; the basic assumption is that the vocabulary and syntax of source-language texts need not be analyzed any more than strictly necessary for the resolution of ambiguities, the correct identification of target-language expressions and the specification of target-language word order; in other words, source-language analysis is oriented specifically to one particular target language. Typically, systems consist of a large bilingual dictionary and a single monolithic program for analyzing and generating texts; such "direct translation" systems are necessarily bilingual and uni-directional.

The second basic design strategy is the "interlingua" approach, which assumes that it is possible to convert source-language texts into representations common to more than one language. From such interlingual representations texts are generated into other languages. Translation is thus in two stages: from source language to the interlingua (IL) and from the interlingua to the target language. Procedures for source-language analysis are intended to be souce-language-specific and not oriented to any particular target language; likewise programs for target-language synthesis are target-language-specific and not designed for input from particular source languages. Interlinguas may be based on a "logical" artificial language, on an auxiliary language such as Esperanto, on a set of semantic primitives common to all languages, or on a "universal" vocabulary.

The third basic strategy is the less ambitious "transfer" approach. Rather than operating in two stages through a single interlingual representation, there are three stages involving underlying (abstract) representations for both source-language and target-language texts. The first stage converts source-language texts into abstract source-language-oriented representations; the second stage converts these into equivalent target-language-oriented representations; and the third generates the final target-language texts. Whereas the interlingua approach necessarily requires complete resolution of all ambiguities in the source-language text so that translation into any other language is possible, in the transfer approach only those ambiguities inherent in the language in question are tackled; problems of lexical differences between languages are dealt with in the second stage (transfer proper).

Within the stages of analysis and synthesis (or generation), most MT systems exhibit clearly separated components involving different levels of linguistic description: morphology, syntax, semantics. Hence, analysis may be divided into morphological analysis (identification of word endings, word compounds), syntactic analysis (identification of phrase structures, dependency, subordination, etc.), semantic analysis (resolution of lexical and structural ambiguities); synthesis may likewise pass through semantic synthesis (selection of appropriate compatible lexical and structural forms), syntactic synthesis (generation of required phrase and sentence structures), and morphological synthesis (generation of correct word forms). In transfer systems, the transfer component may also have separate programs dealing with lexical transfer (selection of vocabulary equivalents) and with structural transfer (transformation into target-language-appropriate structures).

In many older systems, particularly those of the "direct translation" type the components of analysis, transfer and synthesis were not always clearly separated. Some of them also mixed data (dictionary and grammar) and processing rules and routines. Later systems have exhibited various degrees of modularity, so that system components, data and programs can be adapted and changed without damage to overall system efficiency. A further stage in some recent systems is the reversibility of analysis and synthesis components, i.e. the data and rules used in the analysis of a particular language are applied in reverse when generating texts in that language.

Problems and Methods

The main linguistic problems encountered in MT systems may be treated under four main headings: lexical, structural, contextual, and pragmatic or situational. In each case the problems are primarily caused by the inherent ambiguities of natural languages and by the lack of direct equivalences of vocabulary and structure between one language and another. Many examples could be given, some English ones are: homonyms (*cry* as "weep" or "shout", *bank* as "edge of river" or "financial institution") require different translations (e.g. in French *pleurer: crier; rive: banque*); nouns can function as verbs (*control, plant, face*) and are hence "ambiguous", since the target language may well have different forms (e.g. French *contrôle: diriger, plante: planter, face: affronter*). A polysemous word such as English *field* has often many possible translations, e.g. in Japanese: *hatake* (field for crops), *nohara* (open space), *kyougiba* (sports field), *bun'ya* (sphere of activity), etc. In many cases, target languages make distinctions which are quite absent in the source, e.g. *wear* is unambiguous (non-polysemous) for English speakers, but Chinese distinguishes between "wearing clothes, shoes, etc." 穿 , "wearing jewelry, spectacles, etc." 戴 and "wearing a tie" 打 .

In many cases, differences between the vocabulary of the source and target languages are also accompanied by structural differences. A familiar example involves the translation of the English verb *know* into French or German, where there are two verbs which express "knowledge of a fact" (*connaître* and *kennen*) and "knowledge of how to do something" (*savoir* and *wissen*):

(1) I know the man — Je connais l'homme; Ich kenne den Mann.
(2) I know what he is called — Je sais ce qu'il s'appelle; Ich weiss wie er heisst.

Translation into unrelated languages typically involves considerable structural change. For example, the English sentence (3) must be completely reformulated in Japanese (4):

(3) The earthquake destroyed the buildings
(4) Jishin de kenbutsu ga kowareta
    Earthquake-by buildings collapsed
    i.e. "The buildings collapsed due to the earthquake"

Various aspects of syntactic relations can be analyzed. There is the need (a) to identify valid sequences of grammatical categories, (b) to identify functional relations: subjects and objects of verbs, dependencies of adjectives on "head" nouns, etc., (c) to identify the constituents of sentences: noun phrases, verb groups, prepositional phrases, subordinate clauses, etc. Each aspect has given rise to different types of parsers: the predictive syntactic analyzer concentrated on sequences of categories (developed subsequently by Woods as the Augmented Transition Network parser); parsers based on dependency grammar (of Tesnière, Hays, etc.) look for functional relationships; and phrase structure parsers identify the kinds of constituency structures familiar in Chomskyan generative grammars. Each have their strengths and weaknesses, and modern MT systems often adopt an eclectic mixture of parsing techniques, now often within the framework of a "unification grammar" formalism.

The most serious weakness of all syntactic parsers is precisely their limitation to structural features. An English prepositional phrase can in theory modify any preceding noun in the sentence as well as a preceding verb:

(5) The car was driven by the teacher with great skill.
(6) The car was driven by the teacher with defective tyres.
(7) The car was driven by the teacher with red hair.

In (5) the phrase *with great skill* modifies the verb phrase *was driven*; in (6) *with defective tyres* is attached to *the car*; and in (7) *with red hair* is an attribute of *the teacher*. However, these attachments are based on semantic or pragmatic information (e.g. knowledge that cars do not have red hair). But syntactic analysis can go no further than offer each possibility, and the specific relationship has to be identified by later semantic analysis involving lexical and situational context.

To overcome some of these problems, many parsers now include the identification of case relations. Consider, for example:

(8) The house was built by a doctor for his son last year.

In this sentence, the Agent of the action ("building") is *a doctor*, the Object of the action is *the house*, the Recipient (or Beneficiary) is *his son* and the Time of the action is *last year*. Many languages express these relations explicitly, cf. suffixes of Latin, German, Russian nouns (*-ibus, -en, -ami*), prepositions of English and French (*to, à*), particles of Japanese (*ga, wa*); but they are often implicit (as in English direct objects). There are rarely any direct correspondences between languages and most markers of cases are multiply ambiguous in all languages, cf. *with* expressing Manner (5) or Attribute (6 and 7). Nevertheless, there is a sufficient regularity and universality in such "case relations" to have encouraged their widespread adoption in many MT systems, particularly in those with Japanese as source or target language.

There is also some agreement about the use of semantic features, i.e. the attachment of such categories as "human", "animate", "liquid" to lexical items and their application in the resolution of ambiguities. For example:

(9) He was beaten with a club.

In this sentence, the "social" sense (meeting place) of *club* is excluded by the verb-type which requires an "inanimate" Instrument, i.e. it must have the "hammer" or "weapon" meaning.

Similarly:

(10) The sailor went on board.
(11) The sailor was examined by the board.

The "physical" sense of *board* (ship) in (10) is confirmed by the verb-type (motion, *go*) and the preposition of Location (*on*), and the "social" (committee) sense in (11) is confirmed by the verb *examine* which requires an "animate" Agent.

Few operational MT systems involve any deeper levels of semantic or pragmatic analysis, yet the resolution of many linguistic problems clearly transcends sentence boundaries. A common and persistently difficult problem involves the use of pronouns. Consider the following:

(12) The soldiers shot the women. They were buried next day.

We know that the pronoun *they* does not refer to *soldiers* and must refer to *women* because we know that "shooting" implies "killing" and "injury" or "death" and that "death" is followed (normally) by "burial". This identification is crucial when translating into languages where the pronoun must indicate whether the referents are male or female (e.g. French *elles* and *ils*). Such examples demonstrate that the disambiguation and correct selection of target-language equivalents would often seem to be impossible without reference to knowledge of the (non-linguistic) features and properties of the actual objects and events described. Recent advances in Artificial Intelligence (AI) have encouraged the investigation of knowledge-based MT systems, at least for systems restricted to specific domains. For example, in a system designed for translating texts in computer science and data processing the English word *tape* could mean either magnetic tape or adhesive tape. In the following sentence (13), reference to the knowledge base should establish that only the "adhesive tape" interpretation is possible since diskettes do not contain "magnetic tapes" which can be removed.

(13) Remove the tape from the diskette.

In view of the linguistic limitations of MT systems it should be clear that the most suitable texts are either those of a technical or scientific nature, where there is often a high degree of direct terminological equivalence and where problems of homonymy and polysemy can be reduced by the restriction of dictionaries to specific subject domains, or administrative texts with a high degree of repetition, where stylistic considerations are unimportant (e.g. the minutes of meetings, internal reports, etc.) Obviously unsuitable are literary and philosophical texts, where nuances of vocabulary and cultural and stylistic factors play an important role; and equally unsuitable are texts with particularly complex sentence structures, e.g. patents and legal documents. The suitability of texts intended for publication depends on various economic factors, such as whether input texts are in machine-readable form, whether long documents change little between editions (e.g. operational manuals for equipment), whether a great deal of terminology work has to be done, and so forth. In certain circumstances, the control of input text (e.g. restrictions on vocabulary and syntax) can be cost-effective if output is to be in more than one target language. There is now a substantial body of practical experience with MT systems, which can be called upon to assist potential users.

History and Future

Research on using computers as aids for translating natural languages began within a few years of the first appearance of the newly invented "electronic calculators". The major stimulus was a memorandum in July 1949 by a director of the Rockefeller Foundation in New York, Warren Weaver, who described tentative efforts in Great Britain (by Booth and Richens) and in the United States (by Huskey and others in Los Angeles) and proposed various approaches. Within a few years research began at many US universities, and in 1954 the first public demonstration of the feasibility of machine translation (MT) was given (a collaboration of IBM and Georgetown University). Although using a very restricted vocabulary and grammar it was sufficiently impressive to encourage massive funding of MT in the United States and to inspire the establishment of MT projects throughout the world.

The earliest systems consisted primarily of large bilingual dictionaries where entries for words of the source language (SL) gave one or more equivalents in the target language (TL) and some rules for producing the correct word order in the output. It was soon recognized that this "word-for-word" approach was inadequate and ad hoc; the need for more systematic methods of syntactic analysis became evident, and a number of projects were inspired by contemporary developments in linguistics, particularly Zellig Harris' and Noam Chomsky's ideas on syntactic transformations, but also other models such as dependency grammar and stratificational grammar.

Optimism remained at a high level for the first decade of MT research, with many predictions of imminent "breakthroughs", but disillusion grew as researchers encountered "semantic barriers" for which they saw no straightforward solutions. There were some operational systems — the Mark II system (developed by IBM and Washington University) installed at the USAF Foreign Technology Division, and the Georgetown University system at the US Atomic Energy Authority and at Euratom in Italy — but the quality of output was disappointing (although satisfying many recipients' needs for information). In 1964, the US government sponsors set up the Automatic Language Processing Advisory Committee (ALPAC), which concluded in its famous 1966 report that MT was slower, less accurate and twice as expensive as human translation and that "there is no immediate or predictable prospect of useful machine translation."

The ALPAC report was widely condemned as narrow, biased and shortsighted, but the damage had been done. It brought a virtual end to MT research in the United States for over a decade and it had great impact elsewhere in the Soviet Union and in Europe. However, MT research did continue in Canada, in France, in Germany, and in Hong Kong. Within a few years Peter Toma, one of the members of the Georgetown University project, had developed Systran for operational use by the USAF (1970) and by NASA (in 1974/75), and shortly afterwards Systran was installed by the Commission of the European Communities for translating from English into French (1976) and later between other Community languages. At the same time, in Canada the METEO system developed at Montreal University was successfully put into operation for the daily translation of weather reports into French — in continuous use from 1976 to the present day — and in Hong Kong the CULT system (Chinese University Language Translator) began to be used for the regular production of translations of a Chinese mathematics journal into English. METEO is an example of a fully automatic system in a highly restricted "sublanguage"; CULT is a system demanding substantial pre- and post-editing.

In the 1960s in the US and the Soviet Union MT activity had concentrated on Russian-English and English-Russian translation of scientific and technical documents for a relatively small number of potential users, most of whom were prepared to overlook mistakes of terminology, grammar and style in order to be able to read something which they would have otherwise not known about. Since the mid-1970s the demand for MT has come from quite different sources with different needs and different languages. The administrative and commercial demands of multilingual communities and multinational trade have stimulated the demand for translation in Europe, Canada and Japan beyond the capacity of the traditional translation services. The demand is now for cost-effective computer-based translation systems which can deal with commercial and technical documentation in the principal languages of international commerce.

The 1980s have witnessed the emergence of a variety of system types and from a widening number of countries. There are a number of main-frame systems. Best known is Systran, now installed worldwide and operating in many pairs of languages. Others are: Logos for German-English translation and for English-French in Canada; the systems developed at the Pan American Health Organization for Spanish-English and English-Spanish translation; the systems developed by the Smart Corporation for many large organizations in North America; and the recently marketed METAL system from Siemens for German-English translation. Major systems for English-Japanese and Japanese-English translation have come from Japanese computer companies, Fujitsu, Hitachi and Toshiba. The wide availability of microcomputers and of text-processing software has led to the commercial market for cheaper MT systems, exploited in North America and Europe by companies such as ALPNET, Weidner, Linguistic Products, Tovna and Globalink, and by numerous Japanese companies, e.g. Sharp, NEC, Oki, Mitsubishi, Sanyo. Other microcomputer-based systems have appeared from China (TRANSTAR), Korea (e.g. NARA), Bolivia (ATAMIRI), the Soviet Union, etc.

Throughout the 1980s research on more advanced methods and techniques has continued. The dominant strategy is now that of "indirect" translation via intermediate representations, sometimes interlingual in nature, involving semantic as well as morphological and syntactic analysis and sometimes non-linguistic "knowledge bases". There is increasing emphasis on devising systems for particular subject areas and particular specific purposes, for monolingual users as well as bilingual users (translators), and for interactive operation rather than batch processing. The most notable projects have been the GETA-Ariane system at Grenoble, SUSY and ASCOF at Saarbrücken, Mu at Kyoto, DLT at Utrecht, Rosetta at Eindhoven, the knowledge-based MT project at Carnegie-Mellon University (Pittsburgh), the ArchTran project in Taiwan, and two ambitious international multilingual projects: Eurotra, supported by the European Communities, involving teams in each member country; and the Japanese CICC project with participants in China, Indonesia and Thailand.

In the immediate future, there will clearly be continued expansion and improvement of systems for the business and administrative communities. As at present, the MT market will include both microcomputer and mainframe systems. The cheaper microcomputer systems will produce relatively poor output needing substantial revision but which can be applied cost-effectively in commercial services. More expensive mainframe (or minicomputer) systems will be developed on transfer and interlingua approaches with some use of artificial-intelligence techniques. These will be producing higher quality output, which, although still requiring revision for many purposes (e.g. publication), will be satisfying basic information needs without revision.

It is probable that other types of systems will appear. Nearly all systems at present require users to know both source and target languages, generally to the level expected of regular translators. There is clearly a need for systems which can be used by individual non-translators ignorant of the source language in order to get translations giving at least the essential content of documents. At a further stage, these systems should be integrated with other documentation systems (information retrieval, abstracting, paraphrasing). There is an equally clear need for systems for those ignorant of target languages, e.g. businessmen (and others) wanting to convey simple messages to make travel arrangements, to book hotel accommodation, to arrange meetings, etc. Already some research has been done on "interactive analysis" systems: writers would be asked (in computer-initiated dialogues conducted in their own language) for information to resolve ambiguities and to enable the generation of appropriate texts.

However, probably the most obvious area of future development will be speech translation. Research is already in progress (particularly in Japan) on systems for international telephone communication (initially restricted to standard business messages) which combine voice interpretation and voice production with machine translation. Given the problems of speech recognition in addition to the peculiarities of conversational language, operational prototypes are regarded very much as long-term objectives.

Nearly all developments depend on improvements in the automation of the basic translation processes. Many researchers still aspire to the ultimate ideal of fully automatic high quality translation but it seems increasingly unrealistic. MT output suffers still from what appear to be low-level problems: wrong pronouns, incorrect prepositions and tenses, erroneous translations of common vocabulary. Progress is slow, but developments in artificial intelligence, in linguistic theory, in computational linguistics and in computer technology promise future improvements in overall quality.

At a more basic level much progress depends on the continued efforts to standardize terminology both within and across languages, which is of benefit to translators and technical writers generally. More specifically, the wasteful duplication involved in the creation of large MT dictionaries calls for inter-project cooperation, a process which has already started in Japan with the Electronic Dictionary Research project.

The translation of natural languages by machine, first dreamt of in the seventeenth century, has become a reality in the late twentieth. Computer programs are producing translations — not perfect translations, for that is an ideal to which no human translator can aspire; nor translations of literary texts, for the subtleties and nuances of poetry are beyond computational analysis; but translations of technical manuals, scientific documents, commercial prospectuses, administrative memoranda, medical reports. Machine translation is not primarily an area of abstract intellectual inquiry but the application of computer and language sciences to the development of systems answering practical needs. MT is no longer seen as a threatening replacement of translators but as an aid to multilingual communication. The future development of MT rests on fruitful interaction between the researchers of experimental systems investigating new methods and theories, the developers of commercial systems exploiting well-tested methods in cost-effective practical systems, and the perception of the real needs of translators and other potential users of translation systems.

References

ALPAC. *Language and Machines: Computers in Translation and Linguistics: A Report by the Automatic Language Processing Advisory Committee*. Washington, D.C.: National Academy of Sciences, 1966.

Hutchins, W. J. *Machine Translation: Past, Present, Future*. Chichester: Ellis Horwood, 1986.

———. "Recent Developments in Machine Translation: A Review of the Last Five Years." In *New Directions in Machine Translation*, edited by D. Maxwell, *et al.* Dordrecht: Foris, 1988, pp. 7–62.

——— and H. L. Somers. *An Introduction to Machine Translation*. London: Academic Press, 1991.

Slocum, J., ed. *Machine Translation Systems*. Cambridge: Cambridge University Press, 1988.

Vasconcellos, M., ed. *Technology as Translation Strategy*. Binghamton, New York: State University of New York, 1988.

Practical Considerations of Machine Translation

Zhang Liangping
Department of Foreign Languages
Qinghua University, Beijing, China

Research work on machine translation has been conducted for more than thirty years, but generally speaking, its practical application is still limited. A number of "automatic translation" systems or devices available commercially are restricted to narrowly-defined subject fields and language style. Some of them are actually machine assisted translation system, that is, heavy post-editing work is needed and many kinds of application do not allow such human intervention and time delay. On the other hand, with the rapid development of telecommunication technology and tremendous amount of information waiting to be exchanged, people do hope that lots of the laborious, non-creative translation work could be taken over by some translation robot — machine translation.

There are always controversies about the merits of machine translation systems. Computer scientists lay stress on the relief of manual labour by machine translation, while traditional linguists make jokes about some ridiculous translated sentences produced by the machine. The smooth and effective development of machine translation needs a better mutual understanding between machine translation system designers and users.

To get an objective view on machine translation's advantages, limitations and potentials, the following practical considerations might be helpful for both scientists working in the field of machine translation and other people who are concerned about the development of this technology.

Application Areas

In the foreseeable period, it is not possible for machine translation systems to work as a universal translation tool, or to replace the human translators. Machine translation systems surely cannot translate literary works like short stories, novels, poems and plays, etc. In these cases, the translation process not only involves the surface meanings, but also transfers senses, cultural differences, and the beauty of both source and target languages. The areas where machine translation is most likely to have advantages are as follows:

1. Documents that have basically the same format and terminological scope but need to be revised or amended regularly. Manuals, instruction books, product introduction pamphlets, patent application files are some examples of this sort. Translating texts in this category, especially some of them requiring frequent revision for new editions, is very dull. It is both desirable and probable for these kinds of texts to turn to machine translation. Some fully automatic translation systems already exist. All steps, from source text input, translation, to target language version printing, can be carried out by computers.

2. Information scanning and screening on a routine basis. The international information exchange is now a constant flow of very great volume. Most information workers would be substantially relieved if they could get some rough idea about each item of information in their mother tongue. The examples in this area include telegraphic news reports, scientific and technological information, international finance and market reports, magazine and journal articles, etc. Although the translation is not accurate, it helps the editor to focus on the most valuable pieces for elaboration. Quite a few news agencies, scientific information institutes and digest/abstract publishers have already shown their interest.

3. Materials to be translated into or from several different languages. It is very expensive and sometimes even difficult to retain a high quality multi-lingual translation team. Furthermore, the team's working load fluctuates greatly with different periods and languages. A multi-lingual machine translation system would ease the pressure of personnel shortage. The examples here are United Nations, EEC, other international organizations, international conference centres, and so forth.

4. Real time telecommunication translation service without human attendance, such as translating international telephone calls, translating telegram or telex.

Other applications might emerge, but the point is that the clear definition of the fields for machine translation application is essential for the development of machine translation systems and their acceptance by the linguists.

Quality of Translation

As discussed above, the machine translation system should not be seen as an integrated one. According to its specific use, the system would be of different complexity, and the quality of the translation also varies. As a rule, the quality of translation of an machine translation system is mainly determined by the variety of the subject and the style of writing. By use of most sophisticated intelligent computers (e.g., LISP or PROLOG computer) with complicated syntactic/semantic rule base and parsing procedures, the readability of the translated text can be improved. However, up to now, for a general-purpose machine translation system, the best result of translation quality is that only 75–80 percent of the resulted sentences are acceptable without major correction. Meanwhile, the expensive dedicated computer system for machine translation limits its use to very few users. A reasonable compromise should be made here and diverse machine translation systems should be developed.

For the task of only browsing a large amount of materials, the quality standards can be relaxed and the rather simple and cheap machine-translation systems can be used. For the first application area mentioned above, accuracy is very important, so the system should orient itself to the specific subject, terminology, and writing style. For the tasks involving heavy translation duty and many different languages, a preliminary translation is still very helpful, even when post-editing is needed.

Any excessive expectation of the translation quality of machine translation systems or attempt to develop an machine translation system capable of replacing human translators is unrealistic.

Combination with Other High Technologies

The rapid development of microelectronic technology has started a new revolution of information collection, storage, transfer, and processing. Especially in the field of telecommunication, people need direct, instantaneous exchange between speakers of different languages. As mentioned above, the first generation of simultaneously translated international telephone and telegram services has already been put into trial use.

Computer recognition of printed and written characters through optical or magnetic means; speech recognition and synthesis with computers; satellite transmission and optical fibre cables; very large scale integrated circuits; artificial intelligence; natural language cognition; reasoning computers, all these high technologies have created the necessary environment for better mutual transformation between different written or spoken languages. They also call for a most efficient and universal language analysis and synthesis model reflecting the essence of the languages. Close cooperation between computer scientists and linguists will surely promote the development and practical use of machine translation, and finally overcome the language barrier.

Comprehensive Utilizations

A practical machine translation system should be a useful tool in multilingual communication. Users have shown strong interest in the machine translation systems with multiple functions.

Integrated Multi-lingual Electronic Dictionary

Several volumes of different bilingual dictionaries with thousands of pages can be packed into computer storage. By use of the fast dictionary-searching program built in the machine translation system, the user can quickly find out the equivalent words in several languages. Actually, there are a number of portable electronic devices of this kind commercially available. They could be viewed as the by-product of machine translation development.

Flexible Machine Translation System

To meet various needs of different users, the machine translation system should be flexible in its operation mode. It should be able to accept OCR and/or phonetic input, as well as the keyboard input; to produce magnetic form and/or phonetic output, as well as the printed text; to operate under fully automatic, uninterrupted translation mode, or an interactive, screen-editing mode, depending on the user's choice. The latter operation mode is a useful tool and assistant of the professional translators. The traditional tedious hand-writing and repeated typing can be avoided. The resulted text stored on the magnetic media would be sent directly for computerized typesetting and printing.

The system should be able to be used on main frame computers with multiple terminals, so that a translation service company with many staff members can share the function. A helpful machine translation system should also provide bi-directional (i.e., both English-Chinese and Chinese-English) translation function, or even capability of translation between any language pair in a multi-lingual situation.

Derivative Applications

The subsystems of a machine translation system can be further developed into a series of software for languages instruction and text processing, such as concordance analysis, content analysis, language style identification, text readability statistics, automatic checking and marking of writing exercises, etc. It is also possible to develop an automatic abstracting system, which can read an article and recognize the key words and essential sentences from the introduction and conclusions to form an abstract of the paper. Language teaching (e.g., Chinese self-learning) systems for non-native speakers, sounding system for the blind, and displaying system for the dumb are also logical expansions of machine translation development.

Cost

Any potential customer of machine translation system would compare the cost of machine translation with that of human translation. The cost for the latter case is normally a lump-sum, a rather standard price for certain number of the words translated. However, the cost of machine translation should include the initial investment on computer hardware and software, as well as the extra expenses for source text input, operation, maintenance and post-editing. While for a few cases, owing to the lack of qualified translators or the need for promptness, an expensive advanced machine translation system might be feasible, most users at the grass-roots level would only accept a machine translation system with a reasonable price. If the initial investment of a machine translation system is too high, they would rather turn to the translation service people. The unattractive quality of the translation made by the machine further strengthens this hesitation.

To eliminate this economical barrier, the popular-type machine translation system must be compatible with the most popular microcomputers already in wide use, and should make the software system compact enough to reduce the cost significantly. The reasonable price would also prevent unrealistic expectations of the machine translation system. And the user would take it as a basic system which can be expanded and improved by himself.

Easy Maintenance by the User

There are two important conclusions from the machine translation history:

1. Dictionaries should be independent of the program and different functional parts of the program should be separated into modules. This separation is crucial for the maintenance and extension of the system.
2. Any practical machine translation system should aim at some specific subject field and text style, rather than aim at the capability of translating diversified texts.

A skillful translator always learns through his practice. For a machine translation system, it is even more important to have the possibility of being improved. None of the machine translation systems developed by the software designers can deal with all the exceptions to the normal language rules for different fields. The most feasible way is to improve the system through practical use, something like training. The user would get a lot of feedback information during the application of the machine translation system: whether the explanation of certain term is included and proper for the specific field; whether the way of ambiguity treatment should be revised; or whether some target language generation rules need to be added, etc.

A practical machine translation system should offer convenient ways of access to the machine dictionaries, the parsing network and the rule bases, and should allow the user to update the system. In this way, the user would feel that the system is friendly and usable.

This principle is not only an approach to facilitate the maintenance of the system, but also a necessity caused by the immaturity of machine translation systems. User's involvement in the machine translation system maintenance is helpful to the better understanding of the merits and weak points of machine translation. Through wide practice, it is possible to develop a number of testified practical machine translation systems with fairly good performance.

Now the attention of the world is focussed on the fifth-generation, intelligent computer. With the progress of computer science and technology, machine translation will have bright prospects. Many people in this field are expecting the occurrence of a new generation of machine translation system, which is understanding-based and intelligent. However, only with appropriate design philosophy meeting the requirements of the potential market and with deep understanding of the different users' criticism, can machine translation system be improved progressively and become a useful tool in the international cultural, technical, economical exchange and cooperation.

Terminology

Blaise Nkwenti-Azeh
Centre for Computational Linguistics
University of Manchester Institute of Science and Technology, U.K.

Introduction

The word "terminology" is currently used to refer to

(a) a particular theory explaining the relationships between concepts and terms,
(b) the activity of collecting, describing and presenting terms, and
(c) the vocabulary of a special subject field.

In the sense of (a), terminology is now firmly established and widely recognized as a distinct area of study concerned with the vocabulary of special subject languages, in particular, the relationship between concepts, terms and extra-linguistic ("real-world") objects; this study is backed by an established set of clearly defined theoretical assumptions, methodological approaches and practical goals (including application domains).

In the sense of (b) and/or (c), terminology is a component of sublanguage which differs from general language in the functional characteristics of its lexical items. These characteristics include

(a) lexical restrictions in the range of designatory forms;
(b) restriction/specificity of meanings;
(c) overlap between sublanguages;
(d) overlap with general language;
(e) existence of privileged designatory classes (nouns, verbs, adjectives and adverbs);
(f) high frequency of certain syntactic constructions, e.g. Adjective + Noun, Noun + Noun compounding in English.

Concepts

Concepts constitute the starting point of any terminological description. According to ISO 1087 (1990), a concept is "a unit of thought constituted through abstraction on the basis of properties common to a set of objects". Concepts are therefore mental constructs which enable us to classify experience (knowledge and objects) on the basis of some distinguishing criterion. Concept classes are evolved separately for each subject field and are reflected in special languages. In other words, the scope of terminology is restricted to concepts which have been assigned a linguistic referent, i.e. term in some area of specialization.

The division of knowledge into subject fields can be seen as the most generic level of abstraction. There are no doubt general concept classes which cut across subject fields and which serve as essential links between the arbitrary divisions which a scientific community imposes on the totality of knowledge. Nonetheless, the way in which a particular knowledge subspace is organized varies from one scientific community to another: the knowledge domain of physics, for example, is organized differently from that of, say, chemistry or psychology. Furthermore, the way in which entities are interrelated varies from one domain to another: the relationship between the substances *gold, silver, plutonium* and *copper* in the field of geology, are different from those in say, chemistry or economics. These different partitions and relationships underline the fact that concepts rely on a broad consensus among users for the special reference status associated with them, and also that concepts are not bound to particular languages even though they may be influenced by the social and cultural background of the society.

Typology of Concepts

Concepts can be grouped into conceptual classes. Scientific and technological changes introduce different groupings so that words like *entropy, morphology, noise, shell* occur in the vocabulary of such different disciplines as electronics, biology, linguistics, physics with quite different definitions and conceptual relationships. The same real-world object can also be found to belong to different conceptual classes and therefore contract different conceptual relationships with other concepts within a given special subject. These concepts may be of concrete, observable entities, for example plants,

animals, minerals, manufactured products, or they may be of abstract entities, industrial processes, measurements, properties of entities.

Sager (1990) identifies four independent classes of concepts, namely
entity concepts, activity concepts, property concepts, and relation concepts:

(1) entity concepts are obtained from the abstraction of items of our
    experience and reflection perceived as having a separate existence
    in time and place (i.e. separately definable items). This class of
    concepts is required for identification and classification of units of
    experience and knowledge.
(2) activity concepts are obtained from abstraction of separately defin-
    able processes, operations, or events carried out by or with entities.
    The class of activity concepts thus constitutes separately definable
    operations, processes, or activities carried out on or with entities.
(3) property concepts are obtained from abstraction of qualities, dispo-
    sitions, or characteristics of entities or activities. This class of
    concepts is thus a subclass of concepts required for differentiating
    among entities or activities.
(4) relation concepts are obtained from abstracting physical, temporal
    or other ontological relationships among objects, and from logical
    relationships among entities and activities. This class of concepts is
    thus a subclass of concepts which identify the relationships that
    exist or are established between entities, between activities, or
    between entities and activities.

Concept Identification

Concepts can be identified by reference to their characteristics. Any imaginable feature can be used as a characteristic of a concept; however, from
among the vast range of characteristics that can be attributed to a given
concept, only a small subset is isolated and stipulated as being both necessary and sufficient for an identification or fixation of the concept. These are
so-called "intrinsic" or "essential" characteristics, as opposed to the non-
criterial "extrinsic" or "non-essential" characteristics. Evidence of systematic selection of characteristics is readily found in nomenclatures where
parallelism of linguistic forms abound.

The concepts of any one area are fundamentally described in three
ways:

(a) by definition
(b) by their relationships to other concepts
(c) by the linguistic forms, the terms, phrases or expressions by which they are realized in any one language.

In a terminological theory, there are three types of correspondence: concept-symbol, concept-object, symbol-object. The basic correspondence, as far as terminologists are concerned, is that between concepts and terms (concept-symbol); the concept-object relationship is covered by the definition, and the symbol-object relationship is that of proper names.

Terms

A *term* is simply "a lexical item which belongs to a specialized area of usage" (Sager, 1990). This definition implies that terms typically belong to a particular area of knowledge (sublanguage) within which they are assigned a special and often uniquely definable reference. As such, they are functionally different from *names* which refer to "individual, unique" objects, as opposed to "classes of objects"; they are also different from *words* which refer to "classes of general language concepts". In practice, this means that terms are always studied in relation to the conceptual or knowledge subsystem to which they belong and in which they function.

Terms are created for efficient and unambiguous communication, which accounts in part for the parallelism often found between terminological structures and conceptual structures, e.g. a compound term designating a complex concept. However, isomorphism is not always achieved, due to the diversity of term-formation patterns, and the conflict between motivated naming and other desiderata of efficient communication.

Term Characteristics, Formation and Equivalence

Terminology is important for translators insofar as (a) it explains the behaviour of terms, thus leading to or helping in an understanding of their use in sublanguage texts, and (b) it explains the difference between term- and word-formation and, in particular, the scope of neology. Although terms are ideally univocal/monosemous in the sense that each term refers to a unique concept, and there is usually a 1:1 relationship between concept and term, terms occur in different linguistic contexts and frequently have context-conditioned variants.

A major problem facing translation of terms is the identification or recognition of terminological units in text. The precise nature of such variation largely depends on the language in question and on the syntactic, syntagmatic and terminological characteristics of the particular text-type (article, catalogue, glossary, invoice, legislation, taxonomy, etc). Sublanguage texts in English, for instance, exhibit the following phenomena:

(1) graphic variants of compound terms, e.g. *earthstation, earthstation; Earth-to-space link, earth space link, Earth/space link*;

(2) letter-case variation in acronyms and abbreviations, e.g. *FSS, fss; MUSA, musa; e.i.r.p., eirp*;

(3) mixed combinations of abbreviations and full-form words, e.g. *ground-to-air t.d.m., half off-set qpsk, ots satellite.*

(4) reduction of term forms, e.g. *antenna gain* ⇒ *gain; outgoing propagating wave* ⇒ *outgoing wave*;

(5) synonymy, e.g. *backscattering coefficient = echoing area.*

These variations can create difficulties for the translator who is not familiar with the subject. For example, where term-reduction occurs within a text, it is sometimes difficult to differentiate between a broader term used synonymously for a narrower term, and a shorter form of the narrower term. In some cases, it is possible to retain this ambiguity provided the reduction process occurs in both languages (L1 and L2). But, if it only occurs in one of the language pairs, it may be misleading to use the L2 equivalent of L1 hyperonym as an equivalent of L1 hyponym. In fact it is conceivable that there exists a form in L2 which is not a hyponym of the L1 term.

The specific devices for term identification depend to a significant degree on the patterns of term-formation in the field. The following characteristics of terms reflect the formation patterns available to a scientific community:

(1) words which have been taken over from general language or from other fields and reused/redefined in the field, e.g. *absorption, amplifier, amplify, data, footprint, receiver, time-out*;

(2) eponymic terms, containing proper-noun elements (usually, the inventor, discoverer, initiator, etc.), e.g. *Anik satellite, Molniya orbit, Luneberg lens*;

(3) simile, i.e. designations based on extralinguistic association or

resemblance, e.g. *dish, footprint, flat-top antenna, Gaussian shaped beam, loop signalling, fishbone antenna, T antenna*;

(4) compounds resulting from varying combinations of general-language and special-language items into new syntagmatic units, e.g. *crystal clock, satellite propulsion unit, calibrated standard radio frequency signal generator*;

(5) terms formed by affixation with the base forms not also occurring as terms in the domain, i.e. derivatives existing in only one form, e.g. *absorption, dedicated, isolator*;

(6) terms formed by prefixation with neoclassical and standard language prefixes: *on*-hook, *off*-hook, *multi*-address, *trans*multiplexer;

(7) multiple derivation resulting in clusters of derived terms, e.g. *polarization, depolarization, polarized, cross-polarization*;

(8) compression, by freezing syntagms into clearly identifiable terms, e.g. *ACSSB (amplitude companded single sideband modulation), DAMA (demand assigned multiple access)*;

(9) reduction, e.g. *small dish earth station* ⇒ *small earth station* ⇒ *small station*;

(10) conjunction, i.e. the combination of two concepts to form a new concept, e.g. *modulator-demodulator* now reduced to *modem*.

The diversity of term-formation patterns suggests that translators cannot rely on intuition or other ad-hoc methods for resolving the terminological problems of a text.

Definitions

The use of definitions for expressing meanings is well known, but the diversity of typological labels for definitions encountered in the philosophical and linguistic literature attests to the complexity and multifacetted nature of the defining activity. According to the British Standard BS3669 (1963),

> ... by defining a concept is meant determining its position within a system of concepts. The definition is a verbal statement of characteristics so selected as to show (i) what the concept has in common with its related concepts, and (ii) by what attributes it is distinguishable from them. That is, having stated the

field in which the concept occurs, one defines the boundaries of the portion of that field which it occupies.

In a special subject environment, a definition is essentially an equation (or a predication) consisting of two components, the unknown term (*definiendum*) which refers to a concept, and an explanation (*definiens*) by means of known terms and expressions. The major types or forms of definition that are generally acknowledged are *stipulation, ostension, analysis, synthesis, denotation, synonymy* and *implication*.

The objective or purpose of definitions varies with the pragmatic environment in which it occurs. There are at least 3 basic needs for definition:

(1) the initial fixation of the term-concept equation;
(2) the identification of a term by verifying the existence of an independent definition;
(3) the explanation of the meaning of a concept — for specialist users of term banks such as translators and subject specialists, and possibly also laymen.

Within the narrower practical-oriented environment of translation, the stipulative and ostensive categories are inapplicable: stipulative definitions occur only at the time of neologization, i.e. when the objective is fixation of meaning for later reference/use, and ostensive definitions which involve non-verbal pictorial, graphic or other descriptive information fall outside the verbal definition framework. Textbooks, glossaries and technical dictionaries (both human and automated) constitute the most common environment for definitions wherein they serve three main functions:

(a) a knowledge representation function which incorporates fixation of reference of concepts and term, identification of the meaning of terms, and determining the linguistic expression form of concepts;
(b) an ordering function, comprises the classification of concepts and the expression of relationships;
(c) a didactic function, notably, clarification of meaning, and prescription of limited reference.

The primary function of a terminological definition remains that of circumscribing the area of reference of the term. Irrespective of the way in which the definition is formulated — this ranges from the rigorous methods in taxonomies and other highly artificialized languages to the flexible approach in innovative technologies — each definition is (intended to be) self-contained and therefore should adequately describe the concept.

The reality of the defining activity is more complex than would be apparent from a simple listing of types of definition. In the first instance, definitions are rarely monolithic even within a given special subject: more often than not, the modes of definition are combinations of different parts of the types listed above; this results in different types of relationships (usually, ontological plus logical) being expressed in a single definition. Secondly, an examination of practical definitions reveals that definitions take cognizance of their users, and are generally formulated to meet the knowledge requirements of the particular user-environment — definitions in glossaries, printed dictionaries and term banks will emphasize different aspects of the concept.

Even though definitions cannot reflect the full range of conceptual relationships between the elements of a concept, it is recognized that terminological definitions are characterized by a particularly high information content. And, although each definition, in isolation, gives only a partial view of the conceptual position of the definiendum, we can reconstruct a "complete" or "global" view of a concept through analysing a coherent set of definitions.

Working Methods in Terminology and Translation

The compilation of collections of terminologies occurs mainly in a multililingual environment. There is thus some coincidence in the spheres of activity of terminologists and translators since both groups of specialists are information mediators, and both are often required to work — in close collaboration with subject specialists — in a sub-system with which they are not sufficiently familiar. However, terminology and translation function on two different linguistic and cognitive planes and have a different focus.

In terminology the focus is on *concepts* and their linguistic form expressed in *terms* which are extracted from texts. Terminologists isolate single linguistic items and their corresponding conceptual referent from a text; they view the lexicon as many separate sub-systems related to the knowledge of each subject field or discipline.

The linguistic forms in each discipline can be found in a single or several languages. But, for term translation to occur, there would have to be corresponding forms for a given concept in the language pairs of the translation activity (as illustrated in Fig. 1).

Translation is a dynamic process concerned with the movement from the textual substance in one language to the textual substance in another (Fig. 2).

Figure 1 Focus in Terminology

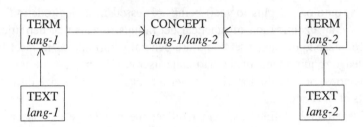

Figure 2 Focus in Translation

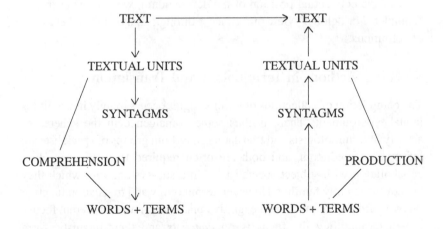

Translators match *units of meaning* as represented in a text. Inside this process there is a procedure in which units of meaning of one culture are matched with those of another before finding their *textually* and *situationally* appropriate linguistic expression. From the point of view of terminology these units lack interest because they are temporary and casual collocations of concepts brought into a particular relationship by a writer.

We therefore observe that translators work with concepts and terms in context, whereas terminologists, on the other hand, isolate terms from context (i.e., decontextualize them) and then associate them to concepts before finally deciding on the appropriate linguistic referent in the target language. Term equivalence focuses on an atomic unit isolated from context whereas translation equivalence focuses on the largest meaningful unit in context. Whatever terminological matching takes place is between term and concept and not between textual unit and textual unit.

In their capacity as readers and writers, translators perform the matching process of units with a high degree of intuition. The extent to which they simply "know" the appropriate units of equivalence depends on their familiarity with the subject matter and with the linguistic expression forms in the two languages involved. In certain cases, such knowledge of the domain has to be supplemented with knowledge of the terminology of the commissioner of the translation, i.e. "firm-specific" or "user-specific" terminology. Only when they need to research meaning and/or form, do translators have to resort to the techniques of terminologists.

Bi-lingual or multi-lingual terminologists need some understanding of the objectives of translation, and only to the extent that it enables them to present the results of their labour in a user-friendly manner, e.g. by making terminology more context-sensitive, or by defining user-specific information classes.

All specialized translators need an understanding of terminology because they frequently have to change roles during the complex decision making process of translation and work in the analytical mode of terminologists before switching back to text production, e.g., when they are faced with decisions concerning the right choice among several alternatives of expression forms or the choice of creating a neologism, a neonym or a paraphrase. Since translators are rarely trained on the basis of their previous specialism in a subject field, but are expected to develop subject specialisms later, they need to have the means to cope with unfamiliar subjects and the techniques of producing reliable work despite their limitations of knowledge.

The essence of terminology for translators is presented in the two diagrams that follow:

Figure 3 shows the monolingual set of variously interrelated concepts, definitions, terms and their variants. It highlights the distinction between terminological-linguistic structure and conceptual structure.

Figure 3 Object-Concept-Definition-Term Interrelation

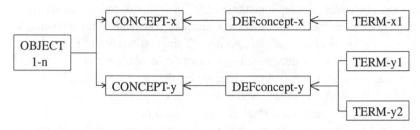

Figure 4 Translation of Terms

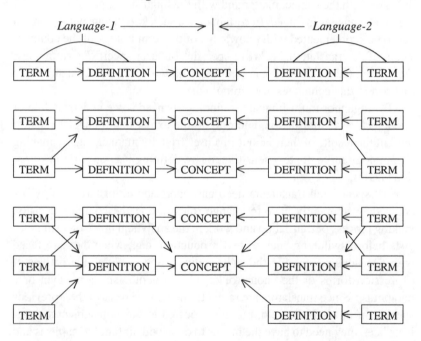

Figure 4 shows how translation of terms takes place between two languages. Here, the focus is on the concept which can be defined in different languages while still providing a common point of reference. It underlines the complete dependence on definitions as the only access point and bridge between concept and term.

Terminological Reference Tools: Term Banks

In the past, translators used dictionaries and other printed reference works for term equivalents; this was supplemented by personal collections of bilingual terminology; industrial organizations compiled collections of terminology of product documentation to be used by in-house teams of translators and technical writers.

The advent of computers has introduced a new range of lexical support tools (e.g. term banks, text databases, CD-ROM dictionaries) which are required to deal with more technical texts, requiring greater specialized know-how or terminological research than even ten years ago. Since terminological research can occupy a considerable amount (up to 60%) of time of specialized translation, it is not surprising that translator training courses now lay greater emphasis on the principles and methods of terminology compilation.

Term banks may be viewed from two theoretical standpoints: either as

(a) as computerized mono- and multilingual dictionaries, containing the various information items found in conventional lexicographic works, in which case they may or may not be in a form suitable for end-use, or

(b) as lexicographic data bases, in which case they contain all the information items to be found in the conventional printed-paper dictionary, thus responding to the immediate requirements of their user-group(s).

Ideally, a term bank should be

a collection of automated specialised vocabularies, including nomenclatures, standardised terms and phrases, together with information required for their identification, which can be used as a mono- or multilingual dictionary for direct consultation, as a basis for dictionary production, as a control instrument for consistency of usage and term creation and as an ancillary tool in information and documentation. (Sager and McNaught, 1981)

Term Bank Evolution

The number of term banks has since grown significantly, from the 12 or so operational systems in the early 1980s. Since their inception in the 1960s, term banks have undergone three major evolutions.

(1) The first generation started off as conventional data bank (i.e., *electronic dictionaries*), and incorporated little or no terminology theory. These "term-oriented" data bases are the predominant type today and include EURODICAUTOM (the term bank of the Commission of European Communities), TERMIUM (Canadian Federal government), TEAM (Siemens A.G.) and LEXIS (Bundessprachenamt of the German government).

(2) The second generation of term banks incorporated some ideas of structure, notably, hierarchies. In spite of advances in computer data management, the few implementations of concept-oriented systems that exist include DANTERM (the Danish term bank, developed at CEBA, Copenhagen), CEZEAUTERM (Université de Clermont-Ferrand, France), and BTB (the British term bank prototype, developed at UMIST, Manchester). Although this is a significant improvement over the first-generation-type term bank, the theory is inadequate to represent the diversity of terminological relationships for any one domain (e.g., *type_of, part_of, cause-effect, process-product, raw_material-product, succession*).

(3) The third generation of term banks is already at an advanced research stage, the prototypical example being the CODE system being developed at the University of Ottawa, Canada. This type of term bank is seen as an expert system in which terminology is viewed as special (-language) knowledge representation and problem-oriented.

Characteristics of Term Banks

The earliest term banks were developed in the mid 1960s and early 1970s by translation departments in large organizations, e.g. LEXIS (1966), TEAM (1967), EURODICAUTOM (1971). Their main functions were:

(a) to supplement printed dictionaries by providing up-to-date multilingual terminology;

(b) to preserve centrally the considerable effort of in-house language specialists, and to make this work more widely available;

(c) to permit greater terminological unity among translations split up among different translators by providing agreed, reliable and unified terminology;

(d) to speed up the translation process by giving the translator a single efficient reference tool;

(e) to serve as instruments for language planning or standardization.

The different orientations of term banks are represented in Table 1.

Table 1 reveals, firstly, that most terminological data banks concentrate on terms, and only a few (TEAM, LEXIS and particularly, EURODICATU-TOM) admit phrases and sentences. EURODICAUTOM accepts whole sentences as entries with some of the terms marked as search-term.

Secondly, all the existing implementations listed above, with the exception of CEZEAUTERM (specializing in the construction industry) are multidisciplinary in their approach since each database collection is drawn from more than one specialised domain.

Lastly, the majority of term banks are term-based and rather than concept-oriented.

Table 1 Typology of term banks

Coverage	Language(s)				Subject(s)		Record		Main Entry	
	bi-		multi-		mono-disc.	multi-disc.	term-based	concept based	term	phrase/sentence
Termbank	D	ND	D	ND						
BTB			+			+		+	+	
BTQ	+					+	+		+	
Cezeauterm				+	+			+	+	
Danterm		+				+		+	+	
Eurodiccautom				+		+	+		+	+
Lexis			+			+	+		+	+
Normaterm		+				+		+	+	
Team				+		+	+		+	+
Termium			+			+		+	+	

BTQ = Banque de Terminologie du Quebec (Quebec, Canada)

Notes: D = Directed (L1 $\Rightarrow$ L2 only)

ND = Non-Directed (L1 $\Rightarrow$ L2)

From the architectural point of view, the vast majority of term banks are characterized by:

(1) an adherence to rigid subdivision of the knowledge base into separate areas, and disregard for interdisciplinary and overlapping subject fields;

(2) a tendency to organize the database linguistically rather than conceptually;

(3) the absence of conceptual relationships, as they are difficult to represent using the network-type database model in use by the systems; even in more recent systems such as DANTERM, CEZEAUTERM, only basic thesaurus-type relationships have been defined;

(4) the tendency to impose a uniform record structure over the whole database. Thus for example, medical terminology (rich in taxonomies) and Data Processing terminology (loose structure) share the same logical record format;

(5) the inability to represent the translation relationship as a many-to-many (m:n) relationship with the consequence that text-type-conditioned variants are entered as separate records.

Within the present term bank environments, one can get responses only to simple queries such as spelling, usage (language variety, context, restrictions, etc.), foreign-language equivalent, definition, context of use, restrictions on use, bibliographic source, (other) subject(s) in which used, and synonyms/abbreviations, all of which require extraction of explicitly-coded information from within individual records.

In a translation environment, users often require information of an inferential/evaluative nature as opposed to factual information, and which cannot be obtained in the majority of current systems, e.g.

(a) Which terms are related to Y (by *part, type, cause, process*, etc.)

(b) What is the nearest foreign language equivalent for X ?

(c) Can term X be used in the context of Y ?

(d) List the immediate conceptual information for X.

(e) What do you call a machine that does Y ?

(f) Has X got any parts ? List them.

(g) List all terms which have parts associated with them.

(h) What is the relation between terms X and Y ?

New Trends in Terminology Management

During the last few years, the main changes in terminographic orientation have been from word-based to concept-based systems, and from technology-influenced, database-dictated, inflexible structures to conceptually-motivated, dynamically generated systems. There have also been significant developments in human-assisted or machine-assisted terminography, notably, research into the use of an integrated package of terminographic and editing tools in the so-called "translator workstation" or "translator's workbench". The basic principle behind the workbench is that the translator's editing suite should include

(a) machine-assisted acquisition, extension and maintenance of collections of terminology;
(b) access to on-line reference sources (dictionaries, text archives, etc.);
(c) customizable text-editing facilities, e.g., different configurations for translators and revisors in a large organization;
(d) mechanisms for manipulating text archives (e.g., examining previous translations and retrieving parts thereof).

Terminology Training for Translation

A foundation in terminology as part of translator training provides among other things an understanding of the nature of term formation and so provide tools for both term analysis and the coining of translation equivalents. Term-formation is important to the extent that the translator is informed about which combinational elements to use for neologism and which combinations are not possible in the domain. Translators/interpreters also need to know where there are conceptual or terminological incompatibilities between their working languages so that they know when a paraphrase or a neologism is necessary. Such incompatibility can only be arrived at either by comparing or through a knowledge of the conceptual structures of the subject field in the different languages.

In designing terminology courses for translators one must be aware of the fact that an understanding of terminology requires a minimum of theory and the conflicting fact that translators have a distrust of theory or theorising. It is therefore important to convince translators that the solution of practical translation problems is assisted by an understanding of the

underlying principles and that a sound methodology for developing terminology must also be based on the same theoretical foundation.

Translators must be able to recognize that they are dealing with a term
rather than a word, thereby narrowing down the search space in the reference works to be consulted. It may be less obvious that terminology, or an
understanding of the distinctive nature of terms, is also useful in the earlier
stage of the translation process which is concerned with understanding a
source text, especially when the subject matter or terminology of the source
text is not completely familiar. Translators must therefore learn to separate
terms from words, identify compounds or other juxtapositions as single
units or casual collocations, recognize variants and have criteria for finding
the standard form, etc.

The core of a course must first of all give a certain theoretical foundation and basic premises of terminology, secondly, a methodology for carrying out research and for compilation of small glossaries and, thirdly, an
understanding of term formation and the creation of neologisms. Practical
exercises give experience in the fundamental terminological activities
which future translators need to be able to perform.

Terminology Pitfalls in Translation

Teachers of translation have expressed concern about the danger which too
much terminological theory poses in translation training. The argument is
that students can be misled by the simplicity of term-concept matches in
pure science to assume a similar simplicity in other fields. Worse, the
direction from meaning to words implied in the onomasiological (i.e.,
concept-linguistic form) approach may lead to the impression that there
should be just one name for each object. It is possible therefore that the
terminological approach may also obscure the fact that conceptual systems
often differ from culture to culture and only numbers, units of measurement
and proper names seem to be context-independent. An over-simplistic
theory of terminology may also introduce a misleadingly sharp distinction
between polysemic words and monosemic terms, thereby obscuring the fact
of terminological synonymy and variants.

Juhel (1987) draws attention to the following specific dangers arising
from an overemphasis (in translator training) on terminological viewpoints:

(1) The translator may be tempted to look only for terminological
     equivalents and translate without due regard for larger units of

meaning. Student translators should, therefore, be led to interpret the sense from its context and if they cannot find an equivalent they should be required to paraphrase in order to maintain the informative content of the source language message.

(2) Translators that have been taught term formation rules may be too liberal in the creation of new terms instead of searching for existing terms in the target language. Therefore, students have to learn that terminological usage is determined separately (a) by the subject field, and (b) by a text with regard to synonymy.

(3) A simplistic view of the world tempts translators to over-produce neologisms based on a rather literal translation of elements when in fact different cultures form terms on the basis of different distinguishing features of concepts and different linguistic techniques.

In spite of these dangers it is evident that terminology can be of great assistance in view of its insistence on the cohesion of the conceptual structures of subject fields and special languages and through the disciplines imposed by the need for definition.

References

BS 3669. *Recommendations for the Selection, Formation, and Definition of Technical Terms.* London: British Standards Institution, 1963.

ISO. *International Standard ISO 1087: 1990 (E/F). Terminology — Vocabulary*, 1st ed. International Organization for Standardization, 1990.

Juhel, D. *L'enseignement de la terminologie: point de vue d'un professeur de terminologie.* In J.-C.Boulanger and A. Reguigui. *L'enseignement de la terminologie à l'université: état de la question*, No. 5, edited by Girsterm. Laval, Quebec, 1987.

Sager, Juan C. *A Practical Course in Terminology Processing.* Amsterdam: John Benjamins, 1990.

——— and J. McNaught. *Feasibility Study of the Establishment of a Terminological Data Bank in the U.K.* British Library R. & D. Report Nr. 5642, 1981.

TRANSTAR: An English-Chinese Machine Translation System

Dong Zhendong
BGL Computer Co. Ltd.
Beijing, China

Machine translation, or automatic translation, is the application of computers to the translation of texts from one natural language into another. The research of machine translation has been of great significance to natural language processing and artificial intelligence. It also contributes much to the theory of translation, which is traditionally considered as humanities, for the achievements of machine translation have convinced us that translation is not only art but also science. After over forty years of arduous work on its research and development, machine translation is now no longer a dream, it is a reality. Especially in the last five years, it has clearly shown that machine translation keeps growing both in width and in depth, and has become so intensive a field of global activity. One of the largest growth areas has been in the marketing and sale of commercial machine translation systems.

TRANSTAR, or 譯星 in Chinese, is the world's first commercial English-Chinese machine translation system. It was released and marketed by Chinese Software Technique Corporation in August, 1988, and has so far been sold over 50 users both at home and abroad.

Historical Review

The research and development of the system can be dated back to the late 70s. In 1977, a machine translation research team was formed in Heilongjiang University, North-east of China. The team began their research on linguistic theory, English and Chinese grammars, as well as techniques of machine translation. The research and development of the system was based on the linguistic theory and language model, called Logical Semantics, which was put forward by Dong Zhendong, the team leader and the chief designer of the system. In 1979 an experimental English-Chinese machine translation system, called MT-H78, was successfully completed. In the end of 1981, two of the team members transferred to Academy of Military Sciences, and a new machine translation research group was then set up and a new project, KY-1, started in the Academy. After four years of research, including pilot system design, prototype testing, trial application and evaluation, KY-1, as a real application-oriented machine translation system was brought into being. The KY-1 system, based on the same language model, naturally inherited much of linguistic strategy and practical technique of MT-H78. KY-1 was acknowledged as China's most successful machine translation system and it was awarded the National Second Prize for Advance in Science and Technology, a top-level prize in China. In 1986 the system was transferred to China Software Technique Corp, in which a language engineering lab was then specially engaged in the commercialization of the system. Much work was done for application testing, translation quality control, vocabulary enlargement, user's interface improvement, etc. In August 1988, a commercial English-Chinese machine translation system, named TRANSTAR, was released.

Current Status

TRANSTAR is a unidirectional (English to Chinese), semantic-transfer-based machine translation system. The system mainly composed of three parts: databank, controller, and maintenance package. The databank contains two types of dictionary, i.e., a basic dictionary and a technical term dictionary, both of which contain an English version and a bilingual version, and two types of rulebase, i.e., a grammar-driven rulebase and a lexicon-driven rulebase. The controller includes three subsystems, i.e., pre-processing and dictionary look-up, source language analyzer, and transfer and target language generator. The maintenance package provides various kinds of software tools for both system developers and end-users, such as databank maintenance, debugging tools, post-editor, etc.

Dictionaries:
(1) basic dictionary — 40,000 words, phrases, idioms and proverbs,
(2) technical term dictionary — 200,000 technical terms, covering over 10 domains, such as computer science, economics, telecommunications, car and tractor manufacture, printing industry, etc.

Rulebases:
(1) grammar-driven rulebase — 3,000 rules allocated in 81 subgram-
    mar bases for source language analysis or for transfer and target
    language generation
(2) lexicon-driven rulebase — 3,000 rules for treating individual lin-
    guistic phenomena such as particular ambiguities, idioms, concur-
    rence, etc.

Equipment:
(1) implementation language — COBOL
(2) minimal memory size — 640 kilobytes
(3) minimal disk size — 40 megabytes
(4) machines available — ranging from any PC's to mainframes
(5) operating systems — DOS

Performance:
(1) speed — varying with machines available, 1,500 word/hr on PC's

Facilities:
(1) a bilingual editor
(2) dictionary maintenance for users

The configuration of TRANSTAR and the translation flow are shown
in Figure 1.

Figure 1

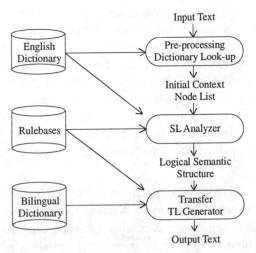

Logical Semantics

It is generally recognized that there are two steps in human translation, that is, understanding and expression. Corresponding to these steps, machine translation may include two stages, that is, source language analysis and target language generation. The depth of source language analysis is critical to a machine translation system. Moreover, the translation between the languages of different families is more difficult than that between languages of the same family. Therefore it is very important to choose a proper analysis depth for an English-Chinese machine translation system. Obviously, since the two languages are of different families, to have a deep analysis of the source language will be desirable. Hence, in TRANSTAR, a semantic structure is taken as the analysis depth or target rather than a syntactic one. The TRANSTAR system is based on a linguistic theory called Logical Semantics, which is defined as a structure of semantic relations and attributes in a language sector (usually a sentence). There are three types of critical semantic relation apart from the denotation of the language units in a sentence. They are the relation between the conceptual entities of the sentence, the relations between the language users (speaker and listener), and the relation between the language users and the entities of the sentence. For example, in the sentence "Open the door, please," the three types of relations can be shown below:

Type 1. <Action> → <Patient>: OPEN → DOOR
Type 2. [Request] → (SPEAKER) → (LISTENER)
Type 3. <Action> → <Agent>: OPEN → (LISTENER)

And in this sentence the word "please" refers to a kind of attribute, i.e. modality of "politeness". The semantic relations and attributes in TRAN-STAR are categorized in different sets, which are illustrated as follows:

(1) Concept relations: Action, Agent, Patient, Member, Existent, Experiencer, Manner, Frequency, Means, Instrument, Scope, Initial State, Final State, Time, Space, etc.
(2) Event relations: Cause, Concession, Condition, Time, Purpose, etc.
(3) Specific relations: Compared, Content of Comparison, Referential, Degree of Comparison, Part-of, Possessive, Quality, Definite, Indefinite, etc.

(4) Sentential attributes: Declarative, Interrogative, Imperative, etc.
    Topic, Focus, Emphasis, etc.
    Comparison, Negative, etc.
(5) Action attributes: Tense, Aspect, Voice, Mood, Modality, etc.

It is well known that every sentence in a written language has two different kinds of structure: the syntactic structure and the semantic structure. In TRANSTAR, it is the semantic structure rather than the syntactic one which both the analysis and the generation are directed to. In other words, the logical semantics is taken as the termination of the source language analysis and the starting-point of the target language generation, or the so-called intermediary representation, while the syntactic structure is merely a mid-way result in the analysis. This argument may be illustrated by the translation of the following two sentences:

(1a) He read the book in the room.
(2a) He put the book on the desk.

Obviously, grammatically (1) and (2) have the same syntactic structure, i.e. SVO with a PP as an adverbial. However, they differ greatly in their semantic structure, as

(1) <Action> → <Agent>, Patient, <Space>
(2) <Action> → <Agent>, Patient, <Final-location>

And the only correct translation of the two into Chinese should be based on their semantic structures:

(1b) 他在房間裡讀書。
(2b) 他把書放在書桌上。 (NOT: 他在桌上放書）

Source Language Analysis

After having input the source language text, the system starts its analysis stage which is most essential and complicated part of the process. The source language analysis of TRANSTAR adopts Constituent Functional Relation Grammar which takes logical semantics as its theoretical basis. Constituent Functional Relation Grammar is characteristic of deterministic algorithm with bottom-up processing in a multi-phase operation. The main steps of Constituent Functional Relation Grammar operations are:

(1) to look up the dictionary and take each word in the sentence being

translated with its information specified in the dictionary into the buffer and thus generate an initial context node list. In TRANSTAR's dictionary each entry is provided with 28 information items to the maximum which are allocated to different information zones, i.e. morphological, syntactic, semantic and transfer zones.

(2)   to analyze the sentence morphologically first, including homograph resolution, the treatment of undefined words, or not-found words, then to start unification operation so as to form various kinds of phrases, e.g. NP, VP, AP, PP, etc. The relations of the heads of each phrase, called constituents, are formed by a two-way link technique so that the children nodes are able to be visited by their parents, and vice versa.

(3)   to generate a logical semantic structure of the sentence. The maximum of information items of each word will then increase up to 57. It should be noticed that the logical semantic structure generated after the analysis by Constituent Functional Relation Grammar is a semantic network with the predicate of the sentence as its root constituent. Figure 2 shows the semantic structure of the English sentence "this desk was easy to make" on the right, and it will be then transferred into more abstract structure which is the real logical semantic structure, in which all the attributes obtained from the analysis of source language will be attached to its head concepts. And the Chinese translation 這張桌子做起來容易 will be generated from this structure. In this sense, TRANSTAR is a typical semantic-transfer-based machine translation system.

Constituent Functional Relation Grammar is executed through a rule-matching mechanism driven by the system's controller. As mentioned above, the rules for analysis are arranged in two types of rulebase i.e. the grammar-driven rulebase and the lexicon-driven rulebase. The former is composed of various subbases according to the various kinds of general problems which the source language analysis confronts, including undefined word processing, homograph resolution, finite and infinite verbs determination, formation of phrases, treatment of clauses, coordination structures, and establishment of logical semantic relationship between constituents, etc. The latter is designed to handle words which have so complicated a behaviour that they need their own particular rules all to themselves.

When the logical semantic structure of a sentence processed is obtained

Figure 2

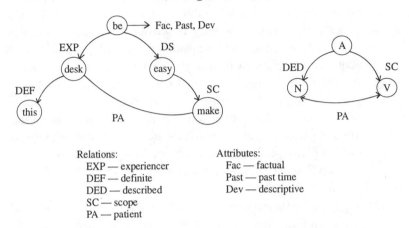

Relations:
  EXP — experiencer
  DEF — definite
  DED — described
  SC — scope
  PA — patient

Attributes:
  Fac — factual
  Past — past time
  Dev — descriptive

after the analysis, it is possible for the system to go to the text stage, that is, the generation of the target language.

Target Language Generation

The implementation of target language generation as well as source language analysis varies with different language pairs to be processed in machine translation systems. The main tasks of target language generation in TRANSTAR are assigned as follows:

[1] to generate target language sentences in proper Chinese sentence patterns and word order arrangements. For example,

(3a) The electric light was invented by Edison.

(3b) 電燈是愛迪生發明的。 (NOT: 電燈被愛迪生發明。)

(4a) Line A is three inches longer than line B.

(4b) 線A比線B長三英寸。 (NOT: 線A比線B三英寸長。)

[2] to use proper Chinese function words, such as 了, 把, 起來, 加以 etc., in the right places into the target language sentence. For example:

(5a) He can swim, too.

(5b) 他也會游泳。 (NOT: 他會也游泳。)

(6a) This cloth is very soft to feel.

(6b) 這塊布摸起來非常柔軟。 (NOT: 這塊布非常軟摸。)

[3] to employ translation skills as much as possible, especially in the

case when they are absolutely necessary, e.g., the conversion of part-of-speech. For example,

(7a) The treatment of meanings by the computer.

(7b) 利用計算機處理意義。 (NOT: 利用計算機的意義的處理。)

[4] to choose natural Chinese collocations of words, especially in the case when they are absolute necessary. For example, *make progress* — 取得進步 , *make mistakes* — 犯錯誤 , *make a decision* — 作出決定 , *make a study* (*analysis, search*, etc.) 進行研究（分析、搜索等）.

All the tasks are performed by two generation packages in the generator of TRANSTAR. The first package is designed to deal with general problems, while the second is aimed at handling special or more complicated problems in target language generation. The general rule in the first package is based on an imaginary Chinese sentence with all the logical semantic relations in their proper order, for example, Concession — Condition — Agent — Time — Space — Action — Patient ... etc. Hence when package is to generate a Chinese sentence with the following logical semantic structure from the English sentence "He read the book in the room after supper":

READ	(Root, past)
HE	(<Agent>, READ)
BOOK	(<Patient>, READ)
SUPPER	(<Time>, READ)

the first package will be called to act in accordance with the general rule and generate the Chinese translation:

他晚飯後在房間裡讀書。

However, just one general rule is far from adequate to tackle all the tasks listed above. The second generation package contains over 500 specific rules allocated in 7 main modules, i.e. generation of verbs in active, passive, nouns denoting actions, numerals, negative noun phrases, negative verb phrases and adjective phrases, and subordinate clause assembly. To take (3a) as an example, the translation of (3a) into (3b) is handled by the module of generation of verbs in the passive. The specific rule for generation a Chinese sentence pattern as (3b) can be roughly interpreted as follows:

Condition part: (1) Tense verb as the root, passive, past tense, positive,
                          not causative
                     (2) Subject as the <Patient>, definite — topic of the
                          sentence
                     (3) Other Logical Semantic Relations as new informa-
                          tion

Action part: (1) To generate in the word order: <Patient> + 是 +
                          <Other Logical Semantic Relations> + 的
                     (2) To mark the Chinese sentence pattern

Although the critical factor in target language generation of TRAN-
STAR is the logical semantic relation, on which the Chinese word order
mainly relies, the attributes in the logical structure obtained from the source
language analysis are also important, which will affect the overall generation. In TRANSTAR, special attention is paid to the integration of all these
factors, as they are usually interdependent. For example, in dealing with the
aspect of verbs as one of the attributes, there is a rule which will add the
function word 了 immediately after a Chinese verb to express "Completeness" in translating an English verb in the perfect tense. For example:

(8a) He has read that book.
(8b) 他讀了那本書。

And in dealing with the word order, there is a rule which will generate in the
following way:

(9a) He put the book on the desk.
(9b) 他把書放在書桌上。

but when we change the tense verb of (9a) into the perfect, and because of
the above rule about 了 , we would obtain a clumsy Chinese translation as

(10a) He has put the book on the desk.
(10b) 他把書放了在書桌上。 (wrong!)

Thus in order to handle properly in this case, another rule must be added to
integrate both the factors of logical semantic relation and the factor of the
verb aspect. It should be noticed that all the clumsy or wrong Chinese
sentences listed in this section are not artificial or imaginary ones, they did
occur when there were some pitfalls in the development of the system.

SCOMT

This is a software tool which consists of two parts. One is a problem-oriented language, called SCOMT language, which is based on a higher-level programming language. The other is an interpreter, called SCOMT interpreter, by which the rule of the system will first be turned into the programming language and then be executed. By the help of SCOMT, the separation of the linguistic data from algorithms is successfully achieved. The separation enables the linguists to concentrate on the resolution of linguistic problems in both source language analysis and target language generation, and the programmers to concentrate on the development of efficient algorithms. The separation can greatly shorten the development period, for it means that rules can be changed or modified without changing the processing algorithm. It also makes it easier to achieve modular design, as TRANSTAR rulebase is divided into 81 modules. The advantage of module design is that any part can be modified and tested without affecting other parts of the systems.

All the rules of TRANSTAR, for both analysis and generation, are written in the SCOMT language. Each of them, as a production rule, is composed of two parts: condition and action, as roughly shown in the previous section. As SCOMT is highly expressive, though very simple, and has a good readability, it is easy for linguists to learn and use.

References

Dong, Zhendong 董振東 . 〈邏輯語義及其在機器翻譯中的應用〉 (Logical Semantics and Its Application in Machine Translation). In 《中國的機器翻譯》 (*Machine Translation in China*), edited by Liu Yongquan 劉湧泉 . Beijing: Knowledge Press 知識出版社 , 1985, pp. 25–45.

———. "Machine Translation Research in China." In *Proceedings of New Directions in Machine Translation International Conference*, Budapest, 1988, pp. 85–91.

——— and Zhang Deling 張德玲 . "KY-I Machine Translation System and Some Linguistic Aspects Concerned." In *Proceedings of 1987 International Conference on Chinese Information Processing*, Beijing, Vol. 2, 1987, pp. 1–8.

——— and ———. 〈語言、翻譯、機器翻譯、兼談 "科譯 1 號" 英漢機譯系統〉 (Language, Translation, Machine Translation and a Discussion of the KY-I English-Chinese Machine Translation System). Paper presented at "Conference on Translation Today," Hong Kong, 17–21 December 1987.

Hutchins, W. J. *Machine Translation: Past, Present, Future*. Chichester: Ellis
    Horword, 1986.
———. "Recent Developments in Machine Translation: A Review of the Last Five
    Years." In *Proceedings of New Directions in Machine Translation International
    Conference*, Budapest, 1988, pp. 7–63.

MASS MEDIA

Translation and Mass Communication

Dirk Delabastita
Department of English
Facultés Universitaires Notre-Dame de la Paix, Belgium

1.

The notion of mass communication covers an enormous domain, including the printed media, film, radio broadcasting, TV broadcasting, music records, and so forth. In addition, different new media and technologies have been developed in the last few years, either as extensions of existing electronic media or not: the compact disk, teletext, home video, the videodisc, cable and satellite television, computer video games, videotex, and so forth. Any of these media can fulfil different functions, such as entertainment, information, commercial advertising, political propaganda, or social control. They are, moreover, all subject to further distinctions. Thus the category of the print media encompasses many different kinds of text with their own specific purpose and place in society, and their own channels of production and distribution. School textbooks, literature, journalistic writings, political pamphlets, etc. each seem to represent a fairly distinct kind of communication. It is therefore hardly surprising that scholars of communication find it difficult to arrive at a clear and universally applicable definition of mass communication, and that research in this field shows so many different approaches, each focusing on another aspect of the whole issue. (For a useful recent survey, see Edelstein *et al.*, 1989, DeFleur and Ball-Rokeach, 1989, or McQuail, 1987.)

So far very little scholarly research has been devoted to the study of translation in mass communication. This can partly be explained by the fact that translated messages in the mass media are often presented and received as "original" messages so that their status as translated texts remains obscured. However, there must be other reasons as well. Thus, the specialists in communication studies all appear to be working with monolingual models. The standard books in the field simply fail to mention matters as multilingualism or translation. One might perhaps have expected a significant contribution from the discipline of sociolinguistics, but it has little more to offer. Its models are, again, predominantly monolingual. In addition, little systematic research seems to have been conducted into the effects of the modern mass media on the social structure and evolution of language in general (Baetens Beardsmore, 1984). Translation studies — of all disciplines — has also largely overlooked the issue. This may be due to various factors. Many translation scholars have been so preoccupied with abstract theoretical problems ("equivalence", "translatability", etc.), that there was no room left for the empirical study of the historical reality of translation. Others have looked into existing translating practice, but preferred to study translations of, or by, canonized literary writers rather than translation as a mechanism of "popular culture". It is, indeed, well-known that the social sciences often select their objects for study on the basis of prestige, rather than intrinsic interest. Another reason may be that many translation scholars have preconceived notions as to what translation "is" or "should be", and that translation in mass communication is often done according to principles which do not come up to such *a priori*, normative definitions. Many critics would thus assume explicitly or (more often) implicitly that the subtitling or dubbing of films is a form of "adaptation" rather than "translation proper" and accordingly exclude these phenomena from the discipline.

There have however been in the last two decades some major shifts in the discipline of translation studies. There has been a tendency for abstract theoretical speculation to be replaced by an interplay between theoretical working hypotheses and practical description. Many scholars have also come to accept that their first responsibility is to study (and not defend, or dispute) the values, definitions, canons and norms found in historical reality. The cultural prestige of certain texts and textual practices, or existing definitions of "genuine" translation can no longer be taken for granted, and have in fact become part of the object to be investigated. These shifts, which are more fully explained in Toury 1980 and Hermans 1985, have made it possible and even necessary for the question of translation in mass communication to be incorporated into the discipline.

A crucial fact of modern mass communication is that it is becoming increasingly international. Formerly the institutions of the mass media were largely patterned on the political map of the world. The national networks for radio and TV are a case in point. While this situation still persists to some extent, and remains predominant in totalitarian states, there has been a general trend towards denationalization, both in the form of decentralized (e.g. local radio and TV) and supra-national initiatives. The latter development, which is obviously more relevant for our purpose, has been going on for quite some time. The "Americanization" of the film industry and film culture started as early as after the First World War. More recently, the advent of new technologies and increasing economic pressures has speeded up the whole trend, leading to enormous power concentration across linguistic as well as political barriers. This has, in fact, created a new situation of multilingualism, viz. one which exists irrespective of the parameters of place and time. Translation is of course only one of the possible solutions to multilingualism, next to e.g. the use of all the languages involved, or the use of one of them or of an artificial language (Esperanto, etc.) as a *lingua franca*. In any case, it stands to reason that the internationalization of the mass media and its multiple consequences deserve to be studied systematically by translation scholars.

This article will limit itself to the presentation of some general hypotheses, and examples will mainly be taken from film (my shorthand for both cinema and TV) translation. As some of the situations described may be valid in the Western context only, the study of the modes and functions of translation in the Asian and African mass media can be expected to reveal many new aspects.

2.

There is at least one level where translation in mass communication seems to differ fundamentally from translation in general, viz. the level of *possible* relationships between source texts and target texts. The public and collective nature of mass communication is based on the property that its messages are materially fixed and reproduced. It is through technical reproduction that they are — at least in principle — accessible to a large and not previously delimited group of people. This material fixation may, however, impose certain restrictions on the translator's options.

This becomes obvious when one compares (the translation of) theatre and film. Both film and theatre establish multi-channel and multi-code communication. They use the visual (light waves) as well as the acoustic (air vibrations) channel, and there is a whole range of codes that give shape to the play or film as a meaningful sign and enable the spectators to make sense of the message: linguistic and paralinguistic codes, literary and textual codes, moral codes, vestimentory codes, politeness codes, and so forth. When it comes to translating such semiotically complex texts, the main difference between theatre and film is that the film translator has to reckon with the more or less stringent material constraints of his medium, whereas the theatre translator has in this technical respect a much greater freedom in dealing with the source text. Such restrictions will therefore determine the range of *possible* translations, and have to form the basis of the theoretical "competence" model of the translation scholar.

From the technical point of view the basic distinction to be made in film translation is between the acoustic and the visual channel. Since this distinction (which pertains to the level of channels, i.e., of material transmission) does not coincide with the distinction between verbal and non-verbal signs (which pertains to the level of codes, i.e., of meaning), we can distinguish between the following four categories of filmic signs:

a. visually transmitted verbal signs (the title, credits, documents shown for perusal, road signs, etc.);
b. visually transmitted non-verbal signs (all other visual information);
c. acoustically transmitted verbal signs (the dialogues, etc.);
d. acoustically transmitted non-verbal signs (music, sound effects, etc.).

It can be shown that this basic classification forms a useful starting point for a theoretical model of possible relationships in film translation (Delabastita, 1989:196–205). Thus, the two best known techniques of film translation — dubbing and subtitling — can be described in the following terms:

dubbing = signs from categories a., b. and d. are copied, while there is a substitution of signs belonging to category c.;

subtitling = signs from all categories are copied, while there is an addition of signs belonging to category a.

Most of the technical aspects of dubbing and subtitling have been fairly well described. The dubbing process appears to be quite elaborate and requires a whole team of experts and actors. Inevitably, the cost of a dubbed version is rather high. The replacement of spoken verbal signs is in varying degrees subject to the constraint of synchronicity, according to which the visually perceptible movement of the actor's articulators and entire body must be in agreement with the audible sound production. This constraint underlies the term "synchronization", which is very often used as a synonym for "dubbing". However, it is dependent, among other things, on the semiotic convention of "realism", and therefore not of an absolute nature. In fact, certain film cultures appear to care very little about audio-image synchronicity. The subtitling of films poses rather different technical problems. Actors usually speak faster than can with ease be represented visually and read on the screen, so that many subtitlers decide to compress the amount of linguistic information in the translation. As a guideline many of them accept the six seconds rule, which means that six seconds are needed for the adequate reading of two full lines of subtitled text (some sixty characters and spaces in total). Another problem that is typical of subtitling is that the *spoken* text of the dialogue has to be rendered by means of *written* language; this tends to create awkward dilemmas on the level of style and register, but these go beyond the strictly technical level.

On closer inspection it turns out that there are many more techniques than dubbing and subtitling, including the mere copy of source film signs belonging to the four categories — "non-translation" — or their deletion. Various consecutive or simultaneous combinations of these techniques are also possible. Considering this wide range of possibilities, one can only conclude that the translation of film cannot be reduced to a process of mere linguistic conversion. The source film usually contains many linguistic signs (e.g., written ones) that are not converted at all, while the process as a rule also involves a direct or indirect modification of non-verbal signs.

The modern mass communications started with the invention of printing rather than with the advent of electronics. Although this is not usually done, it is therefore possible to perceive published translations as an aspect of translation in the mass media. Viewing source and target texts as such in the present context awakens us to the material, i.e., graphic dimension of the print media. Neither in "monolingual" literary and textual studies nor in translation studies is it customary to pay much attention to the material character of texts, as if readers had immediate and direct access to the abstract ideas "behind" the material face of the text. In fact, the typography and lay-out of a text often acts as a signal of a text-type or genre (cf. the specific appearance of a business letter), as a principle of segmentation either symmetrical or not with other such principles (cf. enjambment, which is based on the non-coincidence of graphic and syntactic divisions), and may in general be used to underscore other prosodic, grammatical or semantic text patterns. In more extreme cases of visual poetry graphic devices even become the dominant principle of text structuration. It is probably indicative of our idealist text conceptions that translation scholars have fairly systematically overlooked this aspect of printed mass communication.

There is one particular domain where translation scholars have paid due attention to the material aspect of the print media and to its restrictive effect on possible translation relationships, viz. the case of comic strips (e.g. Spillner, 1980). With comic strips the interaction between the verbal (linguistic) and the graphic (pictorial) level is indeed particularly obvious. Favourite verbal devices of the genre as deixis, allusion, ambiguity and wordplay are very often dependent on contextual clues that can be derived from the visual setting only. This situation imposes major restrictions on the translator's range of possible action, unless he/she is willing to make modifications on the visual level.

3.

The example of the comic strip shows that translators working in the print media may well find themselves faced with some of the technical dilemmas that film translators have to confront. Let us now turn away from the theoretical level of *possible* source text / target text relationships and focus on *actual* translation relationships in empirical reality and on the normative principles that have governed these.

It is well-known that translators can basically chose, or look for a compromise of some kind, between two extreme positions. On the one hand, they may strive for a maximal reproduction of the source text and thus of the stylistic, cultural, etc. norms and values that it embodies. As a consequence, translations of this kind — so-called "adequate" translations — often turn out to be more or less incompatible with the expectations and norms of the receiving culture. On the other hand, translators may attempt to produce a text which is first and foremost an acceptable text according to the norms of the receiving system. Unavoidably, the adherence to the norms of the target pole that characterizes such "acceptable" translations often entails considerable shifts vis-à-vis the source text.

Modern descriptive research has demonstrated that it is possible to make certain hypothetical predictions as to the kind of conditions in which a translator is likely to follow particular strategies. Thus, if the target culture or a segment of it is "weak" (e.g., because it is still in the process of being established, because it is undergoing sudden changes, or has a peripheral position within a larger cultural frame), the translators working in it and for it are relatively speaking more likely to bow to the authority of the original text and welcome it as a new text model, and hence adopt an adequate strategy. However, if the target culture or its relevant segment is "strong" (consolidated, stable, central), translators will show the tendency to fashion translations in accordance with its own existing norms and text models rather than the source text's.

These basic principles seem to apply in the case of the modern mass communication as well. Consider the example of film translation (see also Lambert, 1989). It is indeed possible to describe subtitling as a paradigm of adequate translation, and dubbing as a typical form of acceptable translation. Subtitling can be compared with the bilingual edition of a foreign work, which has the original and the translation on facing pages. In both cases the translation — literally — does not take the place of the original, but is offered as a mere gloss or as supplementary information in support of the understanding of the original text, symbolizing the translator's subservient attitude towards the latter. There is no attempt to reduce or cover up the foreign origin of the original film, quite the contrary. Such an attempt is exactly what characterizes the practice of dubbing. Especially when linked with certain other operations (e.g., the translation of the film's title and of the credits), the technique of dubbing results in bringing the source film much closer to the models of home-made film production. This effect is brought about by making the actors speak their dialogues in the "appropriate" linguistic code and subcodes (dialect, sociolect, idiosyncrasies), but there is again much more at stake than just a linguistic conversion. Comparative research between source films and dubbed versions (e.g., Hesse-Quack, 1967) has shown that in the process many of the cultural signs (names, events, allusions, ideological content, etc.) are modified too in order to meet target pole notions and expectations. The principle that dubbing brings source films very close to the home production of films is even true in strictly economic terms, given the many job opportunities created by the dubbing industry at the target pole and the enormous budgets involved.

In the mass media too the distribution of "acceptable" and "adequate" translation techniques seems to conform to specific cultural principles. Thus, it is a well-known fact that subtitling is systematically preferred by smaller countries, which have a tradition of multilingualism and/or a peripheral position on the world map of cultures; Belgium, the Netherlands, Switzerland, and the Scandinavian countries are typical examples. There are good reasons to assume that this choice of subtitling is not merely motivated by economic considerations, even if dubbing is a far more expensive and time-consuming practice and therefore not very cost-effective in the case of smaller markets. Surveys show that viewers have outspoken preferences for either dubbing or subtitling, and these are to all appearances linked with linguistic and cultural norms. It would be most interesting to compare preferences in matters of film translation with other manifestations of such norms: e.g. the degree of linguistic purism versus openness, the degree of cultural and economic protectionism, foreign language teaching policies, attitudes vis-à-vis internal multilingualism, etc. Conversely, there has been an interesting attempt to view the systematic preference for dubbing in certain countries as "an assertion of the supremacy of the national language and its unchallenged political, economic and cultural power within the nation's boundaries. [...] Subtitling indirectly promotes the use of a foreign language as an everyday function in addition to creating an interest in a foreign culture. No extreme nationalistic society could allow a foreign language to reach the masses so easily and compete with its national language" (Danan, forthcoming).

The picture is undoubtedly more complex than has just been suggested. Thus, even in countries where subtitling is the predominant technique of film translation there exist certain kinds of mass communication where "acceptable" strategies are usually preferred. Advertisements produced by international agencies, or journalistic texts which can be traced back to international press agencies seldom show their foreign origin and status as translated texts (Lambert, 1989:230). The text on a box of cereals may be in four languages, but advertisements for the same product are likely to present themselves as monolingual communication. More research is definitely needed to detect the principles behind such selections.

4.

It appears fruitful to compare translation in the audiovisual mass media with translation in the printed mass media or with translation as a general category. In a last remark I would like to suggest that a careful study of translation in the mass media may actually require us to reconsider and modify one of the most basic models in the entire discipline of translation studies.

Translation scholars very often represent translation by a variant of the following diagram:

$$S1 — \text{Text1} — R1 = \text{Translator} = S2 — \text{Text2} — R2$$
$$\text{Code1} \qquad\qquad\qquad \text{Code2}$$

This representation of translation as an instance of bilingual communication is of course modelled on Bühler's and Jakobson's diagram of the monolingual act of communication. It shows translation as a somewhat more elaborate version of the "standard" communicative act: the translator acts both as a receiver (R1) of the original text (Text1) and as the sender (S2) of the translation (Text2), and in this intermediary position he/she carries out the complex recoding act (from Code1 to Code2). One may disagree with this particular representation, but the diagram nicely visualizes a basic assumption that is almost universally accepted in the discipline of translation studies: source-text communication is prior to target-text communication both logically and chronologically. To put it differently, it is generally assumed that there is a clear distinction between (original) communication and (translational) *meta*-communication, between the "production" of texts and their "reproduction", or between their "life" and their "afterlife".

Such a conception characterizes most traditional theories, which claim, in a rather normative manner, that translation *should* reproduce the relevant features of the original text ("Text2 must be equivalent to Text1"), or the relevant features of the entire communicative act ("S2 — Text2 — R2 must be equivalent to S1 — Text1 — R1"). But it also underlies more recent descriptive and target system oriented theories, which insist that translations are first and foremost facts of the receiving system, since the latter decides — in accordance with its own functional needs — whether there will be import at all, which texts will be selected for import, and which textual form the "reproduction" of the imported communication will take (e.g. Toury, 1980). Indeed, by insisting that import and reproduction policies are determined by the target system, such a theory takes the prior existence of source communication for granted. This is of course arguably justified in a very large group of cases, but not in others. Not only do some cultures follow an explicit and active *export* policy which is more than just the corollary of import by foreign cultures: consider phenomena such as translation prizes, subsidies for translators, cultural boards abroad, "ambassadorial" translations produced within the source culture intended for foreign markets, and the like; in addition — and this is really my present concern — there seem to be trends in modern mass communication which transcend the very oppositions between import and export and between source communication and target communication.

The trend towards growing internationalization referred to above frequently leads to a situation in which the "first" sender in the communicative chain already finds himself/herself faced with a multilingual situation and possibly with a need of translation. Translation is here not something which may, or may not, happen to the sender's messages after these have started to function in an originally monolingual situation, but it is potentially an inherent component of any communicative act he/she may want to perform. This situation could be diagrammed as follows:

S1 — Text1 — R1
id. — Text2 — R2
id. — Text3 — R3
id. — Text4 — R4
etc.

Again we can borrow our example from the world of the cinema (for more information, see Vincendeau 1989, which is my main source for what follows). While translation posed few technical difficulties in the days of the silent movies, problems became more acute with the advent of the talkies in the late twenties and early thirties, especially since American film companies were strongly dependent on European film markets. One of the techniques used in this early period to overcome the language barrier was the production of multiple-language versions of the same film, either in Hollywood (e.g., MGM) or in newly built centres in European places as Berlin, London or Paris (e.g., Paramount). Even though some actors had a polyglot reputation and played in different versions, as a rule the cast in each version was of the nationality of the target audience. The same set and scenario were used for each production, and sometimes the shooting of the different versions by the different crews took place in shifts, up to 24 hours a day. In the course of the 1930s the making of multiple-language versions was gradually superseded by the technique of dubbing, which had been developed alongside. And yet this chapter in the history of film making and film distribution was more than the negligible curiosity that most film historians have taken it for. For one thing, it anticipated one of the directions that international mass communications would take later on — think of multilingual campaigns launched by international advertising agencies, of the role played by international press agencies, etc.

Multilingual activities such as just described cut right across the distinction between source communication and target meta-communication, and thus form a challenge to the traditional two-phase models of translational communication, which present translation as a reproductive act or secondary text of some kind. If the discipline of translation studies wants to be flexible enough to encompass translation in the modern mass media, it may have to lose part of its former specificity and evolve in the direction of a more general theory of text production (Lambert, 1989:217).

References

Baetens Beardsmore, Hugo, ed. *Language and Television*. Special issue of *International Journal of the Sociology of Language*, Vol. 48 (1984).

Danan, Martine. "Dubbing as a Question of Nationalism." *Meta*, (Forthcoming).

DeFleur, Melvin L. and Sandra J. Ball-Rokeach. *Theories of Mass Communication*, 5th ed. New York and London: Longman, 1989.

Delabastita, Dirk. "Translation and Mass Communication." *Babel*, Vol. 35, No. 4 (1989), pp. 193–218.

————. "Translation and the Mass Media." In *Translation, History and Culture*, edited by Susan Bassnett and André Lefevere. London and New York: Pinter, 1990, pp. 97–109.

Edelstein, Alex S., Youichi Ito and Hans Mathias Kepplinger. *Communication and Culture. A Comparative Approach*. New York and London: Longman, 1989.

Hermans, Theo, ed. *The Manipulation of Literature. Studies in Literary Translation*. London and Sidney: Croom Helm, 1985.

Hesse-Quack, Otto. *Der Übertragungsprozess bei der Synchronisation von Filmen. Eine interkulturelle Untersuchung*. Munchen and Basel: Reinhardt, 1967.

Lambert, José. "La Traduction, les Langues et la Communication de Masse. Les ambiguités du discours social." *Target*, Vol. 1, No. 2 (1989), pp. 215–37.

———. "Le Sous-titrage et la question des traductions. Rapport sur une enquête." (Forthcoming).

McQuail, Denis. *Mass Communication Theory: An Introduction*, 2nd ed. London and New Dehli: Sage Publications, 1987.

Spillner, Bernt. "Semiotische Aspekte der Übersetzung von Comics-Texten." In *Semiotik und Übersetzen* (= *Kodikas/Code*, 4), edited by Wolfram Wilss. Tübingen: Gunther Narr, 1980, pp. 73–85.

Toury, Gideon. *In Search of a Theory of Translation*. Tel Aviv: The Porter Institute for Poetics and Semiotics, 1980.

Vincendeau, Ginette. "Films en versions multiples." In *L'Histoire du Cinéma*, edited by Jacques Aumont, André Gaudreault, and Michel Marie. Paris: Publications de la Sorbonne, 1989, pp. 101–17.

Media Translating

Ho Wai Kit
Department of Chinese, Translation and Linguistics
City Polytechnic of Hong Kong, Hong Kong

Media translating refers to acts of translation involving the media or for the media, a common category of translating activity, which enables information transmission and dissemination across linguistic and cultural boundaries.

In this era of information and knowledge explosion, the technical media or mass media are the media translator's main providers of raw material and users of the translations that result. Apart from the usual varieties of the broadcast media, i.e. radio and television, and those of the print media, i.e. newspapers and magazines, mass media here also include books, records, cassettes, discs, films, photographs, pictures, notices, speeches, posters, performances, and other means of communication that serve the general public.

The media translator, often part of the modern institutionalized forms of information production and dissemination, is one of the gatekeepers guarding the channel through which every message the society receives has to pass, because the media translator, like media editors and producers, is responsible for selecting, rejecting or otherwise manipulating items of information in service to the society. The performance of gatekeepers is of fundamental importance since it determines the quality and quantity of information the society has at its disposal.

The strategic position of the media translator as one such gatekeeper requires certain essential qualities of the media translator in order to create satisfactory products of translating.

The media translator at his or her best is a calm fact-reporter, vivid story-teller and tireless culture-seeder. A competent media translator is expected to be accurately and effectively informative and forward-lookingly educational. This competence is the result of having such attributes as (1) A truly sufficient grasp of the source language, and source-text subject matter and background; (2) A very solid or near-perfect knowledge of the target language and profound sensitivity to its uses; (3) Creative faculties of imagination, analysis and reasoning; (4) A high degree of intellectual maturity, curiosity and integrity; (5) Considerable experience of life and a sound understanding of cultures, history and the world; (6) The willingness and capability to get help from appropriate reference sources and people in the know whenever necessary; (7) A firm grasp of sound principles or tried guidelines based on translational experiences in all fields, especially media translating experiences; (8) A good understanding of the purposes of translating the events concerned and prospective receptors' interests and expectations; (9) An eclectic and open-minded attitude towards the changing reality and needs of the translation profession and society at large.

As mass media are manifold, media translating takes multifarious forms , among which news translating is one of everyday importance to the public, hence, worthy of special attention.

News translating, under its primary definition, means renewing in one language significant current information carried by the form of another language. The main requirements of news translating are: (1) accuracy of major ingredients of contextual meaning; (2) timeliness or reasonable speed of production; and (3) comprehensibility to the majority of prospective receptors.

On a practical plane, news translating frequently takes place more or less as part of a mixed bag of translating and editing: many forms of textual renewing, refracting and adapting, possibly involving abstracting, contracting, amplifying, summarizing, and above all, inventive rewriting, etc. It thus often goes beyond the traditional precincts of translating, and therefore, much of what is usually known as news translating may be more appropriately called news translating-editing.

For decades, news translating from English into Chinese has thrived, particularly as a source of information on current international events for the Chinese-language media of the world. It has partly grown out of Chinese communities' apparent over-dependence on Western news supplies, which is, to a certain extent, detrimental to the interests of user communities in the long run. Renewed demands for ideological independence, remarkable economic achievement, and notably advances in journalism and translatology have, however, helped Chinese efforts to redress the balance over recent decades.

On the other hand, news translating continues to complement news gathering and writing, and, when coupled with effective means of dissemination, has constituted a powerful countermeasure against all forms of obscurantism, contributing to the cause of freedom, democracy and human progress in general.

Speed requirements and deadlines often dictate the way media translating proceeds, but there are ground rules or fundamental considerations never to be brushed aside lightly.

One central consideration is the situation of use or the setting for the target text. Usually, the purpose of the translating act and the general interest of the community concerned take precedence over the intent of the source or original author and the wishes of the translator. A conscientious media translator always bears in mind the fundamental interests of the would-be receptors for whom a translation is being prepared. And the success of a translating act is usually measured by the extent to which it satisfies the needs of its target receptorship.

It has to be decided, for example, which parts of the implicit source-text information should be represented by target-text verbal devices so that target-text receptors can comprehend the message as well as expected; some comparison between the target receptorship and the known or imagined source-text receptorship can be important for such decisions. Dealing with a sentence like "The bill has been passed by the House," in a piece about United States politics being translated into Chinese for an Asian receptorship unfamiliar with American affairs, the translator has to consider whether it is necessary to flesh out the sentence by verbalizing certain originally implicit information: "The bill has been passed by the House of Representatives in the United States."

One major objective of media translating is to reach the greatest number of receptors possible in an effective manner. It follows that most of the language used is geared to a general educational level. From time to time obscure and out-of-the-way expressions are replaced with plainer ones, and highly specialized terms and neologisms are carefully explained, if not avoided, for easy comprehension. Overblown vocabularies, poor grammar and excessively elaborate sentence organization can make news less accessible to the average receptor, and therefore media translators as well as writers often prefer conciseness and clarity over complexity and floweriness as long as accuracy and attractiveness are guaranteed. This is particularly emphasized in broadcast-media translating, where structural simplicity on the sentence level is favoured. However, when handling discourses or texts carrying authoritative weight, experienced translators always show due respect for the formal and semantic as well as pragmatic features of the source text, particularly when the news items concerned have legal, political or financial implications. For example, nobody would attempt to embellish the letter or spirit of a blunt declaration of war.

Keeping a target text in line with target-language norms — good grammar and natural usage above all — is another consideration. For example, as any meticulous observer of the everyday Chinese-language and English-language press can tell, one-sentence paragraphs occur far less frequently in the Chinese-language press than they do in the English-language press, so quite often it becomes the job of a media translator working from English to Chinese to consider some formal changes, including re-paragraphing, so that optimal approximation to target-textual ease, idiomaticity and impact can be achieved.

On the other hand, respect for receptorship does not mean delivering everything on a silver platter. Responsible translators do not deliberately translate down to the receptors, nor do they lose sight of the elevating role media translating plays.

As receptors are left in peace quite often while the author is brought to them, it will do the receptors and their cultures a lot of good if authors are left in peace while receptors are brought to authors once in a while. That is to say, for instance, there are times when expressions depicting new things in a source culture need not be replaced by culture-free generic terms or local terms native to the target culture. So the former Chinese Communist Party Chairman Hua Guofeng's 華國鋒 "whateverism" 凡是論 need not be translated into English as "conformism", nor need China's *Renda* 人大 always be translated as "the Chinese Parliament", — for receptors unfamiliar with the Chinese scene, an explanation can always be furnished, in parentheses maybe, when things like *Renda* are introduced for the first time in a news item, — "the resolution was adopted today by *Renda*, the Chinese 'People's Congress'." One reason for keeping source-culture particularities as such is that generic or target-language "equivalents" are not always workable. For example, "conformism" has an European religious ring totally foreign to Chinese Marxism and the usual kind of "parliaments" that exist in parts of the capitalist world are very different from the "parliament" in China's "socialist democracy". *Renda* is preferable just as the Japanese *Diet* and the Israeli *Knesset* are — such culture-specific terms are more descriptive and informative, and less generic and hence less misleading. And in this way exotic formal and semantic elements of the terms can be carried over and assimilated in target-language texts, enabling target-text receptors to get closer to a source-culture situation, understand its true meaning in use, and acquire new knowledge, — always provided that some homework is done on the receptors' part or extraneous explanations such as that suggested above for *Renda* are supplied to help receptors without any homework done. It is in such small ways that translating fulfills its educative responsibility.

The same can be said about translating with "cultural equivalents" or seeking expressions with "equivalent connotation". As cultures differ, expressions depicting different cultures may not always have genuine cultural equivalents. Similarly, connotation is not always universal. There are universal connotations and national connotations, but connotations can also be regional, local or even personal. "The Berlin Wall" may mean "restriction on natural rights" or "resistance to decadence" to different people just as *Tiananmen* may be "a new awakening" or "turmoil" in different eyes. "Dragons" may not always be "majestic", the colour "white" does not always carry a sense of "sadness" in the Chinese culture, and "aircraft" may suddenly become "a curse" instead of a symbol of speedy travel to a person who has just lost loved ones in a plane crash. Differences in connotation and nuances of attitude and taste are especially sensitive matters in political items and media translators have to be on the alert when they try to select the right expression out of what appears to be a group of "alternatives". One such example is the group of "referential synonyms' for China's biggest island — "The Republic of China", "Formosa", the "State of Taiwan", "the Treasure Island", and "Taiwan province". A second example is the common practice of referring to Taiwan or Hong Kong as a "country" or a "nation" instead of just one region, territory or even dragon. Such insensitivity unavoidably changes the impression a receptor gets of a media translation or a news agency; it may even lead to the rejection of an otherwise excellent item.

Respect for media house rules, especially stylistic requirements, is generally encouraged. Special attention is also paid to achieving uniformity of proper names and technical terms as far as possible, so as to enhance communicative efficiency.

Translationism or translationese is yet another major concern. Some English-Chinese translations of media items as well as some media items themselves are clogged with instance of what is generally known as the negative variety of Europeanized syntactic structures. Localized or selective Europeanization in the Chinese language represents what is called the positive variety of Europeanized syntax and has indeed helped strengthen the logical and reasoning capabilities of the language and contributed to linguistic enrichment generally. Many such structures are very useful and will certainly be joined by more of similar nature as intercultural communication and Chinese-language sophistication deepen. Positive examples of European languages lending a helping hand to Chinese can be found in works like those by Wang Li 王力 (1989 and 1985).

However, there is no denying that many instances of Europeanized Chinese usage as seen in the everyday media of Hong Kong, Singapore, Taiwan, the Mainland China and overseas communities, also make very awkward reading. These are frequently a result of too abruptly deviating from usual morphological and syntactical patterns in translational uses of Chinese.

One way to distinguish between the good and natural from the bad and awkward among instances of Europeanized usage in media Chinese is to hone one's sensitivities and to enhance native feel-judgement or intuitive perception of truly idiomatic and refined Chinese by continually studying and mimetically renewing the lively and refined colloquial styles of contemporary mainstream Chinese as exemplified by model discourses or texts from representative authors.

Media translating being so important a means of human communication, enhancing both its operational quality and social status indeed deserves far more attention from society than it has received so far.

References

Anderson, Douglas A. and Bruce D. Itule. *Writing the News*. New York: Random House, 1988.

Chang, Chin 張勤 . 《電視新聞》 (*Television News*). Taipei: San-min Bookstore 三民書局 , 1983.

Chiang, Ching-yao 姜慶堯 . 《新聞英語編譯實務》 (*Journalistic English Translation in Practice*). Taipei: Buffalo Publishing Company 水牛出版社 , 1969.

Department of Extramural Studies, The Chinese University of Hong Kong 香港中文大學校外進修部 , ed. 《翻譯十講》 (*Translation: A Symposium*). Hong Kong: Swindon Bookstore 辰衝圖書公司 , 1969.

Ho, Wai Kit 何偉傑 .《譯學新論》 (*New Essays on Translation*). Taipei: Bookman Books 書林出版公司 , 1989.

Hodgson, F. W. *Modern Newspaper Editing and Production*. London: Heinemann, 1987.

Lan, Hongwen 籃鴻文 and Ma Xiangwu 馬向五 .《新聞語言分析》 (*An Analysis of Journalistic Language*). Beijing: Zhongguo Wuzhi, 1989.

Larson, Mildred L. *Meaning-based Translation: A Guide to Cross-language Equivalence*. Lanham, MD: University Press of America, 1984.

Lin, Xingren 林興仁 .《實用廣播語體學》 (*Practical Broadcasting Text*). Beijing: Zhongguo Guangbo Dianshi 中國廣播電視 , 1989.

Lin, Yutang 林語堂 , *et al.* 《翻譯縱橫談》 (*Essays on Translation*). Hong Kong: Swindon Bookstore 辰衝圖書公司 , 1969.

Liu, Miqing 劉宓慶 .《現代翻譯理論》 (*Modern Translation Theory*). Nanchang: Jiangxi Education Press 江西教育出版社 , 1990.

Stephens, Mitchell. *Broadcast News*. New York: Holt, Rinehart and Winston, 1986.

Wang, Chia-yu 王家棫 and Huang San-yi 黃三儀 .《淺談新聞翻譯》 (*On Journalistic Translation*). Taipei: Taipei Association of Journalists 台北新聞公會 , 1976.

Wang, Li 王力 .《中國現代語法》 (*Contemporary Chinese Grammar*). Beijing: The Commercial Press 商務印書館 , 1985.

———.《漢語語法史》 (*A History of Chinese Grammar*). Beijing: The Commercial 商務印書館 , 1989.

Whetmore, Edward Jay. *MediAmerica*. Belmont, CA: Wadsworth Publishing, 1989.

METAPHOR

Translation of Metaphor

Mary M. Y. Fung
Department of Chinese
University of Hong Kong, Hong Kong

What is Metaphor?

According to Aristotle's classic definition, "metaphor consists in giving the thing a name that belongs to something else," operating "on grounds of analogy" (*Poetics*, 1457b). While taking metaphor to be a figure of speech with the power to surprise and delight, Aristotle recognizes that its function goes well beyond mere embellishment, for the metaphor enables the hearer to "seize a new idea promptly" through "an intuitive perception of the similarity in dissimilars" (*Poetics*, 1459a). His emphasis on intuitive perception is in line with the modern cognitive approach that defines the metaphoric process as involving perception of one thing in terms of another. I.A. Richards proposed what has come to be called the "interaction" theory of metaphor, which can be summed up in the following sentence: "When we use a metaphor we have two thoughts of different things active together and supported by a single word, or phrase, whose meaning is a resultant of their interaction." (*The Philosophy of Rhetoric*, 1965)

Richards' views anticipate George Lakoff and Mark Johnson's ideas of metaphor, which we shall show in the later sections of this article to be most satisfactory in the treatment of the subject. Lakoff and Johnson argue that metaphor, instead of being deviant, is actually pervasive in everyday language, thought, and action. Our everyday metaphorical concepts, of which we are largely unaware, structure the way we perceive of reality and behave in our community. To them, "the essence of metaphor is understanding and experiencing one kind of thing in terms of another" (*Metaphors We Live By*, 1980). For instance, a wide variety of ordinary expressions like "your claims are *indefensible*", "He *attacked* every weak point in my argument", etc. point to the phenomenon that their speakers normally and unconsciously conduct an argument as though they were waging war. Although these expressions are normally considered "literal" or "conventional", they reflect an underlying metaphorical concept ARGUMENT IS WAR. However only some aspects of the concept argument are understood in terms of the concept war, namely, certain aspects are highlighted while other aspects are concealed. Following the premise that metaphorical concepts are partially structured, Lakoff and Johnson distinguish between literal and imaginative metaphor. Literal or conventional metaphors reflect the "used" part of a metaphorical concept. Imaginative metaphors are those that reflect (a) extensions of the used part of a metaphor, (b) the unused part of the literal metaphor, and (c) novel metaphor, that is, a metaphor as a new way of thinking about something. As Lakoff and Johnson's theory is experientially based, it embraces all the relevant disciplines involved in human interaction and presents the most complete scenario.

Review of Literature on Translation of Metaphor

In contrast to the voluminous literature on metaphor in the fields of literary criticism and rhetoric, the translation of metaphor has been largely neglected by translation theorists. Menachem Dagut's article entitled "Can 'metaphor' be translated?" appearing in *Babel* in 1976 was a timely call for attention, which initiated a welcome discussion of the subject. Taking metaphor to be a specific and highly distinctive category of semantic change, Dagut sets out to delimit the exact scope applicable to the term as follows: "Every 'metaphor' in the proper, narrow sense, is an individual flash of imaginative insight, ... which transcends the existing semantic limits of the language and thereby enlarges the hearers' or readers' emotional and intellectual awareness." (*ibid.*) Therefore to him, all metaphors are by definition "original" and "live" and belong to the realm of "performance". They should be differentiated from metaphorical derivatives which, having lost their uniqueness and become part of the established semantic stock of the language, have shifted to "competence". Metaphorical derivatives can be classified into "simplex" (consisting of a single lexical item), forming polysemes (e.g., a *warm* welcome), and "complex" (consisting of more than one lexical item), forming idioms (e.g., *flog a dead horse*). In their final stage of development, polysemes and idioms may form formators (e.g., *in view of*). Dagut feels that since the translation of metaphorical derivatives has to do with two systems of language competence, it is dependent on the bilingual competence of the translator to "find" target language equivalences for them, whereas the translation of metaphor will have to be "created". After analyzing a number of translations of metaphors from Hebrew into English, he concludes that

> "what determines the translatability of a source language metaphor is not its 'boldness' or 'originality', but rather the extent to which the cultural experience and semantic associations on which it draws are shared by speakers of the particular target language." (*ibid.*)

In an article published eleven years later he reiterated the same conclusion only with a slight modification, replacing "the cultural experiences and semantic associations on which it draws" by "the cultural and lexical matrices in which it is set", as he realized that the effectiveness of the metaphor hinges on the ability of the translator to reproduce its cultural and lexical resonances in the target language. (Dagut, 1987)

Raymond van den Broeck's response to Dagut in the form of a conference paper presented in 1978 but published in 1981 (hereafter referred to as van den Broeck, 1981), was the most systematic and theoretically oriented of the ensuing discussions. He uses an operational definition of metaphor as "transferred meaning" with which to examine categories, uses, and functions of metaphor. In accordance with their degree of being "institutionalized", metaphors are divided into three categories: lexicalized, conventional, and private. In explaining his disagreement with Dagut's exact distinction between metaphor and metaphorical derivatives (polysemes, idioms, and formators), he makes the important point that the status of a metaphor is not static but dynamic, so that if there is a shift from "performance" to "competence", there may be a shift in reverse from "competence" to "performance" through which lexicalized or "dead" metaphors may become "alive" again. For translation theory the use of metaphor should be considered in relation to its functional relevance to the communicative situation and further distinguished between creative metaphor and decorative metaphor. He proposes a scheme of three possible modes of metaphor translation: (1) Translation "sensu stricto", when both source language "tenor" and source language "vehicle" are transferred into target language, (2) Substitution, and (3) Paraphrase. In discussing translation problems arising from the use and function of metaphors in texts, he refutes Dagut's assumption that translation of lexicalized metaphors is "an area of translation that can be fully 'mapped' by translation theory, through a contrastive analysis based on the understanding of transferred meaning," (Dagut, 1976) as he feels that the treatment of lexicalized metaphors will entirely depend on their functional relevancy to the communicative situation. Finally, mention should be made of his formulation of a basic law of translatability of metaphor: "translatability keeps an inverse proportion with the quantity of information manifested by the metaphor and the degree to which this information is structured in a text" (*Ibid.*) with further specifications.

Moving from van den Broeck's tightly structured theoretical treatment of the translation of metaphor in its full complexity to Peter Newmark's more pragmatic approach, we have a complete change of scene. Newmark's discussion of the subject appeared as a short article in *Babel* in 1980, later expanded to form a chapter of his *Approaches to Translation* (1981), and further revised when collected in *The Ubiquity of Metaphor: Metaphor in Language and Thought* (1985). The definition of metaphor, not given in the aforesaid discussions, was formulated in his *A Textbook of Translation* (1988) as "any figurative expression: the transferred sense of a physical word; the personification of an abstraction; the application of a word or collocation to what it does not literally denote, i.e., to describe one thing in terms of another." Metaphors, which may be "single" (one word) or "extended" (a collocation, an idiom, a sentence, a proverb, an allegory, a complete imaginative text) are further divided into six types: dead, cliché, stock, adapted, recent, and original (the type "adapted" being added in 1988). Cutting across this categorization, are two others of a different kind: the conceptual metaphor in the Lakoff and Johnson sense, which Newmark recognizes to be basic and universal, and the affective metaphor, which indicates states of mind, whether individual or collective. Drawing on practical experience, he proposes eight procedures for translating metaphor in order of preference: (1) Reproducing the same image in the target language (2) Replacing the image in the source language with a standard target language image (3) Translation of metaphor by simile (4) Translation of metaphor (or simile) by simile plus sense (5) Conversion of metaphor to sense (6) Modification of metaphor (7) Deletion (8) Reproducing same metaphor combined with sense (Newmark, 1985). The above methods, envisaged as guidelines for the practising translator, about exhaust all the ways of handling the metaphor.

Opposing the views of the previous three scholars who recognize the centrality of the translation of metaphor in the theory of translation, Kirsten Mason in her 1982 article in *Babel*, pronounces it is futile to establish a theory of the translation of metaphor after demonstrating that the problems with metaphor and the problems with translation are separate and distinct. To her the translation of metaphor has to be accommodated within a theory of translation which has to allow room for the notion of the purpose of translating each new text. Not discouraged by Mason's misgivings, scholars continue to be fascinated by theoretical problems concerning the translation of metaphor. Mary Snell-Hornby's 1983 paper was conceived as a reaction to Newmark's initial formulation on the translation of metaphor. Her views on the issue have crystallized into a succinct account forming a section of a chapter of her book *Translation Studies: An Integrated Approach* (1988). Of interest is her conviction that "metaphor is text", rejecting Newmark's concept of the "one-word metaphor" in favour of an integrated approach, in particular as regards the phenomena of dimension and perspective. A "one-word metaphor" can be shown to be a complex of three dimensions consisting of object, image, and sense, using Newmark's terminology. In her 1983 paper she quotes Lakoff and Johnson's definition of metaphor, pointing out that metaphors are fundamentally conceptual in nature. In her 1988 book more emphasis is put on cultural differences: "The essential problem posed by metaphor in translation is that different cultures, hence different languages, conceptualize and create symbols in varying ways, and therefore the sense of the metaphor is frequently culture-specific (Snell-Hornby, 1988)." She does not subscribe to watertight categories of metaphors such as dead, stock, etc., but believes that the position of a metaphor shifts with cultural developments. Taking her position that metaphor is more or less translatable depending on its structure and function within the text, she reiterates her view expressed earlier: "As an abstract concept, metaphor might be universal (as claimed in Newmark 1981); in its concrete realization however, being closely linked with sensuous perception and culture-bound value judgments, it is undoubtedly complicated by language-specific idiosyncracies." (1988)

The literature on the translation of metaphor discussed so far was in the form of papers or individual chapters of published works. Alicja Pisarska produced a full-length book entitled *Creativity of Translators: The Translation of Metaphorical Expressions in Non-literary Texts* in 1989. Applying van den Broeck and Newmark's procedures to a corpus of non-literary texts, she tested the adequacy of the two schemes and came up with the finding, not quite unexpectedly, that the translatability of metaphors in the above instances is high, the creativity demanded of translators low, and the problems involved are minimal, as the metaphors examined are chiefly ornamental. Taking the point that the function of a metaphor is directly related to the kind of text in which it appears, she proposes a four way division of metaphors between conceptual and ornamental on the one hand and new and used on the other. Her conceptual metaphors are not used in the Lakoff and Johnson sense as metaphorical concepts which structure our experience but rather in Dagut's sense of true metaphors. Their characteristic appearance in literary texts in which they combine aesthetic, artistic, symbolic, and cognitive values determines the intellectual power and artistry of the work. In the conclusion of her monograph she calls attention to the need for an interdisciplinary approach to the study of metaphor. In this connection she suggests that Lakoff and Johnson's cognitive approach, which has not yet been explored by translation theorists, may open new vistas.

Although the above theorists present conflicting views on the various issues involved (e.g., definition, classification, function, modes of translation, and translatability, some of which will be taken up later), all of them, with the exception of Mason, agree that the translation of metaphor is central to the theory of translation and should be re-evaluated. Moreover there is a tendency in recent studies to favour a cognitive and interdisciplinary approach to the translation of metaphor.

Taking up the Issue from EC/CE Perspective

The translation of EC/CE metaphors, though it has its own peculiar set of linguistic and cultural specific problems, nevertheless falls within the purview of the translation of metaphor in general. Discussions on the subject, especially those written in Chinese, are mostly pragmatic rather than theoretical. Adopting the traditional view of treating metaphor as a rhetorical device, the body of writings concentrate on the translation of idioms, proverbs, and allusions.

We shall use as a working definition Lakoff and Johnson's statement concerning the essence of metaphor quoted in the first section of this article. The translating of metaphor will be considered, translating being taken as a communicative event which is both interlingual and intercultural. Owing to the many provinces of human knowledge and experience it traverses in such human communication, and the various systems, be it socio-cultural, linguistic, or literary, it interacts with, translating must be seen as interdisciplinary and intersystemic. As far as possible, the operation of metaphor will be discussed in context, and subordinated to the constraints bearing on all kinds of writing, namely, collocational, syntactic, and stylistic.

From the discussion summarized in the foregoing section, it seems that theorists cannot agree on the classification of metaphor except for the general notions of the "used" (variously called "dead", "conventional", "stock", "lexicalized", etc.) and the "original" (which Dagut recognizes as metaphor proper and is referred to as "poetic", "private", etc. by others). Lakoff and Johnson's "conventional metaphors" and "imaginative metaphors" would correspond to these two categories, the first of which would be considered "dead" by many scholars. But as I.A. Richards warns, the old distinction between dead and living metaphors needs a drastic re-examination (*The Philosophy of Rhetoric*, 1965). On the whole we tend to see the living and dead metaphors not as polarizations but as forming a cline.

The following quotation from the well-known Qing novel *Honglou meng* 《紅樓夢》 can well illustrate the point:

黛玉聽了這話，如轟雷掣電，細細思之，竟比自己肺腑中掏出來的還覺懇切。

The second part of the sentence reminds one of the idiom 肺腑之言, 肺腑 meaning the lungs and other internal organs of the human body. In Lakoff and Johnson's sense, this is an ontological metaphor: words seen as objects that can be taken out from the inside of the human body. With repeated use throughout the ages the underlying metaphorical concept has worn off so that under most circumstances native speakers coming across the expression would take it to mean words of great sincerity. They would not call to mind human entrails just as the English speaker would not visualize the lower part of the heart on hearing "(words) from the bottom of one's heart", the English counterpart of the idiom. The Chinese text quoted above has revived the image by focusing on the action of 掏出, drawing out (the words).

Compare David Hawkes' translation:

Dai-yu was thunderstruck. He had read her mind — had seen inside her more clearly than *if she had plucked out her entrails and held them out for his inspection.* (Penguin Books, 1977, Chapter 32)

Omitting the very important 這話 (these words), the translator presents a horrible picture of a young lady plucking out her entrails. It has to be remembered that different literary conventions give rise to different effects in the use of the same metaphor. 肺腑 is not an unusual term in ordinary and literary usage in Chinese, as evidenced by numerous idioms containing images of internal organs like 感人肺腑, 五臟六腑, 肝腸寸斷, 愁腸百結, 披肝瀝膽, 推心置腹. In colloquial usage one often says 肺都氣炸了, meaning to explode with rage. All these expressions are habitual ways of conveying intense and deeply seated emotion. However in English writing one's entrails are hardly mentioned except in the anatomical sense. One could envisage therefore that the response aroused by turning the partially resurrected metaphor in the original into a very alive one in the translation would be nothing short of shocking.

The above example is taken from a paper by the author written in collaboration with K. L. Kiu (published in *Babel* in 1987), in which eleven samples each of English and Chinese metaphors in excerpts selected from Shakespeare's *Hamlet* and *Hongloumeng* respectively together with their translations were analyzed. Our aim was to investigate the problems involved when the metaphors cross the frontiers between English and Chinese, languages which neither belong to the same family nor share a common culture. Our comparison of the two sets of data showed that in the case of the English metaphors the image is more often than not retained, whereas with the Chinese metaphors, substitution is frequently used (the above example being an exception). One reason perhaps is that the Chinese audience are more familiar with and receptive to Western culture than the average English reader is to Chinese culture. This observation finds support in the vigorous introduction of Western thought and literature into China since the latter half of the 19th century and the influx of missionaries bringing Christianity into the lives of the common people. There is no counterpart, however, of such an inter-cultural movement in the reverse direction into England. An extralinguistic factor such as the pattern of cultural contact plays a part in influencing the choice of the translator in his handling of the metaphor.

In this and in a later paper by the author presented to a 1991 conference on translation which adopts Lakoff and Johnson's scheme of metaphor as framework for analysis, attempts were made to explore further the intricacies of the problem first formulated by Dagut. To say that the translatability of metaphor depends on the "overlap" of cultural experience and semantic associations in source language and target language, though correct in a general sense, does not seem to do justice to the complex issue. Dagut is apparently dissatisfied with his former statement. In puzzling out "what it is that makes one metaphor effective and vivifying and another jejune, ridiculous, or even incomprehensible," the issue which he thinks, "lies at the heart of the question both of the genesis of metaphor and of its translatability" (Dagut, 1987), he tries to focus on the cultural and lexical matrices in which the metaphor is set and on the reproduction of resonances in the target language.

In our investigations we have found that when the basic metaphorical concepts of source language and target language communities correspond, as in the cases of SLANDER IS WAR and LOVE IS WAR (Fung and Kiu, 92), and THE RELATIONSHIP BETWEEN MEN AND WOMEN IS WAR (*ibid.*), the translation process is normally most efficient. Likewise the translation of Sylvia Plath's metaphors of love into Chinese is greatly facilitated by the existence of similar basic metaphorical concepts in the two cultures such as LOVE IS UNITY and LOVE IS FIRE, which in turn, are grounded in our bodily experience. On this common basis, extensions of the underlying model or novel ways of conceptualization would not be difficult to comprehend, assuming that human beings share a general conceptualizing capacity.

In this connection, we shall discuss the translation of the ring metaphor in Plath's poem "Event":

When apple bloom ices the night
I walk in a ring,
A groove of old faults, deep and bitter.

—— ll. 13–15

The ring metaphor can be seen as a unity metaphor in which the wholeness rather than the integrated parts are highlighted. The lines are built up of a cluster of metaphors: MARRIAGE IS A RING and MARRIAGE IS JOURNEY, the latter of which subsumes ERRORS FORM A GROOVE. The ring as a token of marriage (suggested by its contextual association with apple blossom, symbol of love and weddings) by virtue of its perfect round shape signifies unity, wholeness, and eternity. This is seen against "ring" as a circular path (more specifically "groove") of endless "faults" in the word's double sense of "failings or errors" and "fractures" in the earth's crust. The dissolution of the marriage vow of eternal love has turned the wedding ring into a path of endless repetition of offences and mistakes, in its turn serving to alienate the partners ever more, thus breaking the continuity and unity of marriage. The main obstacle in the translation lies in the absence of polysemy matching the two meanings required in the Chinese equivalents for "ring" and "faults", so that the two trains of thought activated in the metaphorical complex cannot be activated by using one and the same word. The *double entendre* of the former is especially crucial to the existence of the metaphorical complex. Zhang Fenling's 張芬齡 translation, published in *Zhong wai wenxue* 《中外文學》, Vol. 7, No. 10 (March 1979) reads as follows:

在那蘋果花凍結夜晚的地方
我繞圈而行，
古老的過失固定反應著，
深刻且痛苦。

The appearance of 蘋果花 would not bring with it any association of marriage in the Chinese culture, neither would 繞圈 remind one of the wedding ring; the translated lines, syntactically correct, would simply be taken as a literal statement by the reader. Compare this with the version by Zheng Min 鄭敏 (*One Hundred Modern English Poems*, 1992):

在蘋果花冷凍了黑夜的地方，
我踏著戒指的圓圈散步，
一個舊過、深恨磨成的故轍。

Recognizing the significance of the metaphors, Zheng painstakingly retains them by building the two meanings of "ring" into the lines, forgoing the less important geological implication of "faults". By making explicit what is implicit in the original, she sets the whole scenario for the activation of two trains of thought. The similar use of "ring" as a token of marriage in Chinese makes it possible for Zheng to retain the metaphorical dimension in the above example.

At times associations of an image in one culture may be lacking in another one. For instance the "palm" in Western culture is a symbol of glory, victory, and superiority, closely associated with Christianity. The

Shakespearean coinage of "the *palmy* state of Rome" (*Hamlet* 1.1.116) with its rich associations finds no equivalent in the Chinese tropical plant 棕櫚 so that the image of palm cannot be retained in the translation (Fung and Kiu: 1987). More problematic than the lacking of cultural associations is the attribution of conflicting values to an object by the two cultures concerned, as is the classical example of the mythical dragon, an auspicious symbol embodying excellence and good luck in the Chinese folk theory, whereas in English culture it is a fire-breathing monster, representing overwhelming evil power.

Cultural-specific metaphors make themselves felt when allusions are made to the source language's historical, literary, or folk heritage, in the use of myth (taken in a general sense to include fable and legend). According to Colin Turbayne, the myth is an extended or sustained metaphor, consisting of a story that we make believe to be true (*The Myth of Metaphor*, 1962). To put it in Lakoff and Johnson's terms, one may say that when two domains of thoughts are involved, the source domain is taken up by the make-believe world of the myth. The implications of the story generally accepted by members of the culture in which the myth has grown up in part constitute the implicative complex by which the myth will be interpreted. It follows therefore that it may not be understood by speakers of a different culture without the support of the relevant system of implications.

To illustrate this point we shall look at the last two stanzas of Sylvia Plath's "Purdah":

I shall unloose —
From the small jeweled
Doll he guards like a heart —

The lioness,
The shriek in the bath,
The cloak of holes.

A Greek myth is hidden in the last two lines: when her husband Agamemnon, King of Mycenae, returned from the Trojan war with his concubine Cassandra, Clytemnestra killed him in the bath. The speaker in the poem is a woman cast into the role of a jeweled plaything, a treasured possession of her husband, severely restricted in her physical movement and mental development. Yet she has a majestic power in her, whose release will bring about the destruction of her tyrannical master, resulting in her total liberation and transformation. As the myth is alluded to and not fully narrated in the poem, Zheng Min's almost word for word translation of the last stanza can only present a fragmentary picture:

一隻母獅，
那浴室中的尖叫，
那百孔千瘡的斗篷。

(One Hundred Modern English Poems)

Even though the translator summarizes the Clytemnestra story in a note, the implication of the myth to the Chinese reader may well be different from that of his Western counterpart. Rather than being symbolic of female strength, the lioness, especially when it is associated with the image of a wife, may call to mind the idiomatic phrase 河東獅吼 , alluding to the story of the wife notorious for being fierce and jealous. Such qualities, to say the least, are quite contrary to the traditional virtues expected of a Chinese woman, let alone the immoral act of murdering one's husband. The metaphor, instead of signifying the liberation of energy through justifiable revenge necessary for the woman's spiritual resurrection, may to a conservative-minded Chinese indicate moral depravity foreboding damnation.

One must admit that in addition to socio-cultural and linguistic considerations, the translator in dealing with the Plath poems is also influenced by the requirements of the literary text as poetry. In the above two quoted passages, the translations attempt to come as close as possible to the original in form and content, without undue conformity to the target language literary system. This can be accounted for by the fact that modern Chinese poetry since the May Fourth Movement has been greatly influenced by and is still very much receptive to Western poetic models so that innovations coming through translations would not be regarded as deviations from the norm and adversely received.

Though one cannot deny that the receptor's response is a significant criterion in evaluating the effectiveness of a metaphor, it is difficult to anticipate and largely beyond the translator's control. Theorists disagree on the feasibility of literal transferring of images of novel metaphors, on the basis of their own varying estimations of the receptor's response. If we believe that the process of communication and understanding is itself an imaginative experience, it is not impossible to translate metaphors embodying conflicting cultural values as those quoted in our last example, or for that matter, for the translation to be fully understood, as long as the target language readers are willing to readjust their cultural values and to restructure reality accordingly.

We have discussed some of the problems involved and attempted to identify a number of factors concerning the translation of metaphor between English and Chinese with reference to literary texts. We believe that as there are special problems involved in the translating of metaphor, the formulation of a theory of the translation of metaphor is justifiable, just as a theory of the translation of poetry is justifiable, within a general theory of translation. We subscribe to van den Broeck's view that such a task could be approached on a theoretical constituent level, when one aims at identifying factors, uncovering hidden mechanics and regularities before a complete theory is arrived at. The translation of metaphor from a full range of texts in a wide variety of languages will have to be studied before the individual patterns will be seen to constitute a whole structure. The future direction of research on the translation of metaphor as we see it would be interdisciplinary and intersystemic, and in this connection the framework of metaphor proposed by Lakoff and Johnson may be one that could be profitably explored.

References

Dagut, M. B. "Can 'Metaphor' Be Translated?" *Babel*, Vol. 22, No. 1 (1976), pp. 21–33.

———. "More about the Translatability of Metaphor." *Babel*, Vol. 33, No. 2 (1987), pp. 77–83.

Fung, Mary M. Y. "Riddle in Nine Syllables: Translating Sylvia Plath." Paper presented at "Asia-Pacific Conference on Translation and Interpreting: Bridging East and West", 28–30 October 1991, to be published in the Conference Proceedings.

———, ed. *One Hundred Modern English Poems*. Hong Kong: The Commercial Press, 1992.

——— and K. L. Kiu. "Metaphor Across Language and Culture." *Babel*, Vol. 33, No. 2 (1987), pp. 84–106.

Lakoff, George and Mark Johnson. *Metaphors We Live By*. Chicago and London: The University of Chicago Press, 1980.

——— and Mark Turner. *More Than Cool Reason: A Field Guide to Poetic Metaphor*. Chicago: University of Chicago Press, 1989.

Mason, Kristen. "Metaphor and Translation." *Babel*, Vol. 28, No. 3 (1982), pp. 140–49.

Newmark, Peter. *A Textbook of Translation*. London: Prentice Hall, 1988.

———. "The Translation of Metaphor." In *The Ubiquity of Metaphor: Metaphor in Language and Thought*, edited by Wolf Paprotte and René Dirven. Amsterdam/ Philadelphia: John Benjamins, 1985, pp. 295–326.

Pisarska, Alicja. *Creativity of Translators: The Translation of Metaphorical Expressions in Non-literary Texts*. Poznan: Uniwersytet im. Adama Mickiewicza w Poznaniu, Seria Filolgia Angielska Nr 23, 1989.

Snell-Hornby, Mary. *Metaphorical Thought and Translation: Taking a Stand on P. Newmark*. Series A, Paper No. 108, Trier: L.A.U.T, 1983.

———. *Translation Studies: An Integrated Approach*. Amsterdam: John Benjamins, 1988.

van den Broeck, Raymond. "The Limits of Translatability as Exemplified by Metaphor Translation." *Poetics Today*, Vol. 2, No. 4 (1981), pp. 73–87.

MUSIC

Chinese Music

John L. Witzleben
Department of Music
The Chinese University of Hong Kong, Hong Kong

Before discussing the practical problems of translating Chinese musical terminology into English, we need to realize that there is an underlying problem of the "meaning" of these words. That is to say, the implications of a particular term may vary widely according to context, region, genre, or historical period, and even within a specific context. Chinese scholars often differ in their interpretations. The subject is a vast one, and in this article, I will concentrate on only three areas of concern: in ascending order of difficulty, these are musical instruments, titles of musical compositions, and theoretical terms. In the space allotted, it is impossible to cite references or alternate translations for all of these examples. Most of the ideas presented here have developed from problems encountered in the translations found on recordings and in concert program notes, in translations of fiction, and in my own writing in English on Chinese instrumental music.

Musical Instruments

Gradually, the names of the important Chinese instruments are seeping into Western usage, but even for Western ethnomusicologists, the Chinese names are less widely known than those of Japan, India, or Indonesia. As a rule, I favor using the Romanized Chinese names, accompanied by a brief explanation at first occurrence. But what kind of an explanation? For the ethnomusicologist, one should speak of a zither or lute which may be fretted or unfretted, and is plucked, bowed, or struck. The general reader may prefer to hear of fiddles, guitars, banjos, or oboes. Should the translation focus on the instrument's appearance, its sounds, or its cultural function? For modern-day musicologists, the *qin* 琴 is indisputably a zither, but it has been immortalized by R.H. van Gulik as the "Chinese lute." His choice was by no means a casual one:

> In my opinion, however, the shape of an Oriental musical instrument should not constitute the first consideration when selecting an English equivalent; the spirit of the music produced by an instrument and the place it occupies in the culture of its native country are as important factors as its shape and structure ... Since the word "lute" is associated by Westerners with poetry and refined enjoyment, it adequately suggests the atmosphere that surrounds the *ch'in* [qin], while "psaltery" [the term musicologist Curt Sachs suggested to Van Gulik], on the other hand, suggests an instrument doomed to obsolescence since many centuries; moreover many readers would have been unfamiliar with this term. For these reasons I still prefer to render *ch'in* as "lute", giving the inner meaning precedence over the physical form. (Van Gulik, 1969)

The word "lute" is arguably far more evocative than either "zither" or "psaltery," yet in the end the 琴 really has no Western equivalent.

The controversy over the 琴 is perhaps the most famous, but it is by no means the only problem case. The *suona* 嗩吶 (colloquially known as *laba*) is technically a type of oboe (double-reed aerophone), but looks and sounds more like a trumpet to the casual observer. "Shawm" is more accurate, but will send many readers to consult an English dictionary. The 嗩吶 is commonly discussed in fiction and travellers' accounts, where I have seen translations as varied as flute, pipe, clarionet, and flagelot. The sound of the *sanxian* 三絃 approximates that of a banjo, but it has neither frets nor a round body, and the social connotations are misleading: the 三絃 is primarily a "folk" instrument, but it is associated more with the urban storyteller than with rural traditions. The question of social status is a complex one, but should not be passed over lightly. The *erhu* 二胡 and its many relatives are widely referred to as "fiddles," and while an ethnomusicologist would prefer "two-stringed bowed lute," fiddle is a common word in world music. However, calling a Western violinist a "fiddler" is normally considered to be derogatory, implying a lack of formal training or technique. The tendency to use "high art" translations for vocal music and "folk art" translations for instruments has resulted in the incongruous juxtaposition of "opera arias" accompanied by "fiddlers" and "drummers."

Titles of Pieces

Most Chinese instrumental pieces have programmatic titles, so perhaps this area is less technically musical and closer to the translation of the titles of poems or paintings — which is not to say that it is straightforward. A good translation of a title will maintain the literal sense of the original without sacrificing eloquence. One basic difficulty is caused by the fact that many titles consist of a series of nouns which are not linked by verbs or prepositions. The connections between these words are left to the imagination of the reader, or perhaps not implied at all. 〈春江花月夜〉 might best be rendered as "Spring, River, Flower, Moon, and Evening," although constructions such as "Spring River in the Flowery Moonlight" are more commonly encountered. Sometimes, however, literal translation of the words may make excessive demands on the English reader: rendering 〈蕉石鳴琴〉 as "Plantains, Rock, Sound, Seven-string Zither" sounds nonsensical. "Playing the Qin on a Rock in A Banana Grove," although cumbersome, is quite intelligible, but not definitive. But perhaps one should be listening rather than playing, and "Sound of the Qin" is more accurate? 〈蕉窗夜雨〉 may be rendered as "Evening Rain on the Banana Leaves by the Window"; although the title makes no mention of the leaves or the sound of the rain, this is the natural connection among the title's images.

Another layer of difficulty arises when we examine the many programmatic titles which contain implied references to historical events, legends, or traditional Chinese customs. In these cases, should the translator present the literal meaning or attempt to communicate how these words would be understood by an educated Chinese reader? For example, 〈十面埋伏〉 can be translated as "Ambush from All Directions," more literally from "Ten Sides"; 〈霸王卸甲〉 is "The Hegemon King Sheds His Armour," probably best omitting the word "Hegemon." But both of these pieces are universally understood to refer to various events in the battle between Liu Bang 劉邦 and Xiang Yu 項羽 leading to the founding of the Han dynasty. The programmatic subtitles are even more explicitly historical and thus more obscure when translated. The princess Wang Zhaojun 王昭君, who was married to the chief of a hostile state to the West in order to save the Chinese kingdom, is another historical figure referred to in instrumental pieces: in

〈昭君怨〉, or "Zhaojun's Resentment," the reference is clear. 〈塞上曲〉, or "Song of the Frontier," however, reads like a military piece, but subtitles like "〈昭君出塞〉," or "Zhaojun Crosses the Frontier," indicate that it is anything but. The legendary cowherd and weaving girl are clearly the subject of 〈銀河會〉, or "Meeting at the Silver River (Milky Way)." This slightly cumbersome title seems to communicate both the poetic image and the celestial body it stands for. The same couple are the implied subject of 〈雙聲恨〉, also called 〈雙星恨〉, but a satisfactory translation for these titles eludes me, although I have in the past opted for "A Pair of Sorrowful Sounds" or "… Stars," as the case may be. For all of these examples, the problem here is less one of translation than of annotation; that is, no brief translation can hope to convey the symbolism contained in these titles, which is not merely implied but universally accepted.

〈行街〉 is a well-known piece from the *Jiangnan sizhu* 江南絲竹 tradition of the Shanghai area. "Walking in the Streets" is mundane, and most musicians agree that the title indicates the piece's original function of accompanying a bride's sedan chair through the streets. "Wedding Procession" is a common translation; I prefer "Street Procession" which is closer to the actual meaning of the title. Even when a literal translation makes sense, much of its deeper meaning will be lost without an understanding of its cultural background. 〈繡荷包〉 is indeed an "Embroidered Purse," but unless the role of this item in traditional rural courtship is explained, even a song with text makes little sense.

Technical Terms

Under this heading, I am including both theoretical terms and musical genres, and they collectively comprise the most problematical area of translation related to Chinese music. As an experiment, in 1988 I sent a list of twenty-nine musical terms to the members of the Association for Chinese Music Research, a U.S.-based society. The thirteen respondents were mainly faculty or graduate students specializing in Chinese music, some native speakers, all fluent in Chinese and English. The purpose of the survey was to see if there was a consensus among specialists in the field. While I expected some variance in the responses, I was surprised at the near total lack of consensus on some terms. For example, here were some of the translations for two important terms:

qupai 曲牌 : tune, tune-type, aria type (for music), prosodic pattern (for texts), name of the tunes, pre-existing tune with recognized title, tune title, type of melody specific to a genre (especially drama), descriptive music tune, song book.

minzu yinyue 民族音樂 : any ethnic music, Chinese orchestral music (PRC), national music, Chinese traditional music, Chinese music, folk music, minority music, native (Korean, Chinese, etc.) music (Witzleben, 1988:11–12).

Some of these responses are explanations rather than translations, and many scholars expressed their preference for defining Chinese terms and then using romanization rather than a translation. I have used "labelled tune" for 曲牌 , in the sense that it is a relatively fixed short melody which can be set to a variety of texts or used as the basis for instrumental compositions. 民族音樂 is commonly used as a catch-all term for "Chinese music" (as opposed to Western music), but it does more literally refer to the "music of a people"; without futher qualification, this "people" is understood to be Chinese, but references to the 民族音樂 of Japan or the United States are readily understood; thus, the generally accepted term 民族音樂 for ethnomusicology, in the sense of the study of ethnic or indigenous musical traditions, is quite reasonable.

The widely varying responses to this translation survey suggest that it would be futile to strive for standardization in the translation of Chinese musical terms, for their meaning often changes considerably according to context. For example, a simple word such as 板 may have very different meanings in different contexts. It can mean "beat" or metrical unit in titles such as 老六板 . It can mean tempo in expressions such as 快板 , but this refers more specifically to the frequency of the strokes of a clapper, and thus also includes implications of meter (a regular pattern of strong and weak beats). The word also often refers to the clapper itself. 散板 is not really "scattered," and the precision of performance of 散板 passages is far more codified than "free rhythm" indicates. "Rubato" is closer in spirit, but implies a stylistically evocative deviation from an established pulse or tempo, whereas 散板 often opens a piece (as in *qin* music).

Rulan Chao Pian has attempted to penetrate this theoretical density by relating some of these terms to their dramatic function in Peking Opera: "animated aria" 流水板 , "narrative aria" 原板 , "lyric aria" 慢板 , "declamatory aria" 散板 , and "dramatic aria" 搖板 (1970:21). These terms work well for the operatic tradition, and are certainly more evocative than literal translations. However, some of these terms also are common in instrumental music, in which their exact meaning is debatable, but in which dramatic functions are not really applicable. Among the questions still to be answered is whether, in fact, there is an underlying continuity of musical meaning in the use of 慢板 for a section of Chaozhou music and a Peking opera aria.

Conclusion

To return to my opening premise, the names we choose for translating musical terminology must be preceded by a clear understanding of the meaning of the Chinese terms in the specific context in which they are used, and of the musical significance and extra-musical symobolism they communicate to an educated Chinese reader. Chinese music is a complex art, and the cultural translation of meaning is more difficult than the translation of words alone. The challenge for Chinese music specialists is to communicate the sense of both the words and meanings, not only to Chinese music specialists, but to a broader audience of both Sinologists and music lovers.

References

Pian, Rulan Chao. "Rewriting of an Act of the Yuan Drama, Lii Kwei Fuh Jing, in the Style of the Peking Opera: A Fieldworker's Experiment." *Chinoperl News*, No. 2 (1970), pp. 19–39.

van Gulik, Robert Hans. *The Lore of the Chinese Lute*. Rutland, Vermont: Sophia University and Tokyo: Charles E. Tuttle Company, 1940, 1968.

Witzleben, John L. "Chinese Music Translation Survey." *Association for Chinese Music Research Newletter*, Vol. 2, No. 1 (1988), pp. 10–12.

Western Music

Liu Ching-chih
Centre of Asian Studies
University of Hong Kong, Hong Kong

Introduction

Translation of musical terms and phrases not only requires expertise in music, but also involves knowledge of European history, philosophy and aesthetics as well as the theory and technique of translation. Since the beginning of the 20th century, writings on history of music, compositional techniques (harmony, counterpoint, orchestration and musical form) and aesthetics of music had been translated from Japanese, German, French and English into Chinese, by translators including Wang Guangqi 王光祈 , Feng Zikai 豐子愷 , Zhu Sudian 朱蘇典 , Xiao Youmei 蕭友梅 , Li Qingzhu 黎青主 , Miao Tianrui 繆天瑞 , Fu Lei 傅雷 , Zhang Hongdao 張洪島 , Chen Hong 陳洪 , Gu Lianli 顧連理 , Feng Chenbao 豐陳寶 , Zhu Shimin 朱世民 , Qu Xixian 瞿希賢 , Qian Renkang 錢仁康 , Wang Qizhang 汪啓璋 , Wu Peihua 吳佩華 and others. The majority of them were music educationalists by profession, while others were musicologists and historians. There are few full-time music translators at present in China.

Most of the translations were for teaching purposes, especially in the first half of the 20th century during which there were practically no music text books on the development of European music, compositional techniques and aesthetics. In view of this, teachers at conservatories of music and university music faculties had no choice but to compile their own "text books" by rendering articles and books in foreign languages into Chinese or writing their own lecture notes. However, great difficulties were encountered in the work because (1) names of musicians and musical terms and phrases are in Italian, Latin, German, French, Dutch, Spanish, Greek, English, Bohemian, Russian, etc; (2) translators from various parts of China favoured their provincial pronunciation and therefore it was difficult to arrive at uniform transliterations; (3) different foreign languages represented different cultures and different conceptual approaches might be required for the same terms; and (4) the same terms in different periods of historical development might also have different connotations. Translation of terms, phrases and names of composers was therefore more complicated and difficult than people had expected. Despite almost 90 years of experience since the beginning of the 20th century, there are still erroneous, misleading and inconsistent translations.

In the early 1950s, the Central Conservatory of Music compiled 《音樂統一譯名表》; in the 1970s, the Central Conservatory of Music compiled 《俄漢音樂用語匯編》; in the 1980s, the Shenyang Conservatory of Music compiled 《音樂譯名匯編》; in 1988, the Shanghai Conservatory of Music compiled 《外國音樂辭典》; and in April 1989, 《中國大百科全書・音樂・舞蹈》 was published, which is, up to the present moment the most comprehensive dictionary of music and dance published on Mainland China. The translation of musical terms and phrases has been discussed in recent years in Hong Kong and China and a special seminar on music translation was held in Bejing in December 1989. On the other hand, concerted efforts to improve the standards of music translation have been absent in Taiwan since 1962 when the Taiwan National Translation and Compilation Bureau published a pamphlet entitled 《音樂名詞》 in which there are 2,847 terms and names of musicians translated from foreign languages into Chinese. There has not been any revised edition of this pamphlet since then — a lapse of 30 years.

According to incomplete statistics, in the first half of the 20th century (up to 1949), there were 60 translated works on music, of which 33% were on musical education (including rudiments of music), 20% on compositional techniques, and 20% on musicians' biographies, and there were very few on musical history and musicology. From these data, it is obvious that the translations of works on music were not well-balanced. For example, of the seven translated biographies, six were on Beethoven; and there were three translated versions of Romain Rolland's *Vie de Beethoven, viz* 《悲多汶傳》 translated by Yang Hui 楊晦, published by Beixin Bookstore 北新書局 in July 1927; *Beethoven* 《悲多汶》 translated by Chen Zhanyuan 陳占元, published by Mingri Press 明日社 in January 1944, and *A Biography of Beethoven* 《貝多芬傳》 translated by Fu Lei 傅雷, published by Camel Press 駱駝書店 in April 1946.

During the 1950s, there were 300 translated works, excluding reprints. These were 10 fruitful years and the number was six times more than that of the preceding 50 years. Compositional techniques were the most popular subjects, followed by European instrumentation and performing, music education, music appreciation, biographies, music and musicians in general, ethnomusicology, analysis of compositions, rudiments of music, theory of vocal music, musical history, musicology and conducting. During the decade, the existing conservatories of music were expanded and new ones established, and as a result, publications including translations on compositional techniques, instrumental techniques and biographies of musicians were in great demand. Among the 28 translated biographies of composers, the life and works of Bach, Chopin, Handel, Mozart, Schumann, Tchaikovsky, Borodin and Shostakovich were for the first time introduced to Chinese readers. The influence of the Soviet Union was strongly felt and of 29 translated works on music education, 28 were translated from Russian.

During the 1960s, due to the stringent economic and unstable political situation, music translation suffered. In the first six years, there were only 54 translated works published. Translated works on musical aesthetics appeared for the first time during the 1950s and 1960s, such as 《音樂美學問題》 which was translated by Wu Junxie 吳鈞燮 and published by Beijing Art Publishers in 1954, 《音樂美學問題概論》, translated by Wu Qiyuan 吳啓元 and Yu Chengzhong 虞承中 and published by Beijing Music Publishers in January 1959, and 《音樂美學問題》, translated by Liao Shangguo 廖尙果 and others and published by Beijing Music Publishers in November 1962.

During the 10 years of the Cultural Revolution (1967–1976), not a single translated work on music was published. From 1978 to 1979, 27 translated works appeared; however, most of these were mimeographed. From 1979 to 1988, 216 translated works were published. Although European instrumentation and performing still topped the list, more interest was shown in translating works on the history of music, musicology, and other aspects of musical studies, including non-European musical history and ethnomusicology such as Japanese, Arabic and American Negro musical history, oriental music culture in the 19th century, music language, psychology of music and music sociology.

It is rather difficult to gather statistics on music translations in Taiwan. From the translated works published since the 1960s, a variety of subjects has been translated, such as 《音樂的結構與風格》 (translated by Pan Huanglong 潘皇龍), 《音樂美學》 (translated by Guo Changyang 郭長揚), 《從巴洛克到古典樂派》 and 《浪漫樂派》 (translated by Chen Linlin

陳琳琳), 《歌劇、歌曲、華爾滋》 (translated by Chen Linlin), 《音樂七講》 (translated by Xu Changhui 許常惠), 《音樂欣賞》 (translated by Lin Shengxi 林聲翕), etc. The translation of terms, phrases, and names of composers is mainly based on *Musical Terms* 《音樂名詞》. In Hong Kong, music translation is almost non-existent, except in essays on music, programme notes of recitals, concerts, operas, and music critiques, where the use of translated terms, phrases, and names of composers is inevitable, and the translations are inconsistent. There is therefore an urgent need for a glossary to standardize musical terms, phrases and names of musicians, so that writers and broadcasters may apply them consistently.

According to the statistics quoted above, there were about 630 titles of foreign works on music, musical instruments and musicians translated into Chinese from the 1920s to 1988. However, apart from 《外國音樂辭典》 compiled by the Shanghai Conservatory of Music and 《中國大百科全書・音樂・舞蹈》, there do not seem to be any comprehensive publications devoted to musical terms and expressions, as well as names of composers, which can serve as a reference similar to *The New Oxford Companion to Music* and the like. It will be useful to discuss the appropriateness of some of the Chinese translations of musical terms and phrases in the past 60 odd years and to find the closest Chinese equivalents of the relevant terms and phrases.

In the following sections, I will confine the discussion to five aspects: (1) terms which indicate both speed and style of a piece of music, including the names of dances, adagio and allegro; (2) ornaments; (3) terms of compositional techniques, major and minor, and modes and tonality; (4) musical forms; and (5) musical history. The examples used are mainly from the translations of Wang Guangqi and Feng Zikai who represented the 1920s and 1930s, and Fu Lei who represented the 1940s, as their translations, especially Fu Lei's, have strongly influenced the translations of the younger generations of translators. However, the majority of the problems encountered in translating musical terms and phrases have yet to be considered carefully. It will be too ambitious for this article to solve all the difficulties. The purpose of this article is to identify the essential problems and to suggest solutions to them.

Terms and Phrases

This section focuses on the discussion of translating musical terms and phrases which indicate (1) both the speed (tempo) and style of a piece of music; (2) ornaments; and (3) compositional techniques.

Tempi and Styles

Musical tempo, style and expression indicate the speed, the intensity and generally the way of performance rather than the notes and their strict time values.

In November 1930, the well-known musicologist Wang Guangqi completed his 《西洋音樂史綱要》 (*A Concise History of Western Music*) in the National Library in Berlin, which is probably the first book on this topic written in Chinese. In the book, when he discussed the dances of a suite, he translated "tonality" as 宮調, "allegro" as 快板, "grave" as 慢板, and "Pavane", "Galliarde", "Allemande", "Courante", "Sarabande", and "Gigue" as 舞樂:

> 舒怡塔 Suite (Partita) 爲第十七世紀初葉，德國方面所流行之 「樂隊音樂」。其組織，係將「舞樂」若干篇，聯合起來，成爲一部作品，並將各篇「宮調」劃一，以爲維繫全部作品統一之道。最初，內部組織，共有下列四篇 (1) Pavane（意大利舞樂，慢板，4/4 拍子，性質嚴肅）。(2) Galliarde（舞樂名，爲上述 (1) 篇之尾聲，快板，3/4 拍子，性質活潑）。(3) Allemande（德國舞樂，慢板，4/4 拍子，性質 嚴肅）。(4) Courante （法國舞樂，快板，3/4 拍子，性質活潑）。但到了十七世紀中葉之時，其組織略有變更，成爲下列四篇： (1) Allemande。 (2) Courante。 (3) Sarabande （西班牙舞樂，慢板，3/4 拍子，性質嚴肅）。 (4) Gigue（英國舞樂 [Jig]，快板，6/4 拍子，性質活潑）。 (Volume I, p. 76.)

Wang transliterated "suite" as 舒怡泰 and mixed up tempo with the titles of the dances which are frequently used to indicate both the tempo and the style of a piece. In the following paragraphs, I will compare the connotations of the dances with Wang's translations.

> Allemande, of German origin, in four-four time. The mood is rather serious, and a characteristic feature of the piece is a continuous flow of semiquavers occurring throughout. The piece usually commences with a short unaccented note before the first bar.
> (Wang's translation: 德國舞樂, 慢板, 4/4 拍子, 性質嚴肅)

> Courante. There are two distinct types of the Courante, the French and the Italian. The former is a quick piece in an alternating tempo of three-two and

six-four, the Italian being again lively, but in three-four or three-eight time, and consisting of running quaver passages throughout.
(Wang's translation: 法國舞樂 , 快板 , 3/4 拍子 , 性質活潑)

Sarabande is of Spanish or Moorish origin, and forms the slow movement of the Suite. It is in three-two or three-four time, and a characteristic feature is the slightly accented second beat. The mood is serious, and stately, in direct contrast to the preceding pieces on account of its harmonic rather than contrapuntal style.
(Wang's translation: 西班牙 , 慢板 , 3/4 拍子 , 性質嚴肅)

Gigue is of Italian origin, and being the final movement, is very spirited, and lively. It is in compound quadruple time, and contrapuntal in style.
(Wang's translation: 英國舞樂 [Jig], 快板 , 6/4 拍子 , 性質活潑)

In translating the names, characteristics and styles of these dances, Wang oversimplified and tended to generalize the features of the dances with distinct national styles by translating them as 快板 , 慢板 , 性質嚴肅 , 性質活潑 . Since the middle of the 1950s, the word "suite" has been translated as 組曲 , "dances" as 舞曲 , and the names of the dances have been transliterated, *viz* Allemande 阿勒芒德舞曲 , Courante 庫朗特舞曲 , Sarabande 薩拉班德舞曲 , Gigue 吉格舞曲 .

Wang Guangqi was not the only one who tried to avoid translating the terms and who generalized the tempi and characteristics of dance music; the famous translator Fu Lei did the same. In his translation of Romain Rolland's *Jean Christophe*, he avoided translating the word "Adagio":

奧里維嘆了口氣,在鋼琴前面坐下了,很柔順的服從了這個自動挑中他的專制的朋友。他遲疑了半日,方始彈一曲莫扎爾德的B小調Adagio。
(Volume III, pp. 160–61, 1957.)

However, in the 1980 edition, the phrase " 莫扎爾德的B小調 Adagio" has been changed to 莫扎特的B小調柔板 . While 莫扎特 may be closer to the pronunciation of "Mozart" than 莫扎爾德 and 柔板 is more Chinese than "Adagio", it is however not quite appropriate to change the text of the translation, especially after the death of the translator (Fu Lei committed suicide in 1966).

Is it appropriate to translate "Adagio" as 柔板 ? European musical terms can in general be classified into five categories: (1) indicating the tempo of a piece of music such as "allegro", "andante", etc, which are usually translated as 快板 and 行板 ; (2) indicating the style of a piece such as "cantabile", "expressivo", etc, which are usually translated as 如歌地 , 富於表情地 ; (3) indicating both the tempo and the style such as "adagio", "largo", etc. These terms should be translated according to the context, but 板 does not seem to be an appropriate solution; (4) indicating dynamics such as "forte", "piano", etc, which should be translated as 強 and 弱 ; and (5) indicating instrumental techniques such as "con sordini", "pizzicato", etc, which should be translated as 用弱音踏板 and 撥弦 . As mentioned in Category (3) it is obviously inappropriate to translate "Adagio" as 柔板 . According to *The New Grove Dictionary of Music and Musicians*, the word "adagio" has the following three connotations:

1. Tempo designation. Adagio means "at ease", "leisurely" (悠閑地). Praetorius equated adagio with largo and lento, translating all three "Langsam". Purcell said that adagio and grave "import nothing but a very slow movement." By the 19th century, "adagio" was generally agreed to be the slowest tempo, while "largo" was used to suggest something more grand, and "grave" became more serious but was rarely slower as well.
2. Title of a piece, such as Mozart's Adagio in B Minor, Schubert's Adagio in E flat Major, or a movement in a symphony/sonata/concerto. When the term is used as a title of a piece, it not only indicates the tempo, it also suggests the appropriate style the piece/movement should be interpreted, *viz* at ease, leisurely, elegant, etc.
3. Slow movement, such as the coda of Haydn's Solomon Symphony's first movement is marked "segue adagio" (繼續溫文而徐緩地). (Volume I, pp. 88–89.)

Mozart's *Adagio in B Minor* should therefore be played at ease, leisurely and elegantly. It seems that to render "Adagio" as 柔板 is not appropriate, as 柔 indicates a kind of style and 板 denotes a tempo. It is therefore not quite correct to combine 柔 with 板 as a term, similarly it is also improper to translate "Largo" as 廣板 .

It is therefore extremely difficult to handle any terms which indicate both tempo and style. For example, when we translate "largo", "grave" and "adagio", different periods of composition will entail different translations. The possible way out, it seems, is to translate the three terms as 慢板 — 廣闊、從容 , 慢板 — 莊重、嚴肅 , 慢板 — 柔和、典雅 respectively. Although they sound cumbersome, they are at least accurate and clear. These translations can be used as the tempo as well as the title of a piece.

The word 板 derives from the metre and rhythm of Chinese music. From the ancient times to the Southern Song dynasty, Chinese songs were almost always composed one word (character) to one beat, and one beat was divided into the strong 板 and the weak 眼 . We should take note of these characteristics of Chinese music when we translate foreign terms so as to avoid using such erroneous combinations of 柔板 , 廣板 and the like.

The two examples given in the foregoing paragraphs illustrate the difficulties confronting music translators during the three decades from the late 1920s to the 1950s, and explain why they were hesitant when they rendered European musical concepts into the Chinese language. They are indeed difficult to translate, as in the case of the Italian term "allegro" which will serve as the third example in the discussion of translating tempo and style into Chinese. There are for example at least six Chinese versions, which are more or less similar in meaning to one another:

i.   快板：這個字的原意是高興或快樂，奏鳴曲、交響樂或協奏曲的第一樂章，通常都用這種速度。
        （王沛綸編：《音樂辭典》）

ii.   快速的樂章或樂曲。
        （王沛綸編：《音樂辭典》）

iii.   快板：愉快的、高興的、靈活的、迅速的。
        （上海音樂學院：《簡明音樂辭典》）

iv.   快板的通稱。
        （康謳編：《大陸音樂辭典》）

v.   快板：愉快地、愉快的、活潑的。
        （羅詠心編訂：《音樂譯名辭典》）

vi.   快板；活潑：用以表示一個輕快的樂章，往往和其他形容詞或表情術語連用，如 Allegro Moderato, Allegro con brio。
        （汪啟璋、顧連理、吳佩華編譯：《外國音樂辭典》）

The Oxford Companion to Music (tenth edition) defines this term as follows:

Allegro (Ital). "Merry", i.e. quick, lively, bright. Often used also as the title of a composition or movement in that style. The superlative is Allegrissimo.

Is it true that the term connotes the meaning of "merry", "quick", "lively"? If so, then how do we explain why Beethoven used "Allegro con brio" for the first movement of his fifth symphony? According to the definition given above, "Allegro con brio" should be translated as 高興的、

靈活的、熱烈的快板 which do not apply to the mood and emotions expressed in that movement. People who have heard the first movement of the fifth symphony would agree that it is 快板 — 激昂、輝煌 . If we accept such a definition, then not only is the Chinese version questionable, the definition given by *The Oxford Companion to Music* is also doubtful.

According *The New Grove Dictionary of Music and Musicians*, "Allegro" means:

> Allegro (Ital). The literal meaning of this word is "cheerful", and it is in this sense that it is employed as the title of Milton's well-known poem. In music, however, it now has the signification of "lively" primarily in the sense of quick, and is often combined with other words which would make nonsense with it in its original meaning — e.g. allegro agitato e con disperazione (Clementi, "Didone abbandonata" sonata). When unaccompanied by any qualifying word allegro indicates a rate of speed nearly intermediate between andante and presto. There is, however, no other time indication which is so frequently modified by the addition of other words. The word allegro is also used as the name of a piece of music, either a separate piece (e.g. Chopin's "Allegro de Concert", op. 46), or as the first movement of a large instrumental composition, such as symphony or sonata.

I tend to agree with *The Grove's* definition of "Allegro", i.e. 快速而活躍 , but not by any means "merry". The original and correct connotation of the term is not suitable to express the tempo and/or style of a piece of music, and when it is applied to music, it should be defined as follows:

> 快板：活躍而快速，介於原板與急板之間。常與其他術語合用，單獨應用此字時，可作爲樂曲之標題，或大型器樂樂曲如交響樂、奏鳴曲的第一樂章。

It is surprising that so many people have misunderstood such a simple term.

Ornaments

There are mainly four types of ornaments:(1) the appoggiatura family; (2) the shake family; (3) the division family; and (4) compound ornaments.

1. The Appoggiatura Family

The definition in *The New Grove Dictionary of Music and Musicians* is as follows:

In principle, this group comprises those ornamental notes that "lean" (the Italian verb is "appoggiare") on the following, so-called "main" note, which is written in normal notation.

The Chinese translation for "appoggiatura" is based on the word "lean" and is therefore rendered as 倚音 , reflecting the function of this ornamentation. There are quite a few variations in the Appoggiatura family, as follows:

i. The indeterminate appoggiatura, 不確定倚音 , meaning the performer is allowed to have a certain flexibility in playing the main note of the appoggiatura group.

ii. The long appoggiatura 長倚音 .

iii. Unwritten appoggiatura, 不標明的倚音 , indicating that there is no sign of such an appoggiatura and that the performer can insert an appoggiatura at a certain place in the music.

iv. The short appoggiatura 短倚音 .

v. Post-Baroque appoggiatura 巴洛克後之倚音 .

vi. The double approggiatura 雙倚音 .

vii. The slide 滑溜音 .

viii. The simultaneous appoggiatura, 波音式的倚音 , meaning that this appoggiatura should be played at the time with the main note which is a semi-tone apart from the appoggiatura.

ix. The passing appoggiatura 經過倚音 .

x. Acciacatura, there are two Chinese versions: 倚音 and 碎音 . In fact, this term should be translated as 短倚音 .

2. *The Shake Family*

There are several types of "Shake", including tremolo, vibrato, trill, and modernt:

i. Tremolo. There are two Chinese versions: 顫音 and 震音 . According to the effect of this ornamentation on the string instruments and harps, this term can be rendered as 重覆顫音 or 交替顫音 .

ii. Vibrato. There are four Chinese versions: " 揉弦 "、" 顫吟 "、" 振音 "、" 震動 ". In view of the fact that this ornamentation is produced on the string instruments, it should therefore be rendered as 揉弦 or 揉震 .

iii. Trill. There are two Chinese versions: 顫音 and 震音 . It is also called "the Shake". In view of the fact that this ornamentation is between two one-tone notes, it can be rendered as 兩度交替顫音 which is different from 交替顫音.

iv. Modernt. There are two Chinese versions: 波音 and 漣音. According to its nature and effect, it should be translated as 波音. There are two kinds of "modernt": upper 上 and lower 下, and the lower modernt is also called the "inverted modernt" 逆波音. C.P.E. Bach first used this ornamentation in 1750. In 1800 it was called "Schnell", and later changed to "Prall-triller".

3. The Division Family

The word "division" means allowing the ornament to share the time with the main note, and therefore it should be translated as 佔用音. There are five kinds of them:

i. Passing note 經過音 : there are "accented" 強, "unaccented" 弱 and "free" 自由 passing notes.

ii. Changing note, 換音, derived from "Nota Cambiata" 骿枝音.

iii. The Turn: there are two Chinese versions: 回音 and 迴音. It seems the former is a more appropriate translation.

iv. Broken notes 分解音, similar to the term "broken chord" 分解和弦.

v. Arpeggio, 琶音, imitating the sound of a harp.

4. Compound Ornaments 複裝飾音

There are three types, as follows:

i. Appeggio with modernt, trill or turn 琶音與倚音、波音、兩度交替顫音或回音的混合.

ii. Turn with trill 回音與兩度交替顫音的混合.

iii. Double cadence with double relish 終止與雙重潤飾的混合.

I have only discussed the Chinese translation of the terms of four kinds of ornaments which have been frequently used over the past several centuries and put forward my views on the Chinese equivalents or near equivalents, in accordance with the background, functions and practice of these ornaments. In fact, performers, composers, music historians, musicologists, music teachers and amateurs are accustomed to these terms in foreign languages. However, Chinese speakers are not familiar with them and therefore Chinese translations are necessary.

Terms Relating to Compositional Techniques

Since Wang Guangqi's time, Chinese translation of terms for the various disciplines of compositional techniques has been inconsistent and confusing. In this section, I would like to select a few for discussion, including terms related to harmony, counterpoint, orchestration, conducting, major and minor keys, modes and tonality.

In Chinese, the word 學 as used for instance in 社會學 (Sociology) connotes a specific discipline which has been used quite consistently in translation. However, it has not been the case in translating musical terminology such as 和聲學 (Harmony), 對位法 (Counterpoint), 配器法 (Orchestration), 曲體學 (Musical Forms), 作曲法 (Composition), 指揮法 (Conducting). What are the reasons for some to be translated as 學 (-ology) and others as 法 (method), and what are the differences between the two characters 學 and 法 ? It does not seem that there is a distinct criterion to determine the choice of these two characters. These subjects are in fact all specialized disciplines 學問 and each has its own methodology 法 , i.e. the combination of theory (discipline) and technique (method).

In the early 1920s, musical translation was in quite a chaotic state, and translators translated European terminology at random, as in 〈近代二大樂聖的生涯與藝術〉 by Feng Zikai:

> 裴德芬底披雅娜朔拿大共有三十二曲，由二、三、或四樂章成立，所用的拍子的種類有十一，調子數有二十。其中拍子以四分之四的爲最多，得二十六；其次爲四分之二的，得二十五；四分之三的得二十四。調子變E長調的有十二樂章，C長調的有十一，F長調的與變A長調的各有九樂章。又短調的樂章計有三十一，長調的樂章計有七十三。

This paragraph was written in 1927. A few points require clarifications: (1) 裴德芬 (Beethoven) has been translated as 貝多芬 since the late 1940s and 披雅娜朔拿大 (Piano Sonata) has long been translated as 鋼琴奏鳴曲 ; (2) it is considered inappropriate, if not wrong, to describe four-four time, four-two time and four-three time as 四分之四 , 四分之二 and 四分之三 which are mathematical descriptions, not musical; and (3) 變E長調 (E flat Major) has been rendered as 降E大調 , 變A長調 (A flat Major) as 降A大調 , and 短調 (Minor Key) as 小調 .

In music, "major" and "minor" are complementary and contrastive in connotation, and therefore there have been three versions in Chinese renditions, *viz* 長調 and 短調 , 大調 and 小調 , and 陰調 and 陽調 . Feng Zikai used 長調 and 短調 , while Wang Guangqi in his *A Concise History of Western Music* used 陽調 and 陰調 :

德國大音樂家巴赫，於一七二二年所譜之《調和鋼琴曲》中，將「十二平均律」各譜陽調、陰調一篇，共二十四篇。 (Volume II, p. 99.)

Fu Lei in his 〈貝多芬的作品及其精神〉 also used 陽調 and 陰調 for "major" and "minor" respectively (Fu, 1946:148–153). Feng's article was written in 1927, Wang's in the 1930s, and Fu's in 1942. In 1954, Zhang Hongdao 張洪島 in his 《和聲學實用教程》 continued to use 長調 for "major" and 短調 for "minor". In fact, since the late 1940s, "major" and "minor" have been translated as 大調 and 小調 respectively in most of the publications on musical theory.

Among the three translations of "major" and "minor", indeed it is very tempting to opt for 陰調 and 陽調 which sound very Chinese. However, if we analyse the scale structure, we should then translate "major" and "minor" as 大調 and 小調 , as the two scales named after the two terms "major" and "minor" are due to a "major third" (a four semi-tone interval) in a major scale and the "minor third" (a three semi-tone interval). As a result, we have a set of "by-products", including major and minor scales 大小音階 , major and minor intervals 大小音程 , major and minor triads 大小三和弦 , major and minor keys 大小調 , establishing an extremely important major and minor system which influenced European music for several centuries. Since the structure of a major or minor third interval is upward, either vertically arranged (the harmonic pattern) or horizontally arranged (the melodic pattern), it is more logical to translate them as 大調 and 小調 .

The major and minor keys have been the foundation of European music during the past several centuries, and theorists have termed them as "tonality" 調性 . As mentioned above, Wang Guangqi in his *A Concise History of Western Music* used the Chinese term 宮調 for 調性 which is, I think, a very appropriate rendition. 諸宮調 means all the keys in the major and minor tonalities in European music.

Xu Changhui 許常惠 in his article entitled 〈如何了解音樂？〉 (How to Understand Music?) wrote about tonality and modes:

甚麼是調性呢？調性是人生來具備的對聲音的有秩序排列的感覺，換句話說，如果有一項音樂作品要給人聽起來有秩序，它必須具有調性，否則它是零亂的，它不能成爲好的音樂作品。這不是告訴我們：調性是每一項音樂作品的必需條件嗎？

然而，在音樂的世界裏，從古至今，不分民族，我們有無數的調式，儘管以調性和聲爲基礎的大調或小調音階，它的組織可能最精密、最科學，它發揮了輝煌力量，但是它還是無數調性中的一種！(p. 121)

It is apparent that Xu mixed up the two terms of "tonality" and "mode". The major and minor keys were evolved from the "modal system" 調式體系 and therefore the modal system is the basis from which the major and minor tonality, the offspring of the modes, evolved and developed. The writer turned the two terms upside down. Perhaps it is the Chinese translation of 調性 and 調式 which confused Xu.

Since the beginning of the fifth century A.D., religious music in Europe had developed on the basis of the modal system. In addition, folk music in many European countries is also modal in nature. From the tenth century to the sixteenth century, European music continued to develop on the basis of the modal system until the time of J.S. Bach (1685–1750) and G.F. Handel (1685–1759) when the use of the modal system gradually became less popular. It however did not mean that the modes completely gave way to the major and minor tonality, for example, in Beethoven's (1770–1827) *String Quartet in A minor* op. 132, we can still feel the flavour of the Lydia Mode. The influence of the modal system extended well into the twentieth century, as R. Vaughan Williams (1872–1958) used modal scales in many of his compositions.

In *The Oxford Companion to Music*, there is a comparative account of the modes and the major and minor scales:

The difference between one mode and another is not the kind of difference which exists between C major and D major but that which exists between C major and C minor or D major and D minor, i.e. a difference of the arrangement of tones and semitones, and hence, necessarily, of the width of some of the other intervals. It may be called a difference of flavour, so that a keen ear, well accustomed to modal music, should be able to tell in what mode a piece of plain song or a piece of early harmonized music lies.

The twelve modes in the modal system, the twelve "scale patterns" so to speak, are quite different from the tonality concept which is a system of the twelve keys arranged in alphabetical order. In view of this, "Modes" should therefore be translated as 音階模式 , or in greater detail as 宗教音階模式 (Ecclesiastical Modes or Church Modes). As regards the translation of "Tonality", it should be considered together with "key". "Key" means 調子 in Chinese, the term covering the whole system of the keys should then be 調體系 . However, 調體系 is not as concise as 調性 , it is therefore considered more appropriate to translate "tonality" as 調性 . In this way, we will not be confused by "Tonality" 調性 and "Ecclesiastical Modes" 宗教音階模式 .

Musical Forms

"Form of Music" and "Structure and Style" are the two of the many terms for the study of forms, structures and styles of musical compositions, i.e. the musical genres. In Chinese, these terms have been translated as 曲式、曲體、樂式、結構與風格 , etc. There are two distinct aspects to this subject: the formal structure in musical compositions and the styles of the various forms including the evolution of such styles during its development.

In his *A Concise History of Western Music*, Wang Guangqi transliterated such names as Sonata and Cantata. Also in the 1920s, Feng Zikai in his 〈近代二大樂聖的生涯與藝術〉 transliterated violin, sonata, cello, and cantata. He nevertheless translated "String Quartet" as 弦樂四重奏 , "Trio" as 三重奏 , "Concerto" as 競奏曲 , "Overture" as 序樂 , "Missa" as 彌撒 , "Opera" as 歌劇 , and "Symphony" as 交響樂 . For his part, Wang translated "Sonata" as 演奏曲 (as compared with Cantata 演唱曲), "Overture" as 開場曲 and "Intermezzo" as 過場曲 .

During the period from the 1920s to the 1940s, the progress made in translating the terminology of musical forms was negligible. In the case of "Sonata", "Concerto" and "Variation", the Chinese versions of "Sonata" were changed from " 朔那台 " to " 朔拿大 ", mainly due to the dialects of the translators. Not only did Feng Zikai use " 朔拿大 ", Fu Lei also used " 朔拿大 " in his translations of Romain Rolland's *Vie de Beethoven* (《貝多芬傳》, 1942) and *Jean Christophe* (《約翰・克列斯朵夫》).

" 朔拿大 " was still used again in 1943, in J. C. Fillmore's 《西洋音樂史教程》 translated by Wei Bi 韋璧 . It is rather amusing to note that in a biography of Romain Rolland 《羅曼羅蘭傳》 tanslated by Shen Liansan 沈鍊三 published in 1947, the Chinese translation for *The Third Sonata for Piano Op. 10* was 《鋼琴用的第三長曲》 , indicating the irresponsible attitude of the translator. It was not until the late 1940s and early 1950s that translators began replacing 朔拿大 by 奏鳴曲, which can be found in translations such as 《造物者悲多汶》 by Chen Shi 陳實, 《曲式學》 by Miao Tianrui 繆天瑞, 《貝多芬及浪漫樂派》 by Feng Chenbao 豐陳寶, 《巴赫及古典樂派》 and 《布拉姆斯及現代樂派》 by Zheng Xiaocang 鄭曉滄, 《貝多芬九大交響樂解說》 by Yang Minwang 楊民望, etc. This was probably due to the effort of the editor of these books, as the books mentioned above were mostly published by Wan Ye Book Shop 萬葉書店 in 1951. However, as early as 1946, in a publication entitled 《音樂的解放者悲汶》, the term "Sonata" was translated as " 奏鳴曲 ".

The evolution of the Chinese version of "Concerto" has been similar to that of "Sonata". There were several versions between the 1920s and the 1940s: 空澈提 by Wang Guangqi, 競奏曲 by Feng Zikai, probably borrowed from Japanese, " 合奏曲 " by Fu Lei. Since the early 1950s, "Concerto" has normally been rendered as " 協奏曲 ". In an article written by Zhao Zheng 趙正 entitled 〈幾個值得商榷的音樂術語〉, there are two paragraphs commenting on the Chinese translation of "Concerto":

> Concerto 一詞歷來有人翻譯爲 "協奏曲" 及 "競奏曲" 二種，由於 "協奏曲" 一詞通用到如此程度，如果改用了 "競奏曲"，反而不易爲人們所接受了。

> 但必需指出，協奏兩字雖可解作協和演奏，但譯者原意恐只是指協助演奏而已；而此種樂隊協助獨奏樂器演奏的風格，屬於古典及浪漫期之作品而已，而 "競奏" 兩字不但適用於各個時期 concerto 的風格，且符合其原意 "競爭和對比" 的意思。 (p. 77)

The views expressed here sound reasonable. However, before we decide on the appropriateness of the two Chinese versions 競奏曲 and 協奏曲, let us look into the background of this term.

In the sixteenth century, Adrian Willaert (1480–1562) in his church compositions made use of a double choir, as was required by the architectural arrangements in the church over whose music he presided; this was the start of contrast and complementary singing by two groups. Later, Andrea Gabrieli (1510–1586), pupil of Willaert, and Giovanni Gabrieli (1557–1612) (uncle and nephew), Adriano Banchieri (1568–1634) and Viadana (real name Ludovico Grossi 1564–1645) wrote choral music called "concerti ecclesiastici". In this sense, the term "Concerto" indicates some elements of contrasting, comparative and complementary singing since the number in the two groups of the double choir was entirely equal.

However, such a balanced arrangement changed in the seventeenth century. Arcangelo Corelli (1653–1713) applied the "concerti ecclesiastici" type of writing to instrumental writing, with one larger group "Ripieno" and one smaller group "Concertino", which resulted more in contrast than in competition, as there was no equivalence between a larger group and a smaller group of instruments. In the classical and romantic periods, the structure and style of the concerto form were different from their predecessors: its structure was a Sonata-allegro form, and the previous two groups of "Ripieno" and "Concertino" became one solo instrument and one orchestra respectively, thus completely losing all the competitiveness. According to the evolution of this form, in the sixteenth century the "concerti ecclesiastici" could be translated as "競唱曲"; in the seventeenth and eighteenth centuries, the concerto grossso could be translated as "器樂協奏曲"; and in the classical and romantic periods, the concerto could be translated as "獨奏與樂隊協奏曲". The latter two can therefore be simply translated as "協奏曲".

However, Kang Ou 康謳 in his 《大陸音樂辭典》, put forward the following views:

> 最近又有另一個字源的說法, 即是拉丁文的 conserere "聯合", 主要是因為協奏曲一詞偶爾出現過另一種拼法 conserto。

A concerto is a musical composition which provides a musical dialogue between a solo instrument and an orchestra, at times emotional and violent and at times quiet, peaceful and tender. Even though there may be competition of some kind, it will be short and temporary. It is therefore not appropriate to translate the term as "競奏" as it can be misleading.

The term "Variation" is normally used together with "Theme" or "Air" — "Theme and Variations" or "Air and Variations", which makes for more straightforward translation than "Sonata" and "Concerto". In the 1920s, Feng Zikai translated it as 變奏曲; in the 1940s, Fu Lei translated it as 變體曲. In his 〈近代二大樂聖的生涯與藝術〉, Feng had this footnote: "即把主題在節奏、旋律、和聲各面進行種種的變化的而集成一曲的。" (p. 49). Since the Chinese translation of "變體曲" indicates the change of the "form" 體 which is in fact not the case, it is therefore more appropriate to translate it as 變奏曲. In *The Oxford Companion to Music*, there is a very descriptive explanation:

> The Air with Variations. This, which is a dinner of one sort of fish served up in

many courses with different cooking and sauce, is one of the very earliest instrumental forms.

A fish will always be a fish, no matter how you cook it. What has changed is the flavour and not the food itself.

I have only discussed the translation of three musical forms, *namely* "Sonata", "Concerto" and "Variation". There are of course many more which need to be considered, such as "Rondo" 迴旋曲 , Sonata-Rondo 奏鳴曲迴旋曲 , "Fantasia" (幻想曲 or 隨想曲), "Interlude" and "Intermezzo" 間奏曲 . However, it would be too lengthy to include all in this article, and I have therefore only touched upon the few essential ones.

History of Music

Up to now, there is no comprehensive Chinese publication on the history of European music. There are of course a number of factors contributing to this, and one of them is probably the difficulty of translation. The task is colossal, as it covers almost everything, including such subjects as history, literature, philosophy, physics, aesthetics, mathematics, industry and manufacturing, science and technology and theory of music. The first necessary step is to compile a glossary of all the terms and phrases to be used. In this section, I will discuss the Chinese translation of the various periods of the development of European music, so as to avoid the conceptual confusion caused by inappropriate and inaccurate translation.

The periodization of musical history varies as a result of the different schools of thought. *The New Oxford History of Music* divides the development of music into nine periods (volumes 5 and 6 belong to the same period 1630–1750), as follows:

1. Ancient and Oriental Music
2. Early Medieval Music up to 1300
3. Ars Nova and the Renaissance (1300–1540)
4. The Age of Humanism (1540–1630)
5. Opera and Church Music (1630–1750)
6. Concert Music (1630–1750)
7. The Age of Enlightenment (1745–1790)
8. The Age of Beethoven (1790–1830)
9. Romanticism (1830–1890)
10. The Modern Age (1830–1960)

The division seems reasonable, without too many subdivisions of the kind Paul Henry Lang introduced in his *Music in Western Civilization*; some divide it into six periods, such as Hugh Milton Miller in his *An Outline of the History of Music*. The differences in the division of historical periods are subject to the historians' interpretations.

These are just three of the many publications on the history of European music written in English and other European languages. However, works written in Chinese have so far been scarce and the few I have come across are nothing more than pamphlets. Wang's *A Concise History of Western Music*, which may be regarded as the pioneering effort, consists of six chapters:

第一章　　緒言
第二章　　單音音樂流行時代
第三章　　複音音樂流行時代
第四章　　複音音樂流行時代(續前)
第五章　　主音伴音分立時代
第六章　　主音伴音混合時代

單音音樂 (Monophony) refers to the ancient music (unison singing) of Egypt, Babylon and Greece, and the Gregorian Chant of the Catholic Church. 複音音樂 (Polyphony) refers to the simultaneous combination of a number of parts, each forming an individual melody and harmonizing with the others, including Organum, Discautus and Fauxbourdon in the early stage; Conductus, Motetus, Rondeau, Kanon, Madrigal and Ballata in the middle stage; and contrapuntal music (Wang translated as 對譜音樂) of J.S. Bach and G.F. Handel in the later stage. "Homophony" refers to part-writing in which there is a clear-cut distinction between the melody and the harmonic accompaniments or in which all the parts move in the same rhythmic pattern (i.e. chordal style), as opposed to polyphonic (or contrapuntal) treatment. Wang divided 主音伴音 (Homophony) into 分立 (divided) and 混合 (merged) periods which I think is not necessary as they only mark the different stages of the development of homophonic music.

Before discussing Wang's translation of these Chinese terms, let us go through the Chinese versions of these terms by other musicologists and historians. Zhang Hongdao in his 《西洋音樂史》 only translated "Monophony" 單音音樂 and "Polyphony" 複音音樂 , leaving out "Homophony" 主音音樂 ; and he grouped the music of the second half of the eighteenth century together with that of the nineteenth century in Volume II

《複音音樂》, which does not appear to make sense. Liu Zhiming 劉志明 only mentioned 複音音樂 (Polyphony) and avoided mentioning 單音音樂 (Monophony) and 主音音樂 (Homophony) in his 《西洋音樂史與風格》, which comprises 16 chapters grouped into nine parts. Other publications have also failed to clearly differentiate the definitions of these three terms, such as 《圖片音樂史》 translated by Jian Mingren 簡明仁, 《畫中的音樂歷史》 edited by Shi Weiliang 史惟亮, 《西洋音樂史》 written by Li Yang 李陽, etc.

In fact, "Monophony", "Polyphony" and "Homophony" cover three important periods in the development of European music. The development of European music can roughly be divided into four periods: (1) Monophony; (2) Polyphony; (3) Homophony; and (4) Modern Music (20th century music). These four periods can be subdivided into smaller units so as to more or less cover the entire history of European music. It is for this reason that the Chinese translations of these terms should be regarded as a most important job which will affect the accurate understanding by the readers of the styles of the various historical periods.

As I mentioned earlier, "Monophony" refers to unison singing without harmonic accompaniment. It is a term used to indicate the structure and style of primitive and religious music in Asia, Africa and Europe before the tenth century, including ancient Greek music, Gregorian Chant, Byzantine Chant, songs sung by French Troubadours and Trouveres, songs sung by German Minnesingers and Meistersingers, etc. Therefore, "Monophony" is primarily a single melodic line with rhythms, not single notes. It is therefore misleading to translate it as 單音音樂; it should be translated as 單旋律音樂.

"Polyphony" is a term referring to music with several parts moving independently or in imitation of one another which developed during the period from the tenth century to the middle of the eighteenth century until the death of J.S. Bach in 1750. It was a transitional period during which a single melodic line developed from simple two-part and three-part parallel melodic lines to complicated contrapuntal writing, which lasted 800 years. It had a long period of experiments and reached its maturity in J.S. Bach's compositions. In the early stage, Polyphonic music included two-part Organum and Discantus, three-part Fauxbourton, Conductus, Motetus and Rondeau, and the antiphonal-type of Canon; in the latter stage, contrapuntal treatment replaced the simple two-part and three-part writing, such as Oratorio, Cantata, Passion, Fugue and Concerto Grosso. "Poly" means "multi" and "Polyphony" means "multi-voices" music 複聲部音樂 and for instrumental music, it could be translated as "Multi-melodic" music 複旋律音樂 .

"Homophony" is derived from Greek "homophonia", meaning voices or instruments which sound alike. The term was originally applied to unison singing, for example in plainsong, but has been replaced by "Monophony". The main characteristic is that music written in the homophonic style is in two distinct parts: the melody and the harmonic support for the melody, as opposed to polyphony (or contrapuntal) treatment. Wang Guangqi rendered it as 主音伴音 with good reason, although the expression is cumbersome. The homophonic period stretched from Classical and Romantic periods to part of the Modern period. The foundation was laid firmly by Haydn and Mozart, consolidated and developed by Beethoven, and matured in the hands of the Romanticists. The "Sonata-allegro" form and the "Sonata" form were the most important musical genres in the homophonic period, and have been used extensively since Haydn's time until now, though with modifications. From the "Sonata" form, symphonic music, solo concertos, chamber music, choral music and the various kinds of programme music came into being.

By Brahms' time, the relationship between melody and harmonic accompaniments had become less distinctive and the texture of Brahms' compositions such as his Fourth Symphony contains both polyphonic as well as homophonic treatments, which means in this symphony contrapuntal writing merged into homophonic writing and became a kind of a "harmonic contrapuntal" style. Brahms employed more than two independent melodies in his homophonic treatment, thus bringing Bach and Beethoven into one — Brahms' style. It is therefore considered misleading to choose a term of conceptual nature, and the term "homophony" is not entirely suitable to the "harmonic contrapuntal" type of the Fourth Symphony, although most of Brahms' compositions are primarily homophonic in style.

From the foregoing paragraphs, we understand that the distinction between the two terms "homophony" and "polyphony" represents two entirely different kinds of musical textures and styles, although during the late 19th century there were some "polyphony" elements (independant melodic lines) injected into the homophonic texture. The original meaning of the Greek word "homophonia" ("voices or instruments sound alike") was replaced by "monophony" so that it could be used as a term in comparison with the other two, and used "homophony" to indicate music with the sort of texture and style as described above. If the term "monophony" is translated as 單旋律音樂 and "Polyphony" as 複旋律音樂, then "homophony" can be translated as 和聲織體的音樂 (meaning music with a harmonic-texture music). It is not advisable to translate it either as 主音音樂 or 主調音樂, as the former can be misunderstood as "the main tonal music" and the latter as "the main key music".

Names of Composers

Apart from a few well-known composers, the translation of the names of most composers has been inconsistent, partly due to the dialects of the translators. In the 1920s, there were quite a few amusing ones, as indicated in Wang Guangqi's *A Concise History of Western Music*:

> 茲將此時代中，西洋音樂界各種重要主義，簡說明如下：（甲）古典主義派 Klasiker，爲第十八世紀下半期之樂風，其代表作家爲"維也納三傑"：海登 Haydn (1732–1809年)，摩擦耳提 Mozart (1756–1791年)，白堤火粉 Beethoven (1770–1827年)。（乙）羅曼主義派 Romantiker，盛行於第十九世紀之中，其代表作家，爲魏伯耳 Weber (1786–1826年)，許伯提 Schubert (1797–1828年)，史卜耳 Spohr (1784–1859年)，馬耳邪南 Marschner (1795–1861年)，門登思宋 Mendelssohn (1809–1847年)，薛曼 Schumann (1810–1856年)，伯爾柳遲 Berlioz (1803–1869年)，李斯志 Lizst (1811–1886年)，瓦庚來 Wagner (1813–1883年)，史推斯 R. Strauss (生於1864年) 等等；自伯爾柳遲 Berlioz 以下四人，世亦稱之爲"新羅曼主義派"。（丙）印象主義派 Impressionismus，其始創者爲法人德比舍 Debussy 氏 (1862–1918年) …（丁）表現主義派 Expressionismus，其代表作家，爲荀白格 Schönberg (生於 1874 年)。…（戊）無主音樂派 Atonalität … 此派之中，復分爲溫和激烈兩派。溫和派如上述之荀白格 Schönberg 氏以及亨得米提 Hindemith 氏(生於1895年)，史托文思齊 Strawinski 氏(生於1882年) 等等皆是。激烈派則爲好耳 Hauer (生於1833年)，古里邪夫 Golyscheff (生於1895年) 等等皆是。

In this paragraph, Wang translated 19 names of composers and none of these is used today: Haydn is now translated as 海頓, Mozart as 莫扎特, Beethoven as 貝多芬, Weber as 韋伯, Schubert as 舒伯特, Mendelssohn as 孟德爾遜, Schumann as 舒曼, Berlioz as 貝遼茲, Lizst as 李斯特, Wagner as 瓦格納, Hindemith as 享德密特, Stravinsky as 史特拉文斯基, etc. 荀白格 (Schönberg) seems to be quite a close resemblance in sound to the original name; however, translators in Taiwan translated it as 荀白克 which is not quite correct, as the sound of "g" in "berg" should be 格 rather than 克 . Zhang Hongdao translated it as 勳柏爾格 , which is quite close phonetically to 荀白格 .

The Chinese translations of composers' names presently in use are closer to the original sound as compared with those translated by Wang Guangqi whose Sichuan provincial accent might have contributed towards the extraordinary phonetic effects in his translations, e.g. 白堤火粉 for Beethoven which should be pronounced in three syllables Bai-thoh-ven, and the Chinese should therefore be phonetically 貝 - 頭 - 墳 which, although very close to the original sound, does not look very nice in writing, as the second character means "head" and the third "grave". There were several translations for "Beethoven", including 悲多芬 , 悲德芬 , 裴多汶 . In the 1940s, after Fu Lei's translation of *Beethoven*《貝多芬傳》 was widely read in China, 貝多芬 for Beethoven became quite consistent. As regards "Schubert" and "Schumann" both of which begin with "Schu", Wang translated the former as 許 and the latter as 薛 , a sign of his disregard for consistency in dealing with translation of composers' names.

There has never been any guideline or principle for translating "Western" composers' names, and therefore it has always been confusing and misleading, especially when original names are not provided in the Chinese texts. Translators and scholars translated or selected the Chinese names at random, even using different transliterations for the same sound, as in the case of Schubert and Schumann. As mentioned in the "Introduction", the Ministry of Education in Taiwan published a glossary 《音樂名詞》 in 1962, and the Chinese translations of composers' names listed in this glossary were included in quite a few dictionaries of music published in Taiwan, such as 《大陸音樂辭典》 and 《音樂辭典》 .

I would like to discuss the general principles in tackling this issue. Let me select six Chinese transliterations of composers' names listed in the 《音樂名詞》 , and compare them with my proposed ones: (see over page)

The comparisons in the six examples indicate: (1) that translators engaged in transliterations of composers' names must be a competent Guoyu/Putonghua speakers, so as to avoid incredible transliterations such as 曲冰 for "Chopin" in Wang Guangqi's *A Concise History of Western Music* (Volume II, p. 143); (2) that transliterations should be as simple, as concise, and as close to the original sound as possible, e.g. there have been six different Chinese transliterations for "Mozart", *viz* 摩擦耳提 , 莫遮脫 ,

Name	《音樂名詞》	Proposed transliteration
Berlioz [Bair-lyoh]	貝遼士	貝遼茲
Clementi [Clem-en-tee]	克來曼悌	克雷曼蒂
Dvorak [Dvawrr-zjahk]	德佛亞克	德沃扎克
Scriabin [Skree-ah-been]	史克里亞賓	斯克瑞亞賓
Wagner [Vahg-nerr]	華格納	瓦格納
Wolf	佛爾夫	沃爾夫

莫差爾特, 莫扎爾德, 莫扎爾特 and 莫扎特. The differences among the six versions are 差 and 扎, 特 and 德, and with 爾 and without 爾. "Mozart" should be pronounced Mohts-arrt 莫扎爾德, as "ts-arrt" sounds 扎爾特. However, in order to make it simple and concise, it is to be transliterated as 莫扎特; (3) that different languages have different pronunciations, such as "Dvorak" and "Chopin" which are not English and should therefore not be pronounced as such; (4) that it is sometimes impossible to find equivalents in Guoyu/Putonghua for certain syllables in foreign languages. For example there is no equivalent sound in Guoyu for "ski" or "sky"; however, in Cantonese, they could be transliterated as 斯基. Even so, for the sake of uniformity and consistency, we should stick to Guoyu/Putonghua pronunciation; (5) that we should continue to use those which have been in use for a long period of time, even though they may not be very ideal transliterations; and (6) that we should try our best to formulate a general guideline in the light of the discussions in this section, e.g.

li   is to be transliterated as 理, 利 or 李, depending on the syllable, e.g. Salieri 薩列理, Lulli 呂利, and Lizst 李斯特.

bi   is to be transliterated as 畢, 比 or 必, also depending on the syllable, e.g. Bizet 比才.

lei   is to be transliterated as 雷 or 累, e.g. Lespighi 雷斯比基.

rie   is to be transliterated as 瑞 or 銳, e.g. Fauré 佛瑞.

von is to be transliterated as 方 or 芳 , e.g. von Weber 方・韋伯 .

van is to be transliterated as 范 , 範 or 凡 , e.g. van Beethoven 范・貝多芬 .

t is to be transliterated as 特 when it is on the last syllable, e.g. Schubert 舒伯特 , Mozart 莫扎特 , etc.

d is to be transliterated as 德 or 得 when it is on the last syllable, e.g. Field 費爾德 .

Schu is to be transliterated as 舒 , e.g. Schumann 舒曼 , Schubert 舒伯特 , etc.

s is to be transliterated as 斯 or 司 , e.g. Delius 戴流斯 .

z is to be transliterated as 茲 or 茨 , e.g. Berlioz 貝遼茲 .

There is of course a lot more to be discussed. If we are determined to continue with this work, we will eventually be able to compile a practicable and consistent glossary of composers' names. In fact, we do have a few composers whose Chinese transliterations are consistent after half a century's extensive use, such as 巴赫 (there is another commonly used transliteration 巴哈) for Bach, 海頓 for Haydn, 莫扎特 for Mozart, 貝多芬 for Beethoven, 舒伯特 for Schubert, 蕭邦 for Chopin, 柴可夫斯基 for Tchaikovsky, etc.

Conclusion

In the foregoing sections, I have briefly discussed the history and problems of the Chinese translation of musical terms, styles, expressions, musical forms, musical history and names of composers, and this is just the first step towards the more complex and comprehensive work of translation of conceptual and technical terminology. It is therefore necessary for us to make absolutely sure that the first stage of work is done properly before we proceed further.

The views expressed in this article are purely my personal observations and therefore by no means represent definitive solutions to the complex and controversial problems of the Chinese translations of musical terms and phrases. My purpose has been to identify the problems and to find out the possible ways of solving such problems, so as to determine the closest possible Chinese equivalents for the foreign musical terms and phrases. It should be noted that research, teaching, composing and performing will be seriously affected if this work is not properly done.

Perhaps it is useful to reiterate the following points:

1. terms relevant to tempi, dynamics and instrumental playing should be translated as "Chinese" as possible, e.g. try to make use of existing Chinese musical terms, either by fully or partially adopting the Chinese equivalents, or by modifying Chinese musical terms;
2. Chinese translations should be accurate, concise and unambiguous;
3. the background of each term should be carefully considered;
4. the development of individual periods and the styles of music in the history of European music should be taken into account and Chinese translations should be able to show the various periods and styles in perspective; and
5. in transliterating the names of composers, the pronunciation should be based on Guoyu/Putonghua: provincial variants have no place in the transliteration. In this connection, it is considered necessary to compile a glossary of Chinese transliterations of composers' names.

The ideal music translator should be someone who is a musicologist by training; if not, he should at least collaborate with a musicologist. A linguist, no matter how capable, will not be able to tackle the problems encountered in this specialized discipline, if he is not a music scholar himself. Furthermore, music translation should be developed hand in hand with music research, as in the case of literary translation in which research on the social and cultural background of the work and on the writer is indispensable. If we could afford full-time professional music translators, it would be an ideal solution to the problem; if not, musicologists, music historians and music scholars should be encouraged to act as part-time translators.

References

Chang, Jing 常靜 . 〈我國二十世紀音樂翻譯著作一瞥〉 (A Glance at the Translations of Musical Works in the Twenth Century China). 《中國音樂學》 (*Chinese Musicology*), No. 2 (1990), pp. 120–22.

Dai, Mingyu 戴明瑜 . 〈二十世紀音樂研究成果與翻譯〉 (Results of Studies on Twentieth Century Music and Their Translation). 《中國音樂學》 (*Chinese Musicology*), No. 2 (1990), pp. 103–105.

Gu, Wenxian 谷文嫻 . 〈全面翻譯各派觀點的必要性〉 (The Necessity of Comprehensively Translating Viewpoints of Different Schools). 《中國音樂學》 (*Chinese Musicology*), No. 2 (1990), pp. 113–16.

Hirmer, G.S. *Baker's Biographical Dictionary of Musicians*, 7th ed., edited by Nicolas Slonimsky. Oxford: Oxford University Press, 1934.

Jin, Qiu 金秋 . 〈翻譯與研究〉 (Translation and Research). 《中國音樂學》 (*Chinese Musicology*), No. 2 (1990), pp. 118–19.

Ju, Qihong 居其宏 . 〈譯學與當代音樂研究〉 (Music Translation and Studies on Contemporary Music). 《中國音樂學》 (*Chinese Musicology*), No. 2 (1990), pp. 122–23.

Kang, Ou 康謳 , ed. 《大陸音樂辭典》 (*A Dictionary of Mainland Chinese Music*). Taipei: Mainland Bookstore 大陸書店 , 1980.

Liu, Ching-chih 劉靖之 . 〈論音樂翻譯〉 (On Music Translation). In 《翻譯叢論》 (*Essays on Translation*), edited by Stephen Soong 宋淇 . Hong Kong: The Chinese University Press, 1983, pp. 107–36.

———. 〈統一音樂譯名芻議〉 (A Draft Proposal for the Standardization of Music Terminology). Paper presented at "Confererence on Translation Today," 17–21 December 1987, Hong Kong.

———. 〈裝飾音名詞的翻譯〉 (Translation of Ornaments in Music). 《中國語文通訊》 (*Chinese Language Bulletin*), No. 4 (1989).

Luo, Bingkang 羅秉康 . 〈關於音樂統一譯名的 "老生長談" 〉 (Clichés on the Standardization of Chinese Terminology). 《中國音樂學》 (*Chinese Musicology*), No. 2 (1990), pp. 109–10.

Mo, Dechang 莫德昌 . 〈中國音樂詞匯漢譯英的一些問題〉 (Some Problems in Translating Chinese Musical Terms into English). 《中國音樂學》 (*Chinese Musicology*), No. 2 (1987), pp. 118–21.

The New Oxford History of Music. Oxford: Oxford University Press, 1954–90.

Sadie, Stanley, ed. *The New Grove Dictionary of Music and Musicians*. MacMillian Publishers Limited, 1980.

Taiwan National Translation Bureau 台灣國立編譯館 , comp. 《音樂名詞》 (*Musical Terms*). Taipei: Zhengzhong Bookstore 正中書局 , 1962.

Tang, Yading 湯亞汀 . 〈翻譯. 編譯. 編寫. 著述〉 (Translation, Translation and Editing, Rewriting and Composition). 《中國音樂學》 (*Chinese Musicology*), No. 2 (1990), pp. 116–18.

Thompson, Osca, ed. *The International Cyclopedia of Music and Musicians*, 10th ed. New York: Dodd, Mead and Company, 1975.

Wang, Guangqi 王光祈 . 《東西樂制之研究》 (*A Study of Eastern and Western Musical Systems*), Taipei: Zhonghua Bookstore 中華書局 , 1971.

———. 《西洋音樂史綱要》 (*A Concise History of Western Music*). Shanghai: Zhonghua Bookstore 中華書局 , 1937.

Wang, Zhaoren 王昭仁 . 〈國外重要音樂著作翻譯〉 (Translation of Important Musical Works in Foreign Countries). In 《中國音樂年鑒》 (*Chinese Music Almanac*), edited by Huang Xiangpeng 黃翔鵬 and Tian Qing 田青 . Beijing: Culture and Art Publishing Company 文化藝術出版社 , 1987, pp. 292–95.

———. 〈略議音樂翻譯的歷史和使命〉 (A Brief Discussion on the History and

Mission of Music Translation). 《中國音樂學》 (*Chinese Musicology*), No. 2 (1990), pp. 107–109.

Wu, Sen 吳森 . 〈中國傳統音樂研究與翻譯工作〉 (The Study and Translation of Chinese Traditional Music). 《中國音樂學》 (*Chinese Musicology*), No. 2 (1990), pp. 111–12.

Onomatopoeia

Yu Yungen
Foreign Languages University
Luoyang, China

Onomatopoeia, also known as echoism, refers to the formation of a word by imitating the natural sound associated with the object or action involved. It is a simple and primitive word-building process. Words thus formed are called echoic or imitative words, or simply onomatopoeia. Such words abound in every human language known, and have played an important role in the enrichment of their vocabulary. In English, words imitating the sound of metal are *clash, clank, ting, tinkle, clang, jangle, tick-tack, ding-dong,* etc.; words copying the sound of water or liquid are *splash, bubble, fizz, sizzle, splish-splosh, drip-drop,* etc.; *neigh, baa, moo, miao, screech, hiss, cock-a-doodle-do* are a few examples of words imitating the sounds of different animals; and *giggle, chuckle, shriek, snort, sneeze, snigger, smack, whisper, grunt, grumble, mumble, sputter, murmur, chatter, gurgle, whoop* are some examples of sounds produced by humans. Similarly, in Chinese, we have 噹噹、叮嚀噹啷、叮冬、叮噹、嘎嘎、叮叮、噹啷 etc., for metallic sounds; 潺潺、滴滴答答、（水流）瀎瀎、咕嘟、（沸水）嘶嘶 etc., words echoing the sound of water or liquid; 咪咪、喵喵、汪汪、（羊或小牛）咩咩、（豬）咕嚕、喔喔喔 etc., words copying the sounds of animals; and 哈哈（笑）、喃喃（說）、呃啾（打噴嚏）、哇哇（哭）、哼哼（聲） etc., words describing different human sounds.

Onomatopoeia is not only a useful word-formation principle, but also a very important rhetorical device. Used properly, echoic words can appeal to the reader's sense of hearing and deepen his impression of what he is reading. As a result, they are widely employed by writers to achieve certain artistic effects. A famous example in English literature is a stanza from Alfred Tennyson's poem *The Brook*:

> I chatter *over stony ways,*
> *In little sharps and trebles,*
> *I* bubble *into eddying bays,*
> *I* babble *on the pebbles.*

With the help of the words *chatter, bubble* and *babble*, the sound of the little brook is vividly depicted, and it will linger in the reader's mind's ear long after he finishes reading the poem. Another well-known example is taken from *The Cask of Amontillado* by Adgar Allen Poe. In the following few lines, the author uses the word *ugh* 15 times to imitate the cough of his dying protagonist, thus creating a vivid picture in the reader's mind's eye.

> "Niter?" he asked at length. "Niter," I replied.
> "How long have you had that cough?"
> "Ugh! Ugh! Ugh! — Ugh! Ugh! Ugh! — Ugh! Ugh! Ugh! —
> Ugh! Ugh! Ugh! — Ugh! Ugh! Ugh!"
> My poor friend found it impossible to reply for many minutes.

To illustrate this point, two more examples are taken from two famous Chinese novels. One is *The True Story of Ah Q* by Lu Xun, and another is *Midnight* by Mao Dun. The effects produced by the echoic words are self-evident.

> 1. "我總要告一狀，看你抓進縣裡去殺頭 — 滿門抄斬 — <u>嚓</u>！<u>嚓</u>！"
> 2. 一<u>些</u>首飾和銀錢<u>豁拉拉</u>的掉在樓板上了。

As a universal linguistic phenomenon, echoic words in different languages, say, English and Chinese, have a lot in common. For instance, some imitative words in English and Chinese are very similar in pronunciation. The sound made by a cat is *mew, miaow,* or *meow* in English, and 咪咪/mimi/ or 喵喵/miao/ in Chinese; *dingdong* is an English word echoing the sound of metal, and its Chinese equivalent is 叮噹/ding dang/; *hem and haw* is used in English to express uncertainty whether to do something or not, and its Chinese counterpart is 哼兒哈兒/henger haer/. But in most cases, English and Chinese echoic words each have their own characteristics, or pronunciations. A dog *barks, yaps* or *bowwows* in English while it makes the sound of 汪汪/wang wang/ in Chinese; the singing of a cock is *cock-a-doodle-do* in English and 喔喔/wu wu / in Chinese. Another difference is revealed in the following examples. The sound of a gun is *crack*, *bang*, etc. in English and 叭、辟啪、砰 etc. in Chinese. But *crack* can also be used to describe a loud long explosive sound as in *a crack of thunder* or a sudden sharp noise as of something breaking as in *the crack of whip* and so on. Likewise, 叭 and 辟啪 are also used to imitate the sounds of something breaking and applause respectively in Chinese. From this we can see that 叭、辟啦 and *crack* are equivalents in a certain aspect only; they are, in other words, not complete equivalents. Most echoic words in the two languages are of this kind. In addition, English and Chinese echoic words have different grammatical functions. As is often the case, an English echoic word is used as a verb or a noun, functioning as the predicate, subject or object of a sentence while a Chinese imitative word is usually adjectival, functioning as the attribute, adverbial or predicate of a sentence.

Since onomatopoeia is an important part of every language and a useful rhetorical device favoured by literary men, a translator cannot afford to ignore this language phenomenon. He needs to ascertain the similarities and differences of the echoic words in both the source language and target language, and attempt to deal with them properly in the translated text. This article discusses the translation of onomatopoeia both ways, viz, from English to Chinese and vice versa.

The Translation of Onomatopoeia — English to Chinese

Generally speaking, the techniques of translating English echoic words into Chinese can be summarized as follows:

(1) If an echoic word appears in the original text, try to find its equivalent in Chinese and translate accordingly.

    (a) Like interjections, an English imitative word is often used as an independent element, having no grammatical relationship with any part of the sentence. The same is true of Chinese echoic words. Such being the case, the only thing a translator ought to do is to turn the echoic word in the original text into a corresponding one with the same grammatical function in English. Take the following:

        (i) Two heavy guns went off in the woods — BRUMP! BRUMP!

兩門重炮在森林裡開始發射了 —— 轟隆！轟隆！

(ii) *Whee-ee-ee! Whee-ee-ee!* The police whistles shrilled suddenly.

"的！的！"突然警笛響了。

(iii) *Thump*! A table was overturned!

"嘩啦！"桌子推翻了。

(b) While most English echoic words are used either as verbs or nouns or verbal or nominal derivatives, the majority of Chinese imitative words function as verb or noun modifiers. Therefore, as a rule, echoic words in an English text are put into verb or noun modifiers in Chinese. Examples are:

(i) But as the door *banged*, she seemed to come to life again.

可是當門砰地關上的時候，她好像又清醒過來了。

(ii) All was quiet and still except for the distant *tinkling* of a piano.

除了遠處一架鋼琴的叮噹叮噹聲外，萬籟俱寂。

(iii) "What's happening?" he *muttered*.

"怎麼回事呀？"他喃喃地問。

(iv) They heard the *twitter* of birds among the bushes.

他們聽到樹叢發出的喊喊喳喳聲。

(c) As is stated above, a certain echoic word in one language may be used to describe the sounds of several different things. In other words, this echoic word has several equivalents in another language. It is the same the other way round. For instance, *rumble* in English can be the sound of thunder or trucks or the stomach. But in Chinese, the sound of thunder is 隆隆/long long/, that of trucks 軲轆軲轆/gulu gulu/, and that of the stomach 咕咕/ gugu/. Consequently, in translating words of this kind, a translator has to take the whole text or context into consideration and try to find its true equivalent or the echoic word in the receptor language. For instance:

(i) Thunder *rumbled* in the distance.

遠處雷聲隆隆。

(ii) The cart *rumbled* past.

大車軲轆軲轆地駛過。

(iii) His stomach *rumbled* emptily.

他的肚子餓得咕咕作響。

(2) An echoic word in the source language may be done into a non-echoic word in the receptor language.

  (a) To be sure, echoic words can make a sentence vivid and descriptive, but not every echoic word in English should or must be mechanically rendered into a echoic word in Chinese. As we all know, there is a limit to the use of imitative words either in composition or in translation. If overused, they may seem frivolous and superfluous, and weaken instead of enhancing the effectiveness of the writing. Therefore, the translator should deal with them in a flexible way, trying to avoid a mechanical reproduction of these echoic words by replacing them with non-echoic words in Chinese. Here are some cases in point.

    (i) I *clanked* the kettle.
    我<u>敲</u>水壺。

    (ii) The train *puffed* towards Tokyo from Sendai.
    火車從仙臺<u>開</u>向東京。

    (iii) He *slammed* his tea cup down on the table.
    他把茶杯往桌上一<u>頓</u>。

  (b) In English, specific echoic words may be used to describe the normal functioning of nonliving things. But this is not the case in modern Chinese. More general terms like ……聲 or ……響 are used instead. For instance:

    (i) They heard the machines *whirr*.
    他們聽到了機器<u>聲</u>。

    (ii) The train whistle *tooted*.
    火車汽笛<u>響</u>了。

    (iii) The underground train was *humming*.
    地鐵在<u>響</u>。

  (c) English echoic words are often used to imitate the sounds of animals. The same is true of ancient Chinese. In ancient Chinese, there are 狗吠、狼嗥、鶴唳、鵲噪、馬嘶、虎嘯、獅吼、鳥囀、雞啼、蟬噪、猿嘯 etc. But in modern Chinese, especially in colloquial Chinese, these specific echoic words to describe the sounds of animals are no longer commonly used. Instead, more general terms like ……叫 or ……鳴 are used. Take the following:

- (i) The frogs in the fields outside the town were *croaking* cheerfully.

    青蛙在城郊田野裡起勁地叫著。

- (ii) The cock in the yard *crowed* its first round.

    院子裡的雄雞已經叫頭遍了。

- (iii) The moment he rushed in, the hens *clucked* and the dogs *barked*.

    他一進門，雞也叫，狗也咬。

(3) Non-echoic words in English may be turned into echoic words in Chinese to add force to the text.

- (i) The stone *fell* on his head.

    石頭叭嗒落在他的頭上。

- (ii) The child *fell* into the water.

    小孩撲通落到水中去了。

- (iii) The kids are crying loudly.

    孩子們在哇哇大哭。

The Translation of Onomatopoeia — Chinese to English

In the previous section, we have discussed how to translate English echoic words into Chinese. Since the same problem arises when it comes to the translation from Chinese to English, this section is devoted wholly to the discussion of how to translate Chinese echoic words into English. And the following methods may prove to be a helpful guide.

(1) Try to keep to the original parts of speech and grammatical function of the echoic word in the translated text if possible.

- (a) An independent element is turned into an independent element.

    - (i) 拍！—— 一聲響，那枝象牙鴉片煙槍斷成兩段。

        Crack! ... the long ivory opium-pipe broke in two.

    - (ii) 轟 - 轟 - 轟轟 —— 巨大的爆炸聲從山後滾滾而來。

        "*Boom ... boom ... boom-boom ...*" The thunderous sound rolled in from the other side of the mountains.

    - (iii) 嗚！嗚、嗚、嗚；……汽笛叫聲突然從那邊遠遠的河身的彎曲地方傳來了。

        Toot! Toot-toot-toot ... Far up the bend in the canal a boat whistle broke the silence.

(iv) 哈哈哈，這不要緊！

Ha! Ha! Ha! What does it matter?

(b) A verb is turned into a verb.

(i) 一個蚊子哼哼哼。

兩個蒼蠅嗡嗡嗡。

A mosquito *hums and hums.*

Two flies *drone and drone.*

(ii) 秋風颯颯。

The autumn wind is *soughing* in the trees.

(iii) 車轔轔，馬蕭蕭。

Chariots *rumble and roll*;

Horses *whinny and neigh.*

(c) An attribute is turned into an attribute.

(i) 杯筷陳設在各人面前，暖鍋裡發出嗞嗞有味的聲響。

Wine-cups and chopsticks were laid out, and a delicious *sizzling* sound came from the chafing dish.

(ii) 一陣噼噼啪啪鞭炮聲，在官渠岸的小巷裡爆發了。

An explosion of firecrackers erupted in a lane in Guan Creek Hamlet.

(iii) 吱吱嚛叫的獨輪車，三輪大車，載運著米糧、被服和彈藥。

Squeaking one-wheeled barrows and three wheeled ox-carts were transporting rice, uniforms and ammunition, …

(2) Change the parts of speech and grammatical function of an echoic word in the translated text when necessary.

(a) An independent element is turned into a subject, an object or predicate.

(i) 登！登！登！一陣樓板響，匪徒們上樓了。

Then followed a loud *Clump! Clump!* as the bandits rushed up the stairs.

(ii) 一片叫罵聲突然起來，又突然沒有，突然變成了人肉和竹木的擊衝，拍剌！拍剌！

A din of shouting and cursing suddenly broke out, then stopped abruptly, only to be replaced by the *swish* and *thud* of bamboo and wood on human flesh …

(iii) 撥拉！撥拉！黃浦的水怒吼著。甲板上那幾位半酒醉的老闆們都仰起了臉哈哈大笑。

> The waters of the Whampoa *splashed and gurgled* around the laughing, wine-flushed party on deck.

In example (i), the independent element 登！登！登！ is changed into the subject of the translated sentence. In example (ii), the independent element 拍剌！拍剌！ is turned into *swish* and *thud* functioning as the object of the preposition *by*. And in example (iii), the independent elements 撥拉！撥拉！ are put into *splashed* and *gurgled* acting as the predicate.

    (b) An adverbial is turned into a predicate.

        (i) "沒有水了"，他喃喃地說道。

            "No water left." He *muttered*.

        (ii) 一輛騾車軲轆軲轆地走過高低不平的車道。

            A mule-drawn cart *rumbled down* the rough street.

        (iii) 正中的門呀地開了一半。

            The centre door *creaks* half-open.

    (c) An attribute is changed into a predicate or an object.

        (i) 隔壁牢房的鐵鎖響了一聲，接著，傳來推開鐵門的嘩啦啦的巨響。

            A lock rattled and there was a loud *clank* as the door of the next cell was flung open.

        (ii) 河邊一棵歪斜要倒的樹上，有兩隻不知名的灰色羽毛的鳥，不住地朝著他叫著"咯咯呀呀"的難聽的聲音。

            On a leaning, collapsing tree on the riverbank there was a pair of birds whose names he did not know, with grey plumage, keeping up a continual harsh *chatter* at him.

        (iii) 嘩啦啦一聲巨響，一棵大樹倒了下來。

            A large tree toppled to the ground with a mighty *crash*.

    (d) A complement is turned into a predicate or the object of a preposition.

        (i) 北風吹得呼呼的。

            A north wind is *whistling*.

        (ii) 碟子碗子碰得叮叮噹噹的。

            The dishes and bowls slid together with a *clatter*.

(3) The echoic words in Chinese are turned into non-echoic words in English.

    (a) The echoic word functioning as a modifier in the original text may be turned into a non-echoic word.

(i) 早春的清晨，湯河上的莊稼還沒有醒以前，因為終南山裡普遍開始解凍，可以聽見湯河漲水的嗚嗚聲。

Early one spring morning before the peasants living along the Tang Stream wakened from their slumbers, the *sound* of the rising waters became audible: the ice and snow on Mount Zhongnan were beginning to thaw.

(ii) 在咯嚓咯嚓的鍘刀聲中，聽到了死難者英勇的呼聲："共產黨萬歲！鄉親們……報仇"

Even as the chaff cutter *did its grisly work*, the last shouts of the victims rang out: "Long Live the Communist Party … folks … revenge …"

(b) The echoic word functioning as an adverbial in the original text may be done into a non-echoic word.

(i) 她見江華嘆哧笑了，自己也忍不住地笑起來。

Jiang Hua *laughed* at that, and she could not help joining in.

(ii) 歐陽海繫好了保險繩，帶著一股火往上攀。剛爬了四五米，一腳沒踩穩，哧溜一下滑了下來。

Hai tied himself to the safety rope and started to climb rapidly. About five meters up, his foot slipped and he *fell*.

(c) The echoic word functioning as the predicate or an independent element in the original text may be rendered into a non-echoic word.

(i) 我聞琵琶已嘆息，又聞此語重唧唧。

I had sighed when I first heard the lute, and now I heard her story, which made me *lament*.

(ii) 他的話剛完，砰、砰、砰，連著三聲清脆的槍聲劃過寂靜的夜空 —— 這是發現敵人的信號。

Barely had he finished when three shots *rang out* sharp and clear —— the signal that an enemy had been sighted.

(4) Echoic words may be used in the translated text even if no echoic words appear in the original.

(i) 覺來盼前庭，一鳥花間鳴。

When I awoke and looked around me,
I saw a bird *chirping* among the flowers.

(ii) 二十五年以後的一個春天，從關東開進一趟列車，直向保定駛來。

One spring day, twenty-five years later, a train *puffed* towards Baoding from the northeast.

(iii) 木硪一排一排地<u>砸</u>在土裡……

Team by team the wooden rammers *thud* into the earth …

(5) Coinages

Sometimes some Chinese echoic words cannot find their equivalents in English. Apart from the above-mentioned techniques, a new method may be used by the translator, that is, creating new echoic words.

(i) 他們用個斧頭來頂替小錘 —— 所以打鐵的響聲不是"<u>叮噹叮噹</u>"而是"<u>踢通踢通</u>"。

Not having a hammer, they used an axe — which was what caused the *titung-titung* sound instead of the usual *ding-dong*.

(ii) 這樣，他的"<u>汪、汪、斯、斯</u>"的聲音，在牛聽起來，成了溫和可愛的熟人的招呼，自然樂於順從了。

And so his *"wang, wang, si, si"* sounded to the bull like the greetings of a gentle, lovable, and familiar friend, to which it naturally yielded happily.

We have dealt with some questions of how to translate echoic words both from English to Chinese and from Chinese to English. But our solutions are by no means conclusive. A responsible translator should use his own head, take the whole text into consideration, and by making a concrete analysis of concrete conditions, produce the best version.

OVERTRANSLATION

Overtranslation

Alan McConnell Duff
Member
Slovenian Translators Association, Slovenia

Introductory Note

The aim of this article is to illustrate the commonest forms of overtranslation through representative examples drawn from a variety of sources and source languages. In all instances, the target language is English. The source language of each example is indicated in brackets, but the original texts are given only where necessary for clarification.

Finally, it should be pointed out that here we are concerned with overtranslation as a general issue, not as a question specific to any one language.

For the sake of brevity, comments are given mainly in note form.

General

The term *overtranslation* can be broadly taken to mean: the use of more words in the target language than are needed to convey the sense of the source language. Or, the use of words and expressions in the target language which are too strong for the context, i.e. overtranslation of register.

Before turning to specific examples, let us briefly consider some of the main causes of overtranslation.

Defective Source Language Text

The original text may be badly written, loosely worded, ambiguous, repetitive, or inconsistent in thought. These defects are likely to be magnified in translation: (Duff, 1981)

> The concept of basic education, in which keen interest is being shown in the different parts of the world, seems to provide possibilities likely to be particularly useful for the purpose of mass education. (Source language: French)

Literal or Word-for-word Translation

The translator automatically reproduces the word order and wording of the source language text. This often results in overstatement and blurring of the meaning:

> Our workers keep endeavouring to achieve best quality pharmaceutical medicaments, thus assuring references of adequate foreign quality control institutes. (Source language: Slovene)

Mixed Register

The translator may choose a register in the target language which is either too formal: (Duff, 1981)

> An entire street, the Rue du Midi, is devoted to those of you who thrive on philately. (Source language: French)

Or too colloquial:

> The nightspots here (in Tokyo) are open far into wee hours, drawing many night owls. (Source language: Japanese)

Or an awkward mixture of formal and informal:

> In addition to guests who stop over at Otocec only to grab a bite to eat, there are also those who decide to stay longer. Otocec offers a unique combination of a creative experience of nature and a direct link with the world. (Source language: Slovene)

Fixed Expressions

These include standard or formulaic expressions (e.g. *ways and means, aims and objectives,*) rhetorical or "empty" phrases, clichés, worn-out idioms and "dead" metaphors (*the fact of the matter is ..., at the end of the day, all being said and done,*) and routine sentence fillers (*in the context of, at the level of*).

In most languages, close equivalents exist for expressions such as these. Consequently they are often thoughtlessly used, and over-used.

Metaphorical and Idiomatic Language

Metaphors and idioms are notoriously difficult to translate, particularly when they are incorrectly used in the source language text. As here:

> The corruption of the balance of learning makes people into the puppets of their tools. (Source language: English)

Careless use of imagery in the source language becomes even more striking in translation. As here:

> Over the past decades in a number of Latin American countries, no class has been able to tap that reservoir and produce a stable articulation of its components. (Source language: Spanish)

The Untranslatable: "Culture-bound" Expressions

Most languages contain expressions for which no *adequate* dictionary equivalent exists in the target language. These may range from individual words to complete statements. They also include cultural and historical references, popular sayings, and idiomatic expressions. For instance:

> *banzai* (Japanese): "may you live a thousand thousand years"; *glasnost* and *perestroika* (Russian): "openness and restructuring".

This category also includes expressions which must either be adopted in their original source language form, or else explained in the target language. If the source language expression is not adopted into the target language, the translator is often obliged to overtranslate:

> In most central European countries, families celebrate not only birthdays but also *névnapjai* (i.e. name-days, each family member's name corresponds to one on the official calendar of saints).

In such cases, it is often preferable to retain the source language expression, with only a brief, rough translation in brackets.

Specific Examples

We shall now take a closer look at some of the points touched upon above. The divisions used are intended for ease of reference; they are not rigid categories, and there is considerable overlap between them. In certain examples, italics are used to indicate problem areas.

The Original Text

The quality of a translation depends directly upon the quality of the original (source language) text. If the original is vague and inconsistent, as in the example below, the translation will be little better: (Duff, 1981)

> This *tentative* definition, giving a *more precise idea* of what is involved in basic education or, *more accurately* in the basic cycle of education, was bound to be *somewhat general* in character, since the problem was posed in international terms. (Source language: English or French)

The meaning is not clear, mainly because the sentence is full of unnecessary qualifications: *tentative, more precise, somewhat general.* The translator must now decide whether to render the text word-for-word — and risk overtranslating — or else to reduce it to a simple statement: "This definition, though general, gives a more precise idea of what is involved in basic education."

The next example illustrates what happens when the translator opts for the word-for-word approach:

> Regardless of the *form and extent* to which shorter working hours are introduced, whether this *takes the form* of a five-day week or a shorter working day, *or occasional free Saturdays*, shorter working hours mean more free time *from work and in consequence longer rest from work*. (Source language: Polish)

Most of the words in italics are superfluous. The sentence could be reduced to:

> Regardless of how shorter working are introduced — by adopting a five-day week or by shortening the work day — the gain would be the same: more leisure time.

When the source language text contains a mixture of jargon and loose thinking, the translation becomes so diffuse as to be almost meaningless:

> The outmoded *phrase* about the country where the nuts come from (Brazil) has

been substituted by objective approaches to realities that were provincial and distant and *are now worldwide and importantly close to the life of everybody.* (Source language: Portuguese)

How can a *phrase* be *substituted by realities*? And what are these *objective approaches* that are *now worldwide*? We do not know, but we can be sure that the source language text was no clearer than the translation.

Over-writing is common not only in official publications but also in brochures and publicity material. This diffuseness, however, is not always evident to the reader of the original text, because the words are familiar and can be accepted at face value. It is in translation that the diffuseness emerges:

As trade fairs and exhibitions *have been for many years an integral part* of investments *made in the market,* we can say that *such a* planned policy has brought rich returns so far. *With well planned performances* we have achieved important business results, *accompanied by new experience acquired by every new manifestation, which constantly contributed to improve our presentation.* (Source language: Slovene)

If we cut away the excess fat — the unnecessary words — the passage could be trimmed down to:

Trade fairs and exhibitions have long been vital to our planned policy of market investment. This policy has brought rich returns: improved business results, fresh experience, and greater success in our presentations at trade fairs.

Although the re-wording might be questioned, the information given is now clearer and easier to absorb in English.

Literal or Word-for-word Translation

From the examples above, we can see how word-for-word translation may distort the sense of the original, even though the translator cannot be blamed for the weakness of the original text.

While native speakers of English may be able to avoid some of the pitfalls of literal translation, non-native speakers (translating *into* English) may understandably adopt the word-for-word approach as being safer. For instance:

The systemic quinolones can and must be used to make the treatment effective and short-lasting, with as short hospitalization as possible and with lowest costs possible. (Source language: Slovene)

This is acceptable, but the sentence could be "tightened":

The systemic quinolones can and must be used to ensure rapid, effective, low-cost treatment with minimal hospitalization time.

When the translator follows too closely not only the word order but also the choice of words (the tone) of the source language text, the translation is likely to sound even more pompous than the original:

Depuis dix ans, la RATP a lancé *une politique d' animation du métro, propice à la convivialité de quartier, faite* de rencontres et de surprises *au long des rues.*

For the last 10 years, the RATP has practised *a policy of encouraging activities* in the Metro *propitious to the emergence of this neighbourhood conviviality, composed of* encounters and surprises *down the length of the streets.* (Source language: French)

Here, source language influence is particularly marked. The translated sentence still sounds like French, not English. The translator has tried to overcome some of the difficulties — e.g., the lack of a suitable equivalent for *animation* — but the translation remains word-heavy.

Word Order

Although changes in word order do not necessarily reduce the length of the text, they do make it easier to read. If the word order of the source language text dominates the translation, the reader will be slowed down:

Epsamom has a good effect in spastic syndromes, especially in multiple sclerosis. Occurrence of effect is quick already after three days but is of short duration with some exceptions. (Source language: Serbian)

Change to:

... Already after three days occurrence of the effect is rapid but — with some exceptions — of short duration.

As a general rule, a sentence in English should not end on a weak note. This is why *with some exceptions* should come earlier in the sentence.

Two further examples:

Diving with apparatus is permitted in principle, except in some restricted zones where there are military installations (this includes skindiving.) (Source language: Croatian)

Change to: Diving with apparatus (this includes skindiving) ...

The rather tastelessly decorated building on the corner of the (Nevsky) Prospekt spoils the architectural harmony somewhat. (Source language: Russian)

Change to: ... somewhat spoils

Faulty word order may also lead to ambiguity:

In patients with high blood pressure the therapy with diuretics should be withdrawn for at least 2–3 days prior to treatment with ENAP, *if possible*, otherwise the risk of hypotension is increased. (Source language: Slovene)

The words *if possible* do not, in fact, refer to the drug (ENAP) but to the withdrawal of therapy. The word order should be: "the therapy with diuretics should, if possible, be withdrawn ..."

As will be seen from these examples, the overtranslation results not so much from the use of too many words as from misplaced emphasis.

Register

What may be plain speech in the source language may sound like jargon in translation. If it does, this is probably because the registers are not properly balanced, i.e. the target language rendering is too formal, or too colloquial. Two examples: (Duff, 1981)

The hotel offers guests the possibility of making use of special weight-losing cures; guests who *wish to avail themselves of this amenity* have a special menu. The *structure* of the food is varied and *tasty. The duration of the cure is programmed* for *a period of* 18 or 21 days. *The hotel directorate* guarantees that the guest *will depart with four kilograms less if he adheres to the cited programme.* (Source language: Croatian)

The register of the translation is far too formal for the context. This is particularly evident in the last two sentences, which could be reworded simply as:

The cures last for either 18 or 21 days, and we guarantee that you will lose at least 4 kilograms if you follow the programme.

By contrast, the register in the passage below is too informal:

Dear Sir,

We know that AF is well-known manufacturer of computer maintenance products. Our representative, Mrs M. L., contacted you at the CE-BIT fair in Hannover. *We've* tested some of the products *she'd* bought from you, and found them convenient for our market. (Source language: Slovene)

The use of the contracted form — *we've tested, she'd bought* — is too familiar in this context. So too is the abrupt opening: *We know that ...*

In both examples, the register dominates: in the first case it is too formal, in the second case too informal.

In literary translation, too, register is of great importance. We have space, however, for just one example. Compare these two translations of Turgenev's play "A Month in the Country":

a. DOCTOR: But shall we leave the riff-raff, bless 'em, and glance at our own affairs? Well?

   LIZAVETA: Well said the echo ...

   DOCTOR: Would you object to my enquiring why, when one puts to you a simple question, you raise and lower your eyes like a mechanical doll? ... We're neither of us chickens.

b. DOCTOR: Anyway forget 'em. Let's talk about ourselves, shall we?

   LIZAVETA: What did you want to talk about, Doctor?

   DOCTOR: Don't mind my saying so, but why must you be so coy, why suddenly lower your eyes like that? After all, we're not youngsters any more.

If we ask which of the two translations sounds more natural in English, the answer is surely the second. In the first, the Doctor speaks an odd mixture of formal, colloquial and idiomatic language: *would you object to ... the riff-raff, bless 'em, we're neither of us chickens.* In the second, his tone is consistent: *Let's talk about ourselves, Don't mind my saying so, We're not youngsters.* The comparison suggests that the first passage is overtranslated.

Fixed Expressions

Translation into English is often marred by fixed expressions or "empty" phrases transferred automatically from the source language. This "padding" makes the text longer and more difficult to understand. For instance:

> *In the framework of the efforts* to make known our traditional folk art, some illustrated albums have been published, *including the one produced here.* (Source language: Albanian)

This could be reworded as:

> This album is part of a series (of illustrated books) designed to make Albanian folk art better known.

Another "framework":

> *Within the framework of chamber music achievements* the Dubrovnik Chamber Orchestra deserves special attention. (Source language: Croatian)

This means little more than:

> The Dubrovnik Chamber Orchestra has established a well-deserved (international) reputation.

A final "framework":

> *The framework of educational channels must be flexible* and offer freedom of choice in terms of the pathway followed. (Source language: French)

Can a *framework of channels* possibly be *flexible*? And can this flexible framework offer freedom of choice *in terms of* the *pathway* followed? Or is this merely bureaucratic padding for a simple statement such as:

> The educational system must be flexible, offering learners freedom of choice in their studies.

In instances such as these, the overtranslation is clearly attributable to source language influence, or to defects in the original text. As a final example, to illustrate how easily the translator can be lured into overtranslating, consider the following:

> Mais la durée des travaux nécessaires pour adapter une ligne aux materiels sur pneumatiques se révélant trop longue *dans le cadre d'un métro en exploitation*, la RATP a mis à l'étude ...

> But the time necessary for adapting a line to pneumatic-tire trains proving to be too long *in the context of an operational metro*, the RATP undertook the study of ...

It is possible, in English, to say *in the context of* ..., but there are preferable solutions. For instance: But the time ... proved too long for a metro-system which had to be kept running (or, in operation), and so the RATP ...

To summarize: when fixed expressions in the source language are automatically transferred to the target language, there is always a risk of overtranslation.

Metaphorical and Idiomatic Language

The use of metaphor and idiom in literature is too vast a subject to be dealt with here. So, reluctantly, we must limit the discussion to non-literary texts.

Many images are common — in one form or another — to several languages. Of these, many are so familiar that they are generally accepted to be "worn-out" metaphors, or clichés. Nevertheless, they continue to be used. Typical examples would be: *the dawn of civilization, the path of progress, peak achievement, vital role, galloping inflation, the problem facing us,* etc. Likewise, individual words such as: *pearl, jewel, flower, fruit, zenith, dawn, focus, backbone, storm, lightning, flood, star, root, heart,* etc.

Such expressions can usually be translated directly, cliché for cliché. The results, however, are rarely satisfactory. Usually the translation — however faithful — appears to be an overtranslation:

> After it had been chosen among the eight most attractive islands of the world, Korcula *represents a pearl necklace* to all those who love the sea. (Source language: Croatian)

> Zagreb's surroundings are like *a beautiful pearl necklace* around it. (Source language: Croatian)

> Discover this beautiful part of north-eastern Slovenia *the pearl of unspoiled nature* and its friendly inhabitants. (Source language: Slovene)

An island cannot *represent* a "pearl necklace," and mountains and hills and unspoiled nature do not resemble *pearls*. In the source language, the image of the pearl is perhaps an acceptable cliché; in the target language it is not.

When several inconsistent images are used, as in the examples below, the translator has only two choices: to simplify the text, or to reproduce it faithfully.

> The mighty *silhouette* of J.S. Bach *closes* the epoch of the European Baroque style in music *without filling it completely.* (Source language: Polish)

Here we have only one image, that of the *silhouette*, but its effect is three times contradicted by the words *mighty, closes,* and *filling.*

The next example also refers to Bach:

> At the same time *zenith* and *beginning* of a prodigious culture, his work *make up the keystone* of our musical history. (Source language: French)

The images of *zenith* and *keystone* do not match well.

> If one attempts to go beyond the evident *links* existing between food production and nutrition, one has *to sieve through* the economic, social and religious *fields.* (Source language: French)

Again, the images of *links* and *sieving through fields* do not match.

In all the above examples, the images are inconsistent. The translator would therefore be justified in removing them, wholly or partly, from the text in order to avoid overtranslation.

"Culture-bound" Expressions

In all cultures and languages there are expressions which cannot be adequately translated, even with the help of a dictionary. Such expressions may require explanation or clarification, for instance:

— In this work, Kikuchi measured the interpersonal value of *Giri* to *Ninjyo* (obligation and sympathy, peculiar to Japanese) …
— *Brnik* (the airport near Ljubljana)
— *tabla* (Indian musical instrument)
— *baozi* (Chinese filled dumplings)

Brief explanations in brackets do not count as overtranslation, unless the information is unnecessary. Overtranslation does occur, however, when the source language expression is stretched in the target language, as in these extracts from a festival programme:

> Sobota 1.7: slavostna večerja, spoznavni večer
> Saturday, 1 July: festive dinner, *evening for the acquaintance of each other.* (Source language: Slovene)

English has no real equivalent for *spoznavni večer,* but in this context "get-together" would be adequate.

Nedelja 2.7: *kulturni program*, v katerem bodo sodelovala *kulturno-umetniška društva izseljencev, zdomcev*, in *zamejcev*.

Sunday, 2 July: *A cultural programme*, at which the *cultural artistic clubs of emigrants, guestworkers and minorities from abroad* will appear.

Although the words *cultural* and *programme* are acceptable in English, they would not normally be used in this context. *Guestworkers* is a legitimate loan-word from the German *Gastarbeiter*; but *minorities from abroad* is not clear — which minorities? (Slovene?).

Culture-bound expressions are notoriously difficult to translate, particularly when they relate to place-names, dates, rituals, traditions, and local customs and habits. If a suitable target language expression cannot be found, the best solution is often to retain the source language expression (e.g. 清明節) with a brief explanation in the target language ("Pure Brightness Festival": a day in spring for visiting family graves) when the expression first appears.

Terminology

A distinction must be made between fixed and changing terms, particularly in the language of law, medicine, economics, and computer science. In legal language, for instance, many terms are either fixed or relatively unchangeable. By contrast, in economics, finance, and information technology, new terms are constantly being introduced.

In translation, it is essential to know how much freedom may be taken in translating professional terms. In contractual law, for instance, little freedom is allowed. Fine distinctions need to be made between, e.g. *loss* or *damage*, *compensation* and *indemnity, liability* and *responsibility*. Repetitions and qualifications are frequent:

Any *claims or disputes* arising *out of or in connection with* this Agreement shall be submitted to arbitration in London. (Source language: English)

The Managers shall *indemnify* the Shipowners in respect of all *liabilities, damages, claims, expenses, costs* and other *losses* of whatsoever nature which may be *suffered or incurred* by the Shipowner. (Source language: English)

None of the words in italics could be omitted, even though (to the layman) the distinction between *costs* and *expenses* … *suffered* or *incurred* may seem slight. In addition, words which might seem unnecessary, such as *herein, thereto, thereof, stated, forthwith*, should not be omitted in translation.

> If you fail to satisfy the claim or to return the Acknowledgement *within the time stated*, or if you return the Acknowledgement *without stating therein* an intention to contest the proceedings, the Plaintiff may proceed with the action and judgement may be entered against you *forthwith without further notice*. (Source language: English/Chinese)

> 倘汝上述指定期限內對本聲訴不予清償或不將訴狀送達認收書交回或於交回訴狀送達認收書中未列明是否予以抗辯，則原告人得繼續進行其聲訴復可逕向法庭申請判汝敗訴而毋須再行通告。

It should not be assumed that because a Contract or Agreement contains "many words" it has necessarily been overtranslated. The same is true of medical texts, in which fine distinctions (*recuperation* and *recovery*) and necessary repetitions (of words such as *patient, dosage*) are also common.

In other subject-areas, more liberty may be allowed. (Newmark, 1990)

> Lexically, an economic text consists of ordinary language, descriptive economic language, and standard economic and institutional terms. As I see it, a translator is free to simplify or improve the ordinary or economic language, but the standard terms have where possible to be preserved in aspic (!), thus:

> L'indice des prix de gros qui comporte des décompositions par catégories de produits ...

> The wholesale price index, which is broken down in product categories ...

> Des revisions de cet indice doivent intervenir périodiquement ...

> The index has to be revised periodically ...

As Prof. Newmark well illustrates, a literal translation — *The revisions of this index have to made periodically* — would be an overtranslation.

Conclusion

If we say that a text is overtranslated, we are making a subjective judgement. In most cases, there is room for disagreement as to whether too many words have been used, or whether the register is too powerful for the context. In addition, we must consider not only the language but also the *reader*. Is the text aimed at the professional reader or the general public? This question has a direct bearing on the language of the translation. The professional reader may require clarifications which the "general" reader does not need:

> The French word *désir* is used indiscriminately to translate three quite distinct Freudian categories: *Wunsch, Begierde, Lust.*

Although our assessment of a translation may be subjective, there are also objective criteria which may apply. These include:

(1) *Economy*

Are too many words used?

> The hotels offers extreme comfort with suites, a restaurant, skiing instructors, *a service for the rental of equipment and all necessary skiing requisites.*

Reduce to: ... a ski-equipment hire service.

(2) *Accuracy/Clarity*

Is the meaning clear?

> Within the period of the duration of this Contract the contracting parties oblige themselves not to reveal any information entrusted to any third persons.

Ambiguity. Alter the word order to: ... undertake not to reveal confidential information to any third persons ...

(3) *Fluency*

Does the sentence have a natural flow? Is the word order acceptable?

> It is estimated that every year travel 300 million people, of whom 16 million from developed countries to underdeveloped ones, where the risks (of diarrhoea) are very high.

Reword as:

> It is estimated that 300 million people travel worldwide each year. Of these, 16 million move from developed to underdeveloped countries ...

(4) *Appropriacy*

Does the language suit the context?

> In London, in New York, in Mexico City as well as in Paris, the metro is

becoming the *indispensable navigational instrument* of the city dweller of the year 2000.

No. A metro train cannot be a navigational instrument. Change to: ... the metro will be indispensable (for the city-dweller of the year 2000).

(5) *Balance/Register*

Is the tone consistent? Is there a clash of registers?

> The architects had quite a lot of trouble with these columns before the desired optical effect was achieved. *The thing was* that, in spite of the raised pattern, the concrete rods could be seen through the glass.

There is a conflict here between the formal tone (*desired optical effect*) and the informal (*The thing was*). The formal tone is more suitable.

(6) *Idiomatic Consistency*

Do the idioms — or images — make sense in translation?

> Clarifying the problems will *equip the field* with the theoretical *foundations* it has so far lacked.

No. One cannot *equip* a *field* with *foundations*.

More might be added, but I trust that the list — as it stands — will serve as a useful point of reference.

I began by saying that the term *overtranslation* involves subjective judgement and, by implication, decisions which lie beyond the dictionary. This does not mean dispensing with the dictionary but rather relying upon it, and only then upon one's own judgement.

References

Duff, Alan. *The Third Language*. Oxford: Pergamon Press, 1981.
Newmark, Peter. "Paragraphs on Translation." *The Linguist*, Vol. 29, No. 1 (1990).

PHILOSOPHY

Translating Chinese Philosophy

Roger T. Ames
Department of Philosophy
University of Hawaii, Honolulu, U.S.A.

In reflecting on where we are in the translation of the Chinese tradition into Western languages, I want to begin from a blind that has impeded progress on this front from our first sustained encounters with China in the seventeenth century, and which continues to block our way in the present moment.

From the outset, and particularly over the last century, the classical Chinese corpus has been carefully studied by philologically trained translators with adequate, and sometimes exceptional, language skills. Philosophy as a discipline, however, has not entertained the Chinese tradition as "philosophy", and has made its contribution to the introduction of the Chinese tradition to the West only in fits and starts. As a consequence, the major problem confronted by the Western humanist in attempting to use the translated materials lies not as much in the syntax of the translated materials as in the lexicon which informs it — the semantic content of the core philosophical vocabulary is not well understood. Simply put, our existing formula of terms for translating the core philosophic vocabulary is freighted with a cosmology not its own, and thus perpetuates a pernicious cultural reductionism.

There is a circle. The twentieth century Western philosopher's ambivalent attitude toward the Chinese tradition and the reluctance of the discipline to legitimize it as an area of philosophical inquiry, is traceable to the translator's impoverishment of its lexicon. And the inadequacy of the lexicon is in important measure due to the marginalization of culture and history entailed in the positivist's program, which precluded professional philosophical interest in the Chinese tradition. The Chinese texts are neither interesting nor philosophically important when reduced to the cultural importances of our own tradition. Uncritical assumptions about "humanity" as a category and the fear in some quarters that too much difference leads to incommensurability, has disguised and obscured the radical degree of difference we owe the Chinese in observance of their distance from us as an exotic and radically different order of humankind. An alternative inventory of presuppositions has been at work in the growth and elaboration of Chinese civilization, and the failure on our part to excavate and acknowledge this difference in our translations has rendered the Chinese world view deceptively familiar. And when an alternative philosophic tradition is made familiar, and at the same time, is adjudicated on standards of rigor and clarity foreign to it, it can only be an inferior variation on a Western theme.

To *begin* translating Chinese philosophy into Western languages, we must recognize this problem of reductionism, and formulate a strategy for avoiding it. The purpose of this essay is modest: it is only to try to persuade sinologists that we do in fact have a problem.

The degree of this philosophic difference (and indifference) can be anticipated historically. The civilizations that share the Indo-European group of languages are certainly many and diverse, but by virtue of trade, war, population movements, and the imperceptible dissemination of ideas entailed by such contact, they have over past millennia developed a cultural family resemblance. The movement among these cognate Indo-European languages lulls us into a sense of shared conceptual ground that is illusory when addressing the more exotic traditions.

Philosophers such as Nietzsche and Heidegger return to the conceptual clusters of pre-Socratic Greek as a strategy for getting behind the dualistic metaphysics dominant in the received Platonic-Aristotelian-Christian tradition, and for recovering alternative philosophical possibilities. Both philosophers are persuaded that a particular world view is sedimented in the language of a culture and the systematic structure of its concepts, encouraging certain philosophical possibilities while discouraging others. As Nietzsche speculates,

The strange family resemblance of all Indian, Greek, and German philosophizing is explained easily enough. Where there is an affinity of languages, it
cannot fail, owing to the common philosophy of grammar — I mean, owing to
the unconscious domination and guidance by similar grammatical functions
— that everything is prepared at the outset for a similar development and
sequence of philosophical systems; just as the way seems barred against
certain other possibilities of world-interpretation. (Nietzsche, 1966)

In translating Chinese philosophy, we need to guard against universal-
izing assumptions prompted by what we as members of only one language
family, take to be the nature of language itself.

Other Western thinkers who have been self-conscious about side-
stepping the underlying dualistic tendencies of Western philosophy have
produced alternative linguistic strategies. Whitehead and Pierce invented
neologistic categories which could be defined in such a way as to skirt
traditional presuppositions. The phenomenologists proposed an explicit
methodology for precluding implicit metaphysical assumptions. The her-
meneuticists, in challenging "method" itself, have sought to expose "the
myth of the given."

The Chinese, having developed the technology to explore the world
earlier than the European powers, have been resolutely centripetal and
parochial — a "stay-at-home" culture. For them, the Great Wall has over
the millennia served as a man-made reiteration of mountain, desert and sea
to isolate their sub-continent — serving them as much as a cultural screen
as a physical barrier against foreign invasion.

The prominent French sinologist, Jacques Gernet, argues that when the
two civilizations of China and Europe, having developed almost entirely
independently of each other, first made contact in about 1600, the seeming
inaptitude of the Chinese for understanding Christianity and the philosophic
edifice that undergirded it was not simply an uneasy difference in the
encounter between disparate intellectual traditions, but a far more profound
difference in mental categories and modes of thought, and particularly, a
fundamental difference in the Chinese conception of human agency.
(Gernet, 1985) Much of what Christianity and Western philosophy had to
say to the Chinese was, for the Chinese, quite literally nonsense — given
their own philosophic commitments, they could not think it. And the Jesuits
interpreted this difference in ways of thinking quite specifically as ineptness
in reasoning, logic and dialectic. (Gernet, 1985)

The West fared little better in its opportunity to appreciate and to appropriate Chinese culture. In fact, it fared so badly that the very word "Chinese" in the English language has come to denote "confusion", "in-comprehensibility", "impenetrability" — a sense of order inaccessible to the Western mind. The degree of difference between our dominant sense of order and that prevalent in the Chinese world view has plagued our encounter with this antique culture from the start. With Eurocentric savants seeking corroboration for our own universal indices in the seventeenth century, we idealized China as a remarkable and "curious land" requiring the utmost scrutiny. (Mungello, 1985) The engine of the industrial revolution altered this image utterly. Europe and America, accelerating full speed into the nineteenth century under the banner of inevitable progress, lost all esteem for China. The earlier visions of an exotic Shangri-La plummeted from "Cathay" idealizations to the depths of disaffection for the inertia of what, in the comparison with our own industrial and commercial growth, was cast as a moribund, backward-looking and fundamentally stagnant culture.

To begin translating Chinese philosophy, then, we will, at the very least, have to recognize that we are dealing with a fundamentally different world view. As such, we will certainly require a vigilant hermeneutical sensitivity to stave off facile comparisons. And the more distant the lexicon of Chinese philosophy is from our own vocabulary and conceptions, the more likely it is that our own languages will have difficulty in accommodating our discussion of it. After all, each of the world's languages is "specialized" in saying particularly well those things necessary to address the unique features of its own natural and social conditions, and hence, the greater degree of difference among cultures, the greater degree of difference in translating among the languages that express them.

In our recent study, *Thinking Through Confucius*, David Hall and I elaborated a distinction between a logical and an aesthetic sense of order. This distinction has been useful in bringing into contrast certain features of the dominant Indo-European world view and Chinese alternative to it, and can be extended to focus important differences between dualistic and correlative modalities of thinking, and the kinds of "reasoning" that attends them. While some scholars will take exception to the necessary simplification entailed in making the broad characterizations which follow, I would argue that the only thing more dangerous than making cultural generalizations, is failing to make them.

To establish a working contrast, the gross lines of our own sense of order can be sketched in the following terms. Our own cultural experience, going back to ancient Greece, was to deny the reality of change, and to pursue the permanent *arche̅* behind the transitory. In Plato, this proclivity separated an immortal soul from the temporality of physical, sensual existence; it separated the universal and objective form of beauty and justice and all things good from their shadowy reflection in particular phenomena; it separated rational principle as an Archimedean point in the changing world of experience; it separated and elevated "scientific" knowledge (*theoria*) over practical and productive knowledge. With the melding of Greek philosophy and the Judeo-Christian tradition, the immortality of the soul was guaranteed, the universal principles of truth, beauty, and goodness came to reside in God-head, and a rational theology promised that an understanding of the world constructed by the light of reason was consistent with and a complement to that higher knowledge available through revelation and faith. In this tradition, just as God's punishment imposed on human beings for their initial sin was mortality and change, so His reward for obedience is permanence.

The signal and recurring feature of the "archic" sense of order which emerged to dominate the development of our philosophical and religious thought was the presumption that there is something permanent, perfect, objective and universal which, existing independent of the world of change, disciplines it and guarantees natural and moral order — an eternal realm of Platonic *eidos* or "ideas", the One True God of the Judeo-Christian universe, a transcendental strongbox of invariable principles or laws. Behind a seemingly random Nature are the unchanging natural laws that control it. Behind the changing and culturally variable moral standards are unchanging moral principles. Behind the ambiguity of both natural and moral order is an unalterable principle of reason that enables us to pursue clarity and intelligibility. The model of a single-ordered world in which the unchanging source of order stands independent of, sustains, and ultimately provides explanation for the sensible world, is a familiar if not often an unconscious assumption in our tradition.

The pervasiveness of this world view is easily demonstrated. Take, for example, the many different ways we organize and categorize historical data to explain our past. The many alternative periodizations we use to make historical distinctions — Christian, Marxist, Hegelian, or that of modern science — share one feature in common. They are teleological, presupposing some cosmic meaning and design. They assume some determinative beginning and a linear process whereby we achieve some inevitable end.

Our sense of order, then, tends to be cosmogonic, assuming an initial beginning and privileging the primal, unchanging principle that causes and explains that origin and everything that issues from it. There is implicit in this world view a primacy given to some transcendent principle: it is a top-down, disciplining order which can be discerned as unity and intelligibility, whether it exists external to us as Deity or internal to us as the hardwiring of our essential nature. It is a determinative "given" — a source of order independent of our own actions.

The ontological disparity between the transcendent source of order and the world that it orders — the assumption that what is permanent is more real than what changes — generates the familiar dualistic categories through which philosophical reflection has largely been pursued in our tradition: God/world, reality/appearance, knowledge/opinion, reason/experience, mind/body, cognitive/affective, form/matter, essence/accident, nature/nurture, and so on. In each of these paired distinctions, the former member owns a place of privilege and stands independent of the second, explaining the second member while not itself being explained by the second. The shadowy world of appearance is dependent on reality for its explanation, but appearances, far from explaining reality, distort and obfuscate it.

Hegel, himself committed to this familiar notion of a transcendent order, was typical of nineteenth century Western thinkers when in his *Philosophy of History* he said of China

> its distinguishing feature is that everything which belongs to Spirit — unconstrained morality, in practice and theory, Heart, inward Religion, Science and Art properly so called — is alien to it. (Hegel, 1956)

What would possess Hegel, unquestionably one of the greatest philosophers and intellectuals of our tradition, to revile China in such blunt and deprecatory terms? In his account of the Chinese world view, Hegel continues: (Hegel, 1956)

> Moral distinctions and requirements are expressed as Laws, but so that the subjective will is governed by these Laws as by an external force. Nothing subjective in the shape of disposition, Conscience, formal Freedom, is recognized. Justice is administered only on the basis of external morality, and Government exists only as the prerogative of compulsion.... Morality is in the

East likewise a subject of positive legislation, and although moral prescriptions (the *substance* of their Ethics) may be perfect, what should be internal subjective sentiment is made a matter of external arrangement.... While *we* obey, because what we are required to do is confirmed by an *internal* sanction, there the Law is regarded as inherently and absolutely valid without a sense of the want of this subjective confirmation.

This perception of China as a culture internally inert and hence externally animated, is hardly obsolete. In Paul Cohen's *Discovering History in China*, his basic argument is that although more subtly framed, this same perception is very much present in our recent generation of historians who describe China's halting emergence into the modern world as a reaction to the imposed Western challenge. (Cohen, 1984) Cohen takes critical exception to contemporary historians who would apply Western conceptual models such as "impact-response", "tradition-modernity", "undeveloped-imperialist", and so on, as "overarching intellectual constructs", unknowingly inflating our cultural importances to become what is most important for the Chinese experience. That is, Cohen's position is not to deny the relevance of Western pressures, which are real enough, but to call for a balanced assessment of this period which gives significance to the more exotic internal dynamics at work in China's changing dispositions.

How do we escape our own presuppositions, then, to discern and articulate the internal impetus that gives definition to both change and order in the traditional Chinese world view? Jacques Gernet, in comparing the two cultural experiences, observes: (Gernet, 1985)

According to Aristotle, it is normal for all things to be at rest, whereas for the Chinese, in contrast, universal dynamism is the primary assumption.

In describing the largely failed encounter between the Jesuit missionaries and the Chinese intellectuals, Gernet ascribes the mutual misunderstanding to this contrast between externally imposed order assumed in our tradition, and the Chinese assumption that order is immanent in and inseparable from a spontaneously changing world. It is for this reason that the Chinese had no need of a willful God-head:

Believing that the universe possesses within itself its own organizational principles and its own creative energy, the Chinese maintained something that was quite scandalous from the point of view of scholastic reason, namely that "matter" itself is intelligent — not, clearly enough, with a conscious and reflective intelligence as we usually conceive it, but with a spontaneous intelligence which makes it possible for the *yin* and the *yang* to come together and guides the infinite combinations of these two opposite sources of energy.

The Confucian assumption traditionally has been that personal, societal, political, and cosmic order are coterminous and mutually entailing, and further, from the human perspective, this order is emergent in the process of one's own self-cultivation and articulation.

Importantly, the Chinese world view is dominated by a "bottom-up" sense of order. Rather than beginning from some originative principle, it starts from a welter of disparate and competing details, and registers order as it emerges from their interrelationships. It is "anarchic" in the sense that it does not posit the existence of some independent *arché*, some pre-assigned design in explanation of natural order. As a tradition, it is not fundamentally metaphysical in the way so familiar to us from the classical Greeks, assuming as they did that the most basic questions and the highest knowledge is dependent upon a science of first principles. The traditional Chinese world view can in contrast be described as an aestheticism, concerned for the artful way in which particular details can be correlated efficaciously to produce the *ethos* or character of concrete historical events and cultural models. Order like a work of art begins with always unique details, from this's and that's, and emerges out of the way in which these details are juxtaposed and correlated. As such, the order is resolutely immanental — the striations in stone, the coloration that differentiates the various layers of earth, the symphony of the morning garden, the veins in the leaf of a plant, the wind piping through the orifices of the earth, the rituals and roles that constitute a communal grammar.

The Chinese sense of order is captured and represented by several images in the classical tradition. The term, "harmony" 和 , describes a situation in which the myriad of unique things correlate themselves in interdependent relationships such that each of these things, maintaining its own integrity, construes itself in such a manner as to enhance the other environing members of the complex while at the same time benefiting from their contributions.

The relative absence in the Chinese tradition of Western-style teleology has encouraged the perception among Western historians that the Chinese, with libraries of carefully recorded yet seemingly random detail, are inadequate chroniclers of their own past. From the perspective of our more rationalistic world view, the penalty paid for the absence of that underlying metaphysical infrastructure necessary to guarantee a single-ordered universe is the large measure of intelligibility and predictability assumed by Aristotle's *Metaphysics*. The compensation for this absence is a sense of the immediacy and wonder of change, and one's complicity in it — the motive for revering the *Book of Changes* as the ultimate defining statement of the tradition.

Order is not imposed from without, but is inherent in the process of existence itself, as are the rings of the tree trunk, the veins of the stone, the cadence of the ocean. "Causes" are not external to act upon an inert world, but internal to a dynamic process of change in which "that which causes" and "that which is caused" is not a legitimate distinction. If "reasoning" is the discovery of reasons or causes, how does it work in such a world? And how is it different from our own? It is essential we ask this question if only to rescue the Chinese tradition and its corpus from the inadvertent "rationalization" it has suffered from the first substantive contacts between our Western cultures and the Chinese world.

Having attempted to make explicit certain presuppositions distinguishing Western and Chinese cosmology, we can now turn to the project of translating Chinese philosophical texts and reflect on the consequences of having failed to acknowledge this difference. David Mungello in exploring the origins of European sinology contrasts the first Western translation of the opening lines of the *Zhongyong* 《中庸》, one of the Confucian *Four Books*, edited by the Jesuits Philippe Couplet *et al.* in their *Confucius Sinarum Philosophus* (1697), with his own rendering of the same passage. I want to take Mungello as my example here not because of weakness, but because of deserved strength. By current sinological standards, his work is beyond reproach. It is not the work of Mungello, but the current sinological standards, that I take as the object of my critique.

> *Philippe Couplet*:
> That which is placed into man by Heaven (*t'ien ming* 天命) is called the rational nature (*hsing* 性). Because this is fashioned by means of nature and imitates it, it is called a rule (*tao* 道) or is said to be in harmony with reason. Repetition to the point of diligently practising this rule (*hsiu tao* 修道) and one's own regulating of it is called education (*chiao* 教) or the learning of virtue.

> *David Mungello*:
> That which is mandated by Heaven is called one's inherent nature. Fulfilling

one's inherent nature is called the *Tao* (the way). Cultivating *Tao* is called philosophy/religion.

There is no question Mungello's translation attempts to avoid the rationalistic assumptions of the seventeenth century Jesuits, but I would suggest even Mungello's translation, while syntactically accurate and certainly representative among responsible contemporary English versions, is still burdened by a set of essentialistic presuppositions which are not only alien to the Chinese world view, but which distort it beyond recognition. What is the translator's responsibility to the reader? Mungello's translation is not wrong; it is misleading. In what he conveys to his reader, his translation is far closer to the Jesuits whom he critiques than to what the *Zhongyong* itself is trying to say.

Implicit in Mungello's language is a teleological conception of "human nature" which conjures forth in the mind of the non-specialist student of Chinese culture a potentiality/actuality distinction and the Judeo-Christian conception of soul. The tendency will certainly be to interpret 性 broadly as, quoting Donald Munro, "a 'given' that exists from birth" that "cannot be altered through human action." (Munro, 1979) Benjamin Schwartz, in his support for the conventional interpretation of 性 as "a 'heavenly endowed' or 'heavenly ordained' tendency, directionality, or potentiality of growth in the individual," is encouraged by what he perceives to be a "striking resemblance" between 性 and the Greek *phuo* (to grow) and the Latin *nascor* (to be born). (Schwartz, 1985) But it is precisely the absence of cosmogonic beginning in the classical Chinese conception of creativity that renders just such a seeming resemblance deceptive. By formulistically translating 人性 as "human nature", we will prompt in our readers what *we* generally mean in our tradition by "human nature" — the genetically given.

I have argued elsewhere that the prevailing interpretations of 性 have been inappropriately skewed in favor of what is continuous, general, and enduring about the human being at the expense of what is novel, particular and creatively achieved. (Ames, 1991) That is, the interpretative prejudice has stressed an historical "given" as opposed to what the human being makes of himself. A more adequate interpretation of 性 will necessarily reflect the appropriate distance between the familiar conception of human nature as a psychobiological starting point — an internalized, universal and objectifiable notion of human being — and 性 as an historically, culturally and socially emergent definition of person. For classical Confucianism, one's humanity is not decidedly precultural, but preeminently and distinctively a cultural construction. Said another way, 性 does not have primarily a labelling or reference function, but rather requires explanation culturologically as something defined and enacted in community. We can only redress this interpretative problem by highlighting the existential, historical and cultural aspects of 性 which have been undervalued in our standard reading of this concept.

In the translation of 天 as "Heaven," there is an implicit separation between transcendent Creator and creature. Again, the unsuspecting reader, in the absence of any caution, is encouraged to read capitalized "Heaven" as "God". How then, do we import the classical Chinese term, 天, into our vocabulary?

In reconstructing 天, I want to try to recover what has been lost in conventional translation. In studying the Chinese corpus, the translator consults dictionaries that encourage one to believe that many if not most of the characters such as 天 have "multiple" alternative meanings from which one, informed by the context, is required to select the most appropriate. This approach to the language, so familiar to the translator, signals precisely the problem I am most concerned about.

I would suggest that with the appearance of any given term in the text, with varying degree of emphasis, the full seamless range of meaning is introduced. And our project as interpreters and translators is to negotiate an understanding and rendering that is sensitive to both context and to this full undifferentiated range of meaning. 神, for example, does not sometimes mean "human spirituality" and sometimes "divinity". It always means both, and moreover, it is our business to try and understand philosophically how it can mean both. What are the implications of this particular range of meanings? In fact, it is this effort to reconstitute the several meanings as an integrated whole and to fathom how the character in question can carry what for us might well be a curious, often unexpected, and sometimes even incongruous combination of meanings that leads us most directly to a recognition of difference. The inseparability of "human spirituality" and "divinity" would suggest an alternative to transcendent, "independent" Deity is at work here, and would also suggest the possibility of theomorphism: the ascent of the human being to divine status.

In the *Shuowen* 《說文》 lexicon, 天 is defined paranomastically as 顚, "top of the head", "the highest". Etymologically, it is either explained as a "combined-meaning" 會意 character — "the one great" 一大 , or, from the oracle bones and bronzes, as a pictograph of an anthropomorphic deity.

The standard English translations for 天 are: (1) the material heavens, the firmament, the sky; (2) the weather; (3) a day; (4) Heaven, Providence, God, Nature; (5) husband; (6) indispensable. They contrast rather starkly with those provided by the Morohashi: (1) the sky; (2) 氣 ; (3) the movement and pattern of the heavens; (4) the sun; (5) the spiritual/divine 神 ; (6) nature, what is so-of-itself; (7) ruler 君 ; (8) father; (9) indispensable; (10) a period of time; (11) a day; (12) 陽 (as opposed to 陰); (13) one's lot; (14) one's entire process of growth 性 , one's person 身 ; (15) great.

On the basis of these sets of meanings, we can make several observations that reinstate aspects of 天 that tend to be concealed by the translation, "Heaven".

First, the association between 天 and the sky encourages proper notice of the profound temporality and historicity that attends this notion. 天 is inextricably linked to the processes of change. 天 further is a patterned sky. Deity is thus defined as the "day" and the "skies" under which culture accumulates rather than as some more disjunctive atemporal and aspatial "other".

Secondly, 天 as 氣 is psychophysical, making it a hylozoistic deity. 天 is neither pure spirit, nor a material firmament. Rather, it is a psychosomatic sea in which the processes of life are played out.

A third point is that 天 is both *what* our world is and *how* it is. It is both the cosmos itself and order of the cosmos; both creator and the field of creatures. There is no apparent distinction between the order itself, and what orders it. This is a characterization made familiar in related notions of the Daoist 道 and the Buddhist *dharma*. On this basis, then, 天 can be described as an immanental, emergent order negotiated out of the dispositioning of the particulars that are constitutive of it.

Fourthly, 天 is categorial — it is self-so-ing. While it might be argued that it is in some sense cosmological, it is definitely not cosmogonic. There is nothing antecedent to it; there is no beginning to it or end of it. There is no distinction between nature and its power of organization and generation.

Fifth, 天 is anthropomorphic, suggesting an intimate relationship with the ancestor euhemerization that grounds Chinese ancestor worship, and which is the ultimate source of the Shang dynasty's 帝 . There seems to be sufficient reason to assume that 天 is consistent with the claim of the anthropologists, Sarah Allan and Emily Ahern, that Chinese gods are dead people. (Allan, 1979; Ahern, 1981) It is not surprising, then, that the relationship between *mythos*, *logos* and *historia* is radically different from our tradition. Culturally significant human beings — persons such as Confucius — become 天 , and 天 is itself made determinate in their persons.

A sixth point is that 天 is not only culturally specific, but also geographic. The discovery of a new and sophisticated culture would anticipate the discovery of a 天 representative of that culture. One would expect other cultural traditions to have a 天 of their own.

Finally, 天 does not speak, but communicates effectively although not always clearly through oracles, through perturbations in the climate, and through alterations in the natural conditions of the human world. Given the interrelatedness and interdependency of the orders defining the Confucian world, what affects one affects all. A failure of order in the human world will automatically be reflected in the natural environment. Although 天 is not a "personal" deity responding to individual needs, as in the Christian world, it would seem that 天 functions almost automatically and impartially to maximize the possibilities of emergent harmony at all levels.

Mungello, in translating 道 as "the *Tao*" using a definite article and then capitalizing *tao* introduces a notion of univocal Truth which does not belong to the classical Chinese world view on which he is reporting.

道 is not to be "metaphysicalized" as some single, objective and universal truth which one satisfies in the shaping of one's character. The intelligible pattern that can be discerned from each different perspective in the world is 道 — a pathway which can in varying degrees be traced out to make one's place and its context coherent. Rather than a spatial form, it is the determinacy of a temporal flow inherent in the process of change. 道 is, at any given time, both *what* the world is, and *how* it is; *what* is ordered, and *how* it is ordered. In this tradition, there is no final distinction between some independent source of order, and what it orders. There is no determinative beginning. The world and its order at any particular time is self-causing, so-of-itself 自然 . For this reason, explanation does not lie in the discovery of some antecedent agency or the isolation and disclosure of relevant causes. Rather, any particular event or phenomenon can be understood by mapping out the conditions which collaborate to sponsor it. Importantly, these same conditions, once understood, can be manipulated to anticipate the next moment. It is for this reason Confucius would say that "it is the person who extends order in the world 道 , not order that extends the person." Truth, beauty and goodness are not "givens" — they are something done.

Mungello's translation of the *Zhongyong* passage, while foregrounding our philosophical importances, pays the unacceptable penalty of concealing precisely those meanings which are most essential to an appreciation of its differences. This penalty is unacceptable because it is surely the possibility of identifying and appropriating what is not already ours that motivates the translation in the first place. The irony is that we serve clarity in highlighting what makes sense in our own conceptual vocabulary only to bury the unfamiliar implications which in themselves are the most important justification for the translation. My concern, then, is that through the process of translation, we must identify and lift to the surface those peculiar features of Chinese philosophy that are in danger of receding in our reading and interpretation of the texts. A rendering which, although contesting our present lexicon and the kind of formulistic translation that it encourages, is more responsible to the underlying Confucian assumptions outlined above, might be: (Ames, 1991)

> The constitutive relationships between human beings and their world are what is meant by the nature and character of human life; according with and developing this character is called making one's way; and the shaping of one's way is called learning.

In this essay, I have attempted to recover some of those dimensions of the classical terms, 性 , 天 , and 道 that have been concealed by the conventional translations, "human nature", "Heaven", and the *Tao*, respectively. From this exercise, it becomes clear at least that a formulistic translation of these term puts at risk a great deal that is philosophically significant. Our choices of how to resolve this translation problem are several, and yet all seem inadequate. The easiest and most common move has led to our present predicament — we search our inventory of philosophical terms and select that equivalent recommended by our own experience. What has not been properly noticed is this approach often resolves ambiguity at the expense of equivocation and cultural chauvinism. A second option is to muddle through, attempting to do justice to as many of the different connotations as possible by providing novel terminological equivalents. This effort usually leads to clumsy neologisms. On the positive side, given the relative unfamiliarity of these new terms, they sound a warning that we have entered distant and exotic philosophical terrain. If we can rely upon our readers to exercise their imaginations, these neologisms might even bring some novel complex of meanings into relief. More likely, however, such attempts will impress our impatient readers only as mystifications. Finally, we may try to avoid begging the question by simply retaining the original language in the form of a transliterated symbol of the word or character in question as we do with 道 , 風水 , 氣 , and so on. Can we communicate classical Greek philosophy without the bare minimum of *logos*, *phusis*, *nous*, *nomos*, and so on?

While the resolution to the translation problem remains beyond the ambitions of this essay, my purpose has been served to the extent that I have alerted those who must read the Chinese tradition through even the most acclaimed and authoritative of the Western language sources to the very real limitations of this exercise. Until the translators are ready to abandon the current lexicon, and to recognize that, like it or not, we cannot avoid interpreting the Chinese tradition in our translation projects, any such reading in the Chinese corpus can only be an invitation to a tentative understanding. Only by devising strategies to self-consciously factor the basic differences recoverable from the philosophical presuppositions of the respective traditions into the work of translation can we begin to put the myth of "objectivity" behind us.

References

Ahern, Emily. *Chinese Rituals and Politics*. Cambridge: Cambridge University Press, 1981.

Allan, Sarah. "Shang Foundations of Modern Chinese Folk Religion." In *Legend, Lore and Religion in China*, edited by Sarah Allan and Alvin P. Cohen. San Francisco: Chinese Materials Center, 1979.

Ames, Roger, T. "The Mencian Conception of *Renxing*: Does It Mean 'Human Nature'?" In *Chinese Texts and Philosophical Contexts: Essays Dedicated to Angus C. Graham*, edited by Henry Posemont, Jr. La Salle: Open Court, 1991.

Cohen, Paul A. *Discovering History in China: American Historical Writing on the Recent Chinese Past*. New York: Columbia University Press, 1984.

Gernet, Jacques. *China and the Christian Impact*. Cambridge: Cambridge University Press, 1985.

Hegel, F. *Philosophy of History*, translated by J. Sibree. New York: Dover, 1956 reprint.

Mungello, D. E. *Curious Land: Jesuit Accommodation and the Origins of Sinology*. Honolulu: University of Hawaii Press, 1985.

Munro, Donald J., *Concept of Man in Contemporary China*. Ann Arbor: University of Michigan Press, 1979.

Nietzsche, Friedrich. *Beyond Good and Evil*, translated by Walter Kaufmann. New York: Vintage, 1966.

Schwartz, Benjamin. *The World of Thought in Ancient China*. Cambridge, Mass.: Harvard University Press, 1985.

POETRY

Factors of Poetic Translation

André Lefevere
Department of Germanic Languages
University of Texas at Austin, Texas, U.S.A.

Problems in the translation of poetry can be listed, not solved — that is to say not solved once and for all, in an abstract, eternally valid manner. The solution of the problems will always depend on individual translators in their interaction with their time, their literary/cultural tradition, the institutions that mediate that tradition and the power(s) underwriting these institutions. The only rules that can be given in the translation of poetry are the rules of language: obviously translators should know what they are doing; if they do not, they had better not translate. The real work of translation takes place on various levels beyond the linguistic level proper. Except for the occasional aside we shall therefore leave the locutionary aspect of language (understanding, grammaticality, all the things we worry about when we are actually learning a language) out of consideration here, and we shall concentrate instead not just on the illocutionary aspect of language (the level of register, mainly, diction, and style — all the things we worry about when we know a language and when we are able to say more or less anything we want in it, but we are not exactly sure how to,) but also on the other levels involved in the translation process, which are precisely the levels on which the main problems occur.

It would be a mistake to think, though, that the study of the translation of literature and, more particularly, poetry, consists merely of the production of actual translations combined with the production of "how to" books designed to help translators to produce better work. Nobody will dispute the fact that the production of more translations, especially from neglected and emergent literatures is a laudable, and even noble endeavour. Unless poetry produced in these literatures is translated into either English or Russian, it simply does not exist for the world at large. Yet it is increasingly harder to dispute the fact that the "how to" books are becoming increasingly predictable, operating either on a very abstract level marked at every turn by boxes, arrows, dotted lines, circles, and circles within circles, or on a very trivial "don't do this, do that" level. The kind of knowledge they provide is, ultimately, not very productive, if only because it is, again ultimately, neither the translator nor the critic/theorist who decides what a "good" translation of a poem is, but rather the people in the receiving culture (the culture/literature into which the poem is translated) who read poetry. As they change their mind, over the years, so changes the quality of the translation in question.

This aspect of the study of the translation of literature and poetry needs to be supplemented by the study of the part played by actual translations in the evolution of literatures and the cultures in which they are embedded: the translation of Buddhist texts, for instance, changed the face of China for ever, just as the translation of the Bible changed the face of Europe and the Americas for ever.

The level of the "process" in the study of translation — highly predictable, repetitive, and not very likely to shed light on central concerns in the life of a culture/literature — must therefore be supplemented by the study of the influence of the "product." This kind of study touches on problems like power, manipulation, domination, and resistance that can be said to touch the central concerns in the life of a culture/literature much more closely.

The two types of study can be linked in a productive interaction as soon as one abandons an essentially normative point of view, i.e. as soon as one abandons the attempt to prescribe solutions in favour of bringing the problems and their ramifications home to students and scholars of literature and culture. The problems in question can be reduced to four main categories. Those categories are, in descending hierarchical order: first, ideology (the world view behind the original); second, poetics (the idea of what literature is, or should be, that helped shape the original); third, universe of discourse (the collection of concepts — such as Taoism, objects — such as brushes for writing, geographical — such as specific incidents in the life of the

Buddha — a writer or generation of writers, such as the T'ang poets, can draw on); and fourth, language.

Every poet is born into a culture that exhibits these four categories, as is every translator. These categories are not fixed and eternal, even though they may appear so to those who are born into them, and whose life is shaped by them. A simple comparison between two translations of the first line of Wang Wei's short poem 鹿柴 will serve to illustrate this point. In 1919 W. J. B. Fletcher translated 空山不見人 as "So lone seem the hills; there is no one in sight there;" in 1978 Gary Snyder translated the same line as "Empty mountains:/no one to be seen." Obviously the original has not changed, but the poetics shaping the two translations most definitely has; and yet both Fletcher and Snyder were and are convinced that they were/are writing "poetry", and both were/are right, each within the framework of his time.

At first sight the problem appears to be that the categories do not overlap in different cultures, so that direct substitution of one item in a poem produced in literature A by an equivalent item in a poem produced in literature B is eminently impossible. That is perhaps most graphically obvious in the case of the fourth category, that of language, especially when one compares Chinese and English: the very writing testifies to it. The differences are no less marked on another linguistic level, that of morphology: Chinese uses no tenses, no plural, and almost no personal pronoun.

When Chinese poems and their English translations are juxtaposed it becomes immediately obvious that the other three categories mentioned above do not overlap either. Going back to the Wang Wei poem, we immediately see that the world view behind it is very different from the world view behind Fletcher's translation. The difference between the poetics has already been remarked on, and the difference in the universe of discourse is obvious in the invocation of the landscape.

But the problem is not just that the categories do not overlap; rather the real problem is that they must be made to overlap in the translator's person. Translators make these categories overlap, at least for a time, and at least in some more or less productive manner, by means of an activity that is not easy to describe and that will be referred to here by means of the concept of "frame".

It can be said that a culture "frames" another: culture A constructs an image of culture B. That image may be relatively true, or it may be far off the mark, but that matters, if at all, only to specialists. To the great majority of those who participate in culture A the image of culture B that has been constructed and propagated quite simply *is* culture B. Maybe the most obvious example of such a "cultural frame" in relatively recent memory was the construct of the "yellow peril" in the United States, conjuring up the image of vast hordes of evil-looking Chinese intent on destroying the American way of life and usurping all its blessings. The most obvious example of a Chinese way of "framing" another culture is so obvious that it has become part and parcel of the Chinese language itself: non-Chinese were/are often referred to quite simply as "foreign devils".

Cultures "frame" cultures, just as people "frame" people, and they probably do so in order to make life more manageable: a certain degree of prejudice or, if you like, image-manufacturing allows both cultures and individuals to reduce the complexities they have to face. Whether they are right or wrong in doing so, or even right or wrong in particular instances is not at issue here; the fact is that they do so, have done so for centuries, and will go on doing so.

And of course individuals — translators, to name but one group among them — frame cultures as well, their own and that of others, both of which they may accept or reject: individuals may belong to the "right" or the "left" of their own cultures, they may be xenophiles or xenophobes or, much more likely, all kinds of shades in between. Finally, translators frame works of literature, of the foreign literature, both against the background of their own culture and that of the frame of the foreign culture their own culture has constructed. They can frame the foreign work of literature in a way that confirms the frame their own culture has constructed of the foreign culture, or they can frame it in such a way that the frame of the foreign culture constructed by their own culture is undermined, to some extent. Translators can make foreign works of literature fit certain spaces their own culture/ literature has made available for them, or they can refuse these spaces and try to carve out different spaces which, they feel, can do more justice to the original.

Needless to say, all this framing is to a great extent dependent on a series of factors, some more social, and some more individual in nature. The final decision is always made by the individual, but it is not made by the individual in a cultural and historical vacuum. That individual is subject to the social constraint of a world view that can be enforced by the use of power, or even violence, but in most cases that world view is experienced as something like the individual's "natural environment" or socially sanctioned dominant cultural prejudice, if you prefer. It is mediated, not primarily by overt violence or repression, but mainly by institutions, such as education, the media, publishing houses, which are underwritten by dominant powers in the culture, but do by no means always show that power in a blatant manner. In the final analysis the individual can work with or against the dominant world view.

That world view, or socially sanctioned dominant cultural prejudice, which becomes an ideology by the very fact that it is socially sanctioned, is usually at the very root of any translation process: together with the socially sanctioned dominant literary prejudice, or poetics, it determines which texts will be selected for translation in a given socio-historical situation, which texts will be left untranslated, or even, as in the case of China, whether foreign texts will be translated at all. Once texts have been selected translators begin to devise strategies to produce a successful translation — but successful on whose terms? A translation can be highly successful in the translator's mind, and not be acknowledged at all by the audience. This can, of course, be the result of ignorance or lack of craftsmanship on the translator's part, but usually the reason is to be found on a deeper level: the translator wants to go against the cultural/literary grain. Translators who do so must be prepared for the criticism their work will inevitably call forth. In fact, they usually translate in this provocative manner in order to elicit criticism and its attendant notoriety. Translators who are successful on the audience's terms, on the other hand, tend to be so because they disturb their audience's frame as little as possible. Again, what I have sketched here are the two extremes of the scale; needless to say there are all kinds of gradations in between, just as there is the kind of translation of poetry that does not aim to function as poetry in the receiving literature, but rather as a kind of "crib", a help in reading the original, in practice almost a kind of dictionary or vocabulary constructed for one particular text. I want to exclude these kinds of translation of poetry from consideration here, but not altogether, since they are symptomatic of another factor that influences the construction of a cultural/literary frame.

The "crib" translation can look back on a very long and rich tradition in European culture. We should not forget that — as opposed to China — Europe used translation as one of the main tools in foreign language teaching, and for no less than twenty centuries. As a result, every literate European from Roman times to the beginning of the twentieth century grew up with the phenomenon of translation: it was a test, the test of his (very rarely her) knowledge of a foreign language. This institutional fact has left a profound imprint on all thinking about translation in the West: it is ultimately responsible for the normative terms (good/bad, faithful/free) in which translation has always been discussed, for the reduction of the study of translation to the first type mentioned above, and for the consequent relegation of the study of translation to the sidelines of cultural/literary studies, whereas its rightful place can easily be shown to be in the centre.

The "crib" translation always implied the cultural and literary superiority of the original, and as such reflected the relative prestige of the literature of the original and that of the translation, as they were perceived by the people who produced the "cribs". As such, the crib is indicative of the self-image of a culture/literature at a given time, and also of the relative importance that culture attaches to other cultures. Translators in Europe and the Americas have traditionally attached much more importance to the literatures of Classical Antiquity than to those of the Middle or Far East, whose cultural prestige, or ranking, was perceived to be much lower. If culture A sees culture B as inferior to itself, culture A is likely not to take too great an interest in culture B. If and when that is the case, culture A will be content with the current frame of culture B, and culture A will not go to any great length to revise or upgrade that frame. In fact culture B will, in that case, not proceed too far beyond the — to coin a phrase — "chinoiserie" stage: different, exotic perhaps, and therefore mildly interesting, but in the end not really important. In that state of cultural affairs translators will not be moved by any great incentive to try to revise their culture's frame of the other culture, which goes a long way toward explaining why W. J. B. Fletcher made Wang Wei's poem into a rhyming quatrain in 1919. After all, had the quatrain not worked wonders for another poet from the East, Omar Khayyam, not too long before that time? It is very important to stress, at this point, and hopefully once and for all, that neither Fletcher nor any of the other translators whose work will be adduced here to illustrate my own statements on the translation of poetry, did what they did to willfully and wistfully mislead the reader, or to undermine whatever impact Chinese literature might have had in the West. On the contrary: they acted with the best of intentions under the cultural and institutional constraints of their time. The first two lines of Fletcher's "The Form of the Deer" (perhaps not too far-fetched a title in a literature that had produced many a poem and prose work entitled "Portrait of a Lady") may, or may not, in hindsight, translate Wang Wei's

空山不見人，但聞人語響

"well." The fact is that , in 1919, "So lone seem the hills; there is no one in sight there. /But whence is the echo of the voices I hear?" (Weinberger, 1987:8) scan well, and rhyme with lines three and four. Therefore, they must be poetry, since the dominant poetics of 1919 held quite firmly still that poetry should rhyme and allow of scanning along certain metrical patterns. Whatever did not was not poetry. Translating Wang Wei into this kind of "non poetry" would have amounted to doing him a disservice. The audience, inclined to admit that "this chap Wang Wei" was capable of writing "nice" poems on the strength of Fletcher's translation, would most likely have been perturbed by anything else, and dismissed both the poem and the poet.

As soon as we learn to think beyond polar opposites ("well/badly" in this case) therefore, the study of translation begins to be capable of realizing its full potential: we see cultural and personal frames in operation, we are witness to an attempt at acculturation and the attendant manipulation that process necessarily entails, and we can also gauge the extent to which a certain ideology and a certain poetics had been interiorized by both the translator and his audience, in this case to the point where they had become transparent, utterly natural, and beyond all questioning. Three years later T. S. Eliot published "The Wasteland".

Chang Yin-nan and Lewis C. Walmsley give us a fascinating insight into both diction and frame in their translation of Wang Wei's last two lines, which they transpose to the beginning of the poem. The original reads: 返景入深林，復照青苔上 . The translation has: "Through the deep wood, the slanting sunlight/Casts motley patterns on the jade-green mosses" (Weinberger, 1987:16). Sunlight is almost supposed to "slant" in vaguely Arthurian "deep woods" ever since Tennyson's "Idylls of the King". The fact that the translation was published in 1958 but makes use of a diction that is more likely to be identified as belonging to 1910 or 1920 highlights another factor in the translation of poetry: once a respectable number of poems have been translated from the same literature (as was the case for Chinese poems by 1958), the receiving literature tends to construct another frame: the diction of the translation does not necessarily hold pace with the development of the diction of the poetry written in the original litera-ture. The result is often denigratorily referred to as "translationese". But again, translationese is at least as much the result of the construction of a literary/cultural frame as of any conscious decision on the part of translators, witness Soame Jenyns' 1944 translation of Wang Wei's third line as "The slanting sun at evening penetrates the deep woods" (Weinberger, 1987:12). On another level translationese is a not uneloquent tribute to the power of the institutions referred to above: it is not unlikely that translators belonging to the same generation have been exposed to roughly the same classics of their own poetry in school and at university, and that this kind of exposure to "the best" paradoxically tends to have a leveling, rather than an uplifting effect: the classic's unique formulation appears, for that very reason, destined to become the translator's convenient cliché through the unintentional intermediary of educational institutions.

The "motley patterns" of Chang Yin-nan and Lewis C. Walmsley's second line quite obviously belong to the realm of the "chinoiserie": a trifle quaint, perhaps, but not unpleasant. The most obvious, indeed transparent influence of the cultural frame appears of course in the use of the word "jade" to further qualify the "green mosses" in the same line. Of course the "jade" is nowhere in the original, but then again, the original is Chinese, after all, is it not, and China is full of that sort of thing. Needless to say this kind of transparent application of the cultural frame is also indicative of the relative ranking of Chinese culture/literature in the translators' minds. Kenneth Rexroth's translation of Wang Wei's first two lines show us the cultural frame from the opposite angle. Wang Wei's 空山不見人，但聞人 語響 becomes "Deep in the mountain wilderness/Where nobody ever comes/Only once in a great while/Something like the sound of a far off voice" (Weinberger, 1987:22). No downgrading of Chinese literature/ culture is implied; rather it is simply naturalized. The four lines of the original are expanded into eight lines in the translation, and the first four lines of the translation are not unlike the beginning, the setting of the stage for the longer, semi-narrative, semi-meditative poems so characteristic of Rexroth's own oeuvre. The Chinese original is enveloped not just in the contemporary literary frame of American culture, but also in the translator's own personal frame, and the latter may well help to account for the total absence of translationese in Rexroth's translation.

The Chinese cultural frame is in evidence again in William McNaughton's 1974 translation. The first line, an attempt to render Wang Wei's 空山不見人 , reads: "In empty mountains no one can be seen" (Weinberger, 1987:34). Of course the cultural frame itself has evolved over the decades: gone are the jade and the "chinoiseries". The China of the seventies, or rather, the T'ang China of the seventies is that of profound wisdom voiced in a few terse words and obviously wasted on those not attuned to it. The cultural frame is mainly responsible for the fact that the wisdom of the original could be taken for little more than a tautology in the translation.

If McNaughton's translation of 1974 represents a transparent use of the cultural frame from the outside, so to speak, H. C. Chang's 1977 translation represents an attempt to turn that cultural frame to positive use, an attempt to explain it from within. Chang's rendering of the first line: "Not the shadow on [sic] a man on the deserted hill" (Weinberger, 1987:40) makes it quite obvious to the Western reader that there is no one, absolutely no one around, and without resorting to tautology. Chang makes his first line so obvious because he wants the reader to be genuinely surprised at, confused by the "voices" in Wang Wei's second line: 但聞人語響 ; but Chang's "editing" of the first line of the original for the benefit of the Western reader may be too much of a good thing. Still, he is way beyond Fletcher. Fletcher's second line reads: "But whence is the echo of voices I hear?" (Weinberger, 1987:8). Needless to say, the "I" almost never appears in Chinese poetry, but it is the hallmark of Western lyrical poetry since the Romantics and beyond. The speaker of the original may not exactly be wandering "lonely as a cloud," but he ("I") simply has to be "bodily" present in the translation — in 1919 or, more precisely, in terms of the poetics Fletcher had interiorized well before 1919, but to such an extent that they quite obviously guided his hand in 1919.

Ten years later than Fletcher, Witter Bynner and Kiang Kang-hu translate the same line as "And yet I think I hear a voice" (Weinberger, 1987:10), oblivious of the fact that the cultural frame of China current in their time, which already allowed for the half-mad hermits cackling in forests and on mountains, is in total opposition to the ideology the original is based on. It would be hard to find a better example of an instance where the frame, the "image", becomes, usurps the "reality", with total impunity and probably, in the translators' minds, all in the service of a good cause.

The absence of any personal pronoun in the original makes G. W. Robinson's translation of Wang Wei's second line 但聞人語響 even more puzzling. He has: "We hear only voices echoed" (Weinberger, 1987:28). Suddenly the mad hermit has metamorphosed into a merry band of hermits, all presumably more or less mad. This is probably the farthest anyone can get away from the spirit of the original, or the ideology underlying that original. And yet that translation was duly published, and in a very influential series: the Penguin Classics, presumably still one of the more economical ways for any interested lay reader to first make Wang Wei's acquaintance. It is easy for the theorist to pontificate that the use of "we" in the second line makes for a "bad" translation. After he or she is done pontificating the translation not only remains in print, but it probably also remains the translation that is likely to reach the most readers. We are faced, and quite helplessly so, with another instance of the power of institutions, in this case publishing houses, to play a significant role in the dissemination of translations and, as such, in the potential impact of those translations.

Robinson's "we" is also symptomatic of another factor that is not without importance in the translation of poetry, and yet is often overlooked by zealous scholars determined to explain everything by reducing it to a few fixed categories. It is, after all, quite possible that Robinson's "we" may have been, if not a mistake (not quite on the same level as H. C. Chang's misprinted "shadow on [sic] a man" quoted above), at least a personal idiosyncrasy. It is not good to ever forget that it is always the individual translator who makes the final decision, and that the translator, like any other individual, is entitled to his or her own idiosyncrasies. They should be allowed to stand for what they are, and not necessarily always interpreted as symptoms or "traces" of something deeper and more meaningful. Let me also note in passing here that mistakes and idiosyncrasies tend to be conducive to more than a little self-righteous gleeful finger wagging within the context of the first, bipolar, "good/bad" paradigm of translation studies described above, and rightly, though limitedly so. They do not command too much attention within the context of the second paradigm designed to supplement the first. In terms of the second paradigm an isolated mistake is a mistake, and therefore relatively unimportant, even though it should be pointed out so as to avoid repetition; a string of "mistakes" or, if you prefer, a meaningful pattern of deviations, on the other hand, may well be part of a strategy and may, as such, be capable of being linked to something deeper and more meaningful, such as a cultural frame, an interiorized poetics, an indication of the relative standing of original and translated literatures in the translator's mind.

In terms of poetics pure and simple, I have already had occasion to remark on the fact that Fletcher's 1919 translation rhymes and is written to a certain meter, to which elegance is sacrificed in the obligatory last word of the first line: "So lone seem the hills; there is no one in sight *there*" (Weinberger, 1987:8). It is perhaps more surprising that James J. Y. Liu's 1962 translation does so as well. His second line "But human voices are heard to resound" (Wang Wei's 但聞人語響) rhymes with his fourth line: "And falls again upon the mossy ground" (Wang Wei's 復照青苔上). Liu's diction in his last line is definitely not that of 1962, and rhyme did not play a dominant part any more in the contemporary poetics of the receiving literature. Then why rhyme? Like many translators Liu makes use of an inverted cultural/literary frame to command respect for the original. Since most of the canonized poetry of the receiving literature rhymes, the reasoning goes, the mere fact that the translation rhymes in a time when originals no longer rhyme in the receiving literature will automatically draw attention to the canonized status of the original in its own literature.

Both the translation of poetry, then, and the study thereof, seem to be a matter of attempts by individuals to — under certain socio-cultural constraints — either find solutions to problems raised by the failure of such fundamental categories as ideology, poetics, universe of discourse, and language to overlap in different cultures, or to analyze the solutions found with a view to learning more about the processes of both acculturation, seen as the construction of an image of one culture to fit the needs of another, and the manipulation of images within a culture. Needless to say, both of these processes can be seen to influence much more than literature at the present time. Both the translation of poetry and the study of translated poetry are of vital importance for the comparative study of literatures and cultures. Much remains to be done in both fields and neither can be regulated — for long.

References

Weinberger, Eliot and Octavio Paz. *Nineteen Ways of Looking at Wang Wei*. Mt. Kisco, New York: Moyer Bell Limited, 1987.

W. J. B. Fletcher's translation is to be found on p. 8 in Weinberger and Paz, Gary Snyder's translation on p. 42, and Wang Wei's original on p. 2.

Chinese Classical Poetry

John Cayley
Wellsweep Press, London, U.K.

The Translation of Classical Chinese Poetry

Incontestably, the translation of classical Chinese poetry into English has given us a body of work which is culturally distinct from the poetry of its host language but which has immediate appeal, and is often read with intense pleasure, and a deep awareness of its moral and artistic significance. Quite apart from this, for the reader and writer of English, the fascination of translation from classical Chinese poetry continues to be its perennial, uncanny tendency to uncover and set in high relief many of the problems and contested issues in the fields of historical and comparative poetics, criticism, and, of course, translation itself. There are reasons for this which relate in part to the intrinsic characteristics of the Chinese language and script, and the use of this unique, culturally specific medium for artistic and aesthetic purposes. There are also historical and accidental reasons for this stimulating tendency, and these are not without their elements of irony and paradox.

It is not that the study of Chinese poetry has resided comfortably at the centre of Western critical and theoretical focus. The field remains on the margins, under-subscribed and little studied, given its vast original corpus and the cultural significance of that corpus from the perspective of world literature. Neither — with the exception of a small number of contemporary scholars — has the field been dragged to the centre of wider critical attention by students and teachers of Chinese literature in the universities. If classical Chinese poetry has had an unexpected, disproportionate influence on English poetry and criticism — and it undoubtedly has — then this is primarily because of the serious, practical, but chiefly amateur interest of poets and other writers working in English. This can be demonstrated in two simple examples, one famous in literary history, one recent and telling from the realm of criticism. Ezra Pound, controversial giant of high modernism and notorious, often miscalculating, amateur of Chinese, was for T. S. Eliot "the inventor of Chinese poetry for our time". He remains so for the majority of readers and writers of English who share a serious interest in poetry and poetics. Much more recently, one of the best and most challenging critical surveys of translation from Chinese poetry was provided in a review essay by a poet and critic of *English* literature, J. H. Prynne.

A Little History

The early history of English translation of Chinese poetry has been outlined in a critical study by R. E. Teele (see references). Lyric material which filtered back to Europe for three centuries after renewed contact with China in the later sixteenth century was more or less randomly selected, and classic works found themselves jostling together with banal doggerel versions of popular rhymes. The *Book of Songs* or *Classic of Poetry* (long since variously translated in its entirety by James Legge, Arthur Waley, Ezra Pound and others) was transmitted to the West relatively early because of its close association with the Confucian canon (and hence with the proper education of the "true gentleperson"), but it was only in 1870 that J. F. Davis provided English men and women of letters with an intelligent initial assessment of Chinese lyricism (Poesos Sinicae Commentarii: The Poetry of the Chinese). However, Davis concentrated on the "golden age" of what proves to be one particular tradition of classical Chinese poetry — *shi* 詩 and especially *lüshi* 律詩 "regulated poetry" — which matured and flourished under the Tang dynasty (618–906). This vital and seductive period with its strict, formal lyricism has remained a focus for Western (and Chinese) interest and, although it provides an all but inexhaustible source of poetic material, it nonetheless represents one facet of a much larger and even more various whole, other aspects of which are still under-represented in translation. It was not until David Hawkes produced his splendid translation of the *Songs of the South* (Oxford, 1959) that English readers were made fully aware of freer, animistic poetic traditions from the south of China dating, in part, as far back as the *Classic of Poetry* itself. Translators still closer to our own time have opened up the new worlds of the Song dynasty (960–1279) *ci* 詞 ("song words" of variable length lines composed to a "tune"), Yuan dynasty (1260–1368) *sanqu* 散曲 (dramatic lyrics liberated from their original dramatic context), and much other later classic poetry of all types which was written long after the better-known "golden age". At the same time our access is being steadily increased to that poetry which pre-dates the Tang. Anne Birrell has translated a significant body of work from Han dynasty *yuefu* 樂府 poetry (literally, "music bureau" poetry — songs gathered by music bureau officials from the people and later providing a formal pattern for high literary exploitation), ancestor of the classic lyric as much in terms of shared themes as formal organization. She has also given us versions of everything contained in an influential early anthology of private or love poetry, the *Yutai Xinyong* 《玉台新詠》 whose poems date from the second century B.C. to the sixth century A.D. Meanwhile, David Knechtges' continuing project to translate the most famous Chinese anthology of pure literature, the *Wenxuan* 《文選》, in its entirety, has made available more examples of those long rhapsodic pieces, *fu* 賦 (sometimes translated "rhyme-prose"), which are entirely different from the brief, restrained lyrics of the Tang.

The Body of Available Work

Still, today, English readers have access to literary translations of classical Chinese poetry chiefly in the form of anthologies. These anthologies usually cover a vast chronological and cultural spread. It is within the confines of the anthology that academic understanding interacts with literary expertise. The more specialist books like some of those mentioned above, which extend our awareness of Chinese poetry beyond, for example, the Tang dynasty lyric, are mainly produced by trained scholars of Chinese, and their pure literary value as texts in English is secondary. The same is true of the increasing number of monographic works on individual poets, where a critical biographical approach is usually adopted, sometimes accompanied by selected or complete translations. In the existing anthologies, two complementary tendencies come together. On the one hand, the more academic writers apply themselves to literary values; while, in other cases, poets working in English engage those resources of Chinese poetry which have been made available to them. Both struggle to produce English versions which will thrive outside the academic glasshouse with greater or lesser degrees of success. As time goes on, and classical Chinese poetry in translation becomes more and more accepted into an ever more outward-looking English literature, we may expect to find literary values extend to the more specialist works, giving us the genre-, thematic and historically defined collections which we need, not to mention significant selections from the work of individual Chinese voices of real stature, who deserve to be examined with the degree of *distinction* which is accorded to their English compares.

In this world of anthologies, apart from the distinction between collections originated by poets and those originated by scholars of Chinese literature, there is also a distinction between the anthologies produced in the United Kingdom and those produced in the United States. Of the work produced in British English, there is, of course, one figure who stands head and shoulders above all other contributors, Arthur Waley. Waley was unique in being one of finest sinologists which England has ever produced, and also a man with a genuine and more or less original literary sensibility. He was well-connected with the then dominant literary intelligentsia of Bloomsbury in London and produced an important body of work in translation beginning with his *170 Chinese Poems* (1918). He was also the first English translator to give a voice to an individual Chinese poet. His personal empathy with Bai Juyi 白居易 (*The Life and Times of Po Chü-i*, 1936) is well-known, but he also produced the somewhat less sympathetic *Poetry and Career of Li Po* (1950). Li Bai and Du Fu may be the most famous Chinese poets, West or East, but — thanks to Waley — the general English reader has a better chance of hearing the individual voice of Bai Juyi, both man and poet, than any other.

Waley was goaded into producing his versions by the earlier publication of Ezra Pound's sinologically amateur adaptations. Accuracy and faithfulness was important to him as he reacted to Pound's inventions but he also had a literary programme. He applied a form of "sprung rhythm" (Gerald Manley Hopkins' counting of stressed beats in lines with a variable number of syllables) to Chinese verse, attempting to match stresses to the number of characters in the original line of Chinese. Thus Waley's translations make some formal demands. This and his careful diction mean that his versions are properly literary, much more so than the freer and less formal translation of other scholars of Chinese. On the other hand, his versions are rarely striking poetry, as can be seen if one of his most beautiful translations, of Li Yu's (937–978) "Immeasurable Pain", is compared with almost anything else which he produced:

Immeasurable pain!
My dreaming soul last night was king again.

As in past days
I wandered through the Palace of Delight,
And in my dream
Down grassy garden-ways
Glided my chariot, smoother than a summer stream;
There was moonlight,
The trees were blossoming,
And a faint wind softened the air of night,
For it was spring.

After Waley, anthologies of translations in "British English" are of less significance, particularly for their literary value. A number deserve honourable mention. Soame Jenyns produced some "Pre-Raphaelite" renditions of the *300 Poems of the T'ang Dynasty* (*Selections*, 1940 and *Further Selections*, 1944) in a style which has clearly dated. C. J. Ch'en and Michael Bullock (*Poems of Solitude*, 1960) and Richard F. S. Yang and Charles R. Metzger (*Fifty Songs from the Yuan*, 1967) are both examples of collaborative work involving one English poet which have led to very readable final versions and — particularly in the latter case — have both extended our knowledge of the range of Chinese lyricism and revealed much concerning the process of literary translation. Alan Ayling and Duncan Mackintosh produced two fine collections of later lyrics, chiefly Song dynasty *ci*, in unashamedly rhymed verse translations (*A Collection of Chinese Lyrics*, 1965, and *A Further Collection* ... , 1969). A. C. Graham's *Poems of the Late T'ang* (1965) and John Scott's *Love and Protest* (1972) are examples of what latter-day British sinologists have been able to do in terms of making a literary contribution related to their field, though neither comes anywhere near the influence of Waley. Neither, finally, does the small amount of published work by Arthur Cooper (*Li Po and Tu Fu*, 1973, and *The Deep Woods' Business: Uncollected Translations*, 1990), but Cooper's translations deserve a mention because, like Waley, they make formal demands even more closely related to the prosody of the original poetry (in Cooper's case syllable counting — with some further rules concerning the use of feminine or masculine rhythmic feet for line endings — mapped to that of the original line lengths), and achieve even better results in terms of the literary value of the final English version:

Among mountains
where birds fly no more
  Nor have the paths

any men's tracks now,
>   There's orphan boat
and old straw-hat man
>   Alone fishing
the cold river snow.

("River Snow", Liu Zongyuan, 773–819)

For more comprehensive anthologies with a wider range we must turn first to the work of American scholars. While he does not have quite the same literary authority and general appeal, Burton Watson can be seen as something of an American Waley. He has translated a similar or greater range of material; he has the same or greater depth of scholarship (including, like Waley, an active involvement in Japanese literary scholarship), and he has also been careful to try and make his translations more than just approachable for the general reader. Over the years he has produced a number of specialist works on various periods of Chinese poetry or on particular poets and recently he was the translator/editor of *The Columbia Book of Chinese Poetry: From Early Times to the Thirteenth Century* (1984). This anthology was shortly followed by a companion volume, *The Columbia Book of Later Chinese Poetry* (1986) translated and edited by Jonathan Chaves, a younger scholar seemingly very much in the mould of Watson with a similar scholarly record and a similar respect for the readability of his translations. This book has the further advantage of dealing with the neglected later period, so that for the first time the general reader has been able to see examples of the continuity of the tradition of classical Chinese poetry up to 1911.

However, in recent times a rival set of American anthologies have given us the most comprehensive over-view of Chinese poetic writing in English. *Sunflower Splendor* (1975) and *Waiting for the Unicorn* (1987) edited by Wu-chi Liu and Irving Yucheng Lo together cover a similar chronological span but a much larger range of material. They also differ in that they use a number of translators, mostly academic, and while this leads to uneven quality both in terms of accuracy and in terms of the literary worth of particular translations, it does give us a range of voices to hear and introduces some names which may prove important to the influence of Chinese writing on our own literature, amongst which that of Jerome P. Seaton stands out, especially for his versions of Guan Hanqing (c. 1220– c. 1300).

Amongst the American scholars Stephen Owen also deserves to be singled out both for his contribution to the corpus of translated poetry — in a number of collections with commentaries covering different periods — and also for his critical excursions which have done much to bring the appreciation of Chinese verse up to date in theoretical terms. His book *Remembrances* (1986), a piece of sophisticated and creative criticism, is particularly valuable in revealing certain characteristics of the "profundity" often recognized in Chinese poetic writing. Owen quite rightly locates the source of this richness in the Chinese writer and reader's "experience of the past" — in the backward-looking and allusive tendencies of Chinese culture. And so, paradoxically, while this may mean that the translation of a Chinese poem demands an all but impossible translation of its particular allusions and links to the Chinese experience of life and history, it also means that the process of translation or transmission — from past to present, or from "lived world" to the text — is especially appropriate to Chinese poetry, which shares precisely this project and concern (unlike the typical Western text which, as Owen points out, pretends to have absolute boundaries, aspiring to be "a world unto itself").

Finally, for our purposes, there is that strand of English translation from Chinese poetry which winds through the work of poets and writers whose major preoccupation has been their own literature. Before the advent of Ezra Pound and his "invention" of Chinese poetry there had been attempts to render Chinese verse into English metres. But this was of no interest to Pound, who, after all, claimed his central role in the effort to "break the pentameter". Chinese poetry became a crucial influence for him at precisely the moment that Pound was "making himself new" as a giant of Modernism and it is for this reason — because of this coincidence — that a particular interpretation of the Chinese poetic tradition has been disproportionately influential on the development of English poetic writing.

This influence has two fundamental aspects relating to the form and content of the lyric. Paradoxically, the translation or adaptation of what were originally highly structured lyrics seems to have allowed Pound and the writers following on from him (perhaps even including Waley in this respect) to free themselves from the formal constraints of their own poetic traditions. It is as if the atomization of the original poem in the notes and glosses they used to produce their versions allowed them to discover an essential poem underlying any formal structure which could be rendered in free verse as well as in any other form. However, in Pound's case at least, this is not to say that the adaptations produced are necessarily banal or lifeless, or merely prose. Whatever else one thinks of his *Cathay* poems, they are rich in rhythmic and linguistic figures. Formally, they are unmistakably poetry.

The content of this new English poetry was conveyed by the "image", usually a natural image or what Pound came to call an "ideogram" by which he meant a complex or gestalt of images. The image in this sense was not employed as a symbol, merely to stand for something else. At one and the same time the image represented itself, in a real experiential context, and served as the "objective correlative" of the poem's underlying tenor (a complex of emotions, an insight, a human drama, whatever).

Lack of formalism was certainly alien to classical Chinese poetry. Whether the Modernist conception of the "image" is true to the rhetorical principles of Chinese verse is still a matter for some debate. However, it is true that the imagery of Chinese poetry is typically naturalistic and self-consistent. It may represent idealized experiences, but we think of these experiences as natural and real. It is also true that in the best Chinese poetry this imagery leads beyond itself — "beyond the words" as the Chinese critical phrase has it — and attempts to convey those aspects of human experience which cannot be put into (ordinary) language, or which have not yet been, or which can only be conveyed through the words of the poem itself.

Apart from *Cathay*, Pound embedded a certain amount of Chinese poetic material in his monumental *Cantos* and made an extraordinary, complete verse translation of *The Classic Anthology as Defined by Confucius* (1954, *The Book of Songs*) in an frequently folksy style which is often appropriate to the original. Pound remained a controversial figure in literature (not to mention political history), and is still not fully accepted into the canon. Nonetheless he is recognized by the majority of practitioners, more especially on the western side of the Atlantic where his influence can be detected among those poets who took up the translation of classic Chinese seriously. Amy Lowell, depending heavily on the work of Florence Ayscough, was a rival "Imagist" whose versions are likely to date quickly. Witter Bynner working with Kiang Kang-hu produced a complete translation of the 300 Tang poems in *The Jade Mountain* (1929) which is one of better examples of a far more restrained Modernist poetic. More recently Kenneth Rexroth and Gary Snyder stand out as poets of some stature who have produced a significant number of translations and adaptations, admitting Chinese poetry as a formative influence on their original work.

The Chinese Language and the Translation of Classical Chinese Poetry

Poetry is *the* art of language, and the characteristics of the Chinese literary language and its script — so radically "other" in both fact and in fantasy — have provided another focus of interest for poets and translators working in English. The well-known myths — concerning absence of "grammar", the minimal use of apparently vital function words such as pronouns, the predominence of monosyllabic words, the pictographic or ideographic nature of the script — do have some basis in the history and actuality of the Chinese language. However, it is clear that the supposed critical implications of these myths — for example concision and purity of expression, the relative absence of the author's ego, the extra richness of imagery provided by the ideogram — have been greatly exaggerated or, as in the case of Pound's rendition of Ernest Fenellosa's critical speculations (*The Chinese Written Character as a Medium for Poetry*, 1936) have been all but willfully misunderstood in line with *English* literary programmes already well underway and ultimately requiring evaluation quite apart from their relationship to actual Chinese poetics.

The situation is confused by two considerations which are often forgotten when trying to do what Fenellosa attempted. Firstly, we need to remind ourselves that the medium of classical Chinese poetry is *literary* Chinese, that, although poetry is still written in classical forms, the language used bears a similar relationship to the various dialects of modern, spoken Chinese as does Latin to the modern Romance languages. In fact the situation is even more peculiar in that classical poems are most often read — internally or aloud — in modern pronunciations, although they are composed, structured and prosodically understood (and rhymed) according to pronunciations more or less fixed during the sixth to seventh century. The language of this poetry is both dead and living. We must take particular care over our speculations about "the Chinese language and poetry" in this context.

The second source of confusion is that produced by the relationship of a script to its language (not only, of course, in the case of Chinese). Particularly when the focus of attention is literature, there is a tendency to make too strong an identification of a script with its language, to the extent that we look at the script as if it *were* the language and not a graphic record of the language. This is not to say that the nature of the script is of no interest or that its characteristics cannot be exploited by the writers who use it, but we do need to remind ourselves that the expressive stategies and resources of a script — a "system of writing" — should not be identified with those of the language.

But is there anything in these intriguing myths? Taking each one, very briefly, in turn does highlight some of the perceived and real differences between Chinese poetry and our own, and so may help to show what an engaged translation might struggle to carry over into English.

Chinese is — like English but to an even greater extent — an "isolating" language, meaning that linguistic relationships between words tend not to alter the form of the words themselves. Instead, the job of indicating grammatical relationships is borne by special function words and by the order of words within the sentence. In the sense that grammar is not built in or tacked onto the bodies of words, grammar *is* "absent" in Chinese — or rather it is inaudible and invisible since the pronunciation and spelling of words is usually unchanged and the aural and graphical characteristics of function words are basically the same as those of the content-bearing words they link together. This emphatically does not mean that Chinese poetry is formless, unstructured or, as it were, "free" of "unpoetic" grammar. The grammatical stategies of Chinese are different and whether this difference has a recognizable rhetorical effect is very difficult to argue. However, it may allow the enhancement of, typically, metaphorical relationships between nearby words which are not syntactically linked in the strict sense. Certainly, the incorporation of "parallelism' into the formal rules of Chinese poetry (see below) must have been facilitated by these characteristics of the language.

More specifically, much is often made of the relative absence of pronouns in Chinese poetry, especially the (authorial) first person pronoun. But this *is* only a relative absence and is clearly a matter of choice for the poet. Chinese grammar — in most registers including the literary — encourages the elision of a pronoun where context makes the reference unnecessary, and many examples in poetry may be simply explained as good grammar reinforced by the need to express oneself in as few words as possible. The suggestion that the absence of pronouns allows the "universalization" of the poem's content is highly questionable. Poems in any language can make specific reference to persons or things and still transcend their particularity. "Universalization" of a theme depends more on the purposes and skills of the writer than on the linguistic resources at his or her disposal.

The predominance of monosyllabic words in literary Chinese is not a myth. Most free words in literary Chinese are of one syllable and are written with a single character. But the language has no fear of multi-syllable compounds and these are found throughout the literature. In the modern language free words written with more than one character are the norm for a variety of historical reasons. Once more the rhetorical significance of monosyllabism is difficult to assess, although it has had a clear and obvious effect on the rhythmic structures of Chinese poetry.

The question of the script has already come into our discussion. It "conceals" or makes impossible "grammar-as-spelling". It is the outward sign of a monosyllabic regime. But the picto- /ideographic origins of the script — apparent on the surface of the graphs still used today — have held a particular fascination for the non-Chinese reader. In fact, the iconic and symbolic elements of the script were already subordinate to a mature system of writing — meaning that the graphs pointed to "words-as-used-in-language" rather than objects or ideas outside it — in the earliest form of the script known to us, that on the oracle bones of the Shang period. In the oracle bone script many images are clearly recognizable, but many more are already stylized for graphic reasons. In all later forms of the script, stylization based on calligraphic requirements takes over, and in nearly all cases the eye must be trained to recognize the original images. The point here is that the iconic and symbolic material in the script is subordinated to its linguistic function.

Having apparently undermined the myth of the script, it remains to underline its unique and considerable contribution to the rhetorical strategies of Chinese poetry, a contribution which fully justifies the fascination of any interpreter, writer or critic. The fact that the basic, atomic units of the script correspond to "words" in literary Chinese renders them more concrete, individual representatives of the words they stand for than an assemblage of letters. Many poets think of words as living creatures with their own bodies, personalities, histories. In Chinese the "character" of the word is graphically present to both reader and writer, more so, arguably, than is the case with our kind of "spelling". In fact, of course, the words of all languages have images and metaphors — whole histories of usage — buried within them, images and metaphors which the poet often tries to highlight and reactivate. In Chinese the images are *graphically* closer to the surface, although no less subordinate to the common strictures of the language as used in any text, including a poem. Again, it is possible to argue that the nature of the script means that metaphor — in the general sense: the play of images and substitutions for underlying concepts — has a more prominent role in Chinese rhetoric, but this is difficult to argue in detail.

The nature of the script has also allowed the development of calligraphy as the highest — well above painting, for example — of the fine arts in China. The influence of calligraphy on the aesthetics, the presentation and even the composition of poetry is difficult to overestimate, and all but impossible to translate for a culture like our own where calligraphy is very much more of a craft. That a poet should also be a calligrapher, that the aesthetic principles of calligraphy could be applied to verse and that the presentation of a poem in fine calligraphy greatly enhanced and generalized its aesthetic effect — these were things that were more or less taken for granted and which need to be recalled from time to time when Chinese poetry is considered from afar.

The Forms of Chinese Poetry and Their Translation

Apart from structures and meanings of the language itself, there are also formal poetic structures to take into account in the translation of verse. The majority of such features will not carry over as such into a target language, but many translators have attempted to map original formal prosodic elements onto near-corresponding elements of native prosody, or onto newly devised forms based on the original prosody, but designed to be suited to native characteristics of English verse.

To indicate the basic formal elements of classical Chinese poetry we will briefly outline the elements of the most exacting form, the *lüshi* or "regulated verse" of the Tang dynasty. While other forms of Chinese poetry are not governed by the same rules or not to the same extent, the elements of "regulated verse" do give a fair idea of the significant features of Chinese prosody. Of course, as in all poetry, rules may be broken and this may be done by fine poets for the sake of an exceptional poem.

The elements of "regulated verse" are: No character should be repeated in a poem. Lines are of regular length, either five or seven (rarely six) syllables. Lines are nearly always end-stopped. There is a pause after the second syllable of the five character line which should correspond to a semantic and syntactic division. There is a similar "major" pause after the fourth syllable of the seven (or six) character line, as well as an additional "minor" pause after the second syllable. This metrical regularity is modulated by a cadence of tones along each line of verse. The tones are variations of pitch intrinsic to each monosyllable. Only certain arrangements of tones are permissible, giving a basic repertoire of tonal contours to the line. Lines are strictly associated in couplets. The standard regulated poem consists of four couplets. A two couplet form is also common, usually considered to be extracted from a notional eight-line poem, or the result of such a longer piece being cut short, hence its Chinese name, *jueju* 絕句 ("cut-off lines"). Poems with a larger number of couplets may be tonally regulated. Contrasts of tonal pattern serve to keep the members of a couplet in tense opposition. Partial similarity in the tonal patterns of the juxtaposed members of adjacent couples serve to link the couplets together. More precisely than in the case of other poetries, the effect is like a tapestry woven in the elements of verbal music. The last words of each couplet rhyme and the same rhyme is preserved throughout the poem. The lines of many couplets (always the second, and nearly always the third, in the four couplet form) must display a more or less exact and subtle "parallelism" of both structure and sense, involving matching correspondences of particular words and classes of words. The associations and subsequent enrichment of meaning implied by these correspondences may be as important to a poem as its narrative, syntactical or logical development. Thus, the regularity produced by end-stopped lines of equal length is further modulated by a form of language capable of greatly enriching the poem's meanings in directions which may not follow the usual "line of the sentence".

Tonal patterning, the defining characteristic of "regulated poetry" is the only formal feature which it is *impossible* to carry over into English, but non-repetition of words, an evenly stressed monosyllabic metric, a preponderance of end-stopped lines, a regular caesura, a single rhyme throughout a poem — these are all features which are unnatural to English prosody. Parallelism can be reproduced, but not with the degree of "neatness" and sophistication which is possible in Chinese.

Most examples from the existing corpus ignore formal constraint in the translated version. Translation of the supposed sense of the poem overrides other considerations. Setting aside the (usually nineteenth century) versifiers, some translators — Pound, Waley, Cooper, Rexroth — have attempted versions with formal characteristics designed to reflect something of the original form — Waley matching stressed feet to the original syllable count; Rexroth and Cooper counting syllables in the line and rhyming or half-rhyming intermittently; Pound rhyming in the case of his *Classic Anthology* and generally adding an unprecedented degree of poetic energy to his renditions. However, no long-standing formula for the "translation of the forms" has arisen and that feature which, arguably, would most enrich a Chinese-inspired poetic in English, namely parallelism, has not been systematically exploited by those writers otherwise fascinated with Chinese traditional poetry.

The Question of Translation and Classical Chinese Poetry

None of the apparently unresolvable questions in the unending debate on the translation of poetry from any one language to another will be answered with conclusive evidence from the case of classical Chinese poetry as it has been rendered into English. However, the linguistic and formal differences of Chinese and English poetry have very much enriched and broadened this important debate. The differences and huge distances bring into relief one final aspect of the debate. What is the purpose of translation from classical Chinese poetry? And who is it for?

In the academy, it clearly serves to help document the understanding of Chinese literary history which has (or has not) been achieved by Western scholars. The irony is that anyone with a serious interest in such specialized (and up to the present time, marginal) intellectual pursuits should not need and may not want translations of the material they are studying. It is the general reader who requires a translation, along with writers and fellow poets working mainly in English. But these readers need a different kind of translation. They must have the authority of the academy — which, strangely, they must take on trust — but they also deserve translation with a measure of the linguistic and poetic energy and sophistication that was contained in the original, carried over and embodied in the translation. If the ultimate goal of literary translation is the creative interpretation of shared human concerns, underpinned by a faithful understanding of both the form and content of the original, then, up to the present time, it is poets and writers of English — relative amateurs and naives in Chinese studies — who have done the better job of providing us with those translations from classical Chinese poetry which are needed by their true readers.

References

Birrell, Anne, tr. *New Songs from a Jade Terrace: An Anthology of Early Chinese Love Poetry*. Harmondsworth: Penguin, 1986 (1st ed., London: George Allen & Unwin, 1982).

Chaves, Jonathan, tr. and ed. *The Columbia Book of Later Chinese Poetry: Yuan Ming and Ch'ing Dynasties*. New York: Columbia University Press, 1986.

Liu, Wu-chi and Irving Yucheng Lo, eds. *Sunflower Splendor: Three Thousand Years of Chinese Poetry*. New York: Anchor Books, 1975.

Owen, Stephen. *Remembrances: The Experience of the Past in Classical Chinese Literature*. Cambridge, Mass.: Harvard University Press, 1986.

Pound, Ezra. *Selected Poems*, Introduction by T. S. Eliot. London: Faber and Faber, 1928; revised 1948; many reprints. Includes all of *Cathay*. London: Elkin Mathews, 1915.

Prynne, J. H. "China Figures." Originally published in *Modern Asian Studies*, Vol. 17 (1983), pp. 671–804; republished with alterations in the paperback edition translated by Anne Birrell, pp. 363–92.

Teele, R. E. *Through a Glass Darkly: A Study of English Translations of Chinese Poetry*. Ann Arbor: University of Michigan Press, 1949.

Waley, Arthur. *Chinese Poems*. London: Allen & Unwin, 1946; 5th impression, 1976.

Watson, Burton, tr. and ed. *The Columbia Book of Chinese Poetry: From Early Times to the Thirteenth Century*. New York: Columbia University Press, 1984.

Contemporary Chinese Poetry:
Poems by Bei Dao as an Example

Bonnie S. McDougall
Department of East Asian Studies
University of Edinburgh, U.K.

Poetry translation requires special consideration in regard to language and form. In recent years it has become commonplace to claim that in translating a poem the translator should produce a form corresponding as much as possible to the form of the original.

The demand for "corresponding form" is more complex than it may seem. One problem lies in determining what is meant, in specific cases, by "corresponding": for example, whether rhymed verse in one language corresponds to rhymed verse in the target language, and if so, whether the rhyme scheme should be identical and so on. In other words, one may try to "read" the outward form of any poem or group of poems as a text with its own message to the reader. The same is true in genres other than poetry, of course, but not usually to such a critical extent.

The use of rhyme in contemporary Chinese verse can illustrated with examples from *Poems by Bei Dao* 《北島詩選》, which is divided chronologically into three parts: 1973–1978, 1979–1982 and 1983–1986. Of the twenty-two poems in Part I, roughly half are rhymed. These rhymed poems are all written as a sequence of stanzas, usually quatrains but occasionally longer, and the rhyme is conventionally carried at the end of the couplet, with the same or a similar rhyme used throughout the poem. Sometimes the rhymes are only half-rhymes, e.g., in the poem "True" 〈眞的〉. In "The Answer" 〈回答〉, the rhymes are more exact. In contrast to this pattern of rhymed stanzas, the remaining poems fall into two kinds: a short poem without stanza divisions, and very long "sectional" poems where each section is very short and only occasionally further subdivided. The most well-known example of the former is "All" 〈一切〉, where the end rhymes on alternate lines may well be accidental rather than consciously formulated. In another poem with a similar structure, "A Day" 〈日子〉, the rhyme seems even more random and irrelevant to the couplet structure of the poem; in particular, the repetition of 日 seems at least to a Western ear rather disphonious. In the sectional poems, such as "Notes from the City of the Sun" 〈太陽城札記〉, some individual sections are clearly rhymed while others are clearly not; some rhymes are dubious; and some sections consist only of a single line.

It seems to me unnecessary to ask if the poet deliberately intended to create certain effects by the use or non-use of conventional or unconventional rhymes; it is enough to examine the poems themselves and evaluate our own responses. The most obvious correspondence between the more and less conventionally rhymed poems is the more or less conventional structure of the stanzas or other arrangement of lines. It seems in this context irrelevant that the rhymed quatrains are most probably based on Western nineteenth-century versification, since by the time Bei Dao was writing, this form had become thoroughly assimilated into modern Chinese practice. It may be more interesting to speculate on the origins of the sectional verse that features so prominently in Bei Dao's early poetry, but again it is not strictly relevant to the argument here. What is more to the point is that the kind of sectional verse represented by "Notes from the City of the Sun" is, in terms of line structure, a distinct departure from current usage in China since 1949. The absence of conventional rhyme therefore underlines the experimental and unconventional structure of the poem as a whole. Further, it may also be observed — though here individual readers' responses may differ considerably — that the tone of the structurally conventional poems can be distinguished from the tone of the structurally unconventional poems. Thus, the tone of "The Answer" is relatively direct, concrete and even strident, whereas "Notes from the City of the Sun" is indirect, abstract and muffled.

My "reading" of the use of rhyme is this group of poems is, therefore, that it is closely related to the structure and tone of each poem as a whole. It therefore in turn seems desirable that this feature of the poems be represented in the translation of the poems. The question is then whether the appropriate way to do this is to use rhyme in similar measure in the translations.

Contemporary practice on the whole is to avoid rhyme in the translation of poetry. The distorted meanings and trite jingles that are found in most modern rhymed translations are notorious and need no citation.

Nevertheless, there are two cases where I have tried, with success I think, to produce rhymed translations of modern Chinese poetry. The first is in the translation of "Nocturne" 〈雌夜啼〉 by the May Fourth poet Zhu Xiang 朱湘 (1904–1933), (McDougall, 1984) where I have adopted a standard English rhyme pattern, including some half-rhymes as in the original. To achieve the right rhyme I have sometimes substituted a word or phrase with a different literal meaning but with a class resemblance to the original: for instance, translating the word for "leaf" in the second verse as "grass" (both falling into the same class of small green objects in nature). My reason for using rhyme here is that the poem creates a general mood rather than gives specific descriptions of actual scenes or events. Since rhyme is clearly a major factor in the poet's own choice of words, the translator may feel justified in adopting the same criterion in the translation. One might even claim that an unrhymed translation in this case would be inadequate.

Another and rather different kind of example is "Lost Identity" (McDougall, 1983) by Qiu Xiaolong, a contemporary poet who has translated T.S. Eliot into Chinese and attempted translations into English of his own poetry. We collaborated on the translation of several of his poems in the following way. First, each of us prepared independently our own version of the poem. Then we compared our two versions, and I asked the poet specifically which elements could, if necessary, be discarded and which must absolutely be retained. On the basis of this comparison of notes and discussion, I took the third and final step, independently producing a final version. None of the poems we translated together was rhymed in the original, but in "Lost Identity", the rhyme first arose spontaneously, and, with a little extra effort and the agreement of the author, was worked into a regular pattern.

What these two cases had in common was a similarity of tone. The mood might or might not be sombre, and the message of greater or lesser social import, but in both cases the tone was light. In modern English practice, the use of rhyme, whether unconventional or not, usually produces a similar lightness of tone: either drily ironic or frankly comic. It therefore seemed to me appropriate to use rhyme in the English translations to convey the tone of the originals, especially where the poet himself could indicate the parameters in which the translator could work.

In the translation of Bei Dao's poetry, on the other hand, it seemed to me for precisely this reason to be quite inappropriate to employ rhyme in accordance with the poet's own practice. It is well-known that rhyme in

Chinese verse, compared with English verse, is relatively easy to achieve, and even the modern Chinese poets of this century have generally continued to employ rhyme in a fairly relaxed and casual way. Its absence, therefore, creates a strikingly modern effect that is not echoed in the lack of rhyme in modern English verse. Conversely, its incidence in contemporary Chinese verse does not create the same effect of lightness of tone as in English verse. To convey the same sense of difference between the two kinds of verse in Bei Dao's early poems — those more or less conventional in form and correspondingly more or less direct and concrete in tone — the use of rhyme seemed both inadequate and inappropriate.

In the end I hit upon a device quite unrelated to rhyme. The choice between capital or lower-case letters at the beginning of each line of verse — an option that has been available in English versification for the greater part of this century — seems to play a similar function in contemporary English poetry to the use of rhymed or unrhymed verse in contemporary Chinese poetry. That is, the absence of capitals creates the same "modern" effect as the absence of rhyme in Chinese. Since in any case the question of capitals versus lower-case has to be determined in all English translation of Chinese poetry, there is a definite advantage to be gained by their strategic deployment. Where the Chinese poem has a definite and fairly conventional rhyme and stanza structure, as for instance in "The Answer", I have therefore used a capital letter at the beginning of each line; where there is no rhyme and an unconventional structure, as in "Notes from the City of the Sun", I have used lower-case beginnings more or less exclusively; and where the form is more indeterminate, as in "A Day", I have used a capital at the beginning of the first line but not in subsequent lines. I need hardly add that this method has served as a guide rather than as an inflexible rule.

Apart from special cases such as literary allusions and botanical or zoological names, the language of most contemporary Chinese poetry does not necessarily pose major problems to the translator (assuming the translator's familiarity with the characteristic language of poetry in English). On the contrary, many of the abstract terms, cultural allusions and concrete referents in contemporary Chinese poetry are derived directly or indirectly from the West and are directly translatable into English equivalents. The increasing alienation of younger Chinese writers from their own tradition, especially from the popular culture of the countryside, and their increasing assimilation of foreign, especially Western culture, means that strictly intracultural references in poetry are decreasing in quantity. The approximation of contemporary Chinese urban life to contemporary Western urban life, and, even more strikingly, the shared time frame of poet and translator as co-inhabitants of the same world, are both a cause and a part of cultural assimilation and intercommunication. In this aspect the translation of contemporary poetry differs greatly from the translation of Chinese classical and folk poetry (to a lesser extent, even from modern Chinese poetry from earlier this century). Classical, modern and contemporary Chinese poetry, on the other hand, share one general characteristic that makes them to me, at least, easier to translate than fiction: that is, they address the reader in a relatively formal and elevated register. Although the level of formality differs from kind to kind and from poem to poem, even the vernacular poetry of contemporary Chinese writers tends to employ an elevated register, drawing on literary rather than colloquial vocabulary, and on abstract or universal rather than concrete and culturally specific imagery.

Without going into detail about the grammar of modern Chinese verse, it is possible to say that the structure of phrases and sentences has been very much influenced by Western practice, perhaps even more so than in prose. In this aspect, the translation of modern and contemporary Chinese verse offers much less of a challenge than classical poetry. By the late 1970s, Bei Dao had read sufficient Western poetry in Chinese translation (not to mention Westernized modern and contemporary Chinese verse) to be influenced by it, so that his lines on the whole go fairly readily into English. Some Chinese readers complain that Bei Dao's poetry became too Westernized, especially by the mid-1980s. Some lines even seem to read more smoothly in English than in Chinese: contrast

自由不過是
獵人與獵物之間的距離。

with

freedom is nothing but
the distance between the hunter and the hunted

The main problem with line structures is that the prepositional (or co-verb) phrases which in Chinese precede the main verb most naturally follow the verb in English; similarly, subordinate clauses tend in Chinese to precede and in English to follow the main clause. On the whole I prefer the more natural sequence in English, even at the possible cost of losing a sense of climax, since otherwise the overall effect becomes strained of falsely rhetorical.

The grammar of definite or indefinite articles has been a more difficult problem to resolve. The tendency of some translators simply to drop articles from their English versions seems to me unfortunate, producing an unnatural idiom that is neither English nor Chinese. It seems not to be understood by some translators that, for example, the absence of an article before a plural noun in English is equivalent to an indefinite article: it is not, as the Chinese often is, truly ambiguous. Chinese syntax, on the other hand, can be a guide to the use of definite or indefinite articles, though the syntactical variations that sometimes take place in poetry may obscure the code.

In vocabulary also, the translation of Bei Dao's poetry into English presents relatively few problems. In the earlier poems he relies on a very straightforward standard poetic terminology of words such as life, death, love, dreams, stars, clouds and the sun. Of these terms, perhaps only "sun" has a special reference which is immediately understandable to the native audience but not to a foreign reader. Generally in poetry and other forms of writing from the 1970s and 1980s, "the sun" stands for Mao Zedong, whose familiar designation, especially in the Cultural Revolution, was "the red sun in our hearts". In "Boat Ticket" 〈船票〉, for instance, the lines "the sunlight drying out upon the beach/makes one so terribly dizzy" have both a physical and a political reference.

A more famous reference to the sun occurs in the first section of the poem "Notes from the City of the Sun," entitled "Life" 〈生命〉, which reads: "The sun has risen too." This line also embodies a technique familiar to Chinese readers but perhaps not so widespread in the West, that of negative reference. The meaning of the section, including its title, is that the sun is only one phenomenon in life and not the sole progenitor of life. The final section is even simpler: after the title "Living" 〈生活〉 comes just one word: 網 (a net). In the early 1980s, and especially during the anti-"spiritual pollution" campaign, this section of the poem was commonly quoted out of context as a complete poem, and the expression "a net" was read as a description of a life entrapped in a net. The section can take on a different meaning in the proper context of the poem as a whole, where the net is a symbol of the inter-connectedness of all the other aspects of life "in the city of the sun."

In the second and third parts of *Poems by Bei Dao*, the vocabulary becomes colder, even clinical. In Part II, for instance, we find expressions

and terms like "ambulance" and "hypodermic needle" in "The Artist's Life"
〈藝術家的生活〉, "mountains of menopause" in "You Wait for Me in the
Rain"〈你在雨中等待著我〉, "saline-alkaline soil" in "Résumé"〈履歷〉,
and "false teeth", "baldness", "hormone pills" and "a public lavatory" in
"Portrait of the Young Poet"〈青年詩人的肖像〉. In Part III, the language
is not quite as bleak, but we still find "age spots" in "A Blank"〈空白〉,
"an asylum" in "Doubtful Things"〈可疑之處〉, "museum specimens" in
"Starting from Yesterday"〈自昨天起〉, "false teeth" again in "Don't
Ask Our Ages"〈別問我們的年齡〉, "sewers" in "Space"〈空間〉, "a
burning brand" in "Electric Shock"〈觸電〉, "sweating bodies" in "Dirge"
〈挽歌〉, and "an undismantled scaffold" in "The Art of Poetry"〈詩藝〉.
However, just as with the more sentimental imagery of the early poems,
these are universally understandable images and present no problem to the
translator. They may, however, indicate that in cases where English offers
alternatives, the choice may be for "softer" renderings for the earlier poems
and "harder" renderings in the later poems. For instance, I have translated
呼吸 in "Rainy Night"〈雨夜〉, "An End or A Beginning"〈結束或開始〉
and "Untitled"〈無題〉, which occur fairly early in Part II, as "breath" or
"breathing" but 氣息 in "Bodhisattva"〈菩薩〉 in Part III as "respiration".

Contemporary Chinese poetry is largely concerned with modern urban
life, and modern urban life in Beijing (still the centre of Chinese poetry) has
become in many ways similar to urban life in the West. The spurious
doctrine of "proletarian aesthetics", as practised in the past thirty years in
China, means that modern urban life has become overwhelmingly squalid,
ugly, intrusive and cramped. In Bei Dao's poetry, neon lights, billboards, the
graceless pronged lampholders along Changan Boulevard, pedestrian control railings, traffic lights and other street furniture are images of physical
and social oppression. Both the objects described and the atmosphere they
evoke are familiar to Western readers, and the correspondence in vocabulary is usually one to one. Finally, a large number of abstract nouns in
contemporary Chinese are borrowed directly or indirectly from the West
and can be retranslated back into Western languages without loss of meaning or specific association: 世界 (world), 時間 (time) and 自由 (freedom) are
inevitably still the common currency of Bei Dao and his fellow-poets.

One of the major differences between classical and modern Chinese
poetry is the relative lack of allusions to traditional Chinese literature and
history in the latter. This is generally true of the shadows poetry of the
1970s and 1980s — major exceptions being works by Jiang He and Yang

Lian — and more so in the case of the new schools of "everyday" and "nihilistic" poetry that emerged in the 1980s. Allusions in Bei Dao's poetry are as much to Western as to Chinese culture. It is mainly in his long poem, "Daydream" 〈白日夢〉 that the problem of specifically Chinese allusion occurs. In section IX of "Daydream", for instance, the "sick tree" is most likely derived from a poem by Li Qingchao 李清照 ; in section X, the "arrow shot at a gate" is a reference to Li Zicheng's 李自成 challenge to the Ming emperor; and in section XX there occur in close proximity "a straight wisp of smoke" and "a lonely fisherman", suggesting the scholar whose talents are ignored by the emperor. In the first and last examples, Bei Dao may not have been consciously quoting but simply drawing on an imagic vocabulary generally familiar to educated Chinese readers. The non-sinologist Western reader requires some explanation. The problem is how to explain these local references without turning ordinarily accessible allusions into an academic exercise.

The most common ways in which explanations can be given are in a preface, in footnotes or endnotes, in a glossary or by expansion of the original text. Expansion by insertion of explanatory epithets (e.g., "Mount Tai, China's sacred mountain", "Zhang Chunqiao, one of the Gang of Four", "the beautiful provincial city of Guilin") may be useful in non-literary texts, but the method has two serious drawbacks in literary translation. Firstly, it makes the text more verbose, which is particularly unfortunate when most Chinese writing (and most English translations of it) is already long-winded enough. Even more seriously, it inevitably produces the effect of a Chinese writer writing for a non-Chinese audience. Poetry would suffer most from these drawbacks, while the only literary form in which the advantages might outweigh the disadvantages is translation for performance.

In literary translations designed for a general audience, it seems advisable to avoid footnotes or endnotes marked by a number or other sign in the text: both kinds of notes are distracting to all readers, and are felt to be patronizing by some. A preface or introduction which deals with the general social and political context of the original can sometimes be an appropriate place to explain political and social references (for instance, the use of "sun" as an image for Mao Zedong in "Notes from the City of the Sun"). A glossary is most useful for the explanation of specific vocabulary such as the political jargon found in contemporary fiction but less commonly in shadows poetry. Neither an introduction nor a glossary is particularly helpful for the explanation of literary allusions in poetry.

In Bei Dao's case, since these allusions occur rather rarely, my solution in a collection aimed at a general reader was simply to ignore them. A justification for this practice was that a great deal of contemporary Western poetry contains imagery unfamiliar to most of its readers but nevertheless generally published without footnotes or other explanation. A recent example is the poem "Tricky Little Magdalene" by Peter Porter: how many of its literary or academic British readers would know (or care) that several decades ago, Resch's Dinner Ale, a type of bottled beer, was considered marginally superior to most other bottled beers, and that bottled fresh oysters were sold in pubs as a weekend treat in working-class Sydney?

The most significant characteristic of Bei Dao's poetry which makes it relatively easy to translate into English is that the poet's genius is expressed in terms of striking images rather than in elaborate wordplay or sound patterns; an outstanding example is in the lines "freedom is nothing but the distance ..." quoted above. This is true also of other shadows poets like Gu Cheng 顧城 and Mang Ke 芒克 , though some of Duo Duo's early poems, for instance, have complex rhythmical effects which make them difficult to translate literally. Among contemporary poets, however, none has been as widely quoted as Bei Dao, in lines like:

> I don't believe the sky is blue,
> I don't believe in thunder's echoes,
> I don't believe that dreams are false.
> I don't believe that death has no revenge.
> 我不相信天是藍的；
> 我不相信雷的回聲；
> 我不相信夢是假的；
> 我不相信死無報應。

or the following:

> I am no hero
> In an age without heroes
> I just want to be a man
> …
> I will not kneel on the ground
> Allowing the executioners to look tall
> The better to obstruct the wind of freedom

我並不是英雄
在沒有英雄的年代裡
我只想做一個人
〔我〕決不跪在地上
以顯出創子手們的高大
好阻擋那自由的風。

— inscribed on a banner in the student demonstrations in Tiananmen in
April-June 1989 and recited by the student leader Chai Ling in a televised
interview on her escape from China in April 1990.

Finally, Bei Dao's poetry lightens the translator's task by its consistently elevated register: even the occasional passages of dialogue are in
plain colloquial language rather than slang or localisms. Again, this formality is characteristic of the shadows poets in general, as also of the vast
majority of classical and modern Chinese verse. It was admittedly provocative to claim in my Introduction to *The August Sleepwalker* that Bei Dao's
poetry is translatable, and some reviewers wondered if the poet's true
"Chinese" voice had been in fact obscured in the translation. I don't claim
that "all" of the original is there, but I wonder in turn if some reviewers are
looking for an "other" and more exotic voice which may have been lost
forever from Chinese verse written by young urban intellectuals.

References

Bei Dao. *The August Sleepwalker*, edited and translated by Bonnie S. McDougall.
    London: Anvil Press Poetry, 1988; US revised edition, New York: New Direc-
    tions, 1990.
—— 北島 . 《北島詩選》 (*Poems by Bei Dao*). Guangzhou: New Century Press
    新世紀出版社 , 1987.
McDougall, Bonnie S., tr. "Lost Identity." In *Stubborn Weeds*, edited by Perry Link.
    Bloomington: Indiana University Press, 1983, p. 194.
————. "Thirteen Lyric Poems by Chu Hsiang." *Renditions*, Nos. 21/22 (1984),
    pp. 241–51.

English Poetry

Yang Guobin
Beijing Foreign Studies University, Beijing, China

The translation of English poetry in China started around the mid-nine-teenth century. The first English poem to be translated into Chinese, has been traced to Henry Wadsworth Longfellow's "A Psalm of Life", which came out in 1865. That was followed by a long period of silence, however. The great age of translation did not come until the beginning of the 20th century. Today, with the combined efforts of several generations of transla-tors, nearly all the highlights of English poetry have been made available to the Chinese readers.

The first contingent of translators of English poetry were Yan Fu 嚴復 , Gu Hongming 辜鴻銘 , Ma Junwu 馬君武 and Su Manshu 蘇曼殊 . To Yan Fu have been attributed the first lines of British poetry done into Chinese. These were the lines from Alexander Pope's *An Essay on Man* and Alfred Tennyson's *Ulysses*, which Thomas Henry Huxley quoted in *Evolution and Ethics*, and which Yan translated in a famous Chinese version (1898). Gu Hongming, three years Yan's junior and remembered mainly for his English translations of Confucian classics, nevertheless left a lively classical Chi-nese version of William Cowper's *John Gilpin*, while Ma Junwu is known for his elegant rendering of Byron's "The Isles of Greece."

The most accomplished and influential of the four was Su Manshu. Poet, novelist, painter and fighter for national and individual freedom, Su was an avid admirer of Byron. In 1908, he put out a slim volume of five of Byron's poems. Four of these he translated himself, including his own version of "The Isles of Greece." The translations, like those of the other three translators, were done in classical Chinese verse. The rhymes and rhythms were quite different from the original and the diction appeared archaic even in his own day. But then the spirit of Byron was powerfully evoked. The revolutionary ideals, the poetic images and the poetic tone were so successfully conveyed that, as W.J.B. Fletcher says in his preface to Su's volume, these translations "made a desirable addition to the literature of popular liberty in China." No one since has ever done better in classical Chinese translations of English poetry.

A major cause of the decline of translations in classical Chinese is that the language itself was not flexible enough to realize the possibilities latent in a foreign poetry. After 1919, with the onset of the New Culture Movement, *baihua* 白話 , or the vernacular language, gradually replaced classical Chinese as the standard written language. Since then, most translations of poetry have been done in the vernacular.

The first fruits of the vernacular translations came from the pens of Guo Moruo 郭沫若 and Wen Yiduo 聞一多 . Both Guo and Wen were pioneers and masters of the New Poetry, i.e., poetry written in the vernacular language as opposed to regular classical Chinese verse. Like many other writers then and thereafter, both were also well versed in Western literature and actively involved in translation. Guo published, among others, translations of *The Rubaiyat of Omar Khayyam* (1924) and of *Selected Poems of Shelley* (1926), in addition to *Verse Translations of Moruo* (1928) and, posthumously, *Translations of English Poetry* (1981). His translation of *The Rubaiyat of Omar Khayyam*, based on Edward Fitzgerald's English version, was not unfavourably reviewed by Wen Yiduo, although Wen also pointed out many of his inaccuracies. His last book, *Translations of English Poetry*, contains about a dozen American poems. Yet strangely enough, while his own poetry bears clear evidence of the influence of Walt Whitman, he never translated any of Whitman's poems. He was instead best known for his powerful version of Shelley's "Ode to the West Wind."

Compared with Guo's translations, Wen's output seemed meagre, only 21 of Elizabeth Barrett Browning's *Sonnets from the Portuguese*, published in the magazine *Crescent Moon* in 1928. Nevertheless, while Guo's translations are sometimes marred by a sorry mixture of the classical and the vernacular language that too often made awkward reading, Wen's versions were much more smooth. Moreover, Wen set great store by the aesthetic aspects of translation. He was the first to study the possibility of exploiting verse translation as a means of enriching native verse forms. Using translation as a means of poetic experiment, he took special care to keep the original rhyme scheme and to produce verse lines of roughly equal lengths. He succeeded to such a degree that not only did his translations turn out to be excellent poetry faithful to the original in sense and form, but his own poetic writings also became more disciplined and regulated. Even his poetic tone, as for example the tone of his famous poem "Dead Water" 〈死水〉,

the title piece of an influential volume published in 1929, came to be more controlled and measured. Owing perhaps to the relatively small number of his translations and to his much greater fame as a poet, Wen's success and significance as a translator is not fully appreciated, although in 1981 Fang Ping said from his own experience of translating Elizabeth Browning that Wen Yiduo's translations were so good that he found them unsurpassable.

Wen's effort to introduce English prosody through translation became the fountain head of a translation tradition, i.e. the translation of poetry as poetry. In the 1930s and 40s four other poet-translators followed suit and brought out verse translations of a high standard. They are Zhu Xiang 朱湘, Liang Zongdai 梁宗岱, Zhou Xuliang 周煦良 and Sun Dayu 孫大雨.

Zhu Xiang, who drowned himself at the age of 29 in 1933, had a book of verse translations published posthumously in 1936, entitled *The Book of the Myrtle*. The book contains poems from many countries, but the greater part is taken up by English poetry. It was in fact the most comprehensive foreign poetry anthology in China up to his day. Here are found not only such giants as Shakespeare, Donne, Milton, Blake, Wordsworth, Coleridge, Shelley, Keats, Tennyson, Robert Browning and Mathew Arnold, but also lesser figures like John Lyly, Samuel Daniel, Walter Savage Landor, Arthur Hugh Clough, Robert Seymour Bridges and John William Watson. Even more surprising is the fact that Zhu Xiang not only translated shorter poems like the sonnets of Shakespeare and Milton, but also ventured into longer pieces such as Wordsworth's *Michael*, Coleridge's *The Ancient Mariner* and Arnold's *Sohrab and Rustum*. His translations on the whole did justice to the originals, although he sometimes went too far in his efforts to cut his verse lines to equal lengths. For that he sacrificed much of the natural flow of poetry.

Like Zhu Xiang, Liang Zongdai in translating Shakespeare's sonnets was also careful to reproduce the original form. He explained in the preface to a 1936 translation of Goethe, Blake, Shelley, Valéry, *et al.*, that he had followed the originals as closely as possible, out of the "superstition per-haps" "that the language and word order of the original, i.e. the language and word order that were chosen by great poets, cannot but be perfect." This same principle also guided him in his work on Shakespeare's sonnets. The remarkable thing about his translation is that close adherence to the original neither hampered the poetic flow nor prevented him in any way from achieving beauty and exquisiteness in poetic diction. Because of the excel-lence of these translations, many of which were first published in 1943 in the magazine *National Literature*, they were brought together into the first complete translation of Shakespeare's works in 1978, to be published again as a separate volume in 1983.

Two other poet-translators concerned with formal matters in translation were Zhou Xuliang and Sun Dayu. Like Wen Yiduo, Zhou and Sun took up verse translation in order to establish new verse forms for the vernacular poetry. Zhou found the 63 poems in Alfred Housman's *The Shropshire Lad* well suited to his purpose and in about ten years, from 1937 to 1948, completed his translation of them. Only part of these beautiful translations were published then. When the whole volume came out in 1983, it was a long-delayed success. In a long preface to his modest volume, Zhou Xuliang elaborates on his theory of how to build up a regular verse line by the division of "syllabic groups." Basically, his idea is to use one Chinese syllabic group to correspond to one English foot. What is crucial is that these syllabic groups alternate in lengths within a line, and from that alternation comes the vital force of poetic rhythm.

In the preface to an earlier book of translation, Zhou Xuliang's one-time neighbour Sun Dayu outlines his version of a similar theory. This is the preface to his verse translation of *King Lear*. Before him, the playwright Tian Han 田漢 had published in 1922 a prose translation of *Hamlet* — the first of Shakespeare's plays ever to be published in China. However, to Sun Dayu any prose rendering of Shakespeare was anathema. Hence his own verse version of *King Lear*, finally published in 1948. His solution to the problem of metre was to use a syllabic group of one to five characters to correspond to a foot in the English blank verse. However, his verse lines often lacked a sense of rhythm, his division of syllabic groups tending to be inflexible, even mechanical and arbitrary. The task of real verse translations of Shakespeare's plays had to wait for many years to accomplished by another translator.

But there were good prose translations. In 1935, a young man of 23 by the name of Zhu Shenghao 朱生豪 embarked on an ambitious plan of translating Shakespeare's complete works. It took him ten years and his young life — he died of poverty and illness in 1944 — to almost fulfill his plan, leaving undone only six history plays and the poems, an achievement that has not been surpassed. His translations glow with the genius of a master hand. He never allowed himself to be trapped in trivialities, like those attendant on word-for-word equivalence, but, as he says in his preface, always "tries as much as possible to keep the spirit of the original, and when that is unattainable, at least to convey its meaning in plain and smooth language." As a result, in prose but never prosaic, faithful yet extremely readable, his translations have won the admiration of the Chinese audience down the years. When in 1978 the first *Complete Works of Shakespeare* was published, it was Zhu's translations that were chosen as the standard text.

Many other translations of English poetry were published or undertaken in the 1930s and 40s. Mention may be made of Shi Zhecun's translations of dozens of American poems (1934), of Liang Shiqiu's 梁實秋 prose versions of many of Shakespeare's plays (1936, to be completed and published in 1981 in Taiwan as *The Complete Works of Shakespeare*), of the woman poet Zhao Luorui's 趙蘿蕤 translation of *The Waste Land* (1937) and finally of Fu Donghua's 傅東華 rhymed version of *Paradise Lost* (1937).

The 1950s and early 60s saw another translation boom in China. Verse translations in this period include Milton's *Paradise Regained* (1951), Marlowe's *The Tragical History of Doctor Faustus* (1956), Shakespeare's *Sonnets* (1950) and *The Chartist Poems* (1960). Among prose translations of poetry, there were more versions of Shakespeare's plays. *Beowulf* and *The Works of Chaucer* also came out in Chinese prose. This latter, published in 1962 and translated by Fang Zhong 方重, a student of the famous Chaucerian J.S.P. Tatlock, reproduces remarkably Chaucer's humour and conviviality. It is the best of prose translations since Zhu Shenghao's Shakespeare.

However, both in the quality and quantity of poetry translations of this period, the works of the English Romantics topped the list. Many long romantic poems were translated in this period, such as Shelley's *The Revolt of Islam* and *Prometheus Unbound* and Byron's *The Siege of Corinth, Cain, Manfred, Hellas, Childe Harold's Pilgrimage* and a not very adequate version of *Don Juan* (1956). As to Blake, Burns, and Keats, they were each represented by at least one volume of their selected poems.

Out of this translation boom, three outstanding figures emerged. They were Bian Zhilin 卞之琳, Zha Liangzheng 查良錚 (*alias* Mu Dan 穆旦) and Wang Zuoliang 王佐良. Bian published his verse translation of *Hamlet* in 1956. Zha, the most productive of the three, single-handedly put out in two years' time (1957–1958) three books of translations (one each of Byron, Shelley and Keats), besides numerous translations of Pushkin. Wang brought out a volume of Robert Burns in 1959 to mark the poet's 200th anniversary. Even as they were working away at their translations, a political upheaval was in the making. It finally broke out in 1966 as the Great Cultural Revolution that put a stop to all cultural activities. Zha did not survive the "revolution", but all three were to publish, posthumously in the case of Zha, other important works of translation in the 1980s.

This past decade opened with Zha Liangzheng's masterful translation of Byron's *Don Juan*. A poet-turned-translator, Zha had started his work on *Don Juan* in the early 1960s and had persevered throughout the hard years of the Cultural Revolution. When it finally came out in 1980, three years after his death, it was hailed as a milestone in verse translation and replaced the 1956 version as the standard text.

In this work, Zha's difficulties were three-fold. First, he had to keep the original rhyme scheme, the *ottava rima*. To do this for several stanzas would normally present little difficulty. But to sustain it in canto after canto till the very end of that long epic would be a real feat. Zha did it, with very few exceptions, and for that alone he deserves great admiration. But then he overcame another difficulty — Byron's conversational English. Here he had no other examples to follow but his own poetic sensibility and linguistic versatility. With these and his free command of Mandarin, he was able to attain a level of spoken Chinese that corresponds remarkably to the effect of Byron's English. Still, one last difficulty loomed large — Byron's ever-changing moods, by turns meditative, lyrical, sardonic. Zha coped by developing a varied poetic style which managed to reproduce not only Byron's wit but also his rhetorical effects, including his anticlimaxes.

Another translator who aims at the equivalence of effect is Bian Zhilin. A major modernist poet, he turned to translation in 1954. He started with *Hamlet* and went on over the years to *Othello, King Lear* and *Macbeth*, publishing them together in 1988 as *Four Tragedies of Shakespeare*. Bian's version of *Hamlet* was used successfully to dub Laurence Olivier's film version. Published with the translations of the other three plays, it inspired new interest and confidence in verse translation. Bian's success lies in his solution to the problem of the blank verse. In this, he acknowledges his indebtedness to Sun Dayu. But instead of adopting Sun's idea of the syllabic group, Bian comes up with a Chinese verse line consisting of five speech units punctuated by five pauses to correspond to the English iambic pentametre. By the use of what Bian calls "pauses", a clear and steady rhythm is created. Besides, sophisticated poet that he is, Bian is alive to the nuances and subtleties of Shakespeare's poetry and retains most of them in his translation. One need only compare his version of the "To be, or not to be" speech with the many other versions to see his superiority.

Also superior are the translations of Wang Zuoliang. A student of William Empson and F.P. Wilson, Wang is one of the few translators who have combined scholarship with poetic sensibility in verse translation. His translations of Burns, which had been published back in 1959, were revised, enlarged and issued in a new edition in 1985. Wang's approach, like that of many other poet-translators, is to render poetry as poetry. Unlike many others, however, Wang did not allow himself to be bogged down in metrical minutiae. Instead of counting the pauses or syllabic groups of a verse line, he delimits roughly the number of characters in each line according to the length of the original. Thus while following the original verse forms quite closely, he could pay more attention to the more important aspects of stylistic features and the overall effect. He paid special attention to the faithful reproduction of the images and the natural poetic flow. These qualities contribute to the popularity of his translations such as "A Red, Red Rose" and "Tam o'Shanter."

In recent years Wang edited an *Anthology of English Poetry in Chinese Translation* (1988). As no other anthology of the kind existed before in China, this one aimed at comprehensiveness. A book of 315 poems by 64 poets, it opens with verse selections from *Beowulf* and ends with Seamus Heaney. In between are found middle English ballads, Renaissance sonneteers, the metaphysicals, 18th century neoclassicists, major Romantics and Victorians and 20th century moderns. Thus the entire history of the English poetic tradition is represented here. Another notable feature is that considerable space is devoted to 20th century poetry. Besides Yeats and Eliot, there are, for instance, Thomas Hardy, Gerard Manley Hopkins, D.H. Lawrence, Edwin Muir, Hugh MacDiarmid, Wilfred Owen, W.H. Auden, Louis MacNiece, Dylan Thomas, Philip Larkin and Ted Hughes. All this amounts to a handsome selection of the best of 20th century English poetry. Finally, the anthology is also notable for the high quality of the translations chosen. They include the famous pieces by veteran translators, but more are fresh versions by budding young talents. Where no version of an important poem exists, the editor himself fills the gap. Thus he has had to range widely over the whole field of English poetry, translating many items, which, not usually included in an anthology published abroad, have nevertheless a special significance for China, such as Empson's "Autumn on Nan-Yueh." Wang Zuoliang's translations of passages from *Paradise Lost* and some of Philip Larkin's poems, in particular, represent new triumphs after his work on Burns.

Besides the translations of Zha Liangzheng, Bian Zhilian and Wang Zuoliang, there were yet other good poetry translations in the 1980s. Tu An's revised edition (1981) of his 1950 version of Shakespeare's *Sonnets* and Yang Deyu's *Byron: 70 Lyrical Poems* (1981) have won critical acclaim for their faithfulness both to the sense and the form of the originals. Yang, moreover, took up Wordsworth after Byron and published in 1990 a *Selected Poems of Wordsworth*. Wordworth has often been regarded as a difficult poet to translate, because his poetic language is so simple. One may recall, for example, how Zhu Xiang's venture into *Michael* had sacrificed natural poetic flow for orderly-looking verse lines. Yang Deyu is more successful in this respect. For one thing, he is such a serious translator that if he finds a translation unsatisfactory, he will simply leave it out. Thus apart from nine exceptions that deviate from the original verse forms, the 109 poems that he translated for the book all retain the original forms while also recreating the poetic effect.

Apart from individual endeavours, one publishing house in Hunan has launched a large project, the publication of over 70 volumes of foreign poetry in Chinese translation. These include more than twenty volumes of English poetry. Some of these, such as the verse translations of Liang Zongdai, Zhu Xiang and Shi Zhecun, are reprints of editions that have long gone out of circulation. But many more are new translations of such works as Sir Walter Scott's *The Lady of the Lake* (1986), Blake's *Songs of Innocence and of Experience* (1988), *Selected Victorian Verse* (1985), and a new complete version of *Paradise Lost* (1988). This series is by far the most comprehensive of its kind in China and has helped to bring English poetry to a wider audience.

Finally, a brief look at the translations of other English-language poetry.

To begin with, how about translations of the English poetry written in New Zealand, Canada, and Australia?

Although such Australian poets as Mary Gilmore, Roderic Quinn and Hugh McCrae attracted the attention of Chinese writers as early as in 1921 — the famous novelist and critic Mao Dun commented briefly on their poems in the "Newsletter from Abroad" column in Volume 12 (1921) of the *Short Story Magazine* — translations of the poetry of these countries are a fairly new phenomenon. Only in the last decade, with the increase nationwide in the number of translation journals, have there appeared such translations. A quick look at two major Beijing-based journals such as *World Literature* and *Foreign Literatures* shows how rapidly the translators have been catching up. Both journals, for example, have published special issues on Australian literature, representing such names as A.D. Hope, Judith Wright and Kenneth Slessor. Although no individual book of translations of Australian, Canadian or New Zealand poetry has as yet appeared, it is no longer fair for any English poetry anthology to be confined only to British poetry.

Yet what about the translations of American poetry?

In spite of the 1865 rendering of Longfellow's "A Psalm of Life", the real beginning of the translation of American poetry can only be placed in 1930s. In 1934, as was mentioned earlier, Shi Zhecun published his translations of a handful of American poems in the journal *National Literature*. Slightly earlier than that, around 1930, Chu Tunan 楚圖南 started translating *The Leaves of Grass* in order, in his own words, "to introduce some democratic ideas." His *Selected Translations of the Leaves of Grass* was first published in 1949.

Apart from a reprint of Chu's translation of Whitman, and a version of Longfellow's *The Song of Hiawatha* (1957), hardly any translations of American poetry were published from the 1950s to the end of the 1970s, due mainly to China's political situation. Since the 1980s, however, more and more American poetry has been translated, and several anthologies have since appeared. For instance, the poetry translation series launched by the publishing house in Hunan mentioned earlier include *Contemporary American Poetry* (1987) translated by the woman poet Zheng Min 鄭敏 , and *Emily Dickinson: Poems* (1988) by Jiang Feng 江楓 , who is also the editor and translator of *Modern American Poetry* (1986). Some of the poets represented in these anthologies are Edgar Lee Masters, Edwin Arlington Robinson, Stephen Crane, Robert Frost, Carl Sandburg, Wallace Stevens, William Carlos Williams, Sara Teasdale, Hilda Doolittle, Langston Hughes, Mark Strand, John Ashbury, Robert Bly, Kenneth Koch, W.S. Merwin, Sylvia Plath, Gary Snyder and Allen Ginsburg. Other things apart, the list itself represents a good introduction to modern American poetry.

Yet Whitman's influence still holds. Chu Tunan's selected translations, which were revised and republished in 1978 and 1983, seem to be an all-time hit. But then Chu's translations have two problems: they are not complete, and the language appears somewhat old-fashioned to readers today. Li Yeguang tackled the first problem by translating the poems left undone by Chu and incorporating Chu's translations to bring out a two-volume complete edition in 1987. Earlier than that, Zhao Luorui, the erstwhile poet and the first translator of *The Waste Land*, had set out to meet the second challenge. Zhao is a specialist in Whitman studies, and when her new translation of *A Song of Myself* was published in 1987, it was praised for its accuracy and fluency.

Nevertheless, how does Zhao, or Chu, cope with Whitman's wild and unruly free verse? How do they face up to the challenge of the colloquial American language? It is a challenge that translators of, say, Shakespeare or Milton or any other British poet, did not have to meet. Have translators of the American free verse proved equal to the task?

Not quite, as Wang Zuoliang points out in a recent important review article in 《讀書》 (*Reading*) of the *Anthology of American Poetry*. The trouble lies mainly in the translators' inability to appreciate the native American poetic tradition and their incompetence in handling the living Chinese speech. Most Chinese translators, Wang argues, are school-trained: they are too cultured to cope with Whitman's unconventional, common-people free verse. This is perhaps the trouble with Chu, as it is also with the translators of the *Anthology of American Poetry* (Hong Kong, 1976; Beijing, 1989). Edited by Lin Yiliang 林以亮, this anthology contains 110 poems by 17 poets ranging from the 19th to mid-20th century. After a careful study of the translations, Wang Zuoliang finds that the best translations are of poems by such traditional lyric poets as Edgar Allan Poe and Robert Frost, while those written in the colloquial idiom and spoken rhythms are less satisfactorily done, as in the case of Whitman or his latter-day followers; or poets are simply left out, as in the case of William Carlos Williams. The problem is again in translators' incompetent command of the living Chinese speech. That incompetence makes it hard for translators to reproduce the rhythm, tone and rich nuances that are the life force of the American free verse.

The discussion thus comes full circle. The earliest translators of English poetry started by using classical Chinese verse forms and the classical language. After 1919, the vernacular language rapidly took over the ground and the task of translators has since been two-fold: to render English poetry in Chinese vernacular language, and to temper the vernacular language into a resilient and effective means of poetic expression. With the efforts of such translators as Wen Yiduo, Zhou Xuliang, Bian Zhilin, Zha Liangzheng and

Wang Zuoliang, this two-fold task has been fulfilled. But the challenge posed by 20th century American free verse in the tradition of Walt Whitman has yet to be met.

References

Bian, Zhilin. "The Development of China's 'New Poetry' and the Influence from the West." *Chinese Literature: Essays, Articles, Review*, Vol. 4, No. 1 (1982), pp. 152–57.

Editorial Division, *Chinese Translators Journal* 《中國翻譯》編輯部 , ed. 《詩詞翻譯的藝術》 (*The Art of Verse Translation*). Beijing: China Translation and Publishing Corporation 中國對外翻譯出版公司 , 1986.

Ma, Zuyi 馬祖毅 . 《中國翻譯簡史 —「五四」運動以前部份》 (*A Brief History of Translation in China up to the May Fourth Movement*). Beijing: China Translation and Publishing Corporation 中國對外翻譯出版公司 , 1984.

Wang, Zuoliang 王佐良 . "Chinese Translators and American Poetic Styles." 《讀書》 (*Reading*), No. 6 (1990), pp. 43–53.

———. *Degrees of Affinity: Studies in Comparative Literature*. Beijing: Foreign Language Teaching and Research Press 外語教學與研究出版社 , 1985.

Problems of Translating the Han Rhapsody

David R. Knechtges
Asian Languages and Literature
University of Washington , Seattle, U.S.A

The *fu* 賦 is a genre that first emerged and flourished during the Han dynasty. After the Han it continued to be a major form of literary expression, and also developed into several distinct forms, including the regulated *fu* 律賦 , a special form used in the civil service examinations during the Tang and early Song, and the 文賦 or "prose fu", a subgenre of 古文 (ancient style) prose that was favored by such Song dynasty writers as Ouyang Xiu 歐陽修 (1007–1072) and Su Shi 蘇軾 (1036–1101). Because the *fu* has no Western counterpart, a standard English name for the genre does not exist. A common English name for the Han *fu* 漢賦 , in which declamation and recitation were important, is rhapsody. Other English names such as rhyme-prose, prose poem, verse essay, exposition, or poetical description also have been applied to the genre as a whole.

The Han *fu*, which also is known as 大賦 (grand *fu*) or 古賦 (ancient-style *fu*), has the following features: an ornate style, lines of unequal length, alternation of rhymed and unrhymed passages, extensive parallelism, elaborate description, hyperbole, repetition of synonyms, cataloguing, difficult language, a tendency toward a complete portrayal of a subject, and often a moral conclusion. The primary creator of the grand *fu* was Sima Xiangru 司馬相如 (179–117 B.C.), whose "Rhapsody on the Excursion Hunt of the Son of Heaven" 〈天子遊獵賦〉, also known under the title "Rhapsody on the Imperial Park" 〈上林賦〉, is an ornate description of the imperial hunting park of the great Former Han ruler Emperor Wu (reg. 140–87 B.C.). His *fu* is filled with rare words and long catalogues of plants, trees, animals, and minerals and was intended as a tribute to the grandeur and glory of the Han empire. At the end of the Western Han period, Yang Xiong 揚雄 (53 B.C.–A.D. 18) wrote similar pieces, not only about the imperial hunting park, but also the grand palace of Ganquan 甘泉 (Sweet Springs) located north of the capital. In the Eastern Han period Ban Gu 班固

(A.D. 32–92) and Zhang Heng 張衡 (A.D. 78–139) composed even grander display poems on the western and eastern capitals Chang'an and Luoyang. Ban Gu's "Rhapsody on the Two Capitals" 〈兩都賦〉 is a panegyric to the Eastern Han, while Zhang Heng's "Rhapsody on the Two Metropolises" 〈二京賦〉 is both a detailed account of the Western and Eastern Han capitals and a satire of imperial excesses. By the end of the Eastern Han, as imperial prestige declined, the grand *fu* gave way to shorter, more lyrical pieces.

Appearing alongside the grand *fu* is the subgenre termed by the late Professor Hellmut Wilhelm (1957) the "*fu* of frustration." In these highly personal expressions, the poet complains about the evils of his time and his inability to gain acceptance by the ruler and the powerful ministers at court. This subgenre developed out of the 〈離騷〉 attributed to the Chu poet Qu Yuan 屈原 (ca. 340–278 B.C.) and its imitations. Another type of *fu* that eventually become very popular was the 詠物 or "*fu* on things." In such pieces, the poet wrote about a single subject such as a plant, animal, bird, or even an insect. The *fu* on things were often allegorical, and in some examples of the form the object described often represented the poet himself.

The *fu* is perhaps the most difficult genre of Chinese literature to translate. One obvious reason the twentieth century reader finds the *fu* so difficult is that the linguistic and cultural gulf that separates him from ancient Chinese literature is so vast. Even the modern Chinese reader of the *fu* has almost as much difficulty understanding the text of a *fu* as his non-Chinese counterpart. For example, Lu Zongda 陸宗達 has said the following about translating the *fu* section of the *Wen xuan* 《文選》, an important sixth century anthology, into modern Chinese: "To annotate is not easy, and to translate is even more difficult. The thought and subtleties of writers from a thousand years ago are not easily grasped, and their unique qualities are even harder to express."

Because the translator is so far removed from the culture and language of the *fu* writer, he must learn as much as he can about the language and *culture* of ancient and medieval China. Linguistic knowledge alone is not sufficient for a proper understanding of the meaning of a text. Although one may know the literal sense of every word in a line, and be able to explain grammatical function and even reconstruct the putative ancient or medieval pronunciation of the words, such knowledge may not produce a correct translation. For example, in translating the *fu* on capitals, one must first study the historical and archaeological studies of these great cities. One must become familiar with the 《三輔黃圖》 (an early work on Chang'an), the reports on archaeological excavations, and studies of early Chinese architecture. The capital *fu* of Zhang Heng and Ban Gu are replete with accounts of ritual, and the translator must acquire a thorough knowledge of the ritual classics 《禮記》 and 《周禮》 as well as the monographs of the dynastic histories on ceremony and official dress. In order to translate the passages that describe features of buildings, one must learn something about ancient architecture. The *fu* is replete with the names of plants, animals, fish, stones, and constellations, and the translator must become a student of Chinese botany, zoology, icthyology, geology, and astronomy to determine their Western language equivalents.

The type of *fu* that offers the greatest linguistic challenge to the translator is the grand *fu*. Arthur Waley (1923) has characterized the *fu* as engaging in a kind of "word magic" that achieves its effect by "a purely sensuous intoxication of rhythm and language." *Fu* poets such as Sima Xiangru are well known for their long catalogues. For example, the "Rhapsody of Sir Vacuous" 〈子虛賦〉 contains the following rhymed list of names of minerals, precious stones, plants, water creatures, trees, birds, and animals:

> In their soil:
>   Cinnabar, azurite, ocher, white clay,
>   Orpiment, milky quartz,
>   Tin, prase, gold, and silver,
>   In manifold hues glisten and glitter,
>   Shining and sparkling like dragon scales.
>
> Of stones there are:
>   Red jade, rose stone,
>   Orbed jades, vulcan stone,
>   Aculith, dark polishing stone,
>   Quartz, and the warrior rock.
>
> To the east there is Basil Garden,
>   With wild ginger, thoroughwort, angelica, pollia,
>   Hemlock parsley, sweet flag,
>   Lovage, selinum,
>   Sugar cane, and mioga ginger.
>
>   ...

The high dry lands grow:
  Wood sorrel, oats, twining snout, iris,
  Cadweed, nutgrass, and green sedge.

The low wet lands grow:
  Fountain grass, marshgrass,
  Smartweed, water bamboo,
  Lotus, water oats, reeds,
  Cottage thatch, and stink grass.
  So many things live here,
  They cannot be counted.

To the west there are:
  Bubbling springs and clear ponds,
  Where surging waters ebb and flow.
  On their surface bloom lotus and caltrop flowers;
  Their depths conceal huge boulders and white sand.

Within them there are:
  The divine tortoise, crocodile, alligator,
  Hawksbill, soft-shell, and trionyx.

To the north there is a shady grove:
  Its trees are elm, *nanmu*, camphor,
  Cinnamon, pepper, magnolia,
  Cork, wild pear, vermilion willow,
  Hawthorn, pear, date plum, chestnut,
  Tangerine and pomelo sweet and fragrant.

In the treetops there are:
  The phoenix, peacock, simurgh,
  Leaping gibbon, and tree-jackal.

Beneath them there are:
  The white tiger, black panther,
  The *Manyan* and leopard cat.

Although the identification of some of the items listed in Sima Xiangru's catalogue is difficult, the task is made easier thanks to such sources as
Bernard Read's translation of the terms in the 《本草綱目》, the philological notes by Qing dynasty commentators such as Zhang Yun'ao 張雲璈
(1747–1829), Hu Shaoying 胡紹煐 (1791–1860) and Zhu Jian 朱珔 (1759–
1850), and various specialized works on botanical terms. For those terms

that cannot be precisely identified, the translator must invent his own English equivalents. For example, 昆吾 is a stone found in a famous volcanic peak that produced copper and gold. An English approximation might be "vulcan stone." No one really knows what the 砥砆 stone might be, and thus the translator is free to concoct something based on the sound of the word; hence, "warrior stone" (ex 武夫).

For most plant names, the translator can provide the English common name, or give a literal translation of the scientific name. For example, "twining snout" for 苞 is an English translation of the scientific name *Rhychosia volubilis*. When the authorities do not agree on the identification of the plant, one may coin his own term. Thus, the foul-smelling 軒于 becomes stink grass.

Names of mythological creatures always present special problems to the translator. There are established Sinological conventions for the 鳳 (phoenix) and 鸞 (simurgh), but there are many creatures for which one must either romanize the name or create a new English term. Thus, 梟羊 becomes "roving simian", 蜚遽 is "flying chimera", and 鸄鳥 is turned into "canopy bird".

One problematical term is the word *manyan* 蛫蜓 of the last line in the passage translated above. The Western Jin commentator Guo Pu 郭璞 (276–324) explains it as a large beast, eight hundred feet long, resembling a wildcat. Some commentators have argued that the length Guo Pu specifies for this creature is a gross exaggeration, and that it actually was not *eight* hundred, but eight feet long. However, since the *manyan* clearly is an imaginary being, its precise length is of no consequence. Guo Pu perhaps derived his explanation from Zhang Heng, who refers to it the "giant beast eight hundred feet long."

Translators have provided various renderings for *manyan*. Burton Watson simply gives "leopard" with no explanation for his choice. Yves Hervouet calls it a "wolf the length of a hundred meters." In a detailed note discussing the name, he cites the *Shuowen jiezi* 《說文解字》 explanation of 獌 as belonging to the wolf class. However, this word refers to the animal variously known as 猵獌 or 猵犴 , which is possibly the leopard cat. Whatever manner of creature *manyan* was, its name obviously is descriptive of its great length: "long and extended." One could render it as "behemoth", but this name generally applies to the hippopotamus.

In cases where the English lexicon provides no appropriate equivalent, it perhaps it best simply to leave such words as *Manyan* untranslated and to explain the term in a note. The *fu* in fact is one of those learned forms of poetry that require extensive annotation. Even translators such as Arthur Waley and Burton Watson, whose translations are intended for non-specialist readers, have provided at least some annotation. Scholarly translations, such as those done by Yves Hervouet and David Knechtges, have a surfeit of annotation.

In addition to the rare bird, animal, and mineral names that appear in *fu* catalogues, there also is difficult and unusual technical terminology. For example, pieces such as Zhang Heng's "Rhapsody on the Two Metropolises", the "Rhapsody on the Hall of Numimous Brilliance in Lu" 〈魯靈光殿賦〉 by Wang Yanshou 王延壽 (fl. 163), and the "Rhapsody on the Hall of Great Blessings" 〈京福殿賦〉 by He Yan 何晏 (ob. 249) all have extended descriptions of architectural features of palaces. Wang Yangshou's rhapsody contains the following lines:

> In three compartments, four exteriors,
> Eight sectors, and nine corners,
> A myriad pillars, leaning in clusters,
> Ruggedly rising, provide mutual support.
>
> Floating posts, sublimely soaring, suspended like stars,
> Are perilously poised on high, cleaving and clinging.
> Flying rafters, arched and arced, pointing like rainbows,
> Raised aloft, great and grand, soar en masse.
> Layered bearing blocks are precipitously piled precariously positioned;
> Curved bracket arms, bent and bowed, concatenate like chains.
> Mushroom-shaped capitals are thickly arrayed, closely clustered.
> Bracing struts, like bifurcating branches, lean at angles;
> Laterally twisting and turning, they jut sidewards,
> Conjoined and connected, braced and trussed together.

In order to translate passages such as the one cited above, one must become familiar with traditional Chinese architectural terminology and building techniques. The Song dynasty architectural treatise 《營造法式》 by Li Jie 李誡 (1035–1108 or ca. 1065–1110) and Else Glahn's study of Han architectural terms are indispensable to the translator.

There are also some *fu* that employ such specialized vocabulary, the translator is very hard-pressed to discover what the terms mean, let alone devise an English rendering. Fortunately, some of these pieces come equipped with near-contemporary commentaries that often provide excellent guides to deciphering the language. For example, the "Rhapsody on Pheasant Shooting" 〈射雉賦〉 by Pan Yue 潘岳 (247–300) employs a host of terms pertaining to crossbow shooting, pheasants, and hunting blinds. In this case, we are fortunate to have a commentary by Xu Yuan 徐爰 (394–475), who lived about 150 years later than Pan Yue. Xu Yuan gives clear explanations for most of the technical terms Pan uses in his *fu*. Thus, we know that 翳 is a type of blind made of branches and leaves behind which hunters shot the pheasants. Xu Yuan also explains that 鞍 is a term for the plumes "inserted between the tail feathers." Thus, it probably is a term for the coverts. Xu Yuan elsewhere provides a detailed description of the 鷩 or golden pheasant, including information about its "ferocious" 憋 (an obvious pun on its name) temperament.

The most troublesome words of the *fu* are the binomial descriptives 連綿字 . The binomial descriptives are either alliterative or rhyming binomes 雙聲 and 疊韻 . Although they are common in the *Shi jing* 《詩經》 and *Chuci* 《楚辭》 , they are the stock language of the *fu*. The grand epideictic *fu* of Sima Xiangru, Yang Xiong, Ban Gu, Zhang Heng, Zuo Si 左思 (ca. 250–ca. 305), and Guo Pu consist of long series of binomial descriptives many of which were difficult to understand. The critic Liu Xie 劉勰 (ca. 465–ca. 522) comments on how hard it was even for learned men to read what he called "precious words" 瑋字 :

> Furthermore, when rhapsodizing on capitals and parks, most [*fu* writers of the Han period] used loan graphs and phonetic compounds. Thus, the philology of the Former Han largely is concerned with precious words. This was not only because the expressions they created were unusual, but also because they were difficult for most people to understand. By the Later Han, philology became neglected.... In the Wei dynasty writers composed in elegant language, but graphs had a common standard. When they looked back on the Han writings, they found them difficult and abstruse. Thus, Cao Zhi in referring to the writings of Yang Xiong and Sima Xiangru said that their aim was hidden and their import deep, but without a teacher the reader was unable to decipher their language, and without broad learning he cannot comprehend their meaning. This was not only because their talent was far-reaching, but also because the words they used were obscure.

If the learned scholars and writers of the Han and Six Dynasties period found the binomial descriptives difficult to understand, what of the hapless translator who attempts to render the less common of these words into

English? One of course can consult the commentaries. However, the commentaries provide only limited assistance in understanding the precise meaning of these "precious words". First, they do not always gloss individual words, but only provide the general sense of several words in a series. For example, Guo Pu's "Rhapsody on the Yangtze River" 〈江賦〉 contains the following two lines consisting of a series of four binomes:

滴湟忽泱
灂泅瀾淪

The *Wen xuan* commentator Li Shan 李善 explains that the two lines are descriptive of swift movement of water. Although helpful for understanding the general sense, his paraphrase does not provide any information about the meaning of each term. The Qing dynasty philologists have made studies of some of these words, and their learned glosses often contain useful information about related words or variant ways of writing the same word.

For example, Hu Shaoying compares 滴湟 (*gjiuet-guang*) with 律皇 (*ljuet-guang*), which occurs in Yang Xiong's "Plume Hunt Rhapsody" 〈羽獵賦〉 in the sense of "swiftly moving".

Even if one obtains a gloss on a particular expression, either from an early glossographer or a later philological commentary, one still must decide how to render it into English. One solution simply is to provide a paraphrase of the entire line. This is the method generally used by von Zach. For example, he renders four lines of Guo Pu's "Rhapsody on the Yangtze River" into one line of German: "Im Kampfe unter einander stürmen sie rasend dahin."

滴湟忽泱
灂泅瀾淪
漩澴滎濙
溾瀤濆瀑

One method of translating these words is to endow each binome with a English meaning that conveys the sense, at least in context. The translator might try to devise alliterative (or occasionally rhyming) equivalents that convey something of the euphonic effect these words have in the original. Thus, a translation of these same lines reads:

Dashing and darting, scurrying and scudding,
Swiftly streaking, rapidly rushing,

Whirling and swirling, twining and twisting,
Peaked and piled, spurting and spouting.

Another problem that confronts the translator of not only the *fu* but other genres of classical Chinese literature is the difficulty of conveying the rich language and original metaphors of the Chinese original. Consider the following opening lines of the "Rhapsody on Lamenting Those Who Have Passed Away" 〈歎逝賦〉 by Lu Ji:

伊天地之運流
紛升降而相襲
日望空以駿驅
節循虛而警立

The general sense is clear enough: Heaven and Earth are in constant motion, the four seasons alternate, and time swiftly passes. However, to put these four lines into a comprehensible English version that does not sacrifice Lu Ji's rich language presents a great challenge to even the most gifted translator. The words themselves are rather plain and ordinary, and it is often the case that the most difficult passages to render into intelligible English are those that contain the most common words of literary Chinese. The difficulty comes from casting English sentences that represent the phrasing and structure of the Chinese as much as possible. What is the force of the initial 伊? Does one for example give full force to the 之 in the first line? In the *fu* each line is a complete sentence, and thus one should ignore the 之 and construe the basic meaning as 天地運流, "Heaven and Earth turn and flow." The initial particle 伊 may have a rhetorical force, but in this instance it seems untranslatable. It may have some emphatic force as in the following line from Zhang Heng's "Pondering the Mystery" 〈思玄賦〉: 伊中情久信脩, "Indeed, my inner feelings are truly good!"

The second line presents more difficulty. How does one construe the adverb 紛 (which is one of the most troublesome words in ancient and medieval Chinese to render into English)? What is the subject of 升降? Li Shan says that the implied subject is the 氣 (pneuma) of Heaven and Earth. He then cites a passage from the 〈月令〉 of the *Li ji* 《禮記》 to illustrate his interpretation: In early spring the vapors of Heaven descend while the vapors of Earth rise; in early winter the process is reversed. Although 氣 is not in the text, one could supply it for the sake of clarity: "Their 氣 thickly ascends and descends in mutual succession." However, is the translator justified in supplying a word that is not in the original text? Can one devise a rendering that preserves the economy of the original without the insertion of padding words such as *pneuma* that are awkward in an English line? One solution to this problem is that if one must add a word, it should be to the first line, for it really is not Heaven and Earth that "turn and flow" but their 氣 . If the implied subject is 氣 , the verb 運 here does not mean "turn" in the sense of "revolve", or "rotate" but rather "to move in a circular fashion", "to swirl". Thus, one might devise the following English rendering of the two lines:

Oh, how the vapors of Heaven and Earth swirl and flow!
Thickly they ascend and descend in continuous succession.

One supplies the word "vapors" to indicate that it is the 氣 (air, breath, vapor, vital force) that emanates from Heaven and Earth to propel the process of creation and growth. Although the word "vapors" does not fully convey the sense of the term 氣 , it matches well with "swirl and flow". To preserve the vapor image, 紛 is rendered as "thickly". In a note one would explain that the rising and falling of the 氣 represent the cyclical changes in the cosmos. Finally, 相襲 is translated as "continuous succession", a rendering that only partially accounts for everything the word implies in this line. The literal sense, "following one upon another", does not work well in the English line. The meaning here clearly is that the process by which the cosmic 氣 rises and falls goes on unabated. The 氣 of Earth is replaced or followed (襲) by the 氣 of Heaven and vice versa. Again, all of these implications must be spelled out in a note.

The last two lines of the "Rhapsody on Lamenting Those Who Have Passed Away" passage cited above are relatively straightforward. However, 警立 in line 4 is a rather unusual expression that requires some attention. Li Shan explains that 警 is like 驚 "startling", presumably in the sense of startling swiftness. The usual translation of 立 "to stand" or "to establish" does not fit this context, and one must find another English equivalent. The subject of 立 is 節 (season). The sense of 立 perhaps is "begin" or "set in". Since the two lines are parallel, one should attempt to produce nearly parallel English lines. An approximation might be:

Across the sky the sun drives like a racing courser;
Out of the void the seasons set in with surprising swiftness.

Because of the richness of *fu* diction, the translator must attempt as much as possible to retain the surprising metaphors and unusual expressions in the English rendering. For example, the Western Jin poet Mu Hua 木華 (fl. ca. 290) in his "Rhapsody on the Sea" 〈海賦〉 describes the floods that occurred in the time of Yao and Shun as 天綱浡滴. The meaning can be paraphrased as "The Heaven-appointed waterways swelled and overflowed," (Watson, 1971) or even "a mighty flood". However, the Chinese original says nothing about "Heaven-appointed water-ways" or "a mighty flood." The original uses the term 天綱, "mainstays of Heaven", which are the cords that bind the heavenly bodies. The flood waters swelled so high they caused the mainstays of Heaven to "froth and foam" (the rhyming binome 浡滴 describes the seething waters in flood). Although the literal rendering results in a startling statement that challenges our conventional understanding of celestial phenomena (the mainstays of Heaven frothed and foamed!), it is preferable directly to translate Mu Hua's wording than to resort to some bland paraphrase that excises from Mu Hua's line the rich and novel expression that it contains.

Another important feature of the *fu* is the use of parallelism. Although such Han writers as Sima Xiangru, Yang Xiong, Ban Gu, and Zhang Heng made extensive use of parallelism, during the North-South Dynasties period parallelism came to dominate all forms of writing to an extreme degree. Thus, a common name for the *fu* of this period is 駢賦 (parallel-style *fu*). Famous examples are the "Rhapsody on Separation" 〈別賦〉 and "Rhapsody on Resentment" 〈恨賦〉 by Jiang Yan 江淹 (444–505) and "Rhapsody on the Small Garden" 〈小園賦〉 by Yu Xin 庾信 (513–581). In their *fu*, as well as most *fu* that make use of parallelism, the basic metrical unit is the couplet. The couplets may consists of three, four, five, six, or seven syllables. In order to present the couplet structure and more clearly show the parison, the translator may set off the English text by indentation. Thus, parallel lines from Jiang Yan's "Rhapsody on Resentment" can be given the following form in English:

Sometimes there are:
The apprehensive tears of an estranged minister,
The crestfallen heart of a concubine's son,
A banished stranger on the northern sea,
An exile guarding the frontier north of Long.
These men have only to hear the mournful wind swiftly rising,

And bloody tears soak their lapels.
They too
 Filled with bitterness, stifling their sighs,
 Fall into extinction, plunge into oblivion.

The 文賦 or prose *fu* presents fewer difficulties for the translator. Because it is a form of *guwen* prose, there is less parallelism. The language also tends to be much simpler and involves fewer rare words.

The first translations of the *fu* were done by Arthur Waley. His *The Temple and Other Poems*, published in 1923, consists mainly of *fu*. Another early translator of the *fu* into a Western language was the Austrian Sinologist, Erwin von Zach, who translated most of the *fu* of the *Wen xuan* into German (see *Die Chinesische Anthologie*). Although von Zach was capable of producing literary translations, his intended reader was the student of Chinese. Thus, his *fu* translations often read as paraphrases, and in spite of his desire for accuracy, are not always philologically exact. Another European Sinologist who translated a number of *fu* into French was the Russian emigré Georges Margouliès, who devoted an entire volume to translations of *fu* in the *Wen xuan*. The first scholar to set rigorous scholarly standards for the translation of the *fu* was James Robert Hightower of Harvard University. Professor Hightower in his long article on the *fu* of Tao Qian provided faithful, but highly readable renderings that were amply annotated. A good selection of high literary quality is Burton Watson's *Chinese Rhyme-Prose*, published in 1971. This is the best collection of *fu* translation for the general reader. For scholarly, thoroughly annotated translations, the works to consult are Hervouet and Knechtges' translations of the *Wen xuan*.

References

Clark, Cyril Drummond le Gros. *The Prose-poetry of Su Tung-p'o; Being Translated into English*. London: Kegan Paul, 1935.

Hightower, James Robert. "The *Fu* of T'ao Ch'ien." *Harvard Journal of Asiatic Studies*, Vol. 20 (1957), pp. 512–33.

Knechtges, David R. *The Han Rhapsody*. Cambridge: Cambridge University Press, 1976.

———. "Problems of Translating Descriptive Binomes in the *Fu*." *Tamkang Review*, Vol. 15 (1984/85), pp. 329–47.

———. "Two Studies on the Han *Fu*." *Parerga*, Vol. 1 (1968).

————. *Wen Xuan, or Selections of Refined Literature*. Princeton: Princeton University Press, 1987.

Lai, Monica and T. C. Lai. *Rhapsodic Essays from the Chinese*. Hong Kong: Kelly and Walsh, 1979.

Waley, Arthur. *The Temple and Other Poems*. London: Allen and Unwin, 1923.

Watson, Burton. *Chinese Rhyme-Prose: Poems in the Fu Form from the Han and Six Dynasties Periods*. New York and London: Columbia University Press, 1971.

Wilhelm, Hellmut. "The Scholar's Frustration: Notes on a Type of 'Fu'." In *Chinese Thought and Institutions*, edited by John K. Fairbank. Chicago: University of Chicago Press, 1957, pp. 310–19, 398–403.

Sanqu

Wayne Schlepp
Medieval Chinese Literature
East Asian Studies, University of Toronto, Toronto, Canada

General Background

In China the practice of setting words to tunes goes back as far as the earliest poetic literature that survives. *Sanqu* 散曲 takes its place in this tradition following closely the nature and form of the *ci* 詞 of Song times, which is usually seen as the epitome of the literary song.

In the general histories of Yuan (1278–1367) literature the *sanqu* is adumbrated by the drama which is taken to be the representative genre of that period. The drama is made up of songs arranged into sets with dialogue interspersed but many of the tunes in these sets were popular in society and were sung on their own. Singers or writers will have composed their own lyrics to these single songs which were called *xiaoling* 小令 . At times song sets as well were composed but without the dialogue of the drama and were referred to as *taoshu* 套數 . The lyrics of these songs were collected and now make up the corpus of *sanqu*, or "loose" *qu*, which were not bound to a dramatic piece.

Sanqu as a branch of the literary song tradition developed, with the music and verse of the drama, along a relatively independent course in the north. Had the Northern Song dynasty simply continued without interruption, there would no doubt have been similar developments in the song tradition, perhaps through the influx of foreign music and linguistic changes that were taking place in the north. If for some reason northern songs had become prominent enough to be noticed on the general literary scene, most likely the differences will have been treated as a matter of style rather than anything serious enough to warrant establishing a new genre. However, the period from about the beginning of the 12th century to the last quarter of the 13th was marked at points by social and economic disruption. The periods of prosperity that did occur were separated from the mainstream of Chinese culture and developed somewhat independently. By the time China was reunited in the 1270's the semblance of a direct line of development from *ci* to *qu* was obscured. Futhermore, the northern dialect came into prominence for political reasons; it could hardly have had the influence on the literary tastes of the south if the capital had remained in Kaifeng. These factors contributed to a view of northern songs which would later set them apart as a separate genre. It is difficult to trace this branch of the song tradition because the extant corpus of *sanqu* was collected for the most part in the last generation or so of the Yuan and the pieces that could provide a view of the transition are lost or difficult to identify. The best information we have now comes from studies tracing the development of the drama.

This is not to imply that there is hidden somewhere a direct line of development from *ci* to *qu* which must be found out. It is merely to reiterate that the practice of setting words to songs is a continuing process with changes arising from linguistic change, different musical material, and adoption by writers of different skills and purposes and most certainly economic and politcal circumstances. In this respect a transition would have been much as it is in any age. There were *ci* from Song times which continued to be written and some are found in the collected works of Yuan writers, but the greater bulk of what we now call *sanqu* are new songs, songs that had never been heard in the south.

Although *sanqu* is adumbrated in general histories by the drama, it is seen in those same accounts as the representative verse of Yuan times. There are good reasons to question this but if indeed it is true that "the literary vitality of the time went into writing colloquial songs, song-suites, plays and stories," (Waley, 1963:93) then we must admit that the *sanqu* corpus is relatively small. If we adjust for the greater duration of the Tang and Song periods, the number of Yuan *sanqu* preserved is about one-fifth that of verses in the *Quan Tang shi* 《全唐詩》 and one-half that in the *Quan Song ci* 《全宋詞》. However, the broad spectrum of pieces preserved in the corpus is quite remarkable. There is a vigorous, vulgar side coming from its uses, perhaps origins, in the markets, brothels and theatres and at the same time a subtle and refined side which developed in the hands of master poets with more traditional literary skill. In this the *sanqu* probably differs little from patterns of development in the rest of the song tradition though one must remember that after the unification at the end of the 13th century it was imported by the south and was taken up by some members of the literary community in that region and was subject to their literary tastes and practices.

A reflection of what at least some writers thought of *sanqu* in the Yuan is found in the prefaces of two of the major collections of the times, i.e. the preface by Guan Yunshi to 《陽春白雪》 and that by Deng Zijin to 《太平樂府》. They attempt to set *sanqu* in the grand tradition of Chinese poetry, most particularly the *yuefu* 樂府 and, by implication, even so exalted a work as the *Classic of Poetry*. There seems to be reflected in these prefaces a certain air of self-congratulation. Radtke (1984:25) remarks, however, that "not one Korean or Japanese source of (the Yuan) period mentions the *qu* genre in general or the *xiaoling* or the *zaju*. We may take this as an additional indication of the low status that these genres seem to have enjoyed in their time." It was not until later times that *sanqu* tended to be seen as a separate form of the song tradition and was discussed and practiced as a distinct form of verse.

Critical writing, such as descriptions of the rhyme system, discussion of how songs ought best to be written and general commentary on successful songs and the best writers, begins as early as 1324 when Zhou Deqing wrote the 《中原音韻》. This literature grows quite large from the Ming onward and although most of it is dedicated to discussion of the *qu* as it appears in the drama, there is much which pertains to the *sanqu* as well. One of the general qualities of *sanqu* which critics remark upon and which might be of interest to a translator seems to be its "freedom". It is this which distinguishes *sanqu* from other forms of song verse for most critics. Of this Wang Jide says:

> *Shi* (Tang lyrics) do not compare to *ci* (Song lyrics) and *ci* do not compare with *qu*, which tend to conform more to one's feelings. The *shi* is limited to the eight-line (*lü* 律) and the four-line (*jue* 絕) forms, and if the thought is not dealt with completely, one cannot add a single word if one wants to. The *ci* is limited to the tune, and if the expression (of feelings) is not complete, one cannot add a single phrase even if one wants. With *qu*, however, the tunes can be used in tandem and words can be added extra-metrically. *Shi* and *ci* do not allow jokes or dialect but with *qu* anything is allowed, no matter what my mouth would want to say or where my thought would want to go. That is why I say: To satisfy the feelings, one need go no farther than *qu*.

We must take this in its proper context and avoid interpreting it according to recent notions of freedom which in some quarters have been raised to cult levels. Whatever else Wang was talking about, he was not counselling a disregard for tonal form, though he does say that in many colloquial *qu* certain patterns have been violated with impunity. In the Yuan, Zhou Deqing maintained that the prosody of *qu* was stricter than *ci* because, for example, certain positions specified not only the *ping ze* 平仄 tones of classical poetry and *ci* but sometimes distinguished *yang* 陽 from *yin ping* 陰平 and *shang* 上 from *qu* 去 tones. Furthermore, for southern writers the form was restrictive because they didn't always know what to do with the *ru* 入 tones, though it must be granted that some probably did not find this an impediment. It is a fact, of course, that a great many of the most admired lines derive their beauty from decidedly traditional diction and from the effects of tone patterns, and verses which are still most admired as poetry usually show the tautness of classical verse.

Another critical bias which is useful to consider is the concern with "individuality", that is to say, expecting all verse to be unique in expression, to avoid cliché and create a private world as an oblique exposition of the poet's soul. These are a part of our perceptions of modern Western literary verse, a verse which might be characterized as interestingly ingrown and quite different in conception and execution from the *sanqu* of Yuan or indeed from the song writing of our own day. It is easy to see how even the inadvertent elevation of biases to the level of universals will prejudice the view of the corpus.

The *sanqu* have been preserved mainly in four anthologies of Yuan times: two, the *Yangchun baixue* 《陽春白雪》 and the *Taiping yuefu* 《太平樂府》 were collected by Yang Zhaoying (fl. 1300); the other two, the *Yuefu xin sheng* and the *Yuefu chun yu*, are by unknown editors. Of these the *Yuefu chun yu* is thought to be the earliest; the *Yangchun baixue*, in one form or another, appeared before 1324 and the *Taiping yuefu* was published in mid-14th century. Least is known about the *Yuefu xin sheng*. There are Ming anthologies that have preserved some songs beyond these as well. (Schlepp, 1970:11–13) There are many modern editions with annotations that can be of use to translators but the *Quan Yuan sanqu* by Sui Shushen presents the best and most complete text. It is arranged according to author which has certain advantages. Another anthology, the *Yuan ren xiaoling ji* by Chen Naiqian, contains nearly all the *xiaoling* of the Yuan; it is arranged so that all the songs of the same verse form are together which is often useful when problems of meter or interpretation arise.

General Remarks on Communication

As a matter of coming to terms with biases, it is worth any translator's while to consider a basic model of communication. In addition to a Text we recognize an Author and Reader; outside these is the Interpreter who constructs notions of the other three for purposes of dealing with a particular communication. As the text is performed, usually by the Interpreter, there is revealed more about the three basic elements, Author, Text and Reader, and this in turn calls into play more of the resources of the Interpreter. We can say all is in the mind of the Interpreter and is subject to his capacities. This process of generating more and more information suggests there can never be a definitive understanding of the text. This is true, but practical conventions dictating the purposes of social intercourse within the cultural group guide speakers and hearers in limiting the generation of information to fit the purposes of the immediate act of communication.

It is often remarked that the translation of poetry, in distinction to other literary forms, is impossible. By some absolute standard, all communication is equally impossible, for no word, no sentence, no gesture ever means exactly and totally the same to two people. Yet we communicate effectively every day simply because, as we said, the communication is circumscribed by social necessity which establishes an agreed upon context to which each act of communication will apply. The difficulty in translating poetry — or complex prose texts for that matter — is that the contexts, which are implied by any act of communication, are less obvious and perhaps not complete enough to make "poetic" communication as "perfect" as that of simple, everyday speech. When we interpret and translate poetry, we are obliged to depend heavily upon what we can guess of the poet, his readers and the message of the text, something we take for granted in communications whose contexts derive from the immediate situation in, for example, "Please come in and close the door." It is in filling out these "incomplete" contexts that we make the most extended assumptions but unfortunately it is also at this point where the problem tends least to be acknowledged. This has special consequences for the translator.

One of the ways by which the contexts of poetry are generally filled out involves the translator in the functions of the philologist or critic, for he must be able to judge the literary value of the works he translates and must as well be able to set them in the perspective of literary history. He must also know the target literature and its history so that comparable settings can be found or contrived to represent in some reasonable way the native literary setting of works he translates. The literary conventions of a people will always influence literary production and, of course, translation. For example, in the religious traditions of societies, the elements of communication assume a fixed and unquestioned position; the author is divine, the text is immutable and we, the readers, are in need of its instruction and guidance. Clearly this imposes a special kind of interpretation on all the texts associated with that tradition and it does this by circumscribing very strictly the functions that each of the elements of communication may have.

It is possible also to establish a bias toward any one of the elements, Author, Text or Reader, which will influence interpretation in special ways as well. Biases are unavoidable in practice. They will be part of a cultural view of literary communication, such as we see in traditions which uphold the sanctity of the Text, or in another which is enchanted by the genius of the Author, or in yet another which concentrates on the Reader as the centre and source of the Text. It is important that the translator recognize bias both in himself and in critics upon whom he might depend. The purpose is not to eradicate bias but merely to see the effects it has on interpretations of the literary communication and indeed on how it gives society its view of its own literature. If these points are kept in mind when translating or judging translations, it is easier to establish useful points of reference between works which differ owing to different sets of biases. Critical discussion will then have a better chance of being useful.

Author

When we consider a text we invariably assume there was at some time and some place an author. We assume this to be true whether we know little or much about this author, whether it is detailed or sketchy, whether what we know of his times and his place is precise or misty and confused. Any human or human-like trait in our experience can be attributed to this author and at one time or another during interpretation we are likely to refer, tacitly or otherwise, to vast bodies of these traits to help us make some kind of sense of the text.

What this suggests is that we should discover the "myths" which go to make up Author not to replace them with some "truth" or another but rather to see why certain assumptions are deemed necessary by certain Readers and to recognize what effect that will have on interpretation. It is in these assumptions about Author that the Interpreter, and of course the translator, has most need of and is most influenced by a knowledge of the life and times of the historical author. Such knowledge from the Yuan period, as most early periods, is necessarily thin and liable to be stereotyped or subject to extra-literary biases of later ages. Typical is the view first taken by the Ming critics that all *qu* writers were necessarily frustrated officials, educated but unwilling to serve barbarian rulers. This is a questionable generalization and perhaps the best counsel to give the translator is to rely upon good studies which treat the sources critically. It is vitally important to examine the background from which we in the role of Interpreter construct notions of Author, Text and Reader, and care in doing this is a practice in the best of philological traditions.

Histories of literature and of *sanqu* tend to split the Yuan into early and late periods. The majority of the authors of the early period are usually characterized as *haofang* 豪放 , which suggests a free, forthright sort of attitude, not much concerned with the niceties of form. The second period authors are said to be *qingli* 清麗 , which would indicate a more meticulous approach to their craft. A useful division could also be drawn along geographic lines separating north from south. Although the early period would show very few southern writers, a great part, if not the majority, of song production in the later period was owing to them and bears the marks of their literary style. In any event, it is hardly likely that southern writers could know first-hand the changes that had taken place in the north, or always know the patois which northern writers could so easily make use of in their *sanqu*. Most will have brought to this new genre typically southern habits of composition, somewhat literary in style, somewhat removed from the common folk and lacking therefore in some of the robust qualities which are so much admired in the northern writers. But this meant at the same time the introduction of refinement, the very quality which gave the most admired Song *ci* its character. These qualities had best be taken into account as the translator judges each text.

In the *sanqu* corpus there is a small body of anonymous verse, about 50 *xiaoling* and a dozen *taoshu* in *Quan Yuan sanqu* 《全元散曲》 . These are by no means all from lower class writers whose product will be colloquial, rough or vulgar. Authors of which anything is known, on the other hand, seem to come more often from the upper levels of society. (Radtke, 1984:22) This may be owing to the fact that it is this very sort of person who could afford to have his works published. This also means that the greatest writers will not necessarily be the ones that are best represented; Zhang Xiaoshan 張小山 , although a master versifier, is not a great poet, nor was he one who made best use of the genius of *sanqu*, yet he has a greater number of poems preserved than any other, 855 *xiaoling* in 《全元散曲》 , about four times that of the next most numerous. For a genius like Guan Hanqing 關漢卿 , who very likely produced as much verse, only 57 *xiaoling* are extant, which is few even compared to other well known *sanqu* writers. Zhang Xiaoshan was an official with the means to publish his works — or he may have had a filial son to edit and preserve them; Guan Hanqing very likely lacked such means, though possibly also he just couldn't be bothered. There are only about half a dozen others with more than 100 *xiaoling* attributed to them and not all of these writers will have been officials.

Among the writers of *sanqu* were many foreigners, as indeed there were among writers of other forms of verse, notably the *shi*. A few of these are justly famous for their production of verse and the best known of them is Guan Yunshi 貫雲石 , a Ouighur. Among the Chinese writers of *sanqu*, the ones most frequently seen in anthologies of *sanqu* translations are Lu Zhi 盧摯 , Guan Hanqing, Bai Pu 白樸 , Yao Sui 姚燧 , Ma Zhiyuan 馬致遠 , Deng Yubin 鄧玉賓 , Zhang Yanghao 張養浩 , Qiao Ji 喬吉 , and Zhang Xiaoshan 張小山 .

Reader

The Reader as an element in communication can have as many and varied attributes as the Author. Literature that is in the public domain will invarably have an audience that is a group, and this is true even if the addressee of the literary communication is a specific person. The important point to note about an audience of this sort is that it will cross boundaries of time and locale. An Interpreter's notion of the readership will include what might be known or imagined about the social status and times of the Author but it will also include notions of Readers outside this sphere. It will necessarily include an audience which is the translator's own. In addition, one reader will always be oneself as Interpreter of the text, or more likely some abbreviated notion of oneself suiting the purposes of the communication.

It is difficult to characterize the Yuan audience. Again it could have included nearly anyone throughout the social scale but unless we are making a history of the times, it is perhaps less important to know the specific size and composition of the class than who the readers might reasonably have been under certain circumstances. An interesting characterization is found in Metzger and Yang (1967:12) where it is suggested that the readers were predominantly Mongols, Moslems, Tartars and Koreans, and so poets used vernacular rather than literary Chinese in the hope that these compositions would then be better understood and their literary wares more marketable. This is certainly possible but perhaps a broader view is required. One might look again at the Art and Literature section of *China under Mongol Rule* as well as other sections of that book. Again Idema and West (1982), is helpful, especially the first two chapters. Dolby (1971) deals with the circles such writers as Guan Hanqing frequented and Waley in the "The Green Bower Collection" provides visions of the world of entertainers which many writers knew so well. The milieu of entertainers and fellow writers will give an indication of only a small portion of the readership, but it is an important one as it will be a technically proficient audience whose standards will have had to be met. The northern drama eventually spread to the south, but it is worth considering that for many southern writers the circle they would be writing for might be quite different from that in the north. It is therefore useful to distinguish Readers according to region as well. Matters of dialect will enter in. For example, a southern writer who misplaced the *ru-sheng* (entering tone 入聲) words would have had complaints from northern singers though he might not have from southern singers. This is, of course, one of Zhou Deqing's concerns.

Text

A text is a complex assemblage of symbols which may form into arresting groups which we can refer to as textual features, each of which will have some specific function for the initiated. It is the function rather than the form of these that translators should consider, i.e. what function a feature might have in the conventions of both source and target languages. In the following discussion we will consider rhyme, rhythm and meter, syntax and the general balance of these in a poem.

(1) Rhyme

In the hands of a good versifier rhyme, in conjunction with line length, functions to shape discourse in ways that a sentence does in prose. It is sometimes important to retain some of this shaping in the translation and a resouceful translator will find many ways in which this can be done. Ironically, it often turns out that rhyming in the translation usually subverts any effort to maintain a semblance of that shape. If this is the major purpose for rhyming, what we find in translations is too often gratuitous.

Of recent *sanqu* translators, J. I. Crump and Yip Wai-lim most consistently attempt rhyme in their versions and often succeed admirably. Crump has his greatest success with lighter themes such as his translation of Yang Na's verse to a flea. (Crump, 1983:130) One of his more successful ones on other themes is Zhao Yuguei's 趙禹圭 "Remembering Things Past":

1. Oh, I recall the banquet when
2. Among those drifting Clouds of Sunset Hue
3. I saw my fated love and knew
4. She sojourned on this earth again.
5. My trammeled heart can not forget her
6. Even for a single day.
7. Countless times in dreams we've met
8. To no avail, for I have yet
9. To find a single word to say!
   (Crump, 1983:36–7)

1. 記前日席上泛流霞
2. 正遇著宿世冤家
3. 自從見了心牽掛
4. 心兒裡撇他不下
5. 夢兒裡常常見他
6. 說不的星兒話

Comparison with the original shows that the rhymed translation diverges from the general shape of discourse rather more than an unrhymed one would. Though Crump avoids it better than most, there is the inevitable problem of stilted diction which rhyming in English forces upon the translator and it is safe to say that only rarely does rhymed English achieve an appropriate tone in the translation of serious Chinese verse. In this respect, the following by Yip does seem to imitate the effects of the rhyme in the original a bit better. This is achieved with near rhyme though here as well the rhymed words stand out to the English reader as unnatural, an effect that surely does not occur in Guan Hanqing's original:

1. Winds whistle.
2. Rains drizzle.
3. Even the Sleep Immortal cannot go to sleep.
4. Sorrow meshed on heart's tip.
5. Downpour, downpour, tears drop.
6. Chilling cicadas stop, crickets creak.
7. Drip, drip, fine rains on banana-leaves beat.

(Yip, 1976:446)

1. 風飄飄
2. 雨瀟瀟
3. 便做陳摶睡不著
4. 懊惱傷懷抱
5. 撲簌簌淚點抛抛
6. 秋蟬兒噪罷寒蛩兒叫
7. 淅零零細雨打芭蕉

One is drawn to consider how the linguistic facts and the dexterity of Chinese versifiers of the Yuan differ so vastly from the conventions of English and the rather dim appreciation of such skills which present day English speakers have. Almost inconceivable is the custom of *he* 和, writing a new poem using the rhyme words of another poem. Feng Zizhen 馮子振 (1257–c.1328) wrote 42 verses in the Heiqinu song form with exactly the same rhyme words and generally the same theme to a poem by Bai Wujiu 白無咎 (c. 1297 fl.). Even if one could do a passing translation of such a tour de force, it is likely that most English readers would find it a curiosity and wonder why anyone would bother.

Unfortunately most translations get rhymed simply because the original rhymes, but this is not a compelling reason. Perhaps one should always try to rhyme but remember that finding a few ringing words does not always constitute success.

(2) Rhythm and Meter

Rhythm is a sequence of equal intervals of time marked by a beat and it can be generated in a number of ways independent of language. Meter is founded on rhythm. It is a rhythmic system which can enhance the rhetorical effects of language. In *sanqu* it originated in music which was by no means necessarily the same as the spoken meters we perceive in the texts today. Meter is naturally related to syntax which is to say that the two must accommodate one another. The beats would likely be as follows in this poem by Guan Yunshi:

1. 隔簾聽
2. 幾番風送賣花聲
3. 夜來微雨天階淨
4. 小院閑庭
5. 輕寒翠袖生
6. 穿芳徑
7. 十二闌干憑
8. 杏花疏影
9. 楊柳新晴

This does not take into account extra-metric syllables 襯字 nor does it pretend to give the rhythm in which it might have been sung. It marks instead the stress points a modern reader casually reading the text is most likely to make. It does not imply a pounding beat as this is something which is left to the taste of the reader who can shift from a heavy accent on the beat to an emphasis of the off-beat, all without changing the meter. What this means for the translator is that the line is broken into manageable units; a line is not a conglomeration of undifferentiated syllables; its meter is not simply derived mechanically from the total syllable count. It provides a rhythmic pattern which gives the quality of smoothness to verse and which helps to group words into points of focus in the sentence.

Metzger and Yang translate this poem keeping the syllable count of each line the same in the English translation. It is not quite clear why they establish this as one of their standards of "faithfulness" though they hope for some "gain … at least in point of tone." (1967:15) The result can on occasion be quite attractive, as is the following:

1. Gentle winds
2. Waft voices of flower-sellers
3. into my garden after
4. rain. Walking the
5. Flowered path I savour
6. The dampness.
7. Pausing beneath the
8. Blossoms, I think

9. A new Spring-thought.

(Metzger and Yang, 1967:62)

Their accomplishment notwithstanding, this style of translation allows them to be faithful to neither rhythm, nor meter, nor sequence or substance of images, the last of these at least being a point to which they wish to "hold as faithfully as possible." Arthur Waley tried to have as many stresses (beats) in the English line as there were syllables in Chinese. This is arbitrary as well but generally, at least for Waley, worked better though even he professed difficulties with the seven syllable line. One could just as well translate one beat in English for one beat in Chinese, as beats are defined above, e.g.:

1. Outsíde I héar
2. Bréezes bríng a véndor's cáll;
3. The stárs, wáshed last níght by ráin.
4. My quíet gárden,
5. Líghtly, cóld upon my sléeve,
6. The flówered páth,
7. To tóuch the bállustráde;
8. Ápricot in shádows,
9. Wíllow in límpid air.

If we take the most important effect to be line length, as Metzger and Yang seem to, there are other ways to give the impression of the varied lengths and parallel lines of the original without adhering to the number of syllables. One significant difference between this version and theirs is the relation to sense and focus in the original lines. Key words are kept and sometimes they take the stress in both English and Chinese readings, though the last line could not keep within two beats; imagery is reduced somewhat and many translators, I am sure, would prefer a fuller syntax.

As we saw above from Zhou Deqing's concerns, the tone patterns were as important in the composition of *sanqu* as in Song *ci* though practice differed. For the translator attention to them is important for a serious study of *sanqu* as they yield insights into the diction of an author and are useful for purposes of interpretation. The song registers, 曲譜 , set out the patterns clearly and give indications of line structure.

There is considerable theorizing about syntax and its effects in Chinese poetry. Perhaps the first thing that a translator feels is "conciseness" in the

Chinese text. The novice will compare this illusion directly to English syntax and see the two on the opposite end of the same scale. No matter how one feels about it, the fact is that such qualities in one literary tradition are not directly comparable to similar ones in another but have meaning only within the scope of their own system. If the language of poetry in Chinese is noticeably more concise than Chinese prose, we can note this; if the same is true of English, we can say there may be some rough correspondence between the uses of conciseness in Chinese and its uses in English. This fact notwithstanding, there are those who argue that having to state subjects, conjunctions and other relational words in English is a barrier to translating Chinese verse and will in fact block the image creating capacity of language and turn "pure imagery" into "statements about" things. It may well be that English verse tends heavily toward the "statement about"; a brief look through Palgrave's *The Golden Treasury* will tend to confirm this. Still one wonders how syntactically perfect poems like Yeats' "The Lake Isle of Innisfree," for example, can manage to be so evocative of "pure image". Furthermore, a very brief look into even the *sanqu* corpus will reveal an enormous amount of verse devoted to the very kind of intellectualizing and "statements about" that one finds in the English verse in Palgrave's. But even if it is true in some absolute sense that English is over-specific, perhaps it should be recognized as a fact which a translator must cope with. It is important to remember that where the image making is exceptional in Chinese, it is exceptional with regard to the rest of Chinese, and does not say all that much about English. Translating image-making devices, like the other rhetorical devices, must be done within the scope of the target language's literary system. To ignore this is to ignore the conventions that are at work in any culture.

Having said this, we must add that the efforts of Yip and others have been salutary as a contrast to the sprawling lines of some prosaic translations. But again one should be able to use such techniques when necessary and drop them when they no longer have the right effect. As this technique results in a fatiguing telegraphic style, one should use it sparingly. Even the awkwardness of prosaic translation will be more readily accepted, giving the translation a chance to endure among an English readership. One might deplore this but to reach a certain public, one cannot but consider their tastes and perceptions of literature. On the other hand, a full, prose-like syntax need not be laborious as the following translation of a poem by Bai Pu will attest:

1   After a long drink, no barriers are left standing
2   If you don't sober up, what worries can you have?
3   Lees and pickles, they're two titles to fame
4   Hard liquor irons out the ups and downs of all the ages
5   Yeast buries the 10,000 foot ambition of a coloured rainbow
6   The unsuccessful can laugh at sober Qu Yuan's folly
7   But those who know what's what all confirm drunk Tao was right

(Scott, 1972:125)

1. 長醉後方何礙
2. 不醒時有何思
3. 糟醃兩箇功名字
4. 醅淹千古興亡事
5. 麴埋萬丈虹蜺志
6. 不達時皆笑屈原非
7. 但知音盡說陶潛是

Each line of the translation has interest, the lack of metric shape is comparable to the loose rhythm of the original and lines 4–5 rise to the climax. It is in this respect that the translation can be judged faithful to the general spirit of the original. In addition, an English speaker will be able to take a good deal of this kind of writing. The following two translations of a poem by Ma Zhiyuan are worth discussing from this standpoint.

1   Under the afterglow,
2   Wine-flags are slow.
3   Yet to reach the shore — two three boats.
4   Falling flowers, scented water, straw huts in the dusk.
5   At a broken bridgehead: scattering fishmongers homeward go.

(Yip, 1976:453)

1. 夕陽下
2. 酒斾閑
3. 兩三航未曾著岸
4. 落花水香茅舍晚
5. 斷橋頭賣魚人散

The translation seems to take little account of general effects. In the first line is a curious play between "under" and "after" but the expression in Chinese is a cliché and demands no such attention. There is ambiguity in line three but the Chinese line is a masterpiece of simplicity and directness. Line four in the Chinese version clusters the images in ways that suggest the "pure imagery" we mentioned above, however, the translation "falling flowers, scented water" produces the very separation this translation technique is supposed to circumvent; instead of a direct image of flower-scented water simply rising like magic out of the dross of mere words, the English speaker must stop to extract "scented water" from the echoes of magazine ads and cast about to justify its place in this line, finally to realize that "with falling flowers the stream (or water) is scented" is actually the vehicle of the image. The phrase "water scented", as it stands in the original, might have worked better but the tendency to nominalize in this style of translating probably prevented it from being used. Further in this line, the nice sequence "thatched huts, evening" is made into a "statement about" by a preposition and an article. Finally in the last line it is only the distraction of the archaic "homeward go" that keeps us from an image of fishmongers scattering for the nearest bomb shelter. One might ask how one justifies all this unusual language and imagery in regard to the original poem. The "pure imagery" which has inspired this technique of translation occurs in the fourth line but there the technique failed by its own standards to convey it.

1   Evening sun sinks;
2   wineshop banner hangs.
3a   Two, three boats
3b   have not yet reached the shore.
4a   Water fragrant with falling petals,
4b   night comes to thatched roofs;
5   from the old bridge, fish peddlers leave for home.

(Chaves, 1986:35)

There is no intention here to purge the translation of connectives or pronouns but interestingly the loss of just a few articles and a conjunction or two creates the same unfortunate effect yet without any of the advantages of greater compression. The first line is both faithful to the sense and style of the original but it is hard to see why the article "a" could not have been added at the head of the second line. In line 3a the conjunction "or" would have brought a little easier flow to the syntax. Yet in line 3b we find an abundance of function words and see as well that either "have" or "the" or both could have been dropped with good effect. If in 4a the translator could have used "The water is ...," the dactyl in the last three syllabes of this phrase would have balanced the one in "fragrant with" and helped to keep it from obtruding as it does when it stands alone in a line of trochees. Lines 4a and b would do well to be bound together with "and", not because it is one line in the original, though that is a factor, but because the lines in the translation up to this point have too much the same rhythmic effect, something one does not feel in the original. The lack of the article before "thatched roofs" grates somewhat but perhaps not as much as adding it would have. One might say something like "And night descends on thatched rooves" but the translator is probably wise to keep the verb less vivid according to the original, which has merely the juxtaposition of nominals. Also the more legato sound of "rooves" would perhaps be better for this poem. The last line is not striking but then perhaps it ought not to be and although the original is a more interesting line, it is difficult to know what better could be done in the translation.

(3) Balance

In the discussion of the previous two translations we have already touched on matters of balance and general effects. We can continue this with the next four translations with added attention to the questions of allusion, proper names and the like. The following poem was written by Ma Zhiyuan to the tune Bo buduan:

1 布衣中
   cotton clothes among
2 問英雄
   ask-of brave hero
3 王圖霸業成何用
   king plan hegemon achievement accomplish what use
4 禾黍高低六代宮
   rice millet high low six era palace
5 楸梧遠近千官塚
   catalpa paulownia far near 1000 official tomb
6 一場惡夢
   one (measure) bad dream.

A few remarks about "literal" versions are in order. Quite often the English speaker who knows no Chinese will express a certain interest, even delight, in this literary pidgin. A translator should not mistake an infatuation with the quaint for literary taste and be drawn into producing a kind of poetic chinoiserie. The "literal" version is very useful for pedagogical purposes and is necessary in critical discussions aimed at non-Chinese speakers.

This is a very appealing poem and not overly difficult; it has a tautness which the Bai Pu poem above does not have and the rhymes are very effective. The first of the four translations is as follows:

1 Wearing plain
2 Clothes, I ask:
3 What good are palaces? Tombs
4 Of our kings grow Catalpas.
5 Tungs garnish official ruins.
6 Yet nightmares reign!

                                                    (Metzger and Yang, 1967:51)

Having seen the original, one is inclined to declare this version rather free. One tries to imagine what an uninitiated English reader would think. The first three lines will work, after a fashion, but what is to be made of: our kings' tombs growing Catalpas, an innocent enough tree, the "garnishing" of official ruins with tungs, and the reign of nightmares? The reader needs to study a "literal" version before attempting the "poetic" translation but this is not the best way to appreciate verse and the impression left by such great divergence between two versions "of the same poem" is misleading. The following is similar to the Metzger and Yang draft (1967:112), though it is more polished:

1 Clad in humble cotton dress,
2 I ask the heroes:
3 What was the use of imperial designs and ambitions?
4 Rice and millet cover high and low the palaces of Six Dynasties;
5 Catalpa and *wu-t'ung* trees grow far and near on the tombs of thousand (sic) officials
6 — A mere nightmare!

                                                                (Fu, 1975:10)

There may well be disadvantages to this version but none compared to the above. For the general Reader this is a more "faithful" translation despite the fact that it conveys an awkwardness of diction which is not in the original. The following is tighter and by far the most successful of these:

1 Among men of plain clothes
2 ask about heroes.
3 What's the use of plans to be king or hegemon?
4 Grain crops sway on palace sites of six dynasties;
5 catalpa and paulownia grow from tombs of thousands of officials
6 The whole show, one bad dream.

(Chaves, 1986:34)

Successful as it is, more effort could have been made to imitate the stanzaic structure of the poem. Certainly one factor is the difficulty of the proper names and technical terms, and one would suggest that the translation need not mention "hegemon"; king or the like would suffice, as in Metzger and Yang; "imperial designs and ambitions" in Fu's translation is perhaps a bit abstract. Since "rice and millet" is reduced to "grain crops", why not simply "grain" or something similar? And so it could be asked of "six dynasties", whether taken as a proper name or not, which could be made into a more abstract reference to time. The "catalpa and paulownia", hardly convey the graveyard imagery to a Western reader for whom "sad cypress" or the yew has this function.

1 Among common men
2 I wonder at heroes.
3 The ambition of princes — what use can it be?
4 Corn grows now over time and its ruins
5 And cypress, around these thousands of tombs.
6 All — a bad dream.

In this version the stanza shape is maintained, the images are mainly in the original order. The "exotic" terms have been transformed, something many would not condone; still in "poetic" translation patriation of this sort is always a useful alternative to the dead weight of technically correct terms. One reasonable criticism of this version is that it is, by comparison to the original, rather bland. Rhyme would make it stronger. The points at which it might be inserted are at the ends of lines 3 and 6; the half-rhymes of lines 4 and 5 might stand, though they are problematic whether taken as part of the rhyme scheme or not. "Seem" would rhyme with "dream" but replacing "be" in line four with this more concrete modal verb would destroy the balance, taking away the focus of "what use". One could retain "be" and replace "bad dream" with "reverie" but that does not carry the judgment expressed in the original and the sound is forced. The point here is that one should explore the possibility of rhyming but should decide to use it only if it attains an excellence by English standards of versification that compares to the excellence of the Chinese rhymes.

Conclusion

There are many techniques for translating or imitating rhetorical effects and they are all useful to know and indeed to strive for at times. However, in translating poetry one seldom has the luxury of embracing any one technique in all cases for its own sake. It is best to know the techniques well and be able to use them when necessary or at least know how they work if they cannot be mastered. The best translators are those in whom these skills are so well entrenched that they never get pressed under by cultural biases or lost in a welter of theories.

References

Crump, J. I. *Songs from Xanadu*. Ann Arbor: 1983.

Frankel, Hans. "English Translations of Classical Chinese Poetry Since the 1950's: Problems and Achievements." *Tamkang Review*, Vol. 15, Nos. 1–3 (1984–1985), pp. 307–28.

Fu, Sherwin. "Ma Chih-Yuan's *San Ch'u*." *Tamkang Review*, Vol. 4, No. 1 (1975), pp. 1–17.

Idema, Wilt and S. H. West. *Chinese Theatre 1100 to 1450: A Source Book*. Wiesbaden: 1982.

Langlois, J. D., ed. *China under Mongol Rule*. Princeton: Princeton University Press, 1981.

Metzger, C. R. and R. F. S. Yang. *Fifty Songs from the Yuan*. London: 1967.

Schlepp, W. *San-ch'u: Its Technique and Imagery*. Madison: University of Wisconsin Press, 1970.

———. "Tentative Remarks on Chinese Metrics." *The Journal of Chinese Linguistics*, Vol. 8, No. 1 (1980), pp. 59–84.

Scott, John. *Love and Protest: Chinese Poems from the Sixth Century B.C. to the Seventeenth Century A.D.* New York: Harper and Row, 1972.

Yip, Wai-lim. *Chinese Poetry: Major Modes and Genres*. Berkeley: University of California Press, 1976.

POLITICAL WRITING

Translation of Chinese Political Writings

Cheng Zhenqiu
Department of Translation and Interpretation
Ministry of Foreign Affairs, China

A word about Chinese-English translation in general before discussing the topic of this entry. It is generally admitted that with some rare exceptions Chinese translators should render English writings into Chinese, which is their mother tongue. This is because very few people are really bilingual. And if bilingualism is hard to achieve in respect of two languages of the same linguistic family such as English and French, it is undoubtedly even more difficult of attainment in the case of languages as far different as English and Chinese.

However, a large amount of Chinese-English translation is actually going on in the field of political writings in China today. The New China News Agency flashes news and information about China in English to all parts of the world, which are mostly based on Chinese-English translations. The Foreign Languages Press turns out English editions of books, periodicals and other publications. The Central Translation Bureau is in charge of rendering into English the important documents of Party Congresses and National People's Congresses as well as selected works of Party and government leaders. And various government departments have also the need to put some of their official papers into English for the benefit of foreign readers. All this has to be done by Chinese translators to whom English is a foreign language. To make up for the inadequate command of the English language they often carry on their work collectively. There are translators, revisors and polishers working as a team, with the role of the polisher often assumed by native English speakers.

If time permits, the ideal method for Chinese-English translation is perhaps what the translators of Mao Zedong's *Selected Works* call the "confrontation method." Several Chinese and English experts were invited to finalize the translation of Mao's works, and their job was to get together and discuss sentence by sentence the English version of the Chinese original. The Chinese members of the group had to see to it that the meaning of the original was faithfully conveyed, while the English members must ensure that the English version was idiomatic. This was of course a rough division of labour, for English members sometimes raised questions of meaning about the Chinese in the course of reading the English translation, and Chinese members sometimes offered good English versions in the course of explaining the meaning of the Chinese to their English colleagues. The discussion could get quite animated, and sometimes a whole afternoon was spent on a single paragraph. But the effort was not made in vain, and more often than not a version was finally worked out to the satisfaction of all present.

The first requirement of translation is naturally fidelity. Without faithfulness to the original work there is no translation to speak of. But fidelity may mean different things to different people. Some argue that the translator should be faithful not only to the author but also to the reader. Others assert, not without a taint of male chauvinism, that translation is like a woman: if beautiful, it's often not faithful; if faithful, it's often not beautiful. They mostly have in mind literary translation where there may be a grain of truth in the assertion. We are not in a position to go into the relative merits of these arguments here. Nevertheless, one thing is certain: in political translation, the importance of fidelity cannot be overemphasized. Inaccuracies may sometimes lead to grave consequences. And once harm is done, remedies are hard to come by. For instance, we have to be very careful with the word 華僑 which used to be loosely translated as "overseas Chinese." In many cases the correct translation should be "Chinese nationals (or citizens) overseas (or residing abroad)," whose legitimate rights and interests are protected by the Chinese Government. Overseas Chinese is, however, a broader and vague term, and most Chinese living overseas have acquired the nationality of the country in which they reside. This is a very sensitive issue in Southeast Asia, where people of Chinese descent are an important minority. Obviously, failure to make this distinction in translation will cause serious complications.

Very few people are in favour of word-for-word translation. But, whether consciously or not, translators very often come under the influence of the source language, that is, the language they are translating out of. Such expressions as "make achievements," "learn knowledge," "grasp the national banner," "welcome you to fly CAAC," "we had the experience that" and "build China into a modern socialist state" are all wrong collocations, bearing the unmistakable imprint of the Chinese language. They are not English, but Chinglish. In political translation, literalism may sometimes get you into trouble. Take the following sentence for example. 祖國統一後，台灣特別行政區可以有自己的獨立性，可以實行同大陸不同的政策. How should 獨立性 be translated into English? Certainly not "independence." Nor is "an independent or separate identity" a correct rendering. The translator finally decides on "a unique character." (Deng, 1987) Perhaps a better version would be "a distinctive character of its own." In any case, a literal translation is out of the question.

In political translation we should try our best to be faithful to both the letter and the spirit of the original text. We have pointed out the danger of adhering to the letter at the expense of the spirit in the preceding paragraph. But we must hasten to add that there is no spirit without the letter and that departure from the letter may also lead to grave mistranslation. In the translated sentence "Human history is cursed with wars," the word in the original text is "full of," not "cursed with." By this change the translator has not only infused an emotive element into the original sentence which is simply a statement of fact but, more seriously, distorted the position of the writer who is not against all wars but makes a point of distinguishing between just and unjust wars.

Translators in China erred more often on the side of literalism in the past, because they wanted to be very faithful to the author and failed to break the constraints of the Chinese wording. There are signs now that in the effort to make the translation more readable they may go to the other extreme and err on the side of liberalism. Our advice is that we should try to be as literal as possible but must avoid literalism by all means. Perhaps translation is a perpetual tug-of-war between literalism and liberalism. But in political translation at least fidelity comes before beauty and meaning has precedence over style.

To achieve fidelity in political translation we should always take note of the linguistic differences between the two languages. English is the least synthetic of the Indo-European languages, and as a consequence the relationship between different parts of an English sentence is sometimes ambiguous. For instance, "pretty young girls" may be open to two interpretations. The phrase may mean "young girls who are pretty" or "girls who are pretty young." The same is true of "more powerful weapons." You have to decide which is meant from the context. Sometimes a hyphen is used as in "higher-education cost" to eliminate the ambiguity. Chinese is an analytic language *par excellence*, with virtually no inflections. The problem of the relationship between different parts of a sentence, or of what we call "which governs what," crops up again and again. Space does not allow us to go into details here. But this is an important point we must keep firmly in mind in Chinese-English translation.

As an analytic language, Chinese lacks infinitives, participles and gerunds, which are known as non-finite forms of the verb in English. Nor are there relative adverbs or relative pronouns in Chinese. As a result, with very few exceptions the various parts of a Chinese sentence appear to be coordinate with one another without any formal signs to indicate their relative importance. Thus, the sentence 前途是光明的，道路是曲折的 can at least be rendered into three different versions: (1) The future is bright, (*and*) the road is tortuous (2) The future is bright, *but* the road is tortuous (3) The future is bright, *although* the road is tortuous, depending on the exact nuance the author wishes to convey.

A careful reader may note that no connective is used in the Chinese sentence cited above. This is a feature of the Chinese language which distinguishes it from English. Chinese is highly paratactic in structure, which means coordinative arrangement of successive words, phrases and clauses without any connecting word. The English version of the saying 白貓黑貓，抓到老鼠就是好貓 may be either "It doesn't matter *whether* the cat is black or white *as long as* it catches mice" or "*Whatever* its colour a cat is a good cat *that* catches mice." In both cases the English translation cannot dispense with the italicized words (connectives) without breaking up the whole sentence. Quite often a translator who renders Chinese into English has to supply the right connective.

Another feature of the Chinese language is the frequent omission of the grammatical subject. Strictly speaking, it is not exactly an omission for in a Chinese clause or sentence there is often no structural need of a subject. In Chinese-English translation we have in many cases to supply logical subjects, that is, subjects inferred from the context to meet the need of English sentence structure. The problem is further complicated by the fact that there may occur a change of the logical subject in the middle of a Chinese sentence. It is therefore necessary to exercise great caution in the choice of he logical subject in Chinese-English translation. Let us take the following sentence:

一些人幸災樂禍，一些人喪失信心，把這叫做馬克思主義的 "危機" 。

It was first translated as "Some people gloated over the setbacks, whereas others have lost their confidence, describing Marxism as being in a state of 'crisis'." But this is really a mistranslation. Who described Marxism as being in the state of "crisis"? The Chinese is vague but it is clear that people calling it a "crisis" are not just those who have lost their confidence. In the final version the sentence is broken into two which read: "Some people gloated over the setbacks, whereas others have lost their confidence. This is being described as the 'crisis' of Marxism."

As everybody knows, word order is important in both Chinese and English. But there are certain differences. Here we would like to call attention to one major divergence. In English shorter and less weighty words usually come first, a point which is discussed by R. Quirk and others under the principle of end-focus and the principle of end-weight in their *A Grammar of Contemporary English*. The order in Chinese is, as a rule, just the opposite as exemplified in the following sentence:

某些企業要關、停、併、轉，或者減少生產。

There is a complete reversal of order in the English translation: "Some enterprises should either cut production, switch to other products, be amalgamated with others, suspend operations, or simply close down." To place the stronger word before the weaker one would be anti-climactic and violate the rule of English word order.

Besides anti-climax there is the question of personification and metaphor where the two languages differ in usage. While personification has fallen into disuse in English except for poetry and certain specific fields such as stock market reporting, it is very much alive in Chinese. We often come across sentences like: 一種（思潮）以陳獨秀爲代表，認爲…… (This view, represented by Chen Duxiu 陳獨秀, held or maintained that ....). But a view cannot hold or maintain anything, and "held" has to be replaced by "was" to avoid awkward personification. Similarly, in 宗教不得干預政治和干預教育 , we have to translate the sentence as follows: "No one should interfere with politics and education in the name of the religion." In Chinese-English translation we must be on our guard against unwarranted personification.

Metaphor is, in the words of I. A. Richards, "the omnipresent principle of language." (Vallins, 1960) Another writer argues that the question of metaphor is "the central problem of translation." (Newmark, 1981) A general discussion of the problem would not be in order here. But it should be stressed that in Chinese-English translation efforts must be made to steer clear of mixed metaphors such as "handing over responsibilities to the younger generation step by step." In the well-known example of "the backbone of the right wing" 右翼骨幹 , the "wing" in "the right wing" is a dead metaphor, but it is galvanized into life under the stimulus of the word "backbone." Then the phrase calls up an absurd picture in our minds, for the backbone is between the two wings and cannot possibly be *in* the wing.

While linguistic differences between Chinese and English must be well taken care of, the different social and cultural connotations of words and expressions in the two languages present far greater difficulty or challenge to the translator in the field of Chinese-English political translation. Take the word "liberalism" 自由主義 . It is always used in a pejorative sense in China. But the word is used appreciatively in the West where there is a strong liberal tradition. Perhaps the difference in understanding lies partly in the fact that whereas people in the West stress the political aspect of democracy, those on the Chinese mainland lay more emphasis on its economic aspect, arguing that in the capitalist world where there is great disparity in wealth, liberty for the pike is tyranny for the minnow. Despairing of bridging such social and cultural gaps, some translation theorists hold that passages such as Shakespeare's sonnet "Shall I compare thee to a summer's day" cannot be semantically translated into the language of a country where summer is unpleasant. Others disagree, saying that when the reader finishes reading the whole sonnet, he or she will realize that summer in England must be far from unpleasant. We think they have a point. After all, there is no text without context. Words like "liberalism" and "liberalization" have to be understood against the background of different cultures and ideologies.

Another headache is 社會主義精神文明 which is translated into "a socialist society that is advanced culturally and ideologically" or "a socialist society with advanced culture and ideology" in official documents. The phrase is quite a mouthful and does not bear repetition. Though not a very happy collocation, "spiritual civilization" was once used. However, the expression has been strongly objected to for the religious connotation of the word "spiritual" and was finally discarded. But the word is not always used in the religious sense. Surely there is nothing that smacks of religion in the following sentences: "The theatre was her spiritual home" and "The acknowledged spiritual ancestor of Bentham as of Karl Marx was Thomas Hobbes." What is more, probably no one will suspect China of fanning religious fervour when coming across "spiritual civilization" in Chinese articles and documents. Perhaps the term can be reconsidered for its brevity. Lord Acton says, "Compromise is the soul if not the whole of politics." (Bolinger and Sears, 1981) Sometimes, a measure of compromise may not be entirely out of place in Chinese-English political translation, provided it does not impair the essential meaning. The question here is not one of seeking complete equivalence which is well-nigh impossible, but of finding a neat version that comes in handy.

Difficult problems of Chinese-English political translation arising from the social and cultural differences between the two languages are too complicated to be tackled here. We have to be satisfied with the above brief discussion.

To conclude, we would like to recapitulate the main points of our discussion on the Chinese-English translation of political writings. First, it is imperative to bear in mind at all times the overriding importance of conveying the precise political implications of the original text. Secondly, the translators should try their best to guard against both literalism and liberalism. The more carefully written the Chinese text is, the more literal they should be in rendering it into English. Thirdly, it is highly important for the translators to cultivate a sharp sense of discrimination with regard to the linguistic as well as the social and cultural differences between the Chinese and English languages.

References

Bolinger, D. and O. A. Sears. *Aspects of Language*. New York: Harcourt Brace Javanovich, 1981.

Cheng, Zhenqiu 程鎮球 . 《翻譯問題探索》 (*On Problems of Translation*). Beijing: Commercial Press 商務印書館 , 1980.

————. *On Problems of Translation.* Beijing: The Foreign Language Teaching and Research Press, 1981.

Deng, Xiaoping. *Fundamental Issues in Present-day China.* Beijing: Foreign Languages Press, 1987.

Newmark, P. *Approaches to Translation.* Oxford: Pergamon Press, 1981.

Quirk, R. *et al. A Grammar of Contemporary English.* London: Longman, 1973.

Vallins, G. H. *The Best English.* New York: Pan, 1960.

PRAGMATICS

Pragmatics

He Ziran
Department of Linguistics
Guangzhou Institute of Foreign Languages, Guangzhou, China

Pragmatics is a relatively new branch of linguistics, but research on it can be traced back to the periods of ancient Greece and Rome. The word "pragmatics" derives from late Latin "pragmaticus" and Greek "pragmatikos." Traditionally, the term is used to label one of the three major divisions of semiotics (along with semantics and syntactics). According to Charles Morris, pragmatics is the study of the "relation of signs to interpreters" (Morris, 1938:6); it deals with "the origin, uses, and effects of signs within the behaviour in which they occur" (Morris, 1946:218). In modern linguistics, pragmatics deals with particular utterances in particular situations and is especially concerned with the various ways in which the many social contexts of language performance can influence interpretation. The study of pragmatics focuses on an area between semantics, sociolinguistics, and extralinguistic context, but there is neither a unified field, nor a unified view of what pragmatics is or ought to be. According to Levinson (1983), the scope of pragmatics involves the topics of deixis, conversational implicatures, presuppositions, speech acts and discourse structure, but this does not offer any perspectives on a unified and coherent pragmatic theory of language (Cf. Verschueren, 1985). However, there seems to be one constant aspect in the concept of pragmatics viz. the concern with language use, with meaning of language in social and cultural context. Thus, pragmatics deals, on the one hand, with pragmalinguistics, with the context which is formally encoded in the structure of a language, and, on the other hand, with socio-pragmatics, with language usage, understanding and appropriateness in social and cultural context.

Because of this common aspect of pragmatics we find that it can very well be applied to translation, to how a translator is able to interpret a message in the source language and reproduce it in the target language appropriately. Eugene A. Nida (1982) once said, "Translating means trans-lating meaning." The main task of a translator is to convey to his/her reader all the possible meanings of a message. Since meanings are coated with culture and determined by the writer/speaker's intention in a given context, it is quite difficult for a translator to bring out absolutely both the intended meaning in context and the cultural, linguistic aspects of the original mes-sage. Then the pragmatic approach to translation can be adopted to help solve this problem by striving for the pragmatic equivalent effect between the source and target messages.

The pragmatic equivalent effect in translation, as we put it, aims at translating meaning in full, taking full account of differences between the target language and source language in pragmalinguistics and sociaprag-matics.

Pragmalinguistics in translation refers to the study of pragmatic force or language use in context from the viewpoint of linguistic sources. Prag-matic force, or illocutionary force in speech acts theory of pragmatics, is the intended meaning of a given message. There are two major kinds of prag-matic force: implicit, below the surface and unstated, and explicit, on the surface and stated. It is important to identify the implicit forces as they appear in their various social contexts, for frequently the apparent intention of a message is not the same as the actual intent. The following example shows how to analyze the implicit pragmatic forces between the target language and source language.

(1) 寶釵獨自行來，順路進了怡紅院……不想步入院中，<u>鴉雀無聞</u>。
（曹雪芹：《紅樓夢》）

There are two versions of translation for the underlined expression in the original message. One (translated by Hawkes) is "(... The courtyard was silent as she entered it.) Not a bird's cheep was to be heard," from which we might infer that there *were* birds in the courtyard. The other (translated by Yang) is "(... To her surprise, his courtyard) was utterly quiet," which corresponds well with the writer's only intention of describing the amazing quietness of the yard with no people around. It is not important whether the image 鴉雀 has been lost or retained because that was not the actual intent of the writer.

(2) 他只好不再回來，作爲<u>眼不見心不煩</u>。有時候他恨女兒……
（老舍：《駱駝祥子》）

The underlined original message means that if he did not see his daughter it would not trouble his heart. It would be a failure in pragmalinguistic understanding if the message were translated into "out of sight is out of mind," which refers only to one's remembrance: what is not seen is forgotten.

(3) The missiles were already in Cuba, and all we could be doing with a blockade would be *"closing the door after the horse had left the barn."* (Robert F. Kennedy: *Thirteen Days*)

A possible acceptable translation of the underlined expression is " 賊走關門 ," implying that "it is too late to act." If we use a Chinese idiom " 亡羊補牢 ," which bears the implication that "it is not yet late at all," it will conflict with the intention of the original message.

(4) By the winter of 1942 their resistance to the Nazi terror had become *only a shadow*. (Winston Churchill)

By using the expression "only a shadow" the writer intended to mean that "their resistance to Nazi terror" was no longer as strong as it used to be. Thus, the translation of this expression should reveal that hidden intention by " 名存實亡 " instead of keeping the original metaphor of " 僅剩下一個模糊的影子 ."

Pragmalinguistically, the intended meaning or pragmatic force of a message may be hidden in discourse deixis, such as *actually, anyway, after all, still, well*, etc. It is necessary to reveal the force of these deixis in translation, so as to achieve the equivalent effect of pragmalinguistics. For example:

(5) A: I really disliked that man you introduced me to.
    B_1: *Actually*, he's your new boss.
    B_2: *Anyway*, he's your new boss.
    B_3: *After all*, he's your new boss.

B₄: *Still*, he's your new boss.
B₅: *Well*, he's your new boss.

The intended meaning or pragmatic force of "actually" in B₁ is a warning. It suggests that A should consider his statement. So the rendering may be "說話慎重點，他可是你的新老闆." "Anyway" in B₂ is a patient persuasion, suggesting that his dislike is irrelevant. The rendering then becomes "那樣，他是你的新老闆." "After all" in B₃ is a suggestion of not showing dislike for the new boss, so the rendering would be "他畢竟是你的新老闆嘛！" "Still" in B₄ is a well-meaning advice, suggesting that he should make the best of things, and the rendering is "你還是算了，他是你的新老闆呵." Finally, "Well" in B₅ refers to a consolation, because it suggests that A has got problems. The rendering of this could be "好自爲之吧，他是你的新老闆."

Pragmalinguistics in translation includes choosing the appropriate forms of language to convey the intended meaning or pragmatic force of the given message. We should not assume an equation between linguistic forms and communicative functions when we are engaged in translation. From the pragmalinguistic point of view, we should not be misled into thinking that commands are uniquely associated with imperative sentences, and questions with interrogative sentences. Thus, the sentence

(6) Can you speak a little louder?

is conventionally used, though interrogative in form, to make a request. The sentence should not be translated as "你能說大聲點嗎？" but as "請說大聲點." On the other hand, the request is not necessarily expressed in the imperative form, because imperatives are rarely used to make requests in conversational English. Instead, we tend to employ sentences that only indirectly make the requesting. According to context, and in different degrees of pragmatic force, we have one of the following ways to render the message of "請關門":

(7) Can you close the door?
    Are you able by any chance to close the door?
    Would you close the door?
    Won't you close the door?
    Would you mind closing the door?
    Would you be willing to close the door?
    May I ask you to close the door?

You ought to close the door.

I want you to close the door.

I'd be much obliged if you'd close the door, etc.

Judging from the sentence-type, these examples are prototypically the affirmative, interrogative rather than imperative forms expressing a command or a request. Pragmatically, these are indirect speech acts, in which one illocutionary act is performed indirectly by way of performing another (Searle, 1975:60).

In translation, it is important to try to map onto the given message the same pragmatic force assigned to it by the writer/speaker of the target language. Here are some examples:

(8) CLEVELAND (to HENRY): Sir, *How about* coming on our show? We'd be honored to have you. (Herman Wouk: *The Wind of War*)

It is true that "How about ..." is usually used for a tentative suggestion, but the context (Henry is the American naval attaché in Berlin; his daughter works under Cleveland, who is program director) reveals that it is in fact an invitation given with confidence by the speaker (Cleveland). To convey this pragmatic force properly, it is not strong enough to put "How about ..." literally into "……怎麼樣？" The preferable rendering should be "（先生），請您來參加一次我們的節目（您的光臨將會使我們感到十分榮幸。）."

(9) Ouch! Isn't that a little steep for a room this size?

This is not a question at all. A good translation should reveal the strong force of assertion under the surface form of the message: "哎唷！才這麼大一間房，這麼高的房租未免太貴了！"

Sociopragmatics refers to the pragmatic studies which examine the conditions on language use that derive from the social and cultural situation. In translation, this consideration depends on the translator's beliefs as well as his/her social and cross-cultural knowledge. The equivalent effect of sociopragmatics in translation usually occurs when the translator holds a correct conception of the different social institutions or cultural backgrounds between the source language and target language, and adequately represents one for the other. Here are some examples:

(10) "巧媳婦做不出沒米的飯菜"，叫我怎麼樣呢？（曹雪芹：《紅樓夢》）

The two versions of translation for the underlined part are: (a) (translated by Yang) "Even the cleverest housewife can't cook a meal without rice;" (b) (translated by Hawkes) "Even the cleverest housewife can't make bread without flour." The sociopragmatic equivalent effect of these two versions of translation can be evaluated according to the translator's belief and understanding of cross-culture. If he/she believes that his/her translation is intended merely for Chinese readers, version (a) must be understood easily, though it's quite possible even for a Chinese to cook *a meal* without rice. On the other hand, if the translator's work is intended for Western readers of native English, version (b) is a better one, though one can argue that it is hard to imagine that people in ancient China ate Western bread rather than rice for their meals.

(11)　她認爲離開了辦公大樓，離開了政工部門，就是離開了政治，就
　　　聽不到那些閒言碎語了。誰知是離開了鹹菜缸又跳進了蘿蔔窖。
　　　（蔣子龍：《赤橙黃綠青藍紫》）

"鹹菜缸" and "蘿蔔窖" are culture-specific expressions in Chinese; and the intended meaning of the whole message "離開了鹹菜缸又跳進了蘿蔔窖" has nothing to do with its literal interpretation. Here it has the implication of "from bad to worse." If sociopragmatics is taken into account, an English image should be substituted for that typical Chinese image, i.e. "jump out of the frying pan into the fire."

(12)　… for dessert you got *Brown Betty*, which nobody ate … (Salinger: *The Catcher in the Rye*)

To achieve the equivalent effect of sociopragmatics, some culture-specific source items may be translated literally, but it should be replenished with interpretation tags pin-pointing their implied meaning. Thus, "Brown Betty" may be treated as "（……給你上的甜食是）"褐色貝蒂"，一種水果布丁，（不過誰也沒吃過……）."

Likewise, if we want to achieve the same effect and bring out, without using any footnotes, the meaning of a culturally-loaded message, a short and clear interpretation modifier may be added to the translated message:

(13)　… this hopeful young person soared into so pleasing a *Cupid* as to constitute the chief delight of the maternal part of the spectators. (Dickens: *Hard Times*)

Here, the allusion of "插著雙翅的愛神丘彼得" stands for the single

word "Cupid". This will help the reader to overcome the cross-cultural difficulty.

(14)   We would sell the raft and get in a steamboat and go way up the Ohio amongst *the free states*, and then be out of trouble. (Mark Twain)

"The free states" refer to those states of America where slaves were not bought and sold. To reveal the social back ground of the original message, an interpretation modifier is added to the translated version: （……搭上小火輪，順著俄亥俄河往上水去，）到那些不買賣黑奴的自由州去（以後就不用提心吊膽了。）.

Actually, a clear line between pragmalinguistics and socio-pragmatics may sometimes be difficult to draw. The necessity to convey the intended meaning or the pragmatic force of a message may be due to the needs of achieving the equivalent effect in both pragmalinguistics and sociopragmatics. For example:

(15)   There were 60 million Americans at home working to turn out *the thousand and one* things required to wage war.

Culture-specifically, the expression "the thousand and one" in English does not have the literal denotion as the number indicates. Rather, it is a metaphorical use suggesting the idea of manifoldness. We should think of the expression " 成千上萬 " in Chinese, which is exact pragmalinguistically and appropriate sociopragmatically.

(16)   I think he was married and had *a lioness at home*.

Pragmalinguistically, "a lioness at home" in the context refers to his wife, who is the most important member at home. Sociopragmatically, people of the West liken a lion or a lioness to an important person, but Chinese have different images in their minds. To achieve the equivalent effect of both pragmalinguistics and sociopragmatics, " 太太又是一個母老虎 " is perhaps an adequate rendering in this context.

(17)   三個人品字式坐下，隨便談了幾句。

Graphemic resources of different languages may play a part in the overall meaning of an expression. The unique graphic characteristics of Chinese characters are often used in metaphorical language to achieve their visualizing effect. Pragmalinguistically, the expression of " 品字式 " in the

Chinese original sentence is simply a description indicating the position of the seats. To make the reader understand this expression in the target language, we have to give up the visualizing effect of " 品 " as well as its metaphorical image, rendering it into "(The three men sat down) facing each other (and began casually chatting.)"

The pragmatic approach to translation can be summed up in the following:

A. Render the expression literally, if it is possible to feel or recognize in context the same intended meaning or force of the message in the source language:

易如反掌	as easy as turning over one's hand
跑了和尚跑不了廟	the monk may run away, but the temple can't run with him
crocodile tears	鱷魚眼淚
like sardines	像沙丁魚罐頭一樣

B. Render the culture-specific expression into a synonymous one accepted by the reader of the target language to retain an equivalent effect of the message in both the source language and the target language:

外甥打燈籠照舅（舊）	back in the old rut
說到曹操曹操就到	talk of the devil and he will appear
騎驢找馬	hold on to one job, while seeking a better one
kill two birds with one stone	一舉兩得
the early bird catches the worm	近水樓台先得月
there are several straws in the wind	不無蛛絲馬跡

C. Translate a culture-specific expression into an expression of general adaptation in the target language, giving up the specific description of the source language, and retaining only the pragmatic equivalent effect of the message:

carry coals to Newcastle	多此一舉
every Tom, Dick or Harry	一般老百姓
外甥打燈籠照舅（舊）	back to what they were before
情人眼裡出西施	beauty lies in lover's eyes

D. Translate a culture-specific expression literally, but replenish it with brief interpretations, to reveal the intended meaning:

a bull in a china shop	公牛闖進瓷器店 — 肆意搞亂
a skeleton in the cupboard	衣柜裡的骷髏，見不得人的事兒
井水不犯河水	well water and river water leave each other — stay out of things that don't concern you

E. Render the intended meaning or pragmatic implicit force of the message in the source languae regardless of the functions of its surface form:

(1) a. Render the implicit force of a *request* regardless of asking the hearer's "ability":

Can you pass the salt?

Could you be a little more quiet?

Are you able to reach the book on the top shelf?

b. Render the implicit force of a *request* regardless of stating the speaker's "wish":

I would like you to go now.

I want you to do this for me, Henry.

I'd rather you didn't do that any more.

I'd be very much obliged if you would pay me the money back now.

c. Render the implicit force of a *request* regardless of asking the hearer's "intention" or "wish":

Aren't you going to eat the spinach?

Would you be willing to write a letter of recommendation for me?

Would you mind not making so much noise?

Would it be too much trouble for you to pay me the money next Wednesday?

d. Render the implicit force of a *request* regardless of stating a fact:

Officers will henceforth wear ties at dinner.

The dog must die. It's nothing but a wild beast. Only a wild beast would bite a child like that …

I can't see the movie screen while you have that hat on.

(2) a. Render the implicit force of an *offer* regardless of making a
      statement or asking a question:
      Could I be of assistance?
      I can get it for you.
   b. Render the implicit force of an *offer* regardless of asking the
      hearer's "wish" or "intention":
      Do you want me to help you, Sally?
      Wouldn't you like me to bring some more next time I come?
   c. Render the implicit force of an *offer* regardless of stating the
      speaker's "intention" or "wish":
      I intend to do it for you.
      I want to be of any help I can.
      I plan on repairing it for you next week.

The pragmatic approach to translation should not be expected to solve all problems in the process of rendering. It is not realistic to adopt it as the absolute way, for "translation theory is eclectic." (Newmark, 1982:37) Besides, the pragmatic approach is not yet so well-knit as to reckon with all problems of translation. Since pragmatics is the field greatly contributing to the linguistic, social and cultural reflection of translation, the present consideration, as was stated at the beginning, slanted towards a few topics of only one constant aspect in the concept of pragmatics. However, it has its place when it helps one to sort things out when faced with an entangled heap of problems in translation. The pragmatic approach may serve as a varied standpoint from which the translation theorist and translator may benefit. It may also serve as a provoking starting-point for the further studies in this domain of Chinese-English/English-Chinese translation.

References

Cole, P. and J. Morgan, eds. *Syntax and Semantics, Vol. 3: Speech Acts*, New York: Academic Press, 1975.

He, Ziran. *A Survey of Pragmatics* (in Chinese), Changsha: Hunan Education Publishing House, 1988.

Jin, Di and Eugene A. Nida. *On Translation*. Beijing: China Translation and Publishing Corporation, 1984.

Leech, G. *Principles of Pragmatics*. New York: Longman, 1983.

Levinson, Stephen. *Pragmatics*. Cambridge: Cambridge University Press, 1983.

Morris, C. *Foundations of the Theory of Signs*. Chicago: University of Chicago Press, 1938.

———. *Signs, Language and Behaviour*. Englewood Cliffs, N.J.: Prentice-Hall, 1946.

Newmark, Peter. *Approaches to Translation*. Oxford: Pergamon Press, 1981.

Nida, Eugene A. *Translating Meaning*. San Dimas: English Language Institute, 1982.

Searle, J. "Indirect Speech Acts." In *Syntax and Semantics*, edited by P. Cole and J. Morgan. New York: Academic Press, 1975.

Smith, N. and D. Wilson. *Modern Linguistics, the Results of Chomsky's Revolution*. Harmondsworth: Penguin Books, 1980.

Thomas, J. 1983: "Cross-cultural Pragmatic Failure." *Applied Linguistics*, Vol. 4, No. 2 (1983).

Verschueren, J. "Review Article on G. N. Leech, *Principles of Pragmatics*, and S. C. Levinson, *Pragmatics*." *Journal of Linguistics*, Vol. 21 (1985).

PROCEDURES

Cognitive Aspects of the Translation Process

Wolfram Wilss
Universitäte des Saarlandes, Saarlandes, Germany

Translation has become a very important instrument of international communication in recent years. As a consequence there has been an increased commitment to scientific research concerning it. In the last 30 years the science of translation, influenced in no small part by machine translation, has actively contributed to "building the tower of science" (Karl Popper) and broadened considerably the spectrum of inquiry into language, culture, communication, and computer science. This does not mean to suggest that our century is the first to devote intensive thought to translation. Since antiquity translation has repeatedly been the object of theoretical, methodological and praxis-related reflection concerning its various aspects, whether theological, philosophical, aesthetic, anthropological, or psychological (Wilss, 1982).

If we trace the cognitionally motivating interests of the modern science of translation, we arrive at the following conclusions: The question is no longer one of justifying its own position in regard to methodology and prac.ice, as was so often the case in the past. Its goal now is to clarify the principles, structures, and categories of the act of translation. In accordance with the general contemporary perception of the problems involved, the science of translation attempts to establish comprehensive interactional categories and to develop a verifiable representational system to describe and explain the processes and results of translation. This representational system may be characterized as an objectification of reflections on the problematics of translation. It is a difficult undertaking because research in this field has increased in flexibility, complexity, wealth of perspective and preciseness of detail in recent years, leaving the way open to contradictions. As a result, discussion of translation science frequently develops into controversy over the "relevant" points of reference in a particular case and is very likely to lead to endless and heated debate over the correctness of this or that theoretical or methodological perspective.

In contrast with the theories of other scientific disciplines, translation theory has not attained its goal if it is merely free of contradiction and is logical. A body of theory relating to translation should address it in all its manifestations and at the same time leave room for an understanding of the basic sociocultural position and value system of the translator as an individual. In this regard, translation science depends on cognitive psychology in the belief that it contains a scientific "central concept" with both an interdisciplinary and unified research perspective. This perspective permits us to pursue the question of how the more or less structured knowledge sedimented in our memory is activated by external stimuli, i.e. by the text to be translated. The fascination with cognition that we have witnessed in recent years may be explained by the generally conceded integrative capacity of cognitive psychology to describe action and behaviour.

The effort toward cognitive embedding of the translation process finds justification in the fact that translation, like any type of language usage, is a goal-directed action. In the course of this action the translator makes an attempt, or an integrated series of attempts, within the framework of his or her potentialities and limitations to translate into a target language (in a functionally adequate way and for a specified addressee) a text that has been written by a source language "sender" who has a particular communicative intention. In a pragmatic sense, therefore, we may conceive of translation as a particular type of linguistic activity that is dependent upon a given situation, is value-oriented, and subject to time limitation.

Such considerations are relatively new in translation science. The attempt to develop a cognitive argumentation signifies a departure from all the obscure pronouncements that were until quite recently supposed to constitute translation theory. These considerations attest to the presence now of a self-aware standard of current thinking whose concern is to comprehend a field of study particular to it alone.

The science of translation has, to be sure, not come very far in its effort to organize its research, despite a huge and growing flood of publications.

In the judgement of most people, at least, the reason is that translation resists to a large extent the development of particular scientific/cognitive forms and goals relevant to its praxis. People do, of course, accept the fact that the history of translation can be just as much a field of historical study as the history of language or the history of literature. But there is obvious skepticism toward the notion that the translations that one encounters, either as a reader or as a practising translator, should be the object of a science whose results are supposed to be not only theoretical but actually applied. The layman assumes, *inter alia*, that anyone can translate if he or she has sufficient knowledge of both the source and target languages, and consults in case of doubt, a more or less reliable bilingual dictionary. For according to a dictum still frequently heard, it is largely only a question of mechanically reproducing a pre-formulated text in another language, preserving the meaning as consistently as possible.

Any practising translator knows, of course, that translation involves more than just "reproduction". "Reproduction" is merely the final stage of a chain of mental operations in which processes of analysis, interpretation, comparison, analogy, inference, weighing of possibilities, planning, combining, etc. are interactively united. When the translator proceeds in a manner suited to the text, these processes yield a product that can withstand critical scrutiny. All the operations are cognitive and they are intermediary agents between comprehension of the source text and its (re-)production in the target text, and identify the translation process as a cognitive activity (Tommola, 1986). Furthermore, this activity cannot be described with any degree of completeness within the framework of a linear, left-to-right decoding/encoding model. Such a model shows too little differentiation. The empirical approach to translation processes — the "*experimentum crucis*" of any model — proves it to be inappropriate to the object. It does not do justice to the translator's cognitive achievement, either in handling the source text or in the production of an acceptable target text. It also does not give an adequate picture of the mental complexity of the translation process. This complexity can be explained by the fact that two more or less divergent linguistic quantities must be intertextually harmonized. This task forces translators, at least when they are not dealing with interlingually highly standardized texts, to draw upon their cognitive resources; but in any case, the task is only approximately fulfillable, because ordinarily there are, interlingually speaking, no ideal intersections. (The intertextual problem of equivalence was expressed programmatically by Jakobson (1959) and Nida

(1964) in their later much quoted formulations: "equivalence in difference" and "closest natural equivalent".)

If we decide to describe and explain translation processes by means of a cognitive framework of representation and legitimation, this has meaning only if we are prepared to investigate these processes in accordance with operational concepts. Such concepts are action, behaviour, problem-solving, decision-making, creativity, intuition, and the strategies, methods, techniques, and routines of translation. These will be the topics considered in the following discussion.

A definition of the translation process based on action theory might read as follows: translation is an action directed toward both the source text and the reader of the target language. Its procedure is determined by its function and it pursues a goal of enabling understanding between individuals of different linguistic communicative and cultural communities. In other words, translation is characterized by specific actional circumstances and preconditions. The most important actional circumstance is the dependence of the translation process upon the original text, which considerably restricts the translator's freedom of choice. Translators do not work independently, nor are their actions directly attributable to themselves, which makes the definition of their role in the interlingual/intercultural communicative process so difficult; they work within the context of a mediative situation rather than a direct, actional situation. This means that they respond to this situation reactively on the basis of the linguistic extralingual or situational knowledge available to them, and within a framework of more or less binding conditions specific to a certain text and text-type, and to a certain receiver. Translation can be regarded as a specific case of "constituting a common horizon of action" (Stierle, 1981:5585), in so far as the translator accommodates the source text to the reader of the target text. Like every text, a translation is part of an interactive procedural continuum shaped by the particular specification. The crucial determinant of the act of translation is the intent to create common communicative conditions by means of hermeneutic-analytic and synthetical combination of mental operations based on a complex presuppositional situation.

If in such situations the science of translation is to help translators to orient their actions, it must develop theories of procedure on an empirical foundation. Its goal will be to prepare practical, useful, efficient prescriptions for action as well as norms of behaviour supported by background knowledge relevant to action and behaviour. An extreme case of such theories would be a "technological theory" such as that recently proposed by Nida:

> It is best ... to regard translation as essentially a technology in that it is based upon several different scientific disciplines, including especially linguistics, information theory, psychology, and anthropology. It is essentially the application of insights from a variety of scientific disciplines which makes possible both the study of the processes of translation and the development of useful pedagogical techniques for improving translators' capacities for effective translation. One may say, therefore, that translation is essentially a skill, an art, and a technology, in the sense of a related set of techniques derived from the sciences of human behaviour (Nida, 1982:23).

Here we shall not concern ourselves further as to whether this technological understanding does full justice to the nature of the translation process. Our primary goal is solely to establish that translation is a specific form of linguistic activity and behaviour. It differs from monolingual activity and behaviour through the fact that translators carry out "code-switching" processes; they are bound to the procedurality of comprehending the source text and of reproducing that text in the target language.

This double function requires deliberative action. Translators must objectively weigh the reasons for or against a target language perspective, establish anticipatory hypotheses concerning their tasks and the consequences of their actions on the basis of well-reasoned cognitive criteria, and from these draw conclusions for their translating. This course of action is not determined so much by the question "Why?" (discovering causal relationships) as by the question "To what end?" (determining final concepts).

If translation is regarded as a deliberative linguistic process, this means that translators must not follow the path of least resistance or maintain an attitude of complacent opportunism. They must instead act with circumspection and demonstrate that they have the necessary foresight to bring the translation of a text to a convincing conclusion. At the same time the preparation and execution should not take more time than the particular commission allows. When translation is carried on for practical professional purposes, it is usually done on a piecework basis. In many cases time pressure is the primary factor. The professional translator normally does not have as much time as might be desirable for research or for optional interruptions of the reception and revision process, or for completing the work at leisure. Therefore, translators must make a strong effort to develop "minimal strategies", i.e., to produce as efficiently as possible a translation that is acceptable in both content and style, according to the much-quoted motto of Nida and Taber:

> Translation consists in reproducing in the receptor language the closest natural equivalent of the source-language message, first in terms of meaning and secondly in terms of style (Nida and Taber, 1969:12).

In the context of translation procedure this means that the translator must know as precisely as possible the variable of the sender and receiver of the object text in order to establish validity as a dependable communicator with a defined goal of action and a clear assessment of the source text sender and target text receiver as the other two members of the "triangular relationship" characteristic of any translation process. This assessment of the other partners is determined not only by the expectations of the receiver of the target text, as has been stated recently from time to time, but also by the communicative intentions of the sender of the original text. Any translation, even a literary one, should be seen in the context of a "réécriture" referred to an original text, but this does not mean that translators must always have an affirmative attitude toward the text to be translated. Translators work with given linguistic data that can be reconstructed more or less systematically; "[the translator] responds through his actions to the questions and challenges of a text that is itself already a response to the questions and challenges of a situation" (Harald Weinrich, *Frankfurter Allgemeine Zeitung*, 4/20/1968). This process of reconstruction encounters limits beyond which a comprehensive monitoring of results is no longer possible. For this reason, translators should have as concrete a conception as possible of their communicative partners; through this consciousness they are able to identify themselves as linguistic participants without surrendering their own identity.

Translators see what goes on around them and, within the framework of their cognitive capabilities, make observations concerning the facets of this world in terms of the target language. Thus, if we want to know what the connection is between the translator and the text to be translated, we must picture the translator as an observer whose task is to construct — to the degree possible — a "characteristic relationship" (Horst Turk) between source and target texts. I say "to the degree possible", because the results of the translation process are not always coherent and predictable; they depend not only on the source text but also on the translator's mind-set and specific evaluative inclinations.

Every translation is the result of a covariation pattern focused on a person and situation. Aspects of personality theory and situation theory must be interactively involved in determining the translator's role in the translating process. The same is true in localizing from a critical standpoint the factors contributing to the specific form of translation. Any translation theory that abstracts from the person of the translator or is content to define the translator in terms of communication theory as a kind of "super-communicator" is running the risk of falsifying or idealizing its research objective. Translation theory has in fact sometimes made its own task too easy in this regard and fallen prey to the "simplicist fallacy" (for example, in the matter of faithful translation versus free). More recently, however, the theoretical approaches to translation have become more cautious, pluralistic, and also more relativistic. The translation theory of today had distanced itself more than ever from a monistic position. Scarcely anyone would now think of explaining the translator's actions within the context of a homogeneous motivation or a single rigid methodology. The spectrum of relevant texts and modes of procedure and behaviour is too broad for that.

However desirable pluralization may be, I feel that the demand heard now and then for a basic right of codetermination on the part of translators in producing the target text must remain questionable. This demand is justified in cases where a translation must be made acceptable for the culture represented by the target text, but it tends to create the impression that translators either can or even must elevate themselves to judges of the text to be translated and to act in a manner that borders on arbitrariness. I see this danger also in the view "that the literary translation necessarily deviates from its model — in other words, that it articulates different quali-ties" (*Sonderforschungsbereich* 309, 1987, XI). Arbitrariness can be de-fended only to the degree that a differentiation must be made between "arbitrary" and "non-arbitrary" activities according to whether they are intended by "the person performing or experiencing them and have a definite purpose for this person, who examines them for their functionality and corrects them where necessary" (Heckhausen, 1980:2). Translation does not depend exclusively on the evaluative judgements of the translator. Holz-Mäntäri errs in arguing (1984) that the source text has no intrinsic value of its own and is absolutely subordinate to the functionality of the target text (cf. Newmark, 1981, on the differentiation between semantic and communicative translation). In my opinion, the text being translated retains its original binding authority for the translator. This ceases only when it is incompatible with either practical reason or aesthetic principles, that is, when translators, in order to realize their conception and not put themselves in a questionable light, shift from the sphere of "recoding" into that of "new coding" (Kade, 1968) within the framework of their subjective notions of rational action (for example, in the transaction of literary or commercial texts or texts that are specifically sociocultural in character). A good illustration of a sociocultural shifting of the translational perspective is seen in a passage of the German translation of Winston Churchill's autobiographical "My Early Life". Churchill describes as follows one of the aspects of the reception of students at Harrow and Eton:

> The Harrow custom of calling the roll is different from that of Eton. At Eton the boys stand in a cluster and lift their hats when their names are called.

In the published German translation, the second sentence says:

> In Eton standen die Schuler in Haufen beieinander und *lüfteten* bei der Nennung ihres Namens *die Mütze*.

Of interest here in connection with our topic is the translation of "lift their hats". There are two explanations for the use of "Mütze" (cap) as an equivalent of "hat". One possibility is that the translator did not know that Eton boys wear top-hats instead of caps; if so, one cannot avoid criticizing the translator's knowledge of English customs. The second possibility, which is relevant to the principles of translation criticism, is that the translator very consciously transferred the passage in question into the milieu of the German *Gymnasium* of the 19th century, where the students *did* wear school caps. This would then be a case of translating "prospectively" instead of "retrospectively" (Postgate, 1922). It is, of course, also conceivable (as Rudolf Soellner suggested to me) that it was not the translator but the publisher's reader who shifted the perspective.

As a rule translators do not operate with their own coordinate system, but that of others. Their role consists of transmitting thoughts that do not originate with them to an audience they are unacquainted with. Translators are not text producers in the closest sense, but rather recipients *and* producers of a text, even when they are following their own formal, semantic, and pragmatic conceptions. The nature of the often taut relationship between the source text producer and the translator is clarified in the following quotation from Winograd:

> Language is a process of communication between intelligent active processors, in which both the producer and the comprehender perform complex cognitive operations. The producer begins with communicative goals, including effects to be achieved, information to be conveyed, and attitudes to be expressed. These include such things as: causing an action, either verbal or non-verbal, on the part of the comprehender; causing the comprehender to make inferences or have reactions, either about the subject matter or about the interaction between producer and comprehender; conveying information about some thing assumed to be known to the comprehender, getting the comprehender to be aware of some new thing known to the producer; and directing the comprehender's attention to some thing or some of its properties, to establish context for a subsequent utterance (Winograd, 1983:13f).

The situation in which translators operate forces them to undertake actions in which they cannot give primary attention to themselves but to the object text. There is a causal dynamic in the relations between source text, translator, and target language recipient, and these three variable elements influence each other in such a way that the translator is a dependant variable between two independent variables — the source text and the receiver of the target text — and must act in coordination with them. A translation is always a reaction to a precedent text which must form the starting point of the translator's actions. For this reason I believe that the following programmatic statement goes too far:

> Translations are texts "in their own right". They are based on source material, but must function independently of them .... Target texts are produced by a translator under the primacy of the texts' own scope and purpose (Holz-Mänttäri et al., 1986:5).

Translators can be relatively free in their actions when, as indicated, there are no target text models — thus when, for whatever reason, they must personally determine the target text perspective in order to guarantee the functionality of their translation. In such cases, translators find themselves in a macrocontextual determinative situation. This is a constitutive characteristic of every act of translation in so far as the act can be understood as a cooperative undertaking and does not serve the self-profiling of the translator, as Cicero demonstrated in exemplary fashion in his postulate of oratorical translation. With his duality of "ut orator" and "ut interpres" in translation praxis he postulated two classes of equivalence. Apparently from a need for social recognition and a striving for rhetorical creativity, he uncompromisingly embraced the first-mentioned principle.

The function of the translator can be characterized by the question "What does the object text express transactionally (semantically) and inter-actionally (pragmatically)?" (Brown and Yule, 1983). The supplementary question "What do I as a translator have to add?" becomes valid only within the scope of a given task of translation. Under certain circumstances, depending on the degree of professional competence possessed by the translator, the confrontation may induce a feeling of insecurity. In such a case the translator must accept "the risk of having no guarantee of attaining one's goal" (Blumenberg, 1986:12).

How the translator is supposed to handle various work situations is — like the familiar discussion concerning the ever fresh topic of "equivalence" in translation studies — very difficult to conceptualize. For translation is, despite or perhaps even because of its relation to a foreign text, not a bookkeeping activity. Any aspiring translator needs experience, combina-tive imagination, and a wealth of methodological inventiveness to clearly hold his or her work to the parameters of the conditions imposed on it and to disengage it from them in conflict situations. Such situations arise when the translator must grasp the facts and value orientations expressed in the source language and transpose them into actions determined by the target text. Not every translator is equally successful in performing these opera-tions. The act of translation is the function of an operative intelligence founded on varying quantities of linguistic, extralinguistic and situational knowledge.

The question of the degree that alternative possibilities enter into one's consciousness during this process will have to be answered in regard mainly to the specific text-type. In technical texts it is definitely easier for the translator to make hypotheses concerning the function of the target text than in literary texts or texts where the extralinguistic reality cannot be transmit-ted directly but only through a cultural filter. The clearer the externally imposed communicative points of reference become, creating an ever-lower threshold of perception, the greater are the translator's feelings of security during the translation process and chances of creating an intertex-tual consensus that eliminates the danger of a conflict of values. The necessary first phase which prepares the way for this security of action is a comprehensive understanding of the source text.

The processes of textual comprehension can be laborious, but do not have to be so. They are relatively unproblematic when the receiver's capacity to understand converges with the claims placed on one's understanding by the text. I feel that Kaplan's almost apodictic-sounding statement is valid only in such cases:

> Language comprehension, one of our most intricate cognitive abilities, happens so automatically and with so little conscious effort that it is not easily susceptible to scientific observation or introspective analysis. Thus it is not surprising that there is still no satisfactory explanation of how the listener deciphers and assimilates the conceptual relationships that are conveyed by spoken and written language (Kaplan, 1975:117).

Van Dijk and Kintsch use a different argumentation; although they place a high value on the degree to which the processes of comprehension and production are automatized they also speak of possible situations which involve complexities of comprehension:

> ... the production and comprehension of verbal utterances is an automatized activity. Unless an utterance has specifically difficult, problematic, or unusual properties, production and comprehension is not monitored at each step by the language user. If we do not know the meaning of a word, we may apply the strategy of asking somebody, consulting a dictionary, or guessing the meaning of the word from context, and if a sentence structure is particularly complex, we may — in written communication — backtrack and start reading again. Similarly, in discourse, we may have texts that are so complex that various external aids, such as schemata, summaries, or notes, are necessary to control the meaning of the text in production or comprehension. But such devices are rather special: understanding and speaking are usually almost automatic processes (Van Dijk and Kintsch, 1983:70).

The goal of source text comprehension is to reconstruct the actional perspective of its author in a competent evaluative fashion and derive target orientations from it. In doing this, translators often find themselves in an imprecisely defined position between norm and freedom. We can distinguish two extreme situations in this regard: first, the substitution of facts within the context of (culturally) multilingually valid worlds, second, the modification of source text worlds by the transformation of monolingually represented words in the context of the target language's linguistic, communicative and cultural community. Between them is a field of tension produced by varying predispositions concerning which translators must establish as much certainty as possible through an analysis of the source text that prepares the way for their translation. The success of the translator depends very definitely upon a capacity for cognitive calculation, and this calculation is based on translation as a directed linguistic action. This directed action operates, on one hand, between source language, author, and translator and, on the other, between translator and target text reader (or group of readers).

Important factors for effective translation of any type are:

(1) The translator's personal traits and qualifications: mental disposition; horizon of experience in translating; ability to make macro- and microtextual decisions and to recognize regularities of transfer; level of expectations; recognition of textual norms; competence (subjectively assessed) vs. difficulty of the text; interaction between motivation and cognition, etc.

(2) Linguistic and textual elements: compatibility (or incompatibility) of the text; degree of syntactic, lexical, and sociocultural contrastivity between the source language and the target language; variability and flexibility of the target language's potential expression; complexity of the text.

The processes of consciousness that play a part in the course of translation are of differing nature; they can, but do not have to, lead to a homogeneous targeted result. All targeted results are acceptable or at least worthy of consideration as long as the translator can verifiably account for them with due regard to the author of the source text, the target language receiver, and, not least, to the translator.

Verifiability is dependent upon, among other things, the problem-solving competence of the translator himself. In the science of translation there has been little said about problem-solving in the sense of a systematic descriptive method, perhaps because the content of translation teaching and learning has not been clearly established. The subject-matter indexes of Reiss and Vermeer (1984), Holz-Mäntäri (1984) and Vermeer (1986) do not mention the concept of problem-solving, nor is here any reference to it in Snell-Hornby's programmatic introduction to her collection (1986). This does not mean that translation science has not been well aware of problems. There are innumerable titles in the field in which the word "problem" or its equivalent appears. But the understanding of problems that we find in such publications is not uniform, and the proposals for the elaboration of translation problems or difficulties have seemed largely to be one of only passing interest. This statement is not a value judgement but is intended merely to express the thought that the science of translation has apparently had great difficultly in defining an intersubjectively stable research paradigm for problem-solving. This is especially true of problem-solving in its important relationship to the teaching of translation, whose lack of conceptual and methodological certitude was recently discussed critically by Poulsen (1987).

When problem-solving methods are applied to translation, a distinction must be made between macrocontext and microcontext. For macrocontextual problem-solving operations, the translator needs a plan that is oriented to the totality of the text to be translated and excludes arbitrary assignment of meaning. This means that the translator must gain a clear idea of what the content of the text implies, what its communicative purpose is and for what reader or group of readers the target text is intended. Here a rough orientation usually suffices, for which the Lasswell formula, with its seven peristatic determinants can be helpful as a problem-solving schema. It is obvious that texts of a specialized type of linguistic expression, such as technical, commercial, narrative, or literary, should as a rule be received as such. It is not likely that such texts will be regarded differently by the several participants in the communicative process — source text sender, translator, target text receiver. In other words, there exists in general a "constancy of function" between source and target texts, even when they involve different cultural communities. The translator must not undertake any fundamental "reader-based shifts" (Blum-Kulka, 1986:34). Variance of function is the exception rather than the rule.

On the other hand, the handling of microcontextual problems often causes severe or even almost unsurmountable difficulties for even the experienced translator. These include, *inter alia*, singular conditions of the individual text, such as semantic vagueness (but not semantic ambiguity, since the situational knowledge of the translator offers semanticizing assistance), syntactic complexity and syntactic ellipses, the distribution of thematic and rhematic information in sentence relationships, metaphorical expression, ironic incongruities, distorted or ineffective formulations, morphological idiosyncrasies, adjectival-substantive collocations, gerundial and participial constructions, etc. Here it becomes clear that general problem-solving methods as developed by the game theory and normative decision theory are of little help to translators when they encounter a conflict situation in their search for criteria of optimality. The reason is that the solution obtained for a microcontextual translation problem can be generalized only in limited fashion (in contrast with the generalization possible with grammatical rules). In other words, the more unique a translation problem is, the less practicable are any general problem-solving procedures, because the field of translation offers no systematic coordination of individual textual perspectives from general evaluative viewpoints (as exist, for example, in the game of chess). For this reason the problem-oriented science of translation has clearly distanced itself from traditional mechanistic-technocratic planning of translation, with its global conception of faithful *or* free translation from beginning to end.

The problem-solving method that translators select in a specific situation depends on their declarative and procedural knowledge ("knowing that" and "knowing how"). It may be considered certain — hypothetically — that translators do not always attain an acceptable result, at least when dealing with texts that are difficult in content and form, in a single transfer attempt but rather in a series of reflexive transferal attempts, using self-corrective feedback. This is a procedure which Voegelin (1954) was apparently the first to discuss under the term "multiple stage translation", and which is advantageous for the following reason: by means of self-applied (self-regulated) feedback involving a constant self-monitoring process of comparing the interim result attained at each transfer stage to one's own performance standards, the translator can intervene correctively to improve the translation product step by step. All the intermediate stages taken together form an operative scaffolding that facilitates a progress from "minimal transfer" (small textual units) through various "substance levels" to "maximal transfer" (large textual units) (Nida, 1964). The number of approach stages necessary in each case depends on individual experience. It gives the translator the breadth of choice required to apply cognitive methods to difficult transferal situations. This procedure reminds us somewhat of the concept of cybernetics developed by Wiener (1948) — a term that he derived from the Greek word for helmsman, "Kybernetes". A ship cannot sail toward its goal by the shortest route because it is at the mercy of wind, weather, and waves, and the helmsman must constantly change its direction. The result is a zigzag course, which is certainly not optimal but is in any case the second best solution, since the direct way toward the goal is not available.

If we consider the method of "multiple stage translation" a serious possibility in constructing a target language solution, this does not mean, of course, that we can schematically reduce translation problems to individual steps applicable to the translation process — steps that can be simply typified into a standard program with an exactly prescribed instructional sequence. This is not feasible if for no other reason than that a problem-solving method selected by a translator is merely a contingent course of action. It does not need by any means to be the only one possible, or even the best one, especially when the translator, for lack of knowledge, cannot develop problem-solving methods appropriate to the text. Such situations are conceivable at all levels of linguistics relevant to translation — morphology, lexicology, idiomatics and syntax. Any translator can remember occasions in which he or she knew that a translation problem was involved, but did not know at first how to solve it and arrive at the desired result. This is especially the case with texts marked by a wealth of associative and connotative overtones and undertones. Here the translation attains the dimensions of a language game that can no longer be logically defined, calculated, and verified with precision. The situation is different for texts in which the referential dimension is dominant or in which conventions relating to a specific text-type prevail and force the translator to operate within a semiotically restricted procedural context, as in the case of specialized texts with a sharply defined format or in other subtypes of utilitarian texts such as advertisements.

The range of application of problem-solving procedure is especially broad when few conditions are attached to its employment. A case *par excellence* is literal translation, which we can designate microcontextually as an elementary operation. In non-literal translation, on the other hand, the translator applies either syntactical-transpositional and/or semantic-modulatory methods. This means that non-literal translation requires more problem-solving than literal translation, whose importance for translation theory has often been either overstated or understated.

It would of course be an illusion to think that there can ever be a problem-solving model that serves every translational contingency and offers a well-defined institutionalized sequence of problem-solving operations. Such a model would be at most be conceivable in a problem-solving situation "with a closed problem area". But translation is always, or almost always, a procedure "with an open problem area" (Krause, 1982:35). This suggests that translators must learn to develop problem-solving procedures that demonstrate their ability to steer a professional course on which they maintain an acceptable input-output relationship and at the same time produce competent decisions.

Competence in decision-making is necessary because every translator must function in a way that contributes to an expected or prescribed end result. Translation as a conscious and intentional production of a target text is only possible when translators can anticipatorily assess the effect and results of their work on the basis of informed decision-making, taking into account the particular situational constraints. They must weigh the strengths and weaknesses of their work methods and behave in such a way that a plausible, convincing result is attained. To do so, translators must rely upon themselves and their own competence. This competence must be of a quality that enables them to follow their own procedural proclivities as they mediate between the source text author and the target text receiver, taking into account Grice's principles of cooperation (1975) and specifically applying them to translation. In order to make the right decisions for the particular contractual situation, translators must orient themselves to procedurally important variables such as text-type, aspects of content and relationship, as well as stylistic values, in their double role as recipients of the source text and, at the same time, planner/producers of the target text.

We know little about the behaviour of translators in decision-making situations. The science of translation has obviously not yet taken into account the comprehensive literature on decision theory that was produced in the 1960s and 1970s. Whether it can afford to disregard it much longer is a different question. The economic sciences played a leading role in the origination and rapid development of decision theory, but today, because of the broad spectrum of decision-making problems now being addressed, decision theory is a focus of discussion also in the computer sciences and in philosophy, mathematics, information theory, systems theory, and operations research. The aim of decision theory is to ascertain the prerequisites for conscious, well-considered, verifiable, comprehensible, and value-oriented decisions within a framework of alternative actions, and thereby to create the preconditions for rational, goal-directed decisional processes.

In my opinion, procedures for decision-making are not identical to those for problem-solving. But the boundary between them cannot always be clearly drawn, and they are therefore occasionally equated with each other. I personally consider problem-solving to be a more comprehensive concept. Decision-making processes do not begin until the area of decision is sufficiently defined within the structure of problem-solving operation that prepares the way. It then becomes clear what factors and criteria of decision-making are operative in the particular course of action and what weight they will be given.

All this is easier to propose as desirable than to actually transform into reality in a translation. Translators often find themselves in a situation that forces them to progressively filter out, through comprehensive information-processing, norm-deviant variants from the possibilities available in their more or less open horizon of action. They then must select from the acceptable variants the one that most closely corresponds to their conception of an adequate target text. The decision *for* a variant signifies, of course, also a decision *against* all other possible variants, some of which might, under certain circumstances, be just as acceptable.

In doing this, we can distinguish between decisions made under relatively risk-free conditions, and those made under conditions of considerable risk. Decision-making faces many risks when translators are working under uncertain circumstances that prevent them from drafting an appropriate plan of action. Contrastingly, decisions entail few risks when translators have access to a relatively large amount of linguistic and extralinguistic information and can draw upon a large potential of knowledge and experience. Translators can avoid risks most easily (assuming they have the necessary linguistic and extralinguistic knowledge) when they are dealing with the language of technical and utilitarian texts, i.e., operating instructions, weather reports, resolutions, etc. In such cases, one can also use so-called "standard equivalents" based on a regularized relationship between one's own work and the relevant textual factors. This amounts to a routinization of the translation process as far as decision-making is concerned; the translator is operating in an area in which the principle of procedural self-regulation prevails. In translating specialized texts there is no necessity of dealing with multiple textual perspectives and one can operate "without a viewpoint", so to speak.

We do not know whether there is a straight-line, continuous growth from less to more competence in decision-making or whether this accumulative process is amenable to group guidance or, on the other hand, requires individualized translation instruction. To address this question, translation pedagogy would need "longitudinal studies" (Corder, 1973) such as those advanced for some time now by applied linguistics. Such studies are difficult because the determination of the necessary experimental conditions presents methodological and economic problems. In any case, we cannot expect to learn much from simple hypothetical models. We cannot establish an absolute requirement that the translation process be decision-oriented, but must limit ourselves to essentials and rely on our ability to use improvisation and intuition.

As far as the logic of decision-making is concerned, the translator's actions conform to the general experiential finding that every human being imparts a specific configuration to a bundle of perceptions and conceptions. Thus there is such a thing as a covariation between the individual and his or her decision-making behaviour, or an effectivity of decision-making determined by the individual's personal traits, so that a certain text, organized differently and referred to a different "life world", can lead to different translations. Here the question arises whether a typology of translation might be written that distinguishes varying kinds of temperament. The prospective, goal-oriented translator can be contrasted with the retrospective, indecisive one who wavers in the preparation of the target text, exemplifying a state sometimes referred to as the "Pilatus syndrome". We can speak of translator types that are stubborn, skeptical, hesitant, ambitious, sensitive, inhibited, or inconsistent. All of these are behavioural aspects that would have to be discussed from the standpoint of a theory of the translator's personal attributes in connection with the theory of personality developed in motivational research (Heckhausen, 1980). This would likely lead to the finding that many transitional situations are characterized by closely interwoven personal sociocultural, and intellectual dispositions that can scarcely be untangled — a milieu in which translators often can find their way only with difficulty.

Nevertheless, translators must engage their abilities as best they can to create a target text appropriate to the situation. If their sense of responsibility is insufficiently developed, a situation arises in which subjectivism becomes an ever stronger factor in their work and points the way toward arbitrary decision-making. For this reason, decisionistic attitudes that find justification only in themselves should yield to methodological considerations appropriate to the given situation. Such considerations would lessen the feeling of insecurity toward the text to be translated and increase the feeling of mastery, or relative mastery, of the text. This would signal in the translator's profession the growth of a stronger sense of self-legitimation that could remove epistemology, cognitive-sociological, and psychological doubts as to whether objective findings concerning decision-making have any place in the framework of particular communicative interests.

Decision-making is discussed nowadays in discursive and algorithmic terms. The science of translation, oriented as it is toward decision-making, must come to grips with the computer sciences, regardless of whether this agrees with its self-image as an anthropological science. It will, of course, never become an exact science in the sense of scientism; it cannot commit itself to procedures that are radical, naturalistic, prescribed, and non-deliverative, but it can and must develop heuristic methods for making appropriate decisions about translation. What the science of translation needs is not a "conceptual mask" but a theory of practical knowledge.

This theory would include a confrontation with the extraordinarily difficult subject of creativity in translation. Although the idea of creativity is, so to speak, an icon of the present day, the study of creativity is still a problematical area of psychology, with a multiplicity of different research methods, perspectives, and goals. Guilford, who is considered the father of creativity studies (1950), drew attention to this as early as two decades ago (1968), but in the meantime there has been no decisive change in the situation. Creativity is still a "smoke screen"-concept; this is due, among other things, to the fact that we lack clear conceptual and definitional distinctions between creativity, productivity, originality, and imagination. To be sure, it is a matter of question whether such distinctions are possible at all, because of the difficulty in assigning precise meanings to these concepts. Although we know that creativity is an essential part of our life, we are still hard put to objectify the concept of creativity in a scientific way or to investigate the dimensions of human creativity. The reason is, perhaps, that under the influence of systems theory we have acquired a compulsion for epistemological methodizing and regularization.

In modern linguistics, especially in language theory , there has been intensive consideration of linguistic creativity both within and outside of the generative model. Since linguistic creativity expresses itself in certain forms of language use and since translation is a specific form of language use, it would have been incumbent upon the science of translation also to conduct a dialogue on the nature of translational creativity, but such a dialogue has not yet taken place. Creativity remains for the most part "terra incognita". So it is perhaps not surprising that in instances where attempts to define the concept of creativity in translation have been made, the authors exaggerate its complexity by drawing upon ideas from information theory:

> Translation ... is a creative process, consisting of the transformation of the units of (the) language ... in which is encoded the sender's message M, into units of another language ..., reproducing so far as possible a constant information I=I (Ludskanov, 1975:6).

There are several reasons for this uncertainty in defining the concept of creativity in translation.

(1) Translation is a specific form that combines comprehension and invention. In the translation process a specific type of linguistic creativity is manifested — creativity in the individual-psychological sense, not in the generative sense. Translational creativity is by nature an elusive concept. It can neither be grasped conceptually nor exactly measured, weighted, or described. Which of our mental faculties should it be classified under? Creativity is obviously a mental "super-datum", in which reason, understanding, intuition, and imagination work together in an integrative way. Creativity in general, and translational creativity in particular, cannot be predetermined. We cannot predict with any certainty what creative ideas we shall have tomorrow or whether our creative potential will permit us to do justice to our object text.

(2) The opinion may be argued that creativity is in contradiction to the nature of the translation process; its goal is to reproduce a source text in a target language. "The translator must be willing to express his own creativity through some one else's creation" (Nida, 1976:58). In other words, translators must activate their own mental resources of creativity in a specific translational situation to produce a likeness of the source text in its semantic, functional and pragmatic aspects. Translation is a "transformative" activity; its place is basically in the field of tension between creativity and re-creativity.

(3) Translational creativity cannot be completely objectified, either inductively or deductively; no descriptive or explanatory system can be developed for it that will be theoretically founded and clearly verifiable by empirical means. The volatility of the concept of translational creativity appears to be confirmed by the fact that even today there is no definitive opinion as to whether translation is an art, a skill, or a scientific undertaking in the sense of

possessing a methodology related to specific text-types and situations (Nida, 1976:66ff).

(4) There is obviously no homogeneous concept of translational creativity; translation involves various levels, areas, and manifestations of creativity.

We may perhaps approach the concept of translational creativity more closely if we keep in mind the fact that the translator can employ two different procedural approaches which can be subsumed grosso modo under the concepts of translation method and translation technique. In my opinion, these two concepts are not equal in substance (Wilss, 1983). They represent differing stages of consciousness in the context of the action and behaviour involved in translation. The processes constructed on them cannot be given exact limits in respect to each other; they represent, rather, a behavioral continuum ranging from the slow, hierarchically organized, cognitively demanding processes to those that are rapid, associatively accessible, and automatic.

The methods used in translation are always reflexive or "dependent on consciousness". The translator sets them in motion when it is a question, firstly, of utilizing text analysis and transfer procedures heuristically to address the transactional and interactional aspects of a given translation situation, and, secondly, of working step by step toward an optimal and qualitatively verifiable product. A good example of this is the method of "multiple stage translation", as previously discussed.

In contrast with translation methods, translation techniques are procedures characterized by routine and repetition, in which abstract contents of memory are automatically activated in a series of concrete actions. It is based on the principle that in similar or at least comparable conditions a similar or at least comparable result can be obtained regardless of the situation. Translation techniques represent a specific form of standardized information processing. They require a relativization of the concept that in a field of study like translation, scientific criteria such as objectivity and repetition cannot be used meaningfully.

To be sure, it is not logical to proceed toward general rules of translation procedure in every case. On the contrary, the important thing is to grasp the overall situation in each translation project as precisely as possible in all its particulars and to reproduce it in the target language as honestly and as clearly contoured as possible. Translators do themselves a disservice if they restrict their creative potential through premature use of standard procedure and let the source text dictate, so to speak, how they are supposed to react. It is true that our linguistic roles are prescribed for us and that translation too is a kind of linguistic role-playing, but in the very consciousness of this role-playing there are possibilities and perspectives of creative action opened for the translator — creative action which is grounded in one's own experience of the language, the text and the world and which contradicts the conception of translation as a stereotyped "activation of a frame by a frame" (Vannerem and Snell-Hornby, 1986:203).

Whenever creativity in translation is discussed, the concept of intuition must also be considered. Here we see a very similar picture. The concept of intuition in translation has also not been examined by translation science, because it cannot be precisely defined. Intuition has its traditional place where the chain of scientifically verifiable links of knowledge ends. Intuition is not the ability to construct solutions to problems in a rational manner but rather to generate them spontaneously when the situation demands.

Intuition is the converse of prototypical conception. This is true for intuition in translation as well as for any other form of intuition. All translators will orient themselves, whenever possible, toward the procedural patterns that they have acquired in a more or less systemic way, and they will practise a methodologically and linguistically institutionalized form of language usage. But they must always be prepared for situations that lie beyond the normal modes of translation regulated by methods and techniques. This is where the realm of intuitive translation begins.

When textual circumstances permit, translators call upon their intuition (in so far as they possess it and trust themselves to use it) and draw bold formulations that may not agree at all with the work of another translator. Such an approach is of course not without risk, which explains perhaps why intuition is much rarer in translation praxis that one might assume on the basis of the notorious characterization of the translation process as an intuitive linguistic act.

In the taxonomy of translational modalities — word-for-word translation, literal translation, methodologically controlled translation in the sense of a creative and decision-oriented problem-solving strategy, routinized translation techniques, intuitive handling of translation problems — the intuitive approach represents the most differentiated stage in the development of forms of consciousness relating to translation. Intuition applied to translation produced modes of action which translators perform within the frame of their subjective attributes and knowledge apart from the expectancies associated with systems theory.

This circumstance confirms the fact that there is evidently no reliable way to reconstruct, mold, and operationalize the concept of intuition in translation. Reflection concerning cognition and translation cannot enter the scientifically inaccessible realm of intuition. To observe intuition and to speak scientifically of it are two different things, and any attempt to unite these two perspectives to the advantage of both can apparently not really succeed because of the inevitable imprecision of all inward perceptions.

As previously suggested, ideas based on intuition cannot be summoned upon command. They are unpredictable and can also, under certain circumstances, become dangerous sources of error: "Obviously, some intuitive leaps are 'good' and some are 'bad' in terms of how they turn out. Some men are good intuiters; others should be warned off" (Bruner, 1960:60). To this extent we cannot rely upon intuition; it often helps us in an emergency, but without guarantee. Its use may arbitrarily produce results in a very definite situation in a very definite way. But this does not justify a general mistrust of intuition. Advocacy of intuition is not a statement against any clear mental and formulative processes in translating. Intuition stimulates a type of thinking and formulation that does not orient itself toward strictly normative methodology. It is a mode of behaviour that frees one's consciousness from an attachment to technicalized structures, theories, and models such as those that prevail in machine translation. Intuition opens up a world that transcends rationality and yet is founded on it, where translators must find their way just as in the world of rationally controlled problem-solving methods.

References

Blum-Kulka, S. "Shifts of Cohesion and Coherence in Translation." In *Interlingual and Intercultural Communication. Discourse and Cognition in Translation and Second Language Acquisition Studies*, edited by J. House and S. Blum-Kulka. Tübingen: Narr, 1986, pp. 17–35.

Brown, G. and G. Yule. *Discourse Analysis*. Cambridge: Cambridge University Press, 1983.

Bruner, J. S. *The Process of Education*, 1st & 11th ed. Cambridge, Mass.: Harvard University Press, 1960 and 1969.

Corder, P. *Introducing Applied Linguistics*. Harmondsworth: Penguin, 1973.

Grice, H. P. "Logic and Convensation." In *Syntax and Semantics, Vol. 3: Speech*

Acts, edited by P. Cole and J. L. Morgan. New York: Academic Press, 1975, pp. 41–58.

Guilford, J. P. *Fundamental Statistics in Psychology and Education*, 2nd ed. New York: McGraw-Hill, 1950.

―――. *Intelligence, Creativity and Their Educational Implications*. San Diego, Ca.: Knapp, 1968.

Heckhausen, H. *Motivation und Handeln. Lehrbuch der Motivationspsychologie.* Berlin/New York: Springer, 1980.

Holz-Mänttäri, J. *Translatorisches Handeln. Theorie und Methode*. Helsinki: Academia Scientarum Fennica, 1984.

―――, H.-J. Stellbrink and H. J. Vermeer. "Ein Fach und seine Zeitschrift." In *Textcib Text. Translation. Theorie-Didaktik-Praxis 1*. Heidelberg: Quelle and Meyer, 1986, pp. 1–10.

Jakobson, R. "On Linguistic Aspects of Language." In *On Translation*, 2nd ed., edited by R. A. Brower. New York: Oxford University Press, 1966, pp. 232–39.

Kade, O. "Kommunikationswissenschaftliche Probleme der Translation." In *Grundlagen der Übersetzungswissenschaft. Beihefte zur Zeitschrift Fremdsprachen II*. Leipzig: VEB Verlag Enzyklopädie, 1968, pp. 3–19.

Kaplan, R. M. "On Process Models for Sentence Analysis." In *Explorations in Cognition*, edited by D. A. Norman, D. E. Rumelhart and LNR Research Group. San Francisco: Freeman, 1975, pp. 117–35.

Krause, W. "Problemlosen — Stand und Perspektiven." *Zeitschrift für Psychologie*, Vol. 190 (1982), pp. 17–36, 141–69.

Ludskanov, A. "A Semiotic Approach to the Theory of Translation." *Language Sciences*, Vol. 35 (1975), pp. 5–8.

Newmark, P. *Approaches to Translation*. Oxford: Pergamon, 1981.

Nida, E. A. *Toward a Science of Translating. With Special Reference to Principles and Procedures Involved in Bible Translation*. Leiden: E. J. Brill, 1964.

―――. *Translating Meaning*. San Dimas, Ca.: English Language Institute, 1982.

――― and C. R. Taber. *The Theory and Practice of Translation*. Leiden: E. J. Brill, 1969.

Postgate, J. P. *Translation and Translations. Theory and Practice*. London: Bell, 1922.

Poulsen, S.-O. "Fragen und Überlegungen zur Erarbeitung von Übersetzungslehrbuchern." In *Übersetzen lehren und lernen mit Buchern. Moglichkeiten und Grenzen der Erstellung und des Einsatzes von Ubersetzungslehrbuchern*, edited by F. G. Bochum, 1987, pp. 83–89.

Reiss, K. and H. J. Vermeer. *Grundlegung einer allgemeinen Transltionstheorie*. Tübingen: Niemeyer, 1984.

Snell-Hornby, M. *Übersetzungswissenschaft — eine Neuorientierung. Zur Integrierung von Theorie und Praxis*. Tübingen: Francke, 1986.

Stierle, K. "Text als Handlung und Text als Werk." In *Text und Applikation. Theologie, Jurisprudenz und Literaturwissenschaft im hermeneutischen Gesprach*, edited by M. Fuhrmann, H. R. Jau and W. Pannenberg. München: Fink, 1981, pp. 537–45.

van Dijk, T. A. and W. Kintschz. *Strategies of Discourse Comprehension*. New York: Academic Press, 1983.

Vannerem, M. and Mary Snell-Hornby. "Die Szene, hinter dem Text: 'Scenes-and-frames semantics' in der Übersetzung." In *Übersetzungswissenschaft — eine Neuorientierung. Zur Integrierung von Theorie und Praxis*, edited by M. Snell-Hornby. Tübingen: Francke, 1986, pp. 184–205.

Translation Procedures

Peter Newmark
Department of Linguistic and International Studies
University of Surrey, U.K.

Before translation procedures are described, their purposes must be stated. Translation procedures are followed in order to produce accurate and economical translations of segments of a text that are consistent with the style of the text, given the following assumptions:

(1) The more important the language of a text, the more closely the language has to be translated.

(2) The less important the language of a text, the less closely the language need be translated.

(3) The less important the language of a text, the more important its message; the less important its semantics, the more important its pragmatics.

(4) If a text is well-written, that is, if its language closely and accurately reflects its meaning and intention, there is no good reason for not translating it closely, whether it is important or not, provided the translator's purpose coincides with its author's.

(5) Provided that the referential and pragmatic meaning of the original is accurately reproduced, transference (loan words) is normally the closest form of translation procedure, followed by literal translation (of which there are three types), and through or loan translation; the remaining (indirect) translation procedures are of varying degrees of looseness.

(6) The importance of a text is determined by its legitimate use. It may lie in its message or its thinking, its facts or its formal qualities.

Translation procedures may be defined as typical methods of translating various and specific types of segments of a source language text that are shorter than paragraphs, into corresponding target language segments. Being typical, they can be presented extracontextually without much loss; if they were atypical, their context would have to be stated. Thus the French *après l'avoir fait* is typically translated as "after doing it", but the options "after having done it", "after it had been done", "after we/they/she etc. have/has/had done it" are also available.

Translation procedures may be either lexical or grammatical, or they may convert from lexis to grammar, or *vice versa*; single-word or extended; universal (following logic) or language-specific. When a few professional linguists began to study translation in the 1960s, translation procedures were distinguished and enumerated, notably by Vinay and Darbelnet, Malblanc, and Catford and later by Koller, Wilss, Bausch, Vasquez-Ayora and others. Later when translation theorists became engrossed in discourse, these procedures tended to be neglected.

The closest translation procedure is transference, often known as borrowing, that is the reproduction of a source language word in the target language text. When the source language word has approximately the same meaning and currency in the source as in the target language, in and outside the context (e.g., for French and English, élite and restaurant), transference is a mandatory form of translation. Since there is a general economic and social convergence in the developed countries, transference has always been most common for natural and later for cooked food terms (e.g., pizza, paella) stretching across several languages. Where the source language word denotes a new or indigenous product, an unfamiliar proper name, a title of a book or a periodical or an artistic work, or the name of a private or national institution which is not known in the target language, it is customary to transfer it, and to add a gloss where necessary either within or outside the translation. (Up to now, geographical terms have tended to become "naturalized", first in pronunciation (e.g., Berlin), then in their morphology (e.g., Vienna) when they become well known, but this process may decline or be reversed out of increasing national respect (e.g., Beijing). Names of people have not been naturalized since the 18th Century (Linnaeus). Sometimes a word changes its meaning or develops a new sense after it is transferred and acclimatized in the target language (e.g., amateur or *roue*, which is "skilful" in modern French and "debauched" in modern English), and becomes a deceptive cognate or false friend. (The Dutch word "*coffeeshop*" would have to be translated into English as a "dive" or a "caff".) At other times a source language word is transferred by the media before journalists have had time to translate or adapt it (*perestroika*). Even in a time of computerized dictionaries, the experts, the lexicographers, come too late to deal with such difficulties. Official translations of contracts, treaties and laws may produce official versions of terms which are normally transferred (*Bundesrat*, "Council of Constituent States").

The argument in favour of transference is that it respects the source language culture, and when the item is value-free and unique to that culture, it is justified — frequency of use will determine whether it is incorporated in the target language (From spaghetti to tagliatelle). Further, a foreign expression may be neater than its equivalent in the target language, the one powerful argument for using Latin (*ad rem, ad hoc, ad hominem*).

The argument against transference is that it may be used for commercial reasons by vested interests, as French governments have realized for nearly thirty years, taking only partially effective measures against it; secondly, it may be used for fashionable, snobbish and elitist reasons by translators and others who want to demonstrate that "they are with it". In some cases, transferred words (*matador*, killer; *picador*, pricker; *apartheid*, racial domination; *Anschluss*, appropriation; *Volksraum*, national expansion; *Gleichschaltung*, forcing into line) have been perversely used to conceal the truth, and could have been translated literally or with the implicit meaning exposed.

To summarize, transference of names for material objects, when cultures and languages are in contact, is a natural phenomenon, as is naturalization, a secondary translation procedure which may succeed it (*Rosbif, bortsch*). Transference of ideas or qualities associated with individuals or groups, which may be promoted by powerful media instruments (*nouvelle vague, ciné-vérité*), is delicate. It could be maintained that there is little difference between slovenliness and *Schlamperei* (which is not normally transferred), *glasnost* and transparency, which is coming in from French; and *machismo* could have been translated as "masculinity", its literal translation, in a non-pejorative sense.

On the other hand, one could also maintain that transference of words denoting human qualities can fill up the numerous lexical gaps in every language and make them more subtle and more powerful instruments for representing and understanding human characteristics. Why has only German appropriated "fair" in the sense of "fair play"? Neatness and plainness are not particularly English characteristics, nor is the notorious "privacy", but they only exist fully and completely (*in toto*?) in the English language. Arguably national characteristics are declining or converging and reverting to a universal element. But one cannot argue where there is no evidence.

There are three types of literal translation. The closest, word for word translation, follows the source language text and consists of segments of one or more parallel target language words in the same order, each with the same primary meaning. This type may consist of a single word (*jardin*, garden), a group (*un beau jardin*, "a fine/beautiful garden"), a collocation (*faire un discours*, "make a speech"), a clause (*quand cela fut fait*, "when that was done"), a sentence (*L'homme etait dans la rue*, "The man was in the street"), a metaphor or idiom of varying length (*au pied de la montagne*, "at the foot of the mountain").

Secondly, one to one translation consists of a text segment of words corresponding functionally and formally with their source language equivalents, but respecting the target language word order: thus, *cheveux bruns*, "brown hair"; *er sagte, dass er müde war*, "he said that he was tired".

Lastly, there is the generic term, literal translation, which includes the above, and also allows for the addition or omission of grammatical words, and the use of grammatical or lexical words not with their primary meanings: thus *il a brûlé la chandelle par les deux bouts*, "he has burnt the candle at both ends"). Standard collocation correspondences such as *prononcer une conférence* for "deliver a lecture", where the primary extracontextual meanings of one of the collocates diverge (i.e., *prononcer* is not typically "to deliver"); grammatical switches (*etablissement* as establishing or "to establish"; *le vol* as "stealing"; near word for word metaphors (*brûler les vaisseaux*, "burn one's boats") could be placed in this category, which is the broadest form of literal translation.

"Legitimate" examples of all three types of literal translation have been produced — all out of context but all unlikely to be affected by any particular context. The third type, quasi-literal translation, is likely to be more common than one to one translation, and one to one translation will be more common than word for word translation. Quasi-literal translation, which cannot cope with many cultural words, metalingual words (e.g., puns or language-specific linguistic terms) or segments where the reader requires extratextual information (e.g., *Plzen* as "Plzen", familiarly known as Pilsen, the town in Czechoslovakia known for its beer,) — quasi-literal translation shades into "semantic" translation, which is accurate translation at the author's level, which can sometimes cope with these difficulties.

The term "literal" has connotations of science and truth, the letter, the word, the detail, and is often placed in opposition, not to "wrong" or "untrue", but to "figurative", "imaginative", "artistic" and so on.

Nevertheless, translation, and particularly all kinds of literary translation, appears to be becoming qualitatively and perhaps quantitatively more accurate, and therefore more literal, than it was at any previous period in history, except when translation began, probably with literal translation; this in spite of most present-day translation theorists.

Literal translation can also be used as a critical weapon to expose the cultural, literary and linguistic aberrations of many texts or their inadequate translations. Back translation is itself a useful procedure in revising a translation.

The third type of direct translation, which is variously referred to as a *calque*, loan translation or through-translation, consists of the literal translation of the components of a syntactic unit. Typically, this unit is standardized both in the source and in the target language, e.g., *l'Assemblée Nationale*, National Assembly; *Gouverneur-général*; governor-general. Further, any acceptable collocation that translates literally (*tourner la page*, turn the page), is an instance of correct through-translation, whilst a mistaken through-translation (e.g., "turn the page", *die Seite drehen* (should read: *umwenden*) is an instance of translationese, i.e., incorrect literal translation. A translator continuously has to guard against thoughtless through-translation.

Modulation, according to Vinay and Darbelnet, is a translation procedure where, obligatorily or for stylistic reasons, the meaning of a proposition is reproduced, but it is seen from a different point of view. The procedure is mainly exemplified when a positive is replaced by a double negative, or *vice versa*, which is a universal procedure intra- or interlinguistically:

He acted at once; *il n'a pas hesite d'agir.*
He is not stupid; *il est tres intelligent.*
He gave in; *il s'avoua vaincu.*

This procedure typically offers the translator a variety of options, as does any procedure followed for stylistic reasons. Strictly, the double negative is weaker than the positive, but this can be compensated by the ironical or forceful tone of the double negative (e.g., "I am a citizen of no mean city").

Although both irony, hyperbole and understatement are universal expressions of thought, they may be culturally tinged. Traditionally, English is notorious for understatement ("not bad") and Italian for exaggeration, but a translator should only modulate instances when they form part of standard expressions, such as some formulae in letters: *Carissimo*; dear colleague; *agréez, cher Monsieur, mes sentiments les plus distingués*, yours sincerely.

Modulation may be practised by the translator as an intuitive resource when a literal translation is clumsy or stark, and, unlike the original, does not follow normal social usage, or does not quite correspond to the contextual sense of the original. Thus for "He has a guilty conscience", *Il se sent coupable* reproduces "guilty" but loses the end-weight of "conscience", whilst in modulation, *Il n'a pas la conscience tranquille*, "conscience" is preserved, but "guilty" is modulated to *pas tranquille* ("uneasy"). There are also other options: *Il a la conscience coupable* or *lourde* or *chargée*, but the alliteration of the (first) literal translation (which I would prefer) might irritate some translators or readers. An elegant modulation may be preferred to a stark literal translation, but whether it is used also depends on the importance of the precise wording of the original.

Any lexical word can be modulated, usually to conform with normal social usage. Thus, in: *l'économie s'est révelée moins chancelante au cours du quatrième trimestre*, literally, "the economy has proved to be less unsteady in the fourth quarter", the sentence would gain in force if translated as "... has proved to be more stable" in any language. Again, *certes les avis divergent* (literally, "certainly, opinions differ") gives "admittedly, not everyone is in agreement", although this may imply that the dissenters are in a minority.

Some modulations are standard, owing to a lexical gap in one component of a language pair: e.g., "shallow", *peu profond*; "trivial", *peu signifiant* or *insignifiant*. In other standard cases, opposite terms replace the positive/double negative: *assurance-maladie*, "health insurance"; *danger de mort, lebensgefährlich*, where English had a lexical gap, until "danger of Death" became the official term in the United Kingdom.

A second universal form of modulation is active to passive, or vice versa, but the change of focus and stress, and the currency of the use of the passive, always have to be kept in mind.

The other modulation procedures specified by Vinay and Darbelnet, such as "abstract for concrete", "part for whole", "space for time", "change of symbol", etc. are rather arbitrarily selected and illustrated.

Lexical equivalence is the main translation procedure for segments of text where direct translation is not possible owing to cultural differences or lexical gaps in the target language. They may be divided into four types:

(1) Cultural equivalents (pragmatic or cognitive).
(2) Functional equivalents.
(3) Descriptive equivalents.
(4) Componential analysis.

(1) Cultural equivalents replace source language with target language equivalents, and therefore they are *per se* inaccurate. They are used on the ground that where there are cultural differences, they constitute the only procedure for securing equivalent pragmatic effect, that is producing the nearest possible effect on the target language readership to the one obtained on the source language readership. For this reason, it has been suggested by Neubert and Svejcer (respectively German Democratic Republic and Soviet Union translation specialists) that in Shakespeare's sonnet No. 18 (line 1):

Shall I compare thee to a summer's day?

"a summer's day" should be replaced by a cultural equivalent, say an "oasis" or a "palm-tree", when it is to be translated into the language of a country where summer is unpleasant. This view is questionable; in this instance, the relevant readership has to acquaint itself with the connotations of an English summer day, and they will be abundantly assisted by the context of the sonnet, which explains that an English summer is beautiful, but often too hot. The view that translation always requires the conversion of the source language culture into the target language culture is mistaken; where the source language culture is important, it has to be preserved; where it is not, there is a choice between a culture-free universal component as well as a target language cultural equivalent.

Connotative cultural equivalents are more justified in the translation of drama, where an immediate audience reaction is important, and in particular, comedy and farce, where cultural references to say trousers, knickers, bananas, false hair which fail to make the target language audience laugh as the source language audience do should be replaced, preferably by generic and universal rather than by target language cultural terms which would be out of place and incongruous. In other cases, the dramatic context of say "tea", "rice", "sausages" may be so clear that a substitution is unnecessary.

The more effective use of cultural equivalents in translation is explanatory rather than emotional, and particularly for uninformed and not much interested readerships, for example when *Cortes* is translated "the Spanish House of Commons" or *pétanque* as the French version of bowls. However, such cultural equivalents are only successfully used if the reader understands that they are only there to give a general impression, that they are inaccurate in many details, since cultural terms are *per se* peculiar to one language community. In a sense they are a form of metaphor (q.v.), (which is similarly handled), an introduction, where the detailed cultural differences can later be handled cognitively.

(2) Functional equivalents are a partial translation procedure: when "National Trust" is translated as "an organization for preserving historical buildings, monuments and areas of the British countryside", the function is stressed.

(3) Descriptive equivalents reproduce the substance: "the National Trust" is translated as "a national organization which is the largest landowner in Britain, also owning 240 historic buildings". The mention of "ownership" (description) rather than "preservation" (function) could mislead many readers. Normally the title "National Trust" is transferred, but even the full title (National Trust for places of historic interest or natural beauty), which is barely known to non-members in Britain, would not convey the meaning adequately.

(4) Componential analysis is a lexical translation procedure which may be used when a one to one word target language equivalent of a source language lexical unit is inadequate, and the lexical unit is important enough to justify more than a one word target language synonym. Normally, a componential analysis consists of a generic or superordinate term plus one or more specific or subordinate terms, also known as hyponyms, thus, for "lunch", a meal eaten in the middle of the day, consisting usually of two courses (main course and sweet); a formal word mainly in middle class use. (Here the subordinate components have been incorporated into a sentence.) However, a large number of English adjectives of quality appear to translate fairly evenly into two or three components, thus: "neat", *propre, soigné, ordonné*; "plain", *clair, franc, evident, sans ornement*; "gawky", *godiche, gauche*. Componential analysis may be useful for translating institutional terms (in particular sets, series and hierarchies, e.g., public service and military ranks), and idioms. The use of classifiers for proper names is an analogous procedure (e.g., Luneville; Luneville, a city in North-western France; *die Weser*, the river Weser).

Metaphor is a special topic which has its own translation procedures, which can only be briefly summarized here. A metaphor has two aspects: its content or sense, and its form or image, and three main translation procedures: (a) transfer the source language image (the closest procedure) (e.g., "born under a lucky star", *né sous une bonne étoile*. (b) replace the source language with a target language image (e.g., thank one's lucky star (*benir le ciel*). (c) reduce to sense ("a starring role", *un des rôles principaux*.) In the case of a dead metaphor, where the image is barely noticed the image is disregarded in the translation, though it may coincide in the two languages ("in the light/field of human knowledge"; *à la lumière/dans le domaine des connaissances humaines*). Stereotyped metaphors are kept in authoritative texts, but livened up, or more often, reduced to sense, in non-authoritative texts (get a bit of shut-eye; *piquer un roupillon, dormir un peu*). Standard metaphors follow the three main translation procedures. Original metaphors should be reproduced in authoritative, but normalized (conform to normal social usage) in non-authoritative formal or neutral texts; in informal or colloquial texts, e.g., journalism, they should remain arresting. In cultural metaphors, the translator may decide to combine the image with the sense, thus appealing both to educated and less educated readers (e.g., *C'est un renard*; He's as shrewd and crafty as a fox.).

Neologisms and proper names may be subject to a variety of translation procedures; when they have connotations, e.g., in fiction, they should normally be literally translated and then naturalized (e.g., Joyce's "northroomer" becomes *ein Nordzimmerer* in German; Dickens's Mr Veneering becomes "Mr Polituring" in German).

Transpositions, referred to by Catford as "shifts", are defined by Vinay and Darbelnet, who first applied the term to translation, as a procedure through which the signified unit of language, typically a word, a group or a clause, but occasionally a co-ordinate or complex sentence, changes its grammatical category when translated; the lexis remains unchanged by standards of literal or close translation. The universal grammatical structure of actor-action-goal (all may be premodified, as in "The lightning could have struck the white house") is at the basis of all transpositions, but it is sometimes distorted by the formal constraints (e.g., inflexions) probably imposed on individual languages or groups of languages by the relevant national or religious clerisies or intelligentsias. Therefore the precise reproduction of grammatical structures is mainly likely to recur in cognate languages, and not to be particularly common, thus:

> The beautiful woman saw a red flower.
> *Die schöne Frau sah eine rote Blume.*

If the tense is changed to perfect or future, the correspondence no longer holds, and the focus of the transposition switches from the object to the verb:

Die schöne Frau hat (wird) eine rote Blume gesehen (sehen).

Translators can benefit from work in comparative linguistics, which distinguishes typical syntactic differences in semantically approximately equivalent units. However even in standard transpositions, there are often differences in emphasis:

An exceptionally important fact
Un fait d'une importance exceptionnelle.

In the English original, the stress is on "fact", in the French on *exceptionnelle*. In another English version, "a fact of exceptional importance", an unmarked reading would put the focus on "importance", but "exceptional" is one of several words which are likely to attract emphasis in any language. The translator practising a transposition has a number of options, and can put particular stress on any component of the transposed unit by changing word order, or using the standard accentuating devices, in English: "It is ... that" (not so common as in French), "very" (a little old-fashioned), "itself", "myself", etc., "in fact", "in truth", "precisely" (rather German and Marxist), "notably", "even", "remarkably", "just", "exactly", etc.

In many cases, the grammatical options are numerous, varying in semantic strength to allow for varying contexts. Thus, *on ne peut pas* may give: "One cannot"; "we/you/they cannot (can't)"; "it is impossible to"; "there is no possibility of ..."; "the possibility does not exist of ..." The options vary in degrees of formality, insistence and complexity.

The above is a background to transpositions as translation procedures. They can be divided into five categories:

(1) Straight correspondences, without alternatives, for one language pair.

Thus, for noun groups: *un pantalon*, trousers; *des conseils*, advice; *un conseil*, a piece of advice; *la maison blanche*, the white house; for verb groups: *il ne l'aurait pas fait*, he would not have done it.

(2) Unique syntactic structures in the sentence language.

English has a unique capacity, in relation at least to the main Indo-European language groups, to form phrasal words (verbs: "put off"; nouns: "a put-off"; adjectives: "off beat", "off-centre", "off-Broadway"); gerunds denoting states or activities, and replacing nouns or verbs; emphatic present and past tenses ("do/did come"); converting monosyllabic verbs into monosyllabic nouns (cut, hate). Further, it has idioms with grammatical functions ("be about to"; "near to" plus adjective). All the above by definition show up grammatical or lexical therefore semantic gaps in other languages; usually there are translation options. The gerund is often translated by an infinitive, which may be more formal or emphatic. (Compare "the chance of doing it" with "the chance to do it". Again, phrasal verbs are usually more informal than the verbs or nouns that are used to translate them.

(3) Standard transpositions.

Within language pairs, typical conversions of one syntactic structure into another, have become accepted, either for grammatical reasons, where there is no alternative, or for stylistic reasons, where the alternatives are not so idiomatic. Thus, for Romance languages, gerunds preceded by prepositions are treated as follows:

Before working   *Avant de travailler*
After working   *Après avoir travaillé*
Without working   *sans travailler*

The above are standard. When the gerund is preceded by other prepositions ("to", "if", "while", "when", "on"), there are options. Some other standard transpositions for converting French to English are:

a. Noun modified by adjective of substance; noun plus noun: *cellule familiale*, "family unit"; *centre nerveux*, "nerve centre".

b. Adverbial phrases; adverb: *d'une manière bourrue*, gruffly ... (English forms adverbs more readily than French).

c. Verb of motion, accompanied by *en* plus present participle; verb plus preposition plus noun (This is Vinay and Darbelnet's "criss-cross" transposition). *Il traversa la chambre en rampant.* "He crawled across the room".

d. Noun plus past participle or adjectival clause or present participle plus object; noun plus preposition plus noun. *Le complot ourdi contre lui*, "the plot against him"; *la tour qui se dressait sur la colline*, "the tower on the hill". *La tour dominant la colline*, "the tower over the hill".

    e. Participial clause (active or passive) plus main clause; adverbial clause plus main clause. *L'unité française renaissante, l'opinion pèsera de nouveau.* "As French unity revives, public opinion will carry weight again". *Cela fait, je serai prêt.* "When I've done it, I'll be ready".

(4) Transpositions from grammar to lexis, or vice versa, referred to by Catford as level shifts. Here a lexical gap in one language is replaced by a verb group in another. *Après sa sortie,* after he had gone out. *Il a été un des pionniers de ce médicament;* "He pioneered this drug". *Il le cloua au pillori;* "he pilloried him".

(5) Universal transpositions. It is always possible to convert a complex into a co-ordinate sentence, or into two simple sentences. A verb may be translated by an "empty" verb plus a verb noun. *Il lui sourit,* "he gave him a smile". Such transpositions may follow individual style, or the "genius" of the language, i.e., custom initiated by elites in various fields.

A necessary and possibly most frequent form of translation procedure is synonymy. Synonymy is necessary for two reasons: primarily, because of the vast differences in the size of the word stock in most languages. English, for instance, is said to have three and a half times more words than any other language. (The classical example is the number of adjectives denoting velocity: quick, rapid, fast, speedy, fleet, nimble. German has about one and a half times as many words as French, whose word stock appears to have been more strictly controlled than that of any other language. Russian appears to have a larger vocabulary than most other European languages, possibly because of its deftness with prefixes (e.g., in verb aspect) and suffixes.

Whilst languages with restricted word stocks are likely to have more words each with a greater number of recognized senses (particularly French with *assurer*, etc.), this is unlikely to greatly affect their lexical deficiencies or limitations.

Secondly, translations have to make use of synonymy where there are lexical gaps in the target language which are not adequately covered by context.

Generally, the measure of a language's word stock will depend on the number and the depth of its cultural, social and technological contacts with other languages. As in the attested example of colours, the more isolated the language is, the smaller its vocabulary is likely to be. Inevitably, a translator's most important and frequently used aid after dictionaries and encyclopaedias is a target language thesaurus or dictionary of synonyms (grouped with and without distinguishing definitions) and antonyms.

Most translations are more or less synonymous with their originals.

Translation procedures are useful to the translator if they are typical and can be precisely formulated. They may offer a limited number of target language options, whose stylistic differences should be assessed. Such terms as paraphrase, expansion, reduction, adaptation are too general to be adequately exemplified. Translation labels, where new terms are given provisional translations, are particularly useful for relatively uninvestigated and unfamiliar languages. Compensation, where a semantic or a formal feature in one segment of a text is offset in another, a process of undertranslation followed by overtranslation, is an important translation procedure, but it is difficult to systematize.

Translation scholars in text linguistics are apt to forget that most translations are performed in segments, whilst the values of the text that go beyond the sentence (cohesion and coherence) have a regulating function; often they are a form of control or verification. Suzanne Guillemin-Flescher continues to explore translation procedures for French and English, and has provided brilliant and useful insights. Research into many other language pairs would be a service for translators.

References

Catford, J. C. *A Linguistic Theory of Translation.* Oxford: Oxford University Press, 1965.

Guillemin-Flescher, S. *Syntaxe comparée du français et de l'anglais.* Paris: Ophrys, 1981.

Lindquist, H. *English Adverbials in Translation.* Lund: Lund University Press, 1989.

Malblanc, A. *Stylistique comparée du français et de l'allemand.* Paris: Didier, 1980.

Newmark, P. *A Textbook of Translation.* London: Prentice-Hall, 1988.

Vinay, J. P. and J. Darbelnet. *Stylistique comparée du français et de l'anglais.* Paris: Didier, 1958.

Wilss, W. *The Science of Translation.* Tübingen: Narr, 1982.

Psycholinguistics

Wolfgang Lörscher
Institute of Applied Linguistics
University of Hildesheim, Hildesheim, Germany

Preliminary Remarks

Until very recently, translation theory has been primarily concerned with two phenomena (cf. Lörscher, 1991): with translation as a *product* and with translation *competence*:

— Translation as a product, i.e., a written text in a target-language (TL) as the result of a translation process, has traditionally been described and analyzed by a comparison with the respective source-language (SL) text. The relation between the SL text and the TL text has been dealt with in a large number of different and highly theoretical models of equivalence. By and large, these models have been *prescriptive* rather than *descriptive* and of very limited use to the practical translator.

— Translation theory was mainly competence-oriented and focussed on (professional) translators' internalized knowledge. The models of translation were theoretical and speculative rather than empirical and concentrated on idealizations rather than on actually occurring data.

As a consequence of translation theory being product- and competence-oriented, hardly any attention has been given to the *process* by which a translation is produced, and to translators' actual performance (Lörscher,

1991). This narrowing of the object and of the dimensions in which it is investigated have only recently been realized to be a deficiency. As a result, a new, process-oriented, performance-analytical discipline within translation studies has developed (cf. Gerloff, 1988; Jääskelainen, 1990; Krings, 1986; Lörscher, 1991; Séguinot, 1989; Tirkkonen-Condit, 1991).

The *empirical* investigation of the translation *process* seems to be especially important for three reasons:

(1) As far as the psycholinguistic investigation of translation is concerned, it can be expected that only on the basis of empirical studies of translation performance using a process-analytical approach can hypotheses on what goes on in the translator's head be formed. Thus, light could be shed on translation as a psychological process which is still largely unknown and uninvestigated.

(2) As far as psycholinguistic investigation in general is concerned, it can be expected that empirical studies of translation performance will yield general insights into language processing, about aspects of the mental processes of speech reception and speech production and about the mental strategies employed by the language user.

(3) As far as the teaching of translation is concerned, it should be possible to make use of knowledge of the translation process for teaching translation. If certain translation strategies turn out to be successful, it might be worth considering teaching these strategies in one way or other.

My own research, and thus the considerations made in this article, can be located within this newly established field. They are based on a research project which I have been carrying out since 1983. The aim of this project is to analyze psycholinguistically translation *performance* as contained in a corpus of (at present seventy-three) orally produced translations from German into English and vice versa. This is done in order to reconstruct translation *strategies*. These underlie translation performance, operate within the translation *process*, and are thus not open to direct inspection. In the first stage of the project, translation processes of advanced foreign language learners were investigated. The results yielded are contained in my monograph *Translation Performance, Translation Process, and Translation Strategies. A Psycholinguistic Investigation.* Tübingen 1991. The second stage of the project, in which professional translators' and, later on, bilingual children's translation processes are analyzed, is in progress (Lörscher in preparation).

Methodology

As concerns the methodology employed in researching the object of investigation, a distinction can be made between methods and procedures for the *elicitation* of data and those for the *analysis and evaluation* of data.

Methods for Data Elicitation

Among the *methods for the elicitation of data*, the introspective procedure of thinking-aloud (Ericsson/Simon, 1984) is the most widely used. The following six arguments capture what to me seem to be the main points concerning introspective methods in general, and thinking-aloud in particular, as a means for eliciting information about translation processes in my investigation (Lörscher, 1991: 48ff.):

(1) It is generally accepted that subjects can only report what is in their focus of attention. It is only information stored in the short-term memory which can be externalized, and which, by definition, is in the individual's focus of attention.
There is no way of obtaining information about mental processes which are not given cognitive attention by means of thinking-aloud or any other introspective method.

(2) To obtain mainly unedited and unanalyzed data, subjects were asked to think aloud only. In this way, I wanted to make sure that the method of data collecting exerts the least influence possible on the mental processes of task performance.

(3) Thinking-aloud was also requested because it is a type of concurrent verbalization. In contrast to retrospective reports, subjects are not exposed to a memory load, which means that the information they externalize is potentially more complete.

(4) Translation processes mainly operate on verbally encoded data. This seems to be another favourable precondition for thinking-aloud to yield the largest possible amount of information on ongoing mental processes.

(5) In my analysis of translation processes I concentrated on translators' problems and on what they thought aloud when they found

themselves confronted with such problems. There was hardly any thinking-aloud during subjects' automatic, i.e., largely unconscious, substitution of source-language text segments by target-language text segments.

(6) Solving translation problems is often carried out as a series of steps. Generally, subjects do not immediately reach solutions which they consider to be optimal. They rather have to work out optimal solutions. In searching through their memories they activate informational networks thus producing interim solutions, and try to optimize these with regard to their expectation structures. The step-by-step nature of translational problem-solving is a further favourable precondition for thinking-aloud to yield many reliable data on the on-going mental processes.

From all these considerations, it becomes clear that verbal report data are useful for making hypotheses about mental processes if we take into account the conditions under which the data are externalized, and their inherent limitations.

Methods for Data Analysis and Evaluation

The *analysis and evaluation of data* is carried out by means of an interpretive approach, as this is customary in performance analysis. The primary aim of this approach is the hypothetical reconstruction of sense relations. The analyst interprets the collected data with regard to his/her epistemological interest and hypothetical assumptions. In the process of interpretive reconstruction, certain data are interpreted as (observable) indicators of (unobservable, mental) translation strategies. These indicators represent the basis for the formation of hypotheses on the mental translation process. (A more detailed description of these phenomena is contained in Lörscher, 1991: 56ff.)

The process of knowledge accumulation with respect to translation strategies has a dialectical nature. On the one hand, the analyst must have some knowledge of the concept of translation strategy in order to be able to ascribe the status of strategy indicators to certain signs. On the other hand, it is only by their indicators that translation strategies are constituted, so that knowledge of them can, to a very large extent, only be gained by means of strategy indicators. Therefore, the analyst must often proceed in a speculative and hypothetical way. He/She often does not interpret certain signs to be indicators as a result of his/her knowledge of the respective entity or of the relationship between an indicator and a segment of reality, but rather on the basis of considerations of probability. They can be corroborated or turn out to be false in the course of accumulating further knowledge of the phenomena and of gathering more experience in intepretation. The analyst of the translations, which are explicitly monological texts, is possibly in a less favourable position than somebody who has to interpret (dialogical) conversations. In conversations, the communication partners negotiate reality and jointly constitute sense (Mehan/Wood, 1975). This often manifests itself in the text produced and thus becomes accessible to analysis. In (explicitly) monological texts, however, the text producer implies his/her model of reality and does not usually make it explicit. The same probably applies to sense constitution. It is likely to be verbalized to a lesser degree in monologues than in conversations. In order to compensate for these deficiencies, at least partially, the method of thinking-aloud suggests itself. By means of this procedure it is possible to obtain information which is generally made explicit in (dialogical) conversations but which is implicit in (monological) texts.

A Strategic Analysis of the Translation Process

Translation strategies have been defined by me as *procedures which the subjects employ in order to solve translation problems.* (Lörscher, 1991: 76ff.) Accordingly, translation strategies have their starting-point in the realization of a problem by a subject, and their termination in a (possibly preliminary) solution to the problem or in the subject's realization of the insolubility of the problem at the given point in time.

Between the realization of a translation problem and the realization of its solution or insolubility, further verbal and/or mental activities can occur which can be interpreted as being strategy steps or elements of translation strategies. They can be formalized to yield categories of a model for the strategic analysis of the translation process. The model consists of three hierarchical levels. The first and lowest contains those phenomena which can be interpreted to be *elements of translation strategies*, i.e., the smallest detectable problem-solving steps. The second level captures the manifestations of *translation strategies*, and the third and highest level comprises the *translation versions*. (A detailed description of the model can be found in Lörscher, 1991.)

Elements of Translation Strategies

Elements of translation strategies can be distinguished as to whether they are original or potential. The former exclusively occur within strategic phases of the translation process and are thus original elements of translation strategies. The latter also occur within non-strategic phases of the translation process. The 22 elements of translation strategies which could be found in my data corpus are listed below.

Original Elements of Translation Strategies

RP: Realizing a Translational Problem
VP: Verbalizing a Translational Problem
→SP: Search for a (possibly preliminary) Solution to a Translational Problem
SP: Solution to a Translational Problem
PSP: Preliminary Solution to a Translational Problem
SPa,b,c..: Parts of a Solution to a Translational Problem
SPØ: A Solution to a Translational Problem is still to be found (Ø)
SP = Ø: Negative (Ø) Solution to a Translational Problem
PSL: Problem in the Reception of the SL Text

Potential Elements of Translation Strategies

MSL: Monitoring (verbatim repetition) of SL Text Segments
MTL: Monitoring (verbatim repetition) of TL Text Segments
REPHR.SL: Rephrasing (paraphrasing) of SL Text Segments
REPHR.TL: Rephrasing (paraphrasing) of TL Text Segments
CHECK: Discernible Testing (= Checking) of a (preliminary) Solution to a Translational Problem
OSL: Mental Organization of SL Text Segments
OTL: Mental Organization of TL Text Segments
REC: Reception (first reading) of SL Text Segments
[TS]$_{com}$: Comment on a Text Segment
TRANS: Transposition of lexemes or combinations of lexemes
T: Translation of Text Segments
→T2,3,..n: Conceiving a Second, Third, etc. Translation Version
ORG: Organization of Translational Discourse

Translation Strategies

Translation strategies are procedures for solving translation problems. They are constituted by those minimal problem-solving steps I have just outlined. As the data show, the elements of translation strategies combine in specific ways only to build up structures. Accordingly, translation strategies contain one or more of these structures.

Following a model for the analysis of discourse, which I developed in a different context (Lörscher, 1983), a distinction is made between *basic structures*, *expanded structures*, and *complex structures* of translation strategies. This is based on the fact that although translation strategies can be highly complex and thus difficult to document and describe in their manifold forms, they can be reduced to a fairly small number of simpler structures. The application of a generative principle allows the transformation of *basic structures* into *expanded* and *complex structures*.

As regards their description, basic structures are the simplest structural types. This, however, does not necessarily imply that *in the course of the translation* the subjects consider those *problems* which they address with strategies consisting of one basic structure only to be especially easy to solve. As a consequence, the *linguistic* complexity of the analytical constructs need by no means be identical with the *psychological* complexity of the problems, as assessed by the subjects. It can be assumed, however, that, *in retrospect*, the subjects consider those problems to be especially complex, and thus difficult to solve, which they have tackled with linguistically complex strategies requiring a great amount of time and mental effort.

In my data corpus, a tendency seems to be recognizable according to which the subjects generally use (linguistically) simple strategies first, and only when they turn out to be unsuccessful do the subjects employ more complex strategies. This procedure of the subjects complies with the generative principle whereby complex translation strategies are constituted by and can be derived from simpler structures.

The types of translation strategies used by the subjects of my investigations are schematically represented below.

Translation Structures

Five types of *basic structures* occur in my data corpus:

Type I: RP — (P)SP#/SPØ

Type II: RP — →SP — (P)SP#/SPØ
Type III: RP — VP — (P)SP#/SPØ
Type IV: (RP) — (→SP) — VP — (→SP) — (P)SP#/SPØ; at least one →SP must be realized.
Type V: (…) (P)SPa/SPaØ (…) (P)SPb/SPbØ (…) (P)SPc/SPcØ — (…)
Type Va: RP — (→SP) — (P)SPa/SPaØ — (→SP) — (P)SPb/SPbØ — (→SP) — (P)SPc/SPcØ — (…)
Type Vb: RP — (→SP) — VPa — (→SP) — (P)SPa/SPaØ — (→SP) — VPb — (→SP) — (P)SPb/SPbØ — (→SP) — (…)
Type Vc: RP — (→SP) — (VPa) — (→SP) — (P)SPa/SPaØ — (→SP) — (VPb) — (P)SPb/SPbØ — (→SP) —(…)

According to the generative principle, types II to IV can be derived from type I. Type II contains an additional phase of searching for a solution (→SP), type III contains an additional verbalization of the translational problem (VP), and type IV contains both an additional phase of searching (→SP) and a verbalization (VP).

Expanded structures of translation strategies consist of a basic structure which contains one or more expansions. Expansions are defined as additional elements of a strategy itself. So, for example, the strategy RP — VP — →SP — VP2 — →SP — PSP contains a type IV structure, i.e., RP — (→SP) — VP — (→SP) — (P)SP, with two additional elements of the structure itself, (VP2, →SP), i.e., with two expansions.

Complex structures are built up of several basic and/or expanded structures. An example may elucidate this. The strategy VP — SPO — →SP — PSP contains a type III and a type II structure. The former is terminated by SPO, i.e., with the subject leaving the problem aside in order to try and solve it later. The second part of the strategy is the realization of a type II structure. It terminates with a preliminary solution to the translation problem.

The translation strategies, which I have just described, can be represented in the flow chart overleaf.

Explanatory Remarks to the Flow Chart of Strategic Translating

After realizing (RP) and possibly verbalizing (VP) a translational problem, and after a potential search for a solution (→SP), a subject may achieve a

Flow Chart of Strategic Translating

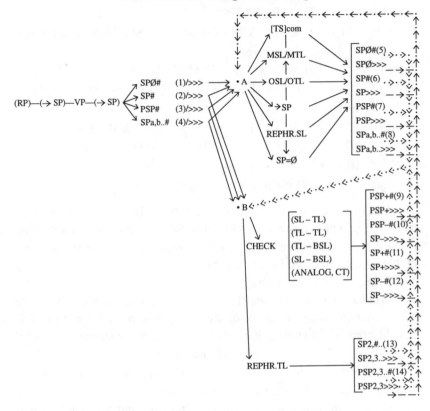

>>> = continuation symbol denoting continuation of strategy; # = termination symbol denoting termination of strategy; elements in brackets ( ) are optional; • A / • B = decision node A / B.

solution (SP, SPa,b..) or a preliminary solution (PSP) immediately (2), (3), (4), in which cases the problem-solving process may come to an end (#). This may also be the case when the subject considers a problem insoluble (1).

Having found a (preliminary) solution (2), (3), (4), the subject may go on dealing with the problem (>>>) and proceed to either decision node A or B (•A, •B). When the subject cannot find a solution (SPØ), he/she can only proceed to decision node A. Having reached decision node A, the subject may try to bring about a solution by monitoring SL or TL text segments (MSL, MTL), and/or by rephrasing SL text segments (REPHR.SL), and/or by (further) searching for a solution (îSP), and/or by mentally organizing SL or TL text segments (OSL, OTL), and/or by commenting on text segments ([TS]$_{com}$), and/or by conceiving a negative solution (SP=∅).

As a result of these problem-solving activities, the subject may either find a (preliminary) solution to the problem (PSP, SP, SPa,b..) or not (SP∅). Here again, the problem-solving process may come to a successful (6), (7), (8) or to an unsuccessful (5) end.

When the subject decides to continue, he/she may either go back to decision node A, which is possible after SP∅, PSP, SP, and SPa,b..; or he/she may proceed to decision node B, which, however, is not possible after SP∅.

Having reached decision node B, the subject continues by rephrasing (REPHR.TL) the respective TL text segment (SP, PSP, SPa,b..) or by testing it (CHECK).

The result of the rephrasing is a new (preliminary) solution ((P)SP2,3.., SPa2,3.., SPb2,3 ...). Here again, the problem-solving process may come to an end, as in (13) and (14), or the subject may proceed to one of the decision nodes again.

After the testing of a TL text segment, the (preliminary) solution may either be corroborated ((P)SP+) or rejected ((P)SP–). In both these cases, the subject may terminate the problem-solving process (9), (10), (11), (12) or proceed to either decision node A or B.

Translation Versions

As my data clearly show, the translation process contains both strategic phases, which are directed towards solving translational problems, and non-strategic phases, which aim at accomplishing tasks. The former range from the realization of a translational problem to its solution or to the realization of its insolubility at a given point in time. The latter start with the extraction of a unit of translation and terminate when it has been (preliminarily) rendered into TL or when a translational problem arises.

Translation versions are derived from a maxim which dominates an entire translation and according to which a translation should not merely convey the sense of the SL text into TL, but should be an adequate piece of discourse produced according to the TL norms of language use.

Whereas translation strategies can, by definition, only occur within strategic phases of the translation process, translation versions can consist of strategic and/or non-strategic components. They can be located within strategies (i.e., intrastrategic versions), between strategies, and can range from one into another strategy. The latter case is called intraversional strategy.

As my data reveal, the subjects often produce several translation versions. They can comprise the entire text or only parts of it (e.g., paragraphs, sentences, clauses, or phrases). The production of several translation versions can have various reasons, of which at least four can be interpreted from the data:

(1) If a subject does not succeed in solving a translational problem at the first attempt, he/she may try to solve the problem *in its further context*. This may require a second, third, etc. translation version which potentially also contains non-strategic parts of the translation.

(2) If, at the first attempt, a subject does not succeed in rendering a strategic or non-strategic part of an SL text into TL in a way which is considered adequate, the subject may try to optimize the TL text production by conceiving a more adequate second, third, etc. translation version.

(3) If a subject, while checking a complex TL text segment, finds an alternative for it, he/she may conceive a further translation version which contains the alternative TL text segment plus part of its context.

(4) If a subject translates a complex SL text segment consisting of several strategic and/or non-strategic parts by successively rendering its components into TL, the subject may produce a further version of the TL text segment. Thus, he/she may become aware of the complex interrelationships between the components of the TL text segment. He/She may realize that the components, in order to make an adequate stretch of TL discourse, cannot be put together in the same way as they were successively translated from the SL.

Application of the Model of Analysis

The model for the strategic analysis of the translation process which I have outlined will now be exemplified by applying it to a segment of a translation of my data corpus. The analyses are reproduced in detail and commented on on the following pages.

The transcribed and analyzed translation segment contains four strategies the types of which can be found below:

S1:   Nos. 6–9/10
        This strategy realizes a type Va basic structure. It is followed by
        CHECK+. At the end of the strategy, a solution to the translational
        problem is found.
        Type: Va + CHECK+ SP#

S2:   Nos. 17–18/21
        Strategy 2 is the realization of a type II basic structure with two
        bound elements, CHECK and REPHR.TL.
        Type: II + CHECK + REPHR.TL SP#

S3:   Nos. 24–36
        This strategy is based on a complex structure consisting of an
        expanded and a basic structure. The expanded structure belongs to
        type Vc and contains three expansions (2VP, →SP) and one embedded element <SPb = Ø>. As a result of the expanded structure,
        PSPb is found. The second part of the strategy is a basic structure
        of the type II. SPb and thus an entire solution to the problem is
        found.
        Type: Vc + 3EX + <SPb = Ø — II SP#

S4:   Nos. 39–40/45
        This is an intraversional strategy realizing a type II basic structure.
        Three bound elements are appended to it: VP + CT, CHECK, and
        REPHR.TL.
        Type: II' + VP+CT + CHECK + REPHR.TL SP#

A Quantitative Analysis of the Translation Strategies

The *qualitative* analysis of my data corpus has yielded a differentiation of types of strategies with different internal structures. In this section of my article, an outline of a *quantitative* analysis of the different translation strategies will be given in order to gain insights into the frequency and distribution of the strategies in the entire corpus and in the translations *from* and *into* the mother tongue. The data corpus for this investigation comprises forty-five translations *from* and *into* English produced by advanced learners

No.	T4　S28 Text	Categories of Analysis		Comments
1 2	Okay, ich les mir den Text erst mal durch	 ORG		The subject organizes (initiates) the discourse.
3	(Reads text aloud)	REC		The first reading of the text is categorized as REC.
4	(2s) Okay.	ORG		This organizing utterance marks the beginning of the translation.
5	Sale of Honours	OSL		The first unit of translation is determined.
6	(2s)	RP ▬▬▬		The subject realizes a translational problem.
7	vielleicht "Ausverkauf von	PsPa ——	S 1	The subject verbalizes the first part of a possible solution.
8	(2s)	→SP		The remaining part of the solution is searched for.
9	ehm Ehrentiteln"	PSPb ▬▬		The remaining part of the solution is verbalized.
10	(3s)	CHECK(7, 9)+ ▬		During this pause, the subject probably checks the two parts of the solution. As the translation proceeds, the result of the checking is probably a corroboration of the utterances 7 and 9.
11 12 13 14 15 16	"There is no possible argument (2s) on which the decision by the congregation of Oxford University to refuse Mrs Thatcher the proposed honorary degree is worthy of respect."	REC		Reading is categorized as REC.
17	(4s) ehm (3s)	RP/→SP ▬▬		The subject realizes a problem and starts searching for a solution.
18	Es gibt keinen (1s) Grund	SP ▬▬▬	S 2	A solution to the translational problem is found.
19	(7s)	CHECK ▪ ▪ ▪ ▪		Here, the subject probably tests the preceding TL text segment.
20 21	ja, oder 'es gibt kein Argument"	REPHR.TL(18)/ SP2 ▪ ▪ ▪ ▪		As a result of the checking, the subject finds another solution to the problem. It is a rephrasing of utterance 18.
22	(8s)	OSL		The next unit of translation is determined.
23	für die Entscheidung (↑)	T		The translation continues.
24	(7s)	RP/→SP ▬▬		The subject realizes a problem and searches for a solution.
25	der	SPa ——		This is interpreted to be the first part of a solution.
26	(2s)	→SP	S 3	The search for the remaining part of the solution goes on.
27 28	congregation of Oxford University	VPb+CT		The remaining part of the translational problem and part of its context are verbalized.
29	congregation	VPb2		The problem is verbalized a second time.
30	(4s)	→SPb		The subject searches for a solution.
31	nicht "Zusammenschluß"	SP=∅ ——		A negative solution is uttered.
32	congregation	VPb3		The problem is verbalized a third time.

No.	T4 S28 Text	Categories of Analysis		Comments
33	(4s)	→SPb	S	and the search for a solution continued.
34	"Versammlung" vielleicht	PSPb ———	3	The subject utters a possible solution.
35	(9s)	→SPb		Nonetheless, the search for a definite solution is continued.
36	oder "Beschlußorgan" (1s)	SPb ■■■		This text segment is interpreted as being the solution to the problem. The translation proceeds without the subject's further searching for a solution.
37	Also nochmal	┌ →T2		A second translation version is announced.
38	Es gibt kein	MTL (20)		Part of the text segment No. 20 is repeated verbatim.
39	(4s)	RP/→SP ■■■		The subject realizes a problem and searches for a solution.
40	mögliches (1s)	SP ■■■	S 4	The problem is solved by producing a TL text segment which was not contained in the first version.
41 42	there is no possible argument	VP + CT		The problem and part of its context are verbalized.
43	(11s)	CHECK (40) ■■ ■		The solution uttered in No. 40 is tested.
44 45	irgendwas mit "wie auch immer"	REPHR.TL (40)/ SP2 ■■■■■■ └ — T2#		As a result of the checking, the subject finds another solution to the problem. It is a rephrasing of No. 40.
46	Es gibt kein	┌ →T3 MTL (38)		The subject starts producing a third translation version. Here, utterance 38 is repeated verbatim.
47	wie auch immer	MTL (45)		Verbatim repetition of utterance No. 45.
48	geartetes	T		The translation is continued.
49	Argument	MTL (21)		Verbatim repetition of utteranc No. 21.
50	(22s)	CHECK (46–49)		The adequacy of the TL text segments 46–49 is tested.
51	Nee	TS (TL) (46–49) — └ — T3#		As a result of the checking, the subject realizes that the TL text segments 46–49 do not represent an adequate stretch of TL discourse but that they have to be combined in a different way.
52 53	Vielleicht fang ich nochmal ganz anders an	→TRANS ┌ →T4		Therefore, the subject announces a transposition by producing a further translation version.
54 55 56	(1s) ehm (4s) Vielleicht fangen wir mal so an mit dem "on which the decision"	OTL <MSL>		The subject mentally organizes the succession of the TL text segments in order to produce an adequate translation.

(xs) = pause of x seconds; ■■ = translation strategy;
— — = translation version; [↑] = rising intonation.

of English as a foreign language. (A more detailed description of the investigation is contained in Lörscher, 1991.)

Basic, Expanded, and Complex Structures

As pointed out in the preceding section, translation strategies can occur as basic, expanded, and complex structures. According to a generative principle, complex structures are built up of several basic and/or expanded structures. The frequency of occurrence of these structures, both in numerical values and percentages, is recorded in the following diagram:

Basic, Expanded, and Complex Structures in the Translations
from **and** *into* **the Mother Tongue**

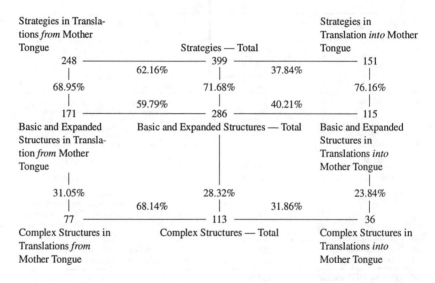

The forty-five translations which constitute the corpus of investigation contain 399 strategies altogether. 248 (= 62%) of them occur in the translations *from* the mother tongue, and 151 (= 38%) occur in the translations *into* the mother tongue. In other words, each of the twenty-five translations *from* the mother tongue contains an average of ten, and each of the translation *into* the mother tongue contains an average of eight translation strategies.

Of the 399 strategies documented, 286 are basic or expanded structures. This is surprising in so far as the subjects employed *linguistically* simple strategies in about 70% of the cases to solve the problems they were faced with during the translations, and only in about 30% of the cases did they use *linguistically* complex strategies. However, what was pointed out in the preceding section must be taken into consideration, i.e., the fact that *linguistically* simple strategies need not necessarily be regarded as simple and *linguistically* complex strategies as complex by the subjects during the translations.

The distribution and the percentages of the basic and expanded structures on the one hand, and of the complex structures on the other yield a further important insight into the translation process. As has already been pointed out, basic and expanded structures constitute complex structures. Therefore, a basic or expanded structure followed by at least one more basic or expanded structure must be produced so that a complex structure can be constituted. Thus, when a subject achieves a solution to a problem or realizes its insolubility by means of a basic or expanded structure, the translation strategy is terminated. As mentioned above, this applies to ca. 72% of all the translation strategies.

When a subject cannot bring about a solution to a translation problem by means of a simple or expanded structure but continues his/her problem-solving activities and produces (a) further basic or expanded structure(s), a complex structure is thus constituted. Therefore, the assumption suggests itself that the high percentage of basic and expanded structures in the corpus indicates the fact that the subjects can either solve the great majority of the problems they face or realize their insolubility after having made a comparatively low strategic effort. Only relatively few translation problems require a high strategic effort before they can be solved or their insolubility be realized.

Of the 286 basic and expanded structures of the corpus, 171 occur in the translations *from* the mother tongue and 115 in the translations *into* the mother tongue. In other words, about 69% of all the strategies contained in the translations *from* the mother tongue and about 76 of all the strategies contained in the translations *into* the mother tongue realize basic or expanded structures.

As shown in the diagram, the percentage of basic and expanded structures in the translations *into* the mother tongue is about 7% higher than the percentage of these structures in the translations *from* the mother tongue. If one additionally takes into account the fact that the translations *into* the mother tongue contain an average of eight and the translations *from* the mother tongue an average of ten strategies, the assumption seems justified that the effort which the subjects must make to solve the problems of the translations *into* the mother tongue is slightly lower than for the problems in the translations *from* the mother tongue.

Further-reaching conclusions about the translations from and into the mother tongue, *in general*, would be of a purely speculative kind.

Types of Basic and Expanded Structures

The basic and expanded structures are distributed over the five structural types as follows:

Type I: RP — (P)SP#; 18 times (= 4.51% of all the strategies)

In the translations *from* the mother tongue, this structural type occurs 6 times (= 2.42%), and the translations *into* the mother tongue contain 12 type I basic structures (= 7.95%).

It can be assumed that the translation problems which are solved by means of these strategies are retrieval problems. By putting the problematic SL item into the focus of cognitive attention, the subject may succeed in making the equivalent TL element accessible to him or her.

As concerns the direction of the translations, it can be observed that type I structures occur about three times more frequently in the translations *into* the mother tongue than in the translations *from* the mother tongue. Thus it is justified to conclude that the subjects succeed better and more frequently in retrieving and making accessible to them items of their mother tongue than items of a foreign language.

Type II: RP — →SP — (P)SP#; 106 times (= 26.57% of all the strategies)

In the translations *from* the mother tongue, this type occurs 56 times, which amounts to 22.58% of all the respective strategies. The translations *into* the mother tongue contain 50 structures of this type, which corresponds to 33.11% of all the strategies in the translations into the mother tongue. Translation problems which are addressed by type II strategies are partly retrieval problems for lexeme equivalents and partly problems for whose solution processes of construction or of syntactic or semantic paraphrasing are required.

Type III: (RP) — VP — (P)SP#; 15 times (= 3.76% of all the strategies)

In the translations *from* the mother tongue, this type occurs 10
times, which corresponds to 4.03%. In the translations *into* the
mother tongue, this type occurs 5 times (= 3.31%).

With a percentage of less than 4, this is the least frequently
occurring type of structure. It differs from type I only by an
additional verbalization of the respective problem. When a subject does not succeed in finding a TL equivalent to an SL item
solely by putting the problematic item into his/her focus of
attention, the subject can verbalize the SL item as a specific
problem-solving activity. The verbalization results in a (further)
mental focussing on the problem.

Type IV: ((RP) — (→SP)) — VP — (→SP) — (P)SP#; 61 times (=
15.29% of all the strategies)

In the translations *from* the mother tongue, this type occurs 38
times, which corresponds to 15.32%. In the translations *into* the
mother tongue, 23 type IV structures (= 15.23%) are contained.
When a subject does not succeed in finding a TL equivalent to
an SL item solely by putting the problematic item into his/her
focus of attention, specific problem-solving activities can follow. The subject can initiate a phase of searching for a solution
(as in type II), or he/she can verbalize the problematic SL text
segment. If both these strategic measures turn out to be unsuccessful, a further focussing on the problem can occur. In the
case of type II, the phase of searching is followed by a verbalization of the problem and perhaps a further phase of searching
for a solution. In the case of type III, the verbalization is followed by a phase of searching. Thus, type IV structures can be
regarded as continuations of type II or type III structures. This is
why they bring together the structural characteristics of these
two types.

Type V: (a) RP — (→SP) — (P)SPa — (→SP) — (P)SPb...#; 41 times
(= 10.28% of all strategies)

(b) RP — (→SP) — VPa — (→SP) — (P)SPa — (→SP) —
VPb — (→SP) — (P)SPb...#; 4 times (= 1.00% of all
strategies)

(c) RP — (→SP) — (VPa) — (→SP) — (P)SPa — (→SP) —
     (VPb) — (→SP) — (P)SPb...#; 4 times (= 1.00% of all
     strategies)

Types V occur 37 times (= 14.92%) in the translations *from* the
mother tongue and 12 times (= 7.95%) in the translations *into* the
mother tongue.

Type V strategies are mainly used to solve complex problems if
these can be split up into parts and solved successively.

Both the lexico-syntactic and the purely syntactic problems reveal a high degree of complexity and require mainly constructive
procedures for their solution. Obviously, the problematic text
segments do not function as units of translation. They are too
large and/or too complex to be processed in one go. Rather, they
are split into parts which can be handled by the processing
system, successively transferred into TL and then joined together
again.

Strategies for Translation into and from the Mother Tongue: A Summarizing Comparison

To conclude this article, I would like to briefly compare the strategies which
my subjects used when translating *from* and *into* the mother tongue.

In spite of many differences, the abundance of individual results which
the quantitative analysis of my data has yielded can be said to coalesce into
quite a homogeneous picture.

The results of the respective analyses show that the subjects generally
attempt to solve problems in the translations *into* the mother tongue by
means of linguistically less complex strategies than problems in the translations *from* the mother tongue. Possibly, they estimate the former problems
to be less serious than the latter.

As the distribution of the basic and expanded structures reveals, their
percentage in the translations *into* the mother tongue is about 7% above that
in the translations *from* the mother tongue. Apparently, problems in the
translations *into* the mother tongue are less difficult and laborious to solve
than problems in the translations *from* the mother tongue. The reverse
distribution is true for the complex structures. The assumption made is also
supported by the distribution of the types of basic structures. The less
complex types I and II occur more frequently in the translations *into* the

mother tongue, whereas the more complex type V can be found twice more frequently in the translations *from* the mother tongue.

On balance, the result of this section can be summarized as follows: Although differences between the strategies of the translations *into* and *from* the mother tongue exist, these differences are of degree, and not of kind. They are partly caused by the different distributions of the types of problems and by the different degrees of difficulty of the respective problems.

References

Ericsson, K. A. and H. A. Simon. *Protocol Analysis: Verbal Reports as Data*. Cambridge, Mass.: MIT Press, 1984.

Gerloff, P. A. *From French to English: A Look at the Translation Process in Students, Bilinguals, and Professional Translators*. Mimeo. Cambridge, Mass.: Harvard University, 1988.

Jääskeläinen, R. H. *Features of Successful Translation Processes: A Think-aloud Protocol Study*. Mimeo. Savolinna: Savonlinna School of Translation Studies, University of Joensuu, 1990.

Krings, H. P. *Was in den Köpfen von Übersetzern vorgeht. Eine empirische Untersuchung der Struktur des Übersetzungsprozesses an fortgeschrittenen Französischlernern*. Tübingen: Narr, 1986.

Lörscher, W. *Linguistische Beschreibung und Analyse von Fremdsprachenunterricht als Diskurs*. Tübingen: Narr, 1983.

————. *Translation as Process: An Empirical Investigation into the Translation Processes of Professionals, Bilinguals, and Foreign Language Learners*. In preparation.

————. *Translation Performance, Translation Process, and Translation Strategies. A Psycholinguistic Investigation*. Tübingen: Narr, 1991.

Mehan, H. and H. Wood. *The Reality of Ethnomethodology*. New York: 1975.

Séguinot, C., ed. *The Translation Process*. Toronto: H. G. Publications, School of Translation, York University, 1989.

Tirkkonen-Condit, S., ed. *Empirical Research in Translation and Intercultural Studies*. Tübingen: Narr, 1991.

Thinking-aloud Protocol

Jacqueline K. M. Lam
Language Centre
University of Exeter, U.K.

Definition

The *thinking-aloud protocol*, a method borrowed from psychology, is used to investigate how translational equivalence is achieved; the actual procedures, strategies, and the successive stages that each potential translator goes through to achieve an equivalent target language word, expression, sentence or a whole text. It involves externalizing the contents of our minds, i.e., what we are currently aware of as we engage in a particular activity, without in any way inferring the mental process or strategies involved. In actual practice, subjects who use the thinking-aloud technique are requested to give simultaneous reports on whatever is in their minds while they are translating.

Historical Background

Much research is done to investigate issues like: How to obtain good translation? What kinds of techniques should be used for teaching new translators?, etc. This research is usually based on the finished product, as Steiner (1975:273) remarks:

> In the overwhelming majority of cases, the material for study is a finished product. We have in front of us an original text and one or more putative translations. Our analysis and judgement work from outside, they come after the fact. We know next to nothing of the genetic process which has gone into the translator's practice, of the prescriptive or purely empirical principles, devices, routines which have controlled his choice of this equivalent rather than that, of one stylistic level in preference to another, of word "x" before "y". We cannot dissect, or only rarely.

However, as scholarly research in language moves into a new era —

emphasis once put on describing linguistic systems now shifts to the investigation of the process in producing or receiving speech — this kind of change is also occurring in the field of translation: research tends to concentrate more on the process of translation. Some linguists, namely Quine, 1960; Catford, 1965; Katz, 1978; Keenan, 1978, regard translation as linguistic science. In this way, they create formal models of the translation process, which enables them to consider better the theoretical aspect. (cf. Gerloff, 1987:136) Then there come "post-process observations", which include "memory for task information", "retrospective reports" and "post-experimental questioning" (cf. Ericsson and Simmon, 1987:40). Through these observations, "retrospective data" on the translation process are gathered. Among all these newly developed methods, the "think-aloud" technique, through which concurrent verbal reports of the translation process are recorded, seems to be a rather reliable method for data collection. The data collected through this method are known as "introspective data".

The introspective technique was not first used to investigate the translation process. In the early period, it was used in the analysis of problem solving by Wurzburg and Gestalt psychologists (Duncker, 1945; Selx, 1913, 1922; Wertheimer, 1945), in clinical analyses of thought (Freud, 1914) and analyses of children's thinking development (Inhelder and Piaget, 1958) (cf. Ericsson and Simon, 1987:24). As I have mentioned above, later on this technique was widely applied in language research, like researching in second language, language learning, language processing, learners' lexical inferencing procedures and learners working on a foreign language test, etc. One of the pioneers who used this skill in translation research was Hans P. Krings. He employed the "think-aloud" technique to inquire "into the structure of the translation process in advanced German learners of French as a foreign language." (Krings, 1987:159)

Value

The use of the thinking aloud protocol in studying the translation process provides a valuable source of data about the sequence of events that occur while translators are performing their cognitive task. The assumption is that while participants in the experiment are performing their translating task they are able to follow their normal sequences of thoughts and concurrently verbalize them. Translating by its very nature is a linguistic process, so the verbalizations externalize linguistically structured information and can normally do without an additional process of verbal encoding. Verbal protocols as they are sometimes called (the use of the subjects' own verbal reports as data) offer an immediate ongoing account of internal language processing as it is actually happening, but it must be stressed here that the data one can obtain with this method largely depend upon the subjects' ability to express their linguistic strategies.

Justification

There are a number of objections to the use of "verbal report data" in psychology; according to Krings (1987), the main criticisms are as follows: firstly, it is argued that most of the cognitive processes are unconscious, so the subjects will have little or no access to them; thus they are not accessible for verbalization. Secondly, it is claimed that subjects may produce verbalizations that are inconsistent with their actual behaviour. Thirdly, it is thought that the verbalization task may alter in the normal course of the task performance. Lastly, the verbalizations are said to be necessarily incomplete even for the conscious part of the processes (cf. Krings, 1987:163) The validity of these objections is argued by some of the researchers, namely Al-Besbasi, Jones, et al. Some of the defences are supported by the researchers' own experience through testing the "thinking aloud technique" themselves. Some inexperienced translators admitted that when they first used the thinking aloud technique, they had been at a loss as to what was actually in their mind. They found that it was difficult to verbalize a single word of what they were thinking. Such a situation seemed to be in accordance with the objection that "the subjects have little or no access to their cognitive processes because most of these are unconscious and, therefore, not accessible to verbalization" (Krings, 1987:163). Nevertheless, reports also showed that after some practice, most of the researchers were able to verbalize their processes of thinking while they were translating. This seems to imply that when a person is made aware of verbalizing his/her thinking, the original unconscious cognitive processes may gradually become more conscious to him/her. There may be still some hidden information, which, in Hölscher and Möhle's (1987:40) opinion cannot be extracted:

> one promising method for observing these normally invisible as well as
> unconscious processes is to make them accessible by means of thinking-aloud

protocols .... Unfortunately, we cannot expect him to verbalize things he is not aware of.

On the other hand, some experienced translators performed differently. Unlike the inexperienced translators, they had no difficulty in verbalizing their thoughts even though it was the first time they were invited to experiment with such a method. Some of them verbalized their thought after they had swiftly finished translating: these kinds of data Ericsson and Simon call "retrospective reports" (as opposed to "concurrent verbal reports": Ericsson and Simon, 1987:40); they further define the former as follows:

> In the ideal case the retrospective report is given by the subject immediately after the task is completed, while much information is still in STM or otherwise directly accessible, and can be directly reported or used as a retrieval cue.

The second objection claims that "the subjects produce verbalizations that are inconsistent with their actual behaviour" (Krings, 1987). Again, some inexperienced translators felt that the thinking-aloud technique was in fact adequately described by Krings: "the thinking-aloud technique is a type of concurrent probing," i.e., "concurrent verbalizations are made while the relevant information is still available from short-term memory." (Krings, 1987:164). These translators argued that since they verbalized every word that appeared in their mind without delay, they might say that their verbalizations were consistent with their actual behaviour. Moreover, according to Ericsson and Simon's findings (1980:224), the validity of verbal report data decreases with the degree of selectivity and abstractness of the verbalization task (cf. Krings, 1987:165) — during their verbalization of thoughts, they found that the thinking-aloud technique required no abstraction, selection or inference processes: what they needed to do was to report whatever came into their mind while they were translating. In this sense, they may say that the thinking-aloud technique is more consistent with their actual behaviour in translation work than other methods, such as the retrospective technique.

The third objection claims that "the verbalization task alters the normal course of the task performance". However, since translating is by nature a linguistic process which requires no additional process of verbal encoding, all a translator needed to do was to verbalize as exactly as possible what he/she was thinking. In this way, according to some translators' self-experimenting experience, they found that the process of translating was not distorted; the only drawback they would relate was that when verbalization was added to the processes of translation, the speed of the performed task would be slowed down.

The last objection states that "verbalizations are necessarily incomplete even for the conscious part of the processes" (Krings, 1987:163). Here, the word incomplete is a bit ambiguous. If "incomplete" means the subjects cannot verbalize everything that they are aware of in their mind, then it may contradict with some of the translators' experience. As translation is a linguistic process, all a translator need do during his/her thinking-aloud processes is to repeat what is in his/her mind, in other words, to speak out simultaneously and accurately what he/she is thinking. During the self-experimenting process, some translators found that once they were conscious of what was in their minds, they would automatically utter the information. In this way, even though the speed of the task performance was decreased, the structure and course of the task processes were not changed. Thus, it seems that verbalizations are not necessarily incomplete, at least not for the conscious part of the processes. On the contrary: it may be said that the data produced by the thinking-aloud technique would appear to show less degree of distortion than other types of probing.

Summing up the above arguments, Krings's point that "thinking-aloud while translating is an almost natural type of activity to which most of the criticism levelled at verbal report data does not apply," (Krings, 1987:166) is strengthened by the assumption that "translating is often accompanied by 'inner speech'." (cf. Krings, 1987:166) This can be verified firstly by some translators' own experience and secondly by the observation of other translators' processes of translating. Some of the translators' experiences showed that while they were translating, they used to verbalize their thoughts unconsciously; for example, some of them said that they had the habit of reading out the original text again and again while they were searching for the appropriate terms. For them, this "reading out loud" process is just an extension of their usual "thinking silently in the mind" practice. This kind of "reading out loud" may be regarded as an expression of "inner speech", which seems to reflect the fact that translating is accompanied by "inner speech" anyway. This argument can be further supported by observing other translators' lips during their processes of work. In many cases, people who are translating tend to murmur or move their lips silently when they are not "speaking": it seems as if they are using an "inner language" to communicate with themselves. Nevertheless, such kinds of "murmuring" may sometimes serve other purposes, for example, it may be a device to aid a translator's short-term memory until a solution is found which is worth writing down. Moreover, "sounding good" is one of the requisite features of poetry, thus translators need to murmur through various solutions. From all the above arguments, it may be said that the use of thinking-aloud technique in translation has a high degree of validity, and this is why more and more scholars use this technique to conduct research in the field of translation.

A Mode of Actual Practice

Usually, the entire thinking-aloud process is recorded by a tape recorder while the subjects are translating the given texts; at the same time the behaviour of the subjects should be recorded by the researcher on paper or other devices, for example, video camera. The main concern of the observation is to find out what is in the subjects' mind while translating; this is obtained mainly through their verbal reports. However, sometimes, when there are lapses during verbalization, it is worthwhile noticing the behaviour of the subjects, since part of their thought may be revealed through body language, whose precise meaning can be obtained by asking the subjects to explain immediately after the behaviour has occurred.

Another suggestion is: after the recording of the thinking-aloud processes is finished, the researcher can ask the subjects to summarize the whole procedure of translating. By doing so, the researcher may know whether the subjects are aware of how they translate and whether they can generalize their own translating methods — and also, whether they have adopted them throughout the experiment.

It is advisable that the researcher should try out the thinking-aloud method beforehand since this will give him/her a general understanding of what he/she may expect from the subjects and of how they may feel when they encounter problems during the experiment session. This enables the researcher to give adequate support when needed while the experiment is being carried out. As for choosing subjects, experiments show that subjects who have no experience in translation are likely to produce more verbalization than an experienced translator, and experienced translators tend to use a kind of "automatic processing" (cf. Bialystok, 1982). In other words, they tend to translate spontaneously, which militates against the gathering of adequate data. If the research is primarily on the problems of translation, then subjects who have no prior experience in translating are able to give first-hand information on what problems a learner translator may encounter.

In this way, learners' initial translating procedures are revealed. The follow-ing is one mode of using the thinking-aloud technique:

A Sample Scheme of Using Thinking-aloud Technique

Creation of a relaxed atmosphere
↓
Explanation of task
(-verbal explanations
-written explanations)
↓
Relating of some basic personal translation experiences
with reference to the thinking aloud technique
↓
Opportunity for practising the thinking-aloud technique
↓
Actual translation experiment
↓
Final interview of subjects

(cf. Krings, 1987:164)

Points of Awareness

It is suggested that before the subjects start using the thinking aloud tech-nique, it is helpful to ask subjects to practise this technique with themselves before coming to the experiment. This will help them to become familiar with the method. However, they will also be given the opportunity to practise it for a few minutes before the experiment as a warm-up exercise.

It is advisable that the translation is done under the normal circum-stances that a professional translator would enjoy. Thus, no restriction on time and language should be imposed on subjects. Moreover, subjects should be allowed to use dictionaries or reference books. It will be useful for the researcher if the names of the dictionaries or reference books are mentioned while the experiment is carried out.

It is also important to remind subjects to retain all their drafts and submit them with their final translation, since prior experiences indicate that researchers usually need to work on subjects' drafts as well as their final translation. This also means that all the crossings out and changes of opinion with regard to finding equivalents constitute an essential part of the investigation.

Method of Analysis

Among the different methods of analysis, the following one seems to be quite common:

Verbatim transcriptions of the tape-recordings

↓

Establishment of transcription rules

(cf. Krings, 1987:164)

The first step of analysis is to transcribe the tape-recordings, and then the researcher has to begin to construct appropriate analytical categories for the experiment. Analytical categories, which include framework of translation, translation problems and translation strategies, are shown in the following diagram:

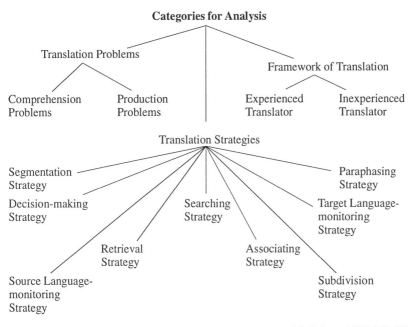

(cf. Krings, 1987:167–73)

Each category is defined as follows:

Framework of Translation

The framework of translation is the procedures of translating employed by subjects. Usually it is the subjects' retrospective report or idealized procedures of translation. It can be produced by both experienced or inexperienced translators. Here is an example suggested by an experienced translator:

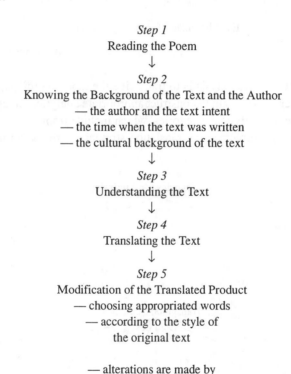

Step 1
Reading the Poem
↓
Step 2
Knowing the Background of the Text and the Author
— the author and the text intent
— the time when the text was written
— the cultural background of the text
↓
Step 3
Understanding the Text
↓
Step 4
Translating the Text
↓
Step 5
Modification of the Translated Product
— choosing appropriated words
— according to the style of
the original text

— alterations are made by
crossing out the unsuitable items, and
by rewriting the translated products
again and again

(Lam, 1991:27)

Translation Problems

The point (i.e., a word, a phrase or a sentence) when the subject got stuck and had to stop to understand or to think of an appropriate equivalent is regarded as a translation problem. It can be categorized as Comprehension Problems which are related to understanding the poem, and Production Problems which are concerned with the production of proper equivalence.

Translation Strategies

These are ways of solving translation problems. An example of suggested strategies is shown as follows:

Segmentation strategy means that subjects obtain the translation equivalences through dividing the source text into different small sections.

Paraphrasing strategy means that subjects obtain the translation equivalences through rephrasing or rewording a unit (e.g., line, sentence, etc.) of the source text.

Subdivision strategy means that subjects obtain the translation equivalences through dividing the words, phrases or sentences of the source text into smaller parts; the biggest unit is at sentence level.

Searching strategy means that subjects obtain the equivalences through monolingual dictionaries, bilingual dictionaries, reference books, computer word finders and source persons, etc.

Retrieval strategy means that subjects obtain the equivalences through experience and instinct, etc.

Associating strategy means that subjects obtain the translation equivalences through combining segmented parts to form a larger component for translating.

Source language-monitoring strategy means that subjects get hold of the meaning or the mood of the text through reading again and again the original text.

Target language-monitoring strategy means that subjects select the proper wording for the translated text by reading again and again the translated product.

Decision-making strategy means that subjects obtain the final translation equivalences according to (1) text intent (i.e., re-arranging the target text into different forms, e.g., poetic forms, with/out rhythm or rhyming etc.); (2) linguistic intent (i.e. semantic analysis, tense, subject, punctuation, sentence structure, etc.).

The above categories for analysis can be established by constructing "Equivalent Seeking Diagrams" (cf. Krings, 1984:171; Lam, 1991:54) of which an example is shown opposite.

With this type of diagram, researchers can have an idea of what happens between the first and last step of translation. Such information seems hardly able to be gathered through the investigation of only the finished product. The above Equivalent Seeking Diagram shows the five steps that a subject takes in searching for the translation equivalence of the term "three minds". The horizontal axis represents the interlingual and the vertical axis represents the intralingual dimension of the equivalent seeking network. (cf. Krings, 1984:170) Abbreviations used in the diagram are elucidated as follows:

Abbreviation	Denotation
BD	Bilingual Dictionary
PE	Potential Equivalence
(H 9:9), etc.	Page Reference of the Transcribed Tape Recordings
O	No translation equivalence is produced

Three Minds

Limitations and Pitfalls

Although "the use of thinking-aloud technique in translation has a high degree of validity", during actual practice, shortcomings can still be detected: the first inadequacy is the boredom caused by the frequency of verbalizing what is in the subjects' head. Such fatigue drives the subjects, on the one hand, to finish their work as soon as possible; on the other, it commits the subjects to producing every detail in their mind. In other words, the longer the time required for translating, the lower the probability of getting accurate and complete data. (Lam, 1991:143)

The second shortcoming is noted by Krings (1987:174), in "The Use of Introspective Data in Translation." He says:

> The information provided by the thinking-aloud data is not equally abundant for all features of the translation process.

For example, some researchers think that it is difficult to construct items like "framework of translation" from the recorded verbal data. Sometimes, researchers may adapt Krings's recommendation (Krings, 1987: 174):

> Wherever the information is scarce (e.g., because the subjects do not focus on these aspects in their verbalizations) the thinking aloud data can be complemented by other kinds of data that provide the missing information.

(Krings, 1987)

Thus, post-interviews have to be carried out in order to accomplish a fuller picture.

Recommendations

Since translation work is a rather idiosyncratic task, it would certainly be beneficial to translators to know how others handle their work. In this way, sincere translators are able to evaluate and to improve their own methods through absorbing others' experiences. "Thinking-aloud" technique provides a good channel for researchers to find out the translation problems and strategies the translators may have encountered and used. As "thinking-aloud data are especially suited to uncover individual differences in the translation procedure of the subjects, thereby avoiding the wash-out effect of large samples," (Krings, 1987:173), it is advisable to use the "thinking-aloud" technique to conduct research of this type.

References

Al-Besbasi, I. "An Empirical Investigation of Some Cognitive Process of Translation between English and Arabic, With Special Reference to the Use of Dictionaries." Unpublished PhD thesis. Exeter: University of Exeter, 1990.

Ericsson, K. Anders and Herbert A. Simon. "Verbal Reports on Thinking." In *Introspections in Second Language Research*, edited by Claus Faerch and Gabriele Kasper. Clevedon: Multilingual Matters Ltd., 1987.

Gerloff, Pamela. "Identifying the Unit of Analysis in Translation: Some Uses of Think-aloud Protocol Data." In *Introspections in Second Language Research*, edited by Claus Faerch and Gabriele Kasper. Clevedon: Multilingual Matters Ltd., 1987.

Hölscher, Anke and Dorothea Möhle. "Cognitive Plans in Translation." In *Introspections in Second Language Research*, edited by Claus Faerch and Gabriele Kasper. Clevedon: Multilingual Matters Ltd., 1987.

Krings, Hans P. "The Use of Introspective Data in Translation." In *Introspections in Second Language Research*, edited by Claus Faerch and Gabriele Kasper. Clevedon: Multilingual Matters Ltd., 1987.

Lam, Jacqueline K. M. "An Investigation into the Process of Translating Poetry from Chinese to English and Vice Versa with Particular Emphasis on What Is in the Translator's Mind." Unpublished MA thesis. Exeter: University of Exeter, 1991.

Puns

Huang I-min
Department of English
Tamkang University, Taipei, Taiwan

Puns are especially important in translating a play because a play is basically made up of dialogues. Often puns or word-plays construct the comic or ironic atmosphere of the whole play. Failure to translate puns can mean failure to translate the whole play. Up to the present time, many translators have struggled with the problem of translating puns and it seems that all of them agree that translating a pun is one of the most difficult problems they have encountered in translation. Yu Kwang-chung 余光中 (1983:156) admits that sometimes a pun is untranslatable and he cannot but give it up. Liang Shih-ch'iu 梁實秋 , with his rich experience in tackling Shakespearean puns, holds the opinion: "In translation puns present great difficulties as they are almost always untranslatable.... So, he [a translator] is left with no alternative but to footnote his translation." (Liang, 1974:13–14) Ching-hsi Perng 彭鏡禧 presents some interesting and good translations of puns in his article "Classical Chinese Drama in English: A Critique of Some Recent Translations" but he does not give us any systematic study on the translation of puns. (Perng, 1982) The only systematic study on the translation of puns that I have been able to find, up to now, is Hwang Mei-shu's 黃美序 "Translating Puns for the Stage." (Hwang, 1980) In this article, Hwang offers three methods: (1) provide footnotes; (2) write explanation into the pun; and (3) resort to invention to preserve the original flavour of the pun.

Expanding on these alternatives, I think in translating a pun or a pun-like word-play, the first consideration should be to try to come up with something like an equivalent to the original in sound and meaning. The second priority is creative transposition, and the last is to footnote, which is at least better than a complete omission, but is of little value in translating puns of a play intended for performance.

First, I want to discuss finding an equivalent to the original pun in sound and meaning. Many translators may think that it is usually just a happy coincidence when a stage translator can hit on the same combinations of sound and sense in the target language. (Chan, 1977) But I think this does not mean that we should not try. It is a very encouraging sign that there are quite a few successful examples of translating puns in this method in classical Chinese drama cited by Perng. (Perng, 1982:392, 414–17) So I believe this strategy should be the first consideration for a stage translator. Only when he cannot employ this method after a careful consideration should he try other alternatives.

I would like to present to you an interesting example of my translation of a pun from Hwang's 〈楊世人的喜劇〉 to illustrate this method. In Act II, when Yang comes home to tell his family what has happened to him, his parents, his wife, and his friends (Dr. Meng and his wife) do not believe him. They begin to argue among themselves about whether there are ghosts or not. Yang's father, finding that the argument is futile and useless and that it is time for dinner, urges them to stop and prepare to eat dinner. At this moment, Yang's brother, Hongren, opens a book and starts to recite Hamlet's famous soliloquy, "To be or not to be...." Hearing this, Yang's mother, who naturally does not understand English, mistakes them for 什麼「吐皮」不「吐皮」的 . The original of this comic episode runs like this:

> 楊恆人：（翻開書） "To be or not to be, that is the question"....
> 楊母：（站起）什麼「吐皮」不「吐皮」的，能吃的都應該吃下去！
> 糟蹋了糧食可是罪過。

And I translate it as:

Hongren (opening the book): "To be or not to be, that is the question...."
Mother (standing up): What is this "to peel or not to peel"? Any food which is edible should be eaten! It is a sin to waste food.

The comic effect depends on the pun on "to be or not to be/ 吐皮不吐皮 ". Although " 吐皮 " means to spit out the skin after eating in Chinese, "to peel" is the best English equivalent in sound and meaning I can think of, since it also catches the mother's sense of "wasting" the food, and echoes the sound of the English "to be".

In translation, especially in translating a pun, one of the major problems that a translator has to consider is how much flexibility he can employ. Two of the very common related practices are:

(1) the translation becomes an interpretation without much attention to the special arrangement of the words or the particular sound effect which is usually the soul of the pun or play on words. Such a translator only aims at transmitting the meaning and context of the word-play. For example, Stanley Munro, in translating the following exchange of dialogue, states that "A strict translation of this exchange, particularly 美不美 and 親不親 would produce confusion. I again opted for feeling and situation rather than structure and vocabulary." His translation reads:

> 祝英台道：「這眞是美不美，故鄉水了。」
> 那相公道：「親不親，故鄉人，太巧了。」

> Yingtai said, "That's perfect! The same stream flows through our villages!"
> "That makes us neighbours!" the young lord said. "What a coincidence."

Although Munro can transmit the meaning or the feeling of the original word-play to the English-speaking audience, the atmosphere created by the word arrangement and sound effect of the original is completely lost. To retain the flavour of this word-play, it seems necessary to stress the parallel word structure and the particular sound effect in which the young lord uses a phrase with equal emphasis upon "home town" to parallel Yingtai's to evoke a sense of "close relatedness." Thus I translate this exchange as:

> Yingtai said, "Whether beautiful or not, it is after all a river of our home town."
> "Whether really close or not, we are folk of the same town," the young lord said. "Isn't that amazing!"

(2) The translator tends to overinterpret or overtranslate the pun so that the special effect and the flavour of the pun or word-play are completely destroyed. In other words, the translator does not trust a reader's ability to comprehend or enjoy the play on words. I would like to bring up three examples from Sung's Chinese translation of *Antigone* for discussion, which, although they are not puns in the strict sense, are pun-like, for they are plays on words which are closely related to our discussion of puns in terms of word repetition, double meaning, and parallel structure:

1. And if you think my acts are foolishness
   the foolishness may be in a fool's eye.
   要是你認爲我的行爲愚蠢，
   那你不過是「貓哭耗子」假慈悲。

2. *Ismene*: But will you kill your own son's promised bride?
   Creon: Oh, there are other furrows for his plough.
   伊：你準備要殺掉你兒子的未婚妻？你未來的媳婦？
   克：天下的女人多的是。

3. I who am nothing more than nothing now.
   我現在還是能算一個人嗎？

T. H. Banks' English translation of the passage cited in Example 1 is "And if these acts of mine seem foolish to you./Perhaps a fool accuses me of folly." Fitts and Fitzgerald translated these lines as "Think me a fool, if you like; but it may be/That a fool convicts me of folly." It is obvious that these words "fool", "foolishness", and "folly" are particularly emphasized in all of the English translations, including in Example 1 on which Sung's Chinese translation is based. It is obvious that the passage strongly conveys the feeling that Antigone believes that her action is right, and holy, while Creon's action is wrong, folly. The repetition of the words "fool" and "folly" will express Antigone's powerful accusation of Creon and will foreshadow Creon's final understanding in the end that he is a fool. Therefore, the ironic and satirical effect is achieved through the play on these words. But in Sung's overtranslation, this effect is completely destroyed. Sung's rendering that "You are nothing but a hypocrite, shedding crocodile's tears" is a careless distortion in which Antigone's poignant accusation of Creon of his folly is lost in his overintepretation. The satirical effect of Antigone's rebuttal is basically achieved through her emphasis upon the pun-like structure of folly and foolishness. So, I revise the translation as " 要是你認爲我的行爲愚蠢，那是傻瓜眼中的愚蠢 ."

In the second example, Sung overtranslated the line "Oh, here are other furrows for his plough," as " 天下的女人多的是 ." Of course, Creon means that. But he does not say, "Oh, there are too many other women for him" in the play as Sung's translation would seem to indicate. And all the other English translations I can find are very similar to Wyckoff's translation as far as this line is concerned. For example, T. H. Banks translates it as "Yes. There are other fields that he can plow." Fitts and Fitzgerald's translation is "There are places enough for him to push his plow." And R. C. Jebb's

translation is "Nay, there are other fields for him to plough." (Jebb, 1938)
Apparently the translators of the English versions are not afraid that their
translations will be misunderstood by an English-speaking audience. Is it
possible that Chinese audience's ability to comprehend is inferior to that of
the English-speaking audience? Besides, the most serious problem of
Sung's overtranslation is that the strong male-chauvinistic flavour of the
original is lost. Because in all of the English translations, women are
regarded as "fields," as "things" rather than as human beings as in Sung's
translation. In a sense, the male chauvinism of Creon is greatly softened.
So, the overtranslation may not only deprive the audience of their right of
imagination, but also may hinder them from making a correct judgement
about Creon. And you may notice that all of the English translations that I
have cited carry a strong sexual connotation. Creon seems to imply that
women are nothing but tools to satisfy men's sexual desire. But in Sung's
translation, this connotation is lost. Coincidentally, there is a Chinese
phrase " 藍田種玉 " (literally meaning "to plant jade in a blue field") which
carries a connotation of sexual intercourse. Thus, I believe that we may
use this phrase as a similar equivalent to translate the English version:
" 不錯，天涯何處無芳草，他要「種玉」，「藍田」可多得是 ."

In Example 3, it is quite difficult to think of a Chinese translation which
can correspond to the English version in sound effect and parallel structure.
But I think Sung's translation is too careless. His overtranslation "Can I be
called a human being now?" is completely different from the English
version from which he translates in both meaning and connotation. Sung's
translation seems to imply that the speaker accuses himself after commit-
ting a moral or ethical sin. But the situation in *Antigone* is that Creon after
learning that his son and his wife committed suicide because of his stub-
bornness and folly, feels hopeless, feels futile in his blind struggle against
fate or the gods. To retain the parallel structure and the atmosphere of the
English version, I can only think of this tentative solution:in which the
emphasis on the repetition of "nothingness" and on the hopeless worsening
situation are preserved: " 我一無所有，現在更是窮途末路 ."

Finally, I would like to deal with a problem which Hwang Mei-shu
raised but left unsolved in his article on translating puns. (Hwang, 1980) In
two classical Chinese plays 〈烏龍院〉 and 〈翠屏山〉, when the hero
accuses the heroine of unfaithfulness, the heroine says, "First I steal
things; ..." Then she stops, finding herself unable to go on. But the hero
forces her to go on. Then she says, " 二不偷人家的 ," ("Second, I won't

steal another's.") implying "I won't steal another's thing".) Familiar with the common phrase " 一不做賊，二不偷人 ," the Chinse audience will be amused at the cleverness of the heroine and laugh at her witty twist of " 二不偷人 ", "Second, I won't steal a man (i.e., commit adultery) into " 二不偷人家的 " ("Second, I won't steal a man's (thing)). Therefore, it is obvious that the fun of this pun is primarily based on familiarity with the original phrase. So, if this pun is literally translated into English, it does not make sense to an English-speaking audience. Thus, a creative transposition may be an effective way to solve this problem. The equivalent of the whole phrasal context must be made up as an attempt to come close to the amusing effect created by the original pun. So, I may offer a tentative solution as follows:

> Woman: First, I don't steal things; Second, I won't steal a man, no, no, no, I won't steal a man's....
> Man: A man's what?
> Woman: A man's THING!!!

Conclusion

Although a completely exact translation is but a myth, especially in the case of puns, I believe that it is the translator's duty to struggle to approximate the stylistic features of the original as closely as possible. It is a real challenge, a special skill, for a translator to try to transfer faithfully the connotative meaning , or the "inner spirit" of a literary work to another language. And I think the fun of translating puns lies in this challenge. Any conscientious translator should deem it his duty to take up this challenge. And in translating puns especially for a play, I think that finding an equivalent in meaning and sound should be given first priority. If this method cannot be used, then creative transposition can be employed. The most important thing to bear in mind in translating a pun is that the fun and spirit of the pun should be preserved to the greatest possible degree. In this sense, much attention should be paid to the special sound effect of the sound and particular structure of the words. A pun should be translated as a pun. Therefore, care should be taken to avoid overinterpretation or overtranslation which can often kill the soul of the pun, leaving for the reader a dead play on words, a play which is no longer playful.

References

Chan, Mimi. "On Translating Chaucer into Chinese." *Renditions*, No. 8 (1977).

Hwang, Mei-shu 黃美序 . "Translating Puns for the Stage." *Renditions*, No. 14 (1980), pp. 73–78.

Jebb, R. C. "Antigone." In *The Complete Greek Drama*, edited by Whitney J. Oates and Eugene O'Neill. New York: Random House, 1938.

Liang, Shih-ch'iu 梁實秋 . 〈關於莎士比亞的翻譯〉 (On Translating Shakespeare), translated by Chau Sui-cheong and Derek Herforth. *Renditions*, No. 3 (1974), pp. 13–14.

Munro, Stanley R. "From Theory to Practice: The Translation of Chang Hen-shui's *Liang Shan-po and Chu Ying-tai*." *Tamkang Review*, Vol. 17, No. 1, p. 20.

Perng, Ching-hsi 彭鏡禧 . "Classical Chinese Drama in English: A Critique of Some Recent Translations." In *Bulletin of the College of Liberal Arts of National Taiwan University*, No. 31 (1982).

Yu, Kuang-chung 余光中 , tr. 《不可兒戲》 (*The Importance of Being Earnest*). Taipei: Great Earth Press 大地出版社 , 1983.

RETRANSLATION

Retranslation

S. P. E. Almberg
Department of Translation
The Chinese University of Hong Kong, Hong Kong

To retranslate is to translate again or to translate back, but retranslation can also imply indirect translation, meaning translating not directly from the original but via another translation in a third language, i.e. a language other than either the source or the target language. Hence the three categories under this entry, namely, back translation, indirect translation and new translation (or multiple translations).

Back Translation

Abbreviated as BTT, i.e. back translation test or back translation of text, this category usually denotes the technique for assessing the semantic range of the source-language text by translating a stretch of the target-language text back into the source language for purposes of comparison and correction. However, this is not suitable in the case of source language or target language lexical gaps, apart from which a translation not corresponding with the *source-language* text may also be justified if a wider context supports the non-corresponding version.

Back translation occurs also under peculiar circumstances as in the case of Lao She's 老舍 novel 《鼓書藝人》. The work was first written in the late forties during the author's stay in the U.S.A. An English version titled *The Drum Singers* and produced by Helena Kuo directly from Lao She's manuscript was published in New York in 1953. Unfortunately, the original manuscript was subsequently lost before it ever went to print. However, almost three decades later, and fourteen years after the author had passed away, 《鼓書藝人》 was "retrieved" and it emerged anew in the form of back translation from *The Drum Singers*. It was published by the People's Literature Press 人民文學出版社 in Beijing in 1980. This Chinese "rendition" was the work of Ma Xiaomi 馬小彌 , daughter of a very close friend of Lao She's, to whom the author had told many stories dedicated to her as a child. Casual readers might well take the novel in this edition for the original, for its cover as well as its title page gives nothing away about the tortuous existence through translation and retranslation or back translation.

In such a case as the above, when the "back-translated" text has more or less to pass for the original, any back translation text will only be secondary. For the primary question here is rather really how close such a version gets to the non-existent original and not merely to the "source language-target language" text. Granted that Ma Xiaomi translates competently from English into Chinese, granted that she had intimate first-hand knowledge of Lao She as a narrator and granted that she has also a sensitivity to his use of language, it still remains a question as to how capable and inspired a literary "impersonator" she is in order to produce a near facsimile of the true original by Lao She. This is indeed a matter of personality, for, by virtue of her task of trying to reproduce a lost work through retranslation, Ma has foregone the freedom of interpreting the source-language text (i.e. *The Drum Singers*) as she sees it for her audience in her own time. She would simply have to "forge" Lao She's with the help of Helena Kuo's version but without a blueprint.

Indirect Translation

This category of retranslation is not only prevalent and often indispensable, especially in older times, but also highly significant in the dissemination of human culture in general. An eminent example would be the Bible until recent days. In the case of *The Rubaiyat of Omar Khayyam*, the original, despite its well-known Persian origin, has been as good as obliterated by Edward Fitzgerald's famous rendition into English from the last century. In a sense, Fitzgerald's has become an original text. The bilingual edition of Huang Kesun's 黃克孫 Chinese rendition of the poem, for example, is one in Chinese and English, not Perso-Arabic. Translations of works from English into Chinese and vice versa are predominantly direct and understandably so nowadays, since English has become the *lingua franca* of the modern world, while Chinese has also become a less unusual foreign language in the West. However, thanks to indirect translations, texts of many other origins have become accessible to Chinese readers and added to the interflow of information exchange world-wide. At the beginning of this century, however, Japanese as a rule, and occasionally German, played a similar role to that of English and served as the "medium" for Chinese translators. Ibsen, for example, reached China this way.

With the study of foreign languages other than English, French and German becoming more and more common, indirect translations are giving way more and more to direct translations. Swedish translators, for example, with very few exceptions, translate directly from the originals including Chinese and even so-called minor languages. Similarly, Chinese translators since the fifties often translate, too, from the originals, though this is not necessarily any guarantee of quality. On the other hand, one Swedish version of Lu Xun's 魯迅〈吶喊〉 and 〈徬徨〉 rendered in the sixties turned out to be excellent, although the translator, R. Ekner, is not familiar with the Chinese language. His indirect translation is not only a scholarly piece of work involving research on the original as well as reference to and comparison of various translations in several European languages but also the product of a creative writer in his own right who has an affinity with the original.

Indirect translation may well deserve more credit than it has got. All controversies notwithstanding, the 《易經》 (or *I Ching*) is a classic case in point. Without indirect translation, this esoteric Chinese text perhaps would never have become part of the cultural consciousness in so many minds of the world.

New Translation (or Multiple Translations)

This, perhaps, is retranslation proper.

Most great classics of the world have been translated more than once. Despite the authorized version of the Bible which has dominated the English scene for over four centuries, new translations of the Book in present-day English have come into existence and become more and more in use. Even E. Fitzgerald's classic (which, to begin with, was by no means the first translation of the Persian poem) has also to give room to new English versions of the *Rubaiyat*. Hence the joint venture of P. Avery and

J. Heath-Stubbs now current side by side with its eminent predecessor. The Buddhist scriptures, too, have been rendered from the Sanskrit more than once into Chinese at various points of the history of Buddhism in China.

Works are retranslated for one or more reasons. Many a time, new translations are made on the rationale that the target language has changed so much since the previous translation that however good this had been, it sounds old-fashioned now. World classics translated into Chinese during the May Fourth period (let alone Lin Shu's 林紓 *wenyan* 文言 versions at the turn of the century) have undergone new translations during the fifties and again in the eighties, which, generally, turn out to be improvements on the unsophisticated though pioneer attempts of the twenties, not only because of the maturing process of *baihua* 白話 itself but also because of a better understanding of foreign cultures concerned. Sometimes, a new translation is called for simply because the existing one is not good enough. There are also new translations that come into being inadvertently in the sense that the new translators are not aware of the older or even contemporary versions. Sometimes, too, new translations are made for the sake of specific audiences. W. J. F. Jenner's and A. C. Yu's versions of the *Xiyouji* 《西遊記》, for instance, show that while the former is mainly eager to keep the flow and get a lively narrative across to a lay audience, the latter is basically concerned with getting things correct with detailed footnotes for fellow-academic readers. But above all, new translations are made on the ground that times have changed and even the original works evoke new interpretations, making it not only justified but actually necessary to have new translations.

Lu Xun, for one, was a staunch advocate of retranslations. In his essay 〈非有復譯不可〉 ("It Is Imperative to Have Multiple Translations"), from 1935, he argues strongly in favour of retranslating important literary works, going so far as to maintain that two or more contemporary translators can knowingly choose to start translating the same work at the same time and that a translator, in order to achieve "perfection", can simply improve upon previously published translations by others instead of doing the work altogether anew. Thus, according to Lu Xun, a work can deserve as many as "seven or eight" translations or retranslations.

Mao Dun 茅盾 was a contemporaneous defender of the same. His critique 〈《簡愛》的兩個譯本 — 對於翻譯方法的研究〉 refutes arguments against retranslations as being "wasteful" and points out that not only have both Chinese versions of *Jane Eyre* turned out to be good works but they also provide materials for us to study and compare different methods of translation.

Today, Lu Xun as well as Mao Dun could have spared himself his battle, for any diehard insisting on one single authoritative translation of any work must have become a rare if not impossible animal by now. Modern literary theories emphasizing the dynamic nature of a text indirectly support the call for retranslations. Mary Snell-Hornby (1988) draws on this and writes, "... the text cannot be considered as static specimen of language ... but essentially as the verbalized expression of an author's intention as understood by the translator as reader, who then recreates this whole for another readership in another culture. The dynamic process explains why new translations of literary works are constantly in demand, and why the perfect translation does not exist."

Also clearly in support of multiple translations, Rainer Schulte put forth the analogy of the performance of a musical piece. Pointing to the changing psychological and semantic presences of language, she says rather specifically, "In general, translations have to be redone in intervals of thirty years." My reference above to the work done since the May Fourth seems ready evidence to bear out this opinion.

Like the works of William Shakespeare in English, much of classical poetry is the source text of retranslations, which reflect not only the particular need and tone of different periods but also the personal style and voice of individual translators. We can easily pick up some five or six English renditions of Li Bai's 〈中山問答〉, for example; and diverse as they are, these provide interesting material, poetic as well as pedagogic, for our understanding and appreciation of this short but pregnant and resounding piece by a great poet-recluse. And, in some way, apart from the Chinese original, these renditions together form also an epitome of the changes in the practice of poetic translation during this past century or so.

References

Birch, Cyril, ed. *An Anthology of Chinese Literature*. Harmondsworth: Penguin, 1967.

Fitzgerald, Edward. *Rubaiyat of Omar Khayyam and Other Writing*. London and Glasgow: Collins, 1953.

Giles, Herbert A. *Gems of Chinese Literature — Verse*, 1922 ed. Taipei: Literature House Ltd, 1964.

Lao She 老舍 . 《鼓書藝人》 *(The Drum Singers)*. Beijing: People's Literature
    Press 人民文學出版社 , 1980.
Lau Shaw. *The Drum Singers*. London: Victor Gollancz Ltd, 1953.
Li Pai. *200 Selected Poems*. Hong Kong: Joint Publishing Co, 1980.

Rhetoric

Yu Lisan
Department of Foreign Languages
Shantou University, Shantou, China

A good use of rhetorical devices is of great importance in doing translation. A figure of speech used in the original makes the language vivid, figurative, and impressive. Sometimes it will make the language sonorous and symmetric so as to show the inner link of the context. Figures of speech can make a piece of writing more forceful, more appealing, or more fascinating. Sometimes they produce association of ideas, provide food for thought, and go deeper in expounding the significance of an event or portraying a character. Therefore, to make a faithful translation, not only true to the original ideas, but also true to the original style, a translator has to convey the original rhetorical devices correctly in the version.

Almost every English rhetorical device finds its Chinese counterpart and vice versa. They are similar to each other in pattern and in rhetorical effects. Only alliteration and assonance do not have any equivalent in modern Chinese, though the former is somewhat similar in pattern to Chinese 雙聲 and the latter to Chinese 疊韻 . In modern Chinese, neither of them is any longer regarded as a rhetorical device. They are a mere play of words.

Since most English rhetorical devices have their Chinese counterparts, it is self-evident that the best translation is a literal one, making the original and the version alike in appearance and in spirit as well. But very often this cannot be realized. To avoid obscurity or misrepresentation, sometimes a translator cannot copy the original rhetorical device, but will have to use a nonequivalent one in the version, or use a different comparison. And, sometimes, it is advisable to use plain language adding a modifier or extending the meaning of the original word.

Literal Translation

In many cases an English figurative expression can be literally translated into an idiomatic Chinese one, similar to the original not only in words and sentence pattern but also in meaning and rhetorical effect. Even if the idea or comparison is new to Chinese people, a literal translation may also be good, so long as it is understandable and readable. The same is true with Chinese-English translation. Sometimes, a good literal translation can become an idiom, though borrowed from another language. For example, the Chinese 武裝到牙齒 is borrowed from English synecdoche "be armed to the teeth", while the English metonymy "save face" is borrowed from Chinese 保全面子 .

There are abundant instances of good literal translations:

Simile	明喻
as quick as lightning	疾如閃電
Metaphor	借喻
crocodile tears	鱷魚的眼淚
Metonymy	借代
The pen is mightier than the sword.	筆杆子比刀劍更有力。
Antonomasia	借代
This is another Munich.	這是又一次慕尼黑事件。
Personification	擬人
Nature has been niggardly with him.	大自然對他很吝嗇。
(Jack London)	
Apostrophe	呼告
O Captain! My Captain!	啊，船長！我的船長！
Our fearful trip is done.	我們的可怕航程已經結束。
(Walt Whitman)	
Irony	反語
We are marching backwards to the	我們正在大踏步退回十六世紀
glorious age of the sixteenth century.	那光輝年代。
(John Scopes)	

Hyperbole
    I was scared to death.

誇張
    嚇死我了。

Litotes
    He didn't try in vain.

含蓄渲染
    他的實驗沒有白幹。

Euphemism
    And, it being low water,
    he went out with the tide.
    (Dickens)

避諱
    正是退潮的時候，他跟潮水一
    道去了。

Innuendo
    After three days in Japan, the spinal
    column becomes extraordinarily
    flexible.
    (Jacques Danvoir)

婉轉
    在日本待上三天以後，脊樑骨
    就會變得特別柔軟。

Contrast
    The fellow was subtle besides being
    naive.
    (J. Galsworthy)

對照
    那傢伙既狡滑又幼稚。

Oxymoron
    She spoke with her disagreeably
    pleasant laugh.

反映
    她講話帶著討厭的媚笑。

Transferred epithet
    I enjoy the cool support of the water.
    (V. Sackville-West)

移就
    我喜歡池水的涼爽漂浮。

Allusion
    I have nourished a viper in my bosom.
    (W. M. Thackeray)

暗引
    我是在胸口養了一條毒蛇。

Paradox
    I am so serious is why I can joke.
    (Ernest Hemingway)

雋語
    正因爲我很認眞才開玩笑。

Repetition
    Oh, the dreary, dreary moorland!
    Oh, the barren, barren shore!
    (Tennyson)

反覆
    啊，淒涼的，淒涼的荒野！
    啊，荒蕪的，荒蕪的海岸！

Catchword repetition
    The smile extended into a laugh,
    the laugh into a roar, and the roar
    became general.
    (Dickens)

聯珠
    微笑逐漸變成大笑，大笑變
    成狂笑，狂笑勾起一陣哄堂
    大笑。

Chiasmus
> Let us never negotiate out of fear,
> but let us never fear to negotiate.
> (John F. Kennedy)

回文
> 讓我們永遠不要去進行談判是
> 出於害怕，但也讓我們永遠不
> 要害怕去進行談判。

Parallelism
> The seed ye sow, another reaps;
> The wealth ye find, another keeps;
> The robe ye weave, another wears;
> The arms ye forge, another bears.
> (P. B. Shelley)

排比
> 你們播下的種子別人收；
> 你們找到的財富別人留；
> 你們織造的錦袍別人穿；
> 你們鑄造的武器別人握在手。

Antithesis
> I deserve neither such praise nor
> such censure.
> (J. Austen)

反對
> 這樣的誇獎我擔當不起，這樣
> 的責備我也擔待不起。

Rhetorical question
> What will not necessity do?
> (W. M. Thackeray)

設問
> 只要是必需的，有甚麼事幹不
> 出來呢？

Represented speech
> "Also you need a haircut."
> "I have my hair cut as it needs it."
> Robert Jordan said. He would be
> damned if he would have his head
> shaved like Golz.
> (Ernest Hemingway)

描述性引語
> "你還需要理髮。"
> "需要理髮的時候我就理。"
> 羅伯特喬丹答道。如果要他也
> 剃成戈爾茲那樣的光頭那才見
> 了鬼了呢。

Climax
> Some books are to be tasted,
> others to be swallowed, and some
> few to be chewed and digested.
> (Francis Bacon)

層遞
> 有些書應當淺嘗輒止，有些應
> 當囫圇吞棗，而有些應當細嚼
> 慢咽。

Aposiopesis
> I agree with you, only ...

跳脫
> 我同意你的意見，不過……

Onomatopoeia
> The ticking of the clock was the
> only sound that greeted him.
> (Thomas Hardy)

擬聲
> 迎接他的只有滴答響的鐘聲。

Change of Image

The fact that most English rhetorical devices have their Chinese equivalents does not necessarily lead to the conclusion that literal translation is valid everywhere. Very often a translator will have to change the image in a figure of speech. This is because an image in a figure of speech may conjure up different associations among English speaking people and Chinese people. For example: Chinese people can never understand how a person could be "as happy as a cow" or "as stupid as a goose". In their mind's eye, happiness should be symbolized as a lark, while stupidity only suggests comparison with a pig. Similarly, when Chinese people describe someone 像老黃牛一樣幹活 (to work like an old ox), English speaking people would not be impressed with his hard-working spirit. On the contrary, they might think that the person in question was lacking in efficiency. In their eyes, the symbol of hard-working spirit is a horse.

Further examples:

English Similes	*Suggested Chinese Translation*
as drunk as a lord	爛醉如泥 (as drunk as mud)
as timid as a rabbit	膽小如鼠 (as timid as a mouse)
like a duck to water	如魚得水 (like fish to water)
like a hen on a hot griddle	像熱鍋上的螞蟻 (like ants on a hot griddle)
like a drowned rat	像落湯雞 (like a hen in hot water)
industrious as an ant	像蜜蜂一樣勤勞 (industrious as a bee)
dumb as an oyster	守口如瓶 (tight-mouthed as bottle)
thirsty as a camel	像一條渴龍 (thirsty as a dragon)
tall as a Maypole/beanpole	像電線杆一樣高 (tall as a telegraph pole)

The list can be even longer.

We can not only find many such examples of similes as listed above, but also cite numerous similar examples with metaphors.

> The night has a thousand eyes,
>   And the day but one;
> Yet the light of the bright world dies
>   With the dying sun. (F. W. Bourdillon)

In the poem the eye is used metaphorically as the image of stars and the sun, but Chinese people can never imagine an eye symbolizing the sun, while they, perhaps, will accommodate such imagery for stars. It is, therefore, advisable to change the image into a lamp when we translate the poem into Chinese.

When a Chinese says someone is 害群之馬, the 隱喻 should not be translated literally into "an evil horse of the herd". The equivalent English idiom is "black sheep". If a Chinese dissuades you from 對牛彈琴, the phrase should be translated into "casting pearls before swine", not "playing the lute to a cow". There can also be a long list of such examples.

Change of the Figure and the Principle of Compensation

To be faithful to the original sometimes a translator has to convert a figure of speech into a different one in the version. For example, "a heart as hard as flint" is an English simile, but one cannot translate it into an equivalent Chinese 明喻 "心如鐵石", for the former means unfeeling and pitiless while the latter means firm and persistent. To convey the original meaning, one has to use Chinese 隱喻 "鐵石心腸", which corresponds to an English metaphor in pattern.

"He made the money fly" is an English metaphor. If we translate it literally, the Chinese reader will be confused. A handy Chinese idiom 他揮金如土 is an exact translation, though equivalent to an English simile in pattern.

In Lu Xun's 魯迅 epigram,

橫眉冷對千夫指
俯首甘為孺子牛

孺子牛 is Chinese 借喻, which corresponds to an English metaphor, but it is appropriately translated into a simile as follows,

Fierce-browed, determined, I defy
A thousand pointing fingers,
Head-bowed, I serve these children
Like an obedient ox.

The change of the figure occurs especially when a translator comes across such rhetorical devices as syllepsis, zeugma and alliteration. Because the range of collocation often differs between English words and their Chinese equivalents, an English polysemous word can never find any

Chinese word that coincides with it in its multivalence, and the two languages differ phonetically. To be content with another Chinese figure, when it is impossible to put an English figure into its Chinese equivalent, is to follow the principle of compensation. The purpose of doing so is to preserve some rhetorical effect — to give tone or atmosphere to discourse, to provide vivid examples, to stimulate thought by startling the reader or listener, to give life to inanimate objects, to amuse, or to ornament.

A handy substitute for such untranslatable figures is a Chinese syntactical device — a 對偶 or a 排比 . For example, syllepsis occurs twice in "Its crockery and atmosphere were thick; its soup and napery thin." (O. Henry) It is advisable to translate the sentence into Chinese 對偶 instead of 異敘 : " 它的碗盞呆笨而氣氛呆板；它的湯味淡薄而餐巾單薄 ."

While zeugma is used in "She was dressed in a maid's cap, a pinafore, and a bright smile", the sentence can be translated into Chinese 排比 instead of 黏連 : " 她戴女僕帽，繫白圍腰，容光煥發，面帶微笑 ."

The case is especially true with alliteration which has no Chinese equivalent. "It was a splendid population — for all the slow, sleepy, sluggish-brained sloths stay at home" (Mark Twain) can be easily translated into Chinese 排比 as follows: " 這是一批卓越能幹的人民， — 因爲所有那些行動遲緩、瞌睡稀稀、呆如樹懶的人都留在家鄉了 ."

Similarly, sometimes an English translator may find it difficult to put Chinese 異敘 or 黏連 into their English equivalents, but easy to put them into alliteration or parallelism or something else. For instance, in 如今人情薄了，這……酒都是薄的 (Wu Jingzi 吳敬梓), the first 薄 means indifferent, the second 薄 weak. Since it is impossible to use one English word to convey both, and form a syllepsis matching this Chinese 異敘 , well, we can translate it alliteratively, "Now men are interrelated indifferently; the wine is incapable of intoxicating anyone." Here the principle of compensation is also brought into play, and the rhetorical effect of the original maintained to some extent.

The Avoidance of Excessive National Traits and the Use of Plain Language

A good translation should be in the idiom of the language that is used, but that does not mean that a translator should try to adopt another national character. Excessive national traits will only make the version clumsy.

Consider for a moment the case of a Chinese reader reading Conan

Doyle. If when Sherlock Holmes says, "He is the Napoleon of crime", the antonomasia were translated into "他是罪犯中的楚霸王," the reader would feel the story neither fish, flesh nor fowl.

When an Englishman says, "I will send for a priest to exorcise the evil spirit", it is no good to translate the sentence into "我要請張天師收妖."

Similarly, when a Chinese says, "這裡簡直是世外桃源," it is unadvisable to translate the Chinese 暗引 or 典故 (allusion) into "The place is simply an Eden." Neither is it good to translate "他是我們村裡的諸葛亮" into "He is the Solomon in our village."

Not only is it incongruous to have something characteristic of Britain in a Chinese story and vice versa, there often exist slight differences in meaning between an English allusion or antonomasia and the similar Chinese expression. "A Trojan horse" is similar in meaning to "鑽進肚皮裡的孫悟空," but the former can be either commendatory or derogatory, while the latter is only commendatory. "A Solomon" means the person is gifted with wisdom and discretion, while a 諸葛亮 means a man of wisdom and tactics.

The way to translate an antonomasia, metonymy or allusion, therefore, is either literal translation (transliteration), if it is well-known to Chinese people, or expressions of plain Chinese. For example, in the sentence "It was then that he became the ranch's old man of the sea," (O. Henry) the allusion "old man of the sea" is unfamiliar to Chinese people. We can neither translate it literally into "海上老人," nor explanatorily into "像長期騎在水手辛巴德背上的海上老人那樣成了牧場上的累贅," for the former is ambiguous and the latter clumsy and ambiguous as well. The best way to translate the sentence is perhaps to put it into plain Chinese: "從那時起他就成了牧場上的累贅."

Similarly, it is advisable to translate the previous Chinese sentence "這裡簡直是世外桃源" into plain English: "The place is simply a haven of peace" instead of "an Eden" or "the land of Peach Blossoms away from the turmoil of the world".

The use of plain language often occurs in translating an English pun or a Chinese 雙關. In these cases a note is necessary. The point is to make a careful choice between the two meanings and put the proper one in the text and another in the note. It is, of course, preferable to choose the one in which the humour or main idea lies (usually the figurative one, not the literal one), as long as it reads smoothly. For example:

Joe was painting in the class of the great Magister — you know his
fame. His fees are high; his lessons are light — his highlights have
brought him renown. (O. Henry)

喬在偉大的麥基斯特那裡學畫 —— 他的聲望你是知道的，他收費高昂，
課程輕鬆 —— 他的高昂輕鬆給他帶來了名望。
注：末句語義雙關，原文 "highlights" 一義高昂輕鬆，另一義爲圖畫
光線明亮處。

Here the figurative new compound "highlights" is chosen to go in the
translated text, while its literal meaning is put in the note, because the new
compound is where humour lies.

The same rule also works in Chinese-English translation. For example:

〈石灰〉   于謙
千錘萬擊出深山，
烈火焚燒若等閒；
粉骨碎身全不怕，
要留青白在人間！

Limestone Song   Yu Qian
It was digging
    chiseling
            cutting

That led me into the world.
What can heating
        burning
                boiling
Do to hurt me, now?
Reduce me to dust, to powder,
I'm not afraid
So long as I remain stainless, and pure.

Note: In the last line, 青白 is a pun, literally meaning "clear white", and
figuratively "stainless and pure".

Again, we find the figurative meaning is chosen to go in the text, while its
literal meaning is put in the note, for it is the figurative meaning that the
author uses to convey his lofty ideals.

Sometimes a different choice is made for coherent writing:

She's too low for a high praise, too brown for a fair praise and too little for a great praise. (William Shakespeare)

她太矮，經不起高度的讚揚；皮膚太黝黑，經不起說她白皙的讚揚；個子太瘦小，經不起大的讚揚。
注：原文語義雙關，"low"一義"矮"，另一義爲"地位低下"；"fair"一義"白皙"，另一義爲"公正"。

Evidently, "low position" and "justice" are what the author means, but they are put in the note instead of in the text. The reason is that the sentence as a whole seems to be commenting on a girl's appearance. The choice is made for coherent writing.

The use of plain language (sometimes with a note) also often occurs in translating a figure of speech like parody, syllepsis, zeugma and so on. As space is limited, it is impossible to cover everything.

Here some rules of translating figures of speech have been discussed, but just like all linguistic rules, there are exceptions to any translation rule, for there is an immense variety of language texture. The task of a translator is to try to be as faithful to the original as possible. If the version is faithful to the original in words, in form, in style and in spirit as well, so much the better. When it is impossible to achieve this, the first choice is, preferably, to be faithful to the original in spirit.

For example, a literal translation would be insipid with the very popular song "Do-Re-Mi". We might as well change the words and their literal meaning so as to maintain its stylistic effect, for many of the original words are homophonous puns and are used only for amusing, not to convey any idea. The following is one of many alternatives:

Do-Re-Mi
Doe ... a deer, a female deer. Ray ... a drop of golden sun. Me ... a name I call myself. Far ... a long long way to run. Sew ... a needle pulling thread. La ... a note to follow sew. Tea ... a drink with jam and bread. That will bring us back to doe.

〈朵 - 來 - 密〉
朵，美麗的祖國花朵。來呀，大家都快來！密，你們來猜秘密。發，猜中我把獎發。索，大家用心思索。拉，快點猜莫拖拉。體，怎樣練好身體，做茁壯成長的花朵。

(Flowers, you beautiful flowers of the country. Come! Be quick, every-one of you! Here is something secret, please make a guess at it. Carry off a prize, if you guess it. Think, just think it through. Don't delay. Please guess it in good time. Health — how to build up your health, and become sturdy flowers.)

Reference

Chen, Wangdao 陳望道. 《修辭學發凡》 (*Introduction to Chinese Rhetoric*). Shanghai: Shanghai Literary Press 上海文藝出版社, 1962.

Feng, Cuihua. *Figures of Speech*. The Commercial Press, 1983.

Holman, C. Hugh. "Figures of Speech." *Encyclopedia Americana*, Vol. II. New York: Grolier Incorporated, 1983.

Yu, Lisan 余立三. 《英漢修辭比較與翻譯》 (*A Comparison of English and Chinese Rhetoric and Translation*). Beijing: The Commercial Press 商務印書館, 1985.

Scientific Translation

Yan Qingjia
*The Institute of Scientific and Technical Information of China,
Chongqing Branch, China*

English is one of the most widely used languages in the world. A special kind of English, the English for Science and Technology (EST), came out in the 1950s due to the rapid development of science and technology. The vocabulary, grammatical construction and ways of expression of EST are different from those of everyday English. Since about two thirds of scientific literature of the whole world (including journal papers, conference proceedings, scientific reports, government publications, dissertations, patents, industry standards and scientific books) is published in English and amounted to more than 1,500,000 pieces a year by the 1990s, great importance is attached to EST by scientists and engineers all over the world. In the developing countries, such as China, scientific literature of English is often translated selectively and utilized widely in scientific research and technological innovation in order to advance the improvement of national economies. Thus, the translation of English scientific texts into Chinese is indispensable.

Translation involves two languages — here English and Chinese — each with its special features. Apart from having a good command of these languages, a translator needs to master the relevant subject or specialization, grasp its specialized vocabulary, and moreover, understand translating techniques and methods in order to make good translations of writing in EST.

The Standards of Scientific Translation

Good translation means that the translated text precisely and perfectly reproduces the meaning and linguistic form of the original text, in so far as the latter is consistent with the norms of the target language. In respect of translating EST texts into Chinese, the standards are preciseness, smoothness and conciseness.

Preciseness

The purpose of scientific translation is to introduce from abroad the advanced science and technology, in which the requirement of accuracy is very strict. Hence the first and the most important standard of scientific translation is preciseness. Preciseness comprises two meanings: accuracy and clearness. The former means that the translated text should exactly report the scientific content of the original text. The latter means that the translation should clearly express the real meaning of the original, i.e. it must not be ambiguous. For example:

> There are cross transverse steady and longitudinal alternating fields.

This sentence shows that there are two magnetic fields, hence its Chinese translation should be 存在著交叉的橫向穩定磁場和縱向交變磁場 . If it is translated as 有交叉橫向穩定和縱向交變磁場 , the translation is not precise, because Chinese readers might understand that there is only one field. As there is no plural form in Chinese, the word for "field" 磁場 has to be repeated.

Smoothness

The translated text should conform with Chinese grammar, be easy to understand, and read fluently. To attain this goal, the translator must be careful in selecting words, making sentences and expressing mood. For example:

> Commercial magnesium ingots were used as received except for acid pickling to remove surface oxide.

This sentence should be translated as 工業鎂錠係在購進狀態下使用，祗是要經過酸洗，以去除表面氧化物 . If its translation is 工業鎂錠祗有在酸洗去除表面氧化物之後才能在購進狀態下加以使用 , it is not smooth. And moreover the focal point emphasized in the original is wrongly expressed. The preparation of the ingots before use is secondary in the original, but becomes in this translation the primary concern.

Conciseness

This means that the Chinese translation should be brief and succinct, without superfluous words. For example:

> Each product must be produced to rigid quality standards.

The translation may be 每件產品均須達到嚴格的質量標準. If it is translated as 每件產品都必須生產得符合嚴格的質量標準, it becomes unnecessarily lengthy and jumbled.

The Regularities of Scientific Translation

Because translation is to translate one language into the other, translation work comprises the two processes of comprehending the original text and composing the translated text. Thus, "to comprehend the original text thoroughly" and "to compose the translated text precisely" may be considered as general rules of translation, which apply not only to the translation of everyday or literary English but also to the translation of EST.

To Comprehend the Original Text Thoroughly

In order to attain this goal, the translator should first clearly understand the grammatical relations of the elements of each sentence through meticulous analysis of the sentence structure, and especially distinguish the parallel relation of two and more modificators (attributes or adverbial modifiers) from the subordinate relation of the modified and the modifying elements. Secondly, the translator must conscientiously elicit the real meaning of every notional word in the sentence, particularly the implication of scientific terms. Thirdly, he ought to comprehend the technical content of the whole sentence from the context. For example:

> Angina pectoris means pain in the chest, a symptom which accompanies any interference with blood supply or oxygenation of the heart muscles.
>
> 心絞痛即胸部疼痛，心肌供血或供氧受到干擾即會引起此症。

In this sentence, *symptom* is the appositive of *pain*, and *oxygenation* is parallel with *blood supply*. Grammatically, however, the sentence could be construed as stating that "interference with blood supply" and "oxygenation of the heart muscles" can give rise to the symptom of pain in the chest; only knowledge of physiology will determine that "oxygenation of the heart muscles" is also governed by "interference with".

To Compose the Translated Text Precisely

After comprehending thoroughly the technical content of a sentence, the translator must express it in Chinese precisely and definitely, perfectly and appropriately, smoothly and concisely. Thus, the translator should compose the translated text meticulously according to Chinese grammar, so that the translation can conform with the three standards mentioned above. In this respect, the translator should pay attention to the selection of exact words, the proper organization of sentences and the elimination of ambiguity, and do his best to make the text brief and concise. However, over-conciseness can create ambiguity. For example:

> The most effective method of removing this acid contaminant is to cool and then neutralize the exhaust gases.
>
> 去除這種酸性污染物的最有效方法，是對廢氣進行冷卻，然後加以中和。
>
> If the translation is 去除這種酸性污染物的最有效方法是冷卻後中和廢氣, although it seems rather concise, it may cause confusion, because the reader might misunderstand the *method* to be *to cool first the contaminant and then to neutralize the gases*.

Methods of Translation

There are four and only four kinds of translating methods, i.e., direct translation, conversion, omission, and supplementation, which apply to the translation of various classes of writings in all languages.

Direct Translation Method

So-called direct translation corresponds to literal translation as generally understood, but it is not simple word-for-word translation, although it is ordinal translation. This method has two characteristics. First, the grammatical structural forms are preserved in the translation, i.e. the order of sentence elements and of clauses undergoes no substantial alteration. Secondly, the apparent meanings of words are directly translated, without conversion or extension. For example:

In chemistry we use formulae to represent compounds.

在化學中我們用分子式表示化合物。

Computers are of great help to our work.

計算機大大有助於我們的工作。

Conversion Method

Conversion method belongs to, but is not the only form of free translation, because the omission and supplementation methods to be described below are also free translation. This method includes the conversion of (1) word meaning, (2) parts of speech, (3) sentence elements, (4) sentence structure, (5) voice, (6) clause order, etc., examples of which are as follows:

1. The *shortest distance* between raw material and a finished part is precision casting.
   把原料加工爲成品的最簡便方法是精密鑄造。
2. Also *present* in solids are numbers of free electrons.
   固體中也存在著大量自由電子。
3. *Gold* has an *advantage* in that it cannot react with oxygen.
   金子的優點是不同氧發生反應。
4. Energy is that which may be converted into work.
   能可以轉化爲功。
5. Sand may be carried many miles away by the wind.
   風可以把砂土帶到許多英里以外的地方。
6. The solenoid can attract scraps of iron, when it is connected to a battery.
   在螺線管接上電池以後，它就能吸持鐵屑。

Omission Method

Omission here means that some word (such as an article, pronoun, conjunction, verb, etc.) in the original is sometimes left out in the translation according to the usual practice of Chinese in order to make the text concise. For example:

The atom is the smallest particle of an element.
原子是元素的最小的粒子。
(All three articles all are omitted.)

If you know the frequency, you can find the wave length.
如果知道頻率，就能求出波長。
(Both pronouns are omitted.)

When the pressure gets low, the boiling point becomes low.
氣壓低，沸點就低。
(The conjunction and link verbs are omitted.)

Supplementation Method

A word which is not present in the original is often added to the translated text with the purpose of clarifying some English word meaning, or rounding off sentence structures to conform with normal Chinese practice. For example:

Resonance is often observed in nature.
在自然界中常常觀察到共振現象。

The first electronic computers went into operation in 1946.
第一批電子計算機於 1946 年開始使用。

This is what we must resolve first.
這就是我們必須首先解決的問題。

Literal Translation and Free Translation; Ordinal Translation and Inverse Translation

With respect to the translation of EST, the best literal translation is free translation, and the best free translation is literal translation. Hence there is no need to argue over which of them is better. Of course, both literal and free translation should be faithful to the original and in accord with Chinese grammar. As for ordinal and inverse translation, owing to the special features of scientific literature, ordinal translation should be preferred in the translation of EST writings into Chinese so long as such translation does not violate the usual practice of Chinese grammar and discourse. Only if ordinal translation cannot produce a sentence up to the standards of Chinese grammar may inverse translation be adopted. Why should ordinal translation be preferred? There are three reasons: (1) Ordinal translation can exactly express the line of thought of the original. (2) Ordinal translation can contribute to correlating the context. (3) Ordinal translation can avoid the mistakes often generated by inverse translation. For example:

There is cupric oxide only in the surface of the boration layer.

This sentence should be sequentially translated as 氧化正銅僅祇存在於滲硼層面中 , and never inversely translated as 在滲硼層表面中祇有氧化正銅 . The latter translation is completely wrong, because the fact is that there is a lot of cuprous oxide in the surface layer besides the small amount of cupric oxide.

To sum up, the translator must appropriately resolve the contradictions between literal translation and free translation, between ordinal translation and inverse translation, and between preciseness (which requires supplementation) and conciseness (which requires omission) as each situation demands.

Reference

Yan, Qingjia 閆慶甲 . 《科技英語翻譯方法》（修訂版）(*Methods to Translate Scientific English* (rev. ed.)). Beijing: The Metallurgical Industry Publishing House 冶金工業出版社 , 1991.

SELF-TRANSLATION

Author as Translator

Joseph S. M. Lau
Department of East Asian Languages and Literature
University of Wisconsin-Madison, Wisconsin, U.S.A.

The process of translating one's own works into a target language can be very educational, as we shall see below. For a gifted polyglot such as George Steiner, the difference between source and target languages is not so acute. As he puts it,

> I have no recollection whatever of a first language. So far as I am aware, I possess equal currency in English, French, and German. What I can speak, write, or read of other languages has come later and retains a "feel" of conscious acquisition. But I experience my first three tongues as perfectly equivalent centres of myself. Tests made of my ability to perform rapid routine calculations in them have shown no significant variations of speed or accuracy. I dream with equal verbal density and linguistic-symbolic provocation in all three.... Attempts to locate a "first language" under hypnosis have failed. The banal outcome was that I responded in the language of the hypnotist.

Philip E. Lewis, who "translated" his own French essay into English, outlines an author-translator's prerogative as follows:

> Thanks to the opportunity to translate freely and expansively, a translator who is also the author of the original can undertake to do precisely what is not possible for the translator who works on the text of another author: in the present case, the author-translator can both interpret according to English and according to French, can shift at will between conventional translation that

has to violate the original and commentary that attempts to compensate for the inadequacy of the translation.

We cannot quarrel with Lewis. Since he is the creator of both the source and the translation, we have no grounds for challenging his *modus operandi*.

When this author-translator issue is seen in the history of Chinese literature, there are quite a few poets whose backgrounds suggest that they may have been bilingual, though we have no evidence that they wrote in any language other than Chinese. The first name that comes to mind is Li Bai 李白 (Li Po, 701–762). "Li Po's birthplace is uncertain," wrote Stephen Owen in a biobibliographical entry for *The Indiana Companion to Traditional Chinese Literature*, "perhaps in Central Asia, and a minor branch of Li Po studies centres on the irresolvable question of whether Li was of Turkic origin." But whatever his origin, the fact remains that, in the popular imagination at least, he is remembered as the Banished Celestial who refused to draft a communiqué in an unspecified "barbarian" language for Emperor Xuanzong 玄宗 unless he was first catered to by Gao Lishi 高力士 and Yang Guifei 楊貴妃 . So at the behest of the emperor, as most of the anecdotes go, the powerful eunuch removed his boots for him, and the beautiful Consort Yang wetted his inkstone and ground ink for his brush.

One could also think of Sa Dula 薩都剌 (?–1355), the famed Yuan *ci* 詞 poet reputedly of Mongol extraction. And as far as bilingualism is concerned, Nalan Xingde 納蘭性德 (1655–1685) was as Manchu as his name. However, "Where one might have expected this poet of alien ancestry to have sounded a different note, that is not the case, for even his *pien-sai* ("border") verse assumes a conventional Chinese view of the northern desert regions as an unfriendly, inhospitable land." Did he try his hand at "translating" his Chinese verses into Manchu? We simply don't know.

A meaningful discussion of the work of the author-translator should focus on the modern period. If we limit our discussion to Chinese-English bilingualism, such poets as Xu Zhimo 徐志摩 , Wen Yiduo 聞一多 , and Zhu Xiang 朱湘 , who had studied in Britain and the United States, would be legitimate objects for investigation, had they attempted to translate their works and if we had access to them. But a bilingual person would not necessarily want to be a bilingual writer.

Before citing specific examples, we must ask ourselves: Is 白話 poetry as impossible to translate as its classical counterpart? It all depends. If we are talking about a text as transparent as Ai Qing's 艾青〈紐約〉"New York" (1980), one would say no. The first two stanzas from the original with a translation by Eugene Eoyang can be quoted as an example:

矗立在哈得遜河口
整個大都市
是巨大無比的鋼架
人生活在鋼的大風浪中

Standing at the mouth of the Hudson River
An entire metropolis
A huge, incomparable framework
Human lives in a maelstrom of steel

鋼在震動
鋼在磨擦
鋼在跳躍
鋼在飛跑

Steel vibrating
Steel rubbing together
Steel vaulting up
Steel flying through

If traditional Chinese poetry "demands from its readers an attention to the details of a poem and an ability to extrapolate certain information from those details", there seems to be no need for such an exercise in the present case. What you see is what you get. Unlike the word 草 discussed in Owen's article, 鋼 is not a "field" word subject to "a set of discriminations". From whatever angle you choose to look at it, it is still "steel" in English.

The verb-phrases in the second stanza offer a range of possibilities for the translator. Along with "vibrating" for 震動, one could come up with other equivalents no less dynamic, such as "shaking", "quivering", "quaking" or "trembling". But in view of the fact that Ai Qing sees New York as a metropolis of acquisitive passion and insatiable greed, Eoyang's choice is a judicious one.

However, any reader who has sampled Kai-yu Hsu's 許芥昱 *Twentieth-Century Chinese Poetry: An Anthology* (1963) is well aware that not all 白話 poetry is written in language as "plain" as the above quoted example. Long before the term 朦朧 was introduced to designate the poetry of young

writers such as Gu Cheng 顧城 and Bei Dao 北島 , modern Chinese poetry
had been notoriously obscure, as in the following lines from Li Jinfa's
李金髮 "Woman Abandoned" 〈棄婦〉:

靠一根草兒與上帝之靈往返在空谷裏
我的哀戚惟遊蜂之腦能深印著

As translated by Kai-yu Hsu, the English version reads:

By way of a blade of grass I communicate with God in the desert vale.
Only the memory of the roaming bees has recorded my sorrow.

This is an impressionist poem charged with striking conceits. By reading 遊蜂之腦 as "memory of the roaming bees" and 能深印著 as "has
recorded", Hsu has taken an approach akin to what Peter Newmark calls
"communicative translation", which "attempts to produce on its readers an
effect as close as possible to that obtained on the readers of the original". On
the other hand, if Hsu had written something like "my sorrow can only be
deeply imprinted in the brains of the roaming bees," the translation could be
labelled semantic, an approach which attempts to "render as closely as the
semantic and syntactic structure of the second language allows, the exact
contextual meaning of the original".

Hence it can be seen that the degree of difficulty facing a translator of
Chinese poetry is not determined by the language the poet employs, i.e.,
whether it is written in 文言 or 白話 . Rather, the idiosyncrasies of the
individual poets make the difference.

Since poets such as Xu Zhimo and Wen Yiduo, though bilingual, did
not translate their own works into English, we would have to turn our
attention to those who publish in Taiwan. Does Taiwan poetry better lend
itself to English translation? Again, it all depends. Since Ji Xian 紀絃 has
been hailed as the "High Priest of modern Chinese poetry" and has exerted
a tremendous influence on Taiwan poets during the 1950s, his poem "The
Star-plucking Youth" 〈摘星的少年〉 is quoted here as the first example:

摘星的少年，
跌下來。
青空嘲笑它。
大地嘲笑它。
新聞記者
拿最難堪的形容詞

冠在他的名字上，
嘲笑他。

Simple enough — if no translation is required. But let's look at how Yu Kwang-chung 余光中 interprets it in English:

The star-plucking youth
Fell down,
Mocked by the sky,
Mocked by the earth,
Mocked by the reporters
With ruthless superlatives
On his name.

The translator's *embarras de choix* concerns the word 它. Ji Xian, being a modern poet, apparently employed it in the 白話 usage as a pronoun in the neutral gender, because he used 他 in lines 7 and 8 to refer to the youth. But if the translator were to take 它 literally, lines 3 and 4 would be exceedingly clumsy: "It is mocked by the sky,/It is mocked by the earth." For fear the reader might not know what "it" refers to, the translator could go one step further: "The whole venture [of star plucking] is mocked by the sky,/The whole venture [of star plucking] is mocked by the earth."

Now suppose that "The Star-plucking Youth" were Yu Kwang-chung's own poem and had been "reincarnated" in English by someone who decided to ignore the difference between "it" and "he". How would the poet feel? Would he prefer this "new life" to sound better in English or would he rather that it keep its natural form despite stylistic clumsiness? A possible answer can be found in his own translation of "The Double Bed" 〈雙人床〉, which first appeared in *Acres of Barbed Wire*. The same poem has been translated by Wai-lim Yip 葉維廉 in his *Modern Chinese Poetry: Twenty Poets from the Republic of China 1955–1965*. Since Yip's anthology predates Yu's by one year, we do not know whether Yu consulted Yip's translation before attempting a version of his own. In any case, it would be instructive to compare the two translations.

讓戰爭在雙人床外進行
躺在你長長的斜坡上
聽流彈，像一把呼嘯的螢火
在你的，我的頭頂竄過
竄過我的鬍鬚和你的頭髮

讓政變和革命在四周吶喊
至少愛情在我們的一邊

Double Bed

Let war go on beyond the double bed,
Lying upon your long, long slope,
We listen to stray bullets, like roaming fireflies
Whiz over your head, my head,
Whiz over my moustache and your hair.
Let coups d'état, revolutions howl around us;
At least love is on our side ... (Yip)

The Double Bed

Let war rage on beyond the double bed
As I lie on the *length* of your slope
And hear the straying bullets,
Like a swarm of whistling will-o'-the-wisps
Whisk over your head and mine
And through your hair and through my beard.
On all sides let revolutions growl,
Love is at least on our side ... (Yu; emphasis added)

By reading 進行 as "go on", 長長的 as "long, long" and 螢火 as "fireflies", Yip reveals himself as a literal translator. While Yu "short-changed" 政變 in line 6, Yip dutifully sticks to the original and gives the term its due: coups d'état.

But what if Yip replaced "go on" with "rage"? Could he be accused of being a "usurper" of a translator? In this connection, it might be helpful to note a recent statement by Jin Di 金隄 and Eugene A. Nida: "The phrase 'dynamic equivalent translation' does not mean that such a translation is merely 'creative' or 'appealing', though in a sense it may be both."

While "rage" is certainly not a synonym for 進行, as "proceed" is for "go on", it is a happy dynamic equivalent sanctioned by the immediacy of the context. And so long as the context is war in the literal as well as metaphorical sense, it causes no disruption to the underlying imagery of the whole poem. A similar result is achieved by equating the adjectival phrase 長長的 with the noun "length". The "slope" in this highly suggestive poem is truly "body language". Unless the person referred to is particularly tall, there seems to be no need for the double qualifier. It can be argued, on Yip's part, that his rendition is a formal equivalent because that is exactly what the Chinese words suggest.

This brings us to the question of rhetoric and idiom in the two languages. In the first place, 長長的 "rhymes" with 床, whereas "long, long" is a cacophonous fellow for "bed". If I were the Chinese author of this poem and were translating it into English, I would have done what Yu Kwang-chung has done, just for the music of it. In the second place, if the "slope" in question refers to the whole body, then the qualifier 長長的 would seem necessary for the sake of clarity. Suppose Yu had written instead: 躺在你的斜坡上. Could he blame his translator if it were translated as "As I lean my head on your breasts?"

As I see it, 長長的 is more rhetorical than functional in the original; "long, long" in the target language is habitually denotative and descriptive. When we say "long, long ago" in English, we do mean long, long ago.

The clear advantage of the author-translator is that he has the licence to tamper with his own writing. At times, this practice can be carried too far to no good purpose. The case in point is Yu Kwang-chung's replacing "fire-flies" with "will-o-the-wisps". Since there is no rule governing the limits of an author-translator's poetic licence, it seems pointless to argue with Yu over his preference for will-o'-the-wisps. But as students of translation, we enjoy no such licence. We can either treat Yu's translation as re-creation or as "creative translation", which ignores what is implied by the terms "source" and "target" languages. If we are to treat Yu's translation as translation, then it is our duty to ask him: what has happened to 政變 in line 6? Did you delete it because you thought "revolution" is inclusive enough to cover "coups d'état"? Or does "On all sides let revolutions growl" sound better in English than "on all sides let coups d'état and revolution growl"? Of course, as the author-translator, he may simply reply: this is strictly a matter of personal preference.

We have seen how closely Wai-lim Yip adheres to the original when he is dealing with another's text. How respectful is he as translator of his own poem? Here is his 〈賦格〉:

北風，我還能忍受這一年嗎
冷街上，牆上，煩憂搖窗而至
帶來邊城的故事；呵氣無常的大地
草木的耐性，山巖的沉默，投下了
胡馬的長嘶

North wind, can I bear this one more year?
Streets shivering along the walls
Romances in cold sorrows the frontiers
Remind me of these:
Patience of mountains Erratic breath of outlands
Chronic neighing of Tartar horses …

〈賦格〉 is a poem of 101 lines, but what is cited above is sufficient evidence that Yip, as his own translator, takes far more liberties with the original than Yu Kwang-chung does. Following his manner of translating Yu, I will attempt to give a literal translation of his poem below:

North wind, can I bear this one more year?
On the cold streets, along the walls, *sorrow drifts in through the windows*
With stories from the border-town;
The great earth heaving its erratic breaths
The patience of the woods and plants
The silence of the mountains, *throwing down* the long neighing of the Tartar horses …
(emphasis added)

Though Yip is listed as the translator of 〈賦格〉, a comparison of the two versions above will show that what he has done is not translating but re-writing. Beginning with the second line, the syntax is topsy-turvy. "Cold streets" (or "deserted streets" if the line were not preceded by "north wind") is changed to "streets shivering". "Stories" is transformed to "romances". "Sorrows" takes on a frosty tone. "Border-town" becomes "frontiers". 草木的耐性 and 山巖的沉默 are lumped together to read "patience of mountains". 投下了 is recast as "remind me". And if we recall how he renders Yu Kwang-chung's 長長的, his preferred equivalent for "long" in 胡馬的長嘶 reveals his true preference: "long neighing" is recast as "chronic neighing".

Arthur Waley, in his "Notes on Translation" describes his experience as an editor of a scholarly volume of translation:

People, in fact, who write very well when expressing their own ideas tend (unless they have been to some extent schooled in translation) to lose all power of normal expression when faced with a foreign text. I once edited a volume in which a number of archaeologists, all of them excellent writers when expressing their own ideas, undertook to translate articles by German colleagues. The matter of the articles was purely technical and concrete; the translators knew exactly what had to be said. But one and all they were unable to produce anything but the most abject translator's pidgin. The sight of German sentences put them completely out of their stride.

In translating his 〈賦格〉 into English, Wai-lim Yip must have had a similar experience. In Chinese he can get away with the ambiguity inherent in 搖窗而至 , but in English he has to pin down his meaning and provide us with an "equivalent". To be sure, Yip's translation can be a model of "literal translation" provided that the text at hand is so terse that it leaves little room for manipulation. Witness his translation of his own poem "Edge of Waking" 〈醒之邊緣〉:

鉸鍊戛戛
停住
又開始
停住
洗碼頭工人的談論
沒入霧裡

The grating of anchor and collar
Stops
And begins
Stops
The talking of workmen on the pier
Recedes into the mist; …

Nothing has been distorted or omitted. The syntax and diction is so elementary that it could not possibly "throw anyone out of his stride". To conclude the case of Yip as translator and author-translator, one may say that he has translated Yu Kwang-chung's "Double Bed" and his own "Edge of Waking", but he has not translated "Fugue". He has just re-written the poem in English. Since the poem is his brainchild, he is free to remould it as he pleases. But to describe the work as a translation is a misnomer. There is no justifying the kind of reconstruction he preforms on his Chinese text.

Echoing Edward Said's sentiments in *Orientalism* (1978), William H. Nienhauser, Jr. has correctly pointed out that most of the so-called translations from Chinese poetry by such practitioners as Kenneth Rexroth are essentially "recreations". For this reason, "these translations are as much a part of American literature as they are of Chinese." Yip is different from American poet-translators like Pound and Rexroth, who had to "re-create" Chinese poetry because of their inadequate knowledge of China and its language. Yip, sanctioned as a bilingual author, makes his Chinese poem read as much like an English original as possible through his own "creative translation".

It is easy to see why bilingual poets like Yu Kwang-chung, Wai-lim Yip, Yang Mu 楊牧 (Ching-hsien Wang 王靖獻), and Zhang Cuo 張錯 (Dominic Cheung 張振翱) have taken it upon themselves to be their own translators. Robert Frost, as we have often heard, defined poetry as what is lost in translation. Even distinguished translators speak of their trade with characteristic self-effacement. David Hawkes, who has given us an exquisite translation of *The Story of the Stone* 《紅樓夢》, ends his introduction to the work with this modest statement: "I cannot pretend always to have done so successfully, but if I can convey to the reader even a fraction of the pleasure this Chinese novel has given me, I shall not have lived in vain."

There are of course exceptions to the rule that translation is at best approximation, or, in Owen's phrase, "an exercise in imperfection". One gains renewed confidence in the profession when it is reported that Gabriel Garcia Marquez, author of *One Hundred Years of Solitude*, "prefers Rabassa's English translation of his masterwork to the Spanish original". But such success stories are rare. Quite frequently, translations from Chinese are either distorted due to miscomprehension or manipulated to suit a translator's whims. We are not talking of translations produced in Herbert A. Giles's (1845–1935) time. Two lines from one of Li Shangyin's 李商隱 (813?–858) untitled poems have been stretched to seven by way of extrapolation in a "translation" published in 1986:

春蠶到死絲方盡
臘炬成灰淚始乾

Just as the silkworm spins silk
Until it dies,
So the candle cannot dry its tears
Until the last drop is shed.

And so with me.
I will love you
to my last day.

Translators are equally irresponsible when they follow what James J. Y. Liu has called a penchant for "barbarization". He provides one such example in Eric Sackheim's "translation" of two lines from Cao Cao's 曹操 (155–220) 〈短歌行〉：何以解憂；惟有杜康 which reads "How to untie grief/There's only the brewer." This is comparable to Julius Caesar intoning to his friends, " 'Let's head for the nearest bar (or pub)' — yet with no sign of conscious parody."

Even if Cao Cao or Li Shangyin were contemporaries of their translators, the poets would not have been able to vindicate the abuses heaped upon them unless they could translate their own works. Authors are truly at the mercy of their translators. It is precisely because of their desire for their work to be reborn into as close an image of their former existence as possible that our author-translators have taken the laws of reincarnation into their own hands. What the author-translator must remember is that in the process of self-transmigration they should refrain from unnecessary self-mutilation lest the Sackheims be encouraged to commit more "barbarizations". If the author-translator wants his work to be "naturalized" so that it sounds like a genuine English poem, he is of course entitled to do so, so long as he informs the reader that the work in question has been rewritten. The "reincarnated" poem, then, will stand or fall on its own merits, and the critics of translations will respectfully make their retreat.

Semantics

Zeng Xiancai
Department of English
Guangzhou Institute of Foreign Languages, Guangzhou, China

Retrospect

Semantics is the philosophical and scientific study of meaning.

Meaning in language is an old as well as a new subject. From ancient times to the present day, many philosophers and linguists have studied it, digging out the "meaning of meaning". They have produced an immense number of articles and books and come up with various theories on it.

In Plato's dialogue "Cratylus" 2000 years ago, one finds the view that the form is a word in a language and the meaning is the object in the world that it "stands for", refers to" or "denotes": words are "names" or "labels" for things. This is the oldest theory of naming. Xun Zi (313–238 B.C.), a Chinese philosopher during the Warring States Period, stated, "Originally a name has nothing to do with an object. It is conventional — through people's long use, the name standing for the object is established." This "name-object" view is similar with Plato's.

In 17th century, John Locke (1632–1704), a British philosopher, put forth the conceptual theory of meaning: "… the function of words lies in that they apparently mark various ideas, and those ideas they stand for are their innate and direct meanings." This view was shared by many modern philosophers and linguists. When speaking on language, Karl Marx and Friedrich Engels stated, "Words and symbols are just the presumed (arbitrary) names for the objective world and they have no essential link with reality." And the modern linguists C. K. Ogden and I. A. Richards developed the conceptual theory into a famous "Semiotic Triangle":

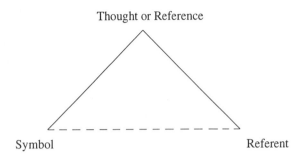

They hold that the symbol (word) has no direct link with the referent (object); the link is established through thought or reference, the concept of our minds. That is to say, the meaning of a word is its abstract and generalized reflection of reality.

At the beginning of the 20th century, the Swiss linguist Ferdinand de Saussure (1857–1913) laid the foundation for modern linguistics with the publication of his book *Course in General Linguistics*. He was the first linguist who introduced the distinction between *langue* and *parole*, between language system and language behaviour.

This theoretical concept is one of the cornerstones in modern linguistics and has had a great influence upon modern linguists, who later put forth a number of new linguistic theories, such as the distinction between semantics and pragmatics by R. Carnap and C. Morris, the distinction between language competence and language performance, between the deep structure and surface structure by Noam Chomsky, the distinction between sentence meaning and utterance meaning, and so on.

In the field of semantics, the British linguist J.R. Firth, who was heavily influenced by the Vienna-born philosopher L. Wittgenstein, initiated the theory of behaviourism, upon which the behaviourist linguist L. Bloomfield developed the theory of "stimulus and response" between the 1930s and 50s. He argues that the meaning of a linguistic form should be viewed as "the situation in which the speaker utters it, and the response which it calls forth in the hearer."

In the sixties, J. L. Austin caught the attention of linguistic circles with his famous speech act theory. He holds that the meaning of language presents itself in the pragmatic force in speech acts — locutionary force, illocutionary force and perlocutionary force.

The generative linguists with Noam Chomsky as their leader excluded meaning of language in their studies of pure form — language structure — in the 50s and 60s. Having met with great difficulties, they began to introduce semantics into their research in the early 70s. Later they developed a number of new semantic theories within the frame of grammar, which include Interpretive Semantics by Katz, the Extended Standard theory by Chomsky, the theory of Generative Semantics by G. Lakoff and others, and Case Grammar by Fillmore.

Up to the present, remarkable progress has been made in the study of meaning, but not every problem about meaning has found a satisfactory answer. Efforts to seek solutions of the problems are being strengthened.

Semantic Meaning and Pragmatic Meaning

In the light of the philosophical and linguistic achievements in semantics, meaning of language consists of two major aspects: semantic and pragmatic. Semantic meaning refers to the static meaning of an expression innate in the language system and independent of context/situation and its user, the speaker/author, hearer/reader, whilst pragmatic meaning refers to the dynamic meaning of an utterance, which derives from its semantic meaning and is dependent on the context/situation and its user.

Semantic meaning consists of:

(1) Conceptual meaning or denotation, which refers to the function of an expression reflecting the objective reality through the mediation of concept of the mind, and which "involves the relationship between a linguistic unit (especially a lexical item) and the non-linguistic entities to which it refers...." (Crystal, 1980). Concept is the basis of meaning whereas meaning is the form of concept in language. They are dependent on each other on the one hand and different from each other on the other hand. First, meaning belongs to linguistics whereas concept, being a unit of thinking, goes to the category of philosophy. Secondly, concept is of generic reference whilst meaning is of both generic and specific references. For instance, the word "cat", being a concept, refers to the kind of carnivorous furry mammal, long domesticated and useful for keeping down mice, including all cats, old and young, male and female,

long-haired and short-haired, black and white and spotted. But the meaning of this word, in addition to its generic reference, can, in a given context, refer to a specific cat, as in "I saw a cat in the garden."

(2) Associative meaning or connotation, which refers to the emotional association or evaluation an expression suggests in one's mind. For example, "mother", with the conceptual meaning of "female parent", generally connotes love, care and tenderness. The word "pig" suggests bad qualities as greediness, laziness and dirtiness. "Confidence" and "slim" have positive evaluation or appreciatory meaning, whereas "complacency" and "skinny" link with negative evaluation or derogatory meaning.

(3) Stylistic meaning, which refers to the features of distinctive uses of language in different situations by different users. Generally speaking, style consists of: (a) writing style, such as common language, literary language, technical language, etc; (b) discourse style, such as colloquial, bookish, frozen, formal, consultative, casual, intimate, etc.; (c) style of times, such as Victorian, modern, etc. (d) style of location, such as dialect, jargon, etc.; (e) style of idiolect, such as Shakespearean language, Dickens' language, etc.

Pragmatic meaning consists of:

(1) Locutionary force, which refers to the function of an utterance conveying literal meaning. The pragmatic meaning of an utterance in a locutionary speech act is identical with its semantic meaning or sentence meaning or propositional meaning.

(2) Illocutionary force, which refers to the function of an utterance realizing the speaker's intention, which includes believing, swearing, hypothesizing, reporting, requesting, predicting, greeting, farewell bidding, inviting, promising, allowing, admitting, threatening, recommending, suggesting, commanding, persuading, announcing, declaring, thanking, apologizing, congratulating etc. For instance,
  1. Hello, how are you? (greeting)
  2. The inflation will increase. (predicting)
  3. I'll shoot if you move. (warning)
  4. Would you like a cup of coffee? (offering)
  5. I am sorry I wasn't at the meeting this morning. (apologizing)

  6. You can play outside for half an hour now. (allowing)

(3) Perlocutionary force, which refers to the function of an utterance bringing about an emotional or behavioural response on the part of the hearer, such as pleasing, angering, causing fear, embarrassing, encouraging, causing tension, drawing attention, distracting etc. For instance,

  7. There's a hornet in your left ear. (causing fear in the hearer)

  8. Miss, Billy swore at me. He told me to piss off. (causing surprise to the teacher, who might reproach Billy)

  9. Come on! The peak is not far ahead. (encouraging the hearer)

(4) Rhetorical force, which refers to the function of a special verbal device (figure of speech) the author/speaker employs to achieve a particular effect on the reader/ hearer. For instance,

  10. Helen knew what Charles was: nothing but a piece of blank clay. (metaphor)

  11. Bill wanted the news like he wanted a hole in his head. (irony)

  12. She had gone to glory when he arrived. (euphemism)

  13. I've told you hundred times. (hyperbole)

  Semantic meaning and pragmatic meaning are interconnected, with the latter deriving from the former. A sentence has a semantic meaning (literal meaning/propositional meaning) and a potential pragmatic meaning as well. In other words, when used in a context/situation, a sentence becomes an utterance and develops a pragmatic meaning accordingly; when used as a locutionary act, it has a locutionary force which overlaps with its semantic meaning; in an illocutionary act, an illocutionary force; in a perlocutionary act, a perlocutionary force; and when used rhetorically, a pragmatically rhetorical force.

  There are two factors which affect the meaning of language in use. One is the intention or purpose of the speaker / author. And it is in this sense that Grice says, "Meaning means intention." The other is the context or speech situation, which includes: (a) the occasion (which may be a casual meeting or an official reception); (b) the social relationship between the participants (which may be that of family members or employer to employee); (c) subject matter (which may be about a football match or a serious political issue); and (d) the mode of discourse (spoken or written). And it is in this sense that Wittgenstein says, "For a large number of cases … the meaning of a word is its use in the language."

Semantic Approach and Pragmatic Approach

Translation consists in reproducing what is expressed in one language in another language. Traditionally, translating the idea (content) of the original text without keeping to its grammatical form is referred to as free translation whereas translating word for word or nearly so is referred to as literal translation.

Modern linguistic theories have opened up new horizons for the theoretical study of translation.

Translation is, in terms of linguistic theory, the process and result of the transformation between the surface structures of the source text and the target text on condition that the meaning remains unchanged. Eugene Nida's compendious remark "translating means translating meaning" indicates that meaning is the main concern of the translator and the starting point as well as the destination of translation. In the light of modern semantics, meaning consists of semantic and pragmatic aspects. Accordingly, translating meaning means translating semantic meaning and pragmatic meaning. In other words, the source text and the target text should be approached semantically and pragmatically in the process of translation.

Semantic translation consists in reproducing the semantic meaning of the source language in equivalents of the target language whereas pragmatic translation consists in conveying the pragmatic meaning of the source language in equivalents of the target language. The former involves the ideational/locutionary function of language and the latter the interpersonal/social function of language. For example,

14. Context is the overriding factor in all translations and has primacy over any rule, theory or primary meaning.
    在所有翻譯中，上下文（語境）是壓倒一切的因素，它比任何規則、理論或基本詞義都來得重要。
15. (a) Wet paint!
    (b) Frisch angestrichen!
    (c) 油漆未乾！
16. (a) How do you do?
    (b) Bonjour!
    (c) 你好！

The original of (14) expresses the view of the speaker about the importance of context in translation and the semantically translated version reproduces the same thought of the speaker. The intended meaning of (15) is to prevent people from touching the object that has been just painted. This communicative purpose is realized with different linguistic devices in different languages: "Wet paint!" in English, "Frisch angestrichen!" in German, and " 油漆未乾！" in Chinese. (16)(a) and (b) are performatives, with their pragmatic meaning (illocutionary force) of greeting each other at a first meeting. Their semantic meaning (propositional meaning) is of little significance here. If they are translated semantically into Chinese: " 你怎麼做？" " 好日子!", the translated versions cannot convey the speaker's communicative intention, because these two Chinese sentences do not have the potential pragmatic meaning (force) of greeting. However, the Chinese utterance " 你好？" is identical in pragmatic meaning with (16)(a) and (b), therefore, (c) is a correct translation.

In semantically equivalent translation the translator's task focuses on content whereas in pragmatically equivalent translation he is concerned with communicative purpose and pragmatic effect. For instance,

17. Language is the direct reality of thought.
    語言是思想的直接現實 .
18. It made my blood boil.
    我肺都氣炸了 .

(17) is a proposition, and the task of the translator is to convey exactly its content but nothing else. The Chinese translation fulfils the task. But it is not the case with (18), in which the speaker intended to express his hot anger. Here the great extent of anger is realized by an image — "blood boils" instead of abstract expressions such as "very very angry", "in the extreme of anger" etc. Its semantic rendition in Chinese " 這使我熱血沸騰 " departs far from the speaker's intention. For these two utterances, "blood boils" and " 熱血沸騰 ", though identical in semantic meaning, are different in pragmatic meaning (pragmatically rhetorical force), the former of which is "extremely angry", and the latter "very much excited". The Chinese " 肺都氣炸了 " has the same pragmatic force as the English "blood boils" does.

Literality, Modification and Adaptation

A translated text — the product of translating — is finally realized on the linguistic level of syntax and text. Based on the practice and experience of countless translators, three kinds of translation have been generalized in terms of methodology — literal translation or literality, modified translation or modification and adapted translation or adaptation or cultural adaptation. These translation methods are closely related with the linguistic and cultural differences, the identity of the source language, and the target language involved in translation.

In translating, the literal method is employed when the linguistic and cultural factors of the source text and target text involved are similar or basically identical, and accordingly the diction, syntax (grammatical structure) and the literal and pragmatic meaning of the translated version are basically equivalent to those of the source text. Sometimes this method can also be used when the linguistic and cultural factors in question are different so long as the translated version will not lead to misunderstanding among its readers. One of the advantages of literality is the introduction of new concepts, new expressions and sentence structures from the source language into the target language. However, this is done at the expense of the loss of smoothness and idiomaticity to some extent in the translated text.

Literality is applicable in both semantic and pragmatic approaches.

When the linguistic and cultural factors of the source and target texts are different and cannot be translated by means of literality, modification is resorted to, in which changes occur in diction and syntax for the sake of the adequate reproduction of the meaning of the original text and the smoothness and idiomaticity of the translated text. Modification is usually realized through a series of translation techniques, which include, among the frequently used, diction, extension of word meaning, conversion of word class, conversion of voice and sentence pattern, amplification (addition and repetition of words), omission of words, inversion of word order, reversion of affirmation and negation, division (splitting a long sentence into shorter sentences) and combination. Take the following examples from English into Chinese:

19. The diplomat holds that mistiness is the mother of safety.
這位外交家認爲含糊其辭最保險。（選詞）
20. The electronic computer is chiefly characterized by its accurate and rapid computation.
電腦的特點是計算準確而迅速。（轉換：詞類轉換、語態和句型轉換）

21. In April 1971, there was a "ping" heard around the world. In July, the ping "ponged".
    1971 年 4 月，全世界聽到中國 "乒" 的一聲把球打了出去；7月，美國 "乓" 的一聲把球打了回來。(增詞)

22. Before you hand in your paper, you have to read it over and over again, and see if there is anything in it to be corrected and revised.
    交卷前，必須讀幾遍，看有無需要修改之處。(減詞)

23. Judgement should wait upon information.
    情況不明，不能妄下判斷。(反譯)

24. "Politics is perhaps the only profession for which no preparation is thought necessary," Stevenson once said.
    史蒂文森曾經說過： "政治或許是唯一的被認爲無須作準備的職業"。(詞序調整)

25. They went out through the revolving doors that made a fairly derisive whistling sound when you pushed them.
    他們推著旋轉門往外走：旋轉門發生輕輕的響聲，像是在嘲諷人似的。(拆譯)

26. He was very clean. His mind was open.
    他爲人單純而坦率。(合譯)

Modification can be applied in both semantic and pragmatic approaches.

When the gap between the linguistic and cultural factors of the source and target texts is too wide for the translator to reproduce the pragmatic meaning of the original text by literality or modification, adaptation is preferably adopted. The translated version thus produced may be quite different from the source text in terms of diction and syntax, but has the identical pragmatic meaning to the original. This is a sort of pragmatic translation, and a cultural adaptation as well. Adaptation is often realized by the following techniques: (1) Reproduce the pragmatic meaning while abandoning the image in the original as in example (27); (2) Reproduce the pragmatic meaning while replacing the image as in (28); (3) Reproduce the pragmatic meaning by replacing the proposition, as in (29).

27. (a) "我剛來，眞是丈二和尙摸不到頭腦 …"
         "Being new here, I'm very much in the dark myself …"
    (b) Birds of a feather flock together.
         物以類聚

28. (a) "你這是寅吃卯糧"

"You're eating your corn in the blade."

(b) The mills of God grind slowly but sure.

天網恢恢，疏而不漏。

29. (a) 他跟老人招呼了一聲："吃過沒有，老爹？"

"Good morning, Grandpa," he greeted the old man.

(b) All sales are final.

貨物售出，概不退換。

Adaptation is preferably applied in pragmatic approach.

The above-discussed translation approaches, methods and techniques and their relationship can be illustrated in the following diagram:

Semantic Level	Syntactic and Textual Level	
Approach	Method	Technique
Semantic Translation	Literality	Basically word for word
	Modification	Diction and extension; Conversion; Amplification; Omission; Inversion; Reversion; Division; Combination etc.
Pragmatic Translation		
	Adaptation	Abandoning Image; Replacing Image; Replacing Proposition etc.

References

Baldinger, Kurt. *Semantic Theory*. London: Basil Blackwell, 1980.

Catford, J. C. *A Linguistic Theory of Translation*. London: Oxford University Press, 1965.

Hurford, James K. and Brendam Heasley. *Semantics*. Cambridge: Cambridge University Press, 1983.

Leech, Geoffrey N. *Principles of Pragmatics*. London: Longman, 1983.

Levinson, S. *Pragmatics*. Cambridge: Cambridge University Press, 1983.

Lyons, John. *Language and Linguistics*. Cambridge: Cambridge University Press, 1981.

Newmark, Peter. *Approaches to Translation*. Oxford: Pergamon Press, 1981.
Nida, Eugene A. *The Theory and Practice of Translation*. Leiden: E. J. Brill, 1982.
―――. *Translating Meaning*. San Dimas, Ca.: English Language Institute, 1982.
Palmer, F. R. *Semantics*. Cambridge: Cambridge University Press, 1976.
Rose, Marilyn Gaddis, ed. *Translation Spectrum*. Albany: State University of New York Press, 1981.

SENTENCE TRANSLATION

English Attributive Clauses

Liu Zhongde
Department of Foreign Languages
Hunan Normal University, Changsha, China

Introduction

In English there are three kinds of complex sentences, namely sentences containing attributive clauses which function as adjectives; sentences containing subject, object, predicative or appositional clauses which function as nouns and sentences containing adverbial clauses which function as adverbs. Among them sentences of the first kind are most difficult to translate. Here it is our purpose to discuss such sentences. First of all, we must know that in Chinese there are attributes which are often translated in the form of attributive clause in English, e.g.,

> 這就是說，我們不但要把一個政治上受壓迫，經濟上受剝削的中國變爲一個政治上自由與經濟上繁榮的中國，而且要把一個被舊文化統治因而愚昧落後的中國，變爲一個被新文化統治因而聰明先進的中國。

The corresponding English version is as follows:

> In other words, not only do we want to change a China that is *politically oppressed and economically exploited* into a China *that is politically free and economically prosperous*, we also want to change the China *which is being kept ignorant and backward under the sway of the old culture* into *an enlightened and progressive China under the sway of a new culture*.

Secondly, we must know that whether a sentence is smooth or awkward does not depend on whether it is long or short, but depends on whether it is well organized or not. The above example is rather long, yet it is smooth both in the original and in the translation. In contrast, the following two sentences are not so long, but their respective translations might sound very awkward if we could not handle them properly.

1. My plan, which I have used many times, is very simple.
   * 我的我已經用過多次的方案是很簡單的。
2. Toward evening, we stopped at an inn, where we passed the night.
   * 傍晚，我們停留在一家我們在那裡過了夜的旅店。

No doubt the Chinese versions of these two sentences both sound awkward because they, on the one hand, violate the law and methods of translating various kinds of attributive clauses and, on the other, do not conform to Chinese usage. The attributive clauses in the above English sentences are both non-restrictive. In accordance with the proper law and methods of translation and the usage of the Chinese language, they should not be translated word for word as they are in the original and be placed before the words they originally modify; at the same time there is no need to get the subjects of both attributive clauses expressed in the Chinese translation. Thus the proper translation of the two English sentences should be like this:

1. 我的方案，已經用過多次，很簡單。
2. 傍晚，我們停留在一家旅店，在那裡過了夜。

As a result, the complex English sentences each with an attributive clause have now been transformed into two simple sentences with a compound predicate.

From this analysis, we can see that a translator ought to forever observe the laws and methods of translating various kinds of attributive clauses. Grammatically, attributive clauses are divided into two classes: restrictive and non-restrictive. But as far as the question of translation is concerned, we have to divide attributive clauses into five classes, as follows: Class I: Restrictive Attributive Clauses, Class II: Non-Restrictive Attributive Clauses, Class III: Adverbial-Attributive Clauses, Class IV: Attributive Clauses Introduced by Relative Pronoun "As", and Class V: Attributive Clauses to Be Treated in Unusual Ways.

Class I: Restrictive Attributive Clauses

The restrictive attributive clause is used to restrict the meaning of the antecedent it modifies. It has three characteristics: (1) It is placed after the antecedent; (2) Generally there is no comma to separate the clause from the antecedent it modifies; (3) The clause forms an indispensable part of the sentence it belongs to in meaning. If you should drop the attributive clause, the sentence might change its meaning or even become senseless, e.g.

1. This is a book (that) I like very much.
2. This is the book (that) I like best.

Without the attributive clause, the first sentence can still stand as an independent simple sentence, but there is a great change in meaning. As for the second, it will no longer make sense, for no one will understand what you mean by "This is the book" without a proper context or conversational situation.

In translating sentences of this kind, generally speaking, we should place the attributives before the words they modify in Chinese. Here we simply use the term "attributives", for in Chinese such modifiers are not necessarily in the form of clauses all the time. Sometimes they may be either in the form of phrases or in the form of words. This applies to all the following Chinese sentences.

1. This is the place *where the Workers' and Peasants' Red Army made the crossing in 1934.*
   這就是工農紅軍一九三四年渡江的地方。
2. A. Do you know the man *who spoke to your father yesterday*?
      你認識昨天對你父親講話的那個人嗎？
   B. No, I don't know who he is.
      不，我不曉得他是誰。
3. Here is the man *you are looking for.*
   你正在尋找的那個人就在這兒。
4. Everything *he said* seemed quite reasonable.
   他說的話似乎都很有道理。
5. That is the first book of the kind *I have ever come across.*
   這是我碰見的第一本這樣的書。
6. She made a list of all the articles *there are on the subject.*
   她把有關這個題目的現有的一切文章列了一個單子。

7. There is no difficulty *we can't overcome.*
   沒有我們不能克服的困難。
8. This is the problem *which remains to be solved.*
   這就是那個尚待解決的問題。
9. That's the way *they study.*
   這就是他們學習的方法。
10. Who is the man *you visited yesterday*?
    你昨天訪問的那個人是誰？
11. Such people *as they are* will never do that sort of thing.
    像他們那樣的人永遠都不會做那種事情。
12. Have you got the same pen *as I bought last week*?
    你已經得到像我上週買的那樣的鋼筆嗎？

In general, such attributives in Chinese are also placed before the words they modify as mentioned above. But in some particular cases, as in those sentences whose main clauses are of the "there is (or are)" pattern, either kind of word order — the attributives placed before the words they modify or the attributives placed after them — sounds all right, e.g.

(1) But there are still people *who have failed to memorize the lessons of the past.*
(2) How many students are there in your class *whose homes are in the countryside*?

Compare the two Chinese versions of each of the original sentences in the following:

(1) 但仍然有人沒有記取過去的教訓。
    但仍然有沒有記取過去教訓的人。
(2) 你們班上有多少同學家在鄉下？
    你們班上家在鄉下的同學有多少？

Both versions are grammatical, but only the former, the so-called pivotal sentence pattern, is correct. The other pattern alters the thrust of the sentence, reassigning the clause underlined, which carries the main point, to a subordinate position.

Class II: Non-restrictive Attributive Clauses

The non-restrictive or continuative attributive clauses are used to give further or supplementary explanations to the words they modify. Generally, there is no need for antecedents and attributive clauses to change places with each other. That is to say, the same word order may remain in the translation from English into Chinese. This applies to sentences from 1 to 8. e.g.,

1. Someone proposed the name of Mr. Smith, *whom we elected as representative.* (= and we elected him …)
   有人提史密斯先生的名,我們選他當了代表。
2. Last week I saw "Modern Times" with Charles Chaplin playing the leading role, *which I think one of the most amusing films.* (= and I think it …)
   上週我看了查理・卓別麟主演的《摩登時代》,我認爲是最有趣的影片之一。
3. His article, *which I have just read,* is very instructive.
   他的文章,我剛才讀過,很有教育意義。
4. Westminster Abbey, *which is one of the oldest churches in Great Britain*, contains the graves of many famous Englishmen.
   威斯敏斯特教堂,大不列顚最古老的教堂之一,裡面有許多知名英國人的墳墓。
5. It rained all night and day, *during which time the ship broke into pieces.* (= and during that time …)
   雨整整下了一天一夜,在那段時間裡,那條船破碎了。
6. Jack is a scholar, *in whose study there are lots of books.* (= and in his study …)
   傑克是個學者,他書房裡有很多書。
7. John won the race, *which made him very happy.* (= and it …)
   約翰賽跑獲勝,這使他很高興。
8. The relations between China and the United States of America have been improved, *which will contribute to our four modernizations and world peace.*
   中美兩國關係已經得到改善,這將有利於我們的四個現代化和世界和平。

So far as the method of translating these sentences is concerned, all such attributives are placed after the words they modify. But the disposal of the relative pronouns is not quite the same. (1) They are usually omitted in the Chinese version when used as subjects or objects (sentences 2, 3, 4); (2) they must be translated when used as other parts. In sentences 5 and 6, "which" and "whose" are both used as attributes. (3) Sentences 7 and 8 have their own characteristics: first, the relative pronoun is always the word "which" and what it stands for is not a noun phrase but the whole main clause; secondly, it always serves as the subject of the subordinate clause and it may often be rendered as the Chinese character " 這 ".

Class III: Adverbial-Attributive Clauses

Such attributive clauses are named semi-adverbial by R. W. Zandvoort in his work entitled *A Handbook of English Grammar*. The term signifies that such clauses are attributive ones in form, but adverbial ones in function and sense. Yao Shanyou 姚善友 calls such clauses "formally attributive clauses functioning as adverbial ones in sense" in his 《英語語法學》 (*A Practical English Grammar*). And I term them as Adverbial-Attributive Clauses in my work entitled 《翻譯漫談》 (*Remarks on Translation*). They may be translated into Chinese as adverbial clauses expressing cause, purpose, condition, etc., e.g.,

1. <u>Premier Zhou</u> *who was busy all day long* never knew what fatigue was.
   周總理雖然整天很忙，卻從不知疲倦。 (concession)
2. <u>My uncle</u>, *who will be seventy tomorrow*, is still a keen sportsman.
   我伯父雖然明天就滿七十歲了，但仍愛好運動。 (concession)
3. <u>Envoys</u> were sent who should strengthen our international position. (who should = so that they should)
   派了使節，以便加強我們的國際地位。 (purpose)
4. <u>Anybody</u> *who should do that* would be laughed at. (who = if he)
   無論是誰，只要做那種事情，都一定會受到嘲笑。 (condition)
5. For further particulars you had better apply to <u>my brother</u>, *who has paid* particular attention to the subject. (who = because he)
   關於細節，你最好詢問我弟弟，因為他對這個問題特別留意。 (cause)

All such attributive clauses can be placed after the words they modify in the Chinese version and connected to them by " 雖然 ", " 以便 ", " 只要 " or " 因為 " etc. Meanwhile, the subjects of the subordinate clauses may be omitted in translation as in examples 1, 2, 3, 4, if they refer to the same persons as those of main ones; otherwise, they should be retained in the Chinese version as in example 5.

Sometimes the subordinating conjunction expressing cause may be omitted in the Chinese version, and the relation between cause and result can still be felt by the reader. e.g.,

6. Our teacher, *who is getting old*, will soon retire. (who = as he)
   我們的老師，越來越老，不久就要退休。 (cause)

7. The citizens' war in Russia, *which inflicted heavy losses on Napoleon's army*, incensed the conqueror, *who had never met that kind of opposition anywhere in Europe*. (which = because it; who = as he)
   俄國的人民戰爭，使拿破崙的軍隊受到重大的損失，激怒了這位征服者，（因為）他在歐洲任何地方都從來沒有遭到過那樣的反抗。
   (cause)

Class IV: Attributive Clauses Introduced by Relative Pronoun "As"

In the following, we will discuss the attributive clauses introduced by the word "as" functioning as the relative pronoun.

When the word "as" alone is used as the relative pronoun in the attributive clauses, there may be five cases with its antecedents.

Here only three of them will be illustrated. Attention should be paid to the function and translation of the word "as" in the subordinate clause.

I. The word "as" standing for the concept of an action in the clause.

1. To write a dull book, as any poor writer could do, was unworthy of him.
   寫一本枯燥無味的書，這是任何一個蹩腳的作家都會做的，但對他來說，是不相稱的。

2. It is absolutely wrong to think foreign languages useless, as quite a few people did before.
   認為外語無用是絕對錯誤的，不少人過去有這種想法。

In sentence 1 the word "as" stands for the concept expressed by the infinitive phrase "to write a dull book" and in sentence 2 for that expressed by the infinitive phrase "to think foreign languages useless". The phrases both serve as the subject, and thus the word "as" is a relative pronoun, which functions as the object of the verb "to do." In such sentence patterns, the Chinese word " 這 " or expression " 這種 " may be used to translate the relative pronoun "as".

II. The word "as" standing for the concept which may be inferred from a similar noun or noun phrase in the main clause.

1. Now many young people wish to be <u>scientists</u>, as (= scientists) it is possible for them to be, on condition that they work hard.
現在許多青年都想當<u>科學家</u>，在自己刻苦努力的條件下，<u>這</u>是大有可能如願以償的。

2. His grandfather was <u>a simple-mannered man</u>, as (= simple mannered man in its plural form) large-hearted and large-minded men are apt to be.
他祖父質樸<u>大方</u>，慷慨而心胸開闊的人也往往是<u>這樣</u>。

3. He seems <u>a foreigner</u>, as (= a foreigner) in fact he is.
他似乎是個<u>外國人</u>，事實上，他也是個<u>外國人</u>。

III. The word "as" standing for the concept expressed by an adjective in the main clause.

1. He was not <u>sick</u>, as (= sick) some of the other passengers were.
他沒有<u>病</u>，其餘乘客有些人倒是<u>病</u>了。

2. He thinks her answer <u>incorrect</u>, as (= incorrect) it probably is.
他認爲她的回答<u>不正確</u>，她的回答大概也是<u>不正確的</u>。

There are two common characteristics in the second and third uses of the word "as": (1) "as" serves as the predicative in the subordinate clause; (2) there is a verb to be in the clause where "as" functions as a relative pronoun. You may either use "這" or "這樣" or repeat the foregoing noun or adjective to represent "as" while translating such sentence patterns.

Class V: Attributive Clauses to Be Treated in Unusual Ways

1. In short, we are for a world *in which every people, rooted in their national cultural values, will be receptive to the abundant benefits of other nations.*
一句話，我們贊成<u>這樣的</u>世界：<u>每個國家的人民都扎根於自己的民族文化寶庫之中</u>，<u>又汲取其他國家的豐富滋養</u>。

2. But it has the big disadvantages that we have no large and disciplined army of socialist leaders *who understand the objectives in all their complexity,* and *who have clear ideas about how to promote the movement towards them.*
但它的一大缺點是使我們缺少<u>這樣</u>一大批受過訓練的社會主義領導

人，他們懂得我們目標的全部複雜含義，<u>並且明確地知道怎樣才能</u>
<u>推動運動朝著這些目標前進</u>。

3. He unselfishly contributed his uncommon talents and indefatigable spirit to the struggle *which today brings them (those aims) within the reach of a majority of the human race.*
他把自己非凡的才智和不倦的精力無私地獻給了<u>這種</u>鬥爭，<u>它今天</u>
<u>已使人類中大多數人</u>可以達到這些目標。

The restrictive attributive clauses in all three examples are not translated in the Chinese structure ending in the character 的 and placed before the words they modify, but rendered as post-positioned explanatory clauses. And at the same time, the English articles before the antecedents should be converted in the Chinese modifiers 這樣的 as in 1, 這樣 as in 2 or 這種 as in 3 in order to show the close relation between the words to be further explained and the clauses which aim to make a further explanation of the original antecedents; we have treated the restrictive attributive clauses in the above three examples in such an unusual way, either because there is more than one restrictive attributive clause as in 1 and 2, or because the restrictive attributive clause is rather long as in 3. If we should translate them as we usually do, the Chinese versions would sound unnatural and unidiomatic.

4. He liked his sister, *who was warm and pleasant*, but he did not like his brother, *who was aloof and arrogant.*
他喜歡熱情愉快的妹妹，而不喜歡冷漠高傲的哥哥。

5. But his laugh, *which was very infectious*, broke the silence.
但他富有感染力的笑聲打破了沉默。

The above-mentioned two attributive clauses are non-restrictive in form, but they are all rendered as pre-modifiers just like restrictive ones. It is because they are short and closely related to their antecedents. They would result in a loose sentence construction and a choppy context if we should translate them as we usually do non-restrictive attributive clauses.

6. We are peoples *that have inherited wisdom, that know the worth of biding one's time and recognized the right opportunity for combat.*
我們的人民<u>繼承了古代的智慧</u>，懂得如何等待並善於抓住戰機。

7. In a word, a true revolution is one *that is devoted to human progress in all domains and that makes human progress the supreme and final object.*

總之，眞正的革命，致力於人的全面發展，並以此作爲行動的最高指標。

8. We live in a world *where relations between states are relations of forces*.
   在我們所處的世界上，國家之間的關係是力量對比的關係。

In 6, 7, and 8, all the attributive clauses are restrictive, but they are translated in special ways: In the first two, they are transformed into predicates of the Chinese sentences with the omission of relative pronouns after the main clauses are compressed into noun phrases serving as subjects of the predicates mentioned above. In the third, the main clause is compressed into an adverbial phrase while the restrictive attributive clause transformed into the SVA Chinese version with the relative adverb already blended in the adverbial phrase at the very beginning of the sentence.

9. He had talked to vice-president Nixon, *who assured him that everything that could be done would be done*.
   他向副總統尼克松談過話。副總統向他擔保，凡是能夠做到的都將竭盡全力去做。

10. He is with his youngest son, *who is accompanying him on his lecture tour in China*.
    他帶著小兒子。小兒子陪他在中國進行巡迴演講。

In these two examples, the actors and sufferers of the action are of the same number and sex. If, in the second clause of the Chinese version, we do not repeat the nouns functioning as the antecedents in the original, the reader will not be clear who is the actor, because there is not the so-called relative pronoun in the Chinese language. Since the nouns have to be repeated, the better way out is to make the second clause independent, which seems more natural and idiomatic in Chinese.

The methods of translating the several kinds of attributive clauses as discussed above are not complete at all, but they are fairly typical. They may be helpful when taken for reference.

References

Gu, Yanling 顧延齡 and Xiong Xiling 熊希齡. 《英漢・漢英翻譯敎程》 (*A Course of English-Chinese/Chinese-English Translation*). Changsha: Hunan Science and Education Language Audio-visual Press 湖南省科敎語言音像出版社, 1989.

Liu, Zhongde 劉重德.《翻譯漫談》 (*Remarks on Translation*). Xi'an: Shaanxi People's Press 陝西人民出版社, 1984.

———.《英語 AS 的用法研究》 (*A Study of the Uses of the English Word "As"*). Changsha: Hunan People's Press 湖南人民出版社, 1979.

Lu, Hongmei 盧紅梅.〈也談英語定語從句的譯法〉 (On the Translation of English Attributive Clauses). Paper presented at the "Conference on Contrastive Studies and the Translation of English and Chinese," Jiangxi, July 1990.

Ma, Zuyi 馬祖毅.《英漢翻譯技巧淺談》 (*On the Technique of Translation from English into Chinese*). Nanjing: Jiangsu People's Press 江蘇人民出版社, 1980.

Mao, Zedong 毛澤東,〈新民主主義論〉 "On New Democracy".《毛澤東選集》 (*Selected Works of Mao Zedong*), Chinese ed. Beijing: People's Press 北京人民出版社, 1952; English ed., Beijing: Foreign Languages Press 北京外文出版社, 1965.

Yao, Shanyou 姚善友.《英語語法》 (*English Grammar*). Beijing: The Commercial Press 商務印書館, 1964.

Zandvoort, R. W. *A Handbook of English Grammar*. Bristol: Western Printing Services Ltd, 1957.

Zhang, Daozhen 張道眞.《實用英語語法》 (*A Practical English Grammar*). Beijing: The Commercial Press 商務印書館, 1981.

STANDARDS

Translation Quality Assessment

Juliane House
Zentrales Fremdspracheninstitut
University of Hamburg, Hamburg, Germany

Introduction

The essence of translation lies in the preservation of the "meaning" of linguistic units as they are transferred from one language and culture to another. In assessing the quality of a given translation one sets out to determine how this "meaning" has actually been preserved in the translated text. The nature of one's conception of the "meaning" of linguistic items — the largest of them being the text itself — will then be crucial in determining the mode of the assessment of the quality of a translation.

Given the fact that translation always operates on concrete instances of language-in-use (stretches of discourse or text), conceptions of meaning based on theories of language in use, which stress the importance of the context enveloping a linguistic unit, are especially relevant for translation. Such views of meaning have been held in several European and North American linguistic schools: the Prague school of language and linguistics with its particular emphasis on functional styles and functional sentence perspective; sociolinguists and sociologists of language investigating the users and uses of language varieties; cross-cultural pragmatic and communication analysts providing descriptions and interpretations of culturally conditioned differences in linguistic behaviour patterns; British contextualists stressing the role of the "context of situation" in linguistic description, and providing delicate analyses of registers and styles.

In the following, a model for translation quality assessment is presented, which is eclectically based on pragmatic theories of language use such as the ones referred to above. Before the model is laid out in detail, a brief review of alternative approaches to judging the quality of a translation is given.

Selected Approaches to Translation Quality Assessment

Pre-linguistic Approaches

There is a long tradition of anecdotal discussions on the subject of translation quality offered by professional translators, philosophers, philologists, novelists and poets. In these treatises and essays, the status and importance of broadly general criteria such as "faithfulness to the original", "retention of the original's spirit" on the one hand as opposed to "a natural flow of the translation" and "the pleasure of the reader" on the other hand were discussed by means of a large array of examples. (Cary and Jumpelt, 1963; Savory, 1968). Vague, subjective and ultimately unverifiable statements of opinions abound in these writings on translation quality assessment suggesting for example that a good translation should not read like one, or pointing to a mysterious connection between the personalities of the author, the translator and the addressees, audience and the resultant quality of the translation.

In general, what characterizes such intuitive and random treatments of judging a translation's quality is the denial of the possibility of establishing rules or principles for translation quality coupled with endless listings of supposedly unique translation examples and expositions of the difficulties of optimal renderings in a variety of target languages.

In the more recent literature, vague if common-sense criteria which obviously render it difficult for the assessor to make transparent and justify his judgment are still being suggested, e.g. by Newmark (1988), who gives overly broad guidelines for evaluating translations, seriously considering "taste" as an important subjective element in arriving at a judgment of a translation, or by Stolze (1982) who is sceptical about the possibilities of objective comparisons of source and translation texts, offering as a (dubious) alternative the translator's participation in the expression of human experience as a general yardstick.

In summary, the tradition of denying the feasibility of setting up criteria for translation quality assessment which are intersubjectively valid and transparent stresses the belief that the quality of a translation depends most importantly on the "human factor", i.e., the translator's personal and subjective decisions based as they are on his (often idiosyncratic) linguistic/cultural intuitions.

Psycholinguistic, Response-based Approaches

As with the anecdotal approach, in this type of studies as well, broadly general principles to be heeded in optimal translations are set up as norms. Nida's three criteria for assessing the quality of a translation are examples of response-based, programmatic and very general criteria: "(1) general efficiency of the communication process, (2) comprehension of intent, (3) equivalence of response" (Nida, 1964). The third, the most important criterion for translation quality assessment is, of course, closely related to Nida's famous and influential principle of the "Dynamic Equivalence of a Translation" , i.e., for an optimal translation, it is posited that the manner in which receptors of the original respond to it must be equivalent to the manner in which receptors of the translation text respond to the translation text. "Equivalent" is different from identical, in that responses can obviously never be the same given different cultural, historical and situational settings.

While it is true that a translation should produce a response which is equivalent to the one elicited by the translation text, it remains an open question whether it is, in fact, possible to empirically test the nature of a response. If this cannot be reliably and validly done, it seems fruitless to postulate the equivalence-of-response principle, i.e., this principle is of no more value than the vague criteria of "fidelity" and "retention of the spirit of the original" cited above. Three similar criteria are given by Nida and Taber (1969): (1) the correctness with which the receptors understand the message of the original, (2) the ease of this understanding as well as (3) the involvement a person experiences as a result of a translation's formal adequacy. These behavioral criteria were made more concrete using the following tests: a cloze test, in which the degree of comprehensibility of a text is related to its "degree of predictability"; eliciting respondents' reactions to several translation alternatives; reading-aloud of the translation text to some other person, who will then be asked to explain its content to several other persons who were not present at the first reading of the text; reading-aloud of a translated text by different persons before an audience when places in the text where readers encounter difficulties in the reading of the text are taken as indicators of translational problems. In all these tests, there is no reference to the original text; consequently, there is no norm or basis for comparative judgments, and, in general, the basic problem of response measurability is not solved.

Other behavioristic methods, in which observable, verifiable responses are taken as indicators of the quality of a translation have also been suggested in the 1960s, e.g., by Carroll (1966) or MacNamara (1967). These methods include the elicitation of the opinions of experts; measuring a translation against a "criterion translation"; asking comprehension questions of respondents who had been exposed to either the original or the translation, and comparing the answers; using rating scales for intelligibility and informativeness as the basis for evaluation.

The limitations of these suggestions seem to be the following: (1) equating overall quality of a translation with degrees of informativeness is somewhat reductionistic, (2) the assumption that a "criterion translation" exists, creates more problems than it solves, since the basic problem of establishing "criteria of excellence" for the criterion translation still remains. Such criteria cannot be taken for granted as, e.g., the tests involving expert judges seem to presuppose; rather their development constitutes the crux of translation quality assessment, (3) no provision is made for a norm against which the results of any behavioral test could be measured. This norm can only be supplied by the source text. Proposals for assessing the quality of a translation by taking into account the peculiarities of the source text will be briefly reviewed in the next section.

Source Text-based Approaches

Wilss (1982) makes the programmatic statement that a model is needed for the linguistic description and analysis of the source text and an evaluation of the translation text in terms of deviations from the source text on syntactic, semantic and pragmatic levels. He maintains that the concept of a "norm of usage" in a language community with reference to a given situational context and the deviations from that norm are of particular significance for translation quality assessment. A translation may then be judged according to whether or not it is adequate vis à vis the normal standard usage of native speakers in the instance of the text on hand. However, the situational context in which the source text was written is unique, and therefore the notion of a norm existing in the source culture is implausible. Even less plausible is the assumption of a norm for this unique text in the target culture. Koller (1983) calls for a three-stage-model for evaluating translations: (1) critical analysis of the source text with a view to transferability, (2) translation comparison in which the methods employed in producing different translations are described, (3) native speaker assessments of the translation according to whether text-specific features established in (1) are adequately realized or not. Unfortunately, these innovative ideas remain programmatic only.

One of the most influential suggestions for taking the source text as a yardstick for translation quality assessment was put forward by Reiss (1978). Reiss assumes that in attempting to judge a translation one has to first determine the function of the source text and its textual type. She claims that different types of texts can be differentiated on the basis of Bühler's three functions of language postulating content-oriented, form-oriented and conative texts. According to Reiss, it is these textual types which have to be kept equivalent in an adequate translation. In order to determine the textual type, the source text must be analyzed carefully. However, despite the numerous examples cited, Reiss fails to indicate how exactly function and type of a text are to be established.

In Reiss and Vermeer (1984), a more extensive "Skopos-theory" is presented, its crucial postulate being that any translation is first and foremost a function of its "skopos" (purpose). Given the primacy of the purpose for which a translation is produced, the most important yardstick in evaluating a translation is the degree to which target culture norms are being heeded. Equivalence and adequacy of a translation are distinguished, equivalence obtaining whenever source and target text fulfill the same communicative function, and adequacy referring to the relation between original and translation whenever there is no functional match between source and target texts. There are no precise linguistic guidelines given as to the method of establishing the presence of equivalence or adequacy, or to the precise relationship between individual parts of the text and its global purpose.

What is needed for intersubjectively verifiable translation criticism is a model which goes beyond programmatic statements and provides guidelines for a linguistic description of whether and how a translation is equivalent with or deviates from its source text. One such attempt at setting up an assessment model (House, 1981) is described below.

A Model for Translation Quality Assessment Based on Pragmatic Theories of Language Use

The Original Model

Translation is defined as the replacement of a text in the source language by a semantically and pragmatically equivalent text in the target language. The pragmatic aspect of meaning has overriding importance in translation, i.e. it is essential to aim at equivalence of pragmatic meaning, if necessary, at the expense of semantic meaning. In this definition of translation, the term "equivalent" is the key term, and the concept of equivalence is also taken to be the fundamental criterion of translation quality. Thus, an adequate translation text is a pragmatically and semantically equivalent one. As a first requirement for this equivalence, it is posited that a translation text has a function equivalent to that of its source text. Such a use of the concept of function presupposes that there are elements in any text which — given appropriate analytical tools — can reveal that text's function.

The use of the term "function" in this context is open to misinterpretation, mainly because different language functions can co-exist inside what will here be described as an individual text's function and because language functions have often been directly correlated with textual types. Many different classification schemes for the "functions of language" have been proposed, but most of them can be reduced to a basic division into a cognitive-referential (content-oriented) function and a non-cognitive (emotive-expressive, person- or interaction-oriented) function. While these two broad functional categories cannot be used to establish a functional-textual typology for translation such that any text exhibits a predominant function (as has been suggested by Reiss and others, see above), they are useful as a basis for providing convenient labels for the two components of a text's function, which are always co-present and will be referred to as the *ideational* and the *interpersonal* functional component (cf. Halliday, 1973).

The function of an individual text is defined rather differently from those "functions of language": it is the application or use which the text has in the context of a situation. Any text is embedded in a unique situation. From this it follows that in order to characterize its textual function precisely, a text must be analyzed at the appropriate level of delicacy. For the particular purpose of establishing functional equivalence between a source text and a translation text, the source text has to be analyzed first, such that the equivalence which is sought for the translation text can be stated precisely. Since textual function was defined as the use of a text in a particular situation, each individual text must be referred to the particular situation enveloping it and for this, a way must then be found for breaking down the broad notion of "situation" into manageable parts, i.e. various "situational dimensions". Crystal and Davy's (1969) elaborate system of situational dimensions may be taken as a starting point for the purposes of correlating situations and texts. An adaptation of their scheme led to the following set of situational dimensions:

1. Dimensions of Language User
   a. Geographical Origin
   b. Social Class
   c. Time
2. Dimensions of Language Use
   a. Medium: simple
                    complex
   b. Participation: simple
                        complex
   c. Social Role Relationship
   d. Social Attitude
   e. Province

The language user dimensions simply relate to the text producer's geographical, social class and temporal origins. The dimensions of language use, however, are less obvious and need some more explanation:

Medium: this category refers to spoken or written language with "simple" referring to the use of either spoken or written language without any switch among the two modes (e.g., written to be read), and "complex" referring to language which is marked by some kind of switch to the alternative mode, e.g. written to be spoken as if not "written" (as in a play) or simply "written to be spoken" (as in a draft of a speech) (cf. Gregory, 1967). In determining features of the spoken mode in a given source text, phenomena such as structural simplicity, incompleteness of sentences, specific manner of text constitution (in particular theme-rheme sequencing), subjectivity (marked e.g. by the use of modal particles and gambits) and high redundancy are taken into account.

Participation may also be simple or complex, i.e. a text may be either a "simple" monologue or dialogue, or a more "complex" mixture involving, in an overt monologue, various means of participation elicitation and indirect addressee involvement manifest linguistically e.g., in a characteristic use of pronouns, switches between declarative, imperative and interrogative sentence patterns or the presence of contact parentheses.

Social Role Relationship is a dimension characterizing the role relationship between text producer and addressee(s), which may be either symmetrical (marked by the existence of solidarity or equality) or asymmetrical (marked by the presence of some kind of authority). In considering the addresser's social role vis à vis the addressee(s), further, account is taken of the relatively permanent position role (teacher, priest) and the more transient situational role (visitor in a prison, speaker at a given occasion).

Social Attitude describes the degree of social distance or proximity resulting in relative formality or informality. Distinctions of different styles such as the classic schema suggested by Joos (1961), which consists of five different levels of formality: frozen, formal, consultative, casual and intimate, provide useful schema for analysis of a text along this situational dimension.

The dimension of *Province* is a very broadly defined one referring not only to the text producer's occupational and professional activity but also to the field or topic of the text in its widest sense of "area of operation" of the language activity, as well as details of the text production as these can be deduced from the text itself (the notion of "register" is relevant here).

Returning to the earlier discussion of a textual function which is to be kept equivalent in translation, it is now posited that the function of a text can be determined by opening up the linguistic material (the text) in terms of this set of situational constraints.

The evidence in the text which characterizes it on any one particular dimension is, of course, itself linguistic evidence. This linguistic evidence is broken down into three types: syntactic, lexical and textual.

The situational dimensions and their linguistic correlates are then considered to be the means by which the text's function is realized, i.e. the function of a text is established as a result of an analysis of the text along the eight situational dimensions as outlined above. The basic criterion of functional match for translation equivalence can now be refined: a translation text should not only match its source text in function, but employ equivalent situational-dimensional means to achieve that function, i.e. for a translation of optimal quality, it is desirable to have a match between source and translation text along these dimensions which are found — in the course of the analysis — to contribute in a particular way to each of the two functional components, ideational and interpersonal, of the text's function. By using situational dimensions for opening up the source text, a particular textual profile is obtained for the source text. This profile which characterizes the function of the text is then the norm against which the quality of the translation text is to be measured, i.e. a given translation text is analyzed using the same dimensional scheme and at the same level of delicacy, and the degree to which its textual profile and function match or do not match the source text's is the degree to which the translation text is adequate in quality.

If a translation text, in order to be adequate, is to fulfill the requirement of a dimensional, and as a result of this, a functional match, then any mismatch along the dimensions is an error. Such dimensional errors are referred to as *covert errors*. These are to be differentiated from those *overt errors* which result either from a mismatch of the denotative meanings of source and translation text elements or from a breach of the target language system. Overt errors have traditionally been given more attention, whereas covert errors, which demand a much more qualitative-descriptive in-depth analysis, have often been neglected. The relative weighting of individual errors both within the two categories and across them is a problem which varies from individual text to individual text.

The final qualitative judgment of a translation text consists, then, of a listing of both covert and overt errors and of a statement about the relative match of the ideational and the interpersonal functional components. The notion that a mismatch on a particular situational dimension constitutes a covert error presupposes:

1. that the socio-cultural norms, or more specifically the norm-conditioned expectations generated by the texts, are essentially comparable. Obvious differences in the unique cultural heritage must, of course, be stated explicitly and discussed in each particular text.

2. that the differences between the two languages are such that they can largely be overcome in translation.

3. that no special second function is added to the translation text, i.e. works translated for special purposes or special audiences are

excluded. Such translations are no longer translations but will be defined as overt versions of an original text. Given these three presuppositions, it is thus assumed that the addressees of a translation text form a basically similar sub-group in the target community to the sub-group formed by the addressees of the source text in the source language community, both being defined as speakers of the contemporary standard language, i.e. that supra-regional variety which is (commonly) used by the educated middle class speaker and which is at the same time accepted by the majority of the whole language community.

In House (1981), the above model of translation quality assessment is tried out with a corpus of eight English and German textual pairs, four belonging to the ideational functional category, and four to the interpersonal functional category. The texts cover a wide range of different "provinces": a scientific text, an economic text, a journalistic article and a tourist information brochure make up the ideational set of texts; an excerpt from a sermon, a political speech, a moral anecdote and a dialogue taken from a comedy belong to the interpersonal set of texts.

Refinement of the Model and Distinction between Two Types of Translation

On the basis of the results of an analysis of these eight test cases, a distinction between two types of translation — which is crucial for the evaluation of translations — is suggested: *overt translation* and *covert translation*.

(1) *Overt Translation*

An overt translation is one in which the addressees of the translation text are quite "overtly" not being directly addressed : thus, an overt translation is one which must overtly be a translation, not, as it were, a "second original". In an overt translation, the source text is tied in a specific manner to the source language community and its culture. The source text is specifically directed at source culture addressees but at the same time points beyond the source language community because it is, independent of its source language origin, also of potential general human interest. Source texts that call for an overt translation have an established worth or status in the source language community and potentially in other communities. Such source texts may be divided into two groups:

a. overt historically-linked source texts, i.e., those tied to a specific occasion in which a precisely specified source language audience is/was being addressed. An example from the test sample mentioned above is a political speech given by Winston Churchill on the steps of the townhall in Bradford in 1942.

b. overt timeless source texts, i.e., those transcending as works of art and aesthetic creations a distinct historical meaning while, of course, always necessarily displaying period and culture specificity because of the status of the addresser, who is a product of his time and culture. Such (mostly literary) texts although timeless and transmitting a general human message are culture-specific because they are marked on the language user dimensions (presence of a particular temporal dialect and a geographical dialect respectively) and because they have independent status in the language community through belonging to the community's cultural products.

Both groups of source texts, historically-linked and timeless ones, then, necessitate an overt translation. The requirements for this type of translation lead to an important modification of the model of translation quality assessment as outlined earlier: a direct match of the original function of the source text is not possible in overt translation, either because the source text is tied to a specific non-repeatable historic event in the source culture or because of the unique status (as a literary text) that the source text has in the source culture.

In cases of overt translation, a similar second-level function, i.e., a kind of "topicalization" of the original function may have to be posited as a criterion for adequate translation. This second-level function is then the function holding for the contemporary standard language speaker of the target culture and frequently also for their potential counterparts in the source culture, who may not be the original addressees either.

In overt translation, the source text as a piece of work with a certain status in the source language community must remain as intact as possible, given the necessary transfer and recoding in another language. On the other hand, cases of overt translation present difficulties precisely because their status in the socio-cultural context of the source language community, which must be topicalized in the target culture, necessitates major changes.

It is this dialectical relationship between preservation and alteration which makes the finding of translation equivalence difficult in cases of overt translation.

(2) *Covert Translation*

A covert translation is a translation which enjoys or enjoyed the status of an original source text in the target culture. The translation is covert because it is not marked pragmatically as a translation text of a source text, but may, conceivably, have been created in its own right. A covert translation is thus a translation whose source text is not specifically addressed to a particular source culture audience, i.e., it is not particularly tied to the source language and culture. A source text and its covert translation text are pragmatically of equal concern for source and target language addressees. Both are, as it were, equally directly addressed. A source text and its covert translation have equivalent purposes, they are based on contemporary, equivalent needs of a comparable audience in the source and target language communities. In the case of covert translation texts, it is thus both possible and desirable to keep the function of the source text equivalent in the translation text.

In the sample texts analysed in House (1981), a scientific text (an excerpt from a coursebook in mathematics), an economic text (a letter written by the President of an international investment company to the shareholders), a journalistic text (an article on anthropology, which appeared in a popular magazine) and a tourist information booklet (advertising brochure on Nürnberg) exemplify the category of source texts necessitating a covert translation. All these translation texts have direct target language addressees, for whom they are as immediately and "originally" relevant as is the source text for the source language addressees.

In the case of the economic text in the test sample, for instance, both source and target language addressees are shareholders of the same investment company, i.e. they differ only accidentally in their respective mother tongues.

While it is thus clear that such texts are not source-culture specific, it is the covert type of translation they require which presents more difficult, and more subtle, cultural translation problems than those encountered in the case of overt translation, where the particular source culture specificity had to be either left intact and presented as a culturally and historically linked monument, or overtly matched in the target culture setting. If the source text and its translation text are to have truly equivalent functions, which is necessary in a covert translation, the translator has to take different cultural presuppositions in the two language communities into account in order to meet the needs of the target language addressees in their cultural setting, and in order to achieve an effect equivalent to the source text's effect. In a covert translation, the translator has to make allowances for underlying cultural differences by placing a *cultural filter* between the source text and the translation text; he has to, as it were, view the source text through the glasses of a target culture member.

Given the goal of achieving functional equivalence in a covert translation, assumptions of cultural difference should be carefully examined before any change in the source text is undertaken. In cases of unproven assumptions of cultural differences, the translator may be led to apply a cultural filter whose application resulting in possibly deliberate mismatches between the source text and the translation text along several situational parameters, is not justified. If a covert translation makes allowance, unwarrantedly and in a patterned way, for the target culture group's different presuppositions about the *Social Role Relationship* and *Social Attitude* of addressees vis à vis the addresser in a particular *Province*, then such a translation is no longer a translation but will be defined as a *covert version*. A covert version is by definition an inadequate translation in that the application of the cultural filter is unjustified.

Covert versions must be clearly differentiated from *overt versions* which result whenever a special function is (overtly) added to the translation text. This special function can involve cases in which the translation text is to reach a special audience (e.g., special editions for a youthful audience with the resultant omissions, simplifications, different accentuations of certain features of the source text etc.) or it can involve cases in which the translation text is given a special added purpose, e.g., resumés or abstracts, where it is the special purpose of the version producer to pass on only the most essential facts.

In the discussion of different types of translation and the distinction between a translation and a version, it was implicitly assumed that a particular text may be adequately translated in only one particular way. The assumption that a particular text necessitates either an overt or a covert translation may, however, not hold in every case. Thus, any text may, for specific purposes, require an overt translation, i.e., it may be viewed as a document which "has independent status" and exists in its own right: for instance, a commercial circular may be cited as evidence in a court of law, or its author may, in the course of time, prove to be a distinguished political or literary figure. In these two instances, the texts would clearly not have an equivalent function in translation, i.e., in both cases an overt translation would be appropriate, and it should be evaluated as such.

Further, there may well be source texts for which the choice overt-or-covert translation is a subjective one, e.g. fairy tales may be viewed as folk products of a particular culture, which would predispose a translator to opt for an overt translation, or as non-culture specific texts, anonymously produced, with the general function of entertaining and educating the young, which would suggest a covert translation; or consider the case of the Bible, which may be treated as either a collection of historical literary documents, in which case an overt translation would seem to be called for, or as a collection of human truths directly relevant to Everyman, in which case a covert translation might seem appropriate.

It is clear that the specific purpose for which a "translation" is required will determine whether a translation or an overt version should be aimed at. In other words, just as the decision as to whether an overt or a covert translation is appropriate for a particular text may be conditioned by factors such as the changeable status of the text producer, so clearly the initial choice between translating a given source text and producing a version of it, cannot be made on the basis of features of the text, but is conditioned by the arbitrarily determined purpose for which the translation/ version is required.

The comparative assessment of different translation texts of the same source text can be conducted on the basis of the evaluative model outlined above to the extent that the relative importance of the individual situational dimensions has been demonstrated in the analysis of the source text. A relative weighting of covert and overt errors can only be achieved through a consideration of each individual textual pair. However, the subgroup of overt errors referred to as "mismatches of the denotative meanings of elements of the source and translation texts", will detract more seriously from the quality of a translation text, whenever the source text has a strongly marked ideational functional component, e.g., mismatches of the denotative meaning of items in a science text are likely to be rated higher than a mismatch on *Social Attitude*.

A detailed hierarchy of errors for any individual case can, however, only be given for a particular comparison of two or more texts depending in any particular case on the objectives of the evaluation.

Conclusion

In translation quality assessment, an overt translation must be distinguished from a covert one, and translations must be distinguished from versions. It is through these different categories that the nature of the equivalence required for a translation of optimal quality can be better understood and described. Although the basic requirement for equivalence of a source text and a translation text is that the translation text has a function which is equivalent to the source text's function, it is only in cases of covert translation that it is possible to achieve an equivalent function in a translation text. In cases of overt translation, a similar second-level function must be posited as a criterion for adequate translation.

The type of text- (or product-) based approach suggested in the assessment presented above has recently been supplemented by attempts to take account of the process of translation, i.e., seeking to access what goes on in the heads of translators by using introspective methods such as asking subjects to think aloud while translating or making them retrospectively reflect on what they had been doing in translating. (House and Blum-Kulka, 1986; House, 1988). Such introspections might be useful in an attempt to substantiate the assessments along the individual situational dimensions provided in the evaluation model outlined above: asking the translator to give reasons for his choices will put the assessor in a better position to differentiate between conscious or motivated translational decisions and unconscious, automatic transfer moves. Especially in the case of covert versions, the occurrence of changes along the parameters of language use might be better understood, explained and/or justified if one attempts to make the underlying process of ongoing source text analysis and translational choices more transparent by asking the translator to produce "verbal reports" of these activities.

This psycholinguistic approach, which relies on methods of investigating what goes on in the minds of translators, is complemented by a cross-cultural pragmatic line of inquiry, where the theoretical notion of a "cultural filter" posited in the assessment model by House (1981) is given some empirical substance in a number of recent contrastive and interlanguage pragmatic analyses (Blum-Kulka, House and Kasper, 1989). A combination of psycholinguistic and contrastive pragmatic analyses is attempted in House (1990), in which cases of cross-cultural pragmatic failure and misunderstandings are traced via retrospective reports to unsuccessful instances of covert translation. For future studies of translation quality assessment, a broad interdisciplinary approach to investigating why and how a translation is good or bad seems to be the most promising one to take.

References

Blum-Kulka, Shoshana, Juliane House and G. Kasper, eds. *Cross-cultural Pragmatics*. Norwood, N. J.: Ablex, 1989.

Carroll, J. B. "An Experiment in Evaluating the Quality of Translations." *Mechanical Translation*, Vol. 9 (1966), pp. 5–66.

Cary, Edmond, R. W. and R. Walter Jumpelt. *Quality in Translation*. New York: Macmillan, 1965.

Catford, J. C. *A Linguistic Theory of Translation*. Oxford: Oxford University Press, 1965.

Crystal, David and Derek Davy. *Investigating English Style*. London: Longman, 1969.

Gregory, M. "Aspects of Varieties Differentiation." *Journal of Linguistics*, No. 3 (1967), pp. 177–98.

Halliday, M. A. K. *Explorations in the Functions of Language*. London: Arnold, 1973.

House, Juliane. "Cross-cultual Pragmatic Failure: From Mistranslation to Misunderstanding." In *Übersetzungswissenschaft. Ergebnisse und Perspektiven*, edited by R. Arntz and G. Thome. Tübingen: Gunter Narr Verlag, 1990, pp. 315–25.

———. *A Model for Translation Quality Assessment*, 2nd ed. Tübingen: Gunter Narr Verlag, 1981.

———. "Talking to Oneself or Thinking with Others? On Using Different Thinking Aloud Methods in Translation." *Fremdsprachen Lehren und Lernen*, Vol. 17 (1988), pp. 84–98.

——— and Shoshana Blum-Kulka, eds. *Interlingual and Intercultural Communication: Discourse and Cognition in Translation and Second Language Acquisition Studies*. Tübingen: Gunter Narr Verlag, 1986.

Joos, M. *The Five Clocks*. New York: Harcourt, Brace and World, 1961.

Koller, W. *Einführung in die Übersetzungswissenschaft*, 2nd ed. Heidelberg: Quelle und Meyer, 1983.

MacNamara, J. "The Bilingual's Linguistic Performance: A Psychological Overview." *The Journal of Social Psychology*, Vol. 23 (1967), pp. 58–77.

Newmark, Peter. *A Textbook of Translation*. New York: Prentice Hall, 1988.

Nida, Eugene A. *Toward A Science of Translating*. Leiden: E. J. Brill, 1964.

——— and Charles R. Taber. *The Theory and Practice of Translation*. Leiden: E. J. Brill, 1969.

Reiss, Katharina. *Möglichkeiten und Grenzen der Übersetzungskritik*, 2nd ed. München: Hueber, 1978.

———. "Quality in Translation oder wann ist eine Übersetzung gut?" *Babel*, No. 4 (1983), pp. 198–208.

——— and Hans J. Vermeer. *Grundlegung einer allgemeinen Translationstheorie*. Tübingen: Niemeyer, 1984.

Savory, Theodore. *The Art of Translation*. Boston: The Writer, 1968.

Stolze, Radequndis. *Grundlagen der Textübersetzung*. Heidelberg: Quelle und Meyer, 1982.

Wilss, Wolfram. *The Science of Translation: Problems and Methods*. Tübingen: Gunter Narr Verlag, 1982.

Translation Standards

Wang Zuoliang
Beijing Foreign Studies University, Beijing, China

What constitutes excellence in translation? The answer made by Yan Fu at the start of a great era of translation in modern China has had a lasting effect. Writing in 1898 in the preface to his own translation of Thomas Henry Huxley's *Evolution and Ethics*, Yan laid down this criterion:

> Translation has to do three difficult things: to be faithful, expressive and elegant. For a translation to be faithful to the original is difficult enough, and yet if it is not expressive, it is tantamount to having no translation. Hence expressiveness should also be required....

> The *Book of Changes* says that rhetoric should uphold truthfulness. Confucius says that expressiveness is all that matters in language. He adds that if one's language lacks grace, it will not travel far. These qualities, then, are the criterion of good writing and, I believe, of good translation too. Hence besides faithfulness and expressiveness, a translator should also aim at elegance. (Luo, 1984:136)

Thus the famous three-point standard for a good translation. What lent authority to the pronouncement was Yan's own success as a practitioner, for besides Huxley's work, he also rendered into elegant classical Chinese Adam Smith's *Wealth of Nations*, Montesquieu's *Spirit of Law*, John Stuart Mill's *On Liberty* and *System of Logic*, Herbert Spencer's *Principles of Sociology*, etc., all basic books of modern Western thought. There is a lot more in the preface — such as Yan's explanation why he did not go in for a word-for-word or even sentence-for-sentence translation but had resorted to paraphrase in many cases — but it is the three points that have come to exert a tremendous influence on almost all later translators and writers on translation in China.

This standard, agreed to by nearly everybody, has nevertheless occasioned endless controversies. Even the point about faithfulness to the original has been disputed. Faithful to what, it has been asked, to the letter or spirit of the original? In the early 1930s, the question was hotly debated between two schools of translators, those who went in for "smooth" rendering and those who practised literal translation. The former found their spokesman in Zhao Jingshen 趙景深, who argued that since readers cared above all for something easy to read, he would not mind a few departures from the original so long as he could produce a smooth version. Thus he would "rearrange Yan's three points in a new order, as follows: expressiveness, faithfulness, elegance." (Luo, 1984:267) The latter included the eminent writer Lu Xun and the communist ideologue Qu Qiubai 瞿秋白, who not only upheld faithfulness as the first principle, but gave it a new interpretation. For they would equate faithfulness with literalness, and literalness included the reproduction in Chinese of the sentence structure and word order of the original — and this for a good reason:

> A literal translation introduces not only new subject matter, but also new ways of expression. The Chinese language, whether written or spoken, is too imprecise.... To remedy that, we will have to undergo a little ordeal, that is, to bring in bizarre ways of constructing sentences — ancient, outlandish, foreign ways, incorporating them into our language. (Luo, 1984:276)

Thus Lu Xun. His friend Qu Qiubai would go even further:

> Our demand is: absolute accuracy and absolute vernacular. By the latter I mean the language used must be intelligible to all when read aloud. (Luo, 1984:276)

He too believed in the necessity of introducing new linguistic elements, but with this proviso:

> To create new ways of expression, they must fulfil one condition, namely, they can all be spoken. (Luo, 1984:281)

This is asserted vis-à-vis the archaic prose used by Yan Fu as well as the sort of half-bookish, half-vernacular, "lackey's lingo" spouted by Zhao Jingshen and others.

Qu also disposed of "elegance", another much disputed point. By elegance Yan Fu had meant the use of "the vocabulary and syntax of the era before the Han dynasty" which he insisted "could express subtle thoughts better than latter-day journalese," though his real purpose was to attract the mandarin-scholars, "those who read ancient classics." This became an untenable position after the language reform of 1919, when 白話 or the spoken language replaced 文言 or classical Chinese in most publications. In any case, if the original is not written in a deliberately archaic style, then any attempt at giving it an antique glow in the translation amounts to a violation of Yan's first principle, namely, faithfulness. Hence Qu Qiubai's observation: "In espousing elegance, Yan wiped out faithfulness and expressiveness." (Luo, 1984:267) Still, the dispute went on unabated about what constitutes elegance and, indeed, whether elegance should be made a criterion at all. Obviously, a good deal depends on the nature of the original. If the original is not elegant in language, stylistic embellishments would be quite out of place. And in certain kinds of writing, such as philosophical works, a translator is often obliged to combat the very idea of elegance. Professor Chen Kang 陳康 , after translating Plato's "Parmenides", sums up his experience thus:

> Faithfulness is our unshakable fundamental principle.... Our translation cannot but be literal. Being literal, it is often inelegant, even unidiomatic. Whenever it becomes impossible to take care of both meaning and language, our self-imposed rule is: keep the meaning even at the expense of the language, not the other way round. True, there is the adage: "If language lacks grace, it will not travel far," but we could add: "If language exceeds substance, the farther it travels the more humiliating it becomes." (Luo, 1984:445)

He, too, has a reason why inelegance is often unavoidable:

> The purpose of translating philosophical writings is to convey ideas unknown to one's native land. However, the words and expressions of a particular language are accustomed to express, as indeed they can only express, ideas already in that language. Hence if we adhere absolutely to the principle of faithfulness and yet want to express in words and expressions already familiar to us ideas that have never occurred in our land, we will be trying to do the impossible. In such cases, either you sacrifice ideas, or you sacrifice language. (Luo, 1984:444)

Substantially the same reason as advanced by Lu Xun, namely, new ideas require new expressions, however inelegant. At the same time, it should be pointed out that in all these disputes, no one went so far as to champion inelegance as a virtue. It may be unavoidable, even inevitable, yet not really desirable. In actual practice, even when translating difficult treatises on literary theory by Soviet ideologues, Lu Xun tried to make his versions as readable as possible.

Elegance, then, must be considered in the context of faithfulness. Later discussions tended to see all three points as interrelated. In a way, that was

Yan's original position; he had written: "All this effort is to achieve expressiveness and to be expressive is really to be faithful" 凡此經營，皆以爲達；爲達，即所以爲信也 . After years of discussion and — even more important — of practice there has emerged a clearer, more integrated view, summed up by Qian Zhongshu 錢鍾書 thus:

> Faithfulness in translation should include expressiveness. Expressiveness gives full scope to faithfulness, and elegance is not just to adorn expressiveness. To convey the meaning of the original in the same style — that is faithfulness. (Luo, 1984:23)

This may be taken as a *modus vivendi*. In recent years, there have been signs of a growing weariness with the perpetual wrangle about the three points and discussions have moved on in two directions. First, the specific standards for different genres of writing. Modern stylistics has shed light on the special features — phonetic, lexical and syntactic — of such different kinds of writing as scientific papers, advertisements, public notices, news reports and such varied utterances as sermons, speeches, sports commentaries, telephone conversations, etc. Obviously each requires a different standard. Sociolinguistics has for its part added a new dimension to the discussion of "equivalents" in translation by emphasizing the social or cultural factor: different speech communities have different ways of addressing people, being polite or rude, crying their wares, showing their approval or displeasure, etc. In such cases, a literal translation would often be misleading, if not fatal, and the suggested solution is: find the usage pertaining to the particular "variety" in the target language.

Second, the total effect of a translation of a literary work. This question came to the fore when some signal successes had been registered in practice — notably the translation of the works of Shakespeare by Zhu Shenghao 朱生豪 and that of the novels of Balzac by Fu Lei 傅雷 . Both are considered models of literary translation — accurate, readable, done in a Chinese that combines vigour with grace. Both translators speak in disfavour of the stiff, word-for-word translation and would strive for "resemblance in spirit" 神似 . Specifically, this means, in Fu Lei's words:

> To strive for resemblance in spirit, not in appearance, the translator must write pure Chinese, not something stiff and awkward, but a language which can be read aloud harmoniously in a rhythm and tempo akin to the original. (Luo, 1984:694)

Here the concern is no longer with the three points, which are taken for granted, but reaches a higher plane where more stringent demands are made on the translator. Two prerequisites stand out: an intimate understanding of the original, all the nuances and overtones in it, and a supple use of the target language. Neither of which is easy to achieve. Fu Lei's striving for "resemblance in spirit" had only a limited success in his own translations — certainly his range of vocabulary and mastery of demotic language falls short of Balzac's rich, protean French — and for most others it has remained only an ideal.

Neither can "appearance" be ignored altogether. For verse translators, there are stanzaic forms and rhyme schemes to consider. Even the sonnet, Shakespearean or otherwise, has been reproduced with its intricate pattern intact. Here certainly the Chinese classical tradition of excellent short poems has helped. The most valiant effort has been made by poets who would not rest until they had translated Shakespeare's poetic dramas into suitable Chinese verse, for good as Zhu Shenghao's versions, mentioned above, are, they are prose renderings. After decades of persistent work, the erstwhile modernist poet Bian Zhilin 卞之琳 has been able to establish a Chinese verse line of five metrical units, punctuated by five pauses, as an equivalent to the English iambic pentameter and with this he started to translate *Hamlet* in 1954, followed by *Othello* (1956), *Lear* (1977) and *Macbeth* (1983), finally published together as *Four Tragedies of Shakespeare* in 1988, a labour of over thirty years. And a crowning success, too, for here we see verse used as Shakespeare meant to use it — as a dramatic medium for dramatic effects. Another recent achievement is the translation by Zha Liangzhen 查良錚 of Byron's *Don Juan*, all sixteen cantos of it in stanzas of eight lines each, with a rhyme scheme close to the original *ottava rima*. Again it is a poet's work, which not only keeps the form or "appearance" of Byron's verse, but manages to catch its spirit too — the wit, the vivacity, the cynicism, the ardour in love and war, the whole spectrum of the young lord's moods and yearnings.

By now we can leave translation standards behind, for we have come to the point where aesthetics takes over.

Reference

Luo, Xinzhang 羅新璋 , ed. 《翻譯論集》 (*Essays on Translation*). Beijing: The Commercial Press 商務印書館 , 1984.

Subtitling

Henrik Gottlieb
Center for Translation Studies and Lexicography
University of Copenhagen, Copenhagen, Denmark

Subtitling in a Historical Perspective

Subtitling as a means of film translation dates back to 1929, when the new sound films reached an international audience. The method of adding strips of translated dialog to moving pictures was invented as an inexpensive alternative to postsynchronization, or dubbing. In subtitling, the original dialog remains an integral part of the film, while in dubbing, it is replaced by more or less lip-synchronous dialog in the target language.

When in the 1930s dubbing became the preferred mode of film translation in the world's big-market speech communities, subtitling proved to be the only viable technique in several minor European speech communities, such as Finland, Norway, Sweden, Denmark, the Netherlands, and Flemish-speaking Belgium. Small countries without a national language of their own — as for example Switzerland and Austria — tended to share their neighbors' pro-dubbing habits.

This division between larger, dubbing-minded speech communities, and smaller ones favoring subtitling, is found even today, after more than four decades of television. Thus, while Italy, Germany, Spain, and Russia still prefer voice replacement techniques, the Nordic countries, the Baltic countries, Holland, Flanders, Portugal, Slovenia, Croatia, and Greece subtitle foreign-language cinema films and TV programs. Outside Europe, Francophone and Spanish-speaking countries tend to favor dubbing, while subtitling is making headway elsewhere. Straddling the fence, Britain has formed a tradition of dubbing foreign-language films and television programs aimed at a mass audience, whereas "art movies" are shown with English subtitles. To a lesser extent, this tendency is found in the US and in France, where intellectual audiences tend to prefer subtitling to dubbing.

Today, the balance between the two rivals of screen translation is slowly shifting toward subtitling, partly for economic reasons: the increasing production and exchange of films and TV programs, combined with the fact that the number of TV channels is outgrowing the number of TV households, calls for a quicker and cheaper method of translation than dubbing. But to viewers in subtitling countries, the economic advantages of subtitling are secondary; retaining the authenticity of the original production is paramount. Once considered a nuisance or a necessary evil, subtitling is now becoming the preferred mode of language conversion for literate film and television audiences worldwide.

Subtitling Defined

Subtitling can be defined as (1) written, (2) additive, (3) immediate, (4) synchronous, and (5) polysemiotic translation.

(1) Being of a *written* — as opposed to spoken — nature, subtitling differs from all other types of screen translation.

(2) The label *additive* indicates that verbal material is added to the original, retaining the source-language discourse.

(3) The term *immediate* refers to the fact that in filmic media, all discourse is presented in a flowing manner, beyond the control of the receptor.

(4) The label *synchronous* reflects the fact that the original work (with or without the original dialog) and the translation are presented simultaneously — unlike 'simultaneous' interpreting.

(5) The term *polysemiotic* states the fact that the target-language rendering only covers one of several parallel channels of communication in the translated product. In the table below, six major types of translation are distinguished, using the five defining qualities of subtitling as parameters:

	Form Written	**Role** Additive	**Reception** Immediate	**Presentation** Synchronous	**Composition** Polysemiotic
Subtitling	+	+	+	+	+
Dubbing	–	–	+	+	+
Consecutive interpreting	–	+	+	–	+
Translated drama	–	–	+	–	+
Comic book translation	+	–	–	+	+
Literary translation	+	–	–	–	–

The Different Types of Subtitling

Linguistically, two main types of subtitling can be distinguished:

(1) *Intralingual subtitling* (in the original language):

    (a) Subtitling of domestic programs for the deaf and hard of hearing. (In countries with very little interlingual subtitling, this variant — sometimes called captioning — is what people associate with the notion of subtitling.)

    (b) Subtitling of foreign-language programs for language learners.

(2) *Interlingual subtitling* (from the original language):

This type I will concentrate on in the following. In addition to the five defining qualities listed above, it has a *diagonal* quality: In interlingual subtitling, the subtitler 'crosses over' from interpreting the spoken foreign-language dialog to presenting a written domestic-language translation on the screen:

	Foreign language	**Domestic language**
Spoken form	Original dialog	—————
Written form	—————	Subtitles

Technically, the main distinction runs like this:

(1) *Open subtitles* (not optional)
  (a) Film subtitling belongs to this category: in cinemas, subtitles are either a physical part of the film, as in feature films for public viewing, or transmitted separately, at festival screenings, etc.
  (b) Interlingual subtitling from terrestrial TV stations is nearly always of the open type. Although the subtitles are stored on a floppy disk, they are broadcast as an inseparable part of the TV signal.
(2) *Closed subtitles* (selected by the individual viewer)
  (a) Most domestic-language subtitling belongs to this category: Subtitles for the deaf and hard of hearing are normally transmitted via teletext, and thus optional. They are selected by the individual viewer on his remote control and generated by a decoder in his TV set.
  (b) Satellite-transmitted television normally uses (interlingual) closed subtitling. This method allows different speech communities to receive different versions of the same TV program simultaneously.

The Media-defined Constraints of Subtitling

Each type of translation comes with a specific set of constraints. These may be caused by a host of different agents in the communicative process from production of the original to reception of the translated version.

In the following, I will look at the constraints determining the characteristics of subtitling, as found in its most common form: interlingual open subtitling for TV.

Formal (quantitative) Constraints

Traditionally, the process of subtitling has not been considered 'translation', and, indeed, seen in isolation, subtitles are often less than a true representation of the original message. With television, this state of affairs has been justified on these grounds:

(1) The width of a TV screen — in combination with the minimum

lettersize legible to the average viewer — limits the number of characters to approximately 35 per row.

(2) The image should not have central parts covered with text. With some TV subtitling systems it is possible to use up to 12 rows of text, but most broadcasters accept one- or two-liners, only.

Together, constraints (1) and (2) establish a maximum of c. 70 characters per subtitle (*space factor*).

(3) The reading speed of the average viewer is considered slower than the talking speed of the person to be subtitled (*time factor*).

However, the space factor is largely irrelevant, since with the available 70 characters, and a large number of subtitles in quick succession, the subtitler would be able to render even complicated expressions in the target language, were it not for the time factor. This factor is crucial for the subtitler when deciding whether a longer, more adequate rendering should be preferred to a more concise, easy-to-read version.

So far, very little research has been conducted in this central field. But according to Swedish studies from the early seventies, the average television viewer needs 5–6 seconds to read a two-liner (of some 60–70 characters). This has since been the rule of thumb in most European TV subtitling departments, reducing the dialog (quantitatively) by about one third. Since the mid-eighties, however, a number of Belgian studies have indicated that a considerable group of viewers are able to read subtitles *faster* than the speech tempo.

If future, larger-scale studies support this notion of a fast-reading audience, familiar with the immediacy of the electronic media, this must result in a total revision of the hitherto prevalent view of subtitling as necessarily reductive. But already now, a conscientious and talented subtitler is able to operate with a minimal loss of semantic and stylistic information, leaving his audience time enough to enjoy the film proper.

	Visual Track(s)	Audio Tracks
Original Version:	PICTURE	DIALOG
		Music & Effects
Subtitled Version:	PICTURE	DIALOG
	Subtitles	Music & Effects

From a receptive angle, subtitles intrude into the picture (1) and challenge the dialog (2). From a productive angle, however, the picture and — depending on the viewers' expected knowledge of the source language — even the dialog may limit the freedom of the subtitler:

(1) The positioning (in space) and cueing (in time) of the subtitles must correspond with both static and dynamic visual features, i.e. picture composition and montage, respectively.

(2) The wording of the subtitles must reflect the style, the speech tempo, and — to a certain degree — the syntax and order of key elements in the dialog, whether informative or entertaining in nature, deliberate or spontaneous in form.

Audience reception of a subtitled TV program is based on the interaction subtitles-picture, with the dialog playing a pivotal role. When viewers understand (some of) the dialog, a heavy *feedback effect* is unleashed.

In a number of cases, such feedback is felt by both subtitler and viewer as negative, for instance when satirical programs present puns referring to for example source-language specific homonyms, or jokes presupposing a detailed knowledge of people, places and events in the source culture.

However, in other situations the feedback from the original version is of a positive nature. As polysemiotic media — where the communicative burden is shared by several channels — film and television present the translator with many deictic solutions to potentially ambiguous utterances: The subtitler can actually see or hear how a certain passage should be interpreted, and this privilege is passed on to the audience.

Subtitling — Strategies of Tightrope Translation

As demonstrated above, constraints in subtitling are not always rocks to steer clear of. Quite often, they prove to be stepping stones in the river of transmission. Benefiting from the support and counteracting the pressure from the array of formal and textual constraints, the subtitler transcodes the uncompromising dialog into strips of graphic signs conveying a maximum of semantic and stylistic information. In this balancing act, the subtitler — consciously or not — utilizes certain techniques, but as with any type of translation, the goal of functional correspondence is not always reached.

To assess the quality of a specific subtitling, the rendering of each verbal segment of the film must be analyzed with regard to stylistic and semantic function in the polysemiotic context.

The following ten strategies will illustrate the different techniques used in professional interlingual subtitling:

Type of strategy	Character of translation	Media-specific type?
(1) *Expansion*	Expanded expression, adequate rendering (culture-specific references)	No
(2) *Paraphrase*	Altered expression, adequate rendering (non-visualized language-specific items)	No
(3) *Transfer*	Full expression, adequate rendering (slow, unmarked speech)	No
(4) *Imitation*	Identical expression, equivalent rendering (proper nouns; international greetings)	No
(5) *Transcription*	Non-standard expression, adequate rendering (dialects; intended speech defects)	No
(6) *Dislocation*	Differing expression, adjusted content (musical/visualized language-specific items)	Yes
(7) *Condensation*	Condensed expression, concise rendering (mid-tempo speech with some redundancy)	Yes
(8) *Decimation*	Abridged expression, reduced content (fast speech; low-redundancy speech)	Yes
(9) *Deletion*	Omitted expression, no verbal content (fast speech with high redundancy)	Yes
(10) *Resignation*	Deviant expression, distorted content (incomprehensible or 'untranslatable' speech)	No

Of the ten strategies, types 1–7 provide correspondent translations of the segments involved. The strategy of condensation is considered correspondent, because in condensating — as opposed to decimating — the subtitle retains the meaning and the stylistic content of the original. Normally, the only loss implied in a condensation is the loss of redundant features of oral disourse, especially spontaneous speech as found in interviews, etc. But even in deliberate speech, ranging from newscasting to TV drama, much of the reduction necessitated by the formal constraints of subtitling is created anyway, due to the diagonal nature of this type of translation. With spontaneous speech, subtitling without *quantitative* reduction (in the number of words used) would produce awkward-looking results.

However, in cases where the reduction is found to be *qualitative*, and the semantic and stylistic content suffer in the process, we are dealing with examples of strategies 8 and 9. These types represent drastic cuts in the original expression, but through positive feedback from the audiovisual tracks, the subtitled product as a whole will often manage in conveying the message.

Unlike types 5–9, which are all more common in subtitling than in printed translation, resignation (type 10) is a strategy found in all types of verbal transmission. In subtitling, this abortive strategy is frequently resorted to, in situations where translators find themselves unable to render tricky idioms or other culture- or language-specific elements because of negative feedback from the non-verbal tracks. Sometimes, even subtitlers are at a loss for words.

References

Delabastita, Dirk. "Translation and Mass-communication: Film and TV Translation as Evidence of Cultural Dynamics." *Babel*, Vol. 35, No. 4 (1989), pp. 193–218.

Gottlieb, Henrik. "Tekstning — synkron billedmedieoversættelse." Prize thesis, University of Copenhagen, 1991.

Growenewold, Sjoerd. "Ondertiteling." Doctoraalscriptie, Universiteit van Amsterdam, 1986.

Marleau, Lucien. "Les sous-titres ... un mal necessaire." *Meta*, Vol. 27, No. 3 (1982), pp. 271–85.

Nir, Rafael. "Linguistic and Sociolinguistic Problems in the Translation of Imported TV Films in Israel." *International Journal of the Sociology of Language*, No. 48 (1984), pp. 81–97.

Reid, Helene J. B. "Literature on the Screen: Subtitle Translating for Public Broadcasting." In *Something Understood: Studies in Anglo-Dutch literary Translation*. Amsterdam: Rodopi, 1990, pp. 79–109.

TEXTLINGUISTICS

Text Typology and Translation: Across Languages

Marilyn Gaddis Rose
Center for Research in Translation
State University of New York at Binghamton, U.S.A.

Some kind of typological identification always occurs in translating. The identification can range from automatic and non-controversial (e.g., when the Canadian meteorological machine translation program does weather forecasts in French and English) to meditated and endlessly debated (e.g., how to translate Arabic *sufiyyas* or Japanese *haiku*). Translating always involves taking into account the text type, even if reproducing or calquing is neither feasible nor desirable.

The assumption, of course, is that if we translators identify the type or genre of text we are translating, we shall translate more intelligently — and, more often than not, better. (Talent, enthusiasm, health, time pressures, information access, etc. can all affect both the translator's ease of translating and the quality his or her translation is judged to manifest.) Certainly translating informed as either a human text-processor or a computer programmer is a value in itself. The underlying premise is that each identification carries with it a set of implicit specifications: if translators know these, they will either know what to expect or what is a reasonable range of expectations. And if translators know what to expect, their minds can prepare even if only quasi-consciously for what will arise. In typology, these expectations use rhetoric as a point of departure. That is, no matter how much the expectations may hermeneutically interact with "real-world" knowledge and situation, they start with the form, e.g., not what the Rev. Billy Graham would be expected to say to a Russian audience, based on our knowledge of his religious views, but what we would expect to find in one of his sermons because it is a sermon and not some other text type.

What classification is used should depend on what is most natural and helpful to the translator. Just now we used "sermon," an important subgenre of oration and one found in most major world religions. When translators label an extended speech act meant to be heard as a "sermon," they immediately cue their inner repertory of expectations. For example, in a sermon we expect a text with dignified, yet stirring diction; in most cases, a predictable organization. The text will be oriented to an audience which has been fairly well defined in advance; Graham's staff in editing and revising his address will accommodate the age range, moral code, education level, and relationship to speaker. In the situation we are using the sermon will be revised not only to make it appropriate for the audience but to make it transferable by simultaneous interpretation. (Further, in a Moscow audience the interpreter will know that bilingual listeners will be present.)

Katharina Reiss in her valuable *Texttyp und Übersetzungsmethode* (Reiss, 1976) would forewarn translators by calling Graham's sermon an "operative" or persuasive text. (The other two Reiss types are expressive, e.g., literary and informative, e.g., scientific and technical.)

Juliane House in her equally valuable *A Model for Translation Quality Assessment* (House, 1977) would say Graham's sermon when delivered to a Moscow crowd is an "overt" translation; after all, the auditors knew they were hearing an interpreter's simultaneous version, even though Graham's voice was audible over the public-address system. But if a newspaper in a Soviet socialist republic published the text of Graham's sermon in, say, unsigned columns of Russian, and Ukrainian, House might want to call the Russian and Ukrainian "covert" translations because the duo of texts would be presented as the same text in two languages (regardless of how many originary issues are raised by the word "same") even if most readers would remember that Graham probably used very few Russian words in his presentation.

James R. Child (Child, 1987), who has linked text typology both to levels of lexical and grammatical complexity and to substantive originality and information depth (1981–1987), might well find all four of his modes touched by Graham's sermon: the Orientation Mode because Graham would be sure to call up real-world situations and present sense stimuli; the

Instructive Mode because Graham would give advice on the basis of the shared information and values of the Orientation Mode; the Evaluative Mode for Graham is certain to move into his personal appraisal; and Projective Mode where Graham describes eventualities based on his religion-cued imagination. Usually, these modes are somewhat consecutive in difficulty, i.e., orientation is level 1 (simple tourist directions); instructive, level 2 (tabloid newspapers); evaluative, level 3 (these can be technical, but the reader is presumed to share the information); projective, level 4 (creative writing, philosophy, etc.).

Eugene A. Nida, who has found clearings in so many taxonomic- or cartographic-thickets since he founded modern translation studies in 1946, proposed a no-nonsense functional typology in 1990 (Creskoff, 1900). He favours a three-level typology which articulates text type with the knowledge required for translating: Level 1: *common* (can be understood by an American high school student, i.e., a 16-year-old who has received formal education since age 6) including novels, commercial texts, newspapers, brochures; Level 2: *broad* (postsecondary education, willingness to research texts), including government reports, magazines and newspapers targeting postsecondary readers, legal documents; Level 3: *specialized* (for field specialists), including complex legal documents, technical journals, and subtle and allusive texts. Even so demystifying a list as this proves that to itemize a nomenclature is simultaneously to trigger exception. For instance, the Bible which has been the focus of Nida's career — is it common since small children can follow it? Or specialized since only scholars can approach the variants among the scrolls?

All of these typological identifications move outward from the text and its formal characteristics although all depend on the author's intention and the reader's response. Many translators will find these classifications clarifying but possibly no more so than the traditional typological classifications of literary, non-literary and scientific/technical; general audience and special purpose; original and formulaic; or the hyper-traditional classifications of genre (not just poetry and prose but very fine-tuned, e.g., ballad, feature-story, first-person narrative etc.) Thus, of Graham's sermon we would say it is in the epic voice (i.e., he is talking *to* the receiver), sprinkled with anecdotes and biblical quotations (which in themselves offer a plethora of rhetorical genres), makes use of phanopoeia (imagery and allusion), and melopoeia (sound), and is organized in the Ciceronian oration style brought to high pulpit eloquence in his own American literature through the Puritan preacher Jonathan Edwards. (There will be a thesis, plan of attack, illustration and development, summation, and emotional closing.) Most cultures which have been visited by Western Protestantism, Evangelical Christianity or Liberation Theology have learned to accommodate all these typological conventions and, hence, having made room for them in their own literary systems, have learned to translate them.

The fact remains that no translator can translate both intuitively and effectively at all time. This means that any typological classification that triggers better analysis and verbal recall is not to be dismissed.

References

Child, James R. "Language Proficiency Levels and the Typology of Texts." In *Defining and Developing Proficiency: Guidelines, Implementations and Concepts.* Lincolnwood, Ill.: National Textbook Company, 1987.

Creskoff, Ellen. "Nida Proposes New Classification." *The ATA Chronicle*, Vol. 15 (1990), pp. 9, 26.

House, Juliane. *A Model for Translation Quality Assessment.* Tübingen: Gunter Narr Verlag, 1977.

Reiss, Katharina. *Texttyp und Übersetzungsmethode.* Kronberg/TS: Scriptor Verlag, 1976.

Textlinguistics

Albrecht Neubert
Department of English and Translation Studies
Karl-Marx University, Leipzig, Germany

The Textlinguistic Approach to Translation

The complexity of translation, which is one of the few things translation scholars agree upon, is mirrored in the great variety of aspects that tend to be focused in translation studies. Among the research topics that in recent years have come to figure at the top of the research agenda one of the most favourite candidates is provided by the textual nature of translation. Of course, translation has always been tacitly understood as involving more than word-by-word or sentence-by-sentence renderings of source language products into target language reproductions. But the translator's primary concern with manageable smaller units of language such as grammatical constructions, lexical items, stylistic figures, etc. has directed the practice as well as the teaching of translation towards how to solve the host of problems arising sure enough from the contrasts and imbalances between source and target languages. As a result translation studies were for a long time regarded as a branch of traditional linguistics dealing with the potential correspondences one can set up between the components and relations of two language systems. It came to be regarded as a branch of contrastive linguistics.

This view was challenged with the advent of textlinguistics in the seventies. Not that the prevalent model of translation as a reconstruction of words and structures, sentences and figures of speech was actually discarded, what is happening is that a new and more complex view is being introduced that will eventually turn out to supplement the more restricted approach. To a certain extent, what the textlinguistic perspective has brought to translation studies is a re-interpretation of "old" grammatical and lexical distinctions as well as an exploration of correspondences beyond the sentence level. Somewhat more bluntly one might say that disregarding the role of the text was like failing to see the wood for the trees. In other words, translating the words and structures correctly does not guarantee an adequate text.

Translating Texts as Wholes and as Members of a Type

In order to judge the contribution of textlinguistics to translation studies one need not specify the various and sometimes conflicting views of looking at texts. It is rather more instructive to list the two areas where translation is sure to profit from an approach that expands its scope beyond words and constructions.

(1) Linguistic utterances are always parts of larger communicative events, i.e., they are integrated into texts.
(2) Individual texts can be grouped into classes of texts that reflect the communicative habits of the speakers of a particular language.

Rephrasing these two textlinguistic insights in terms of the study of translation we get:

(1) Translation in the real world always has to do with whole texts, the solution of individual translation problems being determined by the global function of the target text in relation to the source text.
(2) Translation is always tied up with how other "similar" texts have been translated before, the kind of problems encountered in one text being, normally, instances of the translation of a particular text type.

The research programme of the textlinguistics of translation has indeed evolved around these two key topics. They are, therefore, well suited as a guide to what texts and translations have in common. We will term the first problem area *holistic* translation, and the second *generic* translation. These two together are the two inseparable aspects of we will call textual translation. Since they represent important distinctions relevant for practical translator and translation scholar alike they will we taken up one by one:

(1) Holistic Translation

Translation, however varied its implementation appears in detail, is intricately tied up with the aims of recapturing the message of a source text with the help of a target text. This overall purpose determines the detailed ways and means of rendering the lower-level expressions, that is, their grammatical structuring, their lexical coding, and their stylistic shading. Both the process of translation and its result, the concrete sign sequences in the target language, get their final justification from an assessment of the global textfunction. It is the unifying frame that keeps the various elements or features of a text together and attributes them their share in constituting a unique message. The global function turns the text into a complex communicative signal or event. It is a property of the original, and it has to be re-created by the translator. He/she achieves this holistic aim by continually monitoring his/her work in a "top-down" fashion. On the surface the translation exhibits various forms and grades of cohesion. At the deeper levels indicative of the ordering or at least sequencing of ideas and often also feelings, translations are characterized by degrees of coherence. With respect to the source text and its author a translation attempts to realize intentionality, and with regard to the target version and its readers the desired aim is acceptability. Considering the place of the source and target text in the communicative continuum the criterion of situationality has to be taken into account, with translations often attaining but displaced situationality. Last but not least, translations act upon the cognitive state of the recipients thus supplying informativity, just as the originals had been a source of (not necessarily the same) informativity for their audience.

More importantly, these six features of the source text which have gone to constitute the translation, though in a possibly somewhat "skewed" distribution, form an intricate network. They are closely related to each other allowing, more often than not, one or several factors to be balanced or reconsidered by others. Translations like texts are global systems that exhibit an internal structure. And this structure while corresponding as a whole to that of the original is far from homomorphic. Translations may differ with regard to the standards of textuality enumerated above. To be more specific, what has to be chosen by the translator to implement a particular standard, e.g., acceptability, in the target text, and what strikes the translation scholar as markedly different from the source text, turns out to be the very normal or expected way a speaker of the target language is accustomed to read the text.

Here it becomes immediately evident how the findings of textlinguistics derived, to be sure, from systematic descriptions of texts in one language can be applied most profitably to a comparison of texts in two languages. It is one of the key procedures of textlinguistics to analyze the various ways textfunctions are linguistically implemented in the structure of a text. In response, translation studies can integrate the methodology developed for monolingual texts into a contrastive textual analysis. In taking up this cue translation students have contributed considerably to the enormous empirical work of sorting and interpreting the wealth of detailed information that goes into constituting the global structure of a text.

(2) Generic Translation

Although the insights gained from a close comparison of how the textfunction of the source text is (to be) constructed by the linguistic means of the target text is extremely rewarding to translation research and, for that matter, translation practice, there is an additional or rather complementary line of study which is even more typical of the current interplay between textlinguistics and translation. Indeed, individual translations never exist in a "textual vacuum". Translating one text is influenced by previous translation of other, notably similar texts. Just as in monolingual communication when a speech community converses by means of a network of different sorts or types of text, so in translation or "bilingually mediated communication" target texts have to compete with the norms of a new and often contrasting target textworld. It is characterized by recurrent features that have become hallmarks of certain groups of texts. Translating a text implies translating a member of a particular textclass, which again makes it necessary that the translator takes into account what are the distinctive features of that textclass, if it has any. The result is generic translation, which means paying attention to grammatical, lexical, and stylistic markers characteristic of this whole sort of texts. In translating a particular text one remembers how one has managed to translate texts of the same type before and one takes one's bearings from how others have coped with parallel problems. Generic here also refers to the class of linguistic parameters that help to identify textual norms in a speech society. And this applies to the spectrum of texts in the source language as well as in the target language. More succinctly, before translation of a text is envisaged the translator has to be sensitized to "what is textually the case" in the two languages he/she is working in. In this respect, the findings of textlinguistics are prior to translation. They may be summarized as saying that communication by language is primarily communication by texts. And the system of texts current in a communicative society deserves the same serious study as the system of signs, the linguistic system, used by the speakers of a particular speech society.

Whereas linguistic science dealing with the language system has worked out highly elaborate methods and theories describing and explaining the items and rules characterizing the systemic levels or modules, textlinguistics is still in its infancy with regard to a reliable research methodology, let alone a solid theoretical foundation. That is why the categories available for a systematic study of texts are still underdeveloped. Some linguists even wonder whether textlinguistics can ever achieve the same rigour system linguists are so justifiably proud of.

A case in point is the concept of textclass that also underlies the notion of generic translation. Textlinguists as well as translatologists have made many attempts to establish topologies into which texts can be integrated. This has proved to be extremely difficult. Deductive classifications such as descriptive, argumentative, narrative texts or informative, expressive, directive texts provide frameworks that are not clear-cut enough to serve as practicable guidelines for analysis. But it is doubtful whether a universally applicable system of texttype-constituting features can be devised at all. A much more promising approach practised both in textlinguistics and in translation studies appears to be the inductive method of a cumulative analysis of "similar" texts. It concentrates on the compilation of diverse items and arrangements shared by texts with identical or related textfunctions. As a result the analyst can point out the intertextuality combining a number or group of related texts. On a closer scrutiny, the relationship of intertextuality is constituted to a very significant degree by the incidence and distribution of the textual standards discovered in the course of the holistic procedures. Studying one individual text after another by first singling out the distinctive features which are responsible for their cohesion, coherence, intentionality, acceptability, situationality, and informativity, respectively, leads to a graded characterization of the generic quality of the class of text as a whole. We have to admit, though, that such an empirical classification does not yield a highly satisfactory text typology of the above deductive kind. What is does achieve, however, is a highly informative repertoire of textual data that is amenable to further interpretation by the text theorist as well as to most effective application by the translation scholar and the translator. Judging by the recent advances of translation studies there is some justification to assert that we are now in the midst of a "textlinguistic phase". Many previous views are now rephrased in terms of what they imply in a textlinguistic model of translation.

Textlinguistic Categories of Translation Study

Meaning in Translation

The most striking textlinguistic revaluation of what happens when we translate texts and not words in sentence structures has to do with the handling of meaning. Whereas meaning for the linguist resides in the language system, meaning for the textlinguist is determined by the text. Since languages *qua* systems cannot be translated what counts as semantic currency with which to pay for the meaning of the original in terms of the meaning of the translation has to be of a new or at least different quality. Although the system-specific meanings incorporated into the text are not invalidated, they get reinterpreted by the text. And it is their textual profile that has to be translated. A more suitable term for meaning in translation is communicative value. It denotes the semantic quality of a segment of text which functions as an integrated component of the whole text. The communicative values of a word, a phrase, a sentence, a chunk of text constitute the global communicative value of the text as a whole, also called global text meaning. A criterial ingredient of this global meaning, which is inherited to the lower-level communicative values, is the texttype-specific functionality of the whole as well as of the individual parts. Equally relevant is the "place value" which the textual units and patterns are assigned to in the architecture of a concrete textual token.

Texttype and texttoken, then, model the communicative values in a way that is clearly to be differentiated from the primary conditioning of meanings by means of the linguistic system.

Equivalence in Translation

Communicative values are the proper objects of translation. Or rather, the often-heard dictum that we translate meanings blurs the fact that it is only communicative values that can be equivalent. Meanings just as well as language systems cannot be translated. Equivalence turns out to be a textual phenomenon. It is a relation between texts, source texts and target texts. Textual equivalence, again, is the basis of the equivalence of lower-level units such as partial texts, sentences, phrases, and words. But textual equivalence does not require such a fully-fledged parallelism. In fact, to demand it from the translator would amount to asking for the impossible. So-called "literal translations", which aim at the closest possible correspondence on the word and structure levels, do not attain equivalence. They produce interlinear versions that inform the target reader more about the source language than about the source text. By contrast, textual translation exploits lower-level equivalence as much as possible. But it stops short of any fake word-for-word or construction-for-construction substitutions. The textual perspective of translation equivalence does not support a freewheeling treatment of source items leaving room for subjective and, in principle, biased blurring of semantic distinctions of the source text in the name of the "ignorant" target reader who has to be fed a second-rate version. Textual translation involves the identification of all those source text segments that offer more or less direct transfer to equivalent target text segments. It is the translator's task to test the transfer potential of the various levels and components of the original and to integrate them, i.e. their equivalents, fully and consistently into the target text.

Units of Translation

In the light of the demand for communicative equivalence between texts, the translator's quest for a viable strategy to recode the source text and to build up the target text in a step-by-step-fashion requires a powerful review procedure that informs him/her where to effect the transfer and where not. This is the decisive question: where to locate the units of translation. They are the smallest source items or patterns susceptible of being rendered into a target text. Their main feature is their flexibility. They could consist of single words. But there may be cases where they are of text length. The decision which the translator has to take is prompted by the role played by the segment to be translated in the context of the whole text (cf. holistic translation) or with regard to texttype (cf. generic translation). The same words and phrases may be quite differently translated depending upon the position they have in a particular text the function they have as markers of a certain texttype. Units of translation, though they refer to linguistic items of the source language, cannot be defined without recourse to textlinguistic considerations. They cannot be retrieved from a dictionary or a grammar book unless these sources of reference are put together in such a way that they include the relevant textual indicators supplying the necessary information pointing beyond the place of the word or construction in the language system. Useful reference works of this kind are technical dictionaries or guides to technical writing. They arrange language according to how it is used in technical texts.

Units of translation are not only comprised of signs and sign sequences as such. They may also reside in larger textual structures. They are called macrostructures. Source texts very often show a particular macrostructural order or distribution that is dependent upon certain conventions of a texttype. These conventions governing how textual chunks are coordinated and/or superordinated may differ significantly from the usual way texts are structured in the target community. As a result communicative equivalence may make it necessary that the translator rearranges the internal architecture of texts. This is especially in order if the respective sequence of text components or macrostructures is critical for acceptability of a text exemplar. Not following this procedure might jeopardize the communicative validity of the translation. On the other hand, changing the macrostructure of a source text in the process of translation can hardly be accepted as a general policy. What is to be recommended with certain types of translation will be extremely harmful in others. As is generally the case with units of translation ranging from the word to the macrostructure or even the superstructure of the whole text, the strategy of the translator is a function of the overall assessment of the text in its setting.

Text-bound Translation

The flexibility in the treatment of source texts leads to an equally flexible translational policy. All descriptive and explanatory statements about the nature of translation as well as all prescriptive and methodical guidelines about the practice of translation relate to individual instances or classes of texts. The study of translation is a text-bound discipline. The textlinguistic impact on translatology has resulted in a sober reconsideration of the lofty axioms promulgated by translation theorists. It has strengthened the empirical basis of translation research. But it has also stimulated the teaching of translation. Last but not least, it has enhanced the prestige of translation studies among the practitioners of the profession. Of course, it has also relativized the claims put forward in the name of a general theory of translation. The text-bound nature of translation just as the text-bound character of linguistic communication altogether, postulated by textlinguistics or perhaps rather a science of texts, cannot be fully under-stood by system-bound categories. In fact, for linguistics to cover the complexities of translations it has to be supplemented by disciplines that are in a position to clarify and explain the many-faceted structures and relations embodied and activated by texts in communication. The two most immi-nent disciplines exerting their pervasive influence on translation studies are text analysis and text typology. They contribute to the study of text-bound translation of individual texts and of classes of texts, respectively.

Parallel Texts

Another mine of information about the text-boundness of potential units of translation is the corpus of parallel texts available in both the source and the target languages. Parallel texts have been produced by users of different languages under near-identical communicative conditions. They are not translations but translation-independent products of the communicative cultures or text worlds typical of the source and target languages respec-tively. What makes them ideal sources for translators is their structural patternedness exhibiting unadulterated material that is uniquely suitable for inclusion into a translation. This conveys originality to a text. Parallel texts, i.e. their grammatical, lexical, and stylistic components, may be said to contain "hidden" translation units, which the translator has to identify and store for later use as building blocks when he/she constructs the target version of a source text. In a certain sense, a translator's experience is based on an awareness of what fits into which text. Parallel text files, whether broken down into term glossaries, routinized grammatical correspon-dences, or conventionalized style checking procedures, are part and parcel of the material and mental equipment of the competent translator. It is equivalent to a vast databank and an enormous experience. It opens the road to an extensive knowledge of how texts are structured in different languages and a thorough skill in how this knowledge can be transformed into select-ing the right word or construction for an adequate translational purpose.

Adequateness of a Translation

Adequateness, closely related to the purpose of a translation, is a conse-quence of applying what can be derived from a parallel text to the genuine translation. If a translation can compete with a parallel text then the chances are that it may be said to have a similar status as a text that has been produced by a person who is well-versed in the target textworld. Since we can normally take for granted that the original is equally an adequate source text there is a relation of adequateness between source and target text. It differs from equivalence, satisfying the semantic relationship between original and translation, in that it fulfils the pragmatic requirements for the target text with regard to its source. Adequateness can be subtly related to equivalence in that it can decide whether equivalence is to be achieved at all. If, for instance, a literal translation serves a certain purpose, such as a preliminary work for a poet's creative adaptation of a work of art, or a rough translation for an expert, a non-equivalent translation may be perfectly adequate. Or again, a philologically elaborate translation rich in paraphrases and footnotes, giving much more explicit information for the target reader than was expressed in the original, may be just the adequate solution. But the interpretation of the many implicit features of the source text, which are taken for granted by the source language audience, actually "overtranslates" the text and falls short of communicative equivalence.

Textual Translation and Pragmatic Translation Types

Translation Procedures

As a rule units of translation are of lexical, grammatical or of a complex nature. Reacting to their discreteness facilitates the translator's job. Finding their equivalent correspondences helps to minimize the difference between a translation and a parallel text. A translation reads more like an original. But the distinction between equivalence and adequateness makes it evident that the final criterion is a pragmatic one. Since text-boundness is crucial in translation a decision about what is equivalent about a particular choice is determined by the purpose of the translation at hand. The translator has to know or, at least, he/she has to be informed: What function is the translation to have? Which textfunction of the original is to be kept constant? Which should be changed or modified?

Now the most natural purpose would be that the translation fulfills a communicative need that conforms to the textfunction of the original for the source audience. This "normal" case is communicative translation. Other pragmatic types are literal, philological, and adaptive. Of course, these are not pure types. But there is no doubt about the dominance that can be ascertained. And the assignment of a translation, the situation in which it is carried out, and, most important of all, the aim it is supposed to perform make it imperative that the translator be aware of the pragmatic function the translated text is to play in the target community. The pragmatic type leads to selective procedures. Thus communicative, literal, philological and adaptive are actually translation procedures motivated by pragmatic considerations.

Text Directedness

Since pragmatics has to do with the relation of texts to the user, the translation of texts in practical situations invariably entails further assessments having to do with the aim of the translation in the context of the sender and the receiver. The result is another set of pragmatic translation types that do not focus on procedures but on purposes. Monolingual texts are not normally meant to be translated. They are directed to a source language audience. If they get translated, their pragmatic import is widened, i.e. their directedness is expanded. According to the kind of directedness involved one can distinguish four types of translation. Type 1 is represented by texts that are "double-directed", i.e., they are of equal interest to the source language community and the target language community (e.g., technical texts, instruction manuals, non-fiction books, etc.). Type 2 refers to texts that have a primarily "unilateral" directedness, i.e. they arise from the communicative need of source language readers (e.g., local newspapers, legal texts, insider information, etc.). Type 3, on the surface, is an important subcategory of Type 2. It consists of texts that are deeply rooted in the communicative life-cycle of source language readers. But these texts are at the same time pointing beyond the realms of the source community. They are of general human interest, which make them in a new and important way target-language-directed too (e.g., poetry, fiction, *belles-lettres*). Type 4, by contrast, comprises texts that are primarily directed towards target language recipients. The source texts of this type are merely pretexts for translation. Their sole purpose is to serve as models or memory helps for the target text, which is to reach the world of the target community (e.g. information and propaganda to be circulated abroad).

It goes without saying that translators, in taking these four types into account, have to make and, equally, are entitled to make a great number of textual adjustments. Translation flexibility, the main consequence of the textlinguistic model of translation, is thus a necessity as well as a great opportunity.

Textlinguistic Implications for Machine and Computer-assisted Translation

The textlinguistic approach has enormous consequences for the use of electronic means in translation. On the one hand, machine translation programs are enhanced in their effectiveness if they incorporate the text specificity into their grammatical and lexical database. The empirical work devoted to the discovery and the description of text-bound correspondences between source and target languages is amply compensated by the greater acceptability standard achieved by the latest MT versions. It is perhaps safe to say that further progress is highly dependent upon texttype-specific qualification of source texts. Machine translation, if it is to be profitable, is restricted to particular texttypes. Provided the texts to be translated are fully textually indexed, speed and reliability of the mechanical translation process can be steadily improved. Where this poses insurmountable difficulties, all attempts at machine translation may be counterproductive.

The textlinguistic approach to translation will perhaps be of the greatest effect for computer-assisted human translation. If the computer is used as a workstation providing the translator with a translation-intelligent environment compiled from previous adequate translations, then the actual core component of the program will be a highly sophisticated model of the translational expertise of several or even many gifted practitioners. It is an expert system guiding the user of the workstation in his/her search for the most effective strategies. Since the individual translational tactics are heavily text-bound, the program modules must have a strong textual bias. Empirical research into the textual constitution of the translational process, the textual features of the source and target texts as well as, in particular, the textual matching potential on all levels, will contribute significantly to improve this perhaps most important translation tool of the future.

References

Arntz, R. and G. Thome, eds. *Übersetzungswissenschaft. Ergebnisse und Perspektiven*. Tübingen: Narr, 1990.

Beaugrande, Robert de and W. Dressler. *Introduction to Text Linguistics*. London: Longman, 1981.

Bell, Roger. *Translation and Translating: Theory and Practice*. London: Longman, 1990.

Catford, J. C. *A Linguistic Theory of Translation.* London: Oxford University Press, 1965.

Delisle, Jean. *L'Analyse du discours comme méthode de traduction: théorie et pratique.* Ottawa: University of Ottawa Press, 1980.

Neubert, Albrecht. *Text and Translation.* Leipzig: Enzyklopädie, 1985.

Snell-Hornby, Mary, ed. *Übersetzungswissenschaft — eine Neuorientierung.* Tübingen: Narr, 1986.

Reiss, Katharina. *Texttyp und Übersetzungsmethode. Der operative Text.* Kronberg: Scriptor, 1976.

Van Dijk, T., ed. *Handbook of Discourse Analysis.* Vols. 1–4. London: Academic Press, 1985.

Waard, Jan de and Eugene A. Nida. *From One Language to Another: Functional Equivalence in Bible Translating.* Nashville: Nelson, 1986.

Wilss, Wolfram. *The Science of Translation: Problems and Methods.* Tübingen: Narr, 1982.

THEORY

Translation Theory from/into Chinese

Liu Miqing
Department of Translation
The Chinese University of Hong Kong, Hong Kong

A Brief Historical Survey

To trace the ancestry of the present-day studies of translation from/into Chinese, one must go back to the last years of Huan Di 桓帝 (146–168) of the Eastern Han dynasty, when translation into Chinese from Buddhist scriptures in Sanskrit was just beginning to unfold. After more than half a century of translation practice, the first budding of translation studies appeared some time between 223–224. Zhi Qian 支謙, a productive translator of the scriptures in the period of The Three Kingdoms 三國, initiated a searching criticism of Zhu Jiangyan's 竺將炎 translation. Drawing arguments from his revision of Zhu's translation, Zhi Qian contended that Zhu, as an original translator, "notwithstanding a perfect command of Sanskrit, was rather weak in clear Chinese, which led him to a rather blunt literal translation as the result of direct borrowing or transliteration" 雖善天竺語，未備曉漢，其所傳言或得胡語，或以義出音，近於質直. To this, Vighna 維祗難 offered a rebuttal supported by the audience in which he cited a maxim from Lao Zi 老子 that "beautiful words are not faithful, faithful words not beautiful" 美言不信，信言不美, and asserted that "in rendering Buddhist instructions, what should be accorded with is their original meaning free from any polish" 佛言，依其義不用飾. This contention resulted in a theoretical agreement on the basic principle for scripture translation, i.e. "literal adherence to the original text" 案本. This principle was put by Zhi Qian in concluding his argument as "adhering to the original gist and giving no polish to the language" 因循本旨，不加文飾 , and by Dao An 道安 (314–385) as "literal transferring in accordance with the original text without any alteration at the expense of the original words and sentences" 案本而傳，不令有損言游字 . "From time to time," Dao An adds, "I make some reversions to straighten out the sentence order. Except for that, I follow the original text strictly as it really is" 時改倒句，餘盡實錄 .

This "source-text oriented principle of translation" 案本的翻譯原則 was first challenged by Kumarajiva 鳩摩羅什 (334–413), an Indian immigrant monk and translator, and later by Xuan Zang 玄奘 (602–664), a highly esteemed scripture translator in Chinese history. Xuan Zang used every endeavor to revise the principle of strict literalness by rejecting rigid stereotyping of Sanskrit syntax and allowing for faithful alterations both in sentence structure and expression with a view to improving the fluency of his Chinese translation. Backed up by his ripe experience in translation practice (his translations of Buddhist scriptures in 19 years amounted to 1,335 *juan* or 75 volumes) and direct knowledge of both cultures, Xuan Zang succeeded in upgrading the "source-text oriented principle" to the "principle of faithfulness", an uplift from blunt literalness to the approach of a two-fold requirement, i.e. translation at once faithful to the source text and fluent in Chinese 信達 . The success was justly assessed by Liang Qichao 梁啓超 (1873–1929) as "the peak of perfection in Buddhist scripture translation, thanks to his harmonious regulation of free and literal translation" 若玄奘者，則意譯直譯，圓滿調和，斯道之極軌也 .

The principle developed by Xuan Zang was kept to for centuries until 1894 when Ma Jianzhong 馬建忠 (1845–1900) put forward his principle of "tactful translation" 善譯 , by which he meant an approach to exact translation after "repeated and scrupulous pondering upon the original in order to ascertain its gist and meaning and imitate its spirit and tone so as to achieve an appreciation capable of producing an effect in translation on the reader the same as he would derive from reading the original" 夫如是，則一書到手，經營反覆，確知其意旨之所在，而又摹寫其神情，仿彿其語氣，然後心悟神解……能使閱者所得之益，與觀原文無異 . Four years later, in 1898, Ma's principle was further promoted by the best known explorer and pioneer of Chinese traditional studies of translation, Yan Fu 嚴復 (1853–1921), himself a political reformist and translator of the then Western masterpieces in the humanities and science. Yan's merit is his formulation of the Three-character Criterion in evaluation of the artistry of translation, i.e. "Faithfulness, Expressiveness and Elegance" 信達雅 , which is boiled down from the first sentence of the Foreword to his translation of T. H. Huxley's *Evolution and Ethics* (1883): "There are three ticklish problems with regard to translation — faithfulness, expressiveness and Elegance" 譯事三難：信達雅 . For more than eighty years since its formulation, the time-honored Three-character Criterion has been pondered over, commented on, clarified and followed by generation after generation of Chinese translators. Its lasting vitality and validity lie in the fact that Yan's interpretation, with striking succinctness and incisiveness, conveyed more of the complexity and delicacy of the art of translation than theoretical or methodological implications. It is more like a facile pithy formula, an easy-to-handle "yardstick" for a translator in his attempt to perfect his translation than "a theoretical system", as has been repeatedly elaborated by its advocators. Notwithstanding the obvious ambiguity and limitations, Yan's principle was widely regarded as the most convincing proposition ever made in connection with Chinese translation both in practice and in traditional theory.

Traditional studies of translation in mainland China gained new momentum in 1950s when translation practice and teaching flourished with the founding of the new republic. Based on his broad experience, Fu Lei 傅雷 (1908–1966) reiterated the theoretical point of view of "closeness of spirit" 神似 and "formal closeness" 形似 , an old topic in Chinese classical aesthetics but reasserted for translation studies by Chen Xiying 陳西瀅 and Lin Yutang 林語堂 (1895–1976) in the 1920s and 1930s. Fu's principle was first put as "the endeavor of a translator is to achieve closeness of spirit rather than closeness of form" 所求的不在形似，而在神似 and later, even more explicitly, as "our emphasis must be put on closeness of spirit instead of closeness of form" 重神似，不重形似 . In the light of this principle Fu's translation (chiefly from French literature) is widely acknowledged as a convincing embodiment of "the principle of closeness of spirit", the implications of which Luo Xinzhang 羅新璋 , the addressee of Fu's letters on translation, describes as "an approach to translation based on a penetrating and insightful comprehension of the original" 妙悟原文而爲譯者 , "to achieve equivalence free from the bondage of the form of the original" 離形得似 .

"Closeness of spirit", as a criterion as well as a principle, was most influential in 1950s and some time beyond in the area of literary translation. The result was a noticeable enhancement of the quality of translation compared with that before. This was exactly in conformity to and in keeping with the development of the contemporary Chinese language in fluency and expressiveness, thanks to the increasing language contact. Against this background, Qian Zhongshu 錢鍾書 (1910–　) offered his view of "sublimation" 化境 in literary translation, stating that "the supreme criterion of literary translation, is 'sublimation', by which I mean to transfer the language of a work into another language without bearing any trace of awkwardness or far-fetchedness in translation because of the differences of language usage, and at the same time without losing the slightest flavor of the original" 文學翻譯的最高標準是 " 化 "。把作品從一國文字轉變成另一國文字，既不能因語言習慣的差異而露出生硬牽強的痕跡，又能完全保存原有的風味，那就算得入於 " 化境 ". Qian compares what he defines as "sublimation" to "the transmigration of souls" 投胎轉世 to mean the transfer of the original to the target language as "an incarnation in a different body of the soul that remains unchanged" 軀殼換了一個，而精神姿致依然故我 . And the translator's path to sublimation, Qian asserts, is his obtaining the truest possible feel of the original by means of strenuously digging into it.

With the above description of the historical development as the background, we now move on to an overview of the worthiness and weaknesses of the Chinese traditional studies of translation:

(1) The studies began with a controversy over translation thought 翻譯思想 , centered round the problems of translation principles and criteria. The controversy went through more than 1700 years, falling into four stages, each characterized by a keynote of traditional translation thought: Source-text Orientation 案本 — Faithfulness 求信 — Closeness of Spirit 神似 — Sublimation 化境 .

(2) The four-stage development of the Chinese translation thought give us clues as to what happened in China with respect to the coincident dispute between literal and free translation in Europe. The source-text orientation is literal translation in its strictest sense; it was held to until the middle of the Eastern Jin Dynasty (317–420) or some time beyond. From the Sui (581–618) and Tang (618–907) dynasties, especially from Kumarajiva and Xuan Zang on, the principle of "faithfulness and expressiveness" 信達 was practised with a view to improving Chinese readability. Yan Fu and Ma Jianzhong's studies signify the maturity of traditional thinking on translation, which culminates in Fu Lei and Qian Zhongshu's

aesthetic interpretation of a complementary integration of literal and free translation.

(3) As has been stated above, the traditional approach to translation studies is obviously characterized by its narrowness of theoretical vision and observation. Restricted by historical conditions, it tends to regard translation theory as nothing more than discussions on the controversial topics of translation principles and criteria, usually in terms of literal and free translation. The narrowness in the scope of theoretical study of translation thought lingered on for more than seventeen centuries in China. The limitation has resulted in a legacy or rather a popular assumption in China that "translatology" is but a set of much talked-about principles or criteria such as 信達雅 or 神似與形似. Confined by the assumption, studies of translation tend to look upon of criteria translation theory and translatology as a closed system incapable of opening up new horizons.

(4) Following the beaten track, most traditional studies of translation find it impossible to get out of it. Any theory of translation must draw upon a theory of language (Catford, 1965). However, the study of language in China before the beginning of the 20th century was basically an auxiliary discipline called 小學, meaning the study of the form, phonology and meaning of the written language of ancient China. It concerned itself wholly with "annotation of the classical texts by means of empirical research" 訓詁考證. Since the beginning of this century, linguistics in China has undergone a process of "Westernization", or "Indo-Europeanization" in grammatical studies. Lacking in linguistic backup, Chinese traditional translation studies have been left to stick with classical literary aesthetics, or philological aesthetics, which is almost incapable of providing any theoretical nutriment for Chinese translation theory other than a series of abstract aesthetic values.

(5) In methodology, Chinese traditional translation studies are also profoundly influenced by philological aesthetics. In the analysis of the aesthetic values of "beauty" 美, "elegance" 雅, "embellishment" 文, "substantialness" 質, "spirit" 神, "form" 形, "beauty in sentiments and expressions" 情采, "beauty in spirit and expressions" 姿致, etc., studies rely heavily on intuition, empirical insight and empathy, and therefore tend to be too fuzzy, both

qualitatively and quantitatively, owing to the neglect of structural analysis and logical verification. They are disposed to use "impression terms" 印象性術語 that usually bring about too much fuzziness 模糊性 . A typical case is Yan Fu's 達 and 雅 , for which so far at least eight and fifteen interpretations are on record respectively. In fact, their meanings are subject to every translator's subjective appreciation 了悟 . Fuzziness blurs the boundaries of the logical intension 內涵 and extension 外延 of the terms, hence the difficulty to set scientific norms to live up to them.

Highlights of Modern Translation Theory from/into Chinese

Translation is a science as well as an art. As an art, it has its aesthetic values. As a science, it must be scientifically grounded. Although a storehouse of aesthetic intelligence and insight of outstanding translator-theorists in China over the past centuries, traditional translation studies are obviously weak in scientific groundwork.

To meet the needs of language contact and communication in the contemporary world, it is imperative to guide the Chinese traditional studies of translation toward a science of bilingual and bicultural transferring. To accomplish this aim, modern translation studies must draw up theories from modern linguistics, particularly contrastive linguistics, pragmatics, semantics, textlinguistics, stylistics, and grammatical theories. Contrastive linguistics is of special significance as Chinese and English belong to different language families. Their extreme linguistic and cultural disparities make a good testing ground for the development of translation theories and techniques.

Studies of Fundamental Theory

Fundamental theory of translation concerns itself with the following theoretical topics in connection with CE/EC transfer.

The Essence of Translation: equivalent transfer of meaning from source language (SL) to receptor language (RL).

Taking into account the extreme differences in form between Chinese and English in cases of the letter-system 文字系統 and the linguistic structure, CE/EC translation studies must pay special attention to equivalent transfer of meaning instead of form, and therefore regard it as "the essence of translation" 翻譯的實質 . Since language in communication is stratified into word, phrase, (clause), sentence and text, the meaning to be transferred is, theoretically, composed of the semantic content of all the syntactically grouped components at the above-mentioned levels. And, since language in communication is situationally defined, the semantic content of each component may have multi-dimensional meanings. They are conceptual meaning 概念意義 , formal meaning 形式意義 , connotative meaning 聯想意義 (including figurative meaning 形象意義), stylistic meaning 文體意義 , affective meaning 感情意義 , cultural meaning 文化意義 , and collocative meaning 搭對意義 . In EC translation, special attention must be paid to formal meaning. It is thus clear that meaning transfer is bound to be a multi-dimensional task.

Equivalence: The Basic Criterion of Translation.

The object of the whole process of bilingual transfer (CE/EC) is all the way up to an exact or the most proper RL equivalent of the SL counterpart. To attain this purpose, the translator is permitted to make, by all means, adjustments (Nida, 1964) to fit the language situation in the operation of the following models of bilingual transfer:

(a) Model I   Correspondence   對應式轉換 : e.g. 醫德 — medical ethics
(b) Model II   Parallel 平行式轉換 : e.g. 南瓜 — the Spanish gourd
(c) Model III Substitution 替代式轉換 : e.g. 遺腹子 — a posthumous child
(d) Model IV Confliction 衝突式轉換 : e.g. tango — 探戈舞

Adjustments in CE/EC translation include addition 增詞 , subtraction 減詞 , transliteration 音譯 , rephrasing 易詞而譯 , conversion 詞類轉換 , blending 詞義融合 , combination 聯綴 , etc. Adjustments above the word level include cutting 分切 , reversion 反轉 , splitting 拆譯 , recasting 重構 , etc. The ultimate object of adopting every possible means of adjustment in bilingual transfer is to get the RL equivalent, and the art of translation is the art of selecting the means of adjustment to achieve the best equivalence.

The Formal Mechanism

Given the extreme differences in letter-system, grammar and mode of expression between Chinese and English, equivalence in CE/EC transfer is basically a matter of meaning transferring. That, of course, does not mean that the translator need not pay any attention to the "form" of the language. Rather, it adds complexity to the task of the CE/EC transfer.

First of all, the meaning of the word "form" has to be redefined in a broader sense than that in general linguistics. As Catford points out, "translation between the levels of phonology and graphology — or between either of these levels and the levels of grammar and lexis — is impossible" (Catford, 1965). Translation between these levels is basically ruled out in CE/EC translation theory. It has to exclude "the outward form" or "physical structure" from the meaning of the word "form" as there is no similarity in form to speak of between Chinese and English. At the same time, it does include the semantic aspects in the meaning of "form". In terms of semantics, accordingly, "formal equivalence" in CE/EC transfer is scaled down as described below. Likewise, formal equivalence is possible when it is broadly meant to refer to the distribution patterns of the basic syntactic components (SV, SVO, SVOO, etc.) in SL-RL comparison.

Referential Norms with regard to "formal equivalence" in CE/EC translation theory are as follows:

(1) In the broad context of Chinese translation studies, "form" refers to the basic conceptual meaning and basic syntactic order, or to put it figuratively, "form" refers to the "kernel" rather than the "husk".

(2) Accordingly, CE/EC "equivalence of form" refers to the correspondence of the basic conceptual meaning and basic syntactic order of the SL and RL counterparts.

(3) Formal equivalence between Chinese and English is scaling down as follows:

    (a) Correspondence 對應 (cf. Model I)

        e.g. "by the sixth sense" → 憑第六感覺

    (b) Similarity 類似 (cf. Model II)

        e.g. "by the sixth sense" → 憑直覺 (" 感覺 " 與 " 直覺 " 同類屬).

    (c) Approximity 近似 (cf. Model III)

        e.g. "lack of historical sense" → 缺乏歷史眼光 (" 眼光 " 與 " 感覺 " 近似).

    (d) Non-equivalence in form (無對應 , cf. Model IV)

        e.g. "contrary to all sense" → " 荒謬絕倫 "

(4) In general, formal equivalence in CE/EC translation is also scaling down while the language level is scaling up. Take "proof" 證明 for example:

    (a) Word Level: proof — 證明 (Equivalence is fully maintained)

    (b) Phrase Level: tangible proof — 具體例證 (Equivalence gets looser because of the collocation)

    (c) Sentence Level: They sent over a gift as a proof of regard — 他們送來了一份禮物以示敬意 (Equivalence is scarcely maintained).

Formal equivalence can usually be attained at the word level as shown above, while at the sentence level it is difficult to keep up with the stretch of the semantic structure. Formal equivalence usually peters out at the level of text 語段 :

    (d) A: That's the telephone. 有電話

        B: I'm in the bath. 我在洗澡呢

        A: O.K. 好吧，我去接

This is so-called "Declension of Formal Equivalence" 形式對應的式微傾向 in interlingual transfer.

(5) Dynamic handling of formal equivalence in CE/EC translation is of vital importance. Mechanical formal equivalence, i.e., mechanically sticking to the "kernel" in a superficial "sense for sense" transfer, unavoidably brings about absurdity:

    (a) cat's cradle → ╳ 貓的搖籃 ✓ 翻絞絞

    (b) 過橋的時候，欄杆一定要把穩。

        ╳ To cross the bridge, the railing should be held on to.

        ✓ To cross the bridge, we should hold on to the railing.

It is thus clear that "formal equivalence" is identical to "formal closeness" 形似 in traditional studies of translation. And, as has shown in the above examples, the "form" is the clue that misleads the translator. Adherence to the letter may indeed "kill the spirit" 因詞害義 .

"Function" and "form" are two factors that interconnect each other complementarily in the use of language. The Chinese language is rather weak in "form" (in the sense of outward structural indication), which automatically attaches more importance to function.

(1) Functional Analysis vs Grammatical Analysis

Grammatical analysis of the source language is undoubtedly indispensable both in CE and EC translation. Because of the weakness in form in Chinese, grammatical analysis in CE translation has to give way to functional analysis when no formal/inflectional indication can be employed as the clue for SL structural analysis. Fuzziness in form and ambiguity in meaning can be exemplified by the following sentences:

(a) 被乘數被乘數所乘。
The multiplied is multiplied by the multiplier.

A comparison between the source language and receptor sentence shows immediately the weakness of the Chinese sentence in form. In the English sentence, "the multiplied", and "the multiplier" are different in form, hence they serve to shape up the meaning of the sentence, whereas in the Chinese sentence, the first 被乘數 and the second one are fuzzy in form. Their difference can only be determined by their syntactic function framed up by the structure 被…所… .

(b) 高層官員並不定期會商。

This sentence has two meanings because of the fluid characteristics of 不 . When 並 and 不 are used together, the sentence means "Top level officials do not meet regularly". When 不 and 定期 are put together, the sentence means "Top level officials meet irregularly". The exact meaning of the sentence can only be determined by a stretch of the sentence into a text such as:

(c) 高層官員並不定期會商，以便及時交換意見。
Top level officials meet irregularly for timely exchange of views.

(2) Grammatical Structure vs Semantic Structure

The preceding examples also serve to show the differences of the semantic structures between Chinese and English. In English, the semantic structure must be geared into the framework of specific grammatical structures based on rigorous grammatical norms 語法規範 . But in Chinese, the semantic structure may variably take a very simple form, unnecessary to be put in any grammatical framework other than word order and in some cases "empty words" 虛詞 . Compare the following pairs of SL and RL sentences:

(a) 一胎生了三個孩子。 (Note the use of the time-indicator 了 . No number indicator is necessary)

Three children were born at one birth. (voice, tense and number indicators are indispensable.)

(b) 電報發了。(No voice indication is necessary.)

The telegram has been sent out. (Voice indication is indispensable.)

Unlike English, the semantic structure in Chinese is based on linearity 對接 , sentence formation 句子成形 and sentence aggregation 句子聚集 with linearity as the basic mechanism acting mostly in accordance with the "Principle of Temporal Sequence" (PTS, 時序律) (Liu, 1989). Linearity, sentence formation and sentence aggregation (and sometimes contraction 緊縮) make the Chinese sentence (semantically and structurally) take a very simple form, e.g., 天不怕，地不怕 (SV+SV, here, "S" is a receptor subject, namely, 受事主語). Its English equivalent may be: "We fear neither Heaven, nor Earth". Whatever the equivalent is, it must be grammatically sound to make it semantically complete.

(3) Logical Inference vs Linguistic Sense

Studies into the relationship between linguistic structure and language sense are definitely needed in CE/EC translation theory. Owing to the weakness in form, the Chinese linguistic structure may often fall short of logical grounding (as has been exemplified by 電報發了 and 天不怕，地不怕). This imperfection in grammatical "correctness" and structural "preciseness" is usually compensated by the language sense of the Chinese speaking people. The following examples show the importance of the role of linguistic sense:

(a) 中國隊大勝美國隊 = 中國隊大敗美國隊。

The Americans were beaten by the Chinese in the game.

Antagonism in form and in logic leads to a surprising identity in semantic content. Also:

(b) 這件事好令我傷心 = 這件事好不令我傷心。

I was greatly disappointed in that affair.

More often than not, the use of lexical indications to show the passive voice in Chinese (e.g., 被 , 受 , 讓 , and 叫) is determined by sense of language rather than grammatical norms and logical inference.

(4) Language Situation vs Syntactic Structure

Studies on the relationship between language situation and syntactic structure is another important area worthy of specific consideration and exploration. A typical topic in this connection is the mechanism of word order in CE/EC translation, which is of vital importance in the shaping up of semantic structure of the Chinese at phrase as well as sentence levels. Again owing to the weakness in form, the position of the sentence components can flexibly be shifted without any necessary change in form. Variability in the sentence pattern is basically subject to the pragmatic motivation implied in the text. Take the following examples:

(a) 他甚麼都知道。（他：actor-subject/thematic subject. 即施事主語 / 主位主語；甚麼：receptor subject. 主語）
He knows everything about it.

(b) 甚麼他都知道。（甚麼：receptor subject/thematic subject. 即受事主語 / 主位主語；他：actor-subject.)
He is really knowledgeable.

(c) 他知道甚麼？（他：actor-subject, thematic subject.；甚麼：object.)
What the hell does he know about it?（他知道甚麼？！）

(d) 他究竟知道些甚麼？(ditto)
He knows nothing about it.（他甚麼也不知道！）

A summing-up of the instances cited in the above items (1–4) demonstrates the necessity of the study of the mechanism of function in CE/EC transfer. The covertness 隱含性 of Chinese grammar in comparison with the overtness 外顯性 of English grammar emphasizes the necessity. Full play of the mechanism of function may result in the gradation of CE/EC translation in terms of quality and effect in bilingual communication:

Level A（最高等級翻譯） Top Level Translation	— Semantically exact/Pragmatically appropriate/Semiotically dynamic
Level B（中間等級翻譯） Intermediate Level Translation	— Semantically exact to some extent/ Pragmatically appropriate to some extent
Level C（基礎等級翻譯） Basic Level Translation	— Semantically passable/Pragmatically passable/Semiotically too close

Functional mechanism can also be shown in terms of models of bilingual transfer to achieve equivalence, the basic task of translation:

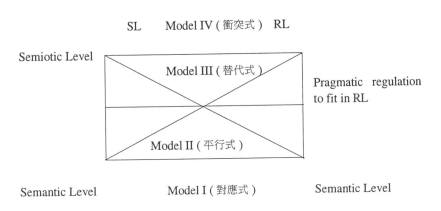

Semiotic Level

SL   Model IV (衝突式)   RL

Model III (替代式)

Pragmatic regulation to fit in RL

Model II (平行式)

Semantic Level   Model I (對應式)   Semantic Level

Cultural Transfer in CE/EC Translation Studies

No language is free from cultural coloration extensively encoded in cultural signs. In other words, no language is free from the imprints of diversified cultural information. As a matter of fact, all human languages stem from their specific cultural matrixes. In that event, no translation is exempt from a cross-cultural transfer. Given the extreme disparities between the Chinese and English cultures, bilingual transfer of meaning can in no way be realized without studying models of cross-cultural transfer in translation theory.

(1) The signalization 符號化 of cultural information in language.
Different languages have different "cultural flavor", or "color", characterized by their cultures. The Chinese culture is what makes the language Chinese. The same goes for English. And, any language can be looked upon as "a tape" 幅帶 carrying a system and its subsystems of cultural signs. Generally, the sign system of a language falls into a series of subsystems of signs encoded on the "tape":

(a) Signs of ethnological ideology 民族思想、意識符號
In Chinese, e.g.: 孝道、官本位、中庸之道
In English, e.g.: sportsmanship, Christianity, keep up with the Joneses

(b) Signs of ethnological institutions 民族典章、政制符號
In Chinese, e.g., 大鍋飯、政協、狀元
In English, e.g., parliament, cop, land agent

(c) Signs of ethnological environment 民族地理、環境符號
In Chinese, e.g., 長城、蓬萊仙境、胡同
In English, e.g., Dover, Big Ben, mall

(d) Signs of ethnological material life 民族物質生活符號
In Chinese, e.g., 八寶飯、旗袍、茶館
In English, e.g., sandwich, cigar, jeans

(e) Signs of ethnological cultural life 民族文化聲象符號
In Chinese, e.g., 信天游、相聲、琵琶
In English, e.g., rock-and-roll, sonnet, poker

(f) Signs of ethnological social customs 民族社會習俗符號
In Chinese, e.g., 開後門、賽龍舟、倒插門
In English, e.g., thanksgiving, honeymoon, coffee break

Needless to say, recognition of the SL cultural signs is the first step to transfer them into the receptor language.

(2) Possibilities for a cross-cultural transfer are realizable on the following grounds:

(a) Identity of cultural cognition 文化認知的同一性 is universal. For instance, people can learn to read music of other lands without much difficulty.

(b) Cultural contact side by side with language contact makes different cultures readily understandable to each other. Cultural contact opens up ample possibilities for language contact.

(c) Psychologically, men are invariably motivated by the desire to crave novelties. This novelty-oriented mentality 求異心態 , (Piaget, 1950, 1953) always makes an alien culture (here, the SL culture) attractive to the minds of the RL readers and hearers.

(d) The message content in a SL cultural sign is usually not difficult to get across by many compensatory means more effective than language. That makes the cultural signs in language more easily decoded. For instance, disco dance makes it very easy to figure out what the word "disco" is all about.

The result of these possibilities ensures the acceptability of a "literal transfer" of the SL culture into the receptor language and justifies the basic norm for cross-cultural translation, that is, the translation must faithfully reflect the SL cultural matrix to the RL readers.

(3) Expediencies for the transfer of the SL culture into the receptor language apart from "literal transferring".

The decoding of SL cultural signs also includes the following expediencies:

(a) Description 描述法 : a means of decoding the sign by way of describing the message content:

e.g., 青紗帳 → the green curtain of tall crops

Scotch → 蘇格蘭威士忌酒

(b) Rephrasing 易詞法 : a means of decoding the sign by way of substituting a more acceptable RL equivalent for the original:

e.g., 殺身成仁 → die for a just cause

chewing gum → 口香糖 (more acceptable than 咀嚼糖)

仁 is a Chinese ethical sign 倫理觀符號 , which is bound to require lengthy yet still incomplete rendering (e.g., "description") if not otherwise transferred. 口香 gives an aesthetic flavor in Chinese. Rephrasing affords a wider margin for social acceptability.

(c) Addition 加詞法 : a means of decoding the sign by way of adding a category or generic word to improve intelligibility and acceptability:

e.g., 二簧 → *erhuang* melodies

Swahili → 斯瓦希里語

Here, the category/generic word serves as an annotation.

(d) Transliteration 音譯法 : a more or less direct means of introducing an alien cultural sign into the receptor language:

e.g., 麒麟 → kylin

taxi → 的士

With the development of cultural contact as well as language contact, equivalent decoding ("literal transferring") of cultural signs has, undoubtedly, good prospects of gaining more and more ground in cross-cultural translation.

Studies of Applied Theory

Applied theory of translation concerns itself with the following topics in CE/EC translation in a theoretical dimension:

Limits of Translatability

Disparities in language and culture between Chinese and English may give rise to extensive obstacles in the channel of bilingual transference. Obstacles can be classified into the following groups:

(a) Obstacles caused by disparities in language structure, especially in the letter-system:

  e.g., 年年難過年年過

     處處無家處處家 .

  Most Chinese antitheses or couplets 對聯 are structured to contain antithetical structures framed up by Chinese characters; some are very cleverly devised. The above couplet is structured with only six characters 年、難、過、處、無、 and 家 , the meaning being "After the bitter year comes another; the homeless makes his home nowhere and everywhere".

(b) Obstacles caused by disparities in the phonological system between Chinese and English:

  e.g., "Life is made up of sobs, sniffles, and smiles, with sniffles predominating." (O. Henry)

  The alliteration in the above sentence (sobs, sniffles, and smiles) is untranslatable into Chinese. For most puns, it is difficult to find an equally witty RL counterpart. In Chinese RL the names of the four unfortunate girls in Cao Xueqin's novel *A Dream of the Red Mansions* 《紅樓夢》 , 元春 , 迎春 , 探春 and 惜春 make up a pun 元迎探惜 → 原應嘆息 , meaning "It's really lamentable."

(c) Obstacles caused by disparities in ethnological cultural matrix:

  e.g., 待字閨中

  Here 字 means 生庚八字 (the date of birth and the eight characters of a horoscope), a superstitious belief in old China, which was supposed to predetermine a girl's marriage. Today the idiomatic phrase may still be in use but is only rendered to mean "not betrothed yet".

(d) Obstacles caused by disparities in nomenclature 命名法差異 :
   e.g., 牛頭鉋床 — shaper (shaping machine)
   Nomenclature may vary from language to language owing to the differences between people's perception of the object. The Chinese 牛頭 (a cow's head) is a figurative while the English "shaper" stresses the function of the machine.

(e) Obstacles caused by disparities in collocative conventions:
   e.g., 吃食堂 (述賓結構 , a VO structure)
   The original collocation, which means "be at mess", would be absurd if rendered literally into English.

A great many Chinese "measure words" 量詞 fall short of equivalence in English, such as 三尾魚 (three fish), 闖一場禍 (to court a disaster), 一片深情 (inflexible devotion), etc. Loss of meaning because of collocative inflexibility also occurs quite often in EC translation.

Remedies to overcome the obstacles vary. As exemplified above, the most commonly used means are substitution 易詞而譯 , decoloration 淡化 , or de-figuration 非形象化 , or simply subtraction.

Studies on Translation Procedures in CE/EC Transfer

Applied theoretical studies in this area involve tasks of analytical and synthetical studies. The whole process can be broken down into three stages:

The First Stage: Analytical Studies, chiefly on the source language:

(a) Morphological/lexical analysis 形態/詞匯分析
(b) Semantical analysis 語義內容分析
(c) Syntactic analysis 句法關係分析
(d) Textual analysis 篇章結構分析

The Second Stage: Synthetical Studies, chiefly on the receptor language:

(a) Word order readjustment 語序調整
(b) Sentence organization 句子組織
(c) Textual arrangement 句段安排
(d) Stylistic polish 文體修飾
(e) Cultural regulation 文化調節

The Third Stage: Check and test routines (including "back translation" of samples and final revising).

Studies on Translation Methods

Applied theoretical studies concern themselves much with a systematic methodology developed in CE/EC translation practice. The system which has been so far described in various surveys comprises techniques including "cutting" 分切 , "combining" 並聯 , "splitting" 拆離 , "converting" 轉換 , "substituting" 替代 , "reversing" 反轉 , "shifting" 轉移 , "extending" 引伸 , "decoloring" or "restoring", 淡化或還原 , "annotating" 註釋 , "adding" 加 詞 , "subtracting" or "omitting", 減詞或省略 , "recasting" 重構 , and "blend-ing" 融合 . Translation methodology (techniques on a systematic basis) is an open-class system awaiting improvement and further development.

Studies on the Basic Model of CE/EC Translation Theory

In the wake of extensive practice and new developments in translation studies in the West and Eastern European countries in recent decades, Chinese translation theorists are beginning to embark on an in-depth study of the basic theoretical model for translation from/into Chinese.

While a great number of translators are still taking 信達雅 as their guiding principle in practice as well as in theory, some theorists have shifted to new approaches based on linguistics. Theoretical principles of J. C. Catford, E. A. Nida, G. Mounin, A. V. Fedorov and L. S. Barkhudarov were introduced. The result is the appearance of different schools of thought. There are advocators of the introduction into Chinese translation theory of the "model of equivalence" (equal value 等值翻譯) and the "model of equal effect" 等效翻譯 . Other theorists advocate a "text linguistic model" 語段 語言學模式 or a model based on CE/EC contrastive studies with a view to the construction of a new model paying special attention to semantic structure and functional mechanism (semantic-function model, 語義 - 功能模式). Explorations in this direction are beyond doubt worthy of serious consideration for the construction of a scientific system of the fundamental theory of Chinese translation and translatology.

References

Jin, Di 金隄 . 《等效翻譯探索》 (*Exploring Equivalent-effect Translation*). Beijing: China Translation and Publishing Corporation 中國對外翻譯出版公司 , 1987.
———— and Eugene A. Nida. *On Translation*. Beijing: China Translation and Publishing Corporation 中國對外翻譯出版公司 , 1984.

Loh, Dian-yang 陸殿揚 . 《英漢翻譯理論與技巧》 (*EC Translation Theory and Techniques*). Beijing: Times Press 時代出版社 , 1959.

Luo, Xinzhang 羅新璋 . 《翻譯論集》 (*Essays on Translation*). Beijing: The Commercial Press 商務印書館 , 1984.

Ma, Zuyi 馬祖毅 . 《中國翻譯簡史 ——「五四」運動以前部份》 (*A Concise History of Translation in China — Before the May Fourth Movement*). Beijing: China Translation and Publishing Corporation 中國對外翻譯出版公司 , 1984.

Qian, Gechuan 錢歌川 . 《翻譯的技巧》 (*Translation Techniques*). Taipei: K'ai-ming Bookstore 開明書店 , 1973.

Wu, Xinxiang 吳新祥 and Li Hongan 李宏安 . 《等值翻譯論》 (*Explorations in Equal Value Translation*). Nanchang: Jiangxi Education Press 江西教育出版社 , 1990.

TRANSFER

Transfer and Translation

Carl James
Department of Linguistics
University of Bangor, Wales, U.K.

Transfer, in its most general sense, is used by learning psychologists to refer to the observation that the learning of task A affects the subsequent learning of task B. When we narrow the scope of the term to language transfer we derive the hypothesis that one's learning of a foreign language will be conditioned in various ways by the language-knowledge one already possesses, which will be, in the limiting case, one's native-language knowledge. We should go on to restrict the scope of the definition of transfer further still, and avoid speaking of global knowledge of say Portuguese or English and think in terms of one's present (native-language) and targeted (foreign-language) knowledge of specific rules and systems.

Transfer and Translation

The tendency of the earlier "classic" writers on the subjects of transfer and translation is to emphasize the similarities between these two processes. Thus Harris writes of the "inherent connection between transfer and translation", while Eugene Nida's "Science of Translation" paper often conflates the two notions, so that literal translation or calquing are equated. One might say that this is also the layman's view of transfer: substituting foreign-language with native-language lexis while keeping the other dimensions of the "original" intact.

Later discussions of the relationship have attempted to find features distinguishing transfer from translation. These features reduce to four types and are listed and discussed by Danchev as follows:

(1) Translation is "conscious" while transfer is "unconscious". The use of this term poses more problems than it solves, taking us into the realm of linguistic metacognition. How can we ever be sure that we were conscious or not, as opposed to having become aware, in retrospect, of our linguistic behaviour? This is the same problem as that which surrounds the protocol analysis of foreign language learning advocated by some researchers. Then there is the problem of specifying what one was conscious of : was it of the fact that one did translation or resorted to transfer, or of the mechanisms how one did these things? To confuse the issue further, one researcher of foreign-language learning, Tarone, describes transfer as a "conscious communication strategy".

(2) Translation is unnatural while transfer is natural. This is clearly Peter Newmark's position, for he speaks of translation as "a complex, artificial, and unnatural process" while Gideon Toury claims that "learners hardly ever translate on their own initiative". On the other hand there is the standpoint of "natural translation" represented by Harris and Sherwood and defined by them as "The translating done in everyday circumstances by people who have had no special training for it."

(3) Translation has broader scope than transfer. This distinction is not wholly clear but the implication seems to be that literal translation or calquing or transfer (all three being synonymous) is only one of many types of translation: it follows that transfer is relatively narrow in scope. The claim is valid only while this inherently restricted definition of transfer is maintained however. As soon as one begins to consider such phenomena as discourse transfer or even lexical transfer, the artificiality of the distinction becomes evident.

(4) Translation is written while transfer is spoken. This is the weakest distinction to defend, since it is manifestly true both that translation can be spoken (in which case we speak of Interpreting) and also that transfer takes place in writing as well as in speaking a foreign language. This is not to deny, however, that unwanted or "negative" transfer can be reduced and positive transfer nurtured more

effectively in writing than in speaking, for the simple reason that one has more time for monitoring one's output in writing. Also, what is said remains said and cannot be unsaid, whereas revisions before commission and committal are feasible in writing, which may undergo several drafts before the author decides on his final version.

What we seem to have in these putative distinctions between transfer and translation is a set of half-truths. In this there is a strong similarity with translation theory in general. It would be preferable to say that there is no inherent relationship between transfer and translation, only the accidental one mentioned in (3) whereby the type of lexical substitution that can lead to poor translation happens to coincide with syntactic (word order) transfer. In fact, much has recently been made of this type of transfer in the Monitor-Model theory of foreign-language learning.

Transfer in Translation

Linguists have had occasion to distinguish two different types of transfer, which we shall refer to here as "primary" and "secondary" transfer. Primary transfer is spontaneous, the untaught strategy of each individual learner, and was described by Einar Haugen as "actual original interference [transfer], not regulated by previous usage". Secondary transfer is by contrast "institutionalized", in the sense that is the property not of the individual foreign-language learner, but of the community in a language contact situation. In the history of transfer studies the focus was initially on secondary transfer. Thus Weinreich and Haugen are respectively descriptions of the linguistic assimilation of Yiddish and of Norwegian toward English in immigrant communities in the U.S.A.

A consideration of the effects of transfer in the process of transfer reveals a further possible distinction to be made. First, and especially if the directionality of translation is native-language-to-foreign-language (or L1 > L2), the translator will tend to transfer the forms and patterns of his native language to his attempted foreign-language production. He will however do this not because he is translating, but quite simply because he is composing in a foreign and thus "weaker" language; and the same transfer — positive as well as negative — would be likely to take place had the individual been writing a letter, describing a film, or having an argument in the foreign language. Since such (native-language) transfer occurs independently of the task and is the result of the confluence, in the speaker's mind, of two knowledge-systems, we could call this systemic transfer. The second type of transfer is unique to the act of translation, owing to the fact that the translator, if she is to translate, must have the source-language text *in praesentia*. Where the source-language text is not present in this sense, the corresponding target-language text is not a translation but an interpretation of or semantic reaction to the source-language text. We can call this kind of transfer translational transfer. As Toury relevantly says, "L1 is directly supplied to him [i.e. the translator — CJ] in encoded chunks … far beyond the abstract system which is stored in the brain and available for activation and use". Certain interesting implications derive from this distinction between systemic and translational transfer:

(1) That transfer from L1 to L2 is likely to be potent during the act of translation. It is potent because it springs from two sources: from the source language text *in praesentia* and at the same time from the translator's systemic knowledge of his L1. The reason why foreign language teaching methodologists have outlawed translation as a learning device is precisely because of their belief that translation is a process that lets in the roughest forces of transfer. I believe, however, that this view can be challenged if we invoke a further distinction that has gained currency in work on foreign-language learning: I refer here to the notion of learner strategy. In this framework, it is claimed that L1 transfer, in common with some other strategies, has two uses for the learner: he can resort to the L1 either in order to solve a problem of L2 learning, or to alleviate a problem in L2 communication. Accordingly, transfer may be either a competence-oriented learning strategy or a performance-oriented communication strategy. One of the big problems with this claim is how to see the wood for the trees: how can we tell when the learner is resorting to transfer as a communication strategy, rather than as a learning strategy? Here research into the act of translation is in a less compromised position than research into L2 learning, for the simple reason that communication is a necessary concomitant of learning a foreign language, whereas in translating one is communicating but not learning. From this it follows that the direct and uncomplicated study of transfer as a communication strategy can be best pursued in studying the act of translation.

(2) A second implication is that translational, but not systemic, transfer will be activated in translation that is L2 > L1, that is into the native language, because here, no less than in L1 > L2 translation, instances of the L2 are again "directly supplied ... in encoded chunks." It may also be the case, as Toury suggests, that transfer goes relatively unchecked in L2 > L1 translation because the translator is over-confident of his command of the translation (in this case his native language) and so relaxes the "normal" monitoring functions which he activates for the inverse directionality.

(3) A third implication is that attempts made by some fashionable applied linguists to banish the Behaviourist-coloured terms "transfer" and "interference" and replace them with the more Cognitivist "ignorance" may be entirely unjustified. I have argued elsewhere that it is possible to find among L2 learners clear evidence of ignorance in the absence of interference as well as vice-versa. Here I would like to refine those arguments a little, suggesting that in the case of translational transfer into the L1 it would be absurd to invoke the notion of ignorance: in this case we quite clearly are dealing with interference in the strictest (and original) sense of the term.

(4) If we now invoke all four of the transfer types identified — original, institutionalized, systemic and translational — a very complex picture indeed emerges for those engaged in translator training. If the trainee is a natural bilingual he is likely to come disequipped for his vocation, that is with tendencies to all four types of transfer. If the trainee is a foreign language learner he will supply the original transfer, his teachers the institutionalized, and the act of translating itself the other two.

Translation in the Study of Transfer in Foreign Language Learning

The classical paradigm for the study of L1 transfer in L2 learning was Contrastive Analysis, as expounded by Lado, and according to which potential transfer could be predicted by juxtaposing descriptions of comparable systems of L1 and L2. So, a contrastive analysis of the determiner or article systems of Portuguese and English allows us to predict that the Portuguese learner of English will tend to say

* The John is in the garden.

since it is a contrastive feature of the respective grammars that Portuguese allows articles with proper nouns while English does not: hence *O João está no jardim*. However, this procedure as we have described it is vulnerable to the charge that we are imposing potentially arbitrary criteria for comparison. While in the case cited the equation of the grammatical categories article leads to acceptable results, this might be largely due to the accident of Portuguese and English being closely related languages: what if we were to compare English with Russian, a language without articles? What if the two languages have categories whose similarity is limited to a cultural accident of shared linguistic terminology? In such cases attempting to use category-membership as the criterion for comparability is likely to run into difficulties.

For these reasons formal and categorial criteria have to be abandoned and semantic-pragmatic criteria resorted to: translation becomes the *tertium comparationis* and we accept as input to a contrastive analysis translationally paired texts, usually single sentences. It is here where the contrastivist encounters just those problems which his colleagues in translation theory have been wrestling with for centuries. The problem is essentially that of the contextual dependency of translational equivalents: what fits one context does not fit another, and the result of forcing is translationese. Another way to explain the same problem would be to say that translation has to be text-specific, whereas the contrastivist, keen to explain L1 transfer, aspires to make statements that are more general in that they cover not just tokens but rather types. One interesting attempt to solve the problem, by resolving the tension between category-comparison on the one hand and token-comparison on the other was Levenston's suggestion for a "translation paradigm":

> A grammatical category from language A is listed opposite all the categories in language B by which it may be translated. Whenever possible, the grammatical and contextual criteria governing the choice of one translation rather than another are listed in notes to the paradigm. The most frequent translation is listed first ...

Here the "A" language is the L1 (Hebrew), so the effect is to list the L2 alternatives in transfer or translation: in other words, there is a one-to-many relationship of divergent polysemy, but of course the opposite directionality could be instructive to diagram in such a "paradigm" also.

The contrastivist's discovery of the complexities of translation equivalence was only the beginning of his realization that the basic approach of classical contrastive analysis would need to be revised: juxtaposing structural descriptions of L1 and L2 is easier said than done, and even when done does not always lead to successful predictions of transfer. It was precisely this repeated failure to predict L1 transfer when it did in fact occur, and the related error of predicting transfer which did not materialize that has led latterly to some hard thinking. Let me sketch in the main thrust of this more recent thought.

Markedness Theory and Transfer

Markedness theory has assumed two forms, linguistic markedness and psycholinguistic markedness. The linguistic approach derives from work in the 1960s on typological universals and got extra boost from Chomsky's "Universal Grammar". Eckman exploited the notion first in contrastive analysis, with his "Markedness Differential Hypothesis", according to which the learning difficulty of an L2 item is determined not simply by its similarity to or difference from the corresponding L1 item but also by whether the L2 item is more marked than the L1 item. The hypothesis explains why it is that Germans learning English find it difficult to maintain the +/– voicing contrast of obstruents in word-final position (as in English [lok]:[log], which get conflated to [lok]): the reason is that word-final is a marked position for the contrast in question: typologically, it is much rarer for a language to have the voice contrast finally than initially or medially.

A second application of Markedness Theory is Zobl, who develops ideas derived from word order typology. He observes that French learners of English do NOT tend to say *"He them likes" by transfer from L1 *Il les aime*, whereas English learners of French do produce constructions like *Le chien a mangé les* by L1 transfer. Note the misprediction that classical contrastive analysis would have made here, for it would have predicted just the opposite. The explanation lies in the fact, according to Zobl, that in both English and French the Subject + Verb + Object (SVO) word order is unmarked or "normal" and it is a marked quirk of French to allow the SOV order provided the Object is a pronoun. So the French learner of English suppresses his urge to transfer a marked feature to the L2 while the English learner of French has no scruples about transferring the unmarked SVO word order to French, even though the Object is pronominal rather than nominal. It seems to me, incidentally, that L1 Portuguese, with its Brazilian and Lusitanian variants of pronominal object placement, would be a good test-case for the refinement to the transfer hypothesis, with English as the foreign language.

And the connection to translation is just as intriguing, invoking as it does the issue of directionality of transfer. In the case of foreign language learning we are concerned with directionality of learning, and with transfer as a learning strategy. In the case of translation we are involved with directionality of transfer as a communication strategy. The implication of linguistic markedness theory is that the strategy will be more successful, and lead to less mistranslation, in one direction than in the opposite.

Psycholinguistic markedness theory suggests that learners have intuitions about what parts of their L1 are candidates for transfer and which are not: they are equipped with a "psychotypology", perhaps derived from folk linguistics and that in turn from universal intuitions of language specificity. Learners will not transfer to L2 items which they feel to be marked, that is items perceived by them as "… infrequent, irregular, semantically or structurally opaque, or in any way exceptional" even if they would in fact successfully transfer. This means that the learner is no longer at the mercy of his L1 as he was assumed to be in the Behaviourist version of transfer theory: he is a discriminator. The implication for foreign language teaching is that techniques need to be developed to sharpen his powers of discrimination, to help him make decisions concerning what he should and should not transfer. Here it is that Translation comes into the picture again. The use of translation as a teaching technique has been banned by the orthodox for many years. However, at the same time we have seen a growing interest in techniques involving "consciousness raising" and "awareness of language", and it might be the case that translation could be about to be reinstated.

Another interesting suggestion concerning the role of L1 in foreign-language learning and one having pedagogic appeal is Krashen's L1 plus Monitor Mode. If the learner discovers that he is ignorant of a particular foreign-language rule to make himself understood, he can always invoke the corresponding L1 rule as a makeshift device. This is essentially a "cosmetic" operation, cosmetic in two senses, first in resorting to the L1 rule in the first place as the bald gentleman resorts to a wig, and second in papering over the obvious cracks in the plaster that resorting to the L1 has laid bare: this is Monitor use. So the two steps are: (1) First, "… plug lexical items of the second language into the surface structure of the first language

... as one would handle word-for-word translation" (2) Then secondly, "... add some morphology and repair word-order". What is truly remarkable about the L1 plus Monitor Mode concept is that its author rejects it out of hand as constituting a mere "hollow victory" for the learner, makeshift repair rather than permanent cure for that ignorance which only further acquisition can cure. While nobody would deny that it is preferable for learners to produce L2 utterances on a direct-access basis rather than through the mediation of the L1, that is in a coordinate bilingual mode rather than a compound bilingual mode, I see no reason for excluding the L1 + Monitor Mode from the skill-getting phase of foreign-language learning. It is true that the L1 + Monitor Mode is no permanent cure for not knowing and that its operation is cumbersome and time-consuming. But the more they are practised, the less effort, time and attention will be called for, since the requisite skills will slowly become automatized: "Repeated performance of the activity ... leads to the availability of ready-made plans in long-term memory for such activities". To this we can add that the production of such construction kit utterances by the learner himself, no matter how dysfluent, creates extra autogenerated "comprehensible input" that is likely to promote Acquisition anyway. I feel that we have here a typical case of the contempt with which most applied linguists view translation as a foreign-language learning device.

References

Danchev, Andrei. "Transfer and Translation." *Finlance*, Vol. 2 (1982), pp. 39–61.
Levenston, Edward A. "The 'Translation Paradigm': A Technique for Contrastive Analysis." *International Review of Applied Linguistics*, Vol. 3, No. 3 (1965), pp. 221–25.
Nida, Eugene A. "Science of Translation." *Language*, Vol. 45 (1969), pp. 483–98.

TRANSLATABILITY

Translatability in CE/EC Translation

Guo Jianzhong
Department of Foreign Languages
Hangzhou University, Hangzhou, China

The problem of translatability is an essential issue in translation theory, and it has also played a prominent role in the modern science of translation. In fact, debate over possibility/impossibility of translation began with the very emergence of translation practice and translation studies in history.

The perennial question whether translation is, in fact, possible is rooted in ancient religious and psychological doubts on whether there ought to be any passage from one language to another. (Steiner, 1975:239)

At a later stage in history the school of impossibility of translation based their theory on the formal and pragmatic conviction that there can be no true symmetry, no adequate mirroring, between two different semantic systems.

This school also holds that meaning can never be wholly separated from expressive form, since all human speech consists of arbitrarily selected but intensely conventional signals. Thus, the style, harmony and force of the language are untranslatable.

Still others hold that there are developed, civilized languages and undeveloped, primitive languages. According to them, what can be expressed in the former cannot be expressed in the latter because the latter lacks the vocabulary and grammatical structures of the former.

There are also some people who based their argument on the

cultural differences. Different nations have their own backgrounds, traditions, customs, religions , philosophies and values, which can hardly be expressed in different languages for the lack of the concepts and the way of speaking about them.

In a word, this school over-emphasizes the differences between nations in language and culture, and approaches the problem from a metaphysical point of view.

The modern science of translation expounds and proves the possibility of translation from a dialectic point of view of unity between thought and language.

First of all, all human thoughts are identical for the cognitive worlds and the way of thinking are universal. A common humanity made translation possible. (Steiner, 1975:246)

Secondly, there is a common core of human experience and the relatable modes of speaking about it. According to many linguists, what unites mankind is much greater than what divides. The view that in principle everything can be expressed in every language is, in fact, widespread in modern linguistics.

The dichotomy of language and speech also provides arguments for the possibility of translation, for what is to be translated is not language system but speech.

The development of text-linguistics shows that individual elements which are untranslatable when isolated, may become translatable if dealt with on the basis of the whole text. It is still an undisputable principle that in translation equivalence can always be established at a higher level of language units.

Last but not least, the modern science of translation also proves that cultural differences should not be an unsurmountable obstacle to communication between nations. Different peoples can understand each other if they hold no prejudice, and there is a universal natural predisposition to language, so that all languages must hold within them the *key* to understanding all languages. So apparent untranslatability brought about by cultural differences of individual speech can be countered with potential translatability.

However, the serious translator believes, in effect, that a perfect translation from one language to another is not always possible, and that there are limitations on translatability.

No communication, even within a single language, is ever absolute … and we certainly cannot expect a perfect match between languages. (Nida and Taber, 1982:4–5)

The translator's language can only be approximate. (Newmark, 1981:7)

Untranslatability occurs due to either linguistic or cultural reasons, as noted by Catford (1965). This classification, though not absolute, provides us with a point of departure for our discussion.

Linguistic Untranslatability

If the form in which a message is expressed is an essential element of its significance, there is a very distinct limitation in communicating this significance from one language to another. It is usually impossible to reproduce this type of "meaning".

In CE/EC translation linguistic untranslatability may occur at various levels.

Graphological Level

In the sentence "You have written 'skill' with a 'c' instead of a 'k'.", the word "skill" and the letters "c" and "k" cannot be translated into Chinese.

Likewise, in the sentence " '八' 字都還沒一撇呢 ," 八 is also untranslatable.

Phonological Level

Accent, either local, social or foreign, can hardly be translated. For example, if in a short story, a certain character speaks English with a Chinese accent, how this can be conveyed in the Chinese translation of the story?

The same is true with dialect. Should we use a southern Chinese dialect in the translation of Black English?

Mispronunciations of an illiterate character in literary works are always difficult to reproduce in translation.

Lexical Level

Connotative meaning may vary from language to language. David Hawkes translated "The Dream of the Red Chamber" into "The Story of the Stone", and when he had to express the idea of "the dream of the Red Chamber", he turned it into "the dream of Golden Days". Likewise, he turned "The House of Red Delights" into "The House of Green Delights", and so on and so forth. It is because he was aware of the different connotations of the two colours. According to him, "red" in the story is a symbol — "sometimes of spring, sometimes of youth, sometimes of good fortune or prosperity.... Unfortunately — apart from rosy cheeks and vermeil lip of youth — redness has no such connotations in English and I have found that the Chinese reds have tended to turn into English golds or greens.... I am aware that there is some sort of loss here, but have lacked the ingenuity to avert it." (Hawkes, 1973:43)

Whether this change is successful or not is another question. Our interest in citing Hawkes is to show the difficulty, sometimes the impossibility, of reproducing connotative meanings in translation.

Few words correspond precisely in two languages. There is no English word corresponding to 親家 in Chinese , nor a Chinese word corresponding to "cousin" in English. And what is more, the individual language determines the segmentation of many physical objects and virtually all intellectual concepts differently.

Take colours for example: "green" in English may be 青 or 綠 in Chinese. Then how is 青山綠水 to be rendered into English? A Chinese feels 酸、脹、麻、痛 , when given acupuncture, but the English-speaking people can only feel a "pain". That is because there exists a world-view centered in individual languages, according to some linguists. Then how is the Chinese phrase 腰酸背痛 to be faithfully turned into English?

It is universally accepted that idioms, idiomatic phrases and proverbs are difficult to translate. This should also include 歇後語 in Chinese, for all of them are products of the national or linguistic characteristics, closely related to historical, cultural and geographical backgrounds. Many a time we can only retain the meaning at the sacrifice of the form.

A very important dimension of fidelity which translators often neglect is comparability in frequency of occurrence, or the relative familiarity of the expressions in the original and the translation. (Chao, 1976:155) A familiar term in one language is an unfamiliar term in the other. This will affect the fidelity even if the translation is accurate in other respects.

For example, 竹 (bamboo) is a familiar term to Chinese, and there are many idioms or expressions associated with 竹 . But it is unfamiliar to English-speaking people. On the other hand, baseball is a popular game in

America, but unfamiliar to most Chinese. There are many idioms and phrases associated with the game, which can hardly be turned literally into Chinese.

Some peculiar expressions or structures in one language can hardly be turned faithfully into another. For example, Lincoln's Gettysburg Address begins with "Four score and seven years ago", which covers the identical time span with "eighty-seven years ago". In the Chinese translation, the flat, colourless and matter-of-fact statement "eighty-seven years ago" has to be used, for the Chinese language lacks the expressive form corresponding to "four score and seven years ago" with its unmistakably biblical ring, appropriate to solemn oratory.

Puns are generally considered untranslatable because of the ambiguities which arise from two main sources, (1) shared exponents of two or more source-language grammatical or lexical items, (2) polysemy of a source-language item with no corresponding target-language polysemy. (Catford, 1965:94) In translating Mao Dun's 茅盾 *Vacillation*, Mr Qian Gechuan 錢歌川 turned 委員 and 桂圓 which are assonant into "committee" and "common tea". This is undoubtedly a successful translation. But according to L. Forster, "What has been rendered — and brilliantly rendered — is the fact of the pun; not the pun itself, which is probably untranslatable." (Forster, 1958:5)

Included in this category are play with words like a riddle about a character or a word, fortune-telling by analyzing the component parts of a Chinese character (glyphomancy), games of forfeits in English, all of which are based on the graphological level, and also play with words like palindrome, deliberately intended ambiguities and play with punctuations, all of which are based on the grammatical level.

Almost all translators and translation theorists regard poetry as untranslatable because the expressive form and content in poetry cannot be separated. Even scholars like R. Jakobson and Eugene A. Nida who insist that anything that can be expressed in one language can also be expressed in another hold that "... poetry by definition is untranslatable. Only creative transposition is possible." (Jakobson, 1959:238)

> In a similar way we cannot reproduce the rhythm of ... poetry, the acrostic features of many poems, and the frequent intentional alliteration. At this point, languages just do not correspond, and so we must be prepared to sacrifice certain formal niceties for the sake of the content. (Nida and Taber, 1982:5)

Grammatical Level

When two or more distinct source-language grammatical items are ex-pounded in one and the same phonological or graphological form, it is (relatively) untranslatable. For example, "Flying planes can be dangerous." The ambiguity of the sentence is caused by the shared grammatical form of "flying" both as a present participle and a gerund. When isolated as a single sentence, it is untranslatable.

Jakobson also discussed different grammatical categories in different languages. It is more difficult to remain faithful to the original when we translate into a language provided with a certain grammatical category from a language devoid of such a category. (Jakobson, 1959:235)

In a word, the more remote languages are from one another and the more different syntactically, the harder it must obviously be to express the same concepts and feelings in both.

Stylistic Level

Generally, style refers to language varieties as well as to historical, national or individual styles, which are considered most difficult to be reproduced in translation. It is a common view that in order to retain the original style, a translator has to strive to retain the expressive forms of the original. Then the paradox of untranslatability recurs here.

But Nida points out: "Though style is secondary to content, it is nevertheless important. One should not translate poetry as though it were prose, nor expository material as though it were straight narrative.... It is usually quite impossible to represent some of the stylistic subtleties of the original." (Nida and Taber, 1982:13) Nida further explains that in trying to reproduce the style of the original one must beware of producing something which is not functionally equivalent, since reproducing style, even on a formal level, may not result in an equivalence, and it is functional equiva-lence which is required, whether on the level of content or on the level of style.

Characteristics of period are one aspect of style. Today's style in one language can of course be best translated by using today's style in another. As for the period of the languages involved, there is no necessity, or special virtue in matching period with period. In such a case, Chao Yuen Ren 趙元任 suggested writing in as timeless a style as possible, though this practice, to be sure, may involve a loss of colour and life. (Chao, 1976:162)

The writer's individual style is reflected in his use of language. The fine shades of colouring either at the lexical level or grammatical level can hardly be reproduced in translation. Just as the saying goes, "The style is the man." So the translator's style, which can hardly be avoided, will become an obstacle to the reproduction of the original style, too.

Another aspect in style is pace, which is perhaps most difficult to render, like rhythm in poetry. The abrupt, fast-moving rhythm of I. B. Singer is almost impossible to be reproduced in Chinese. "To reproduce the pace of the original, the translator has to strike the right key right after he begins his translation."

Cultural Untranslatability

When a situational feature, functionally relevant for the source-language text, is completely absent from the culture of which the target language is a part, cultural untranslatability occurs. This type of untranslatability is, however, less "absolute" than linguistic untranslatability. (Catford, 1965: 99)

If the text describes a situation which has elements peculiar to the natural environment, institutions and culture of its language area, there is an inevitable loss of meaning. (Newmark, 1981:7)

For example, words like "potluck" and "garage sale" could find no correspondence in Chinese simply because there are no such practices among the Chinese. Nor could words like 餃子, 餛飩 and 粽子 find their correspondence in English simply because there is no such kind of food for the English-speaking people.

It is often supposed that certain more "abstract" lexical items of concepts or values peculiar to a certain culture are most difficult to translate, such as 陰 and 陽 in Chinese and "humanism" and "rationalism" in English.

Even the same word may have different connotations in different cultures. 宣傳 is always a commendatory term, or at least a neutral one, to Chinese while "propaganda" is always a derogatory term for the English-speaking people. Dogs are generally regarded as "Man's best friends" in the English-speaking countries while for most Chinese they are always associated with unpleasantness. "A lucky dog", if literally translated, would cause misunderstanding by a Chinese who is ignorant of English culture.

Puns, jokes or humour that are associated with a particular culture are also untranslatable.

A Chinese may describe a crowded gathering by saying "It is like 芝麻醬煮餃子 (dumplings being cooked in sesame paste)." To his foreign friend who has never tasted sesame paste and has never seen 餃子 (dumplings) being cooked, the humour would be lost. To describe a very crowded gathering, Westerners often say "It is packed like sardines". Such a comparison might be understood by some Chinese, but the vividness would be lost, for very few Chinese have ever seen a newly-opened can of sardines, with neat rows of finger-sized fish packed tightly in a small flat container. (Deng and Liu, 1989:10)

Undoubtedly, the greater the differences between the two cultures, the more difficult it is to translate anything from one language into another.

Although untranslatability occurs now and then, a good translator can always find means of compensation. These are called compensation strategies, or compensatory methods of translation. A Russian theorist defines it as a special kind of substitution method by which translation equivalence can be achieved when no equivalent can be found, or no appropriate expressive form can be employed in the target language.

If there is no corresponding word in the target language, we may use loan-words like 麥克風 and 味美思 which are borrowed from "microphone" and "vermouth" in English and "kung fu" and "qigong" which are borrowed from 功夫 and 氣功 in Chinese , or we may use loan-translation like 航天飛機 (also 穿梭機) and 五角大樓 which are borrowed from "space shuttle" and "Pentagon" in English, and "paper tiger" and "lose face" which are borrowed from 紙老虎 and 丟臉 in Chinese.

If some grammatical category is absent in a given language, its meaning may be translated into this language by lexical means. (Jakobson, 1959: 235) For example, the various tenses in English grammar are usually translated into Chinese by lexical items.

Besides, there are various common techniques such as conversion, amplification, omission, negation and repetition which may be employed to reduce the loss at various levels.

Cultural untranslatability may be compensated by "cultural equivalence" or explanatory notes.

For example, the Chinese proverb 謀事在人，成事在天 is translated into "Man proposes, *God* disposes", which is a good example of making use

of "cultural equivalence", for the literal translation would be "Man proposes, *Heaven* disposes".

Shift of position is another compensation method based on the text
level. For example, not all English idioms can be turned into Chinese
idioms. On the other hand, many non-idioms in English may be turned into
Chinese idioms. That provides us with compensation strategies. Suppose
there are 100 idioms or idiomatic phrases in a given English text. 40 of them
may be turned into Chinese idioms. In this case, it is possible to compensate
the loss of 60 idioms by turning non-idioms in English into Chinese idioms,
if not 60, at least as close to 60 as possible. That is why it is said that
possibly, parts of the text are untranslatable, but that there is no text that is
untranslatable as a whole.

Compensation methods show that untranslatability is relative. Besides,
more and more translators and translation theorists have come to realize that
the concept of translation equivalence is a dynamic, relative one, and that
translation is thus and will continue to be a relative concept. For example,
the concept of formal correspondence as a translation criterion is being
replaced by the concept of functional equivalence.

The change in attitude towards poetry translation is another example.
As is mentioned above, up till now, most translators and translation theorists still hold that poetry is untranslatable because they think the rhythm,
rhyme and meters of poems cannot be reproduced in another language. As
a matter of fact, while they approach the problem of translation in general
from a dialectic point of view, they deal with poetry translation again on the
basis of formal correspondence. G. Mounin, however, insists that what
should be translated is poems, not the rules and forms of poetic composition
or metrical patterns of various kinds of poems. It is the content of the poem
and the relation between content and form as a whole that should be taken
into consideration in the translation of poetry. Based on this recognition, a
translator should be able to convey the same content and produce the same
or similar effect in the appropriate form of poetry in another language.
(Mounin, 1963)

From the above statement, we can see that Mounin stands for the
translatability of poetry. Now there may be few who agree with him. But in
the future, who can say that there won't be more and more people who take
a more open-minded view towards the problem of poetry translation?

Furthermore, with the passage of time and with more and more contact
between two languages and cultures, what was untranslatable in the past is

translatable at present; and what is untranslatable today will become translatable tomorrow "through linguistic changes, through a refinement of interpretative means, through shifts in receptive sensibility." (Steiner, 1975:249)

Take for example the above-mentioned sentence "It is packed like sardines". This canned food has long been introduced into China, and more and more Chinese are getting used to this canned food. The vividness of the sentence would remain in its literal translation. And what is more, the sentence has frequently appeared in the literary works of Chinese writers:

> 這車廂彷彿沙丁魚罐，裡面的人緊緊的擠得身體都扁了。
>
> （錢鍾書：《圍城》）
>
> 他和那些風塵僕僕的，在黑暗中看不清面容的旅客們擠在一起，就像沙丁魚擠在罐頭盒子裡。
>
> （王蒙：《春之聲》）

To sum up, translation is possible, but there are limits to translatability. However, translatability is always a relative concept. That is the dialectics of translation.

References

Adams, Robert M. *Proteus, His Lies, His Truth: Discussions on Literary Translation.* New York: W. Northon, 1973.

Brower, Reuben A., ed. *On Translation.* Cambridge, Mass.: Harvard University Press, 1959.

Catford, J. C. *A Linguistic Theory of Translation.* London: Oxford University Press, 1965.

Chao, Yuen Ren. *Aspects of Chinese Sociolinguistics — Essays by Yuen Ren Chao.* Stanford: Stanford University Press, 1976.

Deng, Yangchang and Liu Runqing. *Language and Culture.* Beijing: Foreign Language Teaching and Research Press, 1989.

Forster, L. "Translation: An Introduction." In *Aspects of Translation*, edited by A. H. Smith. London: Secker and Warburg, 1958.

Jakobson, Roman "On Linguistic Aspects of Translation." In *On Translation*, edited by Reuben A. Brower. Cambridge, Mass.: Harvard University Press, 1959, pp. 232–39.

Mounin, Georges. *Les problèmes théoriques de la traduction.* Paris: Gallimard, 1963.

Newmark, Peter. *Approaches to Translation.* Oxford: Pergamon Press, 1981.

Nida, Eugene A. *Customs and Culture.* New York: Harper and Brothers, 1954.

———— and Charles R. Taber. *The Theory and Practice of Translation*. Leiden: E. J. Brill, 1982.

Savory, Theodore. *The Art of Translation*. London: Cape, 1968.

Smith, A. H. ed. *Aspects of Translation*. London: Secker and Warburg, 1958.

Steiner, George. *After Babel*. London: Oxford University Press, 1975.

TRANSLATOR/INTERPRETER TRAINING

Training of Conference Interpreters

Pong Lam Shuk-lin
Toronto, Canada

Who Are Conference Interpreters?

Conference interpreters provide interpretation services at bilingual or multilingual conferences. These could be multilingual conferences with a large number of participants, or private discussions between heads of states or ministers. Conference interpreters facilitate communication between delegates who do not speak, or who do not have a complete understanding of, the language or languages spoken by other delegates.

Throughout the history of mankind interpreters have always provided the link which bridged the language barrier. Conference interpreters, however, first made a name for themselves when consecutive interpretation was provided at the Paris Peace Talks which took place after the First World War. Conference interpretation in the form of simultaneous interpretation was successfully attempted at Nuremburg in 1945. This mode of interpretation had been widely used since the setting up of the United Nations in 1946.

Different Modes of Conference Interpretation

There are two main modes in conference interpretation. They are:

Simultaneous Interpretation — a team of conference interpreters sit in a sound-proof booth and wear headphones to listen to discussions or speeches delivered in the conference room. The interpreters take turns to interpret these simultaneously into microphones. Delegates listen to the interpretation by tuning in to receivers. This mode of interpretation takes place in step with the meeting. Interpretation can be provided simultaneously into several languages if required, without prolonging the meeting. Simultaneous interpretation is now the preferred mode of interpretation in about 95% of all international conferences.

Consecutive Interpretation — the conference interpreter sits in the conference room. He listens and takes notes of speeches to aid his memory. He renders his interpretation after the speaker has finished part or all of his speech. This is the preferred mode of interpretation in negotiations or in meetings between political figures, such as ministers or heads of states. No electronic equipment need be installed, except for large conference rooms where sound amplification may be required. As interpretation is rendered consecutively one language at a time, the meeting time is substantially prolonged, particularly at meetings where more than two languages are used.

Qualities of a Conference Interpreter

The conference interpreter's main task is to bridge the language barrier by putting across clearly, fully and accurately all points in speeches or discussions made in one language into another language. He must have the following qualities in order to function effectively:

Language Proficiency — that this is required is self-evident. It does not mean, however, that a person who is proficient in his working languages will be a good conference interpreter. He must also have attributes enumerated in paragraphs below.

Interpretation Technique — the conference interpreter must be able to master techniques such as breaking up long sentences into shorter units, and rearranging sentences with convoluted structures. He will have to interpret large figures, as well as speeches with parts which are not entirely audible. In the latter case, the cause could be momentary equipment failure or speakers turning away from microphones while speaking.

Analytical Power — this quality is equally important. An interpreter with an analytical mind will be able to readily grasp the main points in a speech and interpret them orderly and accurately. This will also enable him to make sense out of muddled or ambiguous speeches.

Sharp Wits and Power of Concentration — these qualities are required as the interpreter has to listen, comprehend and interpret either simultaneously or consecutively. Whilst interpreting he has to listen and comprehend what is to follow so as to be able to provide continuous and accurate interpretation of the whole speech or discussion.

Wealth of Knowledge — a conference interpreter has to be a generalist with a wealth of knowledge. When an unexpectedly unfamiliar subject matter is discussed, he must be able to draw on his general knowledge and render an intelligent interpretation.

Articulation and Eloquence — a conference interpreter must have smooth delivery and be an articulate and eloquent speaker. These qualities will make his interpretation convincing, pleasant to the ear and readily understood.

Types of Training Offered

Two types of training are offered. Job-oriented training is organized by large international organizations such as the United Nations and the European Economic Community. Trainees are trained with a view to working for the organization upon successful completion of training. On the other hand, there are courses of study, mainly in the form of a master's degree programme, offered by academic institutions such as the École Supérieure d'Interprétation et de Traduction, Université Paris III, the Fu Jen University in Taiwan, the University of Hawaii at Manoa, and the Monterey Institute of International Studies in California. These courses are intended to give students exposure and a good and thorough training in conference interpretation and its techniques. This will enable students, upon graduation, to take up the profession of conference interpreting.

Training of Conference Interpreters

Conference interpreting is a challenging, demanding yet rewarding profession for people with attributes outlined above. Training itself is a very rigorous process, and is generally offered to those who have passed aptitude tests designed to test language proficiency and potential for training.

The objective of a training programme is to polish language skills and to improve interpretation techniques. Trainees should be assisted to overcome stage fright so that they can totally concentrate and render complete and accurate interpretations. Even when hard pressed for time, they should be quick-witted and should use logic and power of analysis in the presentation of ideas. The language proficiency of trainees should be further enhanced; and public speaking techniques further refined. Trainees' knowledge of meeting procedures can be improved through initial practice in the classroom, and later through familiarization visits.

To achieve these objectives, it is best that training be conducted in small groups. Training should be the responsibility of an experienced trainer who is also a practising interpreter. He could call on the help of fellow interpreters for language combinations he is not totally conversant with, and linguists could also advise on linguistic aspects and comment on the interpretation from the audience point of view. There should be access to simultaneous interpretation facilities. Trainees' performance should be recorded on cassette tapes for easy playback and to monitor improvements made over time. Recording trainees' performance on videotape would allow trainees to see their facial expressions, gestures, etc., so that they can further improve on their presentation. Towards the end of the course mock conferences and familiarization visits to meetings provided with interpretation services could be organized. Trainees should be allowed to practise in booths when actual meetings not requiring interpretation services are conducted.

Training should be conducted in a friendly and open manner with full participation by both trainers and trainees. Not only should trainees practise interpretation skills, they should also take turns to improvise and deliver extemporaneous speeches. Towards the end of the course trainees should organize mock conferences where they play the roles of delegates and interpreters. Discussions of performance should be conducted in a positive and constructive manner. There should also be individual sessions where trainer and trainees can discuss progress made, as well as individual strengths and weaknesses. Improvements made by trainees differ at various stages of training, and the same holds true for their response to working under pressure. Patience and understanding on the part of the trainer will go a long way in encouraging aspiring interpreters on the road to further progress and improvement.

Phased Training Programme

Training should be conducted in phases. The initial phase is basic training, which will lay the groundwork for subsequent training in consecutive to be followed by simultaneous interpretation.

From the outset, trainees should be encouraged to gather as much information as possible on what conference interpretation is all about. Trainees would be able to gather first impressions of the profession by attending public meetings provided with interpretation service. They can follow up by reading newspaper reports of meeting proceedings and referring to Hansard copies.

For someone entirely new to the profession , the first major difficulty to be overcome is to be able to speak, and at the same time to listen and understand the speaker without allowing the latter to interfere with one's trend of thought. This is easier said than done. Since childhood one is taught to listen to the full message of the speaker before responding. The *shadowing* exercise will help trainees overcome this obstacle. In this exercise trainees listen to a speech and simultaneously repeat it in the same language. A slow and simple speech allows trainees to warm up before gradually working up to faster speeches on more complex subjects.

The above exercises will also allow trainees to be more spontaneous and articulate, so that they are able to speak as quickly or as slowly as required. For best results, these exercises should take place concurrently with exercises in speed reading and in elocution.

The next phase in training is *at-sight translation*. This is the rendering of interpretation in the target language, as one reads a text in the source language. These are exercises in comprehension. As a start trainees should read the text slowly once or twice and, with the help of the trainer, highlight important points and convoluted structures requiring extra attention. Gradually, trainees are allowed shorter reading time, before doing away with pre-reading altogether. At-sight translation tests are an accurate reflection of comprehension and language proficiency. At-sight translation forms an essential component in recruitment and aptitude tests.

Exercises in *gist extraction* should follow. Trainees, with the help of the trainer, should attempt to extract essential points in a speech to facilitate comprehension and delivery. These exercises help to develop critical and analytical thinking so as to avoid the bad habit of *parroting*, i.e. mechanically interpreting words from the source language into the target language without paying attention to sense and meaning.

After mastering gist extraction, the teacher can then go on to practise *paraphrasing* with his trainees. In this phase of training, trainees are encouraged to express the same meaning or idea in as many different ways as possible. This helps to develop linguistic flexibility and enable the interpreter, while interpreting, to find, with greater ease, appropriate and accurate words and phrases to express the speaker's ideas.

The next stage in training is *consecutive interpretation.* In this mode of interpretation the trainer can start with exercises in interpretation of simple text from memory without note-taking. These are very useful memory exercises. After this has been mastered, the trainer can teach note-taking techniques, as well as discussing with trainees useful symbols used in note-taking. Whilst there is a lot to be said for adopting commonly used symbols, trainees should be encouraged to use other symbols that they find useful. Consecutive interpretation with note-taking can start with simple and short speeches, gradually working up to long and complex speeches. Notes and interpretation should be frequently checked and compared with the original speech to identify areas for improvement.

The final phase is training in *simultaneous interpretation.* This phase should start only when trainees have successfully completed all the foregoing exercises. The trainer should start with slow and simple speeches before gradually working up to fast speeches on complex subjects. Interpretation by trainees should be recorded on cassette tape, and during replay teacher and trainees could analyze and discuss areas for improvement. The interpretation should also be checked against the original to spot mistakes and inaccuracies.

During the final phases of training mock conferences can be organized, with trainees alternatively playing the role of delegate and interpreter. Trainees take turns to deliver extemporaneous and prepared speeches, and to interpret consecutively and simultaneously speeches delivered by fellow trainees or guest speakers.

Conclusion

The prerequisite for a successful conference interpreter is aptitude. However, this must be complemented by intensive training. The training programme should be well organized, and be conducted by an experienced trainer or group of trainers with input from practising interpreters and linguists. As training proceeds, progress made by trainees should be monitored and when necessary, adjustments should be made based on trainees' strengths and weaknesses. This will help to ensure the running of a successful programme to the benefit of all parties involved.

Professional Translator and Interpreter Training Programmes

Seán Golden
Faculty of Translation and Interpreting
Universitat Autonoma de Barcelona, Barcelona, Spain

The first step in translator or interpreter training involves selecting the candidates to be trained. The selection process is complicated by a number of factors: aptitude, prior training in translation or interpretation, knowledge of mother tongue and foreign languages (and number of languages known), prior training in other fields of knowledge, educational level of the training programme (undergraduate or postgraduate), etc.

A clear definition of the objectives to be achieved must be the first step in the selection process. A postgraduate training programme in specialized translation of a specific scientific field for people who have a degree or experience in that field and already speak the source language and the target language well is not the same as an undergraduate training programme for students who have to learn the source language and have no prior training in any field of specialization.

It should also be borne in mind that interpreting and translation are two very different kinds of activity, requiring different kinds of aptitude and different kinds of training programmes.

A proper definition of a translator or interpreter training programme should also take into account the future role of the translators and interpreters. Translation and interpretation might have an important role to play in teaching foreign languages or comparative literature, but a professional translator or interpreter training programme must prepare people to work in a demanding professional market where the texts to be translated correspond to very specific types, and the style, register, terminology and phraseology to be employed must correspond to those that would be employed by professional writers working in a particular field in their native tongue.

Surveys of the professional market for translation and interpreting generally coincide in identifying the two major components of the market as being scientific or technical translation on the one hand, and commercial translation on the other. Legal translation plays a lesser role, generally related to commercial translation (contracts, trade regulations, etc.), followed by translation for the communications media (press, film, TV, etc.) and by literary translation (which holds the smallest share of the professional market).

This analysis of the professional market is extremely important for the definition of a translator or interpreter training programme because it represents an inversion of the commonly perceived role of translation as a literary phenomenon. Translation as an aid to foreign language studies or comparative literature studies or literary translation may have generated a great deal of theory about translation, but the market for professional translators and interpreters is not generally speaking a literary market.

This means that the professors for a translator or interpreter training programme, and the syllabi for their courses, should concentrate on the methodologies and techniques that would be used by professional translators rather than on the special problems of literary translation.

This is so because professional translation usually involves commonly accepted conventions regarding text types, registers, terminology and phraseology, etc., while literary texts are by nature atypical, and the translation problems that literary texts represent cannot be as readily solved by general rules or conventions as can the problems of texts for technical or professional translation.

On the job market, professional or technical translators and interpreters generally divide into *in-house* translators and interpreters or *freelance* translators and interpreters. In-house translators may be found working for translation firms, for large business firms, for governmental bodies or for international organizations.

Freelance translators may collaborate with translation agencies or may work entirely on their own. Studies show that the "productivity" of freelance translators is higher than that of in-house translators, because the former are paid by the page, line or word, while the latter are paid by the hour. Students of translation or interpretation should receive professional orientation as part of their training programme.

The translation/interpreting market is also subject to the attitude of potential clients. Good translators or interpreters are relatively expensive but the quality of their work is guaranteed, while less expensive translators or interpreters, whose work is less satisfactory, may actually be the cause of economic losses for their clients in the long run. A translator or interpreter training programme should take account of this fact and inculcate a serious code of ethics for translators and interpreters while attempting to make potential clients more aware of the need to maintain high standards in translation and interpreting, even though the short term cost may seem to be high.

It is difficult to find detailed studies of the translation market that link correct or incorrect translations to economic profit or loss, but some work has been done in this field, and it has demonstrated that poor-quality translation can lead to serious economic losses (machinery damaged because of translation mistakes in instruction manuals; erroneous — and dangerous — chemical and/or pharmaceutical formulas due to translation errors, etc.), while a farseeing policy of high-quality translation may lead to future profits because the image projected by a business firm is far more attractive when correctly translated, or because the availability of correctly translated information about international grants or about international bidding for contracts, together with correctly translated application forms or bids, may lead to an important increase in profits.

With all of these factors in mind, it might be said that an ideal translator or interpreter training programme would be offered at the postgraduate level to people who have already been trained in the field they are going to translate and who already know the languages they are going to translate from and into. Such a programme would separate translator training from interpreter training and would apply separate admissions standards to each training programme. Candidates for the translator training programme would have to demonstrate sufficient knowledge of each working language, including their mother tongue, and of their field of specialization. Candidates for an interpreter training programme would have to demonstrate sufficient knowledge of each working language and a high level of general knowledge (because they are much more likely to be required to work with a wide variety of specialized fields), as well as a series of psycholinguistic aptitudes that may not be common to translators.

This is a very important point. Translation is an activity that allows time for consultation; simultaneous interpreting is not. Interpreters must have an aptitude for assimilating and processing information almost instantaneously and must develop an aptitude for public-speaking that allows them to improvise a discourse around a series of data without having to hesitate even an instant for link-words or for grammatical structures. Interpreters require a prodigious and agile memory. Even consecutive interpreters, who take notes while someone is speaking, must be able to reconstruct a long discourse rapidly and fluidly on the basis of an extremely schematic system of note-taking (because they have no time for anything more elaborate).

Just as a translator should have the same capacity for writing as a professional writer, an interpreter should have the same capacity for speaking about a subject as does a specialized lecturer or public speaker.

Many, if not most, translator or interpreter training programmes cannot conform to this description and must train translators or interpreters in less than ideal circumstances.

The first factor that complicates the definition of a translator or interpreter training programme is the linguistic level of the student. Under normal circumstances translators and interpreters will translate into their mother tongue. They must be able to use their mother tongue to advantage in order to do so, and training in the use of their mother tongue should be an important aspect of the training programme. Translators who cannot write or speak their native tongue well will not be able to translate into it well either. A sensitivity to language and its usage, as well as a large dosage of common sense, should be elements of selection for any translator or interpreter training programme. Translation errors are frequently based on a misuse of the mother tongue or target language rather than a lack of understanding of the source language.

Knowledge of foreign languages usually depends on the role given to foreign language learning in primary and secondary education. If students enter a translator or interpreter training programme with an insufficient knowledge of their working languages, then the programme will have to reinforce the amount of attention given to language learning as part of the programme. This is an area which differentiates translator or interpreter training programmes from traditional philology or foreign language programmes, because the professional translation market is based on contemporary texts and usage in a variety of specialized fields, while traditional language studies are based on theoretical linguistics, the history of a language and its literary texts. To a certain extent, it could be said that translation studies are primarily synchronic while philological studies are primarily diachronic, and this must be reflected in the language training specific to a translator or interpreter training programme.

If translation or interpreting students must dedicate a large part of their time to language training, they will not have as much time to study specialized fields of knowledge, and the training they will receive as translators will necessarily be more general in nature. Students will have to specialize later, and perhaps on their own.

Another factor to be taken into consideration is the number of languages a translator or interpreter should know. This will depend to a large extent on the specific geographical location or professional market, but it is obvious that a translator or interpreter who can work with more than one foreign language will have more opportunities to work.

Each translator or interpreter training programme should also define the language level to be achieved by the students. Translators may be able to work well with a passive knowledge of a foreign language (i.e., aural and written comprehension) if they are going to translate into their mother tongue only, but this is seldom the case in practice. To be able to translate from their mother tongue into a foreign language, translators must also have an active knowledge of the foreign tongue (i.e., oral and written expression as well as aural and written comprehension). This is especially true in the case of a Chinese language translator or interpreter training programme: the majority of translations from Chinese into other languages is being done by Chinese-speaking translators and interpreters, and this situation will undoubtedly continue to be true in the future.

Language training for a translator or interpreter cannot be divorced from cultural or area studies. The original author or speaker of a text or a discourse works within a specific context that is both material and cultural. So does the original reader or listener. What they share in common from a cultural point of view allows them to communicate. The reader of a translated text does not share the material and cultural context of the original author. The translator shares these contexts to a greater or to a lesser degree, but twice over: with both the original text's author or speaker and with the translated text's reader or listener.

Translators and interpreters who will be working with languages within the same language family as their own mother tongue will probably share a large part of the common cultural heritage of that language family, but when translators and interpreters begin to work with languages that are farther away from their own mother tongue and its language family, there will be much less in common from a cultural point of view, and this must be reflected in the language training they will receive. The further the cultural distance between two languages, the greater the need for extensive cultural studies. In the case of a Chinese language translator or interpreter training programme this is equally true for Chinese-speaking and non-Chinese-speaking translators, and special care must be taken to train students in area studies and in the basic research techniques they will need to be able to continue such studies and to find the information they will need to bridge cultural gaps. Most important of all, they must be made especially sensitive to the fact that there are large cultural gaps to be bridged.

This concept is also related to the degree of difficulty of a text. There are various ways to establish the difficulty of a text to be translated. One has to do with content. General information is less difficult to translate than technical or scientific information because there is no corresponding problem of technical terminology or content that is difficult for a layman to understand. Legal texts require a special kind of knowledge and care because they have legal repercussions. Literary texts are highly individual and atypical and require the translator to have literary skills similar to those of the original author. The difficulty of a text is also related to the relationship between author and reader. A scientist writing for another scientist uses a language that the layman will not understand. The same scientist writing for a layman will use a language that is easier to understand, as will a layman writing on science for another layman. These considerations hold true for the translation of languages that share a great deal of culture in common. When there is a large cultural or chronological distance between the source and target texts the level of difficulty will be higher still.

Thus, language studies and cultural studies must be integrated with translation and interpretation studies, and this requires a general definition of what translation or interpretation must do. One such definition might include the successful transmission of all of the information of the original source language text to a reader or a listener who does not know the source language (and was not the intended receiver), by means of a target language text or discourse that seems natural to a target language reader or listener, while maintaining an effect equivalent to that which the original text or discourse would have had on a reader or listener of the source language.

This definition is based on the application of communications theory and information theory to the process of translation and it can be broken down into various parts. In a normal model of communication a sender (person A) encodes a message that is transmitted — by code and by some means or medium of communication — to a receiver (person B), who decodes the message. If there is no serious interference (or "static") the message can be sent and received. (If there is interference, techniques of redundancy can be used to guarantee that the message gets through.)

Traditional Model of Communications Theory (one Code only):

Sender
    →Encoded Message
        →Means of Communication
           →Decoded Message
             →Receiver

The process of translation is an important variant of this procedure because it introduces a new factor which is not normally envisaged in communications theory: the code used by the sender cannot be decoded by the receiver. This constitutes a radical form of interference that cannot be overcome by any of the conventional means of defeating static in communications theory.

The communications model for translation must posit a Sender A who encodes and transmits message A in one language (code A) that will first be decoded by the translator (Receiver A, who is not the intended receiver of the message), and will then be re-encoded and re-transmitted as message A' (in code B) by a Sender A' (who is not the original author of the text), to a new Receiver A' who will decode message A' in code B (with the expected result that Receiver A' will receive the same information that was intended for Receiver A, that is, that message A' = message A). To be able to do this, the translator or interpreter must be a simulacrum of both the original sender and the original receiver, and must play both roles at the same time. When the text is specialized these roles obviously become more complicated to play and the translator's training must reflect this fact.

Translation Model of Communications Theory:

Sender A
    →Encoded Message A
        →Means of Communication A
           →Decoded Message A
             →Receiver A = Sender A'
                →Encoded Message A'

→Means of Communication A'
→Decoded Message A'
→Receiver A'

The translator must play both roles in this communications model, and the translation must be a reconstruction of a text or a discourse that the translator must first of all understand, as if he or she were the intended receiver, and second of all recreate, as if he or she were the original sender.

To be able to carry out this process, the translator must understand all of the information in the original text in the source language, and re-transmit all of this information in the translated text in the target language, and this requires a very high degree of sensitivity to the concept of information that is explicit in a text and, even more importantly, of information that is implicit in a text.

To be more specific, the translator must understand when information that is implicit in a source language text must be made explicit to the reader of a target language text (because the target language reader or listener is unfamiliar with information that is so obvious to a source language reader or listener that the original text leaves it implicit), and vice versa. This definition of translation places the meaning of a text in an area that is neither purely syntactic nor purely semantic and places a great deal of emphasis on the pragmatics of both the source language text and the target language text.

Development of the sensitivity to implied meaning that is required of a translator or interpreter must also be included in the language training that will form part of a translator or interpreter training programme. This will involve training in a series of reading strategies and methods of textual and contextual analysis that should form part of the theoretical and methodo-logical training of a translator or interpreter, but it will also require comple-mentary training in discourse analysis, pragmatics and reader response theory which, together with training in writing and speaking skills, should enable the translator or interpreter to achieve the goal of successful retrans-mission of the information of a source language text by means of a target language text that seems natural and has an equivalent pragmatic effect.

The books listed in the "References" contain more extensive discus-sions on the subject of translation and interpretation, and some deal specifi-cally with the application of translation theory to translator and/or interpreter training. They also contain extensive bibliographies of their own. The following is a summary of some of the theoretical matters that should be included in a translator or interpreter training programme.

Translation theory could begin with a study of the history of translation and with the history of translation theories. There is an important debate over the role of translation theory in translation or the training of translators. Some people ask whether or not translation theory ever produced a good translation. This is a bit like asking whether or not literary theory ever produced a good work of literature. Translation theory is a very useful means of defining translation problems clearly and of identifying their sources and causes, and it also allows the teachers of translation and interpretation to suggest strategies for solving these problems.

Translation theory combines aspects from a number of other scientific fields. The following elements of theoretical linguistics are inseparable from translation theory: semantics, syntax, pragmatics and stylistics. They would involve specific topics such as lexicography, terminology, language for special purposes, documentation and research techniques, in the case of semantics; case analysis or valency theory in the case of syntax (as a means of identifying elements of implied meaning); illocutionary force, information theory, communications theory and meaning-based linguistics, in the case of pragmatics; and text types, discourse analysis, rhetoric, genre studies, aesthetics and poetics, in the case of stylistics.

The contemporary translator will inevitably need to come into contact with computer linguistics and its applications in the field of translation: natural language processing, machine translation, computer assisted translation, artificial intelligence, expert systems, knowledge bases and the representation of knowledge (as another tool for identifying and understanding the information load of a text).

Other scientific fields such as the philosophy of language, the cognitive sciences, sociolinguistics, psycholinguistics, cultural anthropology, comparative ethnology, comparative literary theory, literary history and comparative literature are also quite relevant for translation studies.

The methodology a translator or interpreter should learn would include applied linguistics in the form of comparative semantics, comparative syntax, comparative pragmatics and comparative stylistics, according to the working language combinations of the students, as well as the comparative analysis of translations. More specifically, students should learn to apply concepts and techniques such as expectancy chains, link words, restricted domains and strategies like the componential analysis of individual words and phrases, propositional analysis, register and degree of difficulty of a text, general vs. specialized knowledge, knowledge of the real world and linguistic common sense, in the field of discourse analysis and text types; composition and oral expression in the fields of pragmatics and stylistics; information management systems, terminological data bases and documentary data banks, in the case of computer linguistics.

Finally, students should be aware of the need to pursue their training on a continuing basis. They should specialize in some aspect of area studies: law, economics, commerce, parliamentary procedures, international relations, science and technology, medicine, the communications media, etc. Continuing education means a constant up-dating and re-cycling of their language and translation or interpretation skills, and further training in additional languages or additional fields of study. And students should be aware that communication and writing ability vary from one person to the next. No amount of training can create a sensitivity to language where it does not already exist. The translation of texts that go beyond the purely technical (where the terminology and phraseology are pre-established and conventional) requires an ability to work with language, to use all of a language's resources, in order to avoid the production of translationese, which defeats the purpose of translation outlined above. The readers of a translation (or the audience of a spoken discourse) want to understand the text as if it came to them as something original and natural in their own language, not as a text whose artificiality distracts the reader from its content. This is a lofty goal to attain, but it is the final aim of good translation.

References

Ballard, M., ed. *La traduction: de la théorie à la didactique.* Lille: Presses Universite de Lille, 1984.

Bowen, David and Margareta Brown, eds. *Interpreting — Yesterday, Today and Tomorrow.* New York: State University of New York at Binghamton, 1990.

Delisie, Jean. *L'enseignement de l'interprétation et de la traduction.* Ottawa: Editions de l'Université d'Ottawa, 1981.

Drescher, H.W. and S. Signe, eds. *Theorie und Praxis des Übersetzens und Dolmetschens.* Berne: H. Lang, 1980.

Finch, C.A. *An Approach to Technical Translation: An Introductory Guide for Scientific Readers.* Oxford: Pergamon Press, 1969.

Herbert, Jean. *The Interpreter's Handbook: How to Become a Conference Interpreter*, translated by T. H. Pan. Taipei: Chung-Hua, 1960.

Ladmiral, J. R. *Traduire: théoremes pour la traduction*. Paris: Payot, 1979.

Larson, Mildred L. *Meaning-Based Translation: A Guide to Cross-language Equivalence*. New York: Lanham, 1984.

Rose, Marilyn Gaddis. *Translation Spectrum: Essays in Theory and Practice*. Albany: State University of New York Press, 1981.

Seleskovitch, Danica. *L'interprète dans les conférences internationales: problèmes de langage et de communication*. Paris: Minard, 1985.

————. *Interpréter pour traduire*. Paris: Didier, 1985.

Slocum, Jonathan. *Machine Translation Systems*. Cambridge: Cambridge University Press, 1987.

Sykes, J.B. *Technical Translator's Manual*. London: ASLIB, 1971.

Tatilon, C. *Traduire: pour une pédagogie de la traduction*. Toronto: Editions du GREF, 1986.

Vendrickx, P.V. *Simultaneous Interpreting: A Practice Book*. Hong Kong: Longman, 1971.

Weber, Wilhelm K. *Training Translators and Conference Interpreters*. Englewood Cliffs, New Jersey: Prentice Hall, 1984.

TRANSLITERATION

Transcription, Romanization, Transliteration

John J. Deeney
Department of English
The Chinese University of Hong Kong, Hong Kong

In a useful bibliography called *Transcription and Transliteration*, Hans Wellisch begins, "This bibliography is an attempt to bring together the widely-scattered literature on a subject which has long been the Cinderella of the library world and of bibliographical control in general: the conversion of one script into another" (Wellisch, 1975:ix). The author goes on to express astonishment at the lack of a "core" of principal journals on the subject. Fortunately, there is no lack of resources when it comes to Chinese.

On the other hand, at times, it seems as if the Chinese Cinderella still has bound feet, so difficult has it been to find an appropriate glass slipper of fitting transcription to match her distinctly Chinese character. In this paper, I will be tracing the rather slow and painful steps that have marked this long process toward partial acceptance of transcription. After a brief section on definitions and distinctions, I will proceed by discussing four main topics: translation and transcription; historical background and 20th-century developments; variety of systems; and special problems related to Chinese transcription.

Definitions and Distinctions

Transcription, transliteration, and romanization are often used interchangeably in a rather indiscriminate way; in fact, strictly speaking, they can and should be distinguished. In Wellisch's words:

Following the established usage of the ISO [International Standards Organization], the term "Transliteration" is employed for "representing the characters (letters or signs) of one alphabet by those of another, in principle letter by letter", whereas "Transcription" is used for the "operation of representing the elements of a language, either sounds or signs, however they may be written originally, in any other written system of letter or sound signs." When both systems are involved, and for general discussion of the whole topic, the term "Romanization" (also following ISO and the Library of Congress) is used, although it is limited to conversion into a particular script and lacks the universality of the German term "Umschrift" [literally, re-formulation] which has no equivalent in English. Conversion into other scripts is consequently termed Arabization, Cyrillization or Hebraization, as the case may be. For conversion into other scripts, no other "ization" terms seem to exist. (Wellisch, 1975:X)

Although I will respect the usage of authors I quote, my own practice throughout this essay will be to employ the term, "transcription", for both conversion processes (Chinese into English and vice versa). For reasons which will become evident as this essay develops, when referring to standard Chinese, I will use two terms: *putonghua* 普通話 (literally, universal language), common vernacular language or popular speech; and *pinyin* 拼音 (literally, spell the sound), phonetic alphabet, for the Chinese language spelling or transcription system as the most practical way of representing *putonghua*. On the other hand, when quoting or paraphrasing from other sources, I will use the writers' preferred transcriptions (which will also assist the reader in appreciating the variety of systems in current use), but I omit all tone marks except for the illustrative examples in my Figures placed later in this paper. I also follow the preferred practice of italicizing all transcribed words (even when omitted by authors I quote), unless they are proper nouns.

Another distinction we have to make is between the languages we are moving into and out of. Moving from Chinese into a foreign language using an alphabet, for instance, presents a different set of transcription problems than moving from the foreign language into the non-alphabetic system of Chinese. The latter process attempts to represent the sounds of foreign terms by characters which represent similar sounds; transcribing Chinese into a foreign alphabet is an approximation of the Chinese sounds for purposes of accurate pronunciation.

For practical purposes, I will restrict myself to problems relating to

Chinese and English (for the most part), although many of the principles may be applied to representing Chinese in other languages. Scholars dealing with a variety of documents from the distant past to the present, cutting across many language frontiers, will frequently have to master a number of other transcription systems in order to decode certain historical materials.

Because of the many dialects and regionalects (De Francis' term) found in China, there are, in fact, a considerable number of ways in which *putonghua* is pronounced. For instance, many people of China's central provinces speaking *putonghua* would pronounce the word for milk, *niunai* 牛奶 , as *liulai*, the word for airplane, *feiji* 飛機 , as *huiji*, and the province, Hunan 湖南 , as Fulan. The meaning of the following sentence — Do you know if he came into the city or not? — would be pronounced in standard *putonghua* as, *Ni zhidao ta shibushi jincheng le*? 你知道他是不是進城了？ But Shanghai people, speaking their brand of *putonghua*, would say: *Ni zhidao ta sibusi jincen le*?

Strictly speaking, *putonghua* refers to a variety of dialectical pronunciations, though it is now commonly understood to be the northern variety (but dropping such peculiar features as the Beijing local expressions, the retroflex *-ri* [*er*] 兒 , etc.). Popularly and officially, *putonghua* is the standard language spoken in China and also in Taiwan although, in the latter area, it is usually referred to as 國語 , the national language, and sometimes as 官話 or Mandarin (the official court language of the Manchus in the Ch'ing Dynasty 1644–1911). Whenever I use the term *putonghua*, I understand it to refer to the standard northern variety, officially decreed as such in 1955 by the Chinese government, and reinforced in 1982 by explicit mention in the revised constitution that the State would promote the nationwide use of *putonghua*.

Translation and Transcription

Translation is an attempt to transfer the *meaning* of a text from one language into another while transcription deals more with the process of carrying over the *sounds* of one language into another. In addition to the problem all foreign readers of Chinese have in finding a relatively accurate transcription method in order to locate vocabulary items in certain types of alphabetized Chinese-English dictionaries (this is not the place to discuss the relative merits of radical- or numerical-based systems), translators also need transcription in order to let their readers know how certain words are pronounced, especially if they are virtually untranslatable. The latter expedient of using transcription as a concise short-hand in translation work, can also serve as a useful and convenient summary to substitute for awkward paraphrases, unwieldy annotations, or verbose explanations.

The obvious advantage of transcription is that it keeps us close(r) to the original, at least phonologically and, therefore, does not allow for misleading or ambiguous overtones to intrude from any single translation attempt. The disadvantage, of course, is the fact that, semantically speaking, transcription does not give the non-native reader the slightest clue to the meaning of the original. Whatever the advantages and disadvantages may be, there is a laudable tendency among many sinologists translating into Western languages, to rely more and more on transcriptions for difficult and complex terms, rather than attempt outright translations which are often inadequate if not downright distortions.

When reversing the process of lexical borrowing and moving from foreign languages into Chinese, we can either attempt to render the meaning (translation) or the sound (transcription). Eugene Ching (1966) claims that the Chinese language is more amenable to translation. All of his examples (a few of which I have omitted), use the Yale transcription system:

> Many of the borrowed items that were originally transliterations were gradually substituted by translations. For example:
> Telephone → *delingfeng* 德靈風 → *dyanhwa* 電話
> Science → *saiyinsi* 賽因斯 → *kesywe* 科學

He then lists five different types of word importation:

(1) Transliteration:
   mi 米 (meter)
(2) Semi-transliteration and semi-translation:
   bingjiling 冰激凌 (ice cream) [*bing* = ice; *jiling* = sound resembling cream]
(3) Transliteration with a denominator or a modifier:
   pijiu 啤酒 ([*pi* = sound resembling] beer)
(4) Meaningful transliteration:
   yinde 引得 "lead to get" (index) [literally, pull out and lead to]
(5) Translation
   a. Word-for-word:
      regou 熱狗 (hot dog)

b. Descriptive:
huoche 火車 "fire vehicle" (train) (Ching, 1966:109)

The distinguished linguist, Chao Yuen Ren 趙元任 (1976), using his *Gwoyeu Romatzyh* (*Guoyu Luomazi*) 國語羅馬字 transcription (see below for explanation) gives some other established examples where the Cantonese dialect comes into play (I have incorporated his footnotes in square brackets):

> When *Oxford* appears as *Nioujin* (牛津) "Ox-ford," it is translation, while *New York* as *Neou iue* (紐約) [*Naoyeuk* is standard Cantonese, but pronounced *Niouyoak* in another southern dialect, presumably spoken by the original transliterator of this name] is transliteration. But when *Cambridge* is rendered as *Jiannchyau* (劍橋) it is half transliterated [in Cantonese is *kimm*:] and half translated. (Chao, 1976:150)

The Oxford example would be the same as Ching's "(5) Translation" category and the Cambridge example the same as "(2) Semi-transliteration and semi-translation."

Ching's final admonition is: "Translation when possible and transliteration when necessary," even though there are some cases where trans-syllabification has certain advantages over translation, e.g., "*lwoji* 邏輯 (or *lwojisywe* 邏輯學) [logic] ... is syntactically much more versatile" than the usual translations: *byansywe* 辨學 , *lwunlisywe* 論理學 , (or *lwunli* 論理), *mingsywe* 名學 , *lidzesywe* 理則學 (Ching, 1966:109–11).

On the other hand, Ching will allow transcription over translation if the latter cannot nuance important distinctions sufficiently (e.g. translating both "cartel" and "trust" by the same expression, *chiye lyanhe* 企業聯合 , fails to show the crucial differences). His tentative order of preference is (Words in square brackets are examples taken from his article, passim):

(1) Translation
   a. Descriptive [*feiji* 飛機 , flying machine (air plane)]
   b. Word-for-word [*mali* 馬力 , horse power]
   c. Homonymic (same as meaningful transliteration)
      [*kekou kele* 可口可樂 , Coca Cola (palatable and enjoyable)]
(2) Transliteration
   a. Meaningful [*you* 鈾 , uranium (where the radical, *jin* 金 , indicates the material [metallic] and the phonetic, *you* 由 , the pronunciation)]

b. With denominator or modifier [*jyouba* 酒吧 , (liquor-) bar]
c. Straight [*shafa* 沙發 , sofa] (Ching, 1966:112–13)

Ching does not include his earlier category, "semi-transliteration and semi-translation" (e.g., Dragunov, the first character of whose name is represented by the Chinese word for "dragon": *Lunggwofu* 龍果夫) in the above list but, presumably, it would fit somewhere between (1) and (2).

In many cases, neither translation nor transcription have proven adequate, for they more often than not tend to modify and even misrepresent the foreign ideas they are supposed to express. To paraphrase Arthur F. Wright's evaluation of both options: Chinese is a singularly intractable medium for translating foreign ideas, not only because of its uninflected nature and its lack of notations of number, tense, gender, and relationships, but also because of the heavy "weight" of meanings and allusions accumulated over the centuries, to say nothing of its limited resources for expressing abstractions and general classes or qualities. Transcription, on the other hand, is awkward, attenuated, treacherous, and uncouth; it destroys compactness, balance, and rhythm (a monosyllabic word in English may require a polysyllabic transliteration, as in a financial "trust", rendered as *tuolasi* 托拉斯).

In an article on "Language Planning in Mainland China", Dayle Barnes also gives some interesting examples from the natural sciences:

> In chemistry, for example, the sound translation for hydrochloric acid becomes [in Yale transcription] *ha-yi-chu-rwo-ke-lwo-li-ke-a-syi-te*. Reliance on meaning translation may not be much more satisfactory: the Chinese meaning equivalent for phenyl-dithio carbonyl is itself an unwieldy seven syllable compound. (Barnes, 1973:44)

Usually when trans-syllabification of foreign sounds is deemed necessary, the Chinese graphs are chosen from obsolete or relatively rare characters or new ones are created. But the characters used as sound syllables tend to retain their original meaning; consequently, it requires a special type of mental gymnastics for foreign readers. They have to do a series of imaginative double-takes when confronted with the following mouthful of sounds, supposedly disassociated from their original meanings (the example is from Wright who transcribes the Sanskrit as): *Ma-ho-p'o-lo-nei-han* [sic] 摩訶般涅槃那 , for the Buddhist term *Maha parinirvana* which roughly translated means passing over into the Great Cessation. Chinese also has a tendency towards dissylabicity and, therefore, often reduces polysyllabic formulations such as Bodhisattva 菩提薩埵 , to shortened forms like *pusa* 菩薩 .

When all these factors are taken into consideration, it should not come as a surprise that Wright (1953) concludes: "It would appear that, as long as the characters exist, their emblematic force will, to some degree, tend to distort the terminology expressed through the characters used as syllables." (Wright, 1953:299)

Generally speaking, Chinese prefer characters used in loans which have some referential significance rather than mere sound similarity. Barnes (using Yale transcription), gives a striking example to illustrate the Chinese loan for mini-skirt, *miniqun.* "Originally a simple sound translation, the characters now used to write *mi-ni* [迷你] combine with *chyun* [裙] (skirt) to yield, appropriately, 'the skirt that captivates you'" (Barnes, 1973:45).

Historical Background and 20th-Century Developments

The translator's need for a satisfactory way of communicating foreign ideas and expressions into Chinese, or native Chinese ones into other languages, has made transcription more than a humble handmaid in the translation process. Historically speaking, there have been three major phases: Buddhism, beginning in the 2nd century; Christianity, beginning in the 16th century; and, for the lack of a better term, Modernism, beginning in the 20th century.

Indian Buddhism was the first great influx of a foreign thought system into China and Buddhist scriptures were probably the earliest translations of a foreign language into Chinese. Initially, the Buddhists attempted to translate the Sanskrit scriptures into Chinese directly by use of existing Chinese characters and expressions from indigenous Chinese philosophical and religious texts, but it soon became evident that the original meanings were being severely distorted. After serious reflection, this led to the ultimate decision to use Chinese characters simply for their sound value in order to represent certain technical terms. Thus, these phonetic loans or character transcriptions for many key terms became an alternative to attempts at translation and the preferred way over the inadequate and frequently misleading direct translations.

From the Chinese point of view, which considered most if not all outsiders as barbarians, there was little compulsion to borrow many words from other languages and cultures. Buddhism presents some interesting exceptions; for example, the term, *niepan* 涅槃 or *nirvana*, which is imaginatively construed by one scholar as "opaque place-of-retirement", is one attempt at what Ching referred to earlier as "meaningful transliteration" but, even so, the characters were undoubtedly chosen primarily for their sound value.

As for Christianity, the most famous of the early Jesuit missionaries to China, the Italian, Matteo Ricci (1552–1610), devised a transcription system based on the Latin alphabet, primarily for the purpose of learning the language and acculturating himself to the court in Beijing. In addition to books in transcription prepared by Ricci on the subject of ink-making and chess playing, there is an excellent example of his Roman letters system in a little booklet of religious materials called, *Marvels of Western Writing* 《西字奇蹟》 (see Fig. 1). Another French Jesuit, Nicholas Trigault (1577–1628), further refined this system into a published textbook (1625), the first of its kind, entitled *The Western Scholars Aid for Ear and Eye* 《西儒耳目資》.

The Protestant missionaries, on the other hand, located themselves in the southern coastal areas and used a variety of transcriptions to proselytize the masses of illiterates. By the end of the nineteenth century, religious materials and Bible translations (in the transcription systems of all the major dialects) were used as a way of "educating" the masses to Christianity.

China's 20th century attempts to modernize have always placed a great deal of emphasis on language reform, beginning in the Republican period with the May Fourth *Baihua* 白話 Vernacular Language Movement in 1919, and continuing with the rise and fall of the Nationalist Party and the eventual Communist Party victory in 1949. Some people even went so far as to suggest replacing Chinese characters with a phonetic notation or even a transcription. Many, including Hu Shi 胡適, insisted that the *baihua* movement of reducing reliance on classical Chinese would have to come before the transition to a phonetic script could be made.

The problems associated with language reform inevitably involved the role of transcription and received the attention of China's top leaders. John De Francis, in his controversial *The Chinese Language: Fact and Fantasy* (1984), makes a number of interesting observations on certain key historical events. For instance, Mao Zedong himself initially advocated Latinization to overcome illiteracy. During an interview with Edgar Snow in 1936, he went so far as to say that characters would be abandoned eventually for

Figure 1. Samples Pages (7–8) from Matteo Ricci's *Marvels of Western Writing**

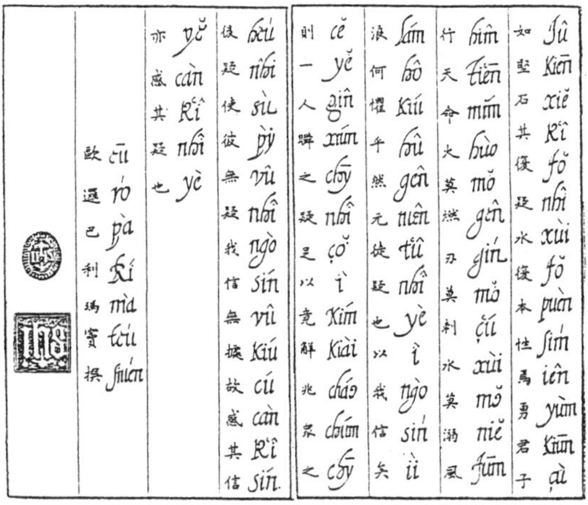

* Serruys provides a useful note to Matteo Ricci's (Li Madou 利瑪竇) *Marvels*: "This was the first latinized alphabetic system in China. The original copy of the Hsi-tzu ch'i-chi is now lost and it is only in the "ink notes" of Ch'eng Chun-fang 程君房 , *Ch'eng shih mo-yuan* 《程氏墨苑》 (*The Ink Garden of Mr. Ch'eng*), that four chapters are reproduced of Ricci's own transcriptions in Roman letters. These four chapters, together with some religious wood cuts, were published by the Peking Fu-jen University on the lithographic press of Wang Ming-hui 王鳴晦 , under the title *Ming-chi chih ou-hua mei-shu chi lo-ma-tzu chu-yin* 《明季之歐化美術及羅馬字注音》 (*Europeanized Art and Romanized Transcriptions of the Ming*). This is a reproduction of the Fu-jen University publication. Matteo Ricci's latinized alphabet contains altogether 26 initials and 44 finals. (1957)" (27–28).

the sake of the masses (De Francis, 1950:247–48). In the 50s, he made simplification of the characters the top priority and urged the adoption of Chinese character stroke combinations or a "'national-in-form' set of phonetic symbols to be used primarily for character annotation but not as an independent orthography." In fact, between 1950 and 1958, there were about 1,700 new alphabet proposals made (another 1,600 were submitted between 1958–1980) but, by the end of the decade the "'national-in-form' scheme was quietly shelved in favour of one based on the Latin alphabet" (De Francis, 1950:262).

Zhou Enlai summarized the issues in the opening sentence of a speech he delivered on January 10, 1958: "The immediate tasks in writing reform are simplifying the Chinese characters, spreading the use of the standard vernacular [*putonghua*], and determining and spreading the use of phonetic spelling [*pinyin*] of Chinese" (Seybolt, 1979:228). De Francis quotes an interview with a former French minister of education, in which Zhou also commented:

> In the 1950s, we tried to romanize the writing. But all those who had received an education, and whose services we absolutely needed to expand education, were firmly attached to the ideograms. They were already so numerous, and we had so many things to upset, that we have put off the reform until later. (De Francis, 1950:258)

From the perspective of the 90s, the three "immediate tasks in writing reform" that Zhou proposed have made remarkable progress though many problems still remain. On the other hand, advocates of alphabetization to replace the characters bewail the lack of top-level support on the part of the government for thoroughgoing reform in order "to overcome the apathy of the masses and the opposition of the entrenched scholarly, educational, and government establishment."(De Francis, 1950:277) The pros and cons related to all these issues are still debated in the many books and journals dedicated to language reform. As De Francis points out, one of the prominent compromises proposed in current debate suggests that "two systems of writing, namely Pinyin and characters, would coexist and have their own spheres of use. This is generally referred to as 'walking on two legs' [a phrase coined by Mao Dun in the early 60s when he was Minister of Culture] or a 'two-track system', and, as we have suggested, might also be called a policy of digraphia." (De Francis, 1950:272) De Francis uses the term 'digraphia' for writing, on an analogy with the term 'diglossia' for speech. In the Chinese context, digraphia refers to the two different systems of writing for the same language: the Chinese character script (albeit simplified in part) and the *pinyin* transcription (for *putonghua*).

Lu Xun's role in the debate is often overlooked, but De Francis dedicates his *Chinese Language* to him and is convinced that the great thinker-writer's approach solves many problems. This is particularly true because of his advocacy of a "phonetic orthography based on the way people actually speak" according to their local dialects or regions (De Francis, 1950:281). According to De Francis, the relevance of Lu Xun's neglected ideas on alphabetization of Chinese need to be reassessed for their true worth. "The importance attached to his support of the New Writing is indicated by a pair of eulogistic scrolls submitted by Guo Morou at the time of Lu Xun's death in October 1936:

> The greatest masterpiece in the world is his *Story of Ah Q*
> But even greater in his life was his activity of Latinization.
> 曠代文章數阿 Q
> 平生功業尤拉化

(De Francis, 1950:250)

In this short space, it would be impossible to cover the many complex arguments Chinese scholars have brought to bear on the transcription question. Furthermore, many of the behind-the-scenes decisions are simply not known, because a large number of the documents have never been published. As De Francis points out in his *Nationalism and Language Reform in China*, the history of the nationalist movement in China, from the end of the 19th century up to the end of World War II, has been marked with controversy and a certain amount of secrecy over language reform. In the following paragraphs, therefore, I will simply describe some of the main issues and touch lightly on the political, cultural, and educational contexts that merit further discussion.

One national language to standardize pronunciation was necessary in order to further unify the country, to communicate among the variety of dialects and regionalects, and to disseminate party directives both orally and in writing. Hence, although the *putonghua* movement has been largely successful up to date as the chief educational tool, local dialects have never been entirely sacrificed in the process. National unity and self-awareness had to be balanced with regional sensibilities and local dialects. The language of the hearth still prevails for home and local use, but *putonghua* is required for a wide range of public activities; for example, education, government service, broadcasting, etc.

Chinese characters have been always acknowledged as one of the chief unifying factors throughout Chinese literate culture, but the intrinsic difficulty in mastering them has also been a major concern for language reformers. This complex writing system was to be simplified, systematically and progressively, in Mainland China (though resisted in Taiwan). By the 80s, the number of characters was reduced by about 7% and reduction in the number of strokes per complex character by about 16.1% (De Francis, 1984:260). But the difficulty in learning and remembering the characters remains more or less unchanged.

Others advocated transcription to supplement (or, in the minds of some radicals, eventually to replace entirely) the characters and speed up the educational process (e.g., teaching children to read or semi-illiterates to recognize road-signs, place-names, slogans, etc.), or to accompany characters in dictionaries as an accurate pronunciation aid for standard *putonghua*. Debate continues, of course, on how much leeway should be given to the growing variety of different transcriptions being used for China's numerous dialects and regionalects. The practice of retaining the characters (which conveniently transcend all spoken dialects except for certain colloquialisms, etc.) as a link to China's long, cultural heritage, is viewed by many as an outdated remnant from the feudal past. On the other hand, using an alphabet seems to smack of subservience on the part of certain "foreign lackeys" to reform the native language system. And, of course, there are objections based on aesthetics or the ambiguities often created by the large number of homophones in Chinese.

There is also the difficulty of choosing the most suitable form of transcription among the many systems proposed. This is why such lengthy debates have occurred over the relative merits of each system; that is, Chinese systems based on character segments versus the foreign Latin or Cyrillic alphabets. The debate finally concluded at the end of the 70s, resulting in the use of *pinyin* which not only facilitates exchange within China but also internationally. Hence, after some initial confusion and normal resistance to change, most members of the international community have accepted *pinyin* as a good way of eliminating the many competing national systems (something the International Orientalist Congress tried and failed to do in 1902), and a useful way of standardizing writing and publication throughout the world.

Variety of Systems

There is a confusing array of different transcription systems for Chinese, and each non-Chinese language usually uses more than one to translate Chinese. Our concern here will be with *putonghua*, although similar systems exist for the speech of the other major regions such as Guangzhou, Amoy, Tibet, Mongolia, etc. Many systems were devised centuries ago when merchants and missionaries first penetrated China. Until recent years, there were around fifty systems in use throughout the world, although these have been gradually reduced as *pinyin* gains more adherents in scholarly publications and in print media throughout the world. My purpose in this section is not to discuss the individual merits of one Latin letter or symbol over another in representing the original Chinese sounds (they are all mere approximations, especially when syllables are pronounced in combination with the tones), but to give an overall view of the major systems used in English.

Five systems vie with one another for acceptance in the English language plus the special case of the *Zhuyin Zimu* 注音字母 which will also be treated below. Rather than attempt a detailed description of the technical aspects of these systems, I will simply illustrate how each one transcribes the same sentence from Chinese characters (see Fig. 2) and make a few comments on each. The sample sentence in Figure 2 along with many of my remarks, have been adapted from I. L. Legeza whose two volumes on virtually all important Chinese-related transcription systems is invaluable, even though his fond hope of putting an "end to the use of adulterated forms of transliteration" (Legeza, 1968–69) will probably never be realized. I treat the transcription systems below in order of current popularity, while the order in Figure 2 is arranged chronologically according to the period when they were first devised.

The *pinyin* system is the official transcription used throughout China and is gaining in popularity throughout the world. An experimental version came out in 1956 and it was officially promulgated in 1958. It was not until 1979, however, that its use was enforced throughout China and recommended to the international community. This decision has caused a certain amount of chaos and consternation, especially among librarians and cartographers but, generally speaking, more and more book, journal, magazine, and newspaper publishers, are turning to *pinyin*.

Internationally, *pinyin* has been a great boon because it is replacing all other widely varying national systems by this one uniform transcription. Linguists may continue to quarrel over its relative strengths and weaknesses but, at least, it has the merit of providing something close to a standard acceptable by the majority of scholars. Hence, a new and necessary uniformity is, indeed, feasible. Virtually all recent Chinese-foreign language dictionaries produced in China (e.g., Wu Jingrong's 吳景榮 1978 *The Chinese-English Dictionary* 《漢英詞典》), employ the *pinyin* system.

Pinyin's main rival, the Wade-Giles system, gained an early and firm foothold in libraries and map-making enterprises in English-speaking countries throughout the world. The system was devised by Thomas Wade

Figure 2. Six Transcription Systems

1. Wade-Giles (WG)
2. *Chu-yin tzu-mu* (CT) 注字字母 (Phonetic Alphabet) or *Chu-yin fu-hao* 注音符號 (Phonetic Symbols)
3. *Gwoyeu Romatzyh* (GR) 國語羅馬字 (National Language Romanization)
4. Yale University (YU)
5. *Hanyu Pinyin* (HP) 漢語拼音 (Chinese Language Spelling)
6. *Jiaanhuah Rormaa Tzyh* (JR) 簡化羅馬字 (Simplified Romanization)

Original Chinese Transcriptions	中	文	大	學	圖	書	館	有	很	多	新	書	嗎 ?
1. WG (1892)	Chung-¹	wen²	ta-⁴	hsieh²	t'u-²	shu-¹	kuan³	yu³	hen³	to¹	hsin¹	shu¹	ma ?
2. CT (1918)	ㄓㄨㄥ	ㄨㄥˊ	ㄉㄚˋ	ㄒㄩㄝˊ	ㄊㄨˊ	ㄕㄨ	ㄍㄨㄢˇ	ㄧㄡˇ	ㄒㄣˇ	ㄉㄨㄛ	ㄒㄣˊ	ㄕㄨ	ㄇㄚ˙
3. GR (1928)	Jong	wen	dah	shyue	twu	shu	goan	yeou	heen	duo	shin	shu	mha?
4. YU (1943)	Jūng	wén	dà	sywé	tú	shū	gwǎn	yǒu	hěn	dwō	syīn	shū	ma ?
5. HP (1958)	Zhōng	wén	dà	xué	tú	shū	guǎn	yǒu	hěn	duō	xīn	shū	ma ?
6. JR (1972)	Jung	wen	dah	shyuer	tur	shu	guaan	yoou	heen	duo	shin	shu	ma ?
Literal Transtation	(In the) Chinese		university		library			are there	very	many	new	books	?
Tone marks:	Ordinarily, tone and other diacritical marks (e.g., WG "hsüeh") marks are omitted in publications unless they are an essential part of the matter under study in order to avoid ambiguity. Many unstressed syllables are toneless or "neutral" (indicated by a dot in the CT system).												

around 1859, and revised by Herbert Giles in 1892, who published his *Chinese-English Dictionary* in 1912. A more modern dictionary using the system was by R. H. Mathews, first published in 1943, which itself has been revised a number of times. In *Mathews' Chinese-English Dictionary*, certain diacritical marks are used in the pronunciation notations, and superscripted numbers are employed to indicate the four tones.

The *Zhuyin Zimu*, or National Phonetic Alphabet system, was promulgated in 1918 and more accurately renamed as *Zhuyin Fuhao* 注音符號 , or National Phonetic Symbol system in 1930. The system does not use Latin letters but something resembling the old Chinese *fanqie* 反切 (phonetic notation for Chinese characters) which is said to have initially inspired the creation of the modern Chinese phonetic symbols. These authentic Chinese symbols are based on the shapes of certain stroke combinations in Chinese characters and are used to represent particular sounds (similar to the Japanese *kana* (假名) syllabary).

The *Zhuyin Zimu* system is claimed by many to be a more accurate reproduction of the original Chinese sound system, but it is a bit clumsy because it divides each syllable into three components — initial, middle, and final sounds. The symbols are placed immediately at the right side of the characters to indicate their pronunciation and in Taiwan, at least, they function as a pronunciation aid rather than an orthographic substitute for characters. The Taiwan government has been using this transcription method in its educational system for over forty years and publishes a large variety of books as well as a daily newspaper in this form. Thus, millions of people in Taiwan have been educated in this system, but it has never gained popularity outside the island. There are a number of dictionaries available in this form such as the monolingual *Guoyu ribao cidian* 《國語日報詞典》 (Taipei: Guoyu Ribao Pub. Co., 1974).

The Yale University transcription system had its beginnings in the 30s and became quite popular in the United States. This was largely accelerated by its usefulness in training interpreters during and after the Korean War, and because of Yale's pioneering series of popular textbooks and its practical usefulness in teaching the spoken language. It is custom-made for American tongues, but it also bears notable resemblances to the *pinyin* system as can be seen in Yale's Institute of Far Eastern Languages publication, *Dictionary of Spoken Chinese* (1966).

Diacritical marks (and, in the case of Wade-Giles, cumbersome numbers) which accompany the first four systems described above, are used to indicate the tones of *putonghua*. Aside from the fact that such tone marks and other diacritical marks disrupt smooth reading, are unsightly, and expensive to set up in type (and, therefore, regularly omitted by most publishers), they also create practical problems in trying to transmit tele-communications, to input words in a computer, etc. Hence, the usefulness of the *Gwoyeu Romatzyh* 國語羅馬字, or National Language Romaniza-tion, an early Chinese system devised by a commission in 1926, which "spelled out" the tones by additional letters. Although officially adopted by the Ministry of Education in 1928, it never supplanted the Wade-Giles system even in government publications.

One of the original members of the commission was Chao Yuen Ren. Chao used this tonal spelling system in his extensive publications and when teaching at the University of California, Berkeley, but gave credit to Lin Yutang 林語堂 for the original idea. In brief, the tones are indicated through orthography; that is, all numbers and diacritical marks are eliminated and replaced by adding certain silent letters. In other words, these tonal letters are not pronounced but they indicate one of *putonghua*'s four tones. This system has been used in a number of dictionaries such as the 1932 *Guoyin changyong cihui* 《國音常用詞彙》 (*National Phonetic Dictionary*) as well as Chao Yuen Ren's and Yang Lien Sheng's 楊聯陞 *Concise Dictionary of Spoken Chinese* (1947).

The *Jiaanhuah Rormaa Tzyh* 簡化羅馬字, or Simplified Romanization system, was a later attempt on the part of Lin Yutang to reduce the complex-ity of the original *Gwoyeu Romatzyh* 國語羅馬字. But this system still remains daunting unless the reader finds compelling reasons to use Lin's *Chinese-English Dictionary of Modern Usage* (1972) in which he refers to the system as "Simplified Romatzyh." Lin compounded the confusion by arranging his *Dictionary* according to an "unforgettable instant index sys-tem" which proved to be an unnecessary and not easily remembered vari-ation on the traditional four-corner arrangement.

Another short-lived system that was championed in the 30s should be mentioned in passing, the *Ladinghua Xinwenzi* 拉丁化新文字 or Latinized New Script. This system was devised by Chinese linguists in collaboration with their Soviet counterparts (who unsuccessfully advocated the Cyrillic alphabet over Latin). It did not indicate tones and, theoretically, was adapt-able to all dialects, but it was violently opposed by some as traitorous in denying that China was a single nation.

Other niggling problems faced by all these transcription systems are deciding upon a logical and coherent set of rules for word division, linking up syllables which constitute a single word, and capitalization. The worst extreme is that which would run whole lines of words together without any break between them as is sometimes seen on signboards in China. Others suggest separating each syllable by a blank space. Still others would use hyphens to connect meaningful units, although there is considerable debate over what constitutes a word. For instance, should *xinwenzi* 新文字 , the "new writing" be written as a single word or separated into two words: *xin* 新 , *wenzi* 文字 ? *Pinyin* simply joins syllables together which seem obviously related, though this can cause some ambiguity. But the problem is relatively simple to solve by adding a diacritical mark when there is confusion between words such as *xian* 仙 (an immortal) and *Xi'an* 西安 (Xian City).

Moving back and forth between these systems can often be quite confusing, so books have been written on the subject and various conversion tables compiled. See, for instance, Legeza; Wellisch (1975:81–93) also supplies a useful list.

Special Problems

Irregular Forms. A problem which complicates transcription practice in modern China is the fact that there is no consistent policy between China, Taiwan, and Hong Kong in the uniform use of Chinese character expressions, let alone the choice of phonetic symbols. Not only do individuals arbitrarily select different Chinese character combinations to represent the approximate sound of the same foreign name (the original pronunciation of which they are not always certain), but often they make no attempt to distinguish the way their dialect represents that sound as opposed to standard *putonghua*. References to Western persons, for instance, in newspapers, magazines, and other publications of these three areas, often result in quite different nomenclature. The relatively simple expedient of including the Western name in its original form, parenthetically, is rarely resorted to as the obvious solution; when employed, it often ignores capitalization and is full of typographical errors.

The confusion is further compounded when foreign words, especially proper nouns, are converted into Chinese characters and then transcribed back into the foreign language again without apparent knowledge of the original name. Whereas back-translation is a positive way of testing fidelity to the original, those who employ back-transcription rarely, if ever, use it as a way of gauging accuracy.

For anyone who has attempted to make an alphabetical index for foreign names represented by Chinese graphs in a Chinese publication, it can be a most exasperating experience. Relatively few Chinese publishers, for instance, will take the trouble to include an accurate spelling of the original foreign name when it first occurs in a Chinese text. Rather, one usually finds a series of inexact Chinese graphs which very loosely fit the original name. For instance, in an index I recently compiled for a casebook publication, there were eight different character combinations for the critic, Rene Wellek; several names had to be simply omitted from the index since no reference book could help to trace the vague approximation of the original. My own name appeared on the title page of one publication as the unhappy hybrid, 約翰 J. 迪尼 (*Yuehan* = John J. *Dini* = Deeney), and on the next page as the author of the preface under my Chinese name, Li Dasan 李達三 ! An additional problem occurs when a Western name is combined with other characters, especially regarding certain -isms. Unless one already knows Chinese, it is often difficult to know where to break the syllables into sense units. How, for instance, at first glance, is one to pronounce, *Makesizhuyi* 馬克思主義 (Marxism)?

Another confusing aspect of transcription policy regards Chinese proper names. When transcribing Chinese characters into English, we not only have the problem of dealing with many established (but mistaken) derivations, but also the intractable problem of covering several major Chinese dialects. In addition, there are the arbitrary concoctions employed by idiosyncratic individuals. An interesting example is the name for Confucius 孔夫子 , which is actually the Latinized name for "Master Kong" whose real name, in fact, was Kong Qiu 孔丘 . Another instructive example is the name for Chiang Kai-shek (Jiang Jieshi) 蔣介石 , a combination of Wade-Giles *putonghua* transcription for Chiang and a Cantonese spelling for Kai-shek.

As for place names, Hong Kong is the familiar Cantonese pronunciation for what, in *putonghua*, is pronounced Xianggang 香港 . Another curious exception is the fact that Peking University still insists on going by the older transcription of its name which was probably determined in the 1936 edition of the *Postal Atlas of China* (along with many other well-established irregular transcriptions); the transcription in *pinyin* is, of course, Beijing 北京 University. Since it will take some years for the transition to take place between some of these irregular but established forms and the new *pinyin*, one can only wait patiently till the indexers, cartographers, and librarians have caught up. Meanwhile one has to learn to locate information in a variety of transcription systems that come one's way and to reproduce them accurately, especially when writing for publication.

Publication. When submitting manuscripts, transcription usage is particularly crucial if one wishes to publish in a journal which may have very specific rules regarding transcriptions in its style sheet policy. Some publishers will not accept Chinese characters at all and require transcriptions plus translations; others will discourage the use of too much transcription; still others will insist on Chinese characters but relegate them to a glossary in the back (identified in the body of the text by superscripted lower-case letters of the alphabet attached immediately following the transcription).

If the publication does not specify, it is always safer to supply more information than less (since it is easier to delete than to add later). Therefore, in documenting footnote or bibliographical data for Chinese publications, the usual procedure is to start with the transcription, followed by characters and, then, the translation (in parentheses if supplied in the original text; in square brackets if translated by you). Supplying bibliographical information in transcribed form not only assists the non-Chinese reader to make an attempt at pronouncing the authors' names and titles, but also facilitates indexing immeasurably. Such a policy would also enable first-rate publications in Chinese to gain their proper and deserved recognition in international bibliographies.

Indexing. In making author and title indexes for books or bibliographies, the alphabetical arrangement, according to *pinyin*, still remains the efficient way, since it is difficult to get complete agreement upon a computer program for Chinese characters whereby names can be automatically arranged according to a universally acceptable character stroke order and number of strokes. A particularly difficult chore has to do with revising already existing indexes to maps of China.

Chinese geographical names have, since 1942, been identified on British and American maps by the Wade-Giles system. Before that period, they followed the spelling of the Chinese Post Office system but, by the early 70s, over 250,000 had been transcribed into Wade-Giles. Although news organizations and academic institutions seem to have coped fairly well in the transition to *pinyin*, geographers and cartographers have found the going much more difficult. The last are particularly desperate. They will have to alter tens of thousands of Wade-Giles transcriptions on hundreds of outdated maps.

Cataloguing. In libraries which have Chinese publications arranged not only according to radical, stroke order, and stroke count of the characters, but also according to a transcription system such as Wade-Giles or *pinyin*, even Chinese can often find information more rapidly through an alphabetical index. This is obviously true for dictionaries as well and explains, perhaps, why so many dictionaries — most of which should be soon available in machine-readable form — are arranged according to an alphabetized transcription system. This need for efficient transcription systems in order to locate data refers not only to academic libraries, but other institutions from hospitals to military units.

But libraries which have been cataloguing their materials according to Wade-Giles during this century are faced with a real dilemma if they wish to convert to *pinyin*. Those libraries which have large collections of Chinese publications (e.g., the Harvard-Yenching Library contains more than half a million cards catalogued according to Wade-Giles), simply do not have the time or resources to make the transfer even though urged to do so, along with other American libraries, by the Library of Congress. Some libraries are trying out a compromise by recording new Chinese books in *pinyin* while maintaining the Wade-Giles system along with it for publications already catalogued. The Committee on East Asian Libraries in America wrote to the Library of Congress policy makers in 1981, strongly urging them not to switch to *pinyin* until such time as more sophisticated machine readable processing would have come on stream for Chinese.

Computers. Just as phonetic writing facilitated the use of typewriters over the slow and cumbersome old-style Chinese-character typewriters, now one of the most interesting phenomena regarding transcription has been the development of computer technology inputting and retrieval. While many Chinese — familiar as they are with characters — prefer working with stroke combinations and touch-typing input systems, most non-Chinese are more at ease with *pinyin*, despite its relative slowness and frequent ambiguity. The computer has taken much of the drudgery out of transcribing characters into one system or another. For instance, there are software programs that can automatically convert the same lists of characters into *pinyin* (for readers in China) or Wade-Giles (for Taiwan and other readers).

There are literally hundreds of software input schemes proposed for

Chinese word processing, data bases, etc., some based on combining character elements or number combinations, but others on the *pinyin* system. This latter method is another important factor which will help to establish *pinyin* as the primary transcription system in the near future, even though the many homonyms (to say nothing of tone markers which are usually omitted) lead to considerable ambiguity in retrieving the exact character sought after. For instance, typing *yuanxing* into the computer could result in the characters for "original shape" 原形 , or "round shape" 圓形 . The computer can eliminate this phonetic ambiguity by presenting, on the monitor screen, a list of characters in frequency order, thus enabling the viewer to select the proper expression. Another problem with *pinyin* for computers is that it requires accurate pronunciation (and spelling), which makes considerable demands not only on non-Chinese, but also on Chinese from different dialectical regions. Nevertheless, Chinese scholars who favour more radical uses of transcription as a tool for rapid modernization, are quick to point out that an alphabetized script is more readily utilized for computer technology than Chinese characters.

As countries in Europe and Asia move closer together in both inter- and intra-national cooperation, rapid communication in the most efficient way possible is an absolute necessity. China's modernization drive is a case in point and its renewed emphasis on transcription is an important part of that march forward. Furthermore, the international problems related to machine translation and the astronomical increase in scientific and technical terminology (particularly medicine), makes instant access through computer highly desirable and this also seems to favour increased emphasis on alphabetization. How else can a modern nation handle its immediate need for scientific and mathematical formulas, abbreviations, indexes, bibliographies and catalogues, to say nothing of assisting handicapped members of society such as the blind, deaf, and dumb?

In an issue as complex as transcription, one must try to put all personal and political preferences aside in order to be objective and practical. China is to be congratulated in taking bold steps for the sake of extinguishing illiteracy and facilitating learning through a more extensive use of *pinyin* transcription. China's willingness to embrace the Latin alphabet is further symbolic of its desire to open itself more to the international community.

As the world approaches the 21st century, it is not likely that there will be any more great changes in transcription policy in or outside of China. It will take decades for individuals and institutions to assimilate the changes that have recently been started. Almost any system used consistently is preferable to the chaos of multiple systems that reigned throughout the world before 1979. For the present and the foreseeable future, *pinyin* has won the field.

References

Barnes, Miller Dayle. "Language Planning in Mainland China: A Sociolinguistic Study of P'u-t'ung-hua and P'in-yin." Dissertation, Georgetown University, Washington, 1974.

―――. "Language Planning in Mainland China: Standardization." In *Language Planning: Current Issues and Research*. Washington, D.C.: Joan Rubin and R. Shuy, 1973, pp. 34–54.

Chao, Yuen Ren. "Dimensions of Fidelity in Translation with Special Reference to Chinese." In *Aspects of Chinese Sociolinguistics: Essays by Yuen Ren Chao*, edited by Anwar S. Dil. Stanford: Stanford University Press, 1976, pp. 148–69.

Ching, Eugene. "Translation or Transliteration: A Case in Cultural Borrowing." *Chinese Culture*, Vol. 7, No. 2 (1966), pp. 107–16.

De Francis, John. *The Chinese Language: Fact and Fantasy*. Honolulu: University of Hawaii Press, 1984.

―――. *Nationalism and Language Reform in China*. Princeton: Princeton University Press, 1950.

Deeney, John J., comp. *Style Manual and Transcription Tables for Mandarin*, 2nd rev. ed. Taipei: Western Literature Research Institute. Tamkang College of Arts and Sciences, 1978.

Karlgren, Bernhard. *The Chinese Language*. New York: Ronald, 1949.

―――. *The Romanization of Chinese*. London: The China Society, 1928.

Legeza, Ireneus Laszlo. *Guide to Transliterated Chinese in the Modern Peking Dialect*. Leiden: E.J. Brill, 1968–1969.

Parker, Franklin and Betty June Parker. "Chinese Language Reform and Language Teaching in the People's Republic of China: Annotated Bibliography." *Journal of Chinese Linguistics*, Vol. 15, No. 1 (1987), pp. 191–98.

Serruys, Paul L.-M. *Survey of the Chinese Language Reform and the Anti-illiteracy Movement in Communist China*. Studies in Chinese Communist Terminology No. 8. Berkeley, CA: Center for Chinese Studies, Institute of International Studies, University of California, 1962.

Seybolt, Peter J. and Gregory Kuei-ke Chiang, eds. *Language Reform in China: Documents and Commentary*. White Plains, New York: M.E. Sharpe, Inc., 1979 (1978).

Wellisch, Hans [Hannan]. *Transcription and Transliteration.* Silver Spring, MD: Institute of Modern Language, 1975.

Wright, Arthur F. "The Chinese Language and Foreign Ideas." In *Studies in Chinese Thought*, edited by Arthur F. Wright. Chicago: The University of Chicago Press, 1953, pp. 286–303.

UNDERTRANSLATION

Undertranslation

Alan McConnell Duff
British Council
Belgrade, Yugoslavia

General

In the general sense, the term *undertranslation* may be taken to mean: the use of too few words in the translation to convey fully the sense of the source language. In the specific sense, undertranslation may also refer to: (a) the use of words or expressions which are too weak for the context, (b) mixed register in the target language, (c) faulty word order and incomplete structures, (d) ambiguity and confused meaning.

The term may also be used in the positive sense to indicate that the translator has consciously removed superfluous or repetitious language from the source language text.

This entry is divided into two main sections: (1) *Language*, (2) *Style and Content*. Under *Language*, we shall concentrate mainly on practical details such as punctuation, word order, sentence structure, and source language influence. Under *Style and Content*, we shall focus more on meaning and register. The section headings should not be regarded as strict divisions, since any given example may illustrate several different aspects of undertranslation.

Finally, it should be added that many of the questions discussed here are also relevant to *overtranslation*, notably the entire issue of source language influence.

We shall now consider in closer detail the points mentioned above.

Language

Punctuation

Faulty punctuation blurs the meaning of a text and leads to momentary confusion. In translation, one of the commonest errors is that of omitting the comma. As here: (Duff, 1981)

> These findings were to lead to research on living organisms and their effect on tumours was investigated very early on. (Source language: French)

A comma is essential after *organisms*, in order to mark the shift in structure from *These findings were to lead* to *their effect was investigated*.
Or here:

> The compounds are brightly lit with torches and tall bamboo poles decorated with small lanterns are donated to the shrine. (Source language: Japanese)

Again, the change of structure requires a comma (before *and*). In technical and scientific writing, one frequently encounters clusters of words — nouns, verbs, adjectives — which need to be separated by a comma. This is especially necessary in sentences beginning with prepositions or adverbs, such as *in, among, after, during*. For instance:

> *Among* the subjective weaknesses mention should definitely be made of the still unsubdued spending and inflation. (Source language: Serbian)

Comma after *weaknesses*.

> *In* experimental studies for the measurement of phagocytosis and intracellular activity PMNL and alveolar macrophages of rodents were used. (Source language: Slovene)

Comma after *activity*.

In legal texts, however, it is common practice to underpunctuate. Commas are more sparingly used, as here:

> If the insured recovers in part or in all from a third party he will need to give credit to his underwriters for that recovery.... On payment the underwriter is subrogated to all the rights and remedies of the assured. (Source language: English)

Commas would normally be expected after *from a third party* and *On payment*, but in contractual law lighter punctuation is acceptable.
Finally, it should be mentioned that there are certain structures in

English, particularly comparative structures (involving words such as *more, less, as, than,*) which require special attention. For example:

> Our findings with the systemic quinolones convince us that they are *as effective or even more effective than* the currently available oral antibiotics. (Source language: Slovene)

... as effective *as* or even more effective than —...

Word Order and Reference

When the word order of the source language is too closely followed, the translation is often disjointed. In addition, words which are *not* present in the source-language text but which are required in the target language may be accidentally omitted. For instance:

> The entire exhibition and sales areas cover about 50,000 sq. m., *while storage areas more than* 120,000 sq. m. (Source language: Slovene)

In English, it would be necessary either to repeat the verb *cover* or to use a synonym, e.g., while storage areas *extend over* 120,000 sq. m.

Although referential words, such as *that, which, it*, are often omitted in English texts, they should not be omitted in translation if there is a danger of confusion:

> A large group of authors accepts the analogy explicitly or suggests more or less clearly in *the formulations they choose agreement* with this position. (Source language: German)

Here, there is a real danger of misunderstanding. For clarity, the phrase in italics should be expanded to: (A large group of authors suggests) *in the formulations* (which) *they have chosen that they are in agreement* ...

In legal and technical documents, precision of language is essential. Undertranslation, or even literal translation, may lead to ambiguity. For instance:

> Within the period of duration of this Contract the contracting parties oblige themselves not to reveal *any information entrusted to any third persons.* (Source language: Croatian)

To avoid ambiguity, the translator might legitimately have reworded the text: ... the contracting parties undertake not to reveal to any third persons *any information entrusted to themselves* (under the terms of this Contract).

Short-cuts

Frequently, translators are influenced by the source language into taking short-cuts which are not acceptable in the target language.

> En 1957, la RATP équipe une première ligne avec des métros sur pneumatiques, *rapides et confortables.*

> In 1957, the RATP put into service for the first time trains equipped with pneumatic tyres — rapid and comfortable. (Source language: French)

French may allow for the condensation of thought in the words *rapides et confortables*, but English requires a fuller rendering. For instance:

> In 1957, the RATP introduced a new type of train fitted with pneumatic tyres. *This innovation made travelling quicker and more comfortable.*

In the second example, the meaning is blurred by awkward wording:

> Automechanika has a tradition of special events. Exhibitions, forums or round-table discussions *have a high reputation as a practically oriented meeting place.* (Source language: German)

More words are needed to complete the structure:

> Exhibitions ... *have earned Automechanika* a high reputation ...

Other typical short cuts include the following:

> This theory is in general analogical, that is to say the researchers apply *theories previously employed* for other illnesses *and which* have apparently succeeded. (Source language: French)

Here, we have two verbs one passive and one active. The distinction must therefore be made clear in the structure:

> the researchers apply theories *which have previously* been employed ... *and which have succeeded.*

When several verbs occur together, they do not always refer to the same subject, as here:

> We make packaging that envelops, protects and attracts the eye. (Source language: Slovene)

This should be expanded to, e.g.

> We make packaging that envelops and protects *the product*, and also attracts the eye.

In certain cases, e.g. in the translation of instructions or directions, short cuts are permissible:

> *Storage.* Capsules should be stored at a temperature not exceeding 25 C, protected from light. (Source language: Slovene)

Strictly speaking, however, this sentence should read:

> Capsules should be stored at a temperature not exceeding 25 C, *and should be* protected from light.

Text Length or "Word-load"

To conclude this section, a brief word must be said about what might be described as "legitimate undertranslation." That is, when the translator deliberately avoids word-for-word translation in order to make the target language crisper, more precise. (See also *Overtranslation*) We begin with an example cited by Professor Newmark (1990):

> Ici aussi, la prise de sang *permet de* réduire très sensiblement ce risque.

The French *permet de* (allows for) is not required in English:

> Here again, a blood sample considerably *reduces* the risk.

Likewise, in the next example, the Spanish expression *En caso de detectar* (lit. In case you detect) could be shortened in translation:

> *En caso de detectar* fuga de gas en un aparato, cierre la llave de paso *del mismo.*

> *If you notice* a gas leak, turn off the supply tap (*of the apparatus*).

If the source language text is "overloaded" with words, as in the next example, the translator may be justified in cutting it down:

> The electric train is a very interesting *technical* toy, *made on purpose for people* who well appreciate educational-*entertaining* toys. (Source language: Croatian)

This could be reduced to:

> The electric train will delight all lovers of educational toys.

Vagueness in the wording of the source language text leads to even greater vagueness in translation. The translator may therefore have to re-think the text, and reduce its length. Compare the two translations — one "full", the other "reduced" — of the French sentence below:

> Si la lecture est enseignée aux petits enfants dès l'aube de leur scolarité, cela ne veut pas dire que l'effort soit facile, cela veut dire simplement que son apprentissage soit fondamental et constitue un préalable à l'acquisition des autres contenus scolaires.

Full (or faithful) translation:

> If reading is taught to small children from the very dawn of their schooling, this does not mean to say that the effort is easy, it means simply that learning to read is fundamental and constitutes a preliminary to the acquisition of other scholastic materials.

Revised (or reduced) translation:

> Although children are taught to read from their first schooldays, this does not mean that learning to read is an easy task. The ability to read, however, is a basic precondition for the mastery of all subjects.

The latter version is shorter and clearer. This is "legitimate" undertranslation.

Style and Content

As was mentioned in the article on "Overtranslation", the style and register of the source language text may not suit the target language. As a result, the translation often seems overemphatic, or "overblown":

> Pure and gentle talcum powder *for the care of very sensitive epidermis. The components* and the slight fragrance of it are *especially indicated* for baby's skin. (Source language: Italian)

Here, there is a clash between context and language. Expressions such as: *sensitive epidermis, components, especially indicated* ... seem out of place on a product designed for domestic (not medical) use.

More rarely, the translation seems too gentle or "low-key" for the context:

Our "Bee and Flower" soap does no harm whatever to your skin. Just try it, and you will see our sincere recommendation is rather convincing. (Source language: Chinese)

The hesitancy of *does no harm whatever* and *rather convincing* is unexpected (though welcome) in advertising language.

In translation, we are dealing not only with language but also with culture. It is often the cultural differences which lead to over- or undertranslation.

Choice of Words — Tone

When the tone of the source language is automatically reproduced, the result may be, for instance:

Departure from the hotel *should be announced* to the reception before 10 a.m. and rooms vacated by 12 noon. *Staying over this time will necessitate payment* of a further day. (Source language: Croatian)

This is a close translation of the original. The language is "correct" but the tone is too formal. Here, undertranslation — i.e. relaxing the tone — might help:

Please let the reception desk know by 10 a.m. of your intended departure, and leave the room by 12 noon. Otherwise, you may be charged for an extra day.

Mixed Register

The tone or register of a text is determined both by the nature of the material (scientific, literary, academic) and by the potential reader. The professional reader is not addressed in the same tone as the general reader.

If the basic tone is formal, the register in translation should be consistent, not mixed:

Both contracting parties are required to *provide* and are entitled to *get* information relating to further product developments. (Source language: Slovene)

In this context, *get* is too informal. Change to: *receive* or *obtain*.

Some of the *major theoretic orientations* in Indian sociology which have shown *varying degrees* of *ups and downs* during the quarter century are: ... (Source language: Hindi/English?)

Here, the expression *ups and downs* is too informal to be matched with *major theoretical orientations*. A more appropriate word would be *fluctuation*.

Occasionally, a change of structure will help to balance the registers:

Pefloxacin, *which patients took orally*, was more efficacious than co-trimoxazole. (Source language: Slovene)

The passive form would be preferable:

Pefloxacin, *taken orally*, proved more efficacious ...

If the basic tone is informal, the translation should not be too word-heavy:

Cocktail parties, private and business meetings, and banquets *can be arranged on your behalf by us*. (Source language: Croatian)

The sentence could begin, simply: *We can arrange ...*

Below is the caption to a photograph:

Difference of opinion among the inmates of the children's camp on Margaret Island. (Source language: Hungarian)

A more natural wording:

Children quarreling at the holiday camp ...

From the examples above, two general points emerge:

1. The tone of the source-language text may become distorted if the words are too literally translated. The translation should aim to sound *as natural as possible* in the target language. For this, some undertranslation may be necessary.
2. The source language text may itself be inconsistent in tone and register. If it is, the translator has the right to correct such defects.

Content

As was mentioned earlier, the meaning of a text depends greatly upon word order. If a translation is difficult to understand (and if the source-language text is not) the reason will often be that the target language word order is defective.

For instance:

The central processing unit *had twenty years ago a size of* about ten thousand,

> *a cost* per million additions of about one hundred thousand and *a speed* of about one to one hundred thousand of *what it has today*. (Source language: Swedish)

As it stands, this sentence (about a computer) is difficult to absorb. A change in word order, and a slight change in wording, makes it clearer:

> *Twenty years ago*, the central processing unit *was* about 10,000 times *larger than it is today*; the cost per million additions was 100,000 times *greater*, and the speed between 1000 and 100,000 times *slower*.

The sentence is now balanced. The distracting time references (*twenty years ago, today*) are shifted to the opening of the sentence, where they belong, and the information is presented coherently by use of the same structural pattern: *larger ... greater ... slower*.

The next example illustrates a similar problem:

> In patients with impaired renal function the quinolones pertain to advantageous drugs for treatment of infections due to their low toxicity. (Source language: Slovene)

At the end of the sentence, the reader is drawn into making a false link between the words *infections* and *low toxicity*. This can be remedied by a change of word order and punctuation:

> In patients with impaired renal function, the quinolones — due to their low toxicity — pertain to advantageous drugs for treatment of infections.

Source language influence on word order and wording is often strong, thus leading to overtranslation:

> The Carrier also retains the right, in case of force majeure of *an insufficient number of passengers being registered* to cancel the journey. (Source language: Serbian)

This could be reworded:

> In case of force majeure or of insufficient *bookings*, the Carrier also retains the right to cancel the journey.

The first version is a replica of the source language text, the second is a translation. It is also a further example of legitimate undertranslation.

As we have seen, the meaning of a text depends not only upon the facts or statements made, but also upon the way in which they are presented. If the longer, "faithful" rendering (the overtranslation) is difficult to understand, then the shorter version (the undertranslation) may be preferred. Undertranslation is not "unfaithful" translation.

Summary

The term *undertranslation* covers many aspects of language, both positive and negative. Among these are:

1. Meaning

Is the translation clear? If not, is it because of defects in the source language text, or because the translator has failed to interpret what is implied but not stated?

2. Syntax

Is the translation difficult to understand because it follows too closely the word order, structure, or punctuation of the original?

3. Style (Register and Idiom)

Does the translation sound natural in the target language? Are there any idioms, metaphors or colloquial expressions which need further explanation?

4. Length

Is the translation too long, or too short? If too long, is this due to source language influence? If too short, is this due to the translator's negligence? And, finally, does the translator have any right to "edit" the source language text?

To continue from the last question, I feel that the translator should have the right to reduce the length of a text if it is clearly overwritten. Such cuts, however, should not be made without consultation, either with the publisher or with the author.

If undertranslation is less common than overtranslation, this may be because the translation is primarily influenced by the source language text, and thus reluctant to leave out anything that has been put down in words. But some of the words may not be needed. It is the translator's job to decide which they are.

References

Duff, Alan. *The Third Language*. Oxford: Pergamon Press, 1981.
Newmark, Peter. "Paragraphs on Translation." *The Linguist*, Vol. 29, No. 1 (1990).

Index